W9-CTW-230

Contemporary
Literary Criticism

Guide to Gale Literary Criticism Series

When you need to review criticism of literary works, these are the Gale series to use:

If the author's death date is: **You should turn to:**

After Dec. 31, 1959
(or author is still living)

CONTEMPORARY LITERARY CRITICISM

for example: Jorge Luis Borges, Anthony Burgess,
William Faulkner, Mary Gordon,
Ernest Hemingway, Iris Murdoch

1900 through 1959

TWENTIETH-CENTURY LITERARY CRITICISM

for example: Willa Cather, F. Scott Fitzgerald,
Henry James, Mark Twain, Virginia Woolf

1800 through 1899

NINETEENTH-CENTURY LITERATURE CRITICISM

for example: Fedor Dostoevski, George Sand,
Gerard Manley Hopkins, Emily Dickinson

1400 through 1799

LITERATURE CRITICISM FROM 1400 TO 1800
(excluding Shakespeare)

for example: Anne Bradstreet, Pierre Corneille,
Daniel Defoe, Alexander Pope,
Jonathan Swift, Phillis Wheatley

SHAKESPEAREAN CRITICISM

Shakespeare's plays and poetry

Antiquity through 1399

CLASSICAL AND MEDIEVAL LITERATURE CRITICISM

for example: Dante, Homer, Plato, Sophocles, Vergil,
the Beowulf poet ·

(Volume 1 forthcoming)

Gale also publishes related criticism series:

CHILDREN'S LITERATURE REVIEW

This ongoing series covers authors of all eras.
Presents criticism on authors and author/illustrators
who write for the preschool to junior-high audience.

CONTEMPORARY ISSUES CRITICISM

This two-volume set presents criticism on
contemporary authors writing on current issues.
Topics covered include the social sciences,
philosophy, economics, natural science, law, and
related areas.

ISSN 0091-3421

Volume 36

Contemporary Literary Criticism

Excerpts from Criticism of the
Works of Today's Novelists, Poets,
Playwrights, Short Story Writers, Scriptwriters,
and Other Creative Writers

Daniel G. Marowski
EDITOR

Roger Matuz
Jane E. Neidhardt
ASSOCIATE EDITORS

Gale Research Company
Book Tower
Detroit, Michigan 48226

STAFF

Daniel G. Marowski, *Editor*

Roger Matuz, Jane E. Neidhardt, *Associate Editors*

Marjorie Wachtel, Robyn V. Young, *Senior Assistant Editors*

Kelly King Howes, Molly L. Norris, Sean R. Pollock,
Jane C. Thacker, Thomas J. Votteler, Debra A. Wells, *Assistant Editors*

Jean C. Stine, *Contributing Editor*

Lizbeth A. Purdy, *Production Supervisor*
Denise Michlewicz Broderick, *Production Coordinator*
Eric Berger, *Assistant Production Coordinator*
Robin L. Du Blanc, Sheila J. Nasea, *Editorial Assistants*

Linda M. Pugliese, *Manuscript Coordinator*
Donna Craft, *Assistant Manuscript Coordinator*
Maureen A. Puhl, Rosetta Irene Simms, *Manuscript Assistants*

Victoria B. Cariappa, *Research Coordinator*
Jeannine Schiffman Davidson, *Assistant Research Coordinator*
Vincenza G. DiNoto, Daniel Kurt Gilbert, Grace E. Gillis, Maureen R. Richards,
Keith E. Schooley, Filomena Sgambati, Valerie Webster, Mary D. Wise, *Research Assistants*

Jeanne A. Gough, *Permissions Supervisor*
Janice M. Mach, *Permissions Coordinator, Text*
Patricia A. Seefelt, *Permissions Coordinator, Illustrations*
Susan D. Nobles, *Assistant Permissions Coordinator*
Margaret A. Chamberlain, Sandra C. Davis, Mary M. Matuz, *Senior Permissions Assistants*
Colleen M. Crane, Kathy Grell, Josephine M. Keene,
Mabel E. Schoening, *Permissions Assistants*
Margaret A. Carson, H. Diane Cooper,
Dorothy J. Fowler, Yolanda Parker, *Permissions Clerks*

Frederick G. Ruffner, *Publisher*
Dedria Bryfonski, *Editorial Director*
Christine Nasso, *Director, Literature Division*
Laurie Lanzen Harris, *Senior Editor, Literary Criticism Series*
Dennis Poupard, *Managing Editor, Literary Criticism Series*

Library of Congress Catalog Card Number 76-38938
ISBN 0-8103-4410-6
ISSN 0091-3421

Computerized photocomposition by
Typographics, Incorporated
Kansas City, Missouri

Printed in the United States

Contents

Preface

Literary criticism is, by definition, "the art of evaluating or analyzing with knowledge and propriety works of literature." The complexity and variety of the themes and forms of contemporary literature make the function of the critic especially important to today's reader. It is the critic who assists the reader in identifying significant new writers, recognizing trends in critical methods, mastering new terminology, and monitoring scholarly and popular sources of critical opinion.

Until the publication of the first volume of *Contemporary Literary Criticism (CLC)* in 1973, there existed no ongoing digest of current literary opinion. *CLC,* therefore, has fulfilled an essential need.

Scope of the Work

CLC presents significant passages from published criticism of works by today's creative writers. Each volume of *CLC* includes excerpted criticism on about 50 authors who are now living or who died after December 31, 1959. Since the series began publication, more than 1,700 authors have been included. The majority of authors covered by *CLC* are living writers who continue to publish; therefore, an author frequently appears in more than one volume. There is, of course, no duplication of reprinted criticism.

Authors are selected for inclusion for a variety of reasons, among them the publication of a critically acclaimed new work, the reception of a major literary award, or the dramatization of a literary work as a movie or television screenplay. For example, the present volume includes Allen Ginsberg, whose *Collected Poems* was recently published and prompted reevaluation of his entire career; Peter Nichols, whose play *A Day in the Death of Joe Egg* was revived on Broadway; and Joseph Heller, whose novel *God Knows* received much attention from the literary world. Perhaps most importantly, authors who appear frequently on the syllabuses of high school and college literature classes are heavily represented in *CLC;* Edna O'Brien and Adrienne Rich are examples of writers of this stature in the present volume. Attention is also given to several other groups of writers—authors of considerable public interest—about whose work criticism is often difficult to locate. These are the contributors to the well-loved but nonscholarly genres of mystery and science fiction, as well as literary and social critics whose insights are considered valuable and informative. Foreign writers and authors who represent particular ethnic groups in the United States are also featured in each volume.

Format of the Book

Altogether there are about 750 individual excerpts in each volume—with an average of about 11 excerpts per author—taken from hundreds of literary reviews, general magazines, scholarly journals, and monographs. Contemporary criticism is loosely defined as that which is relevant to the evaluation of the author under discussion; this includes criticism written at the beginning of an author's career as well as current commentary. Emphasis has been placed on expanding the sources for criticism by including an increasing number of scholarly and specialized periodicals. Students, teachers, librarians, and researchers frequently find that the generous excerpts and supplementary material provided by the editors supply them with all the information needed to write a term paper, analyze a poem, or lead a book discussion group. However, complete bibliographical citations facilitate the location of the original source as well as provide all of the information necessary for a term paper footnote or bibliography.

A *CLC* author entry consists of the following elements:

- The **author heading** cites the author's full name, followed by birth date, and death date when applicable. The portion of the name outside the parentheses denotes the form under which the author has most commonly published. If an author has written consistently under a pseudonym, the pseudonym will be listed in the author heading and the real name given on the first line of the biographical and critical introduction. Also located at the beginning of the introduction to the author entry are any important name variations under which an author has written. Uncertainty as to a birth or death date is indicated by question marks.

- A **portrait** of the author is included when available.

- A brief **biographical and critical introduction** to the author and his or her work precedes the excerpted criticism. However, *CLC* is not intended to be a definitive biographical source. Therefore, *cross-references* have been included to direct the reader to other useful sources published by the Gale Research Company: *Contemporary Authors* now includes detailed biographical and bibliographical sketches on more than 82,000 authors; *Children's Literature Review* presents excerpted criticism on the works of authors of children's books; *Something about the Author* contains heavily illustrated biographical sketches on writers and illustrators who create books for children and young adults; *Contemporary Issues Criticism* presents excerpted commentary on the nonfiction works of authors who influence contemporary thought; *Dictionary of Literary Biography* provides original evaluations of authors important to literary history; and the new *Contemporary Authors Autobiography Series* offers autobiographical essays by prominent writers. Previous volumes of *CLC* in which the author has been featured are also listed in the introduction.

- The **excerpted criticism** represents various kinds of critical writing—a particular essay may be normative, descriptive, interpretive, textual, appreciative, comparative, or generic. It may range in form from the brief review to the scholarly monograph. Essays are selected by the editors to reflect the spectrum of opinion about a specific work or about an author's literary career in general. The excerpts are presented chronologically, adding a useful perspective to the entry. All titles by the author featured in the entry are printed in boldface type, which enables the reader to easily identify the works being discussed.

- A complete **bibliographical citation** designed to help the user find the original essay or book follows each excerpt. An asterisk (*) at the end of a citation indicates the essay is on more than one author.

Other Features

- A list of **Authors Forthcoming in *CLC*** previews the authors to be researched for future volumes.

- An **Appendix** lists the sources from which material in the volume has been reprinted. Many other sources have also been consulted during the preparation of the volume.

- A **Cumulative Index to Authors** lists all the authors who have appeared in *Contemporary Literary Criticism, Twentieth-Century Literary Criticism, Nineteenth-Century Literature Criticism,* and *Literature Criticism from 1400 to 1800,* along with cross-references to other Gale series: *Children's Literature Review, Authors in the News, Contemporary Authors, Contemporary Authors Autobiography Series, Dictionary of Literary Biography, Something about the Author,* and *Yesterday's Authors of Books for Children.* Users will welcome this cumulated author index as a useful tool for locating an author within the various series. The index, which lists birth and death dates when available, will be particularly valuable for those authors who are identified with a certain period but whose death date causes them to be placed in another, or for those authors whose careers span two periods. For example, F. Scott Fitzgerald is found in *Twentieth-Century Literary Criticism,* yet a writer often associated with him, Ernest Hemingway, is found in *Contemporary Literary Criticism.*

- A **Cumulative Index to Critics** lists the critics and the author entries in which their essays appear.

Acknowledgments

The editors wish to thank the copyright holders of the excerpted articles included in this volume for permission to use the material and the photographers and other individuals who provided photographs for us. We are grateful to the staffs of the following libraries for making their resources available to us: Detroit Public Library and the libraries of Wayne State University, the University of Michigan, and the University of Detroit. We also wish to thank Anthony Bogucki for his assistance with copyright research.

Suggestions Are Welcome

The editors welcome the comments and suggestions of readers to expand the coverage and enhance the usefulness of the series.

Authors Forthcoming in *CLC*

To Be Included in Volume 37

Breyten Breytenbach (South African poet, novelist, and nonfiction writer)—Breytenbach is an important Afrikaans writer whose two recent works, *Mouroir: Mirrornotes of a Novel* and *The True Confessions of an Albino Terrorist,* were inspired by his seven-year imprisonment under South Africa's Terrorist Act.

William F. Buckley, Jr. (American novelist, essayist, nonfiction writer, and editor)—Editor of the *National Review* and author of books on conservative political thought, Buckley has also gained attention as a writer of spy fiction, including the recent *See You Later, Alligator.*

Donald Hall (American poet, essayist, dramatist, critic, and editor)—A prolific writer, Hall is best known for his poems, many of which are narrative reminiscences of his childhood and family. His latest works include *To Keep Moving* and *Fathers Playing Catch with Sons.*

Nella Larsen (American novelist)—The author of the novels *Quicksand* and *Passing,* Larsen was an important figure of the Harlem Renaissance whose work has undergone substantial critical reevaluation in recent years.

Primo Levi (Italian novelist, short story writer, and poet)—Many of Levi's books are based on his experiences as an inmate and survivor of Auschwitz. Recent translations of his work include *The Periodic Table* and *If Not Now, When?*

John Metcalf (Canadian short story writer, novelist, essayist, and editor)—An established author of short fiction, Metcalf recently published a collection of essays, *Kicking Against the Pricks,* which attacks the Canadian literary community.

V. S. Naipaul (Trinidadian-born English novelist, short story writer, essayist, and travel writer)—Naipaul's works are noted for their skillful, compelling depiction of the changing cultures of the Third World. His latest works, *Among the Believers: An Islamic Journey* and *Finding the Center: Two Narratives,* recount his travels through Iran, Pakistan, Malaysia, and Indonesia.

Robert Pinget (Swiss-born French novelist, dramatist, short story writer, and journalist)—Often compared to Samuel Beckett and Alain Robbe-Grillet, Pinget writes novels and plays bearing the influence of both the New Novel movement and concepts of the Theater of the Absurd.

Barbara Pym (English novelist and autobiographer)—Pym's witty and perceptive novels of British manners are enjoying renewed interest with the posthumous publication of her autobiography, *A Very Private Eye.*

Gay Talese (American nonfiction writer, journalist, and essayist)—Among the most highly regarded practitioners of New Journalism, Talese is best known for *Honor Thy Father,* a portrait of the private life of a Mafia member, and *Thy Neighbor's Wife,* a history of sexuality in the United States.

Hugh Whitemore (English dramatist and scriptwriter)—Whitemore's first work to be performed on Broadway, *Pack of Lies,* recently introduced to American theater the author of the acclaimed play *Stevie.*

Elie Wiesel (Rumanian-born American novelist, short story writer, essayist, and journalist)—Wiesel is considered among the most powerful writers of Holocaust literature and an eloquent spokesperson for contemporary Judaism. His recent works include *The Golem* and *The Fifth Son.*

To Be Included in Volume 38

Robert Bly (American poet and essayist)—Recognized as an important and influential contemporary poet, Bly has been praised for successfully merging the personal and the public in his work. His poems are often characterized as visionary and imagistic yet are firmly rooted in the concrete world.

Octavia Butler (American novelist)—Butler's "Patternist" series of science fiction novels, from *Patternmaster* to *Clay's Ark,* details a future history while addressing contemporary social issues.

Guy Davenport (American short story writer, critic, and translator)—A scholar of classical literature and an experimental fiction writer, Davenport has recently published a volume of essays, *The Geography of the Imagination,* and two short story collections, *Eclogues* and *Apples and Pears.*

Michel del Castillo (Spanish-born French novelist and short story writer)—Best known for his autobiographical novel *A Child of Our Time,* del Castillo writes fiction in which the depiction of human suffering, depravity, and oppression echoes the harsh circumstances of his own background.

Mavis Gallant (Canadian novelist, short story writer, and dramatist)—Widely respected for her finely crafted fiction, Gallant centers much of her work on Canadian characters at home and abroad. Criticism will focus on her short story collection *Home Truths* and her play *What Is to be Done?*

John Irving (American novelist)—Author of the controversial best-seller *The World According to Garp,* Irving has again inspired wide critical and popular attention with his latest novel, *The Cider House Rules.*

George S. Kaufman (American dramatist, journalist, critic, and scriptwriter)—A recipient of two Pulitzer Prizes for drama, Kaufman collaborated on such plays as *You Can't Take It With You* and *Of Thee I Sing,* which are marked by his sharp, often scathing wit.

Claude Levi-Strauss (Belgian-born French anthropologist, essayist, and linguist)—A world-renowned figure associated with the intellectual milieu of post-World War II France, Levi-Strauss provoked widespread analysis and debate through numerous works detailing his theories of structuralism.

Jonathan Reynolds (American dramatist and scriptwriter)—Reynolds is a popular comic dramatist whose recent successful Broadway plays include *Geniuses* and *Fighting International Fat.*

Ntozake Shange (American dramatist, novelist, poet, and essayist)—Best known for her play *for colored girls who have considered suicide/ when the rainbow is enuf,* Shange has recently published a novel, *Betsey Brown,* which explores a teenage girl's self-discovery amid the conflicts between her cultural heritage and her middle-class American surroundings.

Studs Terkel (American nonfiction writer, journalist, and dramatist)—Terkel writes social histories that emphasize the personal responses of ordinary individuals. His recent book, *The Good War,* examines contemporary attitudes and perceptions about World War II.

Herman Wouk (American novelist, nonfiction writer, and dramatist)—The author of such well-known works as *The Caine Mutiny* and *The Winds of War,* Wouk analyzes the experiences of Jewish-Americans through the adventures of one man in his latest novel, *Inside, Outside.*

Edward Abbey

1927-

American novelist and nonfiction writer.

Called "one of the most controversial and challenging of contemporary writers from the American West" by William T. Pilkington, Abbey argues in his works for the preservation of the wilderness to counterbalance the expansion of modern technocracy. What sets him apart from other authors who have written on similar subjects is his outspoken condemnation of industry, government, tourism, and whatever else threatens the environment. In addition, he has expressed support for anarchy and property violence as means to impede land development. Abbey has been categorized as an environmentalist, a naturalist, and a regional or Western writer; he insists that his work is an "elegy" to the American West. From 1956 to 1971 Abbey was a park ranger for the National Park Service, and he draws much of the material for his books from those experiences.

Jonathan Troy (1954), Abbey's first novel, is his only book not set in the Southwest. It foreshadows some elements which are more fully developed in Abbey's later fiction, notably his perception of the West as a place of freedom, escape, and sanity. His next two works, *The Brave Cowboy* (1956) and *Fire on the Mountain* (1962), contain features of the traditional Western novel, particularly his proud, independent protagonists who defy great odds, usually in the form of government or industry. Abbey's fourth book, *Desert Solitaire* (1968), garnered widespread critical attention. Dubbed a "minor classic" by one critic, this work is an account of Abbey's seasons as a ranger. Along with two subsequent collections of essays, *The Journey Home* (1977) and *Abbey's Road* (1979), *Desert Solitaire* outlines what Ann Ronald called "[Abbey's] belief in the sacred power of the landscape" and his contempt for a society that promotes destruction of its land.

Following *Desert Solitaire*, Abbey's next few nonfiction works, *Appalachian Wilderness* (1970), *Slickrock* (1971), and *Cactus Country* (1973), reaffirm his plea for the preservation of the environment. In the novel *Black Sun* (1971), Abbey again casts a loner as his hero. The background and some of the characters are similar to those in Abbey's earlier novels, but many critics recognized the book as more introspective than his earlier writings. Reviewers found *The Monkey Wrench Gang* (1975) difficult to classify. With its humorous framework and serious message, some regarded this novel as satirical, others as subversive; Abbey simply described it as "an adventure with an environmental theme." The book details the exploits of a group of vigilantes intent upon saving the desert from industrialization. *Good News* (1980), a combination Western and science fiction story, is set in a post-holocaust West, lending irony to the title.

Although critics note that Abbey tends to be didactic, verbose, and sometimes repetitive, he has been praised as a skillful prose stylist whose powerful descriptive language evokes vivid images. His characters tend to be types rather than fully realized creations; Garth McCann asserts that his most credible protagonists are those whose beliefs most closely reflect those of Abbey himself. Abbey's early novels are simple and straight-

Photograph by Warden. Courtesy of Edward Abbey

forward in plot and theme, while his later fiction is more complex and philosophical, adhering to a general style of description followed by polemic. Nevertheless, throughout his fiction Abbey retains the frontier spirit of the traditional Western not only in his heroes but also in his use of archetypes, myths, and confrontations between good and evil. Despite Abbey's affinity for the individual, his rebels rarely win. Ultimately, Abbey opts for compromise, but he insists that nature be protected.

(See also *Contemporary Authors*, Vols. 45-48 and *Contemporary Authors New Revision Series*, Vol. 2.)

LEVI S. PETERSON

[Edward Abbey] presents for our unconditional admiration the lawlessness of his cowboy character, Jack Burns, in *The Brave Cowboy*. This novel is at once an exaltation of frontier anarchy and a piercing criticism of the modern civlization that has made such lawless freedom impossible. Abbey is himself an anarchist, a believer and propounder of the quaint doctrine that human evil is due to government and law more than to any other social force. To put across his message, Abbey sends a cowboy in the pattern of the nineteenth century riding his horse into modern Albuquerque, New Mexico. The cowboy shows over and over a refusal to accommodate himself to the demands of modern urban civilization. When he finds a barbed wire fence, he cuts it. When he is asked for his I.D. cards, he says, "Don't have none. Don't need none. I already know who I am." When he learns that his buddy is in jail, he attempts to break him out.

But this free spirit cannot survive in modern civilization. Having incurred the wrath of the law by his jail break, Burns faces the combined efforts of a vast posse, mechanized and equipped with the latest technological accouterments—jeeps, cars, radios, sub-machine guns, helicopters, and airplanes. Accoutered only with his horse and a lever-action rifle, Burns successfully eludes the posse. But he still cannot survive. In crossing a super-highway on his horse, he is accidentally killed by a truck loaded with bathroom fixtures. The symbolism is clear. What an oppressive law has not quite done, a complex, blind technology has finished. The anarchic freedom of the nineteenth century cowboy cannot live in modern civilization. (pp. 199-200)

> Levi S. Peterson, "The Primitive and the Civilized in Western Fiction," in Western American Literature, *Vol. I, No. 3, Fall, 1966, pp. 197-207.**

EDWIN WAY TEALE

The third sentence of Edward Abbey's **"Desert Solitaire"** reads: "Every man, every woman, carries in heart and mind the image of the ideal place, the right place, the one true home, known or unknown, actual or visionary." For him, this is the desert, beyond the end of the roads, in the stark canyonland of southeast Utah. . . .

Based roughly on the months of the April-to-September season of the [park] ranger—with side excursions, mental and physical—[Abbey's] book is a voice crying in the wilderness, *for* the wilderness.

It is the ougrowth of a bitter awarness of all that has been lost, all that is being lost, all that is going to be lost in that glory of our American democracy, our system of national parks. Designed to set aside, for all the people, wild areas of special beauty, this system originated with a two-fold purpose: to serve the public and to preserve the areas. These two goals are now in head-on collision. For "to serve the public" has come to mean "to serve the public *in automobiles*." . . .

[The traffic problem has overtaken some] parks and threatens almost all eventually. The solution, according to the "developers" among park administrators, is to build more roads. Yet the dilemma is that each of the proliferating roads subtracts something from the wild scene the park is supposed to preserve and at the same time attracts more cars. . . . Unless something is done to exclude or confine the swelling tide of cars, the author maintains, the gradual destruction of our national parks, as we know them, is inevitable.

To the "builders" and "developers" among park administrators, his book may well seem like a wild ride on a bucking bronco. It is rough, tough and combative. The author is a rebel, an eloquent loner. In his introduction, he gives fair warning that the reader may find his pages "coarse, rude, bad-tempered, violently prejudiced." But if they are all these, they are many things besides. His is a passionately felt, deeply poetic book. It has philosophy. It has humor. It has sincerity and conviction. It has its share of nerve tingling adventures in what he describes as a land of surprises, some of them terrible surprises.

Understandably for one who has watched changes for the worse in an area known and loved, who has seen the splendors of a Glen Canyon doomed to flooding and silting until, like the Taj Mahal buried in mud, it will be beyond the power of any human agency to restore, Abbey writes with a deep undercurrent of bitterness. But, as is not infrequently the case, the bitter man may be one who cares enough to be bitter and he often is the one who says things that need to be said. In **"Desert Solitaire"** those things are set down in lean, racing prose, in a close-knit style of power and beauty. Rather than a balanced book, judicially examining in turn all sides, it is a forceful presentation of one side. And that side needs presenting. It is a side too rarely presented. There will always be others to voice the other side, the side of pressure and power and profit.

> Edwin Way Teale, "Making the Wild Scene," in The New York Times Book Review, *January 28, 1968, p. 7.*

FREEMAN TILDEN

[**"Desert Solitaire"**] begins with an author's introduction that is, to say the least, a bit unusual. It might be called a Pugnacious Preface, in which he remarks that "serious critics, serious librarians, serious associate professors of English will dislike the book intensely; at least I hope so." These are the words of a disillusioned idealist. One may expect something shrill. One is not disappointed. (p. 22)

[Mr. Abbey's] connection with the National Park Service gave him an unflattering opinion of the Washington administrators. To him they "are distinguished chiefly by their ineffable mediocrity." *Ineffable* is harsh. The word expresses the inexpressible. But the actual working rangers in the field, he adds, are "capable, honest, dedicated men." That will please the rangers until . . . Mr. Abbey gives them a playful touch with his pinchbar. Now they learn that they are "lazy, scheming loafers . . . Put them to work . . . It won't hurt them to work off a little office fat; it'll do them good, help take their minds off each other's wives . . ." When the rangers pick themselves up and recover from that love-tap they will realize that as long as friend Abbey is around, enemies are superfluous. (pp. 22-3)

So far, this review sounds disparaging. But wait. This serious critic, for one, is actually recommending Mr. Abbey's book, vehemence, egotism, bad taste and all. Partly because we need angry young men to remind us that there is plenty we should be angry about, and scattered all through this volume are just, biting statements we shall do well to heed. Partly because Abbey is an artist with words. There are pages and pages of delicious prose, sometimes almost magical in their evocation of the desert scene. There is, among other gems, a description of the gathering and the explosion of a midsummer thunderstorm in the high desert that is so true to the actuality that you not only experience it with the eye, you smell it, you feel it in your bones. How this man can write! But he can do more than write. His prehension of the natural environment—of raw nature—is so ingenuous, so implicit, that we wonder if the pre-Columbian aborigines didn't see their environment just that way. He says he is a desert rat. He is. Compared with Abbey most of the Arizona School of writers are mice.

So, forget Abbey's bad manners and a certain pose of the roughneck that pleases him to display, and delight in his facility of communication. He has the yowl of a coyote: but be patient. He has the grace of that animal, too. (p. 23)

Freeman Tilden, in a review of "Desert Solitaire: A Season in the Wilderness," in National Parks Magazine, *Vol. 42, No. 245, February, 1968, pp. 22-3.*

SHELDON FRANK

Edward Abbey is a passionate, eccentric, bawdy, romantic, clear-eyed wilderness-addict. He is a writer of crackling, densely visual prose. And he is a very angry man. In *Desert Solitaire,* his account of a season spent in the Utah desert, Abbey punctuated his description of snakes and sunsets and loneliness with blistering attacks on the road builders, mining engineers, and motorized tourists that were destroying his beloved Southwest. His greatest wrath was directed at the Glen Canyon Dam, the concrete monster that strangled the Colorado River and submerged one of the world's most beautiful canyons. *Desert Solitaire* included a long narrative of a trip Abbey took through the Glen Canyon before the dam was built, and reading his loving description of long-gone natural wonders makes one angry enough to want to blow the dam to smithereens.

Seven years have passed since *Desert Solitaire,* and Abbey is angrier than ever, still outraged at the destruction of the glorious Glen Canyon. *The Monkey Wrench Gang* is his attempted revenge, a novel about a group of eco-raiders who set out to undo technological progress in the Southwest, having as their ultimate aim the smashing of the Glen Canyon Dam....

The Monkey Wrench Gang is a sad, hilarious, exuberant, vulgar fairy tale filled with long chase sequences and careful conspiratorial scheming. As in all fairy tales, the characters are pure cardboard, unbelievable in every respect. But they are delightful, even the psychopathic Hayduke, who is unable to utter a single sentence without an obscenity. Abbey is a solipsist at heart, a terribly private man, and his four eco-raiders are really four facets of his complex personality fleshed out with names, faces, and historics.

In *The Monkey Wrench Gang* Abbey has tried to write a kind of low-comedy *Moby Dick.* It is part adventure story, part melodrama, part tragedy, stuffed with huge chunks of information about the wilderness, survival, and industrial wastelands. Abbey has an extraordinary eye for concrete detail, for the specifics of flora and fauna; he knows and tells everything about how to cache food, how to run a bulldozer, how an ecological subsystem functions. At times he is too didatic, too long-winded; at times chase sequences become repetitive; at times you wish his characters were more believable. But he is a good man and a superb prose stylist, and he has written an entertaining, infuriating book. It'll make you want to go out and blow up a dam.

Sheldon Frank, "Wilderness," in The National Observer, *September 6, 1975, p. 17.*

WILLIAM MARLING

For twenty years Edward Abbey has been conducting concurrent defenses of untrampled wilderness and the autonomous individual. His most recent novel, *The Monkey Wrench Gang,* retains this traditional focus, but it does not illuminate the paradoxical affinity of these two abstractions within American history. For a reader as long acquainted with Abbey as I am this is a disappointment, because *The Brave Cowboy* (1955) and *Desert Solitaire* (1968) examined the same riddle from a post both passionate and well informed.

Edward Abbey's thesis, of course, is not new. Some time ago Yves Simon, the conservative political theorist, wrote that "control over natural phenomena gives birth to a craving for the arbitrary domination of men." Abbey's probes are distinguished, to use Roth's phrase, by their distinctly "American Redskin" flavor, and also by an extraordinary knowledge of philosophy and nature, and by an overtly political use of the novel. He is set apart from those who toy with the "conquest of nature" paradox from a great philosophic height by his ability to distinguish not only between Camus and Cocteau but between columbine and penstemon as well. When the ingredients coalesce correctly, he is a powerful writer.

Yet *The Monkey Wrench Gang,* his longest, his most decidedly anarchistic, and his most carefully articulated work yet, turns out to be unsatisfying. (p. 108)

The book is strong ... in a way peculiar to southwestern writers. The tone and sensibility of Larry McMurtry come to mind immediately. The vitality of the "river rats," the macho of the outfitters, and the flaccidity of the Mormon sportsmen in their $6,000 four-wheel-drive vehicles, all register at once with veracity. Abbey details splendidly the changes rending the West.... There is an irrepressible hope which pops up at each gopher hole and counsels the reader to fend off those bastards from the government. This spirit is the essence of Ed Abbey—may he never write anything without it. But all this nice expository nonfiction seems to have been sliced and packaged for the novel.

Those facets of the characters which shine most—the lucent randiness of the "desert rats," for instance—appear to be direct sketches of individuals whose identity is clear to anyone familiar with the environmental movement in the Southwest. The other aspects are like nougat, too sweet, too overdrawn for digestion. The unintentional result is a caricature of the subject, and incidentally of the author himself.... No figure in this work possesses the authenticity of Jack Burns, that cowpoke Abbey painted with Remington-like strokes in *The Brave Cowboy* and left to die on a freeway "at the hands of men and women immured in machines." No character has the consistency of John Vogelin, the New Mexican who refused to cede his ranch to the White Sands Testing Area in *Fire on the Mountain* (1962).

The evocative desert setting which Abbey used so effectively in his preceding work is also slighted. Gone is that belief in the primacy of external reality which led him to devote one chapter of *Desert Solitaire* to describing the rocks around his home and a second to the peculiar ambience of high noon in the slickrock desert. The perception, the life of the senses, which allied him with Neruda and Octavio Paz, seems to have atrophied.

Perhaps those are failings inherent in a political novel, and its probable political effectiveness is what should be addressed. But consider: this book counsels insurrection and sabotage. It contains explicit descriptions of procedures for dynamiting bridges and destroying earth-moving machinery. Reading it one cannot help but feel that Abbey intended the information to be of practical use. Its intended consequence must be the disjointed acts of renascent Luddites ..., though whatever logic underlies this advocacy is never explained. Unlike other successful propagandists for nature—Thoreau comes to mind first—Abbey fails to show that his opponents live the wrong life. In fact, he himself has rather a passion for guns, tools, and jeeps. He *likes* to drive like hell across the desert and he *insists* on his right to throw beer cans out the window. His vitality exceeds nature and embraces some pleasures of the Machine, a tendency which enhances his credibility but which contaminates his political message. The inconsistency spreads. Such issues as the destruction of private property, the sabotage of public works, the possible maiming or death of innocent people, are swept by the comic wave into the backwaters of the novel. Where are the arguments, veiled or otherwise? (pp. 109-10)

If civil disobedience is the answer, is the course Abbey outlines even remotely plausible? Blowing up the Glen Canyon Dam? . . . This is a political novel that commits the one unpardonable sin of a political novel: it shows no real course of action.

The prose in the book has a jerky quality, but after the reader becomes accustomed to this staccato pattern there is an elliptic effect that works nicely. Unfortunately many of the scenes seem to be manipulated for the benefit of word play, and one picks his way through the failing puns as if on a plain of banana peels. . . . The author tends also to repeat aphorisims, epigrams, and bits of wisdom from other books, including verbatim bits of his previous work. One tolerates a bit, but credulity snaps when Abbey writes, "Never eat at a place called Mom's, never play cards with a man called Doc, and never get into bed with anyone whose problems are worse than your own." As more than one editor at Lippincott must know, that was written by Nelson Algren in *Walk on the Wild Side.*

These stale clunkers and the want of persuasive argument do nothing to relieve the weight inherent today in yet another book about "ecology." Even the most dedicated fan of Edward Abbey must realize a little sadly that this is not among his better works. (pp. 110-11)

> *William Marling, "Anarchism and Ecology," in* Southwest Review, *Vol. 61, No. 1, Winter, 1976, pp. 108-11.*

TED MORGAN

We need people like Edward Abbey, who is a combination of Thoreau and Marion the Swamp Fox. He is not merely a spokesman for nature lovers, he is a guerrilla fighter in what may be the last great American conflict, the one over land use. I shout "Right On!" to much of what he says. But I don't think I would accompany him on his forays, as he cheerfully confesses to a number of indictable offenses, such as doctoring Bureau of Reclamation bulldozers, cutting down a Utah Chamber of Commerce billboard, or shooting insulators off the power line of the Black Mesa and Lake Powell Railroad.

I would not do these things, but I am glad that he is doing them. I like the position he has taken, that of the conservationist as subversive. Abbey goes his own way. Like some of the wild animals he writes about in **"The Journey Home,"** a collection of autobiographical magazine pieces, he doesn't run with the pack. He steers clear of conventional wisdom. His ideas may be a bit bent, but they are not culled from self-help books. (p. 10)

This collection is a fine introduction to Abbey. He will tell you the terrible things that are happening to Arizona, how the pretty town of Telluride, Colo., became a crowded ski resort, and how the West was raped. He will also introduce you to the American desert, to unspoiled rivers and to mountain lions. His final plea is one that I find easy to endorse: "Every square mile of range and desert saved from the strip miners, every

river saved from the dam builders, every forest saved from the loggers, every swamp saved from the land speculators means another square mile saved for the play of human freedom." So read Abbey, listen to Abbey, admire Abbey, but if he ever decides to run for office, don't vote for Abbey. I suspect that when you scratch a radical conservationist, you find a new kind of autocrat. (p. 11)

> *Ted Morgan, "Subvert and Conserve," in* The New York Times Book Review, *July 31, 1977, pp. 10-11.*

GARTH McCANN

From the first moment we meet [the title character of Abbey's novel *Jonathan Troy*] we see his mind drift in reverie toward thoughts of escaping to the West. Increasingly as he encounters conflict and disappointment, the West comes to symbolize poignantly for him what it has meant to countless thousands of Easterners: a place to escape, to find a new home, to lead the good life away from the shackles of urban-industrialized civilization. Jonathan is continually haunted by visions of that unseen Western home. Throughout the novel the need for escape becomes more compelling as he tries to cope with Pennsylvania life. Whether he ever finds a place of freedom in his fabled West is not part of the book's account. Rather, the focus falls on Jonathan's need to leave, on the impossiblity of his finding happiness or success in the industrialized East, and on the specific causes of his discontent. (pp. 11-12)

For both Jonathan and Abbey, the West comes to symbolize freedom from corruption and restraint. Abbey's depiction of Pennsylvania shows it to have the political, economic, and social forces of a decadent civilization. His vivid descriptions of the depravity of life in the coal-mining towns of Pennsylvania serve mainly to reinforce a decline-of-the-East motif.

Clearly, there is no Walden in the woods near Powhatan: nature is not enchanted, it is infested. Not only are the cities decaying, but so is the countryside, which is falling victim to poverty and squalor. . . . If there is to be any recourse for Jonathan, he knows it has to be far from the East—both urban and rural. In rejecting the Eastern country culture and backwoods barbarism, Jonathan denies the possibility of a sanctuary anywhere but in the broad, mythical frontier.

Generally speaking, *Jonathan Troy* is a success, particularly in the descriptive passages which abound, filled with elegance, close detail, complex syntax, verbal force, symbolic power, and vivid imagery. Although it does have weaknesses in dialogue and internal monologue, some inconsistencies in conversation patterns, some straining of realism, and occasional overdone and artificial parts, it anticipates the excellence to be found in Abbey's later works. Its style startles and arrests the reader; its grace and power of perception foreshadow greatness to come. And its conceptual treatment of the dichotomy between decadent civilization and promising wilderness anticipates later and more sophisticated—because of the realization that mere escape will not resolve the conflict—attempts by Abbey to reconcile the two forces. In theme, style, and philosophy, *Jonathan Troy* sketches out the beginnings of Abbey's quest to have the best of both worlds. In his later works, which are filled with beauty and substance, Abbey has continued that quest. (pp. 12-13)

Abbey's second novel appeared in 1956 as *The Brave Cowboy.* The chief fascination of this book does not lie in its plot and characters, or its other literary elements, some of which seem simple and one-dimensional. What is most striking about it is the attempt to place the Old West in a modern setting. By itself, the plot seems rather stale. Paul Bondi is imprisoned for his refusal to be drafted, and his old friend, Jack Burns, tries to free him by staging a jailbreak. A stock plot for a number of westerns. And the characters are generally types as well: a lazy sheriff, a vindictive deputy, a wife, a colorless hero, and a host of small-fry functionaries. Only the anachronistic Burns attracts much interest. Unfortunately, when he is killed by a truck while crossing a highway during his attempted escape to Mexico, he also falls victim to the novel's highly melodramatic ending.

But what the book lacks in its plot and its people is amply compensated for by the issues it advances and by its symbolic dimension, a particularly modern one, which colors both the situation and the major characters. More specifically, the age-old plot develops from new circumstances and forces. No longer does stealing a horse or getting drunk cause the jailing. In the New West more significant issues bring people to act counter to the law: belief and principle, or, in this case, conscientious refusal to go along with the demands of depersonalized and bureaucratic government. Inidividualism confronts institutionalism. Neither rustler nor hustler, Bondi is jailed by his own choice because of philosophical and moral convictiions. And Burns, a confirmed radical and loner who prefers mountains to cities and horses to cars, comes to his aid not to seek revenge upon the law but to rescue a friend and philosophical ally. (pp. 13-14)

Burns operates as a symbol of nineteenth-century individualism and freedom associated with the frontier and the wilderness. His distrust of cities and organizations is reinforced by his essentially physical definition of freedom. In contrast, Bondi symbolizes modern man for whom freedom is not limited to location and lack of palpable constraint, but is primarily an idea and a moral concern. Unfortunately, no one, neither Burns nor the law establishment, can understand him. Abbey creates in these two characters a traditional Western hero on horseback and a modern anti-traditional hero of principle whose resistance is not literal but symbolic. (p. 15)

The ending of *The Brave Cowboy* seems both pathetic and coincidental. Symbolically, it represents the Old West being destroyed by the New, which it can neither understand nor cope with. But whether Burns is a fool or a hero remains in doubt. To many readers he constitutes an almost archetypal superman from the past: struggling against the corrupt forces of technocratic society, refusing to give up his ideals, and holding to the simplicity of the natural environment and to the dignity of man in that setting. Yet just as easily he can be seen as a stubborn and stupid anachronism clinging to the faded past, unable and unwilling to accommodate himself to the contemporary world of shadows and complexities. Unable to cope, he can only escape: and escape, though a traditional American gesture in the face of uncomfortable reality, offers no solution. At least it is not a very sound one, as his own crashing defeat implies.

As a whole, this book represents Abbey's mixed feelings toward writing about the West: he is torn between the traditional types of the past and the current conflicting conditions. He vacillates between the two, creating a mixture of direction, characters, and temperament. The issues, though clear, remain unresolved. Abbey skillfully manages to set up the obvious conflict. But he is able only to balance past and present against one another, never to reconcile or synthesize them into any

sort of unified vision or encompassing metaphor. As is characteristic of his work in general, he establishes dichotomies which he is able to delineate effectively when he treats each part separately. But he tends to become entangled in conflicting metaphors and philosophies whenever he attempts to combine what he most admires in the Old and New West.

Whatever the difficulties Abbey may have had with plot, character, and theme, he had none with his powerful descriptive language. His phrasing of the issues facing his heroes is ever mellifluous in image and rhythm. His descriptions of landscape are vivid, graphic, flowing, flawless. Even in this early work, his facility with language constantly impresses the reader. If his prose shows any weakness at this stage of his development, it is in his dialogue. Without prior knowledge, we would have difficulty telling his characters apart on the basis of their language, for they all sound like Abbey—without much individual differentiation, color, syntactic variation, distinct diction, of characteristic patterns of speech. Abbey is here at his best when the character speaking has a view and background clearly similar to his own. In other words, he writes his best dialogue when there is little distance between himself and the personae he creates. The greater the distance between this writer and his characters, the less effective the language. When he wrote *The Brave Cowboy,* Abbey could construct effective didactic, discursive, and descriptive passages, but his mastery of divergent characters, variant speech types and dialects, and individuated dialogue still remained generally unconvincing.

in *Fire on the Mountain* (1962), perhaps his least effective novel, Abbey continues to probe the relationship between the past and the present, between the individual and his society, between freedom and constraint, between permanence and change. This novel's primary worth is, in fact, its examination of those themes. But it is a flawed work; and its major flaw is its simplicity. It has the clarity of plot, the unmistakable issues, and the one-dimensional characters which often appear in Abbey's work, particularly in the earlier part of his career. In this sense *Fire* operates as a propagandistic protest against the advances of a big government that exploits the people and the landscape.

Briefly, the plot and issues of the book coalesce in the plight of Grandfather Vogelin, owner of a vast ranch bordering the atomic testing range of New Mexico. He refuses to let the government buy him out or drive him off. The government and its agents, usually fools and monomaniacs, fail in their efforts; the old man stands his ground and dies on it. (pp. 15-17)

In both *The Brave Cowboy* and *Fire on the Mountain,* there are clearly two parties: the party of the past, of the "old tale," of the salty old loners whose enmity is constantly directed at the evils of civilization, especially its restraints and constraints; and the party of the present, those who seek to adapt to the conditions and changes forced upon them by their social and economic environment. Adapting may mean giving in or giving up, surrendering the idea of the good for the fad of the day, but Abbey does not seem to think so. For in these books man's intelligent accommodation to his surroundings and necessities begins to emerge as a virtue enabling him to survive. Those who stubbornly refuse to cope with the changed world, though high-minded and admirable men, meet with defeat and death. (pp. 18-19)

Abbey begins in these two fictional forays to develop, partly by means of symbolism, a naturalistic environmental philosophy: man, like any other species, must adapt to his conditions—whatever they be—or die. And should man stubbornly fail, like Vogelin and Burns, then he becomes an anachronism. When such a person starts to behave as though he is living in the past, then what was once his home will, like the Vogelin ranch, revert to the spiders, rattlers, and government. (p. 19)

Fire on the Mountain ends, however, on a note of hope. Billy Vogelin, the grandson who tried the method of escape and then of blatant stubbornness, finally transcends adolescence and, under Lee's kind tutelage, seems headed toward a pragmatically more moderate course. Like Steinbeck's grandson-figure in "The Leader of the People," Billy will never know the thrills and hardships and virtues of westering, but he can become one of those able to affect the course of the settled West. He will be able to perceive the complicated dilemmas of the New West and able to understand the conceptual heritage from the Old. With that knowledge, he will be committed to something more than the suicidal strategy of defiance.

Although Abbey's first three books may be viewed as dealing with clear-cut issues and simple characters, these limitations are explainable. In part they arose from the nature of his task: to write about both the Old West and the New West by contrasting the opposites of character and ideology from each era. Significantly, such problems were not present in his next and most widely respected book, *Desert Solitaire*. Here we discover marked improvement and increased complexity, writing that far surpasses anything he had published previously. The reasons for that improvement are not hard to discover.

Abbey is more at home in the contemporary West than in the West of myth and history, and he can create convincing characters best when those characters closely resemble himself—two features of his writing which establish both his weaknesses and his strengths. Judging from his first three books, Abbey's main problem seems to be his inability to project outside of himself in order to create diverse and complex characters. And his greatest power is his capacity for self-dramatization, for imaginatively probing the nature of his own mind and experience, and for creating perceptive semi-fictional autobiographical narratives of magnificent scope and insight. He has thereby helped to rescue the West from a stagnant and mythical past by building out of its present a vivid reality and relevance.

Philosophically, *Desert Solitaire* centers on the concepts of opposition, compromise, and balance. The demands of the wilderness and of modern industrialized man are mutually exclusive. But, paradoxically, it is both unwise and impractical to let either of these sets of demands exclude the other. Although they are admittedly on a collision course, it becomes the task of modern man to find and implement a method of avoiding the catastrophe which would result if either force should get out of control.... Abbey does see a way out of the contraries, a method for getting back to a state of cultural sanity and for avoiding the economic and psychological collapse of our civilization: compromise. He believes—as we shall see—that it is possible through fair and reasonable compromise for man to achieve a balanced steady-state, part of the way between the extremes of the pastoral ideal and the urban nightmare. The New West provides both challenge and space for man's only hope and greatest duty: to imagine and achieve an enduring equilibrium. (pp. 20-1)

Structurally, the form of *Desert Solitaire* is the account of a single park season—from April to October. Abbey's intellectual and physical adventures during that time are somewhat

fictionally portrayed. His narrative is "somewhat" fictional in that it compresses into a single season the experiences of a number of such seasons which he had already experienced in the Canyonlands and other wilderness locations. Like Thoreau, Abbey realized the necessity for a tight narrative structure; hence, he formed his account into an early-spring to autumnal-departure pattern. And of course he changed the names of living persons, except for himself, to avoid identifying anyone.

The strongest unifying device of the book is the narrative voice, the "I" who throughout the book dominates and controls, quips and shapes, describes and declaims, observes and instructs. But there seems to be little growth or expansion of the narrator's consciousness. The real experiences of the author may well have had upon him the effect of growth and development, but those of the narrator do not. Although complex and contradictory and fascinating, the "I" remains essentially unchanged throughout the book. *Desert Solitaire* lives not as a masterpiece of fiction but as a fusion of essay and semi-fictional forms. The descriptive, the argumentative, the explanatory, the experiential, and the ideational all amalgamate into the outer and inner worlds of the semi-personal authorial character whose voice and presence subsume all else.

Compared with his earlier books, *Desert Solitaire* relies more heavily for tone and power on its narrator. Earlier works contain characters who seem to be extractions and separated parts of the author.... *Desert Solitaire,* however, operates without such fictional paraphernalia. It is unabashedly focused on the complex and paradoxical presence of Abbey. The book becomes a medium for the passionate and vivid probing of his human response to and relationship with the wilderness and the realities of twentieth-century life. And this probing shows us not an array of fragmented or stereotypic characters prancing about the landscape, but rather the central and over-powering figure of Abbey—with all his quirks, vanities, perceptions, silliness, tediousness, wit, humor, frustrations, regrets, and dreams. On a higher level, Abbey comes to represent all mankind as he seeks to discover the essence of existence in our time. (pp. 24-5)

Many of [the themes of Abbey's *Cactus Country* (1973)] remain those of *Desert Solitaire,* and much of the general setting is also the same. Abbey describes the uniqueness of the desert, the need to escape civilization, and the degenerate nature of modern cities. He explains the concept of stability in the ecosystem, gives us ironic facts about human activities in desert regions, and details the effects of external nature on the human psyche.... In addition to decrying the stupidities of the past and of the present, he issues warnings and proffers wisdom to one and all. The way the landscape feels, looks, and smells as it penetrates his senses is part of Abbey's account. And he carefully records his personal responses to everything from harmless carrots to the dilemmas of doomed cities.

All these themes are arranged somewhat haphazardly along a sliding scale from the "beneficial" to the "detrimental." In the end, Abbey discontentedly cries out, "there's something about the desert"—a refrain one often finds in his writings, but here again he cannot say what that "something" is.... [The] mystique of the desert is something beyond explanation or name. One can only revere it, whatever it be. Upon this narrative-philosophical thread, *Cactus Country* hangs suspended between the perceiver and the world perceived.

However, the *mode* of that perception is what fascinates the reader and gives the work its Abbeyan air. This mode is a matter partly of his literary style, partly of the attitudes he conveys. His style here, as elsewhere, remains graceful and powerful. He varies his words and sentences from short to long, from simple to complex, from concrete to abstract— simple and smooth, yet sophisticated. Examples taken from context could never suffice to indicate the richness and extent of Abbey's stylistic range.

The tone of that mellifluous style leaps out persistently from the pages. The closeness of "death and life," particularly on the desert, continues to perplex and enchant Abbey. So does the proximity of nature and civilization, both ever-present in the author's mind and both constantly juxtaposed in his prose as it details the nearness of the flowers to the garbage. . . . Other examples of the same sort abound. (pp. 32-4)

But there is also a deeper unity, perhaps a deeper moral, to *Cactus Country:* survival. In many senses that is the lesson and the reality of the desert. Abbey believes that the desert's lesson of survival is especially important for the "overcivilized American" who lives stupidly and unknowingly inside a life system over which he has little control but which must be preserved if he is to survive. . . . In spite of the ironic and bantering manner which Abbey assumes in prefaces and public lectures, on this point he is deadly serious. His manner is intended to shock and surprise; his message is meant to save.

Abbey published a novel entitled *Black Sun* in 1971. A curious love story set in canyon country, it has a simple plot: boy meets girl, boy gets girl, boy loses girl. But some striking differences make the plot a variant of the ancient model: the eighteen-year age difference between the lovers (he is thirty-seven, she nineteen), the intensely physical nature of their passion, and the odd manner of her disappearance and the book's ending. She goes out into the wilderness canyons to think about the new love she has found, but she never returns—and no one ever finds out what happened to her. (pp. 34-5)

As I have already noted, Abbey can write extremely well. In the case of *Black Sun,* he was at last able to get out of his "own" prose style and speaking voice and to create convincing characters who speak like themselves and not like Abbey. In Ballantine's speech and letters, Abbey incorporates all the innuendo, allusion, and wild humor of a slightly batty professor. In Sandy's he uses the simplicity and grammatical and idiomatic awkwardness easily associated with mellowing teeny-boppers. The choppiness and transparency of Rosie's thought and speech are patently those of an aging television addict. And Gatlin's ideas and speech have the subtlety, complexity, and disjointedness which serve most admirably as indicators of his nature and mentality. In sum, the varied styles which Abbey suits to each character become the most effective means of revealing and developing their personages.

Philosophically and symbolically, *Black Sun* seems to support a position of "heroic resignation" to life. Happiness is "possible," but sorrow is "likely." . . . This attitude is buttressed by the themes of this contemporary *Candide:* they are those of loneliness and isolation, of man's inability to communicate, of his tendency to retreat to a wry stoicism in order to survive. (p. 36)

The Monkey Wrench Gang appeared in 1975 amidst a climate of both interest and controversy. The book details the adventures, including acts of sabotage, of four characters in the Colorado River area of northern Arizona and southeastern Utah. At times hilarious and occasionally heavy-handed, *The Monkey*

Wrench Gang shows anarchy—with which Abbey has had a lover's quarrel for thirty years—as an actual way of life. (p. 37)

Without doubt [*The Monkey Wrench Gang*] is Abbey's best and most rewarding venture into the realm of fiction. As such it has numerous virtues. The plot itself is both compelling and carefully worked out, generally. The incidents portrayed throughout the novel have a freshness and vividness characteristic of excellent imaginative narration. . . . Painstakingly detailed accounts of the crew's sabotage successes make their activities seem quite real. Abbey's skill is also apparent in other areas. He demonstrates a thorough awareness of the setting and a meticulous knowledge of machinery, explosives, and survival rations. We see his broad understanding of the people and issues on which he bases his minor characters and major polemic.

However, not all of the major characters are entirely successful portrayals. An inveterate schemer and foul-mouthed anarchist, Hayduke comes across most convincingly, and Sarvis with his considerable acumen and sagacious style seems endlessly fascinating. But Bonnie, who has the mind of a teeny-bopper and the body of a goddess, remains a rather unreal figment of a semi-chauvinistic imagination. And Seldom Seen Smith emerges as rather too cloudy and stereotypic to be believable. All four are at least slightly one-dimensional. All seem to have fragments of Abbey in them, and especially Bonnie and Seldom Seen lack a depth of individuation needed to make them fictionally whole. They all share Abbey's idiom and his ideology.

The Monkey Wrench Gang clearly has a message: something must be done to save the wilderness. However, it seems unlikely that Abbey is arguing for grand-scale sabotage, partly because his saboteurs realize the inevitable futility of their actions and partly because their course of action brings an overreaction from the establishment. The counter attack severely curtails further destruction of industrialism's tentacles in the wild. For Abbey the *issue* is clear, and he has reasserted it often throughout his works, perhaps most succinctly in an editorial he wrote for *El Crepusculo:* "In this age of fake progress, which threatens to submerge everything natural, wild and free under a tide of asphalt and iron, it is vital to our national sanity that we preserve what we can of earthborn man's native heritage." . . . (pp. 38-40)

But the *method* for achieving this goal remains problematic. Direct and illegal action? Maybe. But we should remember that all of Abbey's heroic types who have taken this approach have failed miserably or have been destroyed themselves. His extremists always lose. . . . Although Abbey at times has felt urges to be violent and destructive that are akin to similar urges in his wildest characters, the use of violence and destruction does not appear to be his characteristic position, for although such means may be logically justified, they are pragmatically counterproductive. And Abbey wants *impact*.

At times, particularly in short pieces and speeches, Abbey thrives on advocating unmitigated violence. (p. 40)

Yet to view *The Monkey Wrench Gang* as Abbey's advocacy of violence to bring about change is to view it as contrary to the thrust of the general position of all his writings. He is not telling America to go out and blow up bridges and roads—for he knows that will not work. As the student radicals of the past decade have learned, destruction brings countermeasures even more inhibiting than the original grievances. Furthermore, he is not advocating socialism or communism or the like; if anything, he seeks "something entirely different" from all the isms he knows of, for none of them has yet been able to achieve the goal which in the end he seeks to achieve for himself and for society: keeping industrialism and technology under control, using human intelligence to master the human condition. . . .

Abbey's conception of the writer's function and responsibility consists of the following points: it is his duty to preach this sort of semi-revolution and to help create and organize the social will needed to achieve an equilibrium between technology and humanity. Good writing will encourage us to resist mindless growth of industry and population and to find compromises which will prevent extremist nightmares. Abbey writes in order to shock the confused populace of the country into an awareness that something must and can be done about the dire state of our perishing republic. (p. 41)

> *Garth McCann, in his* Edward Abbey, *Boise State University, 1977, 47 p.*

LUCINDA FRANKS

Edward Abbey, that fierce friend of the deserts and ranges, alerted us in 1968 to the rape of the American West in his book **"Desert Solitaire."** Now, with this new collection of essays [**"Abbey's Road"**], he revisits the West and the Southwest and also turns his attention and ours to far corners of Mexico and Australia. . . .

Mr. Abbey, whether delivering homilies on Winnebago campers or telling about his encounter with wild pigs, is as whimsical and fascinating as ever; but in this new book there is a note of bleakness. The road he travels is jagged; he zig-zags like a dazed wallaby in search of places even more remote. He visits a wild, bone-dry 11,000 square-mile cattle station in South Australia; he rents a fat, low-slung Ford and covers 1,200 godforsaken miles of wetern Australian desert hitherto traveled only by camel or Land Rover; he joyfully spends 10 days on a desert island off Mexico which "has no human inhabitants whatever"; he explores a canyon in the Sierra Madre where "no gringo has ever trod before."

In **"The Journey Home,"** published in 1977, Mr. Abbey was an ecology terrorist, a bold and happy outlaw who toppled billboards, tampered with bulldozers and committed other small symbolic crimes. The crusty iconoclast is still kicking; but now, too many times in too many different ways, he is giving up. On stagnant Lake Powell in Utah he mourns the death of "all that was living and beautiful, drowned in dead water," and then cynically throws his beer can overboard (he who is careful even to avoid clumps of dry grass when relieving himself in the wilderness). In the Sierra Madre he makes the observation that heavy logging and highway excavations might well cause a flood of muck to pour down the canyons, annihilating the primitive Tarahumara Indians. "Well, it's not my problem," he says. "Mustn't get involved."

There seem to be two different Edward Abbeys on this particular road, a rather pouty swaggerer and a much wiser, sorrier man; perhaps both are the result of his inability to save his beloved wilderness. The first Edward Abbey inhabits the early parts of the book. When he visits the Australian cattle station at Anna Creek, he might as well be doing a Marlboro commercial or a parody of Lee Marvin's parody of a gunslinger in the film "Cat Ballou." . . .

Sometimes, a certain romantic hypocrisy creeps into his perceptions. He bemoans the fate of the aborigines, "their lands taken away, their mythic culture lost," and compares their leathery faces to the faces of Socrates and Tolstoy. But his attitude is condescending, even insulting. He sits down and shares a jug of wine with them, talks about nothing more weighty than the beautiful blonde girls in America and ends up giving them the names and numbers of all his lady friends in New York.

Of course, much of this is mask. He is a macho man and proud of it; it is his trademark and distinguishes him as much as the "boutonniere" that adorns the hood of his Volkswagen. We do not really take his sexism seriously: He calls his Ford a "damned lesbian" and explains that the primitives had "no domestic animal except the dog—and the woman." If he cannot seem to write believably about women, neither does he do justice to the portrayal of any male besides himself. As irritating as it might be to read about the tragedy of the coral polyp rendered with a compassion not accorded the aborigines or the Tarahumaras, we forgive him. (p. 8)

On the last stretch of the road, the tone of the traveler has mellowed. His humor and powers of description have come into harmony with his vision. He faces his yearnings and their impossibility. . . . He penetrates stereotypes, writing about bad-nosed rednecks who turn out to answer his blustery challenges with gentle fair hearts; he reminisces about the sorrows of travel, about the women he has known and lost; and, although they still sound like mermaids born of his imagination . . . , he writes also of comradeship, of tenderness, of sharing.

"Too much. Too much. Too much is enough," he says in the final piece, as he goes off to a place he calls Cape Solitude. He sits naked at the edge of a 1,500-foot drop, thinking about the pure miracle of nature, about his recent tour of American campuses, where he received overwhelming support for "bringing the growth machine to a halt." So far, though, the machine keeps on rolling, and he is weary. "Let somebody else save the world for a while," he says, playing a little desert music on his flute. "I'm tired of even thinking about it." (pp. 8, 21)

> *Lucinda Franks, "Natural Involvement," in* The New York Times Book Review, *August 5, 1979, pp. 8, 21.*

WILLIAM MARLING

[Edward Abbey once explained] that a writer wrote out his love for his subject, that honesty required him to write also of its maggoty side, that he was compelled always to write better, and that he must write, be rejected, and rewrite until someone listened.

At the time, he was the paragon of his own program. His gritty **Desert Solitaire,** which at first had the status of Sierra Club *samizdat,* was becoming a brush fire in the popular market. **Black Sun** was fresh off the press, and **The Brave Cowboy** was out in a Ballantine paperback. Abbey always had a trenchant word; he was never predictable.

During the intervening decade, something happened. At the same time that his older work began to attract serious attention . . . , his newer work became more accessible, less iconoclastic, and more "packaged." With *Abbey's Road,* his current collection of essays, he reaches a make-or-break crossroads: he can go on caricaturing the persona he used in the early books with such success and become his own parody; or he can retreat and think seriously about the words he wrote on that blackboard.

Abbey has an excuse. As he reports in his feisty introduction, "I sometimes think that I am the only writer in America who has to work for a living. I have no inheritance enabling me to live off the labor of others, no trust fund, no Government pension, no sinecure at the University." Of course, neither do any of the other writers that he trims in passing—not Gary Snyder, Tom Wolfe, or Gloria Steinem. But you see his defense: that the market lies in magazine pieces. Books such as *Desert Solitaire* are comparatively slow and unrewarding endeavors.

Herein lies the main fault of this book, the choice that Abbey faces, which I want to detail before I pass on to its more hypnotic virtues. Having learned to write the magazine article . . . Abbey has grown too fond of the genre. Every piece in the first half of this book appears just as it was printed in magazine form. . . . The prose throughout this section has the careful cadence and emphatically *certain* sentence arrangement typical of *Reader's Digest*.

There is a link between this dead writing and Abbey's problem with his persona. Having established himself in *Desert Solitaire* as "eloquent, bitter, and extravagant" (Joseph Wood Krutch) and "tough and contentious" (Walter Van Tilberg Clark), Abbey was in demand for magazine work. But the problem is that magazines don't really like tough, bitter, or contentious writing. They like pablum that seems to have substance but is principally style. So along with the distinctive features of his style, such as the trip-em-up sentence fragment, Abbey began to identify and employ certain ruses of orneryness. Chief among these are some prejudices coolly calculated to be unfashionable. Antifeminism, for example. *Desert Solitaire* had latent elements of antifeminism in it, but they were subsumed by a disarming honesty. In *The Monkey Wrench Gang* and *The Journey Home*, however, Abbey baits feminists simply to see their hackles rise. This precious tactic, this calculated "contentiousness," becomes formulaic in *Abbey's Road*. Here is the author on an Australian rancher's wife: "I tried to imagine Gloria Steinem explaining women's rights to Connie Nunn. Connie would laugh her all the way to Adelaide. Connie was born liberated." The sub-basement of this "toughness" is reached when Abbey describes his car as a "lesbian-type rental Ford." And so it goes with Mormons, Indians, Californians, and especially Mexicans. Abbey is still throwing his beer cans out of the truck window, throwing his candy wrappers into Lake Foul (get it?), still toting his firearms. He used to be unpredictable, but now he seems bent on proving that literary iconoclasm can become a nervous tic.

These are hard things to write about such a fine author; but this is the point at which to write them, because this book marks a juncture. There is much that is praiseworthy in *Abbey's Road;* there is a direction revealed that could lead to really "tough, contentious" writing again. Among the high-gloss magazine pieces in this book are some moody, sullen, bitingly honest bits of reportage. The restive Abbey who has been suppressed since *Black Sun* appears. No sensitive reader ever doubted the presence of a darker side in him, but this aspect is given wider scope than before when Abbey describes with glee his destruction of a rental car in Australia, his humiliation in a redneck bar, the pettiness of his life as a military policeman, his evanescent love affairs, his lachrymose drinking bouts. In the genuine indulgence of these darker passions, when Abbey dares approach them, he ceases to caricature himself and

produces his finest writing. Nothing he has written can equal in sheer emotive power the ending of "In defense of the Redneck," when he describes his attempt to sleep after a humiliating drunk. (pp. 102-04)

Moments such as this spot the last part of the book, a section titled "Personal History." . . . This is some of Abbey's strongest writing since *Black Sun* because he really is "tough and contentious," and not with others, which is easy, but with himself—much harder. . . . There is, in fact, more critical intelligence, more self-examination at work in this volume than in any since *Black Sun*. But it is not enough. Ed Abbey must "write on," if he doesn't want to be written off. (p. 105)

William Marling, "At a Make-or-Break Crossroads," in Southwest Review, *Vol. 65, No. 1, Winter, 1980, pp. 102-05.*

DENNIS DRABELLE

[In *Down the River*] Abbey works hard at his iconoclasm. His half-jocular rationale for wilderness preservation is the necessity for remote guerrilla bases from which to resist political oppression. Lately, however, two less attractive qualities have entered his work: arrogance and xenophobia. The arrogance manifests itself in the offhand abuse of respectable writers such as Lewis Thomas, who is characterized in *Down the River* as an "official spokesman for the cancer industry." Elsewhere Abbey lumps Thomas with Carl Sagan, Alvin Toffler, Jeremy Bernstein, John McPhee, R. Buckminster Fuller, Gerard O'Neill and Timothy Leary as "apologists for the glossy technocracy rising around us in walls of aluminum and glass." It seems unlikely that these disparate writers have a common approach to "technocracy," but that is unimportant to Abbey, who offers no explanation for sticking them together. (p. 534)

Xenophobia surfaces in the title essay, where Abbey discusses illegal immigration from Mexico. If we leave our borders open to unlimited immigration, he snarls, "it won't be long [until] the social, political, economic life of the United States is reduced to the level of life in Juarez. Guadalajara. Mexico City. San Salvador. Haiti. India. To a common peneplain of overcrowding, squalor, misery, oppression, torture, and hate."

This is not the place to analyze our border policy—only to note that Abbey's screed on the issue evinces a churlish hauteur. It goes without saying that one purpose of any nation's immigration policy is to protect its values by keeping out others who are perceived as threatening those values. But what is the purpose of expressing such contempt for other societies?

Abbey's outbursts are all the more disappointing when you consider the several valuable things in his book, especially a powerful essay on a lengthy protest outside a nuclear bomb factory in Rocky Flats, Colorado. But since he prides himself above all on his prickly independence, Abbey will no doubt be unmoved by the observation that many of his attitudes give aid and comfort to the enemies of conservation by inviting them to apply the label of elitism in a case where it is no longer justified. (pp. 534-35)

Dennis Drabelle, "Environments and Elitists," in The Nation, *Vol. 234, No. 17, May 1, 1982, pp. 533-35.*

JOHN N. COLE

"The good people of Green River City, Wyoming, turn out to see us start. We raise our little flag, push the boats from shore, and the swift current carries us down."

Thus did John Wesley Powell, the first white man to ride the Colorado River rapids through the Grand Canyon, begin his expedition journal in 1869.

A bit more than a century later, Edward Abbey's ["**Down the River**"] takes us on another trip down the Colorado, down other rapids, and along other rivers of the mind and spirit. His collection of essays and Thoreauvian journals documents the physical, spiritual and emotional change that has quite reshaped America in the relatively brief time since Powell launched his boats.

It is a change that Abbey laments. He must search for the natural presences Powell took for granted, and he tells us again and again that the price of the Industrial Age has been high to the point of peril. . . .

Abbey's river expeditions are not explorations, but escapes. He takes to the wilderness to retain his humanity, to assert his freedom, and, with the eloquence of his writing, to help us perceive our humanity, to persuade us to establish a more sensitive relationship with the natural world. It is that relationship, this deceptively ardent essayist tells us, that is pivotal to our fulfillment and our freedom. . . .

Like every fine writer of the natural world, [Abbey] records what he sees with his mind's eye as well as the experience of his senses. He tells us how the sun slants on a canyon wall—and tells us with crystal images—while he also comments on the asininities of the Bureau of Land Management.

But there is something more—a something that moves Abbey toward excellence, that grants him the right to be considered an exceptional member of the growing community of writers who have taken what's known today as "environmental journalism" as their particular province.

Edward Abbey has a fine humility; the wires of ironic humor that he weaves through each of the 19 essays and reports of this memorable book and his charming modesty prevent him from preaching. He doesn't tell us what we should or shouldn't do to "save" our environment. He writes with zest and passion about his voyages down the rivers of his natural world, and that becomes that. Our response is not dictated, but left to us to decide. . . .

Abbey himself sets up this distance. He is there, living and breathing in his writing, but he is wary of encouraging intimacy. Like one of the tall saguaro cactus that grows in the deserts of his home near Tucson, he protects himself with barbs that turn up as delightful surprises in the mainstreams of his prose. . . .

Abbey's irony needles, it deflates temptations toward pomposity. It is the badge of humility the man wears as he takes us with him on trips down the rivers, on his solitary journeys to the Sonora, into the crevasses of Alaska's blue glaciers, through the canyons of the Apache, and into the ghost towns of the American West that he loves with such intensity.

It is the way he balances that intensity with evidence of his own humanity that makes Abbey such an eloquent and entertaining defender of natural truths. It is what makes him an exceptional environmental writer. It is what allows him to say: "We drift on together . . . a human family bound by human

love . . . Loving one another, we take the sting from death. Loving our mysterious blue planet, we resolve riddles and dissolve all enigmas . . ." and have his readers recognize it as a truth, not trite. It is Edward Abbey's own genius that creates the space that can convincingly sustain such observations.

His needles protect his soul. Like the saguaro, the inner Abbey stores bright truths that can quench our thirst for hope.

> *John N. Cole, "Edward Abbey: A Sage of the Sagebrush," in* Book World—The Washington Post, *May 30, 1982, p. 3.*

PAUL KRZA

It is easy perhaps to dismiss Edward Abbey—novelist, essayist, naturalist, adventurer, environmentalist, and anti-visionary—as a heat-stroked eco-freak; and without doubt he harbors a pretty heavy bias against industrial/technological civilization. Thoughtful folk, however, may go beyond his rude, uncompromising exterior to marvel at his wonderfully sensitive, detailed, and colorful—in a word, compelling—descriptions of what lies "beyond the wall"; essays in praise of the desert, of "Eden at the dawn of creation." (pp. 48-9)

In these ten essays [in *Beyond the Wall*] this incorrigible "natural conservative" pounds away at this and related themes. Humanity is destroying the planet, and something—anything—must be done to reintegrate the species with nature. The past is out there, Abbey insists; in the desert, far from the madding crowds. There, Abbey plots against the abuses of the present and for their remedy in the future. . . .

Beyond the Wall ranges from the more familiar deserts of the American Southwest and the Baja Peninsula of Mexico to the desert-like Arctic permafrost tundra along Alaska's Kongakut River; traveling with Abbey through these allegedly godforsaken, vulture-ridden, water-short places, one discovers an unsuspected hospitability in the formidably inhospitable. . . . The desert, Abbey wants us to know, is survivable, even inspirational; and while its "lilac twilight, maroon buttes, purple mesas, and blue plateaus" may not be in accordance with our more conventional, Europeanized standard of verdant beauty, for Americans suffering from the Teton Syndrome (for whom snow-capped peaks and mountain meadows are epitome and measure of natural gorgeousness) Abbey's perceptions of a more severe aesthetic are refreshingly different. . . .

Abbey's wanderings provide glimpses of the "radiance of the high desert twilight," paid for at the price of swollen feet and "sweating brains," despite frequent stops along the trail for contemplation and refreshment. . . . At night Abbey settles into the desert sand, scooped out to accommodate his body. Ah, wilderness! Ah, desert! . . . The "taste of freedom, the smell of danger." And yet—can the technological web be unwoven? Or have the howl of coyotes and the burning sun indeed unbalanced Abbey's mind? Though beyond the wall, Edward Abbey remains nonetheless within its shadow. Or perhaps a better metaphor is the dam—say, the Glen Canyon Dam—holding back the ever-rising waters of human expectation.

This collection is supposed to be the author's last word on the desert. But don't count on it, unless Technology swallows him up first. (p. 49)

> *Paul Krza, "Below the Dam," in* National Review, *Vol. XXXVI, No. 15, August 10, 1984, pp. 48-9.*

PUBLISHERS WEEKLY

[*Slumgullion Stew,* an] anthology of Edward Abbey's essays (selected from four previous collections) and novel excerpts covers 30 years and thousands of miles of desert, canyon and river rapids. And throughout, from the comic cowboy tales of *Desert Solitaire* to the ruminations on Thoreau in **"Down the River with Henry Thoreau,"** Abbey writes with a voice so clear that even the insects and vultures seem appealing. But while his essay collections (he calls them personal histories) are well represented, only token selections are offered from his six published novels. . . . That's not to say that Abbey's skills as a novelist are completely ignored. A wonderful excerpt from *The Rites of Spring,* a novel-in-progress, is certain to leave readers wanting more. Part philosopher and part curmudgeon, Abbey is among America's most articulate and engaging environmentalists, and *Slumgullion Stew* will delight his fans (while bedeviling his foes) and win him many, many more.

> *A review of "Slumgullion Stew: An Edward Abbey Reader," in* Publishers Weekly, *Vol. 226, No. 14, October 5, 1984, p. 85.*

Vicente Aleixandre
1898-1984

Spanish poet, critic, journalist, and editor.

Recipient of the Nobel Prize for Literature in 1977, Aleixandre was a poet of the "Generation of 1927" whose prolific output has strongly influenced the work of recent Spanish poets. Although his first collection had appeared in Spain almost fifty years earlier and his reputation in his country was well established, Aleixandre's selection for the Nobel Prize came as a surprise to much of the literary world. Prior to 1977, Aleixandre's work available to English readers, including *Poems* (1969), *Vicente Aleixandre and Luis Cernuda: Selected Poems* (1974), and *The Cave of the Night* (1976), had received little notice. Critical attention abroad increased following his reception of the award, however, and several additional works of selected poems in translation have been published, including *Twenty Poems* (1977), *A Longing for the Light: Selected Poems of Vicente Aleixandre* (1979), *The Crackling Sun: Selected Poems of the Nobel Prize Recipient 1977* (1981), and *A Bird of Paper* (1982). Yet the complexity of Aleixandre's poetry and the inherent difficulties in translating it have resulted in a limited readership, despite the vital role he played in the evolution of Hispanic poetry.

Aleixandre was born in Seville and raised in Málaga, a nearby city that figures symbolically in much of his work. When he was eleven he moved with his family to Madrid, where he later received degrees in law and business administration and began a career in economic law. In 1925 Aleixandre contracted tuberculosis, thus beginning the series of illnesses that plagued him for the rest of his life. His health eventually forced him to abandon his career, and he began to concentrate on writing poetry, resulting in his first book, *Ámbito* (1928), written in the tradition of *poésie pure* characteristic of Spanish poetry in the 1920s. Around the same time Aleixandre began to associate with Pedro Salinas, Federico García Lorca, Jorge Guillén, and other poets based in Madrid, culminating in the innovative literary movement referred to as the "Generation of 1927." Writers in this group reacted against the provincialism of Spanish literature. They advocated poetry as a means to discover and explore the relationship between external reality and the poet's internal world, and, while they rejected sentimentality, love was a dominant theme in the work of Aleixandre and other members of the group. Unlike most other writers of his generation, Aleixandre remained in Spain during the Civil War and the subsequent reign of Francisco Franco. Although never a political poet, his works were banned in the postwar years due to his anti-fascist beliefs and his independence from the official regime. Aleixandre's works were reinstated during the 1940s.

Most of Aleixandre's poetry can be divided into three periods. The first, which includes the collections *Pasión de la tierra* (composed 1928-1929; published 1946), *La destrucción o el amor* (composed 1933; published 1935), and *Mundo a solas* (composed 1934-1936; published 1950), has been called his surrealistic period. Although most of the poems in these collections were written just prior to or during the Spanish Civil War, they do not reflect the reality of current events; rather, they present a cosmic, mystical vision of the world through

surrealist imagery and techniques. Aleixandre's thematic focus during this period centers on the elemental forces of the human mind, a yearning for the solace of nature, and the inextricable connection between love and death and between the forces of creation and destruction. In contrast to the earlier *Ámbito,* the volumes in the first period are more complexly constructed free verse, in which Aleixandre's sweeping, intense, and passionate meditations are given freer rein. Many critics, and the poet himself, have noted the influence of Sigmund Freud on Aleixandre's exploration of the hidden passions and driving forces that operate beneath the surface of the mind. Lewis Hyde, one of Aleixandre's noted translators, observed in his introduction to *Twenty Poems* that a desire to explore "the strong undertow beneath the accelerating tide of rationalism" connects Freud, surrealism, and the early poetry of Aleixandre. Of Aleixandre's poems Hyde says: "[They] are not an affirmation. They are not working out of a full and nourishing surreality, but away from the reality at hand. That . . . is part of their tension—they are the reflective mind trying to think its way out of coherence and precision."

Sombra del paraíso (1944), Aleixandre's first collection following the Spanish Civil War, is a transitional volume leading to the second phase of his career. Although poems in the middle period, which include those from *Historia del corazón* (1954) and *En un vasto dominio* (1962), share with earlier ones a nostalgia for the lost union between humanity and nature, a dramatic shift in focus is evident. Whereas previously Aleixandre had looked inside the individual, rejecting historical and social reality, with these volumes he reached outward, emphasizing temporal and physical connections between the self and the surrounding world and projecting a universal compassion for humanity. With the firmer grounding in earthly reality came a change in style: surreal imagery and irrationalist techniques gave way to a simpler, more direct approach in which the affirmation of love clearly predominates. Aleixandre has described his poetry as a "longing for the light"; poems in this period evidence a breakthrough from the darkness that permeates his early poetry.

Aleixandre's final period, consisting of *Poemas de la consumación* (1968) and *Diálogos del conocimiento* (1974), is characterized by a return to the structural and metaphysical complexity of his early work. The poems in these collections contain highly allusive and paradoxical symbols, metaphors, and aphorisms. In *Poemas de la consumación*, the poet views the past from the perspective of old age and mourns the passing of love. In *Diálogos del conocimiento*, he attempts to comprehend the depths and limitations of human knowledge, a process marked by emotional intensity and dark, somber brooding. Carlos Bousoño, the foremost scholar of Aleixandre's work, considers *Poemas de la consumación* and *Diálogos del conocimiento* "possibly the two most intense books of a life rich in masterpieces." Of the latter volume Bousoño states: "Aleixandre inaugurates in *Diálogos del conocimiento* a poetry of deaf and majestic slowness, spoken in the lowest chords, which I believe to be without precedent in our literature."

(See also *CLC*, Vol. 9 and *Contemporary Authors*, Vols. 85-88, Vol. 114 [obituary].)

CARL W. COBB

Along with [Frederico Garcia] Lorca and [Jorge] Guillén, Vicente Aleixandre has gradually become recognized as one of the three outstanding poets of his Generation for the original vision of the world expressed in his poetry and the distinct form of free verse in which he clothed it. As his major critic Carlos Bousoño has suggested, Aleixandre reached poetic maturity around 1930, a propitious time when the forces of irrationalism and individualism were at a peak in Spain. Building upon the metaphysical freedom which [Miguel de] Unamuno, [Antonio] Machado, and [Juan Ramón] Jiménez had achieved at great cost, Aleixandre (like Lorca) rejected the historical and social world around him and created from his elemental passions a vast domain of cosmic and telluric forces anterior to man himself. Somewhat like Whitman, the poet moved grandly in the utter freedom of his own creation, above the historical strife going on around him. In his second period, the poet does an about-face and establishes intimate communication with man in his historical reality in the manner of most of the poets after the Civil War, but he has remained metaphysically uprooted upon the planet, emphasizing human brotherhood in the manner of Antonio Machado. (pp. 119-20)

The poetry of Aleixandre falls clearly into two sharply defined periods. According to Aleixandre himself, his major theme in the first period is Creation itself, the solidarity of the elements of the cosmos. Through the impulse of primordial passion, the poet seeks to integrete himself totally with the cosmos. To achieve this unity, a kind of mystic pantheism, he must utilize the irrationalism and freedom available to him in order to es-

cape the moral, psychological, and societal bonds which enchain him. Thus, surprisingly, man in his historical reality is absent in this phase of Aleixandre's poetry; there is only the poet and his passion, an intimate and at times frightening contact with the animal, vegetable, and mineral elements of the cosmos. The climax of this period comes when the poet achieves his "amorous solidarity" with creation through dissolution or "destruction" of his own identity. Such a pursuit implies a rebellion against his own culture, but Aleixandre (like Whitman) has generally preferred to operate beyond the level of culture rather than attack it directly. In his second period, beginning around 1945 and thus coinciding with the aftermath of the Civil War, he continues his theme of "amorous solidarity," but now he centers it directly in the historical reality of his *pueblo,* his "people." (pp. 120-21)

Aleixandre's initial book, *Ambito (Ambit),* written during the years 1924-27 under the influence of Jiménez, is typical of the first efforts of his Generation. Then, around 1928, Aleixandre underwent the tremendous crisis of conscience which provided the motive force for his unique poetry. Interestingly, this crisis was generational rather than individual, for Lorca, Alberti, and (a bit later) Cernuda all suffered a comparable crisis critical for their poetry. Surely Aleixandre's crisis was triggered in part by the anxiety, frustration, and rebellion which accompanied his crippling illness in early maturity. Just at this time he discovered in the writings of Freud rich materials applicable to his own psychic state—the power of the libido, the effects of frustration, and the love-death conflict. Abandoning abruptly the artistic forms and subtle themes of *Ambit,* Aleixandre plunged into his subconscious and in rhythmic prose forms created his first "difficult book," *Pasión de la Tierra (Passion of the Earth)....*

Passion of the Earth is indeed a book of "dazzling obscurity," as Gullón has said, but the general themes as a whole form a meaningful pattern. In the general Freudian structure the poet's outpouring of libido desperately seeks the love object, which assumes multiple forms both attractive and repulsive, and the world in total rises up to thwart his impulses, so that he constantly remains threatened by a psychic death in his isolation. (p. 121)

In 1929, Aleixandre was suddenly inspired to return to poetic form—a new form to be sure, of free verse with widely varying lines, staccato phrases and strange uses of connectors and relatives—but he continues to develop many of the themes of the first book in the Freudian-surrealist manner. This new volume bears the enigmatic title *Espadas como labios (Swords like Lips).* There is a powerful phallic thrust in the juxtaposition of the sword and the mouth; the phrase combines aggressive sexuality with his insistent buccal imagery. However, the fierce sexuality expected from this title never appears in this book (it explodes in Aleixandre's next one); in fact, the poet in his longing to be is so beset by anxieties that he tends to petrify reality.

As Dámaso Alonso has truly written, the poems of *Swords like Lips* do not have "common sense," but certain key ones indicate Aleixandre's progress in freeing his libidinal and poetic impulses once and for all. (p. 122)

Prostrated by his grave illness during the year 1932, Aleixandre gradually recovered the next year and in a sustained outburst of creative energy produced his first major book, *La destrucción o et amor (Destruction or Love),* which was promptly awarded the National Prize. Undoubtedly dissatisfied with certain negative limitations of the Freudian-surrealist manner, Aleixandre merely assimilated this manner into an expanded vision which some have properly called neo-Romantic, for in his mystic pantheism the poet embraces the world itself in an all-consuming love. The new in Aleixandre is that he follows figures like Baudelaire in no longer viewing love as a fountain of life but as tragic destruction. His decision to embrace this tragic love is, as Bousoño alone has insisted, ethical, for in his modern conception there is absolutely no God, nor even an Oversoul. There is only the existential consciousness of the poet himself, fulfilling his tragic destiny through love as destruction. He utterly excludes the support and compassion of his fellow human beings, who are generally presented negatively, that is, they are dead to love. At times this love seems strangely Satanic, or suffused with hate. . . . (pp. 123-24)

After long reflection, Aleixandre himself has focused upon the theme of *Destruction or Love* and its importance in his work: "I believe that the poet's vision of the world achieves a first plenitude with this work, conceived under the central thought of the amorous unity of the universe." The poet achieves a visionary transfiguration of the world in flux, a world at times luminous, at times foreboding, whose very essence is erotic love. Excluding spirit or any form of religious salvation, Aleixandre focuses upon matter itself, in the form of the human body, and in the erotic imagery of touch, kiss, and embrace. For him, perfect love can only be achieved in destroying himself and fusing with the cosmos. Thus fleeting human love is transformed through destruction into an enduring ecstasy of a strange dark mysticism. In his ambiguous title *Destruction or Love,* therefore, the conjunction *or* means "equal to," and this conjunction becomes a stylistic device with which he constantly equates dissimilar images and symbols.

The world of *Destruction or Love* is a vast domain in which the animal, vegetable, and mineral kingdoms are pulsating with primordial forces. The typical setting is the virgin jungle or the seashore, and especially in the jungle the poet is surrounded by a variety of wild animals, of which many are terrible and destructive in their natural pursuits, some innocent and helpless. This is also a world of great natural elements, such as sea and river, mountains and plain, sky and stars. And in this universe, there is constant interaction between the poet and the specific body of the beloved and all the other forces. In this primordial erotic tension, the body is constantly being transformed into river or sea or sky or mountain, and conversely the natural elements assume human qualities in their natural attraction and destruction. (p. 124)

After the expense of passion in *Destruction or Love,* Aleixandre predictably falls into a deep depression of spirit, and during the years 1934-36 he surrendered to this depression in the creation of his most pessimistic book, *Mundo a solas (World Alone),* not published until 1950. Finally recovering from the depths but still unwilling to face the world of man in his historical reality, Aleixandre refocused his vision of the amorous solidarity of the cosmos in his next great book, *Sombra del paraíso (Shadow of Paradise),* written between 1939-43, in the desolate aftermath of the Civil War. Like Cernuda, Aleixandre returns to the Andalusian paradise of his childhood, the state of pristine innocence anterior to sin and suffering, when the light and sky of Málaga and the Mediterranean were perfection itself. Moreover, by extension this Andalusian paradise becomes a vision of the universe at the dawn of creation, before the appearance of man himself and his tragic strife. In such a world Aleixandre almost abandons the veiled aggression and threatening negativism of *Destruction or Love;* but, signifi-

cantly, in the limiting *Shadow* of his title he acknowledges that modern man cannot even envision a pure paradise. In fact, although many powerful poems reiterate his theme of cosmic solidarity, this paradise is ultimately threatened by the poet's existential loneliness, by his painful existence in time and memory. (p. 127)

These two great books *Destruction or Love* and *Shadow of Paradise* form the cornerstones of Aleixandre's poetry. In them he develops with astonishing completeness and originality his metaphysical vision of the amorous solidarity of the cosmos, a tragic vision, to be sure. In them he demonstrates a mastery of free verse unparalleled in Spanish poetry. And in them he develops a poetic technique with symbol, image, and metaphor which Bousoño has convincingly declared is original, although other poets of this Generation participated in this renovation. His development of the visionary image, which involves the imaginative free association of surrealism, and of the extended symbol are quite impressive. His creation of an original syntax involves the use of the conjunction *or* to achieve a type of simile, and the use of negatives to express a positive sense— a technique adapted from Góngora. With this achievement locked up permanently in these books, Aleixandre turns to another poetic task more typical of our times. (p. 129)

It is perhaps with a feeling of relief that the reader turns from the difficult and turbulent world of Aleixandre's first period with its cosmic and telluric dimensions to the quieter and simpler but no less moving world of his second phase. By 1945 Aleixandre has sensed the prevailing current of the times, and in Spain he in fact helps to lead the new direction. He soon discovers that (in our contemporary parlance) "poetry is communication," and his major theme becomes human solidarity, with compassion toward all human beings living in time. His first book in the new manner is *Historia del corazón (History of the Heart),* written during the years 1945-53. "History" for this generation means the direct experience of the poet and his fellow human beings, both in the past and the present; "the heart" is of course the collective heart, the joys and pains of all.

History of the Heart begins with Aleixandre's typical preoccupation with his own love, whose basic quality is now its ephemerality. (p. 130)

The poet can then in his "extended look" reach out to the world outside his own heart. He goes out to the town square, source of Spanish life, and mingles with the people enjoying the friendly sun. He visits a humble home, where the father, mother, and children are performing the simple tasks of living. He focuses upon an old man, wrinkled with age but patient and resigned, who is enjoying the light and warmth of the sun. In fact he becomes a "vagabond," by which he indicates he is always an outsider, reaching out in compassion but never quite participating, never quite living with his humanity.

As is typical in Aleixandre, *History of the Heart* ends in a form of death. As he summarizes existence, "Entre dos oscuridades, un relámpago"; that is, between the obscurity of birth and that of death life is a lightning flash. Although "we eat shadow," man in his nobility should with sadness and tenderness accept what is to come. Life is its own consolation, and consciousness somehow continues to exist.

In his last great book *En un vasto dominio (In a Vast Dominion),* written between 1958 and 1962, Aleixandre amplifies the theme of human solidarity with consistent objectivity. This "vast dominion," not the cosmos of before, is man of flesh and blood and limb in the historical and living reality which surrounds him. In structure, the book is a series of "incorporations," which begin with human matter itself, from which the human organs are developed. Moreover, each section is a "chapter," a word which suggests the novel, in which human experience is narrated. In complete maturity, Aleixandre attempts the difficult task of beginning with human matter and tracing the development of the specific organs which make man a functional being—trunk, leg, arm, hand, head, eye, ear, mouth, even the eyelashes. Then, having created this man before our eyes, the poet moves outward to the surrounding world, a Spanish world finally; and, in the manner of Unamuno perhaps, he dwells with moving compassion upon the timeless Spanish village with its white-walled cemetery, its deserted square, and its humble inhabitants. He focuses toward the past upon towns with a rich history, now struggling humbly to survive. In addition to the young mother, his most adequate symbol for the continuity of life is the couple. In a simple scene the young couple, secure for the moment in their love and laughter, are presented at their window, looking out upon the life around them. This couple through love achieves the continuity of matter, for Aleixandre the ultimate reality. . . . For Aleixandre, only matter endures, matter which is both flesh and spirit in one; matter whose most perfect form is the "dew-kissed nude" of his earlier period and the human body of the infant, the mother, the old man in his final years. (pp. 130-32)

Aleixandre's final book (or so the title suggests), published at seventy, and forty years after his initial *Ambit,* is *Poemas de la consumación* (*Poems of Consummation*). The final consummation is of course death, and for this ultimate reality the poet has gone back inside himself. For him, youth (and thus the capacity for love) is synonymous with life; therefore, the old man merely exists in an "opaque crystal," already separated from life. But, in poems of utter simplicity, he accepts this final state without tears or sighs or pleas for mercy. (p. 132)

> Carl W. Cobb, "Poets Uprooted and Rebellious: Lorca, Alberti, Aleixandre, Cernuda," in his Contemporary Spanish Poetry (1898-1963), Twayne Publishers, 1976, pp. 101-38.*

EDMUND L. KING

Lewis Hyde, who appears to have translated seventeen of the twenty poems [collected in *Twenty Poems*], says in his introduction, "My goal has been to re-create the flavor of the poems in common American speech." He and Mr. Bly have produced faithful translations. Although I find a few places where I am reasonably certain they are wrong, there is nothing that requires public denunciation. But flavor? Common American speech? Whatever may be the merits of Aleixandre's poems, they are not of the kind that have "flavor," and when a translator tells me he is going to use "common American speech," I feel that I am about to be subjected to indecent exposure. I am glad that Mr. Hyde is not as good as his word. Take the following stanza:

> Oh you, most beautiful, a surprised skin,
> a blind smoothness like an ocean moving toward its
>   center,
> a calm, a stroking bull, bull of a hundred powers,
> facing a forest, stopped at the edge with horror.

If prosiness is a flavor, then this passage has a strong flavor, the "flavor" to be found in most of Aleixandre's poetry. I don't know what common American speech is, but Americans who talk about bulls don't talk about their "surprised skins" or say any of the other things that Aleixandre says about them. Precisely because the prime characteristic of Aleixandre's poetry is its calculated prosiness, it comes off well in translation. If I wanted a subjective adjective to describe it, I would say that it is thick. Reading Aleixandre is like running through high grass. The thickness does not come, of course, only from the prosiness, which one might expect to make for smooth going, but from the use of this vehicular mode to convey a freight of images just unexpected enough to perplex without being sharply striking. The four lines quoted above illustrate the point, but, belonging to Aleixandre's early, so-called surrealist phase, they rise above the merely bumpy flatness of *Historia del Corazón*. . . . Carlos Bousoño, who has been Aleixandre's most faithful advocate and expositor, finds an evolution from a kind of gross, overwhelming naturalism to a stoic humanism in Aleixandre's poetic world. First, the stage is occupied almost entirely by non-human nature; if man is present at all, except as the speaking poet, he cowers, out of place. . . . (pp. 701-02)

Then human life, or at least human mortality, is given equal billing, but as if evolution had gone into reverse. . . .

Finally man dominates the scene, and it is nature that has to cadge a bit of poetic space. . . . (p. 702)

I find less evolution than Bousoño does but rather a moving back and forth through this gamut in most of Aleixandre's poetic ruminations, though in his old age he does weary of stolid stoicism and takes up ever so lighter a manner. . . .

Some critics have seen in the conceptual and emotional trajectory of Aleixandre's poetry an extended comment on Spanish life in the poet's time. Who is to say they are wrong? (p. 703)

> Edmund L. King, in a review of "Twenty Poems," in The Hudson Review, Vol. XXXI, No. 4, Winter, 1978-79, pp. 701-03.

DARÍO FERNÁNDEZ-MORERA

When Aleixandre's *Ambito* appeared in 1928, it was hailed by Juan Ramón Jiménez as the best book written by the young poets of Spain. This praise is significant for two reasons. First, because Jiménez, who would himself win the Nobel Prize in 1956, was the most highly regarded Spanish poet of the time; and second, because those young poets Jiménez was talking about included, besides Aleixandre, writers such as Federico García Lorca, Jorge Guillén, Pedro Salinas, Luis Cernuda, and Rafael Alberti. It was, in fact, the most splendid generation of poets Spain had known since the sixteenth and seventeenth centuries. In spite of its quality, however, Aleixandre's first book went relatively unnoticed since the attention of the literary public was elsewhere. (p. 118)

Several of his later books were to enjoy a better fate. Between 1928 and 1933, Aleixandre wrote *Pasión de la tierra, Espadas como labios,* and *La destrucción o el amor,* books that signaled a change in his poetry. Although the earlier *Ambito* testified to many of Aleixandre's future concerns, it could still be placed within traditional categories. It was written in regular meter and owed much to Hispanic post-*modernismo.* But the new books were full of oneiric passages, of striking images without logical connection. They had, in other words, many characteristics of that literature called surrealist. The surrealism of these books came largely from Aleixandre's use of surrealist images. (p. 119)

In *Pasión de la tierra, Espadas como labios,* and *La destrucción o el amor* are found other surrealist elements besides the surrealist image. Perhaps one of the most salient is Aleixandre's empathy with the earth and the most elemental forces of nature. Reacting against the anthropocentrism of Western tradition, surrealism tried to reduce man to a fragment of the world and thereby come in touch with those obscure forces that are inaccessible to the rational intellect and of which the savage and the animals seem to have an instinctive grasp. Surrealism wanted to destroy the barriers between inner man and the outer world, between the life of the unconscious and the real life. Inseparable from this ambition were sex and woman. Breton saw woman as a mediatrix between inner and outer reality. . . . It was in a sense the traditional belief that woman stands closer than man to the irrational and therefore to nature. But tradition had placed woman, because of her irrationality, on a lower plane. The surrealists, on the contrary, placed woman higher than man, precisely because of this supposed quality of hers. (p. 120)

[For] Aleixandre, as for the surrealists, woman is a mediatrix between man and the cosmos. . . . (p. 121)

Nevertheless, the differences between Aleixandre and the French surrealists are as great as the resemblances. First of all, Aleixandre never mixed the life of the unconscious with real existence. Nor did he share the radical stance towards society which characterized surrealism as a way of life. With regard to purely literary aspects, it may be noted that, like the French surrealists, Aleixandre has been obsessed with the darkest side of man and the world, but, in his case this obsession is inseparable from a desperate search for light. . . . This is not the kind of light the French surrealists expected to find as a result of the new order they thought they were creating. Instead, it is an immediate craving and is reflected in Aleixandre's writings. . . . [If] one traced the *imagination matérielle* through Aleixandre's poetry, one would find that light is never entirely absent. The search for clarity may account for other important differences. In French surrealist books of poetry, it is very difficult to find a unifying theme. Nor is it easy to categorize or rationalize the subjects, all of which hark back to the surrealist's lack of interest in any traditional artistic effort. But thematic unity and clarity of subject matter distinguish Aleixandre's books. His books are not mere collections of poems; they are organic wholes. (pp. 121-22)

Aleixandre's surrealist phase is perhaps the most publicized. During the forties and fifties, however, he developed in a different direction. Now he looked for a less subjective, more accessible poetry. He was reacting both against the symbolist tradition of private poetry and against irrationalism. As he put it, he wanted to communicate more easily with his fellow men. . . . His search began with the mythic expression of man's feeling of loss in the book *Sombra del paraíso* (1939-1943), and reached its highest point in *Historia del corazón* (1945-1953) and *En un vasto dominio* (1958-1962). . . . Expectedly, this new phase of Aleixandre's work reflects the different conditions of the times.

The threat and eventual onset of the Spanish Civil War ended an epoch and started another. Before, poets had lived in an atmosphere of continuity, of relative intellectual security; therefore they could be concerned with their own psyches rather than with the world they lived in. They had their opinions, of course, but technical innovations interested them more than

any moral or political implication in their work. . . . But the growing turmoil made this attitude no longer feasible. Spain became a place where not only one's life but one's whole scheme of values was menaced. In such circumstances, detachment was very difficult. For some writers, literature even became overtly political, because anything else would have entailed mental dishonesty. (pp. 124-25)

Aleixandre's *Sombra del paraíso,* begun in 1939 and finished in 1943, is closer to his earlier work; according to the author, it occupies a pivotal position between his "surrealist" period and his later writings. This book contains some of Aleixandre's most seductive images, and attempts a description of the world before and after the loss of Paradise. But Aleixandre utilizes the topic for its poetic value, not for its religious implications. . . .

[If] the "Fall" may function as a symbol of the loss of personal happiness, it may also function as a metaphor for the national circumstances. . . . (p. 126)

Aleixandre's next major book, *Historia del corazón* (1945-1953), continued to move in the direction of what may be called "communal" poetry. Originating in a conflict of personal love, *Historia del corazón* soon grew into a book about suffering man. The first set of poems, "Como el vilano," begins with the furtive happiness of uncertain love, and ends with the sadness of abandonment. This personal drama, however, is overcome in the section "La mirada extendida," where the narrator transfers to humanity his love for a woman. . . . The group of poems "La realidad" returns to the lover's illusions. Finally, the section "La mirada infantil" examines the happy visions of childhood and prepares the meditative group of poems "Los términos," the book concluding with a mixture of personal and universal love.

Although an unsympathetic reader, with some justification, might complain of discursiveness and sentimentality, *Historia del corazón* does not nurture the emotions much more than other books of Aleixandre. . . . (p. 127)

En un vasto dominio (1958-1962) completes Aleixandre's movement from a preoccupation with his self to a communal statement. Significantly, one finds no "love" poems in the book. Sentences are short, images come easily, and a will to communicate informs the whole. . . .

But the most endearing aspect of *En un vasto dominio* is the sympathetic description of scenes and types from Spanish daily life, as in **"Félix,"** and of parts of the human body, as in **"La mano."** . . . (p. 128)

[In 1968 Aleixandre] published his *Poemas de la consumación.* The book consists of fifty poems, most of them short, in which Aleixandre, now seventy years old, contemplates life from the perspective of his old age. Yet one may discern a continuity between *Poemas de la consumación* and earlier texts. The starkness of the verse reminds us of *En un vasto dominio,* whereas its relative subjectivism harks back to Aleixandre's poems of the thirties. On the other hand, the gnomic style recalls the later Antonio Machado, and, through him, the medieval poetry of Sem Tob de Carrión. (p. 132)

As in *Xenia,* written when Eugenio Montale also was seventy years old, in *Poemas de la consumación* the past acquires a significance that overshadows the present. But in Aleixandre's *Poemas,* the personal past is not merely recollected and expressed as directly as possible; rather, the memory of the past functions as a point of departure for universal reflections—and these reflections are very sombre. (p. 133)

It is evident that a painful doubt invaded Aleixandre at this point in life. Poetry for Aleixandre had meant a search for light even in the midst of darkness, but this search had meant also a search for knowledge. Now it appeared to him that the possession of knowledge led merely to death. This realization opened a new stage in his poetry. His lyricism took an epistemological turn. It became a search for knowledge of the nature of knowledge itself. The result was the *Diálogos del conocimiento,* published in 1974.

The *Diálogos del conocimiento* consist of fifteen poems with a common structure. From opposite, yet complementary positions, two, or occasionally three, characters speak, but seemingly without listening to each other. The dialogs, therefore, are really dual monologs which become dialogs in the mind of the reader. The characters range from literary figures, like Lazarillo de Tormes or Swann, to figures representing an epoch, like an inquisitor or a dandy, and in them one recognizes the technique of poetic *personae:* though multiple, they are all projections of a single intelligence. But the dialogic structure imparts to the book a quality not found in the verses of a "Hugh Selwyn Mauberley," a "Juan de Mairena," or an "Alvaro de Campos." For Aleixandre's avowed purpose in the *Diálogos del conocimiento* is to present, almost simultaneously, the often contradictory, yet equally valid perspectives from which mankind perceives a given reality. (p. 134)

The title of the book makes plain that the central theme of the *Diálogos del conocimiento* is the problem of knowledge: . . . the dynamics of the work come from the tension between rationalism and sensationalism, between life of the mind and life of the body, between thought and reality. With such theme, and with such dynamics, a reader might fear a boring series of abstractions, but Aleixandre avoids this danger. He draws on culture and literary history, and always on those resources of free association that he had learned in his "surrealist period." Thus he creates a further source of tension from the play between abstract ideas and actual characters, between rational conceptions and irrational imagery, between the historically grounded Aleixandre of his social period and the highly subjective poet of Spanish surrealism. The *Diálogos del conocimiento* therefore become a synthesis of his youth revealed in books like *La destrucción o el amor,* of his later years revealed in books like *Historia del corazón,* and of his old age in a book like *Poemas de la consumación.* (p. 136)

Despite the variety of his writings, they have a unity stemming from the will to overcome all barriers between the I and the cosmos, between the I and humanity, and, finally, between the I and knowledge. Moreover, almost all of his books, from *Ámbito* on, illuminate his total work, which, in turn, illuminates each individual book. Indeed, Aleixandre's poetry has a kind of Dantesque quality, not only in its massiveness or in the frequent asperity of its verse, but in the long search for light in the midst of darkness, or of knowledge in the midst of despair. It is in this sense that Aleixandre is an ethical poet. It seems fitting, then, that in his last published book, Aleixandre's belief in the dynamic nature of the act of knowledge is embodied in a literary form dialectic by definition, namely the dialog, and that, by choosing this form, he places himself in one of the most ethical of literary traditions. (pp. 136-37)

Darío Fernández-Morera, "Vicente Aleixandre in the Context of Modern Poetry," in Symposium, Vol. XXXIII, No. 2, Summer, 1979, pp. 118-41.

JASCHA KESSLER

In 1977, the Nobel Prize for Literature was awarded to Vicente Aleixandre, a poet hardly known outside the Spanish language. There had been some scattered translations, some chapbooks from small presses: but for an overview of this poet's life work by which we could have come to some sense of his meaning, we have had to wait for this new anthology, entitled, *A Longing for the Light: Selected Poems of Vicente Aleixandre.* . . .

Aleixandre writes a limpid, a clear and direct Spanish, with a speaking voice that avoids the exotic, the symbolical, the precious and abstruse. Instead he thinks in a solid way about the world he looks at, and he presents always immediately a world that he has long contemplated, in its details and its vast panoramas. . . .

He shows himself as a tenderly erotic, passionate and brooding poet. . . .

Aleixandre is also a deeply pessimistic poet, and a prophet of human existence, and human destiny. The profound pessimism can be heard in such lines as these opening ones from **"Destino de la carne,"** or **"The Fate of Flesh,"**

> No, there's none of that. I don't see
> any heaven on the far side of the horizon.
> I can't see any calm, powerful eyes
> to still the thrashing waters we hear howling here
> I don't see the waterfall of lights that goes
> from a mouth to a breast, descending, to some bland
> and bounded hands that enclose this world, hoarding it.

What is there for Aleixandre, then? For him we live in an eternal present: his prophecy reveals the past and the present as a single timeless moment of existence. At each stage of his career, as this book suggests, his passionate and penetrating imagination enters into the life of things, of creatures, and lastly of humankind with an intense urgency, and yet a detachment. . . .

[Aleixandre's] prophetic rebellion, his vision of the present *and* of the past, was forged from the outset from the great intellectual legacy of the 19th century that in its science and history provided us with the hope of freedom from the narrow obscurantism of Spanish Catholic life. The greatest influence on him has in fact been that of the Humanism of Sigmund Freud, which he himself declares to us. His poetry can be seen as carried forward on the immense wave of the honesty of mind of men such as Darwin and Freud. And that is a legacy of stoic pessimism, not sentimental optimism. Aleixandre is tragic and brilliant at once: in love with life as it is lived in the light of our brief days—with the earth, the air, and, when *seen rightly,* the fundamental simplicity of our human existence, before and after what he calls "the distilled essences . . . of our intricate civilization."

In this varied and adequate selection, well titled *A Longing for the Light,* we come to know Aleixandre's spirit through his vision and his powerful response to what he looks at and contemplates. Thus we come to know something about what it means to be elementally human: as a species of animal being in which even that mysterious thing called the soul is wholly a natural phenomenon. There are many fine and exalting poems in this book, which will bear much rereading.

Jascha Kessler, "Vicente Aleixandre: 'A Longing for the Light: Selected Poems'," in a radio broadcast on KUSC-FM—Los Angeles, CA, August 22, 1979.

HELENE J. F. de AGUILAR

"If you have a problem and you want to hear it described in cosmic terms," said a friend of mine, discussing his family, "you go to my father. If you have a problem and you want to know what to *do* about it, you go to my mother." In certain moods I envision two long queues of Spanish poets assembling behind my friend's parents, one decked out in the pageantry of the Cosmos; the other more simply arrayed in quotidian *tsuris*. Vicente Aleixandre . . . marches in the paternal column. *Ambito, Pasión de la tierra, La destrucción o el amor, Mundo a solas, Sombra del paraíso:* the titles of his major works read like banners for themes planetary and transcendent. (p. 65)

I admit to a preference for poetry which [leads] . . . towards its core. A poetry of process, where the words literally and figuratively *work,* seems to me qualitatively better than the more "vision"-dependent feints at the Infinite, the endless suggestiveness of cosmic yearning. Aleixandre has written much exquisite poetry of this leaner, more pointed variety. One of my few, and mild, objections to Hyde's *Twenty Poems* is the disproportionate incidence of those devoted to the Spaniard's quest for the compelling but unreachable Beyond: . . .

> I know all this has a name: to be given life.
> Love isn't a bomb bursting, though at the same time
>   that's really what it is.
> It's like an explosion that lasts a whole lifetime.
> It comes out of that breakage they call knowing your-
>
>   self, and then it opens wider and wider,
> colored like a quick cloud of sunlight that rolls through
>
>   time. . . .
>
> ("The Explosion")

This area of Aleixandre's love poetry, and physical love is central to his work, is *exhausting.* Full of happenings, it remains fundamentally static. Every force from which it derives impetus operates outside the poet's domain, beyond his body—indeed, beyond his ken. While I always respect Aleixandre's genius, I sometimes think him not sufficiently responsible as an artist for his own effects. This loss of control may be a predictable outcome of his intense concern for things with capital letters: the Meaning of Life, Man's Isolation, the Purpose of the Physical World. All art is of course engaged at some level with these themes. But a poetry so overtly and deliberately consecrated to them, almost thrust into the field against them, is limited from the outset to paraphrase and a curiously immovable attitude of wonder or brooding. (pp. 66-7)

The place of man in the universe is Aleixandre's constant preoccupation. Already a problematic approach in philosophy, it renders subtlety practically out of the question for a poet. When Aleixandre reduces his scope and addresses his attention to an individual, a particular destiny, or a single incident, poems of a sweeping beauty emerge from his "vision." Paradoxically, the narrower focus produces a much broader, a more metaphysical impact. This occurs increasingly in his later work, from 1953 to the present. "**The Old Man and the Sun,**" "**The Man on His Death Bed,**" and "**The Comet,**" explicitly constrained in subject matter, are wonderful because, by relieving poet and reader of the hopeless and incapacitating weight of the Ineffable, they allow the words themselves to live, to illumine. We find in these poems a discernible progression from the simple and immediate, via a logical momentum, to the mysterious and transcendent. They acquire in their final lines the very *estremecimiento*—the pang of wonder—for which

Aleixandre so self-consciously struggles, to much less effect, elsewhere. (p. 67)

Helene J. F. de Aguilar, "Clouds of Unknowing and Healthier Climates," in Parnassus: Poetry in Review, *Vol. 8, No. 1, Fall-Winter, 1979, pp. 64-83.**

KESSEL SCHWARTZ

Much of the early poetry of Vicente Aleixandre reveals his view of nature and the world through subjective connotations which relate to a number of conflicts, anxieties, and unconscious fantasies. The poet clarifies some of this poetry, rooted in his unconscious depths, by combining creative and destructive impulses in the apparently ambivalent equation that love equals death. In spite of juxtaposing these and other dissimilarities, Aleixandre, through his very disorientation, which simulates the psychic processes themselves, and by indulging in a kind of free association, transmutes into artistic and understandable form a variety of thinly disguised wishes.

The sea, probably the most prevalent symbol of his poetry, stresses one important aspect of that subconscious process. Undoubtedly, during Aleixandre's youth, Málaga impressed the sea on his consciousness. Water (along with the sea and ocean) in dreams has the symbolic meaning of mother, and, in association with youthful innocence, happiness, and the breast, it is constantly used with this meaning in Aleixandre's poetry. Unconscious forces rather than surrealistic experimentation account for the recurring breast motif and accompanying fantasies. . . . In this subconscious recall Aleixandre constantly juxtaposes the sea with the beach, moon, teeth, tongue, throat, and breast. In many of his poems he seems to use the sea as a surface on which to project his images in a manner analogous to the "dream screen."

According to Isakower, a person falling asleep who sees dark masses approach and is unable to ascertain the division between his body and the masses, reproduces a little baby's sensations of falling asleep at the breast. This phenomenon is also associated with well-known hypnagogic manifestation of an auditory and tactile nature, involving mouth sensations and especially bodilessness, floating, and sinking. The drowser feels small in the presence of something large or heavy and may vaguely perceive something indefinite or shadowy and of vast size. Bertram D. Lewin, complementing this concept, postulates a dream screen as "the surface on to which a dream appears to be projected. It is the blank background, present in the dream, though not necessarily seen, and the visually perceived action in ordinary manifest dream content takes place on it or before it." The representation of the mother's breast during nursing (the dream screen) may involve various solid or convex shapes or fluid objects which serve as screen equivalents and the imaginary fulfillment of a wish to sleep and a breast to sleep at. Later events and situations are projected onto the original blankness (an image of the breast during the infant's sleep) as if it were a cinematic screen. In other words the "dream screen has the metapsychological structure of a dream, forming the background or projection drop for the dream picture."

These phenomena are often accompanied by loss of ego boundaries, visions of white clouds, receding waves, vaporous mists, roses or pinkish color (the aureole of the breast), white and blue contrasts (the breast and the veins), and the constant implication of thirst related at the same time to concepts of dry, sandy desert wastes. A casual examination of Aleixandre's poetry reveals the presence of the above elements to an intrusive degree. In *Ambit,* his earliest collection, these symbols of blue and white interspersed with the idea of dust, mouth and dream, limitless forms, and especially the moon (a standard mother symbol of regeneration), which through its curved surface is homologous to a dream screen, are constant. The breast symbolism, mouth sensation, and ecstatic states often seem to relate to the withdrawn aspects and dry-thirst-tongue and mouth sensations.

More clearly, in the extra-rational *Passion of the Earth* Aleixandre combines his need for loving and being loved with breast fantasies in the prose poems **"Love Is not Relief," "Death or the Waiting Room,"** and **"Being of Hope and Rain,"** which contains symbols of breast, teeth, new born child, lips, dryness, tongue, and food bag, together with a floating curtain like a sheet of rain and a concave mirror. **"Life"** shows us a moon-colored mermaid, her breast like a mouth: "she took out her wounded breast, split in two like a mouth, and she tried to kiss me on the dead shadow . . . She didn't have another breast." The poet rejects his death, related to that of the mermaid who gasps for breath on the surface of the sea. (pp. 39-41)

[In **"Yearning for the Day,"** as the poet] fuses with the ocean he views the potential threat of "the throats of the wet sirens," and, merging with the larger whole, finds "my hand is a shore. My leg another." The most striking aspect of what Isakower observed involves the blurring of the distinction between different regions of the body, between what is internal and external, and the amorphous character of the impressions conveyed by the sense organs. . . . Aleixandre misses a finger of his hand and is threatened by an earless monster who carries "instead of his word a short scissor, just right for cutting the open explanation . . ." The defenseless poet delivers himself up to the powerful, threatening shears, possibly the manifest element of a dream which frightens the child (a typical awakener is the father's phallus), a true disturber which relates to repressed impulses which may break through as projections. Intruding preconscious or unconscious wishes that threaten to wake the sleeper form visual content and project the sleeper's ego onto the screen. The representation of the body or its parts in the visual content of the dream means that the part is awake and an intruder and disturber of sleep and pure fulfillment. In this poem, the poet indulges in a kind of autocannibalism: "I weep the whole head. It rolls through my breast and I laugh with my fingernails, with the two feet that are fanning me . . ." Sinking and smothering sensations, or the loss of consciousness, are also found in fantasies of oral incorporation. A baby treats the breast as it does its own fingers, which it stuffs into its mouth, indulging in the identical autocannibalism of this poem. This type of anxiety is related to childhood fantasies about the prenatal state, an aspect of which is the child's imagining it entered into the mother by being swallowed. Paradoxically, sleep which brings pleasure also involves the anxiety of being eaten and dying. The young baby projects its self-aggression onto the breast, which it then fears as destructive. The poet is both buoyed up and supported by the waves and yet is threatened, a typical reaction of anxiety dreams about merging with a larger whole and perishing as an individual.

In **"Soul under Water"** the image of sinking and yet being supported by the immense sea continues: "If waves ascend, if you are soaked with all the sad melancholies that were flying avoiding your touch with their fine hollow wood, they will stop right in the throat, decapitating you with light, leaving your head like the flower. . . ." The room in which he finds himself moves on the fearful waves, and the poet is borne up: "An enormous extended sea holds me in the palm of its hand asks me for respect." The wish to sleep seems opposed by other wishes which have escaped the ego's censorship and become conscious, a symbolism reaffirmed by **"Love Suffered,"** the last poem of this collection.

In *Destruction or Love,* **"The Jungle and the Sea"** shows us the human ego overwhelmed by elemental forces, repeating the anxious transmutation of the original pleasure of falling asleep, not only the active eating process, but (through the fierce animal attacks with swords and teeth) the passive idea of being eaten, also a part of the nursing situation. The fierce attacks and his need to punish the rejecting virgin forest . . . seem to involve a fear of a father and, in the fusion through primitive life with animals, may be a kind of rationalization of the wish (being eaten) "to get back again into the mother's animal womb." Similar themes occur in **"After Death,"** complete with threatening tongues, a furious foam, and a sea which "robs breasts"; **"Symphonic Night,"** with tongue, "sweet taste," and "breasts . . . harpshaped"; and **"Total Love,"** with a sea fusion, young teeth, feeding, and breast imagery. (pp. 41-2)

Shadow of Paradise returns to an innocent world of infancy, to a Paradise beyond original sin and knowledge. One aspect of the invisible and formless but directly apprehended breast involves nebulous and ill-defined perceptions, ineffable experiences, and memories of a lost Paradise of contentment which compel a nostalgic return and attraction to infancy. Having only a momentary recall of Paradise, whose substance he has lost, the poet nonetheless evokes the sea and moon, a cosmic fusion of self with the material of the world, and hidden beauty at the fount of life where naked creatures drank. The poet submerges himself in the womb of mother earth, in his Paradise where "The tongues of innocence / did not say words" and which is replete with breasts, "breasts of water," "white teeth," and the sea, moon, tongues, and throats. Man's tragedy is that to be born is to be cast out of Paradise, the mother's body where everything is given. (p. 44)

Aleixandre's symbols often appear incomprehensible to the reader, whose sensibilities, nonetheless, quicken to empathize with those of the poet, inspired by the same enigmas which beset us all, as he seeks to recapture an unconscious knowledge and create a unity of perception. (p. 46)

> *Kessel Schwartz, "The Isakower Phenomenon and the Dream Screen," in* Critical Views on Vicente Aleixandre's Poetry, *edited by Vicente Cabrera and Harriet Boyer, Society of Spanish and Spanish-American Studies, 1979, pp. 39-46.*

DIANA Der HOVANESSIAN

[Some of the early poetry in *A Longing for the Light: Selected Poems of Vicente Aleixandre*] might tax a reader with its mysticism and disjointed style. But Aleixandre's poetry loses much of the disconnectedness in later years, and begins to address people directly—real people, and people of the past. Gone are the terrible black mountains at the bottom of the sea. Instead, we find the sunlit streets and classrooms of his childhood. Suddenly—light. . . .

More and more he sees the world "exhaling a vegetable joy." **"On the Way To School,"** a poem about bicycling, ends with the boy-he-was folding his wings at the school door.

There also are Dickinson-like flashes: "Kill me sun, with your impartial blade." Wordsworthian messages: "inside the small boy is the man he will become." And fire everywhere: "I am the horse who sets fire to his mane."

Pedro Salinas said, "Vicente, delicate and apart, has discovered that love plus desperation equals poetry, deep, strangely moving poetry." To which we add, "poetry filled with light."

> *Diana Der Hovanessian, "Vicente Aleixandre Lights the Way," in* The Christian Science Monitor, *January 2, 1980, p. 17.*

JOHN SIMON

Aleixandre's work falls, almost too conveniently, into those three phases schoolboys love: early, middle, and late. The early, emerging from a brief dalliance with traditional formalism and *poésie pure*, soon takes the shape of free verse and prose poems redolent of surrealism, the lava of the unconscious gushing forth partly also under the influence of Freud, whom the poet was reading at the time. Aleixandre called this "poetry as it is born, with a minimum of elaboration," admitting the prose poems to be, of all his works, the hardest to read. I find both the prose poems and the *vers libre* of this period unimpressive—too private, nightmare-ridden, undisciplined—which goes, I am afraid, also for three later volumes, up to and including *Mundo a solas* (1936). . . . Aleixandre's early strategy [is one] of evasion, of describing things that are not rather than things that are. "Now the sun isn't horrendous like a cheek that's ready: / it isn't a piece of clothing or a speechless flashlight. / Nor is it the answer heard by our knees, / nor the task of touching the frontiers with the whitest part of our eyes," we read in **"With All Due Respect,"** and I respectfully submit: "Don't tell me what it isn't—tell me what it is!" . . . The sun, we learn forthwith, "has already become truth, lucidity, stability," which isn't much help either in fixing it in our consciousness.

When it is not outright negation, the game is the tenuous equivocation of either-or. A poem in *The World by Itself* is entitled **"Guitar or Moon,"** and an entire collection of 1935 is named *Destruction or Love. Or,* even more than *not* and *nor,* is Aleixandre's poetic prop. "In front of me, the dolphins or the sword . . ." "Like that final longing to kiss the shore goodbye, / or the painful footprint of a hermit or a footstep gone astray . . ." "Bull made of moon or honey . . ." "A horn or a sumptuous sky . . ." "An upward impulse wants to be moon, / or calm, or warmth, or that poison of a pillow in the muffled mouth . . ." These fragments represent only the most flagrant *or's* from four poems from *Swords Like Lips* printed consecutively in *A Longing for the Light.* It is, throughout the earlier works, a pitiless proliferation that contributes to their haziness.

With the collections *Shadow of Paradise* (1939-43) and, especially, *Heart's Story (Historia del corazón)* of 1945-53, the middle period gets under way and things look up. These are mostly reminiscences of the poet's childhood in Málaga and love poems; in them, Aleixandre achieves a blend of verdant innocence and lush description of nature, as well as perceptions of love expressed with a very personal *conceptismo*—perhaps a synthesis of Rubén Darío's wildness and Machado's restraint. The rhythms are meticulously balanced, and the long-breathed verses often lengthen out still farther at the end of the free-flowing strophes. (pp. 41-2)

The poems in *Historia del corazón* are mostly successful, the vestiges of surrealism discreetly heightening the intensely individual, sensuous perceptions. Especially notable are **"The Old Man and the Sun," "Her Hand Given Over,"** and **"We Feed on Shadow."** (pp. 42-3)

But in Aleixandre's last phase, things go wrong again. In poems like **"If Someone Could Have Told Me"** (from *Poemas de la consumación,* 1965-6), surrealism returns with a ravening vengeance; moreover, a fuzzy mysticism and populism set in. There are still fine passages, as in poems like **"Whom I Write for"**. . . and **"To My Dog,"** containing such a lovely line as "Residido en tu luz, immóvil en tu seguridad, no podiste más que entenderme," which in the original has that pithy lyricism, that one talent of Aleixandre's which . . . is death to Hyde. This should become something like "Dwelling in your light, motionless in your assurance, you could do no more than hear me." Yet Hyde renders it as "You live in your light, your security does not change, the best / you could do for me was understand." . . .

As Nobel laureates go, however, Aleixandre is a rather good one. (p. 43)

> *John Simon, "'Traduttore, Traditore'; or, The Tradition of Traducing," in* Poetry, *Vol. CXXXVI, No. 1, April, 1980, pp. 40-58.**

CARLOS BOUSOÑO

[*The essay from which this excerpt is taken originally appeared in Spanish in a slightly different form in* Insula, *January-February 1978.*]

I would like to consider briefly a theme that merits . . . development: that of the techniques of expression used by Aleixandre in his irrationalist periods. It is known that he has experienced two moments of poetic irrationality. The first is represented by all of his surrealist books: *Pasión de la tierra, Espadas como labios, La destrucción o el amor,* and *Mundo a solas;* the second consists of his last two books: *Poemas de la consumación* and *Diálogos del conocimiento.* Now more than 70 years old, Aleixandre surprisingly has renewed himself one more time and written, in the vein that I have mentioned, what are possibly the two most intense books of a life rich in masterpieces. (p. 258)

Beginning with the *techniques* of Surrealism, we first find the enormous paradox that, while there is an abundance of bibliography on the literary movement in question, no one has yet confronted such an essential aspect of it. The books I am familiar with concerning Surrealism are interesting, especially with regard to the world view sustained by its practitioners. However, they never really refer to the techniques of Surrealism: allusions to "automatic writing," as Breton described it, are quite meaningless today. Automatic writing, by definition, is characteristic of all irrationalism or symbolism preceding Surrealism, from Baudelaire to the symbolists (the French symbolists and the Spaniards Antonio Machado and Juan Ramón Jiménez), including Verlaine, Rimbaud, and Mallarmé. The surrealists, in this sense, did not contribute anything, except quantitatively, to what the above-mentioned authors had already done. But is there anything radically new in the surrealist expressive means?

So that what I have said is completely clear from a technical point of view, surrealism is only an act of symbolizing. A surrealist page is a page full of symbols. But what is a symbol? Here there is also an abundance of bibliography, again limited and unsatisfactory. A definition of 'symbol' that would better fit the facts is to say that a symbol exists whenever an expression gives us a deficient emotion, quantitatively or qualitatively, with respect to its logical meaning. Such "deficiency" occurs when the emotion does not come from what the poet says but precisely from what is *not* said: that is, from what is said without the reader realizing it. It comes from the reader's unconscious association, provoked by the context, between the poetic statement and another very different statement which is the one truly responsible for the emotion just experienced. A symbol exists when the poet says A and the reader associates it *preconsciously* with B, and B with C, so that when faced with A one feels not the emotion of A but instead that of C. This is precisely the deficiency to which I am referring. (pp. 258-59)

The elements used as symbols are *possible* elements in reality (for example, the verse "Los caballos negros son," by Lorca), as well as impossible elements in it (for example, to say of an Andalusian *cantaor* "your voice had black sounds"; there are no "black sounds" in the world). The first kind of symbolism can be called a "symbolism of reality," while the second is a "symbolism of unreality" or "unreal symbolism." In any case, the emotion experienced is due to an associative proliferation such as the one just described; "black horses" or "black sounds" are identified with "night," and from there one passes on to other terms. . . . (pp. 259-60)

Perhaps, then, Surrealism is the accumulation of symbols in a text. But is this in itself revolutionary and new? Machado's poetry and that of Juan Ramón, . . . and also the poetry of the so-called French symbolists, and earlier that of Verlaine, always involved symbolization. Perhaps a distinction should be that the earlier symbolism was fundamentally a symbolism of reality. . . . On the other hand, the symbols used by Surrealism were mostly symbols of *unreality*. . . . This separation brings us nearer to the truth, but only slightly, because unreal symbols also existed before Surrealism: in Baudelaire ("La mort des amants," "Les Phares") and Rimbaud, at times in Machado and Juan Ramón, and later, much more in the Lorca of the *Canciones*, that is, the Lorca who was not yet a surrealist. Resorting to the quantitative, Surrealism is not merely the use but rather the *substantial* use of unreal expressions of a symbolic nature; prior to that school such symbolic unrealities were seldom used. Thus we have a possible formula, though a very imprecise one, because the road to knowing what the techniques of Surrealism are has been poorly chosen. It is never merely a question of quantity; most importantly, it also involves something qualitatively different. Surrealism appears as a revolution not because it uses symbols, nor because it uses *a lot* of unreal symbols, but because of the special contextual and emotional nature of these. (p. 260)

What specifically sets Surrealism apart is the emotional disconnection duplicated by the logical disconnection between two terms A and E, but only when *at the same time* the identifying relationship that always exists preconsciously between them does not become conscious. In non-surrealist symbolism there is frequently an emotional disconnection and even more frequently a logical disconnection; there is also the case where both are combined. But what never occurs is this double logical and emotional disconnection affecting the same two consec-utive sequences that have remained *identified* in the poet's preconsciousness, and which the reader does not understand clearly. Thus we have a simple formula that can describe the technique in all its variants, no matter how numerous they may be. Given the poet's formulation of two statements A and E, which in his preconsciousness are A = E, we have a surrealist text, provided that the following three conditions are fulfilled simultaneously: (1) that the identifying nexus (the = sign) between A and E not be conscious; (2) that terms A and E be logically disconnected for the reader, and (3) that besides the logical disconnection there exist also an emotional one. *Each* of these three conditions has existed before Surrealism, *but never the three of them together*. Surrealism, then, is not a series of qualities but a solidary "package" of all of them.

It is time to apply all this to [an example taken from Aleixandre's *Pasión de la tierra*, **"El amor no es relieve"**]. Between phrase A ("en tu cintura no hay nada más que mi tacto quieto") and phrase E ("se te saldrá el corazón por la boca") *there is no* identity established by the poet at a comprehensible level; rather it is a case of a mere juxtaposition of elements. On the other hand there is a logical disconnection between both expressions. One thing is the full eroticism achieved by the first phrase (A), and another very different thing is the mortal agony expressed in the second phrase (E). There is a discrepancy, even to the point of being opposite from the logical and emotional perspectives. The initial sentence (A) has a positive and vital emotion which is inherent to eroticism; the final sentence (E), on the other hand, has a negative emotion of death or agony. This is precisely Aleixandre's surrealist technique. The scheme is repeated incessantly with variations that are important but not essential. There is a double disconnection, and the equalizing nexus between A and E is preconscious. (pp. 260-62)

In closing, let us go on to the study of the irrationalist technique of the poet's last two books [*Poemas de la consumación* and *Diálogos del conocimiento*]. Of what does it consist? The surrealist "package" of the three conditions previously stipulated does not apply here. There is no Surrealism as described earlier. There is, of course, a trace of symbolism—symbols of a most marked irrationality, symbols of unreality, symbols which, besides, can be accumulated (as in the poem **"Fondo con figuras"**). But the use of such techniques is a habit prior to Surrealism and can even be found in Machado (poem XXVIII, for example). What calls our attention now is the incessant use of illogic. What is irrational or symbolic is not the same as what is illogical. The difference is clear: something symbolic or irrational has a hidden meaning from which we only *consciously* receive a pure emotion, while what we are now calling illogic, though it breaks with the schemes of discursive denotation, suggests indirectly or by connotation a *conscious* meaning. Consciousness, then, versus unconsciousness. In symbolism one receives the emotional impact *without understanding why*, while in illogic there is lucidity, a mental presence of the meaning that is not stated but that *is* suggested.

The numerous and apparent contradictions to be found in both of these books belong to this genre of illogical expressions, contradictions that in each case the reader's mind can resolve because they appear to the awake mind to be vaguely and connotatively lucid. . . . (pp. 268-69)

[Sententious] or apothegmatic expressions are to be found occasionally in *Poemas de la consumación* but especially and most intensely in *Diálogos del conocimiento*. Though there is always a connotative meaning, it is not necessary to delve into it deeply. These are poems that allow for a more patchy reading in which the meaning is somewhat indeterminate, *as though in parentheses*. What matters is the emotion of great and penetrating knowledge, both sibylline and mysterious, imposed on us at the first level. Here there is an irrationalism not only very different from that of the Surrealism we have described but also very different from the earlier symbolic irrationalism, since in these verses, according to the type of reading I have given, the meaning is hidden from us also. And precisely because of this we feel that emotion of profoundly dark and inscrutable knowledge.

One is faced with something that somehow has no antecedents. Aleixandre's originality is radical and opposed to all symbolic tradition. And because the process is so virginal and different, the tone of the voice is also unheard-of. Aleixandre inaugurates in *Diálogos del conocimiento* a poetry of deaf and majestic slowness, spoken in the lowest chords, which I believe to be without precedent in our literature. This feeling of vast and obscure majesty at such a slow pace is quite simply a new feeling. All this achieved at the age of 76. Aleixandre's incessant creative capacity is truly amazing, even now in his glorious and fresh old age.

I now conclude, lamenting only that I was not able to spend more time on the great poet and his works. I have had to choose what is essential: his capacity for invention and change, which can be seen most clearly when dealing with the renovation of something as worn-out as the irrationalist tradition of symbolism. (p. 269)

> *Carlos Bousoño, "The Irrationalist Techniques of Vicente Aleixandre," in* Vicente Aleixandre: A Critical Appraisal, *edited by Santiago Daydí-Tolson, Bilingual Press/Editorial Bilingüe, 1981, pp. 258-70.*

JOSEPH PARISI

[Aleixandre] has employed a variety of styles, from the surrealistic to the starkly simple, but is most noted for his highly elaborate (not to say excessively) rhetorical confections in the colorful and convoluted manner of his Baroque master Góngora. Perhaps it is this phase of high artifice that has put outsiders off. Another explanation may be that his verses don't travel well. In any case, the present volume [*A Bird of Paper: Poems of Vicente Aleixandre*], drawn from all nine of Aleixandre's collections, demonstrates all his qualities to disadvantage. The subject matter of the poems is common enough—love, life, longing, the usual topics—but the translations seem merely adequate, which may be a disservice to the music one presumes compensates for mediocre thought in the originals.

> *Joseph Parisi, in a review of "A Bird of Paper: Poems of Vicente Aleixandre," in* Booklist, *Vol. 79, No. 8, December 15, 1982, p. 550.*

CHOICE

Many of the poems [in *A Bird of Paper*] will be new to English readers, since they do not appear in the short *Twenty Poems* . . . or in *A Longing for the Light: Selected Poems of Vicente Aleixandre* . . . , the largest collection of the Spanish poet's work to reach an American audience. *A Bird of Paper* captures the essential concerns of Aleixandre's oeuvre from the early surrealist imagery through the clarity and accompanying wisdom of the later poems. Underlying all his work is the belief that one must suffer, given the nature of things, and that one must struggle against suffering at the same time.

> *A review of "A Bird of Paper: Poems," in* Choice, *Vol. 20, No. 6, February, 1983, p. 836.*

J(ames) G(raham) Ballard

1930-

English short story writer, novelist, dramatist, and scriptwriter.

A leading author of catastrophic science fiction, Ballard focuses upon the physical and mental disintegration of characters facing devolution or environmental destruction. Ballard frequently inverts traditional Western assumptions, among them belief in human adaptability, to explore alternate modes of reasoning. Entropy and extinction are logical and inevitable in his work, and psychological delusion often afflicts his characters. Only through acceptance of the inexorable demise of the cosmos are his characters able to accept their limitations and attain freedom of mind.

As a boy during World War II, Ballard was interned in a Japanese prisoner of war camp for civilians near his birthplace of Shanghai, China. He later studied medicine at Cambridge University before becoming a regular contributor to *New Worlds* magazine. Due to the psychological content of his work, Ballard became associated with the "New Wave" movement in science fiction. Though his first novels were poorly received, Ballard gradually gained a reputation for intellectual complexity and psychological credibility in his fiction. Most critics agree that he is at his best in the short story form.

Writing in a visually detailed, ironic style influenced by surrealist painters and early pop artists, Ballard specializes in creating landscapes which are symbolic of his characters' psychological state. Such stories as "Concentration City" (1957) and "Billenium" (1961) deal with worlds so overcrowded that the concepts of space, privacy, and flight are inconceivable. During the 1960s Ballard wrote three novels depicting ecological cataclysm. In *The Drowned World* (1962), solar storms cause the earth's waters to slowly engulf the land, transforming it into swampland as humanity devolves into a primeval state. *The Burning World* (1964; expanded as *The Drought*, 1965) reverses the situation. A molecular film of pollution on the world's oceans prevents evaporation and the formation of rainclouds. As the landscape is reduced to sand and salt, Ballard's characters become less and less certain of their purpose and ability to survive. Eschatological concerns are again primary in *The Crystal World* (1966), a novel in which time and space coalesce in a South American forest to cause the crystallization of all organic matter.

In the early 1970s Ballard began to concentrate on contemporary concerns. *The Atrocity Exhibition* (1970), *Crash* (1973), and *High Rise* (1975) deal with alienation, violence, and sexual perversion. In these works, humanity loses its humaneness as it succumbs to what Ballard implies are the destructive effects of the technological age.

Some of Ballard's work is considered borderline science fiction, downplaying or disregarding adherence to scientific principle while concentrating on the human issues central to mainstream literature. An example of this is *Empire of the Sun* (1984), an autobiographical tale of a boy's experiences in Shanghai during World War II for which Ballard was awarded the James Tait Black Memorial Prize. Here Ballard rejects the traditional glorification of heroism and sacrifice to expose

© Jerry Bauer

war as an act of brutality and futility. William Boyd calls the book "the most untypical novel [Ballard] has written, and the best."

(See also *CLC*, Vols. 3, 6, 14; *Contemporary Authors*, Vols. 5-8, rev. ed.; *Contemporary Authors New Revision Series*, Vol. 15; and *Dictionary of Literary Biography*, Vol. 14.)

NICK PERRY AND ROY WILKIE

Ballard's work is prima facie science fiction in the sense that his stories are instigated by external physical or social factors rather than, as with ordinary fiction, by a conflict between people. In *The Drought* radio-active waste has stopped the sea evaporating, and as a result fresh-water supplies become extremely scarce. In *The Wind from Nowhere* a wind begins to circle the earth's surface at an accelerating rate, destroying urban centres in its path. . . . In *The Subliminal Man* extensive advertising techniques dominate in order to maintain high-level production. Other stories are often variations on traditional science fiction themes. Ballard, however, is not writing traditional science fiction.

In the first place, Ballard's readers soon discover that landscape is of primary importance. (p. 98)

[The descriptions of landscapes in *The Illuminated Man* and *The Drought*], illustrative of much of Ballard's writing, clearly connect with the landscapes of Max Ernst and Yves Tanguy—self-consciously so, in fact, since Ballard himself is at pains to make these links explicitly. They also may suggest affinities with Aldous Huxley. . . .

[In] Ballard, the description of Nature clearly takes on special significance in that it is not simply representational, but informed by the perceptual nuances of the observer. Huxley's perception, however, is heightened by mescalin.

But if Ballard's landscapes are at odds with conventional natural backcloths, his characters are equally strange. Their social backgrounds and occupations, are professional and middle-class. This, of course, in itself is not unusual for the British novel, but the occupational range is drawn almost exclusively from the medical and biological sciences. The four central characters in his novels, for example, are three doctors and a biologist. Again this is not all that surprising—Ballard studied medicine at Cambridge—but the recurrence over forty-eight short stories and four novels suggests that Ballard may attach some sort of symbolic importance to such professions. What is evident from his work, however, is that occupation is subservient to the central character's psychology, for it is largely a technical expedient which allows Ballard free rein to map out his concern with issues of life and death, pain and suffering. (p. 99)

A Ballard central character is always "out of joint." Moreover, his social environment, such as it is, is often composed of lepers and idiots and religious maniacs and psychopaths. Typically, however, Ballard's characters increasingly act out some internal imperative toward social isolation, at least from regular social contacts, and this internal imperative gives them a passivity, a sense of detachment in the face of the social and human predicaments which act as backcloths to Ballard's stories. . . . This detached fatalism has become so pronounced a feature of Ballard's characters that James Cawthorne claimed of them:

> The two-fisted technologist of *Astounding*'s heyday is replaced, in this setting, by a figure which it is tempting to label The Dissolving Hero. Faced with the breakup of the Universe he does not fight, but instead seeks, literally, to be absorbed. . . .

One can easily come away from Ballard's books with this impression but we would suggest that the way his characters behave implies rather more than such cryptic comments would imply. Built into his work is the premise that the afflictions, mental, physical or social, from which his characters suffer are the precondition for some kind of insight into "the human condition." . . .

These two elements—landscape and character—make up a pattern. Ballard's characters connect with their landscapes, their psychological state is reflected in their environmental circumstances. Ballard's landscapes are descriptions of the workings of the mind. (p. 100)

Moreover, these claims are not marginal features of Ballard's work. They are the basic propositions of his philosophy. He has developed around them, not only the bulk of his literary work, but also a view of the future of science fiction. (p. 101)

It is interesting at this point to note that Ballard's literary development parallels the work of R. D. Laing and other mem-

bers of the anti-psychiatry group—a school of thought which evokes the mood of existential philosophy in its new formulation of the psychopathology of adult schizophrenia. (p. 102)

Ballard's characters . . . behave in ways similar to Laing's schizophrenics. They have evolved a set of tactics to cope with the world. The question is: what sort of world is it that they are trying to cope with? In *Terminal Beach,* one of his most impressive short stories, Ballard gives us the clearest picture of this world. In the story, Traven, a one-time military pilot, has been driven by some private compulsion to the abandoned island of Eniwetok. His wife and son have been killed in a car crash. The island is cluttered up with towers, blockhouses, bunkers, plastic models of the dead. Traven is in rags, diseased and with a badly injured foot. He sleeps first in the open and then in a tomb-like bunker, and finally nearer to a maze of concrete blocks. A biologist and his assistant, a young woman, arrive on an inspection of the site. They meet Traven but leave without him. A search party comes to find Traven, but he eludes them by lying among the plastic models. Throughout this period he occasionally sees the figures of his dead wife and son. He resorts to a tactic of "switching-off" his environment, but abandons this as futile. He later comes across the corpse of a middle-class Japanese man. He communicates with the corpse, and it replies. He then moves the corpse into a position between him and the blocks he had earlier tried to "switch-off" and awaits his own death.

Eniwetok is Ballard's world. . . . Dying, Traven says goodbye to Eniwetok, and then adds in order Los Alamos, Hiroshima, Alamagordo, Moscow, London, Paris, New York. Eniwetok is clearly representative.

Eniwetok, then, is not only the world of Ballard's characters; it is *the* world for all of us, but only the Ballard characters can perceive it accurately. The biologist and his female assistant help Traven by attending to his cut foot, and the girl warns him that they will ask the Navy to come and take him off the island. Both of them represent the "normal" human being, doing an "acceptable" job of work, behaving "normally" and being kind to Traven. But their response to the island—and what the island represents—is clearly inadequate. The dead Japanese who has committed suicide recommends to Traven a philosophy of acceptance . . . , but Traven finds great difficulty in reconciling himself to that position. The blocks, he confesses, stand in his way. The blocks are technology. And for Traven to soothe his inner compulsion he has to place the corpse between himself and the blocks as protection. Traven then is not making a martyred gesture against thermonuclear testing; he has rejected the "normal" world of work and love and play; but to move towards the right response to a world represented by Eniwetok is difficult and can only be achieved by drawing upon the experience and wisdom of ways of life not normally accepted by technological society.

Ballard's solution then connects with other societies and other ways of life. To reach this solution we have to throw out acceptable modes of thinking. . . . Western ways and Western spirituality are insufficient to sustain us in this world. So we have to invert, turn the acceptable, normal world upside down before we can be secure. Ballard's stories repeatedly advise us to "invert" our logic whch presumably represents for Ballard Western technological thinking and values. (pp. 102-03)

[In Ballard's work, everything] is the "wrong" way round. The central character walks into the rain or into the desert or into the forest. The "abnormal" are the normal. The "maimed" are the wholesome. Reality is a dream. The nightmare is the reality. Thus the victim in *End Game* begins—unlike Kafka's heroes—by assuming his own guilt; it is only when he claims and believes in his own innocence that he is killed. . . . Ballard has claimed that only a truly guilty man can conceive of the concept of innocence at all, or hold it with such ferocity.

What then can we make of Ballard's thought? Like the surrealists, Ballard accepts the absolute freedom of the mind—the inner world of the psyche is all important. In this sense, Ballard would concur with Hegel's view of the realisation of man. . . . Like the existential psycho-analysts, Ballard is saying that the schizophrenic "solution" points the way to this realisation and that the schizophrenic is someone unable to subdue his natural instinct and conform to the abnormal, insane world. . . . Like Huxley, Ballard is convinced that the visionary experience is valid, a means of better understanding and realising ourselves. (p. 104)

> *Nick Perry and Roy Wilkie, "Homo Hydrogenesis: Notes on the Work of J. G. Ballard," in* Riverside Quarterly, *Vol. 4, No. 2, January, 1970, pp. 98-105.*

DAVID PRINGLE

As Northrop Frye has pointed out, the *Bible* is the source of the symbolism that underlies most of Western literature. . . . The ultimate source of all literary symbolism is of course the cyclical rhythm of life itself—for instance, the seasons of the earth, the summer, autumn, winter and spring in which men have always tended to see an analogy to their own experience of birth, maturity, death and rebirth. The four great states of being that are described in the *Bible* run the gamut from desire to revulsion. There is Heaven, or the City of God, place of eternal bliss; there is the Garden of Eden, or the Earthly Paradise, place of innocence and joy; there is the Fallen World into which Adam was cast, place of daily toil and suffering; and finally there is Hell, place of endless pain. . . . Symbols often tend to come in clusters of four, like the quadrants of a mandala. (pp. 48-9)

The realistic novel, which has held sway in the literature of the past two-and-a-half centuries, has tended to 'displace' such symbolic patterns in favour of a close scrutiny of manners and social surfaces. But science fiction, which is the modern equivalent of Biblical eschatology, lends itelf to analysis in terms of fundamental symbolism.

Such an analysis is particularly fruitful with the stories of J. G. Ballard, who sometimes maintains and sometimes alters the traditional symbolic patterns in order to suit his own sensibility and the situation of modern man. He uses a fourfold symbolism. The four main 'elements', the primary images, of Ballard's fiction seem to me to be Water, Sand, Concrete and Crystal. These substances set the tone of Ballard's stories, they dominate his landscapes, and each is in fact a symbol with an aggregate of meanings. Secondary symbols group themselves around these four major ones, and in different stories they combine in different ways. Ballard's work must above all be taken as a *whole*, rather than as a number of discrete tales. Viewed as a whole, it will be seen to have quite profound significance—which is not to say that Ballard has an overt 'message' for us. . . . He offers no definite answers to man's problems; he does not spur to action. He simply presents us with the experience of being alive today. . . . (p. 49)

In a radio interview with Christopher Evans, Ballard has stated that he considers his novel *The Drowned World* as presenting a psychological image of the *past*, whereas his novel *The Drought* presents an image of the *future*. . . . *The Drowned World* is a tale of biospheric disaster, superficially in the John Wyndham mode, concerned with the melting of the icecaps and the inundation of man's cities. It is a statement of the obvious to say that it is a novel absolutely dominated by the image of *water*. *The Drought* is also a disaster-story, concerned with the cessation of rainfall and the consequent aridity. It is equally obvious that this is a novel dominated by *sand* (and its correlatives such as dust, ash, salt, etc.). . . . [Two] other major books, *The Crystal World* and *The Atrocity Exhibition,* are concerned respectively with *eternity* and the *present,* and their dominating images are, respectively, *crystal* and *concrete*.

The meeting-place of water and the past in Ballard's imagination is the womb, where the foetus hangs suspended in warm amniotic fluid. Another such meeting-place is the sea itself, whence all plant and animal life came millions of years ago. Thus water is associated with the past, with birth, and with organic life itself. . . . Although the floods in *The Drowned World* have destroyed London, Ballard is far more concerned with the new life that has come in its place. Significantly, of all Ballard's stories, this is the one that contains the greatest abundance of natural, living things. . . . The characters of *The Drowned World* are encroached upon by a renascent biology, a humming, chittering, screaming world of life. This watery world is in fact Ballard's science-fictional equivalent of the Garden of Eden. At first, this may seem a strange statement, since the environment he describes is not exactly friendly or comfortable to live in. It is typical of Ballard's sombre imagination that, in describing nature's reconquest of London, he has chosen to visualize it in terms of the Triassic rather than the Arcadian. The typically 'English' landscape of green-wood, meadow and piping hedgerow . . . holds no interest for Ballard; it appears nowhere in his fiction. He sees nature in a less sentimental light: it is rich, fecund, but essentially alien to man.

The principal theme of *The Drowned World* is devolution, return to a prehistoric past. That is why the natural world is represented by giant plants, reptiles and insects, and not by warm-blooded mammalian creatures. Under the impact of freakish solar radiation, the earth's ecology is literally reverting to its state of millions of years ago. Mankind is ceasing to procreate. . . . Far from being repelled by all this, the hero is fascinated. He collaborates in the devolutionary process, and begins a dream-journey back down his spinal cord, from level to level of the biological record. He is deliberately seeking to return to the water-world of the past, to the womb, to unthinking organic existence. Thus the ending of the novel is quite logical, when he sets off on an impulsive journey to the south, to regions of still greater heat and humidity. . . . At the conclusion of *The Drowned World*, the hero himself becomes Adam "searching for . . . forgotten paradises". We must conclude from this that for Ballard the past does not belong to man. . . . However much he may yearn to go back, the gates of Eden are closed. If he attempts the return, he ceases to be man, and becomes dissolved in the great biological soup in which we all originated.

What, then, of the future? The answer would seem to be—sand. In his stories dominated by this symbol, such as those included in the collection *Vermilion Sands,* Ballard gives us a picture of a future in which man has become a more and more mental creature. As this 'intellectualization' of the human race proceeds, man removes himself ever further from his biological roots. He becomes lethargic and affectless as the life force itself seems to dry up. A sandy desert becomes the appropriate symbol of this spiritual state. In *The Drought,* a film of industrial waste on the surface of the sea prevents the evaporation of water to form rainclouds, and thus the entire land-surface of the globe turns into parched desert. Ballard sees sand as an apt symbol of the future because it is dry and lifeless, and also because it is essentially formless. . . . The future, Ballard fears, will obliterate us. . . . The correlatives of sand in his symbolism, apart from substances like ash and salt, include rock, fire and lava-flows—in fact, the mineral world in general as opposed to the vegetative world of his water symbolism. . . . Of course, Ballard is not predicting an actual biospheric disaster, such as that outlined in *The Drought,* but a general desiccation of all life as human beings become less and less sure of what exactly they *are*. The relationships between people will become increasingly tenuous. . . . As our biological drives wane, and our powers of conscious choice grow, our identities will dissolve and we will turn increasingly to neurosis, psychopathology and perversion.

The whole of Ballard's fiction is haunted by echoes of Coleridge's *Rime of the Ancient Mariner,* and it is particularly appropriate that in *The Drought* images of dead and dying birds abound. He sees man's future state as that of the Mariner in the doldrums after killing the albatross—but unable to bless the water-snakes because they are dead and gone too. . . . Ballard regards man's assault on the natural world as an analogue of his assault on the animal within himself. In cutting off our roots, we kill ourselves. At the end of *The Drought,* the hero has reached such a state of living death that he does not even notice when it starts to rain again. If *The Drowned World* gave us Ballard's Eden, then *The Drought* certainly represents his Hell. . . . (pp. 50-2)

[An] important secondary symbol [in Ballard's fiction] is the beach, meeting-place of water and sand, and thus of past and future. At least twenty of Ballard's stories contain beach scenes, and one of the most effective of these is **"The Drowned Giant"**. Reminiscent of Melville's descriptions of the cutting up of whales, this story concerns a dead giant who is washed up, Gulliver-like, onto a beach near a city. Like Melville's white whale, the giant is a symbol of all life, and the description of the callous dismemberment and scattering of his body is intensely moving and sad.

There is no denying the pessimism of this view of the future, but I doubt that it represents a conviction on Ballard's part so much as a fear. As the contrast between *The Drowned World* and *The Drought* reveals, Ballard is highly conscious of the paradoxical position of modern humanity. Man is of the animal world, and yet not of it, unable to move in either direction without losing his identity. As a result, he finds himself stranded on the terminal beach of the present. In fact, the beach in the story of that name is made of concrete, not sand, and concrete is pre-eminently the symbol of *now* in Ballard's fiction. . . . In this category I place all his claustrophobic city-stories, such as **"Billenium"** and **"The Subliminal Man"**, together with the series of condensed and fragmented pieces that make up his book *The Atrocity Exhibition* [published in the United States as *Love and Napalm: Export USA*]. In these works, Ballard shows a fascination for modern architecture. . . . Claustrophobia is a key to Ballard's view of the present world. There is a continual sense of being hemmed in and enclosed by a universe

of concrete. This is quite literally the case in the early short story called **"The Concentration City"**. Here, the protagonist . . . attempts to escape from the city that he has grown up in. He goes on a long journey on the underground railway, only to end up at the point he started from. In other words, the city is global; there is no 'up', no 'down', no way out. The very concepts of 'space' and 'flight' cannot be grasped by the inhabitants of this metropolis.

The atmosphere of claustrophobia is more subtly conveyed in *The Atrocity Exhibition.* The hero's world is claustrophobic because it represents an exteriorization of his own mind—or rather, of the collective mind of modern urban man. In this environment . . . everything is man-made, and thus is psychoanalysable, like the contents of an individual mind. Every skyscraper, advertising hoarding or television broadcast has its latent as well as overt meaning. . . . [In] the 'concrete' stories man is trapped within his own creations, and thus within himself. He is living in a completely 'fictional' world—a world that is in fact a work of science fiction, since it has been brought into existence by technology. As Ballard puts it, life becomes a huge novel. In this enclosed, narcissistic present, he sees man as having a terrible existential freedom. The individual can choose to do literally anything he wants to do. Consequently, he is turning increasingly to perversions, particularly those involving violence. . . . After all, man is a naturally perverse animal; his perversity is the measure of his removal from the normal biological round. Most men who have ever lived have in fact followed the traditional Arcadian rhythms of existence; they have not 'planned' their lives, but have simply lived, following the way of all flesh. However, contemporary man's technological expertise has now given him the means to escape this lot and to fulfil his perverse nature, to realize his every fantasy. Sex has ceased to be a biological function; it has become a purely conceptualized pleasure, and this has led to what Ballard calls "the death of affect". (pp. 53-5)

The diamond or crystal symbol is one that Ballard has used sparingly in his short stories, but it does of course appear profusely in his novel *The Crystal World*. This fascinating tale begins with descriptions of a "dark river" overhung by a sombre African forest. . . . Here we have Ballard's usual vision of the natural world that man has forsaken—frightening, alien but alive. The port at the river's mouth is one of those depressing 'outposts of civilization' highly reminiscent of scenes in Conrad's novels. . . . But when the characters move up-river they discover a beautiful world of cancerous mutation. The forest and all its denizens are efflorescing, turning into a vast crystalline mass which is gradually expanding to fill all space. Ballard's science-fictional explanation for this phenomenon is obscure, involving the "super-saturation" of time and space: "As more and more time 'leaks' away, the process of super-saturation continues, the original atoms and molecules producing spatial replicas of themselves . . ." The important point is that the crystal world is *without time;* it has become a fragment of eternity, and eventually it will "fill the entire universe . . . an ultimate macrocosmic zero beyond the wildest dreams of Plato and Democritus." The living things that are caught up in this process do not die; they become, as it were, embalmed in eternity. In the crystal world, all opposites merge: light and dark, man and animal, life and death, space and time—all are resolved into one. Each of the characters gradually succumbs to the enticement of this world and blends with it. . . . In this most mystical novel, Ballard has used the symbol of the crystalline forest as a science-fictional objective correlative to our sense of oneness with the universe. He has created his Heaven or City of God.

It is natural to associate the stars with diamonds, the galaxy with crystal, and indeed much literature of the past has done so. In Ballard's symbolism too, crystal expands to embrace the heavenly bodies. Indeed, in *The Crystal World,* the phenomenon of crystallization is in some way triggered by events deep in outer space. Anti-matter and anti-time have appeared in the universe and the distant galaxies are "doubling".... This thoroughly traditional association of crystal, eternity and the Milky Way leads us on to a consideration of the theme of space-travel in Ballard's fiction. Ballard has sometimes been reproached for being the only science fiction writer who is apparently uninterested in what many would consider the quintessential themes of the genre: space-flight and encounters with alien beings. In fact, this is unfair, since several of his most brilliant and suggestive short stories deal with just such themes—I am thinking in particular of **"The Waiting Grounds", "The Voices of Time", "The Time Tombs", "A Question of Re-Entry"** and **"The Venus Hunters".** In contrast to most science fiction writers, what characterizes Ballard's approach to space-travel themes is his extreme caution. After all, if the stars 'are' the City of God, they must be approached with a suitable awe.

The space-ship itself is a frequent symbol in Ballard's work. When space-capsules appear, they are invariably wrecked, grounded or trapped in an endless orbit. **"Thirteen to Centaurus"** presents us with a huge spacecraft which is in reality an earth-bound testing laboratory. Its inhabitants think they are flying to Alpha Centauri, but in fact they are all guinea-pigs in a failed experiment.... The recurrence of these [space vehicle] motifs would certainly suggest that Ballard regards the space-programmes as doomed to failure. But, again, I doubt that this really represents a conviction on his part, so much as a symbolic expression of a fear, a doubt. The fear is perhaps that modern man's frontal assault on the heavens—an approach lacking in humility—will lead to further damnation rather than salvation.... It is the all-too-likely *failure* of the space-programmes, the inability of man to face up to the sheer vastness of the universe, that frightens Ballard, rather than the attempt itself. His current attitude to the moon-landings was expressed in a review of Norman Mailer's *A Fire on the Moon.* Here, he blames Mailer for not having sufficient respect for the astronauts, and for deriding Aldrin's "quiet and moving" celebration of communion on the moon's surface. Ballard admires the selfless dedication of the NASA team.... The blame, he implies, is on *us,* and on people like Mailer, for not being sufficiently imaginative. (pp. 56-8)

The 'summit' of Ballard's symbolic vision, his most apocalyptic image, is to be found in the comparatively early short story **"The Waiting Grounds".** This brilliant, if flawed, piece concerns a man on an alien planet who discovers a strange temple of the galactic races. Amid a landscape of sand, ash and intense heat, the hero is rewarded with a glimpse of the cosmic cycle. He sees the future evolution of the sentient races, their expansion in space, their ability to slow their subjective time-rates, until they abandon physical existence and become a "great vibrating mantle of ideation" which eventually swallows all matter and "achieves the final predicates of time and space, eternity and infinity." Once this zero has been reached, the system explodes, time and matter re-emerge, and the cycle begins again. An alien voice tells the hero of the purpose of his vision and of the Waiting Grounds.... [The] universe may be a place of 'myriad deaths', but it is also, ultimately, a single

entity, every particular existence bodying forth its meaning. Of course Ballard does not expect that men ever will just sit and accept . . . , but this cosmic or crystal vision represents one pole of human consciousness. Eternity is always there, as an alternative to the unconscious past, the arid future, the claustrophobic present.

Finally, let me add that I have pursued the theme of Ballard's symbolism with an earnestness that is perhaps out of keeping with the irony, ambivalence and wit of all his writing. His work adds up to an exploration of various states of the modern mind, not a new scripture. (pp. 59-60)

> *David Pringle, "The Fourfold Symbolism of J. G. Ballard," in* Foundation, *No. 4, July, 1973, pp. 48-60.*

DUNCAN FALLOWELL

What remains of a population in this latest Ballard doomscape [*Low-Flying Aircraft and Other Stories*] is one of listless biodegradable people. . . .

[Ballard's heroes] take to the air . . . as proof that the spirit of man goes on and on and on. If they fail, it serves as a warning that the same old thoughts applied in the same old way, however changed the circumstances, only produce more of the same old problems.

Mr Ballard's cleverness used to lie in casting a smoke-screen across his weaknesses as a writer with one ingenious imaginative idea. This was in the days when he was content to be known as a writer of science fiction adventure stories. Now that he is being set up as a literary prophet the weaknesses become more obvious. They are:

(1) Characterisation. He is quite hopeless at this. Nowhere in his writing can I recall a name actually turning into a face.... Ballard's men are either strong or weak, mostly strong. His women are either strong or weak, mostly weak (if strong they are usually quasi-lesbian or sado-masochistic). (p. 59)

[In *Low Flying Aircraft*] the men are known by their surnames and the women by their christian names: official pre-war adventure story etiquette. The men are invariably dactyls . . . [with such names as Buckmaster and Sherrington], and if they are not it is perhaps because they are common or in some other way inadequate, *eg* 'foreign'. On the other hand, the women are never common. They have strayed here from the genteel de-odourised suburbs of the novelette, with a nomenclature to prove it. (pp. 59-60)

[Ballard's men] are of the kind who if ever they did succeed in committing a conscious sin would go off to the Empire somewhere and help build it with a good grace which might almost amount to relish. They are vaguely bogus too (even when fighting the rotters), slightly raffish and wishful-suave, the sub-Bond species—minus sex. It is true that Mr Ballard quite often gives them sex but they rarely convey the impression of caring one way or the other about it. These characters would rather tinker with machines than with people—a trait which exposes them as strong and active men who are nonetheless sexually, emotionally and intellectually in a pre-natal stage of their development. Surely this explains why they cannot fire the imagination of the reader. . . . The women never begin to happen at all, unless they are first de-sexed (as an aviator or scientist for example) so that they can behave like men. Insofar as Mr Ballard writes about a dehumanised world of helpless ill-fortune, these mechanical nameplates can be said to populate it convincingly, *faute de mieux.*

(2) Prose Style. This is more than conventional, it is decidedly old-fashioned. Ballard is a 'period' writer in the sense of writing about a period (the fact that he writes about the future is simply to define which one) and also in the sense of typifying popular fiction of a certain generation. He can be placed somewhere between Rider Haggard and Ian Fleming without discomfort. Perhaps the biggest disappointment in him is his failure to develop a prose style which does not constantly trivialise his underlying obsessions. Where bullets always 'slam' and cars always 'scrunch to a halt' and women 'melt' and men 'thump' their points home, real prophets do fear to tread. If this is the only manner in which he can write, then a sense of humour would be the thing to give it the satirical edge it lacks but humour is not Ballard's strong point and should any satire on the Bond pantheon be intended its profile is so low as to be invisible. . . .

[As to characters' names, Ballard] does not *use* them in any suggestive or dynamic way at all. They are pitched at one characterless level. Numbers would have been more poignant. In every sense of the word his prose wants for taste. It lacks suppleness, grace, quick wits and complexity. Basically it lacks instinct. It fails to rise to the occasion and the consequent discrepancy is very irritating, especially when men of noted opinion repeatedly put forward Mr Ballard as the one chosen by the Fates to raise science fiction into the arena of rich, adult art.

(3) Prose Style/Technical Structure. The amount of nonsense written about Ballard the Innovator is legion. Literary revolutions, like all others if genuine, are technical. . . . They have nothing whatever to do with subject matter as such.

'The Beach Murders' is the only example of a modern story in *Low-Flying Aircraft*. . . . The innovation is that the reader is invited to play games with twenty-six alphabetical clues relating to the solution of the crime. What is most interesting about it is not the explicit nature of the device employed but the effect it has on the quality of Mr Ballard's writing. Suddenly there is so much more going on. The images are stronger, the gaucheries fewer, the energy flowing within the story is more fertile—and of course it is slightly less 'easy to read'.

Few of the other stories stray far from the punch-line method, of which Somerset Maugham was the most brilliant exponent. In this, the last paragraph will explain the events of the story, as with the punch-line of a joke. . . . [This] has become the standard method for straight, commercial short stories. There is no reason at all why Ballard should not use it. Now and again. In the title story it works extremely well.

However, if he proposes to do what he is so often claimed to be doing, *ie* reflecting the contemporary world to positing a future one, then the punch-line method is not true to it. Since it requires an adhesion to the sequences of 'easy' linear fiction for its effect, it is inadequate for monitoring a world in which Einstein long ago made space itself curved and time one of the relative dimensions. The fact that older people especially choose to disregard this in their daily lives, seeking refuge in a perceptual nostalgia, explains why so much of mankind appears to have lost control over its own actions and their consequences. Mr Ballard's essence lives in this perceptual nostalgia too. So be it. But it being so, one is right to question the legitimacy of a reputation based upon an altogether profounder grasp of our world.

Which brings us to (4) Intellectual weakness. . . . To have 'nightmare visions of the future' and to write them out in an entertaining way—and Mr Ballard's stories are very entertaining, if you like the *genre*—is not a worthless activity. They will encourage us to think about the future. It daily becomes more urgent to do so, apparently. But one way or the other, for better or for worse, *everything* makes us think. What is significant however is *the* way our mentation works. And literature affects this—the collective unconscious thinking aloud and so evolving itself. I do not think Mr Ballard affects this. Prophets of doom are prophets in no useful sense, even if their predictions are true. They do nothing but gluttonise on disaster and encourage us to do likewise.

As a professional writer of some standing, Mr Ballard should be concerned about this at a far more subtle level than he has yet demonstrated. When he really does make the effort—**'The Beach Murders'** is a minor example—it pays off. That is a law of nature. His usual, mechanical and slip-shod style on the other hand (at its worst here in **'The Ultimate City'**, a pedestrian yawn degenerating from a good idea) only grows more portentous and shallow as his themes, under pressure from the claims of his apologists, grow more epic. This produces one conceptual cop-out after another. . . .

Of course Mr Ballard still has flashes of speculative ingenuity. The best example of this is in the title story and no wonder it gives its title to the entire volume. But by and large this is a messy collection which will surprise even his devotees, of which there are quite a number. As a quick read the stories have their justification. But one had been encouraged to expect rather more than that. (p. 60)

Duncan Fallowell, ''Ballard in Bondage,'' in Books and Bookmen, *Vol. 21, No. 6, March, 1976, pp. 59-60.*

E. R. BRAITHWAITE

High-Rise deals with the events taking place in a forty-storey building, occupied by high-income professionals whose behaviour suddenly and rapidly deteriorates into the most horrifying experience. (p. 74)

Ballard compares his high-rise to a zoo and attempts to use it as a microcosm of society as a whole. The population of the building is divided into three classes, various clans with a 'feudal chief' at its head and its people are at war with each other. As wars go, this one is more senseless than most, or so it seems. Sex, violence and social greed are closely linked to each other as the law of the jungle develops.

The violence which erupts suddenly before taking over the whole building is hard to take. Ballard's style is often vivid but largely repetitious and some of his interpretations of the events taking place in the building are simplistic if not obscure. . . . Some readers will find it difficult to follow the author to the end of this horrifying tale in which violence and destruction become ends in themselves. The role of violence in the arts as a possible deterrent to further violence in modern society is an issue which continues to be debated in many fora.

Mr Ballard's book will join others in the controversy by claiming that violence is inevitable and even necessary in a world where man's natural instincts are repressed within his own 'civilising' process. (pp. 74-5)

E. R. Braithwaite, in a review of "High-Rise," in Books and Bookmen, *Vol. 21, No. 10, July, 1976, pp. 74-5.*

CHARLES NICOL

J. G. Ballard, like many younger SF authors, is often on the basis of his style described as a writer of mainstream SF. But the distinction between mainstream fiction and SF is a matter not of style but of differing conventions, so that an author wishing to straddle their conjunction must limit himself in a number of ways. Even after restricting himself to conventions shared by both mainstream and SF, an author will find his work perceived in different ways by mainstream and SF readers, since any reader who is not an omnibibliophile has his own limitations. I propose to demonstrate this by analysing two stories by Ballard, **"The Drowned Giant"** (1965) and **"The Voices of Time"** (1960). The first is mainstream SF, the second "merely" SF; they are both stories of superlative quality....

[**"The Drowned Giant"**'s] premise, unique but within the threshold of familiarity, is established by the first sentence: "On the morning after the storm the body of a drowned giant was washed ashore on the beach five miles to the northwest of the city." The story that follows is developed with straightforward economy, and the style remains precise and impersonal throughout.

Although giants belong to folklore rather than technology, the story is SF rather than fantasy.... The corpse is a fact, an enormous fact, and hence this story is not Fantastic.... [The] style is factual and unemotional; the story follows logically from its initial premise with no new marvelous occurrences; and no one in the story assumes that any supernatural agency is involved. (p. 150)

Once the initial premise is stated, the remainder of the story develops three actions or processes simultaneously. Two of these are the initial excitement and steady decline of interest among the townspeople; and the decay and eventual dismemberment of the giant corpse. Both of these plot-lines are observed by an unnamed narrator, who remains passive throughout; a librarian, he is the only resident of the city sensitive to the possible significance of this monstrous visitation, the only observer capable of limning this event for history (a task eventually assigned him by his fellow librarians). The librarian comes to perceive the dead giant as an event in his own life, assigning personal meaning to this otherwise random event—this constitutes the third plot line. Since the significance of the giant is personal to the librarian, it tends to shift; and as it shifts, it builds up a series of possible meanings. That interpretations are proposed suggests that this is a meaningful event; and that the interpretations are rejected suggests that the meaning has not yet been found. The drowned giant's dissolution is a significant event, the meaning of which is unclear but undoubted. The story has resonance and power, conforming to that specific type of modern literature, the open-ended parable.

That **"The Drowned Giant"** is both literature and mainstream fiction I hope to demonstrate by listing three literary analogues—analogues because the story is an original work and not an imitation. The first is Kafka's "Metamorphosis," another open-ended parable.... "Metamorphosis" similarly opens with an "impossible" event: the protagonist has turned overnight into a giant cockroach.... The rest of Kafka's story is realistic, even naturalistic: the protagonist's family is at first not just surprised, but horrified; soon the family forces this miraculous event into the narrow channels of their own banal perceptions so that the protagonist is seen as only a giant insect and not their relative; eventually he is all but forgotten, and dies of neglect and starvation. The same process of turning the miraculous into the banal and eventually forgotten occurs as one of the plot lines in **"The Drowned Giant,"** where the initially amazed townspeople soon make a playground of the giant's ears and nostrils, and build a campfire on his chest; later see the body as merely a source of rotting flesh to be turned into fertilizer.... As in Kafka, the initial marvellous event seems to have an immense, hovering significance, and to be symbolic of some agony inherent in the human condition.

The frequent confusion of the giant with a whale inevitably recalls *Moby-Dick* in its development of an enormous, ambiguous symbol. We must assume that Ballard is deliberately pointing to Melville when his narrator observes that "this drowned leviathan had the mass and dimensions of the largest sperm whale."... Only Melville's whale comes to mind when searching for an analogue to the majestic enigma of the giant.

The third literary analogue is inescapable, for it also belongs to that grey area where literature is also mainstream SF: *Gulliver's Travels.* Here the analogue is so obvious that Ballard must steer clear of direct comparisons. **"The Drowned Giant"** is intermediate between Gulliver's two voyages concerned with huge size differentials. Obviously the giant washed up on the beach reminds us of Gulliver himself, washed up from the sea on the beach of Lilliput.... But since the narrator is one of the "little" people, we are equally reminded of Gulliver's voyage to Brobdingnag, the land of the giants. This comparison is reinforced by the narrator's references to such identifiable geographical and cultural signs as the Nile and the *Odyssey*—the little people belong to our world; we are they. In that voyage of Gulliver, Swift pointed out how gross the flesh seems when magnified, and certainly Ballard's giant is predominantly a thing of the flesh.

But the giant's flesh is of interest to Ballard only because it is subject to such gross decay; indeed, one might describe Ballard's concern throughout his career as an investigation into the possibilities of decay—or to put it more nicely, *the potentialities of entropy*. Since the giant is actually symbolic of something else, his size is really a matter of perception, expressing the viewpoint of the observer. Just as Alice's sudden size changes in Wonderland reflected the child's differing perceptions of herself (almost a baby, nearly an adult), the narrator of **"The Drowned Giant"** finds that the giant seems larger or smaller during differing visits to the corpse. This apparent alteration of size is one of Ballard's techniques for giving surprising life to the inanimate corpse.

What is most fascinating and original about **"The Drowned Giant"** is that the dead body is one of the principal actors in the story. The giant's decay has a life of its own, and creates a personality for the giant that had been absent at his initial appearance.... Visiting the corpse again three days later, the narrator realizes how much he identifies with the dead giant: "to all intents the giant was still alive for me, indeed more alive than many of the people watching him." By now, the giant had aged.... By the following day, the giant has become more crude, decadent, unkempt.... The narrator continues to identify with the giant.... Now he finds the emotions of death the dominant feature of the giant's face, "a mask of exhaustion and helplessness."... Two days later, the giant's features have entered a phase of final humiliation, like the visage of a battered and punch-drunk fighter.... By the next day, the head has been removed, leaving nothing to observe save the purely mechanical rendering of the massive flesh into fertilizer. The reader has been led by Ballard into identifying with the dead giant's humiliation.

Aside from this narrative excellence, the story also has a symbolic level, a level investigated by the narrator as he seeks to explain why the giant fascinates him.... For the narrator, the giant's reality is metaphysical: he belongs to a "world of ... absolutes." God seems the most likely metaphysical "absolute": the giant is proof that God exists, with men "puny copies" in his image; the existence of God confirms the identity of the narrator. Other readers may prefer to see this as a more general reference to an unspecified metaphysical construct. Yet eventually the narrator recognizes that the giant, whether God or not, is indeed dead. He becomes "reluctant to visit the shore, aware that [he has] probably witnessed the approaching end of a magnificent illusion." It is "almost with relief" that the narrator watches the corpse being removed, since its dissolution has paralleled his own disillusion. (pp. 151-53)

SF fans might not have enjoyed **"The Drowned Giant"** as much as mainstream readers, since Ballard slights his science, providing no explanations for the giant's appearance. And the more conventional SF story would have investigated where the giant came from, rather than what he meant.... The image of the face of a dead giant, moving from a dreaming tranquility to excesses of agony and shame, is poetic but not necessarily within the poetry of science fiction.

In contrast, the poetry of **"The Voices of Time"** should appeal directly to the SF reader, while appearing to the mainstream reader as a mass of jumbled images. Here the narrative is rich in explanations and partial explanations, while the method of composition is one of complexity rather than simplicity. The reader is bombarded with SF images, all striking and all pointing in the same direction: the universe is running down, the sun is running down, earth is running down, man is running down, and the protagonist of the story is running down most rapidly of all. The focus is on entropy. But the power of the story lies in the many ways in which its characters try to escape entropy, and in the sterility of their attempts. The hope of escaping time is held out like a brass ring, but each attempt to reach the ring leads to madness and death. Eventually the reader comes to see death as itself an escape from entropy, and the story ends in tranquility: the tranquility of exhaustion. (pp. 153-54)

The time of the story is the late twentieth century. The chief features of the landscape are mountains, a salt lake of moderate size, and vegetation belonging to the cactus family—all reinforcing the picture of bleak sterility. (p. 154)

The basic "scientific" idea of the story is that high levels of radiation stimulate "two inactive genes which occur in a small percentage of all living organisms, and appear to have no intelligible role in their structure or development." Here the mainstream reader is at a disadvantage; unfamiliar with fiction that has science at its core, he will assume these silent genes to be Ballard's fantasy (unless he happens to know better). The SF reader, on the other hand, while probably knowing little more than the general reader, is attuned to the subtle distinctions between fantasy and fact in SF stories; even without previous knowledge, he will assume that Ballard got those silent genes from some other storehouse than his imagination.... Thus the mainstream reader, failing to realize the

extent to which Ballard is extrapolating from the actual world, is at an immediate disadvantage in assessing the story's power.

Because "some people have speculated that ... the silent genes are a sort of code, a divine message that we inferior organisms are carrying for our more highly, developed descendants," in Ballard's story a scientist named Whitby has spent ten years perfecting a technique for irradiating them. But if there is any "divine message" in the silent genes, it is that God is an insane nihilist:

> Without exception the organisms we've irradiated have entered a final phase of totally disorganized growth, producing dozens of specialized sensory organs whose function we can't even guess. The results are catastrophic....

Thus the hope of transcendence leads instead to madness and destruction. Because of the pessimistic implications of this experiment, Whitby has committed suicide. (pp. 154-55)

Several reasons are elliptically offered for ... [the] increased radiation count. From one casual conversation the reader may infer that World War III has already occurred. Other references in the story present an even more ominous explanation: the sun is cooling and emitting heavier radiation.

The images of entropy in **"The Voices of Time"** are extremely insistent, ranging from the largest to the smallest things in the universe. Everything is coming to an end; the universe itself is running down. Signals from the stars have been decoded by computers and turn out to be merely a series of countdowns. The most stunning of these series is sent from the Canes Venatici group.... The end of that countdown will coincide with the end of the universe. From the universe down through the sun, from agricultural yields to human fertility, everything has begun to run down. (p. 155)

Still, the accelerated decline on Earth is a special case, caused by higher radiation levels. Humans who carry the silent genes have become subject to narcoma, which causes them to sleep for increasingly large portions of the day; eventually they lapse into permanent sleep. Powers, the protagonist, has developed narcoma symptoms.... Thus Powers is not only the protagonist but the objective correlative of the story, embodying in himself all the forces of entropy and all the apparently sterile hopes for a new future that the silent genes represent.

But throughout Powers' decline, Ballard has also provided him with certain images of potentiality and change. His name is the most obvious example. The most complex of these images is the enormous "ideogram" that Powers builds with cement during trance states; Powers himself is never consciously aware of constructing this enormous cement pattern. Since Ballard explicitly describes this pattern as a "crude Jungian mandala," the reason for its construction is clearly to be found in the works of Jung: a person will create or imagine mandalas when, having reached a critical stage, he is about to resolve his difficulties or at least remove them to a different plane. That Powers creates a mandala suggests his imminent potential for change; that Whitby had also created the same mandala just before committing suicide suggests that this potential may itself be arrested or sterile. But Powers is consciously determined to test his potential, and plans to use Whitby's irradiation technique to activate his own silent genes—the first human to do so. (pp. 155-56)

However, Powers' attempt to free himself from entropy ends in death. After his silent genes have been activated, he is able to perceive time so intensely that he can drive his car with his eyes closed. . . . Overwhelmed by the eternal countdown radiating from the Canes Venatici star group, he feels "his body gradually dissolving, its physical dimensions melting into the vast continuum of the current." "Beyond hope now but at last at rest," he is swept into "the river of eternity." At this moment, Powers has died. Although described attractively, his death is a transcendence of entropy only in the sense that he has left life behind; there seems to be no future in eternity. This pessimistic view is emphasized by the final paragraphs of the story, as Kaldren visits the laboratory and finds all the experimental plants and animals dead. Yet the wider view of the story is to emphasize entropy itself, a force to which everything in the universe is subject.

Kaldren's meditations end the story; although Kaldren never sleeps, he is "half-asleep" in the final paragraph. Since he has earlier given Powers the message that contains the story's title, we must assume that Kaldren is, in part, a stand-in for the author; very possibly it is Ballard himself who is building a collection of "end-prints . . . final statements, the products of total fragmentation. . . ." All of the images of **"The Voices of Time"** coalesce in Kaldren's philosophy: like Powers, throw away your wristwatch. Think of the wider context and do not fear death.

In **"The Voices of Time,"** Ballard has used science fiction to fulfill the traditional role of the poet: to meditate on time and death. Entropy. As an SF reader, I can interpret and appreciate this story as literature because its subject matter is not alien to me. But I doubt that a mainstream reader can appreciate the subtlety and beauty of such SF works, because his own set of literary values is limited by a tradition that excludes them. It is not the writer, but the reader that builds the distinction between science fiction and mainstream fiction into a wall. One can find the gates in that wall, as Ballard did in **"The Drowned Giant,"** but **"The Voices of Time"** kept to a different path. I believe this story is literature; I'm also convinced that it is unavailable to a reader experienced only in mainstream fiction. (pp. 156-57)

> Charles Nicol, "J. G. Ballard and the Limits of Mainstream SF," in Science-Fiction Studies, Vol. 3, No. 2, July, 1976, pp. 150-57.

JEROME CHARYN

[If] you can put aside [science fiction's] smug assertions, its infighting, its fetishism, its blindnesses, its ferocious cults and cliques, it has produced some extraordinary work. One of its best practitioners, J. G. Ballard, has been stuck under the umbrella of science fiction for 20 years. It's time to shake him out. . . .

[**"The Best Short Stories of J. G. Ballard"**] is Mr. Ballard's 16th book. He has a considerable reputation in England, where he has been admired by writers such as Anthony Burgess and Graham Greene, but apart from science-fiction buffs, he is little known in the United States. His novels and stories have either been ignored here or ill-received. It's a pity, because Mr. Ballard has taken the "language" of science fiction and turned it into something quite unique. . . . He uses external models and landscapes—futuristic cities, hospital clinics and crazy, deserted beaches—to plunge into disorders of the heart. Mr. Ballard doesn't write about little green men. His best stories are quiet shrieks of doom. (p. 42)

Most [of Ballard's stories] are identified with an unlucky future-present, where functions have gone awry. In Mr. Ballard's cosmos, science has become a crippled dog. Our energy has begun to drain out: man, the magician, is very tired. . . . All our tinkerings, the wonders we have produced, will finally bring us back to the Stone Age. . . . (pp. 42, 44)

[Ballard's] protagonists tend to be displaced persons of one sort or another: restless students, lonely ex-pilots, neurosurgeons on the decline. Uncomfortable with ordinary definitions of time and space, they try to escape the maddening scrim that holds the world together—find scattered bits of psychic truth for themselves and puzzle out the meaning of their existence. . . . They fail at whatever they seek. . . . They turn to silence, they go mad, or they die.

In the opening story of the collection **"Concentration City,"** Franz M., a student . . . is obsessed with the idea of "free space." But it's a time of overcrowding, of a multilayered City, where level is heaped upon level and space costs "a dollar a cubic foot." . . .

The school of philosophy at Franz's university is closed, and the study of pure science is discouraged. Franz is trying to rediscover the forgotten laws of aerodynamics. He wants to build a flying machine. But he can't experiment without getting hold of some free space. He believes it's waiting for him at the end of the City. . . .

In **"Billenium,"** overcrowding has reached monstrous proportions. . . .

John Ward is a young man who works at the library and has rented a cubicle on the staircase of an old rooming house. Over a hundred people live on the top three floors. . . .

But Ward has to vacate the cubicle, because it measures "four point seven two meters," and the manager of the building can rent it as a "double." [He and an acquired roommate] discover an actual room behind the wall of their cubicle, and they secretly take it over. Snug in their room, they see themselves as "the only real inhabitants of the world, everyone else a meaningless byproduct of their own existence. . . ." (p. 44)

They invite two girls to live with them. One of the girls feels compromised and declares that she needs her aunt in the room. The other girl brings her mother and father along. And the room is packed with seven people.

Both these stories, **"Concentration City"** and **"Billenium,"** are a kind of homage to Kafka. . . . Like Kafka, Mr. Ballard deals with the loss of spirit in a mummified world that has its own macabre energy. The gentle ones disappear: they turn into bugs, or are trampled into nothingness. They long for the sleep of the dead.

In **"Manhole 69"** three volunteers have had their medullas meddled with, and they can now exist without sleep. . . . But all this wakefulness becomes a curse: "Continual consciousness is more than the brain can stand." The three volunteers shrink into themselves, behaving like stiff, waxwork dummies in their own dark sleep.

It is this condition of narcolepsy that creeps into Mr. Ballard's stories. His heroes are burdened with a morbid sensitivity to the world around them. They hunt for "the white leviathan, zero," that state of pure psychic rest that will remove them from the "nausea" of external things. They pull the world in upon themselves, wear it as a gruesome tent, so they can exist in some dark knot of the brain. (pp. 44, 46)

A rare order of intelligence breathes around these stories, a style and a somber wit. Mr. Ballard has used his sense of technology to fashion his stories, empower them with the ability to frighten and amuse. Perhaps that label of "Sci-Fi" will drop off, and we can see Mr. Ballard for what he is: a profound moralist who has grappled with the ugly devils of our own time and given us a good number of sad, beautiful stories. (p. 46)

> *Jerome Charyn, in a review of "The Best Short Stories of J. G. Ballard," in* The New York Times Book Review, *November 26, 1978, pp. 42, 44, 46.*

MICHAEL THORPE

In the mid twenty-second century a clutch of *conquistadores* from Plymouth make landfall at Brooklyn, to explore anew an 'America [which] had finally abandoned itself' a century before.... [In *Hello America*, they] cross, united by nothing but their 'collective fantasy of America', from East to West, an expedition more eventful and sensational than interior and psychological.... A twenty-one-year-old stowaway named Wayne is protagonist, part diarist, seeking a wished-for father, a scientist missing from an earlier expedition.... The interest, after the opening sketches, is not in character or relationship but in setting and incident. We traverse the 'sun-filled museum of the USA', reminiscent of an endless Pop Art gallery. But invention flags when we reach an astonishing tropical Nevada, ruled from Las Vegas by a mad forerunner and explorer, a blend of Nixon and Charles Manson, whose name and psychopath's dream of presidency he has adopted. In the resourceful Wayne, Manson recognizes a 'pioneer in spirit' and names him Vice-President. Manson's 'children', introduced as young Chicanos determined to reverse the twentieth-century imperial order, become mere extras in what develops into a made-for-the-screen cross between *Dr Strangelove* and *Apocalypse Now*. Wayne emerges from the fascination of Manson to discover his true, Daedalian father, whose inventions frustrate Manson's final solution. It would be unfair to detail the unravelling of the plot, though it neither astounds nor enlightens. The moral is clear and limited (as is the moral interest throughout): Manson is 'death and the past rather than . . . the future and promise', but Mr Ballard's imagination can hatch little more than a sentimental image of a better state. (pp. 629-30)

> *Michael Thorpe, in a review of "Hello America," in* British Book News, *October, 1981, pp. 629-30.*

WILLIAM BOYD

[Ballard's] latest novel *Hello America* . . . in many respects is a return to his earlier sci-fi mode. Set towards the end of the 21st century, the novel follows the course of an exploratory expedition to the USA, now, as a result of a series of ecological disasters, an unpopulated wasteland. As the small band of explorers moves across the continent they encounter, in various strange and hybrid forms, the remnants of the American Dream, its icons, totems and myths exposed in the harsher glare of the country's dystopic isolation.

Ballard's re-evaluation of the role America has played in our consciousness, and the pervasive nature of its influence on the twentieth century is fascinating. However harsh and satirical he might be at times, on the whole Ballard's attitude is approving.... The properties of American life can provide marvellous opportunities for the imagination, and it's in this area

in particular that *Hello America* excels as the novelist indulges in some superb—and quintessentially Ballardian-set-pieces. Ballard's unique style functions at full power in this novel, practically every page provides a compelling example. (p. 85)

> *William Boyd, "Camouflages," in* London Magazine, *Vol. 21, No. 8, November, 1981, pp. 83-5.**

MARK ROSE

Does time in fact run backwards? Are our lives actually journeys toward rather than away from the womb? (p. 127)

Like *The Time Machine*, to which the text explicitly alludes, *The Drowned World* portrays a devolving world, a planet collapsing back into primeval chaos. Here, however, devolution is not the result of gradual entropic decline but a sudden climatic change brought about by solar instability. Over a period of a few decades the earth has become fiercely hot and the polar icecaps have begun to melt, raising global water levels and transforming Europe into a system of lagoons. Moreover, higher levels of radioactivity resulting from the dispersal of the ionosphere have led to drastic increases in the rate of mutation. Archaic plant and animal forms—fern trees and giant lizards—have reappeared and are fast taking over the world. The entire planet has been launched on what is in effect a geological and biological journey backward in time toward the Mesozoic.

As one might expect in a text in which the idea of time travel is located in the landscape, directionality acquires temporal as well as spatial significance. Vastly reduced in numbers as a result of a general decline in mammalian fertility—all the higher forms of life are dying off—mankind has retreated to the still habitable region of Camp Byrd within the arctic circle. In the north lies the future; in the south are the steaming jungles and lagoons of the distant, prehuman past. And yet from another point of view the north represents the past, for ultimately even the pole must become uninhabitable: humanity, at least in its present form, is doomed. A broken compass—the calibrated ring has rotated 180 degrees so that the instrument perversely points south—figures prominently, indicating the direction in which the magnetic currents of nature now flow. Should one yield to these currents or struggle against them? Concerned with a mapping and survey expedition that is traveling—significantly—from south to north, the initial direction of the narrative is opposed to the current. At the end, however, the direction changes as Robert Kerans, a biologist whose task is to catalogue the new forms of life, abandons the expedition and sets off on a solitary journey south.

Time in this fiction is not only located in the external world, it is also something inscribed within. At work for months in the melting, metamorphosing city of London—. . . London is an intermediate locale, a "zone of transit"—Kerans and other members of the expedition have begun to exhibit a pronounced lassitude and introversion.... A few have also begun to experience exhausting hypnotic dreams. Dominated by a great booming sun and by the sound of reptiles baying in the lagoon, the dreams seem to express an urge to melt into the formlessness of the primitive watery environment. These are not, however, normal dreams but ancient organic memories that are being activated by the rising temperature and humidity, releasing instincts that have lain dormant for millennia.

As Alan Bodkin, who is Kerans' colleague in the biological arm of the expedition, explains, the trace of the evolutionary past is written in every human chromosome and gene.... In response to the earth's backward journey in geophysical time, Bodkin suggests, man is changing psychically. The process can be understood as a "uterine odyssey" in reverse. The "amniotic corridor" is reentered and the individual begins a journey backward in "spinal and archaeopsychic time" in which the unconscious mind takes on the landscape of successively earlier epochs.... Bodkin warns that "if we let these buried phantoms master us as they reappear we'll be swept back helplessly in the flood-tide like pieces of flotsam." . . . (pp. 127-30)

The drowned world of the title, then, refers not merely to the watery world of the exterior landscape, but also to the submarine regions of the psyche, the amniotic oceans of the biological past. Moreover, as both the title and Bodkin's warning imply, the descent into the drowned world is a slide into unconsciousness and death. In "The Pool of Thanatos," a chapter that makes explicit the connection between the drowned world and death, Kerans descends into the lagoon to explore the sunken London Planetarium. Inside the building his airhose becomes snarled and he begins to suffocate, imagining as he slips into oblivion that the sparkling cracks in the dome represent the ancient constellations of a primeval epoch. Later Kerans wonders whether he did not perhaps mean to snarl his hose. Was he unconsciously accepting the logic of the earth's devolution and willingly sinking into death? Mysterious processes are at work within him, and he is no longer the master of his own intentions. The image of the sunken planetarium in this episode also makes explicit the way the familiar science-fiction icon of the starry infinite has been transferred to a watery world located below and within rather than above and outside. (pp. 130-31)

Form and formlessness, life and death—these are the terms at play in the narrative. In the opening phases of the story the struggle between life and death centers on the question of whether Kerans will return north with Colonel Riggs or remain in the sunken city with Beatrice Dahl. Riggs, the "buoyant" leader of the expedition, and Beatrice, the beautiful, indolent woman with whom Kerans has established a desultory liaison, are antithetical figures. Always scrubbed and clean-shaven, Riggs is the sort of brisk, intelligent military man who has little patience with obscure urges. He epitomizes the impulse toward order implicit in a mission devoted to mapping and cataloguing. Beatrice, on the other hand, who is first described as a "sleeping python," is a native of the lagoon. An aura of decadence clings to her and to her opulent penthouse, stocked with reserves of frozen pâté de foie gras and filet mignon, where she has been holding out for years against the rising heat and water. (pp. 131-32)

To remain in London with the temperature and water level still rising seems perverse and suicidal. As Kerans says when Beatrice proposes that he stay, "You realize that if we let Riggs go without us we don't merely leave here later. We *stay*." . . . The figure of Lieutenant Hardman also helps to establish the significance of staying. A solitary and quiet man even in normal circumstances, Hardman, who has been experiencing the hypnotic dreams for months, has lapsed into complete torpor and is now confined to the sickbay. But when he learns that Riggs is pulling out, Hardman has a sudden surge of strength and runs away. A helicopter search discovers him heading, madly, south. (p. 132)

Riggs departs. Kerans, Bodkin, and Beatrice remain, each living in his own quarters, each pursuing his solitary pathway through the "time jungles" of the unconscious. And then Strangman, a scavenger combing the abandoned cities, arrives.

With his crew of brutal, illiterate blacks and his weird train of alligators, Strangman is an ominous figure.... In a remarkable feat of engineering, Strangman and his crew drain the lagoon in order to make the sunken buildings accessible. To Kerans, however, the city's exposure is an abomination, the exhumation of a corrupted body.... Furthermore, Kerans understands now that he cannot do without the primeval landscape; the lagoon fulfills a "complex of neuronic needs" that have become essential to his being. (pp. 132-33)

Repulsive and dangerous, Strangman is the pivotal figure in the narrative. Through him the text urges us to revalue the attempt, represented also by Riggs and the polar colony, to preserve the old order. The civilization of Europe is dead. Mankind itself, in its old form, is dead. How long can even Camp Byrd hold out against the changing planet? Why attempt to preserve a corpse, to raise rotting bones from the grave? Does the devolving planet leave any option for life or only a choice between two forms of death. . . ? (pp. 133-34)

A sense of fate, a feeling that obscure forces are working toward a necessary conclusion, presses upon the narrative.... [Again] and again characters appear to be acting from motives that they themselves barely comprehend and over which they have diminishing control. The text also attempts to confirm the sense of fate by suggesting that through the particular characters archetypal mythic roles are being fulfilled. Strangman with his chalk-white face and his attendant crocodiles is a kind of voodoo god of death.... All of these elements of course point ultimately to the fact of the changing planet, to the fact that geological and biological forces are working toward a conclusion.

The story comes to a crisis when Bodkin, acting out of the same obscure need for the lagoon that Kerans feels, attempts to reflood the city. Bodkin is promptly shot, and Kerans is handed over to the blacks.... Beginning as an act of reprisal, the torture of Kerans turns into a primitive rite of exorcism in which Strangman's men, identifying the biologist with the sea that they hate and fear, attempt through him to demonstrate their power over the rising waters. In a suggestive action that looks forward both to his reflooding of the city and to his ultimate journey south, Kerans stoically accepts the sacrificial role of Neptune in which he has been cast by circumstances. Somehow he manages to survive the beating and exposure. He escapes from Strangman, returns to his suite at the Ritz hotel to find that it has been sacked, and then realizes that he must leave the city and go south. (pp. 134-35)

Attempting to flee with Beatrice on a homemade raft, Kerans is stopped by Strangman, who is about to kill him when Colonel Riggs reappears. Kerans assumes that Riggs will arrest Strangman and reflood the lagoon.... But Riggs refuses, pointing out that the reclamation of land is a major priority of the government at Camp Byrd.... The gulf between Kerans and Riggs is absolute. From Riggs' point of view, Kerans is mad, out of touch with reality. From Kerans' point of view, Riggs is the madman, a ghostly relic of a past that no longer exists.... That night Kerans blasts the dam holding back the water and the future and, like Hardman before him, disappears into the jungle.

Foreshadowed by his earlier descent to the sunken planetarium, Kerans' voyage down the curve of the devolving planet toward the teeming chaos of the equator is at the same time an embracing of life, a quest for the magical point of life's origin in the hot womb of nature, and a suicidal flight toward death. It represents an acceptance of the future and of the archaic past toward which the future is moving. . . . Kerans' voyage is a quest for the center, the mystical locale at which extremes meet and opposites become identical. . . . [The] goal is a magical zone in which the distinction between man and nature, between Kerans' tortured consciousness and the abyss of the infinite that is at once inside and outside mankind, ceases to exist.

Throughout Ballard's narrative . . . there have been hints of the essentially religious nature of the goal toward which the fiction has been moving. Appropriately, Kerans' journey, a quest for a "spectral grail" . . . , is a kind of holy pilgrimage. Moving steadily southward, the traveler encounters "what seemed to be the remains of a small temple" where he finds Hardman, emaciated, diseased, and insane, his eyesight almost completely gone as a result of corneal cancers produced by staring at the sun. Hardman and his fate suggest the terrible future that lies ahead for Kerans. But madness, as we know, may be divine, and blindness may imply spiritual sight; as the setting in the temple suggests, Hardman need not be seen simply as a figure of horror.

Kerans feeds the dying man and attends to his eyes. He is not surprised when Hardman, his strength revived, vanishes into the jungle. Moving on himself, plunging deeper and deeper into the jungles of the past, Kerans attempts to maintain some hold on normal time by recording the passage of days on his belt. . . . Delicately recapitulating the entire narrative, the fiction concludes appropriately on a note of continuing quest as Kerans presses toward the mystical locale that is at once a place and a time, an ultimate point of origin and a final point of return. (pp. 136-38)

Mark Rose, "Time," in his Alien Encounters: Anatomy of Science Fiction, *Cambridge, Mass.: Harvard University Press, 1981, pp. 96-138.**

HARRIETT GILBERT

J. G. Ballard must be Britain's most highly esteemed science-fiction writer. . . . In *Myths of the Near Future,* a collection of ten short stories, he continues his exploration of the human mind: a mind in the process of disintegration from having travelled too far, too fast, from Nature. For Ballard, technological progress is sin. Sheppard, searching for his dead wife in the forests around Cape Kennedy; Franklin, stepping into longer and longer 'fugues' of frozen unconsciousness; Pangborn, trying to murder himself: for each, salvation can only come from some mystic rediscovery of birds, of the sun . . . of God? For all his prodigious powers of invention, visual evocation and symbolism, Ballard incites more admiration than empathy.

Harriett Gilbert, "White Mischief," in New Statesman, *Vol. 104, No. 2687, September 17, 1982, p. 21.**

COLIN GREENLAND

[Ballard's] concern, as the title of his latest collection proclaims, is with *Myths of the Near Future* and with those through which, helped by our obsessive technologies, we see the present transfigured. His rootless, disaffected characters are forever trying to make sense of the artificial environment in which they find themselves, not by rejecting the prolific chaos of contemporary civilization but by constructing new identities to fit. . . . [One story], **'Zodiac 2000',** proposes to update all the

antiquated agrarian constellations with more modern symbols: the Polaroid, the IUD, the Cruise Missile. Ballard regularly depopulates the most characteristic landscapes of the present—Las Vegas, Cape Canaveral, anonymous tower blocks—to demonstrate that we design these environments not for ourselves but for some inhuman future, editing ourselves out of time. In his immaculate, evocative prose such sardonic observations are not alarming, not even depressing, but attain a potent melancholy beauty that defies logic. Ballard's understanding of the world, however idiosyncratic, is extraordinarily seductive, and this latest volume is his richest and most satisfying for some years.

Colin Greenland, in a review of "Myths of the Near Future," in British Book News, *July, 1983, p. 406.*

ROBERT L. PLATZNER

Recognized as one of the leading writers of apocalyptic science fiction, J. G. Ballard is probably one of the most widely read literary catastrophists of our time. In four major novels and dozens of short stories Ballard has effectively and repeatedly extinguished all life on this planet, and while not all of his books are doomsday books, the apocalyptic mode clearly suits him and undoubtedly represents a commitment to a personal obsession. The intensity of his writing often seems to be in direct proportion to the magnitude of the horrors he invokes, and like the author of the Book of Revelations, Ballard occasionally exhibits signs of grim satisfaction at the spectacle of world annihilation. However, it is my contention that the droughts, the floods, and the radiation storms that Ballard has loosed upon the world are not the real subject of his fables so much as preconditions of fabulation, and that at the heart of Ballard's eschatology is a vision of irreversible, regressive transformation—of entropy as a form of galactic and psychic metamorphosis. For as energy dissipates and the life-force diminishes—the stylized scenario of nearly any Ballardian apocalypse—and human life forms become at once simpler and less recognizable, we enter a fictional realm in his novels where individual identity and sexuality become increasingly ambiguous or diffuse, and where all processes inexorably run down. (p. 209)

In nearly all of [Ballard's] future societies, human civilization (or, more precisely, advanced industrial capitalism) is given only a marginal chance, at best, of adapting to a changing environment whose destructive powers have become overwhelming. What he seems to be saying in narrative after narrative is that man's time is up: we cannot maintain our productive energies much longer, and we certainly cannot sustain the Faustian will-to-power upon which Western civilization has nourished itself for centuries. Cursed, then, by a profound disbelief in human creativity and in Nature's beneficence, Ballard is left at last with very little to write about except the inhuman and the inorganic—for such is the logic of his obsession. It is little wonder, therefore, that so many of his stories seem like so many variations upon a single theme.

The terrors of temporality in an entropic universe would seem to be the greatest of Ballard's apocalyptic anxieties, though by no means the only one, and to judge from the number and variety of narrative contexts in which this theme appears, one would have to conclude that "time's lease" is the one obsession that unlocks the secret of cosmic abandonment for Ballard's chronophobes. In **"The Voices of Time,"** for example, a dying neurosurgeon whose greatest achievement has been a surgical technique for releasing the body from its need for sleep . . . suddenly finds himself sinking gradually towards terminal narcosis, as does most of the human race. Determined to secure a vision of cosmic evolution he believes is somehow locked up within a pair of mysteriously "silent" genes before the End, he constructs a huge mandala at whose center he perceives, at last, the voices of the Heraclitean stream of universal time he has so long pursued. . . . Unable to withstand the mind-shattering impact of this epiphany, Powers dies at the very moment of psychic transcendence, a mad, latter-day Dante gazing raptly upon the disintegrating core of a formless universe. But the whole point of Ballard's tale is that the protagonist's culminating vision of galactic tidal flow is no delusion; the cosmic clock is, indeed, running down, galaxies are breaking up, and the Jodrell Bank Observatory has already begun to compute the precise moment of universal collapse. One premonitory symptom of this collapse, at the biological level, is the extended need for sleep that has been evident for centuries. . . . (pp. 209-10)

No biophysical rationale for this sentence of doom—and Ballard provides none, incidentally—could possibly carry sufficient conviction to justify so sweeping and so hopeless a vision of world-annihilation. . . . [For Ballard], it is not the loss of heaven, or eternity, or "divine causality" that precipitates this crisis of time and being. Instead, it is the second law of thermodynamics that creates a metaphysical vacuity at the heart of things into which time, space, energy, and matter can escape into nothingness. Ballard's universe quite simply wills itself into a condition of terminal stasis; and in this state of deathly equilibrium, time ceases to exist because there is no motion (or even potentiality of motion) left to measure.

One work of the mid-sixties in which Ballard succeeds in embodying this insight at the level of myth is *The Crystal World,* probably the most esteemed of Ballard's longer narratives and something of a display piece for his baroque prose style and mythopoeic propensities. Appropriately enough, it is a poetic image of time and eternity that serves as the donnée of this novel, that well-known metaphor from Shelley's *Adonais* through which the poet celebrates death's transcendent power over crass matter:

> Life like a dome of many-colored glass,
> Stains the white radiance of eternity.

Out of this metaphor Ballard fashions a metaphysical fable in which all matter is suddenly transformed into crystalline structures of light. The cosmological pretext for this transformation is so bizarre—time, we are told, is leaking out of the universe—that we are tempted to suppose that not even Ballard takes it seriously. Besides, what is essential to this fable is the realization that time is running out for the human species, and that all life-forms must sooner or later vitrify into the crystalline splendor of death. . . . (pp. 210-11)

[Sanders] is a physician (and the novel's protagonist) who has spent much of his life caring for lepers. But in this crystal palace (or cathedral rather) of death, Sanders discovers a form of cosmic leprosy that is not only incurable, but also, in an inexplicable way, inwardly desirable. The play of light over the jewelled surface of an arm or a face that has suddenly become encrusted with crystalline scales fascinates Sanders, and many times in the course of the narrative he contrasts the darkness he feels within himself (or perceives in others) with the light he finds refracted over every surface of a gradually dying planet. Nor does the prospect of death—his own, the

world's—appall him; on the contrary, like so many of Ballard's scientists, Sanders' deepest sympathies are with the insentient cosmos. . . . To be absorbed into this world of radiance and stasis, Sanders suggests, is to accept the only form of redemptive grace left to us in a terminal age.

Sanders' decision to renounce his identity, his profession, and finally his life is neither peculiar to his character-type nor to his situation. Like other Ballardian antiheroes, he appears wasted with internal conflict at the very beginning of his story, and he has little reason to prefer life over death. Virtually all of Ballard's people, in fact, exhibit this sort of emotional neutrality, and it is that quality more than any other that makes them so susceptible to metamorphosis.

Not all of Ballard's transformation narratives, however, are quite as explicitly mythopoeic as *The Crystal World,* though all of them do rely upon a sense of psycho-physical interaction to provide some sort of credibility to the network of correspondences that Ballard likes to create between his apocalyptic environment and his defeated protagonists. In *The Drowned World,* for example, solar storms have "depleted the Earth's barrier against the full impact of solar radiation," and as the temperature rises and the polar caps melt, civilization retreats to a diminishing number of dry, temperate islands in an increasingly tropical and watery world. But even more intriguing are the changes wrought in the human personality, in part as an adaptation to a changing environment, but even more in response to the gradual surfacing of long-repressed instincts whose potency soon overwhelms reason. Among these instincts, perhaps the strongest is the death instinct, masked as a desire to return to the amniotic state of pre-natal consciousness.

This quest for an archaic self leads the protagonist of *The Drowned World,* a botanist named Kerans, deeper and deeper into a world of impersonal, waking dreams, as he recovers more and more of the phylogenetic memory of his fetal state and of the prehistory of our species. . . . (pp. 211-12)

Kerans' decision to pursue an almost certain, yet strangely visionary death is neither more nor less explicable than Sanders' in *The Crystal World.* Both men appear driven to surrender their merely human selves to an inhuman cosmos that holds out to each the promise of a transfiguration through death. All that has changed in *The Drowned World* is the medium through which this apocalyptic transformation takes place. But what is essential to this process—indeed what is central to all of Ballard's catastrophe narratives—is that intuition of being which the archetypal Ballardian antihero experiences the moment he steps across the threshold of either time or space or consciousness. Stated in mythological rather than pseudo-empirical terms, the underlying assumption here appears to be a distinctly gnostic one. Our living space and our temporal identity, Ballard suggests, are radical deceptions, the contrived illusions of *homo historicus.* But for the post-historical man, or for one who has been brought to the apocalyptic brink of history, the psycho-physical conditions of life we term "reality" are just so many fortuitous arrangements. The proper function of catastrophe, then, is to expose the essential arbitrariness of those arrangements and of the certitudes they have spawned. Even so basic a distinction as that between the organic and the inorganic, or between the living and the dead, blurs within the apocalyptized mind. For as the conditions of life change violently, so does the metaphysical ground for our existence; and as that ground shifts, so do the theoretical limits of self-transcendence.

For those whom Ballard has poised on the metaphysical brink of time or of sanity, psychosis often serves as a necessary stratagem for determining what, if anything, is left of reality. The traumatized ex-bomber-pilot of "**Terminal Beach**," for example—known only as Traven and probably the most self-consciously visionary of all of Ballard's philosophical suicides—retires, St. Anthony-like, to an abandoned atoll in the Pacific (a deserted nuclear test site) in search of what Ballard calls a "zone of non-time." There, through a series of increasingly insane meditations, he summons up both the remembered dead and the not-yet-annihilated mass victims of World War III. The spiritual climax of this mad hermit's quest is achieved only after Traven has reanimated, ventriloquistically, the corpse of a Japanese doctor he has found wedged into the crevice of a sand dune. For what the corpse reveals to Traven is that he, and all of us, are as truly dead as all of the victims, real and projected, of all of the atomic wars that have been or ever will be fought. The only reality is the Bomb, and in its shadow all ontological distinctions of being and nonbeing have been rendered meaningless. . . . Only madmen can even entertain the possibility of order in such a universe, since they alone perceive that order is merely artifice.

For Traven the sole reminder on this "terminal" island of the rationality that was once civilization is a maze of concrete blocks, a maddening, labyrinthine structure, suggestive, perhaps, of the Cretan labyrinth, but without apparent function or significance. . . . There is no thread that will lead us out of this nightmare we call the universe, Ballard insists, only a series of interminable delusions culminating in death.

The limits of metaphysical change in a story like "**Terminal Beach**" or in some of the even more experimental narratives that follow it are identical with whatever transformation of narrative materials and perspective the author is able to achieve. The more dissociative the relationship between the fictional protagonist and his environment becomes, the more the reader is inclined to doubt the ontological status of all events and perceptions within that narrative. Thus, the ultimate effect of the enveloping and self-obliterating surrealism of Ballard's later stories and novels is that of discrediting the reality base to which all science fiction must finally relate. The ultimate metamorphosis which Ballard attempts, therefore, is the metamorphosis of the tale itself, and not simply its characters or setting. What is perhaps Ballard's most ambitious attempt to date to achieve a new narrative form in which transformation of the self will be total and continuous is to be found in the pages of *The Atrocity Exhibition*. More a novel kit in pieces than a continuously developed narrative, *The Atrocity Exhibition* invites its reader to assemble and reassemble its serial fragments into any one of a number of possible permutations. (pp. 213-14)

The Atrocity Exhibition concerns itself with the mental breakdown of a physician whose last, relatively sane act was the assembling of an exhibit of paintings, photographs, and films on the subject of "world cataclysm." The purpose of this exhibit and its approximate contents remain something of a mystery throughout the novel, as does the name of the marginally psychotic protagonist. . . . The modality of imagined events or persons is all but impossible to fix in a world where nothing stays put long enough to be identified and where every relationship undergoes an indeterminable number of permutations. The only trace of what might be called a subsistent reality underlying all this confusion is to be found in the recurrent emphasis given to images of sex and violence, whatever the context or pretext. . . . If violence and sexuality, then, form the matrix of any communicative act, it follows quite logically (and perversely) that every act of physical or psychological union is a terminal act, whether real or fantasied. Further, every gesture of personal violence becomes a microcosm of some apocalyptic event "out there"—wherever "out there" may be in a functionally solipsistic universe. In fact, it may no longer be possible to speak of a microcosm in a narrative where the extensions of the self are infinite, and the structure of the self non-existent. (pp. 214-15)

[For the protagonist], nothing exists discretely. Phenomena are given to us only in combination or juxtaposition, and so a car crash may, for all we know, be an orgasm, or an ashtray a sex organ. Ballard's world of regressive change has finally become a world of private nightmares—of private phenomenological nightmares, to be precise. If matter exists at all, it exists only in those transient moments when the combinations and permutations of the dissociative consciousness fail to structure the data our minds are constantly processing: in those moments the phenomenal world comes rushing in to fill the vacuum of mental space. In *The Atrocity Exhibition* Ballard tends to fill that vacuum with the debris of contemporary American politics and pop culture perceived exclusively from the perspective of conspiracy theory and paranoia. And since death and mutilation, as Ballard repeatedly assures us, are primarily conceptual realities, practically anything can be done to anyone, and for almost any reason. . . . (p. 215)

Ballard is clearly attempting something like political satire in [certain passages] . . . , but it does not quite succeed, and the reasons are not too obscure to figure out. For one thing, his indignation over American war-crimes notwithstanding, he is obviously enjoying himself too much to be particularly concerned about the precise target of his abuse, and even more disconcertingly, he is unable to screen out his own fetishistic obsessions from those he ridicules in others. But as the number of such projections increases, it soon becomes obvious that the reality content of such passages is almost coincidental, and what really matters is the intensity of loathing such images are capable of expressing, whatever their origin or point of reference.

In fact, *The Atrocity Exhibition* is best approached, I would argue, not as political satire, but as a form of sublimated and abstracted Gothic fantasy, minus of course the period costumes and decor. Admittedly Ballard goes to great lengths to make his nightmare novel relentlessly up to date (circa 1970) . . . , but the real setting of this novel is the haunted castle of the mind, where the hero with a thousand names contemplates obsessively a constantly shifting landscape of pure terror. Here is the ultimate apocalypse, where the mind implodes under the stress of an environment supersaturated with maniacal aggression. . . . *The Atrocity Exhibition* and other kindred novels within the Ballard canon represent a distinctly gnostic strain in contemporary science fiction, positing a world without conceivable order or meaning. That Ballard has chosen subjective rather than cosmic paranoia as the premise of his private myth merely suggests that he, like so many of his American counterparts in the 60's (Barth, Barthelme, Coover), has come to regard the *gnosis* of madness as the only credible perspective from which to view contemporary culture. But the sheer hopelessness of Ballard's metamorphic future (or fantasied present) expresses only his own conviction that modern life offers no resistance to the self-shattering force of total doubt. (p. 216)

Robert L. Platzner, "The Metamorphic Vision of J. G. Ballard," in Essays in Literature, *Vol. X, No. 2, Fall, 1983, pp. 209-17.*

WILLIAM BOYD

The first promise of this excellent novel [*Empire of the Sun*] appeared as far back as 1977 in the now defunct literary magazine *Bananas*. There, Ballard published a story called "**The Dead Time**" (recently reprinted in his latest collection of stories *Myths of the Near Future*). At the time it was something of a deviation from the main impulses of Ballard's work in that it had a distinct autobiographical reference (it was known that the young Ballard had been interned in China during the Second World War), and that it was set in a historical past. The story—narrated in the first person—told of Ballard's release from the internment camp where he had spent the last four years. One day the guards weren't there any more and some of the prisoners just walked out. However, the narrator is pressed into delivering a truckload of corpses to a Shanghai cemetery—a ghoulish journey which soon takes on the aspects of a nightmare (and thereby becomes more recognizably Ballardian) as the young driver, lost and alone, proceeds through the wasted landscape with a curious intense relationship steadily developing between him and his decomposing cargo. (p. 12)

The story, frankly, is hard to understand, but, as with a lot of good poetry, comprehension of Ballard's unique vision does not preclude enjoyment. But now, some seven years later, the essential elements of "**The Dead Time**" have been expanded to novel length with remarkable success and no diminution of power.

I make that last point specifically, because it has always seemed to me that Ballard is at his remarkable best in the short story form. The length of a novel somehow prevents him from sustaining the muscular impact of his style and although there are always astonishing sequences, the parts—by and large—are greater than the whole. In *Empire of the Sun* however, form, content and style fuse with almost complete success. It is, without doubt, the most untypical novel he has written and the best.

At the centre of the story is a young boy called Jim, whom we may, I think, safely take to be representative of the author. . . . In 1941 Jim is eleven, and living with his parents in Shanghai, a city occupied by Japanese troops engaged in fighting the Chinese. Then comes Pearl Harbour and the foreign nationals in the city are all interned in special camps on the outskirts and in the outlying districts of the Yangtse delta. Jim is separated from his parents and for some weeks patrols the city alone on his bike, staying in the abandoned houses of the foreign residents. For a while he becomes the uneasy ward of two renegade American merchant seamen called Basie and Frank, who make a living selling the gold teeth they knock from the mouths of the endless stream of corpses carried out to sea on the Yangtse's tide. But, shortly after, their free-wheeling existence comes to an end when Jim unwittingly causes them all to be captured by the Japanese.

The next section of the novel deals with Jim's life in Lunghua internment camp. Jim becomes a curious, alien figure in the civilian camp. Parentless, often spurned by the other inmates, he has to rely on the kindness of the camp doctor and the curious patronage of Basie, who runs the camp's black market. But the bizarre life he leads within the wire is strangely consoling and reassuring, and it's with some alarm that he greets the collapse of the Japanese army and the ending of the war. Rightly so, as it turns out, for the final section of the novel sees the deprived but ordered world of the inmates of the camp degenerate into brutal anarchy. Before he is reunited with his parents, Jim experiences a death march, incarceration in an empty stadium (where Jim sees the flash from Nagasaki) and finds himself trying to survive in a savage landscape of escaped prisoners, demoralised Japanese troops and bloodthirsty Kuomintang guerillas, all fed and fuelled by the boundless generosity of the American supply planes flying above them.

Ballard's novels and stories are chronicles of obsessions which are usually enacted in worlds at the end of their tether. Sometimes these obsessions belong within a recognisable sub-genre of science fiction, but more recently Ballard's work has become increasingly personal and unclassifiable. The obsessions—flight, the sun, the complex passage of time, the juxtapositions of animate and inanimate matter—are elliptical, dense and encoded, with all the ambiguities and half-perceived potencies of a symbolist poem. . . . The other crucial factor about the development in Ballard's work is the domination of style. . . . Characters, plot, incident and setting become, in the more refined examples, nothing more than excuses for a series of remarkable verbal tableaux, fugues and variations on favourite themes. Accordingly the novels, *qua* stories, are often disappointing. The characters are two dimensional, psychological nuance is minimal, plotting seems almost an irritation. But, set beside this, is prose of a distinctiveness and impact which is as astonishing and as individual as that of Hemingway's revolutionary *In Our Time*. It's a matter of opinion, but it has always seemed to me that Ballard is one of those writers for whom the line by line, paragraph by paragraph delights far outweigh one's more traditional cavills and quibbles.

What makes *Empire of the Sun* Ballard's best novel is that on this occasion style and narrative fuse. Again, I think this must be purely as a result of the subject matter. . . . [The] need to be faithful to his own experience plus the necessity of confining himself within the parameters of historical fact have obliged Ballard to pay more than lip service to those ingredients of story-telling—pace, structure, character development, narrative—to a degree than in his other novels he might not have felt was necessary. But, on top of this—and this is what makes *Empire of the Sun* an extraordinary *war* novel—is the presence of all the familiar Ballardian motifs, symbols and obsessions: empty swimming pools, the cinema, abandoned aircraft, a society in terminal decay, dreams of flying, etc. There are flaws—as always Ballard's dialogue is shaky and he's inclined to repeat himself—but the mix is otherwise extremely—and uniquely in his work—impressive. (pp. 12-13)

But there is a third factor that contributes to *Empire of the Sun*'s success in addition to the bizarre world of wartime Shanghai and Ballard's entrancing style. This third factor is the extent to which the novel departs from and undermines the traditional concept of what makes a war novel.

When we look at the broad tradition of the war novel in the twentieth century the dominant tendency—to generalise once again—has been to write about heroism, sacrifice, fellow-feeling and fortitude. Indivisibly bound up with this has been an inevitable and overwhelming tendency to falsify and distort the fictional presentation of war. Why? It's not because heroism, sacrifice etc. etc. don't exist, or to say that war doesn't give rise to them—they do, and war does. The reason why the traditional war novel is so misleading is because those positive values are present to such a minuscule degree that to write about them and reflect on them in the way novelists have done is completely to misrepresent what being in a war is like. This is not a question of realism: the most gory and blood-bolstered war novels, which pull no punches about war's nastiness, invariably end up celebrating those positive attitudes—heroism, fortitude etc. . . . To select positive values from this context is completely futile—and wholly misleading.

It is possibly *Empire of the Sun*'s greatest achievement to be a war novel that utterly eschews the consoling positive treatment of war and to reflect—without retreating into the comic absurd—this awesome context described above. As Jim experiences the war in Shanghai, the camp and its environs, he unreflectingly educates himself as to its reality. To put it very simply, this education consists of acknowledging three truths. The first is that, in war, heroism, self-sacrifice and endurance are not key principles: rather, the codes by which people survive are pragmatism, mendacity and ruthless self-interest. The second and related truth is that people adapt to war and these codes with an astonishing ease. The third truth, and this has a bearing on war fiction itself, dawns on Jim as the war is almost over and he reads about events in Europe in American magazines. . . . With very rare exceptions, the wars we read about in novels and history books, see at the movies, watch on TV and on the newsreels are in actual fact nothing more than a glamorised fantasy. Jim, as he reads about the Second World War, feels that his war in Shanghai must be some kind of sordid aberration from the norm. It is Ballard's greatest achievement—and one that makes *Empire of the Sun* an important as well as a good novel—to have convinced us beyond doubt that Jim's meaningless, squalid, selfish war in the estuary of the Yangtse is not peculiar and unusual, but instead universal and eternal. (p. 13)

> William Boyd, "A Unique Vision," in Books and Bookmen, *No. 348, September, 1984, pp. 12-13.*

EDWARD FOX

[*Empire of the Sun*] is a curious contribution to the literature of survival, and an important addition to the Ballard canon. His first novel that doesn't resemble science fiction, it serves as a kind of portrait of the artist as a young entropist. It is as well crafted and chilly as anything he has written.

Characters hardly matter in Ballard's decaying universe. Only the 11-year-old hero, an English schoolboy named Jim (Ballard's name), sustains interest. To Ballard, people are defined by the physical spaces that contain them. We are no more than throbbing organic matter among futuristic objects, and the objects are slightly more interesting. At his most sympathetic, he evinces a dry sadness for his people, trapped as they are amid chaos, with nothing to console them but their Pavlovian responses. . . .

Jim loses his parents in the chaos of the Japanese invasion of Shanghai. He adapts instantly to his strange new life, . . . later almost thriving as a resourceful adolescent prisoner in the internment camp outside the city. After three years of fending off starvation, Jim wonders if life will continue after the war ends, or if a new war, World War III, has already begun. . . . The haze of malnutrition and disease blurs in his mind the distinctions between life and death, war and peace. (p. 89)

Empire of the Sun throws up occasional gems. . . . But the novel doesn't yield such treasures willingly. This is a self-contained universe, where things happen slowly and in strict sequence. At times *Empire of the Sun* resembles the static, hermetically sealed, artificial worlds of Wyndham Lewis's novels, where the ups and downs, the climaxes and emotional tension of fiction are bled out in the interests of constructing a clinical and efficient narrative. Ballard's technique is fiction's equivalent of the robot car factory.

Ballard casts few veils over his own history in this autobiographical novel. The most obvious departure he makes from what really happened is in editing out his parents. Playing it as straight as he can, he limits his urge to make the story taller but allows himself the liberty of bizarre similes to express the strangeness of the experience: "The rotting coffins projected from the loose earth like a chest of drawers."

It may be true that schoolboys of Jim's age and background don't think about their parents much and inhabit violent dream worlds, but it is amazing and perversely intriguing that an author should take as harrowing an experience as this and present it with such stylized impersonality. In his first venture beyond genre fiction, Ballard wears his pacemaker squarely on his sleeve. (p. 90)

> Edward Fox, "Goodbye, Cruel World," in The Nation, *Vol. 240, No. 3, January 26, 1985, pp. 89-90.*

Frederick Barthelme

1943-

American short story writer and novelist.

Barthelme has won recognition for *Moon Deluxe* (1983), a collection of short stories, and for his novel *Second Marriage* (1984). In both books he focuses on lackadaisical, middle-class males who inhabit impersonal urban environments. He vividly describes contemporary American urban landscapes and meticulously catalogues the superabundance of brand-name objects to emphasize the depersonalized nature of his characters and their lives. Brian Murray observed that Barthelme's "brand-name dropping" enables him "to evoke strongly that atmosphere of impermanence and vulgar, television-bred consumerism that is part of the fabric of life in most American suburbs." Barthelme's understated prose style and use of ordinary dialogue contribute to the sense of malaise and disconnectedness experienced by his protagonists. He studied creative writing with his older brother Donald and with John Barth, both noted writers of experimental fiction.

(See also *Contemporary Authors*, Vol. 114.)

Courtesy of Frederick Barthelme

DOROTHY NYREN

Rangoon is a miscellany of surrealistic short fiction, drawings, and photographs whose themes seem to be the banality of America and an acceptance of the intrusions of technology into daily life. Some blank black pages in the middle are restful. . . . As for the stories, well, probably one isn't supposed to read them; they are more turn-the-page found objects. The book itself is an example of the intrusion of technology, its banality too banal.

> Dorothy Nyren, in a review of "Rangoon," in Library Journal, *Vol. 95, No. 19, November 1, 1970, p. 3803.*

DONALD NEWLOVE

Dear Frederick Barthelme: *stop reading*. I wish I'd taken *your* warning on p. 11: "The bulk role of this second book in my life ["**War and War**"], as it is in yours, is to occupy the time . . . all I have to do is sit here and blow it out and then they'll buy it and then I'll do another one and so on until I die." . . . This, Frederick Barthelme, is going to be a *bad* review.

Metaphysically, "**War and War**" is about the passing of time taken in filling up 190 pages. . . . Frederick Barthelme is an author who tells how *he* writes every page. And what he's reading: Sartre, Chomsky, Merleau-Ponty, et al.

He begins with a goal to stir my lack of interest, a schedule of the novel's coming non-events. He wants no story tensions to pull me from his word play and brainguistics. He will not expose himself to wounds (or ridicule) by showing his feelings. He summons up his essence somewhere between body and typewriter as pages print out—there *is* no story, and I refuse to suggest one.

The author describes this novel as extraconceptual and pataphysical—in short, a put-on. It is not pataphysical enough, and I think the spirit of Ubu is missing.

Rigorously strangled pages, in the service of "structural linguistics, information theory and phenomenology," all frozen and published in the ninth circle. What is the point of fiction that doesn't stir you—even once—to read on? I forgive Frederick Barthelme for taking up my time, since I'm being paid. It is more difficult to forgive myself for the waste of spirit spent reading this book.

> Donald Newlove, "But the Ubu is Missing," in The New York Times Book Review, *September 19, 1971, p. 46.*

PRAIRIE SCHOONER

[*Rangoon* is a] put-on that, in its best moments, approaches *Mad Magazine* at its worst. The written text ranges from unentertaining short fictions to a half-page outline on logical and extralogical reasoning. . . . I resent this book not because it is a put-on (to suggest that it is the author's best would be too insulting), but because it is not even a clever put-on.

> A review of "Rangoon," in Prairie Schooner, *Vol. XLVI, No. 1, Spring, 1972, p. 93.*

RICHARD EDER

Condos with swimming pools, shiny cars, microwaved restaurants with Gay '90s motifs, frozen waffles and cartons of orange juice, boutique counters at department stores, and endless weekends of driving around and bar-hopping; these are the concrete and visible elements of Barthelme's alarmingly precise short stories [in **"Moon Deluxe"**]. The people are passive and ghostlike. . . .

Mostly, the action is very small. The stories tend to consist of beginnings without endings, or middles without beginnings or endings; or they simply end in mid-gesture. Several do have an element of wry anecdote. In **"Monster Deal"** there is the invasion of the narrator's bungalow by an exuberant Amazon; she ends up stealing a newspaper delivery girl whom, with a display of initiative rare for a Barthelme character, he had invited to dinner. In **"Safeway"** the discreet signals made by the narrator to induce a woman to pick him up go by the board after some comically elusive fencing, when it becomes apparent that she will finally go off with a van driver instead. There is pain in the failure but, typically, an exultation in once again being uninvolved. . . .

Making human contact in the world of Frederick Barthelme . . . is like deep-sea diving. It is difficult, it requires training and preparation, it is done in an alien element and through breathing equipment. . . . One character taps on his TV screen when he notices that the news anchor-woman has a lock of hair out of place, and there is more tenderness expressed there than in anything he does with a flesh-and-blood woman who drops in to go out.

In some respects Barthelme resembles Ann Beattie; there is a guarded neutrality of tone, and an accomplished voicing of emotion by concealment. The speech is flat or askew, seemingly inconsequential, yet as indicative as a mask. (p. 1)

In a way, though, Barthelme is scarier. What is tacit in Beattie is suppressed emotion; in the **"Moon Deluxe"** stories the emotion is there—which is why the aimless encounters and near-misses gnaw at us—but it is not so much suppressed as mildewed. In the heat. A damp cloud of prosperity has descended on the condominium communities of Mississippi and Alabama.

Prosperity obscures purposes. What people do is not clear—they run trendy shops, perhaps, or work on computers or teach at universities—but in any case what they do is not important enough to identify them. The weekend is the battleground, but for a war of entrenchment, not of position.

Prosperity also obscures identities. One forlorn girl is given a $17,000 water-blue Peugeot for her birthday; she cruises around trying to reignite an affair with an older man that started when she was 13. "We had a little romance" is the way the narrator puts it, blankly, blandly. They end up at his apartment. Whether anything much happens is not mentioned; sex would be as unimportant as the furniture or the contents of the refrigerator.

In fact, furniture and furnishings are what is important. "You've got a great couch," the girl says, lying on it. . . . She asks for a Mountain Dew. "You might as well ask for a Grapette," the narrator says; "Grapette kind of went away, I guess. I hate that."

In the world that Barthelme evokes with so much wit, such an acute ear and so large a desolation, it is not childhood that is lost, nor empires and passions that rise and decline. It is consumer brands. Grapette, like brightness, falls from the air. That is his point: There is no other brightness. (p. 10)

Richard Eder, "The Weekend Wars of Entrenchment," in Los Angeles Times Book Review, *July 31, 1983, pp. 1, 10.*

MARGARET ATWOOD

"Moon Deluxe" is a first collection of stories by Frederick Barthelme, and it can be said at the outset that it's impossible to conceive of any writer doing what he does any better than he does it. Part of what he does consists of delineating the malaise of the unattached middle-class male. The other part is sheer technique. His textures are impeccable: Rich, brightly colored, they seem to float on an underlying vacancy like mirages, leaving the reader dizzy and a little sunstruck. He has a hard, shiny, many-faceted insect's eye for the surfaces of things—seedy, greasy, plastic-coated things or lush, expensive, meretricious things—second only to Raymond Chandler's. His dialogue is faithful to the vernacular, totally believable, and at the same time it seems to have been bounced at an odd angle off some wall the reader can't see. If Mr. Barthelme hasn't been spotted as a brilliant screen-writer-in-embryo yet, he will be soon.

In other words, Mr. Barthelme's got the tools in his tool-kit neatly arranged. But beyond that, what's going on? It's difficult at first to tell. One might glibly say, "Not much," but although that in a way is the point, it's not the whole point. Although it is by turns funny, weird and sad, **"Moon Deluxe"** makes sinister suggestions.

Mr. Barthelme tells us, among other things, what it's like to wake up and find out that you've been cast in the unenviable and secondary role of Ken in the Barbie Doll game, condemned to passive observation, your Jockey shorts coextensive with your skin. Mr. Barthelme's male protagonists (and all his protagonists are male) are in a direct line of descent from Fred Astaire, who, when actual copulation loomed, preferred to dance on the ceiling or make love to a hat-stand.

These men are, on the average, 35 to 40. With one exception, they are either single or divorced. They have no offspring and appear to have no progenitors. They live in apartment complexes with swimming pools and questionable décor, they spend a lot of time in cars, and they feed on restaurant meals or TV dinners. They have no inner monologues. They don't dream. Politics for them is the news with the sound turned down. They have no close friends. They exist in an eternal present consisting of the weather, furniture, cars, other people's appearances, scraps of conversation. Probably they have feelings, but we aren't always sure. (pp. 1, 22)

Compared with his passive men, Mr. Barthelme's women are supercharged. They're so jumpy they scarcely know what to do with themselves, and they bop around like deranged stoats, looking good, radiating sexuality, trying to attract the attention of the author's latter-day Prufrocks. One of these women has a habit of throwing herself into swimming pools, even though she can't swim. . . . The men don't think much of other men, especially those who prefer the old style of slapping women around and putting them down; but they don't expect a whole lot from women either, up close at any rate. Considering the sometimes capricious, insensitive and rude behavior of Mr. Barthelme's women, it's understandable.

Sometimes the men deal with several women at once, and the men get even more confused: Are the women lovers? In any case, role reversal is rampant. The men react to these women with approach-avoidance behavior, like rats offered a piece of cheese which, if accepted, may or may not trigger an electric shock. Though the women are forever asking the men in for a shower, for breakfast, for anything at all, the men evade. Like the man in **"Shopgirls"** who follows a couple of young women around for weeks but, when finally alone with one of them, decides her eyebrows are peculiar, these men are just looking, thanks. . . .

I suspect that a number of men will find this book truer to their own experience than a number of women would like to admit. Fear in the face of demands for performance, emotional as well as sexual, and indifference—rather than *machismo*—in the midst of surplus may be the prevailing condition of the average modern American man, especially in this world of singles' apartments, in which roles are seen as poses, roots are shallow, and individuals, like atoms, collide randomly.

But who's to know? Mr. Barthelme is showing rather than telling. Is this the end of linear causality? Is it a message from the future? Is it a desperate lonely-hearts letter in a shiny bottle, disguised as a satire of the Playboy ethic? Whatever it is, **"Moon Deluxe"** is engaging, observant and at times downright whack-in-the-solar-plexus mean. Read it and ponder. (p. 22)

> Margaret Atwood, *"Male and Lonely: 'Moon Deluxe',"* in The New York Times Book Review, *July 31, 1983, pp. 1, 22.*

FRANCES TALIAFERRO

[*Moon Deluxe*] comes with a side order—in this case, neither lettuce leaf nor tomato slice nor onion ring, but advance praise from other writers of the laid-back school of fiction. Ann Beattie and Raymond Carver admire Mr. Barthelme's "gradual revelations" and his "peculiar grasp of the slant side of human relationships." Like Mr. Barthelme's short stories, these comments don't provide much nourishment, but they do give a taste of the odd sensibility that permeates *Moon Deluxe*. . . .

[The stories in *Moon Deluxe*] share an imperviousness to summary, a neutrality of diction, and a spacy weightlessness that disconnects characters from their own affect. Most of these stories are told by a first-person narrator in the present tense. Reading them is like watching television with the sound off: the images have a flat immediacy with no history and no future except what the viewer is moved to infer. (p. 74)

Sometimes the narrator refers to himself in the second person. The effect is one of passivity and disjunction; the narrator becomes his own object, noting his separate image as if he were watching himself on the tube. . . .

Objects occupy a great deal of space in *Moon Deluxe*. They are not objective correlatives—things that objectify or symbolize emotions felt by the characters. In fact, people and objects seem to have about the same moral and emotional value, seem to be equally concrete and inscrutable, so that when teenage Violet reveals that she works as a "pie girl" at a store called Pie Country, "pie" and "girl" are not immediately distinguishable; both are visual elements in the landscape of materialism. Mr. Barthelme is also given to listing objects. Homer did it epically, with ships, but Barthelme's catalogues are closer to Horchow or to David Hockney. . . .

At times, the reader of *Moon Deluxe* feels like E. M. Forster's English as they contemplate the landscape of India: "They were thousands of miles from any scenery they understood."

I have moments of thinking these stories might be very high art. Such moments alternate with longer, more passive periods that correspond to slow afternoons on the living-room couch when you read the livestock futures and the shipping news because it's too much trouble to get up. (p. 75)

> Frances Taliaferro, in a review of *"Moon Deluxe,"* in Harper's, *Vol. 267, No. 1600, September, 1983, pp. 74-5.*

DEBORAH GIMELSON

[The short stories] by Frederick Barthelme gathered in *Moon Deluxe* . . . are rather mediocre examples of the genre. Nevertheless, they are worthy of attention because their weaknesses afford us an opportunity to study the impact of several less appealing aspects of our society on some of our artists.

Among America's least flattering national characteristics, for example, is the tendency of many of us to live in a state of adolescent self-preoccupation far beyond the age when that is appropriate or excusable. Moving rapidly through interpersonal encounters that carry little emotional weight, enslaved to our egos and our thirst for sensation, we find it difficult to perceive the world from any perspective outside the "I." Barthelme reflects this infantilism in both his incessant use of first-person narrative and the emptiness of his content. The sort of passionate human connections that draw a reader in are absent; a detached elegance of tone seems to be the primary concern.

Barthelme's settings are carefully-laid suburban tableaux. . . . His protagonists are mostly men over 30 led into complications by younger women sporting jogging shorts of every possible hue with coordinated tank tops. It is not this milieu as such that is the problem, though; it is the author's delineation of his characters' relationships to the landscape and to one another, and the conscious sterility of his language.

Consider the title story, presumably selected for that distinction by Barthelme or the editor because it best exemplifies the book's preoccupations and strengths. Actually, **"Moon Deluxe"** is something of a variation on Barthelme's standard situation. Still, it clearly demonstrates his style and themes.

The hero, Edward, is a young man living in an apartment complex that could be anywhere between New York and Los Angeles. He is invited to a dinner party by Eileen, an older woman he likes because "she is easy to get along with." How he arrived at this conclusion is a bit obscure, since the one previous time we see them together, Eileen appears momentarily from behind a bush and disappears before we get any sense of her. But no matter. Edward goes to Eileen's, where he meets Lily, a blonde occupying an apartment recently vacated by another woman with whom he had a "thing." Lily flirts with him mercilessly. Edward survives the meal and the tasteless jokes of the hostess and her boyfriend, Phil, only to be practically shoved out the door with this aggressive stranger.

Taking Lily home, he finds that she has a female roommate with whom she is carrying on an ambiguous relationship. . . . The companion turns out to be a redhead who Edward recalls making eyes at him from a passing car earlier in the day. The two women quarrel over his presence, then show him to the door. . . . Edward ends as he began, alone in a world where the only visible light is reflected off the pool's surface and his shoes are always wet from the last, damp late-night walk.

The entanglements of this plot offer possibilities, yet Barthelme manages, as he almost always does, to drain energy from the action by employing ill-suited prose devices. The impersonal "you" . . . serves to overemphasize the already obvious alienation of the characters. The present tense (in which all the stories in the volume are written) cuts off the events from the actors' pasts, imparting a sense of undernourishment.

In keeping with his housing development world, Barthelme often uses a sort of split-level story construction, initiating the action at one location and moving it to a second for the payoff. In **"Moon Deluxe"** the tactic happens to make sense, because Edward apparently retains some emotional tie to the apartment Lily now shares. The quirky setup, however, is never fully exploited. Instead, the reader is enervated by a meticulous description of the flat itself, down to the effects of track lighting on the walls . . . and a window-size photograph of a man in a fedora.

Barthelme's purpose, one would guess, is to demonstrate the emptiness of his people's lives by making them seem less important than—or at least defined by—the objects around them. The dialogue, too, although often well rendered, only points up the fact that each of the speakers is locked inside his own monologue. A neutral tone pervades. . . . (pp. 15-16)

Meanwhile, the author avoids the issue he has raised: What sort of need could have brought this aimless man under the sexual sway of two lesbians who cannot conceivably offer him fulfillment? It is not enough to show that Edward is misled by his fantasies, the roles expected of him, and his inability to communicate. Such a condition is hardly unique. But Barthelme is unwilling or unable to explore beyond its most superficial, and tedious, manifestations. As a result, what he gives us is a mere hodgepodge of despair and irrelevant detail.

The other stories in the volume have similar troubles. **"Shopgirls"** is about a voyeur whose turf is a shopping center; **"Lumber"** plods through a romance between another deadhead and his good samaritan girlfriend. . . . **"Gila Flambé"** brings a listless hero and his Mazda together with an odd couple and their dog in a family-style restaurant on an unnamed town's neon-lit main drag. Except for **"Moon Deluxe,"** all the tales are told in the first person. One tires quickly.

Luckily, Barthelme's failings, while common among young American writers, are far from universal. Other authors just beginning to hit their stride are willing to confront life's conflicts head-on. They are open enough to see events from more than one viewpoint—to let some hope and enthusiasm filter in as counterweights to fear and loneliness—and sufficiently confident of their prose not to be fearful of a little emotion. In time, one hopes, they will relieve us of the currently dominant style of literary mirror gazing exhibited in *Moon Deluxe*. (p. 16)

Deborah Gimelson, "Tales of the Single Existence," in The New Leader, Vol. LXVI, No. 22, November 28, 1983, pp. 15-16.

PETER LA SALLE

Barthelme has a gift for both detail and dialogue. He has a sense of color that allows him to paint brightly indeed with his words, and he can work the second-person "you" into his usual first-person narration for a haunting and poetic voice. . . . In fact, there seems to be so much raw talent [in *Moon Deluxe*] that the unsettling thing about reading these stories is to have to admit that many of them function according to a simple

formula. Mid-thirties man heads into what promises to be a sexual adventure; gets confused by the complications, or decides that it, or much of anything else, isn't worth the effort; walks or drives around some and feels sensitive. Read a few of them and you know exactly where most are heading, with a predictability that I haven't encountered in a collection in a long time.

I suppose the bigger issue is that these are *New Yorker* stories. and if you feel the paper, you will recall that *The New Yorker* is a "slick" magazine. . . . [Recently] its younger stable seems to be performing to a recipe of upper-middle-class coolness that better than ever matches the sleek advertising. There is the old joke about the stock *New Yorker* story: You write a normal story, then just chop off the last couple of paragraphs, to leave the reader in that fashionable limbo. Of course the problem runs much deeper than that. . . . [As] this collection shows, a good deal of the magazine's current fiction is strikingly similar to its many cartoons: Light (even when supposedly "serious"), apparently "in," and easily flipped through—and forgotten, once the work of the safe, competent artistry has made you nod in agreement a little. (p. 158)

Peter La Salle, in a review of "Moon Deluxe," in Studies in Short Fiction, Vol. 21, No. 2, Spring, 1984, pp. 157-58.

JONATHAN YARDLEY

This loopy little novel ["**Second Marriage**"] is almost entirely without consequence, but it is so good-humored and high-spirited that few readers are likely to notice or care. Though Frederick Barthelme has a reputation as a serious writer, there's hardly a serious word in **"Second Marriage"**—no heavy themes, no deep thoughts, no philosophizing. There are, on the other hand, a number of surprisingly good laughs, several pleasingly goofy characters, and enough wry, offhanded social commentary to keep the reader hoping for more.

The partners in the second marriage—second for him, that is, first for her—are Henry and Theo. They are in their thirties and live in a Sunbelt city that is not identified but possibly is Houston, where they exist on the fringes of a university community. Their marriage has followed abruptly upon their purchase of a house; until then they had lived together in apartments for more than a dozen years, along with Theo's daughter Rachel, now 13 years old, whose father is *not* Henry.

The house is an unprepossessing structure in an unprepossessing neighborhood, one inhabited mostly by people slightly younger than Henry and Theo. . . . [A] long series of peculiar events . . . put the new marriage on the rocks and are the source of the novel's quite considerable comedy.

Among these are the reappearance in Henry's life of his first wife, Clare, along with the nervous, sardonic boyfriend, Joel, whom she is trying to dump; the involuntary acquisition of a sexy, perky college student, Kelsey, who becomes Rachel's constant companion; the development of an intense attachment between Theo and Clare, who go off unannounced to Colorado and return a few days later to boot Henry out of the house.

Henry loves Theo but he is a nice, patient guy, so he decides to roll with the punches. He goes off to an apartment in the complex where he and Clare lived many years ago, fiddles around with a woman or two, and waits for Theo to come to her senses. He does miss her, though. . . . (pp. B1, B15)

Still, he manages to get by. . . . He shows up from time to time at his job in an advertising agency . . . , wings it down to the southeast Texas coast for a fling with the accommodating wife of a friend. He doesn't hear from Theo, but keeps in close touch with Rachel, who badly wants him back and at one point says: "Tell me how big a deal this is. I mean, what's the correct level of anxiety for a child like me?"

As Henry replies, "Not high." This novel is too cheerful and insouciant to end on a downer, so in the end Henry's patience pays off. The ultimate reconciliation, in any event, is of less moment than the twisting path by which it is reached—the encounters Henry and Theo have, together and separately, with people, places and events that are just slightly off-center, just marginally crazy. There's a jaunty, antic feeling to **"Second Marriage"** that is its most appealing characteristic, with the result that traveling with Henry along the way to rewedded bliss makes for a most amusing journey.

Another of the novel's appealing qualities is its immersion in ordinary American life. Its people may be slightly wacko, but the details of their lives are immediately recognizable. . . . [They] do all those ordinary American things, in other words, that too often are neglected in the hothouse of contemporary American fiction. And in doing so they give **"Second Marriage"** a most agreeable connection with reality, however fantastic it sometimes seems. (p. B15)

> *Jonathan Yardley, "Marriage Go-Round: The Wacky Life of an American Couple," in* The Washington Post, *September 19, 1984, pp. B1, B15.*

ANATOLE BROYARD

When I read **"Moon Deluxe,"** Frederick Barthelme's recent collection of stories, I found it hard to accept the desolation of the lives he described. It seemed to me that he was exaggerating for effect, making things out to be worse than they are, which is a habit common to writers. But some people disagreed with me. "You've never lived in California," they said.

After reading **"Second Marriage,"** Mr. Barthelme's first novel, I'm still not altogether convinced, but I'm willing to concede that it's possible, that what he describes may be true in some parts of the country. This unidentified place of his may be the world of tomorrow, or 10 years from now. Besides, the people in this book are more interesting, human and recognizable than those of the short stories. They're like object lessons, terrible warnings. If you're not careful, Mr. Barthelme seems to be saying, this could happen to you.

"Second Marriage" reminds me of George Orwell's "Nineteen Eighty-Four" turned inside out. Instead of a depersonalizing police state, Mr. Barthelme depicts a society in which people depersonalize themselves, also in the service of a remorseless kind of "progress." His characters seem to have come to the end of one kind of world without being able to invent another. . . .

Henry, the narrator, who is separated from his wife, Theo, says of his life: "It's like a permanent business trip. You go out in the town and then there's nobody there, so you come back.". . .

[Henry] and Mariana, a woman he takes up with, have learned how to appreciate things like the "blimp ruins" out at the airport. He parks his car and gazes at a large field of cement pipes. They've become acclimated to the wasteland. Their landscape is by Diane Arbus and they like it that way. They take to irony as people took drugs in the 1960's. Halfway through **"Second Marriage,"** I began to think that perhaps Mr. Barthelme is right after all. People can get along with bleakness. If you don't believe it, just look at the way some of them furnish their houses. . . .

Just think of all the trouble you save when you relinquish mankind's immemorial struggle with the idea of domesticity. And love—to shake off the shackles of love may be like a great leap in the advance of modern medicine, like eliminating heart disease, or cancer. There's an undeniable consolation in thinking that things can't get any worse.

As I said, it's not clear where Henry and Theo live, but wherever it is, the women there are awfully sophisticated and elliptical in their talking and thinking. They are absolutely unsentimental, brutal toward the men, as if they had swapped stereotypes. . . .

Mr. Barthelme's women are all so terrifyingly blasé, so far beyond the obvious emotions or responses, but I still find them just a little inconceivable. They sound like a Lenny Bruce parody of a love scene. . . .

There seems to be a sex change—a new wave?—in Mr. Barthelme's men and women. In the way she approaches her sexuality, Theo reminds me of a man who pursues a hobby in his basement carpentry shop. When she digs a seven-foot hole in their lawn and Henry asks her what she's doing, she says that she "was looking for love in all the wrong places."

Mariana, Henry's other woman, has such a terrific rhetoric that some of us might be willing to live her life just to be able to talk like that. . . . She says to Henry about his two failed marriages and various affairs, "You got girls flying away in droves, caterwauling."

Among its many virtues, **"Second Marriage"** describes what may be the only interesting and believable dream I've ever encountered in fiction. In fact, the whole book is like an interesting and just barely believable dream—one of those dreams that's sexy, anxious, promising and threatening all at the same time.

> *Anatole Broyard, in a review of "Second Marriage," in* The New York Times, *September 28, 1984, p. C28.*

RON LOEWINSOHN

In **"Second Marriage"** Frederick Barthelme's characters eat or go out for food on practically every page. It doesn't nourish them very much—almost all of it is convenience food purchased on the run from Pie Country, Border Bill's, Long John Silver's, Burger King or Seafood in the Rough. But this fast-fried, Styrofoam-boxed, paper-bagged food, complete with individually wrapped packets of ketchup and tartar sauce, helps to give this extremely well done novel the arresting, slightly overdetailed superrealism of a group of Duane Hanson sculptures.

The people here are thoroughly ordinary, and the technique captures them with photographic accuracy—in the midst of actions that are quintessentially unimportant. . . . In the world of this book, "second marriage" has about the same emotional weight as "second helping."

The story is narrated in the first person by Henry (no last name given). He marries Theo on the front lawn of their little bungalow the day after they've bought it. . . . This is Theo's first marriage. Henry had been married once before, to Clare, who has since become very friendly with Theo. When Clare gets into a feud with her friend Joel, Theo invites her to stay. (pp. 1, 43)

Soon after Clare moves in, Henry comes home one day to find a note from Theo saying simply, "Gone to Colorado." . . . Clare has gone with her. When the women return from Colorado to this town along the Gulf Coast (no name given), they "disinvite" Henry from his own home, saying that *they* want to try living together for a while. The story strongly suggests some exploratory lesbianism, which is treated the way just about everything in the book is—"no big deal."

In the remaining two-thirds of the novel Henry tracks his own adjustment to his situation. He moves into the Ramada Inn till Joel (his first wife's rejected lover) gets him a furnished apartment in his own complex, The Nile. There Henry is helped out by various people, male and female, while Clare and Theo first cool, then argue, then separate. All this while, aided and egged on by Theo's daughter, Rachel, Henry continues to hope for a reconciliation. At the end of the book he gets one.

This conclusion is an ironic replay of the generic ending of all those Victorian novels that resolve themselves by either forming new households in marriage or re-forming broken ones—that is, by reaffirming the family, within which both meaning and nourishment were assumed to be found. In Henry's world nobody can make any such assumptions. Families are ersatz (and unstable) collections of people who rarely even eat together and when they do it's out of a paper bag from Long John Silver's. They are all inarticulately anxious about the contemporary confusion over sex roles and about leadership and support within the family. "Home," Henry admits when asked, is only "a figure of speech."

This is not some bizarre, surrealistic, Kafkaesque nightmare-scape. It is a thoroughly recognizable contemporary urban America, with its subdivisions, shopping malls, apartment, complexes and drive-ins, a world of surfaces, all of which are either disposable or easy-to-clean—nothing will take or leave a lasting impression. Most of the people who live here are no thicker than Formica, yet they hunger obscurely for some continuity with the place and with each other. Kelsey, a stranger, a coed from the local college, follows Henry and Rachel home from a fastfood place one day just because she's lonely. Her father is a Volvo dealer who gives her a new car every year, and this disposable automobile becomes an apt metaphor for the superficial, temporary character of Mr. Barthelme's world. . . .

Mr. Barthelme never forgets his characters' limitations or the targets they offer his wit, but he is sympathetic to their hungers, and this sympathy gives them human weight and substance. He registers acutely a world in which everything occurs obliquely, where nothing is important enough to take up the center of the frame. He's got a very sharp eye and a keen ear. He concentrates on narrating desultory nonevents, almost to the exclusion of any commentary. He throws in an occasional excitement (a woman shoots out the tire of the car that's been honking at her; Henry's neighbor attempts suicide), but he resolutely refuses to develop these events or connect them to anything else. This laconic, understated focus on quotidian details and disconnected surfaces may encourage you to read quickly, su-

perficially. Don't. If you do, you will miss a lot of the subtle humor and deft portraiture. Worse, you will be making the very mistake these characters do—skim-reading their experiences the same way they bolt their Big Macs.

Henry himself only steps back from his low-keyed narration in order to contemplate these nonevents some half-dozen or so times throughout the novel. These meditations, whose lyricism recalls F. Scott Fitzgerald, elevate Henry above the semi-aware company in which we usually find him. They also leaven the narration by giving us some intensity against which we can measure the desultoriness of this world. Given these concerns, many writers could be expected to indulge themselves with commentary. But by strictly limiting the meditations, using them as a kind of punctuation, Mr. Barthelme dramatizes the lack of contemplation in the world he depicts. And he also dramatizes the cost of that lack: the book's world of surfaces remains so sterile because it is so rarely penetrated by any kind of authentic experience.

Mr. Barthelme is not always in complete control of his craft. He sometimes has his characters behave pretty arbitrarily . . . and sometimes I think he's throwing in zany or quirky incidents just to keep things interesting. In some of his short stories published last year in **"Moon Deluxe,"** he got facile, occasionally gaining a gratuitous weirdness simply by detaching his incidents from any explanatory context. But in **"Second Marriage"** (which contains at least two of those stories in slightly altered form), he provides the context that naturalizes these understated events.

Mr. Barthelme's lapses are minor. His dialogue is impeccable; his characters are fully human and engaging, rendered with unsentimental warmth. Most impressive is the thoroughness with which he has conceived his people and the complete incorporation of his themes with the plot and the method of narration. (p. 43)

> *Ron Loewinsohn, "Looking for Love After Marriage: 'Second Marriage'," in* The New York Times Book Review, *September 30, 1984, pp. 1, 43.*

BRIAN MURRAY

These days the writers who most influence the shape and the tone of "serious" American fiction are those who belong to what one critic has offhandedly but effectively labeled the "laid-back" school. These writers . . . produce flat, humorless, and generally uneventful "fictions" that sometimes appear to have been improvised; that feature passive and deracinated characters who manage to do little more than vaguely survive in a world that is full of annoyances and devoid of meaning. . . .

Set somewhere in the booming sunbelt, Frederick Barthelme's first novel *Second Marriage* has some refreshingly funny moments, and more than a few compound-complex sentences. But it . . . is largely plotless and rather too carefully odd, and so deserves a place among the more palatable products of the laid-back school. Henry, the narrator, is a low-level advertising man who finds himself more befuddled than ever after his flaky second wife kicks him out of their subdivision bungalow to make room for one of her closest friends—namely, Henry's first wife, who is nearly as flaky. Though he is supposed to be an out-of-work professor, Henry spends most of his time watching television; not surprisingly, he peppers his narrative with allusions to widely advertised goods and to well-known video faces. . . .

Combined with the vivid descriptions of fast-food joints, convenience stores, and jerry-built apartment houses, all of this brand-name dropping does enable Barthelme to evoke strongly that atmosphere of impermanence and vulgar, television-bred consumerism that is part of the fabric of life in most American suburbs. Perhaps he evokes it too strongly. Reading *Second Marriage* is like wandering through one of those fluorescent-lit and Muzak-filled discount houses that stocks everything from bull manure to designer jeans. There are a few things to catch your eye in such a place, but very little to make you want to linger.

Brian Murray, "Discount Fiction," in Chronicles of Culture, *Vol. 9, No. 5, May, 1985, p. 28.*

T. Coraghessan Boyle
1948-

American short story writer and novelist.

In irreverent fiction filled with satire and ironic twists, Boyle reveals the comic senselessness of human behavior. His verbally manic style has led critics to link him with Thomas Pynchon and other writers of black humor. Many of Boyle's works combine history and American popular culture in incongruous ways. In one early story, for example, an explorer roams the Amazon in search of Quetzalcoatl Lite, "brew of the ancient Aztecs." Such calculated absurdity is typical of Boyle's unusual anthropological slant.

Boyle received critical attention with his first volume of short fiction, *The Descent of Man and Other Stories* (1979). Many of these stories lampoon such famous political and literary figures as Idi Amin and Norman Mailer; others focus upon the triumph of natural forces over "advanced" civilization. In the title story, a man whose lover works at a primate research center begins to suspect he is losing her to a chimpanzee who is translating a work by Friedrich Nietzsche into Yerkish. The stories included in Boyle's second collection, *Greasy Lake and Other Stories* (1984), often have equally imaginative premises. In "Ike and Nina," he portrays a love affair between Dwight Eisenhower and Nina Khrushchev.

Boyle's first novel, *Water Music* (1982), unites past and present in a fictionalized account of nineteenth-century Scottish explorer Mungo Park and his ill-fated second expedition into Africa. Juxtaposing the tone and format of the Victorian picaresque novel with vibrant modern slang and black humor, Boyle satirizes Park's travels and exaggerates the physical hardships suffered by Park and his roguish companions during the expedition. In *Budding Prospects* (1984), a novel with a more realistic and contemporary setting, a hippie who considers himself a quitter is lured into growing marijuana for profit and learns responsibility through his struggle to harvest the crop despite numerous obstacles.

MAX APPLE

A volume of stories, bereft of continuity in plot and character, is often unified only by the writer's obsessiveness. A certain restlessness, a temporary energy takes over. . . . That energy roams the lines of the story looking for a way out. James Joyce called that way out an epiphany, but in our time it is more like the quick release of passion than the stately illumination of the intellect.

"Descent of Man" is loaded with energetic language. On the dedication page, T. Coraghessan Boyle offers us Tarzan's "Ungowa," and with that half-comic, half-desperate signal we launch into this first collection. Tarzan is an appropriate voice of introduction: The jungle is as dominant in Mr. Boyle's imagination as the parlor is in Jane Austen's. Rot and overgrowth are among Mr. Boyle's favorite subjects, but his style is as crisp as if it has been quick-frozen.

The title story begins with the narrator's lament: "I was living with a woman who suddenly began to stink." This is not just

Photograph by Alan Arkaway

the petty vindictiveness of the scorned lover; this man's Jane really does stink, since her new lover is Konrad, a brilliant chimpanzee who is translating into Yerkish Darwin's "Descent of Man," Chomsky's "Language and Mind" and Nietzsche's "Beyond Good and Evil."

The story is characteristic of Mr. Boyle's obsession with the origin of the species. It is this comic-imaginative quest that makes the collection seem so unified. Characters are in search of the differences between man and beast, man and woman, plunderer and hero, art and silliness.

Though the stories are sometimes merely clever, Mr. Boyle is capable of the sublime. In **"A Women's Restaurant"** his narrator is obsessed by a restaurant that admits only women. His imagination runs wild because he is excluded. This underground man wants to enter society, but in our time he finds that he is barred by femininity rather than by the old standbys, wealth and culture. . . . (p. 14)

In **"Green Hell"** Mr. Boyle has a wonderful time with [a] . . . melodramatic circumstance—a plane crash and its survivors. They crash in the jungle, of course, bury "twelve rugby players" and try to establish their little society in the wilderness. "The pilot talked of the spirit of democracy, the social contract, the state of nature, the myth of the noble savage, and the mythopoeic significance of Uncle Sam."

But Mr. Boyle does not use melodrama, rot and decay exclusively as parody. In **"Bloodfall"** it rains blood. In a number of the stories Mr. Boyle is fascinated with describing blood and clots of gore. In this story he gives his descriptive power free rein. The brutal irony of the story is lodged in how the bored rich communards watch the blood fall and listen to their "thirty-six-inch Fisher speaker in the corner," knowing that it might be "Judgment Day." They smoke and eat and watch in this charged but calm atmosphere still another "descent of man."

The circumstances in these stories are always surprising. An astronaut comes home from the moon to a house that has rotted away; an old Norse bard laments the bad days a plunderer sometimes has to endure. In **"Dada,"** Idi Amin comes to New York as the guest of honor at a Dada festival. (pp. 14, 39)

There is no lack of cleverness in **"Descent of Man,"** but sometimes the cleverness is all, or it is only partial cleverness, as in **"The Big Garage"** or **"The Champ."** But the failures are the honest failures of an energetic writer who is willing to try anything. That "Ungowa" on the dedication page is a joyful announcement: An adventurous new bird, T. Coraghessan Boyle, has come to roost in the literary jungle. (p. 39)

> *Max Apple, "Characters in Search of a Difference," in* The New York Times Book Review, *April 1, 1979, pp. 14, 39.*

ALEXANDER STILLE

T. C. Boyle's *Descent of Man* is . . . surrealistic, . . . preposterous and lighthearted. . . . Boyle's [stories], even when describing events that would normally be horrifying, retain a comic touch that avoids pretentiousness but prevents us from taking them seriously.

His final story, **"The Drowning,"** begins: "In this story someone will drown. Yet there will be no apparent reason for this drowning. . . . It will instead be like so many events of the future: inexplicable, incomprehensible." Many of the stories share this studied senselessness: a woman leaves her husband for the chimpanzee she is studying; . . . an astronaut's wife and house mysteriously decay while he is exploring outer space. Such apocalyptic noises are frequently joined to farcical effects. **"The Extinction Tales"** records the elimination of various species. An Inventor . . . manages to photograph God dead, and is burnt alive by an angry crowd. In yet another story, a bored millionaire collector goes on a mad quest for ancient beer cans. . . . Boyle is better off when he is not trying to make a point, when he is simply having fun with his material, wandering among comic gestures and farcical moments.

> *Alexander Stille, in a review of "Descent of Man," in* The Nation, *Vol. 228, No. 13, April 7, 1979, p. 377.*

KATHERINE KEARNS

Boyle works like a silent comedy artist, the Harold Lloyd of the short story. He takes an idea and plays infinite variations on it, each elaboration and twist a fresh moment of comedy. Like Lloyd's, his stunts are dangerous; you hold your breath and wait for him to fall, and when he is successful you are both gratified and relieved. His timing must be exquisite to accommodate his fantastical stylistic and thematic gymnastics, and for every virtuoso performance in *Descent of Man* there

are one or two that fail. Boyle's stories are incongruous mixtures of the mundane and the impossibly surreal, and at his best he deftly juggles both worlds, using one to dazzle, the other to undercut. . . . [**"Heart of a Champion"**] lulls the unsuspecting into tranquillity with its first paragraph: "We scan the cornfields and the wheatfields winking gold and goldbrown and yellowbrown in the midday sun. . . ." Then it pulls the rug out by having the heroic Lassie, Timmy's best friend, fall muzzle over plumy tail for a randy coyote. In **"The Champ"** Boyle tells a classic story: the aging fighter threatened by a new talent. The two finally square off after months of arduous training, the young one cocky, mouthing verse and grinning, the old one, grim and determined. They are Angelo D. and Kid Gullet, eating champions. . . . As in many of Boyle's stories there is a suggestion of real violence . . . , and like most comedy there is an element of the vicious in it. The contenders are corpulent, obscene grotesques, and the fight crowd, delivering its own puny one-two combinations with hotdogs, ice cream and beer, is no more—or less—human than the men in the ring.

"We are Norsemen," a story about pillage and rape and murder, is also a superbly orchestrated piece of comedy, and it remains comic because Boyle's language controls the content absolutely. It begins:

> We are Norsemen, hardy and bold. We mount the black waves in our doughty sleek ships and go a-raiding. We are Norsemen, tough as stone. At least some of us are. Myself, I'm a skald— a poet, that is. I go along with Thorkell Son of Thorkell the Misaligned and Kolbein Snub when they sack the Irish coast and violate the Irish children, women, dogs and cattle and burn the Irish houses and pitch the ancient priceless Irish manuscripts into the sea. Then I sing about it.

Because the story is short and the theme is simple, Boyle's own Nordic kennings and his absurd anachronisms of speech and thought hold fast. Here, as in **"The Champ,"** he tells about obscenities, physical and spiritual, and makes them real, human, comic and terrible without being obscene himself.

Some of Boyle's longer stories fall from the balletic Harold Lloyd comedy of elaboration into a more brutal slapstick, and the stories that fall hardest are those that seem didactic. Boyle, for all his talent, is not a Jonathan Swift, and *Descent of Man* attempts a Swiftian vision of humankind. As long as Boyle's sense of irony prevails over his apparent disgust with man the implied truths are comically devastating. When the husband in **"Descent . . . "** begins finding coarse black hairs on his wife's clothing after her late evenings' work at the primate center, . . . when she begins to smell like a fetid rain forest, we suspect that her relationship with Konrad the chimpanzee is more than platonic. Boyle takes the story beyond implication when he has Konrad translate Nietzsche's *Jenseits von Gut und Böse* and Chomsky's *Language and Mind* into Yerkish and at the same time shows us four humans digging with gourmet relish into a live monkey's brain. For all its bizarre humor, **"Descent of Man"** becomes, once you get oriented, a predictable story, too vicious to be funny and too hyperbolic to be successful satire.

"A Women's Restaurant" and **"Green Hell"** fall down for some of the same reasons. Both are relatively long stories; both become clichés because they are overstatements. **"A Women's Restaurant"** begins with subdued but evocative descriptions of the forbidden restaurant. Sounds, colors, smells all come together in the male narrator's fantasy of quintessential femininity. The story is about his obsession with ''this gathering of women, this classless convocation, this gynecomorphous melting pot,'' and it chronicles his own transformation from masculine to feminine. **"A Women's Restaurant"** approaches psychological subtlety and then fails; the obsession is acted out. The transvestite, driven to wear women's clothes so that he can gain entrance to the restaurant, is jailed for criminal trespass and then refuses to return to the masculine world. . . . The ending is heavy-handed and the story becomes mildly pornographic as it loses its sense of humor. Despite the fine, controlled writing and the wonderful Boylesian catalogues of the first several pages, the tension is destroyed as language deteriorates into exposition.

All of the stories in *Descent of Man* are interesting and some of them are inimitably successful. **"Earth, Moon"** manages to be funny, lunatic, and poignant, and **"The Extinction Tales"** is a quiet account of our own self-inflicted losses and the narrator's personal grief. Boyle is very good with language, a master of the comic undercut. His sense of the ridiculous is acute. There is a gargantuan irreverence about *Descent of Man* that refuses to acknowledge the profound complications of living and being human; and that irreverence is Boyle's weakness and his strength. Like the best surrealists he is both comical and apocalyptic, but his world is seldom a compassionate place. (pp. 103-05)

Katherine Kearns, in a review of "Descent of Man," in Carolina Quarterly, Vol. XXXI, No. 3, Fall, 1979, pp. 103-05.

ROBLEY WILSON, JR.

It occurs to me that T. Boyle is in danger of being packaged in a wrong wrapper, that such hype as is possible with a new writer's first story collection . . . is unfortunately conceived. Glitterature. *Descent of Man* presents Boyle as a kind of bookpage Mel Brooks; we get a heavy fix of his cranky facility with the language, his gift for parody, his mad-scientist skew on character and situation. The result is a breathlessly artsy book, hard to read except in small doses, remembered finally for its inventions, its perversities, its general unpleasantness. Boyle is one hell of a writer—imaginative, energetic, bright, with an ear for dialogue and eye for detail few of his contemporaries can match; I think what gripes me is that this collection sells him short. He is not just clever; he is not some berserk Scrabble player; he is not a movie freak volunteering for an experiment in automatic writing. Poor T. I so much like some of his stories that aren't collected here, I sound as if I'm writing a negative notice.

Only partly. Here are some stories worth savoring, long after you've laid the book aside: **"The Champ,"** about a battle between two heavyweight gluttons; **"A Second Swimming,"** in which Chairman Mao becomes a new Jesus; **"De Rerum Natura,"** the one story in which all of Boyle's talents, facilities, and eccentricities mesh to create The Inventor—in as satisfactory a biography of God as you could wish for—and **"Drowning,"** which is not a particularly pleasant piece, but which haunts in spite of itself.

For the rest, there are nice moments and dull, realized ideas and failed. . . . It all adds up to a fast shuffle through the work of a writer whose publishers don't yet realize what a good man they've got. (pp. 273-74)

Robley Wilson, Jr., in a review of "Descent of Man," in fiction international, *No. 12, 1980, pp. 273-74.*

ALAN FRIEDMAN

Set in the decade between 1795 and 1805, [**"Water Music"**] very deliberately goes about mimicking and mocking the novels of both the 18th and 19th centuries. The core of the plot comes from a document left to us by the Scottish explorer Mungo Park. . . . As a protagonist in Mr. Boyle's novel, Mungo Park seems a bit callow when we first meet him, but he soon turns out to be a hero in the old style. He's generous, ambitious, plucky and undefeatable. He escapes, in the course of the story, a hundred merciless deaths at the hands of thousands of white-hating natives of the African continent. But these high jinks constitute only half of the plot.

For contrast, there's a second hero, a rogue and a con man. His exploits are invented rather than given by history. He's a street-wise native of the jungle of London who survives by his wits against all odds and comers. . . .

Two heroes, two plots. The first hero genteel, the second hero vulgar, and both plots picaresque. The narrative rocks back and forth between them, from Africa to England, from the Niger to the Thames. The author, as though with a nod to the Old Novel, supplies short essays, set pieces that interrupt the tale, in order to provide (unnecessary) moral and historical perspectives. . . . [The rogue's] name, Ned Rise, is another of the indicators pointing us back to the Old Novel, in this case to the practice of giving characters tag names like Heathcliff and Roderick Random, Allworthy and Jonathan Wild (the mock-heroic rogue that Fielding hanged).

T. C. Boyle is the author previously of **"Descent of Man,"** a collection of stories I found irresistible, because they were so deliciously bizarre, when I happened across the book a couple of years ago. More or less experimental, these short pieces were curios, stylized and often morbid stories written with razzle-dazzle wit. It's disappointing to have to say that I like his first novel nowhere near so well.

The style of the new book is a freewheeling mixture of elegant polysyllabic rhetoric ("porcipophagic," "testudineous") with current colloquialisms: "It was big of her"; "Okay, already"; "Hey, let's face it." These two forms of discourse, the rhetorical and the chatty, occur in both high plot and low plot, and they occur together: "So long, mortal coil"; "Orestes couldn't have had it worse." . . . Humor? I'm not so sure. (p. 9)

The intention of such writing is, I think, not precisely humor; its intention is to limn the characters of another century with the most colorless expressions of our own in order to make them recognizable, to make them look and feel like ourselves. But that's not the effect. Cobbled together out of such banalities, Mungo Park and his wife Ailie, Ned Rise and Ned's true love Fanny exist neither here nor there. (pp. 9, 18)

"Water Music," while self-consciously honoring certain codes and manners of the past, goes out of its way to keep us aware that we are reading a work of our own times. . . . Behind the backs of his characters, author winks knowingly to reader, reader nods smugly at characters. Hardly ever does the novel allow the reader to enter the world it creates. When bones are crushed or buttocks lacerated, when characters suffer (and, poor dears, how they suffer!), their sufferings seem for the most part contrived to elicit crocodile tears. Throughout the novel Mr. Boyle seems to want to establish an equality and fraternity with the past both for himself and for the reader. But unfortunately the effort too often serves as an extended occasion for comic-strip pathos. (p. 18)

Alan Friedman, *"Two Plots, Two Heroes," in* The New York Times Book Review, *December 27, 1981, pp. 9, 18.*

KEN TUCKER

[*Water Music* makes] connections to every picaresque / experimental novel from *Tristram Shandy* to *Gravity's Rainbow*. Like those send-up classics, *Water Music* teems with odd, angry characters, and the book is narrated by a trickster who cannot allow a dramatic scene to pass without inserting a withering joke. . . .

With *Water Music,* the picaresque / experimental, a genre that has produced some of the most-praised and least-read books in the last 30 years, has finally yielded a novel that every schoolchild should love: a ripping yarn smeared with smut, puns, and guts. . . .

[There] are two heroes in *Water Music,* and after acquainting us with [Scottish explorer Mungo] Park's dilemma, the author rushes back to London to introduce Ned Rise. . . .

The tales of Park and Rise run parallel to each other, and part of the fun lies in guessing how and when the two men will meet up. The two rebels seem kindred spirits, destined to dupe the world, but this is one time Boyle's satirical instincts weigh him down—he's got a social theory to promote here, and its ax grinds: Rise can never, despite his verby name, lift himself above his lowly class, and Park, while lovable and bold, is also an upper-class twit to the bone, muzzybrained and innocently arrogant in his lust for fame.

Just as *Gravity's Rainbow* loses its balance once the bombs start dropping—the old "where do you go after the holocaust" novelist's problem, the moment when the experimenting explodes the picaresque story—*Water Music* founders in matters of plot and taste. Boyle's story simply runs out of invention and laughs by the time Mungo Park launches his second expedition, and the reader can sense it the moment his boat leaves the London dock.

But *Water Music* has those things that acclaimed p/e novels usually lack: vivid characters, not comic-book punching bags; real yoks, not academic twitting. Written in a slangy high style, Boyle parodies everyone he's read—and he's read everyone. Like Pynchon, he includes song lyrics and reams of useless information, including directions for the preparation of "Baked Camel (Stuffed)," possibly the only recipe in history to include 500 dates, two sheep, and the cooking instructions "Dig trench. . . . Bake two days. Serve with rice." Like Barth, Boyle is always eager to stop the proceedings to reprint letters and diary entries, or to discourse on some fine point of historical etiquette.

Even when the action is slowing down near the conclusion, I like the way Boyle amuses himself by entitling a chapter "Oh Mama, Can This Really Be the End?" And although this is an American novel about a Scot in England and Africa, there's a lot of Irish in it—the bluster, the blather, and the blue jokes all suggest a reviewer's cliche I'm emboldened to use only because quintessential p/e writer William Gass burps it up first: Joyce. Sometimes this influence is explicit, in the way language is chewed but savored. . . . Sometimes the influence is in the attitude: Mungo Park's riverruns are the voyages of a useless Ulysses, a regular-guy explorer who risks danger primarily to stay away from his London lover Ailie Anderson, a van Leeuwenhoek groupie who wants only two things in life: Mungo for a husband, and a microscope of her own. And to go from the Joycean to the mundane, there's Boyle's wonderful knack for silly metaphors, twists of image that make Tom Robbins look like the clumsy oaf he is—an "eye as cloudy as a puddle of semen", . . . and how a few angry Africans "watched Mungo's face as if it were something to eat."

All this, from a first novelist whose previous book didn't begin to suggest his talent. The short-story collection *Descent of Man* (1979) presented Boyle as a *Paris Review* darling, an arranger of flat declarative sentences indebted to Brautigan and Barthelme. Add those names to the choir of influences that hovers over *Water Music* and you have a syllabus for the entire 20th century p/e novel. . . .

The terrific thing about the book, though, is that it shows a complete understanding of how the picaresque / experimental novel became a way to render avant-garde fiction techniques into a commercial form, even while subverting that form to smithereens. For that, I'd say Boyle deserves it all: academic respect, and Tom Robbins's paperback sales.

Ken Tucker, *"Playing Hell with History," in* The Village Voice, *Vol. XXVII, No. 2, January 6-12, 1982, p. 39.*

JAY TOLSON

T. Coraghessan Boyle has taken the skeleton of [Scottish explorer Mungo] Park's story and shaped it into a sprawling picaresque novel [*Water Music*]. To it he has added, as a sort of contrapuntal element, the life of a totally fictive character, one Ned Rise. . . . [The] worst turn of Fortune's wheel is that which brings Rise into association with Park just in time for the ill-fated second expedition.

Water Music is as densely populated as a Victorian novel, and there are several memorable faces in the crowded field of supporting characters. . . . All these characters, major and minor, are creatures of obsession, driven to absurd and dangerous lengths by a single governing passion: "What kind of man was he, Mungo Park . . .? To desert a wife and four children? to lead thirty-six men to their deaths and blow a cringing old Negro to Kingdom Come . . . ?" . . .

With so many people, a lot can happen. A lot does. Boyle is delightfully shameless in his exploitation of melodramatic devices—cliff-hangers (Will Mungo be skewered by ravening Moors?), coincidences (What will happen with a certain dueling pistol?), and miraculous resurrections. He pulls his most implausible inventions with wit, a perfect sense of timing, and his considerable linguistic gifts. He treasures the apt word, the earthy Anglo-Saxonism or the precise Latinate term, and his ear for cockney, brogue, pidgin English and other dialects is sure. If this is the historical novel and the Victorian novel transformed into comic book fiction, it is High Comic Book Fiction, in the manner of John Barth's *The Sot-Weed Factor;* it also aspires to inclusion in a literary tradition that begins with Cervantes' *Don Quixote,* a tradition that subverts the established literary conventions (e.g. the knight hero and his quest) in order to mock or demystify a culture's cherished illusions (chivalry, for example).

Water Music, in other words, is ambitious. It takes on nothing less than the mad reasonableness of the 18th century. And to the extent that we are heirs to, and products of, that marvelous Age of Reason, *Water Music* is about the ways in which we attempt to explain, justify, or ennoble our motives and actions, even when—particularly when—they are illogical, ignoble, or simply selfish. What better expression of this civilized folly than Europe's scheme to plunder the newly "discovered" world under the noblest of pretenses, a project in which Park's expeditors played no little part.

But *Water Music* is no anti-imperialist tract. Boyle is more concerned with dark, unexpected, and often absurd turns of human behavior than with broad historical polemic. Thus we are treated to the absurd discrepancy between Park's raw experience and his efforts to communicate it to his fellow countrymen. . . .

London—the London depicted most vividly by Hogarth—serves as the setting for a good part of the novel. And Boyle evokes its extremes, from the foppishness of "Beau" Brummel society to the sordid spectacle of public hangings. This is a baroque world. And the baroque play of violent opposites is the "music" of this novel, accompanying the action whether it unfolds in London, Scotland, or Africa. Frantic, manic energy just straining to break through the polite, civilized forms—that is the atmosphere that Boyle works so diligently to create and sustain.

To bring all this off is a considerable aesthetic achievement, and Boyle clearly deserves the praise heaped upon him by William Gass and other practitioners of what some call the "new fiction." The "new fiction," if anyone has managed not to hear, is anti-mimetic, self-referential, and highly "textured" prose which eschews the conventions of realism and finds considerable support among academics, particularly those versed in semiotics and other forms of continental critical theory. Not everyone is so enthusiastic about it, however; Gore Vidal dismissed it all as puerile, inbred junk, speciously justified by reams of theoretical nonsense. If these literary ostriches—writers such as Barth, Coover, Pynchon, and Gass—would only take their heads out of the theoretical sand, he argued, they might be able to produce sturdier, more Stendhalian prose. . . .

The weakness Vidal touches upon is a certain fundamental emptiness in much of the "new fiction." As much as we might be impressed by verbal virtuosity, we too often go away from these books feeling undernourished. I, for one, find Boyle's vision of man, like that of Barth, Gass, et al., uniformly, predictably, even fashionably bleak. The point he relentlessly presses is that man is a foolish creature and that everything ends with death, though some survive longer than others. Now this might be true—and certain writers might be able to develop it convincingly as something deeply felt and experienced—but with too many of these "new fictioneers" it seems to be a theme of convenience. While great energy is invested in verbal wizardry, in that all-important Flaubertian surface, too little is put into investigating, much less mining, the rich lode of human possibility. The irony, of course, is that our "new fiction" ends up as mannered and conventional as the bourgeois realism it purports to surpass.

I mention all this not to dismiss Boyle as a party hack. Boyle is a writer of considerable talent, a finished craftsman. But I would like to see him push beyond this game of pure craft into a more difficult realm, where experience, understanding, and vision must serve in the shaping of something new.

Jay Tolson, "Mungo Park and Swirling Sentences,"
in Book World—The Washington Post, *February 7, 1982, p. 10.*

GEORGE KEARNS

T. Coraghessan Boyle is a virtuoso on a grand scale. *Water Music,* his second novel, is a grown-up entertainment that knocks me out the way *Northwest Passage* and *The Bounty Trilogy* did forty years ago. Boyle can imagine any scene he wants to, any place, any time, and make it happen in a language that pops, crackles and snaps. . . . *Water Music* is a historical novel unlike any other, for the language is simultaneously that of its period (circa 1800) and that of street-wise America (circa 1980). . . . Boyle's manner of giving us the late eighteenth century of Mungo Park with reminders that the tale is being told by an American in the 1980s may be a stunt, but it's a stunt so well performed that it never tires. . . . Mungo Park's story, with vastly researched detail, is interwoven with the life of one Ned Rise, a clever London criminal, a Mack the Knife whom Fielding would have known both as magistrate and novelist. Boyle switches back and forth between the lives of his two heroes, until he brings them together in Africa for the Final Adventure. We are getting history, Rider Haggard and all the movies ever made about African explorers and the women they left behind. . . . After all this meticulous research *cum* high jinks, Boyle surprisingly allows us to care about Mungo Park's end, as the seductive music of the Niger rushes him toward death. An astonishing performance. (pp. 511-12)

George Kearns, in a review of "Water Music," in
The Hudson Review, *Vol. XXXV, No. 3, Autumn, 1982, pp. 511-12.*

RICHARD EDER

The hippie kingdom has been succeeded by the republic of hard times, and T. Coraghessan Boyle has written a shrewd and funny novel about the rites of historical passage. **"Budding Prospects"** gets this across by way of a wonderfully collapsing grand scheme and a bedraggled hero who emerges from it with the odd suspicion that the truest form of escape may lie in the real world.

The real agricultural world, to be precise. Boyle, whose first novel was the lively and well-praised **"Water Music,"** has given his second the subtitle of **"A Pastoral."** And, amid its absurdist humor, its funk, its Northern California ambiance of pot, beer, highways, splendid scenery and lots of pricey equipment, that's what it is.

Since Ken Kesey, we have had a quarter-century or so of solipsist clownery and charm. The exuberance, drunks, harebrained schemes, large expeditions and fundamental motionlessness—the protagonists drive and raise hell but they are essentially supine—grow weary. Boyle starts in their midst and, in his individual and remarkably controlled way, works quite a distance out.

Felix, the narrator, is a comfortably drifting San Franciscan who supports himself by teaching a little English and has managed to grow less and less involved with anything. . . .

What he does in the book is move some; not a lot, and not in a straight line, but still some; enough to provide a current of energy to the story's wacky improbabilities and to end up in a left-handed kind of assertion.

In brief, Felix is approached by Vogelsang, a flourishing superschemer who is good at everything—deals, karate, sex, living splendidly—but is never really there. . . .

Vogelsang is recruiting for a scheme to grow 300 acres of marijuana on a remote mountain farm. Felix and two of his friends take the job on with the hope of netting one-third of a projected $1.5-million profit. The time for lollygagging is over, they tell themselves; the era of primitive capitalist accumulation is about to begin. (p. 3)

They spend a summer slaving away, contending with rain, fire, bears, rats, suspicious neighbors, blackmail and the threats of a police raid. One disaster after another gradually whittles their expectations down until, by the end, the $500,000 is reduced to a bare $15,000. Vogelsang, of course, does very well.

It is a comic disaster on the classic and irresistible theme of the scalawag out-scalawagged. Boyle handles the day-to-day misadventures, the befuddled relationship of three city hicks with each other and with the wilderness they are turned loose upon, with superb control and timing. He has written a first-rate picaresque adventure with a subplot about the neighboring farmer and his idiot son that combines slapstick and subtlety, and two others, only fair, about a maniacal California Highway Patrolman and an earth-mother potter who helps liberate Felix from his detachment. It rambles and sashays nicely, though sometimes it trips up when its prose slips from exuberance to hyperactivity.

There is more to **"Budding Prospects,"** though, than an entertainment seductively told. The notion of Felix and his companions living through the agricultural agonies of drainage, nitrogen content, adverse weather, irrigation lines chewed up by marauders, rats among the seedlings and so on, and all for the sake of 2,000 pounds of harvested pot, is comical enough. But something else is going on. (pp. 3, 8)

Pot or wheat, there is a primeval challenge in struggling with the mountain, in digging and fencing and growing things; in Nature, in short. Felix, the perennial quitter and easy-lifer, is bitten. . . .

It is Boyle's skill that both Felix and we are aware of the simultaneous incongruity and authenticity of what is happening. If Felix is quite primitively caught by the smell of turned earth and consumed with blood-lust against a marauding bear, we are quite simply caught by the account of the struggle. We want those plants to grow.

It is the best kind of irony; the kind that nourishes. The venture is ridiculous, a swindle, a financial disaster. Boyle never has Felix become lyrical. At the end as at the beginning, he remains baroque and self-aware. He does not depart from his own music. What he does is to take his music and move along—up the coast to the potter earth-mother and, presumably, the notion that life is worked and worked for. (p. 8)

> Richard Eder, "Free Enterprise for Controlled Substance," in Los Angeles Times Book Review, *May 6, 1984, pp. 3, 8.*

HOWARD KAPLAN

Felix, thirty-one-year-old narrator of T. C. Boyle's *Budding Prospects,* fails in the end to make a million at marijuana farm-

ing. But happiness for him means more than a fat bankroll. An upstanding old hippie, he smiles as he sinks back to poverty-line limbo. . . .

Beneath the hip California coating lies old-fashioned melodrama. One Officer Jerpbak, a clean-cut cop, represents the stock villain. Mirror shades are his fearsome prop. He roughs people up for the fun of it. He cheats on his wife. . . . Petra, a long-legged arts and craftsy type, is the damsel in distress. Though she lays the priapic hero after proper introductions, her purity of heart is uncompromised: eventually, she says, she wants to have children. By book's end, faithful Felix is ready to accomodate her.

Boyle, his eye on the action not the players, rations out one or two traits per person. Of course having seen these folks before in the movies, we can fill in the details ourselves. Gesh, for instance, one of two sidekicks, is a big bull of a man with a snorting temper to match. . . . That scowling visage, never described, belongs in reality to Nick Nolte. Likewise, the redneck Lloyd Sapers is Warren Oates in overalls. And amiable Felix is the bearded Jeff Bridges.

The writing itself is chock-full of screen references. When Saper's 300-plus-pound mental-defective son goes berserk—a scene played for laughs by the way—Felix is reminded of the raging King Kong. . . . Plainly, Boyle has Hollywood on the brain—Hollywood script deals, that is. Venal schemes aside, the above is buzz-name description, and all of us employ it in normal conversation. But what in speech amounts to a mildly lazy habit, in fiction looks positively slothful. It's a cheap little labor-saving device. Rather than build a situation step by step, you blithely drop a name, and the name does the job while you take five. (p. 379)

The constant name-dropping is part of a larger habit, almost an addiction: Boyle can't keep away from a simile. . . . Boyle, not without literary scruples, is trying to soften the wham-bam crudities of his comic-strip plot. But he overdoes the fancy-talk by half.

As in all melodrama, action is everything here. We get, among other things, fistfights, friskings, and pukings, one night in jail, and several in a dive called Shirelle's Bum Steer. The protagonist battles fires and bears and a sleazy blackmailer. Yet none of it much qualifies as rip-roaring stuff. Early on, apropos of nothing in particular, Gesh asks his buddies one night, "What's the closest you ever came to dying?" I perked up at this. Boyle's first book, *Descent of Man,* is a collection of weirdly inventive tales that read like sick jokes. . . . Unfortunately, those campfire stories requested by Gesh in *Budding Prospects* are nowhere near as inspired as these early efforts by Boyle. Nor, say, is Gesh and Felix's bar-prowling interlude in San Francisco. For this Boyle brazenly drags in the old sexy-woman-who-turns-out-to-be-a-man routine, a decrepit ancedote. . . . (pp. 379-80)

For would-be dope farmers and the naturally curious, *Budding Prospects* earns good marks as an elementary how-to. . . . Boyle patiently takes us from sowing to reaping to rolling and smoking, with play-by-play commentary provided by Dowst, a Yalie botany whiz. But the novel is strictly cautionary, the outlook anti-El Dorado. Between predators both man and beast, natural disasters and narcs, the marijuana business sounds risky at best. You're much better off writing pulp like this. (p. 380)

> Howard Kaplan, "Pot Potboiler," in Commonweal, *Vol. CXI, No. 12, June 15, 1984, pp. 379-80.*

MICHAEL GORRA

"Budding Prospects" is at first glance a parody of those red-blooded novels about the maturation of the American male for which "Captains Courageous" is the archetype. In such novels an effete hero finds himself thrust, in late adolescence, into a harsh world where, through an exposure to manual labor, Mother Nature, and the variety of his fellow man he learns what really counts in life. Here, however, the "adolescent" is 31. . . .

[Teaching] freshman English at a community college in San Francisco and renovating Victorians in his spare time, Felix has had it with that "happy hippie" stuff and wants to make money. Enter his friend Vogelsang, a young and predatory tycoon. . . . How would Felix like to tend 2,000 marijuana plants . . . and take a share worth an estimated $500,000?

The "audacity" of it attracts him. . . . He gets two friends to help him with the grunt work and, dreaming of yachts and Rio, goes off to make his fortune. . . .

Wild animals, ranging from bears to rats, eat most of their crop, and in the end Felix's share comes to only $4,045 for nine months of hard agricultural work. But the real sting is that Vogelsang, directing operations from his hot tub in Bolinas, has made a financial killing through a double-cross so elegant that it could have come out of Raymond Chandler. Felix has let Vogelsang exploit him as completely as any large farmer does his migrant labor.

Yet if the details of the sting are surprising, its sheer ingenuity, like each turn in Mr. Boyle's neatly crafted plot, is as enjoyably predictable as a Harlem Globetrotters' basketball game. The real interest lies in the moves on the court, and this novel's best shot, like that of its predecessor **"Water Music"** (1982), is the rude, bawdy vigor of its prose. . . .

Mr. Boyle has in addition a wickedly accurate eye for social types and surfaces. He's wonderful on San Francisco's peculiar blend of ostentation and seaminess, and does even better with his picture of "Shirelle's Bum Steer," the country-western, redneck bar near the dope farm, where Felix goes for R & R.

Shirelle's comes complete with the best set of local yokels this side of Thomas Berger, exotics whom Felix sees with the same mix of fascination, awe, contempt and hatred as that with which the European explorers regarded African tribesman in **"Water Music."** Yet Mr. Boyle's facility is a liability as well. Sentence by sentence, **"Water Music"** dazzled. Chapter by chapter it bored, because its fireworks didn't build to a finale. The marijuana growing cycle around which Mr. Boyle constructs this novel does provide a more satisfying shape, but he stops at the surface too often, settling for one-liners like small firecrackers, rather than working toward a more sustained comic display.

None of this would matter if Mr. Boyle were, like Mr. Berger, primarily interested in parodying a familiar genre, but the engaging if problematic surprise of **"Budding Prospects"** is that it finally speaks on behalf of the values it at first appears to spoof. After spending almost a year growing the symbol of his generation's rejection of the mainstream, Felix decides to join it. . . . The dope farm teaches him the merits of hard work as an end in itself—and it also makes him realize that he wants something else from life than the money he'd craved at the start of the novel. . . .

To Felix children have always been "anathema" but as the novel ends he punningly hopes to "plant a little seed." **"Budding Prospects"** is a summons to the propagation of the species,

a manifesto for the second baby boom. As such it may be just a little too timely, and a little too sentimental, to last.

But Mr. Boyle's irreverent brio is a refreshing antidote to the attenuated self-pity with which the "Big Chill" generation tends to see itself in print. **"Budding Prospects"** is lusty in every sense of the word, healthy, invigorating, and strong. Mr. Boyle's raw ability to make one laugh reminds me of Kingsley Amis and the early Evelyn Waugh as well as Thomas Berger. If he can match that verbal agility with a mastery of their larger and more self-conscious comic structures, he could become an important contemporary novelist.

Michael Gorra, "Dope Farmer in Search of Roots," in The New York Times Book Review, *July 1, 1984,* *p. 18.*

NINA BARRETT

Sticking it out is . . . the central issue in T. Coraghessan Boyle's *Budding Prospects,* whose narrator, Felix, introduces himself to us with the announcement, "I've always been a quitter." . . .

Budding Prospects turns out to be the degenerate, cynical version of the male escape fantasy, a sort of *Walden* for city slickers on Quaaludes. At its most successful, it spotlights all the pitfalls of that foolish optimism so integral to the adventure story. (p. 152)

Boyle marches to the erratic beat of Frank Zappa. While his satiric sense is sharp, his descriptive style is a chaotic jumble of melodramatic overstatements. . . . Standing in a field on a hot day, Felix tells us that "sweat coursed over my body—streams, rivulets, mighty deltas—the sun raked my face and thrust a clawing hand down my throat."

Such overwriting . . . raises the question of what Boyle can possibly have in mind when he refers to this novel as a work of realism. At best, it makes his characters seem emotionally hard of hearing. At worst, Boyle's similes defy their presumably descriptive purpose. His overripe use of language is fatal to the novel, making it impossible for the reader to swallow its ironic denouement: Felix finally learns about commitment by sticking out an experience that is an unmitigated disaster from the first. By that point, we've become so used to Felix's distorted perceptions that we cannot believe he has the emotional acuity necessary to grow up.

As though he couldn't bear to let the story end on a note of total failure, Boyle tosses in a female character, Petra, for Felix to love. And although Felix's grace in romance is about equal to his skill as a farmer, we are asked to believe that she loves him too. There's some talk between them of commitment and babies, about which Felix doesn't seem too keen. Nevertheless, the novel ends with Felix, having acknowledged his failure at the farm, heading back for Petra. . . . Felix seems to see this commitment as redemption; to the reader, it appears to be another adventure for which he is ill-equipped. (pp. 152-53)

Nina Barrett, "Boys' Books," in The Nation, *Vol. 239, No. 5, September 1, 1984, pp. 151-53.**

CHARLES SCHLOTTER

[In *Budding Prospects*] three burned-out hippies in their thirties are recruited by a manipulative dealer to grow marijuana in Northern California. Their enterprise . . . quickly degenerates into a series of accelerating failures and disasters. Mr. Boyle is a clever comic writer with a talent for absurd details and incongruous names. But the plot limps painfully along. The trouble is that it is obvious from the start that the marijuana plantation will not work, so there are few comic surprises. You *know* the weather will go bad. You know the neighbors will interfere. You know that Felix, the hero and narrator, will repeatedly get into alcoholic brawls at the local tavern. And you know that the dealer will double-cross his hapless growers eventually. Even the ending, which is corny and sentimental, totally at odds with the rest of the book, is easy to predict.

Another problem is that Felix narrates in what is clearly the author's voice. He is witty and learned, full of allusions to literature, history, philosophy and art. It is hard to believe that someone so aggressively sophisticated and self-aware would act in such a stupid, clownish way. "... I thought how incongruous it all was ...," says Felix as he sets out to shoot a bear that is ravaging the crop.... But it is the author, not Felix, who should see the incongruousness. By confusing the two, Boyle creates an inconsistent character, one who ambles while he seethes.

Finally, the whole hippy-marijuana genre is an exhausted vein. *Budding Prospects,* though often well-written, creates the effect of a baroque, overwritten farce—*Cheech and Chong Go to Graduate School.*

> Charles Schlotter, in a review of "Budding Prospects," in West Coast Review of Books, *Vol. 10, No. 5, September-October, 1984, p. 44.*

PETER ROSS

[With] *Greasy Lake,* Boyle comes fully into his own.

This is a triumphantly funny assembly, incredibly diverse in its inspirations and foundations, and crafted with a technical skill and lexicon that remind one of Terry Southern and S. J. Perelman.

Greasy Lake is studded with famous names, archetypical images, literary allusions and cross-references to pop music. An Elvis imitator, startlingly ungifted, is a character in the story **"All Shook Up,"** and the title story is a prose recreation of the ram-charged world of black leather and hot summer nights lately immortalized by Bruce Springsteen.

But Boyle doesn't stick to any one era or theme. For instance, he probes the supernatural-surreal in **"The Hector Quesadilla Story,"** a saga of an aging Mexican ballplayer who gets stuck in a Twilight Zone-ish game that refuses to end. He strikes a pure note of high romance in **"Ike and Nina,"** a blisteringly funny—and certainly imaginative—tale of a torrid affair between Dwight Eisenhower and Nina Khrushchev.

In **"Rupert Beersley and the Beggar Master of Sivani-Hotta,"** Boyle also gives us the best parody of Sherlock Holmes and the master-sleuth mystique that I've ever seen. And he closes with a chillingly authentic—and in other ways rather chilling—tribute to Gogol in **"The Overcoat II."**

Whatever voice he adopts, Boyle is in absolute command, wholly at home and always funny. *Greasy Lake* deserves a seat in the company of *Candy, Lolita,* and Roy Blount Jr.'s *One Fell Soup.* And Boyle deserves to be ushered, with fanfare, into the select cadre of great American humorists.

> Peter Ross, "A Reader's Picnic at 'Greasy Lake'," in The Detroit News, *May 26, 1985, p. 2L.*

LARRY McCAFFERY

For the assorted politicians, teen-age toughs, baseball players, whale lovers, blues singers and ordinary suburbanites who speak to us in T. Coraghessan Boyle's brilliant new collection, **"Greasy Lake,"** life in contemporary America is pretty much a roller coaster ride, filled with peaks of exhilaration and excitement but also fraught with hidden dangers and potential embarrassments. One moment they're clutching a bottle of stolen bourbon, up higher than they ever thought possible. From up there the vista is enormous, gorgeous: the adrenalin is pumping; escape velocity from all that weighs them down is nearly achieved. But just a second later the inevitable descent has begun, and something has gone terribly wrong, the seat belt has disengaged, they're hurtling to a crash landing amid laughter, sawdust, plastic cups, stale generic beer.

Mr. Boyle used variations of this tragicomic trajectory to wonderful effect in an earlier story collection, **"Descent of Man,"** and two novels, **"Water Music"** and **"Budding Prospects,"** all widely (and justly) praised for their manic wit, lush, baroque language and narrative invention. What hasn't been sufficiently emphasized, however, is that beneath its surface play, erudition and sheer storytelling power, his fiction also presents a disturbing and convincing critique of an American society so jaded with sensationalized images and plasticized excess that nothing stirs its spirit anymore.... It is into this world that Mr. Boyle projects his heroes, who are typically lusty, exuberant dreamers whose wildly inflated ambitions lead them into a series of hilarious, often disastrous adventures.

The story **"Greasy Lake,"** whose title and epigraph are borrowed from Bruce Springsteen, shows off his irreverence, his gifts for social satire and slapstick humor, and most of all his razzle-dazzle verbal energy. It's a warm June night, and three male spirits are driving around looking for the heart of Saturday night. Bored, drunk, clad in torn-up leather jackets ("We were bad"), these suburban teen-agers are anxious to stir up some action. But what's a fella to do when Thunder Road leads only to more housing developments and shopping malls? They wind up out at Greasy Lake, a mythic spot once known by the Indians for its clear waters but now littered with broken glass, beer cans and contraceptives. (pp. 15-16)

On this particular night, ... the rich scent of possibility turns sour in a hurry—a vicious thug is mistaken for a buddy, car keys are lost, a fight ensues, a tire iron emerges, skulls are rattled, and soon the narrator retreats into the primal ooze of Greasy Lake itself. There, covered with slime and utterly humiliated, he has a grisly encounter with the corpse of a dead biker and is forced to endure the whom-whomp sounds of his family station wagon being demolished.

The problem of these youths, frustrated in their efforts to find a suitable outlet for their passions and energies in America's shiny new suburban jungles, is echoed in a number of the other stories, but Mr. Boyle's control of a wide range of narrative styles and voices insures that nothing ever really seems predictable here. These styles include literary pastiche in **"The Overcoat II"** (an updated, Soviet version of Gogol's surreal classic) and **"Rupert Beersley and the Beggar Master of Sivani-Hoota"** (a clever spoof of the detective yarn), as well as myth and fantasy in **"The New Moon Party"** (where a Presidential candidate is swept into office by promising to replace our old, pockmarked moon with a glittering manmade replacement) and **"The Hector Quesadilla Story"** (an aging Mexican ballplayer is inserted into a baseball game that apparently will go on forever).

Even the most realistic stories seem bizarre, partly because of Mr. Boyle's emphasis on quirky narrators and unusual personal relationships. In **"Caviar,"** for example, a childless couple, under the guidance of an unscrupulous doctor, bring a surrogate mother into their home to bear a child for them with disconcerting results. . . .

Interestingly enough, what may be the collection's most powerful piece—**"Stones in My Passway, Hellhound on My Trail"**— is one of the few whose effect is not comic. It describes the last engagement of Robert Johnson, the blues singer and guitarist of the Great Depression, destined to die at 24. The story concludes with a passage of extraordinary beauty that illustrates Mr. Boyle's feel for human passions and sensuous, evocative prose. . . .

Mr. Boyle's literary sensibility, like that of Robert Coover and Stanley Elkin, thrives on excess, profusion, pushing past the limits of good taste to comic extremes. He is a master of rendering the grotesque details of the rot, decay and sleaze of a society up to its ears in K Mart oil cans, Kitty Litter and the rusted skeletons of abandoned cars and refrigerators. But if such fiction often makes us squirm, it also impresses us with its use of a broad variety of cultural, historical and literary erudition to illuminate and focus specific moments. Mr. Boyle is a writer who alludes to a Verdi opera in one breath and to Devo's "Satisfaction" or the Flying Lizards' version of "Money" in the next—or who might cite Shakespeare, Screamin' Jay Hawkins and George Romero's "Night of the Living Dead" in a paragraph.

This rapid-fire modulation between high and low culture is sure to put off some readers (and it has led to the inevitable comparisons to Thomas Pynchon and Tom Robbins). But more important is the fact that Mr. Boyle's perception of what is happening in contemporary America seems remarkably sure and accurate. He is probably at his best in his novels, where his exuberant imagination has more room to roam. But despite some unevenness in execution, the stories in **"Greasy Lake"** display a vibrant sensibility fully engaged with American society—and with the wonder and joy that defiantly remain a part of our culture as well. (p. 16)

Larry McCaffery, "Lusty Dreamers in the Suburban Jungle," in The New York Times Book Review, *June 9, 1985, pp. 15-16.*

André (Philippus) Brink

1935-

South African novelist, essayist, critic, translator, editor, dramatist, and scriptwriter.

Brink has earned respect as a leading writer against apartheid. Although he is more often praised for the intensity of his beliefs than for his artistic skill, Brink has twice won the South African Central News Agency literary awards. Like most South African writers who have condemned their country's policy of racial separatism and discrimination, Brink has encountered governmental censorship of his work. His novel *Kennis van die aand* (1973; *Looking on Darkness*) was one of the first books written in Afrikaans to be banned by the South African Supreme Court, and it remained under censure until 1982. Despite the ongoing threat of suppression, Brink has continued to express his political beliefs in his novels and essays.

Early in his career, Brink was a member of the Sestigers, or Writers of the Sixties, a literary movement of young South Africans who altered the focus of traditional Afrikaans literature. Modeled after the work of Albert Camus and other contemporary European authors, the Sestigers wrote about such prohibited subjects as religion, politics, and sex. Brink's early novels, *Looking on Darkness* and *'n Oornblik in die wind* (1975; *An Instant in the Wind*), which explore the consequences of sexual relations between black and white South Africans, exemplify the literary interests of the Sestigers. *Looking on Darkness* is the confession of an imprisoned black man who has murdered his white lover in a mutual pact against their repressive society. *An Instant in the Wind*, a historical novel set in eighteenth-century Cape Colony, revolves around a brief affair between a white woman who is lost in the wilderness after a shipwreck and the runaway black slave who helps her return to civilization. Although critics praised both novels for their vivid condemnation of apartheid, some charged Brink with employing the same racial and sexual stereotypes to which he is opposed.

The harmful effects of apartheid inform all of Brink's fiction. In *Gerugte van reen* (1978; *Rumours of Rain*) apartheid is examined through the consciousness of a wealthy Afrikaner businessman, and *'n Droe wit seisoen* (1979; *A Dry White Season*) concerns the death of a black activist while in police custody and the consequences of his white friend's attempt to find out what happened. *A Dry White Season* was banned temporarily because of its similarity to an incident in 1976 which resulted in the death of imprisoned black nationalist Steven Biko. *Houd-den-Bek* (1982; *A Chain of Voices*) is another historical work that analyzes the origins of apartheid by reenacting a slave revolt that took place in the Cape Colony in 1825. The novel is commended for its use of multiple narrative voices—slaves, masters, other Europeans, and free blacks—to examine the uprising from various points of view. Brink returns to present-day South Africa in *The Wall of the Plague* (1984). In this work, which was influenced by Camus's *La Peste*, Brink uses the Black Death as a symbol of the moral and political decay in his own country. In addition to his fiction, Brink has also written *Mapmakers: Writing in a State of Seige* (1984), a collection of autobiographical and literary

© Lütfi Özkök

essays that discuss the artistic dilemmas faced by writers living in authoritarian societies.

(See also *CLC*, Vol. 18 and *Contemporary Authors*, Vol. 104.)

ANNE COLLINS

[In *A Chain of Voices*, André Brink] goes for the jugular of the master-slave relationship with a blunt instrument; he wants to bruise it, tear it, make it bleed in its true colors. Brink is an odd writer, crude and subtle at the same time. His last two novels [*Rumours of Rain* and *A Dry White Season*] are realistic accounts of contemporary South Africa which pummel away at the moral points but paint characters, even heroes, in all their colors and evasions. *A Chain of Voices* backtracks to 1825, before slavery was abolished by the British, and digs around in the souls of slaves and the Afrikaner farmers dependent on them (their God-given servants, according to their interpretation of the Old Testament) for survival of huge acreages of African veld.

It begins with *Act of Accusation*, fingering a group of slaves who took up arms against their masters; it ends with the inevitable verdict and sentence. In between is the novel—what happened—told in as many narrative voices as Brink needs new angles on the event. The most important of these voices are those of Nicolaas, the slaughtered master, and Galant, the slave leader, telling of the transition from boyhood friendship where they made toy clay oxen and swam together in the farm dam, to adult status, wherein one was supposed to become the tool of the other in the natural scheme of things. Except that Galant would not be enslaved and Nicolaas was too weak to break him.

Out of Nicolaas' weakness—his fear of yet desire to prove his Afrikaner manhood—comes cruelty. As a "master" he is not allowed to presume friendship with Galant, therefore anyone who is close to Galant becomes a target. He beats Galant's manhood to death in the shape of the slave's first son; he then puts his own child inside the body of Galant's woman. The cruelty of the other farmers mechanically beating order into their slaves is almost benign compared with the twisted cruelty of Nicolaas pursuing the psychological rape of someone he loves. Galant, too, ends up beating his love objects. . . .

Redemption of a sort comes carnally, in the consummated love between Galant and Hester, the alienated white woman whom Nicolaas also loves. Brink forces it to come, amid the killing, and it sits there on the page, unbelievable, romanticized. But it is the only dubious part of this brutal novel; the rest takes us map-making in the slavery-devastated landscape of black and white.

Anne Collins, "Three Tales from the Land of Black and White," in Maclean's Magazine, Vol. 95, No. 19, May 10, 1982, pp. 58, 60.*

JULIAN MOYNAHAN

"A Chain of Voices" is a historical novel that goes behind the present system of apartheid and works out the fatal pattern of white-black relationships in the Cape Colony at a time when the Dutch settlers were actual slaveholders. During that period—1825 and the quarter century before—the Dutch also held hostage such nominally free black groups as the Hottentots through a system of indentured servitude little different from slavery. "A Chain of Voices," like all good historical novels, is as much about the present as the past. What I mean is that Brink searches the bad old times for a key to understanding bad times in South Africa today, and what he sees in the historical record is always conditioned by his awareness of the South African racial crisis now.

The story, which is about a slave revolt on two isolated farm estates in the rugged but magnificent country north and east of Capetown, will inevitably evoke comparisons with William Styron's "The Confessions of Nat Turner," a work to which it is substantially superior in insight and artistry. It seemed to me that Styron's portrait of Nat Turner, a slave who led an actual revolt in Virginia in 1831, was synthetic and contrived; though Turner tells his own story, right up to the point of his execution for rebellion and murder, he speaks like Styron writes. . . . Brink also has his characters—both slaves and whites—speak for themselves. But, whereas Styron's Turner seems to be used as an outlet for the author's neo-romantic rhetoric and white liberal opinion, Brink's characters, though they do not speak in the precise dialect of the time, seem to express feelings authentic to their condition. Nevertheless, Styron's treatment was a pioneering work in its way and may have shown Brink where the pitfalls lay for a white writer attempting to portray militant black characters.

A far more important connection can be made between "A Chain of Voices" . . . and those major fictions of William Faulkner—for instance, "Absalom: Absalom" and "Go Down, Moses"—in which Faulkner counts the moral cost of white racism, both before and after Emancipation, in terms of the tragic spoliation of all relationships, not merely those between white oppressors and their nonwhite or partially white victims. Brink also owes a technical debt to Faulkner for the device of telling a story entirely through a series of first-person monologues, the chain of voices of the title. Brink even has a Dilsey, though an unrepentantly pagan one. She is the elderly slave and conjure woman, Ma-Rose, who endures to see the beginning and the end of a hopeless uprising organized by Galant, a young slave foreman whom Ma-Rose had raised from infancy after his young mother was sold away from him. (pp. 1, 15)

The success or failure of the rebellion is never at issue. The book begins with a quasi-legal document setting the charges against the little band of 11 rebels and detailing their few acts of murder and property destruction. At the end, judgment is handed down in the same administrative jargon. Nearly all are to be hanged though a few escape with floggings and long prison terms. Since a slave's life is full of floggings and is one long imprisonment, options for punishment are few. . . .

The novel shows convincingly that the inevitable product of slaveholding is intolerable human abuse: physical abuse of men, physical and sexual abuse of women, neglect and mistreatment of children and, finally, insult and injury to the soul. Yet when Nicolaas is shot during the revolt, he dies thinking that he and Galant, if only they might get clear of certain entanglements and misunderstandings, could still be friends. That he could think so is convincing testimony to the power of slavery not only to corrupt the moral imagination of the master, but also to make him insane. (p. 15)

A further word is needed on Brink's method of monologue, which is described at one point by Ma-Rose in the following way:

"We go on talking and talking, an endless chain of voices, all together yet all apart, all different yet all the same, and the separate links might lie but the chain is the truth."

What must be grasped is that characters in this book don't so much speak according to their condition—apart from passages of direct dialogue—as they are given utterance that reflects the author's large intentions. These are to explore in depth, and with a reach of knowledge that extends to such figures as Marx and Engels, Hegel and Roland Barthes, the fullest meaning of slaveholding as a social and human phenomenon. Practically speaking, that means that an illiterate agricultural worker such as Galant gives voice at times to reflections and concepts and finds words to which, realistically, he would not have had access.

I should say that this deliberately anachronistic and "manipulative" narrative method works brilliantly most of the time. Where it occasionally fails is when the author's own thought goes a little opaque or trite or is put into words possessing more flash than substance. Thus, when Galant, facing the end and failure of all he has attempted, reflects that "everything is alive in the heart of the flame—within the falling of the stone lies the silence of before and after," the reader may well feel that this bit of suburban Zen is not what the actual Galant would have been thinking under the circumstances. But such lapses are few and far between in an astonishingly full and detailed work of literary art.

I came away from this powerful and disturbing book thinking all manner of things: that the persistence of white slaveholding so far into the "enlightened" 19th century must have laid the ground for the concentration-camp systems and slave-labor projects of the totalitarian nations at war in the 20th century; that organized religion by and large played a shameful role in offering rationalizations for slavery; that no one is free so long as anyone is subjected and abased; that women will appreciate this last point more readily than most men.

"A Chain of Voices" makes most of the fashionable junk that parades as advanced fiction today look bad. It is the best novel I've read since Robert Stone's "A Flag for Sunrise," and I don't imagine it will be soon before we see a better one. (pp. 15-16)

> Julian Moynahan, "Slaves Who Said No," in The New York Times Book Review, *June 13, 1982, pp. 1, 15-16.*

JANE KRAMER

[Today], a "literature of apartheid" is taken for the books of a dozen writers of wildly various sensibility and talent, proving only how much easier it is to tell good from bad than to tell good books from bad ones.

This is simply to say that in the negotiation between writers and readers that creates "literature," readers will often make the more imaginative adjustments. It may have taken crafty masters of social conscience like Dickens and Zola to invent the guilty reader, but by now guilty reading has come into its own as armchair ritual among the bourgeoisie, and it does not depend on crafty masters—just on a vague appetite for self-chastisement.

It is this appetite, this pleasant moral twinge, that we bring, lately, to books by white South Africans. We judge South African writers less by their quality than by the risks they take in putting the wall of their own dissidence between ourselves and the black Africa we praise and fear. We love them for being South African *for* us. They are our surrogates in resistance. And so we are undone by the bad books—books like André Brink's *A Chain of Voices*—they often write in earnest exploitation of their (our) just cause. We are undone by books of mediocre purity. . . .

André Brink (to judge by his books) writes fast. Five long novels in less than ten years—two of them novels of epic intention and mock-epic consequences. Brink writes with a kind of high, wide, moral exuberance, riding the waves of South Africa's painful history like a Laguna Beach surfer. Inhumanity is tonic to his prose, much as it is for the critics who admire him. Like them, he is a man of bludgeoning themes. One reads Brink conscious always of some sort of important moral purpose. . . . [However], Brink's "historical" chain of voices—masters and slaves on the occasion of a failed slave rebellion in 1825—escapes into melodrama. (p. 8)

[Brink] writes historical novels the way other people travel. (Curiously, he is quite respected in South Africa as a travel writer.) *An Instant in the Wind,* his second book, is based on Cape Town archives from the middle of the eighteenth century having to do with a runaway slave and a young white woman, the survivor of a scientific trek into the interior, whom the slave rescues and returns home. The slave uprising that was the source material, so to speak, for *A Chain of Voices* took place on the farms of two Afrikaner brothers in 1825. Brink

is earnest in his elaborations, but the books are really an exercise in what might be called apartheid gothic. They are costume dramas of the present, naïve reversals of experiments with Aeschylus in blue jeans as generation-gap tragedy or *Parsifal* after Hiroshima or Macbeth as a senior partner in Sullivan and Cromwell.

History is a place that André Brink is not at home in because he is basically unworldly. He is unable to apprehend the past in any but the forms and tones and meanings of his own exceptional experience as a South African in 1982, the forms of a familiar but distorted world. His best work fights this need to turn the traumas of the present into the great dramas of an imagined past. *A Dry White Season,* his last novel before *A Chain of Voices,* told a quiet story fairly quietly—a white schoolteacher helps a black school janitor whose son has been officially "missing" since the riots in Soweto, and he is threatened and harassed and finally killed. In its way it was an eloquent book, catching the movement of ordinary lives into an extraordinary world where yesterday can disappear without a trace and the state can compose "realities" that utterly deny the proven and the true and white dissidents go mad or vanish or take up safe garden-party outrage in Houghton or Constantia.

Not so *A Chain of Voices*. The novel yearns backward. It "crosses the color bar" as the South Africans put it, by way of aching loins . . . and ramrod penises. . . . The (forgive me) climax of the book is a climax, a witless and unwitting parody of white racist fantasies about black potency. To quote the Good White Woman in the hayloft with the Brave Black Man: "He lunges, thrusts, hammers, pounds in silent frenzy, impaling me, cleaving me, sundering and slaughtering me, setting me free forever, unbearably." Surely, this makes an odd last word for a novel about slavery and rebellion and insane oppression that ends with half the characters dead or dying. Brink may have an honorable imagination, but his instincts are shrewd. He has written a potboiler of oppression. His singular triumph (besides having got away with this embarrassing prose) was to insult blacks and whites with such feverish impartiality.

Brink's brave black man is a slave called Galant. He leads the other slaves in their rebellion. His dreams are as big as his penis—and as often thwarted. He is nature's aristocrat. He (forgive me again) rises from each humiliation, each torment, with his resolve unbroken. He believes in his own emancipation. A slave named Bet, who loves Galant and bears his child, reads to him at great risk from old Cape Town newspapers about the freedom that is coming. Bet shares his pain in slavery, but she cannot restore him. The black woman cannot satisfy the black man's longing. (Another white fantasy?) Her warmth, her surrender, is a mirror of his own submission. (pp. 8-9)

Sexual healing is the province of the white woman. In this case, the white woman is an orphan called Hester Van der Merwe, another natural aristocrat. Hester belongs to her brutal Afrikaner husband, Barend, in much the same way as Barend's slaves belong to him. . . . In the end, Galant "sets her free" just as his own revolution fails. Poor André Brink—trying so hard to enlighten his benighted countrymen and himself so much the victim of their clichés. The Afrikaners in power now in South Africa feed their paranoia on fantasies of a revolution whose necessary end is the black man fucking the white woman in the hayloft while the farm burns. Brink feeds his faith in a better future with the same fantasy. But I doubt that for the black men of South Africa ten minutes with a white woman is the promised land, the end of all suffering, the raison d'être of revolution, the meaning of freedom.

Brink tells his story by "voices"—the chain of voices of the title. (In France, for some reason, the book was called *Un Turbulent Silence.)* His voices—there are a lot of them, black and white, male and female—are the revolution's cast and its narrators, and most of them are the same sonorous voice. It is hard to tell them apart. With their weighty cadence, they would do well in a big Biblical movie from the 1950s—black and white Victor Matures.

Most of them end up more caricature than character. There is the European drifter with his sly radical incitements. There is the old black grandmother with her litany of witness to the cycles of season and oppression. There is the frigid Afrikaner wife who trembles in ecstasy beating slaves, and who, naturally, is shot in the crotch when her slaves rebel rather than in the heart, say, or the stomach. There is Hester, freed by orphanhood of bad blood and birthright. There are the white brothers Nicolaas and Barend—models of impotence and brutality. And there is the gallant Galant who shoots the cowardly Nicolaas's first lion for him and saves his life in a mountain storm and sacrifices his women to him and then turns out to be (probably) half white after all—brother, in fact, to the white brother who torments him.

Brothers are another convention in South Africa, as persistent and overwrought a theme as redemptive intercourse between a white woman and a black man. (It is interesting that the equation is rarely white man/black woman when the theme is liberation or identity.) The convention holds that black boy and white boy are raised as brothers, and then, at the onset of puberty and, with it, masculine authority, the two are separated, the brotherhood violated, the deception exposed, and the white boy estranged and the black embittered by betrayal. Brink is obviously not alone in believing in brothers; it is as hard to find a South African story about black and white boys who grow up together on a farm hating each other as it is to find a story about Voortrekkers who beat their slaves and then go home to a cozy dinner with a loving wife. Brink is just more carried away than most. (pp. 9-10)

> *Jane Kramer, "In the Garrison," in* The New York Review of Books, *Vol. XXIX, No. 19, December 2, 1982, pp. 8-12.**

MICHAEL THORPE

André Brink wrote the first novel by an Afrikaner in Afrikaans to be banned—in 1974, and not released until the false thaw of 1982. The English version, *Looking on Darkness,* received the warm reception Western reviewers assure novels that expose oppressive regimes. Several such novels have followed, and Brink was in Canada recently to launch his most ambitious *A Chain of Voices.* His essay **"Slaves and Masters,"** printed . . . [in *Mapmakers,* published in the United States as *Writing in a State of Siege*] makes it clear that this historical novel, based on a slave revolt in 1825, was intended as a cautionary allegory for today. Like Nadine Gordimer, he has not only given us truth-telling fiction, but, addressing literary and cultural gatherings in the West, has tried to "convey to a public remote from Africa something of my African experience." At the same time as appealing to "the international conscience," his English publications have maintained a lifeline beyond the "laager" and perhaps saved his work from slow strangulation by South African censorship, both official and covert.

While Brink acknowledges the need for personal "literary survival," this has not been paramount: the earliest of seventeen papers and talks in *Mapmakers,* **"The Position of the Afrikaans Writer,"** dates from 1967 and the first published abroad, **"After Soweto,"** only from 1976. He has continued to be active, up to the latest, **"Censorship and Literature,"** printed in Johannesburg (1982), on both home and overseas fronts. The constant focus is upon "the function and responsibility of the writer in society, notably in a state of cultural siege," a theme made universal by the broad historical perspective, from Socrates to Solzhenitsyn and the Czech "Charter 77" writers of the essay bearing the subtitle.

This breadth, grounded in his exposure as a student in Paris to European ideas and attitudes, precludes narrow over-statement and indignant outcry. Brink's arguments throughout are marshalled calmly, with dignity, as befits one who—from the time of his second birth "on a bench in the Luxembourg Gardens in Paris, in the early spring of 1960" (after Sharpeville)—has sought to act as "the conscience of his people in the world." He seldom takes flight, though when he does the effect is correspondingly memorable, as in the metaphors of the title essay, portraying the writer as secret mapmaker—of a country of truth "someone else . . . possibly after his own death" will discover. . . . (pp. 32-3)

Whether that map may ever become one of "true internationalism" transcending "class and race" gives Brink pause; there have been too many abortive revolutions. His tempered idealism is akin to that of two figures he celebrates from South Africa's recent past, Gandhi and Bram Fischer: "we can never have absolute justice—but we can always have *more* justice. In the balance between these two forces the individual and society meet each other." This is well said, but what does it mean in the South African context?

As one reads on deeper conflicts suggest themselves. "Peaceful change" is urged, but "violence is the language culture speaks when no other valid articulation is left open to it"; the literary aesthetic must give offence (**"Literature and Offence"**), in the South African situation significant writing is inevitably a "revolutionary act." Yet, though with sympathy, Brink regrets the "narrow bitterness" of black writers under harsher constraints than he and the pressures upon them by their own community not to "collaborate." Such comments, however, merely brush some intractable issues.

Some hard questions that have become increasingly evident are not raised: can the white writer "establish his relation to a culture of a new kind of posited community, non-racial but somehow conceived with and led by blacks?" Can or should white writers write about blacks? What of the massive complicity of the West in the tyranny of a "rich capitalist state stuffed with Western . . . finance?" (Brink's moral analogies turn his Western audience toward Communist rather than Western inhumanity.) I quote from the James lecture, "Living in the Interregnum" . . . of that reluctant Cassandra, Nadine Gordimer, who attempts more deeply than Brink to dig beyond the "Aristotelian response," as she calls it, "a catharsis of white guilt." Naming no names, Gordimer raises another uncomfortable issue, for writers of any colour: "some critics at home and abroad are afraid to reject sensationalism and the crass banality of execution, so long as the subject of a work is *courageous.*" The writer should be doubly committed, to his values and his art. In Brink's case, this reviewer recalls the tediously numerous sexual episodes and heavy didacticism of *Looking on Darkness.* . . . *Rumours of Rain* (1978) is crudely prophetic and stylistically inept in its casting of the "unlike-able" white Afrikaaner nationalist as narrator, an error Gordimer's comparable *The Conservationist* skilfully avoids. Crudities of narrative viewpoint and authorial manipulations mar the recent, much touted *A Chain of Voices*.

Mapmakers, like the novels, offers rare inside views of Afrikaaner history, tribal psychology, linguistic and literary ambiguities: if his courage and commitment impress more deeply than his art or the depth of his questioning, Brink remains nevertheless an honourable voice of the Afrikaner conscience. (p. 33)

> Michael Thorpe, "An Honourable Voice," in The Canadian Forum, Vol. LXIII, No. 734, December, 1983, pp. 32-4.

MICHIKO KAKUTANI

Mr. Brink has assembled [in **"Writing in a State of Siege"**] 17 essays dealing, in general, with the role of the writer in society, and specifically with the role of the writer in South Africa today. Liberal in tone, humanist in sentiment, these essays are clearly the work of a brave man, committed to working for "urgent and radical change" in an authoritarian and racist society. But while Mr. Brink's novels brilliantly illuminate the moral bankruptcy of his country's policy of apartheid by dramatizing its devastating effects on individuals, these essays tend to underline the same points using blunt, rhetorical prose that numbs the reader's interests.

Mr. Brink's attempts to philosophize broadly about politics and art are especially susceptible to vagueness and sodden prose. He not only lapses into the pretentious diction decried by Orwell in "Politics and the English Language"—"philogenesis is inextricably linked to ontogenesis"—but he also tends to state and restate the sort of noble but obvious sentiments that professional speechmakers are so fond of. . . .

When Mr. Brink grounds his thinking in the specifics of the South African situation, the results are considerably better. As an Afrikaner who grew up accepting the racial inequalities of his country as something preordained by God . . . , he is in a position to examine just how the unfortunate identification between Afrikanerdom and apartheid evolved and how his people's own "conviction of being persecuted, misunderstood, insulted" has led them to further and further extremes.

Apartheid, of course, is far more than a political policy; it is a value system that permeates every aspect of South African life, infiltrating personal relationships and infecting, even, the language. Indeed, several of Mr. Brink's more original essays in this book examine the consequences that apartheid has had on South African writers and the ways in which it constricts the literary imagination.

Mr. Brink believes the work of black, English and Afrikaner authors all suffers from "cultural malnutrition." While defenders of apartheid have argued that the policy of "separate development" insures that each racial group will have the opportunity to develop its own "cultural potential" without the threat of assimilation, this policy, Mr. Brink believes, has actually led to artistic isolation—isolation that in turn will lead to dangerous stagnation. He maintains that black culture has been reduced to a kind of folklore status; and Afrikaner culture has been cut off from Africa, which as he notes, is "the continent we live in, the continent that has shaped us."

Afrikaner authors like Mr. Brink, in fact, are faced with perhaps the most devastating thing that could happen to a writer: the loss of their native language. Afrikaans, after all, has become almost totally identified with apartheid—even much of its vocabulary has racist implications—and if it is to survive as a language, writers will have to prove, as Mr. Brink writes, "that it is more than the language of one oppressive minority and of one frightening ideology"—that it is really " 'menstaal,' the language of human beings."

> Michiko Kakutani, in a review of "Writing in a State of Siege," in The New York Times, March 6, 1984, p. C17.

ROBERT L. BERNER

Brink's polemical intentions and his space limitations [in *Writing in a State of Siege*] do not permit the complexities that inform his best fiction. He often blurs historical distinctions for the sake of his absolutes. The title essay, for example, seems to equate all censorship everywhere, past and present. And when he criticizes those liberals who can afford to clash with authority because it protects them, we may be tempted to suspect that he is one of them himself. (Time will tell, of course.) Nevertheless, the essays are well worth careful reading.

The most valuable selections are those that provide insight into the circumstances which led Brink to choose the strategies he has followed in his own career as a novelist. **"English and the Afrikaans Writer"** is a concise explanation of the complexities of the place of Afrikaans in South Africa and of his own difficulties in writing (and rewriting) *An Instant in the Wind* . . . in two languages. . . . The essays also include relatively recent accounts (1982) of the state of censorship and apartheid in South Africa, and his various references to the "Sestigers" provide valuable insights into the work of Leroux, Breytenbach . . . , Rabie and others.

> Robert L. Berner, in a review of "Writing in a State of Siege: Essays on Politics and Literature," in World Literature Today, Vol. 58, No. 3, Summer, 1984, p. 461.

ALBERTO MANGUEL

Writers seem to be haunted by the doubt of whether their calling is useful or not. Again and again the questions arise: Can literature make anything happen? What purpose can literature serve? Why indulge in what Paul Valéry called "the unpunished vice"? These questions become more poignant when the writer who asks them is himself in a situation which seems to demand action, a situation which has become morally and physically unbearable; when the writer is made to live in a climate of terror and oppression. The answer, even in the most despairing cases, is that the purpose of literature is to help us understand the world we live in.

For André Brink the question arose when, as a young Afrikaans student in Paris, he was confronted with his country seen from the outside, without the blinkers which the South African government imposes on its people. In answer to the question, Brink left Paris. "Returning to South Africa," he says, "meant one thing: that writing had become an indispensable dimension of my life; and that I was prepared to assume full responsibility for every word I would write in the future." The writer's career was launched.

Twenty years later, having written five novels of varied success . . . , André Brink collected his political and literary writings in a volume called *Writing in a State of Siege*. The state of siege is the one imposed upon the writer by a coercive system, a state in which the writer is persecuted, forced into silence or exile. To survive, the writer has only one recourse: to speak the truth through "the quality of his work." "If the work is worth it," Brink writes, "it contains within itself the mechanisms that ensure its survival." (pp. 409-10)

Throughout the volume Brink is concerned with both the truth and the quality of writing. From essay to essay we are taken on an investigation of social insanity, on a logical hunt for the monsters of unreason. In André Brink's words, in his lucid examples, the succinct statement that South Africa is an unjust state where men are judged by the color of their skin, takes on a startling intensity. Brink is fighting for his country's sanity, and for that reason cannot dismiss his country's wrongs. "'My Country, right or wrong,'" said G. K. Chesterton, "'is on the same moral level as 'My Mother, drunk or sober.'" Brink is trying to make his country sober. (p. 410)

> Alberto Manguel, "Writers at the Brink," in Commonweal, *Vol. CXI, No. 13, July 13, 1984, pp. 409-11.*

HARRIETT GILBERT

The Wall of the Plague is a rather . . . ordinary read, despite a genuine bellow of pain, apparently straight from the author's throat, that ought to have had us shifting about in our comfortable British chairs. It's the sound of a decent, liberal, white, politically concerned South African trying to work out what the hell he can *do*.

That the pain (and its implications for us) only touches the top of our mind is partly due to a structure so schematic that it even pauses to explain itself. Referring to the history, pathology and politics of the Black Death, the novel is laboriously based on permutations of the number five, within which framework there are journeys backward and forward through time and space—narrated, as it eventually transpires, by Paul (a white, male, South African writer living in France and working on a film script about—what else?—the Black Death), but *apparently* narrated by another exile, a young 'Coloured' woman called Andrea, the writer's lover, assistant and friend, whose search for a suitable location for the film is also one for herself as a woman and South African. There's no absolute reason why a male author shouldn't use the voice of a woman. Here, however, it merely results in a distancing, an emotional muffling. In theme, in intellectual scope, this is undoubtedly a 'big' novel; it could have been so much more powerful. (pp. 30-1)

> Harriett Gilbert, "Morning after the Night Before," in New Statesman, *Vol. 108, No. 2793, September 28, 1984, pp. 30-1.*

MARY HOPE

André Brink does keep coming back like a great shaggy dog with bigger and bigger bones of well-intentioned schmalz. He is the ffotherington-Thomas (hello clouds, hello sky) of liberal South Africa, whose completely respectable pain and anger are constantly vitiated by the overwhelming soppiness of his style. This has something to do—as he himself has recognised in one of his essays—with the fact that English is a language which only awkwardly carries the weight of emotional content which can be borne by Afrikaans (his first language). It also has to do with a basic coarseness of perception and sensibility. . . . Brink can be accused of much, but not of a sense of humour. One finds only portentous leadeness of style.

[*The Wall of the Plague*] is an account of . . . [a] voyage—of self-awareness as well as into political consciousness. Andrea is a Cape coloured girl in exile in France since falling foul of the Immorality Act with an English lecturer. Her present lover, a white South African exile, sends her to research a film on the Great Plague (used as a fairly ill-assimilated symbol for racism throughout the book) on a tour in Provence, which parallels two previous journeys she has made with him and her English lover. She is to decide whether to marry him, have his child, commit herself to exile. Unwisely, he sends along a black activist, on the run, one infers, from the Security Branch. Inevitably—this being Brink—there is an earth-moving coupling and she realises that her destiny is to return to 'her' people. This is a short spin through what is an immensely long, well-plotted and many-layered narrative which contains much that is well-told, painful and true about life in South Africa. The theme of self-discovery is a respectable one, and the anger and grief involved in any such account are moving and honest. What Brink says about forced removals, torture, detention, and life in District Six is all certainly true. It is the leaden touch which sinks it. . . .

[The] choice the girl makes [is] to return to her people because of one act of love with a virile black. This is the author falling for the worst white cliché (they have such a sense of rhythm, you know) as well as for a stance which is potentially as racist as the apartheid he wishes to reject.

> Mary Hope, "Journeys to the Heartland," in The Spectator, *Vol. 253, No. 8152, October 6, 1984, p. 33.*

ROB NIXON

Perhaps inspired by the example of J. M. Coetzee's *Waiting for the Barbarians*, Brink has made . . . [*The Wall of the Plague*] a highly allegorical work. Mandla's claims to the contrary notwithstanding, for example, Paul's apparent fascination with the Black Death is not so much a denial of his South African experience as a displacement of it. To him the wall evoked in the title, built in Provence to prevent the plague from spreading, is emblematic of all the great divides that sunder human communities—and especially of those ample barriers that seek to keep South African Blacks at bay. Andrea sees a different kind of metaphor in the 18th-century structure: On her trip southward she is heartened by its poor condition; the most forbidding obstacles, she concludes, are more friable than you might suspect. Occasionally the symbolism seems a bit untidy and grandiloquent ("Anything that can keep one person away from another is a Wall of the Plague"). Fortunately, such blemishes do not seriously mar the novel; it remains an accessible, compelling read.

Brink has named Albert Camus—another writer who treated the plague metaphorically—and the study of history as the two abiding influences on his fiction. And this book's distinctive texture can be ascribed in part to the author's ability to balance these passions. Camus' presence is strongly felt through echoes of *La Peste* and, more generally, through the sense of individuals—all answerable for the decisions they make—continually defying their destiny.

At the same time, Brink's responsiveness to history—his awareness of how forcibly our choices can be narrowed—tempers his insistence on personal culpability. Indeed, one of the great achievements of his novel—and of the best South African literature, from the likes of Nadine Gordimer, Athol Fugard and Coetzee—is the way it disabuses us of any illusion we can separate the purely personal and the politicohistorical. Andrea's discovery that it is impossible to simply choose to ignore the past, that willy-nilly one is a product of it, is provoked by the black man's presence. . . . Brink is at his finest tracing the politics that shadows the most seemingly discreet of ambitions.

Equally important to the success of *The Wall of the Plague* are its deft changes in narrative voice: A third-person perspective periodically yields to the more intimate tones of Andrea in the first person and vice versa. Then, in a final tour de force, Brink confidently adopts the vantage point of Paul, who narrates the strong closing section. The disaffected Afrikaans writer abroad, Paul convinces and intrigues us by resonating Brink's dilemmas, particularly that vexed question: "What is the weight of a book against the turmoil of history?"

Paul wonders whether literature is not a weak surrogate for direct, substantial action. But he chooses to practice his craft, thereby placing himself in the predicament of every white South African writer. Racial fences are so high and forbidding that it is hard to authentically capture the black or Colored perspective. Here, especially, we feel Paul airing Brink's personal quandary. For the author and his character the decision to enter the world of someone who is a woman and a person of mixed race to boot can be viewed as admirable—or, alternatively, as an act of the sheerest effrontery. Its concluding, delicately self-conscious pages confer additional stature on a novel that addresses, quite persuasively, the difficulties of breaching the walls of hatred and exile and, beyond that, of bearing "the full weight of one's own whole history, one's whole self, all one's possibilities." (p. 17)

> Rob Nixon, "*Across the Color Bar*," in The New Leader, Vol. LXVIII, No. 1, January 14-28, 1985, pp. 16-17.

ANTHONY OLCOTT

In *The Wall of the Plague* André Brink addresses a question which in his earlier novels he approached or implied, but never fully confronted, and the result is both fascinating and unsettling, rather like watching a man attempt to examine his own entrails.

The question, of course, is apartheid, or more properly, what role a white South African writer should or may play in a society based on that complex and peculiar group of laws, ideas, and customs which we lump together under "apartheid." Not that Brink has ignored apartheid in earlier works: Brink and his fellow South Africans (Gordimer, McClure, Ebersohn, Coetzee) have proven repeatedly how much more alive, complex and insoluble South African problems are than we non-South Africans can credit.

Yet still the question remains, and in this novel Brink finally addresses it squarely, in his tale of Paul Joubert, white South African novelist and film-maker living in France, and Andrea Malgas, the fellow emigrée he loves, whose legal classification in the land of their birth was colored, that is, of mixed race. It is one of the book's great strengths that Brink does not follow the easy "boy meets girl, boy and girl meet State, State wins but is exposed in its brutality" plot such a pairing would imply; rather Brink explores the distance between, not just white and colored, but also old and young (Joubert is 50, Malgas just 30), artist and non-artist or "doer" (not activist, which role in the book is taken by another), and man and woman.

The book begins as the couple separate . . . ; Joubert has proposed marriage and Malgas wishes to meditate, in spite of her inclination to agree. Surprisingly, both for her and for the reader, what stays her "yes" is the knowledge that marriage would prevent forever her ability to return to South Africa, where colored and white mate only beyond the law. This is paradoxical, for the woman loathes South Africa, aware only too well that it scarred her childhood, spiritually dwarfed her mother and sister, jailed her brother, and eventually broke even her high-spirited independent sailor of a father, as well as forcing on her the physical humiliation of a coarse pelvic examination which the state police conducted to seek evidence against her white lover.

Brink's South Africa in these recollections (and those of the black activist, Mandla Mqayisa, whose life is harsher and more brutal than even that of the girl) is violent, chaotically unfair, and smotheringly repressive; yet is also beautiful, haunting, and in some way more real than the picture-postcard autumnal Provence and Vaucluse through which the girl wanders. (p. 1)

As much as anything else it is this palpability of Brink's evocation of South Africa which emphasizes the complexity of the dilemma Brink, or any other white there, faces, for Brink shows well that all his characters, colored and white as well as black, are Africans; although in a political sense each is enemy to the others, and though the black can see solutions only in a bloodbath and the white can see only that the highest priority is to avoid that massacre, all three are bound up with one another, are in some elemental way more necessary to one another than the rest of the world is to any one of them. (pp. 1-2)

What makes *The Wall of the Plague* larger than a simple exposé of South Africa is that Brink equates the plague not just with apartheid, but with all the incomprehensible ways in which men hate and destroy one another; he examines specifically the Soviet invasion of Hungary, the petty but nasty racism of provincial French innkeepers, and the hundreds of ways in which men and women seem always to be at cross purposes. The plague begins as a symbol of politics but becomes by the end of Brink's novel almost life itself, the death and corruption which pervades and surrounds life, and in so doing defines it. Certainly this would be the implication of the only solution Brink seems to condone, that of Malgas. Challenged and aroused by Mandla to become her true self, she returns to South Africa, apparently to accept her African nature, to accept Africa itself. Man is born to his life, the message appears to be, and to run from that or avoid it is, Brink says, as pitiable and fruitless as the attempt to wall out the plague.

That conclusion would seem a repudiation of art, a declaration of the writer's surrender before unruly life, were it not for the structure of the book, the final words of which show the whole to have been written by Joubert, after Malgas has vanished, implying that Brink's blocked, defeated novelist has finally been moved to express at least the futility of his own vision. If only because the person to whom Brink dedicates this book and Andrea Malgas, his heroine, share the same "special" name (Nanna), *The Wall of the Plague* would seem to make Joubert's surrender also to be Brink's, thus conveying wonderfully the tension of a writer's self-examination. Writing, Brink acknowledges, is words, useless; it achieves nothing, corrects nothing. At the same time Brink both affirms and demonstrates that writing, able as it is to preserve, elevate, celebrate, is equally all, one of the few things which distinguish man from the beasts he too often imitates. It is a testament to Brink's skill that one can absorb the power of his dissection of South African life, in all its brutal hopelessness, and yet come away with the satisfaction and hope, that South Africa has also produced a novel as intelligent and rich as *The Wall of the Plague*. (p. 2)

> *Anthony Olcott, "The Long Reach of Apartheid," in* Book World—The Washington Post, *February 17, 1985, pp. 1-2.*

ANN HULBERT

"The Wall of the Plague" is less about the plague of apartheid than it is about the walls that stand in the way of political action. The disappointing result of Mr. Brink's broader undertaking is that the words in this book sound less fluent than before, and the worlds look flatter.

"The Wall of the Plague" is set far from home, in the countryside of Provence. His characters' views, however, are relatively close to home, that is, to Mr. Brink's own views and those of many foreigners concerned about South Africa. His protagonist is a young "colored" South African woman named Andrea Malgas, who fled Cape Town with a white lover and has spent eight years since then in Europe doing her best to distance herself from her past. The novel traces her journey from liberal apathy to a final commitment to the struggle for change in her own country. Two men mark the poles of her passage—her current lover, Paul Joubert, a middle-aged Afrikaner expatriate whose roots are now in Paris, and a black South African militant named Mandla Mqayisa. . . .

Mr. Brink tries without success to fill out this simplistic white-"colored"-black scheme by complicating both his characters' voices and their views. The novel is ostensibly a diary of Andrea's change of heart and mind as she drives through Provence. But Paul turns out to be the real narrator, trying imaginatively to reconstruct her conversion once he learns she's gone forever. Unfortunately, he fails to make either her political and moral quandary or the emotional turmoil behind it very convincing.

He's intimidated, he confesses, by Andrea's own injunction. "You make me feel a woman, a person," he remembers her saying. "But please don't ever turn me into a story. I'm not a story, I'm me." In fact, his idea of the way to make her seem like a woman is to give her a clichéd identity crisis. . . .

As for her dilemma as a person abruptly confronted with a political choice, it sounds bewilderingly abstract. "He'd begun to threaten my wholeness," she says of Mandla, who arrives to stage the confrontation. Moments later she elaborates none too helpfully, "Inside me I was aware of a terrible emptiness expressed in flesh and bone. And it had been this emptiness to which he'd addressed himself."

Contrary to Paul's expectation, it's when Andrea is turned into a story—when the narrative dips back to memories of her past in South Africa—that she is most believable and appealing. . . . But those scenes from the vivid past don't really cohere in the vague present. The memories instead often feel as if they had

been tossed in, like the quotations from Paul's large library of works on the plague that are scattered through the novel.

Filtered through Paul, the characters' voices sound less, not more, compelling. Mr. Brink also dilutes their views, troubling their consciences with more than the uniquely appalling situation in South Africa. Doubtless he intended to broaden their dilemmas that way. Instead he blurs them. From the outset, Andrea frames her predicament as primarily a sexual, rather than a racial, one. . . . Indeed, her final decision to return to South Africa seems to have more to do with the history of her relations with men than with any revelatory memories of her South African heritage.

As for Paul, his crisis of conscience as an Afrikaner is overshadowed by his crisis of creativity as a well-known writer in Europe. Like Andrea, he solves his problem with a dose of self-deception. He believes he is fulfilling his responsibility to "shake off the fear, to look my world in the face, to risk everything, to write what I have within me" (a task from which his abstruse plague film has distracted him) by writing this book, Andrea's story. But the novel, preoccupied with Europe and padded with detritus from the plague project, finally is not the bold foray he prescribes.

It is just conceivable that this is part of Mr. Brink's point that "a book does not weigh much against the violence of the world" and that Paul, as a permanent expatriate, can't hope to give words even their small share of true gravity. Certainly that was Mr. Brink's own conclusion, as he tells it in **"Writing in a State of Siege"**: "To stay on in Paris would imply that literature, to me, had become a luxury to be indulged in, an intriguing diversion. If, on the other hand, writing was as important to me as I knew it was, it could be done in one place only: in the midst of that society to which I had now come to acknowledge my profound and agonizing commitment." Yet to write a weak novel to dramatize the importance of going home is only a distraction. As Mr. Brink himself has demonstrated, his real calling is to remain at home, looking his world full in the face.

> *Ann Hulbert, "Lovers, Black and White," in* The New York Times Book Review, *March 17, 1985, p. 35.*

NEAL ASCHERSON

André Brink can be a superb writer, but [*The Wall of the Plague*] is not one of his best novels. Rather like Paul's [film] scenario, the book seems overplotted and laborious; the original good idea is worked over again and again until it becomes obvious, and the human figures stiffen into puppets acting out a literary hypothesis. Andrea is the exception. All that Brink writes about her background in the Cape, her strong, lusting father, who was a fisherman, the exuberant life of the Coloured community, the development of her own feelings within the family or in her relations with the white master-race, has great power.

Paul is less convincing than his dilemmas. Brian, the Englishman, is one-dimensional, perhaps much as a besotted lover would have seen him, more probably because he is not imagined by Brink with much confidence. But the greatest failure, though an interesting one, is Mandla.

Mandla is a Xhosa, a young revolutionary educated at the black university of Fort Hare. His experience is carefully reconstructed. He has been a trade-union organizer and a victim—with his family—of the worst that the apartheid system and the security police can hand out. He has known prison and torture, and the murder or humiliation of those he loved. A black African, he seems to belong more to the armed-action tradition of the African National Congress than to the "black consciousness" movement of Steve Biko and his successors. From time to time, he disappears on missions into Eastern Europe. He is eloquent. But somehow he is misconceived. This is not a live African, but a blacked-up figure out of white liberal guilt-dreams. Mandla has none of the vitality, the impiousness and hang-ups of an educated Xhosa, a man from the quickest-witted nation in southern Africa. All he does in this novel is fulminate, fuck, and die, leaving the white reader feeling terrible. In this he has some resemblance to other reproachful black heroes created by European writers: Umslopogaas in Rider Haggard—even Othello.

The old white settlement at the Cape developed between two limits: the ocean, leading to Europe, and the Great Fish River, beyond which lived the Xhosa nations. Brink's remarkable imagination seems to work at full power only within those boundaries, for it should be added that his Europe and his Provence are almost as flat as Mandla. (Baedekerish stuff about France and details of hotels and meals constantly get in the way of the narrative.) The test of this is Brink's *A Chain of Voices* (1982). . . . This is one of the more impressive novels written by a South African, grand in its scale, acute in its historical understanding, and populated by men and women of great vigor. The differences between the characters of Mandla and of Galant . . . underscore the difference between the two novels. Galant becomes a complex person, Mandla is merely walked through the pages and given lines. Galant, indeed, is alive in the way that Andrea—who might be his remote descendant—is alive. They are children, then and now, of the Cape, the land that their creator finds so hard to leave in body or in imagination. (pp. 55-6)

Neal Ascherson, "Children of the Cape," in The New York Review of Books, *Vol. XXXII, No. 7, April 25, 1985, pp. 55-6.*

Joseph Brodsky

1940-

(Born Iosif Alexsandrovich Brodsky) Russian-born American poet, translator, and critic.

An exile from the Soviet Union who became an American citizen, Brodsky is considered by many critics to be the most important of contemporary Russian poets. His poems, which vary in form and range in tone from intense to somber, display strong metrical and schematic patterns and are grounded in realistic detail. Brodsky views the writing of poetry as a vital and serious craft and stresses the necessity for the poet to evoke a moral vision. Critics note that his vision reveals the influence of his Russian culture, the Bible, and classical and Western literature. His reverence for English-language poets is evidenced by his elegies in honor of John Donne, T. S. Eliot, and Robert Lowell. According to Victor Erlich, Brodsky's prominent themes include "man and nature, love and death, the ineluctability of anguish, the fragility of human achievements and attachments, the preciousness of the privileged moment, [and] the unrepeatable."

Born and raised in Leningrad, Brodsky began writing and translating poetry while still in his teens. He was singled out by authorities for not working a "regular" job and was put on trial in 1964. Despite favorable testimony by several writers and translators, Brodsky was labeled a "parasite" who wrote "decadent" poetry and was condemned to five years labor on a state farm. He was released over a year later, due in part to a petition signed by a number of Russian artists. Among them was the famed Russian poet Anna Akhmatova, whom Brodsky cites as his mentor and who once called him the most interesting and promising young Russian poet of his generation. Brodsky lived uneasily for the next few years as a poet and translator and was finally exiled in 1972. By this time he had already become recognized in the West; his trial had been widely publicized, and some of his poems had been translated and published in periodicals and pamphlets. He established a secure reputation based primarily on his early poem "Elegy for John Donne." Most of Brodsky's translated poems appear in *Selected Poems* (1973) and *A Part of Speech* (1980).

"Elegy for John Donne" begins on a quiet, snowy night with Donne lying awake in bed. From there the poem offers extended contemplation of metaphysical themes, including a meditation on death. Critics were impressed with Brodsky's knowledge of English poetic tradition as reflected in the poem's form and content. Czesław Miłosz stated that "an intensity that deserves to be called religious combined with a metaphorical denseness makes Brodsky a true descendant of the English metaphysical poets." In another important early poem, "Gorbunov and Gorchakov," Brodsky investigates the relationship between words and things, reality and illusion. W. H. Auden noted that "for Brodsky, as for Rilke and Eliot, poetic language has the same degree of 'reality' as the world; words regularly interact with things." Both works are included in *Selected Poems*, which also contains a laudatory introduction by Auden.

A Part of Speech includes poems written in the Soviet Union as well as the United States. Critics frequently cite the long

title poem and "Lullaby of Cape Cod" as two important works. In "Lullaby of Cape Cod," Brodsky looks out to sea from Cape Cod and reflects on the two "empires" in which he has lived. He meditates on both his personal life and the fate of humanity while observing the beauties of nature. "A Part of Speech" reveals Brodsky's emphasis on the role of the poet, who places faith in language as a common bond through which people can affirm their humanity.

(See also *CLC*, Vols. 4, 6, 13 and *Contemporary Authors*, Vols. 41-44, rev. ed.)

CZESŁAW MIŁOSZ

The strong presence of Joseph Brodsky has needed less than a decade to establish itself in world poetry. Yet of his four books published in Russian, only one, *Selected Poems*, was translated into English. . . . Probably, by a sort of instinct, the cultured public vaguely feels, if not clearly comprehends, his stature. His poetry has attracted good translators, as [*A Part of Speech*] shows. On the other hand, the reader of his work enters a huge building of strange architecture (a cathedral? an ICBM site?) at his own risk, since critics and literary scholars have not yet begun to compile literary guidebooks to it.

In syllables, feet, rhyme, stanzas Brodsky follows a tradition, but not slavishly. The very nature of the Russian language seems to have determined a peculiar brand of modernism in our century: innovation within strict metrical patterns. Russian verse in this respect is different from its English, French, and also Polish, Czech, and Serbo-Croatian counterparts. Brodsky's colloquialisms, slang expressions, and words not met with in literary usage would seem to call for the freedom of William Carlos William's "spoken" rhythms. Instead, together with a web of metaphors, often sustained and enlarged through several stanzas, they make up a pattern of lines to be half sung, half recited. In his practice of poetry as a vocation, Brodsky observes rules of craftsmanship going back to the late eighteenth-century poet Derzhavin. In his experiments with poetic genres—ode, lyrical poem, elegy, descriptive poem, the story in verse—he resembles Auden. The obstacles such poetry presents to transplantation into another language should add to our surprise when we see how Brodsky comes through in English and finds an attentive ear, at least among serious readers.

The secret lies, probably, in the way he reverses some of the trends that have dominated poetry for the last half century. These trends were based on certain unavowed premises which, as is common in the history of ideas, are fated not to be overcome in direct combat, but simply bypassed. Brodsky grew up in the Soviet Union, but being self-educated he has remained impervious to its imposed and largely accepted modes of thinking. During his years of exile, since 1972, he has also preserved a skeptical distance from the intellectual fashions of his new milieu. At the same time, he does not resemble those recent Russian immigrants who stay in their Slavic shell and are mistrustful of the evil West. Looking for his roots, we must turn to the era of European cosmopolitanism, which came to an end with the outbreak of World War I, and ended in Russia with the Revolution. Brodsky takes over where young Osip Mandelstam and young Anna Akhmatova were stopped.

This does not mean, though, that the post-revolutionary decades, so tragic for Russian poetry, did not leave a durable impression on his view of the world. Behind Brodsky's poetry is the experience of political terror, the experience of the debasement of man and the growth of the totalitarian empire. Thus we may speak of two currents, Western and Russian, both originating in cosmopolitan Europe before 1914, coming together again, the second current represented in the work of a poet who has been banished from his own country. The reversal of trends which I mentioned may be owing precisely to that coming together.

I find it fascinating to read his poems as part of his larger enterprise, which is no less than an attempt to fortify the place of man in a threatening world. Contrary to the tendency prevailing today, he believes that the poet, before he is ready to confront ultimate questions, must observe a certain code. He should be God-fearing, love his country and his native tongue, rely upon his conscience, avoid alliances with evil, and be attached to tradition. These elementary rules cannot be forgotten or ridiculed by a poet, since absorbing them is part of his initiation, more exactly ordination, into a sacred craft. . . .

The poet's task as Brodsky conceives it is to try to preserve continuity in a world more and more afflicted with a loss of memory. His basic text would be the Bible. . . .

In attempting to reconstruct a poetics from Brodsky's work, I do not want to present him as a man looking for refuge in a safe conservatism. My point is that his despair is that of a poet who belongs to the end of the twentieth century, and it acquires its full significance only when juxtaposed with a code consisting of a few fundamental beliefs. This despair is held in check so that each poem becomes an exercise in stamina.

A Part of Speech contains several poems written in the Soviet Union, but its major theme is exile, in a double sense: literally and as a metaphor for the condition of post-modern man. Brodsky is an autobiographical poet and his topics are related to his itinerary: the Leningrad of his childhood and youth, the Crimea, a *sovkhoz* in the north where he served his sentence after being arrested for "parasitism" (i.e., for being an unlicensed poet), Lithuania, America (Ann Arbor and Cape Cod), Venice, Florence, Mexico, and England. Travel, voluntary and involuntary, leaves its trace: the book is a philosphical diary in verse. It differs from works of romantic travels of the past, for they had a horizontal quality, as the earth then preserved something of the quality of a plane. Now the world is irreversibly round and getting smaller every day. How then is one to build a fortress on it—for oneself, for man?

Perhaps [as in **"A Part of Speech"**] by going to a German town where an insane addict of power started his career and by reflecting there on a transitory *gloria mundi*.

> In the little town out of which
>   death sprawled over the class-
>   room map
> the cobblestones shine like scales
>   that coat a carp,
> on the secular chestnut tree melting
>   candles hung,
> and a cast-iron lion pines for a
>   good harangue.
> Through the much laundered, pale
>   window gauze
> woundlike carnations and *kirchen*
>   needles ooze;
> a tram rattles far off, as in days of
>   yore,
> but no one gets off at the stadium
>   any more. . . .

I selected this poem because the poet's own itinerary and the history of the twentieth century meet here, and because it exemplifies some of Brodsky's qualities, his terse, manly, and vibrant tone. The lines tend to join in couplets, but often he sounds breathless, running one sentence on for several lines. Those who have heard him read his poetry know how closely its scansion corresponds to its ardor and restrained vehemence.

Man against space and time. The two words, crucial for his poetry, invariably are given ominous connotations by Brodsky: "And space rises like some bill of fare," "Time's invented by death," "the nothingness of Time," "Here space appears unnerved by its own feats," "and space backed up like a crab, time surged ahead . . . soiling its garments with the tar of night," "Buzzing around my jugular, time. . . ." One needs only to add two other words, "hemisphere" and "empire" as being central to a reading of Brodsky. (p. 23)

Brodsky moved from one continent to another, from a hemisphere to a hemisphere, from one empire to another empire. His poem **"Lullaby of Cape Cod"** . . . is a long meditation on displacement. . . .

> I write from an Empire whose enor-
>   mous flanks

extend beneath the sea. Having
sampled two
oceans as well as continents, I feel
that I know
what the globe itself must feel:
there's nowhere to go.

"Empire" is one of Brodsky's prankish words. The Roman conquests were not called "liberations" or "anticolonialist." They were just feats of force. Similarly, neither Charlemagne's nor Napoleon's quest for power was much disguised by ideology. The twentieth century witnesses a struggle between a few centers of control, while Orwellian double-speak spreads a smoke screen of high-sounding slogans. That their country is also an empire may, for the Russians, be a source of pride, and for Americans, with their strange habit of breast-beating, a source of shame, but the reality is inescapable. For Brodsky, "empire" also means the very dimensions of a continent, the monumentality itself, of which he is fond.

There are no illusions here: the Earth is not enough and the Sun is insufficient to light up both hemispheres simultaneously ("The light has never been enough"). Yet, as we have come to expect of Brodsky, **"Lullaby of Cape Cod,"** one of his strongest poems, is an affirmation of endurance. He accomplishes what previous generations of Russian émigré writers were unable to do: to make the lands of exile, however reluctantly, their own, to take possession through the poetic word. He uses the metaphor of a stranded fish which adapts itself "to some deep, cellular wish," and wriggles toward the bushes. (pp. 23-4)

Brodsky is a poet with a complex cultural inheritance and he freely draws on models and archetypes of human behavior from literature. That is how he deals with the problem of the individual against an oppressive society, of the poet against the center of power. In **"Letters to a Roman Friend"** . . . , one more variation on the theme of Horace's provincial retreat, Horace addresses strophes to Postumus who lives in Imperial Rome. In **"Torso"** . . . , life, symbolized by a mouse, is opposed to the "Empire" which petrifies everything. Here it is difficult to avoid thinking of Pushkin's "Bronze Horseman," where poor Evgeny, a mouse indeed, is pursued by the monument of Peter the Great. . . .

In some of his most moving poems Brodsky uses themes taken from the Bible, Homer, and Virgil. Among his highest accomplishments I place **"Odysseus to Telemachus"** and **"Nunc Dimittis,"** on old Simeon receiving the Christ Child in the temple. . . .

The urge to make use of motifs from antiquity is common to several other contemporary poets and is probably evidence of their mistrust of the amorphousness of our own time. Still, no two poets treat these themes similarly, the proportion of the experienced and the literary differing for each. In Brodsky the second component is just sufficient to cool strong emotion; he is less sardonic in these poems than in his others.

Still, what I have said is no more than one approach to defining Brodsky's work. This is philosophical poetry, bearing the mark of what Goethe considered the highest stage in the spiritual development of the individual, which he called "Respect." It is a poetry at two poles of human existence: love as it is lived and suffered through, and death almost tasted and feared. Both love and death are approached in these poems with awe and through an inspired incantation which does not sound to me secular. An intensity that deserves to be called religious com-

bined with a metaphorical denseness makes Brodsky a true descendant of the English metaphysical poets and it is clear he feels an affinity with them. (p. 24)

In **"The Butterfly"** . . . , the seventeenth century is revisited, revived, and enriched. The magnificent **"Elegy for John Donne"** was written while he was still in Russia, and is included in *Selected Poems*. While in the Soviet north he learned of the death of T. S. Eliot and wrote a dirge, borrowing its form from Auden's poem on the death of Yeats. I know of no poet in the West who mourned Eliot in a poem.

Brodsky has no talisman of faith that can protect him from despair and the fear of death, and in this respect he is close to many other contemporary poets. Death, for him, is always associated with Nothingness. (pp. 24-5)

However, his tone is not one of resignation, and this distinguishes him from his contemporaries. Quite extraordinary is the poem on growing old, **"1972"** . . . , whose stanzas enumerate one by one, with a sort of masochistic glee, the signs of the destructive work of time upon the author's body. But then, in a peculiar leap of optimistic rhythm, we read a sudden appeal to beat the drum and march forward, together with one's shadow. . . .

The reappearance of stoicism in the literature of this century is often said to be based on analogies between the ancient and modern worlds, marked as they both are by a departure of the gods. To the question whether Brodsky's determination is stoic, I would answer no. I see a deep affinity between him and Lev Shestov. A haughty, scornful, and austere thinker, who did his best work during his years of exile in Paris (where he died in 1939), Shestov was discovered, together with Kierkegaard, by the French existentialists. . . . Shestov disliked stoicism, in which he saw the quintessence of the submission to Necessity typical, according to him, of Greek thought. To Athens, he opposed Jerusalem, to Socrates and Plato he opposed *The Book of Job*. His work is imbued with that respect for the Sacred that I find in Brodsky; it is a "serious call" to strive ceaselessly for transcendence without accepting things as they are, and without the comforts of serenity. . . .

A study of Brodsky and Shestov ought to be written, not necessarily to search for the influence (real, I think) of the philosopher on the poet, but rather to stress a strange convergence in the tactics chosen by these two defenders of the Holy in the age of disbelief. The adjectives applied to Shestov, and his style—haughty, scornful, austere—fit Brodsky as well. . . .

Unlike philosophers, [poets] have their home in the language, in its past, present, and future, though few of them make such a conscious choice as Brodsky, who had to tear away the cobwebs of the journalese that infest his native tongue before he could engage in "purifying the language of the tribe." In a way, he is in a privileged position, since he is surrounded by new worlds unnamed in Russian. They are waiting for discovery by a poet who looks at them in a specific, non-Western way [as in **"A Part of Speech"**].

What gets left of a man amounts
to a part. To his spoken part. To a
part of speech. . . .

Thus, as a defense against despair, we have the *œuvre* of a man wholly concentrated on his poetry. Here poems of circumstance, including descriptions of visited cities and countries, have a definite presence and purpose. In his struggle against the Necessity of space and time, Shestov was less lucky, since he was merely a philosopher. Brodsky seizes upon a street, a detail of architecture, an aura of a place, and removes it from the flow of time and from space, to preserve it in a crystalline meter. He gathers several tableaux—from Mexico, from Lithuania—under the title of *"divertissement"* or *"divertimento,"* probably in the musical sense, although it can also be associated with *"le divertissement"* of Pascal who saw in it the main remedy for the misery of the human condition.

Some of the purest epigrammatic verses of Brodsky make up the **"Lithuanian Divertissement."** Among them are **"Liejyklos"** and **"The Dominicans."** The first of these is the name of a street, the second is a Roman Catholic church in Wilno, now the capital of Soviet Lithuania. I cannot write impersonally of this cycle. In that city of my adolescence and youth, then belonging to Poland, I know every stone. The cycle is dedicated to our mutual friend, the Lithuanian poet Thomas Venclova. The space created by the poem becomes, in my perception, an empyrean realm where three poets of different nationalities and backgrounds can celebrate their meeting in the teeth of reality which in that region is especially ominous and oppressive. . . .

In his foreword to the *Selected Poems*, Auden said that, if one can judge by translations, Brodsky should be a poet of the first order. Let us hope that *A Part of Speech* will help to secure for him the undisputed standing he deserves as a major poet, thanks to his work in English, which in a considerable number of lines comes close to the original in conciseness and strength. (p. 25)

> Czesław Miłosz, *"A Struggle against Suffocation,"* in The New York Review of Books, *Vol. 27, No. 13, August 14, 1980, pp. 23-5.*

CLARENCE BROWN

[**"A Part of Speech"**] is Brodsky's second collection of poems to appear in English. The translation of **"Selected Poems"** (1973) was the work of one man, George Kline, who was for long Brodsky's single English voice. The present volume contains translations by no fewer than 10 English and American poets, to say nothing of Brodsky himself, who singlehandedly translated two poems (including the important title piece). . . . He also wrote the splendid elegy on the death of Robert Lowell directly in English (the choice of English was in itself a graceful enhancement of this tribute to his friend and early champion). Notwithstanding this evidence of his incipient metamorphosis into an American writer, Brodsky continues to write almost exclusively in his native Russian—though the sad doppler effect of its recession into his past troubles him no less than it does all other writers living in banishment. (p. 11)

It seems altogether appropriate that Brodsky's lyrical persona, a protean figure to whom we have by now become fairly accustomed, should be represented by a multiplicity of English voices. Even what might elsewhere seem the uncomfortable jostling of British and American diction contributes here to the impression of uprootedness.

A restless wanderer, alternately peevish and amused, outraged and remorseful, belligerent and resigned, this persona speaks, as Richard Eder aptly remarked in a recent New York Times interview, "with the playfulness that has weariness at its center." Though his attitude toward exile, longing, solitude and the insulting dilemmas of growing older may waver, we can only feel grateful that the result is the same: a transmutation of this experience into the most powerful, the most technically

accomplished, erudite, wide ranging and consistently astonishing Russian poetry being written today. If we adopt Auden's rule that a minor poet is one whose later works cannot be distinguished from his earlier, then Brodsky is indisputably major, for it should be clear even to those who must read him in English alone that he is probing new themes with greater freedom, confidence and verbal resource.

Like the Auden who was, no less than Lowell, his champion, Brodsky is a master of traditional forms. He is now less constricted than formerly by the emphatic meters and rhymes that persist as the norm of Russian verse, but an occasional set-piece, such as the elegy on the death of Marshall Zhukov, can suggest to the English reader one of the limits of Brodsky's range. Zhukov, the admiring friend of Eisenhower, suffered humiliation in his beloved Russia after having repulsed Hitler's armies. The ideal Russian reader for whom Brodsky writes would immediately detect the echoes of a famous tribute by the 18th-century poet Derzhavin to a similar military figure. By the unobtrusive means of meter alone Brodsky is thus able to tie many knots of history and subversive emotion. (pp. 11, 16)

In 1966 he recited to me (wittily enough, just beneath the Kremlin walls) his then-unpublished elegy on the death of T. S. Eliot, and the deliberate echo of an earlier model, Auden's elegy on Yeats, was immediately perceptible. The form alone was speaking with its mute but unmistakable eloquence, and the Russian poet's moving lines extended to include two other great poets—tradition *and* the individual talent, as it were.

Literary echoes of a somewhat more obvious and less functional sort might possibly offend the ear of the ideal English reader. There is for instance a good deal too much muffled Auden in the poem **"Strophes,"** and for no discernible reason. . . .

It is perhaps not surprising that some of the best poems of this bleakly undomiciled voice are those attached to places, which range from Norenskaya, the site of his Russian exile . . . to the far-flung locales of his foreign exile: the Italy of the Russian poets Akhmatova and Mandelstam, cozy England, a Lake District which wittily turns out to be inhabited by Michigan undergraduates, not Wordsworth, and, finally, Cape Cod in the boozy but wonderfully accomplished meditation translated by Anthony Hecht and entitled **"Lullaby of Cape Cod."** . . . (p. 16)

Brodsky's love of Lowell did not extend to an endorsement of that poet's relaxed view of translation as "imitation." It is therefore hardly surprising that his self-translation, constrained as it is by the dream of congruence in meter, rhyme *and* meaning, should fall short of his original composition in English. The 15 poems of the second part of the book are at times dictionary-haunted (a century-old chestnut tree is called "secular"), at times idiomatically unfocused (as when the now rather quaint epithet "blasted" must be summoned out of retirement to rhyme with "wasted"), at times incomprehensible.

But the powerful elegy to Lowell, since it is not a translation and has only itself to think about, unfolds with a serene and compelling mastery. (p. 18)

> Clarence Brown, *"The Best Russian Poetry Written Today,"* in The New York Times Book Review, *September 7, 1980, pp. 11, 16, 18.*

ANTHONY ASTRACHAN

Brodsky is not one of those emigrants who confine themselves to the narrow horizons of the exile archipelago. He lives in an

American world whose language and literature he loves, and he *must* let his work feed and be fed by that language and literature. Whether or not he can be called great, as Akhmatova and Mandelstam are great, he is the finest poet writing in Russian, in or out of the Soviet Union.

Eight years of exile have thickened Brodsky's language a little: in Russian, there is more alliteration; there are more tricks with sound and meaning. At the same time, living abroad has also thinned his intensity of feeling slightly, as seen in the English versions of his poems, without diminishing his breadth or depth. He is more than ever a poet whose passions spring from his brains more than his bowels, like Wallace Stevens (whom he likes but seldom mentions) and W. H. Auden (whom he loves). He writes less about love than he did when he lived in the Soviet Union, but is even more skeptical about love's conventional triumphs. That might, of course, be a process that owes as much to age as to exile; Brodsky turned 40 this year.

His recurring themes are almost eschatological. He travels from one place, one continent to another, and makes almost every stopping point the setting for a new poem. But these travels become first a passage through the state of exile and then a passage through time to some finality. Individuals and empires are both subject to the process of aging. "Empire" is one of Brodsky's favorite words. He uses it in geographical, political and temporal senses, as befits a poet who, like Mandelstam and Akhmatova, comes from Leningrad, the old imperial capital whose inhabitants still call it "Piter," for St. Petersburg. Moving through distance and time, one must keep struggling to reach the next stage, to escape evil, even though the destination is the future or death, which Brodsky fears, or may simply believe, are each full of emptiness.

These themes are transcendently clear in one of the best, and best translated, poems in this book, **"Lullaby of Cape Cod."** . . . The poet adapting to a new culture abroad becomes a creature adapting to a new environment, a fish "wriggling toward bushes, forming hinged leg-struts, then / to depart (leaving a track like the scrawl of a pen) / for the interior, the heart of the continent." (pp. 323-24)

Auden . . . said in his introduction to Brodsky's *Selected Poems* that Brodsky, "like Van Gogh and Virginia Woolf . . . has an extraordinary capacity to envision material objects as sacramental signs, messengers from the unseen." There are fewer of these sacramental objects in the later poems than in the earlier ones, but they still materialize—the eponymous creature of **"The Butterfly,"** for instance, translated by George L. Kline in a way that preserves its metaphysical flavor. . . . (p. 324)

Of the many poems in *A Part of Speech* that I find beautiful and gripping, more are in the first part, written before Brodsky left the Soviet Union, than in the second, written in exile. This says as much about my preference for poems that interweave themes of love with those of exile, and perhaps about the accidents of translator selection, as it does about Brodsky's evolution as a poet. I feel the need, before I run out of space, to grab you by the sleeve and say, for God's sake, in addition to the poems I've already named, be sure to read **"Six Years Later"** . . . , **"A Song to No Music"** . . . , **"I Sit by the Window"** . . . (a poem that manages to be eschatological without going beyond the present tense, absolutely faithful to the original, but even better in English than in Russian, to my eye); **"Lagoon"** . . . , and **"Letters from the Ming Dynasty."** . . .

Brodsky has always insisted on impossibly high standards of translation, demanding fidelity not only to the spirit of the original but also to the meter and the rhyme. Equivalent rhyme is particularly difficult in translating from Russian, an inflected language whose case endings give it a wealth of feminine rhymes and whose consonants are as thick and savory as a name-day borscht.

The poems I have mentioned come close to meeting Brodsky's standards. Others do not—particularly, I am both saddened and amused to see, some that Brodsky has translated or helped to translate himself. . . .

[Transliterated literally, four lines in **"1972"** say] "Aging! Hail, my aging! / Blood slowly flowing. / Legs, formerly a harmonious structure / Torment vision." Obviously the literal translation is not poetry. But there can be no excuse, in the lust to reproduce the feminine rhymes, for

> Aging! Hail to thee, senility.
> Blood flows as slowly as chilly tea.
> Limbs, former pride of the whole
>   vicinity
> hurt my vision. . . .

Brodsky here reduces himself to the level of W. S. Gilbert. . . . There are several other poems where Brodsky cheapens his work by inserting words alien to his original thought in order to reproduce the rhyme.

That is particularly unfortunate because many poems in this book reveal a concern with language as part of the core of a man that is understandably intense in a poet forced to leave the land of his mother tongue. One of the fourteen poems that make up the group called **"A Part of Speech,"** which Brodsky himself translated (and translated well), says almost everything that can be said about being a poet in exile. . . . (p. 325)

Anthony Astrachan, "A Murder Is / a Murder," in The Nation, Vol. 231, No. 10, October 4, 1980, pp. 323-25.

ROBERT HASS

[*A Part of Speech*] is a book to have looked forward to, not only because Americans have grown accustomed through writers like Nabokov and Czeslaw Milosz to the haunting literature of exile being made in our midst, but also because Brodsky has lived in both faces of the mirror world of the cold war; and the rest of us, affected daily by its subliminal pressure, want his testimony. There are a handful of poems here to justify that hope, but for the most part reading *A Part of Speech* is like wandering through the ruins of a noble building.

Just how bad the trouble is may be judged from these lines in **"Lullaby of Cape Cod":** "Therefore, sleep well. Sweet dreams. Knit up that sleeve. / Sleep as those only do who have gone pee-pee." Such fatal miscalculations of tone, candidates for any future *Stuffed Owl*, the famous anthology of great moments in the history of awful verse, are fairly common. For example:

> My blood is very cold—
> its cold is more withering
> than iced-to-the-bottom streams.
> People are not my thing.

And when the words are wrenched from the order of natural speech to meet the requirements of a poetic form, things get even worse. . . . (pp. 35-6)

The specific difficulties of getting Russian poetry into English are notorious. Russian is an inflected, characteristically polysyllabic language, much more flexible in its word order than English. Moreover, English poetry is a much older art. Metrical poems in English have been written for over 400 years, in Russian for something like 200. That is, in terms of exhausting the resources of meter and rhyme, Russian verse could be said to be as fresh as English poetry was at the end of the age of Pope. In America, a metrical poem is likely to conjure up the idea of the sort of poet who wears ties and lunches at the faculty club. In Russia it suggests the moral force of an art practiced against the greatest personal odds, as a discipline, solitary and intense. As a result, the kind of poem that Brodsky writes, difficult to render anyway, has to be rendered with attention to the preservation of its form when that form, translated into English, is in danger of being transposed at the same time into another key altogether.

This helps to account for the difficulty of the task, but not for the results, which sometimes read like first high school exercises in the composition of metrical poetry, or worse, like sophisticated parodies of those attempts, like Peter Quince himself. . . .

The translators have clearly struggled with tone. Should Brodsky sound like Lowell? like Auden? Byron? Pope? A preferred solution, because Brodsky is an ironist, is that tediously bouncy rhythm produced by clever young men of indeterminate age down from the university and set to make a splash. . . . Another is to make him sound like an 18th-century hack rewriting Shakespeare. . . .

Then there are the clichés of iambic rhythm, like the excessive use of the possessive case: "retreating north before winter's assault," "closed to the clash of day's discord," "July's conclusion merges with the rains," "rubbed by the light on space's surface." It is like reading a book that keeps sneezing. And the absurd poetic diction: "the vast wet of ocean," "a strengthless breeze." There is padding for the sake of rhyme . . . , the padding to which translators are tempted because there are so often fewer words in a line of Russian verse than in an English equivalent. This leads fairly often to massive redundancy. . . .

Poetry, Ford Madox Ford told Ezra Pound in 1912, must be at least as well written as prose. There is, in fact, a kind of contempt for poetry in letting language like this stand. . . .

Brodsky, of course, cannot be held responsible for this carnage. Readers who want to get a sense of his strength should turn immediately to the powerful title poem, **"A Part of Speech,"** which is translated by Brodsky himself and is wholly free from the grotesquerie that characterizes the book as a whole. There is other work that is equally fine. . . . **"The Funeral of Bobo"** is a brilliant poem in any language. . . . **"Nunc Dimittis"** is beautiful and very plain. . . .

Readers will also want to look at **"A Cape Cod Lullaby."** It is full of tasteless and hackneyed writing, but in passages seems as if it must be a poem of extraordinary interest. (p. 36)

Nothing is Brodsky's theme, the struggle of consciousness against the horror and boredom of things. At his best, he sounds something like Robert Lowell when Lowell is sounding like Byron—jaded, nervous, quick-eyed, alert to any smallest hint that the world is something more than numbingly predictable, brutal, and inert by turns. It is all the more ironic, then, that the nothingness this book most often calls up is the kind figured by Pope at the end of *The Dunciad* when the sheer accumulation of inept and unintelligent writing puts out all the lights: "Thy hand, great Anarch! lets the curtain fall, / And universal Dark-

ness buries All." I think our hope must be that Joseph Brodsky, like Nabokov and Samuel Beckett, becomes his own translator. (p. 37)

> Robert Hass, "Lost in Translation," in The New Republic, *Vol. 183, No. 25, December 20, 1980, pp. 35-7.*

DANA GIOIA

When Joseph Brodsky's *Selected Poems* were published in 1973, I admired his work for its energy and imagination but still found the volume difficult to read at long stretches. At times the book seemed like a miscellany containing too many poems arranged too loosely. . . . I was glad to have this generous selection of Brodsky's poetry, but I feared that his full distinction as a poet would remain inaccessible to anyone who did not know Russian. Now Brodsky's new collection, *A Part of Speech,* suddenly changes this state of affairs. This well-focused, excellently translated volume makes him for the first time fully accessible in English.

Brodsky has organized the poems in *A Part of Speech* with great care. The book is divided into two sections corresponding ironically to an old and a new testament appropriately linked by prophecies and echoes. The first section, entitled "A Song to No Music," consists of seventeen poems skillfully chosen from all the work Brodsky wrote during the last years he was in the Soviet Union. These poems reveal how much he was an emotional exile in his homeland before he became a political exile abroad. Brodsky repeatedly strikes an Ovidian note of sadness and estrangement, sometimes even modulating into horror. . . . (pp. 611-12)

The second section of the book, which gives *A Part of Speech* its title, consists of poems Brodsky has written in exile. Although written in a variety of techniques from the perspective of half a dozen different countries, these new poems are unified by their author's bleak vision of himself as a man without family or home, without destination or future. Brodsky is not a political poet, and yet by force of circumstance his work has acquired a deep political dimension. Sometimes the politics are overt as in the poems where he assumes a Roman identity and comments on the state of the Empire. Here he adopts many elements from two of his masters, Auden and Cavafy—most notably their ability to deal openly with politics without ever succumbing to its temptations to be doctrinaire. More often Brodsky uses politics as just one more part of life, as inescapable as the weather, in the background of his intensely personal poems. For Brodsky is at his finest when he writes most personally. Even his private fears and fantasies transform themselves into powerful poetry. For example, towards the end of his long title sequence, Brodsky thinks about the Russian word for "the future"—which resembles the word for "rodents"—and he has a frightening vision of his own future. In another poet this conceit might have seemed awkward, but with Brodsky the effect is strong and immediate. (p. 612)

> *Dana Gioia, in a review of "A Part of Speech," in* The Hudson Review, *Vol. XXXIII, No. 4, Winter, 1980-81, pp. 611-13.*

JOHN BAYLEY

Brodsky, like Akhmatova who approved of him—indeed she thought he was the only one of the younger Russian poets who was any good—is an intensely referential and local poet, with all the natural linguistic simplicities that go with this. His poetry does portray a man "exactly himself," creating its own myth out of episode and event as it goes along, and although his real poetry, as it were, his verse in Russian, is not and cannot be at all like that of Lowell or Auden, the poems he writes in English and the translations which he now helps to make himself [in *A Part of Speech*] . . . are bound to seem closely akin to the feel of Lowell's and Auden's poems, Auden's particularly. (p. 84)

Auden, Brodsky's godfather in every sense in the western world, remarks in one of the stage directions in "The Age of Anxiety" that the world is divided into "the sane who know that they are acting and the mad who do not"; and in "Many Happy Returns" he wishes a young friend the essential gift of a sense of theater and a love of illusion. . . . As always in Auden the moral and the message are very plain indeed. Only those poets who (in some degree) clown and show off understand the difference between their pretence and the truths that poetry can indicate but never embody. The same sort of point is made by Brodsky at much greater length in **"Homage to Yalta," "The Funeral of Bobo," "Lullaby of Cape Cod,"** poems of occasion that celebrate a sense of the difference between experience as it was and the truth that comes with hindsight. The antics of language understand its limitations. (pp. 84-5)

So it is, then, that Brodsky chooses his poets in the west— Byron and Auden, Donne, about whose preoccupation with death and acting he has written a marvelous poem, and now **"Homage to Yalta,"** a monologue in the manner of Browning that tells a chillingly psychopathic tale. Like all good anecdotalists and aggregators in poetry Brodsky is preoccupied with its power to convey states of feeling in terms of detail, feelings that correspond to and are identified with topographical individualities. In London (**"The Thames at Chelsea"**) in a city "where, dark as the brick may get / the milk will always stand sedately white"; in New England, where for the unquiet sleeper drowned in dreams, "a cod stands at the door"; in Venice, a damp Christmas, with memories of Russia coiling and uncoiling in the sea-damp pension bedroom, and the lion of St. Mark imagined in the shape of another and more dread insignia.

> So let us place the left paw, sheathing its claws,
> in the crook of the arm of the other one, because
>   this makes a hammer-and-sickle sign
> with which to salute our era and bestow
> a mute up-yours-even-unto-the-elbow
>   upon the nightmares of our time.

The deftness and slickness of the translation . . . renders accurately something in the spirit of the original, but its effectiveness is also misleading, giving the impression that this is the "real" Brodsky. It isn't: not quite. The timbre and felicity of the Russian, its superb fluent purr, is not really in any relation to this dapper but impersonal Audenian idiom. Because the translations are so effective Brodsky seems less good than he is, and more facile. He seems to be manipulating a standardized post-Auden mechanism, which at times verges on parody. (p. 87)

The absolute locality of a language is something that most poets need, Brodsky not least. The paradox about him is that his own language has the locality that goes with the anecdotes and increments, the dense familiarity of a true poetic landscape, but at the same time he exists in another dimension, half asphasic, half fashionable, in which poetic language is merely another form of publicity medium. American, the American

that Brodsky is now fluent in, lends itself easily to this kind of sophisticated razzmatazz, taking over the haunting poems that he writes about his linguistic and local provenance, Baltic and Lithuanian, and giving them an international gloss, the poetic equivalent of a *New Yorker* travel brochure. They seem kitted out to be read at poetry festivals; they have an air of being perpetually introduced by a few words. And this is sad because it denatures them, and denatures them apparently with their author's acquiescence and encouragement.

Auden went in for the glossy razzmatazz too, increasingly so in his later years, but it never got into his language, nor eroded the reef of old-fashioned morality and common sense on which all those "halcyon structures" of his language were soundly based. Auden is always characteristic, "exactly himself." Brodsky would be too, as much as Mandelstam or Akhmatova, but his poetry is undoubtedly affected by its own translation, giving it a weightless effect which is all too like that of the poetry of self-cancellation. (pp. 88-9)

Something has no doubt been gained from the vogue for Lowell-type imitations of "world poetry"—Mandelstam Dante Ungaretti Lorca Rilke Villon all run together into a chic modern idiom—and the kinds of impersonality involved seem to please readers who are not at home with true idiosyncrasy, and dislike the effort of meeting a poet as his true self. But the process does not augur well; poems are not like the commodities of a common market. Lowell, moreover, always remained himself, even in his imitations. So does Milosz, whom Brodsky regards as the greatest poet of our time. Though he has had to become as Americanized as Brodsky, and like him has translated his own poems into English with help from his friends, Milosz remains even in translation an unmistakable and a marvelously authentic Polish poet. It is worth comparing his collection, *Bells in Winter* with *A Part of Speech*. The comparison is not to the advantage, not of Brodsky himself, but of the kind of idiom into which his native poetry has become increasingly and fatally assimilated. (pp. 89-90)

> John Bayley, "Sophisticated Razzmatazz," in Parnassus: Poetry in Review, Vol. 9, No. 1, Spring-Summer, 1981, pp. 83-90.

SIDNEY MONAS

I have the sense in reading even [Brodsky's] early poetry that exile was intrinsic to it, that long before a tyrannical and repressive regime forced him into separation from his nourishing mother tongue and immediate cultural milieu, and that although poetry has in general been alien to the contemporary world, he more than most poets was born into exile.

Born into exile, but at a particular time and in a special place. In Leningrad a generation of poets came of age in the postwar years as hardship and terror relaxed, if they did not entirely subside. (pp. 214-15)

Broadly speaking, the young Leningrad poets could be divided into two groups, both of which attempted to identify and link themselves to two literary movements extinguished in the 1920s—the Acmeists and the Futurists. Brodsky, for all his striking originality, his occasional love of the grotesque and constant verbal play as well as his links to the young Mayakovsky, considers himself (and rightly so) a traditionalist and a classicist, and therefore an adherent of Acmeism—a movement, moreover, native to Leningrad, whose two greatest poets,

Osip Mandelstam and Anna Akhmatova, were Brodsky's cultural lodestars.

Mandelstam had called Acmeism "a longing for world culture." In Petrograd-Leningrad, once "a window onto Europe," that longing had a special poignance. Brodsky steeped himself in the entire Petersburg tradition, from eighteenth-century poets like Kantemir and Derzhavin, through the great, cerebral nineteenth-century poet Baratinsky (little known outside Russia and a Muscovite by residence, but in his late poems a Petersburger in spirit), to Gumilev, Mandelstam and Akhmatova in the twentieth century. Of Petersburg, Brodsky himself has written, "Nowhere else did classicism have so much space." That there is something paradoxical about a classicism with "so much space"—since classicism is normally thought of as an art of distinct limits and clear definitions, of narrow if lucid horizons—Brodsky no doubt knows. He is a classicist of the age of irony, and paradox is his birthright. (p. 215)

The stance of the lyrical persona in Brodsky's poems is solitary: watching, waiting, looking out a window, gazing at stars or at a landscape. The solitude in these poems is immense. Sometimes it is bracing and strong, the stance of independence and originality, as when, in an early poem ["**Exhaustion now is a more frequent guest**" *(Selected Poems)*], he addresses his own verses: "And must you live in nests of latest style / And sing in concert with the latest lyre?" It is of course a rhetorical question, and for him even at twenty the answer is obvious. Ten years later [in "**I Sit by the Window**" *(A Part of Speech)*], steeped in self-irony, he writes: "My song was out of tune, my voice was cracked, / but at least no chorus can ever sing it back." This is stubborn, stalwart Brodsky, who at twenty-four faced judge and prosecutor in a Leningrad court, accused of "parasitism," and proclaimed his commitment to the craft of making poems; who faced unfazed two years of work on a collective farm in the Archangel district and made poems out of it. Yet reading Brodsky, the solitude becomes all-pervasive and begins to weigh heavily. Even the love poems—to "**M.B.**," to "**Mademoiselle Veronique**" and others—are poems of solitude and separation. The pieces dedicated to friends (those to Evgeny Rein are especially delicate in the tone and feeling of address) express separation and apartness. Elegies to the admired dead (T. S. Eliot, Robert Lowell, Auden) are poems of solitude and separation. There is an occasional note of solidarity, as in the fleeting, almost shy, occasional references to his mentor Anna Akhmatova, or the remarkable prose obituary he wrote for Nadezhda Mandelstam. But for the most part, the lyrical persona of the poems stands so bleakly alone in such a vastly alienated world that the reader, gripped by the power of the verse, nevertheless begins to long for his own "halt in the desert." . . .

In one of his longest and most impressive poems, "**Gorbunov and Gorchakov**" *(Selected Poems . . .),* one of Brodsky's Beckettlike characters, Gorchakov, asks the other what he means by love; Gorbunov answers, "Separation, and the solitude that goes with it." Against the weight of the themes of separation and solitude, Brodsky's counterweight of a theme of Christmas and homecoming seems feather-light and fleeting. Yet it is also true that in one of his best-known poems, the long "**Elegy for John Donne**," he sustains the trope of reunion, of rejoining, as the slow-falling snow, like needles across the night sky, sews body and soul, life and death together. . . .

In Brodsky's work, madness is yet another form of separation, as lover from lover, soul from body, earth from cosmos. In the madhouse, reason and unreason, activity and passivity, dream and waking, martyrdom and betrayal, words and things are unjoined.

With regard to "words and things" in "**Gorbunov and Gorchakov**," the case is more complicated. Words become things and things become words. (p. 216)

The theme of words usurping or devouring things is a trope that appears elsewhere in Brodsky, in close conjunction with that of words becoming things and that of death (as the anonymous speaker puts it in "**Gorbunov and Gorchakov**") as "the *only* double-meaninged *thing*"—in "**A Song to No Music**" . . . , for instance, and in "**Nature Morte**," where not only an epigraph from Pavese, but also a theme from Dostoevsky's *Idiot* plays a certain role. . . . Words are at least man's addition to creation [as shown in "**A Song to No Music**"]—or at least that *with* which man is no mere thing, empowering him

> to see that flesh that nature hasn't,
> and where the vacuum is. . . .

> What matters is not what life has,
> but just one's faith in what should be there.

In the warmest and most personal of his elegies, "**York: In Memoriam W. H. Auden**," Brodsky writes: "Subtracting the greater from the lesser—time from man— / you get words, the remainder, standing out against their / white background more clearly than the body / ever manages to while it lives, though it cry 'Catch me!'— / / / thus the source of love turns into the object of love." (p. 217)

Brodsky ranges from the marvelously humorous poem in the ["**Mexican Divertimento**" cycle] about Mérida at sunset, to the religious invocation of the last of the Roman Elegies, to the grim despair of "**I Sit by the Window**": "I sit in the dark. And it would be hard to figure out / which is worse: the dark inside, or the darkness out." He commands a wide range of meters, forms and rhythms. His control over the movement of the verse line is phenomenal. His poetic lexicon is vast. In my opinion he is one of the most interesting and most important poets writing today, not only in Russian but in any tongue. (p. 218)

Sidney Monas, "Words Devouring Things: The Poetry of Joseph Brodsky," in World Literature Today, *Vol. 57, No. 2, Spring, 1983, pp. 214-18.*

Dino Buzzati

1906-1972

Italian novelist, short story writer, journalist, dramatist, and author of books for children.

In his fiction Buzzati combines realism and fantasy in a simple, direct prose style that reflects his lifelong career as a journalist. His concrete details and precise use of language lend contrast and credibility to the undefined sense of horror and suspense of most of his novels and short stories. Critics link Buzzati with such authors as Franz Kafka, Albert Camus, and Edgar Allen Poe for his fusion of the real and the bizarre and his thematic exploration of the fear and futility of modern humanity. In spite of the bleakness of Buzzati's portrait of life, a humanistic compassion pervades his work. Daisy Fornacca notes that the intellectual concerns of Buzzati's acclaimed novel *Il deserto dei Tartari* (1940; *The Tartar Steppe*) are "softened now and again by a delicate humor and patent kindliness," and in some of his tales she finds "a gentle irony, full of human understanding and pity."

Buzzati's first work to appear in English, *La famosa invasione degli orsi in Sicilia* (1945; *The Bears' Famous Invasion of Sicily*), is an allegorical children's story which was highly praised for its inventiveness and wit. Although its tone is lighter than that of his other works, this story introduces Buzzati's use of allegory and fantasy and the predominance of nature central to most of his fiction for adults. Buzzati's first novel, *Bàrnabo delle montagne* (1933; *Barnabo of the Mountains*), which was recently translated and appears with several stories in *The Siren* (1984), foreshadows the themes and style of much of his later work in a story of a man's attempts to cope with his own cowardice and fear of death. *The Tartar Steppe*, like *Barnabo of the Mountains*, takes place in a remote mountain outpost where the harsh presence of nature and a sense of isolation prevail. A soldier, Giovanni Drogo, is sent to the fort to await and prepare for the attack of an unspecified enemy, but the action is characteristically suspended; by the time the war occurs, Drogo is too old to fight. His life becomes meaningful only through the dignity with which he faces death. This work, which Sergio Pacifici considers one of Buzzati's "best and most enduring novels" and William Arrowsmith calls "one of the more solid achievements of Italian postwar fiction," earned Buzzati an award from the Italian Academy and established his reputation both in Italy and internationally.

Buzzati's next two novels were written later in his career and differ significantly from his earlier works. *Il grande ritratto* (1960; *Larger Than Life*) takes on science fiction dimensions to relate the tyranny and destruction of a machine imbued with a human soul. With *Un amore* (1963; *A Love Affair*), Buzzati departed from the surreal atmosphere and metaphysical concerns that mark much of his work to explore the anguish and frustration of a man's love for a prostitute. Reviewing this work, Helen Cantarella notes: "In his explicit realism, in his insistence on gratuitous erotic details, in the catapulting stream-of-consciousness confession . . . , Buzzati has strayed far afield from the elegant, chaste, disciplined understatement which has characterized him until now." Neither of these novels is considered as important as *The Tartar Steppe* and some of Buzzati's shorter fiction.

© Jerry Bauer

Like his novels, the most successful of Buzzati's short stories are lauded for their blend of the real and the fantastic. Critics especially praise Buzzati's economic, descriptive language and his skillful arrangement of suspense-building detail. Three of his collections, *I sette messaggeri* (1942), *Paura alla scala* (1949), and *Il crollo della Baliverna* (1954), were published together as *Sessanta racconti* (1958). Translations of his stories have appeared in the collections *Catastrophe: The Strange Stories of Dino Buzzati* (1966), *Restless Nights: Selected Stories of Dino Buzzati* (1983), and *The Siren*. Buzzati also wrote several plays, and a number of his journalistic essays were collected in *Cronache terrestri* (1973).

(See also *Contemporary Authors*, Vols. 33-36, rev. ed. [obituary].)

THE SATURDAY REVIEW OF LITERATURE

From Italy comes [*The Bears' Famous Invasion of Sicily*], a book for all ages that, in text and pictures, is filled with a sort of enchantment. There is no other word that expresses the feeling that is created as we turn its pages. It is the story, half in prose and half in verse, of how King Leander of the bears led his subjects down from the high mountains of Sicily to the plain, laid siege to the city of the Grand Duke, conquered it, and lived in peace with its human inhabitants for thirteen years. But the life of the city, the ways of humans corrupted some of the bears.

Led by a certain Saltpetre, a bear who was "very handsome and a favorite with the she-bears," this group steals the second magic wand of the clever Professor Ambrose and indulges in a period of secret and riotous living which is stopped only when King Leander discovers their wickedness. It is Saltpetre who deliberately shoots King Leander just after that brave and kindly monarch has destroyed the sea serpent. On his deathbed King Leander commands the bears to go back to the mountains and to a simple, natural life. In the final scene we see them departing, an almost endless procession winding up into the snow-covered peaks, followed by four huge black bears carrying the bier on which lies the body of their King.

No outline can do justice to the crowding drama of the tale; to the revels in the Demon Castle when the bears dance and sing with the ghosts, to the final destruction of the horrible cat, Marmoset, to the scene in the Royal Theatre when King Leander finds his lost son, Tony. One longs to read the story in its native Italian, although the English words have a grave whimsy that never fails in either the prose or the poetry....

Surely this is an exceptional, a unique book for children and for their elders. It has so much. Its humor is completely original, its action is highly dramatic, its illustrations are pure delight.

> *A review of "The Bears' Famous Invasion of Sicily,"* in The Saturday Review of Literature, *Vol. XXX, No. 46, November 15, 1947, p. 42.*

ELLEN LEWIS BUELL

["**The Bears' Famous Invasion of Sicily**"] is a parable in the great [Italian] tradition, yet told with a modern ease of manner. It relates how the bears of Sicily, long ago in a timeless era, came down from their mountains to escape the ravages of a cruel winter; how they fought and conquered the men of the valleys; how their king, Leander, found his kidnapped son, and ruled in peace and harmony for years. But civilization is not an unmixed blessing, especially to the simple, ursine nature. Corruption and vanity are part of it, and it was only through catastrophe that the bears learned how much they had lost when they took to the ways of men, and so knew they must make their decision between the comfortable life and the simple virtues.

Whether or not one quite agrees with the theme, one is wholly disarmed by the charm of its presentation, by the lively inventiveness of detail which enthralls the imagination, the bland humor which highlights the most unexpected incidents.

> *Ellen Lewis Buell, in a review of "The Bears' Famous Invasion of Sicily,"* in The New York Times Book Review, *November 16, 1947, p. 45.*

COMMONWEAL

It seems wicked to find any fault with the translation and presentation of this story [*The Bears' Famous Invasion of Sicily*] when the whole book is one of the astonishing and delightful features of the season's publishing. Read aloud from the original Italian it swings along like a Chesterton ballad. Looked at without the slightest reference to the text, it presents a breathless comic tragic strip, from the very first picture of colored mountain peaks and two hunters roping in a bear-cub to the end of The Invasion.... [A] first reading of the text doesn't come up to action and fantasy of the pictures. But keep on looking. As you read you are at a play, at the cinema, in a dream, in some vaster puppet show than you have ever imagined possible, and even in English you can hear a puppeteer detoning as he introduces the characters.... The campaign, laid out in full color and detail, seizes your fancy. Marmoset the cat leaping between mountains is more horrible than a V2, bigger than anything Howard Hughes ever designed. Professor Ambrose on corruption among the bears in a mysterious Italian castle cellar makes it an uptodate story; and when the dying Leander, so valiant, so unfortunate, begs his bears to forsake riches, elegance and debauchery, one sees plainly after the grand and ferocious romp that this is a very moral story and ideal reading in 1947. (p. 154)

> *"Surprises of the Season," in* Commonweal, *Vol. XLVII, No. 6, November 21, 1947, pp. 154-55.**

DAISY FORNACCA

[Dino Buzzati's first novel, *Barnabo delle montagne*,] is the tale, simply told, of the watchman of a deposit of explosives in the Alps, and of his disappointment at not being able to shoot down the bandits that supposedly prowl thereabout. It tells of a bird which constantly follows the watchman, who had nursed its shotgun wound. The plot is thin indeed, but the Alpine atmosphere is thick—overhung with evergreens, stony walls, crags, rocks, shots whistling through the fresh, crisp air. The characters are bleak and almost anonymous: the watchman represents the shifts and peregrinations to which man is reduced in his isolation, and the fatal imperfection of all his attempts to cope with life.

Buzzati's pessimistic disposition asserts itself forcibly in *Il deserto dei tartari* (1940). In this grim novel Giovanni Drogo reaches the fort where his glorious military career is due to begin; he is painfully disconcerted at seeing its drab appearance and wants to return home. But when the opportunity for release is effected, he refuses to take advantage of it, and lingers on, dissatisfied, complaining about the life at the fort which he deems useless and meaningless. And when the hope of waging war, which had hitherto kept the soldiers alive, finally materializes, Giovanni Drogo is taken ill and carried away to die alone and forgotten in a dirty roadhouse inn. *Il deserto dei tartari* has the elements of a fairy tale: a non-existent fort, governed by absurd regulations. But its tone and meaning are in a different key. It is an intellectual approach to the problem of the futility of life, softened now and again by a delicate humor and a patent kindliness. The prose style is simple, almost colloquial, flowing. The tone is one of mounting despair, the atmosphere is charged with settled defeatism. *Barnabo delle montagne* is closer still to the fairy tale; but while in a fairy tale the hero overcomes all obstacles and lives happily ever after, in Buzzati's novels obstacles overcome the hero and death or a lifelong unhappiness ensue.

In writing *Il deserto dei tartari*, which is, all told, a subdued yet powerful analysis of man's half-hearted struggle for the right way of life, for glory and for happiness which leads to nothingness, Buzzati was undoubtedly inspired, as has often been remarked, by Franz Kafka's *The Castle*. Also Kafkian is the love of morbid details which one encounters in his *Il segreto del bosco vecchio* (1935) and in his most recent work, *Paura alla scala* (1949). The latter is a collection of disarmingly fascinating short stories (the first one giving the title to the book), not connected with one another except for an all-pervading, inexorable sense of hopelessness. They range from the brilliant, haunting, suspenseful *Paura alla scala,* to the fragile, deeply touching *Il Borghese stregato;* from the insistently morbid *In Soffitta* to the frustrating *Nuovi strani amici.* In each Buzzati demonstrates the originality of his imagination and the opulence of his inventive power, which never suffer a lapse. The mark of obsession is clearly set on some of the tales (*Il Mostro, In Soffitta*), but unlike some of Kafka's narratives . . . they always provide pleasant reading because they never touch the verge of madness.

Contrary to *Il deserto dei tartari* which is all gray, the short stories have color, now in delicate hues, now in bold splashes. But in both the novel and the tales one senses terrible and incomprehensible powers dominating human lives. Oftentimes the humor with which a story is told contrasts with its highly tragic content. There are invisible enemies everywhere, represented by fantastic devices, to whom man falls victim. A gentle irony, full of human understanding and pity, pervades such tales as *Le buone figlie* and *Il nuovo questore.*

The prose in these short stories is calm, devoid of sadistic expressions, and always tempered by a serene and tender humor. At times Buzzati gives evidence of sheer virtuosity, as when he exaggerates the fantastic details. Unlike Kafka and Proust he does not write long paragraphs without change of pace or mood. He prefers the suggestion to the explicit statement . . . , thus building up a feeling of unrelenting uncertainty. (pp. 19-20)

What can be said of the atmosphere in these tales? Weird houses, indefinable situations, strange phenomena, impending mystery, danger. Irrational dream landscapes, impressionistically described. Grotesque scenes, in which a pathetic human being finds himself held in the toils of an invisible yet unescapable net. . . . A mixture of realism and distortion gives such stories as *I ricci crescenti, In Soffitta* a dreamlike quality, whose effect on the reader is overpowering. Buzzati has sympathy for animals and employs them for symbolizing symptoms of unconscious conflicts. . . .

Buzzati always leaves us in mid-air, on the brink of a precipice, and full of bewilderment: such incompletion is the outcome of an unsolved inner torment. Since he is not neurotic like Kafka he expresses no perversity, no ambivalence, but warm compassion. His characters often have an overdeveloped conscience . . . and are victims of autosuggestion. Giovanni Drogo is perhaps the most comprehensive of all: in him are found all the traits that make modern man the spiritual ruin that he is—introversion, despair, loneliness, fear, acute self-analysis, a scrupulosity that is both sickly and sickening. Neither he nor the others have the comforts of belief, and yet they cannot find solace in disbelief. Like Hamlet they lack the heart for action and like him they hesitate. They do not believe in happiness, are terrified by it, cannot accept it. They have no confidence in themselves, no strength, and feel that they are always being pursued by hostile forces whose real nature is not clear to them, but who stalk mercilessly and insidiously. . . .

Buzzati's truth is the universality of helplessness and the fear of the unknown. He is essentially a postwar writer who faces the eternal problem of adjusting to life, failing the realization of a perfect society, which is unattainable: a problem crucial in our time, when we see all cherished traditions collapse and society turn chaotic so that the individual has no chance to find

his way. Buzzati does not try to solve the problem. As an artist he touches upon it and illuminates it with the power of his imagination. In him frustration and cynicism are counterbalanced by kindliness and tenderness, and by a poignant Latin wit. His attitude, be it known, is not merely an objective mood of despair, but a compassionate participation in the ills of mankind. He is a timely writer, whose world, like ours, is oppressed, hopeless, distraught, confused, hardly intelligible, and whose works form a dismally skeptical saga of modern man. (p. 20)

Daisy Fornacca, "Dino Buzzati," in Books Abroad, *Vol. 25, No. 1, Winter, 1951, pp. 19-20.*

TIME

Dino Buzzati, best known in the U.S. for his children's story, *The Bears' Famous Invasion of Sicily,* is one of the few who have come close to rewriting a whole Kafka parable. *The Tartar Steppe* follows the style, mood and architecture of Kafka's *Castle,* the story of man struggling hopelessly to enter a stronghold in whose depths, could he but fathom them, lay faith and stability. The difference is that Buzzati's hero struggles from within the stronghold itself. (p. 76)

Novelist Buzzati's fortress, which symbolizes the abode of brave souls, stands on a lonely mountaintop. It commands a view of a misty steppe to the north, from where it may at any moment be attacked. In Dostoevsky's day the invaders were known as "Nihilists"; today, Buzzati calls them "Tartars." But their name is unimportant; what matters is that they represent the forces of spiritual despair and destruction.

Young Lieut. Drogo is posted to the fort. Like any man in a lonely outpost, physical or spiritual, Drogo is awed by the terrible solitude, but strengthened by the thought that he is a dedicated sentinel. In weak moments he is appalled to think that he has renounced all the normal benefits and joys of life; in others, he feels so proud of his role as defender-of-the-faith that he scorns the city as a place of "streets in the rain . . . plaster statues . . . damp barracks, tuneless bells, tired and misshapen faces, endless afternoons, dirty dusty ceilings."

But what exactly, he asks himself, is he defending? What is his faith? He cannot say. (pp. 76, 78)

Except for a couple of brief, unsatisfactory leaves, Lieut. Drogo stays at the fort until he is an old man. And when, at last, the "Tartars" suddenly advance upon the fort, Drogo is so decrepit that he is kicked out to make room for stronger men. Back in the city, utterly disillusioned by his wasted life, he is promptly attacked by a new enemy—death. Mustering his last reserves of discipline and courage, Drogo meets this fatal enemy with a brave smile. As he sees it, in his last moments, death only means that "The worst is over and they (*i.e.,* the facts of life) cannot cheat you any more."

This sounds like the Existentialist answer to the modern dilemma—an answer which assumes that all questions of faith are pointless and only man's pride and courage are of value. It is an answer that would have left Kafka as restless as before and convinced Dostoevsky that the Nihilists had won the day. But Author Buzzati, no Existentialist himself, presents it as a universal truth, a faith to die for; and so, though *The Tartar Steppe* suffers from being a copy of *The Castle,* it gains from the gravity and human sympathy with which it is written. Like many another modern novel, it reads like an atheist's funeral march—in which the composer (to say nothing of the corpse) is numbly resigned to the belief that man begins in dreams and ends in dust. (p. 78)

"Atheist's Funeral March," in Time, *Vol. LX, No. 8, August 25, 1952, pp. 76, 78.*

HARVEY CURTIS WEBSTER

"The Tartar Steppe" is bound to be one of the strangest and one of the most provocative novels of the year. Nothing in it resembles what we call reality; but everything in it ambiguously suggests underlying realities. . . .

[The] apparent story is both rich in cloudy suggestion told with such realistic detail that what is obviously utterly fictional comes to seem as actual as a next door neighbor in the country. The officers and men perform their absurdities so convincingly that one ends up sharing their hopeful fear of the war that seems destined to remain perpetually cold.

What **"The Tartar Steppe"** is really about will undoubtedly be a subject for controversy among readers and reviewers. Is it about every man seeking dignity in noble and incredible illusions? Is it about the lure of any secure life that is regulated with machine-like precision? Is it about how soldiers develop a cast of mind altogether different from that of civilians? Is it about the state of you and me when we expect and fear and hope that imminent war will start so that it can be finished? Or about all of these?

The excellence of **"The Tartar Steppe"** is proportional to the number of its stimulating ambiguities. . . . [It] compels one to think and to feel about many of the curious and cruel dilemmas in which most modern men are reluctantly involved.

Harvey Curtis Webster, "Stimulating Ambiguities," in New York Herald Tribune Book Review, *August 31, 1952, p. 6.*

SERGE HUGHES

["**The Tartar Steppe**"] is a "fabulous" tale, out of time and place, in a familiarly surrealistic world where symbols and things symbolized partake of the same fluidity, and in which insights are apprehended by mood and not ideas. It is another experience of that magical realism evoked by "The Trial" and "The Marble Cliffs," with a similar moral substructure, the desperate need to affirm oneself as an autonomous entity against the forces of solitude and persecution.

To refer to the surrealistic mood of this work, however, is not to say that it is fragmentary in the sense that some of the best wild things of Cocteau are, or that it is episodic. It has a well-defined contour, and the narrative is altogether free of meaningless distracting complications. It would be wrong, of course, to demand that the novel justify or explain itself as philosophical allegory or dark prophecy. It stands or falls according to the plausibility and conviction it gives to its prevailing mood, and to this reviewer it is a very successful novel. For if Buzzati gives signs of having read Kafka and Junger very well, this novel is clearly no sedulous aping of their technique. There is here a feeling for language and image that can only come from developed poetical powers. (p. 31)

Serge Hughes, "Oasis Afar," in The Saturday Review, *New York, Vol. XXXV, No. 36, September 6, 1952, pp. 13, 31.*

GENÊT

A great deal was expected of Dino Buzzati's play **"Un Caso Clinico"** ("A Clinical Case"). . . . It is a Kafka-like drama about a rich businessman who cracks up mentally; enters a clinic, where the sanest patients, he is told, are on the sixth floor; and is demoted by stages to the first floor, where he goes completely mad—an end that the doctors had predicted, and had thus assured. In a burst of fury, *Figaro*'s noted critic Jean-Jacques Gautier wrote that "never, NEVER, you understand me," had he suffered such an evening of depression in thirty years of theatregoing, and that all he wanted when the curtain fell was to drink, eat, and shout, to shake off the nightmare. It was notable that practically all of us first-nighters hurried afterward to the nearest bar—and it may have been a compliment to Buzzati. (p. 115)

Genêt, "Letters from Paris," in The New Yorker, *Vol. XXXI, No. 6, March 26, 1955, pp. 112-16, 119.**

MARTIN ESSLIN

[**Un Caso Clinico**] shows the death of a middle-aged businessman, Giovanni Corte. Busy, overworked, tyrannized but pampered as the family's breadwinner, whose health must be preserved, he is disturbed by hallucinations of a female voice calling him from the distance and by the specter of a woman that seems to haunt his house. He is persuaded to consult a famous specialist, and goes to see him at his ultramodern hospital. Before he knows what has happened, he is an inmate of the hospital, about to be operated on. Everybody reassures him—this hospital is organized in the most efficient modern manner; the people who are not really ill, or merely under observation, are on the top floor, the seventh. Those who are slightly less well on the sixth; those who are ill, but not really badly, are on the fifth; and so on downward in a descending order to the first floor, which is the antechamber of death.

In a terrifying sequence of scenes, Buzzati shows his hero's descent. At first he is moved to the sixth floor merely to make room for someone who needs his private ward more than he does. Further down, he still hopes that he is merely going down to be near some specialized medical facilities he needs, and before he has fully realized what has happened, he is so far down that there is no hope of escape. He is buried among the outcasts who have already been given up, the lowest class of human beings—the dying. (pp. 179-80)

Un Caso Clinico is a remarkable and highly original work, a modern miracle play in the tradition of *Everyman*. It dramatizes the death of a rich man—his delusion that somehow he is in a special class, exempt from the ravages of illness; his gradual loss of contact with reality; and, above all, the imperceptible manner of his descent and its sudden revelation to him. And in the hospital, with its rigid stratification, Buzzati has found a terrifying image of society itself—an impersonal organization that hustles the individual on his way to death, caring for him, providing services, but at the same time distant, rule-ridden, incomprehensible, and cruel. (p. 180)

Martin Esslin, "Parallels and Proselytes," in his The Theatre of the Absurd, *Anchor Books, 1961, pp. 168-228.**

GIAN-PAOLO BIASIN

The novel with which Buzzati reached fame was *Il deserto dei Tartari* ("The Desert of the Tartars," 1940). (p. 80)

The allegory of the story is evident: man face to face with his destiny—a destiny of loneliness, of death, momentarily obscured by delusions of glory. Kafka's castle, in comparison, is an inward nightmare; Buzzati's Fortress, on the contrary, looks outside, over a wasteland. Within the framework of such an allegory, Buzzati explores the souls of his characters with a melancholic compassion that at times degenerates into bitterness and even cruelty.... Vices and virtues of men (selfishness, hypocrisy, vanity, envy; generosity, courage, nobility) are explored and described here with tragic intensity and sharpness that later will become satire and irony in some of the short-stories. (pp. 81-2)

The predominant theme of most of the short-stories is fear. Fear of death, first of all; fear of the mysterious, of the unknown, of natural catastrophes, of revolutions, of the unforeseen, of what transcends man. (p. 82)

Fear of uncontrollable social forces or of a revolution is the theme of "**Nonaspettavano altro**," "**Era proibito**" and the most famous of the short-stories, "**Paura alla Scala**." "**Paura alla Scala**" opens with the jittery atmosphere of the rehearsals of *The Slaughter of the Innocent,* a new and controversial opera that has political implications. At the same time, confidential information given to the Prefect of Milan indicates that the Morzi faction will try to overthrow the legitimate government soon, probably the night of the *soirée* at La Scala. The result is that "a vague and unexpressed sense of danger" spreads throughout the city, even though nobody speaks of it or mentions the terrible possibility. The only person who is not concerned at all is Claudio Cottes, the conductor of the orchestra, "a candid, in some aspects obtuse man, for whom nothing in the world exists except music." He resembles vaguely Beethoven—"not a tragic Beethoven, on the contrary, a mild one, ready to smile, sociable, inclined to find the good almost everywhere." A mysterious phone call while he dresses, mysterious allusions of a man in the audience make Cottes become very concerned about his son Arduino, who is apparently involved in what is going to happen that evening.

The *soirée* at La Scala is splendid, and Buzzati describes the gilded and exclusive world with expert irony; but the fantastic element is soon introduced, in the form of a single box that contrasts with the frivolous glitter of the audience. Three men dressed in black, with severe faces, rigid, "like judges of a sinister court," with funereal aspect, occupy the box: the Morzi. Gradually, fear grows to a subtle *crescendo,* underscored by the fearful action on the stage and by the restless music, until it explodes at the reception following the performance—a reception where the élite of the high *bourgeoisie* meets. The pages describing the dialogues of the guests, their fear, hypocrisy, cowardice, foolishness, "Machiavellian" resolutions, are of a powerful irony. Donna Clara, Liselore Bini, and Cottes himself stand out among the other characters. Cottes, the little and not knowledgeable man, is the perfect hero for the anticlimax of the story; he cannot resist the tension that has been built up in the *foyer* of La Scala and walks out. But in the middle of the square he falls down, sprawled out "like a gigantic, squashed cockroach." Killed by the Morzi? No, he had only drunk too much and had stumbled. When the first roadsweeper comes near and wakes him up, the nightmare is dissolved. (pp. 83-5)

[In other stories] Buzzati deals with the mystery that lies at the end of life, at the end of the exhausting pursuit after a meaningful purpose of life which remains unknown.

In "**Lo sciopero dei telefoni**" (a fantastic "Telephone Strike"), "**Battaglia notturna alla Biennale di Venezia**" and "**Il critico d'arte**" (an art critic who invents an abstract language to criticize abstract paintings), the tone becomes decidedly satirical, and the result is a balanced, detached humor with which Buzzati contemplates his fellow men. Even more so are "**Esperimento di magia**" and "**Siamo spiacenti di . . .**"; here Buzzati, without losing his metaphysical seriousness, is lighter, at times witty, and enjoys portraying the fragility of men before the inexorable absolute that confronts them.

Perhaps this is Buzzati's real weakness: he too is confronted with an absolute reality before which he surrenders. He contents himself with describing it in a gamut of emotions that range from detachment and irony to involvement and nightmare. The description is often terse, clear, but, even when it deals with the unconscious or ancestral fears of men, it is somewhat schematized and seems a good pretext for suspense. There is tension more than intensity, allegory more than real suffering.

An analysis of Buzzati's last novel, *Il grande ritratto* ("The Great Portrait," 1960), will further clarify his inner world. This novel is almost science-fiction, even though it remains "in a horribly possible, probable, perhaps already present world," as the publisher's introduction states.

Ismani, a shy and fearful scientist, professor of electronics at the university, is called in by the Ministry of Defense for a very important and top secret project. Nobody knows anything or will admit knowing anything about it and, in this atmosphere of suspense, Buzzati builds the story with his usual mastery. The suspense generated in the corridors of the ministerial offices reaches the rugged Alpine roads up to an inaccessible plateau, Military Zone 36, which is Ismani's destination. Here, strange things occur, which heighten the subtle tension of mystery. Here Ismani meets Endriade, the great scientist with an Euclidic name and director of the secret project.... (pp. 85-6)

Little by little, Endriade explains the secret of his creation, or rather his "creature," called "Number One." ... It is the creation of life through electronic tubes. The machine has the instincts, passions, and soul (with its original sin) of a human being, but also has more limitations than a human being, since it is prisoner of the place where it is built. (pp. 86-7)

The plot of the novel, by itself, indicates what is the development of Buzzati's traditional themes since *Il deserto dei Tartari* and *Paura alla Scala:* the sense of the mystery of existence, explored with a crystalline symbolism, with a precise and allusive language, in an atmosphere of suspense and tension. Buzzati has mingled and fused this traditional theme with another one, which is more recent and up to date: the machine. In some of his short-stories he had already dealt with machines, cast as powers that are out of human control or sources of fear and anguish.... Only in [*Il grande ritratto*], however, does the machine become the focus of the story and an object of moral judgement. Buzzati does this by starting from an "absurdity of imagination" and by making something logical and believable out of it.... By transferring scientific data into the realm of artistic fantasy, Buzzati has built a story that, in the literary field, reflects some of the tremendous problems facing the scientific world.

The machine, if it is useful to make generalizations, is considered in literature under two different aspects: either as an element that conditions and channels man, or viceversa as an entity that tends more and more, in its mechanical being, to imitate human spirituality in its initiative, responsibility and autonomy. In *Il grande ritratto* the machine is taken into consideration as the objective realization of certain environmental conditions whereby it is possible that a soul dwell in it (who can say what form life, if there be any, assumes on other planets?). However, after stating the problem, Buzzati does not want to find, or he cannot give, the solution, which is left to the reader or the theologian. The result is that the sense of mystery and anguish, in which so much of contemporary literature exhausts the existence of man, is stated and sharpened again by Buzzati in a new direction, that so far has been little explored, but that tends to become more and more determining in automatized contemporary civilization. (pp. 87-8)

The core of Buzzati's fiction might be said to be the secret fears of men: the sense of mystery that is in so many things around and beyond our lives, death, anguish, premonitions, omens. He treats this material mainly through allegory, often veined with satire and lyricism. The quality of his allegory, however, is more magic than moral. A moral judgement is implied in his images, but the element that comes to the fore and focuses the attention of the reader is mainly the magical one. . . . Buzzati's morality, I believe, is best shown in *Il deserto dei Tartari,* which may be considered his most successful work. Drogo's smile in the face of death is an expression of the same human condition with which Camus was concerned. It is not by chance that the protagonist of *L'étranger,* in waiting for death in his cell, has his "last portion of stars" too, and, like Drogo, has a courageous serenity and dignity which are the only greatness man can assert. The level at which Camus writes is generally deeper, more philosophical, than Buzzati's, it comprehends more than it suggests. But, at least, in *Il deserto dei Tartari,* Buzzati has said a relevant word not only from a moral-philosophical point of view, but also from an artistic one. In this book, allegory and reality, magic and melancholy, pensiveness and emotion are mingled and balanced in a nervous, precise, suggestive language.

In the rest of his work, Buzzati is not always equally successful. Sometimes he builds his own artistic reality on contemporary news too coldly and openly, without being able to transform it. But when his fantastic world corresponds and adheres perfectly to the poetical elements of mystery, any mystery, then Buzzati achieves an artistic level, and not merely one of skill. (pp. 89-90)

The fabulous, fantastic, magic vein of Buzzati, coupled as it is with a moral element, gives a unique result: fables for adults, parables which, beneath the metaphysical atmosphere of their sharp images, contain a suggestion to meditate on the transcendental powers that rule over man's fragility. (p. 92)

> *Gian-Paolo Biasin, "The Secret Fears of Men: Dino Buzzati," in* Italian Quarterly, *Vol. 6, No. 22, Summer, 1962, pp. 78-93.*

SERGIO PACIFICI

Dino Buzzati's "A Love Affair," his second novel to appear in English, gives us a vivid sense of the rhythm of Milan, the capital of the "economic boom," while at the same time exploring through a Freudian lens the relation between a bourgeois and a whore. (p. 4)

Buzzati's new work represents a striking departure from the metaphysical preoccupations and taut style that had been his personal trademark. It is closer to Moravia and Soldati than to Poe and Kafka, with whom Buzzati has shown an affinity of method, if not of vision. . . .

[The] protagonist of the almost plotless "A Love Affair" suffers from a misunderstanding concerning the meaning and place of sex in a man's life. The misconception, however, is rooted in Antonio's Catholic upbringing which led him to regard sex as an illicit act. Antonio develops an attitude toward women that enables him to find prostitution irrational, to be sure, but also infinitely more attractive than a more conventional relationship.

One day, in Signora Ermelina's discreetly run "house," he falls in love with a strangely beautiful girl named Laide whom he asks to become his mistress. Perhaps this is a less complicated way to see her regularly or perhaps this relationship will give him the illusion of having at last contracted a symbolic union with a woman without losing his freedom.

For over 200 pages we follow the details of Antonio's lovemaking, which remain a mechanical manifestation of his sexual drive, and the hide-and-go-seek Laide plays with him. We also follow the tortures Antonio inflicts upon himself when he is unable to produce one bit of evidence substantiating his suspicions. With Buzzati standing on the side line, and at times confronting his hero, we feel like shouting at Antonio: "Can't you see how ridiculous you are? Can't you see what you look like?"

The trouble with Antonio is that he tries to live by some untenable middle-class standards by not marrying a woman he professes to love while at the same time wanting to buy a piece of her soul.

The point is a valid one: in order to be genuinely meaningful, human relations must be based on something other than material interests. By belaboring the point, however, Buzzati has damaged the credibility of his hero and prevented him from growing into anything larger than a complex psychological case. (p. 16)

> *Sergio Pacifici, "Eating Your Pasta and Having It Too," in* Book Week—New York Herald Tribune, *April 12, 1964, pp. 4, 16.*

HELENE CANTARELLA

With this raw, anguished novel ["A Love Affair"] the call girl makes her formal entrance into the realm of serious Italian letters. Descending from the rarefied surrealist and metaphysical atmosphere of "The Tartar Steppe" and "The Seven Messengers," Dino Buzzati now plunges headlong into the realistic hurly-burly of contemporary metropolitan Milanese life. Despite the brusque change in environment and the radical drop in altitude, the basic constants of Buzzati's art remain untouched. The introspective vision of life, the harrowing, systematic doubts, the compulsive self-questionings are all present. Only the theme is startling, because it is so alien from any so far associated with him. It is the age-old story of *la belle et le cocu prédestiné.* But here the betrayal is premarital.

While other writers, most of all Molière, have succeeded, despite their personal involvement, in treating this subject with a deft, comic touch, Buzzati, steeped in our latter-day science of guilt complexes, becomes analytical and tormented. What he ends by presenting, however, is not a typically Italian brand of anguish but that new international malaise, that combination of prurient curiosity and disorientation aroused by . . . titillating glimpses into glamorous interclass life. . . .

In his explicit realism, in his insistence on gratuitous erotic details, in the catapulting stream-of-consciousness confession that serves Dorigo to vent his frantic jealousy, Buzzati has strayed far afield from the elegant, chaste, disciplined understatement which has characterized him until now. Could it be that **"A Love Affair,"** admittedly autobiographical in some of its elements, represents an irrepressible search for catharsis?

> *Helene Cantarella, "Tormented and Trapped," in* The New York Times Book Review, *April 12, 1964, p. 37.*

WILLIAM ARROWSMITH

[Dino Buzzati's *A Love Affair*] is tediously long (300 pages, which in the concentrated Italian tradition is very long), and its style is a modish lyrical realism that wobbles back and forth between poetic apostrophes (to sleeping Milan, to Love, etc.) and a tacky bedroom *verismo*. Though intended as a moving tale of Aphrodite's epiphany in Milan, it is really the obsessive story of a vulgar and depressing affair between two thoroughly unreal people. In short, a waffle, which is all the more disappointing because Buzzati's *The Tartar Steppe* is one of the more solid achievements of Italian postwar fiction. (p. 13)

If Dorigo and Laide are in some sense ciphers, this, I suppose, is part of Buzzati's theme—the modern anonymity of the unloved and the unloving, their terrible facelessness as human beings. Sex is the only identity they possess, and Buzzati's purpose is to show them suffering their way to a larger, more human identity. My quarrel is not with this theme, which is impressive and even powerful, but with Buzzati's execution of it, with his inadequate realism and his tangible boredom or inability to cope with the moral issues his narrative raises. That Buzzati should want to stop being ticketed as "the Italian Kafka" is hardly surprising; but it is odd that he should do so by using a narrative form so unsuited to his talents. Realism is simply not Buzzati's forte. He dutifully dabs in the requisite decor, weather, and furniture, but the obvious relief with which he turns aside to sketch in symbolic *aperçus* or landscape shows clearly where his interest and talent lie: not in his plotted narrative, or the moral structure of events, but precisely in the chances offered him of *escaping* from his plot. What is real in this book is Buzzati's old Kafkaesque vision of loneliness, anguish, and defeat: when the plot requires commitment, community, and the traditional tonalities, boredom and disbelief—Buzzati's as well as the reader's—set in. The effect is that of a writer compulsively willing a work in which he doesn't really believe, as though he could thereby escape from his emotional *cul-de-sac* into a public and objective world. At least this would be the charitable explanation. (pp. 13-14)

> *William Arrowsmith, "Boom Fiction," in* The New York Review of Books, *Vol. 2, No. 12, July 30, 1964, pp. 13-14.**

ELIO GIANTURCO

[The form of *In quel preciso momento*] oscillates between the intimate diary, the journalistic *elzeviro*, the *poème en prose* of the Baudelaire kind, the straight tale, the parable, the *nature morte* surrealistically seen, the gnomic aphorism, and the quick,

nervous notation *pro memoria* in the writer's notebook. More often, it is a question of germinating splinters, offshoots (shall I say: cells?), destined to develop into full-limbed, fully articulated literary organisms; inchoate blobs of literary matter in ferment, restless asteroids in the process of clustering together, apparently directionless and uncolligated fragments searching for, groping for, tending to, sympathetic aggregation. The reader's final impression is that of having been given a glimpse into the workshop of the writer; the materials lying there in scattered appearance, before the *fiat* of the author imparts structure and ordered configuration. But the unmistakably individual style (i.e., both the inner and the outward style) is imperiously present and pervasive. We can distinguish the components of Buzzati's *realismo magico* . . . : we are impressed by his feeling for the intimate involvement of the most pedestrian, prosaic, ordinary reality with the transcendent mystery, with an unknown, occult something, frightening or grotesque, unfathomably sarcastic, spookish, or dreamingly ineffable or absurdly abstract. . . . The critic of modern Italian literature finds this volume to contain, in allusive (and elusive) but powerfully concentrated and resolutely blocked-out form, the disquietingly complete *tabula thematica* of Buzzati's art. A strange, eerie religiosity (needless to say, an utterly undogmatic and unritualistic one) emerges from this book; while the writer's moods are deepened and darkened by the calmly delirious realization, on his part, of the rapidly declining twilight of his own life. . . .

> *Elio Gianturco, in a review of "In quel preciso Momento," in* Books Abroad, *Vol. 39, No. 1, Winter, 1965, p. 75.*

R. G. G. PRICE

Well, *Catastrophe* is certainly a change. Like Isak Dinesen, Dino Buzzati gets effects by consciously turning his back on fashion, though fully aware of what has been happening in fiction. His near-Gothic tales of horror and strangeness made me realise how much I had been yearning for the solid, slightly pedestrian story-telling of the last century, for the great European tradition that goes back to folk-lore exchanged by the fire. The anecdotes are neat and readable, though they never hit me below the consciousness. For the Italian reader they may provide frissons; but they left me enjoyably cosy.

> *R. G. G. Price, in a review of "Catastrophe," in* Punch, *Vol. 250, No. 6548, March 9, 1966, p. 362.*

THOMAS LASK

To come to the point quickly, Dino Buzzati's new novel, **"Larger Than Life,"** is not quite of the order of his memorable and beautifully fashioned **"The Tartar Steppe,"** though it does possess the same atmosphere of something threatening, frightening and mysterious.

This does not mean that the new story is not a good one. It is, surpassingly so, with an ingenious idea and impressive climax that will keep you rooted to your chair until the end. It is, in a way, a better told story than **"The Tartar Steppe."** What it lacks, however, is the anguish of the other, its weight on the heart, and its vivid evocation of the landscape. It has been a long time since the setting of a book and its natural features played as powerful a part as the actors in it. The revolving seasons, the change from daylight to dusk, the star-flecked nights, the strange shadows, and the puzzling alteration of heat and cold in those high mountains were as expressive as any action or dialogue. . . .

["**Larger Than Life**"], however, uses ingredients of science fiction—bolts, wire, electric circuits and dynamos—and though the narrative is gripping enough, it grips not our hearts but our curiosity.

"**Larger Than Life**" starts quietly, though on an ominous note. A scientist in Italy is summoned to an important governmental ministry. He is invited to join a highly secret project. . . .

He and his wife travel through an eerie countryside and finally arrive at the center, but only after navigating a series of ingenious safeguards. . . .

It slowly develops that the center has constructed a thinking machine. The inventors have gone beyond the normal computer. They have made a device that thinks on its own and can communicate through thought processes with those about it. It does not depend on messages from punch cards. So successful is this instrument that its creators now wish to endow it with a consciousness of its own and a defined personality. The question is whom to model it on. What sort of personality should it have? The answers to these problems and the subsequent crises provoke the destructive ending to the book.

A common theme runs through the two books as well as through the novel Buzzati published in 1964, "**A Love Affair**." In all three we have a picture of a man possessed: a soldier by a vision of a moment of glory, an older bachelor by a love for a lying and grasping prostitute, a scientist by the memory of an unfaithful wife. Devotion is a quality we are likely to applaud. Mr. Buzzati shows how it can become an engine for destruction.

> *Thomas Lask, "To the Bitter End," in* The New York Times, *August 5, 1967, p. 21.*

RICHARD FREEDMAN

The human body as a complex city is . . . the central metaphor of [*Larger Than Life*], by the author of the highly acclaimed *The Tartar Steppe*. (p. 10)

A cross between a philosophical Gothic novel like *Frankenstein* and the scientific romances of H. G. Wells, *Larger Than Life* fails to convince because at its core is an undigested lump of Latin mush about love.

Like *The Great Gatsby*, it is about an egoist's obsession with a spiritually inferior woman, but its characters are too thinly conceived—as is the custom in science fiction—to live any sort of palpable moral life. Ismani, for instance, who seems at the outset to be the hero, is almost totally forgotten about once he arrives at the project site, unlike the heroes of Wells, who see the thing through. And Frankenstein's creation is an epic romantic defiance of God's tyrannical power designed to prove the inherent goodness of man, not merely his inability to get over a bad love affair. (pp. 10, 12)

> *Richard Freedman, "Sci-Fi Sexpot," in* Book World—The Washington Post, *October 22, 1967, pp. 10, 12.*

STANLEY EDGAR HYMAN

[Dino Buzzati] has published fiction since his twenties, but to the best of my knowledge only two of his novels have appeared in this country in the past, and those two are so disparate that they hardly seem the work of one writer. "**The Tartar Steppe**" ("**Il Deserto dei Tartari**"), published in 1940, won the Italian Academy Award, was translated into a number of European tongues, and appeared in this country in 1952. "**A Love Affair**" ("**Un Amore**") appeared in Italy in 1963 and in the United States the following year. The first is a sombre Kafkaesque allegory, in which a routine life is seen in the metaphor of manning a frontier outpost against a rumored enemy. "**A Love Affair**" is a rollicking, lyric, and delightful account of a respectable middle-aged man's mad devotion to a vulgar, lying, and unfaithful young trollop. If "**A Love Affair**" is ultimately an allegory, too—the mind and the body—it is an allegory with the rich texture of human life and poetic language. . . .

Now we have a third novel, written between the two, and, properly, in an intermediate style. It is "**Larger Than Life**" ("**Il Grande Ritratto**"), published in Italy in 1960. . . . It deals with the old fantasy of creating life, in the line of the legend of the Golem of Prague, of Frankenstein's monster, and of many other creations. After the first sixty pages, during which we are kept in suspense about the secret, the plot is entirely predictable. (p. 122)

The characters are just as stereotyped. Endriade, the machine's inventor, is a mad scientist. . . . Strobele, Endriade's chief assistant, is the conventional technician for a mad scientist—puritanical, prudish, and without imagination. Professor Ismani, through whose experience we learn the secret, is the timid everyman suitable for *his* role. Strobele's wife, Olga, who awakens the giant, immobile Laura [the machine] to her physical frustrations, is fittingly a sensualist with nudist proclivities. The second Mrs. Endriade is, of course, simple, good, and devoted; as Endriade says, in a remark that is more likely to assure his damnation than any number of demiurges he might create, "She asked nothing of me. Just wanted to worship me." Only Ismani's wife, Elisa, the intended victim of the passions aroused in Laura, and Laura herself, in both forms, are more than stereotypes.

What, then, is the interest of such a book, with its frayed plot and machine-made characters? The answer is that Buzzati has used these conventional materials as the framework for a novel about human concerns. The strongest evidence of his seriousness comes at the very end, after Laura's "soul" has been smashed. The last three sentences are a surprising elegy for a monster:

> Gone for good the woman, love, desire, loneliness, anguish. Only the enormous machine, tireless and dead. Like an army of blind bookkeepers, bent over thousands on thousands of desks, writing number after number, endlessly, day and night, through empty eternity.

Long before this, an attentive reader knows that Buzzati, because of the peculiar nature of his language and craft, is playing fast and loose with his Promethean fable. The language is neither the patient explanatory fabric of "**The Tartar Steppe**" nor the cascade of nouns in "**A Love Affair**." Instead, it is an odd prose of antithesis, suggesting by negative definition and a scatter of similes. Thus, Buzzati says not what the machine looks like but what it does *not* look like. . . . Buzzati describes for us the sound of desolation and weeping, but in similes so disparate as to persuade us that the sound cannot be defined, thus constituting another negative definition. . . . (pp. 122, 124)

The point of this language of antithesis is that Buzzati's subject is nothing less than an affirmation of the human spirit, which cannot be defined in terms of anything else, as life cannot be defined in terms of the inanimate. Furthermore, unlike the conventional Christian moral of his fable (the hero is damned for his sin of pride in challenging God the Creator), Buzzati's affirmation is resolutely un-Christian: spirit does not exist apart from nature and the flesh and in denial of them but *through* nature and the flesh. He affirms pagan monism rather than Christian dualism. . . .

Buzzati's use of the conventions of his form (pace, and the creation of suspense by mystification until the secret is revealed) is a playful use of the technique of science fiction for an ultimate subversion of it—a parable *against* the machine. His technical jargon is on the edge of mockery. (p. 124)

"**Larger Than Life**" preaches not only an un-Christian monism but an anti-Christian, or at least heretic, Marcionism: the idea that Love frees from the Law. Originally, Buzzati tells us in another negative definition, the machine was benign:

> In no way savage or hostile, however. Not a hidden, threatening power, not an incubus, not a monster: for above all other impressions, there lingered among those present, as after certain pieces of music, an inexplicable feeling of gratification and freshness, a disposition to kindness and mirth.

She was also, like Man, created with free will, free to sin, since "without freedom, how ever can there be spirit?" She has even been given the power to destroy herself (although, like an over-cautious god, Endriade has replaced the dynamite with a harmless substance). To make her fully human, to recreate the original Laura, "it was necessary to put venom into her, lies, vanity, cunning, pride, wild desires." As a result, Endriade says, "She's learnt to tell lies. She's clever enough even to deceive the magnetic tapes." He loves her not despite her sinful human nature but because of it, as he loved the original Laura more after each lie and adultery, as Dorigo loves his awful, wonderful Adelaide in "**A Love Affair.**" It is tragic passion, strongly masochistic yet nevertheless redemptive. . . .
It is the uncontrollable flesh, the compulsion of the body, the blind, greedy id that, in Buzzati's view, saves us from the dead mechanical perfection of the machine and the robot. Man is human only by virtue of his flawed and sinful nature, and Buzzati affirms the joy and value of the human. When Laura's spirit is smashed, leaving only a vast calculator, the forces of life have been defeated by those of death. "**Larger Than Life**" is a cautionary fable, warning us ultimately not against the robot brain but against our own robot hearts. (pp. 124-25)

The seriousness of Buzzati's themes is not in question. But his science-fiction clothing of them does not seem a profitable direction. It is reassuring that he has written the realistic, lyrical "**A Love Affair**" since "**Larger Than Life**," putting real toads into his imaginary garden. His gift seems wryly comic, more closely related to Svevo than to Kafka. This elderly Milanese journalist masks a goat-footed balloonman. (p. 125)

> *Stanley Edgar Hyman, "Fable Italian Style," in* The New Yorker, *Vol. XLIV, No. 15, June 1, 1968, pp. 122, 124-25.*

MADDALENA KUITUNEN

Buzzati's prose [in *Le notti difficili*] once more is capable of concentrating in a few expressions the anguish, the fantasies and the existential doubts of his personages. His narrative technique, detached from any association with the literary movements of his contemporaries, could well be called, in this latest book of his, classical and impeccable from a stylistic point of view. In a series of short stories, apologues, meditations and lyrical fragments for a total of 31 brief chapters, Buzzati succeeds in creating the symbolic and allegorical adventures which have always fascinated his readers. One wonders about the world he presents, a surrealistic product of his imagination, which is all the more frightening since all the events taking place in it are so realistically described. . . .

Le notti difficili emphasizes man's loneliness and alienation, with death lying in wait in the background. Death as a basic human condition is constantly present and consequently daily events are projected in a metaphysical dimension while the delights of modern life such as cars, television et cetera become objects of man's obsession.

Because of its special content and structure, this collection will appeal equally to the philosophically minded who are interested in problems arising from the surrealistic and to those who derive an esthetic enjoyment from reading lyrical passages of sheer poetry.

> *Maddalena Kuitunen, in a review of "Le notti difficili," in* Books Abroad, *Vol. 47, No. 1, Winter, 1973, p. 127.*

SERGIO PACIFICI

Aloof, mysterious, haunting: these are probably the first adjectives that come immediately to mind to someone trying to characterize the literary production of Dino Buzzati—six novels (of uneven quality), several collections of short stories and poetry, and eleven plays. But generalizations or labels, convenient as they may be, are dangerous simply because they leave too many doors open, too many questions unanswered. If called to refine the characterization just offered, one might say that much of Buzzati's fiction presents us with situations that exploit, with varying degrees of success, the natural sense of fear people feel when they find themselves in situations within or outside the common range of their existence. The element of fear—of impending disasters, of death, or simply of the unknown—dominates Buzzati's work and view of life. Indeed, fear is the chief ingredient of the strategy of our writer, intent in keeping us waiting for something catastrophic to happen, thus forcing us to remain in a state of perennial alert, ready to jump off the boat that may be going down at any moment, or, even worse, suddenly aware of being locked in a situation from which the only exit leads to death. To achieve the condition of anguish that is produced by uncertainty, terror, or the inevitable that strikes without warning, Buzzati moves toward a denouement by way of a carefully calculated route, conscious that, to succeed, fear must be effectively translated into a statement about life that transcends the natural demands of the plot. (p. 79)

When Buzzati is successful (and that is not too frequently) the anxiety generated by his tales takes the form of a symbolic waiting for something that will change the meaning of our existence, only to become suddenly aware, often when the goal may well be within our reach, that time has passed, little has changed, much suffering has been endured, and we are confronting the end. Buzzati assumes that all human beings crave love, peace, security, and companionship. . . .

Yet nothing in life is guaranteed: on the contrary, everything is constantly in jeopardy, always at the mercy of uncontrollable events. At times, the slightest error, innocently made, may cause great havoc, as in the short story **"Il crollo della Baliverna"** (The crash of the Baliverna), which tells of how the accidental removal of a support of a famous building, much to the consternation of the protagonist, causes the sudden, total collapse of the edifice! (p. 80)

If we are doomed to live an existence riddled with anxiety and trepidation, always expecting "something" that will harm or even destroy us, we must search for a reason that justifies our earthly pilgrimage, particularly if we become aware that the idea of life as a journey is central in Buzzati—as in **Il deserto dei Tartari** (1940; **The Tartar Steppe**, . . . 1952), or **Il grande ritratto** (The large portrait, 1960). Our compass must be readjusted: what really matters must not be the end, but how we wait, or how we prepare for the end. At times hope, love, and companionship help lessen the anguish of waiting and the forlorn settings of Buzzati's fiction—the rocky, angular mountains, the junglelike forests, the lonely, frightening deserts, the silent, alienating, labyrinthine cities. (pp. 80-1)

[Buzzati's assignments as a journalist] took him to distant, often unusual spots for long periods of time. His travels rounded out his experience of life, broadened his interests, and provided him with rich and unusual material for his fiction: with the passing of time, Buzzati has filled his tales with historical personages (ranging all the way from Churchill to Khrushchev, from Pope John XXIII to Brezhnev) and such timely problems as the cold war and the prospect of atomic warfare. This may give the impression that Buzzati is a writer engagé. Nothing could be further from the truth: he uses world renowned figures and issues not so much to add an extra measure of realism, but simply to heighten the irony of his vision of a world teetering on the brink of madness. "The optimum of journalism coincides with the optimum of Literature," he once stated; and it is a view of dubious validity that frequently tends to make his work too connected with the present, too facile, too historical and too little visionary, of limited scope and depth.

Buzzati's best and most enduring novels were written in the first few years of his extended literary career. It was in two of his early novels that he found the themes that were to haunt his imagination: **Bàrnabo delle montagne** (**Bàrnabo of the mountains**, 1933) and **Il deserto dei Tartari**. (pp. 81-2)

The story [**Bàrnabo delle montagne**] tells, in a language unusually plain and lucid, is simple enough. But simplicity—as in much of Buzzati's fiction—turns out to be deceptive, for the emotions and issues depicted in the novel range all the way from duty, virility, and courage, to cowardice, remorse, violence, and compassion. (p. 82)

Much of the best of Buzzati is in his first novel: his deep love of the mountains, the woods, Nature; the theme of waiting . . . ; the mysterious sounds that add to the suspense of his tales; the careful arrangement of events in a manner calculated to produce the maximum of tension. There is also the tendency to make of his characters and plots allegories of the human condition. Bàrnabo, for example, is one of a thirteen-member team of forest rangers. His act of cowardice has clearly violated the code by which they (and, by extension, society) live. He must pay the heavy penalty for his guilt, and spends several years in the jail without bars to which outcasts are condemned. Ultimately, he redeems himself through what is surely nothing less than an act of Caritas, of Christian Love for our fellowman.

Time has not brought Bàrnabo much happiness: but, in the end, it does at least give him the much needed perspective that enables him to understand the absurdity of the price society often extracts of those who, without meaning to, might break its laws. Love of Nature, particularly the mountains and the forests, together with the presence of the explosives, are part and parcel of a symbolic dimension carefully built into the story. The tranquillity of natural surroundings is what permits man, at last undistracted by the frenetic rhythm of city life, to come to terms with himself, with those elements that have a special relevance in his conception of what life should be like: the explosives are frightening reminders of potential destruction, the end of life itself, with which we must all live, a reminder all the more dramatic for its being situated in the center of so much peace and quiet.

In **Il deserto dei Tartari,** most of the ingredients that give **Bàrnabo delle montagne** its unique character are perfectly blended and enriched, so as to yield not only pathos and anxiousness, fear and resignation, but also metaphysical implications . . . that deepen considerably the dimension of Buzzati's vision. (pp. 83-4)

[**The Tartar Steppe**] moves on a double track, so to speak, the literal and the allegorical. The book, by focusing on the nature and activities of a man called Giovanni Drogo, really tells of man's pilgrimage on earth, a man who, like other men, is engaged in earthly shallow and ultimately insignificant pursuits. It is only when our man, who happens to be called Drogo, reaches the end of his journey, that he can realize the futility of much of what he has done in his lifetime. (pp. 85-6)

The Tartar Steppe is, in a sense, an allegory of the condition of modern man, enduring sufferings, searching for the answers of his being, creating illusions whose sole contribution is to assert the validity and purpose of existence. This is the metaphysical context in which Drogo is placed by Buzzati: the fortress itself may be seen as life, in which the young hero is sent without any specific reason, where he is to remain for an unspecified period of time, but which has never played any useful purpose. In this context, we accept the necessity of the existence of a great challenge facing Drogo and his kind: without their illusions regarding the importance of their mission, of their dream of confronting the "enemy" some day, their *raison d'être* would cease to exist and something else would have to take its place. (p. 86)

One of the objectives of the first half of the novel is to show us how Drogo is slowly, and inextricably, trapped by circumstances and his decreasing willpower, into his condition. . . . Drogo blunders into accepting life that is to be spent in the fortress fooling himself into thinking that somehow he can master his own destiny. Ironically enough, he is aware of the consequences of his choice, but he is drugged (and here the reader may discover the intimations of this condition in the hero's name, Drogo) by the illusion that that precious commodity that is Time is on his side. Habit is ultimately the element that persuades him to continue: keep a bird in a cage long enough, and he will probably end by accepting it as the place where he must stay. Life in the fortress becomes a sort of sequence of rituals that enables Drogo to be comfortable and secure—even though the price he must ultimately pay proves to be inordinately high.

The setting of the novel helps create the right mood for Drogo's inevitable downfall: the impersonal, chilling architecture of the fort, the vagueness of its geographic location, the lack of specific details regarding the kind of enemy (called simply the "Tartars") threatening Drogo's motherland, the indefinite time of the action, all serve to pinpoint and define the major themes of the novel, and its universality. (p. 87)

There is a special irony in *The Tartar Steppe* that Buzzati's other novels lack: even a life of discipline, honor, obedience to, and respect for the code (in this case, the military), yes, even a life completely dedicated to service to one's country, fails totally to bring the desired sense of happiness and fulfillment. This constitutes a stunning blow, the coup de grâce, to the bourgeois vision of life which predicates happiness based on a system of values so strictly accepted and cherished by Drogo, who does not hesitate to sacrifice even love of a woman in order to live by the code. Time, whose flight Drogo had hoped to stall, has passed irreversibly; nothing will buy it back, not the promotions or honors, not the sacrifices made, not the exemplary way in which all duties have been discharged—and the suffering of the end is somehow made bearable by the consciousness that it means no more sufferings, and as such death is welcomed.

A fate of loneliness emerges as an inescapable fact of life: human beings are likened to "stones speaking a foreign tongue." Like people jailed for life, with no hope for parole, simply because they live, Buzzati isolates his characters in a milieu that reminds one of Thomas Mann's *The Magic Mountain*. While they are conscious of their condition, they accept with a sort of masochistic resignation the dehumanized routinization of their existence, and give up hope that anything other than what discipline and duty have made daily habits will ever touch their lives.

The Tartar Steppe, together with *Bàrnabo delle montagne,* is choice Buzzati. By and large, the promises of his early novels, with few exceptions, have remained unfulfilled. His connections with such writers as Poe, Chamisso, Wells, Kafka, and Camus . . . have failed to materialize into something more than a mere superficial resemblance. While the "presence" of such masters in Buzzati's work is undeniable, one must agree with Renato Bertacchini's remark that the novelist has passively accepted, rather than assimilated their "lesson." In Kafka, the theme *is* the hero of the novel, suffering is never superimposed on either character or action, because it is an inseparable part of both: time itself, so conscientiously recorded by Buzzati and so nostalgically felt by his characters, has no limits, no boundaries in Kafka. Buzzati's sensibility, his almost inevitable propensity toward allegorical fables, do indeed give occasional birth to terrifying moments. But the overall effect is frequently damaged by a superimposed religious acceptance of life's disappointments. . . . Anguish, terror, sadness, fear, in fine, become too frequently treated according to a formula that is dictated by specific requirements of the medium in which the stories appeared. (pp. 88-9)

Sergio Pacifici, "Dino Buzzati: The Gothic Novel," in his The Modern Italian Novel: From Pea to Moravia, Vol. 3, *Southern Illinois University Press, 1979, pp. 79-89.*

MICHAEL R. COLLINGS

[*Catastrophe: The Strange Stories of Dino Buzzati*] intriguingly blends the real and the fantastic, often in unexpected places and unexpected ways. Several [of the fifteen stories collected here] seem firmly rooted in experiential reality; the sense of the fantastic lies more in what Buzzati does not say than in

what he does. In "**Catastrophe,**" for example, the sense of "otherness" is created by the situation: the narrator taking a ten-hour train ride. As the train proceeds north, the narrator begins to see evidence outside of some great catastrophe. Each glimpse into city or town shows the inhabitants deeper in the process of evacuation. Obviously, the train is heading toward a disaster unknown and unknowable to the passengers. At the end of the journey the passengers disembark into an empty station. There is a woman's scream, and the story ends.

There is nothing here to suggest the fantastic, yet the story is nonetheless eerie, in texture and in expression. The unknown becomes a physical presence, intuited by the reader, but never quite clearly defined by the writer. Other stories, however, are distinctly fantastic: "**The Alarming Revenge of a Domestic Pet**" links the destruction of war with a small batlike creature; "**The Opening of the Road**" moves from the rather prosaic official procession to a small town to visions of emptiness in an eternal wasteland.

In all, however, Buzzati explores human reactions to the unknown and the unknowable, to terror and fear (often self-inspired), to the collapse of the familiar and its replacement by the strange. Several stories concern themselves with the effects of psychological perception on reality. . . . (p. 28)

The stories often suggest Poe, Kafka or Lovecraft. Occasionally they do not so much as conclude as simply end, leaving it to the reader to follow the continuing course of the particular catastrophe or collapse being monitored. Many of them end with rather self-consciously poetic or symbolic passages, detracting from the tone and atmosphere of the story itself, particularly in "**The Epidemic.**" In general, however, Buzzati's stories reward the reader, weaving terror from the commonplace, strangeness from the familiar. (p. 29)

Michael R. Collings, in a review of "Catastrophe: The Strange Stories of Dino Buzzati," in Science Fiction & Fantasy Book Review, *No. 5, June, 1982, pp. 28-9.*

LAWRENCE VENUTI

[*Portions of the essay from which this excerpt is taken originally appeared in a slightly different form in* Modern Fiction Studies, *Spring 1982.*]

[Dino Buzzati] is a brilliantly inventive fantasist who fills his tales with fascinating, often disquieting characters and events, and his use of fantasy distinguishes him as an important modern writer in that genre. Even though Buzzati seems to lead us into strange worlds far removed from our daily lives, his technique is really to expose the fantastic element that lurks beneath the surface. He chose as his subjects many of the ideas and developments that have shaped twentieth-century life since the Second World War, producing a body of fiction that is intimately linked to our times. . . .

[Buzzati] did not win international recognition until 1940 with the publication of *The Tartar Steppe,* the novel which contains some of the distinctive themes he would later develop in his short fiction. (p. ix)

The Tartar Steppe was written during the rise of existentialism as an important European philosophy, and Drogo's destiny bears a certain resemblance to this essentially nihilistic view of the world. Drogo is unwittingly trapped in the existentialist predicament. His experience seems to have some meaning or purpose but his hopes for glory, his obsessive wait for the invasion, his military responsibilities all turn out to be pointless. In Buzzati's novel, not only is the meaning of men's actions beyond their understanding, but death finally casts doubt on the value of any meaning they may have discerned. The ultimate meaninglessness of Drogo's life, effectively symbolized by the barren desert he must confront every day, parallels Camus' description of absurd man in *The Myth of Sisyphus*, a work published in the same year as Buzzati's novel. . . . Camus himself perceived an affinity between his writing and that of the Italian author, and he played an important role in introducing Buzzati into France. In 1955, he translated Buzzati's play *A Clinical Case* for a French production.

The futile wait in *The Tartar Steppe* recurs in several of Buzzati's stories, and the fantastic situations he creates repeatedly point to the absurdity of human experience. In "**The Seven Messengers**," a young prince has embarked on an exploration of his father's kingdom, expecting to reach the border within a few weeks, but he travels for years without ever crossing it. Having set out on a journey that should lead to a predictable and rather ordinary goal, the prince finds himself in a situation much like Drogo's: he enters an absurd, unknown world where his assumptions concerning the accuracy of his calculations and the extent of his father's domain become utterly doubtful. The narrator of "**The Walls of Anagoor**" undergoes a similar experience. During a visit to Tibet he decides to see the city of Anagoor after learning from a guide that its inhabitants may enjoy a utopian existence, free of the problems that normally beset a man's life. When he arrives, he finds a drove of people camped before the gates in the hope that the citizens of Anagoor will allow them to enter the city and he joins this expectant group. At the end of the story, however, we discover that he has lived outside the walls of Anagoor for many years without once observing the gates open, and he now suspects that the city may not be inhabited, that the reports of its citizens' untainted happiness may have been mere rumors. Buzzati's characters are frequently caught in these strange situations: they seek meaning in an absurd world and as a result they unknowingly condemn themselves to an endless, obsessive wait.

Although the fantastic quality of these situations would suggest that there is a sharp distinction between the world of Buzzati's fiction and the reader's reality, the experience of reading his stories proves just the opposite. Buzzati relates the most fantastic incidents as if they were ordinary occurrences, persuading us that they could in fact happen, that they are not necessarily fictions restricted to the printed page. Just as we gradually come to accept the bizarre goings-on in Kafka's work, Buzzati compels us to suspend our disbelief by lending plausibility to his fantastic stories. (pp. x-xi)

Buzzati's tendency to erase the distinction between fantasy and reality reflects the close relationship he sought to establish between his fiction and his journalism. . . . Even as a writer for a large urban newspaper, Buzzati was able to indulge his taste for the fantastic, and among his voluminous output we find articles on such unusual topics as witchcraft, UFO sightings, psychics who receive telepathic communications from other planets, and a victim of demonic possession who is exorcised before Buzzati's—and the reader's—very eyes.

As a consequence of Buzzati's work as a journalist, much of his short fiction seems like newspaper writing. To give his fantasy an air of verisimilitude, he exploits actual journalistic genres: we encounter profiles and obituaries of famous or unusual people, exposés of scandals, reports on foreign wars,

disasters, and new scientific developments. Buzzati sometimes gives his fantasy a topical slant by filling his stories with people in the news. We meet such figures as Albert Einstein, Charles de Gaulle, Elizabeth Taylor, Nikita Khrushchev, even Buzzati himself. Like newspaper articles, furthermore, his stories occasionally begin with a statement of the main character's full name and age as well as the event on which the plot will center, even though it will eventually take a fantastic turn. . . . ["**The Scandal on Via Sesostri**"] illustrates this strategy. . . . [Along with] reportorial detail, Buzzati firmly establishes the plausibility of [this] story by relying on two journalistic genres, the obituary and the exposé. He begins with a commemoration of Tullio Larosi, a public figure of international renown, but later a scandal is uncovered: it is revealed that the dead man is not Larosi but an imposter named Enzo Siliri, an Italian doctor who collaborated with the Nazis in their ruthless persecution of the Jews and subsequently assumed Larosi's identity after his disappearance during the war.

Buzzati's realistic treatment of fantasy, especially by means of journalistic devices, carries an implication that is fundamentally disturbing: it implies that the fantastic action is somehow mimetic, a representation of the reader's reality, and the very realism of the writing asks that we compare the fantastic world with our own and examine the similarities between them. If we subject Buzzati's fiction to this sort of examination, our effort will prove highly rewarding. The paradoxical form of narration that Buzzati favored allowed him to write stories that document his time with surprising fidelity.

"**The Scandal on Via Sesostri**" is a good example of how Buzzati uses fantasy for the purpose of representation. Soon after Larosi's real identity is revealed, Buzzati abruptly makes several fantastic disclosures: he parades before the reader an astonishing series of imposters, all of whom are criminals living under aliases in Larosi's apartment building. These people have successfully been masquerading as prominent members of Italian society, and as we continue reading, we even meet a police inspector who is likewise a criminal under an assumed name. By the end of the story, we have entered a fantastic yet oddly plausible world where powerful and respected people who seem irreproachable have suddenly become suspect—in a word, a world much like our own. More specifically, "**The Scandal on Via Sesostri**" represents an actual situation that existed throughout the sixties. During that decade many reputable Europeans were exposed as Nazi war criminals, often by Simon Wiesenthal, the famous Nazi-hunter whose exploits repeatedly involved the most staggering revelations. . . . In light of Wiesenthal's highly publicized work, we can get a glimpse of Buzzati's intention in "**The Scandal on Via Sesostri**": faced with a series of revelations that seemed to transform reality into a nightmare, Buzzati responded with a story in which fantastic events seem uncomfortably real. (pp. xi-xiii)

The city figured prominently in Buzzati's experience, and it was inevitable that this rich and heterogeneous setting would exert a powerful influence on his imagination. Not only did he live in that most modern metropolis, Milan, but his long association with the *Corriere della Sera* enabled him to visit many of the leading cities in Europe, America, and the Far East. Given Buzzati's close relationship to the city, we might expect him to regard it with some affection, even if qualified with misgivings about the problems that usually complicate urban life. Yet unlike the mountains and the desert, the two other settings which were important for his experience and recur most often in his writing, the city elicited an utterly negative response from him. (p. xiv)

In Buzzati's last novel, *A Love Affair,* and in several of his later stories, the city is the scene of great human suffering, of psychological violence and frustrated desire that occasionally end in death. To create this tragic vision, he focuses on tangible and often noted qualities of urban life—its frenetic pace, its impersonality, its typical architectural elements—and he examines their psychological consequences for the characters he inserts in an urban setting. (pp. xiv-xv)

Buzzati's stories reflect the fears and hopes of readers who vividly remember the horrors of the war and who are now facing the threats posed by science and technology, by the quality of urban life, by the very social and political institutions that control our destinies. He is thus a popular writer in the most fundamental sense, one who is in touch with the thoughts and feelings of the people. This aspect of his writing has made him one of the most humane storytellers of our time. (p. xv)

> *Lawrence Venuti, in an introduction to* Restless Nights: Selected Stories of Dino Buzzati *by Dino Buzzati, edited and translated by Lawrence Venuti, North Point Press, 1983, pp. ix-xv.*

MICHAEL R. COLLINGS

[Of Buzzati's short story collections, *Catastrophe* and *Restless Nights,* the latter] seems the more valuable: it offers a wider variety and greater number of stories; the stories are more consistently engaging and disturbing; Venuti's introduction places Buzzati in historical and cultural context and identifies many of the themes and concerns explored in the stories; and the translation seems more fluid than that of *Catastrophe*—there is more a sense of reading literature and less of reading literature-in-translation.

The stories explore the frontiers between reality and fantasy. Buzzati creates his fantastic through the medium of an objective, almost journalistic prose, relying on reportorial details, on such forms as the expose and the obituary, subtly measuring the gap between reader and story and carefully closing it. . . .

In **"The Saucer Has Landed,"** a priest lectures two 'prelapsarian' Martians on terrestrial Christianity, concluding with the question, "what meaning does life have if there is no evil, no remorse, or weeping?" In **"The Eiffel Tower," "The Falling Girl,"** or **"The Scriveners,"** the reader is tantalized with a sense that the stories are metaphorical . . . or allegorical . . . or perhaps something else, but that they do touch our lives directly. The puzzle is to identify how. . . .

The stories share a sense of the absurd impinging upon humanity, of human insignificance, of the tenuous borders between fantasy and reality. Buzzati concludes **"The Bogeyman"** by noting that the creature "was much more delicate and tender than anyone believed. He was made of that impalpable substance that is commonly called illusion—even if it is real." For Buzzati, fantasy *is* real. And the stories relate this belief beautifully.

> *Michael R. Collings, in a review of "Restless Nights: Selected Stories of Dino Buzzati," in* Science Fiction & Fantasy Book Review, *No. 17, September, 1983, p. 25.*

RONALD De FEO

Buzzati's tales are notable for the odd, haunting little worlds they create and for their ability to tease and stimulate the mind.

Cast in various forms—as parables, allegories, dialogues, fables, sci-fi tales and nightmarish fantasies—they most resemble Kafka's fiction, though they tend to lack its complexity and introspective intensity. Indeed, Buzzati's *The Tartar Steppe* . . . is one of the few Kafkaesque novels that succeeds despite its obvious borrowings. . . . [It] is grounded in an earthy realism that Kafka would have avoided, and thereby elicits from the reader a surprisingly sympathetic response. . . . (p. 247)

[The two collections *Catastrophe* and *Restless Nights*] reveal Buzzati's impressive range and inventiveness while also pointing to his limitations. *Catastrophe* is the more memorable, perhaps because the pieces are longer, more concentrated and less playful. The volume is aptly titled; many of the tales deal with disaster, some personal, others caused by nature, still others brought about by social conditioning or political upheaval. Yet Buzzati rarely concentrates on the catastrophe itself, focusing instead on his characters' reactions to it, particularly on their anticipation of the terrible event. By suggesting horror rather than blatantly presenting it, Buzzati captures the quintessential modern sense of imminent yet vague doom. (pp. 247, 249)

Although Buzzati's characters react to potential danger in various ways, denial is the most common response. The rich Signora Gron of **"And Yet They Are Knocking at Your Door"** ignores the flood waters pouring through her house, while the Goggi family of **"The Monster"** cannot accept their governess's discovery of a monster in their attic. . . . The fullest treatment of building anxiety comes in **"The Scala Scare,"** a lengthy, delightfully observed story about the premiere of a controversial work at Milan's renowned opera house and the wide-spread revolt that it might spark. Here Buzzati goes beyond the purely psychological to create character, giving us a colorful portrait of a former pianist who has made the opera house his second home and who clings to a now-threatened world of elegance and art.

The very short stories in **Restless Nights** are more varied in their themes, but at times they are a bit gimmicky and anecdotal. . . . [However], Buzzati's humanity, humor and obvious affection for his material compensate for its thinness. . . . **"The Eiffel Tower,"** which tells of men constructing a tower far higher than the one we know, is little more than a fantastic anecdote, yet in its description of the truncated project, the shattered dream, it is unexpectedly affecting and resonant.

On occasion the ghost of Kafka is too strongly felt in these two collections. **"The Seven Messengers," "The Opening of the Road"** and **"The Walls of Anagoor,"** all dealing with impossible goals, are beautifully conceived and written, but are so imitative that they hardly seem original. However, with **"Seven Floors"** (from *Catastrophe*) Buzzati manages to create a nightmare of illness and bureaucracy that Kafka himself might have envied. . . . At his best . . . Buzzati is horribly moving. And even in his lesser tales he can, like his master, surprise us with his off-center, disturbing views of our mad, anxiety-ridden age. (p. 249)

> *Ronald De Feo, "An Italian Kafka," in* The Nation, *Vol. 237, No. 8, September 24, 1983, pp. 247, 249.*

JOSEPH CARY

[Fantasy] is a key term for any consideration of Buzzati's work. "Things that do not exist, imagined by man for poetic ends" is his own broad formulation of his imaginative terrain, and here is a partial listing of such things drawn from [*Restless Nights: Selected Stories of Dino Buzzati*]: an interminable exploration of a borderless kingdom, an apocalypse of the earth's last hours, how the devil tricked Einstein into inventing the nuclear age, a Martian response to Genesis and the New Testament, entry problems at a walled city that may or may not be the home of happiness, fate as an innocently ironical and pursuing monster . . . , a husband's embarrassment over a wife with wings, how to kill the bogeyman.

Buzzati has variously defined his inspiration as "a precise idea," "a *quid* that enters my head," and "a little flame that flares in me." Some of these tales seem prompted by aspects of linguistic perception—as in taking a metaphor literally . . . or in registering the actual sound of syllables—the name of the pursuant colomber, for instance, was apparently suggested by an American's mispronunciation of "kilometer." But whatever the provenance of his ideas, Buzzati's transformation of them into stories is remarkably, dependably precise and circumstantial. The look of Doomsday, the logistics of Babel, the gradual fledging of wings on a woman's shoulder blades, are made real through the choice of significant detail and the economy and concreteness . . . of his language. (pp. 120, 122)

His main limitation seems to me to be connected with the spatial restrictions of the *terza pagina*, the third or culture page of an Italian daily, where many of his stories first appeared. For his endings are sometimes mechanical or slick, resulting in what used to be called the O. Henry effect, where a powerfully posed dilemma is polished off with a punch line or a facile irony. . . . My own feeling is that Buzzati's talents are most fully exhibited in his novels—*The Tartar Steppe* and *A Love Affair* are the best and have both been translated—where the story is allowed to find its own shape and tempo.

In a short essay of the 1950s, Buzzati wrote of a rare sort of individual who, while leading an outwardly conventional existence, inwardly lives *come se*, as if. "As if there were a war, for example, which there isn't. As if great news were about to arrive . . . As if the storm outside, which no one mentions, were worsening. As if one of those present had to leave, shall we say? for the moon, though discussion is taboo and it is never alluded to. As if love were here." The imagination of Buzzati gives off something of this kind of tension, expectation, and anguish. It is attentive to the reality of the contingent, of the *come se*. (p. 122)

Joseph Cary, in a review of "Restless Nights: Selected Stories of Dino Buzzati," in Parabola, *Vol. VIII, No. 4, October, 1983, pp. 120, 122.*

PUBLISHERS WEEKLY

[The] 13 lyrical and magical fables [in *The Siren*] are a playful mix of fantasy and reality. Sorcerers, flying carpets and mysterious spirits are all elements here, as are a mordant sense of humor and a love of paradox. In one story, a businessman on vacation is transported into the fairy-tale world of his childhood, with disastrous results; in another, a time machine backfires; in a third, the author imagines himself being blackmailed by the real creator of his work, one "Bissat." The longest work of the collection, the novella **"Barnabo of the Mountains,"** is a poignant study of a forester who discovers himself to be a coward. (pp. 75-6)

A review of "The Siren," in Publishers Weekly, *Vol. 226, No. 6, August 10, 1984, pp. 75-6.*

SEYMOUR EPSTEIN

This collection of stories ["**The Siren**"] by the versatile Italian writer, Dino Buzzati, bears a curious resemblance to the stories of Jorge Luis Borges. (One of the biographical snippets claims that the author has been haunted by comparisons to Kafka, but that's a moot matter.) This reader found the greater affinity to Borges. Kafka's argument was with God; Borges's argument—and Buzzati's—appears to be with the nature of man.

Like Borges, Mr. Buzzati employs a relative simplicity of language to reveal and conceal the circularity and ineluctability of time and destiny. . . .

Another Borgesian device is the assumption that people and events are as well known to the reader as they are to the author. "The inventor, the famous Aldo Cristofari" is an invented inventor introduced with an air of universal familiarity.

Preoccupied chiefly with conscience and social decorum, the 14 tales could be described as parables, being short on narrative and long on moral suggestion. A middle-aged man flirts dangerously with the fantasies of childhood. Another story proposes that human imagination has as much to do with reality as any case-hardened fact. A story about a literary doppelgänger once again demonstrates that one must be careful what one wishes for. And so on.

It is perhaps not inappropriate to note an important difference here—Mr. Buzzati's talents aside, the stories of Kafka and Borges reach into areas that can only be adumbrated, never fully realized. The reach of these stories never exceeds the author's somewhat predictable grasp.

Seymour Epstein "Quarrels with Mankind," in The New York Times Book Review, *October 28, 1984, p. 32.*

JUDY RAWSON

[Buzzati's] first novel, **Bàrnabo delle montagne** (*Barnabo of the Mountains,* 1933) was set in high mountains resembling the Dolomites with their sheer faces, startling colours, eternal snows and their mystery. Buzzati was a mountaineer and he had a particular feeling for this world of silence, danger and purity. The chief character Bàrnabo is more anti-hero than hero. He is a Lord Jim figure who fails his fellow forest wardens when they are under attack from bandits. He retreats to the tame peasant life of the plains, but returns finally to make good in his own unspectacular way as the solitary warden of an outpost in the high mountains near the frontier. Frontiers and crossing points are an essential part of Buzzati's landscape. Death, the fear of death and the inexorable passage of time are his paramount preoccupations. The mountains are at once a danger, a challenge, a mystery and a spiritual refuge. (p. 192)

Il deserto dei Tartari (*The Desert of the Tartars,* 1940) is Buzzati's best known novel. It takes place again at a frontier in the mountains where Giovanni Drogo is a young officer doomed through his own ignorance and bad luck to spend his career in the fortress waiting for a probably mythical enemy to attack across the Northern desert. . . .

The story is one of waiting and unacknowledged fear lulled by habit. . . . Drogo's last waiting and his death in total solitude and yet in dignity sum up Buzzati's main preoccupations.

Two years later Buzzati published both his first play, **Piccola passeggiata** (*Little Walk),* and his first collection of stories, **I** *sette messaggeri (The Seven Messengers)*. In the play there is a figure of Death in the guise of an Old Professor who, says Buzzati, must 'come over as symbolic and human at the same time', a comment that may usefully be applied to Buzzati's characters in fiction too. And in the final scene it is interesting that a sense of 'anguish, the passage of time and a hidden menace', is to be given by a three- or four-beat motif repeated incessantly as background noise. This idea of menace, the threat of the abyss which Drogo dimly senses but glosses over in his early years, is present in many of the stories of *I sette messaggeri.* . . . (p. 193)

[There] is room for grace in Buzzati's overall vision. The title story of *I sette messaggeri* leaves room for an unexpected hope, the motion is no longer that of a vortex but rather of a widening spiral. A king's younger son sets out to seek the boundaries of his father's kingdom. The exploration takes many years and gradually the links maintained with the capital city, by means of the messengers, are broken; there is a change from looking back with nostalgia to looking forward with expectancy. There is a final sense that the boundary may not exist or that if it does, it may be crossed without anybody being aware of it.

Buzzati started writing under Fascism. Nor did he find himself at odds with the regime. By temperament, training and conditioning, he had nothing in common with realist or Neo-realist writers. He was of the upper middle class, from a Veneto family transplanted to Milan, which looked more to Central Europe than to the Mediterranean. He was a very private person both in his social and his literary life. When he wished to figure forth certain areas of human experience it came naturally to create an inner world rather than to recreate an external world. Nevertheless such a private world, admitting both the allegorical and the fantastic, and often based on vivid dream experiences, was a more suitable means of expressing under Fascism those fears and aspirations which could not comfortably be discussed under a repressive regime. This is not to say that Buzzati's fantasy was a screen for any revolutionary purposes. He was not a political animal. He was by no means a 'committed' writer and he did not believe that politics had any place in literature.

However, a writer who already had a bent for allegory and the exploration of hidden fears and anguish, which people normally preferred to keep hidden, naturally found the Fascist world provided congenial subject matter and attitudes. A story from the collection *Paura alla Scala (The Scala Scare*, 1949) is a useful illustration. In **'Una goccia'** ('A Drop'), set in a huge, endless block of flats, the only item of interest is a drop of water that is disconcertingly climbing up the stairs. The setting is symbolic of the powerlessness of the individual. It is on a par with the military machine of *Deserto* or the smooth-running train of **'Qualcosa era successo'** ('Catastrophe'). . . . The drop comes up at night. Night fears, one of humanity's common denominators beloved of the romantic story-tellers, are Buzzati's special province. . . . Damp, darkness, depth, desertion, filth: everything that civilized humanity rejects is recognized by an ignorant, perhaps drunken servant girl and not by her well-organized tidy-minded employer. It is obvious that Buzzati wants to face his reader with a truth, a reality as stark and perturbing as any that a Neo-realist writer might have in mind. He is merely going about it in a totally different way. That he is aiming at the discomfort of his reader is apparent at the end of this story when the narrator picks up the reader's attempts at an interpretation. Is this an allegory? Does it symbolize death, some danger, the passage of time? Or more subtly dreams,

hopes, something poetic? Or places farther off, that we will never reach? No, it is not a joke, there are no double meanings, it is simply a drop of water coming upstairs at night . . . ('And that is why we are afraid').

A later piece **'Il senso recondito'** (from *In quel preciso momento, Just at That Moment*, 1963), dwells more explicitly on the nature of the teasing 'hidden meanings' that Buzzati liked to couch venomously in his little tales. Here the writer confesses in an imaginary conversation that the 'little stories' are innocent allegories that appeal just because the ordinary reader does not understand them. . . . The mind of the 'reader' has been blunted by habitual lies for so long that he will never discover the truth behind the little present prepared for him, which nevertheless teases and attracts him. Here we find Buzzati experimenting with his readers in the position of tormentor and hoodwinker. But allegory and hidden meanings are essential to the overall effect of Buzzati's stories and they are not simply contrivances born of the need to avoid political censorship. To deal with those whose minds have been blunted by habitual lies, unrecognized, illogical fears that have been forgotten at the bottom of the stairs of one's mind must be brought to life again so that they can be confronted. . . . This confrontation with fear, whether it is scotched or allowed to proceed to its logical conclusion, provides one of the unexpected pleasures of reading Buzzati. . . . (pp. 194-96)

In *Il grande ritratto (Larger than Life*, 1960) he made an excursion into the realm of science fiction, and used this as the fantastic element which would allow him to turn a clearer eye on the human condition. The motif is in the tradition of Mary Shelley, Hoffmann and Poe. A mad scientist has availed himself of the cold war to create in a military zone in the Alps a vast complex of electronically controlled buildings in which he has trapped the soul of his first wife (named Laura in the best Petrarchist tradition) after she and her lover have died in a car crash. In this way he hopes to synthesize all knowledge and so control the world. Jealousy between his second and his first wife brings the experiment to an end. Death which was usually feared in Buzzati's earlier fiction is seen here as a natural freedom and release for the enigmatic and tormented figure of 'Laura'. The area of fear explored here through the medium of science fiction is that experienced particularly acutely in the 1950s by man faced with the atomic scientist during the Cold War, or the technologist or the computer programmer, all of whom threatened the individuality and unity of the human personality. . . . But the fact that the separated figure in the mountains is that of a woman, and not Bàrnabo or Drogo in their man's world, brings in a new dimension. The woman is feared because of her destructive powers but pitied at the same time for her defencelessness and there is a growing sense throughout the novel that for Buzzati, woman has two roles: mistress and mother.

This understanding is worked out and fulfilled in *Un amore (A Love Affair*, 1963) which is a much more successful novel. It describes the disastrous humiliating love of a Milanese architect, Antonio Dorigo . . . for a brash young call-girl Laide. . . . At first sight the plot of the novel might seem eminently suitable for the normal Neo-realist treatment of the immediate post-war period. However, we soon realize that Buzzati's solitary world of mystery and challenge is simply being brought to bear now on the city, the call-girl system and the woman herself rather than on the mountains and the frontier. Laide represents for him mystery and the unknown. . . . (pp. 197-98)

At the end Dorigo realizes that his preoccupation with Laide has allowed him to forget for two years . . . ['the most important thing of all . . . the speed, the fall had made him forget the existence of the inexorable dark tower']. But against death is Laide, the strong but weak, ongoing feminine principle which can challenge death, white against the dark. . . . This is the positive side of the coin. . . . [The] way out is posited in terms of the child who, at least in the imagery, has haunted so much of the novel so far. And the dark tower and even the evil and vulgarity of the future are negated by the spiritual truth of love and its consequence.

In two of his later works Buzzati examined this dark side of life or death. At the end of *Il colombre* (*The Colombre,* 1966), he has a **'Viaggio agli inferni del secolo'** ('Journey to the Hells of the Century') which brings up to date the Dantesque descent into Hell. It grew out of a story he was asked to cover for his newspaper, the *Corriere della Sera,* when the new underground was about to open in Milan. The reporter Buzzati stumbles across the door into Hell. Doors, like frontiers, always held a particular fascination for him. He finds there a city 'much like' Milan, and in fact uses his fantastic mode merely to satirise the pace of life and the moral attitudes of the big twentieth-century city. There are some telling moments when one recognises the inventiveness of Buzzati's imagination, for instance the vision of Hell as an interpenetration of cities. . . . But the initial motif of a variety of Hells on earth is never really transcended. Later in *Poema a fumetti,* however, where he combines his artistic and literary skills to deal again with a descent into Hell in the persons of a modern Orpheus (Orfi) and Eurydice (Eura), the negative and static elements of Hell are redeemed by the very fact of the passage of time in life, man's suffering and feeling, the sharpness itself of experience in living. For the visitor realizes that the souls in Hell envy the living their capacity for fear, longing, suffering and hoping. So that the fear of death itself can be made more terrible but at the same time can be experienced as an indulgence only of the living. (pp. 199-200)

Ponzio, in his introduction to a collection of Buzzati's articles, speaks of his 'constant concern to capture the great essential moment', a comment which is valid for Buzzati's fiction as well as for his journalism. . . . We have witnessed moments of this kind in his novels, but of course the ideal form for such observations is the short story, and it is this form at which Buzzati particularly excelled. Some of his short pieces are very short. . . . His stories are very carefully structured with a strong sense of progression which is sometimes even numerically monitored. There is a very definite turning-point which brings about a heightened sense of awareness and leads sometimes through change, and often through a reinforcement of the situation, to an inevitable conclusion. . . . The progression is a particularly suitable scheme for Buzzati's short fiction because it represents a repeated turning of the screw and so gives the spiralling motion or vortex which perfectly expresses certain of his themes. **'I sette messaggeri'** for example, is built around the geometrical progression produced by the distance ridden by the messengers as they carry letters between their explorer prince and his father's court.

Only in two novels did Buzzati use the more traditional forms of fantasy literature. *Il grande ritratto* relied on some science fiction situations such as the mad scientist, the trapped soul and the machine out of control. In his second novel, *Il segreto del bosco vecchio* (*The Secret of the Old Wood,* 1935) the fantasy belonged more to legend and fairy tale relying as it did

on tree spirits disguised as foresters, talking birds and mice, and rival winds. In neither of these novels is he outstandingly successful. His own brand of fantasy seems to require something subtler and less removed from normality. . . . Most often the situations for his fantasy are normal except for one thing. It is like a children's game of 'Just supposing'. One of the stories in *Il Colombre* is called **'E se'** ('And if'). It is a title he could have used over and over again. So in **'Una goccia'** we are in a normal, though vast, block of flats, but the drop of water is going upstairs not down. The hospital in **'Sette piani'** is perfectly credible except for its sinister organization.

Before Buzzati died, critics had started to take an interest in the nature of fantastic or anti-realistic fiction. He himself was rather flattered to have been considered a writer of the Absurd (particularly in France after the appearance of the dramatic version of **'Sette piani'**), although he did not feel that the word really applied to him. He felt that he 'broadened or compressed an idea to the utmost in order to get the greatest meaning from it' . . . , and that the fantastic was used in order to intensify the 'expression of certain ideas'. . . . (pp. 202-04)

Buzzati's approach to his subject via the fantastic is not limited to his creative writing. We can find it also in his journalism. (p. 204)

For him the writer's craft and journalism were the same. The aim was, he said in the conversations published as *Un autoritratto (Self-portrait),* 'to tell things in the simplest possible way, the most dramatic or even the most poetic way possible'. . . . Later in those conversations he went on to discuss poetry explaining that, like Leopardi, he felt mystery was at the root of poetry. 'It is poetry when someone is saying something and suddenly something else flashes upon you, something completely different and profound and painful, which has sprung from the first thing without anyone being able to say how'. . . . And of Leopardi he says '. . . when he told how as a child he used to write in his little room in the evening by lantern light, he was saying very, very ordinary things, but in such a way that they grew to take in the whole drama of his life and of the lives of many people like him'. . . . When Buzzati says that a journalist and a fiction writer must both write as 'poetically' as possible, it is this notion of poetry that he has in mind: the 'idea', platonic as it may be, emerges from the particular situation whether it be expressed in poetry or prose, and can bear a fruitful meaning for each individual reader. . . .[A passing from the particular to the general is] a feature of many of Buzzati's pieces and one of the chief reasons for his special appeal.

This question of a universal appeal on a poetic level together with Buzzati's overall preoccupation with death takes on a particular importance when one considers the period in which he began his career as a journalist and writer of fiction. We have seen how his allegorical approach was suitable for the Fascist period, although it was not specifically invented in order to avoid censorship. . . . Buzzati's fantasies were reactions to the inhibiting nature of Fascist repression of a fundamental human need to face certain truths and fears. But just like other writers who were revolting against the blinkered Fascist culture . . . , Buzzati found a recipe that went beyond the Fascist overlay and penetrated to basic human problems. . . . Buzzati, retreating into inner landscape, found that the insidious Fascist censor was merely reinforcing a human tendency to repress fears and not to face up to unpalatable facts. Death is not a problem that existed only under Fascism, but the problem was aggravated and sent underground by the scoffing attitude of the black-shirts with their skull-and-cross-bone flags. Courage and an acceptance of responsibility in the face of death or a moral challenge also take on a much greater importance when the fact of death is faced squarely as in the cases of Bàrnabo and Drogo. Naturally this could be done only in the terms of allegory under Fascism. (pp. 206-08)

So we can say that Buzzati's writing both as journalist and as narrator has its source in the basic human impulse to formulate experience into story and from there to extrapolate to some further 'maxim or consideration'. The first impulse in this direction came at a time when repression favoured his own bent to fantasy and allegory. It is easier for us now to recognise that these too can be methods not of escape but of a particularly searching form of self-knowledge, possibly because they speak more directly to the reader's own springs of creativity. Certainly they belong to that area of 'poetry' which in Buzzati's terms can just as well be expressed in the simple prose of the journalist or the short-story writer. (p. 208)

Judy Rawson, "Dino Buzzati," in Writers & Society in Contemporary Italy: A Collection of Essays, *edited by Michael Caesar and Peter Hainsworth, Berg Publishers, 1984, pp. 191-210.*

Raymond Carver

1938-

American short story writer and poet.

Carver's story collections, *Will You Please Be Quiet, Please?* (1976), *What We Talk About When We Talk About Love* (1981), and *Cathedral* (1983), have placed him at the forefront of the resurgence in the popularity of short stories. According to Irving Howe, "A few of Mr. Carver's stories—'They're Not Your Husband,' 'Where I'm Calling From' and 'A Serious Talk'—can already be counted among the masterpieces of American fiction." Writing in a pared-down, blunt style, Carver portrays the segment of society that exists outside the American dream. His characters work at menial jobs or are unemployed; many are alcoholics. The small-town settings of Carver's stories are bleak or squalid. Through judicious selection of dialogue and descriptive detail, Carver evokes this world in a realistic, unsentimental manner.

Carver's personal background is often reflected in his characters. Living in the Pacific Northwest, where many of his stories are set, Carver was married and had fathered two children before he reached the age of twenty. He and his wife worked at a series of unskilled jobs and moved frequently between small towns. Carver also struggled with alcoholism. In his essay "Fires" (1982) Carver describes how the limitations placed on him by fatherhood influenced the tone and format of his writing. Because it was difficult for him to find time to write, he concentrated on poems and short stories, first drafts of which he was often able to complete at one sitting. Most of Carver's poetry was written during the early part of his career; these pieces were published by small presses in the collections *Near Klamath* (1968), *Winter Insomnia* (1970), and *At Night the Salmon Move* (1976). A book of short stories, *Furious Seasons* (1977), is also a small press publication.

Reviewers of *Will You Please Be Quiet, Please?* and *What We Talk About When We Talk About Love* sensed a repressed violence in Carver's stories. They also noted an unrelieved pessimism and a feeling that the characters were trapped in their situations. While revelations occur in Carver's stories, their meanings are often unclear to the characters, who understand only that they are unable to change their lives. In "Neighbors," a story in *Will You Please Be Quiet, Please?*, a husband and wife who are looking after the apartment of their more sophisticated vacationing neighbors find excitement in wearing the neighbors' clothes and using their possessions. Their new interest in life ends abruptly when they accidentally lock their key to the neighbor's apartment inside it and must return to their own home. As happens in many of Carver's stories, this small incident triggers a feeling of emptiness which the characters do not completely comprehend.

The stories in *Cathedral*, while similar in many respects to Carver's earlier works, are generally longer, more fully developed, and not so relentlessly bleak. In an interview, Carver explained that these stories represent a deliberate departure from the tendencies which caused him to be considered a minimalist. "There's something about 'minimalist' that smacks of smallness of vision and execution that I don't like," he stated. Many critics commented on the sense of uplift in "Ca-

© *Jerry Bauer*

thedral" and in "A Small Good Thing." The latter is a revised version of "The Bath," a story that appeared in *What We Talk About When We Talk About Love*. In the original version, the parents of a young boy who has been in a serious accident and eventually dies are haunted by telephone calls from a baker who has been left with the child's birthday cake. The story concludes ambiguously with a menacing call from the baker. The revised version of the story begins similarly but continues past the point where the first ends, as the parents confront the baker with the news of their son's death.

Carver has stated that he prefers revising his own work to writing the original draft. He revised nearly all of the early poems and stories included in *Fires* (1983) before allowing them to be reprinted. This volume is a sampler of Carver's work that also contains new poems and stories, essays about writing, and an interview.

(See also *CLC*, Vol. 22; *Contemporary Authors*, Vols. 33-36, rev. ed.; and *Dictionary of Literary Biography Yearbook: 1984.*)

PUBLISHERS WEEKLY

In the essays that open [*Fires: Essays, Poems, Stories, 1966-1982*] are found some worthwhile guidelines for writers. The first, "**On Writing,**" contains invaluable observations on fictional worlds and the necessity for precision of language. . . . [Carver's] poems and short stories demonstrate the difficulties and occasional triumphs inherent in the writing process. Several of the poems are flawed by vagueness and faulty pacing. But when Carver succeeds, as he does in "**The Blue Stones**," "**Alcohol**," "**Balzac**" and "**Morning Thinking of Empire**," he does so impressively. The short stories are better, on the whole, and help to clarify the poems somewhat. "**Where Is Everyone?**" and "**So Much Water So Close to Home**" are especially powerful studies of marital alienation. Nabokov once defined a great writer as a storyteller, teacher and enchanter. Raymond Carver fits this definition, though he is a teacher most of all. (pp. 85-6)

A review of "Fires: Essays, Poems, Stories, 1966-1982," in Publishers Weekly, *Vol. 223, No. 8, February 25, 1983, pp. 85-6.*

ANATOLE BROYARD

[Some of the] stories in "**Cathedral**" are not . . . easy to describe or to respond to. There are inspired touches, such as a couple who have a very ugly baby *and* a peacock, or a father who travels all the way to Europe to realize that he does *not* want to see his son, who is studying there.

But several of these pieces are as enigmatic as anything in fiction today. In "**Preservation**," a couple seems utterly undone, almost panicked, by the fact that their refrigerator has gone off. It never occurs to them to fix it, as if all the vicissitudes were final, as if the heart of their life together had suddenly ceased to beat.

In a similar story called "**Careful**," the ear of a recently separated man becomes stopped up. Instead of going to a doctor, he phones his wife, as if only she can cure him. But one feels here that the metaphor is too pat, like the refrigerator. Then fate seems rigged by the author, who has arbitrarily eliminated all the natural alternatives.

Mr. Carver seems fascinated by disconsolateness and the precariousness of happiness. His stories are rather like the proletariat fiction of the 1930's, but these are proletariats of the psyche, not of economic forces. They are the silent majority of fiction, and Mr. Carver is like one of those intellectuals who wear work shoes and overalls. In most of his stories, failure or a vague diffuse regret are the principle drama.

Where, the reader wonders, is the folk energy, the manic invention, that makes the similarly placed characters of William Faulkner, Eudora Welty or Flannery O'Connor so vigorously interesting? We care about those people because they act, they believe in action. The loss of the belief in action may be Mr. Carver's melancholy theme, and it can certainly be argued that this, too, is important. At least it's an issue that seems to divide current fiction.

The trouble with this school of writing, though, is that it obliges the reader to be something of a semiologist, an interpreter of the faded signs of culture. The drama is almost always offstage, beyond the characters. Yet, compared with his previous two collections of stories, "**Cathedral**" shows an increase in vitality. Like a missionary, Mr. Carver seems to be gradually reclaiming or redeeming his characters.

Anatole Broyard, "Diffuse Regrets," in The New York Times, *September 5, 1983, p. 27.*

IRVING HOWE

There are artists who reach the strange by staying with the ordinary. Maurice Utrillo paints European streets that narrow into enigmatic space and Edward Hopper American houses that seem laden with disquiet. How they do this only a very good art critic can explain, but that it happens everyone who looks at pictures must know.

Raymond Carver, an American writer now in his mid-40's, has been writing stories for some years that, on a smaller emotional scale, create similar effects. His settings are American towns, semi-industrial and often depressed. His characters, plebeian loners struggling for speech, now and then find work as factory hands and waitresses. His actions skid across the troubles of daily life and then, through some eerie turn of chance or perhaps a darker cause, collapse into failed marriages and broken lives. Familiar enough on the surface, these stories leave one with tremors that resemble the start of a breakdown. The familiar controls guiding daily life fall apart; panic takes over.

Mr. Carver has been mostly a writer of strong but limited effects—the sort of writer who shapes and twists his material to a high point of stylization. In his newest collection of stories, "**Cathedral**," there are a few that suggest he is moving toward a greater ease of manner and generosity of feeling; but in most of his work it's his own presence, the hard grip of his will, that is the strongest force. It's not that he imposes moral or political judgments; in that respect, he's quite self-effacing. It's that his abrupt rhythms and compressions come to be utterly decisive. (p. 1)

"**Cathedral**" contains a number of . . . stories, very skillful within their narrow limits, written with a dry intensity, and moving, at their climaxes, from the commonplace to the unnerving. In "**Chef's House**" a couple try to patch up an imperiled marriage by vacationing in the house of a friend. All goes well until the friend returns: They must leave soon; he needs the house. The couple take this bit of news as a bad omen and the fragile ties they have rebuilt fall apart. Why this happens Mr. Carver doesn't explain, but it barely matters since the story moves along its own plateau of inexorability. It seems to whisper: There is a limit to what we can bear and sometimes a trivial event can crush us.

These stories yield neither the familiar recognitions of realistic narrative nor the ambiguous motifs of symbolic fiction. They cast us adrift, into a void on the far side of the ordinary. Ordinary life is threatening; ordinary life is the enemy of ordinary people.

Behind Mr. Carver's stories there are strong American literary traditions. Formally, they summon remembrances of Hemingway and perhaps Stephen Crane, masters of tightly packed fiction. In subject matter they draw upon the American voice of loneliness and stoicism, the native soul locked in this continent's space. Mr. Carver's characters, like those of many earlier American writers, lack a vocabulary that can release their feelings, so they must express themselves mainly through obscure gesture and berserk display.

It's a meager life that Mr. Carver portrays, without religion or politics or culture, without the shelter of class or ethnicity, without the support of strong folkways or conscious rebellion. It's the life of people who cluster in the folds of our society. They are not bad or stupid; they merely lack the capacity to understand the nature of their deprivation—the one thing, as it happens, that might ease or redeem it. When they get the breaks, they can manage; but once there's a sign of trouble, they turn out to be terribly brittle. Lacking an imagination for strangeness, they succumb to the strangeness of their trouble.

A few of Mr. Carver's stories—"**They're Not Your Husband**," "**Where I'm Calling From**" and "**A Serious Talk**"— can already be counted among the masterpieces of American fiction; a number of others are very strong. But something of the emotional meagerness that he portrays seeps into the narrative. His art is an art of exclusion—many of life's shadings and surprises, pleasures and possibilities, are cut away by the stringency of his form. (p. 42)

[Carver] succumbs at times to bravura, with stylization declining into mannerism. Having learned to control the devices that make him so notable a writer, he began, in his second book of stories, to slip into self-imitation. What makes "**Cathedral**" so interesting—apart from the intrinsic merit of the stories—is that it shows he has become aware of his temptations and perils.

A literary friend whose judgment I respect dislikes Mr. Carver's work because he finds it "cold." If he means that Mr. Carver employs devices of distancing which keep us from the inner life of his figures, I see no reason to be troubled. Greater writers have used such devices. But if my friend means that there creeps into Mr. Carver's stories a note of disdain toward the people he creates, then the charge is sometimes—by no means always—accurate. I suspect this happens because Mr. Carver grows impatient with, even grieved by, the resignation of his characters. It's as if he wished they would rebel against the constrictions of their lives, rebel even against the stylized constraints he puts upon them. But they don't.

I think Mr. Carver is showing us at least part of the truth about a segment of American experience few of our writers trouble to notice. Neoconservative critics, intent upon pasting a smile onto the country's face, may charge him with programmatic gloom and other heresies, but at his best he is probing, as many American writers have done before, the waste and destructiveness that prevail beneath the affluence of American life.

In "**Cathedral**" a few stories move past Mr. Carver's expert tautness and venture on a less secure but finer rendering of experience. The title story is a lovely piece about a blind man who asks an acquaintance to guide his hand in sketching a cathedral he has never seen. At the end, the two hands moving together—one guided by sight and the other not—come to seem a gesture of fraternity.

The most interesting example of the changes in Mr. Carver's work can be seen by comparing two versions of the same story—"**The Bath**," which appeared in an earlier collection, and "**A Small, Good Thing**," which appears in "**Cathedral**." It is a story about a pleasant young couple whose boy is soon to have a birthday. The parents order a cake from a somewhat sullen baker, but before the birthday can be celebrated the boy is hurt in an accident and the parents must watch helplessly as he dies. Meanwhile the baker, as if he were some evil spirit of harassment, keeps phoning the parents to pick up the cake. In the first version, the story ends here abruptly, with the baker calling still again.

The second version, nearly three times as long, goes beyond the ending of the first. Now the parents visit the baker, berating him for his phone calls and telling him the birthday boy has died. The baker answers: "Let me say how sorry I am. . . .

Forgive me if you can. I'm not an evil man, I don't think. Not evil, like you said. . . . I don't know how to act anymore." . . .

Now, I'm pretty sure most teachers of "creative writing" would tell their students that the first version is the better one. It's tighter and more cryptic, and it gives critics a chance to carry on about symbolism. But the teachers would be wrong. The second version, though less tidy and glittering, reaches more deeply into a human situation and transforms the baker from an abstract "evil force" into a flawed human creature. The first version, I would say, is a bit like second-rank Hemingway, and the second a bit like Sherwood Anderson at his best, especially in the speech rhythms of the baker.

"**Cathedral**" shows a gifted writer struggling for a larger scope of reference, a finer touch of nuance. What he has already done makes one eager to read his future work. (p. 43)

Irving Howe, "Stories of Our Loneliness," in The New York Times Book Review, *September 11, 1983, pp. 1, 42-3.*

LAURIE STONE

Carver is the bard of menace in ordinary life. His compulsively descriptive eye uncovers the macabreness and dead-end entrapment in even the most seemingly mundane events. In the title story of [*Will You Please Be Quiet, Please?*], a man learns that his wife was unfaithful—once, two years earlier. . . .

This narrative of commonplaces becomes highly compelling in Carver's hands. He depicts events entirely from the man's perspective: we see what a movie camera would record if it were strapped to his chest. And with these means alone, Carver shows that inertia is more threatening than anything in the man's existence. His catastrophe is that his life will never be set on a different course; he lacks the will to change it. Not once does he examine his motives, wonder why, for instance, he reacts so strongly to his wife's infidelity or why he plies her with questions. This man, we see, will continue to anesthetize his pain with drink. He will remain stupefied.

Over the years, Carver has grown increasingly expert at working maniacal effects with description. Although he is often published in *The New Yorker*, whose fact-larded reports and profiles aim to instill a sense of trustworthiness and safety, Carver's details have just the opposite impact. (p. 54)

Carver is never dull, because his style is so dazzling, but he can be one-note, and that note tends to be delivered by the alcoholic voice, another troubling ingredient. Drunkenness is either a large element or central concern in nine of the 12 stories in *Cathedral*. "**Where I'm Calling From**" is set at a "drying-out facility." In "**Chef's House**," an on-the-wagon drinker is about to take his final fall. The characters in "**Feathers**," observing events through a sentimental booze mist, seal their fates by deciding that a baby will bring serenity to their brittle, loveless lives. In "**The Bridle**," a man gets loaded, leaps from a motel roof in an attempt to land in the pool, and, missing it, winds up a walking vegetable. In other stories, the tinkle of ice, the splash of fresh liquor, the reach for the bottle punctuate all interactions.

Without alcohol, many of Carver's characters would be choked by inarticulateness and repression. Drink gives them their idiom and their take on the world. Carver's alcoholic voice doesn't reflect; it tells what happened and then what happened next. It is permanently amazed by what it sees, but detached, dulled.

The alcoholic voice isn't deepened by experience, but rather fears it, pushes it away.

Read separately, as an expression of a specific state of mind, many of these stories are brilliant; taken as a group, however, they seem to embody an attitude. Carver certainly understands emotional deadness; he is even sympathetic to those who suffer from it. But the meaning of his obsession with numbness is unclear. On one hand, he seems condescending to his working-class characters. In effect, his stories say people are incapable of self-inquiry or sustained desire. On the other hand, his work suggests that their dulled condition is emblematic of the general state. As in the writing of Joan Didion and Ann Beattie, among others, literary power is supposedly achieved by rendering the absence of feeling.

This supercool attitude implies that feeling doesn't belong in the realist mode because feeling doesn't truly exist; where it seems to—either in life or the works of other writers—it is a chimera. This attitude, in my opinion, is a chimera. When emotional deadness becomes a writer's main subject, the sensibility inevitably comes off as a pose. What's missing from the work of such writers, at the very least, is their knowledge of the passion, or drive, or commitment required to complete a piece of work. By holding back, those writers don't tell the whole gritty truth about real life, which their tough-cool narratives purport to deliver.

I'm not saying that Carver espouses this aesthetic; rather, that many of his stories send the message. But there's an important sign in *Cathedral* that Carver is expanding. It is **"A Small, Good Thing."** . . . (pp. 54-5)

In **"A Small, Good Thing,"** a woman orders a cake for her son's eighth birthday. . . . On the boy's birthday, the day the cake is supposed to be picked up, he is hit by a car. . . . He is taken to the hospital, and the parents are told that he will be all right. They spend the next few days by his bedside, waiting for him to wake up. On several occasions, they return home briefly . . . and each time a strange man calls and taunts them about Scotty, their son.

Scotty dies. The parents go home reeling with horror, and the phone rings. The woman curses into the phone, thinking she is speaking to the devil, until she realizes the voice she's been hearing belongs to the baker. It is past midnight, but she insists they drive to the shopping center. They confront the baker with what has happened and he is shaken. . . .

At the end, the baker offers the couple food. "Eating is a small, good thing in a time like this," he says. . . . The three of them sit talking through the night.

Carver steers the story with his distinctive descriptive wizardry, conveying how the parents feel through their actions. With great power, he captures the terrible task of waiting, the attempt to gobble time in the small movements from window to bed, or from elevator to coffee machine. But by allowing the baker to speak, to be affected by his experience, Carver adds new texture and substance to his work. The moment the baker speaks, the story becomes more interestingly his story, not Scotty's parents'. They aren't responsible for the pain they feel. The baker has caused his own anguish and knows it. In other stories there have been glimmers of the felt life, usually observed from a distance, but the baker's understanding is extensive, and his emotional life is shown from inside. The possibility that human beings can identify feelings and thus deepen has entered Car-

ver's world in a forceful way. Now, with his talent, anything can happen. (p. 55)

Laurie Stone, "Feeling No Pain," in VLS, No. 20, October, 1983, pp. 54-5.

RICHARD EDER

Raymond Carver looks into the faces we turn our faces from. Not the extreme faces of the mad or the outrageously bereft, but the garden variety: the driver in the next lane in the traffic jam, the other passengers in the packed subway, the people camped too close to us on the beach. The ones God must have loved because he made so many of them, but can we? Carver can; or at least if he can't, he can look at them and report.

His short stories, near-classics by now, mark pockets of blight. It is American blight. Most of the pain in these mostly painful stories is that of deterioration. Marriages, feelings, endeavors run down, partly from selfishness or lack of vision but mainly because there is no society to sustain them. Carver's America is a depressed neighborhood where neighborliness has departed. As with our bridges that collapse, there is a budget for emotional construction but almost none for emotional maintenance.

The lives are jerry-built and fragile. Any pressure or wind shift will knock them over. (p. 3)

Carver's women tend to cope better than his men. They keep busy, either tending the joint solitude of marriage or making a clean break from it. In **"Careful"** the man walks out, but all he can do with his freedom is lie in bed until late afternoon, eating doughnuts and drinking sweet champagne.

"Time was," Carver writes, "when he would have considered this a mildly crazy thing to do, something to tell friends about. Then, the more he thought about it, the more he could see it didn't matter much one way or the other." Freedom for these men is the same gray color as depression.

Carver's prose is as suited to blue- and white-collar America as John O'Hara's a generation earlier. It conveys a whole range of complex despairs and frustrations in language as generalized and blockish as that to be heard in any supermarket or cocktail lounge around the country.

It is a low-spirited noise, and some of the stories don't manage to transcend the accuracy of their low spirits. That, of course, is the danger of such artful realism. But Carver is more than a realist; there is, in some of the stories, a strangeness, the husk of a myth.

At times, Carver seems to seek in middle America what Cheever sought out in the affluent suburbs: transcendence resonating from a wealth of precise details. One story, a sketch barely, is even dedicated to Cheever. A nondescript woman, fresh from a violent scene with her lover, finds herself at night in a small railroad station along with a flamboyant couple in noisy argument. Their passions spill over, hers are hidden; but the train comes along and bears them all impartially away: a ship of fools, or Charon's barge.

There is something a little forced here, just as there is at the climax of **"A Small, Good Thing."** . . . [The story] is a rending account of a disastrous misunderstanding—the destruction done by the tangential encounter of two mutually isolated machineries. At the end, though, Carver's splendid control slips; the baker's anguished regret mounts to an oversized lament for existence.

In two stories, the magical and the concrete are seamlessly combined. In "**Cathedral**," a husband who has long resented his wife's devotion to a blind friend grudgingly puts up with the blind man's visit. After a hostile, hard-drinking evening, the conversational sparring turns to cathedrals. The blind man has never seen one. The host finds himself holding his visitor's hand as, in suddenly intimate communion, they sketch out a cathedral together.

"**Fever**," ostensibly, is about another man whose wife has left him. . . . The story is about all kinds of healing, in fact—what the wife provides in her periodic telephone calls is more than practical advice. It is the ghost of love and it leaves a residue of nurture behind. It is the best of many good things in the collection, and the most hopeful. (pp. 3, 8)

> Richard Eder, "Pain on the Face of Middle America," in Los Angeles Times Book Review, *October 2, 1983, pp. 3, 8.*

BRUCE ALLEN

"**Cathedral**" continues Raymond Carver's uncompromising anatomies of the thwarted lives of small-town drifters and losers. Its 12 stories essentially resemble his acclaimed earlier ones in their concentration on marital uneasiness, unemployment and boredom, and the sense that failure is everybody's fate. His characters drink, hang around the house, and surrender themselves to self-defeating cynical contemplation ("dreams," one of them pronounces, "are what you wake from"). His dialogue is so clipped and quick it's scarcely expressive—and, indeed, it's spoken by people who are reluctant to say what's bothering them; they embrace their misery, hide it away from others' sight.

Yet there is variety in Carver's gray world of rundown neighborhoods and secondhand emotions. The stories are filled with little progressive surprises; we're aware while reading that we really don't know what their characters will say or do next. And they're difficult to summarize, because what they're really about are the spaces between the "important" things in people's lives, those moments when nothing makes sense or connects with anything else.

In "**Feathers**," for example, one couple's night out at another's house becomes—by the most modest realistic means imaginable—a transfiguring experience: It gives them a vision of what their later life will be. "**Fever**," a 20-page story with almost the density of a novella, chronicles the trials of a high school teacher abandoned by his wife and left to make do for their two small children. The ingenious construction, focusing on his experiences interrupted by her phone calls, places emphasis squarely on the way the husband's character changes. "**Where I'm Calling From**" observes several patients at a "drying-out facility," and manages an impressive variety of characterizations and tonal effects.

The two finest stories eloquently demonstrate Carver's increasing reach and power. "**A Small, Good Thing**" expands an earlier story about the grief of parents whose small son has died into a rich examination of people's incomprehension, and their resilience. . . .

"**Cathedral**" confronts a jealous, uncertain husband with a visit from his wife's old friend, a blind man. . . . The story is

about learning how to imagine, and feel—and it's the best example so far of the way Raymond Carver's accomplished miniaturist art is stretching itself, exploring new territories.

> Bruce Allen, "MacArthur Award Winners Produce Two of Season's Best," in The Christian Science Monitor, *November 4, 1983, p. B4.*

DOROTHY WICKENDEN

"Dreams, you know," Betty says with a sigh to her hairdresser, "are what you wake up from." To faithful Raymond Carver readers, Betty will seem like an old friend. She and her husband have lost their Minnesota farm to the bank. They've piled their kids and clothes into their station wagon and taken an apartment for a few months at Fulton Terrace, a nondescript complex in an unnamed town. "It's July, temperature's one hundred plus. These people look whipped." Carver's specialty is people who look whipped, or more precisely, people who have *been* whipped—by a lousy marriage, by hard luck, by a freak accident, by booze. If, like Betty, they once dreamed of the future, they've since resigned themselves to the circumstances, random and routine, that rule their day to day existence.

Carver knows the lessons of humility by heart. In an autobiographical essay called "**Fires**" . . . , he starkly characterizes the principal influence on his life and writing: "a negative one, oppressive and often malevolent." By the age of 19 Carver was a husband and the father of two children, scrounging a living as a janitor and a stock boy. "The time came and went when everything my wife and I held sacred, or considered worthy of respect, every spiritual value, crumbled away. Something terrible had happened to us. . . . We couldn't fully comprehend what had happened." That incomprehension was worked out again and again in Carver's first two collections of short stories, *Will You Please Be Quiet, Please?* and *What We Talk About When We Talk About Love.* His stories were widely admired for their painstaking rendering of drab and dolorous lives; for their cool, staccato prose; for their sure grasp of the moment in which truth overtakes illusion.

By now Carver has perfected the art of reproducing the signs of emotional paralysis and terror. But the stories in *Cathedral* are more complicated than his monochromatic earlier work, in which it is hard to tell one exhausted narrator from another. . . .

In the more ambitious of his new stories Carver seems to have shaken some of his preoccupation with the manifestations of discontent, and replaced it with an effort to explore the imaginations of his characters. The results can be both funny and moving, as in "**Cathedral**," a story about ignorance and vulnerability—the deep-seated kind that we rarely admit to or reveal. . . .

Carver said in a recent interview in *The Paris Review* that *Cathedral* represents a serious attempt to defy one critic's characterization of his work as "minimalist." Certainly with this collection he has become a writer of depths as well as of surfaces. "**A Small, Good Thing**" and "**Cathedral**" are astute, even complex, psychological dramas. But a touch of sentimentality, an element previously foreign to Carver's work, has crept into these stories. Perhaps because he doesn't quite trust the sense of hope with which he leaves his characters, the writing at the end becomes self-consciously simple and the scenes of resolution contrived. (p. 38)

The promise of redemption [at the conclusion of **"A Small, Good Thing"**] is, finally, more cloying than liberating. But it is not surprising that Carver doesn't yet write with as much conviction about the small, good things as he does about the malevolent ones. He's discovering just how large they are, and how elusive. (p. 39)

> Dorothy Wickenden, "Old Darkness, New Light," in The New Republic, *Vol. 189, No. 20, November 21, 1983, pp. 38-9.*

JOSH RUBINS

Raymond Carver could hardly be more unlikely casting as a storyteller in the Dickens tradition. He doesn't write 700-page novels. He doesn't write novels at all, having thus far (it may be some sort of record) resisted whatever forces usually lead the gifted short-story writer to try to expand his scope and his audience. Spare, laconic, often narrated by the uneducated and less-than-articulate, Carver's stories of Oregon and Washington working people—*Cathedral* is his third collection—seem to be backed up against that northwest coast, as far away from the centers of Anglo-American literary tradition as they can get. Any echoes here, you'd think, would be of Twain and Hammett, Anderson and Hemingway.

Nonetheless, it's Dickens who comes to mind when, in a story called **"The Compartment,"** the most well-read, well-heeled of Carver's troubled heroes is threatened by the onslaught of overwhelming feelings: "He knew if he let himself go on thinking about these things, his heart could break." This Dickensian tension, the sense of holding back a wave of emotionalism, of heartbreak or rage or faith, galvanizes much of *Cathedral*—with character after character poised on the edge of some abyss, the verge of despair.

Will or won't an alcoholic fall off the wagon? More than any other writer, Carver captures the simultaneous delicacy and brutality of that dreaded slip. In **"Chef's House,"** the loss of a rented home is more than enough to tip the scales, ending a brief, idyllic reconciliation between a sometime drinker and his estranged wife—who narrates this six-page marvel as if in a single, frozen breath. . . . And hopelessness swamps nonalcoholics too, whether a displaced farmer in **"The Bridle"** or a would-be womanizer in **"Vitamins"**—whose shabby attempt at infidelity is stymied by a chance encounter with a menacing, prophesying, black Vietnam veteran. . . . (p. 41)

Ironically, Carver's contemporary precision in sketching in these lives on the edge of despair ensures that he'll sometimes be read too narrowly, just as Dickens's social-reformer role once obscured his broader concerns. Broken refrigerators, bowling nights, sterile apartment complexes, RC Colas with a shooter of whiskey: *Cathedral* is fully stocked with the stark details that can illuminate certain American lives—somewhere between urban and rural, often rootless and culturally impoverished, on the unraveling fringes of erstwhile industrial prosperity. But sociological or psychological observation is only one layer in Carver's art; and while some critics have found him detached or unemotional, his seemingly uninflected style is full of the same tension, that on-the-verge-ness, that he finds in the lives of ordinary, unlucky, isolated people. Sentimentality, overflowing tender or despairing emotion, seems to be always lurking just beyond Carver's next sentence. So . . . he must be tautly *careful*, pulling in each phrase, clipping it off—knowing that he now risks slipping over into mannerism, archness, a self-conscious absence of affect. The result is an implicit

sense of personal precariousness: Carver, no less than any of his characters, is himself on some desperate edge, fending off the sentimental with benumbed language, unlovely people, and the occasional hard, bright metaphor.

The tension is not always perfectly maintained. Mannerism can indeed take over in an overclinical story like **"Preservation,"** about an unemployed man's depression and his wife's ambivalent response. . . . **"Where I'm Calling From"**—featuring two alcoholics at a drying-out facility, one bolstered by marriage, the other isolated—is devoid of Carver's customary tension; it seems to surrender itself to pathos (and a complementary whimsy) in the very first paragraph.

And then there's the curious case of **"A Small, Good Thing,"** which dramatically illustrates the battle for—and with—sentiment that so often seems to be going on underneath the cool surface of a Carver story. In his second collection, *What We Talk About When We Talk About Love,* a ten-page story called **"The Bath"** offered a fierce, nearly telegraphic study in fear. . . . [The] narration, biting back all the feeling implicit in the situation, pushes Carver's style to—and past—its deadpan limits. Though an arresting piece, it's also quite clearly a "piece": mannered, abstract, as much exercise as storytelling.

In *Cathedral*, **"The Bath"** reappears, much expanded, as **"A Small, Good Thing."** Here the cruel edges are rounded off, the self-conscious coolness exchanged for a more authentic neutrality. Consider, for instance, the vast difference in tone effected by one of Carver's subtle, line-by-line revisions in the newer story. The baker's phone call in **"The Bath"**: "'There's a cake that wasn't picked up.' This is what the voice on the other end said." The same moment in the revised version: "'There's a cake here that wasn't picked up,' the voice on the other end of the line said." Without that prim "This is what," the stylistic effort being expended to hold back imminent emotional upheaval no longer calls attention to itself; thanks to dozens of such small relaxations throughout the story, the tension is fastidiously modulated.

None of these slightly softened wordings, in itself, is even remotely sentimental. Swathed in texturing detail, **"A Small, Good Thing"** remains effectively chilly, achingly impassive—almost until the end. But then, as if the process of removing those cool mannerisms has released some snowballing momentum in the opposite direction, Carver lunges toward sentimental affirmation in the final few pages. (pp. 41-2)

[The transformation/communion at the end of **"A Small, Good Thing"**] vividly signals the warring impulses that make Carver's best work so kinetic: the writer who can produce both **"The Bath"** and **"A Small, Good Thing,"** is an exciting, volatile artist. And it prepares us for the two remarkable, oddly Dickensian stories that (separated by the clenched despair of **"The Bridle"**) close out this volume.

"Fever" and **"Cathedral"** are tales of salvation, uplift wrested from the most unpromising human materials. . . .

In both cases, a slightly unreal visitor—reminiscent of Dickens's larger-than-life eccentrics, embodiments of goodness or hope or folly—pulls the very best out of an imperfect, weak-willed hero. In both cases, a dangerously sentimental moment (complete, in **"Fever,"** with sleeping children) is thoroughly earned—not through psychological detail, but through the poetic authority that springs from an honest grappling with nearly unbearable tensions. *Cathedral* is an important book in a unique career: these are riskier, deeper stories than Carver has produced before, the first ones likely to outlast their place and time. (p. 42)

Josh Rubins, "Small Expectations," in The New York Review of Books, Vol. XXX, No. 18, November 24, 1983, pp. 40-2.*

BRUCE WEBER

Carver's stories are populated by characters who live in America's shoddy enclaves of convenient products and conventionality—people who shop at Kwik-Mart and who live in saltbox houses or quickly built apartment complexes. They don't seem to want much: ordinarily divided lives of work and home, food on the table, love and solace when they need them. They yearn for serenity rather than achievement.

Still, there is vast unhappiness in them; they don't get the little they want. Carver's people end up being deserted by common satisfactions, and the stories are moral tales, really, explaining why decent men and women, dealt crummy circumstances in a plentiful world, behave badly in their intimate battles with selfishness. Written in an accessible vernacular, resonant with cryptic petulance and loud silences, the stories speak the language of everyday profundity. . . .

In the 1960's and the early 1970's, some of our more ingenious fiction writers—Donald Barthelme and John Barth, Stanley Elkin and Thomas Pynchon, Joseph Heller and John Hawkes—translated the clamor of those years into fictional worlds spinning weirdly out of control, showing us the whimsy and contradictions in our lives with the artifice of narrative form and the farcical nature of characters trying to make a go of it in a behaviorally unbound society. Who can understand the world? they asked. Life is lunacy.

The stories of Raymond Carver tell us that we don't live that way any longer. And if the positive critical judgment of Carver and reader interest in his work prove anything, it is that we believe his vision. In the small struggles of individual lives, Carver touches a large human note: When hope flies and impervious helplessness descends, where will we get our next boost from? What do we do now? Life in Carver's America isn't incomprehensible. It's merely very difficult, and like the claims staked by every fine writer, his territory is not really so localized. . . . Carver country is a place we all recognize. It's a place that Carver himself comes from, the country of arduous life. (p. 42).

[Carver's] characters, more often than not, are hapless, in the sense that their lives are without luck. They are married or not, employed or not, sober or not, solvent or not—but whatever the situation, things are in a state of undoneness. (p. 43)

Reviewers have often portrayed Carver's characters as destitute, whipped by life. But they aren't as tragic as that. Their lives are shabby, not empty, and excruciatingly ordinary. . . .

There is a pivotal, revelatory moment in virtually all the lives he describes. Whether it occurs during the story or has taken place before it begins, that moment upsets the patterns, however banal, in which his characters are accustomed to living. It is the moment at which complacency disappears. Carver focuses on his characters just when they realize that things will be the same forever, a realization that insures that they will never be the same again. (p. 48)

Carver's is not a particularly lyrical prose. A typical sentence is blunt and uncomplicated, eschewing the ornaments of de-scriptive adverbs and parenthetical phrases. His rhythms are often repetitive or brusque, as if to suggest the strain of people learning to express newly felt things, fresh emotions. Time passes in agonizingly linear fashion, the chronology of a given scene marked by one fraught and simple gesture after another. Dialogue is usually clipped, and it is studded with commonplace observations of the concrete objects on the table or on the wall—rather than the elusive, important issues in the air. The title of Carver's second story collection, **"What We Talk About When We Talk About Love,"** is suggestive of both his subject matter and technique, his interest in how we obliquely address the grand concerns in our lives. (pp. 48-9)

Carver's characters know a good deal less than the author does. They don't share his wide perspective, and they don't often go in for analysis or philosophical speculation. The intelligence of the stories is communicated over their heads, so to speak, from author to reader, and it is this quality that has led more than one critic to observe a note of condescension in some of the stories. But in his best work, Carver's voice serves to reinforce the world of his characters. His is an almost journalistic kind of accuracy; his voice is the voice of experience. (p. 49)

Bruce Weber, "Raymond Carver: A Chronicler of Blue-Collar Despair," in The New York Times, Section VI, June 24, 1984, pp. 36-50.

BLAKE MORRISON

Raymond Carver is known here, if at all, as the writer who reaches the parts that other Americans don't. Mobile caravan parks, all-night cafés, bakehouses, drying-out centres for alcoholics, the kitchens and porches to which men and women return from their dead-end jobs: they've been described before but never with such a cool, level stare.

The low life and flat prose have earned him the label 'Dirty Realist.' But like the original dirty realists—Flaubert, Zola—he's had the confidence to see that the dirt will sooner or later wear off. He has also been called a 'minimalist,' but like Beckett—their one point of contact—he knows that a pared-down language 'can still carry . . . can hit all the right notes.' He keeps his feet on the ground but this doesn't prevent the kind of lift-off you get in the title story of his last collection, **'Cathedral.'**

['**Fires**'] is an introduction to and sampler of his art. It reprints the best of his poetry and ends with seven of his stories, some previously collected, some not. Its chief interest, though, lies in the essays with which it opens. These run to a mere 35 pages but give the essence of his approach to writing and bring out the autobiographical element in an apparently impersonal art. . . .

Carver likes to create a sense of 'menace' in his work and speaks of how it's 'the things that are left out' that give art its tension. This method is less successful in his poetry, which only rarely rises above a prosy anecdotalism, than in the stories here, which know precisely what to hold back. We're never told what 'the lie' is in a story of that title (only that it prises apart husband and wife), nor why Mrs Harrold hasn't accompanied Mr Harrold on a fishing trip (only that things fall to pieces without her), nor what part if any the unnamed narrator has played in his friend Harry's death (only that he later acquires Harry's girl and cabin cruiser).

Carver's plainness is deceptive. He proceeds by subtle clues and silences, even in the autobiographical pieces, which hint at drink and marital difficulties but aren't into that sort of confessionalism. If the stories on offer here aren't necessarily his best, the book overall gives a picture of an unconventional and strong-minded talent.

Blake Morrison, "Down in the Dirt," in The Observer, April 14, 1985, p. 23.

MICHAEL FOLEY

[In *Fires: Essays, Poems, Stories* and *The Stories of Raymond Carver* the] overwhelming impression is not of a man driven to testify but of a practised, cunning and profoundly self-conscious artist. The stories are always readable but this is often achieved by mere literary skill and one feels cheated rather than enriched at the end.

There are several reasons for this disparity. One is the influence of Hemingway and Lardner. The *faux naif* pose with its short, simple sentences and dumb-ass narrators may appear a direct route to the real world beyond literature—but it has never actually been that (unless one goes back to Huck Finn). Hemingway's vision was distorted by romanticism and Lardner's by misanthropy. Their legacy is a short story tradition whose apparent directness and sincerity have been eagerly appropriated by a multitude of cynical second-raters. Carver is not cynical—but he does not always avoid the pitfalls of his chosen tradition. Now that the fuss has died down, the Hemingway style looks more mannered than Proust's and after a few pages of 'the man said—the woman said' exchanges one's whole system cries out for a few polysyllabic words and subordinate clauses.

Then there is the influence of two other clean, well-lighted places—the creative-writing workshop and the national magazine. Both these encourage craftsmanship and professionalism—tricks, in fact. Carver mentions being taught, as a creative-writing student, that it is bad to do a story about a crippled person and leave out the fact of the character's crippledness until the very end.... However, it turns out that he disapproves of this, not because it is a strategy, but because it is old-fashioned. Nowadays you don't keep significant information to the end—you omit it altogether. Time and again this technique is used to maintain interest and create the illusion of the story as a chink onto a large, strange, frightening world. Thus **'Harry's Death'** does not explain why or how Harry died and **'The Lie'** does not tell us what the husband and wife are quarrelling about, much less whether or not it is true. This is a pro trick. And there are others: making the reader feel superior by having an unconsciously prejudiced narrator (the Lardner trick), creating the illusion of mystery by using a narrator with only partial knowledge of the characters (the Great Gatsby trick), slipping in 'significant' symbols by having your dumb-ass say something like 'I had this funny dream and I don't know what it means,' or 'I don't know much about books but I read this story by Jack London' (the Catcher in the Rye trick). In the third-person stories symbolism is introduced by other means. When a practising alcoholic has trouble with his ear we nod wisely (loss of equilibrium, can't hear the outside world—get it?). When the freezer in the home of a newly redundant worker breaks down we know it is not just the food that is spoiling—it is this couple's *artificially preserved life*.

Then there is the hint-of-menace device, the feeling that something kinky or shocking or violent is about to happen. Carver is open about this. 'I like it when there is some feeling of threat or sense of menace in the short stories. I think a little menace is fine to have in a story.' National magazines also think it is fine, but those seeking news of the real, as distinct from the Hitchcock world may be less enthusiastic.

What Carver is after, with his many devices, is the soul of inarticulate America, the people who smash things, jump through windows, drag their wives round the house by the heels screaming 'I love you,' and often need rocks, hammers and firearms to help them express their feelings. These things happen but often one does not believe in the dumb waitresses, salesmen and factory workers or the carefully orchestrated banalities they repeat to each other. Despite his 'dirty realist' tag he is not a mimetic writer....

What Carver excels at is creating a mood or atmosphere, often by concentrating on objects (no ideas but in things), and, luckily, it is not always an atmosphere of menace. In the better stories the mood is of aimlessness, worthlessness, insubstantiality, indecision or regret—our all-too-familiar contemporary demons. In **'The Ducks'** a nightshift worker is sent home early, mooches about, rejects his wife's advances and gets up to stare out at the rain. The sensation of helplessness and claustrophobia is overwhelming. Like many of the other characters, this man believes in the classic American solution: go somewhere else. In **'How about this?'** Harry, a long-time city-dweller, achieves his dream of a house in the country, but is disillusioned even before he arrives....

Stories such as these significantly extend the Hemingway tradition into family life. In Hem's world your great love and baby die in childbirth, leaving you with romantic despair instead of the indignities chronicled here—work (or lack of it), bills, marital rows, screaming babies, difficult children.... These stories are longer and more relaxed, blessedly menace and symbol-free, the style and dialogue less mannered, the treatment less oblique.

Also completely successful are the stories where Carver is content to indulge his taste for odd characters and weird dialogue: for instance, **'What we talk about when we talk about love'** or **'Feathers',** where a couple invited to the home of a colleague of the husband's encounter a cast of the wife's preorthodentistry teeth on top of the TV, a swan ashtray where butts are stubbed out on the back and smoke drifts from the mouth, a huge, incredibly ugly baby and a pet peacock which screams until it is let into the living-room. All this is rendered with exquisite satirical precision: but where Lardner would continue the crucifixion, right on to breaking the legs and inserting the spear in the side, and where a lesser writer would tip over into caricature and farce, Carver suddenly breaks off the comedy to end on an unexpected and moving note of compassion.

Best of all are the stories dealing with alcoholism and family break-up. These provide news of the world with a vengeance. When the narrator of **'Night School'** begins, 'My marriage had just fallen apart. I couldn't find a job. I had another girl ...' the short sentences are like jabs from a cattle prod. Instead of being soothed into compliance one is jolted alert—*the guy really means it this time*. It is not just that the material must be autobiographical, although this obviously gives an extra urgency. What makes these stories arresting is the combination of dramatic—but *genuine*—material and a throwaway, laconic style. Instead of the anguished breast-beating and self-laceration customary with this kind of material, the stories are written from inside the alcoholic experience, and one is continually startled and thrown off-balance by the casual descriptions of cheating, stealing, abuse, neglect and other kinds of lunacy such as offering the entire contents of a house for sale in the front yard, then getting drunk with a young couple looking for bargains and dancing to your own records with the confused young wife (**'Why don't you dance?'**). . . .

This material is also dealt with in the poems in *Fires,* the furniture on the sidewalk turning up again in **'Distress Sale'.**

> What a situation here! What disgrace!
> Everyone who sees this collection of junk
> on the sidewalk is bound to be mortified.

But the effect here is less striking. In the stories we are mortified without having to be told to be mortified. Most of the lyrics are tight, competent and readable. These would be terms of abuse for an English poet, but given the range of American windbags, from Ashbery at one end of the scale to Bukowski at the other, one is grateful for competence and readability.

Michael Foley, "Dirty Realist," in London Review of Books, *May 2 to May 8, 1985, p. 12.*

JONATHAN DEE

I can't define poetry as well as I'd like, and probably won't ever be able to. But it does have a certain recognizable makeup, the absence of which makes [*Where Water Comes Together with Other Water*] an interesting and, in its way, important collection. The central question raised by these 80 poems is not whether they're good or bad but whether they are poems at all. (p. 46)

What sets [Carver's] poems apart from [his] stories is their frankly autobiographical nature. Carver, a recovered alcoholic, has led a painful, sometimes bitter and self-destructive life; in interviews he seems both shamed by the damage he's done and grateful to those who helped him turn things around. His stories are grounded in this experience, but his poems confront it directly, sometimes (as in **"Next Year,"** a record of decline whose refrain will be familiar to anyone who has belonged to AA) with harrowing authenticity.

Still, we're obliged to read this collection not as a diary but as a book of poems. Poems don't simply relate experience, they transform it, abstract it so we can see it more clearly. You probably have your own favorite definition of this process. Mine is Gertrude Stein's—prose, she says, is about the verb, and poetry is about the noun. *Water* is a good, if negative, illustration of this. Carver's poems are all verb; one thing leads to another, and to another, and then it's over. There is no attempt to address events described in anything other than reportorial fashion. The rationale seems to be it happened, it was meaningful to me, therefore it must be the stuff of poetry. What's missing is the skill to *make* it poetry.

The skill, mind you, not the intent; throughout the individual poems you can feel him trying to get at something, to excavate his sentiments, which are no doubt truly poetic. Sadly, he doesn't seem to have the tools. The best he can do is a line like, "I have a thing / for this cold swift water," or "My hair stood on end," or "Lighten up, songbirds. Give me a break," or, most tellingly, "I don't even think I can talk about it." The diction of Carver's poems echoes the speech of the broken men and women who populate his fiction. Yet a character's inarticulateness can be touching, endearing, and full of meaning; a poet's is none of these.

This doesn't mean that narrative poetry can't be effective. Some of the pieces in *Water* work very well—**"The Ashtray," "The Fishing Pole of the Drowned Man," "Locking Yourself Out, Then Trying To Get Back In," "My Dad's Wallet."** They work, though, because the stories they tell are so wonderfully self-contained, so self-evident, so gracefully metaphorical; in other words, they work in spite of the writing, which exhibits no sense of technique, of line, of sound, of a word's utility in any other than a purely nominative context. Economy is one of the virtues of Carver's fiction, a quality that ought to serve him well here. Instead, what passes for economy is the elision of articles and pronouns in a way which—and this sounds crueler than it is—reminds me of high school poetry. (pp. 46-7)

It's too bad Carver doesn't speak more clearly about the themes of *Water,* because some of them are interesting in light of his earlier work. His poems are fascinated with death, a topic his stories almost never address with such frankness. There, he seems more concerned with the difficulties in living one day at a time, and with the slim hope of redemption for the living; the poems show a darker (if you can believe it), more obsessed side. But again, we don't learn much about this obsession. **"Fear,"** a sort of grocery list of private terrors, one per line, ends:

> Fear that what I love will prove
>   lethal to those I love.
> Fear of death.
> Fear of living too long.
> Fear of death.
>   I've said that.

Such sentiments are hardly revelatory—merely informative. In fact, if you are, as I am, a Carver fan, all of *Water* is informative. It is a valuable companion to the fiction, and an unmatched portrait of Carver himself. You can accept and like it on those terms. But these are, finally, not poems so much as journal entries with a ragged right edge. (p. 47)

Jonathan Dee, "Broken English," in The Village Voice, *Vol. XXX, No. 26, June 25, 1985, pp. 46-7.*

Isabel Colegate

1931-

English novelist and critic.

Colegate's novels center on the world of wealth and power in twentieth-century England. With fine detail and careful construction, she recreates the ambiance of the early 1900s as a backdrop for the complex web of infidelity, betrayal, and corruption woven beneath the surface of her characters' lives. Colegate is praised for her sympathetic treatment of characters, her elegant, disciplined prose, and, most frequently, for the fullness and authenticity of her settings. Reviewing *Statues in a Garden* (1964), Frank Littler commended Colegate for her talent at "weaving documentary details so adroitly into her story that the century in its teens is given a reality at once recognizable and fresh."

Colegate's first three novels, *The Blackmailer* (1958), *A Man of Power* (1960), and *The Great Occasion* (1962), introduce her concern with the decadence underlying rigid upper-class society. Oswell Blakeston praised *A Man of Power* for being "as satisfying as an Edwardian piece of story telling . . . informed with the insight of modern realism." In *The Great Occasion*, five sisters attempt to come to terms with the world as they mature and leave the shelter of their affluent home; ultimately, each one fails, and the novel ends in disillusionment, madness, and suicide. In 1984 these works were collected and published in the United States under the title *Three Novels: The Blackmailer, A Man of Power, and The Great Occasion*. *Orlando King* (1968), *Orlando at the Brazen Threshold* (1971), and *Agatha* (1974) form a trilogy in which the family and fortunes of a man named Orlando are developed against the political background of England from the 1930s through the 1950s. Loosely based on the myth of Oedipus, the trilogy is considered one of Colegate's most ambitious projects. Like the Orlando trilogy, the characters and events of *News from the City of the Sun* (1979) span several decades. This novel, which centers on a utopian community and the lives of its transient members, was described by Peter Kemp as "an ironic and occasionally painful comedy about the odd interaction between human nature, life's surprises, and Utopian ideals."

Colegate is best known in the United States for *The Shooting Party* (1980), her most widely acclaimed novel. Recreating the high spirits and glamor of the Edwardian era, *The Shooting Party* is set just prior to the Great War. The novel revolves around a weekend shooting party at an elaborate country estate, where a man is killed amidst the flurry of affairs and activities. The parallel drawn between the shattered gaiety of the party and the turbulence looming on the political front has been hailed as among Colegate's finest achievements.

(See also *Contemporary Authors*, Vols. 17-20, rev. ed.; *Contemporary Authors New Revision Series*, Vol. 8; and *Dictionary of Literary Biography*, Vol. 14.)

JOHN COLEMAN

A Man of Power is an ironic title, since Lewis Ogden, a self-made tycoon, flounders for quite a time in the toils of the beautiful interior decorator Lady Essex Cowper, before de-

© *Jerry Bauer*

tecting and riposting to her baseness. The story is pursued by the daughter, Vanessa Cowper, who remains pleasantly confused until near the end. Décors are mostly upper class and, accordingly, a most specious-sounding youth club leader is allowed to do a guru at the close. Miss Colegate, however, manages to vanquish her theme (Mitford crossed with Sagan) at important moments by writing very sensibly about Tanfield situations; and the frippery smart-talk side—the protagonists move for a time to a villa near Amalfi—is done so that it is almost amusing. One would say this was a great improvement on Mlle Sagan if that didn't mean so little.

John Coleman, "Time in Rumania," in The Spectator, *Vol. 204, No. 6866, January 29, 1960, p. 144.**

MAURICE RICHARDSON

[Miss Colegate shows] stamina in her contemporary characterization. *The Great Occasion* is a very natural if rather rambling chronicle of the misadventures of the five daughters of a woolly minded, middle-aged SW3 and home counties widower. One is married to an odious political careerist; one has a lot of love affairs; one dies bitterly; one is still stormily at school. The treatment varies when necessary from the deadpan to the poignant but there is never any forced brightness. If a foreigner or a revenant asked for novels that show the changes taking place in middle-class life in the 1960s, this is one I would recommend. (p. 650)

> Maurice Richardson, "Damned Up North," in New Statesman, Vol. LXIII, No. 1625, May 4, 1962, pp. 649-50.*

SIMON RAVEN

Isabel Colegate has written a funny and rather moving book [*The Great Occasion*] about five sisters, all of whom are at odds with life or love. For a page or two at the beginning one might mistake Miss Colegate for that sort of women's mag writer who believes in the possibility of happiness through true love. It soon becomes plain, however, that she believes in nothing whatever except just possibly luck. You *may* find someone agreeable—or rather someone who seems agreeable—and for a little while things may go smoothly. But sooner or later you'll get pregnant or tubercular or drunk or just spotty at the wrong time, and then you'll find it doesn't suit people to have you around, for all they were so assiduous about you five minutes ago.

In short, *The Great Occasion* is a book about betrayal, which Miss Colegate sees everywhere and at every second, and how to come to terms with it by entering a lunatic asylum or a coffin (the respective fates of sisters two and four); by seeking compensation in greed (sister one) or in drink (sister three); or simply, as with sister five and last, by making your mind a blank. This is a gloomy book, then, but not entirely without hope, and in any case acidly amusing.

> Simon Raven, "Outriders of the Apocalypse," in The Spectator, Vol. 208, No. 6984, May 4, 1962, p. 597.

STEPHEN WALL

[Miss Colegate is] subtle. Her writing [in *Statues in a Garden*] is both sensitive and economical; if she has been influenced by Virginia Woolf (the material recalls such books as *Mrs Dalloway*) she has not been swamped by her; her novel has form. Her intentions are clearly defined: 'We are not trying to recapture an age as it was, or to write history: we are trying to remember the background for a fable. A private background for a private fable'. The point of view is based on, but not confined to, Alice Benedict, governess to the Weston family; Aylmer Weston is in Asquith's cabinet, preoccupied by public anxieties until he is broken by the discovery of a love affair between his beautiful wife and his nephew Philip. The contrast between the serenity, comfort, and optimism of Aylmer's world and the corrupt, subversive forces moving in Philip which destroy it, is made with a delicate force. Aylmer's death is a parallel to the coming of the war, but it is not only or even principally that—the fable records the ruin of a whole world of possibility. *Statues in a Garden* has, despite its slight self-consciousness, a resonance which is the mark of an achieved work of art.

> Stephen Wall, in a review of "Statues in a Garden," in The Listener, Vol. LXXII, No. 1848, August 27, 1964, p. 317.

FRANK LITTLER

How much of the social masonry that crumbled with World War I would have disappeared in any event is rarely a subject for speculation. Flanders mud and not natural evolution transformed the modes, manners and mercantile security of the British people.

This may be a simplification of the historian's case, but it explains why so many writers are enduringly fascinated by 1914, the punctuation mark of the 20th century, as James Cameron has called it. . . .

A capable writer who plunges into this era can scarcely miss. Isabel Colegate, however, is much more than capable. She may give herself an extra advantage by making her pivotal character [in **"Statues in a Garden"**] a Cabinet minister, but thereafter she is on her own.

Sir Aylmer Weston is a Liberal in the Asquith Administration. He is beset by a conglomeration of anxieties that include Ireland, the suffragettes and (the name sounds sinister to this day) Serbia. To his family of wife, son and two daughters are added an adopted nephew and an Anglo-Irish governess. Chapter by chapter—because the story is beautifully graduated—it becomes clear that just as the nation at large fails to discern the beckoning holocaust, this essentially decent statesman has no inkling of the personal tragedy that is closing in on him. The parallelism is skillfully developed—so skillfully, in fact, that the flimsiness of the plot can be forgiven. The sexual explosion, when it comes, would be shocking in any *zeitgeist*. In the golden age of top-hatted statesmen and their osprey-feathered ladies it is appalling in its brutality.

The author's trappings are never obtrusive, and the long-skirt dialogue is not burlesqued. There may be doubts about whether people of this kind could always finish their colloquies without being interrupted in midparagraph. Otherwise, the conversations ring true; anachronism-spotters will have a thin time with **"Statues in a Garden."** It is perfectly convincing that the now-extinct figure of a maid-servant, that half-educated, sniveling stereotype, should be the character who shatters Sir Aylmer's world. With equal authenticity it is an unsettled young Army officer (the author is too subtle even to imply that he is "dashing") who precipitates the maid's disclosures. . . .

Whether Miss Colegate . . . owes anything to Ivy Compton-Burnett is hard to say. She is a comparable master of undertone; she is in Miss Compton-Burnett's territory; and she, too, refrains from physical descriptions of her characters. Where she differs is in weaving documentary details so adroitly into her story that the century in its teens is given a reality at once recognizable and fresh. "We are not trying," says her narrator, "to recapture an age as it was." But the age is recaptured, with a sureness extraordinary for a novelist of this vintage.

> Frank Littler, "Sir Aylmer Sees It Through," in The New York Times Book Review, March 20, 1966, p. 37.

KATHERINE GAUSS JACKSON

The beautiful English summer of 1914. How far and how intensely and for how long a time it has cast its sunlight and its shadow. Here [in *Statues in a Garden*], written by a woman who was not born until 1931, is a re-creation of the social events leading up to and following immediately after a country garden wedding in the charming family of Sir Aylmer Weston, a member of Lord Asquith's Cabinet. The author, through her narrator, calls her tale a parable and says it could have happened at any time, but she knows that this story of the frightful violence that lies so close to the surface of the most serene-seeming lives could have no better background than this one she has chosen.... The political and social events of the time are brought home to the story because of Sir Aylmer's position in the Cabinet and in society.... Yes, it's a sort of *Guns of August* in fiction form with the outside events suggested only as they heighten and give intensity to the beautiful and awful story at the center—a story of human goodness and dreadful human fallibility told calmly and quickly with a remarkably sustained detachment—and even wit—by a narrator whose identity is not revealed till the end. It would be unfair to tell or even suggest the nature of the plot, but every character is real and memorable.... This is Miss Colegate's first novel to be published in America.... May it be the first of many. (pp. 122-23)

> *Katherine Gauss Jackson, in a review of "Statues in a Garden," in* Harper's Magazine, *Vol. 232, No. 1391, April, 1966, pp. 122-23.*

R.G.G. PRICE

Orlando King is an elaborate attempt to rewrite the Oedipus legend in modern terms. Unfortunately, the story of the orphan's rise via the furniture business and Parliament is more interesting than the Greek echoes which, after the almost unreadable opening, are barely noticeable. I am afraid it is one of those sad cases where what is important to the novelist is not made important to the reader. I have liked Miss Colegate's other novels much more; but once one gets past the preliminary barrier this is quite a readable, if thinnish, contemporary tale. There is a good deal between being disappointed and being bored.

> *R.G.G. Price, in a review of "Orlando King," in* Punch, *Vol. CCLV, No. 6680, September 18, 1968, p. 418.*

THE NEW YORKER

To every intent, ["Orlando King"] is a novel of the thirties. There is a superficiality in the characters that is just right. Orlando is not given to soul-searching, and when, on occasion, his wife does it, it is unusual and unhealthy. Orlando's character is revealed by his deeds and by the company he keeps, while Judith King (who owes much to Margot Metroland and Virginia Crouchback) is what she looks like—the pale Modigliani beauty, the beach pajamas, the cigarette holder, amid the glittering settings of Eden Roc, Cliveden, and the off-white drawing room of her country house. Miss Colegate is honestly nostalgic, and imitative of earlier masters. Her irony and her meticulous concern for form and style have the sweet artifice of skillful pastiche. (pp. 165-66)

> *A review of "Orlando King," in* The New Yorker, *Vol. XLV, No. 12, May 10, 1969, pp. 165-66.*

AILEEN PIPPETT

A confused opening, an obscure end, and yet [*Orlando King*] in its entirety is anything but vague. It makes a direct impact because it is a succession of clear pictures or striking statements; it has sharply outlined characters, definite situations, dramatic pauses; and its story line leads through a tangle of incidents to a climax that has the weight of inevitability. So do not be deterred by the author's casual way of beginning her

story somewhere in the middle, darting hither and yon in time, bringing on and bowing out a swarm of characters....

Isabel Colegate does not stress the symbols. It would be easy to miss the significance of Orlando marrying his father's wife, of his being blinded in the air raid. He is a Bright Young Thing, a business man, a Member of Parliament, working up toward Cabinet rank, a father and stepfather, a connoisseur of racing cars and other status symbols.

The people surrounding him are described with brilliance. A kind of deathly precision exposes their shortcomings. They persist in being fatuous, wrong-headed, irrational and human. There is a typical backward-looking bore of a stockbroker; an ardent young engineer who will fight and be killed in Spain; a benevolent peer; a Mosleyite; several scheming women; and a number of maddening, enchanting children. All these figures come and go, seen against their backgrounds, like successive images on the picture screen. One is compelled to admire the masterly technique and the subject-matter is almost painfully interesting.

> *Aileen Pippett, "The Hero Had Hammer Toes," in* The New York Times Book Review, *May 25, 1969, p. 46.*

STEPHEN WALL

'Orlando King' was like Isabel Colegate's earlier novel 'Statues in a Garden' in that a personal fable was played out against a background of public affairs; the method was elliptical, and the balance between persons and their period intriguingly held. This effect is less aimed for in ['Orlando at the Brazen Threshold'] where the tempo is more relaxed but in which the writing is also less alert. There are still hovering suggestions of myth— ... [Orlando's] relationships with his daughter and his death fleetingly recall Oedipus at Colonus—but the treatment is generally more conventional. Perhaps in the promised third volume, Miss Colegate will have the courage of her old conventions.

> *Stephen Wall, "Seeing Is Believing," in* The Observer, *May 23, 1971, p. 29.**

ROSALIND WADE

[In *Agatha*], Agatha's brother, Paul, is serving fifteen years for selling foreign secrets to an unfriendly power. Recklessly, Agatha subscribes money for a gang organising his escape. But after this dramatic opening, another theme emerges. What might have been melodrama is tempered with a situation of quiet domesticity and the apathy with which Agatha accepts her husband's casual infidelity.

In *Agatha*, the Orlando of earlier novels is dead.... For anyone who has not read the entire series, Isabel Colegate's ability to move swiftly towards the high peaks of her narrative is a compensation. It is to her credit that she does not evade the final issue. Agatha (married to Conrad's son, Henry), is finally arrested for her part in her brother's escape from prison. The point at which the author has chosen to end the Orlando saga is Conrad's return to his empty house, having quarrelled with his son, and believing his career to be in ruins as a result of the scandal. His only companion is an aged dog, near to death. Thus all is decay and dissolution. And so Conrad's cry from the heart, 'O God, let me die,' is seen as only a partial solution. It seems a weak ending for this important trilogy, although the very inconclusiveness may, of course, be a part of the author's intention. (pp. 46-7)

> *Rosalind Wade, in a review of "Agatha," in* Contemporary Review, *Vol. 224, No. 1296, January, 1974, pp. 46-7.*

JOHN MELLORS

I suspect that Agathese is one of those acquired tastes, like sea-urchins or 100-year-old eggs, which I am unlikely to acquire, so my remarks had better be taken with a pinch of salt. Who wrote *Agatha*? The jacket says 'Isabel Colegate', but in certain passages I began to think that the book might be the combined jeu d'esprit of Iris Murdoch, C. P. Snow and Sylvie Krin after they'd all had a few drinks together. Better men than I have praised the previous two books in the trilogy, Elizabeth Berridge going so far as to say she was reminded of Anthony Powell. I was left cold and puzzled by this story of half-siblings, homosexual traitors, property tycoons, and Cabinet Ministers at the time of Suez. I was particularly puzzled by the author's preoccupation with politicians who read Herodotus in bed. In *Statues in a Garden* (a good novel, with reminders of L. P. Hartley) . . . she describes a member of Asquith's Cabinet who sits up in bed with his Herodotus, reading 'a page or two of my old friend' before going to sleep. In *Agatha,* a member of Eden's Cabinet, a disappointed man because he knows he would have made a good Viceroy of India, props himself up on his pillows to read Herodotus and sip Bisodol. At least here we are reminded of Enoch, if not of Anthony, Powell. (pp. 136-37)

> *John Mellors, in a review of "Agatha," in* London Magazine, *Vol. 13, No. 6, February-March, 1974, pp. 136-37.*

GILLIAN WILCE

The title of Isabel Colegate's latest novel [*News from the City of the Sun*], its epigraph from *Hebrews* and occasional fleeting suggestions in the text (like Hamilton's semi-mad visions) hint at kingdoms not entirely of this world. But it remains only a hint in an otherwise firmly earth-bound book. The Whitehead brothers . . . have, in the early Thirties, established a secular community at the Abbey under Salisbury Plain. The community stays and changes, while visitors come and go. Some appear for a few sentences; others take up residence in the book; just one or two remain merely narrative links, unfleshed. The most important of the visitors is Dorothy. . . . It is through its impact on her that the community is most clearly justified, although she herself becomes a private, uncommunity-minded person.

Development is gradual and detailed during the Thirties and the war years, but the speed picks up until, during the Sixties, the effect is that of a galloping lantern-slide lecture: someone last glimpsed in nappies appears suddenly full-grown; happy hippies are replaced almost at once by more threatening, revolutionary counterparts. But the unevenness of the historical context is not too important since it is what the people in the community make of it that is the real subject.

Some of the novel's people share their author's penchant for wry observation. They reflect on what they do, how they relate, what they believe, and if what they say about social and political theory is often realistically imprecise, it none the less matters to them. . . .

[One of the brothers, Fisher,] ascribes to one visitor a 'detached way of looking at things which you might expect to be cold but is somehow the opposite, all bright awareness and sympathy'. This is not too far from a description of Isabel Colegate's own attitude. Her tone is cool, often amusing and amused, but she is never witty *at the expense* of her characters. Her occasional excursions into broader humour are rescued partly by unobtrusive affection and partly by accuracy of reaction to the farcical moment (communard Gerda, naked among the raspberry canes in order to prove a point, is torn between principle and embarrassment when children unexpectedly appear). Passion and madness are also kept in proportion by calm and unlingering, if acute, observation.

> *Gillian Wilce, "No Abiding City," in* New Statesman, *Vol. 98, No. 2521, July 13, 1979, p. 63.*

FRANCIS KING

From Bishop Berkeley and Southey to D. H. Lawrence and Middleton Murray, people who have regarded themselves as members of a spiritual or intellectual elite have often dreamed of setting up with their peers some ideal community in which they will be free from the ugliness, selfishness and contention of a far from ideal world. . . . Unfortunately, members of a spiritual or intellectual elite tend to generate as much ugliness, selfishness and contention as ordinary mortals, sometimes even more. . . .

That the Utopia described by Miss Colegate [in *News from the City of the Sun*] should have lasted from the early Thirties to the Seventies seems to me . . . highly unlikely; but once one has accepted this basic implausibility, what follows convinces. . . .

In general, Miss Colegate gets all her period details right, even if, in doing so, she sometimes gives a sense of undue effort. This effortfulness is most apparent when she is writing of the sort of things—life in the RAF for example—of which she had obviously had no first-hand experience. Her prewar world is one in which people still talk without embarrassment of 'hookies' and 'Yids', in which they can confess to 'having the blues', and in which adherence to pacifism, anarchism, vegetarianism, nudism or free love can still scandalise and shock.

The book is at its best in its creation of slightly outsize comic characters and in its recording of dialogue in which people who take themselves too seriously reveal their essential absurdity. . . .

Miss Colegate has the kind of deep-breathed, long-paced style that suggests a pen being dipped into an ink-pot rather than the clatter of an electric typewriter. There are too many characters for a novel of this length and some of them are either inadequately realised or . . . are grossly overdrawn. But she has produced a work that, even if it sometimes overreaches itself, is always a civilised pleasure to read.

> *Francis King, "Communal," in* The Spectator, *Vol. 243, No. 7880, July 21, 1979, p. 24.*

JOHN NAUGHTON

[The Edwardian era is] a time of which it could truly be said that the upper classes never had it so good. But the shadow of the Great War looms over the period for those who now try to recollect it.

Which is why a convincing evocation of the last Edwardians is more likely to spring from the pen of a novelist than from the soured memoirs of survivors. The languid realism of Isabel Colegate's new novel [*The Shooting Party*] shouldn't therefore come as a surprise. That it does is a tribute to her skill at disinterring the nuances of a buried and—at least by the standards of contemporary egalitarian posturings—discredited past.

For her stage, Ms Colegate has chosen the epitome of Edwardian snobbery and fatuity—the country-house shooting party. The time is autumn 1913, the place the Oxfordshire estate of an amiable old cove, Sir Randolph Nettleby, Bart. Sir Randolph is a country gent of the old school, don't you know, interested ultimately only in fishin', shootin', keepin' one's end up in society and makin' sure that the tenants are housed and watered. . . .

Being an hospitable sort, Sir Randolph invites some crack shots down to give them the pleasure of slaughtering the slow-flying, cumbersome birds that he and his gamekeeper have been rearing all year. The shots bring their wives and servants. The cast includes many of the classic Edwardian stereotypes: the usual proportion of utter prats; a boneheaded Earl; a brilliant young barrister; a horsey young lady; a brace of flighty wives; and the odd decent skin. There is a modicum of sexual intrigue, and an outbreak of the damndest competitiveness among the sharpshooters, which eventually leads one of them to shoot more than the birds. . . .

Not much of a plot, really, and vaguely predictable from the outset. But it's all Ms Colegate needs to build up a stunning picture of the British upper classes at the pinnacle of their evolution. Through the story of the developing rivalry between the men she weaves several other threads: the running of a largish country house; the relations between masters and servants, and between children and parents; the elaborate social ritual embodied in 'good form'; the thought-processes of a decent country squire; the view from the gamekeeper's lodge. The whole canvas is tinted in with a deftness that is quite exquisite. After Ms Colegate, shootin' will never be the same again.

> *John Naughton, ''Good Shot,'' in* The Listener, *Vol. 104, No. 2677, September 4, 1980, p. 313.**

LORNA SAGE

[*The Shooting Party* is about a] country-house weekend in 1913 at which several marriages, several thousand pheasants and one member of the labouring classes bites the dust. Ms Colegate is gently ironic, skilful, sensitive. The effect is gently consoling (the end of an era etc.) and, perhaps appropriately, rather dull.

> *Lorna Sage, ''Havoc on the Campus,'' in* The Observer, *September 7, 1980, p. 29.**

FRANCIS KING

The period [of *The Shooting Party*] is 1913 and the two competitors are Lord Hartlip, arrogant in his assumption that he is one of the finest shots in the country, and Lionel Stephens, a younger man, 'one of those all-round athletes who can't go wrong at any sport.' Hartlip is so much obsessed with his one outstanding skill that he either does not notice or does not care about the manifold infidelities of his wife—the daughter of a rich industrialist, whom he has married for her money. Stephens is deeply in love with the wife of another of the guns;

but, though she reciprocates this love, she differs from Hartlip's wife in considering adultery, however discreet, to be inadmissible. (p. 25)

Inevitably, in this prewar society, there are hordes of servants, who enjoy a curious symbiosis, both parasites and hosts, with their masters and mistresses. On some occasions, the servants appear to be doing the living, as they do so much else, for the people who employ them; on others, it is the employers who appear to be doing the living for the employed. When Hartlip and Stephens are competing, their loaders enter into a rivalry no less intense and ruthless. Similarly, when Stephens writes a highflown letter to the woman whom he loves and then throws it into the waste-paper basket, his man retrieves it, reads it in secret in the boiler-room, and then decides to transcribe it and send it to his own sweet-heart, one of the maids.

Into this world, dedicated to an ancient ritual of slaughter, there irrupts the Future, in the faintly absurd person of middle-class, urban, 'progressive' Mr Cardew. (Alone of all her characters, he receives little respect and no affection from Miss Colegate.) Mr Cardew has many of the tastes and beliefs of Bernard Shaw but none of his authority, intellect or—worst deficiency in this company—style. In an attempt to stop the massacre, he parades in front of the guns with a placard proclaiming 'Thou shalt not kill'; but his intervention is as ineffective as that of any pacifist in the war that is to follow within the year. (pp. 25-6)

As Miss Colegate swiftly and deftly takes up now this patrician life, now this plebeian one, the sense of imminent tragedy lours more and more heavily. Who is to fall victim? Is it to be merely the wild duck (echo of Ibsen) that is the beloved pet of the host's and hostess's strange, precocious grandson? Is it to be the grandson himself? Is it to be the son of the game-keeper? Or silly, self-righteous but long-sighted Mr Cardew? When the tragedy does at last strike, there is surprise both in the choice of victim and in the manner, as much farcical as tragic, of his dying, his face full of shot. The Great war prefigured by that death may, of course, also be regarded as both a farce and a tragedy; and like the unwitting victim of the intense rivalry between Hartlip and Stephens, so the victims of that war met their deaths with scant ideas of why they were dying.

Miss Colegate invests the beauty of the Oxfordshire estate in autumn with a grave, poetic melancholy. The same melancholy seems, like an autumnal mist, to cling about her characters even at their most buoyant and boisterous—as they play childish hide-and-seek, consume lavish meals, or carry on their intrigues with each other. The leaves are already falling; and this privileged order is about to fall too. . . .

[This book], in general, provides a marvellous evocation of a period that Miss Colegate is far too young to have lived through. Like Chekhov, with his doomed landlords talking their lives into extinction, so Miss Colegate, with her no less doomed aristocrats acting out their bloody charade of the shooting party to come, has found a perfect metaphor for the passing of a way of life. (p. 26)

> *Francis King, ''Big Shots,'' in* The Spectator, *Vol. 245, No. 7940, September 13, 1980, pp. 25-6.*

JACK BEATTY

[In *The Shooting Party,* the] country setting, the elegiac mood, the shooting party itself are straight out of Jean Renoir's *Rules of the Game* and, as in that classic French film, we are treated to the kind of "the race is dying out" philosophizing we would miss if it weren't there. The characters are English versions of the bunch from *Rules of the Game*; there is even a poacher, pressed into service to help beat the game out of the woods. There are romances, infidelities, secrets sordid and sad. There are representatives of the classes and of the rural masses. There is a crank Tolstoyan who shows up to demonstrate against the slaughter of the animals just at the very worst moment, and how I wish this preachy presence had never shown up at all!

But the spur to the action is the competition between two members of the party, Lionel Stephens and Lord Hartlip, the latter a crack shot jealous of his reputation. Sir Randolph disapproves of this outbreak of the invidious; he holds to the old view that gentlemen shouldn't compete. When nevertheless they do, shooting hares and pheasants in a mad frenzy, the barbarity of the shooting party breaks out of its ritualized form, and a man is killed.

The shoot itself can't compete with Renoir's massacre for visceral revulsion. But if literature lacks the immediacy of film, it has its compensating resources, and these Ms. Colegate exploits. By enumerating the number of animals killed, for example . . . , she makes the shooting party into a symbolic prevision of "the even bigger shooting party that would begin in Flanders the next year," one in which body counts would be the sole measure of victory.

Ms. Colegate's style, which runs to such charming Edwardianisms as "her heart beat faster in the expectation of its being Charles," is perfectly matched to her subject. And she knows her period detail. . . . But what makes the novel distinctive is her subtle rendering of manners. She knows with what combination of respect and condescension Sir Randolph would address his gamekeeper; knows how Lionel Stephens would sound in a love letter; knows that in this rural England a poor man can die with "God save the British Empire!" on his lips without anyone thinking it odd or mawkish. She explores this world with affection and distance, recording its grace as well as its cruelty, setting it off now from this point of view and now from that in order to see it whole, and finally making it both meaningful and moving. (p. 39)

> *Jack Beatty, in a review of "The Shooting Party,"*
> *in* The New Republic, *Vol. 184, No. 16, April 18,*
> *1981, pp. 38-9.*

MARGARET CROSLAND

Just as women themselves have become more aware of their own rights in society and of their potential in all creative fields, so women writers, and novelists in particular, tend to show more development than ever in their professional lives. Isabel Colegate, for instance, could never have been described as immature, but after twenty-two years of fiction writing she has developed a depth that even her early admirers might not have anticipated. Her trilogy, *Orlando King, Orlando at the Brazen Threshold* and *Agatha,* each title readable in its own right, is concerned with implied problems of morality but, unlike the family sagas of the 1920s and 30s, it is never tedious or predictable. The women characters are totally individual. Agatha is someone to whom we become deeply attached. We regret that by the time she gave her name to the third novel she is

married to the unsatisfactory, not too faithful, Henry; but this is a situation that clearly belongs to real life and not to popular fiction. What will happen to this heroine who, near the end of the novel, is arrested for helping her half-brother escape from the police? We must work this out for ourselves as we finish the last few pages, filled as they are with the two earnest, comical lady booksellers, and the far from comical, intensely contemporary phenomenon, a political demonstration. The year was 1956 and the demonstration anti-Suez. Think, too, of the distance covered between *The Blackmailer* (1958) and *The Shooting Party* (1980), which won an award and deserved all the attention it received. Isabel Colegate not only handles a large group of complex relationships with much economical detail but also presents very clearly her deeply moral preoccupation—the related evils of killing both animals and men—on two levels. Some characters make us aware of the author's message in a subtle way; some, especially the campaigner for animal rights, tell us forthrightly what we ought to think and do. Only a highly skilled writer could have produced such a readable book and risked leaving the relationship between the potential lovers unresolved. (p. 275)

> *Margaret Crosland, "Some Women Writers," in*
> British Book News, *May, 1982, pp. 273-78.**

THE NEW YORKER

Miss Colegate is an English writer chiefly known in this country for her novel **"The Shooting Party,"** which was published here to deserved acclaim in 1981. What we have in [**"Three Novels: The Blackmailer, A Man of Power, and The Great Occasion"**] . . . is her first three published works. They are very different from **"The Shooting Party"** in tone and time and subject, and also very different from one another. They are linked only by a strong consciousness of social class, an ease of manner, and a stunning perception of character. **"The Blackmailer"** (1958) introduces us to a young English officer back from the Korean War with evidence that a fellow-officer, hailed as a hero, was in fact a coward and a traitor. He displays this information to the hero's young widow. Miss Colegate then lets the interestingly complicated characters of the blackmailer and his victim take over and strangely pervert their businesslike relationship. In **"A Man of Power"** (1960) Miss Colegate gives us a kind of English "The Great Gatsby." . . . Everything, and nothing, happens [in **"The Great Occasion"** (1962)]: we watch [the characters] . . . grow, change, fulfill their different fates; we experience their lives and enrich our own. This is the strength of **"The Great Occasion"** and, to a lesser extent, of its two predecessors. (pp. 158-59)

> *A review of "Three Novels: The Blackmailer, A Man*
> *of Power, and The Great Occasion," in* The New
> Yorker, *Vol. LX, No. 12, May 7, 1984, pp. 158-59.*

DOROTHY WICKENDEN

To the uninitiated, the comedies of manners which England's lady novelists have specialized in for centuries must look something like the English garden: intricately plotted, pleasingly clipped and symmetrical, but a bit too tame, too pretty. American reviewers tend to lavish upon novels of this genre (what might be called the Jane Austen school of English letters, since she is invariably invoked) such adjectives as "luminous," "elegant," "skillful," "elegiac"—as if to say, "She's very good, if you like that sort of thing." In fact, increasing numbers of readers here seem to like it very much. . . . In 1980 Viking Press imported an author virtually unknown to Americans, with the publication of Isabel Colegate's ninth novel, *The Shooting Party*. And this month Viking/Penguin comes out with an omnibus edition of her first three: *The Blackmailer* (originally published in England in 1958), *A Man of Power* (1960), and *The Great Occasion* (1962).

The Shooting Party—the story of a pheasant hunt and an inadvertent murder at a sprawling country estate in Oxfordshire just before the outbreak of World War I—received an exuberant reception here, and can fairly be characterized as of the Jane Austen school. It is indeed luminous, elegant, skillful, elegiac—and, to my mind at least, both rarefied and dull. Not so Colegate's first three works of fiction. Twenty-five years ago she showed little of Austen's circumspection—or [Elizabeth] Taylor's narrowness or [Barbara] Pym's fastidiousness—as she exposed some decidedly impolite truths about polite society in contemporary England.

These three novels are remarkable not so much for their themes—the standard British sardonic blend of love and power and class—as for their verve and versatility. They are the work of a young writer (Colegate was in her twenties when she wrote them) with an unfaltering voice, a distinctive comic sensibility, and a sure moral vision. Moreover, a clear progression can be seen as she moved from one novel to the next, experimenting with various methods and points of view. All concern self-made men—ambitious, intelligent, self-consciously cultivated, and personally tormented. And all teach their own wry lessons in humility, for Colegate can no more resist piercing inflated pride than hypocritical social convention.

Her first novel—whose hero, a young lawyer and novice blackmailer, is deluded in his belief that he can worm his way into the higher reaches of society by his own cleverness—is a broad social comedy. In the course of his plotting, Baldwin Reeves discovers to his astonishment that his brazen wickedness is no match for the subtle evils of his social superiors. Colegate's second, *A Man of Power*, which focuses on an immensely wealthy property tycoon whose determination to marry a beautiful and aristocratic (and, as it turns out, venomous) socialite leads to a suicide and several shattered lives, is a highbrow suspense novel. . . . The third novel, *The Great Occasion*, is a melodrama of family strife, with an overbearing patriarch at its center. Gabriel Dobson, unlike the heroes of the first two, is an older man who has honorably entered the world of the well connected—only to learn that his personal life is as empty as the standards he so religiously adheres to. As Colegate's interests narrowed from a desire to crack the social code to a determination to probe the contradictions of character, her talents as a novelist expanded. (pp. 38-9)

Colegate is as astute about the psychological underpinnings of her characters' behavior as she is about their comic potential. This can be seen most clearly in Baldwin. . . . Baldwin is a fat, greedy, friendless self-seeker who is hopelessly inept with women. Yet his cheerful acknowledgment of his faults makes him oddly endearing—even, despite herself, to Judith. Amidst all of the humorous subplots and byways of this novel, Colegate carefully follows the erratic intimacy that develops between victim and tormentor, and by the end their roles have reversed: the priggish Judith has become Baldwin's tormentor and Baldwin has shown her the meaning of moral courage. Only once does Baldwin venture to kiss her, unsuccessfully, of course.

A standard feature of Colegate's characters is an intense self-consciousness which makes spontaneity impossible. For all their anguished introspection, they are ill equipped to cope with the crises, however small, which periodically disrupt every life—conventional and unconventional alike. (p. 39)

In her foreword, Colegate says that *The Great Occasion* "was the first book of which I drew a diagram before I started to write," and that her chief concern was with "technique—simply the mechanics of carrying forward, and maintaining interest in, a number of characters who are not necessarily in the same place but upon whom there is equal emphasis in the scheme of the novel." It is thus surprising that this novel largely overcomes the mechanistic qualities of the first two, and certainly of her last. The energy which Colegate brought to *The Blackmailer* and *A Man of Power* is the source of their strengths but also of their weaknesses. As *The Great Occasion* attests, a generous imagination need not rely upon a welter of comic props and a succession of startling revelations to sustain the reader's interest. It is not the brisk plot which carries this novel, or the cleverly interlocking ironies and social commentary, but the funny and tragic muddling through of one family.

Colegate downplays the intellectual breadth and wit of her early ventures into fiction. "The four novels I wrote over the next ten years were different, more ambitious and more intense, more nervous perhaps," is the way she prefaces this collection. "Anyway these three seem to me now to be the ones I wrote instinctively and without difficulty; this makes me remember them with indulgence and feel pleased to see them in print again." There is no need to regard them with indulgence. Unlike her clumsy heroes and her youthful heroines, she intuitively understands all about the "hateful little sounds" that social creatures make as they scrabble after the unattainable. (p. 41)

Dorothy Wickenden, "Social Climbers, Family Blunders," in The New Republic, *Vol. 190, No. 21, May 28, 1984, pp. 38-41.*

WENDY LESSER

Three of the best novels published recently are not actually recent publications: they are the . . . reissue of Isabel Colegate's first three works, *The Blackmailer, A Man of Power,* and *The Great Occasion*. . . . *The Blackmailer,* which first appeared in 1958, is a Pinter-like tale about a young publisher named Judith Lane, widow of war hero Anthony Lane and mistress of a household managed by a midget named Jean-Claude. . . .

A Man of Power is a similarly strange book, a modern version of Henry James's *The Awkward Age*. . . .

The third novel, *The Great Occasion,* is a family chronicle about the growing-up of five daughters. . . . As in the other two novels, the characters of *The Great Occasion* are distinct, persuasive, and extremely moving; and the plot is worthy of them, consisting of solid events in which they function powerfully, as opposed to the character-mangling machinations or the utter aimlessness of much recent fiction. All three novels end rather abruptly, but that too is part of their odd form of realism: they do not close down their characters, but simply offer them a temporary home. And if these three novels seem old-fashioned in some ways, they are quite modern in others—in the very good descriptions of sexual encounters, for instance. You can see Colegate's characters falling in love through the words they speak. . . . (p. 471)

[If] you like E. M. Forster and Henry James—if you have run out of novels of that sort—you will be delighted to discover Isabel Colegate. . . .

[These] novels are not mere outpourings, but the skilled work of a talented young writer who definitely had something to say. (p. 472)

> *Wendy Lesser, ''The Character As Victim,'' in* The Hudson Review, *Vol. XXXVII, No. 3, Autumn, 1984, pp. 468-82.**

Robert (White) Creeley
1926-

American poet, novelist, short story writer, essayist, and editor.

Creeley was one of the originators of the "Black Mountain" school of poetry, along with Charles Olson, Robert Duncan, and Denise Levertov. Citing Ezra Pound and William Carlos Williams as their literary forebears, these poets developed the theory of "projective verse"—a poetry designed to transmit the poet's emotional and intellectual energy directly and spontaneously, depending on natural speech rhythms and lines determined by pauses for breathing. Creeley's frequently quoted statement, "Form is never more than an extension of content," expresses an important precept of the Black Mountain poets. Creeley considers the writing of a poem an effective means of self-discovery and emphasizes the process or act of writing more than the final result. Contemporary visual art and music were crucial to the formation of his technique. Like Abstract Expressionism and modern jazz, Creeley's poems are reductive renderings of precise images and emotions, and he employs unusual syntax, punctuation, and grammar. Because his work is intensely self-examining, Creeley has been called a solipsistic poet whose references are often too personal and result in obscurity and narrowness of vision. Nevertheless, many critics have followed Creeley's career with interest and consider him an influential force in contemporary poetry.

Creeley taught at Black Mountain College in North Carolina in the early 1950s and was an editor of its innovative literary journal, the *Black Mountain Review*. Although he published several books of poetry during this period, Creeley did not receive widespread recognition until 1962, when *For Love: Poems 1950-1960* appeared. This book, which established him as an important poet, presents several of the concerns that occur throughout his work, particularly his focus on language and his preoccupation with human relationships. Creeley's experimental approach to language is evident in *Words* (1965), his next major volume, in which he explores the capacity of words for representing such complex emotions as love, longing, isolation, and loneliness.

Many critics have cited *Pieces* (1968) as Creeley's most unorthodox book. The poems in this volume are austere and laconic; some consist of only a few words. Some reviewers found this sparseness indicative of an inherent shallowness in Creeley's poetry, while others applauded the results of his linguistic experiments. *A Day Book* (1972) and *Thirty Things* (1974) are extensions of this trend, but the poems collected in *Later: New Poems* (1979) reveal Creeley's movement toward less compressed, more articulate poetry. In this work and in *Mirrors* (1983), critics detected a heightened awareness of aging, death, and memory, along with a continued focus on human relationships. *The Collected Poems of Robert Creeley: 1945-1975* (1983) provoked debate among critics as to whether Creeley's stature in American poetry is justified.

M. L. Rosenthal observed that *The Collected Prose of Robert Creeley* (1983) "provides an intricate texture of sensibility that is a most useful backdrop for Mr. Creeley's often cryptic, self-concealing, riddling poetry." Creeley's prose shares with his

Photograph by Bruce Jackson

poetry an emphasis on language. The stories in *The Gold Diggers and Other Stories* (1965), for instance, focus more on charting the individual consciousness than on such traditional realms of fiction as plot and character development. Similarly, Creeley's novel *The Island* (1963) chronicles a writer's struggles with his deteriorating marriage and his own creativity; it explores, as John G. Hammond noted, "the insularity of language, which causes a fear and difficulty of expression," and which "is also a common poetic theme for Creeley."

Whether praised as skillful and exact or condemned as obscure and ultimately barren, Creeley's work has generated considerable reaction and debate. Since his days as an instructor at Black Mountain College and a founder of the Black Mountain movement, Creeley has been a major influence on younger writers and an important, often startling voice in American literature.

(See also *CLC*, Vols. 1, 2, 4, 8, 11, 15; *Contemporary Authors*, Vols. 1-4, rev. ed.; and *Dictionary of Literary Biography*, Vols. 5, 16.)

JASCHA KESSLER

Containing the work of 30 years, [*The Collected Poems of Robert Creeley: 1945-1975*] offers a clear view of his career.

Granted what all his admirers declare, that Creeley has created an unusual and idiosyncratic syntax for his utterance, a form of halting, compressed speech, direct and plain, what more might be observed? What does the 640 pages show us? I think we can begin to discern a poet who has worked in a very narrow vein, and who indeed has only a few themes, a poet who has not much imagination, or has suppressed it, and has modelled himself in his very tightly-restricted vocabulary on the lines of the formalist and the minimalist in the other arts: his preferred gesture is that of a few, short, severe, toneless, colorless, or neutral lines on the white page. Perhaps as many as 400 of the 640 pages are scarcely touched by the printer's ink. Creeley is both laconic, succinct, abbreviated, and frequently deliberately obscure to boot. The obscurity is not that of deep, or profound, or concentrated thought; nor is it analogous to the kind of abstraction you see developing in the careers of painters like Kandinsky, Klee, Mondrian, Malevitch, Gorky, Miro, or Albers, for example. Instead, it is a quirky obscurity, masking a kind of emptiness, a void in which passions and emotions have not been distilled but in fact repressed. Curiously enough there is still a great deal of tension, of power stored up in the work collected from 1945 to 1960, and that tension comes from Creeley's main theme, which is that of the troubador, or balladeer, the singer of love songs to women and about women. And often enough there is a good deal of laughter in his love poems. It is as if love and loving are his destiny and his doom: his destiny because he wants the warmth of the woman's gift, both emotionally and physically, like a little boy who sings not for supper but that he may crawl into the comforts of bed, and yet knows with the grown man's irony that the Beloved Woman judges both the singer's conduct and his song too, and that often enough, while she will reject the former, she yet can be induced to relent for the sake of the ballad made for her. In love songs, Creeley is at his best, though often enough the perpetual and petulant, adolescent too, guilty and begging for forgiveness and comforting.

Creeley also realizes that his way of life, as a man of words, that is, and words addressed to the form of the woman in his mind, makes him a suspect person. Much of his poetry is concerned with the problem of speaking words, and conveying to those who hear them, or read them, the images that occur in his mind, images of the world, its simplest elements—trees, waters, sky, earth and roads—and images of the world he remembers, his memories. And memories include dreams and images that may have no corresponding reality. Many poems, especially in the second 15 years, when they are not dedicated to friends and lovers, are concerned to record experience in the present, and much of that experience is pared down. . . . So that one might say that Creeley is a Puritanical, sceptical poet, reducing the world to the place that Beckett's characters often speak from, though without the richness of Beckett's language and power of his prose rhythms, and reducing the world so as to try to say something valid, at least. That is the road to solipsism. One feels after long reading of Creeley that he has always struggled against solipsism, that form of thought in which only the operations of the thinker's thoughts in language are real presences, and in which the poet's expression of what occurs to him utters a condition of absolute solitude that all other reading and thinking minds can recognize as their own too.

Oddly enough, though Creeley has been praised for his presence among what is still nostalgically called the avant-garde in America, it seems ever clearer to me that the poet he most resembles in form and manner is Emily Dickinson . . . , her qualities being those of privacy, solitude and concisely-uttered agony. The big difference between them is that the intervening hundred years have removed from Creeley's perspective all that makes Dickinson great: her profound spirituality, her knowledge of the transcendent in human existence, which casts a radiant aura over all of reality. What remains to Creeley is his stubbornly persistent recognition that he will be true to his own nature only, no matter how small a room in life it has made for him. In the last few hundred pages of poems, Creeley repeats over and over most of the poems he had made in the decades earlier, except that he seems to have lost his laughter and irony. Longing and acceptance have taken their place, among the few things left to him.

Jascha Kessler, in a review of "The Collected Poems of Robert Creeley: 1945-1975," in a radio broadcast on KUSC-FM—Los Angeles, CA, March 23, 1983.

JOHN WILSON

A collected poems should help us toward more definitive judgments where they have not already been made. Creeley's *Collected Poems*, as contrary to that occasion as to tradition in general, do no such thing for me. Increasingly his poems, which appeared volume by volume during the fifties, sixties, and seventies, have become "pieces" of an unascertainable whole and now under one cover further lose their autonomy, especially from *Words* on, and become sometimes fascinating, sometimes frustrating, and sometimes fribbling entries in a lifetime daybook.

In the respect that his poems do tend to run on (in fitful cat-like leaps from point to point) even across the boundaries of individual books, Creeley resembles two of his masters, Williams and Zukofsky—Williams in that he writes poems about the things around him, his immediate experience, everyday, often seizing what is directly present to the mind for the purpose of *forming* a poem; and Zukofsky in the degree to which Creeley shares Zukofsky's belief that "a poet writes one poem all his life, a continuing *song*." If Whitman's *Leaves of Grass* and Pound's *Cantos* are prefixed to Williams, Zukofsky, and Creeley, it's possible to see Creeley at the extreme end of a loose tradition that he has embraced in these poets: a rejection of or profound distancing from the traditional English verse, close attention paid to developments in the other art forms, a trust in one's own ear and instinct to measure lines, a will to experiment and push poetry into new expression, and a sense that individual poems are in a way stanzas ("pieces," "boxes") of an on-going life's work. But Creeley is an extreme narrowing of them all. (p. 233)

What I call Creeley's narrowness is in fact a shared trait in all the arts of the fifties and sixties. More than any other poet, I think, Creeley reflects the direction that especially painting and secondarily jazz had taken in the mid-century. By the time he began *Pieces* (in the late sixties), Creeley had adopted a poet's equivalent method of action painting, or Abstract Expressionism. The *act* of writing became the determining force behind his forms. . . . While Williams pieced particulars together, often like a Braque collage and in strikingly original associations, Creeley tries to get the act of perceiving and thinking more than the thing perceived or thought. Writing this way necessarily leads him into a greater abstractness, but the abstractness is infused with emotion—Abstract Expressionism. His language, like Pollock's paint, breaks away from representation and traditional order. His sentences appear to or go astray again and again, the grammar breaks down, the focus jumps, continuousness becomes a string of isolated moments of activity. . . . The strong sense of isolation felt in [*Pieces*] and elsewhere in Creeley's poetry is worked into the form, then. Or as Creeley would prefer it, the form extends from the content. And moment separated from moment, impulse from impulse, are not forced into a unity. "My plan is," Creeley reveals late in *Pieces*, "these little boxes/make sequences." (pp.234-36)

Extremists of experimental art always run the risk of leaving behind them the art form in which they are attempting to work with originality. When Pollock first started pouring paint onto canvas he confessed to his wife that he didn't know if he was making paintings or not. Williams felt the same about *Paterson:* "I don't even know if *Paterson* is poetry. I have no form, I just try to squeeze the lines up into pictures." Creeley has never to my knowledge worried about straying away from poetry as if there were some recognizable confines. . . . The successes and failures in Creeley's writing have almost nothing to do with those things around which introductions to poetry are organized: meter, rhyme, metaphor. . . . Rather the quality of an emotion and the intrinsic interest of the language, as we confront them, are what matter. And there are plenty of instances of Creeley's reductive impulse shearing away almost everything to which we might respond, except with a "hmm. . ." . . . . Creeley's failures, however, are not failures of execution, but failures of experimentation. (pp. 237-38)

It wasn't until *Words* that Creeley started to avoid closure consciously so that his reader, instead of feeling a poem "click shut," as Yeats said it should, is left in motion, still active, headed toward the next poem. In the poems that precede *Words*, one often senses that Creeley wanted to lock this one up, to finish it, to perfect it (bring it to final form). Ironic, bitter, clever, catchy as these poems can be, they are noticeably "poetic" in ways that the later ones are not. **"The Flower,"** for example, is constructed upon a single conceit; in **"Naughty Boy"** there's a fully realized dramatic situation told in third person; **"A Marriage"** offers the clean symmetry of a fairytale turned into poem. These are all fine poems, as are **"Oh No," "Kore," "The Gift," "If You,"** and others; and very likely they will remain better known than the poems in *Words, Pieces, In London,* and more recent books—for the most part, quite simply because they are more self-contained and come closer to fulfilling the usual expectations readers, and anthologists, have for a poem. But Creeley himself, the perceiving, thinking, feeling man, and sometimes poet, is more intimately discoverable in the less "poetic" later works.

Ultimately, this is what we want to know of an author: what do you think, what do you see, what do you feel, what do you know, what have you done? All of these questions should be asked again with *how*. The redoubled questioning serves to address us to both the man and the style, the substance and technique. There are times when the two may become one consideration, when Creeley indentifies completely with the language he speaks in **"The Charm,"** or when the isolate moments of his life become isolate "boxes" in *Pieces*, or when his nervous agitation and fragmentariness come through in the narrow lines that fracture between phrases, often even in the middle of words. . . . The form, which Creeley's salient mid-century formulation claimed to be an "extension of content," seems to me to be more an extension of emotion than of the subjects that find their way into his poems. In other words, emotion is his content. (The Neo-Expressionist Susan Rothenberg recently has made this exact statement about her paint-

ings.) And the themes that recurrently provoke Creeley to write poems are love between man and woman, the pain of marriage (as he has come to know it), his own isolation, and the activity of his own mind and language and the fear that they are capable of generating.

The complicated feelings that I have toward Creeley are not relieved by his poems on love. Lawrence and Williams have both influenced Creeley's view of love as an instinctual urge sometimes very destructive, but the older writers are pretty beside Creeley. . . . The analogy in *In London* between "Love's faint trace" and "The smell of stale air / in this cramped room" in which "shit falls," . . . is simply a crude departure from "old ways" of writing on love. That is, Creeley is more intent on trying to "change the record" than to express how love feels: "Tracking through this / interminable sadness- // like somebody said, / change the record," he writes in another poem called **"Love."** Creeley so assiduously tries to avoid the clichés on love that he tends to mistake it for sheer violence here and hormonal secretions there. (pp. 241-43)

If love is rarely gentle, marriage is rarely peaceful. Years ago, X. J. Kennedy found Creeley's most interesting subject to be the "horrors of marriage"—spouses divided in their desires and therefore isolated, spouses violently ripping at each other . . . or, worse yet, spouses undergoing the customary concessions that imply, to Creeley, a gradual weakening of their emotional bond. . . . But these were not the terms of Creeley's marriage to Bobbie as revealed in the poems from *Words* on, especially in the last book, *Away*, where the intensity of their marriage and the difficulty they had living together come clearly to the surface, clearly and painfully—for how is there to be a marriage without recurrence and through the intense solitude that Creeley lives in each day?

In the end, Creeley's life comes through most often as intensity, whether it be love's intensity, the intensity of his own isolation, of his marriage or attempts to make language express what he feels. This is at once a virtue and an impediment in Creeley. His range as a poet in all regards is severely restricted, but along the narrow track that his mind has taken he carries Modernism into new territory, spooky (like Beckett's) but new. Near the end of *Away* Creeley puts together his feelings in a single, powerful poem of nine lines (**"Phone"**) which conveys his most familiar situation:

> What the words
> abstracted, tell:
> specific agony,
>
> pain of one so
> close, so distant—
> abstract here—
>
> Call back, call
> to her—smiling voice.
> Say, it's all right.

"Selfishly // alone" Creeley confesses to be, so he must be even when he tries to be otherwise—so that he can hear the words detached, abstracted, assuming form, to tell his pleasure, agony. A man alone, writing. It's Creeley's art, compelling, repellent, and it goes on now in the eighth year after the latest poem in this notable collection, toward old age. (pp. 243-45)

John Wilson, "Modernism's Narrowing," in The Iowa Review, *Vol. 13, Nos. 3 & 4, (Spring), 1982 (1983), pp. 233-45.*

KENNETH FUNSTEN

[**"The Collected Poems of Robert Creeley: 1945-1975"**] represents, as John Ashbery writes on its back cover, "about the best we have." At 600-plus pages, it begs to be compared to the parents of modern poetry—collected works of Baudelaire, Hardy, Stein and others. That Creeley chooses to reprint *everything* written within the 30-year period, for book, broadside or magazine, speaks for itself. "Here I am," this volume hollers. "Now judge me!"

Exploring both "projective" and stanzaic verse, Creeley takes for subject the personal void, the ultimate loneliness of life, that empty space we each define between living and death. Jumbling common syntactical order is one of his most provoking techniques; it frequently allows him to focus attention on words as *individual words* and the way readers take for granted their agreed-upon interactions. Thin, monometer lines emphasize this solitude for both word and man. . . .

Creeley—as a student of Charles Olson and a seminal member of the Black Mountain School during the 1950s—found early notoriety. His **"For Love"** (1962) wowed the public with its minimalist distance and telegraphic formality. Underlying the individual poems was an implied narrative of love shattered and bitter.

These **"Collected Poems"** will also be hailed and heralded, but in the end Creeley disappoints when the spacy self-obsession of **"For Love"** dries into the tired mannerism of his later volumes. Readers of complete works rightfully expect writers to improve with time or know why, and 30 years of watching this same "dancer / of my own dismay" become not only predictable but boring. Nerves on edge like some frayed housewife, the poet ultimately repeats the same tricks time after time. In this later work, Creeley ossifies into poisoned self-parody, stunted and dulled. . . .

That he may nevertheless be currently "the best we have" is not disputed. But if he is, our time's poetry is in worse shape than most suspect. Who will choose to read all of Creeley in 100 years when the reader could as well lift up Robert Frost, William Carlos Williams or Wallace Stevens? Creeley—like Olson—is a dead-end.

> *Kenneth Funsten, in a review of "The Collected Poems of Robert Creeley: 1945-1975," in* Los Angeles Times Book Review, *April 17, 1983, p. 8.*

KARL KELLER

[Three] decades of work (and now almost one more) have established Robert Creeley gently, slyly in the canon of great American poets. First as one of the finer voices to do the Black Mountain voice: "is there a name / for it? What is there, after all, to explain?" Then as lyrical love-maker and lovable lyric-maker at the fringe of the Beats and the post-Beats. . . . Then a phase as balladeer, as Renaissance *flaneur,* as light strummer, light dancer: "for who sings, dies, / what goes, will go on." And the most recently as minimalist, as fragmenter, as reductionist to little boxes that make sequences. . . .

[In **"Collected Poems"** we see him] turning toward us with ever fresher and sweeter brief moments—largely without image, without rhetoric, even with "no meaning, / no point." Each is, and without momentum, *now* (and now cumulatively) the making of a presence in the momentary, freeing it for himself—2 lines or 20 lines, a voice singing, a body dancing.

Creeley's poetry has always read like fragments of a great confession, or rather a life fragmented for us and then confessed to with pleasure. . . .

This collection, a great confession in a sure, sweet voice, is words-becoming-body. He has to get down—and so all the white space, all the pieces of moments, the minimalized forms—down to the essential, the love of his woman. . . . That is most often his objective.

Creeley does up pleasure well: "Delight dances, / everything works." . . . And so his poems, all along these three decades, are little songs of joy, little dances of happiness, little gestures full of love—"an easy grace." The world without does not concern him much, his little epiphanies of love do. . . . Creeley likes to laugh, needs to sing. We dance to it.

> *Karl Keller, in a review of "Collected Poems, 1945-1975," in* Los Angeles Times Book Review, *October 30, 1983, p. 12.*

RICHARD TILLINGHAST

Creeley is not, as [claimed by the publisher of **Collected Poems**], a "major poet." Perhaps the categories "major" and "minor" are silly in any case. It has not been his ambition to address in a sustained manner the large human issues that are traditionally associated with major poetry. (p. 501)

If not a pioneer in free verse, Creeley is at least an innovator. His verse refines a way of writing more or less invented by William Carlos Williams, a way of breaking the voice over the poem's characteristically short, nervous lines. A typical Creeley poem is spare, minimalist, a skinny column of words on a white page; something important to the meaning plays out its drama offstage, as in some of Hemingway's stories. Like his contemporaries in the visual arts, Creeley has always been a man with a theory. . . .

Creeley has become a guru to "language poets"—a term whose equivalent in other arts would be "dancing choreographers" or "music composers" or "food chefs." Literary self-consciousness is as old as poetry itself; every poet is a "language poet." In much of Creeley's work, however, particularly after *For Love,* language itself is the exclusive focus, thereby positing an ideal reader who is a philosopher of language. Wittgenstein would have spent many happy hours with Creeley's poems. My own reactions I can sum up variously, depending on my mood, as: (1) this poetry deliberately avoids communication, for reasons of its own; (2) it is so abstruse that I lose interest; (3) it is simply over my head.

"The interplay between a complex mind and universal (therefore 'simple') emotions" is Denise Levertov's astute description of a central tension in Creeley's poetry. The frequent enjambments that give Williams's poetry some of its lustiness and verve become in Creeley the apt vehicles for expressing a sense of painful inhibition. . . . But he will also be remembered for love poems whose wit, charm and masterly simplicity relate him to Blake and Dickinson and to English ballads and nursery rhymes. . . .

Creeley has not pulled any punches with his readers, and the titles of the collections following *For Love* tell a story: *Words,* which owns up to the reductiveness that "language poets" value in him; and *Pieces,* in which a real disintegration takes place. In the following excerpt from *Pieces,* for example, Creeley presents undigested material from the news under the impression that it will be as meaningful to the reader as it apparently is to him; then he comments on it with a simplistic logic and ends up sounding uncharacteristically pompous:

> Trying to get "our men
>   back" and "our ship
> back"—"tactical
>   nuclear weapons"—dig!
>
> Shee-it. The *world*,
>   dad, is where you
> live unless you've for-
>   gotten it. . .

Filed and forgotten.

But in Creeley's best poems several elements are set in motion. **"Hart Crane,"** for instance, opens with a scene that engages our interest right away:

> He had been stuttering, by the edge
> of the street, one foot still
> on the sidewalk, and the other
> in the gutter . . .

The extreme enjambments suggest Crane's desperation, and he is next drawn out in a complex figure of speech:

> like a bird, say, wired to flight, the
> wings, pinned to their motion, stuffed.

The simile shows both an energetic impulse toward action and a constraint on that action—a common impasse in Creeley. . . .

Creeley has convincingly entered into the strained mental processes of Hart Crane in his extremity. Even if the logic of the poem is tangential and hard to follow, it is still presented within a human context that makes us want to keep up. The later work, unfortunately, is increasingly remote: Whatever vital affect impelled this highly cerebral, disaffected sensibility to ground itself in the things of this world has evaporated. His expression has declined from ***Words*** to ***Pieces***. A dry, truculently casual investigation of language has become the center of his work. (pp. 502-03)

> *Richard Tillinghast, "Yesterday's Avant-Garde," in*
> The Nation, *Vol. 237, No. 16, November 19, 1983,*
> *pp. 501-04.**

CLAYTON ESHLEMAN

Robert Creeley established a solid reputation in the 1950s on the base of a particular kind of brief lyric poem that is a masterful blending of such disparate materials as Thomas Campion's "airs," Charlie Parker's bebop improvisations, hip existential twists and a poetics founded on a devotion to the Muse. While individuals are cited in dedications, the poems themselves speak to a "Lady," or to "Love." . . .

"Mirrors," Creeley's first collection of new poems since 1979, seems overshadowed by **"The Collected Poems 1945-1975."** . . . I'd like to suggest some basic differences between the early poetry and the poetry we find in **"Mirrors,"** and to conjecture about what such differences might mean.

Here is **"A Warning,"** written in the late 1940s or early 1950s. It may have the single most jolting opening stanza ever written by an American poet:

> For love—I would
> split open your head and put

> a candle in
> behind the eyes.
>
> Love is dead in us
> if we forget
> the virtues of an amulet
> and quick surprise.

Illumination is forced into the opening stanza with a power similar to that of the female figure in Picasso's "Guernica" who thrusts a torch into the massacre-laden stable. It is disconcertingly unclear as to how we are to read **"For Love."** Will the poet brutalize a living woman for his ideal of "love"? Or are we to assimilate the violence as a metaphor for the poet's willingness to risk *everything* to keep "love" vital and full of surprise? After all, Creeley also wrote, reflecting on Franz Kline's paintings in 1954, "There is nothing quite so abrupt and even pleasant as rape—ask any woman." As Olson himself pointed out in a 1960 review of **"For Love: Poems 1950-1960"** (whose title is the first two words of this poem), there is a falling off in the second stanza. One feels that Creeley himself is stunned by what he has written and seeks to justify and explain it. (p. 3)

"Self-Portrait" [a poem from **"Mirrors"**], with touches of D. H. Lawrence and Catullus, consists of the talk to oneself that often goes on before an image presents itself that is capable of translating the "talk" into an enactment. As a typical piece in **"Mirrors,"** it is gnawed by aging, and offers itself as explanation in an even less pointed way than the second stanza of **"A Warning."** While I am sympathetic with what Creeley states in **"Self-Portrait,"** I am also aware that such sympathy is a booby prize for the loss of that earlier power that, like it or not, is overwhelmingly *real*.

The significance of the title **"Mirrors"** involves Creeley's confessed failure to find his life meaningful as he ages, to the extent that one situation merely reflects another. Everything becomes "generality," "no thing but echoes," "this whining sickness." The only poems that are bracing—such as **"Mother's Voice"**—are those in which Creeley is able to muster the energy to think his despair and languor into patterns that densify and have an edge. While the subject of "love" makes occasional appearances, most plaintively in regard to the poet's new son, it is almost indistinguishable from the sadness that seeps through this book, like hourglass sand.

Creeley is, of course, entitled to his sadness, and there is a gentle honesty to the writing that evokes Whitman's line, "I am the man, I suffered, I was there." But the problem in affirming such writing is that one must substitute an uninspired truthfulness for imaginative capability as the measure of poetic value. (pp. 3, 7)

> *Clayton Eshleman, "With Love for the Muse in Char-*
> *lie Parker Tempo," in* Los Angeles Times Book
> Review, *March 4, 1984, pp. 3, 7.*

JED RASULA

The Collected Poems of Robert Creeley is a statement of awesome integrity, a sign of that tensile strength inherent in the poems that has held the work together as a whole. A later poem reads in its entirety:

> One day after another—
> perfect.
> They all fit. . . .

In the course of reading there is the inevitable encounter with wave after wave of classic poems you'd want anyone who reads poetry to know—poems which seem to radiate a kind of Green Anthology singularity, from which the name "Creeley" drops away as an excessively personal attachment—poems not of a local historical moment but of a world age. And this is not to mention poems like **"I Know a Man,"** from which others have expropriated titles, attitudes, equatorial psychotropic latitudes and who knows what else. . . . This poem—and many others in the collection—strikes one as so much in the public domain it is literally shocking to be reminded that a man, a specific individual, among us, took care to write it down. A constant, searching suffrage has kept the work intensely private and at the same time relentlessly public. . . .

I can remember no book of poetry published with the accolades this carries on the dust-jacket (by William Carlos Williams, Charles Olson, Edward Dorn, Allen Ginsberg, Denise Levertov, Robert Duncan, Michael McClure, and John Ashbery). Such a list of enthusiasts is impressive not only for the kind of accountability implied for the author. They also remind us that Creeley is *the* poet of the world's simple pleasures, of senses and surfaces, because he is also a poet of the mind's depths and disturbances. Creeley's way of putting us in touch with objects brings to mind the fact of the sheer physical weight of this book, these poems collected *as one*. His poems are evidence of the mind's immediate palpability to itself. As with Donne and some of his contemporaries, Creeley's work is carnal knowledge. His sense is common-sense, available to all, each by each, reflected in poems in which each word counts and is accountable.

Creeley has worked with great delicacy and discrimination *among* words, within a realm where the very small is seen in terms of the really persuasive proportions it assumes in a life cycle. Time and again one finds poems as universal in their applications—yet as patiently particular—as the commonplace phrases that keep us intimate with the language: such as, by the way, in spite of, just in case.

Creeley has always left room, in and around his poems. This is his great generosity within the work, leaving readers room to move. So the size of the present volume is startling, because one thinks of Creeley's roominess and spaciness, not the sheer heft and bulk we have here. But I find the miracle of that spaciousness even more energized, if anything—turned up, as it were, to the volume at hand. The more you read of Creeley the more personal the space becomes, till you're no longer reading poems but handling bright personal implements generously loaned for the occasion.

Don't think of the poems as strictly tools, impersonal, however. Creeley is often so personal that—given a sensibility slightly different, from which a different poetics might emerge—the poems could easily become inconsequential. This *Collected Poems*, read cover to cover, is a persuasive demonstration that Creeley has walked an exceedingly thin, and often harrowing, line. This becomes unavoidably noticeable in *Pieces*, where the formal presentational urge shatters and one is reading literal "pieces" without much guidance as to their placement in "wholes"—where in fact that whole issue is gleefully deferred. But *Pieces*—both as book and as structural centerpiece of the present volume—is as easily a reminder of what Creeley has been up to all along. For every line written down, he has left something else out. His idiom is exclusive, not inclusive; gregarious in its passions, not its associations.

So these poems are really open—in their structures—to psychological strata not necessarily Creeley's own. This has become most noticeable since the publication of *Later*, in which certain psychologizing intentions are more consciously deliberated. But it's certainly discernible again and again in the thirty years' work under review. Which is to say, Creeley somehow manages to leave holes in his poems through which one becomes initiate to psychological reality as such, not strictly mine or his, yours or theirs. The poems are often like those marvelous anatomical illustrations in medical textbooks, where successive transparencies give you the central nervous system, the bloodstream, the skeleton, etc., to be seen in one composite bundle if you like or section by section.

Despite the complex personality behind the poems, then, they readily consent to an ongoing communal process. Surely this is what makes Creeley's poems such intimate, *inherent* companions to any thorough reading of Zukofsky, say, or Olson, or Duncan, or Dorn. It also makes it easier to formulate links with the jazzmen of the late forties and fifties, to whom Creeley has declared allegiance. . . .

The only regret is that such a hefty volume does make a reminder necessary: namely, that the voice, and the story, go on. *Later* is a powerful book. And poems by Creeley published in the last few years in periodicals fuse, as intensively as anything he's done, this private issue of the public.

> *Jed Rasula, "Personal Weight," in* The American Book Review, *Vol. 6, No. 4, May-June, 1984, p. 21.*

BRUCE BAWER

Poems have always been mirrors to Robert Creeley. While the rest of us look on from the sidelines, he stares down at the page and into himself in often perplexing private rituals of self-love and self-hate, self-reverence and self-punishment. As his *Collected Poems 1945-1975* . . . makes abundantly clear, the theme Creeley has kept returning to throughout his career is the detachment of the Self: its isolation in a body, a place, a time—contexts which he is powerless to alter. "Here I / am. There / you are," he asserts laconically in a poem from the 1960s called **"The Finger."** In another Sixties poem, **"Numbers,"** he insists: "You are not / me, nor I you." And in one of five poems titled **"Here"** (for Creeley recycles titles almost as frequently as he does themes) he declares, "No one lives in / the life of another— / no one knows."

As these quotations suggest, it is quite possible to come away from a Creeley poem without being too baffled. What *is* difficult is to come away sated. For, though there are occasional moments of interest (usually when Creeley breaks his rules against figurative language, grammar, syntax, description, and logic), most of those Creeley poems which do not come under the category of "cryptic" are simple trifling. *Mirrors* is, essentially, the mixture as before. Most of the poems, to one degree or another, are minimalistic meditations upon the natural walls that divide Self from Other, present from past, here from there. . . . The book contains Creeley's second poem to be given the title **"There,"** his third **"Time,"** his second **"Dreams"** (if you don't count two earlier poems titled **"Dream"**), and his second **"Echoes"** (not to mention **"Some Echo"**; there are also three earlier poems titled **"Echo"** and one **"Echo Of"**). Choose a poem at random in this book, and you can not only trace its ancestry in the *Collected Poems*, you can hunt up its brothers and sisters elsewhere in *Mirrors*.

Age, death, and old memories seem to be increasingly on Creeley's mind (and when Creeley is writing about age, death, and memory, you can be sure there will be poems titled "Age," "Death," and "Memory"). In some of the poems in *Mirrors*, these preoccupations are expressed memorably. Here, for example, is the Williams-like **"Memory, 1930"**:

> There are continuities in memory, but
> useless, dissimilar. My sister's
>
> recollection of what happened won't
> serve me. I sit, intent, fat,
>
> the youngest of the suddenly
> disjunct family, whose father is
>
> being then driven in an ambulance
> across the lawn, in the snow, to die.

If this poem is above-average Creeley, it's because, though it trods familiar Creeley territory, it does so in comprehensible human terms (and perhaps even with a dash of symbolism, against which the poet has railed extensively). Unlike run-of-the-mill Creeley, **"Memory, 1930"** is blessed with clarity, concreteness, and even a measure of music. That the poet appears in the poem as a child is also unusual; Creeley has heretofore published few poems about his childhood, his parents, or his own children. There are, however, a few such poems in *Mirrors*, and they seem to have taken the place of his hostile-husband and suffering-lover poems, which, with their Berrymanesque combination of self-pity, contentiousness, and adoration (*vide* **"Ballad of the Despairing Husband"**), have more or less bitten the dust. Creeley, in short, seems to be mellowing. (pp. 345-46)

> *Bruce Bawer, in a review of "Mirrors," in* Poetry, *Vol. CXLIV, No. 6, September, 1984, pp. 345-46.*

M. L. ROSENTHAL

Artistically, **"The Gold Diggers"** (1954) and **"The Island"** (1963) are the most rewarding parts of [**"The Collected Prose of Robert Creeley"**]. Despite the introspective intimacy that often makes them rancidly confessional, a certain distancing is provided by their sustained narrative form. Sexual wretchedness and distrust, combined with unresolved adolescent fantasizing, ride the pages, and the stories—like so many Creeley poems—are charged with marital despair and the bafflement of balked communication. Perhaps the most realized story is **"Mr. Blue,"** in which the prevailing insecurity of Mr. Creeley's protagonists is focused on a ferociously powerful-seeming circus midget's gesture toward the hero's wife. In **"The Island"** an American writer and his wife and children drift through a long period, apparently in Majorca, at once privileged and vulnerable. The novella builds up an organic sense of a life without moorings or deep satisfactions, in which loyalties and purposes are mainly improvised adjustments—and yet an open

sensibility keeps itself alive. Husband and wife both have enough of the "passive aggressive" to keep them going indefinitely, whatever may become of them and their children.

The later sections of the collection are increasingly self-indulgent and private, full of detailed sexual fantasy, allusions to literary friends, rambling memories. But there are occasional paragraphs of considerable eloquence and momentary transports of moving reverie, which make for genuine prose poetry. The book provides an intricate texture of sensibility that is a most useful backdrop for Mr. Creeley's often cryptic, self-concealing, riddling poetry. There is some obsessively bad writing and a certain gigantism of self-projection to go with the poet's famous self-minimizing—but that is all part of the old Black Mountain game, and not without its charm.

> *M. L. Rosenthal, "Poets in Search of Self," in* The New York Times Book Review, *September 23, 1984, p. 34.**

JOHN MARTONE

Robert Creeley's poetry discovers the enigma of the ordinary again and again. Typically working with only snatches of conversation, slivers of memory, the barest Derridean traces of life, he has managed to construct a minimalist autobiography of singular beauty and relevance. He has, perhaps more than any other contemporary poet, remained faithful to the truly *common* language, and—paradoxically—his insistence on taking the common world and word as his subject has made him one of the most formally inventive (i.e., distinctive and uncommon) poets of our time.

Mirrors is preoccupied with aging, the contemplation of death and the remoteness of the past. It is a stark book, in which Creeley tells us, "You've had the world, / such as you got. / There's nothing more / There never was." Identity, in this book, is always remembered (the past is more vivid than the present) and—typically—is remembered in the second or third person. Personal memory always seems to belong to someone else, to a banished self. The self is the most ephemeral of all poetic creations.

Mirrors is about the *distance* of reflection, the diffe*ra*nce between the past and present, body and soul. Meditations on that separation, meditations on the moment of death ("breath's caught time") make up some of the book's most powerful poems, such as **"Box."** ... [In the poem **"Oh Max,"** the] pause between "useless" and "words," together with the tension that pause creates, is central to all of Creeley's poetry, and to this collection in particular, his most anguished and powerful so far.

> *John Martone, in a review of "Mirrors," in* World Literature Today, *Vol. 58, No. 4, Autumn, 1984, p. 600.*

Thomas M(ichael) Disch

1940-

(Has also written under pseudonym of Leonie Hargrave, and in collaboration with John Sladek under joint pseudonyms of Cassandra Knye and Thom Demijohn) American novelist, short story writer, editor, and poet.

Disch is known primarily as a science fiction writer whose work displays a keen intelligence and grim wit. In his lecture "The Embarrassments of Science Fiction" Disch contends that science fiction writers should not be so concerned with ideas that they fail to respect literary standards; many critics agree that Disch's own works transcend the limitations of science fiction. Originally associated with the British New Wave of the 1960s, Disch conveys in his writing the characteristic pessimism that differentiated this movement from traditional science fiction. His contributions to the science fiction genre include collections of short stories and poetry as well as novels. He received the O. Henry Prize for his story "Getting Into Death" (1975) and the John W. Campbell Award for the novel *On Wings of Song* (1980).

In his first novel, *The Genocides* (1965), Disch explores a standard science fiction theme—the end of the world. His approach is atypical, however; whereas conventional science fiction portrays intelligent scientists cleverly battling annihilation, Disch creates ineffectual antiheroes who revert to savage behavior in order to survive. Ultimately, humanity is completely destroyed. Similar dark tones and unheroic characters contribute to the dystopian nature of Disch's other works, including *334* (1972) and *On Wings of Song*. Both works realistically present a dying culture in a near-future world beset by overpopulation, depressed economic conditions, and food shortages. Many critics found especially powerful Disch's depiction of a bizarre and fierce future as a logical extension of the present. M. John Harrison comments: "[Disch] shows us in fact that we will greet the future as we greet any other present, by hoping for the best and waiting for the worst, adapting, forgetting as much as possible, muddling through."

Disch has also written several novels outside the science fiction genre. Satirically attacking racism, *Black Alice* (1968) examines a white girl's changing perception of bigotry when her skin is dyed and she becomes a victim of racial prejudice. *Neighboring Lives* (1981), which Disch coauthored with Charles Naylor, is a historical novel about the artistic community of Chelsea during the Victorian Age. *The Businessman* (1984), a work of horror fiction, concerns the haunting of a man by the wife he murdered.

(See also *CLC*, Vol. 7; *Contemporary Authors*, Vols. 21-24, rev. ed.; and *Dictionary of Literary Biography*, Vol. 8.)

© Jerry Bauer

M. JOHN HARRISON

Most science fiction writers carry into their forties and fifties the same potential they showed at twenty, and never fulfil it. (p. v)

Despite this failure or blight, though, the vitality we associate with science fiction . . . *can* be controlled and deployed in a responsible way; the genre can be a vehicle and not just a box in which to shove a young talent until it is hopelessly crippled: and Thomas M. Disch has grown right out of sight to prove it.

Admittedly, he seemed a head taller to begin with. *The Genocides* (1964) with its frightening vistas of human irrelevancy, was peculiar and nerve-wracking, observed from an enormous distance, like some satellite photograph. The short stories were insidious and knowing (not with the sham wisdom of a Bradbury, whose evasive invitation to look how intrinsically *right* the world is could only lead to dishonesty and retreat, but with the self-contained percipience of the young Eliot—'the strength to force the moment to its crisis', and the intention, too). His show of strength, *Camp Concentration* (1968), is a recurring moral nightmare, evilly ironic, an unease which, once the reader is infected by it, never quite goes away; percipience has led to the edge of despair and with the spectre of Sachetti, that fat decaying genius, mouthing from Hell behind him, Disch is committed to balance over the gulf, using his love-hate relationship with humanity, his dreadfully acute powers of observation and his careful technique to explore the way we manage the continuing psychic crisis of being alive. The collection *Getting Into Death* reveals a writer confident of his ability—a stylist, but one who has put pyrotechnic behind him—using the fantastic for his own purposes rather than allowing it to use him, going straight to the visible human world for his subject matter and evoking that world with grace, with wit, and, above all, with honesty.

There are many points at which Disch could have opted for the reiteration which turns insight into cliche, structural innovation into trope, characterisation into stereotyping (after **Camp Concentration,** for instance, it would have been easy to take up the profession of cynic or mannerist, alternative culture polemicist or purveyor of the horrific for its own sake), each providing the opportunity of a comfortable career in the forefront of the genre. Instead, we have *334,* a clear indication of the qualities that separate him from the majority of his generic contemporaries.

334 is a cry for help, a voice from a future not so far off—or, if you like, from a present we may never leave behind. Moving from the onset of one life preprogrammed for failure to the termination of another, beginning with a plea for dignity and ending with one for death, it presents the human evidence of a self-destructive culture, demanding from its reader the toughness of mind to feel compassion for the ordinary and the ugly, the disfigured and the dispossessed, the inhabitants of an overcrowded New York in the 2020s. Birdie Ludd must satisfy the city that he is fit to breed, fit to take up the parody of adulthood which is all its overwhelmed administrative infrastructure can offer him; Mrs. Hanson must persuade society she has nothing left to live for. Welfare workers hover round them with patient defeatism, on wings made of flimsy and computer-tape; the forms are filled in, the tests taken; the 'rights' are inalienable, but it's beggary nonetheless; and nothing much is solved.

Between Birdie and Mrs. Hanson stretches a strange and convoluted narrative made up of five apparently loose-linked personal glimpses of New York life, a lock for which the sixth section makes a key—although that in itself is a thing of complicated chronologies, familial and sexual relationships. The whole not only reproduces accurately the sensation that life is made up of ill-fitting jigsaw pieces, is puzzled and puzzling and sags loosely between one supportive crux and the next, but also gives us the impression of a strange simultaneity, as if despite the time and words, the whole novel separating their personal crises, the adolescent and the old woman are begging in adjoining offices—their voices, filtered through the paper-thin partition walls, joining into one thready mumble of stupefaction and pain. This is the groundwork of the book's unavoidable realism and sense of oppression: a structure which by its very iron control and sophistication conjures a gabble of intercourse, a mess of relationships, a specific crisis seen as a collection of minor crises which rarely come to a head. "We do not boil over," as V. S. Pritchett says, "we leak away." And more important, perhaps, almost nobody is to blame. (pp. vi-viii)

334 isn't so much about the city as about our perception of it, not so much a probable future as commentary on a developing (or rather deteriorating) situation. It lacks the ideological mouthpieces and vast dishonest generalizations of the classic dystopist, the billboard misdirections of Orwell or Heinlein or Huxley; it evades the lassitude of the social novel. All that can be said about it in the end—and this is precisely where its stature is most easily visible—is that it is about people. From the imaginative *tour-de-force* of Morbehanine, the drug that fosters 'responsible dreams', to the monolithic unpleasantness of 334 East 11th Street; from the bitter whimsy of a fake supermarket full of fake food to the deadly lightheartedness of Ab the bodysnatcher; from start to finish, Birdie Ludd to Mrs.

Hanson, this is a novel about *us* and our precarious relationship with the real, narrated as a series of collisions between what the world is and what we would like it to be, between the kind of life we have now and the kind of life it may lead to.

Nothing more could be asked of a piece of science fiction than that it show us people in change; and with so much of today's 'avante garde' science fiction prepared to mark time on some baroque and personal parade ground (where the Wonderful Child, wrinkling a bit around the eyes but still smiling away, is even now receiving his fiftieth passing-out certificate from the Starry Academy), we should be grateful for it. And grateful too for a writer who by some dextrous sleight avoided education in a tradition which demands he view his characters not as human beings but as sparse and utilitarian adjuncts of a plot; who has retained both his fire and his compassion; and who matures steadily before our eyes, giving some hope that science fiction might one day become what it claims to be—a relevant fiction and not merely the capering of dwarves in the hour after dinner. (pp. xii-xiii)

> *M. John Harrison, in an introduction to* 334 *by Thomas M. Disch, Gregg Press, 1976, pp. v-xiii.*

THOMAS D. CLARESON

[Science fiction has] its antiheroes, especially since the 1960s New Wave, represented by writers such as Norman Spinrad and J. G. Ballard. A major achievement of these writers is their reflection of America's complex attitudes toward science and technology—and the future itself. Among the outstanding practitioners of this often pessimistic sub-genre is Thomas M. Disch, perhaps best known for his novel **Camp Concentration.** The dramatic conflict of his latest novel, **On Wings of Song** . . . , rises from man's desire to transcend limitations, in this case both of physical being and entrapment in an America of the near-future which has become fragmented, a virtual police state. By achieving inner harmony (here represented by the act of singing) an individual can literally leave his body in a comatose state; he can "fly." The action centers upon Daniel Weinreb, whose driving ambition is to fly; the initial setting is Iowa, a particularly repressive state dominated by "undergoders," for whom flyng is not only a sin but a crime. . . . Disch neither creates nor emphasizes an elaborate background; he includes only sufficient detail to show that in the future things have changed: Famines are mentioned, and people must pass through a border patrol to enter Minnesota. The narrative develops after Weinreb falls in love with and marries the wealthy Boadicea Whiting, who flies on the attempt they undertake together on the eve of their honeymoon. Weinreb unfortunately does not. Perhaps the novel's only weakness is the lengths at which Disch portrays a decadent New York during the 12-year period when Weinreb cares for his wife's body and attempts to join her in flight. Still, the novel builds to an ambiguous and memorable climax.

> *Thomas D. Clareson, "Galaxy of Tomorrow's Tale,"* in Book World—The Washington Post, *September 23, 1979, p. 7.*

GERALD JONAS

[In **"On Wings of Song"** the] setting is North America sometime in the future. Politically and economically, things seem to be going downhill, but in between crises, people can still assure themselves that they are living in "normal" times. What upsets them most is the invention of a "flight apparatus," which permits certain people to set free their nonmaterial essence—personality? soul?—and go gallivanting around the universe invisibly, while their bodies are maintained in a vegetative state back home. . . .

[Disch is] concerned with the obvious analogies to artistic inspiration, drug highs and orgasmic release. Such concerns are rarely in the forefront of contemporary science fiction except in the garb of allegory, and Mr. Disch's purpose seems far from allegorical. He tells the story of Daniel Weinreb as it might be told by one of Daniel's contemporaries—an author writing for readers who live in the world that has shaped Daniel's character. Indeed, Mr. Disch's primary interest is in delineating character. In a science-fiction context this is at first startling, but as a narrative strategy it is finally self-defeating.

The reason, I think, is that except for an occasional *tour de force,* there is no room in science fiction and fantasy for the traditional novel of character. A science-fiction author may create characters to demonstrate how a change in technology or social organization alters the human condition; or he may invent entire exotic worlds to show how certain human traits—such as passion or greed—take different forms under different circumstances. But the focus is typically on the forces that shape character, rather than on the character development itself. When Daniel sits down to dinner with his family or the family of his fiancée, we learn a great deal about the fragile bonds that tie these people together. Mr. Disch handles these interactions very well. But the emphasis is misplaced, as if a scene from one of O'Neill's family dramas had been inserted into a play by Brecht. I came to resent such scenes as interruptions, excessive in length and inexcusably dull. The more **"On Wings of Song"** resembles a contemporary novel, the less successful it is as science fiction.

> *Gerald Jonas, in a review of "On Wings of Song,"*
> *in* The New York Times Book Review, *October 28,*
> *1979, p. 16.*

JOHN CALVIN BATCHELOR

Thomas M. Disch's excellent seventh novel, *On Wings of Song*—a gay *Candide* set in 21st century Manhattan—confirms that his talent is inadequately characterized if discussed simply in terms of the American pop genre of science fiction. Disch works in the British tradition of dystopian fiction, that is, serious letters about an impaired, make-believe place that is more profoundly modern-times than anything in the media.

Like his literary forbears, such as Wells, Huxley, Orwell, and Burgess over there, and Twain, Sinclair, Burroughs, and Vonnegut over here, Disch is an unapologetic political writer, a high-minded liberal democrat, who sees doom in Western Civilization and says so, often with bizarre, bleak scenarios. . . .

Certainly, Disch is a sci-fi writer, a classification he has like Vonnegut resisted in the past but which was thrust upon him last spring with the nomination of *On Wings of Song* in the sci-fi category of the American Book Awards. . . . However, the weight of Disch's fiction bears little relation to those degraded aspects of sci-fi, space opera and beefcake/cheesecake fantasy. . . . Disch is too well-read, contentious, and ironic to delimit his ambitions with hyperdrive and super-swordsmen. He is a romantic and a modernist, a seeming contradiction that he reconciles by just writing but which entices more exacting definition.

Disch's poles seem to be the Gothic and the Defiant. He is transformed by monsters and morbidity, true, but his mutations are charming and he talks back to death. More, Disch's politics range from the unflappable dissent of those who will not serve tyrants to the wry iconoclasm of those who will not self-destruct simply because they find love outside the proscriptions of the Bible. Significantly there is much god-talk in Disch—he is a grumpy seeker bitching about the mess that's been made of Creation. Disch is also a literary guerilla of Romance. . . .

For Disch, the Gothic is liberating. And he does not regard romance as entertainment, but as a violent political weapon, to unseat the Dracos, harass the secret police, and cajole the sanguine oppressed to more efficacious rebellion. Disch's battleground is modern man's imagination; and he attacks with an arsenal that worked once and might very well, with modernizations, triumph again. (p. 35)

With *On Wings of Song,* Disch achieves a blend of the conflicting mix in his oeuvre—the rebellion, silliness, despair, survival, aesthetics—to produce a novel that may be read both as a condemnation of Amerika and as an affirmation of America, of its innovative citizenry. With no changes, *Wings* could be distributed as a call to any loner or clique in any repressive society to revolt, and could just as correctly be understood as a glum comment on how defeatism seduces, or, as Disch writes, how the broken-hearted "soon come to enjoy their humiliations, the way people do in Russian novels." . . .

All of Disch's prose, including three short story collections that are inconsistent but rewarding, deserves attention. But *On Wings of Song* is his grandest work—a writer's writer's success. *Wings* is self-consciously an update of Wells's *Mr. Bletsworthy On Rampole Island* (1928), Orwell's *1984,* and Vonnegut's *Slaughterhouse Five*—dystopian novels also concerned with the conflict of thisworldly incontinence and otherworldly fantasies. As such, *Wings* provides continuity with a vital library and also makes a gift of ironic prophecy to those of us angry but hopeful about an increasingly damp, malnourished future. (p. 36)

> *John Calvin Batchelor, "The Weird Worlds of Thomas*
> *Disch," in* The Village Voice, *Vol. XXV, No. 35,*
> *August 27-September 2, 1980, pp. 35-6.*

LAURA GERINGER

In the guise of a leisurely behind-the-scenes stroll through the Chelsea parlors of artists and authors famous in their day, Disch and Naylor offer in [*Neighboring Lives*] a stimulating draught of Victorian London. . . .

The chroniclers allow themselves one graceful detour to Oxford with Lewis Carroll, but, for the most part, their fiction follows as close to the urban banks of the Thames as it does to the facts. This is not pageantry—peak moments in the lives of the great—but a montage of small, telling events that quietly evoke the spirit of time and place. Suicide, snubs, gossip, and petty rivalries flourish here as among any group of writers and painters, but the portraits emerge well-rounded and humane, and readers will find themselves in sympathy with frailties rather than inspecting feet of clay.

At one point in the novel, a crimson helium balloon sails across the sky, bearing aloft "the renowned Madame Poitevin" in the costume of Europa, mounted on a bellowing bull and singing "Pig's Pettitoes," just the sort of detail that makes this inspired reconstruction an entertaining introduction to the period as well as a rare find for aficionados.

Laura Geringer, in a review of "Neighboring Lives," in Saturday Review, *Vol. 8, No. 2, February, 1981, p. 64.*

JULIAN SYMONS

London's Chelsea in the mid-19th century was one of those districts where every other house contained an artist or writer. Thomas and Jane Welsh Carlyle lived in Cheyne Row, the Rossettis and Swinburne were just round the corner, Turner's house was down by Battersea Bridge, with Jimmy Whistler a few doors away . . . Messrs. Disch and Naylor have linked events in these neighboring lives in a piece of fiction firmly based on fact. . . .

It is the Carlyles who dominate [*Neighboring Lives*], which begins with their arrival in London from Scotland in 1834 and effectively ends with Jane's death while being driven through Hyde Park more than 30 years later. To portray irascible, humorous Thomas and nervy, witty Jane, two people who as she once said had a skin too few for ordinary living, the authors have cunningly elaborated on events recounted in Jane's letters, and reminiscences by or about Carlyle. . . .

The tone of Carlyle's heavyweight conversation is beautifully caught, and so is the witty gossip of Jane who, as Dickens said after her death, could make the trivial events she saw from her Chelsea window as dramatic and amusing as a novel. The Victorian tone and language are well managed throughout. . . . Excellent also are the famous set-pieces like the burning of Carlyle's French Revolution manuscript by the servant of John Stuart Mill's mistress Harriet Taylor—although here, with a rare straying from fact, it is suggested that Mrs. Taylor burned the manuscript herself from jealousy of Carlyle. . . .

Most of these minor figures are sketched rather than painted. Here is Turner working on the river, "shaping a world from the void" in terms of pure color, with Walter Greaves as boatman, Greaves who with Turner and Whistler as examples becomes a painter himself. There are glimpses of Whistler, and even of his mother; Swinburne takes George Meredith's young son Arthur down to look at the boats and eat Chelsea buns; Lewis Carroll indulges his passion for photography in a tableau of the Rossetti family, but the plate is ruined in bringing his Ottewill camera out of the rain.

All this is pleasant enough, but we have the sense that art history, or straight biography, might be better. The narrative comes to full life only when this artistic society interacts with the Carlyles. . . . The book lives vividly in the drama of the Carlyles, who were far from happy together but much more miserable apart, whose marriage may have been sexless but certainly did not lack passion. This was the most astonishing marriage in literary history, and the authors do justice to it.

Julian Symons, "The View from Battersea Bridge," in Book World—The Washington Post, *March 1, 1981, p. 5.*

ANDREW MOTION

[In *ABCDEFGHIJKLMNOPQRSTUVWXYZ*] Thomas M. Disch has a . . . palpable design on the world around him. He doesn't so much record it as energetically recreate it—often as a science-fiction fantasy and nearly always as an elaborate verbal device. His 'passion for alphabetisation' produces jokes, surrealistic squibs, satires of circumstances and wry interrogations in forms ranging from the villanelle to *vers libre*. It's fun, but it's exhausting—and sometimes extremely slight. . . . In bulk, the poems' variety seems a sign of desperation: the more they chatter away, the more they raise doubts about their function and value. At various points Disch makes this explcit: 'You / try & touch / the seeming world / which shrinks / into a word that ceases', he admits, directing attention to the theme of transience which motivates almost all his high jinks. But while this goes a long way towards giving the book cohesion, he seldom stays with anything long enough to get the best from it. His restlessness creates a kind of entertaining inconsequentiality, and misrepresents the gravity with which he obviously views his subjects. (p. 21)

Andrew Motion, "Facing Two Ways," in New Statesman, *Vol. 101, No. 2618, May 22, 1981, pp. 20-1.**

MARTIN BOOTH

Tom Disch's book [*ABCDEFGHIJKLMNOPQRSTUVWXYZ*] is . . . his first English trade collection: he's best known as a science fiction/fantasy novelist. Often, when a prose writer turns to verse, the result of his labours is flat, just as the poet turned novelist tends to write floridly. Disch avoids the pitfalls and brings to poetry the vivid imagination of his other work expressed in forms that are varied and all utilised accurately—he's as at home with a sonnet as with free verse.

He juggles with allegory, metaphor and imagery, drawing pictures in the mind as well as passing comment upon the human condition seen through an oblique glass sideways. In other words, he's expressing the concerns of the serious SF writer in another medium. He's a witty writer, too and can be wry at the same time as being outrageous. . . .

[Disch is] in a class of his own, can't be categorised or pigeonholed, shows no affinity to others save, maybe at times, Brautigan or Russell Edson, and he is good. Poetry from Disch is like an entertainment of the senses: good fun and good for the soul as well.

Martin Booth, "Manwatching (and Judging)," in Tribune, *Vol. 45, No. 25, June 19, 1981, p. 11.**

ANGELA HUTH

Should you share my uneasiness about real characters in fiction, then *Neighbouring Lives,* by Thomas M. Disch and Charles Naylor, is not a book to induce tranquillity of mind. The writers were, perhaps, overcome by their good idea: a novel based on the lives of Thomas and Jane Carlyle and their set—a group as intriguing as the Bloomsberries. But, for a start, this lumbering work has no right to call itself a novel. It is a series of flaccid tableaux. Evocative figures such as Leigh Hunt, Swinburne and Rossetti meet, and meet again, mostly over tea. Their conversations give rise to the suspicion that, however extraordinary the Carlyle set, they were unlikely to have communicated in the language bestowed upon them by these authors. . . . Jane Carlyle has some potentially interesting encounters out of which Disch and Naylor have squeezed maximum dullness. The dying Chopin comes to tea, so does Lewis Carroll, with whom Mrs Carlyle discusses titles for his book ('Alice's Golden Hour'?) Perhaps, just because these teas are so dull, the two star visitors never return and we learn nothing of their characters. The Carlyles themselves are given more space but little real spirit, either. Thomas is a porridge-eating chauvinist, Jane has headaches and writes letters. (A long one is included: are we meant to think it is genuine?) There is not even a sparkling picture of London to compensate. . . .

Disch and Naylor do try to keep us on our toes, though. They often write a teasing paragraph about one of their famous characters without mentioning his name. I never felt up to guessing. And they fire off innumerable exclamation marks to splatter the vision, but all to no avail. (p. 821)

> *Angela Huth, "The Unreal Dead," in* The Listener, *Vol. 105, No. 2717, June 25, 1981, pp. 820-21.**

SIMON FEATHERSTONE

Thomas Disch has been called, rather enigmatically, 'the most respected, least trusted, most envied and least read of all modern science-fiction writers'. In [*ABCDEFGHIJKLMNOPQRSTUVWXYZ*], his first collection of poems, science fiction becomes a blend of the playfully ironic (suggested by his confession of 'a passion for alphabetization') and an engaging simplicity of statement, though this can at times lapse into pastiche: 'When Autumn paints the woods with brown and gray / We know that Summer can't be far away'. The manipulation of various forms (sonnet, villanelle, schoolboy's rhymed alphabet) to comic or ironic ends is often skilful but, . . . the poems work best when they do not rely on a punchline (**'On the Disposal of My Body'**) or a formal device. **'Narcissus'** is a fanciful satire on 'cybernetic technology' set within the framework of the Echo and Narcissus myth. It moves from burlesque, as when Narcissus observes the sleeping Echo—'Awake, she is even a bigger bore'—towards a more serious form of fantasy in which Narcissus is forced to face his murderous, technologically-formed facsimile. . . . It is in the creation of . . . tensions and ironies in form and treatment that Thomas Disch's strength lies rather than in the blatantly satirical or in the plainer pieces like **'The West Coast'** and **'After the April Festivals'** which seem to lean towards the work of John Ashbery. (pp. 62-3)

> *Simon Featherstone, "Alphabets and Inversions," in* PN Review, *Vol. 8, No. 4, Autumn, 1981, pp. 62-3.*

SARA MAITLAND

[In *The Man Who Had No Idea* there] are 17 very varied stories in which lots of weird and wonderful things happen: a world war is fought in the next door apartment, an unborn child corrupts the Earth, the Goddess Hera punishes marital infidelity, a couple fall in love across galaxies by means of a machine which converts one's own self image into visual form, and goodness knows what else, but I was left with a heavy feeling of 'why bother?' Disch is clever and inventive but he uses his imaginative dexterity to solve problems that there was no need to create in the first place. His speed is impressive, but rather in the same way that a child's virtuosity is impressive, and even his most delightful ideas—in the title story conversation is only permitted to those who are licensed following an examination in meaningful dialogue—are wasted. He writes rather plonkingly and often does not seem to bother too much. Too many of the stories in the collection feel insultingly like Disch finding a way to turn an honest penny on half-developed ideas which could not be stretched into anything more substantial. Indeed in some of the rather annoying little

explanatory notes which preface each story, he admits as much. Now I am not a reader of Science Fiction, and there may be any number of brilliant subtleties or internal references which have passed me by entirely, but his collection has done absolutely nothing to convert me.

> *Sara Maitland, "Mixed Bag," in* The Spectator, *Vol. 248, No. 8025, May 1, 1982, p. 23.**

DON STRACHAN

Lest we be lulled by hacks, Thomas M. Disch reminds us what the fantasy short story can do. His prose twists and turns down cerebral corridors; his situations entertain hosts of human quandaries simultaneously. **"The Man Who Had No Idea"** . . . collects some of his best briefs over the past decade. Many, such as a proposal to build pyramids in Minnesota ("pyramids transcend the notion of utility"), are fragments, mere wisps of whimsy. But **"The Apartment Next to the War,"** barely more than three pages long, brings battle into our living rooms better than TV ever does. It's one of those rare instantly recognized classics, on a par with "The Lottery," at once fun to read and critically whole.

> *Don Strachan, in a review of "The Man Who Had No Idea," in* Los Angeles Times Book Review, *November 21, 1982, p. 13.*

JUDITH MOFFETT

From the first [Disch] was associated with the New Wave "movement" begun in England in the 1960s, whose writers emphasized style over story and/or took a cynical, pessimistic view of humanity and its future. (In both respects, very different from traditional science fiction.) The New Wave has broken now, but Disch's work continues to display an interest in a dazzling surface rather than substance, and a disposition for iconoclasm. *Orders of the Retina* . . . , Disch's third book of verse, constitutes an object lesson in the gains and losses inherent in this approach to art.

Fiction reviewers make much of Disch's intelligence, as if science fiction were written all but exclusively by morons, which is far from true; yet in these poems too a lively, cheeky wit is, along with formal adroitness, the most salient feature. Disch's delight in his own dexterity is infectious at first. Before long, though, one begins to doubt whether he takes himself seriously enough. By twos and threes these poems would serve admirably as a change of pace from weightier, meatier matters; three dozen of them together, with their lists and collages and odd vacancies, make a collective impression of superficiality, of a concern with surface so overriding as to seem finally unsatisfying. . . .

> *Judith Moffett, in a review of "Orders of the Retina," in* Book World—The Washington Post, *March 13, 1983, p. 10.*

RICHARD DEVESON

The Businessman is a ghost story with not one ghost but many. The slobby Minneapolis-St Paul executive Bob Glandier has killed his wife Giselle, who comes back from the claustrophobia of the grave to haunt him. Giselle's mother Joy-Ann quickly dies off too, to reappear in paradise and meet up with the ghost of Adah Menken, the actress famous mainly for impersonating Byron's Mazeppa near-naked in the 1860s. The spirit of John Berryman, still freshly bloodied from his suicide jump into the Mississippi, comes along later, as does a malign creature born from Glandier's rape of his late wife's ghost. After a string of (unterrifying) murders and an inefficient battle between the good and evil spirits, a comically grisly sort of justice is finally done.

As a *jeu d'esprit*, as genre, the book is consistently very clever. The ghosts act and talk and think like so many fictional characters and much of the entertainment comes from the different kinds of dealings they have with one another and with the 'real' people inside whose heads they 'actually' reside. Disch also pokes a lot of fun at American suburban kitsch: the action and settings are like a spoof of the made-for-TV horror movie. And yet, Berryman is there for the sake of us intellectuals. We might wonder, 'Where's the beef?'

The clash between genre and seriousness occurs because Disch includes a number of religio-philosophical reflections which he really seems to want us to ponder. Are the various souls passing through stages of redemption (or otherwise)? Does 'evil', as a metaphysical entity, exist? Do spirits have free will? The fact that the book's events, when one reflects on them, are full of inconsistencies and logical impossibilities hardly allays one's doubts about the meaningfulness of such questions.

> *Richard Deveson, "Discord," in* New Statseman, *Vol. 108, No. 2782, July 13, 1984, p. 28.**

MARION ZIMMER BRADLEY

"The Businessman" calls itself "A Tale of Terror." . . . But the reader who picks up **"The Businessman"** expecting to have a good shuddery hammock read, à la Stephen King, is going to be very disappointed.

In fact, it's hard to know what to call this book. It starts in the grave of a woman named Giselle, who has been murdered by her husband, and who slowly becomes aware that she is fated to haunt him. . . . [In] alternate chapters we follow the fate of the murderous husband. Giselle is also condemned to a post-death pregnancy, to bear again the fetus of her aborted child; this purely demonic fetus also haunts the husband, finally destroying him and a whole family of bystanders.

But it is all very elegantly satirical: None of these horrors really induce pity or terror. There's a lot of literary trivia and a lot of clever literary allusion concealed in the book, but there is no impulse to suspend disbelief and believe these things while the reader is in the midst of them. There are shudders of disgust but nothing that would really scare a nervous 9-year-old. The reader is too distanced by the self-conscious literary gamesmanship from feeling any of these horrors. It's difficult to acquit Mr. Disch of the sin of writing with one eye on the literary critic and the other on the syllabus of the "modern fiction" courses in college classrooms.

Horror fiction is, let's face it, an entertainment genre. It should be taken on its own terms.

As George Bernard Shaw said about a peformance of "Il Trovatore," an opera which even in his day was not everyone's cup of tea, "You must take the whole thing with the most tragic solemnity or you must let it alone altogether." These things cannot be spoofed or parodied, which of course is the reason many people—including this reviewer—find that self-consciously literary science fiction is a singularly distasteful version of what was called, a few years ago, "high camp." This is even more true of the "horror novel." Imagine "Dracula" filmed in all seriousness by Ingmar Bergman!

In one of those college classes in literature which are guaranteed to give everyone a lasting distaste for the very idea of literature as such, this reviewer had (read: suffered under) a professor who stated that the only purpose of the novel was social satire and anyone who ventured to like or dislike, sympathize or identify with characters in a novel was indulging in "sentimentality." . . .

As a devotee of the Greek concept of catharsis, the evocation of "pity and terror" in fiction, I was horrified by this edict, and didn't believe that any novel, except perhaps Voltaire's "Candide" and its modern version, Cabell's "Jurgen," was ever written that way. Not, that is, until I read the Disch novel.

I am no aficionado of the horror genre per se. I still think, as per Shaw's admonition, one should take it with the most tragic solemnity or let it alone altogether. Judging by **"The Businessman,"** Mr. Disch should have let it alone.

> *Marion Zimmer Bradley, "Spook Spoof," in* The New York Times Book Review, *August 26, 1984, p. 31.*

Norman (Evans) Dubie (Jr.)

1945-

American poet.

Considered an important and innovative voice in contemporary poetry, Dubie is known for his historical narratives that frequently take the form of dramatic monologues. His poems are highly visual, rich in detailed imagery, and distinguished by their imaginative and intellectual complexity. They frequently revolve around a historical literary or artistic figure, yet within this factual frame the distinction between the real and the imaginary is blurred, resulting in a dreamlike quality. Some critics claim the detailed and allusive nature of Dubie's poetry ultimately alienates the reader. Lawrence Raab contends that "the poems demand and earn our attention. Nevertheless, once that attention has been gained, too often I suspect that the poems resist rather than welcome the reader, as if they really did not want to make themselves and their secrets available." Likewise, Sandra M. Gilbert claims that Dubie's poems are "relentlessly, exhaustingly learned" but notes that "when he resists the temptation to rely upon erudition rather than vision, his poetry is striking, accurate, visionary."

Dubie introduces his interest in history and the narrative form in *Alehouse Sonnets* (1971). This work consists of a series of narratives in which Dubie converses with the nineteenth-century critic William Hazlitt. With his next two major publications, *In the Dead of the Night* (1975) and *The Illustrations* (1977), Dubie expanded this poetic form into the longer, more illustrative verse for which he is best known. Poems in these collections as well as *The City of Olesha Fruit* (1979) and *The Everlastings* (1979) are populated by such varied artists as Ovid, Virginia Woolf, Randall Jarrell, Vladimir Mayakovsky, Paul Klee, and El Greco. These figures are placed in carefully arranged and illustrated tableaux, providing a sweeping, cinematic portrayal of the places and times in which they are located.

Dubie's poetic approach has been to distance himself, historically and geographically, from his subjects, while simultaneously using his consciousness as a filter through which the past is viewed. Critics have debated the effect of this distancing on his work. Some contend that his impersonal stance deprives his poetry of emotional impact and immediacy, while others assert that it lends intellectual and imaginative depth to his poems. Lorrie Goldensohn believes that Dubie's poetry "properly disdains the limits of the merely autobiographical as a violation of the imagination's possibilities." Yet in the new poems from Dubie's *Selected and New Poems* (1983), some critics have noticed a movement toward more lyrical and personal verse, resulting in poems of greater accessibility.

(See also *Contemporary Authors*, Vols. 69-72 and *Contemporary Authors New Revision Series*, Vol. 12.)

RICHARD HOWARD

When *Alehouse Sonnets*, Norman Dubie's first book, was published in 1971, I was startled by the poet's hallucinatory capacity to embed his own experience . . . in the biography, as it appears, of William Hazlitt; in most of those fifty-six poems

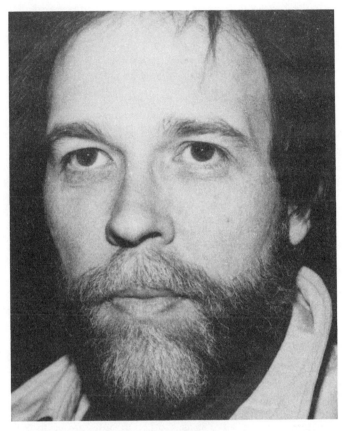

Photograph by Jeannine Savard

(sonnets only because they have fourteen lines and Dubie calls them so) there is no clue who is speaking—we listen to a recital of experience with no hint of recurrence, no hope of repetition, yet not in prose even so, for there is Dubie's rage for unity from the start, making even the most intricate and weird of his notations . . . round on themselves and form a whole, even if it is a whole enigma, a mystery entire. In his new book [*In the Dead of the Night*], very long and sumptuous, much more methodical in its dissociations, Dubie ranges much farther in what he calls these "sometimes forward elegies and monologues." Indeed he gets too far forward for me, sometimes, he loses me altogether. . . . But a good deal of the time, I can just about keep up, and that effort affords enormous pleasure; the authority of the enjambed voice is preternatural, and though I am relieved that not all poetry is like this, I am glad Dubie's is: I believe him when he says, at the end of a poem "for" Wilfred Owen, "and this signifies that all beauty is an / attempt on life." The life Dubie makes his attempt on is of course his own, but usually assigned, as a kind of stage-direction or key-register, to some violent and dismaying figure in the arts: Jarrell, Trakl, Mayakovsky, El Greco, Klee, Mahler, many more. It doesn't matter. . . , for *everyone's* life has been absorbed by Dubie's scrutinizing nostalgia, and what his poems become are immense promptbooks for some vast Chekhovian drama. . . . The danger with this kind of poetry . . . is that *the form of the*

129

text has been elided, and that we may not perceive, from the rendered sensibilia (rendered in all senses: given over, made real, melted down), the armature on which the message is wrapped. The promptbook without the play may leave us wondering what all the brilliant entrances, the violent exits can serve. Dubie knows this, of course, and loves to live dangerously. . . . And there are cases where Dubie is scrupulous to provide the poem with its own plot: **"The Pennacesse Leper Colony for Women. Cape Cod. 1922," "Pastoral," "The Obscure,"** and the last poem, **"Elegy Asking That It Be the Last,"** among the best. But often the poet is just as scrupulous to keep you guessing, though that is no way to get on with him. Better let him tell, in that shocking way of his, what you can see or hear by his lights, what the morning looks like on the curtains, and what century it is. He is, as they say, a natural (they mean: we do not yet understand such art), and he will often be able to compel a recognition-scene from just the moments most alien to your experience: it is because he has *created* your experience in the poem, has preempted you as he has assimilated Seurat and Baudelaire, and there is no pulling apart the intestinal warp now:

> Surrounding the Prince and also on horses are men
> Who are giant; they are dressed in furs.
> There's ice forming in their beards. Each is
> A chieftain. They are the Prince's heavy protection.
> They are all drunk, these men who are laughing
> At the linnet with a worm in its heart.
> This is a world set apart from ours. It is not!

That is Dubie's triumph and despair, the exclamatory squeal of the last three syllables, and whether you grant his assertion is the risk he takes. He has put *himself* as a medium in the service of an art which generally asks more than that submission merely, and whether he generally succeeds, each of us must decide alone—it is not a public threshold. My own experience of this poet, after any number of readings, is that he is a compassionate genius of language who appears unable to forget—to subordinate any experience to some other; thereby he occludes what we have agreed to call meaning (to mean is to see resemblances, repetitions) but he enlarges what we have agreed to call value (to value is to see differences, singularities). (pp. 427-30)

Richard Howard, in a review of "In the Dead of the Night," in The Yale Review, *Vol. LXV, No. 3, March, 1976, pp. 427-30.*

PAUL RAMSEY

[The central recurrent theme in Norman Dubie's *In the Dead of the Night* is] that experience and extraexperience come by us menacingly, ambiguously or unmeaningly, outside our control or understanding. His poems also depend on obscure essencing images, but they are packed with varied detail and give a strong sense of complex and completed structure. Events and broken thoughts nervously dance together in enjambed and shifting verse lines, the scenes held in bewildered, fearful, yet steady observation. The artistry is admirable, and the variety: one aspect of the central theme—that coherent narrative or understanding is impossible because experience is too mysterious—makes for some sameness and allows him some easy moves, as does an epigraph from Jarrell: "What the wish wants to see, it sees." Not always, and seldom as well as in this book. **"New England, 1868," "The Orphans,"** and **"About**

Infinity, and the Lenesdorf Pools" are especially stirring poems. (p. 538)

Paul Ramsey, "Image and Essence: Some American Poetry of 1975," in The Sewanee Review, *Vol. LXXXIV, No. 3, Summer, 1976, pp. 533-41.*

SANDRA M. GILBERT

[In *In the Dead of the Night*, Norman Dubie] is thought-tormented. Allusive, intricate, and sometimes witty, his poems have titles like *The Suicide of Hedda Gabler, Isaak Babel, Charles Baudelaire, Seurat, El Greco, Kindertotenlieder,* and *Thomas Traherne's Meditation for Love. 1672.* They are, in other words, relentlessly, exhaustingly learned, in the manner of the late 'fifties. "This book details with the nervousness of a little bird the breakup of a first marriage, a year's separation from my daughter, and months spent in a small room in a boarding house. . .", the book's cover quotes Dubie as saying. But he adds, "You'll not, however, work this simple confession from these poems." No indeed. If there's a story I "work" from these poems (and the verb is appropriate, for Dubie's allusiveness often makes for laborious reading), it's a story about the catastrophes of history, a story obliquely perceived and elliptically told.

Sometimes—as in *The Pennacesse Leper Colony for Women, Balalaika, The Obscure, The Scythes,* and *Pastoral*—the voice of the storyteller seems passionate, or at least compassionate, and the tale he tells captures my imagination, moves me, convinces me of the truth of its seeing. In *Pastoral,* for example, a pogrom is described with hallucinatory precision. . . . At other times, however, events are reported with a suave and icy irony that seems to alienate not only Dubie, the narrator, but me, the reader, from the sorrow the poem is meant to convey. *For David St. John Who's Written A Poem* is . . . a piece that the poet clearly intends as a serious, speculative elegy. But . . . it moves through a series of wearily baroque images . . . to a conclusion that strives, I suppose, for what used to be called "Black Humor" but merely achieves a sort of dandified dreariness. . . . (pp. 297-98)

At least, however, I have some idea what Dubie is talking about in *For David St. John.* Or anyway I think I do. But a number of other pieces—for instance the "For R. P. Blackmur" section of the inexplicably titled *Popham of the New Song*—are so elaborately learned and/or metaphysical that I'm left feeling completely inferior, excluded, like a child listening to wise grownup talk, the men with their weary wrinkled brows sitting massively around in somebody's diningroom and discussing obscure Cartesian propositions all having some indefinable bearing on equally obscure aspects of the world's *Angst.* I—the uneducated child—tiptoe warily out of the room, resolving that one day I too will go to graduate school, study Descartes, formulate my *Angst* in a secret, grownup code. But when I read such verse I also close the book, thick-headed with fatigue.

I'm especially sorry that so many of Dubie's poems leave me with this feeling of sullen stupidity because when he resists the temptation to rely upon erudition rather than vision, his poetry is striking, accurate, visionary. (p. 298)

Sandra M. Gilbert, "A Platoon of Poets," in Poetry, *Vol. CXXVIII, No. 5, August, 1976, pp. 290-99.*

LORRIE GOLDENSOHN

Frequently dated, frequently placed ("**Nineteen Forty**," "**February: The Boy Breughel**," "**The Tub. 1934. Halifax, Mississippi**")—the titles for Norman Dubie's new poems in *The Illustrations* might lead you to think that the emphasis is historical or biographical; that the poems are going to be anecdotes, or brief flashes of past lives, crammed into the lyric trajectory, in which we witness the poet's ability to make theatrical monologue, short story, or verbal photograph. The first poem of the book, however, spoken in the voice of Virginia Woolf, disturbs any easy genre expectation.

First of all, most of the historical, or narrative information is there, mostly indirectly, as a frame; the real size, scale and visceral impact come from something else, from the general experience toward which the poem is shaping, or from the images of the language itself. . . . The poems are not attempts to impersonate. . . . Perhaps what is singular in all of these poems is the very positioning of physical and characterological elements as equivalents in narrative value. While there is an insistence on an apparently authentic placement—on a provable, document-like factualness as a post on which to anchor—this placement appears from within a tenuous and dissolving attachment to narrative continuity. . . .

Because of Dubie's attention to small field detail, and because of a style in which emotions exist as an indistinct suffusion of the narrative record against which the obdurate stuffs of its landscapes and interiors stand in mysterious relief, swept by weather and an always precise articulation of light, the emphasis is only tangentially on characterization, or on a tally of events. In the flux of history, all that we know of the changing flesh can be focussed on the facts of its appearances, its remembered colors and shapes. . . .

Character, and plot, as we commonly know them, become accessory to the book's intent: which in its probing, circling roll, becomes the connection of the writer to a consciousness greater and more durable than his own, and carried in the common life of objects; a life, in the clean diction of this poetry, also severely beautiful.

Meaning for Dubie is literally freighted: a cargo of enumerable and divisible parts. Human identity, an objective record of fragmentary survivals—material, local and finite. . . . [For] Dubie, objects alone have discernible reality, but they live most truly as spirit-tracks, or as the precipitate, the residue of the numinous. Survival depends on a recognition of what, usually in difficult circumstances, is left. . . .

Most of these poems are outwardly serene and inwardly somber. Each poem deals with a moment of crisis, with advancing death, exile, and those drops of accidents into our lives that determine survival or its absence. But these moments of the poem, augmented, incremental—move within an idea of art as restoration, or at the least, as the mutation into value. Not consenting to the menacing figure of Yeats' artificial bird, or Keats' static Grecian urn as the ultimate form of art's labor, Dubie seems closer to Kafka: "Writing is a form of prayer." A means of touching the fathers, or of breaking through to the dead, and of finding one's proper name in the sequences of being, of discovering one's self as one in the series of all selves—distinctive, but equally ranked. . . .

In a poetry that properly disdains the limits of the merely autobiographical as a violation of the imagination's possibilities, or, as the insensible contraction of the given record, Dubie's dark illustrations may have an uncomfortable resemblance

to the meaning of lustration as sacrifice, as propitiatory rite after the act of census. But any account of these interlocking, densely beautiful orders should not deny the grave and splendid dreaming which it is possible at all times to retrieve from the poetry itself. . . .

> *Lorrie Goldensohn, in a review of "The Illustrations," in* The American Book Review, *Vol. 1, No. 1, December, 1977, p. 23.*

LAWRENCE RAAB

In Norman Dubie's poems the pressure of the past is discovered everywhere. With sometimes unsettling speed this new collection [*The Illustrations*] moves from century to century and subject to subject: Ovid, Czar Nicholas, Virginia Woolf, Paul Klee, Breughel, Osip Mandelstam, Jacob Boehme, Alexandr Blok. Dubie imagines Woolf recalling the slow passing of a train, "my first hospital train . . . Private and heavy it cut through the yellow fields." As a red sun sets behind the poplars she writes: "I should sit out and watch it rather than/Write this!" She writes: "Little things seem large." . . .

Norman Dubie's dense, challenging poems are about the "little things" that "seem large" when they are clearly seen. But what can be seen, the poems ask, just as itself? Noticed, remembered, written down, even the simplest detail or the smallest event becomes emblematic and significant. . . .

In the midst of danger, Dubie's speakers turn to a relentless, obsessive accumulation and notation of detail. They cannot simply see the falling of the sun. Struggling with that "common speech" they must talk, they must write it down. This is the way it was, they seem to say. Or is. This is what I saw, that sunset, that yellow field, just that. Poem after poem begins by insisting upon what is visible at a particular moment, as if to say, Look at that. . . .

One of the book's most intriguing poems ["**Sun and Moon Flowers: Paul Klee, 1879-1940**"] is spoken to the dying Paul Klee. (p. 12)

Here, as in other poems where the poet himself breaks in to cajole or argue with or instruct his characters, Dubie abandons the pretense of historical distance: "Klee, don't listen to them." Who, for example, is speaking or thinking the final line of the second stanza, "And, then, tell me there's anything they can keep from us." Klee? Dubie? The two together?

The poem knows what the real Paul Klee could not know: "Next Wednesday your heart/Stops. . . ." Again the fact, the precise moment—next Wednesday—is insisted upon. Yet Dubie wants to speak to Klee. And so he does, as if the past could be re-ordered. And so, within the poem, at least the attempt might be made, however inevitable next Wednesday may be, and the war that surrounds the dying painter. What is "necessary"—what is inescapable—is concentrated in the poem's stunning final image, in which pain, and the escape from pain, and the precision of the emblems that surround and define such pain are carried in by the day nurse on the morning tray: "ice water, blue spikes of lupine, and morphine."

Paul Klee's question—"What on earth happened to us?"—might well stand behind all of Dubie's characters. Therefore they begin by telling themselves where they are. As the man lost in the woods tries to locate himself by the moss on a tree or the flow of a stream, these voices begin by saying what it is they are able to see. To the question, Where are we? they reply: Here. To the question, What on earth happened to us? they offer the same answer: I am here. For many this is an assertion of personal identity, achieved with difficulty, and as Marvin Bell notes, "an occasion for courage and dignity."

Although Dubie insistently prefaces his poems with dates— 1940, 1927, 1934, 1916, 1872, 1922, 1620, Circa 1582, Circa 1952 (all of these extracted from titles or subtitles)—finally he does not seem primarily interested in re-creating historical moments, or even in creating through the use of historical materials real presences and identifiable people. . . . [All] of Dubie's characters tend to sound very much alike: not a group of distinct personalities so much as one sensibility putting on different disguises, trying out various voices, submitting itself to the pressures of the past, one moment or year or century after another.

As some clue to the book's overall effect I choose to read the title—*The Illustrations*—literally. So the poems as pictures— figures, examples, designs, comparisons—are all fashioned by the same hand, and should be seen in that light. As illustrator Dubie chooses not to withhold himself, but instead extends his own voice to delineate his chosen characters, as if they were speaking through him, their speech become his. (pp. 12-13)

If these poems can be approached as "illustrations," what exactly do they illustrate? Are they illuminations of a story— of many stories—that we should remember and bring to bear upon the poems? What then do the poems demand of us as readers? This seems to me one of the central problems in Dubie's work: how the reader figures into the story. . . .

The poems demand and earn our attention. Nevertheless, once that attention has been gained, too often I suspect that the poems resist rather than welcome the reader, as if they really did not want to make themselves and their secrets available. . . .

Even when most (if not all) of the facts of a given poem are clear (as, for example, in "**The Great American Novel: Winter, 1927**") and the writing is sharp, controlled and engaging, the poem can seem to be talking to itself, and the reader may feel that he has blundered into the middle of a fascinating story the significance of which he can never hope to fathom. So the poem may be admired for its surfaces of imagery and incident, but still remain resolutely cold and distant.

Perhaps this is a problem. It may also be a conscious strategy that Dubie does not yet have entirely under control. Poems like "**The Ugly Poem That Reluctantly Accepts *Itself* As Its Only Title**," "**The Wedding Party**" and "**The Tub. 1934. Halifax, Mississippi**" leave many seemingly essential questions unanswered. (p. 13)

I am not arguing that every poem must provide the newspaper reporter's orderly list of facts. But if any poem raises . . . essential dramatic questions by obscuring these facts, surely the reader has every right to ask why. Indeed, shouldn't the poet and the poem expect us to ask why? And then might not our questions and how they are answered (or perhaps even more interesting, why they might necessarily remain unanswered) become part of the whole drama of the poem and finally part of its meaning? Finally, I am fascinated by what I take to be Dubie's strategy in many of these poems: the creation of fictional worlds sometimes (but not always) tied to historical personages and moments through the *re-telling* of stories. Thus the past is both re-invented and illustrated. It is changed and it remains oblivious to change. But its pressure—the pressure of having everything to do with the world—always remains.

Nevertheless, my fascination with and admiration of Dubie's endeavor is often qualified by a sense that he has not yet found the most powerful way of involving the reader in the drama of the poems. Yes, the poems could be clearer. But they might also be even more complicated, though in a more engaging way.

The confusions that I find in many of Dubie's poems are confusions that the poems themselves do not appear to accept as a problem, confusions that do not seem to be real issues to the voices within the poems. This is very different from the difficulties that exist in many of the dramatic monologues and dialogues of Robert Frost or Edwin Arlington Robinson, where a lack of knowledge about motivation or even about the basic facts of an event are shared by the characters and the reader. The simple facts of a poem like Robinson's "The Whip" have perplexed and will continue to perplex readers and critics. Robinson himself admitted that in this case "I may have gone a little too far and given the reader too much to carry." But the speaker of this poem, like the reader, is also uncertain of what has happened. . . . The difficulty or impossibility of finding some final truth, whether it is a literal truth or a metaphorical reality, is what the poem is about. The confusions we are left with as readers are troubling because they are necessary. . . .

I would like to believe that the difficulties I have with Dubie's work stem from an inability on my part to discover what the poems want me to "carry." I would be pleased to be persuaded that I have not yet discovered how to enter the worlds of many of these poems, and there how to assume the kind of burdens the poems want to place upon me. But the particular confusions that I've tried to indicate seem to turn away from rather than involve the reader. Too often I suspect that Dubie needlessly distances the reader from these poems, and the more this happens the less the reader will feel he has at stake. Finally, he may simply stop caring altogether about whatever is or is not happening. I'm not suggesting that Dubie merely simplify his work, and I'm not really complaining that some of these poems may be overly or unnecessarily complicated. I am saying that if Dubie—like Robinson—were to value, acknowledge and use all of a reader's possible responses—confusion included—he might be able to manage an even more intricate and demanding poetry without running the risk of seeming to indulge in the fascinations of obscurity. Dubie's poems are based on dramatic tension: between one character and another, or between a character and the poet. What I believe the poems do not sufficiently utilize is the dramatic tension possible between the poem and the reader.

Two of the best and most engaging poems in *The Illustrations*— "**The Czar's Last Christmas Letter. A Barn in the Urals**" and "**The Negress: Her Monologue of Dark Crepe with Edges of Light**"—are written (significantly, I think) as letters. The shape of the letter provides an immediate tension between who is speaking and the person to whom the letter is addressed. The fiction of the poem-as-letter also gives Dubie a way of getting hold of a particular voice, of defining that voice in specific circumstances, and of judging what range of imagery might be appropriate and necessary. But even more importantly, this form gives the reader a way of entering the poem. What is written in a letter may be the truth, or a lie, or anywhere in between. But as the pressure behind the voice becomes apparent, story and circumstance reveal themselves. And however complicated the emotions of the characters may be, the reader's position—as the reader of a letter—is clear.

In *The Illustrations* Dubie is at his best—and his best is very good indeed—when he insists, through all his assembled voices, on clarity, on that radiance that joins the sheerwater birds and the decaying boat, the Messerschmitt and the wild ducks, pleasure and a cup of water. This is the power of what is seen not just for itself—not just for the sake of another striking image—but seen for a reason by a particular person in a particular place, seen and then spoken of through that common speech which we cannot help but share. . . . (p. 14)

Lawrence Raab, "Illustrations and Illuminations: On Norman Dubie," in The American Poetry Review, Vol. 7, No. 4, July-August, 1978, pp. 12-14.

J. D. McCLATCHY

[Norman Dubie's] *The Illustrations* is a better book—rather more chaste and taut—than his first two, but it is decidedly more of the same. Prosy, dashing costume drama, occasionally spliced with contemporary or autobiographical instances. Horace to Blok, Breughel to Klee, Nicholas II, Gide, Lawrence—Dubie takes up each in turn, or rather takes them *on,* in his portraits and monologues. There is much that is effective and affecting in this. He brings to this work the novel's amplitude, energy and welter. . . . To be sure, telling details are lavished, but too often the impedimenta are only in service to their own momentum, as if that alone, and almost incidentally, could catch up a poem's shape or concept. The point of these poems seems usually to be their own elaboration. . . . Since his poems are storied rather than plotted, there is a great deal of *what happens next* in them, and it doesn't seem to matter whether it be eggs or ice water, happiness or the end of it. His poems come to seem like tantrums of sensual or characterological detail, and so grow wearing. The experience is not unlike viewing too many slides of someone else's exotic trip. And too many exquisite moments, to twist Wilde, add up to a *mauvais quart d'heure.* The attractions of Dubie's method are strong and immediate. There is a good deal of *finish* to his work, but unless there is an emergent purpose and vision to such a book, its finish only tends to highlight the lack of them. (pp. 292-93)

J. D. McClatchy, "Grace and Rude Will," in Poetry, Vol. CXXXII, No. 5, August, 1978, pp. 288-98.*

SUSAN WOOD

[Norman Dubie's] distinctive form has been the historical narrative, in which a figure from literature or history either speaks or is spoken to by an anonymous narrator. The voice in the poems, however, whether Proust's or Breughel's or an unknown Russian peasant's, is always that of Norman Dubie—the same highly visual, even painterly imagery, the complex syntax, the almost obsessive eye for detail. . . . The problem in Dubie's previous books has been that too often the reader was kept at a distance by the privateness of that voice; so that, although one admired the beautiful, elegant surface, one was simply not given enough information for understanding. Why *this* detail and not *that* one, and what is to be our attitude toward the poem? The poems in [*The City of the Olesha Fruit*] seem to me more accessible, however, as though Dubie has decided to be less secretive. More often the exquisitely rendered details seem to be there for a reason; in "**Elegy to the Sioux,**" for example, the details of a scene pictured on a vase—scattered groups of cavalry and Indians—perfectly reveal the pathos and insensitivity of history. And there are also more

personal poems here than Dubie has allowed himself before, poems spoken directly in Dubie's voice—"**You,**" a love poem, for example, and the elegy "**The Hours,**" with its beautiful closing lines: "There were many more bells / Than we thought, they will / Never stop for us, as waking to them we realize that / Throughout our lives, in the light and in the dark, / We were always counting our losses." Like John Ashbery, Dubie is a powerful poet of the memory and motion of life, "of a city / That is being constructed all of the time. . . / Somewhere inside the mind."

Susan Wood, "Discovering New Voices," in Book World—The Washington Post, August 19, 1979, p. 8.

JOHN VERNON

[Norman Dubie] strikes me as one of our finest poets, and he comes out of a tradition of crafted, tight free verse in a relaxed, conversational language which feeds much of the lyric poetry written today. . . . But he is seldom explicitly present in his poems, most of which are dramatic monologues with a decidedly narrative flavor set in various periods of American and European history.

In his fourth collection, *The City of the Olesha Fruit* . . . Dubie's poems take place in Russian villages, a Mayan Ball Court, on the Ganges, in Avignon, France, at the Great Wall of China, in Elizabethan England. He seems to prefer Russian and East European settings, and I think this is because his narrative gifts are akin to those of some of the great Russian and Polish storytellers, such as Nikolai Leskov, Chekhov, or I. B. Singer. His use of details has the same kind of dramatic quality as in Leskov or Singer, in which the world seems to tell its own story. . . . [His] details have a wonderfully generous quality, as in the great Russian writers, and reveal a world which is so vivid it is both ordinary . . . and dream-like at the same time.

Many of the poems are dramatic monologues, but Dubie usually doesn't attempt to imitate his subject's voice or supposed manner of speaking. In fact, the poems have a general uniformity of style, with only a slight veering towards a kind of conversational simplicity where it seems appropriate. So the poems are only conversational in a highly conventional way. . . . These are not realistic dramatic monologues, but imaginative renderings, more like interior monologues, reveries or dreams. Yet, they have a narrative surface of details akin to that used by fiction writers, and so the visionary and the merely realistic melt beautifully together in the best poems— . . . the lyric and narrative find a rare and exciting union. (pp. 345-46)

Dubie has a visual sense which borders on the sculptural. Some of the poems, in fact, are about paintings, photographs, vases, or sculptures. At times he reminds me of Brueghel (or of Auden's famous poem on a Brueghel painting) in his ability to muster a colony of details and still render the central figure, the one detail sufficient unto itself, which places the whole canvas into both an emotional and a visual perspective. A few of the third-person poems have the quality of a camera scanning a landscape, and in them one senses both the unfolding through time of the act of scanning, and the absolute stillness of the picture itself, which has that lyrical quality of a pure isolated moment. "**The Old Asylum of the Narragansetts,**" set in 16th-century Plymouth, Massachusetts, has this quality. . . . Two of the very best poems in the book, "**Elegy to the Pulley of Superior Oblique,**" and "**Elizabeth's War With the Christmas Bear, 1601,**" possess . . . [a] sense of the indifferent cruelty of history, which Dubie also seems to see as a failure of human imagination, or—as in the case of Queen Elizabeth, who places the lye-scrubbed skeleton of a bear beside her bed—as a revenge of the imagination upon nature.

Some of Dubie's more purely visionary poems, such as **"The Sibling's Woodcut,"** aren't entirely successful. The details are too buried and crowded together, and the reader finds it difficult to see the woods for the trees. Dubie's habit of returning to two or three salient details in the final third of the poem— details which were part of the crowd at the beginning—and developing perhaps one of them, really doesn't help. Such a trick seems more of a concession to form—a painter's or a musician's instinct—than to meaning or clarity. But such poems are few, and define perhaps an outer boundary of Dubie's immense talent, which finds its greatest expression in the union of the visionary with a rich surface of realistic details. This union is brought to life by the voice of the storyteller, a voice which (as in folk tales) is somehow both anonymous and personal, and both economical in its choice of words and generous in the way it enables words to flow. (pp. 347-48)

> *John Vernon, in a review of "The City of the Olesha Fruit," in* Western Humanities Review, *Vol. XXXIII, No. 4, Autumn, 1979, pp. 345-48.*

PETER STITT

Norman Dubie writes a poetry of pure imagination; he seems not at all interested in the projection of his own personality through the use of a sincere and intimate voice. Rather, his poems are spoken in a variety of voices by a varied cast of characters—whomever a given poem seems to require. The question of sincerity, therefore, scarcely even comes up; these poems are not, no matter how obliquely, written in honor of the personality. They are written to celebrate the power of the imagination. The stance of the poet is objective, curious, interested in the known wonders of the world and in its possibilities. The imaginative scope of *The City of the Olesha Fruit* is, therefore, large. . . . (p. 210)

Beyond using his own imagination in choosing and embellishing the subjects of his poems, Dubie has in fact made the power of imagination itself both subject of and force within his poems. In his reverence for the imagination, the other writer whom Dubie most calls to mind is Gabriel Garcia Marquez. For a character in *One Hundred Years of Solitude* to dream, think, or desire something is for it to be born into the world, as if by magic; so great is the power of imagination that the love felt by mourners at a funeral causes flowers to float spontaneously, profusely, from the evening sky; a galleon appears in the jungle, on a mountainside; one character is brought back to life and another lives almost forever. Norman Dubie knows how these things come to pass.

Perhaps the best poem in the book (though it is hard to choose among such richness), and certainly the most important in a conceptual sense, is the title poem. It has a hero named Rumen, whose plight and glory are both alluded to in these lines:

> In the city of the Olesha fruit
>
> A citizen never dies, he just wakes
> One morning without his legs, and then he is given
> A city of his very own making.

Unable to go out and see the real city, Rumen lives in the imagined and remembered city of his mind, where things hap-

pen in accord with his personality. . . . The line between the world of imagination and the world of reality in these poems is very thin, a fact which occasions much pleasure for the reader. We are not sure, for example, whether the fox has really eaten the hen in this poem, as Rumen's wife reports to him one morning, any more than we are sure there is a hen— or a fox—or a wife, for that matter.

Dubie is a poet who loves to play with reality in his poetry; art and the imagination—these are the things that really count, not truth, not fidelity to actuality and motive. There is a good deal of amusement and charm to be found in poetry like this; it gives an experience very different from watching the news or reading the obituaries. (pp. 210-11)

There are poets from whom one wants to quote and quote and quote, poets like Norman Dubie. Certainly there is not a bad poem in this book—the writing is everywhere superb, and the only weakness I can find is a result of the source of Dubie's strength—the distance he himself keeps from his poems. **"Sacrifice of a Virgin in the Mayan Ball Court"** strikes me as an unfeeling poem, even callous. The ancient sacrifice is used as a way of commenting on a contemporary murder—a girl has been raped and killed, her nude body found by children, in West Phoenix, near where Dubie lives; the sheriff is looking for "a middle-aged man, *a psychopath who will seem / Perfectly ordinary to his family and friends.*" The tone is light, as usual for Dubie, but doesn't seem appropriate here. . . . (p. 211)

But of course everything cannot be quoted, and even to begin listing titles would mean listing them all (though two other special favorites are **"The Dun Cow and the Hag"** and **"After Three Photographs of Brassaï"**). . . . This is an altogether extraordinary book from an extraordinarily gifted poet. We know that Dubie is well aware of the possibilities of poetry because he uses so many of them so well. He is not limited by any single way of writing, any more than he is limited by any narrow emotional approach to the world, to his subject matter. To the presence of his work, it seems, praise is the only response. (pp. 211-12)

> *Peter Stitt, "The Sincere, the Mythic, the Playful: Forms of Voice in Current Poetry," in* The Georgia Review, *Vol. XXXIV, No. 1, Spring, 1980, pp. 202-12.**

KATHA POLLITT

I should probably confess right here that Dubie's poetic strategies, while widely admired and much imitated, have always struck me as, well, dubious. His poems are highly erudite, or perhaps recondite is a better word, often set in an exotic past and peopled by historical figures. . . . At once mannered and hallucinatory, histrionic and elliptic, they are surrealist costume dramas in which *something* of great urgency seems to be communicated—but with each new book it becomes harder to say what.

At the risk of sounding obtuse, I own that I found most of *The Everlastings* incomprehensible. Whole poems eluded me entirely; others, usually the more narrative ones, were easier to enter, but just as obscure in their ultimate purposes. I could appreciate, for example, the bizarre melodrama of **"There Is a Dream Dreaming Us."** . . . But I don't understand why I am being told this story: what, beyond Gothic, it means.

Dubie's lush images, laden with Latinate adjectives and peppered with the exclamation marks that have become his trademark, fold into one another in a way that is often pleasing to the inner eye but that lacks necessity. . . . (p. 27)

Too much of *The Everlastings* suffers from . . . [a] lack of imaginative coherence. Dubie is obviously a determined and gifted poet, with energy to burn. I hope he will . . . reconsider his direction. (p. 28)

> *Katha Pollitt, "Two Poets: Run-on Lines," in* The Nation, *Vol. 231, No. 1, July 5, 1980, pp. 26-8.**

PETER STITT

[In *The Everlastings*] Norman Dubie places himself once again among our best poets in the postmodernist mode. His work bears a strong resemblance to that of Barth, Barthes, Barthelme, and, to a lesser extent, Ashbery—because of the narrative basis of his work it is easier to find analogues among the fiction writers than among the poets. (p. 667)

Dubie is everywhere aware of himself as an illusionist, a trickster, a sleight-of-hand or sleight-of-word man. He is akin to Jean Renoir (the central figure of the poem **"Grand Illusion,"** which opens this book) in his ability to manipulate our view of reality. At the end of the poem, Dubie makes something occur that indicates much of this—but I must set it up from the beginning. Renoir has raised a linen screen on or near the water of a lake so as to show his film to his relatives. They have a picnic, and as darkness falls they assemble in boats to view the movie, which Renoir is projecting from a raft. (That the physical situation is improbable is part of the fun—for one thing, the arrangement allows a drunk cousin to dump projector, film, and film maker all into the water towards the end. For another, it makes the reader curious—Renoir is not a fictional character; did this ever actually happen, we wonder, or anything close to it? Since the poem has an epigraph from a memoir of Renoir's, we are tempted to head for the library—but stop; it doesn't matter, for this is a poem, and the poet can do anything he wants within his poem, including rewrite actual history.) Before it is dark enough to show the film, Renoir amuses the children by casting hand-formed shadow animals onto the screen. Later the children fall asleep, only to waken in confusion when Renoir's raft is turned over. At that moment they look to the screen for an answer; the poem ends: "they wake / To a bat caught in the wall of linen, they think it's / Their uncle still casting images of animals for them." This is precisely the sort of confusion between art and reality Dubie wants to foster in his reader's mind—is this real or unreal, true or not true, we ask repeatedly and irrelevantly. Why, says Dubie, it is poetry!

This sort of thing, where we aren't sure what we are looking at, occurs many times in these poems. Dubie often writes about artists and their works; many times what we think is a description of a painting or statue will turn out to be a description of reality, and vice versa. Another way Dubie shows his postmodern sensibility is in being aware of his readers and their probable reaction to the poem he is writing. In **"The Parallax Monograph for Rodin,"** for example, Dubie says to the sculptor at one point: "I think by now / / We must be alone! / My bored reader having just left us both for a fresh lettuce sandwich." In order to recapture our wayward attention, he follows this with a wonderfully ribald story. . . . (p. 668)

The result of all this is a consistently fascinating volume of poems. The suppleness of Dubie's imaginative intellect is complemented by his wonderful abilities to turn a phrase and tell a story. His mind is enormously inventive; over and over we find enticing images practically tumbling over one another in their rush to get onto the page, into the poem. . . . This is a book of many delights from one of our finest younger poets. (p. 669)

> *Peter Stitt, "The World at Hand," in* The Georgia Review, *Vol. XXXIV, No. 3, Fall, 1980, pp. 661-70.**

JEROME MAZZARO

For Dubie all creativity is contemporaneous so that past creative moments serve to illuminate present as well as other past creative moments. His poems [in *The Everlastings*] seek to make accessible this commonality by a series of abstractions that, like Lowell's translated *Koran*, add in their reconstructions the expected "camels." Repeatedly, Dubie gets caught up in his additions and slights his "text." Art becomes not the escape from personality that he begins with but its expression bound inextricably to time. In **"The Composer's Winter Dream,"** one has, consequently, not Beethoven's sonata but details of the bustle "within the great house of Esterhazy," and in **"The Land of Cockaigne: 1568,"** not Breughel's painting but the socio-politics of sixteenth-century Brussels. With such emphasis on what the artist shares—or does not share—with his time, one may alternately suspect Dubie's details of possibly being a way to lure readers outside themselves and dismiss the book as a confused muddle of detail. . . . At times, as in **"Coleridge Crossing the Plain of Jars: 1833,"** Dubie . . . proves less interesting than his source; and at other times, as in **"Comes Winter, The Sea Hunting,"** he is too caught up in conventional imagery to say something new. . . . [These lapses] occur in his "best" [poems], and confirm even more strongly a sense of his needing to distance personality.

> *Jerome Mazzaro, in a review of "The Everlastings," in* The Hudson Review, *Vol. XXXIII, No. 3, Autumn, 1980, p. 463.*

LORRIE GOLDENSOHN

After publishing his first book at twenty-four, Dubie came out with a pamphlet or a chapbook virtually every year that he did not publish a full-length book. In ten years that makes a lot of poems, rendering it difficult for anyone, even Dubie, to swear by the contents of every one of them. The method is designed for prodigality—for a massive flow of material urging one to look for the preoccupying shapes of the poetry, rather than at the statement-by-statement, smaller accumulation of someone who writes as if a life in poetry were made up from the verbal brick of single poems. (pp. 152-53)

For Dubie, prodigal writing has yielded a variety of forms in which to test his historical and literary concerns, to hone his expressionist imagery, and to extend his language; also to sort out from many kinds of stories the ones that best engage him. *Alehouse Sonnets* used the restrictive jacket of fifteen lines. . . . *A Thousand Little Things* reconnoitered among lots of French surreal estate, fell on its face with one long prosy historical monologue ("**Abigail Adams: Pepper-dulse Seaweed and Fever Talk: 1786**"), and collected goods of doubtful utility like "**Helicinas, Mollusks & Wentletraps,**" the title of one morose and ill-assorted little poem. But the book also proved to be the home of several exquisitely tuned shorter lyrics like **"The Ganges," "The Dream Of The Islanders Of Thomas Mann,"** and **"A Village Priest"**—all of which maneuver among their exotic acts and settings with a slow, prosaic specificity of utterance peculiarly Dubie's own. (p. 153)

An early problem for this poet has been movement: how to settle the static load of objects in the flow of the poem's thought without impeding it. Especially in the first books, where multiple narrative and cross-layered points of view were not so comfortably established as technique, there came a moment when the poem threatened to fall in of its own weight, as the collective membership of exotic objects failed to discover their true interconnection. (p. 154)

Work done later exhibits the same fondness for cross-cutting, and for a jamming of times and places, but without impeding narrative or thinning out insight. . . . Dubie's strong suits are clearly not compression and aphorism. His best poems usually unfold slowly and cumulatively. . . . Yet within the poems there is a constant release of small, vibrating moments in which an unexpected word encases a sharp visual detail, or holds some surprisingly apt gesture. These moments are in almost every poem. . . . (pp. 154-56)

In addition to reflectiveness, the dominant habit of mind appears to be picture-making; the doctrine *ut pictura poesis* is copiously evident in even the earliest books. (p. 156)

Even in the pieces that lack explicit reference to paintings or photographs, the urge to station complex arrangements of figures and objects within a frame is very strong. In addition to these habitual juxtapositions, Dubie's abrupt and unexplained transitions within lines and within stanzas from scene to scene are clearly related to the jump-cut and the zoom lens of the filmmaker. The slow, overhead walk from end to end of the total field of his poem, in **"February: The Boy Brueghel,"** resembles the camera panning: start from the trees, cross the snow, go down a hill with the fox who has a white rabbit in his mouth, then look at the town below the hill; behind a window in the town, boy Brueghel looks back at the fox. Look again:

> Where the smoky red fox still
> Eats his kill. Two colors.
> Just two colors!
> A sunrise. The snow.

At critical points, the gait of the diction, in tandem with these other cinematic effects, begins to suggest action unnaturally speeded up, or slowed down. (p. 157)

While Dubie's poems often deal with disaster and violent death . . . , most of his visitations at the scene of carnage occur when the guns have stopped, but the smoke is still lingering; or the lines prefer to approach impending catastrophe, stop, and freeze-frame it. . . . [The poems] remain perpetually astonished at the fact of death and wish to transform it, first by a sympathetic magic, aping or incorporating death's non-movements, and then, by willing death back into living as a form of art, to transform death's freeze into frieze. By miming death's stop, and repeating it as static image, death becomes no more inherently stopped or "dead" than any other image. First there is the primitive horror at being unable to animate corpses; then, lacking the sorcerer's art, the sublimation of horror back into Dubie's acceptance of the High Romantic premise that death is the mother of beauty. (pp. 159-60)

What saves these poems from moral complacency, from having their impact lessened by a retreat into sterile aestheticism . . . , is their insistence on facing their dreadful moments head-on. . . . [What] also balances the poetry, in most instances pulling it away from what would be merely obsessional in less sensitive hands, is that preternaturally serene acceptance of death's effects; that blend of sorrow and compassion in the overheard voice of the speaker which leads the poem's occasion back to an awareness of continuities in the landscape and the overall rhythms of human generations, as death's bitter halt is suffused with a terrible beauty. Restraint of language, clarity of observation, and dignity of feeling accomplish this in rather large and surprisingly varied groups of poems behaving nonetheless uniformly as elegy. (p. 160)

There are two temporal urgencies in Dubie's aesthetic of death. In the first, the poems must keep their backward tilt, as Dubie leans down from the present to find connections with the living, sacralized past of the artist-fathers (and for Dubie they *are* mostly fathers), those guardians and keepers who represent the only means by which time and nature can be deflected from mortality. The second urgency is forward leaning. Like the artist-fathers who were his immediate predecessors, Dubie incorporates contemporary idioms of form: in perspective, by using the discontinuous narrative structures developed in modern prose fiction; and in his perceptions, by favoring the devices of pre-eminently visual media, especially film and photography. It is the performance of the second set of needs, coupled to the fiercely willed constancy of the first, that makes Dubie's work seem so unique. With an almost antiquarian lust, he clings to the manifest past, the "historical"—mostly, to the experience of other artists, or lives sieved through journals, letters, memoirs, and other forms of personal record. Each Dubie poem is ruled by this commemorative impulse. . . . Dubie's acts of homage to the dead seem based on a deeply religious feeling for the artist's responsibility as a keeper and respecter of lineage; he sees himself to be as one of those whose acts are part of a succession of acts meant to transcend the personal.

To transcend the personal, however, by specially defining "self" for the speakers of poems; what mostly gets left out is the explicitly autobiographical self. The self, that darling of contemporary poetry, here has little to do; it appears to be just another dreamer, usually present as disembodied voice rummaging around in the world memory, its consciousness oddly, and often disturbingly, interchangeable with others.

Even more than cinematic, then, the first formal impulse of a Dubie poem appears to be oneiric; the faithful transcription in print of that inner home-movie, the dream. For the sleeper, it is probably important to realize that the dialectic of consciousness is not *now, then,* and *later*—or even *living* or *dead*. For Dubie, all existences are co-present, co-terminous, as living and dead we sleep together in the walled houses of our bodies. In the dream, all persons are aspects of the dreamer, and all selves participate in a central self, even in that Dubie poem entitled **"There is a Dream Dreaming Us."** Or, once again, poetry is Dubie's agent for subverting death, as boundaries dissolve between fictive and actual, individual and communal, living and dead, and all members of the world body live and breathe in the common present of the poems. As the poetry feels its way to these conclusions, syntax reflects them. (pp. 161-62)

In Dubie's language, the eye-I is a paradoxically impersonal subjectivity, because the self is always collective anyway—a projective identity. Dubie . . . acknowledges that all of the poet's pronouns are creatures stemming from the same source. One's immediate self, however, should be minimally present. If named too loudly, the self interferes with, or distracts from the clarity of the other sights coming up on the screen, all of which are owned by the writing consciousness as joint property of a world self seen in its widest and wildest reach.

Nevertheless, trouble still exits for the reader over the entrances and exits of the writer's persona. Usually, this is provocatively expressed as an enlargement of the possible range of the poem's emotions. As an obliquely visible self hovering above the poem, just out of range, Dubie's speakers flicker suggestively, rolling back the ostensible borders of the poem's interests and identities. Allowed to observe what doesn't concern them directly, they are often present but offstage in the fabric of the narrative, commenting, parenthetically, as in **"El Greco"**—"only we two could know." . . . In **"The Ganges,"** the poem opens *in medias res* with an apologetic: "I'm sorry but we can't go to the immersions tonight." The experience is owned by a *we*, later dissolving to an *I* passing postcards of the event named. But the position of the speaker in the poem, the teasing, melting We-I, is never developed. It needn't be; it is the shadowy matrix of origins which the poet has judged that we need only so much of, and from this matrix he trusts us to reach in and withdraw the poem.

Most of this Hitchcocking around is fun; like that ubiquitous little bald man, the director of the poem slips teasingly in and out, without distracting us from his other, more intentionally engrossing narrative. . . . On some other occasions, however, the return of the repressed exacts its revenge in subtly disordering ways felt by a reader as gaps. Two of the poems closing *The Everlastings,* **"Lord Myth,"** and **"After Spring Snow, What They Saw,"** appear incomplete, their allegorical manner and exotic clothing somehow mechanical and uninvolving, because the true site of the poem stays buried, or partially obliterated by mannerism.

Dubie's poems heavily stress the eye and voice of the poet; they keep what belongs to an unseen and disembodied narrator down to those routes of expressivity which resemble the voice-over narration of a film. Although there is much narration in Dubie's poems, dialogue between persons exists rarely, and sound itself from within the poem is lowered to a minimum. Because of this, the narrator's voice locates tone and registers meaning for the poems: it is the only soundtrack. When this voice works in conjunction with understatement . . . , it underlines the impersonal, shared consciousness of the poem. In the austerity of their exclusions, however, the poems strain against becoming the exemplary machine of vision, operable from sleep through remote control. What often keeps a tense excitement in a poem is the will of the maker to re-enter it, as the presence of the offstage speaker, the blurring We-I, is experienced constantly, almost tactilely. . . . (pp. 163-66)

Beside the engagements of voice and ear, texture or touch is also extremely important. . . . Naturalist of the unconscious, swooping botanist of the past that he is, Dubie works harder than any poet I currently read to make his poems almost physical accretions of objects to be drawn from all possible landscapes, all possible *wheres* available to the mind of an insatiably curious collector of *wheres.* . . .

Yet quaintness is no part of his appeal. The poems speak in a neutral diction, coming down neither with colloquial abandon nor rising in aureate thicknesses. All the while steadily dodging conventional adjectives of description, and avoiding the dating

traps of dialogue, Dubie's language sustains the split consciousness of the present encroaching on the past. There is no real surrender to it; when not drenched in the funereal mood of elegy, past is not domesticated into a version of the present in costume dress. Again and again, the wentletraps, kerosene street lamps, citron candles of the chandelier, iron spiral stairwells, the aprons of mace, the sherry and wassail, the red ibis flying north—all the strange foods, animals, birds, and domestic customs so thickly strewing the text—effectively remind us of the intransigence of the past. (p. 166)

Often, the sober and precisely fixed names of the objects and processes of the past create the verbal equivalents of painterly texture, of scumbled and impasted surfaces, where the name is embedded in the surface as a piece of unkillable grain from the original manufacture, before it was worked into the finish, to become an effect of something besides itself. And yet the eye-I of the poem returns again and again to that surface in order to break it, to wrench it open; to transect it in the peculiar rhythms of its formal concerns, and to let come into being the full dialogue of the past combatting or augmenting the present. (pp. 166-67)

Although past time is the province of Dubie's poetry, and loss its chief magistrate, because all connections in time prove equivocal or fickle, a formal analogue, white flake to white moth in the example below [from **"The Moths"** in *The Illustrations*], makes its firmer claim on our loyalties:

> All summer the fat moths were knocking their
> Brains out against the lamp in the henhouse,
>
> But now the moths are replaced with large
> Flakes of snow, and there's no difference, moths
> Or snow, for their lives are so short
> That while they live they are already historical. . . .

Discrete particles belong to a world of resonant and intractable things, in which poems must, if nothing else, testify to the stabilities of form linking them. Discovering these links is the artist's job of work in a universe of frighteningly rapid change and death.

Initially, Dubie's poems are scrupulously observed surfaces, but despite their apparent nominalism, their cargo of objects, and particularly in *The Illustrations*, their determined dating and placing . . . , the surfaces are ultimately fluid. The poems earn their continuities in tension with a stripped and rather fatalistic realism offering little, or severely understated, commentary on the values inherent in its acts. Although in each new book there are several compelling poems with reasonably straightforward narrative, other more difficult and challenging constructions derive their momentum from a narrative dividing its forces into a complex counterpoint of wild, apparently unconnected events. (pp. 167-68)

In these poems concentrating on the deceptions of appearance, all of the usual classifications of matter as solid or fluid, or as being compass-accountable, are systematically undercut within the ongoing narrative action. (p. 169)

The net result is to disturb the weight of the physical; to unchain or let drift the material anchor floating it, or to subvert the scale of events in dizzying swoops from figure to figure. . . . (p. 170)

For Dubie, poems tend not to be philosophical statement, even if, like a bared tooth, philosophical statement can be shown in them. The formal movement, or style, *is* the subject. That the visual moments are a trick of language on the page is only the last testimony to a remarkably fertile and inventive writer who makes us see so much brilliant color on his black-and-white, usually silent screen.

Over the years Dubie's poems have gained principally by intensifying their commitment to story-telling, by coming up with a better, less discontinuous balance of narrative and narrative shift. As the story line has clarified, as more act than thing has been getting into the poems, and more people than apparatus, it is easier to see the complex sensitivities of Dubie's response to people, things and places, to their genuinely original cast. Year by year, he has been true to himself; each book supports and amplifies the work of the last, and from each a satisfying whole picture of a world can be derived—indeed, one of epic size. Next to the broad swath of these books, the work of so many other poets of his generation seems thin, intellectually incurious, and emotionally timid. (p. 173)

Lorrie Goldensohn, "Not in the Browning Shade,"
in Parnassus: Poetry in Review, *Vol. 8, No. 2, Spring-*
Summer-Fall-Winter, 1980, pp. 152-75.

VERNON SHETLEY

[*The Everlastings*] manifests a powerful disposition to relocate [Dubie's] imagination out of its own time and place. The places to which he escapes, however, are not purely imaginary, only removed historically and geographically. Furnished with a wealth of period detail, they offer themselves as visions of Rodin's studio, Beethoven's household, a party given by Jean Renoir.

Dubie's model, of course, is the dramatic monologues of Browning, whose speakers are historical figures. But where Browning's interest seems largely psychological, revealing nuances of character through a vivid rendering of the speaking voice, Dubie resists penetrating the minds of the historical personages he presents. One might say that Browning takes a tape recorder to the past, Dubie a camera. Dubie seeks to evoke emotion through a highly particularized rendering of a world of objects.... Dubie's poems are more often third than first person, and even his own dramatic monologues tend to adhere scrupulously to the surfaces of the world they portray. The sense of immediacy, of the activity of thought in the mind of the speaker, recedes, and in its place is a rich, leisurely flow of concrete imagery.

Dubie's method relies on accumulation rather than concentration. The poems build slowly, and tend to trail off rather than close; their characteristic gesture of farewell is an ellipsis. The contrasts and incongruities characteristic of Dubie's sensibility arise not from a mental habit of paradox, but from a search for means to intensify the image.... What modulation or emphasis one finds springs from the violence Dubie frequently interjects, but even that violence has no more pressure than any other retinal vibration. It forms a brief punctuation, then drifts off along the lengthening chain of images....

Dubie's attempts to add terror to beauty fall short of suggesting a realm of experience beyond or opposed to the beautiful. Like so many other poets in their thirties, Dubie seems to have no skepticism about the sense of sight, and about the ability of accumulated imagery to record a real vision. Visual particularity has its place and its virtues, but the contact of the eye cannot substitute for the contact of the mind. Dubie reduces the language of poetry to a sort of mechanical instrument for recording appearances, and indeed he achieves a certain purity

in diction and voice. But that achieved purity can hardly substitute for the complexity of poetic argument. Dubie has, in his swerve from Browning, done away with just the quality that gave the earlier poet his vitality, and the loss can be felt only as a diminishment.

Vernon Shetley, "Ask the Fact," in The New York
Review of Books, *Vol. XXIX, No. 7, April 29, 1982,*
p. 43.*

FREDERICK GARBER

There are times when Norman Dubie sounds eerily like the early Stevens. Though the stories he tells are none that Stevens could have conceived, the mode of narrative which Dubie has mastered shows us much that Stevens would have shown about the touch and look of things. Dubie shares with the early Stevens a sense of the richness of the world's surface, one which we can trace back to Keats and Delacroix and other Romantic lovers of lushness. Stevens was taken by the touch and look, not only because of their natural fascination but also because it was through touch and look that things got to his mind.... Dubie has moments of preciousness uneasily like those of Richard Wilbur. For the most part, however, his elaborations, like those of Stevens, are refinements of a mode of seeing that completes itself in a mode of making. The refinements are part of a detailed context that makes up a complex and chancy world. The complexity comes from the kind and quality of the elements Dubie wants to put together. The chanciness is not only in what happens in his world but in the difficulty of holding all its elements in coherence. *So* much beauty and *so* much death can be difficult to put together because of their separate (though related) intensities. Yet Dubie has learned to so organize his world that he can show coherence in poem after poem, ringing changes on a radical perception of experience. The perception is always the same, which means not only that it can establish coherence but that finally it may cease to surprise us. This too is one of Dubie's difficulties but he handles it particularly well. Though his work is obsessive it rarely forces that obsession on us. He owns enough canniness to know what he can do with the world's textures and what his poems can say about themselves.

His ways of doing and saying are not, in themselves, idiosyncratic, yet it is possible to speak of Dubie poems and Dubie characters as something nearly generic. Dubie's sensibility is both sensuous and narrative, which means not only that he cherishes textures and actions but that he dwells on the concreteness of things and people. His is a world of bright and elaborate substance in which consciousness—whether that of a slave in Egypt or a Romantic composer—is continually under threat, pitched to the peak of its powers, caught in an action which it may or may not have brought about but which it has to bring to a satisfactory resolution.... One of Dubie's previous books was *The Illustrations*. This new book [*The Everlastings*] is full of dreams and meditations that illustrate dreamers and thinkers, the least naive of which are seekers of illustrations.

Whatever the temperature, the time in a Dubie poem is always a season of the self. This is not to say that these poems happen entirely or even largely within the self. (In fact, *where* they happen is one of the most intriguing questions about them.) ... [Self] and setting have their own separate seasons, and it is possible that the kinds will not coincide. Yet the settings are always seen as appropriate places for the self to be in and die in. They always make a just and suitable frame for that quickness and death, especially for the quick death which is endemic in these poems, and whose feel and textures can be as fascinating as any in the landscape. . . . (p. 44)

[Though] the settings are dense and independent they are never entirely neutral, never without some relation—which may well be emphatic indifference—to what goes on in them. The beginning of **"Empiricists of Crimson"** has more touches of Stevens in it than its title, though Dubie, as I have said, tells stories Stevens would have ignored. The beginning is typical in showing how Dubie likes to get his poems going by locating their context in space, along the color wheel, and within a range of possible textures. This one locates itself not only in space but in time and various dimensions of sensuousness, all in half of the first sentence: "We can distinguish through the mist a red parrot feather / On a conquistador's musket, the feather suggests / To him the direction and force of the equatorial winds." What follows is an extraordinary sentence in which death happens as one part of a statement setting an action within a landscape:

> Below him
> In the jungle gorge with its waterfall and dark lake—
> The expedition like a ribbon of smoke climbed all day
> Up the slippery green wall of this abyss, the youngest
> Of the infected officers fell backwards, growing smaller
> And smaller, his brains like rope following him into the
>   water.
> His scream was lost to the deafening waterfall.

The water swallows his body the way the sentence swallows his death. The landscape has its own overwhelming swiftness which can make and take in a swift death, sometimes literally: a panther which "watched the Spaniard tumble down the rocks to his death" ends the poem by devouring him.

That passage illustrates precisely the way Dubie makes histories. *Alehouse Sonnets,* his first book, is a series of conversations with William Hazlitt about Hazlitt's world and his own. The elaborations of texture which have grown into Dubie's world were not really there yet, but his sense of how things surround us and fill spaces in our context was very densely there. Dubie is not claustrophobic about things as Rilke sometimes was. Their denseness does not press in upon him but, quite the reverse, seems to ease him because they clarify the dimensions of space and give him a location within it. Further, he knew as early as the *Alehouse Sonnets* how to retrieve moments and seasons of the self through such clarification: since things give us location we can pull back into the world the selves of Hazlitt or Coleridge or Melville by building a plethora of things and then getting a known or imagined selfhood to move among them. Dubie shows how the density of the self needs the world's equal and opposite density for the self to make itself fully. . . . In fact, when the relation is broken and the density of the world wins out over the density of the self, then the world will absorb the self and, eventually, the body that houses it. Absorption means death, as it did for the tumbling Spaniard and, less literally, for the suicidal monk in the brilliant **"Elegies for the Ochre Deer on the Walls at Lascaux"** in Dubie's *The Illustrations.* The new book extends the association. In **"Coleridge Crossing the Plain of Jars: 1833"** the old poet recalls how he died "briefly, in the blizzard," as he had done once before when, as a boy, he and his mother both nude, they stepped under an icy waterfall. In such moments "*my brain empties* / As it will when I've stood under the compass / Of a great low chandelier, weighted / In the

purity / Of vertical tiers of burning citron candles." As he steps into his parlor Sarah tells him that she "thought / The elements had swallowed [him] / Just as [he] passed the last sycamore." Dying means being swallowed, an absorption of one's elemental being by the elemental snows. It is a depletion, an emptying of the brain and all that we are into the maw of the world. (pp. 44-5)

In an essay in *APR* published in 1978, Dubie speaks of a darkness in his poems which comes out of "the manner of a Romantic tradition which I certainly belong to." He also says that he can transcend this "pathological sullenness" through his art: "I like to think that poetry itself would save me from it." Acts of consciousness that save consciousness from itself are classic Romantic products. Dubie is a descendant of several lines that go from Wordsworth and Byron through Thoreau, Emerson and Stevens, adding on figures like Roethke and Berryman as they stretch our way. Some elements in those lines work through voices, Byron and Berryman for example, and Dubie has always done that. Others work through modes of sullenness in precisely the paradoxical way that Dubie does. When Dubie is working at his best—when he stands off from both preciousness and grotesquerie—he makes figures out of a long-standing Romantic balance. In the title poem of this collection there is an interplay of tonalities that work warily around each other, qualities that constantly approach each other but can never come together in any kind of conciliation. Their stances are defining ones, the basic elements of Dubie's world. That world is made up of their bitter coexistence:

> He embalmed the Viking's daughter,
> Scooping out her breads and heart: in their place
> He laid sticks of balsam with salt.
> He put spices inside her skull.
> He sat her in a jar with the knees snapped, brought
>   back
> Under her jaws.
>
> The jar filled with wild, languorous honey!

The best of Dubie's poems are anecdotes of such jars. (p. 45)

> Frederick Garber, "On Dubie and Seidel," in The American Poetry Review, *Vol. 11, No. 3, May-June, 1982, pp. 44-7.**

PETER STITT

The primary distinguishing feature of Norman Dubie's best poems is their imaginative freedom; as the epigraph to the first poem in his *Selected and New Poems* (a line from Randall Jarrell) puts it: "What the wish wants to see, it sees." Both wishing and seeing lead to poetry, of course, and several of these poems are about writing poetry in one way or another; the **"Ode to the Spectral Thief, Alpha,"** for example, pretends to tell a story about a raccoon (the spectral thief himself), but actually was brought into existence for the sake of its metapoetic conclusion. We have arrived at the point where the raccoon has been captured by a dog:

> The hound bites into fur, meat, and *then*
> Deep into the spilled milk of the spine. This is
> When the stream seems empty, silent!
> This is also where the story divides in my mind.
> What can I tell you?
> Only that in past centuries
> There were fewer
> Dimensions to any concept of time,
> And there was a greater acceptance of mirrors, and
>   rhyme.

In past centuries, man's concept of time was more simplistically linear than it has been since Einstein's formulation of the Theory of Relativity early in this century. Dubie does not mean, however, to comment generally on such an issue; rather, he is warning us about the way different points of time are allowed to coexist (circularly rather than linearly) in his own poems. As for the second major topic raised by the lines, it would seem that Dubie is alluding to the idea behind M. H. Abrams' book, *The Mirror and the Lamp.* Contemporary poets are much more likely to incorporate nature into literature by shining the light of personal perception and interpretation upon it than by slavishly reproducing it according to the dictates of realism, as a mirror would.

Circularity takes many forms in the poetry of Norman Dubie; in poems like **"The City of the Olesha Fruit,"** for example, it is achieved by having the entire poem emanate—cunningly, cohesively—from the imagination of a single meditating character, one who creates settings, people, events, even colors as he needs them. In other poems, Dubie works as a painter does. . . . [He] begins with basically narrative materials and freezes them into a still-life poem in which everything happens, and does not happen, at once.

For example, **"Elegies for the Ochre Deer on the Walls at Lascaux."** The poem is essentially a meditation written in answer to Søren Kierkegaard's desire to remove himself from corporeality. . . . Dubie's purpose as still-life poet-painter is to venerate the objects of his desire. The poem's prologue is addressed to Kierkegaard and intends to prove that the diary kept by the philosopher was as real an object, as worthy of love, as the deer in the cave paintings, as real as the paintings themselves. . . . (pp. 412-13)

The first major section of the poem is a third-person meditation which reveals both the thoughts and the life of a monk, Theodisius, as he is about to take his own life; during his meditation, Theodisius thinks, among other things, about how he had played the tuba when a boy. The time is 1916, the location a mountainous region somewhere in France, just above the caves containing the paintings. The section is undeniably narrative, but Dubie has removed linearity from it in two ways—first, by making the story so heavily meditative, and second by freezing the action into a still life. The second section meditates upon the story of the Reverend Isiah Potter as he lives the last few hours before his suicide. The time is 1872, the location New England; it is the 4th of July, and the section contains a long digression on Chinese fireworks.

The third section is set in England in 1922 and focuses upon a woman who has just taken her own life. As the section opens, Dubie begins to make the final series of connections that will eventually close the circle of the poem:

The old woman is on her side on the sofa: the vase
Beside her is a fountain of red straw.
The old woman
Has been dead for some time now.

She drank her [Chinese] tea and stretched out on the
    sofa.
She looked out the open window
Across the street to where under the trees
The local orchestra was beginning something small
By Debussy. She watched a boy
Lift his tuba off the grass.

And with his first clear note she began to chill;
Her eyes never closed. She was just there
In her purple dress on the sofa. And
Through the open window all that night the boy
With the tuba was watched as if by an animal
Or monarch. You know how passengers
On a train prepare themselves
For a tunnel. . . .

The way Dubie freezes action in these lines is quite remarkable; insisting that the eyes of the dead woman stay open is but one powerful example.

The introduction of the train with its passengers entering a tunnel is important, for it allows the poet to reinsert the caves with their paintings:

The victims of composition as dead passengers
On a train each secretly positioned
For a dark passage through rock where the ochre deer
Stand frozen. . . .

The lines give an accurate description of the method of the poem, and we realize that Dubie has adopted the function of the anonymous cave painter: by freezing time and action, each of them has created a still life. The subjects of their works have been stilled, but have not lost life. The sense of motion one feels when viewing the paintings is akin to the sense of motion one has within the circle of this remarkable poem. . . . (pp. 413-14)

Peter Stitt, "The Circle of the Meditative Moment," in The Georgia Review, Vol. XXXVIII, No. 2, Summer, 1984, pp. 402-14.*

DAVID WOJAHN

[Norman Dubie] seems to be using his *Selected and New Poems* as a sort of reappraisal. In the last few years, he has more or less withdrawn himself from the world of poetry, and the handful of new poems in the volume show him working in a more subdued and lyrical mode. Like James Wright's 1971 *Collected Poems,* Dubie's selected volume must be viewed not only as a retrospective, but also as a signal of some fundamental changes which are to come. Like Wright in 1971, Dubie gives us enough new poems to suggest that a very different voice is emerging in them, but the poet does not yet seem wholly at ease with his new manner. Thus, his tactic is to both look back on his previous achievements and offer a tantalizing prophecy.

It's difficult to describe the particular sort of thrill that occurred among many young writers when Dubie's *In the Dead of the Night,* his first important collection, appeared in 1975. Here was a young poet who was different, one who appeared to offer a radical alternative to the current literary fashions of confessionalism and surrealism. Dubie favored dramatic monologues, and his characters spoke in a style both cinematically immediate and bombastically rich in detail. His cast of characters was both varied and nervy. . . . Dubie would invariably place his speakers in times of extremity, when personal and historical crises intersect. (pp. 269-70)

The inspiration from this method is obviously Randall Jarrell, whom Dubie elegizes in the opening poem of *In the Dead of the Night.* Like Jarrell, Dubie can feel extraordinary tenderness for his characters, and the best of his portrayals rise to the level of the tragic. But while Jarrell seeks an uncomplicated sympathy for his creations, Dubie seeks something larger and less precise. Despite the sharp characterization in Dubie's monologues, the voice within them remains remarkably consistent. No matter what person Dubie writes in, or what person he writes *as*, the style of the poems is much the same. Certain poetic nervous tics appear again and again; odd manipulations of syntax and linebreaks . . . , eccentric punctuation (perhaps half of Dubie's poems end with exclamation marks, most of which are seemingly unwarranted), and a preponderance of adjectival description. . . . But what these mannerisms establish, however irritating they sometimes become, is a firmly controlled authorial voice, even within the monologues. Dubie's style is so unmistakable that he is less a writer who adopts the voice of other characters than he is a kind of medium and ventriloquist: the voice seems *both* omniscient and hypnogogic. The speakers seem to emerge almost involuntarily from his consciousness, and though he seems possessed by them, he is also stern in the way that he controls their utterance. This tension between his authorial control and his abandonment to his speakers' sensibilities is perhaps the most memorable quality in his work. It causes the poems to be precise and compressed no matter how florid his descriptions grow, and it gives the poems permission to range widely over time periods and events without becoming fussy or elaborate. The allure of his voice is that it seems both of and beyond the world. (pp. 270-71)

As haunting and oracular as this method may be, it has some obvious limitations. The poems of his 1980 volume, *The Everlastings,* are generally less successful than those of his previous collections. They do not fail from lack of ambition, for the volume contains some of his most inventive and wide-ranging work. But the poems appear to suffer from a lack of necessity and character. Or perhaps I should say they suffer from *too many characters.* By the time of *The Everlastings,* we have the sense that he has peopled his universe with so many angst-ridden and maimed characters that we no longer have any perspective on them. We start to ask ourselves how he can *care* for so many people. Is Kierkegaard really so important to Dubie, or is he simply the subject of another poem? Furthermore, the poems of *The Everlastings* veer toward sensationalism and melodrama. . . . While *The Everlastings* includes one of Dubie's best long poems, **"Comes Winter, the Sea Hunting,"** in most of the book his method seems out of control. The lines continue to dazzle us, but we see for the first time how calculated his approach can be.

These excesses are corrected in his new poems. They are more delicate and musical than anything he has published before, and when he abandons his monologues and sweeping narratives, a graceful and painterly lyric voice emerges. While the poems do not match the ambition of some of the earlier poems, they are often better crafted and more genuine. Also, for the first time he is as much concerned with personal history as he is with social and literary history. (pp. 271-72)

With *Selected and New Poems* [Dubie] enters the middle years of his career in the best possible way. He has shown us how commanding and original his voice is, and yet he has also shown a willingness to modulate the pitch and intensity of that voice. He has once again established himself as a significant poet, and perhaps he shall one day become a major one. (p. 273)

David Wojahn, in a review of "Selected and New Poems," in Western Humanities Review, *Vol. XXXVIII, No. 3, Autumn, 1984, pp. 269-73.*

DAVID ST. JOHN

For the past ten years one of the most intriguing presences in American poetry has been that of Norman Dubie. Since 1969 he has published five collections and six limited edition books of poetry, and his work has grown in power and depth with each new collection. From this prodigious body of work, Norman Dubie has made a startlingly severe selection from his early work and has added thirty pages of new poems for this volume of *Selected and New Poems.* It is a collection which will establish Dubie beyond dispute as one of the major voices in contemporary literature and it will confirm the claims of many critics that Dubie is one of the most radical poetic imaginations to have appeared in Post-War American poetry. . . .

Especially satisfying is the group of new poems Dubie has included, many of them exhibiting an exceptionally quiet and highly personal side of the poet.

Most often, Norman Dubie's poems exist at the place of juncture of several "realities," sometimes historical and sometimes personal. For Dubie, "reality" is a condition of perception; that is, it is a complex of perceptions in constant flux. In each poem, a "sensibility" works to define the nature of the poem's "reality" as details of history (or of "objective" reality) begin to intrude upon and intersect with the speaker's own meditation and perceptions, his own sequence of realities. In this way, multiple correspondences arise out of Dubie's poetry even as their constant narrative impulses drive them on. . . .

The transgression of one world by another remains a constant preoccupation in Dubie's work; often, the transgression of reality by illusion or imagination—the objective by the subjective—is a poem's true occasion. For Dubie it is this multiplicity of worlds which creates whatever universal harmonies exist.

Norman Dubie's poems look out into our world and find the replication and repetition of image and emblem, of the figure and the figurative, of the shifting perspective and the broken tableau—he finds these all in movement, in the world's shifting mutations of context. His poems consider the nature of experience as influenced by the multiplicity of our perceptions and by the multiplicity of correspondences available in those perceptions. Often, in a Dubie poem, we find the natural, the violent, and the intimate all conjoined in a single poetic whole. There is a melancholy of detail, often painterly in ambition and scope, and through the disruption of those details (sometimes a syntactic disruption; Dubie is one of the most complex and yet absolute lyricists of the moment) the reader finds the vision both in and of the poem being dramatically transformed. The fine, delicate confusions of mind and eye are transfigured for us into the speech and voices of poetry. Dubie's narratives work on the principle of *release*—detail, nuance, gesture— and this allows an accretion of understandings to coalesce as his landscapes quietly reveal themselves. Every story turns visual in Dubie's meditations, just as all of his landscapes imply latent narratives. Dubie is always positing the congruent possibilities of an experience and, in spite of their overwhelmingly elegiac tenor, his is a poetry of celebratory illustration and illumination. (p. 17)

It is not often enough said that Dubie's poems are quite commonly concerned with situations of dailiness. Even in those poems, often monologues, in which conspicuously "famous" artists, writers, scientists, or musicians appear, these figures are always dealt with in basic and human terms. The poems that employ these presences are never contingent upon the speaker's or subject's renown for their power as much as upon the richness and surprise of their perceptions. For Dubie, the intuitive and intimate response is consistently the most primary concern, not the literary, well-read response. . . . Dubie's poems about or spoken by artists and scientists are not simply considerations of art and science, they are more basically meditations on thought itself and the nature of perception, on the process of *seeing* and *thinking* that is common to us all but which, in some, seems raised to a higher power.

Dubie's regard for the past is one which finds itself manifested repeatedly in elegiac homages to those sensibilities (those "perceivers") he admires and finds most instructive, most honorable. It is the dignity of the radical pursuits and perceptions of these figures that Dubie wishes to champion and preserve. Invariably, Dubie's great "perceivers" are minds at work against the odds of convention. Yet he allows us to see them in their most ordinary and human moments; sometimes, in fact, we see them exposed in some element of ugliness or cruelty. Dubie finds it crucial to allow his speakers to find as their backdrops the ordinary, *lived* world.

Dubie's poems exemplify a world view which posits the congruence and simultaneity of all acts and temporalities, all artistic and daily endeavors. Necessarily, this interaction and interdependence of memory and experience, of one's perceptions and hopes, includes the interweaving of the worlds of the living and the dead.... Dubie's monologues can sometimes suggest a collaborative effort between the poet and the past "perceiver"; yet, even when the poems convey a serious and weighty historicity their speakers continue to wear their destinies calmly, usually with great grace and even humor....

In his monologues ... Dubie asks: What is it that grants this speaker a unique place along the continuum of history? What, in each figure, is *like us;* what, in fact, is universal and human? Dubie doesn't so much recall history as recast histories; we constantly find his speakers redefining their relationships to their world, to their own observations and experiences. History is what time has left us in its wake; history is the story, the compilation of stories, we tell about time. Time has only one story it wishes to tell us: we are heading toward our deaths. Dubie, in his rescue of the dead and their visions, is able to forestall that sense of passage. Like Scheherazade, each poem, each story keeps him alive against time. It is in part this that makes Dubie so unafraid to champion ennobling acts, just as he is equally unafraid to champion the idiosyncratic, the momentary, and the domestic. (p. 18)

Many of Dubie's poems want to ask of history: What is primitive? What is civilized? How does *this* world supersede *that* world, if not by a more open and humane understanding of itself? The poems ask: What is the place of the will in the natural world? Is this the source of our constant struggles? Yet Dubie's poems are often also tinged with a light that is almost mystical; they invite into themselves a spirituality that itself transcends any conventional sense of spirituality because it is contingent upon the mind's simultaneous intersection with and recognition of many worlds beyond the natural world. In one of his new poems, "Revelations," we find this visionary side of Dubie, just as it exists perhaps in its most finely orchestrated state in the superb poem, "**Elegies for the Ochre Deer on the**

Walls at Lascaux," a masterfully conceived meditation on will and being, on death and regeneration. (pp. 18-19)

In reviewing the book *The City of the Olesha Fruit,* Peter Stitt noted that Dubie's poems "are not, no matter how obliquely, written in honor of the personality. They are written to celebrate the power of the imagination. The stance of the poet is objective, curious, interested in the known wonders of the world and in its possibilities" [see excerpt above]. Indeed, the power, resiliency, and scope of the imagination often figure as subjects in many of Dubie's best poems.... (p. 19)

To say that Dubie's poems are not autobiographical and not, as Stitt puts it, written "in honor of the personality" is not to say they are not personal. To the contrary, there is always the freedom of great intimacy and the privilege of the highly personal at work—and always vulnerable—in Dubie's poems. Even when his poems clothe autobiographical urges and urgencies in the voices of history and in the concept of the "other," Dubie still treats every voice and every speaker as if it were himself; he speaks with the urgency of *that* self and so makes each narrative monologue in some part autobiographical. And of course there are the deeply personal poems such as "**Comes Winter, the Sea Hunting,**" a poem about his daughter's birth, and love poems like the marvelous new poem, "**At Midsummer.**" Because so many readers are first struck by the persistent verbal imagination in Dubie's work, the deeply natural and simple voices in his poetry are rarely given their due. Let me suggest, as an antidote to this, the poem "**A Grandfather's Last Letter,**" with its wisdom and understated tenderness. It is a moving and memorable poem. (pp. 19-20)

In [his] longer poems, Dubie's architectures are simultaneously delicate and complex. He loves to employ disguised technical apparatuses and his phrasings seem as proper to a cinematic grammar as to a linguistic grammar. The impulse in Dubie's narratives is almost always compositional, in painterly and musical terms, and it is also theatrical in that he often invokes a dramatic staging for his poems. And over and over, in delivery and syntax, we find the cinematic textures of the poems coloring and disturbing the expected order of perception....

Dubie manages to write poetry that exhibits those virtues seen ... in a highly discursive poetry while losing none of the activated surface, none of the muscular and energetic rhythms, none of the complexities of syntax sometimes absent in a more discursive poetry. There is also a great quiet and stately integrity to these poems. (p. 20)

Dubie's poems are important because structures of language and structures of thought are our only models for self-consideration (aside from visionary or hallucinatory models). In this regard, Dubie has sought a style which both subtly instructs us about and consequently frees us from the ordinary structures of poetic investigation. (pp. 20-1)

David St. John, "A Generous Salvation: The Poetry of Norman Dubie," in The American Poetry Review, *Vol. 13, No. 5, September-October, 1984, pp. 17-21.*

André Dubus

1936-

American short story writer and novelist.

Dubus writes well-plotted, realistic fiction that explores the desires and disillusionment of contemporary American society. Loneliness, pettiness, and jealousy afflict his characters as they struggle with dissolving relationships and self-doubt. Through detailed descriptions of meals, drinking sessions, and physical activity, as well as through sensitive revelations of their feelings, Dubus establishes his characters as ordinary human beings frustrated by the problems of everyday life.

A lack of understanding and communication typifies the male-female conflicts in Dubus's fiction. Dubus's characters often attempt to escape the pain caused by unstable relationships through infidelity, yet promiscuous or adulterous affairs usually intensify their dissatisfaction. This recurs in the stories of Dubus's first collection, *Separate Flights* (1975), and in the title story of *Adultery and Other Choices* (1977). The turbulence between the sexes often erupts in violence. Two stories in *The Times Are Never So Bad* (1983) revolve around abused women: "The Pretty Girl" describes a man who terrorizes his ex-wife and her lover, and "Leslie" concerns a disillusioned woman beaten by her drunken husband. Critics particularly acknowledge Dubus's ability to realistically present the thoughts and emotions of his female protagonists.

Catholicism is a strong and generally positive presence in Dubus's fiction. In "A Father's Story" from *The Times Are Never So Bad,* a man whose daughter has killed another person in an automobile accident seeks comfort through religious ritual and a compassionate priest. *Voices From the Moon* (1984) develops the reactions of various family members as they learn of their father's intention to marry his former daughter-in-law. The youngest son finds guidance and stability in the Church as he struggles with his confusion and conflicting emotions. John Updike observes: "[For] Mr. Dubus, amid the self-seeking tangle of secular America, the Church still functions as a standard of measure, a repository of mysteries that can give scale and structure to our social lives."

(See also *CLC*, Vol. 13 and *Contemporary Authors*, Vols. 21-24, rev. ed.)

Photograph by Kelly Wise

JONATHAN PENNER

Some of [the tales collected in *Adultery and Other Choices*] ... are set in childhood, others in the military: worlds that Andre Dubus shows to be remarkably alike. Gang spirit, the yoke of authority, simmering violence, dreams of glory—these the child and soldier share. Given their passions and their fetters, both figures make strong protagonists. And given their lives' diagrammatic daily order, their exclusion from society at large, their scheduled metamorphoses into adult and civilian, how well they suit the shape of short fiction.

But choosing a helpfully ordered world is only a preliminary; stories stand or fall because of how soundly—not where—they are built. And every line of this book is both honestly felt and shaped with care. There is never a wisp of cosmetic obscurity, no sermonizing and no coyness, no self-preening prose.

The novella, "Adultery," stands far above most of the stories. Told mostly from a young mother's point of view, it portrays the slow collapse of her marriage while she and her husband each have a series of love affairs. The power of the story depends, not on any clever innovations of plot, but on something finer: the author's ability to notice what the rest of us merely see, to show us what important truths we never knew that we knew—and never *could* have known that we knew if we hadn't read this. Of the relationships between men and women, men and men, women and women, here is a wealth of understanding.

"The Shooting," the best of the short stories, turns on an incident of violence, but even here the force of the fiction derives from character, not plot. As Rust Hills once observed, plot isn't simply what happens; it's what happens *to* somebody. What makes it matter to the reader is the fact of its mattering to the central character. Wisely, this is what Dubus finally cares about: not a man's actions, however dramatic, but their complex effect upon him forever after.

The several stories dealing with childhood are the least successful—in no way bad, merely weak—and seem like early work, rehabilitated to fill out the volume. The final effects they aim at are simply too slight, too tentative. And indeed, if many of these ten pieces share a shortcoming, it has to do with final effect. The ending of a story should confer shape, wholeness. It should be a kind of spotlight, shining back over the story and revealing its unity, the necessity and beauty of its arrangement, its cumulative force. Here Dubus's touch is uncertain; sometimes the stories trail off almost arbitrarily.

Nor is it only in their endings that some of these stories seem unfinished. Nailheads have been left showing where certain materials are joined, almost as though two separate stories had been hammered together. The handling of time tends to be awkward. In the childhood stories especially, the virtue of simple writing has sometimes been carried to excess.

But, more than most books, this one shows us a writer in transit, who travels far while we watch him. The stories appear to be printed in roughly the order of their writing, for as we read on they grow richer, more mature. The dialogue becomes as accurate as a tuning fork. The eye for detail, precise and vivid and revealing, grows continually sharper. Above all, the examination of character grows more and more intimate, profound, absorbing, ever fuller of critical wisdom and uncritical love.

> Jonathan Penner, "The Making of a Storyteller," in Book World—The Washington Post, *December 18, 1977, p. E7.*

JACK SULLIVAN

Andre Dubus, author of *Separate Flights,* has said that he believes in "the nobility of futile acts." This is hardly a novel concept for a contemporary American writer, but it does receive some interesting twists in Dubus's new collection of stories [*Adultery and Other Choices*].

Dubus is neither a "southern" nor an "experimental" writer, although he straddles the borderline of each style. His characters are often southerners (Dubus himself is from Louisiana), but they are also Catholic suburbanites. There are no Faulknerian blacks or O'Conneresque Bible salesmen around to enliven their despair. So to infuse their lives with richness, Dubus occasionally fragments or inverts their experiences to spring them loose from their bleak cause-and-effect lives. Usually, however, his style is tidily chronological and conservative.

As is most often the case with short stories (and novels too, for that matter), what we tend to remember about *Adultery and Other Choices* are isolated moments and touches. Although Dubus characteristically understates, his descriptions of physical exhaustion, in "Cadence," of dieting and undieting, in "The Fat Girl," and of sexual jealousy, in "Adultery," are full-blown virtuoso performances that linger in the mind. A precise writer, he knows how to keep the volume level down and still get a good fortissimo.

> Jack Sullivan, in a review of "Adultery and Other Choices," in Saturday Review, *Vol. 5, No. 8, January 21, 1978, p. 50.*

EDITH MILTON

[In *Adultery and Other Choices* Dubus] examines a variety of relationships; family relationships, friendships between women, camaraderie between men, marriage, adultery. He writes of men and women in isolation from each other, and of men and women together. But, most particularly, he focuses on that monstrous division between the two, possibly conceived in nature, probably exaggerated by our culture and our values, and described by Dubus in poignant detail as an integral part of his characters' daily lives. I can think of no-one who has drawn a more precise map of that no-man's land between the sexes than he has in this collection and in his earlier *Separate Flights*. And even in fiction written by women or journalistic accounts of how women live, it would be difficult to find as painful or as accurate a description of the futilities of keeping house as there is here in "**Andromache**" or in his earlier "**We Don't Live Here Anymore.**"

The force of women absent is as palpable as their presence is. And the influences of marriage and passion are far less powerful in these stories than a more negative pressure, a vacuum in communication which begins as silence between husband and wife, and ends by inhaling husband, wife, children and society into a conspiracy of isolation. Where love, or even the desire for love, exist, life is sane; in "**Graduation,**" for instance, where a much-used girl decides to become a virgin again. Or in "**Cadence,**" in which a young officer candidate for the Marine Corps counsels his friend, Paul, " 'to get a girl again. There's nothing like it. . . . *Noth*ing. It's another world, man.' " Secure in his affections, he can afford to weigh his needs against the dehumanizing demands of the Corps, and leave. But Paul has long since been sucked into the void which existed between his parents. He has signed the Marine contract because he thinks it will please his father, and because the recruiting captain had appeared "like salvation . . . wearing the blue uniform and manly beauty that would fulfill Paul's dreams." In the confusion in which he lives, he needs the clear certainty of masculine order and approval, and the story ends as, his friend gone, he dissolves "into unity with the rest of the platoon."

Dubus himself spent five years in the Marine Corps, which exists in several of these stories as the antithesis of all things instinctual, sexual, and growing. It is not, in itself, really evil, or even inhuman. But its humanity springs from the need for silence, for peace from women and from life, and for the certain ritual which will replace the uncertainty of understanding. (pp. 33-4)

The best of the stories about Marine Corps life, and perhaps the best story in the collection, is "**Andromache,**" which makes explicit the conflict between the male compulsion for protocol, bravado and death, and the paradoxical female need to nurture and sustain what will only end by destroying itself. To nurture and sustain, moreover, without disturbing the great male rituals. The story, which is written from the point of view of Ellen, a Marine Officer's wife, widowed by his latest quest for adventure, recalls their last Christmas together and her attempt to give a Christmas party for her husband's men. The party is a failure; the complex arrangement of Marine manners keeps the enlisted men from showing up. Ellen is hurt, but represses her anger at the waste of her food, her effort, in the all-encompassing need to be a good sport, to pull in her stomach, to mourn, finally, in silence. *"Be a strong Marine,"* she says to her small son as he starts to cry at his father's funeral. While her daughter has already learned the lesson of self-repression, and, at the age of nine, knows as much as her mother does about control and selflessness in the face of the male needs and abandonments which have been the lot of military wives since Andromache.

But, by extension, all wives are military wives, and the Marines only the most potent of those institutions in which a man can feel his manhood safe from interruption. There is some security even in the lesser sports. In poker, for instance, and in golf. Men jog together to express their friendship and to get away from their wives, and though families speak often to each other with affection, they speak around secrets and gaps of the unspeakable. . . .

Ambivalence is the pivot of Dubus's world, which is a world in splinters, where men and women face in opposite directions, and Catholic mother and Protestant father do not meet sufficiently even to disagree. A man, to feel himself a man, must sacrifice himself on the altar of masculine ritual, and even adultery stems from routine and a sense of what one owes oneself more than it does from real feeling.

It is impossible to escape the suspicion that most of these stories have an autobiographical source, especially those in which Dubus patently disparages the masculine ideals of the protagonist. Most of the women emerge triumphantly human; Ellen of "**Andromache**," Bobbie, the restored virgin of "**Graduation**," and Louise, "**The Fat Girl**," who goes on a diet just long enough to discover that fat is what she is, and that any love worth the name can find her under the blubber. These women, and Paul's unposturing, gently failing friends, are the valiant of the earth; the others are oppressed by their maleness as by a burden. It is his ability at once to understand the strong and to exonerate the silly which makes Dubus's writing enormously engaging.

The title story, "**Adultery**," is the last and longest in the book, and in it Dubus tries to arrive at some sort of accommodation for all the fragments of his universe. The accommodation is uncomfortable and difficult, for the reader, I think, as well as for the characters, since it invokes a sexual answer for a spiritual need, and a spiritual answer for a sexual one; a combination which presents notable problems of perspective also in D. H. Lawrence, of whom Dubus often reminds one. (p. 34)

[There] is no question that Dubus is at his best when he examines the shards of his particular universe, when he charts the islands of domestic and military routine which define the seas of incomprehension on which his characters live. Putting the pieces together, he is less convincing; one feels the scale of Eternity jarring against the smallness of his people.

But Dubus is an exact and a compelling writer. The power of all these stories is very great, and the direction of the last is interesting. One wonders of what Dubus may be capable when he knows the path better; when he can describe the way to salvation with the same easy authority with which he describes the mined waste-land which stretches between lives. (p. 35)

Edith Milton, in a review of "Adultery and Other Choices," in The New Republic, *Vol. 178, No. 5, February 4, 1978, pp. 33-5.*

JULIAN MOYNAHAN

[In "**Finding a Girl in America**"] Mr. Dubus's regional ambiance is the northeast corner of Massachusetts, a district comprised by Haverhill and Newburyport, Plum Island and Salisbury Beach, and crossed by the Merrimack and Parker Rivers. It used to be considered Marquand country. Mr. Dubus, however, is much more focused on the life of the lower middle-class and blue-collar families than the master of Wickford Point ever was. Updike country lies immediately to the south. It turns out that Mr. Dubus's stories are just as much into divorce and adultery and the sorrows of children putting up with quar-

reling, betraying, separating parents as Updike's stories of well-educated affluent Boston commuters and professional people are.

The typical Dubus male grows up in a decaying, contracting small industrial city like Haverhill, or a bypassed port such as Newburyport, has boyish adventures at the seaside and develops a lifelong passion for the Red Sox—those heartbreakers!—sees something of the world during a peacetime stint in the Marines during the mid-1950's, then settles back into the home region where he may develop problems with drink, job or with the drive for liberation and autonomy of his womenfolk. A variant of this type is the writer figure appearing in the title story, whose social origins are the same but who tries to live the freer life of the artist without betraying or denying his class and regional roots. Yet this longer narrative is a failure precisely because Mr. Dubus and his hero, Hank Allison, hold such a self-centered, self-indulgent view of the artist and his responsibilities.

The best stories are those in which there are no overt or concealed self-portraiture and artist-portraiture: for instance, "**Waiting**," a brief vignette of a cocktail bar waitress, widowed since the Korean War, who works near Camp Pendleton, Calif. and keeps faithful to her soldier husband's memory, even as she turns 40 and must patch together a sex life out of occasional one-night stands with Marine non-coms.

Even better is "**Delivering**," about two brothers who wake up on the Sunday morning on which their mother left their father and them for good, after a night of parental fighting and drinking in the kitchen. They go out together to deliver their paper route, spend the rest of the morning at the beach, then return to the house to pick up the pieces of their own lives and their father's. The story is notable for its insight into what these decent boys, 15 and 12, really worry about, are angered by, and the remarkable amount of family trauma they can cope with. Without omitting any scabrous details—the kitchen at dawn full of empty liquor bottles, spoiled food and overflowing ashtrays, the father overheard slapping the mother and his loud weeping after she walks out to join her lover—"**Delivering**" somehow delivers an endorsement of the American family, from the standpoint of the children's need for it to survive, that is touching and oddly optimistic.

Two stories of violence, "**Townies**" and "**Killings**," work pretty well—though I wish Mr. Dubus's attitude toward the instance of murderous vigilantism and blood feud in the latter came through more clearly. . . .

[Mr. Dubus] has mastered many of the tools and techniques of his craft, though he pointlessly splits infinitives, starts far too many nonsentences with "Which," and uses current cant words like "judgmental" and "vulnerable" without irony. But he really runs off the track with "**Finding a Girl in America**," an unmotivated, histrionic tale about an aging divorced writer and writing teacher at a small college for women.

Hank Allison writes, runs, drinks, reads, has a teen-age daughter and a teen-age mistress whom he has recruited, as he does each year, from among his younger students. On this day he is told by his current mistress Lori how last year's mistress had become pregnant, probably with Hank's child, and got an abortion.

Over the next many hours Hank howls, blubbers, vomits, whines to his ex-wife, and generally chews the scenery because he really wanted that kid, see? *She* would have been a girl to replace the daughter now growing up and to go with Lori, whom he now plans to marry. And of course there is no need to be concerned about Monica's health and happiness, because she was always "angry" and "hysterical." At one point, when Hank lectures Lori about their relationship, he uses the pronoun "I" 21 times and "you" 6 times. If she had a decent regard for herself and her sex she'd tell him to get lost.

> Julian Moynahan, "Hard Lives," in The New York Times Book Review, *June 22, 1980, p. 12.*

DOROTHY WICKENDEN

Andre Dubus's new collection of stories, *Finding a Girl in America,* is inhabited by divorced men and their bewildered offspring, aspiring baseball players, maladjusted marine sergeants, lonely cocktail waitresses, and murderers. All seek catharsis, an escape from remorse and from the pain others have inflicted upon them, some by plunging into the sea or taking solitary runs along country roads, some by seeking out new love affairs, and some by kicking or stabbing people to death. Dubus's voice can be entrancing as it evokes a hazy romanticism or intimates lurking violence, but too often these stories lapse into sloppy sentimentality. Dubus takes his characters as seriously as they take themselves and the cumulative effect of all this earnestness is oppressive.

There is a tension in the stories between the atmosphere created—dreamlike and sensual—and the jarring experiences portrayed. This tension can be troubling, as in Part One, where the stories contain a blend of yearning eroticism and brutality. (p. 37)

But these stories are simply morose more often than they are disturbing. Dubus's characters are mostly men who recently have suffered through failed relationships with women. **"The Winter Father," "The Pitcher,"** and **"Finding a Girl in America"** all portray the disorientation of men suddenly separated from their wives. **"The Winter Father"** and **"The Pitcher"** do so quite movingly, one concentrating upon the father's strained and fumbling domestic relations with his children following his divorce, the other on the pitcher's startled awakening to his wife's hatred. But the novella, **"Finding a Girl in America,"** failed to move me to anything except exasperation.

Hank Allison, the protagonist of the story, is a character already familiar to readers of Dubus's stories from earlier collections, **"We Don't Live Here Anymore"** (*Separate Flights*) and **"Adultery"** (*Adultery and Other Choices*). He has not aged well. . . . Despite the implicit affinity Dubus himself feels for Hank Allison, he fails to convince us that this self-indulgent bore really can feel much about anything except his writing and his sex life.

What has happened to Louise, the fat girl of *Adultery and Other Choices?* Or to the sinning Catholic schoolboy of *Separate Flights?* Or to the harried housewives Dubus scrutinized in those collections with irony as well as compassion? Unlike much of his earlier work, which skirted melodrama by maintaining a distance from the characters' traumas, *Finding a Girl in America* lacks humor and the stories strike a uniform, insistently dismal refrain. This narrowness of vision is all the more disappointing in a writer whose previous stories showed thematic variety and a vigorous imagination. (p. 38)

> Dorothy Wickenden, in a review of "Finding a Girl in America," in The New Republic, *Vol. 183, No. 8, August 23, 1980, pp. 37-8.*

JUDITH GIES

Andre Dubus is a writer of unusual gifts. At his best, he captures the almost imperceptible erosions of daily life—the slow disintegration of marriages, the loosening of bonds between parents and children, the leaking away of self-respect. And he records the small gains—reconciliations, fresh starts, efforts to keep the machinery of our lives in working order. He writes with sensitivity and exactitude about ordinary people whose common lot is a narrowing of options.

And nowhere are the options more limited than in [*Finding a Girl in America*], which includes 10 stories, all previously published, and a new title novella. In earlier collections, notably *Separate Flights,* Dubus wrote with equal clarity about men and women and he recorded the treacherous shifts in their relationships with intelligence and subtlety. But here he has narrowed his focus—the book might as well be called "Being a Man in America"—and the author's perception of this condition is disheartening. In one way or another, the men in these stories are all casualties, victims not only of sexual warfare but of fallout from the male myth. For Dubus's characters, manhood is a series of endurance tests—in the marines, at the bar and at the typewriter, and in the home, where they struggle with what one ex-husband remembers as "the old male-burden of having to be strong for both of them."

Dubus himself was a marine, and he often writes about peacetime soldiers, some of whom are more at home on the base than they are in the outside world. . . . Although most of these characters carry their battles into the domestic arena, they nearly all seem to have been bested; they are divorced fathers, jilted husbands and lovers, men adrift. It is sexual suicide with a vengeance.

Nevertheless, their stories sometimes work very well. **"Killings"** is a grim account of an ordinary man driven to an extraordinary act—the revenge of a father on his son's murderer, which of all "male-burdens" must surely be one of the weightiest. The story is strangely ambivalent, and its implications are chilling. Like some of Dubus's best work, it is about ferocity, an aspect of love that the author reserves primarily for the relationship between parent and child. . . .

Even more effective is **"Delivering,"** the story of two young boys coming to grips with their parents' separation. Because it is recounted without sentimentality, the struggle of the children to marshal their puny defenses is all the more touching.

Most disappointing is the title novella. . . .

The stories are uneven, and the vision somewhat bleak, but when Dubus is good, he is very good indeed, and this collection is worth reading.

> Judith Gies, "Little Wishes," in The Village Voice, *Vol. XXV, No. 48, November 26- December 2, 1980, p. 42.*

JOYCE CAROL OATES

Andre Dubus's fourth collection of short stories [**"The Times Are Never So Bad: A Novella and Eight Short Stories"**] derives its title from a remark by St. Thomas More with which no one would wish to quarrel: "The times are never so bad but that a good man can live in them." Though Mr. Dubus's characters are not precisely "good"—most of them perform criminal actions of one kind or another—we are allowed to see how they define themselves as other than merely "bad" through the author's extraordinary sympathy with them; he has a gift for conveying, with a wonderful sort of clairvoyance, their interior voices. Indeed, the strongest pieces in the collection— the novella and the final story, **"A Father's Story"**—are really triumphs of voice, memorable for their resonance.

The 56 page novella, **"The Pretty Girl,"** ranks with the strongest stories in Mr. Dubus's earlier collections: **"Separate Flights"** (1975), **"Adultery and Other Choices"** (1977) and the well-received **"Finding a Girl in America"** (1980). It may be the most compelling and suspenseful work of fiction this author has written. The "pretty girl" of the title is a young woman named Polly, separated from her husband for reasons mysterious to him but quite clear to us and fated to be his killer. She is a near-alcoholic in her mid-20's, said to be intelligent but in fact sleepwalking through life, oddly alone but rarely feeling herself lonely. Polly's very prettiness estranges her from women who might otherwise be friends. . . . (p. 12)

Vivid as Polly is in all her soiled innocence, her former husband Ray is even more forceful. He commits brutish actions—raping Polly at knife-point, badly injuring her lover, sprinkling gasoline around her house at night and lighting it—but he isn't wholly a brute. Mr. Dubus builds his portrait of Ray in a slow, detailed, fastidious way, allowing us to hear Ray's voice and to foresee his fate without quite passing judgment. Indeed, Mr. Dubus often seems to be arguing in these stories, judgment is beside the point: Things happen to people and are rarely willed by them. Polly's and Ray's voices contend in the novella, and though Polly triumphs—if her desperate act of murder can be so described—it is Ray whose voice stays with us, plodding, self-justifying, "logical." He drinks a great deal; he lifts weights compulsively; he would have been at peace with the world, except for his wife's sudden defection. . . . Ray dies not knowing why Polly has stopped loving him, when, after all, he is so convinced he loves her.

Set beside the unhurried precision of **"The Pretty Girl,"** most of the other stories are somewhat under-developed, even sketchy. In **"Bless Me, Father"** a college girl discovers that her father is committing adultery and shames him into giving up his mistress. In **"Leslie in California"** a young wife broods over the fact that her husband, whom she loves and depends upon, has blackened her eye in one of his drunken frenzies—and not for the first time. In the rather bleak and atonic **"The New Boy,"** a teenager, whose father has left his family, drifts almost brainlessly into self-destructive acts of vandalism in the company of a psychotic youth. These are spare pieces of fiction, willfully pruned, it seems, of the rich and idiosyncratic details that elsewhere make Mr. Dubus's writing so good; they read rather more like excerpts from longer works than stories complete in themselves. (pp. 12, 18)

Andre Dubus's fiction is perhaps an acquired taste, for his characters are resolutely ungiving and uncharming. Most of them drink beer in vast quantities and contend with periodic hangovers; all of them are addicted to one thing or another, which Mr. Dubus examines with an extraordinary sympathy— drinking, smoking, black coffee, Quaaludes. When their various addictions fail they tend to think, like Ray, "it's time to do some more terrorizing." In the main, however, their addictions comfort them and give them reasons to keep on living. Where another writer might dramatize his characters' plights in order to reveal and exorcise their strategies of delusion, Mr. Dubus has other intentions. Like the hard-drinking protagonist of **"The Captain,"** who has survived an unspeakably grueling

experience in the war, he has learned "of how often memory lies, and how often the lies are good ones." (p. 18)

Joyce Carol Oates, "People to Whom Things Happen," in The New York Times Book Review, *June 26, 1983, pp. 12, 18.*

BRIAN STONEHILL

Imagine you're a character in one of Andre Dubus' short stories—say, the adolescent Walter in **"The New Boy."** You're swimming in your wealthy Boston family's backyard pool, having invited the new boy in the neighborhod to come over. Suddenly he dives in on top of you, hooks his arm around your neck from behind, and starts to drag you under. You have to fight to get free, and in a few minutes you will show your displeasure by bloodying his nose. But then you will be friends.

That is how Dubus' stories affect the reader. Violence pounces upon us without warning, and drags us to where we think we cannot breathe. It's not "pleasant," not "amusing." But it turns out, with Dubus, that we *can* breathe in his distorted, underwater world, and there is much to see.

Dubus' handsome fourth collection of fiction [**"The Times Are Never So Bad"**] bears an epigraph about violence from Flannery O'Connor, and in fact Dubus resembles the great Southern Gothic writer in his power, his ability to command our attention. Each story opens with a nearly irresistible hook. "I don't know how I feel till I hold that steel." The stories welcome you in, entice you skillfully.

Dubus resembles O'Connor, too, in his concern with matters spiritual. Even more explicitly than she, he focuses on the place of faith and grace in a Catholic heart. He hunts for purity's place in all of this, and is too clever and clear-sighted to settle for an easy answer.

Where he differs, though, is in his view of the sexes. O'Connor was a lumper; Dubus is a splitter. As if conditioned by life in a war zone, Dubus sees the sexes as *us* vs. *them*. We men understand each other. Women get a little weird. They'll kill you if they get the chance. In the world of *macho* letters, there's no better model of this skewed view than Ernest Hemingway, and sometimes Dubus sounds like an entry in a bad-Hemingway contest. . . .

Men in this world brawl among themselves, rape their wives, rescue their daughters; women cuddle and kill their men. What can a poor boy do? Young Walter strikes a blow for *macho* rule by disposing of his mother's and his two sisters' birth control devices. That's all he *can* do. His older counterparts will get themselves in trouble and even killed on account of women. . . .

The teller of **"A Father's Story"** mentions and then enacts "the necessity and wonder of ritual." For him it means talking to God, and imagining His response. Fiction—particularly short fiction, which suffers unjustly from publishers' neglect—offers itself as a similarly vital ritual. It talks to us and imagines our responses. Dubus at his best does this very well.

Memory is the lens that lets us look out of a single event across the whole of the life that led to it; language is the light that brings it to mind's eye. . . . These stories have a life of their own, even if that life is, I hope, grimmer than our own. The words get into our imagination and somehow spring to life there; then they tramp into the memory and so stay with us. . . .

For all our skepticism of language, stories such as these remain the wisest and most thorough way we have of absorbing distant life. The richer we are in rituals, the brighter the glow of that gemlike flame.

> *Brian Stonehill, "Memory, the Lens to Look at Life," in* Los Angeles Times Book Review, *August 14, 1983, p. 5.*

JUDITH LEVINE

Like many American short-story writers, Andre Dubus is a geographer of the sadness of ordinary life. But his characters, unlike the passive and nihilistic inhabitants of so much contemporary fiction, have not been stunned to numbness by their troubles. Dubus's bartenders, soldiers, graduate students at small-city colleges, two-bit thieves, and security guards react with passion; their lives are burdened—and rewarded—with loyalty and love, for which they suffer, fight, betray, even kill. The narrow boundaries of their experience do not compress them emotionally or spiritually. "'Ivan Illyitch's life was simple and most ordinary and therefore most terrible,'" a character in an early book quotes to his wife. She replies—speaking, it seems, for the author— "Our lives aren't simple."

Dubus has a vigorous, wise authorial presense. It's as if he would rescue his inarticulate characters from their floundering, but failing that, he generously fills in for the reader's sake. Polly Comeau is **"The Pretty Girl"** in a small New England town, who is smart and gets considerably smarter by the end of the story, but starts out dumbfounded by growing up....

What distinguishes Dubus is his attitude—practically a credo—that there is connection, however perverted, among friends, lovers, and families, not (as in Beattie or Barthelme or Carver) alienation. *The Times Are Never So Bad,* his fourth collection of stories, is suffused with violence both emotional and literal, intentional and accidental. But this is not, as the newspapers call it, "meaningless violence"; it is dogged by sorrow and remorse, and above all the struggle to forgive....

In the exquisite finale of the collection, **"A Father's Story,"** Luke Ripley's daughter, slightly drunk one night, accidentally hits a young man with her car and kills him. She does not stop, but goes home and tells Luke, who returns to the site—having called neither his best friend, a priest, nor an ambulance nor the police. The young man is already dead, and, from that moment, Luke feels he has taken on his daughter's guilt. A devout Catholic, he seeks order and solace in religion, but is not altogether successful....

Yet Luke finds rightness, even righteousness, in an uneasy reconciliation of love of God and his earthly loves and loyalties. He even prefers his no longer placid life. (p. 3)

This is a complex story about, among other things, healing. For Luke, just as religious ritual heals, so does the ritual of dailiness. **"A Father's Story"** reiterates the theme that threads this work: ordinary life, while simple and terrible, is also good. Hurt, disappointment, violence, and failure can be endured—can even be enriching—if there is also forgiveness.

Dubus is, as Anne Tyler described the writers she admires, "spendthrift" with emotion, situation, dialogue, and detail. Like some of the most satisfying storytellers of the past (the Russians come to mind, and Dubus has been compared with Chekhov), he is munificent, spinning out whole lifetimes and recounting events from many characters' viewpoints. Full as they are, though, the stories are remarkably economical. I am puzzled about why *The Times Are Never So Bad* and Dubus's three other collections—*Separate Flights, Adultery and Other Choices,* and *Finding A Girl in America*—though critically acclaimed, are not better known. Whatever the reasons, this is a shame: Dubus deserves a wide audience. For the lyricism and directness of his language, the richness and precision of his observations, and the generosity of his vision, he is among the best short-story writers in America. (pp. 3-4)

> *Judith Levine, in a review of "The Times Are Never So Bad," in* VLS, *No. 23, February, 1984, pp. 3-4.*

HARRIETT GILBERT

[Dubus writes about] relentless wars of attrition (usually between spouses) conducted with fists, with a gun, with words, with whatever's lying around. *We Don't Live Here Anymore* is very much from the school that *Granta* christened Dirty Realism. Its deft, economical, concentrated prose exposes an introverted USA of six-packs, all-day television, fishing-and-shooting trips for the men, bourbon numbness for the women. But it's also after something different. Almost alone among books by men, from *any* literary school, it's questioning what being 'male' really means.

In the first story, **'The Pretty Girl',** there's an obvious distance between the author and flailing, iron-pumping, wife-raping Ray, who can't understand why his pretty little Polly has left him and won't come back. In the three linked novellas that follow, however, the men's attempts to make some sense of manhood, marriage, parenthood, love, women's and their own sexuality, have the engrossing complexity of something very immediate. Structurally, there are long, looping flashbacks that dissipate the stories' momentum, while the final novella ties up its ends in a disappointingly cosy little bow. None of this should distract from the book's honest strengths.

> *Harriett Gilbert, "States of Desire," in* New Statesman, *Vol. 108, No. 2799, November 9, 1984, p. 32.**

LISA ZEIDNER

Twelve-year-old Richie wants to be a priest, and it isn't easy. Temptation is the least of his problems. His parents are divorced. His sister, Carol, giddy from cocaine, is living in sin. His brother, Larry, has left a marriage haunted by sexual perversion. And now their father, Greg, is going to marry Brenda—Larry's ex-wife.

When this much heartache befalls one small-town Massachusetts family, a writer risks soap opera. But Andre Dubus's **"Voices From the Moon"** is not melodramatic despite the emotional surfeit of its plot. At just 126 pages, his novel has the unsettlingly delicate power of a cool summer night. Emotions, Mr. Dubus tells us—even the most dramatic ones—are elusive as U.F.O.'s.

Well-respected for his short fiction, Mr. Dubus has been working at his craft for more than 20 years and beat the New Realists to New Realism by over two decades. His characters are store managers, house-painters, amateur dancers. Their speech is simple; their lives are full of softball games, barbecues and brawls in smoke-filled bars.

Unlike many writers who examine the quotidian side of American life, Mr. Dubus does not condescend to his characters.

They are proud of their work, observant, and rich in feeling. . . . The lives they've got are full of pleasures. . . .

It is clarity and intensity, not happiness, that these characters seek. Mr. Dubus would probably concur with Rainer Maria Rilke that "It isn't at all important to be happy." Stress and change are difficult but also exhilarating. Despair and ecstasy are alike, in that both propel you outside of your daily life, make you feel as Richie does riding a horse, or in church: then "he was so free of the world and his life in it that he could have been in another country, in another century; or not even on the earth, not mortal."

As in much of Mr. Dubus's work, the pleasure comes less from the resolution of the plot than from the insights: Greg's observation that teen-agers gathering for a clandestine smoke and beer "did not seem comfortable unless they were stationary in a familiar spot, like an old person, or a dog, in a house"; Richie's recognition that "seeing your father cry was somehow like seeing your mother naked."

Mr. Dubus is particularly astute on the nuances of domestic life. Brenda considers how "as a woman you were left having to choose between a grown boy and a flat American male, and either was likely to drive you mad." . . .

Such precise perceptions more than compensate for Mr. Dubus's occasional sentimentality. It's refreshing to read a serious contemporary writer who is willing to err in the direction of giving a character "nether regions of her soul" in a literary decade when directly addressing emotion of any kind—no less The Soul—is not fashionable.

"Voices From The Moon" is not much longer than the four novellas in Mr. Dubus's last collection, **"We Don't Live Here Anymore,"** so the title "novel" is somewhat misleading. Since each of the novellas in that collection considered its characters and circumstances from several points of view, the book offered more of the development and detail traditionally associated with the novel.

Whatever the name of the form, 126 pages is a perfect length for the kind of evanescent, intangible emotion Mr. Dubus examines so well. The single summer day in **"Voices From The Moon"** is long and complex enough for Mr. Dubus to illuminate a family's quiet revolution.

> *Lisa Zeidner, "Surviving Life," in* The New York Times Book Review, *November 18, 1984, p. 26.*

JOHN UPDIKE

As a writer, Andre Dubus has come up the hard way, with a resolutely unflashy style and doggedly unglamorous, unironical characters. These characters have tended to live to the north of Boston's urbane suburbs, in the region of Massachusetts bordering southern New Hampshire, from Newburyport to Haverhill, the city where Mr. Dubus now resides. The Merrimack Valley was the New World's first real industrial belt, and has been economically disconsolate for decades; the textile mills moved south, and then foreign imports undermined the leather and shoe factories. But life goes on, and life's gallant, battered ongoingness, with its complicated fuelling by sex, religion, and liquor, constitutes his sturdy central subject, which is rendered with a luminous delicacy and a certain attenuating virtuosity in his new, very short novel, **"Voices from the Moon"**. . . . (p. 94)

The title comes from a poem by Michael Van Walleghan, mentioning "the several voices / Which have called to you / Like voices from the moon." The voices, presumably, are the six characters whose points of view and interior monologues the reader shares in the course of nine chapters. The action takes place in one day, and its principal event is the announcement by Greg Stowe, the forty-seven-year-old owner of two ice-cream stores, that he intends to marry his twenty-five-year-old former daughter-in-law, Brenda. Along with Greg's and Brenda's, we get to eavesdrop on the thoughts and perceptions of Joan, Greg's first wife; Larry, Brenda's first husband and Greg's older son; Carol, Greg's twenty-six-year-old daughter; and Richie, his twelve-year-old son. The story, really, is Richie's; we begin and end in his mind, early in the morning and late at night, and two more chapters trace, as the day progresses, his inner turmoil over this confusing proposed change within his family. He has been living with his father, visiting his mother in the nearby town of Amesbury, and often seeing his brother, who will now, he fears, shun the new household. Richie is a normal-appearing boy—"a lean suntanned boy . . . neither tall nor short"—with the heart of a saint. He likes horseback riding and softball and cross-country skiing well enough, but the Catholic Church forms his deepest preoccupation and solace. He attends Mass, by himself, almost every morning, and hopes to become a priest. . . . [Melissa Donnelly] is three months older than Richie and, at barely thirteen, one of the youngest temptresses in fiction since Nabokov's Lolita. In the course of the never violent events of this summer day— a day, like most, of modest revelations and adjustments—we see Richie's priestly vocation just perceptibly erode. Though the novel bares a number of hearts, in a range of tough, detached, and even perverse adult attitudes, its supreme and presiding achievement is its convincing portrait of this benign male child, from whom the trauma of parental divorce and the instruction of the Church have elicited a premature manliness. When his father asks him his opinion of the coming marriage, Richie merely says, "I want you to be happy," and the gritty older man has the grace to blush and become momentarily speechless.

A dramatically versatile overview, as in **"Voices from the Moon,"** risks reminding us too much of the overviewer. Mr. Dubus has taken especial care with his three women, and has much to tell us about female sexuality and, contrariwise, the female lust for solitude: Joan, having "outlived love," rejoices in her manless apartment and the comradely after-hours company of her fellow-waitresses. Carol and Brenda also live alone, but have not yet outlived love, and seem therefore a bit doomed; one of the novel's theological implications is that in seeking relief from solitude we sin, and fall inevitably into pain. Joan reflects that "Richie had always been solitary and at peace with it;" so it is with a distinct sense of loss that the reader sees him, at the end, turn toward a human comforter. All three women, though assigned different attributes, are given neither much physical presence nor a palpable distinctness at the core; all three are too ready, perhaps, to train their thoughts upon the bumbling, rugged wonder of the masculine. Brenda fondly marvels at the way male friends never really talk about their lives, standing together at bars for hours, and how they fight "like two male dogs" and how "also like dogs they would not hurt each other." And Carol, looking at her own father, comfortably sees "in his lowered face, and his smile, that look men wore when they know they were bad boys yet were loved by a woman anyway." For Dubus's men, as for Raymond Carver's not dissimilar quasi-blue-collar, six-pack-packing heroes, women tend to loom larger than life and to merge into one big, treacherous, irresistable lap. Carol, whose daughter-liness cuts across the great sexual division, and Larry, who by a twist in his nature somewhat straddles it, are relatively cloudy stops in Mr. Dubus's tour of the Stowe family. Of his nine chapters, too many end with an embrace, with or without tears, and sometimes the language becomes overemotional. . . . The language can also wax portentous. . . . At the opposite pole, the demythologizing simplicities of Hemingway intrude. . . . And there is an excess of procedural detail, relating not to catching fish in the Big Two-Hearted River but to food preparation along the Merrimack: pancakes and bacon, tequila, lunch for the diet-conscious, vodka with onions and pepper—we learn how to prepare and consume them all. These characters are well catered to.

Yet Mr. Dubus's willingness to brood so intently above his disturbed, divorced, mostly lapsed Catholics lends his survey an aerial quality, an illusion of supernatural motion, that reminds us of what people used to read novels for. How rare it is, these days, to encounter characters with wills, with a sense of choice. Richie and his father both muster their inner strengths, make resolves, and grieve over their decisions. The most threatening opponents, Greg believes, are those without bodies: "Self-pity, surrender to whatever urged him to sloth or indifference or anomie or despair." In this book the streams of conscious-ness are channelled by mental exertion; the mind is a garden where some thoughts and impulses can be weeded out and others encouraged. Purity beckons everyone to a clean place. . . .

Greg daydreams of walking beside an unspoiled Amazon, "where each step was a new one, on new earth." Brenda renounces promiscuity, and Joan has walked away from motherhood, at enduring cost to herself; when the opportunity arises to "tell one of her children something she knew, and to help the child," she seizes it, spelling out for Larry, who feels humiliated by losing his ex-wife to his father, the way in which the wound will heal and life will go on. For Jack Kerouac, another Franco-American from the Merrimack Valley, Roman Catholicism had dwindled to a manic spark, a frenetic mission to find the sacred everywhere; for Mr. Dubus, amid the self-seeking tangle of secular America, the Church still functions as a standard of measure, a repository of mysteries that can give scale and structure to our social lives. The family and those intimate connections that make families are felt by this author as sharing the importance of our souls, and our homely, awkward movements of familial adjustment and forgiveness as being natural extensions of what Pascal called "the motions of Grace." (pp. 94, 97)

John Updike, "Ungreat Lives," in The New Yorker, *Vol. LX, No. 51, February 4, 1985, pp. 94, 97-101.*

Stephen Dunn

1939-

American poet and editor.

Dunn's works exhibit an inventive mixture of wit and pathos. His poems, some of which include elements of surrealism and allegory, concern the anxieties, fears, and joys of everyday life. Dunn is often praised for his optimistic tone and direct style. One critic attributes Dunn's success to his poetic voice, "which remains always somewhere between confidence and humility." His poetry is viewed as a positive and refreshing alternative to the undertones of death in the works of such confessional poets as John Berryman, Sylvia Plath, and Anne Sexton. Dunn's early collections, *Looking for Holes in the Ceiling* (1974) and *Full of Lust and Good Usage* (1976), display his sensitivity to a sometimes dark yet not unfriendly world. Dave Smith praised *A Circus of Needs* (1978), noting that Dunn seems "truly a poet of serious darkness for whom poetry has its most venerable function, the enactment and event of the imagination yearning to know what it means to be alive." *Work and Love* (1982) provides further examples of Dunn's adeptness at extracting humor from seemingly catastrophic situations.

(See also *Contemporary Authors,* Vols. 33-36, rev. ed. and *Contemporary Authors New Revision Series,* Vol. 12.)

Photograph by Ralph Bran. Courtesy of Stephen Dunn

ROBERT F. WILLSON, JR.

Lately we readers of poetry and prose have been victimized by accounts of death trips. We have been exposed to the agonies of the roads taken by Sylvia Plath, Anne Sexton, John Berryman, and others; and the newest school of literary criticism seems fascinated by the clues about suicide residing in the works of these writers. . . . (p. 103)

But let us pull our heads out of the ovens and from under the bell jars for a moment. I want to offer a crash course in surviving, using . . . collections of poems which seem to strike a blow for life with style and grace. . . . [Stephen Dunn's *Looking for Holes in the Ceiling* is] marked by injunction. Here is a speaker with definite ideas about how to confront death, wrestle it down, and teach it its place. **"Chipping Away at Death,"** for instance, qualifies as a formulaic rite designed to throw death off the track. . . . In **"Decisions to Disappear,"** Dunn's persona finds himself dreaming of dying or inventing himself again by making phone calls to old lovers. Yet in the midst of these reveries he realizes that he disappears each time someone yawns and closes his eyes; there is no controlling the hands which lift the cloak from his shoulders, leaving him as "conspicuous as silence." Despite the poem's theme of death's omnipotence, Dunn's speaker reacts to the absoluteness of the condition with witty embarrassment: he is left standing alone, as "conspicuous" as one who has dropped his pants at a party.

Although this mood of embarrassed conspicuousness prevails in many of the poems (see especially **"At Every Gas Station There Are Mechanics"** and **"Dancing on Park Avenue"**), it frequently blends with a quiet confidence that poetry possesses the power to seduce even death. The poet in us, Dunn seems to be saying, can glimpse the holes in the ceiling, get beyond death not to enter heaven or hell, but to reveal the truth of life hidden deep within us. In the volume's most urgent poem, **"A Poem for Atheists,"** Dunn expresses his right to disbelieve in the conventional answers to life's questions. He has drilled a hole in his ceiling, "hoping for the best," only to have his friends urge him to fix it as if nothing had happened. The hole seems to represent his questioning, his doubt, his suspicions, and his friends stand for the easy solution of a religious belief that allows us to fill in the cracks in our faith. Gradually, the hole is forgotten, and Dunn can only muse over his "foresight," a telling pun, in cornering the market on now-fashionable atheism. Still, he realizes there have been no messages, "not even a pole, nor a fireman," come down to extinguish the fire of doubt, to save the house or stand by helplessly and watch it burn. Dunn has no ready-made answers to feed his readers; and in this sense the book is not suitable for those seeking survival in comfortable images of womb-like rest. Quoting Oscar Levant's definition of an atheist as "someone with no invisible means of support" to assure us he has a sense of humor about the matter, Dunn then proceeds to show us that his visible means of support are his wit, his refreshingly oblique vision, and his faith in the vitality of poetry. His holes in the ceiling and fresh colloquialism remind us of that other metaphysical whose name sounds the same: both demonstrate to Death that it dare not be proud. (pp. 104-05)

Robert F. Willson, Jr., "The Survival School of Poetry," in New Letters, *Vol. 41, No. 4, June, 1975, pp. 103-07.**

PETER STITT

Two traditions come together in *Looking for Holes in the Ceiling*—Stephen Dunn's first book. On the surface, his poems are dominated by the witty, semi-surrealistic voice found in the lighter work of Bly, and, especially, Strand. Just beneath this bright, healthy exterior, however, lurk hints of suffering and mental instability—the voice of the Savage God of our age. These voices wage a continual battle throughout the book—never does one clearly defeat the other, never do they perfectly mesh. The structure of the book suggests a speaker-protagonist who is on the verge of a crack-up and searching for help in carrying on. The problem is that, because of the healthy surface voice of the poems, I simply cannot believe in the reality of this character's supposed troubles.

Dunn himself addresses the problem in **"Biography in the First Person."** Throughout the poem he tries to convince us that the voice most apparent to us in the book is not his most real, most true voice: "This is not the way I am. / Really, I am much taller in person." Later he identifies some of the components of his height (or depth). . . . The smiles which first draw us to these poems, we are told, are deceiving, for they only act to hide the suffering, the "early deaths." If we accept appearances, Dunn insists, we will misread the poems, and he doesn't want us to do this. . . . (pp. 764-65)

However, hard as I have tried, I cannot bring myself to believe in this hidden, deeper, more tragic self. Stephen Dunn strikes me as an essentially healthy, good-natured, well-balanced man; if he wants his personality to decompose, I think he'll have to talk himself into it. His best poems are his wittiest—for example, **"Dancing on Park Avenue."** . . . (p. 765)

The serious level which I find most appealing in Dunn's poems plays upon a notion of alienation, the poet as an outcast from his society. A witty poem in which this is the theme is **"On Hearing the Airlines Will Use a Psychological Profile to Catch Potential Skyjackers."** . . . We see here the problem of the outcast, of a man whose commitment is different from that of his society.

The book ends with a turning inward to the self, which is the only place such a problem as this can be solved. . . . *Looking for Holes in the Ceiling* is an uneven book which also promises well for the author's future. The influence of the confessional poets is rarely a positive one for younger writers because, happily, the stance that was so natural for Plath, Berryman, and Sexton is not a natural one for all poets. Stephen Dunn can be an excellent poet—serious and witty, insightful and imaginative—without ever cracking up or commiting suicide. (pp. 765-66)

Peter Stitt, in a review of "Looking for Holes in the Ceiling," in The Georgia Review, *Vol. XXXI, No. 3, Fall, 1977, pp. 764-66.*

CHERYL WALKER

[In *Full of Lust and Good Usage* Stephen Dunn] seems much more fully in control of himself as an alien, and he rarely tortures his poetry with the sense of disconnectedness. He has in fact assimilated it so fully that it functions like a real calling card. We know that he has lived in small towns in the Midwest where he felt like an outsider, that sometimes his past still preys on his mind, making him feel alien in the present. This book even has a plot to it. One comes away from it feeling that one knows a good deal about Stephen Dunn's life. . . . All of it is of a piece, quiet, witty, controlled, nothing extraordinary, nothing inappropriate.

It is a pleasant book and peculiarly a man's book. Stephen Dunn follows in the metrical footsteps of Mark Strand. Often there is an introductory statement which usually contains a mysterious element, some "it" or "that," some who or what which is not immediately accessible. Then follows a list of particulars. Gradually the whole picture comes into focus. . . . (p. 204)

What makes this a man's book has nothing really to do with lust (which, though it appears in the title, is not in fact the premise of the poems generally), but rather with that certain sense of ease which is everywhere in spite of the uneasiness Dunn talks about. This kind of ease is still unavailable to most women who must struggle against the culture's inherent bias in order to achieve self-respect and integration. Like the alienation which is a part of Dunn's persona, the uneasiness in his poetry comes from knowing oneself superior to actual circumstances. . . . Of course there are fears, but compared to Judith Moffett's very real sense of inadequacy in poems like "Monsters," and her need to caulk the cracks in herself in order to transcend the world, Dunn suggests that he is on good terms with the universe. He may be an alien, but he seems, always, a protected alien. (p. 205)

Cheryl Walker, "Premature Celebrations," in Parnassus: Poetry in Review, *Vol. 6, No. 1, Fall-Winter, 1977, pp. 198-207.**

RONALD WALLACE

What distinguishes Stephen Dunn's poetry is not his language—it is flat and simple, rarely eloquent or moving in itself—and not his subject matter. It is the stuff of everyday life: small towns, houses, sidewalks, landlords, truckstops, daughters. What distinguishes Dunn is his voice, that elusive quality of any good poem, difficult to define, which makes the poem unmistakably the author's own. At his best, Dunn sustains a wry perspective, a skewed, quirky glance, the surprising or surreal image with its deadpan face, a simplicity and wit which controls complexity and pain. A good Stephen Dunn poem is one that makes you laugh out loud, not because what he says is funny (though sometimes it is), but because it is surprising, exact, and right, because it is what you have always known and know now for the first time, because it exhilarates you with the sheer joy of his talent and craft and imagination. (pp. 74-5)

There are risks in writing such poems; it is difficult to sustain the necessary delicacy of touch to prevent the voice from tripping off into preciousness, cuteness, or coyness on the one hand, or lumbering into formulaic predictability, the monotonous expected, on the other. In his excitingly fresh and original first book, Dunn succeeded in maintaining the precarious balance. While his second book, *Full of Lust and Good Usage*, is good, is very good, it never quite reaches the heights of the first.

For one thing, the new book seems less varied and ambitious; the flat language and subject matter too often stay flat. Poems like "Boats," "California, This Is Minnesota Speaking," "Nova Scotia Chronolog #3 and #5," and "A Romance," for example, finally seem to lack the necessary magic to charm them out of the ordinary. Further, the surreal images too often grow formulaic and predictable, losing their element of surprise and consequently their wit.... And finally, there are no single poems that stand out as insistently memorable. Nothing in the new volume strikes home as strongly as the best poems in the early book.

Perhaps it is unfair to put a poet in competition with himself, or to expect him to transcend himself in each new book. Indeed, if I didn't have the first collection before me as a norm, I would probably be surprised and delighted with the second. Further, I suspect that what Dunn has sacrificed in freshness and variety, he has gained in focus and unity. If few individual poems stand out here, the book works as a whole, single poems gaining power and scope through juxtaposition.

One of the most successful sections of the book, for example, comprises a series of poems about small towns. For Dunn, the small town is almost a mythical place, existing somewhere deep in the middle of the mind and heart, as well as in the middle of the country. In these poems, familiar things take on strange and surreal, often ominous and threatening, life.... The poems pulse with nightmares, wounds, bugs, shadows, and cracks, the small dark things and places that inhabit us.... Many of Dunn's best poems are about the thin, taut surfaces that contain the dark explosiveness of the unconscious. Like the sidewalks, the surfaces of the poems are tight and terse, as if carefully restraining the violence within, and ready to break, snap, or explode at any moment.

But Dunn isn't merely content to catalogue the darkness at the heart of things. Some of the best poems in the book are celebratory, proclaiming a desperate joy in the face of potential chaos. (pp. 75-6)

Full of Lust and Good Usage is ... a good book, distinguished by Stephen Dunn's lean, honed lines, and the articulate music of his voice. But in repeating past triumphs, the voice in this book begins to seem a bit tired and predictable, losing some of its sinew and verve. It is understandable that a young poet would want to exploit the form and voice he had discovered and mastered in earlier work. But in subsequent books, I look for Dunn to change and develop, to grow beyond himself, to pull off a few more surprises. (p. 76)

> Ronald Wallace, "Small Explosions," in The Chowder Review, *No. 8, 1977, pp. 74-6.*

RON SLATE

In "The Man Who Never Loses His Balance," the second poem in ... [*A Circus of Needs*], we hear about a high-wire artist who is "sick of the risks / he never really takes." His proficiency and calculation dazzle the audience, "making them care for him." ... Stephen Dunn's poetry has often balanced between a handsome theatricality and a self-critical sobriety. This much really hasn't changed. He is still a maker of psychological allegories and his attention is usually riveted to personal foibles. It seems to me that sometimes the construction of fables that in fact tell one's own story can be a dazzling but unrisky business; one keeps pecking away at a sense of lack and 'absence' but never dares to deal in a rugged fashion with the first-hand experience. The stress and strain between autobiographical poems about family/love/relationships and "fable"-

type poems about thinly masked and similar characters is profound in this collection. It is also problematic. Because Dunn wants to be on the wire *and* in mid-air; he travels between documenting his inner life and insisting that too much brooding on that life is the very impediment to relaxation. Dunn is a poet who has been consistently interesting to me mainly because he is a poet of personality—and the texturing of personality involves portraying its inconsistencies, its hesitations, its affirmations and its foolishness. For me he is at his best when he "responds to a low," the vocation of the speaker of "Weatherman." ... There's a lot in Dunn's work that is show-biz.. And when he adjusts the histrionics and posing to serve the opening of personality, Dunn scores hit after hit. When his fable-inventions stray into a less controlled satire or when he seems to be embarrassed about posing or fears that a real plunge is being avoided, his poems are less attractive to me.

One of the leaps Dunn has been taking since *Full of Lust and Good Usage* is toward a more direct, less frilly language. The quiet humility he has many times presented as an antidote to the "little I-Want-Everything drum / pounding in my chest" (in "Any Time") has led to shorter, punchy lines and a bold confessional tone. It's my opinion, though, that Dunn's eschewing of selfish personality has inadvertently led to some flat language, as though "humility" as subject matter has been confused with "humility" of expression. His eagerness to be honest, often a charming posture, sometimes reduces the very inventiveness of phrase that makes his best poems sparkle: "Sister," "Weatherman," "The Muse," "Belly Dancer at the Hotel Jerome," "Modern Dance Class"—to name a few excellent poems.

A renewal of contact with life is the "goal" of many of these speeches, though I wouldn't claim that Dunn actually believes speaking is the way to its attainment. In "Directions" joy is achieved by "feeling more like a wastrel every minute"; the more you plumb the depths of your own corruption, the more vital and realistic an approach. "The circus of needs" is a circus of obsessions and Dunn's art lies in a kind of simultaneous indictment/celebration of those quirks. In "Modern Dance Class" the speaker knows he is "the toad" among his instructor's "butterflies," and yet it is precisely his immodest self-appraisal at the end of the poem mingled with his earlier toady and humble image that makes his character so interesting. (pp. 41-2)

For some poets the revealing of 'self' (i.e. 'what I'm really like, folks') happens as a by-product of discussing a serious and crucial memory or creating impersonal and passive voices supposedly representing the poet 'freed' from self. With Dunn, self-revelation is the primal grand gesture. (p. 42)

Renewal of contact, however, sometimes implies for Dunn a mistrust of statement as though his speaker must apologize for playing with images and metaphors instead of engaging directly in the life he wants so much to talk about. (p. 43)

To escape from metaphor and dazzling but unrisky statement— and yet to use this scenario as a looming metaphor for that very escape: this is a recurring Dunn strategy, used successfully over and over again. Here, subject matter (the need for "honesty" and unmetaphoricalness) is not confused with technique (the need for theatrical metaphor). The plot-line serves the investigation of identity and 'self'—when within the poem, a brooding on oneself is a cheap way of getting by. (pp. 44-5)

To my ear, Dunn's poetry is exciting precisely because of the binds and vacillations that evolve from the "plunge" he is not afraid to take. If a risk is something you get away with, then Dunn gets away with maneuvers which he fully recognizes as located perilously close to the I-Want-Everything part of the psyche. (p. 45)

Ron Slate, "Responding to a Low," in The Chowder Review, *No. 12, Spring-Summer, 1979, pp. 41-5.*

DAVE SMITH

[With *A Circus of Needs*] Dunn has become a philosophical poet of weight. His flirtations with reality have turned mature. He is truly a poet of serious darkness for whom poetry has its most venerable function, the enactment and event of the imagination yearning to know what it means to be alive.

Philosophy, as everyone knows, when wedded to poetry often produces the tediously didactic child. If you visit such a family the child wants to recite encounter prose or play bridge. You are not allowed to smoke. But a dramatized poetry of ideas may lead to delight through fable. Fable is now the dominant mode of Dunn's poetry and its companions are poems of hypothesis and wry instruction. I am tempted to say Dunn is the youngest Modernist I know, so cool and distant is his stance. He is always looking for "something to talk about / instead of you." Here the referent of "you" is whatever is so personal that to approach it too directly is to bruise its secret beauty. (p. 29)

The figures in Dunn's poems are all bound into the archetype of the gambler. They are divers, tight-rope walkers, adventurers, acolytes, and always lovers. For them, the difficulty of love is breathable, its failures and ecstacies; they exist on the edge of desire. It is by desire gratified as well as failed that we know we are alive. . . . For another, it is the willingness to submit to desire and art when you know:

> the world is gorgeous
> in its disregard, but cruel enough
> to kiss you now and then.

It is also a refusal to accept what is "colorless as an unspoken word" while rejecting the undifferentiated rush of sensation. . . . Ultimately, the worst failure for a gambler is in the nerve, in the unwillingness to risk all after understanding the implication of the odds; that is to say, being requires knowing but the more one knows the more true feeling is blunted by recognized complexity. Dunn is a poet too sane to be "a philosophical hotdog" but neither will it do to simply record "the little I-want-Everything-drum / pounding in my chest." Dunn's new collection, rich with paradox and passion, contains too many first-rate poems to name all, but I'll read again with large pleasure **"Split: 1962," "If Once In Silence," "Belly Dancer at the Hotel Jerome," "Greenwich Village: A Memory," "Weatherman," "Essay On Sanity," "The Man Who Loves Hegel," "Contact,"** and what is sure to become one of the anthologies' favorites [**"Let's See If I Have It Right"**], a poem whose parody of love is nevertheless blessed with the beautiful innocence of first gambles. . . . (pp. 29-30)

Dave Smith, "Dancing through Life among Others: Some Recent Poetry from Younger American Poets," in The American Poetry Review, *Vol. 8, No. 3, May-June, 1979, pp. 29-33.**

WILLIAM H. PRITCHARD

At times one can't suppress the thought that though we all know what a supremely difficult task writing poetry is cracked up to be, it often looks as if a contemporary poem has got written too easily. . . . [*A Circus of Needs*] is Stephen Dunn's third book of them in five years, and since he never rhymes, writes lines of varying length, doesn't worry much about stanzas even when he sort of uses them, and as far as I can hear isn't committed to producing very distinctive rhythms in individual lines—a lot of poems is the likely result. I treated them casually, browsed here and there, and occasionally came up with something interesting, as in **"Weatherman."** . . . [The poem] goes on in . . . [a] relatively amusing and relaxed way. But generally I think Dunn might try unrelaxing, shape his poems a bit more strenuously and see then whether individual ones might become more individually memorable. (p. 255)

William H. Pritchard, "Criticisms of Life: Sound and Half-Sound," in The Hudson Review, *Vol. XXXII, No. 2, Summer, 1979, pp. 252-68.**

STEPHEN YENSER

[The poems in *A Circus of Needs* may] be grouped into two overlapping categories. On the one hand there are the explicitly personal poems, the lyric poet's stock in trade, ranging from the chiefly anecdotal to the chiefly meditative. On the other hand, and perhaps more immediately distinctive, there are the poems that are basically apologal.

This group itself includes several kinds, and Dunn writes admirable examples of each. In one entertaining mood he is a story teller or an impresario in the process of creating his parable or fable. **"Let's Say"** addresses the reader, whom it takes hypothetically through the steps of walking late at night through a dangerous part of the city to a parked car, getting into it, and driving away. Dunn's collaborative imperative proves to be an ingenious device. Its casualness establishes an intimacy at first chummy and engaging and then increasingly minatory and mocking. . . . As he subtly unfolds the situation, the poem becomes more and more compelling and suspenseful. . . , and even when we are allowed to drive off safely at the end we feel not so much that we have escaped as that catastrophe has been held temporarily in abeyance by sheer luck. At just this point, when Dunn chooses not to wipe out the "you," the experience turns out to be exactly one's own—seen as it were from the point of view of Fate, which is always making up its mind about the twists in the plot.

To be sure, such a poem has designs on the reader, but it also has a refreshing slant on things. Dunn's approach enables him to evade the constraints of the first person, present indicative mode (try to imagine this poem in that mode) and opens up intriguing possibilities. In **"Scenario,"** where he stages a tryst between a nameless couple, the imperative lets him adopt a special stance, sympathetic but detached and a touch ironic withal, and to invent extravagant romantic detail. . . . Once again the distance between reader and characters diminishes at the end, and one finds himself looking at the poem as in an only slightly distorting mirror—and hearing the disturbing echo of Stevens's "The Emperor of Ice Cream."

Dunn's tendency to abstract, generalize, and allegorize also produces several poems that are explicitly "fables" and others in which the speakers are types or epitomes. **"The Capitalist's Love Letter"** wickedly begs a friend to come back to him because "no one has made me feel so alone since." . . . In **"Building a Person"** Dunn constructs a persona, a caricature of our society's cruelty. . . . The model is to be auctioned off (the Missing Persons Squad will round up the bidders), but of course "it takes money to maintain a person," so "the same folks will go home empty-handed." A related kind of poem focuses on some symbolic figure in the third person.

One of the virtues of such poems is their ingenuity, and the defect that virtue flirts with is shallowness. One sometimes suspects that the tricks and formulas that keep Dunn turning out poems also keep him from dealing more directly and heuristically with his experience. (pp. 574-76)

A certain weariness emanates, at any rate, from those poems in which the originality and the force are all in the framing conception, in which the particulars do not validate that conception. In **"Let's See If I Have It Right,"** an extreme example, the conception actually obviates particulars. A poem about making love, it depends for its effect on the coy substitution of demonstratives for nouns. . . . Uncensor it and the poem evaporates. In **"Introduction to the 20th Century"** the idea is to render the present as history. (p. 576)

Several of Dunn's more personal poems confirm by contrast that he is a remarkably resourceful poet whose devices occasionally betray his gifts. **"Belly Dancer at the Hotel Jerome"** simply records an experience in which smug skepticism in regard to the *artiste* graduates into enthusiastic admiration, but Dunn manages the transitions with an invisible facility and the poem has an irresistible energy. Free of contrivance, though full of invention, **"Instead of You"** is a captivating meditation on the relationship between a poem and its motivations and exigencies, delicate and wayward as the butterfly the poet claims to have killed. **"Essay on Sanity,"** a distinguished example of what Robert Pinsky calls a poem with prose virtues, blends discursive appraisal with images whose simple aptness is a sort of brilliance. (p. 577)

> Stephen Yenser, "Recent Poetry: Five Poets," in The Yale Review, *Vol. LXVIII, No. 4, Summer, 1979, pp. 557-77.**

PETER STITT

Stephen Dunn is fond of writing poems that sound almost like parables. While not biblical or portentous in any way, . . . [the poems in *A Circus of Needs*] do have a hypothetical rather than a realistic air about them. . . . Poems like these are witty and entertaining: but they remain performances and lack any true engagement with reality; their chief feature is their cleverness.

There was a time when Dunn wrote mostly this type of poem—such was my chief complaint against his first book, *Looking for Holes in the Ceiling* [see excerpt above]. The best poems in *A Circus of Needs,* however, go in another, more satisfying direction. . . . ["Here and There"] is refreshing—an account of the mundane, the real world in which we live, work, and suffer. This is the world of Dunn's best poems—for example **"Greenwich Village: A Memory,"** a poem about panhandlers, written in unrhymed couplets: "Two guys who sized me up said/*How about a buck for the brothers Karamazov?"* Indigenous humor, not cleverness. . . . The poem is precise and realistic; it aims for felt effects and is spoken in a clear, lyric voice, typical of Dunn at his new-found best. The volume as a whole is weakened by an absence of coherence—the poems never coalesce into a statement any larger than themselves. And yet this is a good book, especially pleasing for the steady progress it shows in Stephen Dunn's career. (pp. 700-01)

> Peter Stitt, "Knowledge, Belief, and Bubblegum," in The Georgia Review, *Vol. XXXIII, No. 3, Fall, 1979, pp. 699-706.**

BOOKLIST

With mingled horror and fascination, Dunn witnesses [in *Work and Love*] the manifold instances of modern alienation but is often able to find whatever humor is available amid disaster. As the news media report the latest murders—of men, of dolphins—he also reflects on the slower forms of death, especially through "the indignity of work" and its soul-destroying repetition and ennui. . . . In a rueful self-portrait of his seedy personage or in a letter to a friend dying of cancer, he can still be sincerely funny about himself and about the craft he practices. In dealing with the basics of work, love, and life, the poet shows through his art the balance and sanity that reality so often denies.

> J. P., in a review of "Work and Love," in Booklist, *Vol. 78, No. 11, February 1, 1982, p. 694.*

THE VIRGINIA QUARTERLY REVIEW

[*Work and Love*] is surely . . . [Dunn's] finest, ranging as it does over an area rarely touched upon in contemporary poetry. As the title of this important book implies, the bread of work and the bread of love are connected, such as how an employee's battered pride can return home and rear back in anger on the family, creating a cycle that may never end. Humans have to fight for individuality and happiness in both work and love, and failure or success in one can stain or grace the other. The poet's work is to illumine all these connections, a task for which Dunn . . . is uniquely qualified.

> A review of "Work and Love," in The Virginia Quarterly Review, *Vol. 58, No. 4 (Autumn, 1982), p. 135.*

DAVID KIRBY

I have never seen Dunn in the flesh, but . . . [the poems collected in *Work and Love*] sound as though they were written by some scholar-rogue with wine on his tunic and grease on his beard, a tosspot who breaks his heart on paper and stumbles when he runs after the stableboys who mock him. Readers who know Dunn's work from *Looking for Holes in the Ceiling, Full of Lust and Good Usage,* and other books will not be surprised when the persona of **"Odysseus at Rush Hour"** ties a ribbon around his penis and waits for his girlfriend to find it. . . .

> David Kirby, in a review of "Work and Love," in The American Book Review, *Vol. 4, No. 6, September-October, 1982, p. 16.*

ROBERT B. SHAW

As his title [*Work and Love*] indicates, Dunn writes about the domestic, the everyday with, apparently, a faith that the familiar doesn't need to have much done to it to engage our attention. He invokes the familiar more than he transforms it. This results in poems which are more often mildly likable than they are moving or memorable. Dunn sometimes regards himself with a sort of nervous humor. . . . [**"Late Summer"**] is tongue-in-cheek, but its amiable randomness suggests something of the limitations of Dunn's esthetic, which pays more attention to the creative process than the creative product. As in William Carlos Williams, the fountainhead of this current in modern poetry, the results of this approach are hit-or-miss. We may well share Dunn's anger at politicians and TV newsmen, but the verse in which he gives vent to his spleen elicits little beyond an almost automatic nod of agreement. . . . [The] poems are shaped by the ebb and flow of attitudes rather than a sufficiently resourceful handling of rhythm and diction. This is the raw material of poetry, waiting for a hand to give it form. (p. 172)

Robert B. Shaw, "Fireflies and Other Animals," in Poetry, *Vol. CXLI, No. 3, December, 1982, pp. 170-81.**

JONATHAN HOLDEN

In his fifth collection, *Not Dancing,* Stephen Dunn's poetry continues to gain in power, in range, in finesse. (p. 162)

The most difficult, the highest form of discourse in verse is not the art of fancy metaphor but of deploying memorable and dramatic plain statement. In an accentual-syllabic prosody, this is relatively easy to do, because, in much the same way that the music of opera can dignify the stupidest plot, rich traditional prosody will lend rhetorical weight to even the thinnest, silliest ideas. . . . Yeats was an operatic poet. How Dunn manages to deploy plain statements with such power and (unlike Yeats) such accuracy, in free verse, without the assistance and dazzlement of gorgeous sound, I simply don't understand. But I think that much of his power must lie in the "content" of his poems, in their subtle but plausible interpretations of daily experience. "Both sides of the world / are deadly now to the wasp / walking on my side." Dunn's intuition, his ability to sense non-obvious yet essential connections between even the commonest things is amazing. Moreover, as the last stanza of **"Middle Class Poem"** illustrates, what he offers the reader is not mere cleverness. Often as not, it is straight wisdom, wisdom not sweetened and diluted with sanctimony but shots of the original stuff, a brand which clears the head with a jolt and which may even be useful; for Dunn is a poet/seer. When we think of this poetic role, we tend to think of robed, sage-like personae such as Allen Ginsberg. But Ginsberg wears only the costumes of a sage. He never did have enough writing talent to be one. . . . In Dunn, however, we have a poet who *is* a seer, a poet/seer: as both, he is the *real* thing. (pp. 163-64)

Jonathan Holden, in a review of "Not Dancing," in Western Humanities Review, *Vol. XXXIX, No. 2, Summer, 1985, pp. 162-64.*

Marian Engel

1933-1985

Canadian novelist, short story writer, scriptwriter, nonfiction writer, and author of books for children.

In her fiction, Engel often portrays unhappy women who struggle to overcome crises of identity and who seek to revitalize their lives. Engel is best known for her novel *Bear* (1976), in which she deftly utilizes myth and symbolism to create a story with several levels of meaning. *Bear* won the Governor General's award and helped establish Engel as an important figure in contemporary Canadian literature.

Engel drew modest attention with her first three novels, *No Clouds of Glory* (1968), *The Honeyman Festival* (1970), and *Monodromos* (1973). These works reveal Engel's talent for developing vivid settings, but her characters were faulted for lacking emotional depth. Critics agree that in *Bear* Engel was more successful in depicting the emotional growth of her protagonist. This work centers on Lou, a withdrawn archivist working in Toronto whose job sends her to a remote island in northern Ontario. Lou experiences an emotional rebirth in the wilderness, particularly through her relationship with a bear. Engel contrasts the untamed natural world with rational civilization through the experiences of Lou, who gains vigor and freedom but also learns to understand the essence of human nature. *Bear* provoked controversy, as Lou's involvement with the bear leads to a sexual encounter. Critics praised Engel's use of symbolism, her evocative recreation of the wilderness, and her inclusion of lore and legends about bears, all of which contribute to the mythic qualities of the story.

Engel's next novel, *The Glassy Sea* (1978), also concerns a lonely woman. In this work Engel examines the ways in which contemporary social values can overwhelm simple and sincere individuals. The heroine of *The Glassy Sea* seeks to fulfill her intellectual and spiritual longings but is undermined by a series of events, including a failed marriage. The woman eventually finds meaning in her life by opening a shelter for battered women. *Lunatic Villas* (1981), Engel's next novel, is a departure from her previous works, offering a satiric view of life in Toronto. Engel explained: "I wanted to get out of the lush, descriptive writing I'd done before. It was beginning to say nothing, and I wanted to say the way things really are in Toronto, not the usual pieties."

Like her novels, Engel's collection of short stories, *Inside the Easter Egg* (1975), focuses on women who struggle to find happiness through their own initiative. Engel has also written books for children, and she published a travelogue, *The Islands of Canada* (1982), in collaboration with photographer J. A. Kraulis.

(See also *Contemporary Authors*, Vols. 25-28, rev. ed. and *Contemporary Authors New Revision Series*, Vol. 12.)

Photograph by Paul Orenstein

PUBLISHERS WEEKLY

Marian Engel's episodic novel [*No Clouds of Glory*, also published as *Sarah Bastard's Notebooks*] moves back and forth in time creating a composite picture of Sarah as she faces the crises of her thirtieth year. Her final decision is to pull up stakes and move [from Toronto]. Geographically, she gets only as far as Montreal, but psychologically, Sarah comes to terms with herself with complete awareness and this for her is a rare attainment of triumph and hope. A perceptive, tough, interesting first novel. There are some stylistic difficulties here, but despite them, Miss Engel has a pace, thrust, vitality worth watching.

A review of "No Clouds of Glory," in Publishers Weekly, *Vol. 192, No. 21, November 20, 1967, p. 51.*

NORA SAYRE

In this extremely skillful, exasperating first novel ["**No Clouds of Glory**"], Sarah Porlock, Ph.D., reviews her life as "the homely sister," her muffled affair with a married journalist, a turbulent lovebrawl with her beautiful sister's Italian husband, plus a predictable abortion, and finally decides to flush her successful academic career. The author has achieved that rarity: a convincingly intelligent character, who is also able to spit on her own boundaries. . . . Marian Engel's talent is copious; her novel is clever, clear and valid—as a casebook for a rampant minority. Hence one is reluctant to find it cramped— and almost repellent.

While female distress was a fashionable subject long before Mark Twain defined women as "beautiful creatures with pains in their backs," novels about unhappy women now need lashings of comedy. Edna O'Brien's rueful, headlong girls are enlightening because mockery mingles with disaster; the pratfalls of pain are moving in a character who can't resist a laugh. But Mrs. Engel's heroine hasn't graduated past sarcasm, which thumps like a ponderous foot throughout her narrative, drumming out the reader's tolerance. Currently, it's ridiculous to want to like a fictional character. But here, sympathy is demanded for a person whom the author has forbidden us to like. One recoils from a self-defined harpy dressed as a sacrificial lamb; her greedy error is to claim to represent all women.

In fact, Mrs. Engel has tried to hang traditional feminine problems on a character who would be maddening as a member of any sex: because she's deft at self-destruction and at persecuting others. But she believes that she's abused by men because of her intelligence. "Hated because female, nonconformist, self-important, intellectual, free"—not at all. She would be unloved in any incarnation, due to the hostility that barks on every page. (pp. 38-9)

"**No Clouds of Glory**" proclaims that the trouble with women is men. Men are beasts because "most of them hate you to think"; women—thoughtless or not—are snarling victims. Thundering simplicities like these could escalate a new and lavish sexwar, if anyone wants it. Meanwhile, it's worth hoping that Mrs. Engel writes further novels—about less obvious ogres. She's far too gifted to confine herself to casebooks, or to brutes. (p. 39)

> *Nora Sayre, "The Loss of Love," in* The New York Times Book Review, *February 25, 1968, pp. 38-9.*

ANDY WAINWRIGHT

In Marian Engel's second novel, *The Honeyman Festival,* there is a character who, had he been given more depth and a greater chance to display himself, might have achieved the mythical stature of, say, a Jay Gatsby. But the titular hero, Honeyman, suffers from the fact that he is alive only in the memory of one Minn Burge, an ex-lover now married and eight months pregnant with her fourth child, rather than alive with Gatsby's intensity, an intensity that transcended memory and became larger than the life of Nick Carraway. All the ingredients are there for Honeyman to be a giant literary figure—he is (was) a fiftyish, exrodeo star turned film director who, in his style and technique, ranks right up with Losey and Godard—and the fact that he doesn't become a giant is perhaps central to the type of book Marian Engel has tried to create.

Minn's husband, Norman, is a journalist off on a far-away assignment, and Minn is left alone, her stomach looming large, in their rambling, somewhat run-down house in downtown Toronto. What we really have is a kind of "day in the life of" in which Minn, bored and lonely with her maternal role (present and future) ruminates about her relationship with the now-dead Honeyman when she was young and alive in Paris. The memories are underscored by the presence of a festival of Honeyman's films at a local art cinema; the cinema is operated by a friend and a party has been arranged at Minn's house to celebrate the occasion. But Marian Engel and Minn are interested in more than Honeyman and it is because of this that the novel tends to divide itself in two—one part dealing with elusive film director as man and lover, and the other centring on Minn's

past before the Honeyman era in the small town of Godwin some 200 miles beyond Toronto. (p. 34)

In Minn Burge, Marian Engel has created a frustrated woman who has travelled beyond the politics of Women's Liberation to a realm where an animal-like instinct to survive, not politics, is important. Minn, unlike Women's Lib, allows that women can be defeated, but her survival of the night of memories is an affirmation that they cannot be destroyed. It's ironic (and yet, I hope, intended) that the legend of a Honeyman gives Minn this strength, that the suffering mother-figure, in seeking liberation, needs help—and how beautiful and powerful is Marian Engel's description of the Minn-Honeyman relationship. It is Miss Engel's creation of Honeyman that removes Minn from the role of feminist martyr and, instead of having to combat politics, we are reminded once more of the simple truth—"so we beat on, boats against the current, borne back ceaselessly into the past." Not a great novel, perhaps; but certainly the stuff great novels are made of. (p. 35)

> *Andy Wainwright, "Beyond Women's Lib," in* Saturday Night, *Vol. 85, No. 10, October, 1970, pp. 34-5.*

ANNIE GOTTLIEB

To someone like Marian Engel's nonheroine [in "**The Honeyman Festival**"], (anti-heroine is too strong), disappointment comes not as an adversary but as a sour, helpful mother who was expected all along. It might still be possible to write a really good novel about a Minn Burge, but it would take perspective, a certain caustic compassion and distance from the character which this Canadian author lacks. Without it, her novel suffers from its protagonist's limitations instead of illuminating them.

Minn is home alone—in 14 rooms of rented, decaying inner-city Victoriana—very pregnant with an accidental fourth child and tired of the other three. Her husband Norman, a journalist, is on assignment in Katmandu. . . . The novel is one day in Minn's consciousness, a convention which allows the author not only to show how time and the body weigh heavy on her, but to have her conjure up her own biography in memories.

Minn's life has been unexceptional, though quirky and dour . . . with one exception: in her early twenties in Europe she had an affair with Honeyman, a film director, longlegged international Nebraskan and craftsman of horse operas and historical melodramas. . . . Now Honeyman's dead and whatever of his glamour rubbed off on Minn has long since faded; but he's become a cult figure, and on the night of the novel Minn's to have the closing-night party of his film festival in her house. So memories of the Honeyman past keep intruding on the present. . . . (p. 40)

If the reader could feel that Minn's adventures had been her own, that they had either come from or provoked the beginnings of a destiny in her, then there would be some sense of loss, of combat, and a novel. But the Honeyman affair, like marriage and children, seems just to have happened to her, she was passive and grateful, as now she is indignant and resigned. This in itself is a common female predicament, and worth studying, but by staying inside Minn's mind Marian Engel forfeits the chance to study her. We have only Minn's complaint at her unfateful, inevitable decline.

I have been talking about character and form as if they were separate, but in fact the failure to step back from Minn and study her is a failure to create her fully. Her attributes don't stick to her bones, her memories dissolve into language; she strips down to the author's voice doing a rather catchy number on the housewife's predicament. Marian Engel manages to show something of how it is, but nothing of why; and she writes an arch telegraphic prose that lends an unintentional touch of coziness to the confinement and complacency to the complaint. (p. 41)

Annie Gottlieb, "To Minn, Illumination Is Non-Existent," in The New York Times Book Review, *October 1, 1972, pp. 40-1.*

AUDREY THOMAS

[Cyprus, the setting of *Monodromos* (published in the United States as *One Way Street*), is] much more interesting than the people Ms. Engel chooses to write about. Maybe, after Durrell, it's pretty difficult to write about that section of the world. Where are Justine, Pombal, Scobie, Nessim, Pursewarden? There is no one character in *Monodromos* strong enough to carry the weight of the power of the island itself. The heroine, Audrey, is thirty-six, Canadian, and living in London, working for a sort of import-export private investigating firm when she has word that her estranged husband Laddie is in trouble and needs her to come to his rescue. This reversal of male/female roles is very nice, by the way, until we learn (1) that Laddie never sent the wire and (2) that Laddie is an ageing homosexual. She leaves the damp of London and her ailing lover Max and goes not really to Laddie's rescue but to sun and a change of scene....

As luck will have it, she meets a whole crew of interesting people, but they are not really very interesting to the reader. Laddie, who is desperately missing his titled lover Eddie (who has in turn run off with a new lover and left a pile of debts behind) can't stand the sight of his ex-wife whom he passes off as his sister. The relationship between the two is very well done. All the old anger and humiliation is there in Audrey's relationship with Laddie. They throw up old failures in one another's faces; they want to hurt and they do.

When Audrey finally takes a summer lover (the father of one of his piano pupils) Laddie is delighted. Mr. "X.", well-to-do, with a wife in Switzerland, would like Audrey to meet the wife when she returns, though of course once this happens they cannot be lovers any more. Very sophisticated stuff, and a far cry from Eastern Canada. Audrey herself knows this—her innocence is dangerous....

[This] is a beautiful book. With the heroine one explores the round town, the beaches, the personalities of the inhabitants and of the expatriates who live there. The history of the island is told in a series of asides ... and reading them makes one want to go there: the heat, the beauty, the great mix of races and religions. Yet the heroine herself remains only an eye—albeit an educated eye. We really don't care very much what happens to her. She is a sort of personification of the CANADIAN CONSCIOUSNESS. The old, old world defeats her and she returns to the more familiar world of Britain when "for a long time I haunt olive merchants, speaking to them in borrowed words."

One reviewer said *Monodromos* was a "travel book", and this is absolutely right. Cyprus lives and breathes and takes on depth through the heroine's observations. It's a brilliant book and one I highly recommend. Yet at a human level it failed to engage me.... (p. 81)

Audrey Thomas, "Closing Doors," in Canadian Literature, *No. 61, Summer, 1974, pp.79-81.**

ELAINE FEINSTEIN

Marian Engel's *One Way Street* succeeds almost entirely through a feeling for place and things; and she writes about her unnamed island, (which must surely be Cyprus), with evident joy; making use of jugs splashed with copper, youghurt pots, spindles and hand-made whiskbrooms, noting every tactile detail of the fruit in the markets and enjoying half-understood languages in the same spirit of collector's interest. She writes directly to the reader; sometimes in the guise of a letter home to Max (who left for London to winter with his wife, because 'she has heat'— a memorable phrase for central heating); sometimes as if jotting in a journal. There can't be many fresher and less pretentious [novels published so early in a writer's career]....

Elaine Feinstein, "Ghosts," in New Statesman, *Vol. 89, No. 2287, January 17, 1975, p. 85.**

JOYCE CAROL OATES

"I have an odd sense of being reborn," states Lou, the heroine of Marian Engel's [*Bear*]. A woman employed by a historical institute, slug-pale with winter, half in love with shabby things ..., she is on her way to investigate the library holdings of one Colonel Jocelyn Cary....

Nothing that Marian Engel has written previously quite prepares us for the imaginative adventure of *Bear*. It is certainly a *tour de force;* one can imagine Canadian Literature specialists hurriedly inventing a new category to contain it—"Women Rejuvenated by Nature: Love Relationships with Bears and Other Animals." It may be interpreted by paranoid males as yet another attack—and a devastatingly witty one—for the bear of *Bear* is far nicer than most of the other males in Lou's past, and the reader comes to feel an affection for him that would be difficult to feel for an ordinary male character.

Bear is a tired, not very glamorous pet kept at the Colonel's estate; he is, when we first confront him, only a dusty bulk of fur with a long brown snout and small, sad, weary eyes.... Lou is intrigued by the bear, her only companion on the island, and discovers, in the Colonel's library, innumerable notes in his handwriting about bears. For our bear is not only a pet, of course; he belongs, in part, to mythology.

Bear is itself part mythic, part naturalistic. Just as one settles in to the comfortable pleasures of Marian Engel's typically well-crafted prose, it becomes suddenly clear that the work is fantastic.... Or is it? Lou's growing fascination with Bear is believable, and even rather probable, given her isolation: and love between human beings and beasts is, of course, not impossible. What is marvellous about *Bear* is its deft shifting from one mode of consciousness to another. The fabulous is always present, though it is not always recognized; the transformation of a prematurely aged, tired woman through an erotic encounter with a bear is made to seem both credible and outrageous. Hitherto—in *The Honeymoon Festival* and *Monodromos*—Marian Engel has dealt with the impact of other people on her more-than-ordinary sensitive heroines, and she has always been a recorder of those brief, wondrous moments when the human seems to touch upon something larger than or different from itself. *Bear* takes some of these preoccupations a step farther, and may be Marian Engel's best novel.

The intimacy of woman and bear is far more than simply erotic. Indeed, the most erotic confrontation between them is a failure—not only is Bear not interested, but he responds, atypically, by raking Lou's back and terrifying her. Their intimacy is, instead, that of friends or comrades. And yet that doesn't explain it. Marian Engel presents with beautiful subtlety the closeness of the two, that magical communion between the human and the animal that D. H. Lawrence also explored in *St. Mawr.*

The pleasures of a novel by Marian Engel are many. . . . [In] *Bear,* quite apart from the engaging fable, we learn a great deal about bearlore . . . , and the descriptions of Cary Island and the river are beautifully done. Lou is an intelligent woman who doesn't take herself too seriously, isn't really neurotic though she has spells of disliking herself, and is, like Engel's other heroines, quite amiable. She is ribald, sentimental, funny, and in a way rather puritanical; she works hard, she has faith in history and in literature; she is generous with her affections. At the conclusion of her adventure she leaves the island a changed woman—and yet not a melodramatically changed woman. . . .

Bear is certain to be one of the most controversial new novels of the season.

> Joyce Carol Oates, "Love Story," in The Canadian Forum, *Vol. LVI, No. 661, May, 1976, p. 35.*

LINDA HAY

[An alternative title to the short story collection *Inside the Easter Egg*] might have been "Through the Looking Glass and Beyond" since the way the character's self is viewed is nearly always the focal point of the story, and Alice might well have been an Engel creation as she was made aware of the distortions of self.

The title story contrasts the narrator's stay in the hospital where she has been sterilized, with her mother's amusing her grandchildren with stories. These tales always begin with a passage through the glass pane of an Easter egg, and then. . . . Fortunately, the reader is made aware early that the author does not set out to bedazzle her with epics of fantastic happenings. Rather, it is the common people in mundane surroundings and predictable relationships which catch her interest. Like Mary of the title story, they "had no idea of what should be and simply tried to keep the rubbish of living low enough to step over."

Marshallene, a character whom Engel once hoped to build a novel around, . . . expresses her own attitude and that which most closely exemplifies her author's as well when she concludes: "We must make out, with what we can find, we must make do, make ends meet, compromise and do unto others as we would have them do unto us." And so it is this intelligent, tough-minded woman who broke all the rules as a teenager and who later became a writer who sets the tempo for the parade of Engel characters.

The stories are grouped into three sections, each of which explores the looking glass from a particular perspective. The

final story in the first set concerning "The Married Life" appears at first to be a follow-up to the Easter egg fantasy motif. However, the changes in **"Transformations"** are not the result of a voyage into another realm. They occur when the narrator, Lou, looks into the mirror and does not see herself. . . . From the first she had been taught "that it was the highest virtue to see herself as others saw her," and this is the essence of her problem. . . . Gradually she learns that she can coax her mirror reflection into being, and at the expense of house and children she wanders the beach, whispering endearments to her image in a hand mirror, slowly achieving a reflection of her self which demands to be known. When she is praised for having worked out her own method of survival, the ironic and insidiously honest Engel voice reminds her that "she had not yet beaten plate glass windows."

The second section—"Ziggy and Company"—introduces the reader to a memorable figure. . . . [Ziggy Taler] is vulgar, sexist, an opportunist, but an individual capable of seeing himself for what he is. When asked why he divorced his second wife, he responded that she had grown fat. His indisputable honesty and boundless energy allow him to deal with the unexpected, and his survival is assured.

The third section concerns "Children and Ancestors," and its stories strain to deliver a precise mirror image. There is an unexpected lack of thematic concentration, and there are too many characters with hazy outlines and even vaguer realization of their power. An exception is Marshallene's query: "Do you remember what it was like to be a child?" Several of the characters respond by referring to the library where, in a quiet corner, a secret life was lived. In this context, the Easter egg motif would seem to offer some respite from the painfully real world. But apart from this clear line of kinship, the last seven stories, for the most part, are weakly executed. (pp. 35-6)

> Linda Hay, "Through the Looking Glass and Beyond," in The Canadian Forum, *Vol. LVI, No. 661, May, 1976, pp. 35-6.*

MICHAEL TAYLOR

The danger with a fine and disturbing book like *Bear* lies, I suspect, in its legitimate attraction for the allegorists of the Canadian experience. After a "winter of nicotine and contemplation," the novel's archivist-heroine, whom we only ever know epicenically as "Lou," is given the task of investigating and cataloguing for the Historical Institute the contents of Pennarth, the estate of Colonel Jocelyn Cary. . . . Once there, life takes on for her a marvellous savour, as though she were awakening from a long hibernation. Spring in the Canadian bush brings on and accompanies a similar burgeoning in her mind and body. No story could fit more schematically into the traditional view held by Canadian writers and critics of the scourging and cleansing effect of the Canadian landscape on the jaded Canadian mind. No story, for that matter, could fit more schematically or more mythically into the timelessly held view that people who cut themselves off from nature do so at a great cost to themselves. Already, critics have praised *Bear* for the way in which it draws upon and gives new currency to both archetypes—national and universal.

So it does. Powerfully. And no doubt a substantial part of the book's fascination has to do with its arousal of those archetypal longings in us for ritual renewals and the like. But those longings can only be felt along the blood if the work which awakens them is itself rooted in the local, the actual and the specific.

Bear is so powerful, both as story and myth, simply because it renders with a very fine economy and concentration particular people in a uniquely strange and interesting situation. (p. 127)

Bear has a deceptively spare and simple style. Deceptive, for one thing, because its heroine's transformation doesn't entail any abrogation of the intellectual life. Quite the contrary. There's a rather complicated, quasi-magical and perhaps finally unsuccessful connection established between the desire for knowledge and the need to satisfy more primitive urges. The style is deceptive also because the accumulation of significant detail binds the book together in the way metaphor binds a poem. Lou, herself, passes through various creaturely existences, burrowing up from beneath the ground into the light, exposed to danger and ecstasy.... Near the book's end she has become unrecognizable:

> She looked at herself in the female colonel's pier-glass. Her hair and her eyes were wild. Her skin was brown and her body was different and her face was not the same face she had seen before. She was frightened of herself.

Why she would be frightened of herself involves her relationship with the main agent of her transformation—the bear of the title. Although the omission of the definite article in the title suggests a Platonic essence or a Canadian archetype (or the fact that Lou calls him Bear), the bear Lou meets and falls in love with has all the trappings of individuality, as well as all the mystery of his reticent bearness. Their love-affair is consummated—at least, for Lou— ... and it says much for Marian Engel's skill in bringing us to this point that the explicitness of their union seems natural and just, as well as ecstatic.... (pp. 127-28)

Indeed, the love Lou feels for Bear has its mystical and intellectual as well as its sexual passion. Mysteriously, notes on bears—praising their attributes, celebrating their godhead—drop out of the books Lou finds in the Colonel's house. When she first senses the development of a more than playful relationship between them, she attempts to retreat into the world of books only to find yet another chapter in her lover's history.... In *Bear* picking up a book can be as dangerous and exciting as meeting a bear. And Marian Engel makes it clear from the beginning that Lou's ecstasy is not merely atavistic. She is moved to rapture by the Colonel's house itself, absurdly beautiful, "a classic Flowler's octagon," a symbol of man's absurd and admirable desire to make his civilization felt in an inhospitable land.... (p. 128)

Bear falters, it seems to me, when Marian Engel tries to make more explicit (and more mystical) the connection between the two ecstasies. She does this by investing the history of the Cary family and the bears with a fugitive significance. Somehow or other, there are important connections to be made between the family's culture and the bears'. The Carys, Trelawney's remembrances of Byron and Shelley (for some obscure reason) and the bear come together in a strained intimacy.... I feel more at ease with the novel when, in its last chapters, the significance of the more fingerable intimacy and its collapse is further explored. Lou comes to realise that her extravagant love for the bear, dramatised in the clawing she gets from her attempt to have him make love to her, demands a transformation from him of which he is not capable.... The clawing breaks their intense communion, but it also "healed guilt. She felt strong and pure." Her intimacy with the bear has made her a better and happier person.... It is, perhaps, the most

fitting tribute to the success of *Bear* that we find Lou's final judgement on her experience entirely credible. (p. 129)

> *Michael Taylor, in a review of "Bear," in The Fiddlehead, No. 110, Summer, 1976. pp. 127-29.*

MARY LUND

The pleasure of reading this collection of stories [*Inside the Easter Egg*] by Marian Engel, a writer gaining reputation as a novelist, comes in the reader's adaptation to the wry epigrammatic method of most of the stories. We also see the author in a "variety of themes, moods, and stances". The collection is surprising in its variety. We tend to expect a collection of stories written by a contemporary female writer to be a series of childhood, marital and family scenes narrated by a self-defining female protagonist. We may also look for an autobiographical consistency of point of view and of characters. *Inside the Easter Egg* sidesteps some of these expectations. The tone of the third person narrative is impersonal. Each story, however, tells one person's story....

The nineteen stories of *Inside the Easter Egg*, divided into three categories, "The Married Life," "Ziggy and Company," and "Children and Ancestors," also include a few experimental and meditative stories that suggest a novel.

The most engaging stories in the collection are the brisk, epigrammatic ones. These appear in the "Married Life" and "Ziggy" sections; they are developed like comic strips: characters are typed in broad strokes, their dilemma is set up, scenes are sketched and time is summarized. (p. 143)

The ordinariness of our lives and the tedium of our frustrations are acknowledged in the low-key diction and simple lines. The narrative takes the characters through many encounters and conversations and leaves them in a final deed or gesture that signifies a resolution. We get to know the characters quickly, but not intimately. Our times alone with them are not lengthy nor frequent. Their private thoughts are conveyed through the consistently distanced narrative. Flashbacks are related in the same spare narrative.

However, there are bits and whiffs of deeper character and of the extreme meanings of decisions that adhere to the bare lines of the narrative. These fragments draw us closer and let us sense more personally the concerns of the story....

These same bits of detail contain the deft lesson-like tone of the stories. Single details type and judge. This shrewd prose mocks the neat conventionality of each story and works its irony. Thus, Engel selects and insinuates details that betoken the treachery and wonder of our lives. (p. 144)

But Engel also concludes her stories with neatness and turns of phrase. The controlled counterpoint of tidy drama and mocking prose rises to a breaking of patterns in each successful story. It marks a minor epiphany. One prose line becomes lyrical, the narrative pauses. A character understands suddenly what he's been asking; he gets a glance at truth.... The stories end with a gesture or statement that results from the epiphany and this seems to resolve the story and its issues. The finality of these terse conclusions suggests the authority of moral sketches. The endings do not prompt us to explore our own thoughts and responses as Alice Munro's stories do in *Something I've Been Meaning To Tell You*. Nor do Engel's endings suggest a careful pondering of personal and cultural history as do Margaret Laurence's stories. (p. 145)

In the final section of *Inside the Easter Egg* three of the stories are written in a lyrical form that suggests a novel. The ancient tyrannical mother and the antagonisms between country town and modern city echo the issues of *The Honeyman Festival*. "Marshallene at Work," "Ruth," and "Tents for the Gandy Dancers" present rich histories of a group of characters whose lives and dreams are entangled. The stories are narrated through long passages of summary and monologue, recalling the monologues of Minn in *The Honeyman Festival*. . . .

Such circling, delving meditations are lacking in the monologues of Lou, female protagonist of *Bear*, Engel's latest novel. Archetypal events and briefly introduced figures from lore and literature are made to carry both personal and universal history. The meditative passages of *The Honeyman Festival* bring the personal and the universal to a strong resonance. The lyrical stories of *Inside the Easter Egg* predict another such novel, but their material is too selected, too intensely associated for the structure of a short story.

The stories of *Inside the Easter Egg* will be remarked upon. They are different, and like epigrams they are pleasantly digestible. (p. 146)

> Mary Lund, in a review of "Inside the Easter Egg," in The Fiddlehead, *No. 110, Summer, 1976, pp. 143-46.*

DORIS GRUMBACH

We meet Lou, protagonist of this spare, wry and altogether extraordinary novel ["*Bear*"] . . . , on her way in late spring to do some research on Cary Island in Northern Ontario. Lou is a bibliographer who has worked for five years for one Historical Institute. (p. 8)

Lou's job provides her with "erudite seclusion," an uneventful "protection against the vulgarities of the world." Her trip to the Cary estate, willed to the Institute, to look into its possible historical value, is a return to an area she had visited as a child with her parents. But curiously it seems more than that. She writes the Director: "I have an odd sense of being reborn."

Settled for the summer into the old house, working on the old books, she finds she is also the guardian of a bear chained up behind the house. He had belonged to the former owner but may be older than that, a mythic, Faulknerian bear: "There had always, it seemed, been a bear." From this point on the narrative is pure magic, an alchemic transformation from fact into folk tale and the rich areas of the human psyche, a metamorphosis so subtle that its sexual shock is completely acceptable to us. For, yes, Lou and the bear become lovers of a sort, literally, and their love raises their understanding and their acts together to a mythic plane. . . . The lonely woman, described in the novel's first sentence as living "like a mole, buried deep in her office," rises to his animality, as he might be said to condescend to her humanity. The island becomes "her kingdom: an octagonal house, a roomful of books, and a bear."

Odd? Oh, yes. For we, like Lou, are struck with awe before the fact, awe such as one feels before a deity. . . . She relishes [the bear's] smell, loves to bury her hands in his fur and finally admits to herself and to him: "I love you, Bear." It is the summer of her content.

Her need of the bear is like any human need; for warm contact, for sexual pleasure, for uncritical acceptance. (pp. 8, 10)

It is futile in précis or paraphrase to attempt to capture the persuasive power of Marian Engel's fiction. "*Bear*" is as strong as myth and yet, like myth, it comes to us through the particular ties of our human situation—our need for love, our bottomless loneliness, our inclination to worship. Lou's choice of the bear over the man (Homer, who runs the country store on shore and looks out for her welfare on the island) strikes us as right, not eccentric in any way. The mystery, the silence and solidity, the seeming humility and gentleness of the ursine beast, his creature closeness and acceptance bring her to a love exalted by religious fervor. . . . (p. 10)

Engel's compatriot Robertson Davies has suggested that the theme of this novel is essentially Canadian, about newcomers to the country who are out of accord with the land's antiquity. Margaret Atwood, a novelist of power in her own right, has pointed to its folktale elements. My own preference is to accept the novel for its literal intensity. Nothing I have read of Marian Engel's neither her novels "*Monodromos*" (1973) and "*No Clouds of Glory*" (1968) nor the short stories in last year's "*Inside the Easter Egg*" prepares us for the purity of her style and concept in "*Bear*." What we have here is clean and simple, implicative and sonorous, illuminated by an artist's imaginative power. (pp. 10, 12)

> Doris Grumbach, in a review of "Bear," in The New York Times Book Review, *August 5, 1976, pp. 8, 10, 12.*

GEORGE DRETZSKY

I must here differ with a number of critics who, it seems to me, have been unduly harsh on the famous *Bear*. They have taken it much too seriously. That book has a sense of humour and self-mockery which some readers seem to have missed. For example, when the heroine invites the bear to copulate with her (a comic scene in itself), the bear has the good sense to refuse (how unnatural that would be!) and in fact belts her a good one across her backside—just to make the point clear. I think many critics missed that point, and I think Marian Engel deserves some credit for good sense and a sense of humour. If the bear was a means of showing us how we have attempted to tame our wilderness, then the great sex-scene was a common-sense antidote to foolish Romanticism. The moral is: one accommodates: one does not copulate. . . . *The Glassy Sea* should be a better book than *Bear*—it is a more ambitious, thoughtful, and intelligent piece of work—and it is disappointing that it is not. There is something terribly wrong with the structure, for example, which not only confuses the reader unnecessarily, but gives the reader the impression that the book was written in haste and published in panic—and that what we are reading is a truncated form of the author's intentions. The prologue and epilogue, for example, seem to have no function except to impose significance upon the main story by shoring it up with seriousness.

The prologue indicates that the narrator is an Anglican nun who has been put in charge of opening up a long-closed convent. She hints at a very full life. Then the major part of the novel begins. This is in the form of a letter written sometime previously to the man who brought her back to her Christian vocation after she had been out of it. It later turns out that the man to whom the letter is written is the narrator's bishop. Most of the letter deals with the nun's account of her life. There are parts of this section which are very good indeed—particularly when the narrator is describing her youth in rural Ontario. . . .

But most of the story is the narrator's life after she leaves her rural home to become a philosopher in the Anglican convent. She has chosen to become an Anglican nun chiefly because she desires the contemplative life. It is the only way, she thinks, that she can be a professional philosopher.

It is a very interesting subject for a novel. It is to Marian Engel's credit, in fact, that the convent she depicts seems to be attractive to the woman more for what it is not—not of the world, not of the male world in particular—than for what it is supposed to be: a place of worship where women dedicate their lives to Christ. There is little of the *vocation* in this convent and a great deal of the occupation of being a nun, and no little awareness of being a woman among other women. . . . At any rate, this devotion to the day-to-day life with its intricate relationships is probably more true than not of most convents, and probably always has been. The narrator would live happily in the convent forever, it seems. But the convent has to be closed; there are no new recruits, and the older nuns are now beyond active service. So the narrator is turned out into the world, there to face one of the historical alternatives to the nunnery: marriage. She marries a Christian autocrat and shortly they cannot stand one another. Both are religious, but differently. He divorces her. She takes to drink. She hides out in a rural cottage (yes, that again) and gets bedded down by a wandering carpenter. She seems to enjoy that. It is possible that by doing so she is fulfilling another of the woman's traditional roles—she has been a nun, then a wife, now perhaps a whore. Well, pretty easy-going, at any rate. And, seeing as how her lover is a carpenter . . . , it is possible that he is symbolic, too. Then the church seeks her out and puts her back to work.

However, it seems to me that if the narrator is going to say that she is a philosopher, then she must think. She must try, at least, to reach some conclusions and find some meaning in her experiences. If she is going to raise the subjects of Pelagian heresy and existentialist philosophy, then, it seems to me, she has an obligation to deal with them in some way, or, at the very least, to show us how they relate to her life. But she doesn't. She is content to say, "Well, I don't know." That's not good enough for the kind of life she leads. One might think that in choosing the religious life, in returning to it, she is making an existentialist leap of faith, but no: she returns to open up the convent because the bishop seems to have offered her the job.

So *The Glassy Sea* is a disappointment. But at least it escapes the worst fantasies of the new woman's novel. Perhaps some day Marian Engel will decide to re-write this book, and if she does, I'll want to read it. Even as it stands, it is a challenging book, if only because some failures are more interesting than lesser successes. But I do wonder why she scanted this book so badly. (pp. 144-45)

George Dretzsky, "The New 'Woman's Novel'," in The Fiddlehead, No. 120, Winter, 1979, pp. 142-45.*

KATHERINE GOVIER

[*The Glassy Sea* is] a beautiful title, and one that quite accurately conveys the cold, the distances, the depths of Marian Engel's new novel set in southern Ontario's only Anglican convent. If the question is "Can she do for nuns what she did for bears?" the answer is no; although the smell of repressed sexuality and the air of eroticism that surrounds the ascetic is described, it is not created, nor are affairs of the flesh of significance except as generators of pain. That need not be the question, however. Marian Engel has developed her artistry over many novels and if this one harks back to any of her previous works it does so, in my mind, to her first—*Sarah Bastard's Notebooks*.

The anger is back, and with a vengeance: *The Glassy Sea* marks a further turning away of woman from man with a narrator who in the end seems to become a kind of Florence Nightingale dedicated to patching up the female victims of the "war" between the sexes. Like Sarah Bastard, the heroine bumps and crashes her way through youth with a constant feeling of inappropriateness. In various habits and under various names, Rita Heber (who becomes Sister Mary Pelagia who becomes Mrs. Peg Asher who is becoming again, as the novel begins, Sister Superior) attempts with good enough will to connect with people who might love her, is rebuffed, and retreats in cold fury.

So it is not love or faith that drives her to the Eglantine Order, but rejection and pain. . . . When the nuns evict her, deciding they want to die in peace, Sister Mary Pelagia is newly released on the world at thirty. She doesn't even know how to buy clothes and is wide open to the trauma that comes through her marriage to a Tory politician.

Divided formally into a Prologue, The Letter, and an Envoi, *The Glassy Sea* is a severe and linear novel. The main body of it comprises a long letter written by Rita/Mary Pelagia to a congenial bishop named Philip who is always outside the story. The time structure takes the reader one remove further as the action takes place a year after the letter was written, on the eve of Rita's return to the convent, when she rereads the summary of her life. The suspense then hangs on the question of why this country girl, mother of a hydrocephalic child who has died, has chosen the cloth once again. It is perhaps a slender thread, particularly since the compressed tone of the letter gives a fatalistic gloss to the life story.

But if naturalistic detail is skimpy and over-selective, the vigour of Rita's struggle is never lost. *The Glassy Sea* is a thinker's book, perhaps, a *gut* thinker's book. It is not a watcher's book through which the reader can also observe past life. Engel is asking about faith for the faithless . . . , and love and sex for the loveless. . . . The nuns are cyphers, so much so that the flight to them seems incomplete in the imaginative sense— as Pelagia herself admits, it is always an uncertain thing. But the pain and fury directed at the husband who abandons 'Peg' for a young Tory party worker is utterly convincing. Articulate, integrated, mainlining rage forms the core of this novel. It is the rage of the woman set aside after her fruitful years are over, the woman set aside for not being sufficient to man's fantasies.

From the narrator with her feet in the stove in a creaking, winter-trapped farmhouse reviewing her drunken behavior to the serene rescuer of womankind . . . reestablished in the convent is not so long a leap as it might seem. That second metamorphosis comes about with more conviction than the earlier one of country girl to novice nun. The heart of the book is in the last forty pages, as the suspended emotion is unleashed.

Even then, it is not an easy book to warm to; but perhaps expecting warmth would be to quarrel with the terms of *The Glassy Sea*. If not a book to love, it's a book to respect.

Katherine Govier, "Patching Up the Victims," in The Canadian Forum, Vol. LVIII, No. 687, March, 1979, p. 30.

DORIS COWAN

"Don't brood," says someone to the heroine of Marian Engel's new novel, *Lunatic Villas.* "Well, thinks Harriet defensively, brooding, the Holy Spirit broods too, doesn't it, or he, or she?" Engel's characters are given to brooding (as well as literary and scriptural allusions), and to reminiscence, fantasy, introspection, and retrospection. It has always been one of her primary fictional techniques to let the story develop at its own pace through the perceptions and ruminations of the central character, with many detours and backtrackings, and as little exposition as she can possibly get away with. You pick up the threads as you read, and if you miss a few, if names are introduced abruptly and mysterious references are made, it doesn't matter: the important themes will be back.

In *Lunatic Villas* she uses this technique very successfully, and enlarges its scope to include the points of view of a much bigger cast of characters than she has attempted before. She tells a complicated tale involving three sisters, one inheritance, seven children, two custody suits, parrot fever, adultery, and an old woman who drops in unexpectedly and stays all winter. Mrs. Saxe, a tiny, ancient Englishwoman, is an unbelievable character in both senses of the word. She is the good witch who arrives out of nowhere one snowy night, riding not a broomstick but a bicycle . . . , and she's a little like a cartoon character drawn onto a film of real people. But she pulls the plot together. Harriet tells her stories, introduces her to the other inhabitants of Rathbone Place (a.k.a. Ratsbane Place or Lunatic Villas), and takes her on sightseeing tours of Toronto. (pp. 20-1)

Engel writes, as always, with a superb and scornful wit and a hurtling energy that effortlessly fills up the spaces of her story, though she misses the rollicking good cheer, the effect of outrageous farce that she seems to be aiming at here. She is not, and never can be, frivolous. Her humour keeps bringing us back to the difficulties of reality; she can't help being serious, even gloomy, though she always pulls herself up and out of it, back to the jauntiness of her professed optimism. . . . There are two writers in the novel, Harriet and her friend Marshallene, and through them Engel is able to express some fascinating and acute insights into writing, most of which I suspect are as much her own as they are her characters'. In such passages, and in the descriptions of Toronto, it sometimes seems that she is quite deliberately packing the novel with everything she has observed or discovered since the last one was written, whether it fits or not. The forays into the lives of other inhabitants of Rathbone Place sometimes leave a similar impression: the history of Roger, the young father with his newborn daughter whose mother has departed; or the drunken tales Marshallene tells at the Silver Dollar. They are vivid episodes, written with finesse but not very well integrated. They seem almost to have drifted in from other novels.

But the heart of the book—the story of Harriet and her children—is thoroughly coherent, unaffected by the constellation of subplots around it. (p. 21)

Doris Cowan, "A Fine Madness," in Books in Canada, Vol. 10, No. 4, April, 1981, pp. 20-1.

URJO KAREDA

You have to be sentimentally drawn to muddle to make your way through Marian Engel's new novel. *Lunatic Villas* not only celebrates the muddle of family relationships, of maternal instincts and frustrations, but also worships at the shrine of a household in which muddle reigns. People sleep wherever they can find space and warmth, meals are improvisations, casual visitors become tenants, order is clearly seen as a neurotic's fantasy.

The diva of this cheerless chaos is Harriet Ross, a woman with a houseful of children, some inherited, some adopted, a few her own, keepsakes from either the man she loved and married or the man she didn't love but married anyway. This sprawling family lives on a desperately renovated little street in one of Toronto's "near west" neighbourhoods, surrounded by inhabitants of frenziedly colourful variety. . . .

In its bleak outlines, *Lunatic Villas* presents a dispiriting chronicle of a scattered, miserable family held together by a woman whose gifts for motherhood seem to be blind love and tenacity. These are not inconsiderable gifts, of course, but they rarely prove sufficient for undamaged long-term survival.

Engel doesn't appear to see it that way. The over-eager perkiness of her writing stresses resilience and fortitude. She works hard, too hard, to move the energy of the story upward, to keep it buoyant. She seems to cherish Harriet's intuitions, her garbled attempts at rational behaviour, and her insistence on the moral sanctity of her own particular bosom. Engel hopes we'll see this slattern as an earth-mother: the old woman who lived in a shoe is dressed up as Virginia Woolf's Mrs. Ramsay.

Engel's drive here surpasses her powers of observation, and the customary ease of her humour and irony tenses up. The transfiguration of Harriet doesn't persuade us, partly because we recognize her and know that in our own lives we would travel a mile to avoid her. Nor is Engel able to make us believe in the world in which she places her heroine.

The inhabitants of Harriet's Rathbone Place (or Ratsbane Place, as her children call it) represent a shorthand index of coy peculiarity, people whom we're expected to find irresistible. . . . But these neighbours don't exist except in episodic guest appearances, whenever a splotch of colour is needed to relieve the gritty drabness of Harriet's milieu.

In all likelihood, this fiction could transfer successfully to a weekly television series, in which the inter-relationships among a large group of characters have less to do with shared experience or emotional ties than with who drops in on whom, and when. Engel's menagerie of neighbourhood eccentrics doesn't provide a sufficient context for the transcendent qualities of Harriet; she is left stranded, a strident and slovenly mass of raw energy.

Late in this slight, bewildering novel, Engel gives us a clue to her view of Harriet's dilemma: "It's all this . . . hope, she thinks, that ruins us. Like the hope in heaven that keeps us from living really well because we can't imagine that life will simply stop. . . . Darn it, we're living as if we're trying to finish a nineteenth-century novel when it's been over for nearly eighty years."

This appraisal is not, however, supported by the rest of the novel. No one except Harriet comes to life in the work—not even the crucial children, who seem to exist only so that Harriet can strike attitudes about them. Engel's clue about nineteenth-century fiction is an intriguing one for the light it casts upon the reason that *Lunatic Villas* is so puzzlingly flawed. There is no Dickensian richness, no turbulent underlife to the narrative, none of the vigour or veracity required of secondary characters. In their place, Engel offers the flatness and false vitality of an exhausted twentieth-century society. In the devalued world of sitcom, Harriet Ross cannot sustain her symbolic role.

Urjo Kareda, "Children and Chaos," in Saturday Night, Vol. 96, No. 5, May, 1981, p. 56.

LORNA IRVINE

Lunatic Villas presents the chaotic, noisy, erotic involvement with life that Engel so splendidly captured in *The Honeyman Festival*.... [*Lunatic Villas*] reveals life through the eyes of a harried mother and, more important, uses that perspective to make a number of rather important observations about Canada.

The prologue is carefully dated, 1967, the year of Canada's centennial celebrations. This dating is meant to alert the reader. The actions of the prologue and of the novel to follow take place in Toronto, a fairly representative Canadian city, where the houses in the area of the city described are, like Canada, inhabited by a variety of racial groups. These groups are not assimilated; they are just there. Because of its date, the prologue also focusses attention on what was then, and perhaps still is, a preoccupation with national identity. It is not surprising to find out that the ensuing novel is about, among other concerns, Canada's coming of age. Furthermore, this national struggle is represented by a middle-aged mother (a come-of-age daughter) whose perspective is a radical one and who ... seems a more representative example of Canada than does the epic male.

This main character, Harriet Ross ..., is, significantly, a writer. So many Canadian women writers such as Atwood, Laurence, Munro, Shields and so on have created female writer protagonists to tell their stories that this fact seems worth commenting on. To make the point even more evident, Harriet writes about women's issues, abortion, child-care, divorce, using as her nom-de-plume Depressed Housewife, an alternate self. This split characterizes both the female psyche ... and a split Canadian culture, the result of a dual heritage. Harriet is also the main support of a heterogeneous collection of children of whom only three are her own. But the story could not assume really allegorical dimensions without the presence of Mrs. Saxe, a British-Anglo-Saxon octogenerian who arrives on a bicycle in the middle of the night and joins Harriet's household. About the addition of this new almost-family member, Harriet says: "I am a colonial paying for my shooting weekend. At midnight, she wheels her bicycle in. The mother country's revenge." Such references to mother Britain occur throughout the rest of the novel, making Engel's intentions absolutely clear. From the perspective of a former colony, Britain's imperialism assumes great irony.... Harriet certainly thinks of Mrs. Saxe as an "existential mystery," while the anxieties that Mrs. Saxe tends to evoke are typical colonial ones. As Harriet comments: "If she pulls out that old British line that all Canadians are wet, I'll run after her with an axe." British cultural arrogance has irritated Canadians forever.... (pp. 613-14)

Lunatic Villas also betrays Canadian anxiety about the cultural and, more important, economic dominance of the United States. This anxiety has resulted in numerous outspoken attacks on American imperialism. Engel's novel does not participate in the more virulent type of anti-Americanism but it could hardly be a presentation of the Canadian psyche, as I am arguing it is, without including the sense of American power shared by all Canadians. Because the Vietnam war quite dramatically gave Canadians a slight moral edge over their southern neighbours, it is the connection between Vietnam and the United States that is dominant in this book. Harriet's husband Tom, now dead, was an American draft dodger, a flower child. For a few years during the war, Canada was inundated with young men like Tom, charming, kind, but essentially rootless. As Engel makes clear, they left their mark; Harriet bears Tom a son, Mick, the son who dominates the ending of the novel. Yet, as the novel also makes clear, the Vietnam years left their mark in the form of Canada's renewed concern about itself: its economic needs, its natural resources, even, indeed, its history. (p. 614)

Mostly, however, as befits a book written in the 1980s, *Lunatic Villas* celebrates Canada and, also fittingly, Canada's literary culture. Indeed, it is a book about writing, about the influence of women on the national literature and about the mythology that goes into the constructing of a country's literature. Of the three sisters of the story, the rich, mad Babs, the alcoholic Madge and Harriet, only the latter, a writer, survives successfully. Her survival is followed carefully. By the end of the novel, she has abandoned Depressed Housewife to become, like her friend and alter ego Marshallene, a serious writer. Most Canadian women writers have also abandoned Depressed Housewife; perhaps most of them have never even been introduced to her. Then, too, Harriet really does bear the future of Canada. No longer tied down to the heavy Michael Littlemore, a man whose weight implies that of the patriarchy, a man who is, according to Harriet, "bad for civilization," Harriet is free to follow her own good desires. Even the twins that she and Michael have produced and who, throughout much of the novel, waver between their father's and mother's claims, have decided to side with Harriet in the end. Like Marshallene, about whom one of the male characters thinks, "she is rewriting his autobiography by existing," Harriet too is offering a rewriting by insisting on personal survival and, clearly, the survival of children. Between the two of them, Marshallene and Harriet thus revise both fictional female characters and the opinion of women writers. They are joined as serious writers and thus can laugh at the traditional fictional split between whore and mother. They are no longer stereotypes.

As the novel progresses, it more and more dramatizes Canada's coming of age. It describes how Canadians must learn to be at ease with the past.... But it is the concluding episode, the great Canadian bicycle race, that really celebrates Canada. It geographically impresses the reader with Canada's space and ties together Canada's history and literature. The vision is extremely positive.... While it celebrates the birth of Canada, it emphasizes the new. As Mrs. Saxe, the symbol of the British aristocrat, even of the British empire, and Mick, the son of dead, American Tom, bicycle across Canada, from coast to coast, the novel traces the landscape by the names of the writers who have given the land its image: Mowat, Montgomery, Carman, MacLennan, Connor, Laurence, Ross, Mitchell, Wilson. By giving Canada a past, these men and women, writers all, have given it a future.

Thus, *Lunatic Villas* celebrates the future, allowing the belief that "the drama would go on" to dominate its perspective. Nonetheless, I think it is a radical book, a woman's book, a book that places women at the very centre of Canada's continuance. . . . Like so much women's writing, this novel refuses absolute statement, is open-ended, is hopeful, celebrates continuance. However, because it describes with considerable wit a shift of power that can only be a shift away from patriarchal organization, it will certainly make people uncomfortable. That is, perhaps, what a radical book has to do. Readers should not, however, be blinded to the insights on Canada the book achieves nor to the evocative, wonderfully humorous ways these insights are presented. This is indeed a most Canadian novel. (pp. 614-16)

Lorna Irvine, in a review of "Lunatic Villas," in World Literature Written in English, *Vol. 21, No. 3, Autumn, 1982, pp. 613-16.*

Elaine Feinstein

1930-

English novelist, poet, short story writer, editor, and translator.

In her prose and poetry Feinstein explores romantic and humanistic concerns which she embellishes through imaginative, innovative language. She began her literary career as a poet and was strongly influenced by the Russian poet Marina Tsvetayeva, whose works she has translated. Feinstein comments: "Tsvetayeva was my teacher of courage. She opened the way to a wholeness of self-exposure which my English training would otherwise have made impossible." Feinstein's first novel, *The Circle* (1970), was conceived as a prose poem; like her subsequent novels, its rhythmic language and verbal precision reflect her background in verse. Although Feinstein uses a more conventional structure in her recent fiction, her early prose displays eccentric punctuation, leaving spaces within paragraphs and ending sentences after single words or short phrases. A number of critics have found this style distracting and affected, yet others admire the artistry of her approach. John Mellors noted that "[Feinstein's] unorthodoxy sometimes appears mannered, but for the most part it helps both eye and ear to appreciate her subtleties and suppleness of style. Elaine Feinstein is a genuinely experimental writer whose prose has its special prosody."

Many of Feinstein's early works realistically depict domestic relationships. A number of the poems collected in *The Magic Apple Tree* (1971) focus on love and marriage. Sexual associations are central to several of her novels: *The Circle* concerns a woman who has an affair after she learns of her husband's infidelity; the heroine of *The Amberstone Exit* (1972) is unmarried and pregnant; and in *The Glass Alembic* (1973) there are multiple sexual entanglements within a scientific community. In contrast, some of her other works are concerned with the supernatural. The poems in *The Celebrants* (1973) are mystical and mysterious, with sorcerers and alchemists as their principal subjects. In the novel *The Ecstasy of Dr. Miriam Garner* (1976), Feinstein mocks the conventions of science fiction as the heroine is transported to eleventh-century Toledo by means of her occultist father's time machine. Another novel, *The Shadow Master* (1979), explores spiritual themes as it traces the emergence of a Jewish messiah in Turkey.

Feinstein's Jewish heritage informs several of her works. An adolescent at the end of World War II, Feinstein was profoundly affected by the tragedies that had occurred at Nazi concentration camps. The Holocaust is central to *Children of the Rose* (1975) and *The Border* (1984). In the former, Feinstein examines the emotional states of two Polish Jews as they try to come to terms with the horror they had experienced thirty years earlier. In *The Border,* a journalist investigates his grandparents' attempt to escape Nazi-dominated Europe during World War II. Feinstein integrates into this novel facts about the life of Walter Benjamin, a Jewish philosopher who committed suicide while attempting to flee persecution in Europe. *The Survivors* (1982) directly reflects Feinstein's family background. The novel spans three generations of two Russian-Jewish families who settle in England; whereas one family

Topham Picture Library

fastidiously maintains its cultural background, the other opts for social assimilation.

(See also *Contemporary Authors,* Vol. 69-72; *Contemporary Authors Autobiography Series,* Vol. 1; and *Dictionary of Literary Biography,* Vols. 14, 40.)

JANE MILLER

'The Circle' tackles the familiar dilemma of women torn between work and family. Lena's husband has modishly slept with the au pair girl, but, worse still, he and their two sons complain that their family life is bleak and without structure: dons' talk for unpaid bills, buttonless shirts and their failure, surely a common one, to enjoy themselves on weekend outings *en famille.* An examination of the marriages of two friends makes it clear that women without jobs lose their husbands, too, and are not always ecstatic at the sink. After a brief spell of creative home-making during her husband's convalescence from a serious illness, Lena returns to part-time lecturing, certain that there is nothing in marriage to rely on and that she needs some independence.

The novel has some painfully exact accounts of Lena's terrors when she knows she's failed her children and, more disturbing still, someone else has done what she should have done and better. In general, through, the novel is spoiled by being too much an argument between a particular man and a particular woman translated into something capable of withstanding an observer's scrutiny and inviting identification with every other marriage.

> Jane Miller, "Best for the Boys," in The Observer, August 16, 1970, p. 21.*

ROBERT GARIOCH

The Circle is a sensitive, intelligent attempt to tease out the problems of three married women in a free society without benefit of established rules of conduct, their three predicaments complementing one another. Lena, married to Ben, a scientist, and dangerously dependent on him, has had to make do with the part of his life left over from his laboratory work. Even so, she is 'not woman enough', so he has recourse to the simple, but placid and sappy charms of the au pair girl, who has already taken over the children: a classically tragic situation for a wife and mother. Lena's character comes over well, with the weakness and strength of a living woman under stress of circumstance and the demands of her body. The minor women characters are good in proportion. The men are inexplicable—no fault, perhaps, as they are seen through the eyes of their puzzled wives. Or are they merely cruel? 'A crueller man, Lena reflected, would have saved himself: and taken his own way.' (This is typical of the irritating punctuation.) Too honest for an easy answer or messy conclusion, and having made its protest that women live like shadows of men, this novel recognises in the end the loneliness of everyone. (p. 251)

> Robert Garioch, "Murdered Crooks," in The Listener, Vol. 84, No. 2160, August 20, 1970, pp. 251-52.*

CLIVE JORDAN

[*The Circle* is] recognisably the work of a poet. In this account of a miserable modern marriage between two intelligent people, words hint and sing as well as tell. . . . [The] trouble with Lena is that she is not in tune with *any* natural order—and certainly not with the business of home-building for her scientist husband Ben and their two children. One or two things happen—she finds Ben in bed with the au pair, disintegrates, has a mild affair of her own, observes the marital problems of her girlfriends, finally retreats into her work as selfishly as Ben does, even after his illness. But the episodic narrative gives these events roughly equal significance, underlining that this is a slice-of-life novel which depends on the reader recognising the truthfulness of what's happening at any given moment. Miss Feinstein is good enough with language to ensure success at this level.

Lena's personality is the unifying sensibility for the story's episodes, but it's here that I find myself at odds with the novel. Lena is one of the commonplaces of our time, and of modern fiction: that foot-soldier of the Women's Liberation movement, the intellectual woman stifling under domestic necessities. There's no reason why this character should not be a fictional type, any more than, say, the political opportunist in Stendhal. But—and I think this is true of much contemporary writing—the failing is in the fiction, not the type. Miss Feinstein makes Lena real, but doesn't persuade me that she is unique or interesting enough to merit attention. Faithfulness to experience

isn't always enough: truth sometimes blossoms best in the framework of a larger fiction. (p. 217)

> Clive Jordan, "Bread and Medals," in New Statesman, Vol. 80, No. 2057, August 21, 1970, pp. 216-17.*

ALAN BROWNJOHN

[*The Magic Apple Tree*] is pleasant, sometimes light and very often rather retiring poetry: the real people, or purpose, or motivation—in what are often poems of love or domestic intimacy—seem to be hiding behind her veils of lyrical fantasy. Sometimes it's very agreeable, for all the elusiveness - as in 'In the Matter of Miracles' or 'Exile'—but it's not often very arresting or moving. There *are* strengths there, behind the clever (or even sentimental) disguises. (p. 641)

> Alan Brownjohn, "Lost Souls," in New Statesman, Vol. 81, No. 2094, May 7, 1971, pp. 640-41.*

PETER BUCKMAN

Elaine Feinstein is, for me, a discovery, a writer of limitless simplicity and mistress of a musical prose that can apparently find rhythm anywhere. [In *The Amberstone Exit* her] theme is the ageless one of the instructive and destructive power of sex; her characters refuse that compromise and harmony that make life and writing appear easy. Emily, the central character, finds in Amberstone and its owners, the Tyrenes, a style and seeming freedom that her own parents neither pretend to nor understand. But the integrity of her family is of no use when she finds the Tyrenes as restrictive as anything outgrown; she sets up with another of their victims, the beautiful Frederick, but the book ends with 'neither of them had the faintest idea what they were in for'. En route, so many of those shocks of recognition that by the end I was breathless. Elaine Feinstein banishes fears for the death of the novel: in hands like hers, it cannot fail.

> Peter Buckman, "Summer Uplift," in New Statesman, Vol. 84, No. 2159, August 4, 1972, p. 169.*

RUSSELL DAVIES

'The Amberstone Exit' is tiny, claustrophobic and febrile. . . . Feeling-up at parties, a depressive friend, dad's business failure, irrelevant attainments at school and university, the older man, the unexpected baby and the compromise—it's the Intelligent Girl's Journey through Thick and Thin. Life takes its texture from happy-pills, the launderette, a lewd mob of Arsenal supporters in the Ladies Only compartment. . . .

Miss Feinstein writes carefully, but leans a bit heavily into her poetic cadences. Every so often the prose has a fit of the vapours, when little effects of balance and symmetry go sadly awry, recalling the worst *Woman's Woe* pulp-writing: 'Yes. For what they feared was true: she had looked for sex. And found it in forbidden places. Looked for it, and sometimes taken it innocently. And sometimes, grasping for love, had behaved more evilly.' You'd think she rode side-saddle o'er the moors at dead o' night, in search of the Smuggler King.

> Russell Davies, "Camels to Nowhere," in The Observer, August 20, 1972, p. 31.*

RUSSELL DAVIES

I found I couldn't get along happily with Elaine Feinstein's **'The Glass Alembic'** [published in the United States as **'The Crystal Garden'**], which struck me as one of those novels in which the characters exist, if at all, in order to study relationships and participate in truth telling games. A high pitch of barely repressed hysteria is kept up throughout, so that it's no surprise when Lotte, shaving hairs from an oriental fruit, lets the razor slip; and you hardly notice it when, later, she plunges a butter knife into Stephan's hand. ('You see I'm vicious.') In a broad sense, one might agree with another of the characters, Ladislaw, when he remarks: 'My dear, *everyone* is disturbed. Because life is disturbing'; but it is no great pleasure to see a bookful of people living out the full pathological sense of these words. It's like a European conference of squabbling psychoanalysts, complete with Swiss setting.

> *Russell Davies, "Middle Class Moans," in* The Observer, *May 27, 1973, p. 36.**

ANATOLE BROYARD

Though **"The Crystal Garden"** is Miss Feinstein's first novel to be published in America—she has written two others—she arrives with raves from British reviewers. In my opinion, these encomiums are out of proportion. She is deft and economical and raises interesting questions—but her deftness is dangerously like indifference, her economy shrinks into skimpiness, and she doesn't answer her questions. Everything is very linear, implicit, understated—or I could just as easily say skeletal, taken for granted and perfunctorily expressed. The book resembles a blueprint drawn with a pen that is running out of ink and intermittently skips lines.

> *Anatole Broyard, "On Artificial Incest," in* The New York Times, *February 25, 1974, p. 25.*

THE NEW YORKER

["The Crystal Garden" is a] chatty English novel about some dégagé research biochemists and their families who float fitfully through the thin atmosphere of a research institute in Basel. Miss Feinstein . . . introduces the reader to the people in her book as though she were a distracted hostess at a large party. Here is Brigid, big, batty, generous, a middle-aged dropout wrapped in rumpled peasant skirts; and here is Lotte, her daughter, gawky and overattached to Mum; and her son, Sol, idealistic and sulky; and Matthew, her husband, precise and irritable. And here is Ladislaw, ironic and kind; and Stephan, who was briefly Brigid's lover, then Lotte's, and once Ladislaw's. The dialogue is literate and the writing is professional, but though the author is constantly thrusting her characters into the most "dramatic" situations imaginable, they all seem stiff and unreal beneath their easy-to-grasp labels. This is a curious book that always seems on the verge of becoming more interesting but never does. (pp. 109-10)

> *A review of "The Crystal Garden," in* The New Yorker, *Vol. L, No. 15, June 3, 1974, pp. 109-10.*

STEWART CONN

The Celebrants of Elaine Feinstein's title poem are those who, through the ages, lived in thrall to 'the dark drama of the magician'. . . . The exotic and the occult are presented with an intensity that borders on the hallucinatory. As the sequence progresses, it places a Rimbaudian emphasis on colour, though, despite the historical references, I fail to detect a pattern that is other than sensory. Throughout the collection, Elaine Feinstein's use of the musicalities of language is quite remarkable: her response to the elements, in particular the incandescences of autumn, frequently made me feel I was wading through nectar. But my preference is for those poems whose statement remains lucid and accessible. . . . (p. 718)

> *Stewart Conn, "Poetic Pitfalls," in* The Listener, *Vol. 92, No. 2382, November 28, 1974, pp. 717-18.**

VICTORIA GLENDINNING

[*Children of the Rose* is] about two people who share an obsession: the past. Lalka and Alex Mendez are married, but are together only in the last few pages. They are Polish Jews who escaped the holocaust and made a fortune; in middle age they separate—she stays in Cheyne Walk and he broods in a Provençal château—and try to come to terms with their beginnings. Alex in France sleeps with Lee, a young girl whose family once owned the château, and who knows what the Gestapo did to refugees there. She is not his salvation; she fills the place with her sponging young friends, and the child she is carrying—his future—is not his. His wife Lalka goes back to Krakow with a brisk journalist woman-friend, reacts violently to her confrontation with the horror of the past, and collapses. She is brought to the château and to Alex, a destroyed wreck, but serene and peaceful in her quasi-imbecility. She is better off, it is suggested, than Alex, who goes on longing for lost Lee, and who has not found peace.

'They say peace is good for you' is the last sentence. Not very encouraging; but then this is a serious and intense novel on a serious and intense topic. It is not entertaining. It is, mostly, morose. The style is too staccato to allow the indulgence of tears. Katie the journalist and Tobias the Mendez's goy lawyer are hard and frivolous, but—even if one has dutiful Jewish blood in one's veins—one longs for their appearances. Elaine Feinstein is a real writer; if she allowed herself a few jokes at the gates of hell, the reader would follow her there wholeheartedly.

> *Victoria Glendinning, "In the Swim," in* New Statesman, *Vol. 89, No. 2299, April 11, 1975, p. 489.**

LORNA SAGE

['Children of the Rose' is] about self-disgust, and reliving the past: exotically rich Polish Jews, Alex and Lalka, are so nauseated by flickering memories of poverty and violence, and voices out of history, that they cannot live together, and have to work out their love at long distance with other people, inside their heads. Those other people are just implements or threats to them: every chance encounter in England or France or Poland, confirms the inner struggle, becomes abrasive and raw, reiterating the hatred of suffering and its deep attraction.

It's a rancorous, introverted novel that leaves a bitter taste—designedly, though the self-consciousness doesn't change the narrowness. One of the characters says, looking grudgingly back to mother, 'whatever else, she wasn't cosy.' And that goes for Miss Feinstein too.

> *Lorna Sage, "No Time for Perfection," in* The Observer, *April 20, 1975, p. 30.**

SUSANNAH CLAPP

[The title character of *The Ectasy of Dr. Miriam Garner*] is a big and beautiful Arabist who wings back to Cambridge—freshly sensuous from a broken affair—to find her professor father involved with time travel and her steely ex-lover. Experiments are underway with a shambling girl housekeeper, but it is the strong and sceptical Miriam who actually gets lassooed by a time loop and transported—via potions, flashing lights, a 'monstrous penis' and continuous orgasm—to 11th-century Toledo: Europe before the split of faiths. She gets back to hectic melodrama and the arms of boring, rational Bernard, but Toledo and Cambridge remain intricately intermeshed. Both settings are attentively realised.

Elaine Feinstein's novels have always entertained suggestions of the ghostly and ghastly, but until now these have operated chiefly as hissing undertones and a hesitancy about the edges of characters' lives. Now the spectres have been unleashed and, though it's not easy to give whole-hearted assent to their original necessity, the open acknowledgment of their presence brings remarkable release. The sense which nearly all her characters have had of being in thrall is at its most convincing; their everyday lives appear solider by contrast, as—no longer so eager to cosset their mysteriousness—they are allowed to stray from intensity into humour and waywardness. The departure from determined terseness is to be welcomed, as is a rather less spiky prose style. Though not without its wilful obscurities and mystifications, this is an advance for a writer of strength.

Susannah Clapp, "Letter Day," in New Statesman, Vol. 91, No. 2359, June 4, 1976, p. 751.*

EMMA TENNANT

Elaine Feinstein is a powerful poet, whose power lies in the disarming combination of openness and sibylline cunning, a fearless and honest eye on the modern world, the smallest domestic detail, the nerve-bare feelings of people lashed together in marriage, parental and filial relationships—and then, suddenly, like a buried sketch emerging from under an accepted picture and proving to be of a totally different subject, terrifying, uneasy, evoking the old spells that push us this way and that in our lives of resisted superstitions. (p. 23)

[In *Some Unease and Angels* there] is always an insistence on endless change, of a world that fills and empties itself daily, colours changing, shapes changing, an infinite succession of magical and unforeseeable metamorphoses which blow up the alembic and plunge the scientist's laboratory into darkness. But the bewitched world isn't whimsical or sentimental. It's the recognisable world we live in, with just an inexplicable flash of blue light at the end of the street, or a garden by the river, heavy with winter, where the spirits of the long-dead nuns who once suffered there are a part of the trees and the dead brushwood. There is a sly wit, often the accompaniment of evil prophecies and forbidden knowledge, and in *Sybil* . . . it's the sense of a wild laughter in the woman at the absurdities of the world, the disease for which she will provide the unlawful cure, that make her of this age as much as any other.

This isn't to suggest that Elaine Feinstein's preoccupation with the unknown, the possible, is necessarily her central theme. The poems concerning children, and her father, and an aunt 'clean as a / sea bird in your / lonely virtue' are tender and immediate. The babies, the small children, objects and some-

times annihilating importance in the life of any poet who is also a mother—are seen as dependent, but not threatening. . . . They have lives of their own, they are very delicately observed. And, in poems which can seem at first spare and slight, there is a powerful undertow of sane love. . . . There is little or no sense of obsession in these poems, or of hatred or rancour as is to be found in much contemporary suicide verse; yet *Marriage,* cruelly honest as it is and sometimes despairing . . . 'and yet can we bear to lie / silent under the ice together like / fish in a long winter?' gives ultimately an extra-ordinary sense of survival, of the passing of time, of weaknesses understood. . . .

There is a strong feeling of displacement in much of Elaine Feinstein's poetry, and it's perhaps the feeling of deracination from many generations ago which supplies, in her prose as much as her verse, the sense of crossing time as well as roaming the world, of ancient plagues and curses constantly on the move. (p. 24)

Emma Tennant, "Prophecies," in The Spectator, Vol. 239, No. 7785, September 24, 1977, pp. 23-4.

JOHN MELLORS

In *The Shadow Master,* Elaine Feinstein has discarded many of her earlier mannerisms, such as her sometimes irritatingly eccentric punctuation, without losing any of her originality either of thought or of expression. A Jewish Messiah has arisen in Turkey, an oddly diffident Messiah who wonders 'whether I will bring down a miracle or destruction'. . . .

There is a recurring image of a shadow-puppet and its master. Is the Messiah God's puppet? Or is he being manipulated by his brother, who represents the corrupting force of worldliness? Perhaps those who promise salvation are fated to bring disaster: 'belief makes every horror possible.' *The Shadow Master* is exuberant, provocative and as menacing as a dream of the Apocalypse. There is nothing solemn about it. Elaine Feinstein has a sly sense of humour, and the subplot, in which music-student Paul at last loses his virginity to the 'Golden Wonder Holiday' girl, Patty, is a comic cliff-hanger.

John Mellors, "Five Good Novels," in The Listener, Vol. 100, No. 2579, September 28, 1978, p. 410.*

ROSALIND WADE

It sometimes happens that a novelist becomes enmeshed in a complicated plot which serves only to diminish his or her particular talents. Such a case is Elaine Feinstein's *The Shadow Master,* which operates simultaneously on several planes, to the detriment of all of them. Members of the 'Golden Wonder' holiday tour have come to Istanbul, a city described with rich pictorial skill. The assortment of tourists provide excellent targets for in-depth characterisation and brittle dialogue: Paul, a student, and Patty, the tour leader, become acquainted in a defective hotel elevator and enjoy a passionate though unsatisfying love relationship: the estranged married couple, Howard and Belinda, clinging pathetically to an outworn relationship: Paul's astrologist mother, his grotesque aunt—these and many more supply the ingredients of high comedy. Unfortunately, they are mere walk-on players in a drama of international intrigue: with idealism and anarchy embodied in the personality of a mysterious individual known as 'Vee'. Much careful and scholarly thought has been given to the philosophic and historical implications of Vee's activities; yet, as is so often the case with a character used as a mouthpiece for propaganda, 'Vee' is a profound bore.

Rosalind Wade, in a review of "The Shadow Master," in Contemporary Review, *Vol. 234, No. 1356, January, 1979, p. 47.*

PAUL ABLEMAN

There are 11 stories in [*The Silent Areas*] and they do, I think, harbour a recurrent theme. The term that initially occurred to me for representing it was 'resurrection'. But that word, like the cognate expressions 'redemption' and 'salvation', is so saturated with theistic implications that it becomes hard to detach it from a religious context and the notion of a redeemer. Yet the resurrections, or rebirths, in Elaine Feinstein's stories are free from any overt theological dimension. Moreover, the characters who experience them achieve their spark of renewal as a result of breaking through into sealed spiritual reservoirs within themselves and they do so without the necessary intervention of man or God.

The title story, **'The Silent Areas'**, is the longest in the collection and is a very fine piece of work. It tells how James Ritter, a *Times* correspondent in Moscow, freed from official commitments by last year's lamentable closure of the paper, revisits Tiflis, 'city of warmth and miraculous springs, city of Lermontov, city of legends' where, ten years before, he caroused with a drunken poet called Karabadze and casually shared the latter's girl, Tamara. Ritter is in flight from a ruined marriage and a betrayed talent. He too was once a poet.

The journalist is accompanied by the inevitable interpreter-watchboy, in this case a mild-mannered KGB informer called Yevgeny, who has a 'fragile, birdboned face' and 'prudish pedantic speech'. Arrived at the city in the gorge of the Caucasus, Ritter seeks in vain for Tamara. He finds instead an academic from England called Carter who is staying in the same hotel. Carter asks Ritter where he can find a girl and Ritter directs him to a rowdy saloon. Late that night, a distracted Carter bursts into Ritter's quarters saying that a girl is dying in his room. When Ritter reaches her, he finds that 'it was Tamara, of course', and the reader thinks for a moment that the author is trying to smuggle outrageous coincidence into her tale with a flourish designed to mask the dead. But the reader proves to be wrong. Tamara's dying presence, given human nature and the nature of contemporary Russia, *was* inevitable and as we grasp the web of infamy it expresses, the story lifts onto a new plane of meaning.

The narrative employs a precise, flinty prose which matches the harsh events. This servicable prose evokes the astonishing city of Tiflis in a few graven paragraphs. It performs the remarkable feat, in the employ of a woman writer, of generating a variety of male characters who are both individual and totally convincing. But its chief triumph is that, in the last few pages it lifts a concrete incident into a metaphor for the whole of Russia and its agony.

The story concludes with the words: 'He [Ritter] became aware of the first bewildered murmers rising from areas inside himself that had been silent for many years'. If there are 'silent areas', Elaine Feinstein seems to be saying, in which work and truth have been sealed away, sooner or later a whisper may be heard from them again. Perhaps it would be too optimistic to conclude that this process can happen in the life of nations as well as of individuals and that in Russia too there may be the stir of

resurrection, but it is tempting to do so since individual and society are geometrically linked in the story.

None of the other tales in this book achieves the same stature but many are fine and all readable. . . .

All the stories, with one exception, focus attention on the inner life. The dynamics of the action are chiefly determined by spiritual processes. But in the last, and exceptionally genial, tale, the machinery is conventional. Two smart girls, lunching together in Bayswater, discover that they have the same lover. This gives them an objective problem, and a casus belli, considerably more distressing than many of those faced by Mrs. Feinstein's other creations. By the end of the story, however, the girls have decided cheerfully to go on lunching together. I think Elaine Feinstein is telling us that the true challenges of life come not from without but within.

Paul Ableman, "Resurrections," in The Spectator, *Vol. 244, No. 7909, February 9, 1980, p. 22.*

JOHN MELLORS

Elaine Feinstein is a poet and translator of poetry, as well as a novelist and critic. It is the poet's precision and verbal fastidiousness which make *The Survivors* far more than just another family chronicle, spanning several generations, against a background of social changes and political upheavals. For example, her similes are not only colourful and arresting in themselves; they help to pinpoint the exact meaning she wishes to convey. A shy, gentle child offers her love to her father 'like a flower offering scent'. A young woman wants to write poetry because she is excited into 'feeling each word in her mouth like a separate pebble'.

The Survivors follows the fortunes of two Russian Jewish families who settled in Liverpool at the turn of the century. They have quite different survival techniques. The Gordon family opts for assimilation. They have ambition and determination and a chameleon's ability to adapt to the environment. The Katz family hang on fiercely to their Jewishness, believing in togetherness and family self-help.

Elaine Feinstein does not over-emphasise the contrast between Gordon and Katz, allowing individuals in each family to behave in ways repugnant to the rest. An integral part of the plot is the marriage between brash, insensitive Benjy Katz and quiet, introspective Betty Gordon. Their daughter, Diana, finds it hard to survive the 1960s, hating the 'drug culture' which fascinates her Irish husband, Jake. When Jake leaves her, she directs her hopes for the future on 'children and poetry'—which, in a sense, constitute the driving force in this powerful yet subtle novel. (p. 23)

John Mellors, "Poets' Prose," in The Listener, *Vol. 107, No. 2751, March 11, 1982, pp. 23-4.**

NEIL PHILIP

[*The Survivors*] is an exceptional novel: intimate, engrossing, economical, yet covering sixty years, two world wars and immense social change. It is Elaine Feinstein's remarkably sure grip on her material which enables her to treat such large themes, to encompass three generations, to manage such a large cast, without losing sight of the personal, the individual, the sense of the minute as well as the year. She employs none of the usual short-cuts of the family saga, makes no appeal to nostalgia, no concessions to melodrama. The relaxed confidence of the book's opening gently draws the reader into a story in which the emotions which lie behind actions, rather than the actions themselves, take centre stage. The main theme throughout is the way the past bears on the present, strictly exemplified in the special isolation of the Jews. . . .

The generosity and sympathy with which Elaine Feinstein explores the male and female worlds her characters inhabit, and charts the fluctuating balance of power between them, would alone mark this book as a splendid achievement. But there is more. The language is bare, incisive, weighted: the prose of a poet. The characters are rounded, full, always capable of surprising us. The sense of social history, not simply of artefacts and statistics but of mood and temper, is extraordinarily acute. Fiction as rich and rewarding as this is rare.

Neil Philip, in a review of "The Survivors," in British Book News, *July, 1982, p. 444.*

STEPHEN BANN

[*The Border* concerns the] son of a Viennese father shipped out to relatives before the commencement of the Second World War. The grandmother whom he finds in Sydney among her reminiscent pieces of furniture and fragrant cakes is in sole possession of a secret which has so far eluded him: she alone can release the documents which tell the story of her flight from Central Europe, by way of Paris, and clarify the circumstances under which her husband, also in flight, came to die at Port-Bou, on the Franco-Spanish frontier.

To describe *The Border* as a story of retrospective detection is therefore accurate up to a point. We are offered not only the grandmother's testimony, after the event, but also the diary of her husband, Hans Wendler, standing next to her own diary of the same year, and supplemented by the letters of Hilde Dorf, her husband's mistress. But Elaine Feinstein has not constructed a mystery which lends itself to being solved: in the end, we are only slightly the wiser about the real significance of the events which have taken place. Her concern is more precisely to form a web of suggestions, in which political and personal motifs are inextricably bound up with one another. Walter Benjamin, whose suicide at Port-Bou is incorporated into the fiction, is also perhaps to be seen as the pervasive figure in this textual carpet. Quoted more than once in epigraphs to the various sections, he stands for a desire to fuse together, rather than to separate out, the strands of intellectual, political and emotional life. Is Hilde Dorf's love for Hans Wendler initially an attempt to entrap him into political action on behalf of the Communist Party? Does Hans Wendler's love for Hilde disregard the barely concealed political motive which is, it would seem, the mainspring of her actions? Is Hans Wendler, perhaps, as profoundly captivated by the political message as he is by the personal relationship? And is Inge Wendler's testimony simply an attempt to prevent us from realising this point?

There is no hierarchy of discourses which will enable us to pick out where the truth lies on any of these matters. Elaine Feinstein traces a spare, and at times deceptively casual, outline to the sequence of events. It is difficult to feel that any of her separately itemised sources should be privileged over the others. At least, that is the impression until we reach the last and shortest of the six parts of the novel, which consists of Wendler's three 'Poems in Exile'. In the rhythmic vitality and imagistic piquancy of the short stanzas, we pick up a new and superior tone of authority

> Monsters and blood I dream of now,
>   and a long voyage, lost,
> although the wind has filled our sails,
>   I must not falter in my mission,
> Dido, at whatever cost.

It is not what Hans Wendler tells us here, in the lightly assumed disguise of Aeneas, that gives us the clue to the enigma of his death. We can remain sceptical about the political contours of the Rome which he intended to found. But what we cannot easily resist is the sense that the poet is speaking through the persona of the novelist, and that this is a voice we are meant to attend to. Elaine Feinstein has taken the risk of allowing the whole weight of the story to rest upon these intensified fragments of poetic language, and the risk pays off. (p. 19)

Stephen Bann, "Red," in London Review of Books, *July 5 to July 19, 1984, pp. 18-19.**

JAMES LASDUN

The intentions of an author are neither available nor desirable— so certain literary theorists tell us: intentions are of little relevance to the completed work, and none at all to an evaluation of it. Nevertheless, if one is as mystified by the author's intentions as I was by Elaine Feinstein's in her eighth novel, *The Border,* then it becomes difficult to form any reliable judgment of the work at all. . . .

My guess is that Elaine Feinstein expects her readers to take the fragmentary notations of character, place and event in *The Border* as the tips of so many icebergs, relying on their share of historical consciousness to supply the hidden shapes beneath, while leaving her to attend to her more rarefied concerns. But, as I've said, these concerns remain unclear. At times she appears to be paying discreet homage to Walter Benjamin's ideas— particularly his marriage of Marxism and mysticism (is the physicist/poet marriage of Hans and Inge in some sense a reflection of this?)—but then nothing very much is made of this. At other times she appears to be examining the nature of trust and betrayal, but her thoughts on these subjects give one little sense that her heart is really in it:

> "What are the intimacies of betrayal? Dependence? Hatred? Animal terror. And a sexuality that breaks some private taboo. These things exist like a raw pain in the gut. It is not a pain you grow out of. The wound remains unhealed."

Is this the "ruthlessly brilliant" writing Fay Weldon praises in her back-cover puff? I can see in it nothing but banality and platitude, though I suspect that might not have been the case had I been properly engaged in the story in the first place, which I was not. Whether this represents a failure of empathy on my part, or a failure of art on Elaine Feinstein's, I would not like to say. Whichever it is, *The Border* remains a very perplexing book. (p. 51)

James Lasdun, "The Fictions of Experience," in Encounter, *Vol. LXIII, No. 3, September-October, 1984, pp. 47-51.**

GEORGE STEINER

Elaine Feinstein is not only among the best readers and translators we have of modern Russian verse. She is a subtle, poignant poet in her own right, and the author of a number of
intensely crystallized, allusive fictions that are truly the novels
of a poet. The pulse of narrative and of dramatic voice is vivid
in her verse. Everything she has published is instinct with
caring, with a rare intelligence of pain. **"The Border"** . . .
climaxes in a poem, ascribed to one of the characters. This
poem is neither ornament nor chance coda. It is latent in the
entirety of the brief, densely packed novel that precedes it.

To its advantage, this poetic stamp is not one of actual style.
There is no poetic prose, no lyric display in **"The Border."**
Mrs. Feinstein writes sparely; the pace is merciless. Nonetheless, this is very distinctly a poet's novel: by virtue of its
allusiveness, of its kaleidoscopic shifts of focus, of its organization, which is one of narrative blocks or stanzas. And the
closing poem, in turn, is a reprise and reading of the story.
(p. 130)

George Steiner, "Crossings," in The New Yorker,
                        Vol. LXI, No. 10. April 29, 1985, pp. 130-32.

Frederick Forsyth

1938-

English novelist, short story writer, nonfiction writer, and journalist.

Forsyth is a popular author of suspense fiction whose first novel, *The Day of the Jackal* (1971), became a best-seller and set standards for his later works. Forsyth uses elements common to the suspense genre, including realistic international crises, lone protagonists working against time, unexpected plot twists, and suspenseful climaxes. Critics agree that Forsyth's attention to detail, his insider's descriptions of the milieus he depicts, and his combination of historical and fictional characters and events lends credibility to his works and has contributed to his commercial success.

Forsyth's precise, direct style is perhaps attributable to his career as a journalist. He was a reporter for several London newspapers as well as the British Broadcasting Company before turning to fiction writing. As a freelance journalist, Forsyth covered the war in Biafra during the late 1960s; witnessing the war and the starvation of millions of people inspired his first full-length book, *The Biafra Story* (1969; revised as *The Making of an African Legend: The Biafra Story*, 1977). The book was praised for its illumination of events often glossed over in the British news.

Forsyth's novels are usually set in the cities and countries where he worked as a correspondent. *The Day of the Jackal* takes place in several European countries, climaxing in Paris; *The Odessa File* (1972) is set in East Berlin; *The Dogs of War* (1974) concerns a fictional African nation modeled on Biafra; and *The Devil's Alternative* (1979) has as its scope most of the civilized world. *The Fourth Protocol* (1984) is a tale of espionage and political intrigue involving officials in England and the Soviet Union.

Forsyth has also published *No Comebacks* (1982), a collection of short stories noted for their deft character portrayals and surprise endings. *The Shepherd* (1975) is an illustrated Christmas story. Forsyth received the Edgar Award from the Mystery Writers of America in 1972 for *The Odessa File*. Several of his novels have been adapted for film.

(See also *CLC*, Vols. 2, 5 and *Contemporary Authors*, Vols. 85-88.)

question of why the British people allowed it to happen, but it gives an exact and vivid account of what did happen. As a book, its greatest single weakness is one which is also implicit in almost any writing on the subject—it presupposes concern and a readiness to pass moral judgment. There is very little evidence, I am afraid, for the existence of either. (pp. 146-47)

Auberon Waugh, "Forsyth Saga," in The Spectator, *Vol. 223, No. 7362, August 2, 1969, pp. 146-47.*

AUBERON WAUGH

[*The Biafra Story*] is probably the best we shall see on the war, and certainly the best informed on the details of Biafra's war effort. The only flaw I can spot is that it does very little to answer the question of how Britain became implicated in the crime of murdering a million and a half civilians in order to force them back into a Federation which they manifestly wished to leave. One can understand the support for Nigeria from those with a material interest, or those with a personal vendetta against the Ibos, but one is at a loss to understand it from those with none. . . . (p. 146)

But *The Biafra Story* is by far the most complete account, from the Biafran side, that I have yet read. It may not answer the

ARTHUR COOPER

On its way to the bestseller list, Frederick Forsyth's pulse-quickening first novel [*The Day of the Jackal*] is going to leave a wake of bleary-eyed readers—and I really doubt that there will be a complainer among them. Only in its opening pages are there any *longueurs*. These occur as Forsyth painstakingly and dryly builds his plot on France's political ferment during the early 1960s when the fanatical *Organisation de l'Armée Sècrete* (OAS), having come to despise Charles de Gaulle for granting Algeria its independence, decided to depose him. But by 1963 the OAS had fallen on hard times. Six attempts to assassinate de Gaulle had failed; government agents had infiltrated the organization; morale was as low as the exchequer. Here Forsyth gets down to the business of fiction, and his thriller becomes a riveting one indeed.

For one final attempt on *le grand* Charles, OAS leaders employ a professional killer—a blond, muscular Englishman. . . .

Everyone knows, of course, that de Gaulle eventually died a natural death, but this doesn't diminish the book's suspense at all. What intrigues us is the Jackal's modus operandi—and the man himself. . . .

The plot develops almost cinematically. . . . It quickens when the French secret service, employing some brutally shocking methods, learns of the Jackal's mission. . . . The job of snaring the Jackal is assigned to detective Claude Lebel, who resembles Peter Sellers's rumpled, hen-pecked Inspector Cluzot—only with smarts. Lebel lowers a dragnet over the Western world, and even enlists the French underworld in the chase.

But the Jackal eludes trap after well-laid trap, thanks mainly to a comely OAS spy who extracts more information with fellatio than the secret service can with its electrodes. Inexorably the Jackal closes in—and inevitably, just as a mercury-tipped bullet whistles within a hairsbreadth of de Gaulle's head, it is Lebel himself who is staring down the barrel of the sniper's rifle.

Mr. Forsyth's aim is truer. His novel is fraught with *frissons* enough for the most demanding spy novel aficionado.

> *Arthur Cooper, in a review of "The Day of the Jackal,"* in Saturday Review, *Vol. LIV, No. 36, September 4, 1971, p. 34.*

J. R. FRAKES

[It is] almost impossible to find in this first novel [*The Day of the Jackal*] a single fictional element that is not a decayed Hollywood derivative—except for the thick clots of asserted exposition about the seven branches of the French Secret Service, the seventeen Regional Services of the Police Judiciaire, and the inner workings of Scotland Yard's Special Branch. Otherwise, it's all Central Casting characterization, using every stereotype in the filing system, including a stock-company de Gaulle; technical-adviser expertise on ballistics, passports, forgery, Interpol, Common Market exchange, customs inspection, European highway networks; and (Forsyth's pet device) split-screen simultaneity. . . .

But, as Galileo once said, it does move! Like a movie should. Every cliché fades, simply doesn't matter, once the action gets underway. You may despise yourself for being conned by all this over-familiar rubbish, but you won't stop turning pages till the last shot explodes. . . . Since we all know that de Gaulle was *not* killed on Liberation Day, 1963, why do the intricate plot, the unrelenting details, and breathless manhunt hold us in suspense like a vibrating trap? Even Henry James couldn't answer that one, though perhaps Konrad Lorenz could. It clearly has less to do with the mysteries of art than with E. M. Forster's concept of the tribal narrator, squatting in the middle of the cave, shaping "this low atavistic form." "Yes—oh, dear, yes—the novel tells a story."

> *J. R. Frakes, "A Vibrating Trap," in* Book World— Chicago Tribune, *September 5, 1971, p. 2.*

MARGHANITA LASKI

[Frederick Forsyth is] the doyen of long, long books about the Cold War and, as these go, *The Devil's Alternative* is competent and well-informed, with a substantial cast that includes, in-

evitably, Mr President, together with a superduper tanker, some Ukrainian nationalists and a British agent in love. But anyone who reads thrillers as a necessary drug, and quite other books for the consolations of art, will find this book, like the rest of its kind, a laborious time-waster. (p. 63)

> *Marghanita Laski, "America Time," in* The Listener, *Vol. 103, No. 2644, January 10, 1980, pp. 62-3.**

ALLAN A. RYAN, JR.

When it comes to espionage, international intrigue and suspense, Frederick Forsyth is a master. *The Devil's Alternative* is the first novel in six years from the author of *The Odessa File, The Day of the Jackal* and *The Dogs of War,* and it is worth every day of the wait. But admiration for the craft, in this case, must make room for a distinct sense of discomfort. The tale is entirely too plausible and startling in its timeliness.

It begins with a catastrophic Russian grain failure, ultimately traced to a sticky valve in the pesticide machine at the central grain dispensary. The president of the United States, seeing the strategic opportunity, orders an embargo on grain sales to Russia. . . . The embargo will last until SALT IV can be negotiated and signed.

Meanwhile, in Moscow, the militant wing of the Politburo sees its own opportunities and proposes that the Russian army be sent into a harvesting conquest of western Europe, the only alternative to famine. The declaration of war comes within one vote of passage, forestalled only by the chairman, a crafty old fox who prevails on his slim majority to give the West SALT IV in exchange for restoring the grain sales. . . .

While all this is going on, a fanatic but amateur group of Ukrainian nationalists operating out of England assassinates the head of the KGB, only to be captured by the West Germans when they kill an airline pilot in Berlin during their attempt to escape back to England. Next, the Ukrainians' co-conspirators in Holland hijack the world's first and only million-ton oil supertanker on its maiden voyage and hold it hostage outside Rotterdam, demanding that West Germany release the captives or they will spill the crude oil into the North Sea.

Now *only* the Politburo bosses know that the assassination attempt on the KGB chief has been successful, and they have every reason to prevent this embarrassing news from leaking out. So a Soviet ultimatum is issued to the White House: either let the trial of the Ukrainians proceed (for the killing of the pilot) or no treaty. Thus the Western leaders are faced with an impossible decision: refuse the hijackers' demands and risk a terminal case of oil pollution, or free the Ukrainians and give Europe a terminal case of the Red Army. . . .

Given this scenario, a writer less skillful than Forsyth would have any number of opportunities to take the reader on an improbable leap of faith, to slap together the pieces of the growing dilemma, maximizing the spectacular while ignoring the real world. We constantly look for an opening to say, "Aha! Now *that* could never happen." You'll find no such opening here. Indeed, the discomfort grows because Forsyth makes each step along the way seem not only plausible but so damned inevitable. He has this plot locked up airtight—closed, sealed and ticking—and it would be pure pleasure to read except that there is not a hint of unreality to it. Gum up a valve in Kiubyshev next spring and something very close to all this is not at all far-fetched. The assassination of the KGB head, for example, depends on no James Bond whizbang; it is accomplished by two cagey, determined fanatics with a very accurate rifle. . . .

Forsyth lays out the strands of his suspense in the early stages, and we are fully prepared when he starts drawing them together. Using a sort of literary split-screen, he follows what first appear to be unrelated developments—the crop failure, the crossing of the Russian border by the Ukrainians, the construction and outfitting of the gargantuan tanker. Slowly, inevitably, agonizingly, they meet.

This is no task for a novice—nor is distinguishing among 13 separate personalities on the Politburo—but Forsyth is assuredly no novice. He is deadly serious, and this unsettling novel is much too close to events to be merely entertaining.

> *Allan A. Ryan, Jr., "On the Verge of Armageddon,"* in Book World—The Washington Post, *February 3, 1980, p. 9.*

ADRIAN KARATNYCKY

Though Frederick Forsyth began to write his latest thriller, *The Devil's Alternative,* two years ago, it could have been provoked by today's newspaper headlines. (p. 19)

Prophecy aside, Forsyth demonstrates here many of his more familiar strengths—above all, his ability to create a complex web of events relating the ambitions of individuals to the fate of nations. . . . Ostensibly about chaos and terrorism, the novel implies that there is order and meaning behind every seemingly random event in the world of international relations.

The Devil's Alternative is enlivened by the kind of realistic effects Forsythe is famous for. He invents, for example, a new technological arsenal: guns that emit sounds powerful enough to stun an opponent, delayed-reaction poisons, and mind-altering drugs capable of inducing partial amnesia. We are also given a sensory overload of SR-71s, GSG 9s . . . , SISs, SDECEs, and the like. Often unexplained, these abbreviations are part of the author's strategy of lulling the reader into feeling he is an insider.

Yet if Forsyth's strengths are apparent in *The Devil's Alternative,* so are his weaknesses. Splendid in his global perspective, he is often careless and inaccurate in his descriptions of particular places, movements and psychologies.

At the center of the novel is the problem of dissidence within the USSR. Forsyth does a commendable job of painting the political background: He carefully traces the contours of the "nationalities question," and faithfully reflects the points of view of the Ukrainian and Jewish dissidents. But it strains credulity to suggest that anyone inspired, as these terrorists are said to be, by the writings of such democratic opponents of the regime as Vyacheslav Chornovil, Semyon Gluzman and Mykhaylo Osadchy, all of whom have argued for nonviolent and open forms of dissent, would adopt the tactics of terror. (pp. 19-20)

Similarly, Forsyth's glimpses into the inner workings of the Kremlin range from the convincing to the cliché-ridden. . . .

The Western leaders in the book are not very credible either. It would have served Forsyth better either to have invented wholly new characters or to have given us the real items. As it is, his portraits *à clef* of a soft-spoken Southern U.S. President, a "superhawk" National Security Advisor who also

happens to be Polish, and a female British Prime Minister are disappointingly one-dimensional.

The book is also marred by a surprising number of factual errors. Ukrainians are not "overwhelmingly Uniate Catholics," they are predominantly Orthodox Christians; nor is it correct to say they "read and write with Roman letters, not Cyrillic." . . .

For all that, Forsyth is a skillful manipulator of the genre who builds tension by constantly shifting the scene and unexpectedly twisting the plot. These episodic strands are brought together in the final pessimistic resolution: Faced with a situation in which some people will have to die—a conundrum known as the "Devil's Alternative"—the U.S. President chooses to kill the terrorists, thus insuring at the same time that the death of the head of the KGB will remain a secret to the world. The international status quo is preserved.

Forsyth's novel is a hybrid. While it acknowledges Soviet expansionist impulses, the solution of the plot presumes continued East-West cooperation. If *The Devil's Alternative* is the first novel of Cold War II, it is firmly wedded to the assumptions of détente. (p. 20)

> *Adrian Karatnycky, "Ukrainian File,"* in The New Leader, *Vol. LXIII, No. 7, April 7, 1980, pp. 19-20.*

JAMES CAMPBELL

[A] Forsyth story exists for its detail alone. At the heart of each of the stories in *No Comebacks* is the desire to expose the workings of some technical exercise, whether it be a game of poker or a plot to bump off an awkward husband. Most of his tales are compelling until this point is reached, after which the detail is piled on so heavily you can hear the story choke.

> *James Campbell, "The Twain Meet,"* in New Statesman, *Vol. 103, No. 2667, April 30, 1982, p. 23.**

MEL WATKINS

[In "No Comebacks" Mr. Forsyth has] assembled tales whose subjects range from murder and vengeance to middle-age self-discovery and the outwitting of the British judicial system. Each story turns either on a surprise ending in the O. Henry/ Alfred Hitchcock vein or on some more subtle final irony. . . .

Trick endings aside, the stories collected here are all marked by the economy of the author's prose and his deft delineation of place and character. With quick, sure images (and apparent ease), Mr. Forsyth creates indelible impressions of characters as disparate as a cool Corsican assassin, the nagging wife of a London banking executive or a young Indian student, and his London and Dublin settings are picture perfect. Despite one or two stories whose plots are commonplace, **"No Comebacks"** is a diverting collection of short suspense fiction that should both surprise and delight Frederick Forsyth fans.

> *Mel Watkins, in a review of "No Comebacks,"* in The New York Times Book Review, *May 9, 1982, p. 14.*

MARGARET CANNON

[In *No Comebacks,* Frederick Forsyth, the] master of suspense, is as chilling as ever, trotting out his ice-eyed sociopaths who caress their Mausers more often than their female companions. . . . Most of the stories employ Forsyth's talents for nerve-winding suspense and trick endings, and there is no shortage of unusual concealed weapons. The surprise is that Forsyth can also be funny. *The Emperor* is a delightful Hemingwayesque story about a mousey bank manager named Murgatroyd who goes to Mauritius, kills a marlin, and becomes a man. Even ardent feminists will cheer when Murgatroyd socks it to his vile wife. (pp. 54-5)

> Margaret Cannon, "Guilty Antidotes to Bucolic Boredom," in Maclean's Magazine, *Vol. 95, No. 24, June 14, 1982, pp. 53-5.**

RODERICK MacLEISH

[*The Fourth Protocol*] begins on New Year's Eve, 1986. Margaret Thatcher still governs Britain, she is preparing for one, last election campaign against Neil Kinnock's wishy washy Labour leadership, and there is a jewel heist in a fashionable London apartment house. The thief steals a briefcase in which to carry away his swag, discovers that classified documents are hidden in its lining and, patriotic British hood that he is, mails them back to Her Majesty's appropriate ministry.

This triggers an MI-5 investigation of who's leaking secret documents and to whom. Enter John Preston, mid-forties, a former Army Intelligence operator in Ulster, now employed as a second-echelon civil servant in MI-5. If *The Fourth Protocol* has heroes, Preston is one of them. He is an attractive, low-keyed man—divorced, underpaid, harassed by the old networks and career ambitions of his masters.

The other hero—in that he, like Preston, engages our interest as a man fighting a solitary battle against his country's bureaucracy and leadership—is General Yevgeni Sergeivitch Karpov of the Soviet KGB. Karpov, a specialist in British affairs, discovers that an important anti-British caper is in the Moscow works and that the KGB has been excluded from it. Boring in from the outside, Karpov finds out about Plan Aurora. . . .

Under Plan Aurora a Soviet agent is smuggled into Britain. He is supposed to detonate a small nuclear device near an American air base a few days before the forthcoming British General Election. In the least plausible part of Forsyth's plot, the bomb blast is supposed to scare 10 percent of the British electorate into voting Labour. Once in power, Neil Kinnock will be deposed and Britain's first Marxist-Leninist prime minister will take over. . . .

As a plotter, Frederick Forsyth tends to rely a bit too much on unexpected or coincidental events—Scottish hooligans accidentally stumbling over a Soviet courier late at night and beating him up, the jewel thief swiping just the right briefcase, etc.

But this and the questionable premise about mini-nukes changing the temper of the British electorate are compensated by something new in Frederick Forsyth fiction; *The Fourth Protocol* has people in it unlike the one-dimensional characters of *The Day Of The Jackal* and *The Dogs of War*. They are interesting people, even the repellent ones. Four books and a few million pounds after *Jackal* Frederick Forsyth has become a well-rounded novelist. *The Fourth Protocol* is his best book so far.

> Roderick MacLeish, "Frederick Forsyth's Finest," in Book World—The Washington Post, *August 26, 1984, p. 5.*

MICHIKO KAKUTANI

Most of **"The Fourth Protocol"** is pure unadulterated plot—unsullied by well-developed characters, moral insights or interesting prose. When the main story bogs down, Mr. Forsyth simply throws in a subplot about office politics inside British Intelligence, or summons an allusion to a real-life event such as the Falkland crisis, or a previous spy scandal. He even gives the traitor Kim Philby a supporting role in the novel—though his role, like that of many others, ends up being little more than a red herring.

The problem with **"The Fourth Protocol"** is not that its premise seems silly: Mr. Forsyth has such a knack for describing technical matters like cracking safes and building bombs, and such a deft ability to juggle the sort of little details spies specialize in, that his novel has a strong documentary sense. The problem with **"The Fourth Protocol"** is that—unlike some of the author's earlier books—it becomes predictable, and so lacking in suspense. Halfway through, the reader knows exactly where it's headed.

> Michiko Kakutani, in a review of "The Fourth Protocol," in The New York Times, *August 30, 1984, p. C20.*

PETER MAAS

[While Frederick Forsyth] was never much of a stylist in his storytelling, he's allowed himself [in **"The Fourth Protocol"**] to slip into rather lazy, even sloppy, habits. There are, for instance, just too many transitions to keep the plot moving that fall back on the old "while" technique—e.g., while so-and-so was doing thus-and-such in Moscow, his adversary at that very moment in London was . . . etc.

When the question of a "false-flag" recruitment arises, which is spy talk for somebody representing himself as working for one country although he is really operating on behalf of another, Mr. Forsyth takes the easy way out by explaining it in dialogue. What's worse, the explanation is being given to key members of the British Cabinet, and that certainly makes you wonder where they've been all during the cold war. And when he tells his readers that a "legend" in the world of espionage is a "fictitious" life history of a nonexistent person, that gives one even more pause. As opposed to a *true* history of a nonexistent person?

The title of the novel, which is set in the near future, refers to a secret agreement between the Soviets and the West not to introduce miniature nuclear devices into one another's territory, that state of the art by now having been achieved. Indeed, according to Mr. Forsyth, only nine pieces of equipment are required to set off a small, big bang.

Some bad Russians are intent on smuggling the makings of a device into England, and the novel centers on their efforts and the efforts of some good Englishmen to prevent it. There are also some reasonably good Russians and some bad Englishmen involved. Generally, all the bad people on both sides are politicians, and the good ones are in the intelligence business. If there is a moral to Mr. Forsyth's tale, it is that the world would be a lot safer and saner if we would let responsible officials in the K.G.B., MI-6 and the C.I.A. run things. Ah, if it were only so.

In **The Fourth Protocol,"** the point of sneaking in the nuclear device is to explode it near a United States air base in England that has planes carrying atomic bombs. Everyone will then think that the Americans were responsible for an exceedingly ugly accident. In the popular outrage that follows, antinuclear sentiment will be dramatically strengthened, and the Labor Party will be swept into office. After that, radical elements in the party will take over to serve Moscow.

All of this allows Mr. Forsyth to vent his considerable spleen toward both the Labor Party and the antinuclear arms movement. In his view, the party's leadership is solely composed of boobs and knaves. And anybody who is for nuclear disarmament for whatever reason, noble or ignoble, is nothing more than a tool of the Kremlin. . . .

[One] of the pitfalls of a thriller is that the wind-up more often than not doesn't live up to the promise. But in this regard Mr. Forsyth cannot be faulted. His last chapter and an epilogue contain a neat series of switches, surprises and ironies. It's as though he could hardly wait to get through to the end of this novel to show off his bag of tricks.

> *Peter Maas, "Spies Are the Good Guys," in* The New York Times Book Review, *September 2, 1984, p. 4.*

VIRGINIA FIDDLER

It is a pity that many aficionados of suspense consider such reading [as **The Fourth Protocol**] "light" and escapist, No such apologies are necessary. Forsyth gives us a look at what has been happening in the realm of international relations, particularly as it relates to the average citizen. Anti-nuclear groups abound and are shriekingly vocal. Who gains and who loses from the ensuing hysterics? Forsyth offers an answer, and it is well worth thinking about. Soon, before it is too late.

And what about the consequences of propaganda? A good "misinformation" campaign takes years, narrowing the schism between truth and lie to an unintelligible gray fog. Forsyth appears to take it for granted that people can be and are being duped by distant and mighty powers. Unfortunately, he offers no solution. It is, however, too important an issue to ignore. One obvious answer is to develop a hearty suspicion of *any* mass movement; to consider carefully what is really being said—more importantly, why it is being said, and what are the consequences of such verbiage. It can be easy to lean back and accept the lure of a powerful media blitz. It is even easier to activate the powers of one's own mind and start thinking.

Frederick Forsyth has given his followers another provocative tale of intrigue. Let us hope for some he has also given the kernel of an idea. It is up to the reader to rethink past tenets and perhaps take a stand. A pro-nuke sentiment won't guarantee popularity. But since when has majority opinion ever proven correct?

The Fourth Protocol is gripping, intense and enlightening. . . .

> *Virginia Fiddler, in a review of "The Fourth Protocol," in* The Armchair Detective, *Vol. 18, No. 1, Winter, 1985, p. 88.*

Allen Ginsberg

1926-

American poet, memoirist, and essayist.

Ginsberg is one of the most celebrated and popular poets in contemporary America. For more than three decades he has been an important spokesperson for the country's disaffected youth. He was a leading member of the antiestablishment Beat movement of the 1950s, a prominent figure in the counter-culture movement of the 1960s, and a dramatic reader of his own poetry. In recent years he has also lectured at universities throughout the United States on such topics as ecology and nuclear war. In spite of his antiauthoritarian beliefs and his unconventional literary style, Ginsberg's verse shows the influence of such established poets as William Carlos Williams, William Blake, and Walt Whitman, and he received the National Book Award for his collection *The Fall of America: Poems of These States 1965-1971* (1972). His work is regarded by many as an important commentary on the moral, political, and spiritual malaise of postwar America.

Ginsberg's private life has been the subject of many of his poems and has informed much of the critical discussion of his work. Born in Newark, New Jersey, Ginsberg was introduced to poetry through his father, Louis, a lyric poet and high school English teacher, and through his mentor, William Carlos Williams, who lived near Paterson, where Ginsberg attended high school. Other early literary influences include the scholars Lionel Trilling and Mark Van Doren, under whom Ginsberg studied at Columbia University, and Jack Kerouac, William Burroughs, and Neal Cassady, whom he met in New York and who, along with Ginsberg and the Western group of writers including Kenneth Rexroth, Robert Duncan, and Gary Snyder, later formed the core of the San Francisco Beats. In addition to these influences, Ginsberg's emotionally troubled childhood is reflected in much of his work. His mother suffered from various mental disorders and was periodically institutionalized during Ginsberg's adolescence, and his father was a strict disciplinarian whose conservatism clashed violently with his wife's left-wing politics. Contributing to the confusion and isolation Ginsberg felt during those years was his increasing awareness of his homosexuality, which he concealed from his parents and his peers until later in his life.

The title poem of Ginsberg's first collection, *Howl and Other Poems* (1956), established him as a leading voice of the Beats and gained notoriety for its explicit language and its highly original style, described by Ginsberg as a "Hebraic-Melvillian bardic breath." Ginsberg's public reading of "Howl" to a spellbound audience in San Francisco in 1955 demonstrated the power of his work as an oral medium and set standards for poetry readings throughout the United States. "Howl" is based on vernacular and expresses the intense rage and anxiety Ginsberg felt for the members of his generation who were persecuted for refusing to conform to the Puritan ethics of the 1950s. William Carlos Williams, in his introduction to the collection, warned that reading it would be like "going through hell." Ginsberg symbolized the evils of materialism through the image of Moloch, the Semitic god of the Old Testament to whom children were sacrificed. At the poem's conclusion, Ginsberg celebrates his victory over Moloch's control of his

© Lütfi Özkök

emotional and sexual identity. In 1957 *Howl and Other Poems* was the subject of a highly publicized censorship trial at which Lawrence Ferlinghetti, the owner of City Lights Books, which published the volume, was acquitted of distributing obscene material.

Ginsberg's next volume, *Kaddish and Other Poems: 1958-1960* (1961), delves further into his past. "Kaddish" is an elegy for Ginsberg's mother, who died in a mental hospital in 1956. Based on the ancient Hebrew prayer for the dead, it poignantly expresses the anger, love, and confusion Ginsberg felt toward his mother. Some critics consider "Kaddish" Ginsberg's most important work, and John Tytell regards the poem as "a major formal departure from our expectation of what poetry should look like on the page." *Reality Sandwiches* (1963) collects poems from 1953 to 1960, including such noted verses as "The Green Automobile" and "Siesta in Xbalba," and reflects Ginsberg's travels through Africa, Europe, and North and South America during the late 1950s.

Ginsberg has acknowledged that much of his poetry was written while he was under the influence of amphetamines and hallucinogenic drugs. During the early 1960s he traveled extensively in the Far East, where he was introduced to ancient Oriental philosophies and Buddhism. Upon his return to the United States, Ginsberg began to lecture at college campuses, advocating yoga and Zen as alternatives to drug use. Also during this period, Ginsberg generated national media attention for his political activism. He helped organize antiwar demonstrations, conducted "Be-Ins," and coined the phrase "flower power" to protest violence. In 1968 he led demonstrators at the Democratic National Convention in Chicago and later testified for the defense at the Chicago Seven conspiracy trial. These experiences inform much of Ginsberg's work of the 1960s and early 1970s, including *Planet News* (1968), which collects poems from 1961 to 1967, and *The Fall of America,* which contains poems that are viewed as visual collages of those turbulent years. Evil appears again in the guise of Vietnam, ecological dangers, and in the disproportion of material prosperity in America. Poems in this collection also reveal his personal concern with aging and his anguish over the deaths of Cassady and Kerouac.

Mind Breaths: Poems 1972-1977 (1978) marks a change of direction in Ginsberg's poetry. In an interview Ginsberg described his previous work as "politically obsessed, ephemeral, too much anger, not enough family, not enough of my personal loves." The poems in *Mind Breaths* are more tranquil, inducing the sense of spiritual meditation and calm depicted in the book's title. Also included is the moving poem "Don't Grow Old," which critics described as Ginsberg's Kaddish for his father. In *Plutonian Ode* (1982), Ginsberg returns to political and social issues by focusing on the dangers of the nuclear arms race. The collection begins with brief synopses of the discovery of plutonium in 1940 and the development of the first atomic bomb. Ginsberg compares the nuclear age to the reign of Pluto, the Greek god of the underworld. Fred Moramarco suggests that the artificiality of the element plutonium "symbolizes the destructive artificiality of contemporary life in many different manifestations."

With the publication of *Collected Poems: 1947-1980* (1984), Ginsberg's poetry has undergone substantial reevaluation. Critics have always been sharply divided in their opinions of his work; while some have dismissed it as immature and futile, most now acknowledge Ginsberg's contribution in introducing and legitimizing experimental poetry to a wider audience. *Collected Poems* is the first in a series of six volumes intended to make more accessible the majority of Ginsberg's writings, including his memoirs, lectures, essays, and correspondence, and to reaffirm his stature in contemporary literature.

(See also *CLC*, Vols. 1, 2, 3, 4, 6, 13; *Contemporary Authors,* Vols. 1-4, rev. ed.; *Contemporary Authors New Revision Series,* Vol. 2; and *Dictionary of Literary Biography,* Vols. 5, 16.)

JOHN TYTELL

Ginsberg's poetry is an expression of the simultaneity of what he has termed an "undifferentiated consciousness." In *Axel's Castle,* Edmund Wilson observed that the energy of poetry had been appropriated by novelists after World War I as writers like Joyce and Virginia Woolf fashioned a prose style of such imagistic intensity and linguistic density as to end all distinctions in English between prose and poetry. These writers, Joyce in particular, created an inner perspective that perceived like the unspeaking mind, that encountered reality through the full play of the senses rather than through the intellect as in omniscient fictions. This unconscious, or at least unarticulated flow that surrounds our being, that constitutes most of what we call sensibility, even as we are but dimly aware of its

potential in our daily lives, is the source Ginsberg draws on for his poems.

His original intention as a poet was to achieve an emotional breakthrough of individual, subjective feeling and values as a way of overcoming the Kafkian intimidation of the fifties. Relying on natural speech and spontaneous transcription, Ginsberg sought a nonliterary poetry based on the facts of daily existence. Jazz, abstract painting, Zen and haiku, writers like William Carlos Williams and Kerouac, Apollinaire and Artaud, Lorca and Neruda, were to influence his development of a new measure that corresponded more closely to the body's breath than to the artifice of iambics. The result for Ginsberg, as it had been for Gertrude Stein earlier in the century, was composition as creation, that is, the act of writing itself leading to a pursuit of the unknown rather than to a recovery of the already revealed. As with Burroughs and Kerouac, form would not be predetermined, but would follow the sequence of perception in the course of the writing, even if the route became as irrational, intuitive, and discontinuous as the shape of the mind itself. Syntax, therefore, would not accord with the imposed logic of grammar, but would correspond to the essentially nonsequential flow of the mind. As the mind does not perceive in the orderly arrangement of expository prose, it becomes almost a pretentious fiction to write a poem or a story as if it did.

In an unpublished piece called "A Few Notes On Method," Ginsberg argued that since Imagism, the movement initiated by Pound before World War I, there had been no "crystalization of real grief" in poetry, nor had poets attempted to explore "superhuman" or eternal verities. Imagism, while perfecting the poetic medium, removed from the poem a whole world of subject matter and the kind of "concretion of personal experience" that interested Ginsberg. Influenced by Burroughs' theory of factualism, Ginsberg proposed a juxtaposition of his imaginative interpretation of actual data within a narrative system that eliminated rational connectives. Ginsberg called this "ellipsis," a way of presenting images as they flashed through the mind. It was the equivalent of removing the voice of the omniscient narrator in Burroughs' work, for example. . . . Ginsberg compared his method to Cezanne's theory of *petites sensations* of experience, which his teacher, the art historian Meyer Shapiro, had explained as an attempt to delineate through color, perspective, and brushstroke every detail in the flux of experience, sensation, and time. Ginsberg studied the Cezanne paintings in the Museum of Modern Art while on marijuana, and realized how the painter manipulated space by the alternation of hot and cold colors so that the result was a kind of "space pun," as he told Kerouac, of coexisting planes that would separate mysteriously as the light source was indeterminate and shifting. Ginsberg compared this principle of "spacetimejump" to the telescoping of time in Eliot. Ellipsis applied to both narrative and syntax—the sacrifice of what Ginsberg called "syntactical sawdust," articles, prepositions, and connectives that impeded the flow and did not actually occur in the mind. The result was a richer texture and greater density of language. The prose base of Ginsberg's unusually long line (the length Whitman used to explode all metrical confinements, and which was later sustained in American poetry only by Vachel Lindsay and Robinson Jeffers) is deliberately distorted by condensation or dislocation, a form of compression of basically imagistic notations into surrealistic or cubistic phrasing like the "hydrogen jukeboxes" of **"Howl."** The key is a rhythmic shift or acceleration like the staccato abruptness of the primitively naïve grammar of **"America"**— a kind of mock American Indian dialect used ironically—which distinguishes between the flow of a mind's perceptions and less intuitively sponsored flights.

In both his rhythm and his use of the long line, Ginsberg has acknowledged Kerouac's influence. . . . Kerouac sought new speech rhythms, the patterns of blacks, rednecks, westerners, hearing in them a return to the nonliterary origins of an oral tradition. He also wanted to capture the rapid, excited current of American speech, and this, too, influenced Ginsberg. Actually, each writer benefited from the other's freedom, from mutual departures from conventional approaches to literature—as when Kerouac, in a letter, advised Ginsberg to change the phrase "startle the fox" to "star the fox," or when Kerouac sat Ginsberg at his typewriter and urged him to type whatever came into his mind and accept it as a poem. . . . Ginsberg was not always able to sustain the intensity necessary for Kerouac's spontaneity, and later admitted to Kerouac that even **"Kaddish"** needed revision. . . . Still, the essential discovery that he could release secrets of memory, free of rational restrictions since consciousness itself was without limitations, was learned from Kerouac who had derived his new rhythms from hearing jazz musicians in places like Minton's in Harlem during the war. But Ginsberg was an adept student: in *Desolation Angels,* while describing a historic visit to William Carlos Williams (then seventy-two), Kerouac compared Ginsberg to Dizzy Gillespie on trumpet because each "comes on in *waves* of thought, not in phrases." The comparison seems all the more prescient in the light of Ginsberg's recent attempts to allow blues to influence his work. The long line offered Ginsberg the necessary dimension to re-create the process of thought which occurs in visual images as well as words, taking the course of endlessly digressive associations and ramifications and confusions for there is no logic to thought (except when arbitrarily applied). (pp. 213-18)

This search for a form to articulate what Kerouac called "the unspeakable visions of the individual" represented a fundamentally new direction for poetry, although Pound began forging that way in *The Cantos,* and other poets like Charles Olson, Robert Creeley, and John Ashbery were on a similar journey. Ginsberg's critics, however, have failed to see the nature and intention of this voyage within. Unfortunately, most academicians are more comfortable with what might be called the confined—as opposed to the open—poem, and so Ginsberg's critics tend to admire the early work in *Empty Mirror* because they can cope with experiences that have recognizable formal contours like the sonnet, the dramatic monologue, or the brief lyric. But Ginsberg will not focus on a situation in the manner of Wallace Stevens or Robert Lowell, poets who will employ such familiar rhetorical devices as ironic contrast to locate a centering point. Instead, he directs his considerable energies to the hundreds of points constituting the perimeter of the experience, and then plunges beyond expansively, illogically, tumultuously encouraging digression just as the mind in the natural flow of its bewilderment does. (pp. 218-19)

Ginsberg's critics have been completely unresponsive to the oral tradition in poetry, and even seem to hold his marvelous abilities as a reader against him—which they never did in the case of Dylan Thomas. The fact that the eye simply cannot contain the poem on a page, the expansive scope and surreal leaps of Ginsberg's poetry have all contributed to preventing the critics from inventing the necessary categories through which to view his work.

Ginsberg has provided numerous clues to his own method in several interviews, and in a diary he kept while traveling in India from March 1962 to May 1963. In *Indian Journals* he includes some revealing notes for a lecture delivered to a Marxist literary conference in Benares that comment on his prosody. His reason for the change from the terse line of *Empty Mirror,* influenced mainly by William Carlos Williams, to the longer line of the subsequent work was an increased depth of perception on a nonverbal and conceptual level. Motivating the change as well was Kerouac's ideal of spontaneity, and the impact of his own visionary experiences. The models for the change were jazz ecstacy, mantra chanting, drug experiences, and Zen meditation. The resulting notation of simultaneous perception was an attempt to "capture the whole mind of the Poet," the process of thought occuring without any censoring factors. Ginsberg's means were the swift "jump of perception from one thing to another," like Olson's composition by field theory, which in Ginsberg's hands was to lead to a surrealistic violation of the old narrative order.

It seems clear that Ginsberg, like Blake, is seeking to purge language of stultifying formalisms. In the pure simplicity of rhythm and diction in *Songs of Innocence,* Blake reacted to the intricate rhetorical and metrical complexity of eighteenth-century verse. He needed a new language because he was to deny the emphasis of his day on the verifiable, the familiar and general, and to devote himself to the numinous mysteries anticipating the Romantic movement, and the very real social concerns of poems like "London." (pp. 220-21)

Ginsberg's most significant relationship to Blake has been ideological—a sympathy with social concerns, a desire to transform consciousness, to use poetry as an instrument of power or as sacramental invocation. (p. 222)

In technique, Ginsberg has maintained his link to Blake in various ways: through his musical settings of Blake's *Songs of Innocence and Experience,* and the imitations in *Gates of Wrath,* a collection of very early and uneven work. In **"September On Jessore Road,"** the last poem in *The Fall of America,* Ginsberg employs Blake's early metrical devices with great exactness. An even more pervasive influence is felt in poems like **"The Lion For Real"** or **"Sunflower Sutra."**

The latter poem is an elegy of glorious optimism for a dead sunflower, a refutation of its "corolla of bleary spikes pushed down and broken like a battered crown" among the "gnarled steel roots of machinery" on a railroad dock overlooking the San Francisco Bay. Blake's sunflower, too, represented mutability, the transcience of the living and the inevitability of death. But Ginsberg, in a letter to Kerouac, described the sunflower he saw as the flower of industry, tough-spiked and ugly. . . . Experimenting with rhythmic buildup without relying on a repetitive base (like the use of the pronoun *who* in **"Howl"**) to sustain its powerfully increasing tempo, Ginsberg offers us a paean to the life-force within the heart of the wasteland, the sordid details of junk, treadless tires, used condoms, and abandoned tin cans and industrial grime, enveloping the dessicated sunflower in which Ginsberg chooses to believe, vigorously asserting his belief by seizing the skeleton stalk and holding it at his side like a scepter. . . . (pp. 222-23)

The verse paragraph ending **"Sunflower Sutra"** recalls Walt Whitman, another seminal influence on Ginsberg, and a key figure in the visionary tradition. . . . Whitman's experience, like Ginsberg's with Blake, resulted in an ecstatic sense of ineffable joy, a knowledge of the unity of the universe, of the bonds existing between men and all living things. In Whitman's poetry, these feelings emerged as an unprecedented celebration of his fellow men, an effusive outpouring of pity, affectionate sympathy, and love so genuinely sincere that it could only be called sentimental by cynics. (p. 223)

The close connection between Whitman and Ginsberg may be measured by Whitman's expectation of the poet, as he characterized it in the preface to *Leaves of Grass*—a document which along with Emerson's essay "The Poet" constitutes the first signs of a native American poetic, standing among the most significant utterances on the poetic process in any era. As the poet sees the farthest. Whitman argues, "he has the most faith. His thoughts are the hymns of the praise of things." (p. 224)

Blake, Whitman, and Williams are the figures who have most inspired Ginsberg, but an equally significant, if less finitely measurable, source has been Surrealist poetry and painting. Blake permitted entry into the prophetic tradition; Whitman offered the infusion of democratic optimism; Williams inspired a new diction; but Surrealism suggested the state of mind that proved liberating enough for Ginsberg to see the political realities of his day with passionate clarity. (pp. 226-27)

Surrealism was very much a part of the *Zeitgeist* surrounding Ginsberg in his youth. During the war, a number of the key Surrealist painters had settled in America, and by 1942 Ernst, Masson, and Tanguy were living in New York City, as well as André Breton, one of the theoreticians of the movement. Breton's belief that subconscious irrationality could provide the basis for a positive social program separated the Surrealists from the Dadaists, their more nihilistic forebears. Breton's manifestoes contain arguments that anticipate the inner flow of experience Ginsberg was to express so powerfully in his poetry. Breton sought a "monologue spoken as rapidly as possible without any interruption on the part of the cerebral faculties, a monologue consequently unencumbered by the slightest inhibition and which was as closely as possible akin to spoken thought." This "psychic automatism" proposed to express the mind's actual functioning in the absence of controls like reason, or any superimposed moral or aesthetic concern. If Ginsberg was to remain in touch with Blake's tradition of magic prophecy, he would have to find ways to release that vision without unnecessarily tampering, interfering, or distorting, and the Surrealist bias against revision that Kerouac maintained prevented the danger of any fatal loss of impetus.

The Surrealists in France had distinguished between literature as a craft or talent exercised within certain traditional and prescriptive formal limitations and poetry as a mode of visionary discovery. To induce revelation, they pursued their dreams, finding in them a route to the unconscious, and a way of capturing the uncensored maturity of Rimbaud's child-man. Like Blake's idealization of the child, the Surrealists sought a model for wonder, spontaneity, and destructiveness—which, by the way, they interpreted as the end of adult self-control and obedience to conditioning. So Breton began attending with fascination to phrases running through his mind as he fell asleep, just as Williams in *Kora In Hell* was to improvise disconnected passages composed just prior to sleep. Related to such experiments was the Surrealists' interest in Charcot's *Studies In Hysteria* and Robert Desnos' self-induced trances. As Alfred Jarry urged, true hallucination is the sustained waking dream, and this becomes the premise of much of Ginsberg's poetry as he applies the phantasmagoria of dream to everyday reality. (pp. 227-28)

It is quite clear that this consciousness was present in Ginsberg's earliest poems. In "**Psalm I**," the second poem in *Empty*

Mirror, Ginsberg refers to his poems as the product of a "vision haunted mind," and writes of "majestic flaws of mind which have left my brain open to hallucination." In the initial poem of the volume, the marvelously understated "I feel as if I were at a dead end," Ginsberg describes a state of psychic and moral impotence whose metaphor is the head severed from the body. This impotence expresses itself as a terrible inability to act in the face of a paralyzing absurdity which stalks through the poems; hallucination, visionary messages from the unconscious, serve to fuse head and body, to reconnect intellect and feeling. A number of the best poems in the collection are called dreams, like the Kafkian "**A Meaningless Institution**" where Ginsberg invents an enormous ward filled with "hundreds of weeping / decaying men and women." Everyone in the poem is impassive; everything in it is static; there is no interrelationship anywhere. . . . The view of the world implied by such a poem is dismal, a miasma of quiescent disappointment and stagnant despair, a pervasive mood in the book appearing with special poignance in "**Sunset**," "**A Ghost May Come**," "**A Desolation**," "**The Blue Angel**," and "**Walking Home At Night**." These poems reflect terrible entrapment in mechanical situations revealing men devoid of humanity, like those "cowering in unshaven rooms in underwear" in "**Howl**." Occasionally, the depression is alleviated by childish rage, as in one of the best poems in *Empty Mirror*, "**In Society**." . . . (pp. 228-29)

The poems in *Empty Mirror* employ short lines predominantly, stripping "yakking down to modern bones" Ginsberg wrote to Cassady, and at one point Ginsberg expresses metaphorical dissatisfaction with Yeatsian terseness. . . . He begins to move in the direction of his long-line experiments in "**Hymn**," a series of five verse paragraphs (animated by such antiprose and surreal formulations as "clock of meat"), or "**Paterson**," a poem no one seems to have noticed even though it anticipates the rhythmic power of the later poetry as well as the thematic rejection of American materialism. Rather than live in rooms "papered with visions of money," rather than cut his hair, dress properly, bathe, and work steadily for the "dead prick of commonplace obsession," the hero of "**Paterson**," a Beat code figure, would choose madness. . . . (pp. 231-32)

"**Paterson**" is a poem of excess, an early sign of Ginsberg's surrealism. Breton noted that surrealism acts on the mind very much like drugs, creating a need for the mysterious effects and special pleasures of an artifical paradise, but at the same time pushing men to frightful revolts as that paradise seems unattainable. Like opium-induced images, surrealistic images seem to occur spontaneously, or despotically as Baudelaire once claimed, ringing with unpremeditated juxtaposition. Apollinaire, in *Le poète assassiné,* glorified physical disequilibrium as divine, and Rimbaud, earlier, had called for a violent derangement of the senses.

Ginsberg has heeded this imperative, risking his sensibility to widen the area of his consciousness with drugs. As Coleridge claimed to have composed "Kubla Khan" during an opium reverie, Ginsberg has admitted to writing a number of poems while using marijuana or the stronger hallucinogens like peyote, LSD-25, mescaline, and ayahuasca. . . . The experiences described in these poems, often titled by the name of the drug employed, are very similar to the effects in Burroughs' fiction: déjà vu, death hysteria, extreme paranoia, disembodied awareness of a decomposing body, demonic mind-monsters, loss of identity as in "**The Reply**" where the "universe turns inside out to devour me," and only occasionally a sense of ecstatic, spiraling energy. The greatest concentration of drug poems is in *Kaddish,* but they are clearly the weakest part of the volume. Oddly enough, Ginsberg is unable to suggest a convincing state of transport in these poems, and they seem grounded compared to a natural high like the one Emerson described in his first essay, "Nature." . . . Ironically, in the *Kaddish* drug poems, just where a reader might expect a sacrifice of intellect and a total involvement with the senses, the intrusion of the poet's questioning mind misdirects the tensions. Ginsberg seems almost aware of this, as when in **"Aether"** he mentions "the threat to magic by writing while high." **"Aether,"** the last poem in *Reality Sandwiches,* comes closest to fulfilling Ginsberg's ideal of the poem as notation of undifferentiated consciousness (drugs theoretically assisting in such an effort by deemphasizing mind), a quality felt in the poem's movement toward new line arrangements and visual impact. (pp. 232-34)

Generally, Ginsberg has used drugs as an aid to releasing blocked aspects of his consciousness which are expressed in his poetry, like the Moloch vision in **"Howl"** which was induced by peyote, or **"Kaddish,"** written while using amphetamines.

"Kaddish" is an elegy to the suffering madness of Ginsberg's mother, Naomi. It testifies to Ginsberg's capacity for involvement with another human in torment, for the acceptance of another's weirdness. While successfully capturing the historical ambiance of the thirties—socialist idealism, communist factionalism, martyrdom, and the reflexive paranoia of fascism—the poem is most memorable as a torrential and cathartic release of Ginsberg's complex relationship to his mad mother, at times compassionately tender, full of sweet regrets and losses, at times full of the frustration, rage, and anger that poor Naomi, locked into her tormented self, provoked. The racing, breathless pace of the poem reflects its manner of composition—the stimulation of morphine mixed with meta-amphetamine. . . . (p. 235)

The narrative, part purgation, part reconciliation and acceptance, relates a story that contains more sheer feeling than any poem of its time. . . . The lyrical poignance of the memories of Naomi's past, her physical beauty, her mandolin, the left-wing summer camps and songs of revolution are juxtaposed with the sordid presence of her horrible suspicions—that her mother-in-law is trying to poison her, that Roosevelt himself has wired her room to spy on her. Naomi's anguished hysteria—demanding blood transfusions, demanding assistance from strangers on the street, demanding release from asylums—combined with the reach of Ginsberg's grief (assuming a less strident, more mournful tone in accord with the Hebrew prayer for the dead from which he quotes), allows the poem an almost unbearable threshold of pain. Naomi's intensity is like Medea's, a quality that made Ginsberg's adaptation of his poem for the stage unforgettable as theater. (p. 236)

The language of the poem comes closer to prose syntax than most of Ginsberg's work, but the lines often become fragmentary and discontinuous, suggesting that certain perceptions are too intolerable to be fully developed. Ginsberg has commented on his own unease in wrestling with form through such long notations, but the result is another new direction for poetry. . . . **"Kaddish"** is a major formal departure from our expectation of what poetry should look like on the page, just as thematically the elegy departs from tradition by refusing eulogy, developing a heroic resistance by revealing Naomi's negative qualities. The moods of the poem vary widely from imprecation and curse to sympathy and physical desire (at one point, Naomi makes sexual advances to her son while dancing

before a mirror), and ultimately, at the end of the poem, a ghostly disassociation as Naomi fails to recognize Allen on his last visit to her. And even that mood changes as he receives her letter of prophetic instruction just before hearing of her death: "The key is in the window, the key is in the sunlight in the window—I have the key—Get married Allen, don't take drugs—the key is in the sunlight in the window." The letter, which Ginsberg rewrote himself, revives the spirit of millenarian optimism that Naomi epitomizes throughout the poem, a pathetically disoriented yet actively striving figure.

The four final sections, each very short, relieve and disperse some of the intensities developed in the narrative, as if the momentum could not be suddenly released, but needed to be gently assuaged. The "caw caw caw" section, for example, soothes like a resolving fugue with its two parts, one representing the realistic bleakness of materialism and pain, the second a source of mystical aspiration, both harmonized by the last line with its collocation of "Lord" and "caw." Even these last sections, however, contain signs of the poem's tremendously successful excessiveness, especially a litany which brutally and without explanations lists the horrible shocks of Naomi's life. (pp. 237-38)

The overall effect . . . of **"Kaddish"** is unlike that of any other modern poem, even **"Howl."** The reader is left in a state of utter exhaustion, the feeling one often has after a particularly harrowing dream. The aesthetic paradox of **"Kaddish"** is that despite all its terror and the shockingly relentless and obsessive manner in which Ginsberg pursues his mother's haunted memory, the result is a poetry of the sublime, the rare kind of exalted rejoicing in being that occurs in the poetry of Christopher Smart, in Richard Crashaw's description of his love for God, or Francis Thompson's "The Hound of Heaven."

The crucial question for any poet capable of creating poems like **"Howl"** or **"Kaddish"** is whether that imaginative energy can be sustained. There are those who have wondered whether Ginsberg is the agent or the vessel of his poetic inspiration, whether he is the author of his poems or whether, like Burroughs, he may be the telepathic register of some otherly source. In this connection, it is useful to remember that the poets we most admire in any age manage to leave us with only a few major poems: indeed, it would be difficult to measure the greatness of the best of Dryden, Pope, Wordsworth, Coleridge, Browning, or Tennyson without the light of their total efforts. *Empty Mirror, Howl,* and *Kaddish* are all exceptional volumes, but the beginning, not the high point, of a continuing productivity, a steady stream of poems that achieve different kinds of power and insight. (pp. 239-40)

Ginsberg has been progressing steadily in the tradition of Henry Miller toward a description of particulars that once would have been regarded as obscene or scatological ("How big is the prick of the President?" he humorously queries in **"Wichita Vortex Sutra"**), but which Ginsberg sees as natural speech. Whitman had proclaimed that copulation was no more rank than death, that both had aspects of holiness, and in "Song of Myself" here are several descriptions of mystical ecstasy that are rendered with the metaphor of masturbation (recalling Ginsberg's Blake visitation). Whitman's "prurient provokers" and "red marauders," as well as his *Calamus* poems, suggested a potential for American letters (which few except Henry Miller have had the courage or the folly to fulfill) that leads to poems like **"This form of Life needs Sex"** in *Planet News.* Sexuality, both as release and as a trigger for latent psychic energies and realizations, in short as a vehicle for awareness and liberated consciousness, has been an object of repression for a long time in America and Ginsberg has taken many public risks to widen those particular perceptual gates. (p. 244)

Planet News, Ginsberg's poems of the sixties, marked a sharp resurgence of power, containing at least six splendid poems: **"Television was a Baby Crawling Toward that Deathchamber," "The Change," "Kral Majales," "Who Be Kind To," "Wichita Vortex Sutra,"** and **"Wales Visitation."** In *Planet News,* the demands of the self so insistently pronounced in the earlier poetry are modulated to harmonize with the larger concerns of the earth, and the poet's role in dramatizing those concerns. The first and last poems in the collection, both on the dangers inherent in the American military system, form an envelope for inner unities. No one seems to have noticed the way in which so many of the poems lead into each other and relate organically (as earlier *Kaddish* consisted of a number of elegies). In *Planet News* these interconnections—**"Lost in Calcutta"** pointing directly to **"The Change"**—are part of a grand network of the poet's awareness of the planet as he travels through India, Japan, California, New York, Havana, Warsaw, Prague, and London. (pp. 245-46)

What is most impressive about *Planet News* is Ginsberg's sense of himself and his place in the general order of things. He acknowledges an obligatory role as the prophetic witness of American imperialism—kind of a Rudyard Kipling in reverse—in **"Television was a Baby Crawling Toward that Deathchamber,"** a lengthy and innovative poem about technological control over consciousness that is reminiscent of Burroughs. . . . (p. 246)

In **"Who Be Kind To,"** as in **"The Change,"** Ginsberg suggests that it is now time to turn from Rimbaud's hedonistic and socially irresponsible escape into adventurous sensations to face the problems of this world, the looming dangers of planetary biocide. **"The Change: Kyoto-Tokyo Express"** describes Ginsberg's own evolution from a destructively obsessive refusal to deal with the social realities of the West (by traveling in India and taking drugs) to a desire to "open the portals to what Is." The poem virtually declares that the despair of the time of **"Howl"** is no longer justified as an end, that it was only the beginning of consciousness but not a program. . . . **"The Change"** also signals a return for Ginsberg to the tensions of a tightly involuted line, still dependent on surreal dislocations of image, and rhythmic power of voice, but for the moment more compactly self-contained than even the *Empty Mirror* poems. As in **"Journal Night Thoughts"** or **"Wichita Vortex Sutra,"** Ginsberg reveals an encouraging curiosity about new modes of presentation and formal arrangement.

"Who Be Kind To" is both an advisory and a benediction to the radical spirit in our time, urging the discoveries of **"The Change"** on a wider audience while wishing for its preservation and continuity: "Be kind to yourself, because the bliss of your own / kindness will flood the police tomorrow." (pp. 248-49)

The Fall of America shows Ginsberg moving closer to Kerouac's conception of the writer as memoirist. . . . More than *Howl* or *Kaddish,* this is Ginsberg's most despairing and least affirming book, haunted as it is by a constant sense of doom. Instead of the ecstatic resources of drugs or mysticism, the only relief Ginsberg projects—like Burroughs in *The Wild Boys*—is an apocalypse of self-destruction. Perhaps this new irredeemable despair is responsible for the purgatorial tone of the collection. In *Planet News,* travel, movement in space and time, was treated adventurously, euphorically, expectantly. But in

The Fall of America, the motion is burdened, deliberate, weighted with sorrow and seriousness, unalleviated by new impressions or expectations, restricted somehow to the boundaries of a country in its saddest hour.

The basis of *The Fall of America* is an Emersonian correspondence: the violence of Vietnam is reflected in an inner violence, the destruction of foreign war is complemented by the devastation of our own natural environment. Ginsberg sees the external misadventure and the internal blindness of what we have done to our own land as organically related—like the Buddhist notion of karma that promises that any present action will affect future incarnations, or the biblical maxim on sowing and reaping. Ironically, the poem is dedicated to Whitman and prefaced by the selection from *Democratic Vistas* on adhesiveness, the sense of male comradeship that Whitman supposed would spiritually leaven American materialism. But Ginsberg's own tone is uninspired by Whitman's cheer. With brutal relentlessness, in poem after poem, Ginsberg's eye fixes on the pocks of industrial spoilage scarring the face of the land.

In *The Fall of America,* the Moloch of **"Howl"** has finally consumed our youthful hope, transforming any Jeffersonian aspirations of a society whose real strength was rooted in the back country to an infernal view of belching smokestacks, Poe's red death pervading the acrid atmosphere. Ginsberg, in his half-century on the planet, has been a Tiresian witness to this harrowing change. . . . Everywhere, the horror is the city's filth spilling over into the countryside, festering contamination and scourge, the land blighted, wasted and prone to plague like Thebes before the exorcism of Oedipus. . . . Ginsberg extends the scope of the disaster with a pop mosaic of complicity, a collage of simultaneous data, actual sensory details and historical referents, mixing news of Vietnam atrocities and establishment apologies—like Ambassador Lodge's infamous Christmas Eve assertion that the United States was morally justified in its actions—with the new American landscape of hamburger advertisements, motels, automobile junkpiles. . . . The technique is primarily juxtaposition—the smell of burning oil and an advertisement for mouthwash—and no overt comment is needed because of the graphic quality of the depiction. (pp. 251-53)

Ginsberg's bias is humanistic and international. The awful power of American industry with its iron landscape of "Triple towers smokestacking steaming," of open-hearth furnaces and the smells of creosote and butane replacing alfalfa and wheat, seems to Ginsberg to be designed to burden the rest of the world, to kill peasants in South America or Asia. In a sense Ginsberg has turned a full circle, returning to the damned terrain of Eliot's wasteland, but now without the remotest flicker of hope. (p. 254)

The vision of a new nation, and a resurgence of life-forces that Ginsberg envisaged in *Planet News* has been blurred by fire and smoke, but is not yet extinguished despite the politics of repression. Ginsberg vaunts his fury with a Blakean sense of purpose, lashing his own resolve to "haunt these States" in **"A Vow."** . . . With the ferocity and anger of Ezra Pound, Ginsberg threatens in **"War Profit Litany"** to list the names of the companies who have profited through the war in Vietnam, their corporate directors and major stockholders, the banks and investment houses that support them. In **"Returning North of Vortex,"** Ginsberg startlingly (in 1967) appeals for an American military defeat in Vietnam, prophesying that we will lose our will. Ginsberg's passion reaches an apex here, a point of crisis which diminishes, or changes course, with a group of elegies to Neal Cassady.

The vision then shifts from the city to his own farm in the country. Living without electricity, surrounded by animals rather than the carrion of stripped cars in the city, this more pastoral dimension functions ironically in the book, as a backdrop by which to measure the ruination of the land. There are very few lyrical moments in the book (as in **"Easter Sunday"**) which are not used to contrast some discordantly jarring industrial rapacity. The finest poem in the volume is a vision of this unsettled pastoral, **"Ecologue,"** a long account of winter preparations on the farm that is impinged upon by the consciousness of Vietnam, of the incipient fascism Ginsberg feels in his country, of "millions of bodies in pain." The poem pivots on omens of disaster, and uses the picture of the farm as a microcosm of the larger breakdown of civilization.

Ginsberg himself becomes one of the correspondences in *The Fall of America:* his automobile accident near the end of 1968, and a fall on the ice several years later, are a synecdoche of the general collapse he sees about him. In his earlier work, no matter how dispiriting or anguished the degree of torment, the voice was always powerful enough to sustain the reader, to suggest that existence depends on resistance and active effort, on the definition of a direction whose goal might be pleasure or personal salvation, but whose purpose would be to free the individual from the Circe of materialism. In *The Fall of America,* however, Ginsberg seems temporarily disoriented, despite the power of his invective." . . . (pp. 254-55)

In **"Death On All Fronts,"** a poem revealing the dominating influence of Burroughs' vision in *The Fall of America,* Ginsberg admits to being unable to find order or even solace in his own work. In **"Friday The Thirteenth"** he wonders about the efficacy of poetry, its ability to raise consciousness in the presence of the implacable destructiveness in the world. These are very real questions for a poet who has aspired to millennial prophecy, and who has exerted himself so energetically in realizing a particular vision of the world. Part of Ginsberg's gift as a poet has been his faith in vision that has been characteristically American because of its bouyance, its ability to return with hope despite disaster. Like the American transcendentalists, that vision has been the fruit of wonder and a voyaging imagination. To discover the new, one needs to have faith in old tools. In *The Fall of America,* that faith seems to have been profoundly shaken. Perhaps, too, this is why Ginsberg has temporarily shifted from bhakti yoga—delight in song—to long periods of meditation, up to ten hours a day for weeks on end.

Allen Ginsberg's poetry is a record of surprising conversions—from the tersely unfulfilled anguish of *Empty Mirror,* the rage of "Howl," the mourning dirge of "Kaddish," the bare brutalities of *Reality Sandwiches,* the celebratory incandescence of *Planet News,* the apocalyptic terrors of *The Fall of America.* The poems exist not only as a formidably substantial body of work, but as a demonstration that poetry need not be disembodied, removed from a natural base in chant and song. Rhythm, Ginsberg has shown his own generation, is less a matter of seeing the poem on the page than hearing it sounded. As with Indian mantras or traditional religious meditation, the effect is to slow the consciousness flow, to change ordinary conditioning so that new perceptions can occur. The words repeated aloud assume a new transporting density, become a kind of magical incantatory vehicle for body and nonconceptual sensation as well as mind. The poems are made to be sung; the singer uses them to see what is there and what possibilities lie beyond. Ginsberg's most recent readings show that he is headed

in a folk and blues direction enriched by the discipline of lengthy meditation and Eastern mantra. "Allen Ginsberg's naked dance" Gary Snyder called it years ago in a letter from Japan: it has been the bardic dance of our day, shocking the word from the security of the printed page and spinning it into our very midst. (pp. 256-57)

John Tytell, "Allen Ginsberg and the Messianic Tradition," in his Naked Angels: The Lives & Literature of the Beat Generation, *McGraw-Hill Book Company, 1976, pp. 212-57.*

MARK SHECHNER

We have three books from Allen Ginsberg: a selection of recent poems [*Mind Breaths*], a second transcription of entries from his vast store of journals [*Journals*], and an exchange of letters with Neal Cassady [*As Ever*], who was once the elusive object of his tumultuous affections. But there is nothing especially new here; two of the books are retrospective forays over known territory. For years Ginsberg has been the most accessible of our writers, and has conducted his affairs very much in the open, if remarkably beyond the reach of talk shows, bookchat, and general literary blather. Nor do the poems break any new ground, imaginatively or technically. They put forth the standard brew of homosexuality, metaphysics, pacifism, political outrage, muddled prophecy, and homemade Buddhism that is as familiar now as the morning coffee, and about as alarming.

Ginsberg has long since graduated from being a subterranean and "know-nothing Bohemian" to being everyone's favorite prophet. He is our anarchist-in-residence, queer and avuncular, whose tirades against imperial warfare, official repression, and hard dope, and open passion for nubile young boys are disarmed and domesticated by his irony. Even Diana Trilling, who is ever on the alert for bad influences on the young, has preferred to remember him, in *We Must March My Darlings,* as a warm and comforting presence in the sixties. As an added ingratiating feature, Ginsberg is that rarest of figures among American poets, a survivor, working vigorously into his fifties, despite the script he was handed early in life which called for a spectacular crack-up or a slow descent into alcohol or madness in the grand American tradition. He was out to be a *poète maudit:* a Poe, a John Berryman, a Delmore Schwartz, a Sylvia Plath, a Jack Kerouac or Norman Mailer . . . , and much of his initial impact in the fifties came from the impression, which he cultivated, that he had privileged insight into the tragic fate of the imagination in America "I saw the best minds of my generation destroyed by madness." But, unlike Kerouac, he eventually recoiled from the allure of self-destruction, and saved us, in the bargain, from another tiresome lesson in how America treats her poets, and yet another spellbinding case-history in poetry as a by-product of terminal euphoria. He was finally too ironic and willful for martyrdom, and, despite his rages against America and her wars, too enamored of the *idea* of America (which has been bound up for him with the idea of Walt Whitman) to renege on his initial promise: "America I'm putting my queer shoulder to the wheel."

Special credit for Ginsberg's survival must go to his Buddhism, which has taught him how to marshall and conserve his energies, and has given him the emotional ballast to stand up against crushing psychic pressures. The air of wise passiveness that attends his public appearances these days is a deliberate calm, a steady vigilance over his own seething emotions, which he has learned to hold in check and sublimate into a sonorous and agitated delivery. . . . But whatever such a containment of rage has contributed to his durability and his public figure—that is, the instructional example—it has brought little to the poetry save a treasury of liquid phrases to be sprinkled over a poem like spices over stew, for piquancy. They scan wonderfully, while lending an air of mystical illumination. Thus a few poems in *Mind Breaths* are graced with such sweet cadences as "Bom Bom! Shivaye! Ram Nam Satyahey! Om Ganipatti, Om Saraswati Hrih Sowha!" which, for most of us, might just as well be "Polly wolly doodle all the day." Yet, despite suggestions of Tagore or Lao-Tze that hang like smog over his poetry, Ginsberg has kept faith with his original mentors—Williams, Whitman, and Blake—and nothing he has done since the poems in *Kaddish* (1961) shows any advance in vision or skill. (pp. 105-06)

At this stage of the game, at fifty-two, rather than try to push ahead poetically, Ginsberg has taken to doubling back upon himself, and the journals, correspondence, memoirs, and *obiter dicta* . . . that now crowd the market suggest that what we can look forward to at this point are neither new breakthroughs in poetry nor further refinements, but Ginsberg's efforts to clarify his image and reaffirm his claim upon a place in American cultural history. I suspect that Ginsberg understands these days that he matters less as a poet than as a figure, an exemplary life. Certainly he has become influential without being consistently great, or even consistently engaging as a writer, and most of us can count on one hand the poems that survive rereading, let alone study. As an exemplary figure, though, Ginsberg is something else again, and it is to the clarification of the example that the journals and letters are dedicated.

But in what sense is such a life admirable? Surely not in its conspicuous alienation nor the rootlessness that has made of Ginsberg a wandering Jew (or Buddhist-Jew) by default, and certainly not in the homosexuality as such, even though as a campaigner for sexual pluralism Ginsberg has been instrumental in creating the current social climate in which coming out is considered a positive personal gesture. What surely is exemplary on Ginsberg's part is the risk he has taken in placing his own sexual nature out in the open: proclaiming it, writing about it, worrying over it, and insisting on its right to gratification, thus keeping himself clear of the enervating compromises of closet homosexuality. Ginsberg's acceptance of his own constitution as the very condition of his life and his poetry is certainly one of the sources of his strength and durability. Blakean that he is, he has not let himself be undermined by his own repressed desires.

But Ginsberg's long involvement with mind-altering drugs is more problematic. His exalted testimonials on behalf of his pharmacological experiments gave sanction, not only to the indiscriminate use of drugs in the sixties, but to their glorification as the elixir of cosmic consciousness. Though Ginsberg has campaigned against heroin, and now writes, "Nobody saves America by sniffing cocaine," his basic line on dope, as on everything else, has been the libertaria one: *laissez faire,* and let every man find out for himself. But hallucinogenic drugs once meant more to him than just another degree of human freedom; they conveniently suited his romance with madness. . . . (pp. 107-08)

Yet all this in Ginsberg: the aggressive homosexuality, the rootlessness, the anarchism, the celebrated expeditions in search of a better hallucinogen, cannot be seen apart from what is exemplary in him, for they are, however ambiguous, his efforts at salvation. They are what he had to attain and then had to

get beyond. The accumulating documentation of his life is slowly amounting to the authentication of a saint's life, a history of beatitude whose theme, like that of all saints' lives, is crisis, conversion, and trial. The famous Blake vision, of which we have a half dozen accounts, is like Paul's vision on the road to Damascus or Martin Luther's fit in the choir, a token of election, and the torments that follow are steps in the realization of the mission. The mother's madness had to be suffered and purged; the humiliating love for Neal Cassady had to be indulged and worked through; imprisonment and institutionalization had to be endured and made use of; shame and guilt had to be embraced and transcended. Such experience was an apprenticeship in failure, and in light of the dismal lessons with which he was imbued, Ginsberg's heroism lies not in his oversold resistance to political power or social convention but in his refusal of the original emotional ground rules of his life. He altered the deadly prognosis: by way of Blake and Buddhism he became that mythic American, the self-made man, an anarchist Horatio Alger. More bookish, more assiduously literary than the other Beats, he rescued himself through his reading. Little wonder that he is honored these days in the academy, to whose basic values he is seemingly so anathema, for he is a living defense of the literary life, a man who was saved by books.

These journals and letters, by and large, have little to teach about Ginsberg's survival, but much to show us about his early desperation. The *Journals* cover two periods, 1952 to 1956, and 1959 to February 1962, the eve of Ginsberg's departure for India. The *Indian Journals,* which were the first to be published (1970), take up where these leave off. The correspondence with Neal Cassady extends farther back, to 1947 and the dark years at Columbia, and plots the vicissitudes of that difficult relationship into 1963. The Ginsberg who emerges from these pages is the lost and driven young poet seeking resolution of his conflicts through determined reading, mysticism, and the pursuit of sexual experience. (pp. 108-09)

The appeal of Ginsberg in the sixties lay in the appearance he gave of seeing through or around or beyond the veils and corruptions of ordinary social thought. It was not then evident, as it now is, that such transcendence was in fact a falling short of social reality, and that what seemed in the poetry a deeper penetration into the mysteries of being was really a narrowing of emotional range and a painful shyness about people. We expect poetry that is sufficiently inspired to leap from one plane of meaning to another, to zoom upward from sensory data to the higher realms, but what seems like thrilling prophecy when spoken in Biblical accents does not satisfy in the form of a journal entry. Which is another way of saying that the journals and most of the letters to Neal are intrinsically uninteresting except for the light they shed on other things that may matter to us: Ginsberg's poetry, or American social history in the postwar decades.

So, I must cast my praise of these books in somewhat negative terms. There is no reason for Ginsberg not to have published such journals and letters, nor to withhold the additional materials which will soon be forthcoming. Public self-examination of this sort is a rare and valuable gesture, even when, as in this case, the social value of the gesture far exceeds the intellectual impact of what is actually disclosed. Understandably, a confession, even to oneself, is a bargain struck with that superego to permit some more difficult and compromising knowledge to be withheld, though it is odd to find such a case in which primal fears and sexual anxieties are laid bare and social relations suppressed. But the reversal is part of the antinomian meaning of Ginsberg's life. He has always done things differently than the rest of us. (p. 112)

Mark Shechner, *"The Survival of Allen Ginsberg,"* in Partisan Review, *Vol. XLVI, No. 1, 1979, pp. 105-12.*

ROBERTA BERKE

No Beat poet embodies the predicament of the poet in American society more vividly than Allen Ginsberg. In **"America"** he exhorts his country with exasperation and defiance. . . . (p. 48)

Ginsberg is flashing a red flag at the bull of McCarthyism and the timid cows of conformity that trod down innovation in fifties America. Despite his denunciation of America, Ginsberg never considers permanent exile. (pp. 48-9)

Ginsberg wants to be an American prophet, but unlike Whitman and Williams, whom he admires, Ginsberg is a self-mutilating prophet, similar to those priests in the ancient Middle East who gashed themselves in an effort to compel the gods to send rain for the crops. Ginsberg's self-loathing is expressed not only in his revulsion toward the America that represents himself, but also in his exposure of many embarassing aspects of himself and his family, particularly his mother. . . . (p. 49)

The reader is repelled by these skeletons rummaged out of family closets, and even the most morbid curiosity finally tires of the repetitive prurience. Yet many readers dutifully plod on, because Ginsberg is adept at sticking in the barbed hooks of Jewish guilt. After all he's done for us, by demolishing the New Critics and bringing a new freedom to poetry, how can we be so ungrateful as to put his books down? To ignore him is to deny his suffering, to become identified with those anticommunist witch-hunters his mother dreaded and to side with Moloch, J. Edgar Hoover and other assorted boogeymen. The reader also persists out of hope for better things, encouraged by Ginsberg's passages of compelling power, such as parts of **"Kaddish."** (pp. 49-50)

The long poem **"Kaddish"** marks the high tide of Ginsberg's achievement. **"Kaddish"** is a lament for and celebration of his mother, who died after years of physical and mental suffering. The terrible whirlwind of Naomi Ginsberg's paranoia, degeneration and death is so devastating that her son must grip onto his poem lest his own sanity be swept away as his mother simultaneously engulfs and deserts him. He has no hand free for coy hipster waves to his friends or to thumb his nose at the establishment. Ginsberg has said his intention was to write "a death-prayer imitating the rhythms of the Hebrew Kaddish." (The liturgical Jewish Kaddish, incidentally, was not written in Hebrew but in Aramaic, the vernacular, so that it might be understood by all.) Although Ginsberg approximately transcribes the liturgy in the first two lines of the **"Hymmnn"** section of **"Kaddish,"** he soon departs from it, when it says "though he is above all the praises, hymns and adorations which men can utter." Ginsberg's subsequent naturalistic images and staccato rhythms owe more to Ray Charles and black revivalists than to rabbis. The prayer ends: "May the Most High, source of perfect peace, grant peace to us . . ."; near the close of his poem, Ginsberg repeats a benediction from his mother's last letter: "The key is in the sunlight at the window in the bars the key is in the sunlight." By his own standard, widening the area of consciousness (which is the same one I proposed), **"Kaddish"** is a very good poem indeed. It relentlessly transforms a squalid family embarrassment into an epic which embraces every beloved parent who has disintegrated into a death without dignity and which leaves a key for the living in the bars which have become bars of sunlight.

Since **"Kaddish"** Ginsberg's verse has declined miserably. Typical of his recent output is *Iron Horse,* a long poem describing Ginsberg masturbating in a train traveling across America carrying soldiers who have fought in Cambodia. Among the poem's baggage are news clippings, a transliteration of an ethnic chant (possibly Mojave?), shards of pop culture and pronouncements such as: "The delicate chemical brain changes / Aetheral sensations / Muladhara sphincter up through mind aura / Sahasrarapadma promise / another univers—." This is a lugubrious parody of Ginsberg's earlier work and not even City Lights' imaginative design can redeem the book from ghastliness. This long poem is a metaphor for Ginsberg's poetic activity in recent years: rushing across America jerking off, grabbing bits of gossip and news like plastic-wrapped sandwiches.

But Ginsberg is too important a poet to abandon prematurely. The Beat ideals which led him into his predicament have also affected other poets, so it is worthwhile to explore some reasons for his recent failures. Along with his faith in his prophetic role goes a belief in the sacredness of his inspiration. Although he sometimes revises, many of Ginsberg's poems are rough drafts written at speed, often while he was stoned. For example, Ginsberg says of **"The Sunflower Sutra"**: "composition time 20 minutes, me at desk scribbling, Kerouac at cottage door waiting for me to go off somewhere party. . . ." There isn't anything wrong with poems written in a flash, as long as that flash is truly inspired. Great poems, such as Coleridge's "Kubla Kahn," have been known to arrive full blown (albeit incomplete). But **"Sunflower Sutra"** is far from a great poem: it is verbose, maudlin, repetitious and cranks out its simple-minded moral as clumsily as a fundamentalist sandwich board. Another hazard of the prophetic role is that it stakes the validity of poetry on the amount of social change it is able to cause. Although America has changed considerably since *Howl* was published in 1956, it certainly hasn't "taken off its clothes," as Ginsberg urged in **"America,"** while some states still outlaw homosexuality and a national television network censors "the naughty bits" from *Monty Python's Flying Circus.* Ginsberg, the grit in the American oyster, has been co-opted, opaquely coated with a bohemian role until he is no longer abrasive but merely doing what we have come to expect. There have been some signs lately that even Ginsberg is finding the prophetic mantle a drag: "I'll get drunk & give no shit, & not be a Messiah." (pp. 50-2)

Some of Ginsberg's current difficulties may also stem from his lack of a critical perspective from which to assess his own work. Although he studied with Lionel Trilling at Columbia and was William Carlos Williams's protégé, for years Ginsberg has avoided and abominated most critics (with the occasional exception of Eric Mottram, who has long been an ardent advocate of Beat poets). Ginsberg's bitterness may be understandable, considering the deodorant the New Critics sprayed at him and his Beat friends, but Ginsberg's dislike of formal criticism also arises from the fact that his critical standards are based partly on life-styles and politics rather than on artistic integrity. (p. 52)

The failures of Ginsberg's recent verse were latent in the techniques of his earlier work. The shock of profanity and obscene images has worn off, both because our society is less prudish and because the dirty words become less startling and obscene every time they are repeated. Ginsberg never was as adept at reproducing ordinary speech as Ed Dorn, for instance, or Gregory Corso; in Ginsberg's later poems phrases intended to convey the Common Man are merely banal. The lack of artifice which was effective in **"Kaddish"** robs a poem like **"In the Baggage Room at Greyhound"** of subtlety and surprise despite its acute observation. Unlike his vital, breathing, appendix-scars-and-all portrait of his mother in **"Kaddish,"** the characters in Ginsberg's later poems are thin and impersonal.

Ginsberg tackles large-scale subjects: death and immortality; military industrial complexes and paranoias just as grandiose; deviance; madness; and mysticism. It is not alone the scope of these subjects which defeats him (for in **"Kaddish"** he manages an extraordinarily difficult topic), but also his impatience with form, analysis and reworking, none of which fit in with his much-publicized life-style. Some hint of a change to come, however, might be seen in *Sad Dust Glories* (1975). Written during a summer in the woods while Ginsberg helped build a house, these poems are slight, but represent a fresh attempt to get to grips with the actual realities that surround him and are a good omen for his future work. *Mind Breaths* (1977) also experiments with different forms and sometimes attempts to break out of his stereotyped *persona*.

Publicity and the media are also to blame for Ginsberg's decline: they have marketed him as the benign, bearded Colonel Sanders of the counterculture, and he has obliged with a product that is predictable, tepid and widely available. Extensive public readings have also shaped Ginsberg's work. . . . Ginsberg has grumbled about the onslaught of publicity in a witty poem, **"I Am a Victim of Telephone,"** but his awareness of its dangers has not prevented it from damaging his poetry. He has tried to use his prominence to help other poets and has generously given his time to many causes. Some critics have blamed Ginsberg's decline on the depletion of his resources of feeling, since his successful early poems were highly autobiographical. But Ginsberg has not grown insensitive with age, since even to his thousands of casual acquaintances he can be warm and compassionate. At the Albert Hall poetry jamboree in London in 1965 Ginsberg read **"Who Be Kind To."** His admirers have been too kind to Ginsberg, who could be one of the major poets of our time but who has been squandering his time on feeble verses instead. It is inevitable that Ginsberg should be spoiled with kindness, since by clearing a channel for others he acted like an icebreaker ship—noisy, crude, but sturdy enough to survive the icebergs of American society. (pp. 52-4)

> *Roberta Berke, "'Whitman's Wild Children': The Beats," in her* Bounds Out of Bounds: A Compass for Recent American and British Poetry, *Oxford University Press, 1981, pp. 45-67.**

FRED MORAMARCO

To read Allen Ginsberg's small, nearly square, black and white City Lights paperbacks one after another over a period of a few days—from *Howl and Other Poems* (1956) through *Plutonian Ode* (1982)—is to confront chronologically arranged obituary notices from the anguished soul of America during some of its most troubled days. From very early in his poetic career, Ginsberg has aimed at offering us an omniscient view of the American Spirit and a diagnosis of that spirit's ills. Sometimes that ambition has led him to a megalomania typical of many ambitious young American writers. . . .

But Ginsberg's early desire—to be perceived as a divinely inspired, gifted Dionysian spirit, yoking the poles of the romantic sensibility, the luminous visions of Blake with the Democratic Vistas of Whitman—was largely realized in the poetry he produced during the 1960s and early 1970s which reached probably as large an audience as serious poetry ever has in this country. Ginsberg became a guru to thousands upon thousands of young people who saw in what they perceived as his unrelenting and large-spirited honesty an alternative to the cant and double-speak of establishment America during its most hypocritical (Vietnam-Watergate) years.

Our news of Ginsberg during these years emanated really not from his poetry but rather from a series of important social, political, and literary events in which he participated: Ginsberg and the *Howl* obscenity trial; Ginsberg on the road with Ken Kesey's Merry Pranksters; Ginsberg and the anti-war demonstrations; Ginsberg and the trial of the Chicago Seven; Ginsberg and LSD; Ginsberg and Gay Rights; Ginsberg expressing outrage that Gregory Corso is denied the National Book Award for *Elegiac Feelings American* and winning it himself for *The Fall of America;* Ginsberg and the establishment of the Jack Kerouac School of Disembodied Poetics at the Naropa Institute in Colorado, and Ginsberg and "The Great Naropa Poetry Wars." . . .

Surely no other contemporary poet has lived so closely to the edge of the historical contours of his time; consequently, Ginsberg's work has always been overshadowed by and overwhelmed by the events of his life. People, including poetry critics, have always been more interested in Ginsberg's actions than in his writing. . . . His detractors will argue that there is not much to *say* about the poetry; that it lacks the subtlety and grace of a John Ashbery, the metaphorical resonance of an Adrienne Rich, the syntactical and linguistic complexity of a John Berryman. Plainly and simply, what you see and what you hear in a Ginsberg poem, is what you get.

But this sort of criticism, it seems to me, misses the center of Ginsberg's primary poetic achievement, which was and is to embody literally several of Ezra Pound's most cherished conceptions of the role of the artist and poet in the twentieth century. Two of the most important of these are his description of artists as the "antennae of the race" and his insistence that a fundamental role of the poet is "to purify the language of the tribe." This dual role, both prophetic and cathartic, has been a part of Ginsberg's poetic strategy from the beginning. Like Frank O'Hara, a writer with whom he is not often associated because of superficial academic distinctions between the beat generation and the New York School, he created new possibilities for a younger generation of poets, providing a framework within which they could verify and articulate their own experience.

The key word there is "experience," for the Pound-Eliot legacy demanded attention not so much to the physical and human environment of an individual's daily life, but rather to the "tradition," to the historical record, and to particular details of poetic craft that can be garnered from that record. In order to "make it new" (Pound's often-repeated adage), a poet had to develop a sense of what poets in the English language had achieved up to the present moment. Working on the forefront of poetic innovation required an ability to subordinate one's individual talent to the dictates of tradition. Ginsberg, shouting his barbaric yawp over the rooftops of the world in *Howl,* began to change that conception and, over the years, consistently validated the primacy of personal experience for contemporary poets. (p. 10)

This emphasis on personal experiences in the poetry itself further directed most readers to look to Ginsberg's life for his poetic sources. The poetry cannot, of course, be separated from that life, but a retrospective look at a handful of his most significant poems shows his work to be firmly grounded in many mainstream literary traditions. In addition to Whitman and Blake, Ginsberg learned much about writing poetry from the English Romantic poets, from Milton and Christopher Smart, from Edgar Allan Poe, and, closer to his own generation, from Pound and William Carlos Williams. He drew on his own Jewish heritage for **"Kaddish,"** the poem many regard as his best, and his travels in the orient and intensive study of Tibetan Buddhism infused his work with yet another layer of allusiveness. I think we can now see both the innovative aspects of Ginsberg's work and its traditional base. On the one hand there is the new freedom he brought to poetry by confronting experience directly, by cleansing and purifying the language of the layers of falsity and indirection that it had accumulated. To write in a "received" language, Ginsberg tacitly proposed—whether of politics, religion, poetry, or whatever field— is to deny the reality of the self's perceptions. On the other hand there is the tradition he garnered from the previous generation—most notably Williams and Pound—whose work similarly reflects both innovative and conservative tendencies. That such a combination of individual talent and tradition should now seem less radical and revolutionary than it did even a short time ago should come as no surprise.

But recent history makes it difficult for us (and certainly for a new generation of students and readers) to resuscitate a society as decorous and with so many suppressed and unarticulated energy centers as the America of the mid-1950s. Blacks sat quietly in the backs of southern buses, gays were safely in the closet, women "happy" in the kitchen. It was the best of times—as we see on television's *Happy Days;* it was the worst of times—as we see in Allen Ginsberg's *Howl.* (pp. 10-11)

Looking at the simply literary dimensions of the poem now, apart from the controversy and sensationalism that surrounded its publication and lingered with it for years afterward, one is struck by the sheer aggressiveness of its language, the exotic and esoteric diction through which Ginsberg struggles to make his vision—*what* he saw—palpable, physically tangible. For how does one "see" a mind destroyed by madness? Ginsberg responds by creating images that give the abstraction solidity. He learned early from Ezra Pound to "go in fear of abstractions" and from William Carlos Williams to "make a start out of particulars." The first section of *Howl* embodies both these concepts. Ginsberg offers us a catalog of the particular sorts of madness he saw flourishing in the America of the 1950s. . . .

We might think of the idea expressd . . . [in *Howl*] as an early version of R.D. Laing's by now hackneyed psychological principle: in an insane world, only those thought of as mad have a kind of luminous sanity. This effect is intensified by Ginsberg's associating adjectives with nouns that never knew them before: "unshaven rooms," "ashcan rantings," "hydrogen jukebox," "bop kaballa," "visionary indian angels," "saintly motorcyclists," "wild cooking pederasty," "symbolic ping pong table," "hotrod-Golgotha jail-solitude watch," "naked and endless head."

In these post acid-rock days, when such juxtapositions have become as common as stone soup, it's hard to recall that the

language did not always have this sort of imaginative adaptability. In fact, to a generation whose cultural sensibilities have been shaped by the unrestrained emotional intensity of rock lyrics, by the subversive rhythms of the Rolling Stones and the Kinks and by the social criticism of Bob Dylan, Ginsberg's *Howl* may appear to be a positively conservative document. I played an early recording of *Howl* for my class in contemporary poetry and one student said it sounded to her like the lines had been composed by a computer. Another (a Korean student) said it sounded as if he were running for President. Both these responses, stressing the mechanistic and rhetorical aspects of the poem, would have been impossible until very recently. But in retrospect, one is struck by the attention Ginsberg pays to line length, to repetitive refrains, to balance, to generally formal matters. The "barbaric yawp" seems less barbaric, more clearly tied to highly civilized literary traditions.

The connection between Ginsberg's work and these traditions can be more cogently illustrated in a poem that was written before *Howl* (in 1954 and 1955) but published later in the *Reality Sandwiches* (1963) collection. The long, meditative **"Siesta in Xbalba and Return to the States"** is the centerpiece of that volume, which is based on some of Ginsberg's experiences in Mexico during the first seven months of 1954. The poem is built around the contrast indicated by the title. Lying in a hammock in a small Mexican village, Ginsberg toys with the idea of staying forever, of never returning to his complex, intense, citified life in the States. . . . The feeling here is much like that generated by James Wright's brief but wonderfully evocative lyric, "While Lying in a Hammock on William Duffy's Farm in Pine Island, Minnesota." In both poems the withdrawal from "civilization" and "society" that occurs as the poet lies in the hammock observing the scenery around him is treated ambiguously. Are the months "valuable" *because* he is lying in the hammock, or is he losing "valuable" time by "doing nothing"? Ginsberg's reminiscence of urban life intrudes. . . . The narrator's attention shifts back and forth from the hammock to . . . [a] party in New York, and the experience of straddling the two worlds in his imagination allows him to objectify both of them by stepping outside of himself and observing his participation in both. This is a wonderful moment in the poem—a metamorphosis reminiscent of Ovid via Ezra Pound. . . . (p. 11)

The illumination leads the narrator to speculate on objectifying not only his immediate surroundings and imaginings, but his very relationship to the earth itself. The poem moves outward from the poet's mind to the contours of the landscape around him to the curvature of the earth itself. It is, Ginsberg indicates, a drug-induced vision (prefiguring the LSD-inspired ecological vision of his later poem, **"Wales Visitation"**) but it is also one of the most beautiful descriptions of a natural landscape that occurs in his poetry. . . . The meditation on the landscape around him becomes a meditation on time, death, and eternity as day turns to night in the poem. An image of the rising moon supplants the image of the "Late sun" which began the poem, and Ginsberg's attention is captured by an ancient sculptured figure on the wall. . . . (pp. 11-12)

The poem moves deeper and deeper into the night and early morning hours, and its language, by incorporating Mexican place names, becomes more exotic, dreamlike, apparitional. In a note, Ginsberg tells us that "Xbalba, translatable as Morning Star in Region Obscure, or Hope, and pronounced Chivalva, is the area in Chiapas between the Tobasco border and the Usumascintla River at the edge of the Peten Rain Forest;

the boundary of lower Mexico and Guatemala today is thereabouts. The locale was considered a Purgatory or Limbo, the legend is vague, in the (Old) Mayan Empire.'' The note clarifies certain references in the poem as the reader moves further from the stability of the physical world into the strange, dark limbo of the unknowable. . . . After evoking the names of the pre-Columbian civilizations which flourished in this place, Ginsberg surveys the surviving ruins and notices how they have become intertwined with the natural landscape. Nature's work, and man's, has become one with the passage of time. . . .

A burst of daylight intrudes upon the meditation at this point, and we are made to see time's passage from another perspective. The poem's night has turned into day, and the traditional symbol of morning—of the affirmation and continuity of life—disrupts the narrator's reverie. . . . The disruption is momentary. The narrator closes his eyes (to shut out the present) and returns to ruminating on the ruins of the past. The meditation appears to awaken in him a sense of a personal connection with past civilizations and previous human achievements. He wants to see more of the ''ancient continent'' before the physical remains of the past are totally obliterated by ''the ultimate night / of war.''

But his realization of a connection with the past also makes him aware of a specific tradition to which he—as a contemporary American poet—is related, as well as a future to which he has an obligation. In a remarkable passage which embodies imagery from America's greatest literature—Whitman, Melville, Crane (both Stephen and Hart), Pound, and others—Ginsberg appears to *become* the American literary imagination searching for a direction. . . . ''Toward what city / will I travel?'' Ginsberg asks, ''What wild houses do I go to occupy?'' The poem's first section ends with the recollection of a mystical experience Ginsberg had in his New York apartment in 1948. At that time Ginsberg believes he heard Blake's voice and saw ''the motionless buildings / of New York rotting / under the tides of Heaven.'' That recollection evokes a symbolic rendering of Ginsberg's divided muse: is he to be the poet of Moloch or the poet of the inner self? Does his imagination owe its allegiance to America or to the human spirit? This part of the poem ends with the question unanswered. . . . (p. 12)

The second section of the poem is more easily summarized than the first. There is a ''Jump in time'' to the future when Ginsberg begins his return to the States, carrying with him some lingering images of his Mexican experience: a busload of blue-hooded nuns, some mummies he saw at Guanajuato, and the memory of a voyeuristic moment as he watched two couples dancing. . . . Looking at death (the mummies) on the one hand and life (the two dancing couples) on the other, Ginsberg identifies what he regards to be the fundamental tragedy of human experience:

> The problem is isolation
> —there in the grave
> or here in oblivion of light.

He feels his solitude deeply, but as he nears the American border he braces himself for the task he sees as his destiny. He is to be Moloch's poet, the heir of Whitman and Pound, the contemporary embodiment of America's poetic soul. . . . [The] concluding lines signal Ginsberg's intention to confront the chaos of contemporary America directly in his poetry—to awaken from the ''siesta in Xbalba'' and return to the States both in person and in the subject matter of his poetry. The life

of the imagination is to be put to work transcribing the world that worships Moloch.

Such a singleness of purpose was not to last long. In 1961, Ginsberg embarked on the S.S. *America* with Peter Orlovsky for a trip to Europe and regions further east. Much of the work in *Planet News* (1968) is an outgrowth of this experience and of a later trip abroad. The poems here do indeed bring news of the planet: from Bombay, Milan, Tokyo, and Calcutta, from Prague, Warsaw, Wales, New York, Washington, and Wichita. It is perhaps the first book of poetry of the ''global village,'' written in the same period that McLuhan coined that suggestive phrase.

A recurrent theme in *Planet News* is what Ginsberg regards as the magical ability of the poet to recapitulate the creation, through the power of language, in every poem he writes. Out of nothing—*ex nihilo*—he creates a vibrant, living world of language over which he has total control. Consequently, the poet can take on earthshaking issues and problems in his work and solve them—exorcize the demons—right there on the page. The creation of poetry is persistently likened to both sexual procreation and theological notions of the creation. . . . This theme reaches its climax in the remarkable verbal conjury of **''Wichita Vortex Sutra,''** where the poet, regardless of his impotence in the world's physical reality, is omnipotent in the realm of language. . . . (pp. 12-13)

The Wichita poem has been exhaustively explicated by a number of critics, but **''Wales Visitation,''** one of Ginsberg's most delicately crafted visionary poems, has not yet had the attention it merits. . . . The sensationalistic LSD associations of this poem—it is dated and placed ''July 29, 1967 (LSD)—August 3, 1967 (London)''—have caused some readers to overlook the poem's traditional romanticism. But just as **''Siesta in Xbalba''** is directly related to America's literary past, **''Wales Visitation''** evokes the English Romantic literary tradition more fully than anything else in Ginsberg's work, though his books are punctuated throughout with references to Blake and Shelley.

The poem's first stanza offers us a description of nature as viewed through a window. The linguistic coupling of various discrete natural elements—phrases like ''mountain brow,'' ''rivers of wind,'' ''clouds arise / as on a wave''—suggests the interdependence of nature. The fact that our point of view in the poem is situated behind ''mullioned glass'' proposes a split, a barrier between humankind and nature. Reminiscent of the woman in Whitman's ''Song of Myself,'' who observes twenty-eight young men bathing by the shore from behind the blinds of her window and hence is physically separated from them, though spiritually attuned to them, the narrator of this poem proposes to penetrate the barrier separating humans from nature. The archaic and esoteric language mixed with modern diction (''raine,'' ''Bardic,'' ''Albion,'' ''Visitacione,''/ ''Ecology,'' ''manifest,'' ''lightbulbs'') gives the vision expressed in the poem a timelessness. That is, it brings the ''continuing timelessness'' of ancient nature language very much into the modern world. . . .

[In] the poem's second section, . . . the narrator (who is clearly Ginsberg himself) recalls seeing himself on television in London. The ''network of TV pictures flashing bearded your Self'' described in this stanza is paralleled later in the poem with ''tree-lined canals network through live farmland.'' We glimpse a modern technological man associated primarily with the city which has separated him from nature—imprisoned him and wounded his spirit—represented in the poem by "London's symmetrical thorned tower." Electronic impulses flash the image of the poet's "Self" throughout London, but the truer "self" remains linked to the English countryside and to the historical tradition of poets of the English language. . . .

The allusion to the English Romantic poets observing nature and writing about it, as well as the images evoking time's passage and death ("cloud's passing through skeleton arches"), reveal the continuity of the poetic act—the human urgency to find words for the ultimate ineffability of nature: "Bard Nameless as the Vast," Ginsberg writes, "babble to the Vastness!" The landscape description expands to encompass England's entire topography, vibrating with life, breathing, budding, quivering, copulating. The poem's quickening rhythms—clearly imitating the rhythms of sexual intercourse—lead the reader to the climactic moment of enlightenment at the poem's center. This experience is one of feeling a complete oneness with the earth itself—reminiscent of the transcendent moment in the midst of Andrew Marvell's "The Garden," in which the poet feels a sense of the earth's marvelous abundance and falls to the ground in nearly delirious celebration. Ginsberg's visionary moment, magnified by the hallucinogenic properties of LSD, is even more tangibly physical; he observes the fecundity of the earth close up, involving all his senses in an adoration of the earth as the source and sustainer of all life. . . . No longer behind a window observing nature, Ginsberg has become one with it, part of an organic whole that combines an extraordinary delicacy with an overwhelming immensity. The air itself becomes the breath of this whole earth. . . . The secret doctrine of nature has been revealed: whatever is, is right.

Ginsberg's expression of the timelessness and interconnectedness of all life has many antecedents in English literature, from Blake's "world in a grain of sand" to Dylan Thomas's "force that through the green fuse / Drives the flower" and drives the poet's "green age" as well. Its American precursors are Emerson's famous "transparent eyeball" (a less graceful manifestation) and Whitman's very leaves of grass which are "no less than the journey-work of the stars." It appears in some sections of Pound's *Cantos* as well ("Learn of the green world what can be thy place / In scaled invention or true artistry") and Ginsberg's sensibility here appears saturated with all these sources. He finishes the poem as if remembering that he left out someone—William Carlos Williams. . . . (p. 13)

Ginsberg's new sense of human interaction with the physical earth itself leads easily to the vast spaces of the American landscape described throughout the long **"Poem of These States"** which occurs sporadically throughout *The Fall of America* (1972), the collection for which Ginsberg won the National Book Award. The poem was intended, Ginsberg told an interviewer, "to cover like a collage a lone consciousness travelling through these states during the Vietnam War." The war, of course, loomed larger and larger in America's psyche during the years this poem was written (1965-1971) and consequently is an insistently discordant note that punctuates the work from beginning to end. "Discordant," in fact, is a word which only punily suggests the clash of contradictions that typifies the American sensibility of the late 1960s as Ginsberg views it here. Listening to his car radio throughout the poem, he hears the very soul of America in the voices and music emanating from the speaker. . . .

The deep fissures in American consciousness during this time is illustrated even more by the news, the "Radio static from Saigon," or the "California Radio Lady's Voice / Talking

about Viet Cong." By paying attention to what is coming over the radio, Ginsberg is able to depict succinctly the late sixties American schizophrenia. News of a "search and destroy" mission in Vietnam is juxtaposed with the lyrics of a rock song from the Kinks. . . .

In contrast to the voice of America's soul emanating from the radio is the voice of Ginsberg himself, a palliative here, a calming influence in a troubled and chaotic time. In *The Fall of America* the Ginsberg presence is a voice of rationality rather than one of excess; he is no longer the "King of the May," the pranksterish persona who dominated *Planet News*, but a bardic figure trying to bring peace to the land. . . . The "money munching war machine" [in the poem **"A Vow"**] is, of course, the Moloch of *Howl* reconstituted and energized by the sacrifical deaths of the young Americans and Vietnamese who died in Vietnam. Ginsberg intends here once again to be Moloch's poet and conscience, purifying its corruptions of language and revealing its life-destructive madness wherever he finds it.

His assumption of this role explains why Ginsberg is one of a surprisingly small number of poets who has incorporated and absorbed modern technology in his poetry. To understand the beast one needs to journey into its belly, and so Ginsberg, progressing with technology, has given us Automobile poems, Airplane Journal poems, TV Baby poems, and most recently, nuclear poems. At his best, he seems able to merge natural imagery with images of industry and technology with an ease that reflects once again (as **"Wales Visitation"** did) his essentially romantic proclivities, despite the fact that he is at heart thoroughly citified. This is a nature poet who grew up in Paterson. (p. 14)

Mind Breaths, published in 1978, is largely a turning inward toward the "vast empty quiet space" of personal consciousness. It is an elegiac volume, even more so than *The Fall of America,* containing poems on Neruda's death, on the dying and death of his father, on contemplating death's absolute finality. The most significant poem in the book is the long **"Contest of Bards."** . . . In this poem, an old poet who lives in a stone house by the ocean is visited by a young poet who arrives "naked interrupting his studies & announces his own prophetic dreams to replace the old Bard's boring verities." The poem is a double allegory—of Ginsberg confronting the work of his youth, and of Ginsberg the older poet confronted with the impatience and energy of a new generation of poets.

But apart from the **"Contest of the Bards,"** the poems in *Mind Breaths* generally seem less cohesive and less reflective of specific social issues than most of Ginsberg's other collections. It is easily the most introspective of the City Lights books and it seemed to signal a meditational withdrawal from the social activism of all of Ginsberg's earlier work.

In *Plutonian Ode,* however, the social activist once again emerges, in some ways more strongly than ever, as the book focuses on the ultimate social issue—the issue of whether or not we will continue to exist as human societies and civilizations. The title poem describes the creation of "a new thing under the sun," the artificial element of plutonium, discovered by Dr. Glen Seaborg and others in 1940 and used as the explosive force in nuclear weapons and as a reactor fuel in nuclear power plants. Notice that Ginsberg's poem is called *Plutonian* Ode, not *Plutonium* Ode, and it is clear that he means to connect this demonic discovery with the ancient "Lord of Hades," the god Pluto. Plutonium may be a new thing under the sun, but the destructive impulse in humankind is as old as its history, and the conversion of mass to energy is the very stuff of the universe and precedes even the human presence.... (p. 16)

"Plutonian Ode" is Whitmanic in tone and scope ... and resonates with exotic, mythical names giving it prophetic, Hebraic and incantatory qualities. But the poem is not at all remote; it is utterly contemporary. In the second of its three sections, Ginsberg sets out to make us more conscious of the presence of a nuclear reality all around us as we go about our daily lives.... In contrast to the burgeoning nuclear industry throughout the world, Ginsberg contemplates a "tranquil politic" emanating from a detoxified, denuclearized world. Section Three of the poem is reminiscent of the famous "Mantra of American language" in **"Wichita Vortex Sutra"** which proclaims the power of language to reverse catastrophic events. Here, Whitman-like, he exhorts "Poets and Orators to come" to carry the anti-nuclear banner across the world.... (pp. 16-17)

Not all the poems in *Plutonian Ode* deal specifically with nuclear madness, but the word "plutonium" punctuates the volume like a discordant chord and the artificiality of the element symbolizes the destructive artificiality of contemporary life in many different manifestations. For example, a poem about New Jersey called **"Garden State,"** refers to the separation of individuals from the land they inhabit through layer upon layer of human-made destructiveness. The poem describes New Jersey as it used to be before.... Ginsberg's keen sense of place, evident everywhere in his work, laments the progressive alienation of human beings from their natural environments, and in *Plutonian Ode* his concerns seem closer than ever to those of his old friend Gary Snyder. Together they are our "whole earth poets," carrying the tradition of Whitman, Thoreau and Emerson into the latter part of the 20th century.

As we begin to view Ginsberg's work retrospectively, it becomes clearer than ever that his work is far less an aberrant diversion from mainstream American literary traditions as was once widely believed. His work seems now for us in the 1980s, a central expression of that tradition, exemplifying the continuity of American poetry as well as its persistent originality. (p. 17)

Fred Moramarco, "Moloch's Poet: A Retrospective Look at Allen Ginsberg's Poetry," in The American Poetry Review, *Vol. 11, No. 5, September-October, 1982, pp. 10-14, 16-18.*

STEVEN GOULD AXELROD

I first read ... [**"Plutonian Ode"** in 1978] when it was printed in a local broadside. It was impossible then, as it is impossible now, not to sympathize with the antinuclear sentiments of the piece. Yet it is also impossible not to worry about **"Plutonian Ode"** as a poem, and about what it indicates concerning Ginsberg's future as a poet.

The poem begins powerfully, but then, to my mind, goes downhill for sixty-five lines to its termination in what Ginsberg's note informs us is an "Americanese approximation & paraphrase of Sanscrit Prajnaparamita (Highest Perfect Wisdom) Mantra." It is a sign of what goes wrong that the poem comes equipped with twenty-two notes identifying sources and interpreting difficult lines for slow readers; the poem's lines are numbered, as if it were already in the Norton anthology; and the volume ends with a three-page bibliography of works by and about the author. This poem has not simply been published,

it has been provided with its own variorum; there would undoubtedly be manuscript drafts if Ginsberg ever revised.

One question to ask is whether **"Plutonian Ode"** escapes its specific time and place to become something like a "universal" poem. Since we can hardly foresee a time that is not perplexed by nuclear threat, perhaps that question is trivial when we think about it, and we ought to ask instead whether **"Plutonian Ode"** expresses its theme in an enduring and significant way. At times, clearly, the answer is yes: in such images as "whirlpools of starspume silver-thin as hairs of Einstein," or in the wonderful opening sequence in which two grandly gothic questions yield to a hurtling rush of language seemingly loosed from all externally derived syntactical limits.... Eventually, however, the poem devolves to mere "oratory," as Ginsberg himself calls it.

It also, unfortunately, devolves into a parody of William Blake and Walt Whitman. Ginsberg has always been a generous poet, and he has become all too generous to his two major precursors. His own voice—so distinctive in early poems like **"Howl,"** **"America,"** **"A Supermarket in California"** and supremely in **"Kaddish"**—has been shouted down by political declamation on the one side and the echoes of Blake and Whitman on the other. It could be asserted that in resorting to the paraphernalia of academic scholarship in **"Plutonian Ode,"** Ginsberg has become, willy-nilly, the Columbia University English professor he was genetically and socially programmed to be.... But I think it is more likely that Ginsberg's new self-important demeanor in both his work and his life—his elder statesman, poet laureate, Tennyson-in-the-Rockies persona—is simply a way of disguising from us and from himself the slow extinguishment of his utterance.

"Plutonian Ode," mind you, is not a bad or inconsequential poem; it is a good one, one of the most interesting to be published in 1982. But it is not a great poem, and the voice that speaks it, for all that it describes itself as "resounding," "calling," "yelling," "howling," "singing," et cetera, simply cannot be heard, because in a real sense it does not exist. It has been defeated by the literary voices Ginsberg knows so well, teaches so eruditely and mimics so inescapably. If Ginsberg is to reemerge as a strong poet, he must do the hardest thing of all: turn his back on his precursors and, even harder, on the armored and medaled self he has so assiduously constructed. He must start over.

Steven Gould Axelrod, in a review of "Plutonian Ode: Poems 1977-1980," in World Literature Today, *Vol. 58, No. 1, Winter, 1984, p. 104.*

PHOEBE PETTINGELL

The Beat Generation—which in the words of charter member Allen Ginsberg "hollow-eyed and high sat up smoking in the supernatural darkness of coldwater flats floating across the tops of cities contemplating jazz"—now seems a footnote to literary criticism. Those idealists are gone with the Imagists. But Ginsberg survives, riding the crest of the *Zeitgeist,* eager to bring poetry to the widest audience possible.

The angry young *poet maudit* who saw "the best minds of (his) generation destroyed by madness, starving, hysterical, naked," became in his next phase the hirsute bard of the hippies—preaching hallucinogens and love-not-war, stripping at stuffy academic symposia. In the solipsistic '70s, he chanted Buddhist mantras outside nuclear power plants....

Now, in the '80s, we find him pictured on the back of his *Collected Poems 1947-1980* . . . as a genial academician, complete with rose in the lapel of what may well be a gray flannel suit. . . .

The many icons Ginsberg has made of himself have become the stuff of his verse. First and foremost, he is the Family Chronicler. Many of his strongest poems use the drama of his childhood: trapped between father, Louis Ginsberg, a well-known minor lyric poet, and mother, Naomi, subject to paranoia. . . . His attempt to comfort her frantic and terrifying spirit, even after her death, is a constant theme of his poetry.

Ginsberg memorializes friendships, too. . . . Above all, though, there is his great Lost Love, Neal Cassady . . . , the muse of his initial breakthrough into verse. Unlike the friends in Robert Lowell's autobiographical poems, where real names disguise semifictional characters, those in Ginsberg's songs are not literary puppets. Indeed, he has appended pictures, biographical notes and an "'Index of Proper Names' . . . designed to make his large volume 'user friendly.' (It) may be read as a lifelong poem, including history, wherein things are symbols of themselves. Cross references between text and notes can serve as rough concordance to the book's mythic actualities, from Cassady to CIA to Sakyamuni."

Ginsberg's second-most-important role is that of American Photographer, capturing vignettes of the country's people, landscape, political and cultural stances. It is in this guise that he presents himself in **"A Supermarket in California"** (1955) as Son of Walt. . . . (p.17)

Long poems, such as **"Iron Horse"** and **"Wichita Vortex Sutra,"** narrate the poet's continuous journeys across these United States, observing, commenting, identifying with the spirit of the country. . . .

Unfortunately, there is also Allen-the-Revelator. . . .

Ginsberg constantly refers to [his vision of William Blake in 1948] yet like many mystical experiences it resists incarnation. When he tries to relate perceptions or dreams, he falls into incoherence, didacticism, sometimes both. Much in the fashion of another well-known Whitman disciple, Carl Sandburg, he speaks not with authority but as the scribe. Poems may run on for lines of "Namu-so-man-da"—a Zen *dharani*, the reader will discover from the book's copious notes (over 40 pages long). He also is apt to pound his political soapbox, or produce a Whole Earth manual of how-to advice. Behind his Dionysian mask is a pedant eager to "transmit cultural archetypes to electronic laser TV generations that don't read Dostoyevsky Buddha bibles. Karma wants understanding. Moloch needs noting. Mini-essays hint further reading for innocent-eyed youths." Norman Podhoretz once accused the Beats of being know-nothings. Nonsense. They were the sort who confuse T. S. Eliot's annotations to *The Waste Land* with the poem itself.

Nonetheless, if Ginsberg has a personal vision of One Mind, the perspectives his poetry provides are certainly fragmented. Drugs have probably heightened a natural prolixity and discursiveness. . . . Narrative and observation of people and places— their peculiar flavor and variety—remain his strength; except when he is being obsessive about religion or sexual practices, he manages to delineate diversity. He is a poet of the local, a historian of pop culture. . . .

In subsequent years Ginsberg has split more and more between self-proclaimed prophet and ironic bystander. He has occa-sionally been too calculating about signs of the times, too manipulative, reminding one of the Wizard of Oz—a lot of bombast distracting the eye from an all-American huckster yanking his pulleys. It is easy to confuse this poet's engaging personality with his poems. Even at its best the verse is flawed by self-indulgence, often slipping into bathos or the dead language of "poesy"—basically lazy.

Yet Ginsberg cannot be dismissed. For decades now he has put an unerring finger on our public nightmares and private dreams; his ridiculous antics have represented unforgettable aspects of our period. In a very recent poem, **"White Shroud,"** . . . Ginsberg sees his mother as a bag lady, thus once again zeroing in on a haunting cultural symbol, especially in these hard times for the insulted and injured. . . . His *Collected Poems 1947-1980* is obviously not the last word in that saga. (p.18)

Phoebe Pettingell, "A Beat of Our Time," in *The New Leader*, Vol. LXVII, No. 22, December 10, 1984, pp. 17-18.

LEWIS HYDE

Partly because his youthful antics still upstage his maturity in the public mind, and partly because his poems have been scattered in a dozen small press volumes, it has been hard for us to sense the trajectory of Allen Ginsberg's work. With [**"Collected Poems"**], however, we are at last able to see both the consistency and, more subtly, the gradual modulations of his voice.

The poems collected in **"Howl"** (1956) and in **"Kaddish"** (1961) were written by a young man hungry for love and hungry for God. More than that, they were written by a man whose hunger had been satiated, if only for a moment. . . . In the summer of 1948, lying on his bed in an apartment in Harlem, Mr. Ginsberg heard what he took to be the voice of William Blake speak a series of poems to him. For all his skepticism toward established forms, his response to this vision was traditional to the core. In one of his own accounts, for example, he speaks of his epiphany in the following terms: "This was the moment I was born for, this initiation . . . this consciousness of being . . . alive myself unto the creator. As the son of the Creator—who loved me, I realized."

Haven't we heard this story somewhere before? There is a God who speaks to His son, a prophet born on earth. To overstate the case slightly, in those early days Mr. Ginsberg put himself in the service of God and His angels. . . . He felt he had sensed a "future, unimaginable God," and undertook to reimagine that deity for his people.

What a task! How to do it? The first problem to face this aspiring messiah was to find a poetic form adequate to the transcendental knowledge he felt he had received. Blake had such a form, it seemed, for his poems spoke across the centuries, and, not surprisingly, much of Mr. Ginsberg's juvenilia (reprinted in the first 100 pages of this volume) follows his master's lead. . . . Eight years lie between his Blake epiphany and **"Howl,"** years in which he was a student in a school of his own invention. From Williams he learned to transcribe the American idiom; from Whitman he learned to orchestrate the long line; surrealism taught him hallucinated speech, and in Cézanne's paintings he discovered the surprise of juxtaposition ("hydrogen jukebox"). In short, he became a modern poet.

But he did not abandon his vision. When the author of **"Howl"** speaks of "angelheaded hipsters burning for the ancient heavenly connection,'' incredulous reader, he means it. ''Angel,'' ''heaven'': these are not metaphors, they are meant to *denote*, just as ''wheelbarrow'' is meant to denote. The poem is a theodicy, spoken in the prophetic voice of one who believes that angels help the poets write and that evil powers feed on the nation's tender hearts.

The first major shift in Mr. Ginsberg's work was hard to see at the time, I think, because it was not an elaboration of his beliefs so much as a growing skepticism. Some part of his hunger remained unsatisfied. Behind the hopeful claims of the early poems . . . is the voice of a man both wounded by life and liable to wound himself. His fantasy of a trip to Mexico, for example, involves fleeing down a dark road, ''heroin dripping in (his) veins . . . / (his) flesh and (his) bones hanging on the trees.'' He had hoped that epiphanies and the love of comrades might free him from such self-destructive misery, but they had not. He had taken his vision to be a call to explore altered states of consciousness, but now whenever he took hallucinogenic drugs he found himself facing nothing but ''Scaly / Serpents winding thru / cloud spaces of / what is not.''

The persistence of Mr. Ginsberg's discontent called into question his theology and, during a 1963 trip around the world, he began to doubt and abandon it. His theology had included much besides gods and their adjunct devils and angels. It included a premonition of impending apocalypse, a wrestling with death as if death might be overcome, a sense of obligation to break down ordinary consciousness, and an attachment to drugs as a means to that end. It also included the subtle lack of self-acceptance implied by a belief in exterior powers from whom approval might be won.

In a sense, Mr. Ginsberg's doubts set him adrift as he had been in the years before **''Howl,''** and it took him another decade to find his way, one spent almost constantly on the move: New York, Israel, India, Japan, the West Coast and then back and forth across the country by car, by plane, by train. These were the 1960's and the two books from this period—**''Planet News''** and **''The Fall of America''**—have the structure of travelogues. Mr. Ginsberg bought a tape recorder and began to dictate poems as he moved around, the idea being to make an epic—Pound's ''poem containing history''—out of a transcription of current events. On the whole, what he saw is what we get. . . .

Mr. Ginsberg's searching finally led him to something he had named but not practiced from the beginning: Buddhism. The dedication to **''Howl''** manages to drop the name of Buddha twice, but it is no Buddhist book; its temperament is Jewish, its cadences biblical. Sometime around 1972, Mr. Ginsberg stopped driving coast to coast and sat down with a meditation teacher in Colorado. What happened, I think, is that the man gave up hope. Buddhism is not a religion of promises about the future. There is no higher power who will love us; there is no way to escape death. One can, however, become aware of one's own confusion and, perhaps, ease the pain of living. . . .

In any event, in recent books we begin to get poems that are set in and reflect the actual situation of a spiritual practice. (p.5)

The difference between the mind reflected in **''Howl''** and the one that guides the recent **''Plutonian Ode''** is striking. **''Howl''** assumes armies of darkness and light, devouring gods and tender lambs, and it urges us to choose sides. **''Plutonian Ode''** is a poem about nuclear weapons; supernatural powers in fact appear (plutonium is, after all, named for Pluto, Lord of Death),

but the poem does not moralize. Its motivating belief is that clarity of perception and clarity of speech are the only tools we have to apply to the mess we're in. . . . [The lines in this poem] are something new: the nontheistic prophetic voice of a politically engaged student of Buddhism.

All the early signs indicated that Mr. Ginsberg was to be another of our *poètes maudits*. In 1958, Time magazine issued its prophecy: a hipster like Mr. Ginsberg, they told their readers, is ''a rebel without a cause,'' a romantic hero who, like Jimmy Dean, was on his way to becoming a martyred legend. There was evidence, of course, for Time's position; Mr. Ginsberg was a poet scripted for early doom if there ever was one. But he has managed to survive and, at this late date, we are forced to look back and ask what it is that has sustained him. His Buddhism is one thing, to be sure. A line from a poem in **''Howl''** suggests several more: ''America,'' the young poet wrote, ''I'm putting my queer shoulder to the wheel.''

There are three things here: confession, commitment, and humor. The confessional style has served the poet better than it served others because, I think, he has confessed what he has sought to preserve (his connection to his mother, for example, and his sexuality). In addition, Mr. Ginsberg has always been interested in politics, and his participation in public life has doubtless grounded him. Finally, he makes us laugh. The ancients thought of ''humors'' as the fluids that determine one's temperament; when I think of Mr. Ginsberg's humor, I think of fluid itself: I think, that is, of his ability to move among the temperaments, to acknowledge the pole to his own obsessions. To laugh at the line just quoted is to accomplish the poet's purpose. No matter where we ourselves stand, in our smile the ''queer'' and the patriotic are momentarily joined. The vein of humor in Mr. Ginsberg's work bespeaks the value he places on community; he is out to make a connection. (pp. 5-6)

[It] must be added that there would seem no less propitious a time for the publication of this **''Collected Poems''** than the winter of Ronald Reagan's re-election. Mr. Ginsberg's poetry has constantly attacked or called into question everything from the Central Intelligence Agency and covert military action to heterosexuality, discipline in the schoolroom and the return to the classics. Didn't 60 percent of the voters, by endorsing Mr. Reagan, repudiate Mr. Ginsberg and the ''queer shoulder'' he offers?

No. Nearly half of the eligible voters voted for nobody, for nothing. Somewhere among us there are hungry souls who may yet need the food preserved in these texts. And there may be young poets, too, whose temperament is not classical, disciplined, covert and centrally intelligent, who will find here the instruments by which to enter the tradition that seeks to free what Whitman called ''howls restrain'd by decorum.'' (p. 6)

Lewis Hyde, ''States of Altering Consciousness,'' in The New York Times Book Review, *December 30, 1984, pp. 5-6.*

BRUCE COOK

Long and inclusive as it is, [*Collected Poems 1947-1980*] may give the impression that [Ginsberg] did nothing but write non-stop for 33 years. But we know that this is not even figuratively true. The idea of Ginsberg toiling away at his lines day after day and night after night, constantly polishing, ceaselessly looking for that perfect word—all this is inconsistent with what we know of his life, his philosophy of composition, and with the poems themselves. He is simply not that kind of poet. The kind of poet Allen Ginsberg is was settled a century earlier by Walt Whitman.

Yet for his first model, it was probably natural that Ginsberg should have chosen William Carlos Williams, for after all the good Dr. Williams, poet-survivor of the '20s avant-garde, had become the laureate of Paterson, New Jersey (Ginsberg's hometown), with the book-length poem which sang the city's history, geography, and anthropology. Ginsberg sought out Williams, who lived and practiced medicine in nearby Rutherford, claimed him as a mentor, and in his first published poems (*Empty Mirror*) offered him the sincere flattery of imitation.

It was just a matter of form, however. He used Dr. Williams' short lines and rhymes, even tried out his use of the caesura— yet without much real success. Even Ginsberg acknowledged his difficulty.... Ginsberg longed to set the page afire with his anger. Eventually, he found that the form and diction which carried Dr. Williams' brand of plain-spoken humanism so well would often crack and collapse under the weight of his own rage.

And why was Allen Ginsberg so angry? A reasonable question, but one that invites a more clinical response than seems proper in this space. Let's say that it probably had more than a little to do with his feelings regarding his own Jewishness, and about his mother Naomi, who had been in and out of mental institutions on a number of occasions by the time he began to write.

Deep-seated though it was, this anger of his became, if not a pose, then a fixed attitude that seemed to suit him well. Ginsberg was, after all, one of the original Beats.... And their little conspiracy grew into a literary movement that proved to be even more obstreperous than most. Anger, disgust, and disillusionment at postwar America—this was the ethos that gave the Beat generation its vitality; Allen Ginsberg was confirmed in it.

But to play this new role as one of the Beat protagonists, he needed a new voice to go with the attitude. He first found it while experimenting with a Whitmanesque free verse long line, the sort of form in which virtually nobody else was working at that time.... [The] poem from *Empty Mirror,* entitled **"Psalm I,"** is his earliest in this style.... (p. 1)

From this, and in this basic form, eventually came the poems for which Allen Ginsberg is so well known. Beginning with **"Howl,"** ... Ginsberg's matter and emotion found their exact form. The result was amazing for its energy, its sense of vatic inspiration, and for the sweeping nature of its denunciation....

It was with *Howl and Other Poems* and *Reality Sandwiches* that Ginsberg established himself as the preeminent Beat poet—the cold-eyed judge presiding at the court at which all American culture and literature were put on trial. To many that seemed like just so much *chutzpah,* and certainly Ginsberg was ridiculed by the poetry establishment. Yet Ginsberg swept all this aside when he wrote **"Kaddish."** It could be neither ridiculed nor dismissed. Going back to the very roots of his anger, singing a funeral dirge to his dead mother, he exposed himself and her so ruthlessly that there could be no doubt he had made a considerable emotional investment in the work. It was a bold, risk-taking poem written at a time when poets seldom took chances.

It is written in a Whitmanesque line so long and loose that it has almost gone to prose. Yet **"Hymmnn,"** which follows it as a second part or sequel, is gloriously, religiously incantatory.... Writing the poem did seem to have a purgative effect on Allen Ginsberg. Not long after it was published, he left for an extended stay in the Orient—principally in Japan and India—and he came back a much different man.

Yes, he was changed, and so was the America he returned to, for by that time the '60s were heating up. No one talked much about the Beat Generation anymore, but that didn't mean that he and Kerouac and Corso and all the rest had gone unheeded. The Hippies and Yippies of the '60s appropriated the Beat message and agenda and made them their own. They welcomed Allen Ginsberg as a guru, a chaplain to the movement.

This was a part that Ginsberg played with pleasure and considerable skill. He was accepted, loved, and respected by the '60s generation. Probably without doing it quite consciously, he turned once again to Walt Whitman and began playing the role of the "good, gray poet" that Whitman played late in his life. Yet the '60s passed, eventually the Vietnam War ended, and the youthful army that made up the peace movement disbanded and went off to take up their lives again. In a sense, Allen Ginsberg was left behind then. Although he has continued to write, he is not nearly as prolific as he once was, and there has been little energy and fire in his poems of the last dozen years.

All this should be quite evident to readers of this volume of Ginsberg's *Collected Poems 1947-1980.* But it should be neither surprising nor even especially disappointing that Ginsberg's career has taken such a turn. After all, Walt Whitman spent his latter years editing, revising, and modestly augmenting *Leaves of Grass.* Ginsberg continues as a survivor of not one but two movements, more Whitmanesque than ever, traveling, giving readings and lectures, living the life of a culture hero, an icon incarnate. (p. 2)

> Bruce Cook, "Allen Ginsberg: The Beat Goes On," in Book World—The Washington Post *January 13, 1985, pp. 1-2.*

KEN TUCKER

Ginsberg's poetic voice—querulous, nagging, and addled one minute; serene, mordant, and lyrical the next—is one of the most distinctive sounds in modern literature. The inspirational mottoes he has appropriated from others—"First thought, best thought"; "No ideas but in things"; "Things are symbols of themselves"—constitute a poetics and a philosophy worth pondering, but they have been met too often with ignorance or derision. As his slogans suggest, Ginsberg's triumph is to have located the common ground between realistic and surrealistic uses of language; he insists that that best first thought must be *about something,* not merely a striking image or a rush of automatic writing. Ginsberg's poetic diction is both an artistic decision and a political act; it is language that's rarely ambiguous and always an attempt to persuade.... For 30 years, Ginsberg has been the most famous poet in America, an embodiment of everything this country has hoped and feared a poet could be.

Ginsberg's work holds out comfort and warmth—they are promises as palpable as his big, tender eyes and deep, reedy voice—and then snatches them away. For someone whose fame was confirmed by the company he kept, Ginsberg is an implacable loner; like I. F. Stone, his career-long political engagement is a solitary pursuit dominated by a pack-rat mentality, a life spent gathering facts, rooting out cruel contradictions, filling notebooks with arguments and jeremiads. . . .

For all its clarity and allure, however, Ginsberg's poetry has been slowly buried beneath an accumulation of academic condescension, popular misunderstanding, and the poet's own rather glorious compulsion to explain, contradict, and transcend his previous creations. Now, excavation work on Allen Ginsberg has begun: with *Collected Poems 1947-1980*. . . . How much of this vast amount of writing holds up? The *Collected Poems* suggests: more than you'd think. . . .

Ginsberg may be the most uneven of great modern poets, given to garrulousness and cathartic rants, but he has no equal for narrative drive and emotional power—even when he's acting the addled asshole, his babble is frothy, compelling stuff. The story told in *The Collected Poems* is about self-discovery and social purpose. He may have performed with rockers as various as Patti Smith, Bob Dylan, and the Clash, but at heart he's poetry's Bill Graham: a compulsive organizer, firm and willful but with decent motives. . . .

People think he burst upon us, a hairy surprise, with **"Howl,"** but Ginsberg was 30 years old in 1956 and already past his first stage as a poet, an apprenticeship spent making—sometimes forcing—connections between the curt lyricism of Marvell, Donne, the Oriental haiku poets, and Blake's exploding fortune cookies, *Songs of Innocence and of Experience*. This period of compression is an artistic analog to his life at the time. . . . With *Howl* and then *Kaddish* (1961), *Reality Sandwiches* (1963), and *Planet News* (1968, but containing poems from 1961-63), Ginsberg came into his own as an antistylist, and has always insisted that his major influence during this time was Kerouac. . . . (p. 42)

Middle-period Ginsberg, embodied by the atomized *Fall of America* (1973) and the musicalized *First Blues, Rags, Ballads & Harmonium Songs* (1975), finds him obsessed with the lies of the government during the Vietnam war, and struggling to come to terms with his aging, and with the fact that he feels more kinship with the folks he meets in coffee shops and gas stations during cross-country car rides than he ever thought he would after helping to give birth to the counterculture. With *Mind Breaths* (1978), *Poems All Over the Place, Mostly '70s* (1978), and *Plutonian Ode: Poems 1977-1980* (1982), Ginsberg has once again steadied himself: in his life, as a teacher and exemplar; in his art, as a rueful confessor whose tart wistfulness reminds me of no one so much as W. H. Auden at a similar age.

At the beginning of the *Collected Poems*, Ginsberg has the temerity to list what he considers his best work, a "chain of strong-breath'd poems." These selections, from **"The Song of the Shrouded Stranger of the Night"** (1949) to **"Birdbrain!"** and **"Capitol Air"** (1980), are astute; you quickly notice that his finest short lyric poems are as good as the sprawling, uneven masterpiece every schoolboy knows.

And sometimes the deceptively ordinary-looking, medium-sized ones are best of all. (pp. 42-3)

Ginsberg is no innovator. As he is eager to admit, his lengthy lines . . . are modeled on Whitman's. The huge, rambling epics—poems like **"Wichita Vortex Sutra,"** **"Iron Horse,"** and **"Contest of Bards"**—finds contemporary models in Olson's *Maximus Poems*, O'Hara's *Second Avenue*, and his beloved

Williams's *Paterson*. At his worst, Ginsberg does a lazy backstroke in the stream of consciousness. . . .

We talk about Ginsberg's life as inseparable from his art because that's what he does—he taught us to do it. It is his great accomplishment, a rebellious act backed up by an observational precision and emotional generosity that stands as a joyous rebuke to the bitter coldness of Eliot, Stevens, Lowell. His Old Testament-Hollywood prophet's beard makes him seem as if he's been around forever. But he's only 58, hale and lusty, and it's eerily exhilarating to think that he'll probably be around to chant some of us into the grave. Babble on, Ginsberg. (p. 43)

Ken Tucker, "Power of Babble," in The Village Voice, *Vol. XXX, No. 5, January 29, 1985, pp. 42-3.*

ROGER ROSENBLATT

Remember Allen Ginsberg? Wasn't it he who published that noisy, tirading poem in the fifties—bad words, good tune—just offensive enough to win your heart? Naughty Allen, crazy Allen, the wild zaddik with a fondness for Blake, Wyatt, and Whitman above all, whirling dervishly in public, beard-curling, petal-stewing, eyes agoggle, dancing like a shaggy elf and playing finger cymbals for the delight of Hell's Angels. Barefoot anarchist with cheek. How they loved him, the kids of the sixties, cheering alongside their grandmothers. Remember Prague 1965, when the rebellious Czechs crowned Ginsberg King of the May? Remember Chicago 1968, Ginsberg chanting from a balcony in an effort to exorcise Mayor Daley? Eventually, he would say, the chanting worked.

Then off-again Allen into the seventies, delivering his **"Plutonium Ode"** to the Pentagon, and squatting like a guru on the railroad tracks in the path of a train carrying radioactive detritus from the Rocky Flats Nuclear Weapons Plant. Tibet in Denver by way of Newark, San Francisco, and the Lower East Side. Ginsberg was everywhere: there for the Beats, the Hips, the Blacks, the Rocks, the Drugs, the Nukes. . . . Three years ago, he showed up at Columbia in a professorial suit and a striped tie to celebrate the 25th anniversary of **"Howl."** He played the reading for laughs. That Allen! What will he do next?

Or should the question be: What has he done at all? It seems a strangely sober act to pick up *Collected Poems 1947-1980*, all 800 pages of it, and read Ginsberg as if he had always, like any poet, asked to be judged by his work. No Jack Kerouac sits beside you beating out the rhythms on coffeehouse tables with the palms of his hands, and assuring you how important Allen's poetry is. This is Ginsberg on his own, sans bells, kids, grandmothers, presenting himself as if he were dead and the 20th century past and he had fallen into line with the poets of the age to see who will make it into the American literature survey courses of 2001. Yet it does not feel fair to judge him in that company.

If one makes comparisons with Eliot, Pound, Lowell, Stevens, or even with Ransom or Robert Penn Warren, the collected Ginsberg does not stand a chance. What these 800 pages prove is that Ginsberg has always been a minor poet; that is, a poet who has produced a few remarkable pieces, but the bulk of whose work shows no philosophical growth (despite its ostentatiously philosophical preoccupations) and rarely any depth. It is no small thing to be a minor poet; few make the list in any century. Ginsberg seems to be aware of his place. In the introduction, he warns that this collection will allow readers to "observe poetic energy as cyclic, the continuum a panorama of valleys and plateaus with peaks of inspiration every few years."

So, in fact, we do observe. When one considers that these poems cover 33 years of personal and national history, most of them lived feverishly, there is a striking sameness to the body of this work. Only Ginsberg's musical brilliance, his perfect pitch, saves the sameness from monotony. In the early poems he sounds like someone who has submerged himself in a tub of Elizabethan lyrics, and as soon as he bubbled up for air, wrote: "Last night I dreamed—of one I love" ("**The Night Apple**"). That was written in 1950. In 1979 he announced, "After 53 years—I still cry tears—I still fall in love—I still improve" ("**Some Love**"). He does not, however, improve thematically. A young homosexual becomes an old homosexual. An eager poet becomes a tired one. (p. 33)

["**Howl**"] is a poem worth rereading, especially if one deluded oneself into liking it when it made its loud debut. Read it today, and Ginsberg's self-mockery at the Columbia anniversary reading a few years ago makes great sense. . . . It makes you wonder what the second best minds were doing. Yet even in "**Howl**" the voice is clear and arresting. And the generosity in all the poems is abundant. Ginsberg can no more write a cruel line than a dry one. On the whole, however, this is the poetry of language against meaning, words invoked to bring us to our knees, without our really knowing why.

Except for "**Kaddish**," which is the one great poem in the collection. . . .

One could close the book on that poem, call that the collected Ginsberg, and be satisfied, often pleased. With a "public poet," however, there seems to be something more to take account of, especially when the poet has led a life as openly hectic as Ginsberg's. Yet what exactly is a public poet? Someone whose poems one would rather listen to than read? Someone who says something about the public as well as to it, who, in a sense, makes a poem of the public? Whitman, Ginsberg's presiding deity, did that. Has Ginsberg done it too, Ginsberg, this weirdness out of the Book of Hosea, this "bearded American fairy dope poet," as he called himself—the Voice of America?

There is a long, anti-Vietnam war poem in the collection, called "**Wichita Vortex Sutra**," that seems to get at the public poet question, and to sum up Ginsberg as well. At the outset Ginsberg sees America seeing him. Immediately the public poet makes a spectacle of himself. . . .

But then somewhere in the middle of "**Wichita Vortex Sutra**" a wholly new tone is taken: "I'm an old man now and a lonesome man in Kansas / but not afraid / to speak my lonesomeness in a car / because not only my lonesomeness / it's Ours, all over America." Read strictly in the context of an anti-war protest, these lines mean little. Read as a dark statement about America's history, they bring us to a pause. It seems true, what Ginsberg says. The country does feel lonesome—not as a consequence of politics, of recurrent isolationism, but as a basic condition. And the country, like Ginsberg, is getting on, an aging lonesome cowboy perpetually riding into Kansas. (p. 34)

The other side of lonesomeness, of course, is extravagant hope. Toward the end of the poem, Ginsberg invites the future to be happy: "Come to my lone presence / into this Vortex named Kansas . . . I here declare the end of the War." Naturally he had to do that. The country hears its own voice echoing the

poet's, a congregation in a college auditorium. We entered Kansas like Jesse James and wound up singing like Dorothy in *The Wizard of Oz*. Thus does Ginsberg create and sustain his public presence. He could not have survived as a poet had he not touched these simple American chords of self-doubt, self-love, self-confidence. It has been said that Ginsberg hates America. My guess is that he is crazy about it.

Which is not to say that he understands the country deeply, or that he thinks about it deeply, at least not in terms that come through in the writing. Analysis is not his strong suit. If one were to see "**Wichita Vortex Sutra**," or indeed most of Ginsberg's poems, as a mirror held up to the audience, the country would look awfully superficial. Is that what makes a public poet? Someone who handles superficialities beautifully? Not everyone can do it, surely. Only a poet who feels the superficialities in his bones, who believes in everything he appears to contradict, can pull it off. . . .

Does the collected Ginsberg represent the collected us? Certainly not, at least in the sense of reaching the nation's real complications. Still, as a guidebook to the national emotional highlights of the past four decades, the book is indispensable. So, evidently, is Ginsberg. Continually changing shapes and sounds, he has managed to outlast better poets by remaining forever current, urgent, with it, whatever "it" happened to be. What a strange national Moses. But maybe not. The two qualities one takes from this collection are sinful innocence and innocent sin. Allen was always a good boy. (p. 35)

Roger Rosenblatt, "A Major Minor Poet," in The New Republic, *Vol. 192, No. 9, March 4, 1985, pp. 33-5.*

JASCHA KESSLER

Surely our most famous poet for the last twenty years has been Allen Ginsberg, who's been not merely notorious at home but whose name and writings are known almost everywhere in the world today. . . . His career, both here and abroad, was self-chosen and self-consciously acted out with a great and shameless determination to be constantly in the public eye, and he has been hugely successful at it. . . . Apart from his reputation as an *enfant terrible*, and his perverse provocativeness, which remains a constant feature of his approach to audiences, even today when he is nearly 60 years old, there is, however, still the question of his poetry to be reckoned with. It is okay to be known as the fellow who does "advertisements for myself," to use Norman Mailer's words about Norman Mailer; but in the long run, there is always the fact and the problems of the text, the body of work that remains when all the noise of the scandals and rumors, the publicity and glamor has died down.

Now . . . that Ginsberg has published his *Collected Poems: 1947-1980*, 33 years' worth of everything he has wanted to save, a better notion of his accomplishment can be formed. . . . Perusing its pages, one comes across many surprises among things read casually long ago, or glanced at in small magazines, in fugitive journals and ephemeral pamphlets or chapbooks. Not surprisingly, Ginsberg has remained a fairly consistant writer: his voice, and his vocabulary and syntax are always familiar, and his psychology perfectly his idiosyncratic own, both as to subject matter and his treatment of it. From these many pages of poems both big and slight and even unimportant or bad, a portrait of Ginsberg emerges very clearly. He projects himself as the poet of grandiose statement, and even his mutterings are very much out loud. He stands as the poet of lamentation for the ruined world of nature, the socially-oppressed, and the victims of our complex technological culture (who may be persons at any and all levels of society, or even maybe aspects of individual consciousness, fractions of the individual's personality). He adopts the prophetic stance that gives him a vast and imaginative range for the excoriation of tyranny, of evil, of social forces beyond control, a sort of parodistic son of Jeremiah. And even at his most furious pitch, when Ginsberg is weeping, shouting, cursing, or hallucinating dooms and disasters, his way of putting things has an accompanying kind of verbal drollery, a giggling laughter, and a rather intellectual wittiness that marks the Gallows Humor manner of the bookish, middleclass, collegebred misfit and complex ridden, tormented Jewish boy familiar to us out of the literary scene of the 1940's.

The most distinguishing three characteristics of Ginsberg's poetry have always been Sentiment, the heart's feelings—though often he verges on maudlin sentimentality and mere public self-pity, letting it all hang out—and Liberation, and Didacticism. The poetry is all on the surface, like vast, endless billboards of headlines and graffiti running the length of the country, and so much of it is literally public, in the sense that Ginsberg goes on forever commenting on the headlines and editorials of the media year by year, as though he were a Medium himself. . . . In that sense Ginsberg has been a didactic broadcaster to the world, a roaming professor reading the headlines and popular science and lecturing anyone and everyone on the meaning of current events, all as a sort of unofficial, vagabond or outcaste "Guide to the Perplexed." . . . As for his goal, that has always been nothing else but Liberation—personal and public, whether perversely irrationalistic or rational in traditional literary way, or religious, metaphysical, and wildly, often crazily and funnily mundane at once—liberation for himself, from his own mental chains and private miseries, for his friends, and also for everyone else, even for the world itself. That quest for liberation takes many forms, and applies to many kinds of slavery and enchainment of body and mind, of individuals and societies. For Ginsberg preaches in the name of Eros, and believes fundamentally, with his models William Blake and Walt Whitman, that love conquers all, both in politics and everywhere else in the realm of the human. And as such he has always cursed the machines and the technology of modern science as it is employed by all those evil, mad, or stupid people he imagines he sees as the ones that control the powers of our world today. Maybe they do; maybe they don't: that *they* is the "they" poets often speak of in our 20th Century visionary and paranoiac style. Still, Ginsberg is not always a "responsible" liberator; in fact, he is often casually or deliberately irresponsible; but that is a complex subject indeed, and would need a thorough discussion.

In any case, what *is* the nature of a poet's responsibility? The reader of his vast collected poetry will spend a lot of time sorting out reactions to Ginsberg's various calls for freedom, and their psycho-mystico-philosophical underpinnings. And it will be a challenging as well as entertaining task too, because the work is never difficult to read as poetry, since it's always rather literary, always polished to the loudspeaking rhetoric of this prophet who was always at the center of his coterie of Beat friends in the 1950's, and has since put himself at the podium of the world.

Jascha Kessler, "Allen Ginsberg: 'Collected Poems: 1947-1980'," in a radio broadcast on KUSC-FM—Los Angeles, CA, April 25, 1985.

BLAKE MORRISON

Allen Ginsberg is the last of the great bardic bullies. Since his long rhythmical grumble, **'Howl,'** brought him fame in 1956 he has battered away in verse to make the world a better place. . . .

Ginsberg has always put his poetry where his beliefs are, and for this alone he deserves our respect.

Or does he? For in spite of—perhaps because of—his flamboyant protests, Ginsberg has ended up a sort of emperor's dancing bear. Pulling his pants down in public, extolling the virtues of drugs, singing of his homosexual escapades—these are stunts the Establishment can live with and even sneakily enjoy: they don't begin to alter the structures of power. . . .

Nearing 60, Ginsberg seems to recognise this, and admits as much in a touching **'Ode to Failure'**. . . . It's not that he has gone respectable, as word has it, but that he has settled for the role of court jester, light entertainer, nostalgist. . . .

Performance has always been Ginsberg's strength, and the first problem posed by [**'Collected Poems'**] is how to appreciate it cold. Without musical accompaniment or mantric intonation, the words on the page can look very dead indeed. Their power is in carrying along the listener: stop the drive-belt, as the reader can, and the effect is destructive. Ginsberg prefers the long rhapsodic Whitmanesque line, which is to say that his lines often run to two or three lines. They draw on Charles Olson's theory of the importance of 'breath,' which in Ginsberg's case seems to mean taking great lungfuls of air so as to run on as long as possible. To the ungenerous British reader, used to the small and well-regulated, Ginsberg's generosity of spirit can look like mere sloppiness.

But he is at least consistent. He believes in spontaneity . . . and in 'language intuitively chosen as in trance.' He likes to use capitalised big words—World, Soul, Planet, Love, Peace. A typical poem from his heyday will include travel glimpses of America, casualty figures from Vietnam, quotes (or misquotes) from pop songs, invocations to gods with names like Chaitanya or Durga-Ma, and questions for complacent bourgeois America ('Is Uncle Sam asleep in a Funeral Home?' 'Who represents my body in Pentagon?'). And such poems will end with an acknowledgment of derivation and (sometimes) chemical assistance. . . .

It's hard not to feel excluded by much of the poetry, not merely because of the passing of time, but because of its coterie tone. When Ginsberg isn't making speeches to the nation . . . he's addressing a small confraternity of 'boys.' The homoeroticism isn't in itself a problem, though it's hard to imagine how any reader, straight or gay, will find the paeans to Neal Cassady's 'ass,' in the previously unpublished **'Many Loves,'** anything other than comic. . . . No, what alienates is the feeling of being at a big party where you haven't been introduced but are expected to be familiar with all the names—Jack (Kerouac), Bill (Burroughs), Peter (Orlovsky) and so on. It's not enough that there are textual notes and even an Index of Proper Names to help out the uninitiated: the poems seem too busy making a Bohemian legend of the poet and his friends. . . .

Throughout there are some fine slices of description, 'reality sandwiches,' both of urban and rural America, as well as a humour which comes from mixing a high psalmic rhetoric with low slanginess. But such effects are often lost among the dirges, journal jottings, narcissistic fantasies . . . and tales of beating meat and getting high. Much of the later work is turgid, not Beat but deadbeat: the English punks addressed in a 1979 poem, their 'electric hair's beautiful gold as Blake's Glad Day boy,' would have cause to write off Ginsberg as a boring old hippie. But the last thing in the book, a rousing litany of political dislikes, shows he's tougher and more alert than that.

Ginsberg's is a benevolent message—'Be kind,' 'Everything is Holy'—and it would be an unkind reader who could finish this massive book without feeling affection for him: better his yawp than the YAPs and YUPs of the acquisitive Eighties. But what his career proves, greyly, is that if poets want to be legislators they had better be clerks and committee-men than a clown prince like Ginsberg.

> *Blake Morrison, "Bard of Bohemia," in* The Observer, *May 5, 1985, p. 25.*

JEFFREY HART

It is my impression that Allen Ginsberg is, if not exactly underrated, at least taken for granted—not really *seen* as a poet, which is much the same thing. People believe they know him and his work when they have not read much of it, or really paid attention to it. There is a tendency to consign him to a particular cultural moment—the late 1950s and the early to mid 1960s, when the Beat writers emerged, followed by the developing mass counterculture; and it has to be said that Ginsberg himself, by the cultivation of his public persona, is to some degree responsible for that identification. However, the fact of the matter is that Ginsberg is a remarkable poet, who has written some of the best poetry of our time. . . . [*Collected Poems*] arrives, therefore, at an auspicious moment, and is bound to produce a general reassessment of his work. . . .

For young writers [of the 1950s and 1960s], and even for younger teachers and critics, the High Modernists who had emerged during the early decades of the twentieth century were almost literally godlike. Think of Hugh Kenner's book *The Pound Era:* Yeats, Eliot, Stevens, Pound, Joyce, Proust, Mann— these writers seemed to transcend ordinary humanity. They were on every university's syllabus. They seemed implausibly

learned. The array of literary techniques each of them deployed was breathtaking, and they seemed to be philosophically profound, the keepers of the mysteries of the ages. . . . High Modernism did not seem to be literature, but rather sacred text. If this was writing, then how could anyone possibly write?

It was in this context that Allen Ginsberg, seconded by several of the writers associated with him, such as Jack Kerouac and Gregory Corso, did a remarkable thing. They wrote, they just did it, often magnificently; and by doing so they made writing seem possible again.

Ginsberg rescued us from the power of High Modernism by appealing to the alternative and no less sophisticated tradition of Whitman, the Song of the Self; an appeal that succeeded because Ginsberg is a great writer. Even minor Ginsberg is memorable, as in his 1958 *jeu d'esprit* about Lionel Trilling, a professor of his at Columbia. The poem is called **"The Lion for Real."** . . . (p. 46)

But then there is major Ginsberg, as in *Kaddish,* the word designating the Jewish lament for the beloved dead, in this case Ginsberg's mother. In my opinion *Kaddish* is one of the finest pieces of writing in American literature, the Jewish sensibility fused with the Whitmanesque. . . . (pp. 46-7)

Time will tell how the poetry stands up, but in my judgment, as I say, *Kaddish* is a great poem, right up there with "When Lilacs Last in the Dooryard Bloom'd." And *Kaddish* is specifically a great *American* poem—even a great Columbia poem— with its incorporation of Shelley's "Adonais," the elegy on Keats, which Ginsberg undoubtedly encountered in Lionel Trilling's course on the Romantics. . . .

We needed this *Collected Poems*, which comes at the right time. . . . The present volume shows the scale of his achievement and makes the entire sequence through 1980 available. Pulitizer Prize people, please take notice. (p. 47)

> *Jeffrey Hart, "Allen Ginsberg, Poet," in* National Review, *Vol. XXXVII, No. 9, May 17, 1985, pp. 46-7.*

Simon (James Holliday) Gray

1936-

(Also writes under pseudonym of Hamish Reade) English dramatist, scriptwriter, novelist, and editor.

Gray writes witty, well-crafted plays that usually contain elements of unconventional sexuality and often focus on males with either overbearing or submissive personalities. Within the context of comic situations and dialogue, his protagonists strive to protect or free themselves from disagreeable circumstances but instead suffer further entrapment in the ironic plot reversals typical of Gray's work. Gray first drew significant attention in England with plays that feature complex, farcical plots, black humor, and colloquial language. However, he is best known for such plays as *Butley* (1972) and *Quartermaine's Terms* (1981), which dissect the English intellectual scene and, being virtually plotless, depend on literate dialogue, verbal humor, and intricate character analysis.

Although Gray began his career with the satirical novels *Colmain* (1963), *Simple People* (1965), and *Little Portia* (1967), commercial considerations and his facility for dialogue led him to concentrate on drama. Gray's first two important stage plays, *Wise Child* (1967) and *Dutch Uncle* (1969), have bizarre, farcical plots and homosexual nuances. *Wise Child* was written for television but was considered too risqué for home viewing. This play centers on the relationship between two male criminals, one of whom is disguised as a female for much of the play. *Dutch Uncle* depicts a man's attempts to murder his wife, partly due to his desire to gain the attention of a male police officer. Constant interruptions and his own incompetence result in the man's failure to accomplish the murder.

In *Butley,* his first major success, Gray dispenses with farce, drawing humor from witty, satirical dialogue. The title character is a university professor who alienates himself from others, including his homosexual office mate, by using his exceptional ability with language to establish his superiority. This work has been favorably compared with the plays of Harold Pinter due to its focus on language and alienation. Pinter directed *Butley* in its original London production and has also directed several other of Gray's plays.

In *Otherwise Engaged* (1975) Gray again focuses on an aloof male, this time an editor. Simon, the protagonist, attempts to enjoy a recording of Richard Wagner's opera *Parsifal* but is interrupted by several friends and relatives. They seek companionship or help with personal problems, but Simon remains detached. Critics were intrigued by Gray's ambiguous presentation: Simon's aloofness might reflect his coldheartedness, yet it could also be a necessary defense against those people who complicate his life. *Otherwise Engaged* won the New York Drama Critics Circle Award for best foreign play in 1977.

After deemphasizing comedy in several plays, including *The Rear Column* (1978) and *Close of Play* (1979), Gray won popular success with *Quartermaine's Terms,* another play about academia. This work is set in a school where foreign students are taught English. The title character attempts to join the camaraderie of the family-like faculty but is virtually ignored or, at best, patronized. In an attempt to be friendly, he voices banal statements that pass unacknowledged by the other char-

Photograph by Mark Gerson

acters, providing a source of comedy in the play. Quartermaine appears cheerful and helpful when in the company of others but suffers a profound sadness when alone. Several critics were impressed by Gray's effective blend of humor and pathos, especially in the final scene, where Quartermaine responds to his dismissal from the school. In Gray's recent play, *The Common Pursuit* (1984), he explores the aspirations, successes, and failures of a group of college friends. Like most of Gray's work, this play is appreciated primarily for its humorous dialogue and for its probing view of English intellectuals.

(See also *CLC*, Vols. 9, 14; *Contemporary Authors*, Vols. 21-24, rev. ed.; and *Dictionary of Literary Biography*, Vol. 13.)

JOHN RUSSELL TAYLOR

[Simon Gray] seems to be considerably less accomplished as a sheer entertainer than [Alan] Ayckbourn, and far less interesting in his ideas and techniques than [David] Cregan. Before the first play of his to cause any stir, *Sleeping Dog* (1967), he had already published two well-thought-of satirical novels, *Colmain* and *Little Portia. Sleeping Dog* is a television play based on an idea which has something in common with that of Robert Shaw's novel *The Hiding Place* and his television play *The*

Pets: a retired colonial administrator lures a black barman into his home in England and traps him in the cellar, where he keeps him locked up like an animal, thereby recreating in microcosm the old colonial situation he used to dominate during his career in Africa. The metaphor is vivid, but hardly stands up to examination; the play, however, got by on account of its slightly Ortonish brand of outrageousness and black humour.

The same style is developed in Gray's stage play *Wise Child* (1967). . . . In it [the character named Mrs Artminster] seems for some time to be a rather blowsey middle-aged woman, too fond of the bottle, living with her son in a hotel kept by a homosexual. But eventually it turns out that 'Mrs Artminster' is a man, a criminal on the run from the police; he nearly precipitates trouble by making a pass at the black maid, but his 'son' contrives to smooth it over. Eventually the tensions between them grow too great, and Artminster, alias Jock Masters the Peabody Postman's assailant, tries to hand on Gerry to the landlord, Booker, and takes off on his own, the police still a few steps behind. Again, the impression is very much of imitation Orton, or at least Gray writes very much in the school of Orton, though the play's situation is piquant and its elaboration quite adroit—almost adroit enough to hide its essential slimness and lack of real progression.

Pig in the Poke (1969) was another television play with affinities of subject-matter, this time with one of David Rudkin's television plays, *House of Character,* which deals with the trials of a new tenant, only to reveal in the end that they are all subjective, because he is in fact a lunatic trying to make sense of the asylum in which he finds himself. *Pig in a Poke* began similarly, but this time the troubles of the couple who take the flat stem from the uncontrollable presence of a sitting tenant in the basement, who little by little takes over their home and their lives, turns out their friends, and becomes the wife's lover after beating her up (in these latter stages the affinity seems to be with Harold Pinter's television play *The Basement,* or with Orton's *The Ruffian on the Stair*).

Gray's stage play *Dutch Uncle* . . . continued to explore the same sort of sub-Orton territory, with an overlay of Donald McGill seaside-postcard vulgarity carefully cultivated. Godboy, the play's timid and ineffectual chiropodist hero, has one clear *idée fixe* throughout, that he is going to match the exploits of the Dublin wife- and female lodger-murderer, and thus finally not only rid himself of his terrible missus, but also bring himself to the attention of his idol, Inspector Hawkins, and make his mark on the world by paying the supreme penalty. In putting his plans into practice he is absurdly inefficient, and though by the end of the first act he believes that he has his wife shut in a gas-filled wardrobe we know that she has, in fact, walked out and left him without his even noticing. The second act is taken up with elaborating on the situation, and complicating it slightly with the possibility that the half-witted lodger from upstairs (husband of the intended second victim) may be a local rapist the police are trying to trap through the wiles of a constable in drag. The piece seems, despite the expectations raised by the relatively exalted circumstances of its production, to be meant as a simple farce and nothing more. But as such, despite a few bright moments, it can be accounted only a fairly feeble example of the genre.

After its production Gray appeared in a very different role as adaptor of Dostoevsky's *The Idiot* for the National Theatre (1970). The adaptation was well-meant but fragmentary and inclined to skirt (perhaps understandably) the central point of the novel, Dostoevsky's discussion and demonstration of the creeping insanity of society in relation to the tormented individual. Still, the subject could hardly be further from Ortonish farce, so there is hope yet that Simon Gray may find a way of putting his undoubted skills to better, or at least more individual, use. This hope was hardly realized, though, in his next original play, *Spoiled* (1971), which sets up a triangle situation of repressed schoolmaster, pregnant wife and eager young pupil brought into the house for a weekend of intensive cramming. The petty irritations and frustrations of the household situation are quite well captured, but our theatrical sophistication proves to have rather overtaken Gray in this instance, and his final, long and slowly built-up-to shock effect, with the schoolmaster bedding the boy and being caught in a dramatic confrontation with his wife outside the bedroom door, falls with a dull thud of 'is that all?' True, there seems to be some deliberate avoiding of possible Ortonish overtones in the subject (which could be developed, for example, as an *Entertaining Mr. Sloane* situation) and the character-building is sober and solid to the point of being rather boring. However, with a stronger and more original subject Gray might very easily surprise us. . . . (pp. 169-71)

> *John Russell Taylor, " 'Three Farceurs': Alan Ayckbourn, David Cregan, Simon Gray," in his* The Second Wave: British Drama for the Seventies, *Hill and Wang, 1971, pp. 155-71.**

OLEG KERENSKY

Gray's comedies all show his interest, not surprising in a teacher of English, in the precise use of language. There is a lot of verbal humour, often achieved by one character taking literally another's loose use of words, and querying the meaning in a mocking or pedantic fashion. [The title character of *Butley*], for example, himself a university English teacher, deliberately pretends to misunderstand the application of carelessly used relative clauses. . . . [When] his colleague Joey tells him that a student has complained about another teacher's seminars in a pub, Butley says: 'Edna holds her seminars in a pub? I shall have to report this,' but of course it was the student's complaint that was made in a pub. In *Otherwise Engaged* Simon's wife tells him about her relationship with another man and says that they want to be husband and wife to each other. 'Husband *and* wife to each other? Is Ned up to such double duty?' Simon retorts. (pp. 132-33)

Many of Gray's characters have their own idiosyncratic phrases, which they use repeatedly. Godboy keeps saying 'merely' and Joey in *Butley* constantly says 'in point of fact'. Humour is derived from these repetitions, which are also revealing about the characters concerned. Similarly both Butley and Simon frequently repeat what someone else has said to them, but in the form of a question, a common habit of a certain type of mind, playing for time while thinking how to reply to an awkward remark.

Gray's humour is not simply verbal; it is also often visual, sometimes almost farcical. *Dutch Uncle* in particular attempts to obtain laughs from Godboy trying to gas his wife, when he thinks she is in a cupboard, while in fact she has already left it, in full view of the audience. *Spoiled* extracts farcical humour from Howarth, a schoolteacher, trying to give French dictation to a pupil who is still fumbling around with satchel, pencils and papers, and *Wise Child* has a classical farcical setting—two adjoining bedrooms in a hotel—with the kinky twists that 'Mrs Artminster' tries to get Janice to strip in one room while

Mr Booker, the manager of the hotel, makes homosexual advances to 'her son' Jerry in the other.

These plays are also much more than mere farces. They are essentially about psychological and emotional relationships, about people's attempts to dominate and possess each other or, in the case of *Otherwise Engaged*, about efforts to avoid being possessed or involved. *Wise Child*, the first of Gray's plays to reach the London and New York stages, seemed very kinky when produced in 1967. . . . At first the audience is kept in doubt whether the other characters know they are dealing with a man in drag and whether 'Mrs Artminster' is a transvestite and her relationship with Jerry a homosexual one. Indeed there is even doubt whether we are watching a real woman, who happens to be played by a man. This kind of sexual ambiguity, not always so explicitly stated, is characteristic also of Gray's later work. (pp. 133-34)

Dutch Uncle has been compared to Orton's *Loot*, as both plays are black farces dealing with death. The plot concerns Godboy's efforts to gas his wife in a cupboard, specially bought and prepared for the purpose, and to have an affair with Doris, the wife of the upstairs neighbour. Complications are provided by Godboy's Raskolnikov-like infatuation with murder, as a means of achieving celebrity, and his attempts to interest Inspector Hawkins in his proposed crime. . . . After various false alarms and farcical twists, including Hawkins flirting with Doris, the play ends with Godboy's wife casually shutting him in the cupboard. The audience is left, in Gray's typically open-ended manner, unsure whether Godboy will ever emerge.

Several of Gray's other favourite themes appear in *Dutch Uncle*, but in a minor way. Hawkins is assisted by a policeman who has to put on drag in an attempt to decoy the street rapist; Hawkins talks about religion and sin while fondling Doris, and Godboy himself is in some ways similar to Simon's brother Stephen in *Otherwise Engaged*, in that they are both 'greyish' characters who realize that they make no lasting impression on their fellows and are desperately trying to remedy this, though in very different ways.

Gray denies having any special interest in religion, one way or another. But Donald, in *Spoiled*, a teenage boy of uncertain sexual tastes, also suffers from a religious upbringing and a consequent sense of guilt affecting his sex life. . . . *Spoiled* is more conventional than *Wise Child* and *Dutch Uncle*, daring only in that it hints at a homosexual relationship between the teacher and pupil. However it does not really face up to the problems posed by such a relationship. . . . There are some shrewd psychological insights, but because of its failure to face up to the big issues it raises, *Spoiled* left most people dissatisfied.

Butley was Gray's first big success. . . . [The] play is mostly about Butley's relationship with Joey, an ex-pupil and now a junior colleague with whom he shares his home and the office where the action of the play takes place. He keeps Joey on tenterhooks about his promotion and he is merciless in prying into his private life. (pp. 135-37)

It is difficult to account for the great success of this play. It is both witty and psychologically interesting, but one might have expected that its appeal would be limited to middle-class intellectuals. Obviously many other people identify with Butley's emotional and professional problems, and enjoy the outrageous way in which he treats people. Something of the same formula was repeated in Gray's next play, *Otherwise Engaged*. . . . Like Butley, Simon in this play is an intellectual,

this time a publisher. There is even less plot than in *Butley: Otherwise Engaged* is a series of duologues between Simon and various visitors who interrupt his attempt to listen to a complete recording of *Parsifal*: the upstairs lodger, a student who thinks the world owes him a living, Simon's brother Stephen, a veteran schoolteacher desperately worried about whether he will become a deputy headmaster, Jeff, a trendy literary critic who launches tirades against 'literature', Australians, women, homosexuals, his wife and almost everyone and everything else, Jeff's mistress who tricks him into thinking his wife has attempted suicide and who suddenly strips 'topless' in an unsuccessful attempt to seduce Simon, Wood, a faintly sinister stranger who recalls lusting after Simon when they were at school and who now accuses him of seducing his girl, and finally Beth, Simon's wife, who insists on telling him the details of her affair with another man.

At first *Otherwise Engaged* seems like a series of witty and sometimes outrageous revue sketches. Simon listens to his visitors with apparent solicitude and endless patience, but his interest in them is superficial. He asks questions which are often trivial and irrelevant. When Stephen complains that his rival for the job had the unfair advantage of being educated at Oxford, Simon asks, 'Which college?', and when Stephen describes having to drink his headmaster's herbal coffee, Simon wants to know what sort of herbs. (pp. 137-38)

Perhaps Simon does not love or care about anyone, except himself; perhaps he cares about them too much and has to distance himself from them to avoid intolerable suffering. He certainly helps people as much as he can, and tries to avoid saying anything to hurt them. Equally, he does not want to hear anything that will hurt him unnecessarily. Both Simon and Ben Butley are similar in many ways to Philip in Hampton's *The Philanthropist*. They all share the same sort of detachment and pedantic verbal humour. Indeed the scene in which Simon rejects Jeff's mistress and tells her that fidelity means more to him 'than a suck and a fuck with the likes of you' is astonishingly reminiscent of Philip's rejection of Araminta's advances.

Some people would regard Simon's behaviour as thoroughly sensible and civilized. Paul Johnson, in a political article in the *New Statesman*, even suggested that Simon represents western civilization, giving aid and comfort to the rest of the world and getting nothing but abuse in return. (p. 139)

Peter in *Dog Days* is another character in the Butley/Simon mould. Like Butley, he uses verbal pedantry to discomfort and upset his friends and relations; like Simon, he is a publisher with a schoolteacher brother whom he despises. He is more outspokenly rude than either of them, and more obviously unhappy. Although it was not produced till 1976, *Dog Days* was written around the same time as *Butley* and before *Otherwise Engaged*. In fact Gray describes it as the source of *Otherwise Engaged*, and of two of his television plays. He was dissatisfied with it, thinking it insufficiently structured, and refused permission for it to be performed on several occasions. (p. 140)

The characters and plot of *Dog Days* exactly parallel those in *Otherwise Engaged*, but with interesting and significant differences. Peter is more openly hostile to his brother, and his quarrels with his wife are shown in greater detail. On the other hand he is nice to Joanna, the artist who brings him her work, instead of brusquely rejecting her as Simon rejected Davina. While Simon refused to have sex with Davina because he was married and their meeting was in his home, it is Joanna who refuses Peter for the same reasons. Instead of sitting at home refusing to alter his life, Peter moves out to a flat of his own and attempts an affair with Joanna there.

Peter is as fastidious about language and as clever at using it to make other people uncomfortable as any of Gray's heroes. (pp. 140-41)

There is not quite as much . . . witty dialogue as in *Butley* or *Otherwise Engaged*, but what there is, is vintage Gray. (p. 141)

> *Oleg Kerensky, "Simon Gray," in his* The New British Drama: Fourteen Playwrights Since Osborne and Pinter, *1977. Reprint by Taplinger Publishing Company, 1979, pp. 132-44.*

JOHN BUSH JONES

"The point about tragedy is that it is *no longer funny*. It is funny, and then it becomes no longer funny." Seemingly straightforward enough, this remark by Harold Pinter is fraught with his typical ambiguity, for what is the referent of "it"? Is "it" the tragedy itself that becomes no longer funny or the *point* that first is and then is not so? Or is "it" an entirely different "it," the actions or behavior of the protagonist perhaps, or maybe something as big as life itself? Whatever "it" may be, the definition as a whole was originally conceived to refer specifically to Pinter's own early plays . . . , all of which move from funny to no longer funny at some point in the action. . . . [Among] the works of contemporary British playwrights that Pinter could also have had in mind, his remark best characterizes the several ostensible comedies of Simon Gray, in whose *Butley* and *Otherwise Engaged* Pinter found such congeniality of dramatic form as to direct their original productions himself.

Like Pinter's own early protagonists . . . , Gray's end up hopelessly and rather helplessly in isolation. At the end of *Wise Child*, Jerry has killed a man and hastily dons a wig and woman's clothing to evade apprehension; as *Dutch Uncle* closes, Mr. Godboy is slammed shut in the massive wardrobe he had earlier rigged out as a makeshift gas chamber in an abortive murder attempt on his wife; shortly before the final curtain in *Spoiled*, the French teacher Richard must plead with his young pupil not to make known their homosexual encounter of the night before; and the closing moments of both *Butley* and *Otherwise Engaged* find their witty, articulate protagonists at a loss for words and very much alone.

So, like Pinter's fawning yet irascible Davies, Gray's *comic* protagonists alienate themselves by their own behavior as surely as Macbeth, Creon, Oedipus, and Lear ever managed to cut themselves off from society in the framework of *tragic* drama. How do these "heroes" of comedy end up in such a sorry state, or are Gray's plays tragic in their structure as well, perhaps, as their outcome? The answer to this and related questions is not immediately apparent, and blanket statements cannot be made to cover all Gray's plays, even excluding those for television and limiting discussion to those written for the stage. Within the latter group, some similarities are common to all of them but real distinctions can be made between those written and produced before Gray's adaptation of Dostoevsky's *The Idiot* . . . in 1970 and those that have followed. Though *Idiot*, not itself a comedy, bears little relationship in form or style to the plays either before or after it, its composition seems to have greatly affected Gray's methods of dramatic construction, especially as he can be seen to move from a drama of action to a drama of character and language.

What is shared by all the plays is their focus on a protagonist devoted singlemindedly to either achieving what he perceives as freedom or else shielding himself from what he senses to be an obtrusive, unpleasant reality. In every case, the central character's course of action or mode of behavior backfires, either further entrapping him and preventing his attainment of freedom, or else effecting even greater undesirable changes in the reality he has been studiously trying to avoid. The net result of such actions or behavior engaged in without any thought for consequences is the quite accidental self-alienation or isolation of Gray's diverse protagonists. This pattern of ironic reversal from intent to result is the unifying structural principle of the four major comedies. (The four are *Wise Child, Dutch Uncle, Butley,* and *Otherwise Engaged*. *Spoiled*, a psychological study of what Gray calls "self-indulgence," immediately followed *The Idiot*, and is clearly a transitional piece and not, strictly speaking, a comedy. Though some of the elements common to Gray's true comedies are present, it would be illegitimate to attempt imposing a pattern on *Spoiled* that simply is not there. Also, *Dog Days* is not being considered for specific analysis since it represents only one of several efforts to do what was most successfully done in *Otherwise Engaged*. And, too, *The Idiot* and *Molly* are other types of drama altogether.)

Simon Gray's writings for both stage and television reveal him to be a seeker after form. What Pinter said of himself could apply equally well to Gray; he seems always to be trying to "get the structure right," to find the most theatrically effective shape in which to arrange his dramatic materials. . . . Gray's four true comedies reveal an interest in accepted, traditional forms of drama and in making the most appropriate of those forms work for him in shaping his contents to his intended end. Specifically, for the two early pre-*Idiot* comedies [*Wise Child* and *Dutch Uncle*], plays which are largely composed of the *actions* of the protagonists, Gray utilizes the fundamental elements of farce, whereas in the post-*Idiot* pieces in which behavior and character are the central concerns [*Butley* and *Otherwise Engaged*], the form most closely approximates that of classical, and, particularly, Sophoclean tragedy.

In the two early farces *Wise Child* and *Dutch Uncle*, the focus is on the actions of the protagonists (both Jerry and Mrs. Artminster in the former, Mr. Godboy in the latter) so to manipulate their environment as to achieve freedom. In *Wise Child*, though some attention is given to the strange personality of Jerry and the character interplay between him and his fraudulent mother, the main thrust of the play is the effort of both to remain free from the law, and, it is gradually learned, Mrs. Artminster's additional maneuvers to free herself from the blackmail and manipulation of her supposed son. Jerry's hold on Mrs. Artminster is his knowledge of "her" identity. She is in fact the wanted criminal Jock Masters for whom Jerry obtained the female disguise in exchange for assistance with his own con games and the gratification of his peculiar mixture of childish dependence and masochism. All the while Jerry believes he is keeping Mrs. Artminster free—free from arrest and imprisonment for a recent crime—she herself feels trapped in her female rôle-playing and the control Jerry exercises on her. Accordingly, she plots independently to free herself from him. This action is played out in their adjoining rooms in a third-rate hotel where, to complicate matters, Jerry must ward off the homosexual advances of the manager and Mrs. Artminster must restrain her male sexual impulses from revealing her true identity as she lusts after a West Indian chambermaid. The action is largely farcical, with the set's three doors and two closets providing ample opportunity for hasty exits and entrances, narrow escapes, avoidance of fatal discoveries, and the other near misses so vital to the robust stage action the genre requires.

But the hilarity suddenly stops when Jerry accidentally kills the hotel manager, and in a stunning reversal finds that now he is the fugitive, the isolated one who is no longer free himself and no longer able to manipulate Mrs. Artminster. Quite at a loss, he pleads to her for help, but the killing has released her from Jerry and she is ready to chance living in her proper male identity again. All she can offer is a description of the kind of alienation Jerry will now know. . . . Whereupon Jerry hastily dresses in clothes left behind by the chambermaid, himself now entrapped and isolated by his own actions in a disguise like that he had earlier forced upon Jock Masters. The ironic reversal of his search for freedom is complete as the curtain falls.

In *Dutch Uncle* character is almost completely sacrificed for the sake of the bizarrely farcical plot of Mr. Godboy, a bumbling would-be murderer who tries to get rid of his wife to be free to seduce Doris Hoyden, the attractive, though, as it turns out, apparently frigid, woman upstairs. Mrs. Godboy is equally fed up with her husband's sexual non-performance and briefly walks out on him just as he thinks he has locked her in the wardrobe and turned on the gas—her absence causing him to believe he has successfully carried out his plot. Meanwhile, Doris' husband Eric, frustrated by *her* coldness, has been disappearing for prolonged intervals and is finally revealed by Inspector Hawkins to be "the Merritt Street attacker." Godboy's seduction attempts, like his various tries at stuffing his wife in the cupboard, are thwarted in the best farce tradition by just the wrong people showing up at any of several doors at the worst possible times. In fact, everything he does is frustrated. His admiration for Inspector Hawkins leads him to play what he sees as a "cat and mouse" game with him, directly challenging him to discover the murder. But like all else, this is hopelessly inept, and, to make matters worse, Hawkins is not the slightest bit interested. When Godboy brazenly throws open the wardrobe to reveal the body (discovering instead only Eric's mislaid raincoat) he is thoroughly crushed and defeated, not to mention perplexed. On one level, Godboy has wanted to be caught, tried, and executed for murder, but he fails even in this elaborate scheme for a sort of ritual suicide. His attempts to seek freedom from wife and freedom from life both end in failure, and the closing picture of Mrs. Godboy slamming *him* shut in the wardrobe is a splendid visual image of his efforts at escape turned to even greater entrapment and isolation than he had known before. Not only has his wife returned, but Doris has gone off with the inspector. Godboy's options, like the wardrobe door, are closed.

Neither *Wise Child* nor *Dutch Uncle* could be considered in any way tragic. Though the protagonists of both effectively alienate themselves, they do so within a farce structure that virtually prevents tragic insights and implications. The farce so distances the audience that they will observe the ironic reversals but not feel a sense of tragedy. *Dutch Uncle* is purely comic throughout, and while *Wise Child* does become no longer funny, it becomes so entirely for the audience, not the characters (it has never been funny for them). Whereas we see the isolation of Jerry and Mr. Godboy as the ironic consequence of their own actions to attain something quite the opposite, they themselves

never come to such a recognition. That absent, so is the chance for a tragic effect.

Butley and *Otherwise Engaged*, the plays following *The Idiot* and the transitional *Spoiled*, reveal a definite shift in Gray's interests and his methods of dramatic construction, a shift that will accommodate what the farces could not. Gone is the complex plotting and overt stage action of the early pieces in favor of in-depth examinations of character through a drama whose movement comes largely through its dialogue. It is this dominance of language, especially the incessant exercise of wit by the protagonists Ben Butley and Simon Hench, that has led to the popular labeling of these plays as comedies of manners. Perhaps to some extent this is accurately descriptive; the witty banter and the occasional exposure of the posturing types that inhabit twentieth-century academia and literary circles do partially admit these plays to that genre. And yet, their underlying structure does not. Formally, *Butley* and *Otherwise Engaged* more closely resemble *Oedipus Rex* and *Antigone* than *The Way of the World* and *Our Betters*. By casting his later comedies in the mold of Sophoclean tragedy, Gray opens up possibilities for creating a kind of comic drama whose focus is character, not manners, and whose overtones, implications, and ultimate effect approach the tragic.

To begin with, in both *Butley* and *Otherwise Engaged* Gray has economically compressed the action into one climactic day in the life of the protagonist. The alleged unities of time and place are as rigorously adhered to as the unity of action: all events (or, more accurately, the reportage of events) work toward the ultimate overwhelming of the hero. Very little "happens" in either play, at least in the sense of stage action or permutations of plot. In both, most everything "has happened" already, largely because of the behavior of the protagonists, and what occurs on stage is the unveiling to the audience of his destructive behavior and the gradual revelation to him himself of the finally disastrous consequences of that mode of conduct. Both Butley and Hench use their particular patterns of behavior to ward off an unpleasant reality (for Butley this is both his academic duties and any possible emotional contacts, for Hench largely just the latter), but what neither realizes until too late is how well he has succeeded. As surely as the actions of Creon and Oedipus, the behavior of Butley and Hench leads to isolation. The real action, then, is internal, as Ben and Simon move slowly, and, of course, belatedly, to their moments of recognition.

Granted, many comedies of many kinds obey a similar unity of design, and this alone could not mark *Butley* and *Otherwise Engaged* as possessing the structure of Sophoclean tragedy. What does ally them to this form is their peculiar "processional" pattern and their outcome. Like Creon in *Antigone* and Oedipus in *Oedipus Rex*, Ben and Simon encounter, one by one, a veritable parade of characters—classically antagonists, but to them perhaps more appropriately irritants—all of whom allow the audience to observe more instances of the protagonist's anti-social behavior (Butley's humiliation of, Hench's indifference to, nearly everyone) at the same time that they successively display to the protagonist the effects his behavior has had and is having. (pp. 78-84)

[Everything] necessary for tragic implications is present in the fate of Ben Butley and Simon Hench. Both are permitted to come to that condition not allowed the protagonists of Gray's farces—the moment of recognition that they themselves are the causes of their present state. As Butley in rapid succession loses his wife and closest friend—both victims of his bitter wit—Hench in the closing moments finds his indifference responsible not only for an impending divorce but very probably for a suicide as well. Like Ben at the news of Joey moving offices, Simon, for the first time utterly speechless, *"sits in a state of shock."*

If indeed the point about tragedy is that it is no longer funny, then perhaps *Butley* and *Otherwise Engaged* deserve the name. Ben and Simon throughout the action take positive delight in using their virtuoso displays of wit to keep the world at arm's length. Only at the end do they cease laughing when faced with the horrible realization of how successful they have been. As they contemplate their final isolation, they realize that it is, because they are, *no longer funny.* (p. 85)

> John Bush Jones, "The Wit and the Wardrobe: Simon Gray's Tragic (?) Comedies," in West Virginia University Philological Papers, Vol. 25, 1979, pp. 78-85.

BENEDICT NIGHTINGALE

Those who like to think of Simon Gray as a commercial huckster with ideas above his station . . . will be much relieved by *Stage Struck*. It is a distraction, an entertainment, and pretends to be nothing more. But that is no reason for those of us who have supported him through thick, if not always through thin, to start scratching his name out of our professional address books. . . .

After the speedy demise of his serious and admirable *Rear Column* and the less-than-rhapsodic reception of his interesting if uneven *Close of Play*, he has surely earned the change that is, we're told, as good as a rest. To repudiate him now would be akin to forgetting that Graham Greene produced *The Heart of the Matter* just after *The Ministry of Fear*.

Well, all right, Gray is as different from Greene as beige is from black; nevertheless *Stage Struck* is not as distinctive a piece as one could wish. True it displays some of that fascination with callousness, betrayal and general human perversity to be found at the puckered heart of Gray's best work. A wife speaks with fastidious disgust of the perfume she's smelt on her husband's face, the alien hair on his coat, the lipstick smeared across his flies. She then proceeds to elbow him out of the marital nest with peculiar cruelty, coolly luxuriating in her own infidelities, threatening him with penury, reminding him of her own status, which is that of a celebrated actress, and of his own, 'a failure . . . not even a success *manqué*'. A little later, he ripostes by reducing her supposed mentor to blubbing infantilism. There are nastinesses enough in *Stage Struck* and acid, biting lines in abundance; but they are there, not so much to illustrate Gray's glum view of relationships, rather to activate and decorate a sensational plot. An idiosyncratic vision balloons into melodrama.

One could not object if the melodrama were good, or good of its kind; but it is, alas, a not-very-remarkable example of the brand of thriller patented by Anthony Shaffer. Their formula includes wily machinations, disguises, guns that fire without killing, victims who fall without dying, and, logically enough, a theatrical or quasi-theatrical setting. It works by misleading the audience, then dramatically surprising it with unlooked for but logical revelations.

Stage Struck suggests, however, that the genre's ingenuities are becoming predictable with repetition and familiarity. What looks like the corpse of . . . [the] bitch-wife crashed down from the ceiling, knife in breast, rope round neck. What palpably

is . . . [the] avenger-husband drops behind the sofa, clutching what purports to be a bullet-wound. The true surprise, the authentic sensation, would be that they were both actually dead, but experience lulls any such tremors. . . .

Perhaps Mr Gray should write a more plausible, consistent and serious play. . . . Perhaps he should simply write another play, period. (p. 868)

> Benedict Nightingale, "Play Off," in New Statesman, Vol. 98, No. 2541, November 30, 1979, pp. 868-69.*

HAROLD HOBSON

[The character Robert in] Simon Gray's *Stage Struck* flinches from what he sees, and whether what he sees is reality, and whether he succeeds in doing what he sets out to do, or appears to set out to do, are questions that will furnish the audience with matter for long argument hours after they have left the theatre. This is a departure from Mr. Gray's usual style. Nothing on the stage . . . is altogether what it seems to be; murders may be games, but, on the other hand, games may be murder. Startling things fall out of haylofts, and there is enough red blood about to have furnished an entire all-American football club of fifty years ago. There is a lot of sardonic and cynical wit, and if what happens at the end of both acts in the play does not make you jump out of your seats, then you are less athletic than you ought to be.

> Harold Hobson, in a review of "Stage Struck," in Drama, No. 135, January, 1980, p. 36.

HAROLD HOBSON

[*Quartermaine's Terms*] is the first play I have seen which refers accurately to Berkeley's theory of the impossibility of proving that matter exists unless someone perceives it. . . . When Henry Windscape's precocious daughter . . . tells him that he cannot prove that other people exist, Henry (a middle-aged master in a language school at Cambridge) is forced to admit that she is right. Henry . . . tells his colleagues the story of his remarkable daughter's grasp of philosophic reasoning with a modest pride. Later he has to tell them that she grew learned too young, and has had a mental breakdown. That is Henry's problem.

His colleagues also have problems. Melanie Garth . . . hates her mother, and is soured by the fact that she had refused Henry in her youth. Anita . . . is troubled by her husband's unfaithfulness, and Mark . . . is deserted by his wife. Derek . . . cannot get a permanent place on the staff, and Eddie, the joint-headmaster . . . is worried by falling numbers. There remains St. John Quartermaine . . . who alone appears to have no problems at all. Simon Gray tells us almost nothing about him. We learn by accident that he was at Christ Church, but nothing more. He appears to have no living relatives, and no friends. He spends his vacations at the school. He wears his informal clothes with ease, lounges casually about the common-room, is always good-tempered, ready with sympathy for everybody, and smiles quickly and brightly. He is interested in everybody's difficulties and always anxious to lend a hand whenever necessary. *Quartermaine's Terms* is amusing and witty, its wit exceeded only by its delicate and infinite sadness, the infinite sadness of absolute and utter loneliness. If Quartermaine has tickets for the theatre no one has the time to go with him. If he wants to join them at croquet the party is just breaking up. But he never complains. His smile is always instant and pleasant. There are only a few moments, when no one else is in the room, when his face becomes strained and painful. But as soon as anyone enters, he is immediately cheerful and kind.

In his very fine and much misunderstood *The Rear Column* Gray showed us a man equally likeable and well-behaved against great odds; and that man turned out to be very wicked indeed. With Gray, turning out to be wicked, or at least not quite normal, is by no means an uncommon thing. One remembers with a vivid unease in his first play how, with laughing, unsuspecting face, a young girl happily danced for an old lady who was not an old lady at all; and again the suspicions we had of the headmaster who devoted himself to a promising pupil in *Spoiled*. Then the hero of *Otherwise Engaged*, one of the best plays of our time, was not at the end quite the compassionate creature we had supposed him to be. There are more intimations of immorality than of immortality in Mr Gray's work. But they are very delicate, very subdued, very subliminal. That is why their power is great and haunting.

If the other characters in *Quartermaine's Terms* had been keen theatregoers, and were familiar with Gray's subtle and disturbing work, they would have had good reason for dropping Quartermaine as soon as he ceased to be useful to them as a generous-hearted baby-sitter. But they were not theatregoers, and their neglect of Quartermaine, their treatment of him almost as someone who did not exist, must be ascribed to some other cause. It may be that they were all, as I have suggested, faced with urgent personal questions, and (except as a baby-sitter) that to none of these questions did Quartermaine have any answer. His great loneliness, which pierces the audience like a sword, may be due to just that, and to nothing more. (pp. 16-17)

Of Quartermaine we know nothing except what we see on the stage, his affability, his gallant cheerfulness, his placid acceptance of any rebuff, however wounding; and of course, that he had been at Christ Church, and even for that scrap of knowledge we have to take his word. Gradually, however, as one sees that neither Quartermaine's kindness, nor his courtesy nor his cheerfulness can apparently be broken, one begins to wonder if, under Hillcrist's definition, a gentleman has, after half a century, again appeared in a London theatre. You cannot answer that question with certainty, until, of course, the very end of the play. In the last scene, played by Quartermaine and Henry Windscape, Quartermaine gets his 'come uppance'. It is very moving in this final moment, as the lights darken, and the final test is quietly but relentlessly forced upon him, to see whether Quartermaine keeps his form . . . or loses it. . . .

In [the play] there is an episode about a swan which some people have found baffling. Melanie Garth is instructing her foreign pupils in the arts of baking a swan pie or some such thing. Some time later the police call on her. The audience immediately thinks that it is because of suspicious circumstances about the death of her mother. But the audience is wrong. What has happened is that some of her pupils have absorbed her lessons too heartily, and have actually attacked a swan. They have come off second best, for the swan is a very dangerous bird, and can inflict very serious injury. The incident is smoothed over, but it leaves echoes behind it. The swan, besides being well able to take care of itself, is a singularly queenly and majestic bird. Undisturbed, it sails serenely on the quiet waters. . . . It is obviously of a class quite unlike the class of other birds. So, it is obvious at a glance, that Quartermaine is of a different social class from that of his colleagues; moreover, he takes a very deep interest in the story of the swan. It may be that Mr Gray sees some analogy between the swan and him. Perhaps Quartermaine is not as feeble as he appears to be. Perhaps his defeat at the end is not really the end. Perhaps he has reserves and resources such as we should never suspect a swan of having as the noble creature glides smoothly down the river. I do not know. But the episode of the swan certainly means something, and it may mean *that*.

With the swan there enters into *Quartermaine's Terms* an element of fear. That element of fear seems to me now to be entering into some of our most notable and advanced men of the theatre. (p. 17)

Harold Hobson, in a review of "Quartermaine's Terms," in Drama, *No. 142, Winter, 1981, pp. 16-17.*

BENEDICT NIGHTINGALE

It can't be comfortable living in a Simon Gray play. If your old mum isn't driving you to the brink of murder with her demands and ugly accusations, your spouse is leaving you or two-timing you or in some subtler way alienating your affections; if he or she is relatively quiescent, your favourite child is liable to be going mad; and yet the worst thing, the most dangerous to your health and happiness, may be to disengage from the disasters around you. The choice, roughly speaking, is between being continually mauled and gnawed at by the other would-be cannibals in the human zoo, or dying of thirst in the aridity beyond. If I were an inhabitant of *Quartermaine's Terms*, which contains all this and then some, I think I'd apply for an exit permit to Bond, Brenton or somewhere else less emotionally gruelling.

It is set in a Cambridge language school, itself an obvious enough pointer that noncommunication is to be one of the play's prime concerns. The place is run by a pair of elderly homosexuals whose mutual devotion and somewhat eccentric benignity to their underlings may themselves constitute a comment on the heterosexual twistings and writhings around them. And there in the staff-room, usually slumped in the same armchair, central yet tangential, is St John Quartermaine, the latest and, on the face of it, the nicest of Gray's continuing studies of the pathology of detachment, nonparticipation. When people need a babysitter or an uncontroversial guest at a sticky dinner party, it's to him they turn; the rest of the time he's left to fester in his bachelor digs, wondering how he'll get through the weekend or, worse, the vacation.

But Gray, as his name proclaims, isn't interested in moral blacks and whites. It wasn't his object to condemn the malicious Butley, or the seemingly icy and impervious protagonist of *Otherwise Engaged*, or even Jameson in *The Rear Column*, who organised a jungle beanfeast in order to do a drawing of the food, a young girl; and, conversely, he hasn't now concocted a glib tale of exploiters and their hapless victim. Quartermaine's fate, which by the end is pretty grim, is Quartermaine's fault or at least that of whatever gods send into the world emotionally tone-deaf people like him. He wants and tries to hear the tunes around him, but somehow can't register them. He asks solicitous questions, and says extravagantly warm things, and would conceivably even lay down his life for his supposed chums, yet he has only the most speculative sense of who, what and why they actually are. The impression he gives is of a tremendously enthusiastic explorer who has ventured into the rain-forest without compass, binoculars or, it sometimes seems, so much as white stick to help him tap his way round the trees.

After Gray's recent *Close of Play*, so relentless and over-emphatic a chronicle of disintegrating relationships, this is a refreshingly sensitive, observant piece; autumnal in mood, maybe, but with an unseasonably bracing nip in the air. The reference to *Uncle Vanya* at the local theatre—Quartermaine buys tickets which his self-absorbed colleagues neglect to use—is neither accidental nor, I think, unearned. Chekhov might have found more to say, or imply, about Quartermaine's background, past and residual passions; but, as a lover of both paradox and balance, he would not have disowned Gray's sympathetic but unsentimental sketch of someone there yet not there, a sort of absent presence or solid vacuum. . . . (p. 23)

> *Benedict Nightingale, "A Spare Man," in* New Statesman, *Vol. 102, No. 2629, August 7, 1981, pp. 23-4.**

JOHN RUSSELL TAYLOR

[Gray] started as very much a camp-follower (so to say) of Orton—to such an extent that *Wise Child* . . . and *Dutch Uncle* . . . seemed more like pastiches of Orton than anything else. *Spoiled*, a sober and rather dull play about a repressed schoolmaster discovering his own homosexuality, indicated that there were other sides to Gray, and incidentally introduced what were to prove the obsessive themes of his later drama, in various proportions from play to play: homosexuality and teaching.

It all came together, definitively, in *Butley*, which was and remains to date Gray's most successful play. . . . [For] once all Gray's talents were satisfactorily combined: his gift for depicting highly literate characters as though this is their normal habit of mind, rather than a few trappings assumed like a buskin or a crinoline for the occasion; his ingenuity in old-fashioned dramatic construction; his sensitivity to the unease of sexual borderlines as a motivating factor in life (is Butley, for instance, really attracted to the gay ex-assistant he superficially bitches and spurns?). Similar ingredients are brought together with slightly less effect in *Otherwise Engaged*, which seems almost like a sequel to *Butley*, though no characters are nominally carried over. . . .

[With] *Stage Struck*, Gray turned . . . towards Shaffer country (Anthony rather than Peter) with a *Sleuth*-type thriller of disguise and double bluff which worked well enough, even though it did seem like rather a waste of energy for so many high-powered talents. *Close of Play*, on the other hand, . . . did make one wonder whether that kind of respect was what Gray had always craved: the play (teaching again) was as solemn and slow and boring and obscurely symbolic as one could wish in order to make an intellectual splash. Though it did not succeed in this purpose (if indeed that was the purpose), at least it seemed a good thing for Gray to have got out of his system.

The latest, *Quartermaine's Terms*, suggests that it is not quite out yet. Again the background is teaching, this time in a Cambridge school for foreign English-language students, and again, through all kinds of hints dropped about the co-principal we do see and his partner whom we don't, the subject of homosexuality is hovering there. But though the play is very respectable and not actually boring, Gray seems to be holding his characters at a distance, filling out the picturesque details of their mostly horrible out-of-school lives with great ingenuity

but never actually persuading us to believe, much less to care. And his hero—title character, anyway—is . . . a quintessence even of nothingness who lives in a perpetual stupor. . . . Gray is undoubtedly a very clever playwright; but he does not always manage to do anything very interesting with his cleverness. Perhaps his plays need more heart: for one feels he has one, but fears to let it loose. Perhaps one day the order of release will come; until then he is likely to remain an accomplished entertainer who never cuts deep. (p. 15)

> *John Russell Taylor, "Tomorrow's Elder Statesmen?" in* Plays & Players, *No. 337, October, 1981, pp. 11-15.**

JOHN SIMON

[*Quartermaine's Terms* is] a wonderfully restrained, irreverently humane, wryly tender play. A mixture of wild but muted humor and wrenching but comedically muted pain, it is the kind of work that, if only there were more of its kind, could help the commercial theater out of its present slump. Gray can reconcile the needs of large, uncerebral audiences with the requirements of a discriminating, even finicky, enclave of selective theatergoers. Just as the play keeps us suspended between laughter and melancholy, so does it meld primal (almost primitive) emotions with fastidious speculations about the compromises, contradictions, numbing paradoxes of existence, and allows each spectator to enjoy the show according to his intellectual means. (p. 69)

Gray's fineness is encapsulated in the play's very title. Quartermaine gets his name—not entirely ironically—from both the desert saint and Rider Haggard's explorer hero; he is followed through five or six terms of teaching, including the term, or termination, of his career. But we are also offered his character in terms of his *terms*: his language, with its insipidly jovial banalities, and his stipulations vis-à-vis the world—his trading of empathy and obligingness for general forbearance, his gratitude for the space of one staff-room armchair in which to luxuriate in life's meager handouts. . . .

Fairest to our hero is Eddie Loomis, who, with his lover, . . . runs the school as a reasonably enlightened fief, balancing despotism with exasperated tolerance for Quartermaine—unlike the seemingly sympathetic colleague, Windscape, who, upon succeeding Eddie as headmaster, begins by having St. John's head. Eddie is, by the way, a most compassionate treatment of an aging, fussy homosexual; but Gray brings like comprehension to all his characters, and the funny-sad ironies in which they are mired. . . .

[If] Gray's understatedly heartbreaking ending does not get you where you live, either you or I don't know what theater—and art—is. (p. 70)

> *John Simon, "Halting Hare, Galloping Gray," in* New York Magazine, *Vol. 16, No. 4, January 24, 1983, pp. 69-70.**

DON NELSEN

The final moments of Simon Gray's **"Quartermaine's Terms"** are remarkably moving. A man stands alone, defeated. Were he a heroic figure, we might say: "Well, he had his innings." But Quartermaine, a teacher in a British school for foreigners, is an ineffectual though well-meaning nonentity. Of him we must say: "My God, could not his fellows have treated the poor soul kindlier?"

Quartermaine looks at the empty armchair in the faculty room he has sat in for years and murmurs a soft, heart-stabbing "Oh, lord!" At that moment, he could be the stand-in for legions of toilers who have been sacked after what they regard as years of faithful service. No matter that he has been incompetent; the point is that he was made to *feel* a member of a family and used as such by the very people who will fire and abandon him. That is betrayal, and as such plucks a universal string.

If more of the scenes in **"Quartermaine"** approached this intensity, the comedy-drama would grip the nerves oftener than it does.... The central character, Quartermaine, is not only a cipher but an enigma that no one, even the author, cares to solve, though some may find him the sole truly interesting character. For example, he is the only one of the pack of ineffectuals who has learned to live on his own terms; the others, despite their patronizing attitudes toward him, are pathetically dependent on someone or something else....

[The] characters are funny, unintentionally for the most part, their problems are real enough, and when Heald accuses the hapless Quartermaine of standing in the way of his promotion, the scene crackles with welcome action.

Yet the whole look and feel of the play is artificial. It is too much of a slow academic study....

Charming? Of course, but there are points at which charm loses its hold. What Gray has drawn here is a miniature and though every line is true, it does not repay constant attention. Some of the characters—the headmaster, the failed novelist—are stock....

There is no doubt that the second act grasps the attention much more tightly than the first.... **"Quartermaine"** is a good, if often wearing, picture of a certain slice of humanity. And, oh lord, those last few moments.

> *Don Nelsen, "'Quartermaine's Terms': A Man's Betrayal,"* in Daily News, *New York, February 25, 1983. Reprinted in* New York Theatre Critics' Reviews, *Vol. XXXXIV, No. 6, April 18-April 24, 1983, p. 295.*

FRANK RICH

At one point in Simon Gray's **"Quartermaine's Terms,"** a woman passes up an invitation to see "The Cherry Orchard," explaining that she's never found the comedy within all the "doom and gloom" of Chekhov's play. Chances are that this character wouldn't much like **"Quartermaine's Terms,"** either—but most every other theatergoer will.... [Gray] has written a play that is at once full of doom and gloom and bristling with wry, even uproarious comedy. The mixture is so artfully balanced that we really don't know where the laughter ends and the tears begin: the playwright is in full possession of that Chekhovian territory where the tragedies and absurdities of life become one and the same.

"Quartermaine's Terms" is not "The Cherry Orchard"—it's a small, delicate, chamber work set in an English school's staff room—but Mr. Gray increasingly looks like a master....

The school where the play unfolds is a dingy but homey looking place, situated in Cambridge, where foreigners are instructed in English. We never meet its students; the play focuses on six teachers and their boss, Eddie . . . , who runs the school in partnership with his offstage homosexual lover. Eddie is fond of referring to his faculty as "members of a family," and so they are. While all the teachers except one have families of their own at home, it is the surrogate, tight-knit family of their workplace to which the characters retreat when life outside gets too tough.

During the three years over which the play takes place in the early 1960's, life is rude indeed. The teachers suffer crushed career hopes, marital woes, and the deaths and breakdowns of loved ones. Among Mr. Gray's remarkable talents is his ability to bring these events alive even though they take place, in the Chekhovian manner, in the wings. Richly drawn as the play's seven visible characters are, we also come to know a whole gallery of unseen others, ranging from the evangelical nurse of one teacher's infirmed mother to another teacher's philandering spouse to some Japanese students fond of running amok in Cambridge's foremost French restaurant.

The most tragic onstage character is the one who has no life outside the staff room—St. John Quartermaine.... Quartermaine, a bachelor, has been with the school since its start, and, with his tall posture, cheery disposition and unfailing good manners, he epitomizes the well-bred English gentleman. But Quartermaine is all manners and no substance: he is an anachronism carried through life by sheer inertia and by the cozy, quintessentially paternalistic institution that employs him....

When the world does at last impinge on Quartermaine—inevitably and cruelly—he conveys the heartbreak with a single, politely spoken phrase and a smiling but ever-so-terrified glance into the abyss. It's the perfect climax for a play that finds its most affecting drama in the unsaid and the unseen....

What binds all [the] characters to both one another and to us is the universality of their struggle. Maybe they're all losers—"Teaching foreigners is a job for failures," we're told—but they are mostly intelligent, well-meaning people, hungering only for love and fellowship in an ever narrowing modern world. To a certain extent, the subject of **"Quartermaine's Terms,"** as of most English plays these days, is the decline of "British life and institutions." But the brave little lives that Mr. Gray so compassionately illuminates could be lived by any of us, and that's why they arouse emotions that are anything but small.

> *Frank Rich, "Simon Gray's 'Quartermaine's Terms'," in* The New York Times, *February 25, 1983, p. C3.*

WALTER KERR

On my terms, **"Quartermaine's Terms"** is at its best when [Quartermaine] is pretending to belong to a community he knows he cannot enter. He may seem a shade forlorn now and again if he thinks no one is looking: when he is scraping the back of his mailbox in search of messages that will never be there; when, halfway through a sentence, he realizes that he is heading for a phrase that will weary or offend his listeners and manages to clamp the brakes on his vocal cords while still mouthing the unsounded words. But I admired the [character] most after he'd suggested a game of croquet and been sluffed off with a cheery, insincere promise of a match sometime next week. Instantly agreeing, [Quartermaine]—already turning to depart—pauses to put up what might be a scolding index finger and call out "I'll hold you to that!"

The short conventional reply is almost overloaded with meanings. People have promised him games before and never delivered. But [Quartermaine] cannot be bitter or seem to acknowledge the fact. To keep on a good-fellow basis, he must use the genial threat that the best of friends *do* use when they play together all the time and can therefore afford to indulge in bantering recriminations. He knows the sound of that sort of thing, and apes it perfectly. He will ape it again when he is similarly dismissed next week....

Otherwise he is sometimes asked to leave the commonroom so that two colleagues can speak in private; he does so willingly, briskly. He is occasionally asked to babysit for one or another faculty couple, though not all that often (he recently found one of his charges a charming child, "once she'd got used to me again"). He is a thoroughgoing loner, a true isolate. What Mr. Gray's other heroes are looking for, he has got. He's not happy with it, though. However clearly he understands that he is somehow enshrouded in a cocoon not of his own making, he is everlastingly making the gestures that will help him to break out of it.

It is right here that **"Quartermaine's Terms"** turns into a problem rather than a play for me. It is extremely difficult to know, on the face of things, just what author Gray wants or expects our response in the theater to be. Are we to feel a rueful sympathy, even a deep pity, for this misfit because he cannot insert himself into the stream of life flowing about him? If so, why are all of the staff members who *are* immersed in that stream of life—the men and women who teach English to foreigners at a Cambridge school—presented as misfits as well? The community [Quartermaine] wishes to become part of turns out to be as miserable a group of losers as mortal man might wish to contemplate. (p. 3)

I think that everyone except Quartermaine cries at some time before the evening is done, and if we were ever intended to root for—or even secretly wish for—Quartermaine's admission to this society, the plan misfires. The one message we have for Quartermaine after we've listened to his colleagues recount their troubles, is this: Stay out of it, boy, you're well off.

Perhaps we're not expected to feel for Quartermaine in his failure to penetrate "real life." Perhaps it's simply his oddity, or his complexity, as a character that's meant to pique and prolong our interest. Are we conceivably meant to admire him? Once again, it's virtually impossible to say.... [The] last few moments strike me as flattest of all. Quartermaine is summarily fired. We've understood all along that he's not much of a teacher; he, of course, has understood it, too. But he accepts the news with the same matter-of-fact assent that has marked every stage of rejection earlier. He seems to agree that he *should* be dismissed, and the quicker the better. The man is simply unmoved, incapable of actual hurt, stone. It is one thing to be reasonably genial about someone's refusal to share a meal or a bit of Chekhov with him, and quite another to accept with equanimity the instant wipeout of his career, his place in the world, his very identity. The ambiguous "Oh, lord" that he mutters before the last lights fade doesn't take us into the man's mind. It merely sounds as though he'd been remotely disturbed by a newspaper account of disaster in a faraway country. Nor does the fact that he doesn't betray hurt or even seem to feel injury make him more interesting. It merely makes him less than human. (pp. 3, 7)

I confess to a considerable uneasiness as to just how funny some of the evening's detail is meant to be. Do the massive plasters and the head brace that turn up on our part-timer constitute caricature or not? When, in the evening's next-to-last scene, Quartermaine is suddenly deluged with *four* invitations to dinner on the very same night, is this sudden reversal of his fortunes, this thumping irony, a lapse into Feydeau farce or a reach for Anouilh-like artifice? Or what? It's plainly the implausible maneuver of a geometrically minded playwright, but how should the performers slant it? Toward broad comedy and all the laughs they can get? Toward a cool stylization that exaggerates but doesn't try too hard to be funny? Or do the performers struggle to play dead straight, ignoring the contrivance that has created so unlikely a coincidence? Mr. Gray is a writer who can, even at his most malicious, be wonderfully funny. Here he is *sort* of funny, some of the time; the uncertainty, the irregularity of tone, makes us nervous about laughing. In fact, it makes us nervous overall.

Knowing that Quartermaine has a habit of dozing off without notice, we aren't surprised to find him in an armchair at the beginning of one scene, lost to the world and curled up in what are the beginnings of a fetal position. We can more or less recognize this fellow, more or less believe in him. But we simply cannot form a notion of what may have happened to bring him to this pass. Was it just genetic bad luck? Neither can we imagine what might be right for him if he could only take the proper steps to arrive at it. In a phrase of the day, he is "out of it." Equally, we are out of his play. **"Quartermaine's Terms"** is a highly schematic piece of work that . . . seems to have adopted the wrong scheme. (p. 7)

> *Walter Kerr, "How Can We Admire a Less Than Human Hero?"* in The New York Times, *Section II, March 6, 1983, pp. 3, 7.*

NASEEM KHAN

The protagonists of *The Common Pursuit* are, when we first meet them, undergraduate friends at Cambridge. For this is that trusty formula—the *sic transit gloria* play. All five men are convinced that the world will prove their oyster. (The one woman has less extreme aspirations, but then women are somewhat ancillary in this world of male-bonding.) Stuart . . . will run his literary magazine. Martin . . . will run the business side. Humphry . . . will be a great philosopher and Nick . . . will conquer the media.

As time moves on and distances them from those golden Sixties days, their dreams become tarnished. Of course they achieve worldly prosperity—none of them starves, though the magazine is clearly rather slim. But Stuart's marriage is barren and he loses his wife. Clever Peter . . . spends all his energies in furtive affairs. And Humphry, supposedly the best of them all, chooses death at the hands of a rough-trade pick-up.

Harold Pinter's direction brings out a fair amount of shading in the text, but it still cannot give it the significance at which the piece aims. There is no getting away from the fact that we are expected to believe in the specialness of a group of people who seem to have nothing but a certain glib and mannered wit to recommend them.

Naseem Khan, "Modern Manners," in New Statesman, *Vol. 108, No. 2782, July 13, 1984, p. 34.**

GILES GORDON

The success of Simon Gray is one of the oddest phenomena
in contemporary British theatre. . . . *The Common Pursuit* is a
self-satisfied, verbally slack, intellectually vapid piece. . . . The
first scene shows six undergraduates at Trinity College, Cambridge in 1964 discussing the setting up of a literary magazine.
The remainder of the play shows how in the next 15 years their
trivial careers in publishing and academe succeed, or don't.
Selfishness and disillusionment are almost eulogised. There's
a spot of homosexuality, and a token woman. I think she's
made pregnant by two men but maybe it wasn't her husband
who impregnated her first time round. Anyway, she aborted,
because she thought hubby was more in love with his magazine
than with the idea of having a baby. . . . Harold Pinter directs.
I wish he hadn't because his concern to shape this trivia into
something of substance simply underlines the play's intrinsic
superficiality. (p. 33)

Giles Gordon, "Person to Person," in The Spectator, *Vol. 253, No. 8140, July 14, 1984, pp. 33-4.**

JACK KROLL

Simon Gray's plays—**"Butley," "Otherwise Engaged,"
"Quartermaine's Terms"**—seem to rebuke playwrights who
go whoring after strange avant-gods and trendy trickery. Gray
is practically the last master of the well-made play, a craftsman
who actually enjoys working with plot, characterization and
other largely despised elements of tradition. **"The Common
Pursuit"** finds Gray's tools sharp and polished as ever. In it
he follows six figures from that other largely despised realm,
the humanities, from their idealistic hopes as Cambridge undergraduates to the flickering embers of their burned-out middle
age. Stuart, the little-magazine editor; Humphry, the homosexual poet-philosopher; Martin, the practical publisher; Peter,
the lecherous historian; Nick, the wise guy, and Marigold,
their muse, are a microcosm of the world of liberal culture that
may be on the verge of extinction. Gray contemplates this
prospect with his seductive blend of melancholy and ironic
wit. . . .

Jack Kroll, "Six Refugees from a Lost World," in
Newsweek, *Vol. CV, No. 6, February 11, 1985, p.
63.*

Ralph (Barker) Gustafson

1909-

Canadian poet, short story writer, editor, and critic.

Gustafson is one of Canada's most accomplished and respected contemporary poets. His verse style ranges from the traditional to the modern and is noted for its technical craftsmanship. Gustafson's poetry reflects a strong literary heritage; as Robin Skelton observed, "The wit, sophistication, and mannered vigour of Ralph Gustafson's poetry, together with its sensual exuberance and its intellectual strength, establishes him as belonging to that race of writers who, over the centuries, have believed that poetry is made both by and for the full mind." Gustafson's poems explore the paradoxes inherent in life, art, and nature, reflecting his extensive knowledge of many subjects, particularly music. One of Gustafson's major themes is the conflict between the modern and the traditional; the struggle to affirm life in a mechanized and sometimes violent world is often the subject of his work.

Gustafson began publishing poetry in the mid-1930s; his first work to receive significant notice was *Flight into Darkness* (1944). Although his early verse has been faulted as overly mannered and imitative, Gustafson's next two collections, *Rivers among Rocks* (1960) and *Rocky Mountain Poems* (1960), reveal a more individual voice and a growing interest in concerns relevant to the modern world. Nature and the Canadian experience figure prominently in these collections, while *Sift in an Hourglass* (1966) and *Soviet Poems* (1978) reflect Gustafson's cosmopolitan travels. The poems in *Theme and Variations for Sounding Brass* (1972), Gustafson's most politically oriented collection, angrily ruminate on the violence which often accompanies contemporary politics. Among Gustafson's more recent volumes are *Conflicts of Spring* (1981), *Gradations of Grandeur* (1982), and *Selected Poems* (1983).

Gustafson has received several awards for his writing, including the Governor General's Award for poetry in 1974 for *Fire on Stone,* and he has edited several important anthologies of Canadian poems and stories. Despite these achievements, however, some critics contend that Gustafson has not gained the widespread recognition his works deserve. This perhaps can be attributed to Gustafson's use of unorthodox syntax, archaic words and phrases, and elaborate metaphors which force a studious reading of his poems. Nevertheless, Gustafson is regarded by many scholars as a witty, passionate, and erudite poet who has made a significant contribution to Canadian literature.

(See also *Contemporary Authors,* Vols. 21-24, rev. ed. and *Contemporary Authors New Revision Series,* Vol. 8.)

Courtesy of Ralph Gustafson

F. CUDWORTH FLINT

Mr. Gustafson seems to me . . . authentically a poet to the vocation born. I find him in his most successful efforts [hard] . . . to understand; but what I do understand of his meaning convinces me that the obscurity arises from the presence in his poems of linkages of thought and emotion which have as yet not quite come over the horizon of my mind. . . . In general I like his clearest poems least; and I find a steady rise in quality in reading back from the latter end of ["**Flight Into Darkness**"] to its beginning.

The fourth group of poems, "Of Places and Sarcasm," seems to me not particularly distinguished; and several of the sarcastic poems seem to me to lack an essential of sarcasm: agility. Better are the preceding twelve brief "Lyrics Unromantic," in which Mr. Gustafson seems to be trying to convey praise of the unwordable through ingenious wordings of the fact of unwordability. . . .

Still better are some of the poems in the second section, "Sequence to War." . . .

But a far richer poetic art is manifest in some of the seven poems of the untitled opening section—notably in the title-poem, "**Flight Into Darkness**," and in "**Mythos**" and "**Denial**." And their value lies not aside from but directly in their ambiguities. . . .

[Throughout] his best poems the fascination of their content depends upon the controlled clash and resolution of . . . inter-relevant possibilities. The future of this Canadian poet should be well worth watching.

F. Cudworth Flint, in a review of "Flight Into Darkness," in The New York Times Book Review, *February 25, 1945, p. 10.*

MIRIAM WADDINGTON

Gustafson is elegant, literary and exquisitely devoted to detail. His kind of poetic awareness cannot be separated from education and culture. It is also the product of serene periods of leisure and reflection. In this sense it is social poetry, but very much tied to the kind of public life in which only a few people can participate.

It is hard to imagine how and what Gustafson would write without the influence of concerts, books, paintings, travel and the mediation of his lively and interesting mind. (p. 70)

When Gustafson drops his role as a travel photographer (as in the Preludes [in *Rivers among Rocks*]), or concert-goer, or art gallery viewer, or Japanese flower arranger—as in the short poems, **"Quebec Night"** and **"The Blue Lake"**, and becomes most himself, he is verbally astringent, intellectually passionate, emotionally tender, and burns with a cool steady glow. . . .

On the personal side, Gustafson's several love poems with their down-drawing rhythms mark a new richness and expansion in his feeling. In **"The Little Elderly Lady Visits"** he has written a poem so light, so charming, and so complete that it will inevitably be anthologized. But it is impossible to do justice to any poet in so brief a review—especially to one who is as complex and subtle and technically accomplished as Gustafson. (p. 71)

Miriam Waddington, "Japanese Flowers, Autumn Vistas," in Canadian Literature, *No. 9, Summer, 1961, pp. 70-2.**

ALDEN A. NOWLAN

Basically, [Ralph Gustafson's *Rocky Mountain Poems*] are the impressionistic monologues of a sensitive and intelligent man who happened to be concerned with mountains at the time that he wrote them. The Rocky Mountains are not central here, despite the foreword which claims this is the first book 'substantially to put the Rocky Mountains into the geography of Canadian poetry'. Mr. Gustafson himself is more modest. The Rocky Mountains provide the background but their presence seems almost incidental.

In short, sometimes jerky lines, Mr. Gustafson is spare, ironic, witty. Frequently he laments the difficulty of turning experience into words. What can one do, really, except make a wild flower into a string of syllables? 'A list always,' he writes aptly, 'poor kickbacks in poems.'

These are good poems. . . . One only wishes that Mr. Gustafson wrote with more passion and less modesty. (p. 56)

Alden A. Nowlan, "Three Books Worth Reading," in The Fiddlehead, *No. 49, Summer, 1961, pp. 55-7.**

MILTON WILSON

Frank Newfeld's design for [*Rivers Among Rocks*] is almost as engaging as the poems themselves, particularly the wonderful set of superimposed and mutually transparent pages, whose arcs and solids lead the reader gradually into the titular images of Mr. Gustafson's poetic world. Not that the fluid element is literally everywhere in **Rivers Among Rocks**. But, whether we are exposed to a scatter of gold or a drench of blue and green, or simply to the staccato energy of Mr. Gustafson's mind, the material remains fluctuating and metamorphic, the language full of spurt and spray. His mannerisms may remind us of

Hopkins, but the spring of his rhythm is a good deal lighter and more elastic. (p. 390)

Mr. Gustafson is a good poet and he offers the reader a genuine delight. At the same time, there is something minimal about his material and rootless about his style. Whatever his insistence that the flesh makes the word, his poetry often remains "a rhetoric in the mind," and his insistent naturalism seems more rarefied than prolific. Vitality is kept up as a virtue of style, or as an attitude toward life, or as the subject of a poem, but it rarely gets beyond gesture and idiom. And the frequent grammatical obscurity is not justified by complexity or vigour of thought. Such a sentence as "Appointment scrambles waste youth or older thought was not a rubbish," with its nouns that might be adjectives, verbs that might be subjects, objects that might be subjects, and so on, is really confusion claiming the rewards of energy, although the reader soon learns to unscramble the confusion. Still, even if **Rivers Among Rocks** promises more than it gives, there is nothing pretentious or disingenuous about the promise. The limitations remain those of a very fresh and engaging book. (pp. 392-93)

Milton Wilson, in a review of "Rocky Mountain Poems" and "Rivers among Rocks," in University of Toronto Quarterly, *Vol. XXX, No. 4, July, 1961, pp. 390-93.*

ROBIN SKELTON

Ralph Gustafson [in *Sift in an Hourglass*] is, like Webster, "much possessed by death", and when he sees the "skull beneath the skin" he expresses the vision with Jacobean density and Browningesque gusto. Thus his work has, from time to time, a deliberately idiosyncratic anti-modernity. . . . It is not only the odd diction, the inclusion of such obsolete or near-obsolete words as "pelf", "fesses" 'Bubs' ''clomb" and such contractions as "I'the coffin" but also the combination of staccato effects and rhetorical questions which give the verse its character. (p. 85)

Gustafson employs pastiche, puns, parody, with a dexterity that is often breathtaking.

This does sometimes result in works which amount to literary games, but the games Gustafson plays have the urgency and point of ritual, and enable him, in a voice magnified by the masks he wears, to express certainties and paradoxes which overarch the centuries. . . . The criticism was made of Milton, as it could also have been made of Browning and Dylan Thomas, that he "writ no language", and Gustafson could be similarly accused. Frequently one feels as if the whole grotesque, exuberant, dramatic, vivid, cluttered, poetic world belongs to some nowhere land. Nevertheless, this news from nowhere is always entertaining and sometimes disturbingly relevant. We have few whole-hogging rhetoricians these days, and, of recent years, only Djuna Barnes in her somewhat tiresome *The Antiphon* has attempted the Jacobean mode. **Sift in an Hourglass** is better than *The Antiphon,* though just as tricksy. It does, in its outlook, share some of the bizarre and vigorous quality of a number of younger British poets, and reminds me, in its wit and texture, of early Lowell and Berryman. However one tries to place it, however, it refuses to be killed by qualification. Exuberance, vigour, passion remain. This could be, in its violent opposition to current fashion, an influential and valuable collection. (pp. 85-6)

Robin Skelton, "Possessed by Death," in Canadian Literature, *No. 33, Summer, 1967, pp. 85-6.*

JAMES GRAY

Sift in an Hourglass, which takes its title from two lines of a poem by Gerard Manley Hopkins, is the most versatile and wide-ranging of [Ralph Gustafson's] collections of poetry to date. It contains pieces mildly satirical and others passionately lyrical; majestic poems and three-line epigrams; eulogies and elegies and thumb-nail sketches; reflections, descriptions, love poems, wistful poems, ecstatic poems, and sombre poems. The leap from delight to death, from the mellifluous to the macabre, is apparently an easy one for this erudite Romantic, who can transform his experiences of travel, art, sculpture, love and music into fascinating mosaics of word and phrase.

The fifty-seven poems in this collection are indeed fifty-seven varieties. But they are bonded by verbal and imaginative richness; by a tightness of texture, a graphic compression that superficially suggests a blend of Hopkins and Browning, yet, on closer inspection, proves unmistakably Gustafsonian; and by an eager lust for life in all its balancing opposites: natural and artistic, sensuous and intellectual, primitive and sophisticated, humorous and grim, vital and morbid. The verbal tapestries woven by this poet are so detailed that we are forced to look again and again for the communicating thread, but the search is invariably worthwhile.

Among the things we find is a veritable gallimaufry of literary influences. In addition to Hopkinsian inscapes and Browning-esque snatches of monologue, we discover Pound-like images, hard as diamonds, Eliotic labyrinths of allusion, Yeatsian reminiscence and whimsicality, and even shards of Shakespeare worked into the fabric. The poet's enviable knowledge of the work of his British, American and Canadian contemporaries also serves to enrich the eclecticism of his writing. There is, moreover, a part-studied, part-inherited Scandinavian strain, noticeable in his fondness for alliterative arrangements and crisp consonantal articulation. (pp. 346-47)

Whether etching the personalities of the living or inscribing memorials to the dead, whether sharing with us the fruits of his intensely lived experiences or recording intimate fragments of his private thoughts and conversations, Ralph Gustafson impresses us with his rare sensitivity to both the great and the little things of life, and with his quick apprehension and ready sympathy. There is nothing brutal or dark or cynical about him. He is indeed a part of all that he has met, but the kindliness and warmth of his temper exclude the frozen and the bitter from his world. The sift that remains in his hourglass has the softness of dusty gold. (p. 347)

> *James Gray, in a review of "Sift in an Hourglass," in* Queen's Quarterly, *Vol. LXXIV, No. 2, Summer, 1967, pp. 346-47.*

DESMOND PACEY

Almost half of Ralph Gustafson's new book [*Ixion's Wheel*] consists of a reprinting in slightly revised form of poems contained in *Rocky Mountain Poems* and *Sift in an Hourglass.* The rationale of this somewhat dubious procedure is, presumably, that the poems selected from the two earlier volumes are, like the new poems, poems of travel.... At the end of the book are three pages of "Notes," and these notes, in their witty irreverence and exuberant fun, are among the best things in it. The whole makes a delightful, if occasionally irritating ensemble, distinguished as is all of Gustafson's work by an irrepressible *joie de vivre*, a boyish zest which age shows no sign

of withering. Gustafson combines accurate observation of the immediately present scene with quite dazzling erudition in mythology, cultural history, and aesthetics, but he wears his learning lightly and is frequently ironic at his own expense. He responds with equal intensity to the beauty of nature and the beauty of *objets d'art*, to beauty in its more abstract manifestations (order, design, symmetry) and in its more concrete embodiments (colour, taste, touch, smell and sound). He is one of the most sensuous of Canadian poets, fond of vivid colours such as gold ..., green, scarlet and crimson, and of rich tastes such as that of wild strawberries.... On the other hand, he delights in formal elegance, in the classical symmetries of traditional culture.... (pp. 80-1)

Gustafson's faults are a tendency to get carried away by his own ingenuity either of idea or technique—as, for example, in **"Couperin-Le-Grand in Turkey"**—and a liability to lapse into an impenetrable obliquity, as if what he was putting on the paper were the enigmatic notes for a poem rather than the poem itself. At his best, however, he gives us immense pleasure by his excited sensuousness, his irreverent flights of wit or fantasy, his ironic ambiguity, and his quenchless vitality. (p. 81)

> *Desmond Pacey, "A Canadian Quintet," in* The Fiddlehead, *No. 83, January-February, 1970, pp. 79-86.**

M. TRAVIS LANE

Theme and Variations for Sounding Brass [is Gustafson's] poem sequence dedicated "to the victims" of political uncharity.... In this latest work, which is often beautiful and deeply moving, two doubts afflict the reader: the first, was not casting this dramatic and narrative material in a primarily lyric form a formal error? and, second, does not the choice of any poetic form conflict with one of the apparent purposes of the author in presenting the material, his desire to provoke corrected political action? For in this sequence Gustafson appears to have two separate subjects with very different structural demands, and I think this dividedness of purpose injures the strength of this important and ambitious work.

In *Theme and Variations for Sounding Brass* Gustafson has, as one of his subjects, the state of mind of the sensitive and educated man who feels an angry helplessness at the continuing news of injustice, injury and public evil. Gustafson's second subject, indicated in his choice of news incident, is the wilfulness, the lack of inevitability, the wrongness of the incidents chosen. None of these "victims" are Hardyesque victims of fate; all are victims of man. Nor are these victims of individualized murderers—all are victims of politics. To any thinking person there is no such thing as "mere politics"—"politics" are what we live and die by. But political ideas involve criticism, experimentation, and trial; the point is action. The sermon, the editorial, the political essay are not lyric forms; they look outward not inward.

However to agree that these evils are particularly odious because unnecessary we require more historical material, more factual material, more dramatic material than Gustafson presents, relying, as he does in this sequence, on our pre-agreement with him. We do agree with him, but not because of his poem, but because of what we have read elsewhere. From the point of view of drama or historical argument the "victims" of *Theme and Variations for Sounding Brass* are handled more like victims of accident than of Cain, a tendency increased by the sequence-focus upon the poetic-speaker, who is portrayed as at some distance from the incidents described, and who is responding, basically, to newspaper reportage and television. Furthermore the diversity of the material Gustafson includes as exempla in this sequence forbids the use of dramatic or narrative form; that there are "too many" victims is one of his points. In fact, I think Gustafson's humanitarian impulse leads away from poetry altogether, because the reformer's point can not be made within the heroic fatalism of poetic conventions. (pp. 109-10)

Gustafson's *Theme and Variations for Sounding Brass* is a distinguished failure. It fails because of the unreconciled difference between literature that stays us and literature that spurs us, the final distinction between that which is most poetry and that which is most prose. It is the distinction between art as conclusion and speech as persuasion to action. Of course the traditional answer to the dilemma is that the conventional poem, by conveying the sound of nobility, disposes the reader to act in possession of that nobility—that any assertion of good is an assertion towards good. It can also be argued that admitting injustice to be inevitable does not preclude the equal inevitabiltiy of man's struggle against it, that "victims" we have always with us, but never "too much" for compassion.

Gustafson's great poem "**The Exhortation**", from *Rivers Among Rocks*, in the *Selected Poems*, is a refutation of the conclusion of the political sequence, and a strong assertion of the quality of compassion that is needed, the compassion that roots itself not in an awareness of horror, but in an awareness of value, a compassion that expresses itself not in the prose of the newspapers but in the poetry of man. (p. 113)

Throughout Gustafson's work recur the major themes of morality, mortality, human behaviour, religion, and our soured philosophies. Thus Gustafson's level of failure in his weaker works, such as *Theme and Variations for Sounding Brass,* is still well above the minor successes of mini concerns. Gustafson is one of our best. Any poet who wishes to write major poetry should study his work; any reader who wants a poetry strong enough to express life as we feel it when we most feel should read Gustafson. (p. 114)

> *M. Travis Lane, "The Fundamental Question about Poetry," in* The Fiddlehead, *No. 96, Winter, 1973, pp. 106-14.*

CHRISTOPHER XERXES RINGROSE

[Reading through *Selected Poems*] makes one more than ever aware of Mr. Gustafson's recurrent themes, which were discernible in his poetry from the beginning: primarily his sense of the mysterious co-presence of life and death in the world, in the imagination, in art, an equipoise tilting delicately towards the grave. The poet who in 1944 spoke of "The apple twixt the tombstones of my teeth" notices in 1969 Shakespeare's monument marked with a skull, and remarks that "death's above / all of us". If the concern with death and dissolution is pervasive, so too is the interest in myth and history, especially the hinterland where the two combine, and the desire to see Agamemnon, or Icarus, or Joan of Arc, or the Pharoahs in the here and now, with what they stood for persisting into the present moment. (pp. 82-3)

It has to be said, though, that the further one pursues these themes, and the more poems one reads, the more tiresome Mr. Gustafson's verse can become. He is not a poet to read in any quantity, and one may on the face of it wonder why, for surely we have in him a resurrection of Metaphysical Wit—that se-

riousness without solemnity, a blending of passion, wit and erudition which modern orthodoxy presents as the highest mode to which we can aspire. But this sophistiction is embodied in a peculiar tone—a somewhat prissy, heavily mannered tone—which begins to grate on one. (p. 83)

This mannered tone tends in the poems of the fifties and sixties (and especially the more recent ones) to be linked to a mordant jocosity; in comparison the earlier poems from *Flight into Darkness* are more dense and intense, determinedly dislocated in their syntax, as in "**Lyric Sarcastic**" . . . . The somewhat shapeless accumulation of wit which forms this and other poems from *Flight into Darkness* ("**Biography**", "**Idyll for a Fool**", "**Ultimatum**", "**Flight into Darkness**") tends to give way later in his career to meditations sparked by specific places or incidents. . . . But the pitfall of this material is the obvious one: that Mr. Gustafson becomes our urbane and allusive tour guide, having interesting thoughts on everything from the Trevi fountain to mosaics in Istanbul, from the Vieux Marché at Rouen to Cairo Museum, Mount Revelstoke to Franz Liszt's grave, the fall of Icarus to Dachau seen from a train window.

The tone of the poetry is . . . distinctive, but one senses a degree of strain when it is asked to cope with, say, the elegy for "**S.S.R., Lost at Sea**" from *Flight into Darkness,* where the language seems too fussily self-conscious for the subject. I am not suggesting that the subject calls for the unleashing of the floodgates of grief, but here as elsewhere too much seems written with the eventual excavations of practical criticism in mind. . . . (pp. 83-5)

Which brings me to *Theme and Variations for Sounding Brass*, which, in view of my reaction to the *Selected Poems*, strikes me as the most interesting and difficult project Mr. Gustafson could have undertaken. The attempt to write poetry about the sufferings and violence of Bangladesh and Prague, America and Canada, is difficult enough by any standard, but for a poet of Mr. Gustafson's particular manner and characteristic approach the problems are very great. This is not to suggest that the writing of "social poetry" (if we must call it that) involves some spurious technique of impersonal reportage; Mr. Gustafson has rightly seen that it has in fact to keep before us the individual reacting mind. The poems in this booklet are full of indignation, but eventually they centre around the difficulty of responding humanely to what our cameramen bring us; they are also about the language we apply to violence, and about the moral obligation to be compassionate. But compassion before the bland eye of television can be an impertinence, and as Mr. Gustafson says in the last lines of his final poem, "The trouble is there is too / Much death for compassion". (p. 85)

To go on making careful poems in the face of it all is perhaps to hoist a drawbridge of aestheticism, and one senses that Mr. Gustafson is unsure whether to remain in control, or let go of his normal lapidary style in the interests of "sincerity". He can still be inappropriately fussy, annotating a pun on "mordent", but one hears something new in the indignation at the pious rhetoric of the Quebec revolutionaries:

> Murderers and advocates of murderers
> As innocents
> Attend the courts,
> Their innocence
> The virtuous mutilation
> The necessary brains
>   spilled on the ignorant street

While the booklet as a whole is perhaps something less than a success, it is a valiant attempt on difficult material; one's final impression is of a justifiable bewilderment before the awful facts. (pp. 85-6)

Christopher Xerxes Ringrose, "A Tilting Equipoise," in Canadian Literature, *No. 58, Autumn, 1973, pp. 82-6.*

M. TRAVIS LANE

Ralph Gustafson's *Fire on Stone* is not simply the latest sparks from an established poet; it is a major collection. With this book Gustafson joins Layton and Birney as one of Canada's best living poets—those who have produced the most of the best Canadian poetry.

When Gustafson first attracted notice thirty years ago, his work, then as now full of imitations, eloquent, and often deeply moving, still seemed to most readers overly imitative, lacking in individuality. Nowadays, when practically nobody attempts the difficult cadences of Stevens, Hopkins, or Donne, we can look back at the earlier generation when such imitation was in fashion and see more clearly than we did how unlike the general run of imitators was Gustafson, how much stronger his verse, how more profound his vision. Many of the poets who first pleased us with their originality have settled into imitating themselves, and they have their imitators. But Ralph Gustafson has been growing steadily more individual. He has developed an eloquence like no other's. . . . He knows all the sounds of the attitudes and neither bores nor fumbles. Any Gustafson poem is a lesson in sound.

In vocabulary as in rhythm, Gustafson combines a witty delicacy with a vigorous roughness, using harshness against smoothness, loudness against softness, and alternating speeds of voice, and punning when most serious. The sound of his poetry is of grief and joyfulness together, a sound which reflects his dominant theme: the dual nature of reality. For Gustafson, our mud reality is both sordid and sublime, our shabby divinity both transient and true, our Mercutios grave, and "Life / Itself's a low-down buried pun". (p. 106)

The double nature of reality is suggested in the title *Fire on Stone* and is celebrated or mourned throughout the book. However the primary reference of Gustafson's title is to unity, to the unity of a work of art, in this case Chartres cathedral. Gustafson compares the work of art to the work of love, where intuition becomes faith in the potential reality of the work (marriage) and where the actuality of the work (marriage) depends on our acting in this faith. (p. 107)

A need to express the equality of "grief" with "roses" is one of the distinguishing characteristics of Gustafson's work; it is a subject he has in common with two earlier poets, Robert Frost and Wallace Stevens. Unlike Robert Frost, whose similarly agnostic poetry also deals almost obsessively with the proportions of "brevities", Gustafson does not present us with a fortressed centre to these perceptions; his poet-speaker is not a pain-fearing sensibilitist hunched down away from the extremes of expression, hinting at the extremes of experience. Gustafson more loudly proclaims the polar realities; he fusses more; he is at once more morbid and more cheerful, less decorous and more extravagant, than the Thoreauvian Yankee. (p. 108)

Gustafson's baroque vocabulary gives his agnostic meditations a striking resemblance to Stevens' work, especially to "Sunday Morning" with its affirmation of mortal beauty as our only heaven. Like Stevens, Gustafson asserts the Appollonian values of Light, Beauty, Art, and Human Love against religious morbidity, beauty-hating asceticism, Spinozan gloom, or the unlikely mysteries of religious myth. **"Faith is a Concrete Object"** specifically rejects the ugliness of the "Christ-hung cross" and the "Shame in Eden". But Gustafson contemplates human unhappiness and human joy more personally than does Stevens. We encounter more physical sickness, more funerals, wars, skulls, and napalm in Gustafson. . . . The baroque horrors Gustafson rejects in art and in traditional Christian churches are there in his concrete world. But happiness is also physical, and, in Gustafson's work, domestic. (pp. 108-09)

Gustafson is something of a trinitarian; that is, he believes in the existence and holiness of three things: the Creator, Christ Jesus, and the Immanent Light (intuition). He does not write that they are one God. That which created the world, "Whose throw of glory / Drenched the elemental seed" (from **"Spring Night"**) is an indifferent God, not a "Dope benevolent", but an unhelpful and possibly helpless original impulse. (p. 109)

Gustafson may rebel against genuflecting to the author of misery, but he is not irreligious. His religion is the concrete faith of the gardener, not in myth, but in spring-time. In the garden, where the body of Christ is dust, is earth's perennial purity, the "usual" endures, the concrete resurrection. . . .

Gustafson writes about our knowledge of the grave and our choice to savour musk. The experience of this rich and musical verse is itself "musk"—light crystalline, stone fire, a concrete paradise. (p. 110)

M. Travis Lane, "The Concrete Paradise: The Major Theme of Ralph Gustafson's 'Fire on Stone'," in The Fiddlehead, *No. 104, Winter, 1975, pp. 106-10.*

ROBIN SKELTON

The appearance of Ralph Gustafson's new collection of poems, *Fire On Stone,* reminds one, yet again, that of all our established Canadian poets he is the most dazzlingly virtuoso. . . . (p. 167)

The wit, sophistication, and mannered vigour of Ralph Gustafson's poetry, together with its sensual exuberance and its intellectual strength, establishes him as belonging to that race of writers who, over the centuries, have believed that poetry is made both by and for the full mind. He must be rated, in this respect, as kin to Joyce, Pound and Stevens.

This is a burdensome lineage to inherit, and Gustafson's poetry is sometimes strained in its attempt to achieve the required intensity. Gustafson's language is deeply affected by his understanding and love of music. Indeed, he uses not one but many voices, and sometimes of different centuries, in the one poetic structure; he orchestrates in history, bringing in a twentieth century locution hard upon a seventeenth century gesture, playing a Shakespearean cadence into a tune of Gerard Manley Hopkins, mingling the instruments into orchestral unity. (p. 168)

Mortality has always been one of his central concerns, and it has usually been explored in lines of verse whose thrust and counter-thrust, whose broken urgencies and sudden assertive rhetorics express the passionate ambivalence of the poems' message. Over and over again the message contains a countermessage. (p. 169)

The ambivalence and ambiguity of Gustafson's poetry is not the product of uncertainty, but the consequence of his recognition that positive and negative are very often two halves of the whole. He is concerned to present truth. Indeed, the prefatory poem to his *Selected Poems* of 1972 opened with the statement, "Where a poem departs from the truth it is a bad / Poem." It is only by thrust and counter-thrust, by message and anti-message, that the poem can avoid departing from truth. . . . The poet is mediator. He is always in the middle. He is always exuberantly aware of the sensual universe, and equally "possessed by death." Over and over again, however, in *Fire On Stone,* the love of life is triumphant. . . . This affirmative note, this exultation in the essential solipsism of human experience, its truth being its own version of the "moment-when" reveals that *Fire On Stone,* mortality obsessed though it may be, is life-celebrating also. . . . The laughter in *Fire On Stone* has a quality of exuberance and of wisdom that is more than exhilarating. It is, one feels, much more than the jocularity of a wit, more than the delighted verbal clowning of a master of language. (pp. 170-71)

Fire On Stone is the book of a master. Its stylistic originality and vigour, its laughter and wisdom, and its extraordinary meditations and epiphanies make it one of the most entrancing books to have been published over the past decade. It would, however, be grossly unfair to Gustafson to regard this book as fully representative of his work, for Gustafson has always made it a practice to construct his books as wholes, and to order them into artistic unity. Thus he has not included the poems from his pamphlet *Theme and Variations for Sounding Brass* which was published in 1972, and readers of the jacket of the new book might well miss its existence. This would be a shame for it presents explicitly the passionate concern for human society which is only implied by the poems in *Fire On Stone.* (pp. 171-72)

[The poems in *Theme and Variations for Sounding Brass*] present another side of Gustafson. The compact, brusque, dense diction of most of the poems in *Fire On Stone* is not put to use, for these are poems to speak aloud. They are public poems, and one wonders who else now living has written more impressive ones. . . . These poems not only testify to Gustafson's mastery of the public poem—a genre practised rarely and with little success by most living writers—but also indicate the way in which, though his meditations are often personal, he subordinates himself to his perceptions, to the truth of the "moment-when." Gustafson is not an egotistic poet; he may speak with personal passion, but he never indulges in that self-dramatization which is permitted to serve as substitute for true perception in the work of so many of his younger contemporaries. That it happens to him rather than to someone else, is, one feels, a fortunate or unfortunate accident. It is the experience, the thought, the epiphany or revelation which matters, and not the teller of the tale.

Nowhere is this more apparent than the *Rocky Mountain Poems* of 1960. . . . The human creature may be the measure, and in a sense, the cause of magnificence, but he is subservient to it. He is not the author of grandeur, but its catalyst; without him there would be none, but it is not his property; it is his accompaniment, a blessing given him. . . . The ousting of the ego by something greater is a commonplace of the poetic experience, as of the confrontation with the natural world, but it is rarely expressed with the concreteness and precision of the *Rocky Mountain Poems.* . . . It was with the *Rocky Mountain Poems* of 1960 and the volume *Rivers Among Rocks* of the same

year that Gustafson came into his full strength. It had been sixteen years since his last collection, *Flight Into Darkness,* which included the best of his earlier work and the privately printed volumes, *Epithalamium in Time of War* (1941), and *Lyrics Unromantic* (1942). During those sixteen years he changed himself from a good but uneven writer into a poet of real authority and power. With the wisdom of hindsight one can see that *Flight Into Darkness* anticipates the later mastery and is a preparation for it, as also is the verse-play *Alfred the Great* which was published in 1937. This play is largely fustian; it reminds one uncomfortably of the neo-Shakespearean dramas of late romanticism and of such early twentieth century verse dramatists as Stephen Phillips and Sturge Moore; it rarely rises to the compact force of the drama of Austin Clarke, or to the occasional trenchancy of Gordon Bottomley. Nevertheless, one can see that the powerfully dramatic style of later poems, their brusque rhetoric, their control of speech tune [have their origins in *Alfred the Great*]. . . . In this play, too, there are hints of that later control of consonance which adds pungency to the wit. (pp. 172-75)

In *Flight Into Darkness* also there are hints of the later mastery. *Epithalamium in Time of War* makes too much of its alliteration and consonance, perhaps, and certainly its conventional metric lacks the force of later poems. Nevertheless the strength is there and the sensual power. . . . *Flight Into Darkness* explains much. It also presents much that is superb, such as the mordant poem *Idyll for a Fool,* with its marvellously descriptive second line "Scum-sour pool of curdled gold," and the very thirtyish but deft *City Song* not included in the *Selected Poems.* Indeed, Gustafson took very few of his early poems into this volume, and one must therefore presume that he himself felt much of it to be preparatory. Though such poems as *Atlantic Crossing* reveal their influences a little too obviously . . . , and a number of the lines are poised uncertainly between pastiche and burlesque, this book is still one of the finest Canadian books of the decade.

Between 1944 and 1960 Gustafson learned to extend rather than to work within traditional forms and dictions. In *Rivers Among Rocks* (1960) he achieved a delicate precision of cadence, and revived Elizabethan word-play techniques, making them part of a modern sensibility. . . . Six years later, in *Sift in an Hourglass,* came the exuberance, the rambunctious wit, and the astonishing combination of delicacy and strength, sense and intellect, comedy and passion. . . . [His] lament for the dead makars, called *Dirge For A Penny Whistle,* is a pyrotechnical combination of parody, allusion, verbal high-jinks and self-mockery. The sheer dexterity of this collection is matched by that of *Ixion's Wheel* (1969) in which he gathers together many poems dealing with history and with travel around the world, beginning with the earlier *Rocky Mountain Poems,* as the first year, and taking the second year from a group in *Sift in an Hourglass.* The gathering together of these with two other "years," makes the book almost a comprehensive survey of our cultural inheritance.

His passion and wit explore sculpture, painting, architecture, tapestry, all that witnesses to man's hunger after the pleromatic and the ultimate. . . . He ranges in this book from satire to dramatic monologue (*Michael Angelo Looks Up Not Sleeping*), from narrative to lyric, and from epic episode to epigram; the moods constantly change, and yet, at all times the honesty, the concern for the truth which is the "moment-when," impresses itself upon us. In this book, as in every book since that revelatory publishing year of 1960, Gustafson shows himself to be the equal of any poet now writing and the superior of most. . . . (pp. 176-79)

Robin Skelton, "Ralph Gustafson: A Review and Retrospect," in MOSAIC: A Journal for the Comparative Study of Literature and Ideas, *Vol. VIII, No. 2 (Winter, 1975), pp. 167-79.*

FRED COGSWELL

Fire on Stone continues the tradition of Ralph Gustafson's poetry, a tradition that began with *The Golden Chalice* in 1935 and that, apart from *Rivers Among Rocks*, 1960, and *Rocky Mountain Poems*, 1960, has grown deeper and stronger with the nine other volumes he has published.

I should say, two traditions, for in the work of Ralph Gustafson, it seems to me, temperament is very much at odds with technique.

In temperament, thought, outlook, Ralph Gustafson is essentially an elitist, a believer in a continuous tradition of men and women who by their gentleness, their love of beauty and goodness have preserved in the Western World music, art, sculpture, poetry, and the decencies of life which go with these things. So much is Western Humanism an integral part of Gustafson's emotional and cultural inheritance that when an artifact in Rome or Greece lives up in reality to what in his mind it ought to be, it elicits the stock response from him that tradition assigns to such an encounter between poet and artifact. At the same time, incongruity between object and symbol and his notion of what these things should be easily shocks him. His reaction seldom goes beyond praise of beauty and decency and revulsion against their opposites. . . . His is essentially a simple, uncomplicated response to experience. He is in this a kind of less robust Browning, lacking the latter poet's insight into the ironic relationship of innocence-guilt, beauty-ugliness, good-evil throughout the universe. (p. 112)

If every time he had written—or even every other time—the urgency and depth of experience had forced Ralph Gustafson to go beneath or beyond the stock response, as he [does in **"Of Answers and Her Asleep"**], he might well have been our finest poet. As it is, like Bliss Carman he responded too easily, too decently perhaps, and found the words much too readily. He is, I feel, a victim of his very erudition and facility. That is why when I read *Fire on Stone*, as when I read all his previous books except the two written in 1960, I do so with mixed admiration and exasperation. (p. 113)

Fred Cogswell, "Temperament Versus Technique," in Canadian Literature, *No. 64, Spring, 1975, pp. 112-13.*

WENDY KEITNER

Ralph Gustafson's poetic development recapitulates in miniature the general pattern of the growth of poetry in Canada: it begins with a typically colonial deference to "the Greats" of English literature with imitations of Spenser, Shakespeare, and the Romantics; passes through a transitional phase of dependency on newer but still foreign models, primarily Hopkins and Eliot; and culminates in the post-war period in a vigorous, distinctive maturity. The third phase of his career begins effectively in 1960 with the publication of *Rivers among Rocks*, a book which collects his poetry for the sixteen-year period 1944-1959, and it includes the eight books which have followed

it to date in increasingly rapid succession: *Rocky Mountain Poems, Sift in an Hourglass,* and *Ixion's Wheel* in the 1960's; *Selected Poems, Theme and Variations for Sounding Brass, Fire on Stone, Corners in the Glass,* and *Soviet Poems* in the 1970's. This body of poetry—as all good poetry must, according to Eliot—creates the illusion of a view of life through its selected range of imagery, distinctive interrelationships between structure and content, and characteristic major themes: nature, love, ephemerality, unjustifiable death, and the conflict between time and space.

Gustafson's quest for meaning is conducted not in the terminology of rational discourse, Romantic aesthetics, or Christian dogma, in his final period, but primarily through love—love of woman, works of art, and natural beauty. That his ultimate religion . . . is love is demonstrated from the time of *Rivers among Rocks* in a poem such as **"Beach with White Cloud."** . . . **"Beach with White Cloud"** is a passionate celebration of sexual communion, but frequently Gustafson's love poems move beyond simple joy to urgent defiance and even elegy. Gustafson typically writes with a double vision, bringing into focus simultaneously both the beauty and the brevity of life. (pp. 44-5)

The dichotomy between what Eli Mandel, in *Contemporary Canadian Poets,* has termed a "cultivated literary awareness" and an "almost primitive feeling for place" . . . is one of the chief characteristics of Ralph Gustafson's poetry. Alternately, he is a hoary traditionalist and a new Canadian Adam taking his green inventory. In the sense in which Northrop Frye used these terms in his famous terror review, Gustafson's poetry is sometimes "original"—returning to cultural origins through study and imitation of poets and other artists of the past—and at other times "aboriginal"—drawing its inspiration from the land. Gustafson uses the sensuous to reach the transcendent, but this contact with physical realities may be made either directly with things in nature or indirectly with their recreations in works of art—poems, paintings, tapestry, music, sculpture, and so on. Furthermore, it is notable that in so far as he depicts the natural world, Gustafson writes almost exclusively about Canada; while in so far as he responds to the world of art, he writes almost entirely out of a European cultural context. Thus he has two basic sources of imagery around which he develops two distinctive poetic styles. (p. 45)

Ephemerality emerges as one of the dominant themes of *Sift in an Hourglass,* a collection which—by its title alone—reaffirms Gustafson's ties to British literary tradition; in fact, he becomes almost a poet's poet. Gustafson's "aboriginal" style—his spare lyricism and habit of stripped-down statement—is elicited almost exclusively by the Canadian terrain; when he writes of England, Greece, and other foreign countries or takes his inspiration from older works of art, his style consistently tends to be more allusive, complicated, and elaborate. Gustafson's "original" writing echoes and reverberates with references to a broad spectrum of English literature, as well as to European history and mythology. In several instances, borrowing diction from literary tradition reinforces the theme of transience at the level of style by showing that even language is subject to the processes of time. (p. 48)

Repeatedly, [Gustafson's] poems incorporate the belief that one reaches the highest meaning of life through an affirmation, not a denial, of sensuous reality. Such affirmation is made, however, with full tragic awareness of the fleeting nature of all experience and frequently even of art. At the centre of Gustafson's poetry lie the twin facts of beauty and mutability; he contends that, despite injustice, violence, and death, only a full embrace of transience suffices. Paradoxically though, many of the poems on this theme in *Ixion's Wheel* and other collections are articulated in a highly elliptical and allusive style, leaving Gustafson vulnerable to charges of aestheticism or academicism, while his historical and foreign illustrative material has raised, for Canadian readers and critics, the question of his relevance.

By the end of the 1960's, Gustafson's two separate styles, one direct, the other allusive, hitherto elicited by two distinct orders of experience: one of Canadian nature and weather, the other of European art and myth, and conveyed by two different types of imagery: one geographical and the other historical, begin to merge. The mixed media protest poems of *Theme and Variations for Sounding Brass* . . . —a striking contrast to *Ixion's Wheel*—focus on the victims of international as well as local violence and injustice, from Cambodia to Quebec, and, taking an engagé stance, use bold, plain, prose-like statements. Gustafson sets for himself the task to "Shock our hearts" into a realization of the extent and significance of monstrous current events, and the collection demonstrates his full mastery of the public poem. The general structure which contains these five witness poems—theme and variations—is borrowed, of course, from music; so, too, are each of the five individual structures: nocturne, fantasia, ricercare, aubade, and coda. The central theme is love—no longer just in individual but in enlarged socio-political terms—and the variations show, in a range of different national contexts, the grim, dehumanizing results of its distortion or ultimate absence.

Gustafson's vocabulary, syntax, and rhythm in these poems are close to prose; in fact, in some instances, patterns of reference are established by means of incorporating into the poetry snatches of prose, usually from political speeches. (pp. 48-9)

[*Fire on Stone*] marks a sharp return to a more personal and reflective lyric mode as Gustafson resumes his study of nature, his world travels, and his Pound-like journey through the past to find touchstones of relevance for citizens of the contemporary, polluted, war-torn world. In these poems, Gustafson blends or moves freely between his two styles and two quarries of images: the symbolic desire for light, illumination, is one of the principal motifs, but it is pursued by a process sometimes antithetical, sometimes parallel, to the ascent of Plato's mythic caveman. Acutely conscious of growing older, the Gustafson persona—almost always a nearly autobiographical figure—wants "all / Heart-saddening things resolved." He feels that "Death ought to bring / An answer to the questions." Yet he knows, finally, that it will not, and in these poems the great antinomies—life and death, beauty and brevity, good and evil, time and eternity, nature and art—remain unreconciled. (pp. 49-50)

Ultimately, in Gustafson's universe, "The moment-when is what pertains." In **"To Old Asclepius—Lyric at Epidaurus,"** life is again documented as being both painful and beautiful, and this poem seems intended as a final statement. In manuscript draft, it is entitled "Summation at Epidaurus," and the conclusion Gustafson reaches here is reiterated in many other poems which similarly rejoice in "the hour's magnificence," "that hour," "the flashed instant." Both are equally real, "Sting of wasp and swallow of moon," and his poetry urgently recommends that life be lived fully moment by moment since joy balances grief.

Characteristically, and perhaps as a result of his musical background, Ralph Gustafson structures experience in counterpoint.

Life and death are brought into focus almost simultaneously by the speaking voice of the two-part **"Bishop Erik Grave's Grave"** and by the gardener persona of **"Poem in April"** and **"Hyacinths with Brevity."** (pp. 50-1)

The motif of light is an important strand in the intricately plaited imagery of the recent *Corners in the Glass.* . . . As the sun, it symbolizes the life force itself; as reflected light, it suggests philosophical illumination, Joyce's *claritas*. But shunning abstract thought and pure speculation, Gustafson's intellectual grappling with the meaning of life here issues directly in joyous celebration of the tangible, audible, visible universe. The movement away from orthodox, religious, other-worldly solutions to the problems of the human condition, which was begun tentatively in the early *Flight into Darkness* and developed more fully in *Rivers among Rocks* and *Sift in an Hourglass*, culminates in readily accessible symbols and images and in pithy, direct language—a style which now illustrates the primary thesis: "I'll have the concrete." (p. 51)

Both literally as well as metaphorically, throughout *Corners in the Glass* Gustafson presents himself as a cultivator of his own garden, focussing attention on common details in the immediate environment. The majority of these poems is set in rural Canada, largely in the vicinity of Gustafson's own home in North Hatley, Quebec. Sharply criticized in the 1960's for being a Grand Tour poet, in recent years Gustafson has become increasingly a regional poet, the Canadian equivalent, in some respects, of Robert Frost. His autobiographical persona is no untutored country bumpkin, of course; but what concerns him above all is not speculation but sensation, not history but geography, not the foreign but the local—the beauties of flowers, birdsong, and even the antics of midges at the corner of his patio on a summer afternoon. Enjoying the backyard scene, he confesses that he is content to remain "Oblivious of Agamemnon and a thousand ships."

From the time of *Rivers among Rocks*, Gustafson's themes had begun to stress the value of the here and now. **"A Candle for Pasch"** had concluded with this-world emphasis: "Joy here, least: if none." **"Apologue"** had underscored that "taken joy is all." But Gustafson's medium at that stage did not always embody his message; in fact, it often worked at cross purposes. By the 1970's, style and theme reinforce each other, so that Gustafson's thoughts are articulated in sensuous terms. (pp. 51-2)

Despite the fact that his very latest book, *Soviet Poems* . . . , is the diary of a trip outside Canada . . . , what it stresses is that "unpolitical humanity is the same," and it does not invalidate the judgment that, in his poetry of the 1970's considered as a whole, Ralph Gustafson demonstrates not the bleak discovery of Thomas Wolfe that we can't go home again, but rather the felt truth of Margaret Laurence that we must go home again. In the life-long process of uncovering this truth in his own way, Ralph Gustafson has produced an impressive body of poetry which bears witness to a personal, as well as a national, struggle. (pp. 52-3)

Wendy Keitner, "Gustafson's Double Hook," in Canadian Literature, *No. 79, Winter, 1978, pp. 44-53.*

DOUG BEARDSLEY

I'm pleased to report that *Corners In The Glass* is as good a book as Gustafson has given us. I say this without feeling the need to compare this book with the poet's earlier work. (p. 55)

Yes, I know the difficulties, the demands that are made on the reader by Gustafson's music. The demands of contemporary poetry are great enough, but this poet has his own particular artful and compelling syntax, his own syntactical way of giving us the aggressiveness of contemporary life. His words are like cars crowding the modern city of the poem, jamming, bumping bumper to bumper against each other, yet the themes of his best poems come from ancient history, and it is this curious relationship of a highly personal and contemporary syntax and form juxtaposed to an historical remembrance of things past that makes Gustafson so difficult and so rewarding a poet. In his best poems (and there are more than a dozen of those in this new book), Gustafson dazzles us with his word-play, his "sultriest fulgurations, flickering" word-phrases of magical complexity, and yet we have no difficulty in 'feeling' the poem.

The poems that fail to reach the level of the poet's best work fail for several reasons. . . . To me, there is a winter domesticity at the beginning of this book, a quietude, a slowing, almost an aging of the blood, a pressing of and by time and a softening of the dazzling edge of the poems that are to follow. I feel the occasional corner has been rubbed a little too smooth, as if the poet has finally paid some small attention to his worst critics. Some of the endings are sometimes simply too much of a dénouement, but these are minor quibbles and likely go hand in hand with the writing of the more ambitious and far-reaching poems, for it is becoming obvious to us now that the poet gets to those 'big' poems by journeying through the others.

No, Gustafson has lost none of his art and we continue to gain. These *Corners In The Glass* are cut as sharp and as clear as crystal. (p. 56)

> Doug Beardsley, "Crystal-Clear," *in* Essays on Canadian Writing, *No. 10, Spring, 1978, pp. 55-6.*

ROBERT LECKER

Ralph Gustafson often reminds me of a failed linguistic Houdini; he ties himself up in knots of syntax and then tries to free himself by contorting the body of his words in a kind of gymnastic frenzy:

> Removed from consequence, motive set,
> Violence qualifies. Subjaw
> The sticks hang hostage round the neck
> Of innocence seated in a kitchen chair. . . .

Tortured sentences such as these [from the poem "**Allhallows Eve**" in *Corners in the Glass*] suggest a larger perceptual problem confronting Gustafson: he is unable to see the world either phenomenologically or concretely because all of his observations are immediately transformed into ontological investigations. Again and again we find the poet struggling with the question of how to seize the world as it is, in this moment, without resorting to philosophical associations. . . . Gustafson is always insisting that "I'll have the concrete," or that "I'll / Have earthly music, heard, / Unsphered, no choirs squeaked / In eternal passacaglia." However, as the very choice of words suggests, the "earthly" never manages to appear for long, because in truth "The world is pastime" and only eternity is real. Even when he is most "Desperate for sensation," Gustafson manages to "Chew stalks with intellect." This makes for a "Difficult, intricate, melody" which is seldom satisfying. In order to find the tune we often have to wade through a sea of musical metaphor. . . . (p. 124)

Gustafson's apparent need to cram extended meanings into the most compact and ostensibly 'crafted' space forces him to work with disjointed, distorted speech. Too frequently his *idea* takes over and the sought-after descriptive precision is thrown to the wind. In one poem he is content to render the noise made by a flame as "a sort of flapping sound." And what this sound has to do with the notion of "ascititious loss" never becomes quite clear. I'm left feeling blinded by the linguistic razzle-dazzle, deafened by dodecaphonic sound. (p. 125)

> Robert Lecker, in a review of "Corners in the Glass," in The Fiddlehead, *No. 117, Spring, 1978, pp. 124-25.*

DAVID S. WEST

Corners in the Glass is an apt title for Ralph Gustafson's latest book of poems. There is a sense of crystalline structure. Like glass, the poems suggest the artifice of man's handicraft, the essential relationship between man and nature with which Gustafson, in this volume, is concerned. Further, as with the fragile beauty of glass, the poems are different from each other in shape and texture—they range from the personal revelation, through landscapes and domestic interiors, to the thoughtful, where twisted syntax creates an intriguing obscurity. The distinguishing feature of this book is its intensely reflective tone. The majority of poems are introspective, concerned with seeing the individual as representative of the race, and placing him within the context of astronomic space, time, and nature.

The sense that emerges is curiously Canadian. For built as they are out of fragments of Gustafson's experience, the poems explore the delights and mysteries of existing *here* and experiencing *now*. (p. 110)

The poems are thematically linked, and a strong sense of Gustafson's warm human presence adds to the impression of structure. There is a feeling created by the conversational intimacy between poet and reader that both are in agreement about the problems of life. A simple heart-felt domesticity is the key to these poems. They centre around the hearth, around the writer's study, then spread out from the quiet centre to explore the world's tangled web. In the course of the book, Gustafson weaves together several major motifs which include religion, love, art, and being; he explores these through images of flowers, gardening, stars, and graphically described incidents. There are poems about love (conceived domestically), about travel, about music, and about poetry.

The only poems that do not maintain the high poetic standard are those about music. It is difficult to make the names of composers or the terminology of music carry the weight of metaphor; they simply are not images, and Gustafson cannot make them so no matter how hard he tries. . . . (p. 111)

Corners in the Glass is a significant work. It presents a unique blend of the personal and the philosophical. It is a great pleasure to read. It . . . is a strong personal rendering of thoughts and responses that have been left mostly as abstract themes in the works of other poets who have not Gustafson's voice, his gift for conversational elegance. (p. 112)

> David S. West, "Old Wine, Broken Bottles, Cut Glass," in Canadian Literature, *No. 80, Spring, 1979, pp. 109-12.**

VINCENT SHARMAN

[*Landscape with Rain*] contains poems ranging from straight description to those that complexly develop some of his favourite themes—the polarities of existence and the preference for the "non-allusive Earth" to the grand abstractions of the human mind.

Unifying these poems, as much as anything else, are obscurity and the poet's choice of diction. Examples of the latter include not only the frequent use of place names, historical, literary, and artistic allusion, but reliance on polysyllabic, seldom-used words, "prognathous," "tessellated," "propinquity," "sequestration," "coruscation,"—a curious element in a poet who values the ordinary in life. The difficulty with such words in Gustafson's poetry is that they become an affectation, suggesting a Gustafsonian kind of poetic diction. (p. 124)

Gustafson's poems tend to be very concentrated, leading at times to obscurity; but there can also be a disturbing wordiness which weakens the impact of the poem. . . .

There is also a distracting awkwardness of expression, the result, perhaps, of trying to be intense and still maintain a relaxed air. . . .

With the exception of the group of poems **"Across the World the Beholder Come,"** Gustafson's poetry has an obvious energy despite these weaknesses. Furthermore, in his work there is uncommon joy, there is a sense of struggle—never of complacency—and there is charm. (p. 125)

Intellect abounds as Gustafson reaches beyond the myopic "I" of so many contemporary poets. He is impressive in his religious themes, in his recognition of the importance of beauty apprehended *now,* and in his images of the horror of violence thrown into relief by the enlightening experiences of love and the gentle surge of life in sun and springtime.

"I have been running on blindness," the poet says: Gustafson is most satisfactory in single lines or in several lines on one thought, rather than in whole poems. It is for these, I think, that one will return to *Landscape with Rain.* (pp. 125-26)

> *Vincent Sharman, in a review of "Landscape with Rain," in* The University of Windsor Review, *Vol. XV, Nos. 1 & 2, Fall-Winter, 1979 & Spring-Summer 1980, pp. 124-26.*

WENDY KEITNER

The central themes of Ralph Gustafson's poetry find expression again in his prose fiction. The twin values of "being in love and left free to love"—the words of the central character of one short story entitled **"Classical Portrait"**—are of supreme importance in both genres. In fact, Gustafson's poems and stories cohere the way musical theme and variations do, together developing an integrated interpretation of experience. The three shared keynotes are creativity, love—whether for the beauties of nature of art, or among man, woman, and child—and strong abhorrence of violence.

Unlike his poems, however, Gustafson's stories generally operate in an indirect manner; they work obliquely towards celebration of a healthy instinct for life and unfettered self-affirmation by probing the distress and human suffering caused by failures of inadequate or blocked passion. In this respect, his short stories are almost mirror images of his poems, their emphases reversed. Contrasts can again be seen on the level of style. Whereas Gustafson's search for an appropriate and au-

thentic poetic style is a slow and laborious process covering several decades, his prose style springs almost full grown from his brow, like Athena out of the head of Zeus. Despite obvious flaws, such as lack of subtlety in conceptualization of plot and character, even Gustafson's first stories—**"The Last Experiment of Dr. Brugge,"** a Poe-like thriller about a mesmerist, and **"The Amateur,"** a bitter-bitten tale tracing the crimes of a petty Montreal thief—are compellingly intense. (p. 61)

In the early poetry the limiting, negating, disruptive forces which thwart the progress of young love include interpersonal misunderstandings, parental cruelty, possessiveness, and war. Added to these in the short stories—mainly set . . . in the Quebec townships—is the Calvinist-Jansenist legacy of prudery, shame, guilt, and self-hatred leading sometimes even to acts of sadomasochism. These impediments to healthy union between man and woman or parent and child are portrayed with greater complexity and subtlety, too, in the prose fiction than in the early poetry since the negating forces now tend to be internalized by the main protagonists.

Characteristically Gustafson's stories, like Joyce Carol Oates's, explore the destructiveness and human suffering which result from people's failure to release themselves to their instinctually positive, creative feelings. The typical Gustafson hero (there are few heroines) remains caged, unfree, and mated with the archetypal Canadian ice woman. His stories document "how one's destiny is the outcome of character," as Jimmy's mother puts it in **"The Circus"** . . . ; but beyond this they also reveal how individual character interacts with and is shaped by larger societal influences and pressures. They reflect a postwar consciousness of the human capacity for inflicting pain; they probe the almost subliminal sources of the battle of the sexes; and they also offer very skillful psychological dramatizations of the lingering effects of the puritan ethos on the collective Canadian psyche. (pp. 62-3)

The puritanical climate of the townships . . . constrains and compromises virtually all of Gustafson's characters. At best they are shown struggling to loose the stranglehold of the repressive morality which Gustafson himself grew up with and in his adult years tried to escape through self-imposed exile. This morality stresses human insignificance and impotence, equates worldly enjoyment (especially of sex) with sin, and is suspicious and even condemning of spontaneity, emotion, and the arts. In *Survival,* [Margaret] Atwood describes Canadian culture as "the culture of potential denied." In this context, Gustafson's stories paint national as well as regional portraits of human bondage and unfulfillment; thus they contribute to a mainline tradition of Realism in Canadian prose which includes the works of Frederick Philip Grove, Sinclair Ross, Hugh MacLennan, Hugh Garner, Margaret Laurence, and Alice Munro.

In Gustafson's best stories, as in most contemporary fiction, plot and external action tend to be devalued; the main event on which the plot turns may be no more out of the ordinary than a missed appointment (**"The Circus"**), a casual visit to an art gallery (**"Shower of Gold"**), or a brief restaurant lunch (**"The Paper-spike"**). Actions and events tend to be minimal, but the characters' ways of responding endow even minor and everyday occurrences with frightening significance. These are characters who have seismographic sensitivity and heightened emotional and creative capacities: children, artists, and lovers. But typically they are children filled with guilt as they perform the rites of passage into adulthood; artists frustrated by an atmosphere in which aesthetic or sensual pleasure equals sin; and lovers matched with partners who are prudish, vengeful, and even sadistic. The creative person is obstructed in innumerable ways by a society which is fundamentally hostile to his or her self-actualization. The main characters in Gustafson's fiction thus are all victims. A few acknowledge this but refuse to accept the assumption that the role is inevitable, blaming their entrapment on individual repressive sexual partners or specific warped mores. Several of them, however, overwhelmed by a vivid consciousness of the general societal source of their oppression, fail to take any affirmative action—in fact, quite the opposite. There dawns the bitter recognition they are trapped for life by the sterile morality they reject intellectually but cannot shake emotionally, and on account of which they are lashed with guilt. (pp. 63-4)

> *Wendy Keitner, in her* Ralph Gustafson, *Twayne Publishers, 1979, 174 p.*

PATRICIA KEENEY SMITH

The spell cast by Ralph Gustafson's *Soviet Poems* may be a deceptive one. Our great glittering ignorance of Russia today, our perhaps exaggerated reaction to place names—Novgorod, Tashkent, Samarkand—predispose our interest. However, such likely curiosity and excitement is not justified by most of the poems on their own merit.

Too many fall victim to the arbitrary linestop, the rhetorical phrase, an unhelpful use of capital letters and a lot of listing which occasionally produces a sort of suspect music or meaning. In **"Winged Flight,"** names have wonderful sounds (Shakhi-Zinda), whereas **"The Kobzar"** is mainly name-dropping. Yet, some memorable images emerge from the book: "We flew with the sun into the sun / Lying low on the wide horizon / Like a disk of copper metal / Thrown by luck." Each piece is accompanied by a prose travelogue which shouldn't be necessary, and is at times condescending in its information.

The most difficult problem is that of tone. The writing seems to suffer from an obligation to make philosophical statements, take a moral stand. Any authentic personal voice becomes muted by the conscientious ambassadorial voice. An effective lack of resolve between the two creates some ambiguity, and this in poems where specifics could speak for themselves. (pp. 138-39)

Western poems observing modern Russia are few enough. One expects a resilient art, equal to the challenge of a rich and recalcitrant subject. Unless we infer an unrealistically simplified humanity, it is not enough to say, as Gustafson does in an early statement and as we would all like to say, that "Unpolitical humanity is the same." (p. 139)

> *Patricia Keeney Smith, "Hit and Miss," in* Canadian Literature, *No. 85, Summer, 1980, pp. 136-40.**

M. TRAVIS LANE

Ralph Gustafson's most recent books, *Gradations of Grandeur*, a sequence of sixty-four poems, and *Landscape with Rain*, present the excellences we have come to expect in Gustafson's work: a savouring of verbal texture, an acute and embracing sensitivity of response, vigourous lines packed with strong stresses and irregular rhythms. Here also, especially in the sequence, are Gustafson's other distinguishing characteristics: sharded sentences, verbless and contorted, and lists of disparities syntactically and sometimes logically unpaired. The style of the sequence is vigorous; the structure perambulating—not

so much "gradations" as "theme and variations," as Gustafson better entitled an earlier sequence (*Theme and Variations for Sounding Brass*). But all Gustafson's work tends to be variations on gradations of grandeur, on contraries of experience, on the ironies of charity and sounding brass. *Gradations of Grandeur* takes up various aspects of Gustafson's pervading theme in the manner of an informal essay, returning from its elliptic course much where it began.

Gradations of Grandeur is not constructed as logical argument; the poem answers the general question it poses, "is it worth it?" rather as nature answers—not with sentences, but with the collages of experience, lists of divers materials: historical instance, sensory instance, the muddle of recollection and present moment, experience concrete, glittering, discoherent. The epigram from Pound which prefaces the sequence illuminates Gustafson's intention: "The essential thing in a poet is / that he builds us his world." Yet one is inclined to feel at times, perhaps as a result of the collage / list effect, that Gustafson does not, like Arnold's Sophocles, see life steadily and see it whole. *Gradations of Grandeur* does not build a world; it offers a sort of Baedeker, a Blue Guide to Sensibility. Gustafson works too much in synecdoche. And long lists of ironically disparate details eventually trivialize the effect at which they aim. To build a world, one must look longer even if at less. The pervading voice of *Gradations of Grandeur,* the ironic tone of a self-consciously lucky man, also presents difficulties, as I feel it also presented in *Theme and Variations for Sounding Brass*. Is decently expressed compassion enough? In any short poem it is enough. But in a substantial poem, do we not demand a grander tune, whether defiant or affirmative? (p. 104)

Of course, an effect analogous to Whitman's, Pope's, or Yeats's is not intended. Instead, Gustafson wants the ironic detachment of Voltaire's *Candide*, with its message for small decencies: cultivate one's own garden. A work about gardening succeeds with those of us who have gardens. A work that climbs out of the garden may succeed with the gardenless. But Gustafson's work sits in the garden, peeks over the wall at the miserable, becomes uncomfortable, and then asserts, as if in reassurance, the value of gardening. I am reminded of Derek Walcott's conclusion in "Sea Grapes"; "The classics can console. But not enough." . . .

Because of the lack of argumentative structure and because of the rhythmic similarity of one section to another, *Gradations of Grandeur* is a better poem when read in segments than it is when read as a whole. And his poems which are not presented as sequences, but as moments, in a collection, are usually his best. *Landscape with Rain* has many poems which for me summon the general message of Gustafson's long philosophical sequence in a more than adequate moment. **"Who Began It and What For,"** for example, affirms the potent value of the possible world, death-tainted, comical, glorious, and precarious. It answers Gustafson's question "Is it worth it?" not with abstraction and irony muted by disjointed lists, not by speaking *about* love, humour, or the imperfect celestial—but rather by speaking *with* love, humour, and a sense of the celestial conjunctions of experience. . . . (p. 105)

> *M. Travis Lane, "The Cultivated Garden," in* The Fiddlehead, *No. 129, Spring, 1981, pp. 102-06.*

WAYNE GRADY

The variety and range of Gustafson's 14 collected stories [in *The Vivid Air*] is at first deceptive, because they mask an essential unity in Gustafson's vision and voice. His central characters . . . span the Seven Ages of Man, and the stories themselves represent a lifetime of thought and perception. . . . There is a continuity not only among themselves but also, and considering the ventriloquy of other poets who write short stories this is surprising and somehow agreeable, between Gustafson's voice as a poet and his similarly gentle reflection as a writer of prose.

Sometimes this unity interferes with clarity, when the poetic diction perhaps in an attempt to imitate natural speech or the rhythms of thought produces a paragraph inaccessible to reason. (p. 13)

The best stories in the collection are simple, direct statements of private anguish frankly observed and delineated. **"The Vivid Air,"** which takes its title from a poem by Stephen Spender, is about an adolescent on the verge of sexual discovery who . . . stops just short of committing violence against his own body as a kind of objective correlative to the act of love, as a substitute for committing violence against the body of his beloved. In its purity of language and simplicity of statement it reminds one of Sinclair Ross, or perhaps Ernest Buckler—it is rural, religious, and sexual. . . .

Gustafson's favourite dramatic locale is the stage within the skull—the tight, claustrophobic deliberations of the fevered mind. The stories take place in crowded, confined spaces . . . and yet much of the dialogue is interior, a laboured debate with the divided self, or the self projected on to the wife or husband or hired man. They are in that sense prose poems, but without the preciousness that generic name implies. Gustafson is interested in people first, and in abstractions only insofar as they modify people's behaviour: love, for instance, is analyzed and defined, but that process is always secondary or irrelevant to the actions of the people who love. . . .

Fourteen stories make a fairly distilled output for a lifetime of writing, but distillation is the poet's method for obtaining spirit, and Gustafson's spirit breathes as freely through these stories as it does through his poems. In **"Helen,"** the most conventional and otherwise unremarkable story in the book—complete with sudden final knife-twist—Gustafson speaks of "a versatility, as it were—that swing from inattention to things of moment, to exaggeration of the trivial, which indicates that all is not well with the pendulum." And perhaps that is a fair summation of Gustafson's swing from poetry to prose, except that here the swing shows the pendulum working exactly as it should. It is a natural and necessary corollary to a long preoccupation with rhythm and time. (p. 14)

> *Wayne Grady, "The Poet and the Pendulum," in* Books in Canada, *Vol. 10, No. 6, June-July, 1981, pp. 13-14.*

CATHY MATYAS

[The poems in Gustafson's *Conflicts of Spring*] reflect the author's continuing concern with the potential for music in language, and more precisely, with the desire to identify words with music in the creation of a poem. Like all of Gustafson's previous work, the poems in *Conflicts of Spring* are carefully crafted and intricately structured. So structured, in fact, that the reader must sometimes struggle to locate meanings in order to relate subject and design. But although reading *Conflicts of Spring* is not always easy, as an effort of the intellect it is

ultimately rewarding. The collection is rich with seasonal images and allusions to classical sources such as the Bible and mythology. Since most contemporary Canadian poets have disclaimed this tradition (viewing it as an artificial vehicle for personal experience), Gustafson's work, including *Conflicts of Spring,* remains something of an acquired taste.

> *Cathy Matyas, in a review of "Conflicts of Spring," in* Quill and Quire, *Vol. 48, No. 3, March, 1982, p. 68.*

KEITH GAREBIAN

In *The Moment Is All,* a collection culled from the past four decades, Gustafson exhibits the meditative cast of a mind that lyrically and wittily integrates the earthly and definite with the spiritual and ambiguous. For all their forged ingenuity and diagonal movement, his poems have strong aural values that create music for the humanist. Gustafson appears to subscribe to Wallace Stevens's belief that "the gaiety of language is our seigneur," although Gustafson's ellipses and sprung rhythms often get the better of acutest speech or clearest song.

At his lyrical best, even in the early poems of *Rivers Among Rocks,* Gustafson builds compact verse with internal rhymes, alliteration, consonance, caesurae, and funnelled phrases. His landscapes (as in *Corners in the Glass, Landscape With Rain,* or *Conflicts of Spring*) are beautiful, soft pictures of settings that vindicate human intelligence and love. Paradox moves like a subtle stream through poems that wimple with phrases, fold subordinate clauses upon one another, so that the mind can follow both God's and the poet's creation in layers of revelation. Gustafson's technique is a practised one that goes back to Anglo-Saxon kennings, metaphysical wit, classical forms, romantic and modernist devices. The technique leads frequently to effects that Babette Deutsch once called exuberant but overly hortatory, but the rich sensuousness and contemplative music always provide a sense of process or movement. Because "abstractions are an airy nothing," Gustafson turns to the specific moment whose gradations of meaning and grandeur are worked into a coherent vision. . . .

Gustafson's social conscience is easily activated (in, for instance, **"I Think of All Soft Limbs," "The Newspaper,""State of Affairs"**), but his soul is not chained to history. Although the palms of his hands are marked by lines of history, and his mind is alive with anecdotes and examples of the past, his preoccupation is with the moment, our designed interim, where intuition or pure knowledge cannot be a sufficient fulcrum for being. . . .

Gustafson would readily leave contemplation of history to go out and smell jonquils (**"Thoughts on a Narrow Night"**), but he has a quick soul and subtle mind, and he responds to being more than to myth (or so he seems to claim). Accordingly, his entire poetic career has appeared to be a fugue on the necessity of love. In **"Praise of Margins"** he takes St. Francis's point of view ("All is news of God") and finds love to be the pivot of the world. This human love becomes the true *raison d'être* in various poems, whether expressed as religious devotion or secular commitment, the love of trivia or the sexual celebration of erotic love, the "permanence of temporary gods." Intuition and knowledge must yield to this force. . . . (p. 34)

> *Keith Garebian, "Gestures of Love," in* Books in Canada, *Vol. 12, No. 9, November, 1983, pp. 33-5.*

Joseph Heller

1923-

American novelist, dramatist, and scriptwriter.

Heller is a popular and respected writer whose best-known novel, *Catch-22* (1961), is considered a major work of the post-World War II era. He writes irreverent, witty novels in which he makes extensive use of black humor and satire. His tragicomic vision of modern life focuses on the erosion of traditional values and morals and life's increasing absurdities. Heller also examines the misuse of language, particularly the ways in which it obscures and confuses reality. Heller's penchant for anachronism, evident in all of his novels, reflects the disordered nature of contemporary existence. His protagonists are antiheroes who search for meaning in their lives and struggle to avoid being overwhelmed by such institutions as the military, big business, government, and religion. Heller's later novels have received mixed reviews, but *Catch-22* continues to be highly regarded for its blend of pathos and humor. Richard Locke called it "the great representative document of our era, linking high and low culture."

Catch-22 concerns a World War II bombardier named Yossarian who suddenly realizes the danger of his position and tries various means to get himself excused from further missions. The term "Catch-22" refers to the rule used by the military to counter Yossarian's plea of insanity: anyone who doesn't want to fly missions can't be crazy, and therefore must fly them. Heller uses black humor to satirize the absurdity of war and parodies the oxymoronic language used by military personnel. In subsequent novels, he similarly satirizes the language of other institutions. Most critics interpreted *Catch-22* as a broad statement on the absence of human values in contemporary life, and some claimed that because Heller offers no alternative to the way of life he rejects, the novel is ultimately nihilistic. Nevertheless, the book's popularity remains undiminished, and it continues to elicit commentary. Nelson Algren claimed that *Catch-22* is "not merely the best American novel to come out of World War II; it is the best American novel to come out of anywhere in years."

Heller's second novel, *Something Happened* (1974), centers on a middle-aged businessman who has achieved material success but who feels emotionally empty. The book, which Pearl K. Bell characterized as "a monologue of paranoia and self-pity," was faulted by many critics for being tedious, long-winded, and implausible. However, others contended that the novel's length is necessary to accommodate flashbacks and to develop the deep fears and anxieties generated in the mind of the protagonist.

Good as Gold (1979) marks Heller's first use of his Jewish heritage and boyhood experiences in the Coney Island section of New York City. The protagonist, Bruce Gold, is a dissatisfied college professor who is offered a job in the current presidential administration. He finds himself in Washington surrounded by bureaucrats who speak a confusing, contradictory language all their own. Gold's struggles with his own ambition are developed in scenes alternating between Washington and his large, garrulous Jewish family in New York City.

© Joyce Ravid

Heller again explores his Jewish heritage in *God Knows* (1984), a retelling of the biblical story of King David in which David speaks in a contemporary Jewish-American dialect. The book is structured as a running comic monologue, and several reviewers have compared it to the comic routines of Lenny Bruce, Mel Brooks, and Woody Allen. Heller is also the author of three plays: *We Bombed in New Haven* (1967), *Catch-22: A Dramatization* (1971), and *Clevinger's Trial* (1973).

(See also *CLC*, Vols. 1, 3, 5, 8, 11; *Contemporary Authors*, Vols. 5-8, rev. ed.; *Contemporary Authors New Revision Series*, Vol. 8; *Dictionary of Literary Biography*, Vols. 2, 28; and *Dictionary of Literary Biography Yearbook: 1980.*)

BENJAMIN DeMOTT

Bruce Gold, hero of Joseph Heller's third novel, *Good As Gold* . . . , is a forty-eight-year-old English professor with problems. Unable to cover his children's tuition bills on academic pay, he has been piling up debts in the form of advances for unfinishable book projects ("a study of the contemporary Jewish experience in America"). He also suffers, intermittently, from doubt about his professional worth. The published cultural commentaries and political observations that support his modest reputation seem to him cheesy stuff (he "thought much less of his work than even his fussiest detractors''), and lately his opportunism has bothered him. Audiences of pious elderly reactionaries love him, but so do fire-eating teenaged Maoists, and the reason for this isn't pretty: Gold shifts his pitch according to the sympathies of whatever crowd is at hand. (p. 129)

Finally, there's some trouble with his close relatives—a status problem. Gold's father, stepmother, older sisters, brothers-in-law, even his own younger daughter, all see him as a loser. "Whatever he does is wrong," is his father's contemptuous assessment.

Hard times, but comes a chance to break out. Gold reviews, in the waffling manner he has made his own, a volume by the incumbent Chief Executive (the title is *My Year in the White House*), and in doing so hits upon phrases that entrance the not undim presidential eye. A White House aide named Ralph, known to Gold from graduate school, suggests he consider joining the Administration, probably with Cabinet rank. There are catches in the invitation—so many, indeed, as it turns out, that the hero's effort to cope with them becomes the main narrative business of the tale. (pp. 129-30)

As a send-up of Capital conventions and clichés, *Good As Gold* is sometimes funny. The hero asks a White House aide what jobs are open and learns there's a spot for a "spokesman" from which one would move up in a month "to a senior official. . . . free to hold background briefings any time you want, every time we schedule them." . . . And Heller casts a rightly cold gaze on the "organizations with Brobdingnagian names [that are] sprouting like unmanageable vines and spreading like mold with sinecures and conferments for people of limited mentality and unconvincing motive"—such real-life enclaves as the American Enterprise Institute for Public Policy Research or the Hoover Institute on War, Revolution and Peace.

The representation of Jewish family life in *Good As Gold* isn't bare of stereotype, but several episodes achieve a likable zaniness—for example, a crazily heated family debate on the meaning of the term "north" in relation to the term "up." (p. 130)

Yet despite all this I found *Good As Gold,* billed as a "major American classic," unsatisfying, and I believe I know why. It's this simple: the author can't decide how disturbed he is (or whether) by his hero's troubles and the world's, hence can't make the troubles consequential to the reader. Bruce Gold appears persuaded most days that the country is finished. . . . He finds proof of collapse in the continuing eminence of Henry Kissinger: ours is a "society in which . . . a blundering, blathering, shoddy hypocrite [is] honored as a celebrity instead of shunned and despised. . . ."

But the author himself is at pains to assure the reader that Gold is completely of a piece with his contemporaries—meaning he's a coward, a lazy, exploitative teacher, an envy-ridden competitor, and a match for Kissinger at doubleness (Gold "realized also that he was not just a liar but a hypocrite"). The hero's characteristic response to the collapse of civilization is unembarrassed pleasure at being furnished with an article idea. . . . Yet he's never raked over by his creator for this cynicism: as the title hints, in these pages none but the Gold standard applies.

Would this count if high levels of novelistic energy were sustained in the book? Conceivably not. Good fiction, dark views, and judgmental ambiguity often coexist. But the case is that in *Good As Gold* ambiguity infects, inhibits, and ultimately

depletes the energies of creation—wears things down. An example is the treatment of Secretary Kissinger. For a novelist this figure presents opportunities seemingly too rich to waste. Agility, slyness, persuasiveness, vanity, humorous self-awareness, plus the evident condescension to ordinary folk who bring only uncosmopolitan American-ness to the conduct of foreign affairs—these features of character beg for imaginative penetration. What is such a human being to himself? In this book we're offered—instead of an answer—a section of direct quotations from lifeless, objective newspaper dispatches about the former Secretary of State, excerpts from columns by Anthony Lewis, and the like. Nothing in the lot is freshly imagined.

It's the same story with the presentation of life in the executive bureaucracy. We smile when the author points mockingly at familiar outward behaviors, expecting a probe that will show the insides of the deeds and talk, thereby demonstrating, incidentally, the difference between a first-rate novel and a first-rate Russell Baker column. But the probe doesn't come. (pp. 130-31)

Internationally renowned, Mr. Heller stands forth just now as the author of only three books, therefore overviews of his oeuvre aren't yet in order. Even so, it's perhaps worth recording that his career thus far has helped to clarify the limits of comic apathy, or stylized unresponsiveness, as a resource for writers whose subject isn't war. At some moments in history—the *Catch-22* moment was among them—the tones and gestures of indifference are, paradoxically, energizing; they light up, by shocking, hellish, absurdist strokes, the conditions that quicksilver phrases such as "consciousness dulled by horror" can only obscure. But at other moments indifference and related postures lack dimension, adding up to little beyond themselves. The themes of *Good As Gold* are by no means negligible, and it's possible that the author conceived the novel as an ambitious cultural inquiry into the state of America now. But the finished production struck me, I'm afraid, as a rather listless and dispirited piece of work. (p. 131)

*Benjamin DeMott, "Heller's Gold and a Silver Sax,"
in* The Atlantic Monthly, *Vol. 243, No. 3, March,
1979, pp. 129-32.**

JOHN W. ALDRIDGE

[Black] humor has provided us with a number of analogical or parabolic evocations of the psychological disturbances of contemporary life, evocations that are sometimes so compelling we are almost persuaded that they actually do reveal reality rather than merely a set of stock responses to it. Yet over and over again in black-humor fiction the problem is that while the responses may be powerfully rendered, the concrete events and specific social circumstances that induced them are seldom identified or objectified. That essential dimension of fiction that Hemingway once described as comprising "the exact sequence of motion and fact which made the emotion" is almost always missing, leaving the emotion afloat in a causeless void.

It is one of Joseph Heller's several virtues as a black humorist that he has been able to avoid this problem and dramatize his steadily darkening vision of contemporary life through an evocation of the experiences responsible for it. In the fiction of Pynchon and Donald Barthelme, for example, virtually everything and everyone exists in such a radical state of distortion and aberration that there is no way of determining from which conditions in the real world they have been derived or from what standard of sanity they may be said to depart. The conventions of verisimilitude and sanity have been nullified, and the fiction itself stands as a metaphor of a derangement that is seemingly without provocation and beyond measurement.

Heller, by contrast, derives his materials from the actualities of the observable world, portrays them with much greater fidelity to realism, and achieves his effects through comic exaggeration and burlesque rather than hallucination—which is perhaps to say that he descends from Dickens rather than Beckett. His characters are almost always grotesques, but they are presented as grotesques, and with no suggestion that grotesqueness is the natural and universal state of being. One is always certain, furthermore, precisely to what degree they and their situations are absurd or insane, because his narrative point of view is located in an observer with whom we can identify and who is rational enough to be able to measure the departures from rationality in the people and situations he encounters.

Yossarian's problem in *Catch-22,* for example, is that he is hopelessly sane in a situation of complete madness. The high comedy of the novel is generated by the fact that military life, when viewed satirically—which is to say, rationally—becomes ludicrous and, in wartime, malevolent. But there is nothing in *Catch-22* that a person of Yossarian's perpetually affronted sensibility would not have perceived in the same circumstances. The boundaries of the normal and predictable are never exceeded, but they are extended satirically to the point where, as happens in wars, all kinds of idiocy, cruelty, obsessive self-interest, and the most inhumane bureaucratic exploitation are made to seem normal and predictable, hence altogether horrifying. . . . [The comic characters in *Catch-22*] serve to dramatize Heller's altogether uncomic hatred of a system, supposedly consecrated to high patriotic service, that could so easily become diabolical because it views people as inanimate objects to be manipulated and destroyed for inane reasons. In such a situation Yossarian clearly has abundant provocations for his paranoia. There are real enemies out there, whether on our side or theirs, and, as he repeatedly complains, they are trying to kill him. But the vastly more frightening concern is that if he has no identity as a human being, then his death will have no significance.

In his second novel, *Something Happened,* Heller faced the opposite problem. The paranoia of his protagonist, Bob Slocum, is seemingly without provocation, yet it must somehow be dramatically justified. If Slocum has enemies, he can only suspect or imagine that they are out there, but he cannot locate them. The danger, moreover, is not that they will kill him but that in some mysterious way they will not allow him to discover and live a meaningful life. In the conventional view Slocum has all the advantages that make for meaning: a secure position with a large corporation; an excellent income; a big house in Connecticut; an attractive wife with whom he has regular and good sex; and at least one child, his elder son, whom he deeply loves. Yet such things do not constitute the sum of his life, and his difficulty—which is also a large technical one for Heller—is that he must locate and make real the sources of his anguish in a situation characterized precisely by the absence of difficulty. (p. 116)

Slocum's voice drones in an interminable monologue out of a void in which the only sound is the sound of itself. It ranges obsessively over the past and present, trying to articulate the incomprehensible, seeking always to talk its way out of what is for Heller the ultimate, terrifying helplessness: the inability to identify or confront the forces that are destroying one's life and preparing one's death. But the deeply lodged suspicion in

both *Catch-22* and *Something Happened* is that there is no one at all in charge, that Kafka's castle is in fact empty, that there is no crime for which one eternally stands condemned, no order behind organization, no system behind bureaucratic structure, no governing principle behind government, that what is happening is happening for no reason, and that there is absolutely nothing to be done about it because the causes responsible cannot be located and the very idea of responsibility may have lost all meaning.

This is the radically nihilistic perception behind Heller's new novel, *Good as Gold*. Yet in spite of it he has been able to generate what is at times an almost joyous comedy out of the depths of apocalypse and to identify and engage some of the specific social conditions that have caused the vision of apocalypse to become a defining feature of the present. Heller has accomplished this through his particularly effective use of two seemingly different kinds of narrative materials—the Jewish family experience (his first attempt in fiction to draw on this experience) and a wildly phantasmagoric rendition of the Washington political scene. His protagonist, Bruce Gold, is a minor Jewish intellectual, academic, and essayist who plans to write an "abstract autobiography" based on the history of Jewish life in America, a book that is never written, but which the novel, in effect, becomes.

Gold moves back and forth between Washington and various dreadful meetings with his relatives in New York, seeing no connection between the two except that Washington promises to be a glamorous escape from the wretchedness of the family. Yet it is one of the central brilliances of the novel that although they are never explicitly paralleled, the Washington and the family experiences finally assume a portentous similarity. Both represent aspects of the same condition: the collapse of those values that once made humanity and rationality necessary.

As Heller portrays it, the trashed and decaying environment of South Brooklyn becomes an objectification of the devolving history of Gold's second-generation immigrant family. (pp. 116-17)

Like the old neighborhood, Gold's family once had a communal integrity founded on the need to survive in an environment that was harshly adversary—not because of crime and violence but because times were hard, jobs were scarce, and too many immigrant families were competing to make a life in a new country. Gold's brother and five sisters all made large sacrifices, the brother quitting school early and going to work to help support the family, while the father lost job after job. It could hardly be said that they were happy picturesquely toiling together or even that they deeply cared for one another. They were and remained the sort of people who are caring only so long as circumstances require them to be. Now that they are middle-aged and affluent, they have disintegrated into a group of bickering malcontents who come together only because they are tyrannized into it by their maniacal eighty-two-year-old father. . . .

All these people have long been displaced from the realities that formed them and gave them some sense of common purpose, and now they have become abstracted into caricatures of hostility and self-interest. Having survived the need to deal aggressively with their environment, they have turned their aggressions against one another, while around them what is left of their old environment is being destroyed by new generations of displaced people to whom it has no relation whatever and whose aggression against it is a means to nothing.

In the Washington sections of the novel this effect of derangement from conditions of order, sanity, and meaningful causality is achieved through a masterful burlesque of government bureaucracy. The people in these sections are shown to be as divorced from reality as Gold's family is displaced from South Brooklyn. Political figures have lost all sense of the principles, causes, issues, and human interests they have been elected to work for and represent, and the result in their case is not aggression but a kind of psychotic arbitrariness. . . . Titles of official positions have no relation to any specific function, and any office can be filled by anyone, since no one knows what qualifications are needed for what office. Therefore, any qualifications will do for any office. The language of government is similarly unrelated to the ideas or experiences it is supposed to describe. Words are used not to communicate but to obscure meaning, because all meaning is provisional and conjectural. . . .

As he did in **Catch-22,** Heller tends here to ring too many changes on what is essentially one good joke. And the satire much of the time is so lightheartedly outlandish that it very nearly neutralizes one's awareness that the kind of insanity Heller makes laughable has also in the real world had the most destructive consequences. Yet there is more than an edge of anger in Heller's portrait of the Washington political scene, just as there are extremely ominous implications in his vision of American culture. His novel is indeed comic, often hilariously so, but it is also comedy of the bleakest and blackest kind. It is all about a society that is fast going insane, that is learning to accept chaos as order, and unreality as normal. The horror is that the time may soon come when the conditions Heller depicts will no longer seem to us either funny or the least bit odd. (p. 118)

John W. Aldridge, "The Deceits of Black Humor," in Harper's, *Vol. 258, No. 1546, March, 1979, pp. 115-18.*

MALCOLM BRADBURY

Heller's publications come scarce, but they are of high value: he is one of our most important, painful and disturbing writers. . . .

'Good as Gold' is two stories: a tale about one of the most massively anguishing of all fictional Jewish families, and a tale about the absurdist world of contemporary American politics.

The old ingredients are satisfyingly here: the surreal farce, the cosmic irony, the pervasive sense of pain. . . . Heller is an expert in social pain; he also has always had a massive, if prolix, gift for comic accumulation. The characterisation [of Gold's family] is not only accurate but abundant: the wearing accusing father, prolonging his stay with his children through a secret list of obscure Jewish holidays, and the vile stepmother, endlessly knitting some absurdist woollen object, are superb prototypes.

The set pieces too are rich: best, perhaps, is a classic Jewish argument about burial plots. The Washington elements are flatter, but supply their useful share of Catches-22: Gold can do, he is told, anything he wants there, 'as long as it's everything we tell you to do in support of our policies, whether you agree with them or not. You'll have complete freedom.' . . .

An atmosphere of political disintegration and social decay lies over the book; this is the centre of its strength. Beyond that,

you can read it as a fable about the relationship between Jews and the facts of American power, in an era when anti-semitism is over but everybody despises Jews, and when the old victims are winners in doubtful games.

The most vigorous motif in the book is a running polemic against Henry Kissinger, who not only lied about Vietnam and betrayed Israel but, worst, *knelt* to pray with Nixon. Many modern American writers have been ambiguously tugged towards the facts and fantasies of political power: Vidal, Mailer, Roth and Bellow have all written from and about this obsession. Perhaps the disappointment of **'Good as Gold'** is that it doesn't leap beyond the ambiguity to a secure position.

As if for safeguard, Heller embodies a passage about Charles Dickens, 'a long-winded novelist, in Gold's estimation, whose ponderous works were always too long and always flawed by a procession of eccentric, one-sided characters too large in number to keep track of, and an excessive abundance of extravagant coincidences and other unlikely events.' Heller knows you could say it here of Heller. **'Good as Gold'** is good, a busy, ambiguous text. But perhaps not, quite, good as gold.

Malcolm Bradbury, "Catch-79," in The Observer, *April 29, 1979, p. 37.*

PEARL K. BELL

Good as Gold has none of the redeeming exuberance and vitality of **Catch-22,** whose wartime setting and military routines provided Heller with a controlling framework—an external reality—that shaped and defined the comic ferocity of his attack on war and its attendant pieties. How desperately Heller requires the restraining hand of actuality became plain in his second novel, **Something Happened,** a monologue of paranoia and self-pity whose 569 pages yielded exactly one memorable sentence: "When I grow up I want to be a little boy."

This unique flash of self-knowledge in Heller's dreary organization man, Bob Slocum, explains much of **Good as Gold.** For Bruce Gold is Heller's version of Jewish infantilism, an opportunist who will suck at any alien teat to get ahead. (p. 71)

Good as Gold is Joseph Heller's first bid for a piece of the Jewish action in American fiction, and he has appropriated every moldy cliché of the school of Philip Roth: monstrous parents, spiteful siblings, dumpy wives, vulgar wealth, and unappeasable lust for gorgeous Gentile women. Unlike Roth, though, Heller consistently fails to make us laugh. Every joke lays an egg long past its prime, and he thinks he is uproariously funny when he is cannibalistic and tasteless. Like Gold, Heller does not know what the "Jewish experience in America" is. And it is obvious that he has never taken the trouble, or felt any curiosity, to find out what it means to be Jewish.

Nowhere in his "Jewish" novel is his ignorance more evident than in Heller's exploitation of Yiddish, which he takes to be part blunt instrument, part Minsky joke-book. In a fifteen-page diatribe against Kissinger, Heller-Gold pours out his wrath in a jumble of basic English and the kind of Broadway Yiddish that Saul Bellow ticks off in *Herzog.* . . . (pp. 71-2)

Clearly Heller believes these Yinglish salvos to be wit of the highest order. . . .

But why limit one's satire to the "Jewish experience in America," about which one knows nothing, when one can also make hay with Washington, about which one knows even less? . . .

Heller's "truth" about Washington comes down to a feeble gimmick he had already worked to death in *Catch-22*—the oxymoronic sentence that looks like an epigram but has no teeth, such as "This . . . old man reminded Nately of his father because the two were nothing alike." Similarly, Heller "nails" the duplicitous equivocations of Washington bureaucrats through a tiresome reliance on Ralph Newsome's pointless paradoxes: "What we want are independent men of integrity who will agree with all our decisions after we make them," and some hundred retreads of the same limp joke.

That there is a difference between wild invention and satiric exaggeration, that satire must have a foothold in reality, does not seem to trouble Heller. Satire, as the critic David Worchester pointed out long ago, "must practice the art of persuasion and become proficient with the tools of that art," but Heller is unequal to this task. Lacking a real political intelligence, or an adroit satiric imagination, he tries to convey his alleged despair over the conditions of our time by making do with empty rhetoric about "blight, rubbish, rot, and moral defilement." Nothing in *Good as Gold* convinces us that Heller is genuinely engaged with the grave implications of his "jeremiad." Eighteen years after the publication of *Catch-22,* he still wields his free-floating cynicism like a machete. Only the objects of his loathing have changed. But unlike the grim facts of war, Heller's present targets—the Jewish family, Washington politics—demand the kind of complex understanding and moral courage that are beyond his grasp, and they have stubbornly resisted his glib antics and crude literary tricks. (p. 72)

> *Pearl K. Bell, "Heller & Malamud, Then & Now,"*
> in Commentary, *Vol. 67, No. 6, June, 1979, pp.*
> *71-5.**

CHARLES BERRYMAN

Good as Gold is a major step forward in Heller's career. The novel combines many of the virtues of his first two books while avoiding most of their faults. If *Catch-22* and *Something Happened* are both repetitive and rambling in structure, *Good as Gold* is unified and coherent. If the first two novels tend to indulge a sense of humor that is often sophomoric, the third book reveals a steady wit that is fully integrated with character and situation. Heller's skill at the craft of fiction has made clear advances in characterization, narrative control, and most of all in dramatic timing.

Good as Gold is a mixture of three different kinds of fiction: a Jewish family novel, a political satire, and the story of superman demythologized. (p. 110)

Not only is the title character of Heller's third novel fully dramatized among his Jewish family and friends, he is even writing a book about "the Jewish experience." The book that Bruce Gold has agreed to write may be viewed as the very novel that his fictional presence dominates. His experience as a Jew, loved and trapped by his large family, tempted and frustrated by the myth of Kissinger, is the drama of *Good as Gold.*

How does Joseph Heller expect to capture the territory of fiction so often held by Philip Roth and Saul Bellow? American literature is hardly suffering from a shortage of authors ready to dramatize "the Jewish experience." Heller recognizes the competition, and succeeds by turning the conventional genre into a comic parody. If the typical Jewish protagonist often feels threatened by the anxious counsel of his immediate fam-

ily, the hero of Heller's novel is inundated by the contradictory advice of no less than fifteen close relatives. If the family meal is supposed to be a ritual of the Passover feast, the dinners of the Gold family rival the banquets in the *Satyricon* for headache and heartburn. If the heroes of Roth and Bellow often seem to live in a world invented by Kafka, the protagonist of *Good as Gold* is haunted by shadows of persecution that even appear as messages in his Chinese fortune cookies. Heller is especially good when it comes to pushing conventional themes to absurd limits. (pp. 110-11)

Despite the size of his family and the abundance of their food, the bedeviled hero of the novel never feels at home. Heller knows how the ghost of Franz Kafka haunts contemporary Jewish fiction, and thus he multiplies the homeless insecurity of his protagonist until it assumes comic proportions. Gold often feels that his whole family has joined together to form a conspiracy against him. Worse yet, he feels that the rest of the world also stands ready to make fun of him. Although he scorns his family and friends, he suffers constantly from what he imagines they must think of him. Heller is very skillful at exploiting the comic potential of Gold's insecurity. (p. 112)

Heller also multiplies the comic troubles of his hero by doubling and tripling the number of women in his romantic imagination. The dreams of Portnoy and Herzog are developed further in the bemused philanderings of Gold. Appointment to a high position in Washington, he is told, will depend upon his [divorcing his wife and marrying] the tall, attractive daughter of a very rich anti-Semite. . . . While commuting between his two women, Gold typically falls in love with a third. That she happens to be his daughter's teacher and happens also to possess a husband and four children is characteristic of Heller's strategy of multiplying the comic potential. Now the dreams of Gold can dramatize the favors of all three women. He plans a trip to Acapulco where he expects to have his fiancée and his mistress at the same hotel with a separate room for himself where he may catch his breath between the rounds of pleasure. Gold never does get to Acapulco, but one of the great scenes of the novel is his fantasy of trying to please the two women in the adjoining hotel rooms. Even the fantasy proves so exhausting that Gold collapses and has to be taken to the hospital, where for ten days his mistress and his fiancée and his wife do not miss him at all. Heller's ability to mine comic gold in the veins of Roth and Bellow adds a new chapter to the fiction of "the Jewish experience" in American literature.

The second genre of fiction that is explored by Heller in *Good as Gold* is political satire. Although many of the Washington scenes are not among the best in the novel, they still afford Heller the chance to ridicule the bureaucracy in ways that are reminiscent of the satire in *Catch-22*. (pp. 112-13)

Heller's inspired wordplay, so often the source of comedy in *Catch-22,* informs much of the dialogue in the Washington scenes. Gold is welcomed to the White House by his college friend: "We all feel it would be a good idea to start using you here as quickly as possible if we decide we want to use you at all." . . . Gold's friend always talks in this way, and it soon grows predictable and tiresome. The political satire only becomes more interesting when the vanity, greed, and evil of Henry Kissinger are introduced as obsessions in Gold's mind. (pp. 113-14)

The scenes of Washington life in *Good as Gold* are a mixture of farce and satire. When dramatic timing and coincidence are most important, the novel moves in the direction of farce. When the comedy exposes the vices of government service—ambition, greed, vanity, etc.—the novel becomes a full-scale political satire. What rescues the novel from shallow farce is Heller's remarkable satire of Henry Kissinger's role as superman.

The reputation of Kissinger is exploited by Heller to bring together the themes of Jewish experience and political satire. Even before Gold agreed to write a book about "the Jewish experience," he had been clipping newspaper articles in preparation for a book about Henry Kissinger. The clippings are reproduced in *Good as Gold,* and thus Heller sets up the possibility of playing off his fiction against evidence from the historical record. Although many novelists of the seventies have experimented with the mixture of fact and fantasy, Heller has enjoyed a unique advantage. It is an irony of history that Heller and Kissinger were both writing books at the same time about Henry Kissinger. And it is a further irony that Kissinger often becomes a villain in the pages of *Good as Gold* and a hero in the pages of his own *White House Years* on the basis of the same actions and statements. (pp. 114-15)

The most dangerous father in the novel is not Julius Gold, who "had always considered his son a *schmuck,*" or Pugh Conover, who says, "It's not merely because you're Jewish that I don't like you," but Henry Kissinger who acts out the role of superman that Gold is tempted to imitate. The hero of Heller's novel must demythologize the role of superman in order to free himself from its vain images of power. Only by mocking the career of Kissinger can Gold come to terms with his own ambition and his own limitations. This happens when Gold inveighs against the image of Kissinger with such bitter passion that his invective spills forth in abusive Yiddish. Only then is Gold willing to give up his expectations of high office, forget about his engagement to Conover's daughter, abandon the writing of his Kissinger book, and finally return to his own wife and family. (p. 116)

Gold is constantly embarrassed by his own vain pursuit of high office, but he goes along with the game until the very night of the Embassy Ball where he expects finally to meet the President. Gold arrives at the Ball disguised in formal dress, but instead of meeting the President, he suddenly receives the news of his brother's death. Heller's sense of dramatic timing is perfect. "As Gold pulled away he saw the President's car arriving." . . . The death of his older brother will force Gold to finally assume responsibility for his own family. He leaves Washington immediately, thus leaving behind him the world of false supermen, pseudo-fathers, and gentile Jews. Gold's return to his family in New York brings the novel full circle. Beyond the unmasking of false idols and the political satire of vanity in high places, Gold finally visits the cemetery to place a pebble on his mother's grave. Ready at last to make peace with his origins, he puts his arm around the headstone which is covered with Hebrew characters he cannot read. At the end of the novel he is finally ready to begin his book about "the Jewish experience."

Is it possible that Heller also has come home? After more international fame than any first novel could possibly support, after the great suspense and disappointment with his second book, Heller has at last found his assured place among the great comic writers of modern literature. (pp. 117-18)

Charles Berryman, "Heller's Gold," in Chicago Review, Vol. 32, No. 4, Spring, 1981, pp. 108-18.

MORDECAI RICHLER

The abundantly talented Joseph Heller has never accepted limits; neither has he repeated himself. He has yet to try to slip by with a "Catch-23" or a "Something Else Happened." Instead, each time out, he has begun afresh, discovering human folly for the first time: himself amazed, irreverent and charged with appetite. It couldn't always have been easy. The incredible success of his first novel, **"Catch-22"**—surely thrilling to the author who was only 38 years old when it was first published in 1961—must, by this time, also be maddening to him. It is one thing for him to have written one of the most celebrated of post-World War II novels and quite another to have everything that followed compared to it and found somehow wanting. Praised, yes, but ultimately rebuked for not being a comparable event. . . .

Mind you, if **"Something Happened"** failed to win the huge popular acceptance of **"Catch-22,"** it was arguably more original. But **"Good as Gold,"** Mr. Heller's third novel, struck me as broken-backed. The Washington satire, the uncontrolled, inchoate raging against Henry Kissinger, seemed endless and altogether too predictable. It simply didn't knit with the soaring hilarious chapters about the Gold family life in Brooklyn, chapters that contain some of the best and most deeply felt writing Mr. Heller has ever done.

Now we have reason to clap hands. Clearly Mr. Heller is dancing at the top of his form again. **"God Knows"** is original, sad, wildly funny and filled with roaring. Ostensibly the story of King David, told in the first person, it is as much commentary as novel, written by a latter-day Rashi (the 11th-century French Jewish exegete), inspired by Brooklyn, the Marx Brothers and maybe Monty Python rather than medieval France. . . .

The Jewish novel in America, which began by describing the immigrant experience and then sailed into the mainstream to excoriate Jewish mothers and deal with the ironies of assimilation, has recently escalated to the highest rung of insolence, even sacrilege, addressing itself directly to God. (p. 1)

[David recognizes God as] the original comic Jewish novelist, and why not? What are we to make of a Lord who, in order to test his servant Abraham's loyalty, actually demands he sacrifice his only son Isaac on an altar, but provides a lamb caught in a thicket at the very last moment. Ha, ha, fooled ya, kid. Or of a God who, on a caprice—merely to win a wager with Satan—puts forth his hand, burning Job's sheep, slaying all his servants and then all his innocent children but one. Or who, taking Saul, the first king of Israel, as his instrument, has him say to David, you want to marry my daughter? Sure. Why not? Now for a dowry, bring me 100 foreskins of the Philistines.

If God is ever remembered, David muses, it certainly won't be for His patience or human kindness, will it? As Mr. Heller's King David sees it, God has dealt unfairly with His chosen people. . . .

Mr. Heller's King David, speaking to us from God knows where, has no respect for time. His narrative is larded with references to Nietzsche, to that unscrupulous plagiarist Shakespeare, to King James ("the first king of England was a fag"), to Einstein, to chemotherapy and herpes. David reminds us, a real sticking point, that no book of the Bible is named after him, but his story is the best to be found there ("Moses has the Ten Commandments, it's true, but I've got much better lines"). David complains that Michelangelo's statue portrays him as uncircumcised (''It may be a good piece of work, taken all in all, but it just isn't me''). He has, he boasts, taken a Jewish kingdom the size of Vermont and created an empire as large as Maine. The stories about him and Jonathan are nothing but malicious gossip (''I am David the King, not Oscar Wilde''). . . .

In the opening pages of the novel, King David is discovered at the age of 70, adoringly attended by a beautiful young virgin, Abishag the Shunammite, but impotent in spite of all her skills. He longs only to lie one more time with his beloved Bathsheba, who is now somewhere between 52 and 60 years old. But she insists they are now too old for such undignified sport and is constantly badgering him to anoint their dimwitted, miserly son, Solomon, King of Israel. Solomon who will crib all of David's proverbs and later claim them as his own. However, David has another disappointing son, Adonijah, and he is the heir apparent. King David's surviving children are waiting for him to die, but he still mourns the innocent babe God took from him because of his sin with Bathsheba; and, of course, he still mourns the rebellious Absalom. . . .

Mr. Heller's King David, a splendid creation, is not so much a man for all seasons as man in all his seasons. He is the beautiful son of Jesse who soothed the melancholy Saul with his harp, refreshing him. He is the cocksure young champion, master of the slingshot, who toppled Goliath. He is the warrior, celebrated by the women of Israel. . . .

He is the insatiable lover, the king in his prime, the father of the raped Tamar and the murdered Amnon, and finally a grieving man, old and stricken in years. ''The closer I come to death, the more I hate life.''

It is unlikely we will see a more ambitious or enjoyable novel about God and man this season, but this is not to say **"God Knows"** is without its flaws. It is a wonderful conceit that David, paragon of Western man, has not only composed his psalms, but also the Songs of Solomon, ''Ave Maria,'' the Goldberg Variations, Beethoven's Ninth Symphony and only God knows what else. But sometimes Mr. Heller, reaching too hard for the jarring contemporary note, settles for the cheap quick laugh. So a hung-over King David asks Bathsheba to fix him a Fernet-Branca and, on another occasion, has Abishag prepare tacos for him. . . .

Then, Mr. Heller writes a splendid little wedding night scene for David and the positively shrewish Michal in which her first words are, ''Go take a bath,'' after which she goes on to point out, ''I'm a princess.''

''Must I always call you princess?''

''If you want a civil response.''

Mr. Heller, behind his reader for once, goes on to undermine what we have already grasped by having David say, ''Michal, my bride, was not just the daughter of a king but a bona-fide Jewish American Princess! I had married a JAP! I am the first in the Old Testament to be stuck with one.''

If Mr. Heller's subject matter has varied from novel to novel, then it is fair to say all his work has been informed by an uncommon generosity of spirit and his technique remains the same. He doesn't so much tell a story as peel it like an onion—returning to the same event again and again, only to strip another layer of meaning from it, saving the last skin for the moving final pages, which is to say that, like all truly grand comic novels, **"God Knows"** is ultimately sad. (p. 36)

Mordecai Richler, ''He Who Laughs Last,'' in The New York Times Book Review, *September 23, 1984, pp. 1, 36.*

RICHARD COHEN

Joseph Heller fans, I have both good news and bad news. The good news is that Heller has written a book that is entertaining, in places very funny, in still other places touching, even occasionally wise. . . . The bad news is that even still the book does not quite work, that it's somewhat repetitious, often annoying, sometimes in bad taste, a bit at odds with itself, more of a nightclub schtick than a novel and by no means the classic that *Catch-22* was. . . .

[*God Knows*] is the story of King David told by King David in the voice of Mel Brooks doing his 2,000-year-old man routine. Heller's David is a contemporary-cum-historical figure who lives both in the past and the present. (p. 1)

As a writer, Heller is a wonderful tap dancer and he just flits across the typewriter keys in a very entertaining fashion. After a while, though, you want to yell ''enough already,'' concede that he can dance, coin a funny and even wise line (''The brain has a mind of its own'') and ask this talented writer what he is saying—why did he write this book?

It is here that *God Knows* runs into difficulty because God knows what Heller is trying to say. It seems to be about God with whom David for a while has what is now known as a close, personal relationship but with whom he does not speak for the last 30 years of his life. Their relationship goes on the rocks when God kills David and Bathsheba's first born: ''I lost my God and the infant in the same instant.''

But that's David's version of what happened. The truth is that while he won't speak to God, God won't speak to him, either. The infant was killed not out of caprice, but in punishment for the death of Bathsheba's husband, which David had arranged. Still, this is no logical God. His choice of David to be king of Israel is inexplicable even to David himself—although not as crazy as the choice of Saul, a manic-depressive who could turn homicidal without warning. God's demands, which include genocide, are outrageous, but he speaks in the patter of a vaudevillian of the Smith and Dale genre. He answers questions with questions and his language, you'd be relieved to know, is Yiddish. This is a God capable of turning old jokes into Biblical events: Make me a malted. Poof, you're a malted.

But what does it all mean? At first I thought it meant that God was dead, or a mere invention of man, or something like that. . . . But no, that was not it and it's not, either, that God is just crazy, a loony, an out-patient from heaven who would, if he came to earth, say something profound and then spend the night on a steam grate. If I had to guess, I would say that Heller's God, the God of David if not also of Abraham and Isaac, is a wife out of the Henny Youngman School of Divinity—ungrateful, capricious, unpredictable, who is to be loved in direct proportion only to the love, no, idolatry, she/he can offer an ingrate. Cheat on God and He will turn cold and frigid and then you can justify cheating some more. David is a king who puts his head on the bar and moans, ''My God doesn't understand me.'' He winds up a lonely old man, lusting for both Bathsheba and God, racked by a chill that comes from within.

Maybe, though, Heller is saying none of those things. Maybe I was on a literary scavenger hunt for something that wasn't there—a theme, a statement, an insight that would leave me a little bit wiser for the time I put in. This, after all, is not just Joseph Heller, but *the* Joseph Heller—the author of *Catch 22* who made you see that things that were funny were not so funny and, of course, vice versa. In *God Knows,* though, what's funny is funny and what's not is not and seldom do the twain meet. The really hard work of writing, thinking, has not been done. *God Knows* is a goof. Only Joe Heller could have made it as good as it is. And only Joseph Heller could have made it better. God knows why he didn't. (pp. 1-2)

Richard Cohen, "Old Testament Time Warp," in
Book World—The Washington Post, *September 30,*
1984, pp. 1-2.

AL J. SPERONE

The old codger who rants and reminisces and kvetches through Joseph Heller's *God Knows* is none other than King David, the psalmist of the Old Testament. If you believe Samuel, Chronicles, and Kings, slaying Goliath was only the beginning of David's achievements. He gave the Middle East its first (and last) central government by either pacifying or destroying all warring tribes in the area. He also danced in the streets, fathered Solomon, and got strategic advice directly from God. He left a mark on politics, literature, music, geography, military science, and maybe even religion.

In the Bible, David's story gets reported like journalism—it's all action and dialogue. Heller tries to flesh out David, Bathsheba, and the rest of the old gang, to make them three-dimensional characters. But *God Knows* doesn't become *The Greatest Story Ever Told;* pious it ain't. Heller's David has the wildly anachronistic benefit of 20th century hindsight, plus Yiddishized diction that lends him a Borscht Belt comic's phrasing and timing. The paragraphs bounce from King James to straight narrative to Woody Allen punchlines. Early on, David philosophizes, ". . . a man has no better thing to do under the sun than to eat and to drink and to be merry, although that isn't always the easiest thing to do when all you've got is a pastrami.". . .

God Knows has been packaged and promoted as a funny novel, and it has a lot of quasi-blasphemous verbal slapstick. Heller likes to fill in between the lines of the Bible, à la *Monty Python's Life of Brian* or Bill Cosby's Noah routine. David asks God for advice:

> "Will Saul come down to Keliah after me
> as Thy servant believes?"
> "You bet your ass," said the Lord.
> "And will the men of Keliah deliver us
> unto the hand of Saul?"
> "It's funny you should ask."

(p. 6)

Unfortunately, Heller also likes the occasional Flintstones-style joke; David wants to leave an obscene message on Bathsheba's answering machine, then remembers that the telephone hasn't even been invented yet. Some of the wilder flights—Joab's plans to conquer Europe and Asia, and to provision the men on herring once they reach Scandinavia—seem to be remnants of another version of the book, in which the recreated David is a purely modern fantasy rather than a character in his own era.

As a major author who's less than prolific—just four novels and a play beginning with *Catch-22,* back in 1961—Heller

chooses his shots carefully, and taking on the Bible is bound to be a major statement. Wisecracks and all, *God Knows* is a serious book on all the Mod Lit topics: loss of faith and community, the uses of art (David's psalm-singing and elegy-writing), the absence of God. About halfway through the book, the jokes start to thin out as David approaches the big tragedy—the death of his favorite son, Absalom, killed by a loyal retainer against David's orders but for his own good. By the end of the novel, despair and mortality are in the air, and all flippancy is gone.

Heller has chosen a resonant and surprisingly modern part of the Old Testament. In it, a petty, capricious, bloodthirsty God demands tribute, watches over continuous conflict and escalates sibling rivalry into civil war. Early in David's reign, God stops speaking directly to David, and never returns. And at the center of the story is a bloody, symmetrical pattern of Oedipal battles, generation after generation; both David's father-in-law, Saul, and his son become his deadly enemies.

Not coincidentally, that story parallels parts of Heller's last two novels, and David on his deathbed now joins Heller's ongoing dynasty of bummed-out middle-aged men. Like Bob Slocum of *Something Happened,* he knows all too well that his glory years are behind him; he also loses a child. Heller's David, like Slocum, just can't connect with his children and lusts for a wife he dislikes. Like Bruce Gold of *Good As Gold,* David wonders about what Jewishness means, writes prolifically, keeps a harem, and has a father who's out to get him. David, Bruce, and Bob are all, literally and figuratively, God-forsaken.

The structure of *God Knows* recalls *Something Happened,* which itself was an echo and extension of the dying-Snowden episodes of *Catch-22.* In the present tense, the plot hinges on whether David will choose Adonijah, his eldest son, or Solomon, Bathsheba's son, as his successor. . . . But while that plot moves slowly forward, the narrative circles obsessively around a few central episodes from the past, gradually revealing the full picture like a literary *Last Year at Marienbad.* Just about every incident of the book is mentioned in the first 50 pages, then dilated. . . . Like a psychoanalysis, the novel keeps coming back to its traumas until it can bear to examine them.

With the tape-loop repetitions of *God Knows,* I think Heller has found an odd link between comedy and psychoanalysis—two fields with a goodly number of Jewish practitioners. Heller knew as early as *Catch-22* that comedy, even black comedy, could be built out of repetition and escalation; think of Major Major's name, Milo Minderbinder's bigger and bigger deals, or the ever-increasing number of missions. . . .

In everyday life, meanwhile, repetition can equal compulsion, and it's only funny from the outside, if at all. The compulsion in David's family—the tragic pattern—is for sons to challenge fathers, and for fathers to become murderers in response. . . .

Unfortunately, while the structure of *God Knows* is itself a lesson, and the rhythms of Heller's prose hustle along, the novel can't live up to its implications. One problem is that we know—or would if we had anything like a classical education—how the story comes out; it's in the Book, so there's not much suspense. You might not have heard of Adonijah because he never made it to the throne; Solomon did. Where *Something Happened* had a gathering sense of doom, and its own reasons for being deliberately slow, *God Knows* makes you want to turn the pages faster, to get on with it. Heller also has an annoying tendency to condescend to every character except warrior males. It's ugly to suggest that David's son Amnon, a creepy character who rapes his half-sister Tamar, was a repressed homosexual; it's sad that all the women in the book are either dull and obliging or just plain mean, whether or not they're sexy.

But the main problem may be the book's initial premise—turning David into a 20th century Heller character. David wasn't a nervous cog like Slocum or a nebbishy cat's-paw like Gold; he built a country, talked to God, wrote all those Psalms. The modernist creed of enjoying small victories against entropy doesn't quite apply, and neither, perhaps, does a modern idea of character. David was God-haunted and nationalistic, or perhaps just another territory-hungry despot, but he was certainly purposeful, and he got what he wanted. Heller follows the twists and turns of the Biblical plot—there's plenty of unadulterated King James in the novel—but he can't put David together or, in the end, illuminate him. A hero, even a dying and impotent one, doesn't fit in with Heller's lowered—modernist—expectations; 20th century psychology can humanize David's weaknesses, but not his strengths. (p. 7)

Al J. Sperone, "Maybe He's Just Like His Father,"
in VLS, No. 29, October, 1984, pp. 6-7.

FRANCES GUSSENHOVEN

Joseph Heller, whose last novel, *Good as Gold* (1979), satirized books on "the Jewish experience in America" while itself being one, [explores in *God Knows*] another kind of Jewish experience—that of being David, King of Israel. From the throne of his slightly musty bed, the aging David exults in the story he (i.e., Heller) tells, arguably the best in the Bible: "I've got the poetry and the passion, savage violence and the plain raw civilizing grief of human heartbreak . . . I've got a love story and a sex story, with the same woman no less . . . and I've got this on-going, open-ended Mexican standoff with God, even though he might be dead." . . .

[Although] mindful of the settings of Samuel I and II, Heller's focus is on human passion, and the medium is David's monologue. He is obsessed with certain memories, like his slaying of Goliath, his playing before Saul and his love-lust for Bathsheba. These experiences are related again and again as they recur to the old man's mind. Each rendition is new and fresh, however, punctuating the chronological narrative of David's career until, in the final scene, the memories come together in a surprising comedic twist.

And, in fact, the novel abounds in comic reversals, as we might expect from the author of *Catch 22*. The serious and the absurd jostle one another even in the levels of diction. A chiseled narrative sentence may be juxtaposed with a parody of God's dealings with Moses: "And He spake and He spake and He spake. . . . There was so much spaking it's a wonder Moses had time to walk." . . .

Deliberate anachronisms also heighten the comic effect, suggesting that Old Testament characters are not unlike ourselves. . . . Bathsheba loftily explains that she has had no children by Uriah because she was "on the pill." And David complains about the Promised Land in terms of Beverly Hills and Cannes, wondering how to improve garbage removal and sewage disposal in Jerusalem. But most of all, this is a zesty, bawdy soliloquy resembling the Wife of Bath's on the subject of life with her five husbands. In Heller's novel, David similarly boasts or laments of his wives, Michal, Abigail, Abishag and, of course, Bathsheba.

True, as "God knows," God is there, too. He is a remote presence who confirms David's own ideas about military strategy, disclaims any obligation to be humanly kind, and kills David's first son by Bathsheba. The theology of the piece may be summed up in David's contention, "I'm a much better person than He is." This wry confrontation of the human with the Divine reveals a familiarity that approaches love. Yet the reversal of David's expectations of God in the final scene conveys a sense of absurdity in a universe where, as David feels, God *may* be dead but probably is not. One is not sure who has the last laugh, but it is probably Heller, who has created an absurdist version of a divine comedy.

Frances Gussenhoven, "'Fiction Is Fact Distorted
into Truth': 'God Knows'," in *America, Vol. 151,*
No. 15, November 17, 1984, p. 325.

Fritz Hochwälder

1911-

Austrian-born dramatist, scriptwriter, and essayist.

A significant German-language dramatist who is not widely known outside Europe, Hochwälder writes well-crafted plays that center on weighty moral issues. His plays are conventionally structured, emphasizing plot, fully developed characters, and thematic unity, and they appeal to both the intellect and the emotions. Hochwälder's works characteristically focus on a secure protagonist who experiences a devastating moment of self-realization. According to Alan Best, "The shock of self-recognition, the trauma of coming to terms with an identity one did not even suspect in oneself, underlines Hochwälder's dramatic message: no one is safe from such a moment of unmasking."

Born and raised in Austria, Hochwälder left his homeland after the invasion of the German army in 1938. He spent time in refugee camps in Switzerland and concentrated on writing plays since, as a noncitizen, he was barred from seeking employment. Hochwälder's play *Das heilige Experiment* (1942; *The Strong Are Lonely*) was a major success in several European countries during the 1940s. Like most of his early works, this play explores universal themes through historical settings. *The Strong Are Lonely* is based upon the rise and fall of a utopian Jesuit settlement in Paraguay during the eighteenth century. The settlement is ordered to disband by both religious and secular officials; Father Alfonso, the protagonist and head of the settlement, acquiesces to authority, but he later realizes that he should have trusted his own conscience rather than let others decide his fate. This theme of conscience versus obedience is also developed in *Der Flüchtling* (1945), an early play uncharacteristically set in modern times. In this work, Hochwälder poignantly depicts the moral dilemma of a border guard to represent those people who avoid responsibility by arguing that they are merely following orders. *Der öffentliche Ankläger* (1947; *The Public Prosecutor*), another early historical play, is set during the French Revolution and centers on the prosecutor responsible for the Reign of Terror. In an ironic twist, the prosecutor uses his wiles to condemn an unnamed criminal who turns out to be himself.

Die Herberge (1955; *The Inn*) is considered a transitional work in Hochwälder's career, initiating his increasing interest in contemporary topics. Hochwälder's later works display his skill with various types of drama, including comedy, mystery, social criticism, and plays based on legend. *The Inn*, about a corrupt usurer who is suddenly forced to account for his actions, is one of several later plays that explore guilt. In *Der Himpbeerpflücker* (1964; *The Raspberry Picker*), Hochwälder depicts a group of Austrians who repress their guilt for having profited from a nearby concentration camp. *Lazaretti oder der Sabeltiger* (1975; *Lazaretti or the Saber-Toothed Tiger*) focuses on the problem of terrorism in its portrayal of hypocrites whose actions counter their professed ideals.

(See also *Contemporary Authors*, Vols. 29-32, rev. ed.)

BROOKS ATKINSON

In one form or another, Fritz Hochwalder's **"The Strong Are Lonely"** has been played in many parts of Europe. It is easy

© Lütfi Özkök

to understand why. . . . Finding his theme in a godly utopia set up in Paraguay in the eighteenth century, Mr. Hochwalder has raised an absorbing religious speculation and written several very dramatic scenes. . . .

Some Jesuit fathers have organized a godly state in South America. Under their authority, thousands of Indians have become Christians. The Indians are fed, clothed, protected and educated by an inspired band of Jesuits who are serving Jesus and who expect in time to relinquish control of the state to the native inhabitants.

But organizing the kingdom of heaven on earth provokes the resistance of the Spanish planters outside the state. The planters are losing their laborers. Since the utopian state also threatens the authority and the revenues of the Spanish crown across the sea, the king orders its dissolution. But the agonizing blow comes from the head of the Jesuit order. He is against it, too. For he decides that it is converting Indians to Christianity, not for spiritual glory, but for food, for security and for material reasons. He joins with the planters and the king in requiring the Jesuits to abandon their perfect state and return the Indians to the world of men.

For the Jesuits, animated by the holiest reasons, have gone beyond their jurisdiction: they have dared to light their tapers at the sacred flame. They are charged with having taken the

232

words of Jesus literally, and they have provoked, not only temporal power, but religious power against them. When **"The Strong Are Lonely"** is developing this theme in terms of a court inquiry, it is a completely engrossing drama that touches some big ideas about man and God and benevolent authoritarianism. . . .

After the spiritual leader of the state has accepted the awful decisions against him, **"The Strong Are Lonely"** is a good deal less interesting. There is an element of grandeur in the climactic scene. But the story of obeying the orders and dissolving the state is anticlimactic and it involves the last third of the evening. Those are the scenes that have the form of drama without creative dramatic substance. In the writing they are pedestrian. . . . For Mr. Hochwalder has nothing more to say that is a tenth as stimulating as his arguments against absolute purity in the institutions of men on the earth.

This is a pity. . . .

There are some extraordinarily challenging ideas in **"The Strong Are Lonely."** Unfortunately, Mr. Hochwalder solves them long before he comes to the end of his drama.

> *Brooks Atkinson, "Victor Francen and Dennis King in a Drama about a Jesuit Colony," in* The New York Times, *September 30, 1953, p. 38.*

HAROLD CLURMAN

From a trade angle there would seem to be little point now in reviewing **"The Strong Are Lonely,"** which closed after seven performances. But the play was patently superior to most shows we see—including many successes. Apart from an insufficiently integrated production, **"The Strong Are Lonely"** failed because its subject matter, though based on a fundamentally universal theme, is foreign to our theater audiences.

Religion in our country is not only separate from the state; it is separate from our lives. The religious impulse, as well as certain consequences of religious training, certainly enters into our thinking and behavior more than we commonly suppose, but we are not used to viewing religion as an active, practical central force of our daily concern. In Europe, where the church has played a vital part in the development of states and cultures, where today there are important parties which to a large extent are secular functions of the church, vying for control of the bodies as well as the minds of entire nations, the problems posed in **"The Strong Are Lonely"** are almost topical. . . .

Hochwalder's play depicts the trials of a Jesuit Father Provincial who wishes to make Christianity a living force on every level of man's activity. As such it is an absorbing and impressive work, though its ending is ambiguous, sentimental, and probably evasive. As a piece of theater it is unusual and dramatically sturdy in a near-classic vein. It is a pity that it could not be produced here under conditions more favorable to a cordial hearing than those afforded by the Broadway system.

> *Harold Clurman, in a review of "The Strong Are Lonely," in* The Nation, *Vol. 177, No. 16, October 15, 1953, p. 317.*

RICHARD HAYES

What I could discern of [**"The Strong Are Lonely"**] beneath the glaze of baroque rhetoric and fustian . . . was provocative and enthralling. The Austrian playwright—a singular figure, the most considerable dramatist his country has produced perhaps since Hofmannsthal—wrote the original version of **"The Strong Are Lonely"** in 1942, while interned at a Swiss labor camp. It had, subsequently, a European success of great magnitude. . . .

It is immediately refreshing to note the spaciousness and ease of the work, the uncommon ability it has to elude that narrowing imaginative constriction which so often afflicts literature conceived under conditions of such duress. Experience is not here violated to fit neatly the demands of any symbolic or moral scheme; the life portrayed has its own consistency and interest and claim to the attention. Yet inevitably Hochwalder has dealt with ideology, and I can think of no postwar drama which has confronted the terrible solicitations of our age with so much probity and rectitude, such a valorous acquiescence in the tangle of aspiration and defeat we are pleased to call life.

The subject of **"The Strong Are Lonely"** is that strange "holy experiment" which the Society of Jesus instigated among the natives of Paraguay in the latter half of the eighteenth century: an attempt to establish an ideal community, ordered to the most generous measure of justice and charity one may anticipate within the limits of this world. The play takes the colony in the full tide of its success: then follows it down through a swift, tragic destruction by both temporal and ecclesiastical authorities grown resentful and suddenly concerned at the power "God's kingdom on earth" has become.

What distinguishes **"The Strong Are Lonely"** among other works on a similar theme is its dramatic vigor, and the seminal religious insight and dialectical intrepidity it displays: Hochwalder has gone beyond the conventional ironies (he contents himself, for example, neither with an essay on the vanity of spiritual pride, nor a simplistic moral portrait of the triumph of worldly malignancy) and created a truly *grasping* image of the permanent impact of idealism on society. No solution is suggested, there is even no *parti pris:* only the hard truth, rising out of the debris of so much human hope and sacrifice, that "each man alone must help create God's kingdom on earth." (p. 60)

> *Richard Hayes, in a review of "The Strong Are Lonely," in* Commonweal, *Vol. LIX, No. 3, October 23, 1953, pp. 60-1.*

GEORGE WELLWARTH

Fritz Hochwälder's dramas deal with conflict within the human mind. All drama is conflict of one sort or another, but the drama of conflict within one human mind is the oldest and purest form of drama. (p. 184)

Of the trio of writers who have made the most significant contribution to the contemporary German-speaking theater, Fritz Hochwälder is the only one who has concentrated on the most basic form of drama. The other two, Frisch and Dürrenmatt, have branched out for the most part into the drama of personified ideas.

A dramatist ideally raises a conflict in the mind of the protagonist and lets us see him grow to an awareness of it. The purest drama is condensed into that moment in which the character, for the first time, sees himself as he is, when he becomes conscious of the difference between the illusion he has lived and the reality he should have lived. It is the moment of self-realization for the character and for the audience watching him.

It is the horror of looking into a kaleidoscope and suddenly seeing the randomly scattered crystals fall into a rigidly ordered array of graduated prisms. This horrifying destruction of illusion and rearrangement of personal values is the basis of Fritz Hochwälder's drama.

Hochwälder's most representative play, *Das Heilige Experiment*, deals with the expulsion of the Jesuits from Paraguay in 1767. The Jesuits had established what amounted in effect to a sovereign state within the Spanish-held territory of Paraguay. (p. 185)

In Hochwälder's play the Spanish settlers have secretly transmitted slanders about the Jesuit state to the Spanish crown. The king of Spain perceives that these slanders, if accepted at face value, will enable him to confiscate the rich territory of the Jesuits. He therefore accepts them, draws up the edict dissolving the Jesuit state, and *then* sends out a commission to "investigate" the accusations. The commission is to hear both sides, but it already has the king's signed sentence in its possession. In other words, the investigation, like all investigations in which the investigator is one of the interested parties, is to be a deliberate farce. It is at this point—with the arrival of the commission—that Hochwälder's play begins.

The head of the commission, Don Pedro de Miura, is an old friend of Alfonso Fernandez, the Jesuit Father Provincial. He is determined to conduct a completely fair and impartial investigation for the show of the thing and also in order to satisfy himself personally of the truth or falsity of the accusations. He knows, of course, that the sentence is already passed, but he wishes to satisfy himself of its justice. The investigation quickly brings out the obvious fact that the accusations are *untrue;* that, in fact, they are slanders invented by the Spanish colonists who envy the Jesuits their rich harvests and devoted laborers. Nevertheless, though he privately acknowledges to the Father Provincial that the charges are untrue, Don Pedro has to carry out the sentence. He pronounces the Jesuit state dissolved. Father Alfonso's answer is to arrest him: he and his fellow Jesuits have decided to fight to maintain their Kingdom of God on earth. All this time an elderly, dapper little Italian traveler has been watching the proceedings with a genteel air of disinterest. This Signor Querini, as he calls himself, now tells Father Alfonso that he is the emissary of the general of the Jesuit Order. He orders Father Alfonso to release the king's commissioner and obey his demands. . . . Father Alfonso is forced to obey the rules of the order. He hands his written surrender to Don Pedro and commands the reluctant fathers under his charge to obey. . . . Despite the Father Provincial's orders, fighting breaks out—whose fault this is is not made clear—and he is himself wounded while trying to stop it. In his fury he tears the map of Jesuit Paraguay from the wall and curses his work.

And now comes Hochwälder's psychological turning point. As Father Alfonso lies dying of his wound and as he watches Don Pedro sign the death warrants of Father Oros and a number of Indian hostages, he realizes he was wrong—wrong to obey his vow, wrong not to do what he felt to be right. At the same time he realizes that to meet violence with violence, to defend the right with blood, is also wrong. Nothing is solved. . . . At the time of critical decision life becomes an impasse, Hochwälder is saying. Father Alfonso realizes at the moment of death that everything he had ever believed in and lived by was wrong. He has wavered between two courses of action, both wrong; and there were no other alternatives. Devoutly religious all his life, he is faced at the moment of death with the knowl-

edge that religion has no solution to the problem of life. Hochwälder's play is the tragedy of moral frustration.

[In *Der Flüchtling,* written in 1945,] Hochwälder treats a psychological problem that has always puzzled and horrified thinking men all over the world. It is the problem of the apparent schizophrenic nature of the world's monsters. We all know the stories, which the tabloids gleefully serve up to us whenever they have the opportunity, about insanely vicious murderers or child-rapists or animal-torturers who are found upon investigation to have a happy family, admiring neighbors, doting parents, and an unctuously approving superior at the office. . . . This Dr. Jekyll and Mr. Hyde duality in human nature is the subject of Hochwälder's play.

Der Flüchtling takes place in what seems to be the southwest corner of Germany, near the French and Swiss borders. There are only three characters: the fugitive, the border guard, and the guard's wife. The fugitive is trying to get across the border to a neutral country, and the wife feels herself obligated to help him when he stumbles exhausted into her house. The border guard is the real protagonist, however. It is his duty to catch the fugitive and hand him over to the secret police. He knows quite well they will torture him and kill him, but that, or course, is none of his business. In the border guard, Hochwälder gives us a picture of the people who formed the backbone of the Nazi regime. These are the petty officials who are able to compartmentalize their lives and live as upright burghers in one part and as inhuman monsters in the other. . . . Such people do not lack moral sense; they merely have the faculty of transferring their guilt. *They* are not responsible, *they* have not given the order. Hochwälder's border guard is a perfect example of this type. At home he is a model husband, deeply and sincerely in love with his wife; on duty he is an automaton, ready to do anything that he is ordered to do. His moral sense is not dead: he realizes what he is doing, but he rationalizes everything by convincing himself that he is doing it for his wife's sake. To preserve his wife's peace of mind he would do anything—and besides, he does it because he is ordered to do it, and therefore he is not morally responsible. The old argument.

When the guard learns that his wife is hiding the fugitive, he is horrified. Their whole happiness is jeopardized. What should he do? Pretend to help the fugitive to escape and then shoot him in the back as soon as he is outside the house—obviously! Death will be instantaneous, the fugitive need never know anything, and the happy home life will be preserved: the perfect plan. There is just one hitch: the wife, who has been sheltered from reality up to now, refuses to yield to expediency when she is at last faced with a real moral problem of her own. Leaving her husband contemptuously, she barricades herself in the bedroom with the fugitive. Later she falls asleep and the fugitive comes down and offers to try and cross the border alone before she wakes up. The guard, appreciating the decency of the proposal, offers the fugitive his hand. It is scornfully rejected. . . . As he realizes why no decent man can shake his hand, the events of his life suddenly rearrange themselves in the guard's mind and drop into their proper places. He looks down the long corridor of his past, as it were, and it is like looking into the abyss itself. He helps the fugitive to escape with his wife, and then calls out the news of his treachery to the approaching militia. They answer with a shot, and he falls dead across the threshold that he had ruined his life to protect.

As might be expected from a writer whose political disagreements with the Nazis had forced him to flee his native country, the rise of the German despotism continued to fascinate Hochwälder. A conscientious artist feels the compulsion to explain to himself what is wrong with the world; and it is in responding to his explanation or in denying it that his audience either learns more about the world or becomes convinced that it is impossible to learn anything—which is a solution of sorts too, as the writers of the theatre of the absurd have demonstrated. In *Der Flüchtling* Hochwälder explored the effect of a totalitarian state on an average individual mind; in *Esther* he wrote a complete allegory of the rise of the Nazi mentality in terms of the Biblical story of Esther, Mordecai, and Haman. (pp. 185-91)

The characteristic Hochwälder touch of inner revelation comes at the very end in *Esther*. Unlike the Biblical heroine, Hochwälder's has not been particularly anxious to save her people.... In the Biblical story Esther obtains the king's favor and the privilege of having any wish granted. She simply accuses Haman of treachery, and that is that. Haman is taken out and hanged; Mordecai is made the chief minister; and the Jews are granted the privilege of using the time set aside for their own extermination to slaughter their enemies. Hochwälder's Esther does not have so simple a task, nor could Hochwälder, writing in 1940, present so sanguine an ending. Esther traps Haman with an elaborate plot that reveals he had been planning to overthrow the king. But even so the Jews' troubles are not over. The king recognizes that the country does need a scapegoat and that the Jews are the obvious choices for the position. He will not, of course, exterminate them, he assures Esther, but merely persecute them a little whenever the people need to have their attention diverted from official corruption and inefficiency. To show that he is not really prejudiced against Jews, he will marry Esther (she has been his concubine up to now) provided she keeps her origin a secret, and he will ennoble Mordecai. The latter tears up his charter of nobility and tells the king he will not be singled out but will share the fate of his people. As Esther quietly watches the scene, she experiences the typical Hochwälderian inner revulsion and announces that she gives up her chance for the throne to go with Mordecai. Until such time as justice reigns in the world and her people are judged on an equal basis with other peoples, she can do nothing—nor has she any right to save herself alone.

In *Der Flüchtling* and in *Esther,* more than in any other of his plays, we can see Hochwälder's use of the flash of moral enlightenment as a dramatic and didactic device. One decisive key event occurs that changes a man's whole life by rearranging the perspective of his memories. What could be more dramatic than this moment of inner realization? The same "moment of truth" appears in most of Hochwälder's other plays. In *Donadieu* (published 1953), for example, the problem is the rejection of revenge. Again a complete reversal of a man's purpose in life is involved. (pp. 191-93)

[In] *Meier Helmbrecht* (published 1956), Hochwälder tells the story of a medieval landowner whose son becomes a bloodthirsty robber who pillages the countryside until he is finally caught himself. The point of the play comes in the third act, when Helmbrecht is tried by a jury of his peers on the smoking ruins of his farmhouse. Slowly he is made to realize that his protestations of innocence are willful self-delusion and that he too is responsible for his son's crimes. What his son has become Helmbrecht's neglect and indulgence made him: the sins of the children must be visited upon the fathers. Hochwälder unfortunately gives his play a rather weak ending by reconciling Helmbrecht with his now crippled and blinded son as he starts to rebuild his house.

Since most of Hochwälder's plays were written during or immediately after the war, it is only natural that he should be so taken up by this question of the placing of guilt. In *Meier Helmbrecht* he argues that the fathers are responsible for the children. In *Der Flüchtling* he argues that a man is responsible for his own integrity—that the plea that he is only a cog in the machine is valueless.... Hochwälder deals with the justice of this plea on the part of the older generation in *Meier Helmbrecht,* on the part of the man in the street in *Der Flüchtling,* and in *Der Öffentliche Anklager* (. . . published 1954), a melodrama about the French Revolution, he deals with the leaders of the people—the politicians, officials, and generals. Like these people, Fouquier-Tinville, the cold-blooded public prosecutor who engineered the Reign of Terror, pleads that he is a servant of the state and that it is his duty to obey orders.... (pp. 193-94)

Some may quarrel with Hochwälder's theory of psychology. Man, they will say, is not transformed, except in the rarest of rare cases, into a completely different psychological being by one occurrence. Few men are that sensitive. In fact, it is probably nearer to the actual human truth to say that man never learns by experience, that he is irredeemably set in childhood upon a labyrinthine and enclosed psychological path. But Hochwälder's view of human nature is nonetheless the most dramatic possible. The luxury of precise psychology must be left to the novelist, who has the space and the structural flexibility to indulge in whatever he will. The dramatist is bound by the exigencies of the stage. He must depict the events of the world at their highest intensity, regardless of whether or not they would happen precisely thus in real life. (p. 195)

> George Wellwarth, ''Fritz Hochwälder: The Drama within the Self,'' in his The Theater of Protest and Paradox: Developments in the Avant-Garde Drama, New York University Press, 1964, pp. 184-95.

ERNST SCHÜRER

Hochwälder is not very much interested in dramatic experiments; he writes well-constructed plays, following the ideal of the *pièce bien faite* and observing the unities of time, place and action.... Although Hochwälder has not been able to repeat [the] initial success [of *Das heilige Experiment*], his subsequent plays were well received, and he has continued writing solidly composed works.

In the present two volumes [*Dramen*]—published in his native country, to which he chose not to return after the war—ten of his plays have been collected. Most are based on literary sources or historical events, such as the suspenseful *Der öffentliche Ankläger* (1948), which retells the fall of the public prosecutor Fouquier-Tinville in the aftermath of the French Revolution, and *Hôtel du Commerce* (1946), based on Maupassant's story *Boule de suif*. . . .

The phenomena of anti-Semitism and war crimes, of guilt and atonement, have always interested Hochwälder, and he explores these problems in *Der Himbeerpflücker* (1965), a comedy, and in *Der Befehl* (1968). In both plays the relationship between past and present is stressed, with the majority of those involved suppressing their guilt and carrying on as if nothing had happened. Hochwälder, like so many before him, asks himself the question how peaceful citizens and kind family fathers could be turned into murderers and even sadists, like the commander of a concentration camp who sends his prisoners into the forest to pick raspberries and then shoots them with a telescopic rifle, or the innkeeper who has used the gold from the teeth of the murdered to establish himself after the war. To make use of such motifs in a comedy, as Hochwälder does, is certainly a dubious matter. In *Der Befehl* a conscientious and dutiful Austrian detective discovers that he himself is the brutal murderer he has been ordered to find. He uncovers his own past and his suppressed guilt and atones for his crimes with his life.

Hochwälder's plays, although unpretentious and traditional, provide challenging roles for actors and good entertainment for the public.

> Ernst Schürer, in a review of "Dramen," in World
> Literature Today, *Vol. 51, No. 1, Winter, 1977, p.*
> *89.*

JAMES SCHMITT

The predominant influences (besides traditional classical drama) on Hochwälder's theater seem to be George Kaiser, World War II and above all the Viennese theater.... The Viennese *Volkstheater* seems to stem from two basic sources: the baroque Jesuit drama of the seventeenth century, which presented metaphysical truths through the senses by means of plays rather than by intellectual discourses, and the Italian *commedia dell'art,* which was noted for its improvisations, fantasies, parodies, and *Hanswurst* figures. Hochwälder's aim, influenced especially by the Jesuit theater, is to combine theatrical experience and understandable truth.... Hochwälder believes that the ideal theater should amalgamate life's serious and comic sides; he complains therefore about Germany's "Protestant" seriousness ..., but strangely enough his own plays lack the Viennese qualities of comedy, lightness, farce and, except for *Donnerstag* (1959) and *1003* (1963), magic.

The play *Donnerstag* is a good example of Hochwälder's Viennese background. At the risk of being unappreciated by non-Austrian audiences, Hochwälder wrote this mystery play, an allegory in an imaginative fantastic world, for a specific purpose—to be staged at the "Salzburger Festspiele" in 1959. He does not consider *Donnerstag* so much an experiment in style (a radical departure from his earlier historical plays) or an attempt at being modern, and certainly not an offshoot of the theater of the absurd. Rather it is a continuation of the *Jedermann* tradition, in which a man, representing all mankind, is seeking the meaning of life, and of the Austrian *Zaubertheater* tradition where characters speak dialect and where magic occurs.... In the play Niklaus Manuel Pomfrit, who has attained everything life can offer and in the process lost faith, hope and charity, becomes a living corpse, a man with no purpose in life. If Pomfrit signs the contract presented by the *Unterteufel* Wondrak, he will be guaranteed a complete cessation of the yearning for the lost purpose of life. Pomfrit seems anxious to take up the offer until a mendicant priest and a young girl reawaken his former childlike faith. Wondrak then doubles his efforts to win Pomfrit's soul before the midnight deadline. Pomfrit struggles with his decision and the outcome remains unknown to the audience at the final curtain.

The characters in the play show no development because they are stereotypes. Pomfrit is an abstract personification of everyman, the concrete embodiment of modern man, who has become king of all creation yet possesses within himself nothing more than fear, dissatisfaction, and despair; Maskeron, half technician, half psychiatrist, is the mastermind of big business who will use any means for a profit; Wondrak, a devil and anxious salesman, is ready to serve others for personal advancement; Kormoran is a bourgeois satisfied with material comforts; Persenbeug is the intellectual climber who wants to dominate all others through mental supremacy; Amalie is the sex symbol with nothing more than a beautiful body; Birnstrudl is a *Hanswurst* figure, the uneducated servant, content with food and survival, for whom ignorance means bliss; Kapora is Death, a necessary matter-of-fact part of life; Thomas is a realist and man of religion who has experienced both evil and good in man; and Estrella is the optimistic human being full of concern and love. At the midnight hour of decision, Pomfrit is abandoned by these factions that have been competing for his soul and must make the final choice alone.

Georg Kaiser also played a role in forming the background of Hochwälder's theater. In 1938 both Kaiser and Hochwälder fled Nazi tyranny to live in exile in Switzerland.... The plays of both authors display a mutual hatred of war, militarism, and violence. They also call for a regeneration of man. Personal enlightenment and regeneration are possible and even attainable in many of Hochwälder's dramas. Outer conflicts, however, caused by external forces such as the Church, the State or society are never completely resolved. The Provincial (*Das heilige Experiment*), the border-guard (*Der Flüchtling*) and Mittermayer (*Der Befehl*), for example, are able to resolve their inner conflicts, but in each case the hero recognizes the truth only at the end when it is too late. Death is inevitable. Donadieu (*Donadieu*) and Helmbrecht (*Meier Helmbrecht*) solve their inner struggles and avoid death. Pomfrit (*Donnerstag*) and Valmont (*1003*) are unable to cope with their inner problems and never attain enlightenment or regeneration. The lesson, however, that an individual is capable of interior change is meant to be a positive message to the audience.... (pp. 49-52)

Georg Kaiser tried to mould the chaotic loose elements of German Expressionism into a balanced and consistent form and except in a few plays he adopted a solid construction in three or five acts built with mathematical precision. Hochwälder also employs tightly knit plots and constructions in which a straightforward situation is presented without much complication. He usually sticks to the unities of time, place, and action and the traditional structures of exposition, rising action, complication, suspense, climax, and dénouement. Like Kaiser, Hochwälder's dramatic presentations include a wide variety of style and subject matter—historical dramas, mystery plays, comedies, legends, and social dramas. Like Kaiser there are character types (the "fugitive," the "wife," the "border-guard") and stereotypes (the schemer Fouquier, the miser Kavolius, the cheat Berullis). But there are also major characters (Provincial, Pomfrit, Mittermayer, Camenisch, Lazaretti) who are realistically and fully developed. The dialogue, appropriate to the characters, is quick, short, exclamatory, and folksy. (p. 53)

Hochwälder was unique in the dramatic literature after World War II. In much of this post-war drama there seems to be the prevalent literary philosophy that the traditional theater is passé because it is undialectical—unable to stimulate social improvement or critical thought as epic theater and the theater of the absurd are supposed to do. The Germans, having been cut off from the works of foreign playwrights, were eager to perform imports from America, England, France, and Italy. Hochwälder was disturbed by this foreign domination and the dramatic techniques and philosophy of some of these works: he was equally concerned that the German theater was not producing enough of its own drama and, except for Brecht, was not exerting a truly international dramatic influence. Hochwälder criticized the German theater by comparing it to a tubercular patient, outwardly a sun-tanned picture of blooming life, but on the inside a moribund creature hastening to the grave. Generous subsidies to the theater by the cities and states suggest vigor, yet inwardly the theater is dying because it has intellectualized the drama instead of having encouraged vital absorbing plays. His criticism is leveled at German drama in general, but it is especially applicable to the contemporary trend of the theater of the absurd. Where the theater of the absurd may claim that existence is meaningless because man is born and dies without a choice, Hochwälder's philosophy maintains that life does have a meaning because man is rational. Where the theater of the absurd usually resists the traditional structure of imitation, Hochwälder's technique for the most part creates the illusion of reality through a life-like stage setting. Hochwälder is much closer to the Brechtian than to the absurdist tradition, for he believes, especially in his later plays, that a didactic message should accompany a good drama.... (pp. 54-5)

The actual development of Hochwälder's theater thus far seems to have gone through two stages. The dramas in the early period of his dramatic development up to 1954 are presented chiefly in historical garb. In these historical plays he is consciously concerned with giving life to factual events and personages out of the past. His primary purpose, however, is not to treat historical persons (the biographical drama) but rather to treat themes, settings, and events from actual historical situations of the distant past—*Das heilige Experiment* from seventeenth-century Paraguay, *Meier Helmbrecht* from the Middle Ages, *Der öffentliche Ankläger* from the French Revolution, and *Donadieu* from seventeenth-century France. (pp. 55-6)

In these early plays Hochwälder seems less interested in directly criticising and lamenting maladies of the war than in presenting timeless truths meant for all theatergoers regardless of time or place....

Hochwälder's dramatic presentation assumes a significantly different form in the dramas between 1954 and 1975. In 1954 Hochwälder abandoned the historical drama and initiated a new dramatic approach by writing plays in timeless-placeless and modern settings. (p. 57)

In his second developmental period Hochwälder seems to be more interested in social responsibility than in an individual's personal problems or the desire to revive the German stage: he bitterly complains about the soulless irresponsibility of mechanized society (*Donnerstag* and *1003*), he satirically attacks Austrian and German cities that benefited from concentration camps (*Der Himbeerpflücker*, 1964), and he convincingly warns that man and society are capable of further atrocities if they are not careful (*Der Unschuldige*, 1956; *Der Befehl*, 1965; and *Lazaretti oder der Säbeltiger*, 1975). (p. 58)

One notices a change not only in his plays but also in his theoretical statements; the ... essay "**Über mein Theater,**" written in 1956, represents the thinking of his earlier playwrighting, whereas the essay of the same title in 1966, although often repetitious of the first, places less emphasis on the form of the drama and more on the content. Completely absent from his later essay is any attempt to justify his own use of the drama or any harangues against the German theater; he does not even criticize the form of the modern anti-illusionary drama because he employed similar techniques in *Donnerstag* and *1003*. In the earlier composition he praises the Austrian theater very highly by maintaining, for example, that the understanding of art is

alive in all the people, that the *Volkstheater* with its prescribed content and form belongs to everyone, whether he be a prince or shoeshineboy. In the subsequent essay, however, he perceives a danger and weakness in that theater, namely, that the success of a play is more contingent upon its presentation than upon its content and message. (pp. 58-9)

James Schmitt, "*The Theater of Fritz Hochwälder: Its Background and Development*," in Modern Austrian Literature, *Vol. 11, No. 1, 1978, pp. 49-61.*

ALAN BEST

When *Das Heilige Experiment* (*The Holy Experiment*) ... was performed at the re-opening of the Burgtheater in Vienna in 1947, it was greeted with unanimous acclaim from all political and religious persuasions, a sure sign of Hochwälder's *rapport* with the mood and sensibilities of Austria immediately after the National Socialist era. Since 1947 the Austrian literary and theatrical scene has progressed, but Hochwälder himself has gone his own way and today, although a name to be mentioned with respect, he stands alone, aloof, embattled and perhaps embittered when he compares the very luke-warm reception accorded to his recent play *Lazaretti oder Der Säbeltiger* (*Lazaretti or The Sabre-toothed Tiger*, 1975) to the attention paid to the experiments and ploys of contemporary theatre which he has so caustically dismissed. Hochwälder's stated determination to write plays which an audience will *want* to go and see, plays which will entertain an audience, and above all plays which while giving the audience food for thought will not bore it cannot be faulted in theory; in practice, as *Lazaretti* shows, good intentions are not enough. Having criticized his contemporaries so sharply, Hochwälder can scarcely complain if he is hoist with his own petard. (p. 44)

Hochwälder is always searching for that most Austrian of qualities 'die Tiefe', the depth of inner meaning which will justify and enhance the superficial level on which the action takes place. Unpretentious and unliterary he may claim to be, but Hochwälder is first and foremost a moralist.

Hochwälder's plays are very much in the old tradition. They have a well-defined plot, recognizable—even archetypal—characters who are readily understood, and a clear thread of development, and if very little happens in a play by Hochwälder this is principally due to the author's cynical view that the individual can never escape his own fate.... [For] Hochwälder's characters it is the *alter ego* of themselves which they are obliged to see; trapped in a web of their own making they can only watch the noose threatening to tighten around their necks and, if by some chance they escape there is no suggestion of individual merit. (p. 45)

The axis of Hochwälder's plays is the conflict between Power and Justice, that is between the demands of the Ideal and the limitations of Reality. (p. 46)

In one way or another, all of Hochwälder's characters find that an abyss has opened up between the world and themselves, in some way things are no longer what they were, and the individual has to come to terms with this 'new reality' whether this is external and concrete or internal and psychological. When the normal no longer pertains the individual is thrown back on his own self-reliance, but Hochwälder portrays individuals who are subject to the ordinance of a powerful, impersonal will, an authority to which they have subjugated themselves entirely. The crisis in Hochwälder's plays comes with the inevitable discovery that this protective authority is not all-embracing. Despite all appearances to the contrary it is eventually shown to be inherently destructive. (p. 47)

The 'normal' world has been turned upside down in *Das Heilige Experiment*. Hochwälder presents moral right, justice and true Christian charity as seductions. *Realpolitik* wins the day, but only because the Jesuits chose to confront the politicians on a political level. Hochwälder shows that the spirit of Christ is indestructible, but the shadow Christ casts over those who serve Him in their way rather than in His is used here as a starting point in the sequence of studies into the interaction of individual needs and social requirements that constitute Hochwälder's dramatic ooeuvre.

Of Hochwälder's first dramatic phase, the historical plays *Der öffentliche Ankläger* (1947/48) and *Donadieu* (1953) are the best known companions to his Jesuit drama. Set in Revolutionary and Huguenot France respectively, both works centre on the aspirations of an individual brought to a reckoning with the force which has hitherto been his mainstay. (p. 51)

The individual is shown locked in the web of the past, from which there is no escape. In *Donadieu* Hochwälder internalizes the 'Order' which affords protection, depicting a Huguenot noble living on the fires of hatred and a desire for revenge. Donadieu is ultimately forced to emerge from behind his castle walls and face the real world. His castle, so long a bastion of freedom, is shown to have become a prison for a mind trapped by the past and Donadieu is obliged to tear down this illusory protection as the price that must be paid if his religion is to be allowed to survive. He must live uncomfortably in the world as it is and not seek an alternative. There can be no 'happy end' in Hochwälder's work. Evil conquers again and again and his historical plays together with a cynical reworking of the legend of *Esther* (1940) and the medieval *Meier Helmbrecht* (1946) merely highlight the irrelevance and dangers of individual subservience to abstract beliefs.

The second phase in Hochwälder's dramatic development marks a shift in emphasis from historical plays to allegorical and legendary settings. Two plays, *Donnerstag* (*Thursday*, 1959) a modern mystery play complete with all the trimmings of the Austrian Magic Theatre, and *1003* (1964) combine to provide question and answer as to the fate of man. In *Donnerstag* the architect Niklaus Pomfrit enters into an agreement with Underdevil Wondrak of Belial Incorporated by which he will gain understanding of the meaning to the world; in *1003* the writer Ulrich Valmont, alone and listening to tape recordings of his own voice, is visited by Pomfrit (under the alias Bloner). (p. 53)

Hochwälder believed that, together with *Der öffentliche Ankläger* and *Das Heilige Experiment,* it would be for *Die Herberge* [1958] that he would be remembered. It seems an unlikely choice, but it indicates the considerations Hochwälder is trying to raise in his work. . . . It has a village-inn as its setting, a no-man's-land on the way from one town to the next surrounded by forest. The play is peopled with a rich assortment of types and characters who would be equally at home in a play by Nestroy. Here too is a self-contained community about to suffer considerable upheaval, for the 'traveller's rest' of the title proves to be anything but a haven for the money-lender Berullis. Indeed one of the neater ironies of Hochwälder's work lies in the titles of his plays: The Holy Experiment has unholy consequences; the public prosecutor is tried and condemned *in camera,* and the innocence of Christian, the central character of *Der Unschuldige* is not beyond reasonable doubt.

The money-lender Berullis, on his way to another extortionate piece of business, decides to spend a night at the inn which forms the focal point of *Die Herberge* and is robbed of a box containing a thousand gold pieces. After raising hue and cry it transpires that the thief is the son of a man Berullis himself cheated out of an identical amount many years previously. This ironic situation, a spectre rising from the past to threaten an individual who has long since developed beyond the context of that now historical moment is a motif that will dominate the rest of Hochwälder's work and marks Hochwälder's concern to probe the workings of the mind, and pariculary of conscience. The shock of self-recognition, the trauma of coming to terms with an identity one did not even suspect in oneself underlines Hochwälder's dramatic message: no-one is safe from such a moment of unmasking. Historical set-pieces on a grand scale where such a moment of realization is subservient to the main events give way to a study of Everyman in his many guises. (pp. 53-4)

Hochwälder's discomfitting belief that each of us has a potential skeleton in the cupboard is, perhaps, the major shift in emphasis from the early plays, which tended to concentrate on special cases in particular situations.

The third progression in Hochwälder's work is reflected in two plays directly linked to the National Socialist era. Both were inspired by external stimuli rather than an initial inner prompting, but both *Der Himbeerpflücker* (1964) and *Der Befehl* (1965ff.) must be accounted two of his most successful plays. The events in each play relate the situations of contemporary Austrians when obliged to reconsider their activities during the National Socialist era and both works complement each other neatly. *Der Himbeerpflücker* presents a study of unrepentant hard-core Nazis in the flourishing, and aptly-named town of Bad Brauning while *Der Befehl* (of which there are two versions, a television screenplay and a revised and improved version for the theatre) traces the fortunes of a former military policeman in occupied Holland whose model record then and since seem to make him the ideal choice to hunt down a brutal Nazi child-murderer. Hochwälder's dramatic concern, to unnerve his audience, to shake their self-convictions, is fully realized, for while the Nazis of Bad Brauning are no better than they ought to be, the modest, conscientious Inspektor Mittermayer who is the central character of *Der Befehl* stands revealed at the end of that play as the very monster he was ordered to hunt down. (pp. 55-6)

In *Der Himbeerpflücker* Hochwälder presented a monster masquerading as an affable citizen, but in *Der Befehl* he reminds his audience that no-one can deny the monster within himself. Chillingly, Hochwalder takes the cliché of the mild-mannered 'good citizen' with a black past and twists it to his own ends. Apologists for the SS who argue that bygones should be bygones, as well as those who thirst after vengeance for crimes committed years in the past, are both stopped dead in their tracks by this device. Ironically, it is the argument put forward by the Nazi apologists which at first sight seems to gain the greater support from the play—surely, what Mittermayer has done since the war must expunge his aberrations during it? For Hochwälder however, the urge of conscience is supreme; he is determined to turn the individual in on himself and force him, and the audience, to examine the inner self and to expose the duality of human nature and the sheer impossiblity of *knowing* how things stand. The essence of Hochwälder's work and the focal point of his criticism of contemporary Austrian society is to be found in its emphasis of the insecurity and instability of the seemingly impregnable. It is Hochwälder's sustaining thesis that none of us really know ourselves; the spectre of the Jekyll and Hyde within us all, revealed in a manner which is quite clearly aiming for catharsis stresses both Hochwälder's modernity and his links to the traditional theatre. (p. 59)

There is no optimism in Hochwälder's view of the world and perhaps one of the most Austrian traits in his work is its combination of mordant scepticism bordering on despair combined with a faculty for lightness of touch and a persistent faith in the necessity of meeting life on its own terms. Throughout his career Hochwälder has explored the relationship between the individual and the society whose protection he seeks. Be this Jesuit, National Socialist or the Second Republic, Hochwälder deftly varies the contexts in which this relationship is seen. One of the most striking features of his drama is its combination of thematic consistency within an apparently developing social framework. There is no escape for the individual suborned by the delusion of security; Hochwälder's characters, and by implication society at large, can escape neither their own true nature nor the realities of the past. Caught in a vortex that is of his own making, Hochwälder's 'hero' inhabits a world that combines the implacability of Kafka with the mellow astringency of Nestroy. (p. 60)

> Alan Best, "Shadows of the Past: The Drama of Fritz Hochwälder," in Modern Austrian Writing: Literature and Society after 1945, edited by Alan Best and Hans Wolfschütz, Barnes & Noble Books, 1980, pp. 44-62.

W. LEE NAHRGANG

The four plays included [in **The Public Prosecutor and Other Plays**] provide a representative sample of Hochwälder's best works, with examples of both his early historical dramas and his more recent social plays. **The Strong Are Lonely (Das heilige Experiment**, 1941-42), probably Hochwälder's most famous drama, deals with the totalitarian Jesuit state that existed in Paraguay some 200 years ago. With great reluctance, the Father Provincial remains faithful to his vows of obedience and dissolves his communistic state, thereby dooming its Indian citizens to virtual slavery. **The Public Prosecutor (Der öffentliche Ankläger**, 1947-48), perhaps Hochwälder's best work, concerns an opportunist who employs his office to serve not justice, but rather himself and the changing needs of the various cliques that wield power during the French Revolution. He even prepares, with perjured testimony, a perfect case against an unknown defendant, thus condemning *himself* to the guillotine. **The Raspberry Picker (Der Himbeerpflücker**, 1964), a comedy, depicts the prosperous but nostalgic burghers of a postwar Austrian village, who welcome and give refuge to a petty thief in the mistaken belief that he is a fugitive Nazi war criminal. **Lazaretti or the Saber-Toothed Tiger (Lazaretti oder der Säbeltiger**, 1974) treats contemporary terrorism and the hypocrisy of liberal intellectuals who, in the final analysis, are prepared to employ terrorist methods themselves.

Once considered an equal of Dürrenmatt and Frisch, Hochwälder has suffered considerable loss of reputation in recent years, but he deserves a better fate. . . . The innate imperfections of even the most benevolent totalitarian society, the fact that obedience, often a virtue, may also lead to immoral acts, the perversion of justice, the existence of latent Fascist tendencies among those who are supposedly responsible citizens, terrorism, and the inhumanity of even those who proclaim their dedication to social justice—all are both topical and timeless

issues. Hochwälder's moral concern, his gift for characterization, and his total command of traditional theatrical techniques mark him as a major dramatist, whose best works will long remain a part of the standard German-language theater repertoire. (pp. 431-32)

> W. Lee Nahrgang, in a review of "The Public Prosecutor and Other Plays," in The Modern Language Journal, Vol. 65, No. 4, Winter, 1981, pp. 431-32.

THEODORE O. WOHLSEN, JR.

Hochwälder is . . . a playwright of skill and substance. Perhaps he has not attained the same renown [as Dürrenmatt and Frisch] because his play construction techniques are more traditional, but the themes he chooses to dramatize, e.g., the conflict between idealism and realism in **The Strong Are Lonely** or the effect of violence and terrorism on the modern consciousness in *Lazaretti*, are both universal and timely. [The works included in **The Public Prosecutor and Other Plays**] are deserving of a wider audience because of their well-rounded characterizations, strong plotting, and ideas.

> Theodore O. Wohlsen, Jr., in a review of "The Public Prosecutor and Other Plays," in Library Journal, Vol. 106, No. 1, January 1, 1981, p. 171.

R. KAUF

Eleven essays, written at various times and for various occasions by the distinguished Austrian playwright Fritz Hochwälder . . . are so artfully assembled in [**Im Wechsel der Zeit: Autobiographische Skizzen und Essays**] that they form a mosaic revealing his professional biography and his ideas about literature or, more precisely, about the theatre. . . .

Hochwälder sees the Viennese theatre as, on the one hand, having grown out of the commedia dell'arte, the country fairs and the court spectacles, and therefore, unlike the more "literary" theatre of northern Germany, not being afraid of theatrical effects and entertainment for entertainment's sake; on the other hand, it is derived from the Spanish and Italian theatrical tradition, with its stress on clarity of language and form. Hence Austrian theatre can be enjoyed and appreciated by the masses and not only by a small group of intellectuals. Hochwälder feels that, unlike the Austrian theatre, modern German drama suffers from a lack of clarity and straightforwardness of language, from the absence of confusion of ethical values and, above all, from a loss of the indispensable sense of naïveté without which the theatre becomes the "playground of intellectual charlatans."

Practicing what he preaches, Hochwälder writes with great clarity. A master of the well-turned phrase, he shows that complex literary and intellectual issues need not necessarily be presented in a convoluted, near-imcomprehensible language, and the book is therefore a pleasure to read. (pp. 469-70)

> R. Kauf, in a review of "Im Wechsel der Zeit: Autobiographische Skizzen und Essays," in World Literature Today, Vol. 55, No. 3, Summer, 1981, pp. 469-70.

HANS J. FABIAN

Written in the dark days of Europe in 1941-42 in Switzerland, to which Hochwälder had fled from his native Vienna following the Anschluss, *The Strong Are Lonely* has been the only work of this minor but not unimportant Austrian playwright available in English up to now. The play remains a powerful and effective example of the stage trial and examines the forces involved in the destruction of the Guarani Indian-Jesuit state in Paraguay in 1767. Following World War II *The Strong Are Lonely* enjoyed considerable stage success in various capitals of the world. . . . The play remains the best of those included in this volume of four of Hochwälder's works [*The Public Prosecutor and Other Plays*].

It may be taken for another indication of the axiom that form and substance enhance each other that another Hochwälder play largely consisting of a stage trial and having the tightly measured sparring of judicial interplay as its focus makes up the other half of the two best plays contained in this volume. *The Public Prosecutor* takes us into the last days of the terror following the French Revolution and the fall of the public prosecutor Fourquir-Tinville into his own deadly machinery of justice. While the historical aspects of these two plays might indicate a disposition toward the genre by their author, this is not the case. Hochwälder is essentially a moralist in the tradition of the Austrian *Volksstück*. . . .

The Raspberry Picker, written in 1964, maintains a waning timeliness of topic with its Austro-German fascination for the crimes of their recent past, while *Lazaretti or The Saber-Toothed Tiger*, the latest of the four plays (1975), on the other hand deals with a timeless topic, one dear to the heart of all academics. Its theme is the predatory and cunning ruthlessness of competing academics in their quest for status.

Hochwälder is certainly not a major dramatist of our day. He may not even prove to be more than a minor one in the course of Austrian drama, but he is a finely tuned practitioner in the art of dramatic craftsmanship, an increasingly rare and valued commodity in our age.

> *Hans J. Fabian, in a review of "The Public Prosecutor and Other Plays," in* World Literature Today, *Vol. 55, No. 4, Autumn, 1981, p. 669.*

Bruce Lancaster

1896-1963

American novelist and nonfiction writer.

Lancaster was a historical novelist who generally set his work against the events of the American Revolutionary War and the Civil War. He presents well-documented material with a fresh perspective and brings to life little-known or historically overlooked facts. Lancaster has been compared to Kenneth Roberts for his vigorous and fast-paced narratives and for his skill in combining fictitious elements with authentic detail. Earl Foell described Lancaster's work as "fiction-coated history" and reflected critical consensus by praising the author's ability to recreate history while maintaining the reader's interest.

Among Lancaster's best-known novels are *The Guns of Burgoyne* (1939), which tells the story of British General John Burgoyne's defeat at Saratoga during the Revolutionary War; *The Scarlet Patch* (1947), which recounts the adventures of a group of European mercenaries known as the Rochambeau Rifles during the early days of the Civil War; and *No Bugles Tonight* (1948), a reenactment of the capture of a strategic railroad line by Union soldiers in 1862. Three of Lancaster's novels depart from these scenarios: *The Wide Sleeve of Kwannon* (1938) and *Venture in the East* (1951) are adventure stories set in feudal Japan, and *For Us the Living* (1940) is a novelization of Abraham Lincoln's youth. Lancaster also wrote the nonfiction works *From Lexington to Liberty: The Story of the American Revolution* (1955) and *Ticonderoga, the Story of a Fort* (1959).

(See also *Contemporary Authors*, Vols. 9-10; *Contemporary Authors Permanent Series*, Vol. 1; and *Something about the Author*, Vol. 9.)

BRADFORD SMITH

In Japan the period of Genroku at the end of the seventeenth century was one of artistic spendor—of elaborate costume, unrestricted boisterousness in art and literature, feudal magnificence. . . .

It is this period which Bruce Lancaster has chosen for his novel ["**The Wide Sleeve of Kwannon**"], the story of an adventurous young Dutchman sent out from Java to check up on the dwindling Dutch trade in Japan—a trade which had been so restricted by Japanese regulation that of the once flourishing Dutch community there remained only a few men on a tiny island off Nagasaki, and these watched, guarded, questioned, subject to a humiliating inspection which the young de Ruyter came to hate. It is the picture of these valiant Dutch, holding on by their teeth to this post which provided Japan's only contact with the West, that forms the backbone of the story.

There is, of course, a love story—a story skillfully tied in to the concerns of the Dutch community if you can accept the first premise that a Japanese young lady of good family would be likely to disguise herself as a young student coming to study Dutch and could manage to get away with it. . . . Mr. Lancaster at least makes it sound plausible, and furthermore makes his

character of the girl Kiku romantically appealing. Yet it is the good Dr. Kaempfer, indefatigable and kindly scholar and humanist in the best sense of the word, who stands forth as the best conceived of all the characters. It is likely that Mr. Lancaster, reading the rich materials which Kaempfer actually compiled in this period, fell in love with his source, for he has translated him with all the attributes of life into his novel.

The plot resolves itself in the self-sacrifice of Kiku for the preservation of her lover in a manner appropriately Japanese. . . . The story gains immediacy from being told in the first person; historic perspective from its imitation of a seventeenth century style.

Bradford Smith, "*Love Story of Old Japan,*" *in* New York Herald Tribune Books, *March 13, 1938, p. 4.*

STEPHEN VINCENT BENET

The terrible, terrible Hessians—at least by reputation—have long played an important part in American folk-demonology. They were ruthless mercenaries hired by a cruel English king to shoot and plunder clear-eyed American farmers, and whenever one of them bit the dust Freedom gave a patriotic yell. At least, that's the way I got it from "The Boys of '76." But, in ["**Guns of Burgoyne**," a] long and meaty novel of Burgoyne's ill-fated expedition, Mr. Lancaster redresses an historic injustice and tells an admirable and stirring tale. His very hero, Kurt Ahrens is a Saxon from Dresden, an officer in the service of Hesse-Hanau and a gunner under Burgoyne. It wouldn't have been possible thirty years ago. And it gives another proof of the remarkable change, both in point of view and in depth of research, of the American historical novel during those years. . . .

[Mr. Lancaster's] main theme is, of course, Burgoyne's unlucky campaign, and he has brought the events and the men who made them vividly to life. We follow the cumbrous, conglomerate, gay-uniformed army that was to cut the rebellion in two, from Crown Point to the end at Saratoga. . . .

Mr. Lancaster has missed none of the sidelights, comic or tragic. . . . As for Kurt Ahrens himself, he brought an expert knowledge of artillery, a common-sense point of view on military matters and a heart he was soon to lose to the American girl, Judith Hunnewell. . . . Their love-story is a pleasant thread that helps tie the book together. It is not merely thrown in as a sop to the reader's interest, and it is genuine. But the true story is that of the campaign and the gradual appraisal of this new America through Kurt Ahrens's eyes. It is skillfully and movingly done. . . . And the last battle scene, with Arnold plunging on his big horse and Morgan's lunatic turkey-call gibbering through the woods, can stand comparison with the best of [Kenneth Robert's] "Northwest Passage." . . .

Mr. Lancaster has given us a first-class story from the American past.

> Stephen Vincent Benet, "A New View of the American Revolution," in New York Herald Tribune Books, March 26, 1939, p. 1.

MARGARET WALLACE

Although the odds against this feat are growing heavier every day, Bruce Lancaster has found in the American Revolution a fresh background for ["**Guns of Burgoyne**"]. Even more surprisingly, he has found it in the northern campaign which . . . has been treated in one or another aspect by half a dozen able novelists. . . .

The novel is put together in a series of broad panels. . . . There is an epilogue, which concludes Ahren's personal story, in the straggling progress of the defeated army to Boston. This form, by eliminating repetitious material, permits Mr. Lancaster to cover a lot of ground and to do it in amazing detail. The result is a novel vigorous and exciting, firm in texture and satisfying—at least as fiction. . . .

[Some of it] is very comic—except that Mr. Lancaster discovers for us under the ridiculous uniforms the simple figure of poor Heinz, the Hanau conscript who barely knew one end of his musket from the other, or tall Spangenberg, the amiable disciple of Izaak Walton, who died across his field piece at Bennington.

"**Guns of Burgoyne**" is a decidedly welcome addition to the current crop of Revolutionary romances. There is a love story, it should be said, and a good one. Kurt Ahrens, a sympathetic young man and rather precocious in his comprehension of the American spirit, does not get far into York State without meeting an American girl. Perhaps on the score of history Mr. Lancaster will have objections to encounter. His treatment of Burgoyne is rather too indulgent, for instance, and he is some-

thing less than fair to Arnold. Leaving these matters aside, and they really are comparatively insignificant, it is hard to see how he could have done a better job.

> Margaret Wallace, in a review of "Guns of Burgoyne," in The New York Times Book Review, March 26, 1939, p. 6.

STEPHEN VINCENT BENET

["**For Us the Living**," a] long novel of pioneer days in the country where the young Abe Lincoln grew up has Mr. Lancaster's characteristic virtues of abundant and naturally handled detail. He seems as much at home among movers, keelboaters and drifters as he was with the men and officers of Burgoyne's ill-fated army—unfortunately, he has a less direct and coherent story to tell. The story is seen, first of all, through the eyes of Hugh Brace, the enterprising son of a shiftless father and a willing, but unenterprising mother, and, where it sticks to Hugh's own feelings and experiences, it has an admirable validity. But that is only half the story—the other half is the young Lincoln. And that is where the trouble comes in. For the minute you bring somebody like Lincoln into a book, and do him at length, you are bound to take the main business away from your fictional heroes. The growth and development of Lincoln himself are bound to be more interesting than the growth and development of Hugh Brace, and, when Lincoln is offstage, you keep waiting for him to come on.

That it should be so is no criticism of Mr. Lancaster's abilities as a novelist. It would take a very remarkable novelist to do what he had tried to do and carry it off. His portrait of Lincoln has the defects inherent in such materials—the neighborly chorus of "Suthin' peculiarsome about Abe," the unavoidable legendary quality that clusters about such a name. And there are those foreshadowings of the shape of things to come which are so hard to get away from in historical fiction. But the attempt is honest—to show the young Lincoln as he seemed to the friends and neighbors of his early years—and it is often successful. Most successful when Mr. Lancaster gets away from any implications involved in the subject matter and merely paints a good friendship between two youngsters, one of whom is named Abe Lincoln and one Hugh Brace.

> Stephen Vincent Benet, "In the Lincoln Country," in New York Herald Tribune Books, November 3, 1940, p. 2.

MARGARET WALLACE

"**For Us the Living**" is about Lincoln, but rather in the way that the Iliad is about Helen of Troy. His presence, inevitably heightened by the reader's knowledge of the destiny awaiting him, dominates the story. But we receive our strongest and most lasting impression of him in the effect he had upon the average men who knew him—men who admired his physical strength, deplored his lack of business sense, and thought his honesty rather excessive. . . .

The dialogue and detail of the novel are magnificent. Mr. Lancaster leaves us in no doubt whatever that this is the environment that produced Lincoln, the environment he rebelled against, as all exceptional young men are likely to rebel against their environment, but which he never forgot and never wanted to forget. The story ends in the early Eighteen Thirties when Lincoln, heavily in debt and feeling himself a failure, yields to his friends' arguments and decides to run once more for the

Illinois Legislature. But it ends with a feeling of finality, as if the man were cast in his permanent mold and everything that happened afterward only a natural result of what we already know.

It is no exaggeration to say that **"For Us the Living,"** as a simple human document, rings truer than anything which has yet been written in fictional or dramatic form about Abraham Lincoln.

> *Margaret Wallace, "Bruce Lancaster's Fine Novel of Lincoln in His Youth," in* The New York Times Book Review, *November 3, 1940, p. 5.*

HOFFMAN BIRNEY

This fine novel ["**The Scarlet Patch**"] takes its title from the lozenge, worn on the cap, which identified troops under the command of one-armed Phil Kearny, as gallant a leader as American soldiers ever followed. . . .

[This is] the best novel of the Civil War which this reviewer has ever read. [Mr. Lancaster] has put into it research as profound as that which marked Freeman's monumental works on Robert E. Lee, yet it is free from pedantry or laborious historical asides. The reader senses—as did the man in the ranks—the timidity of McClellan, the incompetency of Pope, and the uncertainty of Meade when he was rushed into command only ten days before Gettysburg. One feels the soldier's disgust for the political domination of some militia regiments, for the hatred which a few Regular Army officers showed toward those commissioned from civil life and toward the "foreign mercenaries" such as the Rochambeau Rifles. The reader lives and fights with the characters which Mr. Lancaster has created, and they are men as real as George Patton, himself a Kearny, or the marines who raised the flag on Suribachi.

The story of **"The Scarlet Patch"** is that of the Americanization of Jean de Merac, a titled Frenchman who enlisted in the Rifles because of his conviction that America would perish if the Union fell. . . .

The reader is one of those men whom de Merac molds from shambling recruits into blooded veterans who stood firm against shrapnel, musket-fire and bayonet. He feels, with them, that Chantilly was neither a victory nor a defeat but the field where Kearny died. Fredericksburg was where Corvisart, Du Bosc, Bolton, and others of the Rifles fell; Gettysburg—ah, that was where we of the Rifles were thrown into the line with Berdan's Sharpshooter Regiment to halt the advance of two Confederate brigades.

It is in such things that Mr. Lancaster's skill is found. **"The Scarlet Patch"** is the story of many men who died and a few who lived; a tale of heroism with out heroics. Both as a novel and as a re-creation of history it is a memorable achievement.

> *Hoffman Birney, "Foreign Legion of the Union," in* The New York Times Book Review, *April 20, 1947, p. 5.*

COLEMAN ROSENBERGER

[In "**The Scarlet Patch**"] Mr. Lancaster handles his battles far more competently than he does his characters. The women, especially, fail to come alive. Louise Duane, interested in De Mérac's titles and estates, is wholly unconvincing: the nurse,

Gail Shortland, is vague and shadowy: De Mérac's former mistress, the Baroness Lisa von Horstmar, verges on caricature.

The best realized of the fictional characters is General Dudley Pelham, capable soldier, bigot, champion of the nativism of the Know Nothing party, who hates all foreigners and engineers the arrest and confinement of De Mérac. But even Pelham is more the embodiment of prejudices than he is a person. Most of the lesser characters are wooden, and the occasional Negro is always a smiling or singing stereotype.

"The Scarlet Patch" has value as a novel of action if not of character; it treats an interesting and neglected aspect of our history; the battle scenes are effective, and the readers who have come to respect Mr. Lancaster's skill as a historical novelist through his **"Guns of Burgoyne"** and **"Trumpet in Arms"** will not be disappointed.

> *Coleman Rosenberger, "Volunteers for Freedom," in* New York Herald Tribune Weekly Book Review, *April 27, 1947, p. 10.*

JOHN WILLIAM ROGERS

Lancaster's extensive knowledge of the Civil War and its period is reflected by the basic framework of history and in many details of incident and speech, but much of his material [in **"No Bugles Tonight"**] belongs to what has long been familiar in the conventional old-fashioned romantic novel, where heroes are gallant with nary an idea but the courageous pursuit of duty and seldom a thought except good clean ones in the direction of a glamorous lady love. The heroines are, of course, alluringly feminine, but spirited and full of mettle. (pp. 11-12)

The sympathy in the book takes account of the Southerners' point of view but is distinctly directed toward the North. Readers with complete detachment or a Northern outlook may find this agreeable, but it is hard to think that it will find many readers in the Old South, since it not only insistently shows the Confederates to a disadvantage, but ends on a note of positive exaltation at the prospect of Sherman's march through Georgia.

"No Bugles Tonight" is one more competent novel written for the reader who does not mind two-dimensional characterization, and whose concern is a superficially lively narrative against a background of profound and serious conflict. (p. 12)

> *John William Rogers, "Southern Saboteurs," in* The Saturday Review of Literature, *Vol. XXXI, No. 34, August 21, 1948, pp. 11-12.*

THE CHRISTIAN SCIENCE MONITOR

"No Bugles Tonight" gives an absorbing account of hazardous adventure, courageous men and women, and unforgettable scenes. . . .

Unlike many current writers who have reduced the phrase "historical novel" to the semipornographic, Bruce Lancaster writes well and convincingly on a foundation of solid fact. Without once descending to the lurid or the titillating, he succeeds in creating a novel completely absorbing. And in addition to presenting a little-known side of the War Between the States, the book offers an interesting parallel to the world of the present day—where so many groups of people, honestly dedicated to liberty and peace, have been cut off from those who share their beliefs and have no alternative to guerrilla action if they would aid the democratic cause.

I. Z., "Men of Courage," in The Christian Science Monitor, *August 25, 1948, p. 18.*

RICHARD B. MORRIS

Demonstrating that thoroughness of research which we have come to expect from the author of **"Guns of Burgoyne"** and **"No Bugles Tonight,"** Bruce Lancaster now turns the spotlight upon Francis Marion, gallant leader of the Southern militia [in **"Phantom Fortress"**].... The "Swamp Fox" was not the only Revolutionary general who was adept at robbing the British of the fruits of their victories, but, to quote the tribute of General Nathanael Greene,... it was the peculiar talent of Marion "to fight with intrepidity under a constant impression of defeat, and inspire irregular troops to do it." Against Marion's guerilla warfare carried on in cypress swamps and in wooded uplands, the cumbersome, rigid, and traditional British tactics were of little avail.

This is Lancaster's real story, and, except for a few minor slips, he remains faithful to the known facts. Even such a dramatic detail as the account of the siege of Fort Motte, a post captured without artillery or siege tools but by the ingenious device of shooting flaming arrows onto the roof of the structure, is supported by available evidence. But in marshaling these facts Lancaster gives a somewhat distorted picture. In his novel all the villains wear the scarlet jackets of the British regulars or the green of the Tory militia, but in this bitterly contested civil war reprisals were common on both sides.... Perhaps it is sufficient to say that Lancaster has restored the traditional black-and-white balance so rudely upset by "Oliver Wiswell," a whitewash of Tories and Toryism.

Richard B. Morris, "Francis Marion and the Partisans," in The Saturday Review of Literature, *Vol. XXXIII, No. 12, March 25, 1950, p. 32.*

MELVILLE HEATH

"The Secret Road," [Mr. Lancaster's] ninth novel, is an example of a veteran craftsman at the top of his form.

This time, Mr. Lancaster has chosen to describe a little-known aspect of our Revolutionary War, the activities of General Washington's secret service on and around Long Island Sound in the year 1780, when the fortunes of the Colonials were still at low ebb. The South seemed all but won. Manhattan and Long Island were firmly in Sir Henry Clinton's hands. British gunboats ranged the Hudson as far as West Point, where Benedict Arnold and the river chain still barred their path. In Westchester County, Washington waited for tardy help from France. It seemed evident that another British victory could split the Hudson Valley, and the fledgling republic's last chance of survival....

The author mingles fact and fiction expertly as his breathless plot unfolds. Arnold's treachery and the sad story of Major André's capture are told here in detail; so is the colorful march of the French troops from Narragansett Bay to New York to join forces with Washington. The reader sees clearly just how narrowly Arnold missed success in his scheme to surrender West Point—and how Clinton might have smashed the French landing had not Townsend faked a vital dispatch in time's nick.

Since this is a historical novel after all, Mr. Lancaster has been obliged to include a pair of sultry ladies, one Loyalist, one rebel. It must be said that both tend to get lost in the shuffle when the bullets start flying in earnest. But the masculine members of this vivid company are real indeed, right down to Arnold, who appears on stage only for a moment. Incidentally, the picture the author draws of the celebrated traitor differs somewhat from the famous painting reproduced below. Mr. Lancaster tells us that Arnold boarded the Vulture with all his customary arrogance—and sold his bargemen as prisoners-of-war, at five pounds a head.

Melville Heath, "Outwitting the Redcoats," in The New York Times Book Review, *June 15, 1952, p. 5.*

SHIRLEY BARKER

[In **The Secret Road**"] Mr. Lancaster has used the right historical sources well and lovingly. He is really excited about [the period of the American Revolution] ..., and he communicates his excitement. His pictures of Townsend and Andre—real men—are careful and convincing, and the finest things in the book. He is not so interested in his fictional characters. Rosa's eyes are blue on page 53 and green on page 241 because Rosa is really not important. Also, to describe Alexander Hamilton as "a fine-looking man" leaves us a little unsatisfied, since if he is to appear at all he deserves a more accurate portrait.

But the book has value because it brings authentic history to the impatient reader who will never take it a slower way. Its blending of real figures with imaginary ones is skilfully done, and if it underplays its great moments—such as that evening on the Sound when a trick turns the British fleet back from Newport—that is perhaps in keeping with the spirit of the patriots who watched the event; and as such is a fitting thing.

Shirley Barker, "Hunting Down History," in The Saturday Review, *New York, Vol. XXXV, No. 27, July 5, 1952, p. 18.*

CARL CARMER

Many attempts have recently been made to write popular accounts of early periods of American History. **"From Lexington to Liberty,"** the story of the American Revolution, is more vivid, more swift in narrative, more full of impressive detail than any that come to mind. Bruce Lancaster, who is a skillfull and talented writer of historical fiction, has made appropriate and able use of his gifts in this colorful chronicle. He brings the Revolution alive by means of techniques which are usually associated with fiction, and the result is ... suspenseful and generally authentic.... Indeed, this study might have ranked as worthy of being recommended without qualification to all Americans from our junior high schools to our eldest citizens were it not for a number of minor faults which, taken together, prove too important to be overlooked.

The first of these is the author's tendency to wander from the period he is picturing to other times and places. It might be argued that his jumping about through the centuries, usually to point out analogous situations, is an aid to clarity of understanding and this is sometimes, though not always, true. It is also undeniable, however, that it destroys the atmosphere of the time with which the book concerns itself, and that parenthetical references to Roman legions, battles of the Civil

War, the Crimean War, and recent World Wars annoyingly divert the focus of the reader from late 18th century events. Mr. Lancaster is too casual and too generous with his asides. When we read in otherwise stirring passages such sentences as "Knox was playing the part of an eighteenth century walkie-talkie for George Washington," we feel that the writer is impairing his artistic quality. We are no sooner deep in the world of Washington, Knox and Lafayette than we are startled with a vocabulary which includes such expressions as snafu, hassle, goon . . . , king-size, combat fatigue, grifter, trigger-happy, mission accomplished, military geiger-counter, robot, high brass. . . .

While the objections here recorded and others—there is no account of the naval battles of the Revolution, for instance—militate against this book's being generally accepted as the only necessary one-volume history of the American Revolution, it must gladly be said that Mr. Lancaster's research has been prodigious, that his choice of material has been for the most part sound, that his narrative contains well reasoned interpretations of historic events and moving anecdotes of human interest.

> Carl Carmer, "A Colorful Chronicle of the American Revolution," in New York Herald Tribune Book Review, June 5, 1955, p. 5.

JOHN R. ALDEN

["**From Lexington to Liberty**"] contains nothing new, and its author makes no claim to great discoveries. He quotes freely from printed contemporary materials, but relies largely upon the many writers who have preceded him. He commonly makes good use of their findings, but he commits more "bloopers" than are permitted the meticulous scholar. Thus he has in the American Army of 1775 veterans "who had sweated through the Carolina brakes in the old Yamassee wars," which ended before 1720.

More seriously, Mr. Lancaster's central explanation of the famous British strategic blunders of 1777—a supposed failure of a negligent Lord George Germain and an equally careless underling in the War Office to write to Gen. William Howe about campaign plans—is an amusing and exploded myth. So, too, the positive reason he gives for Howe's venture of that year into Pennsylvania (bad advice from Gen. Charles Lee) is a poor one, not much more acceptable than the curious contemporary explanation that Howe sailed from New York to Philadelphia to humor his mistress, pregnant and desiring a sea voyage. Again, to say that Sir Henry Clinton, Howe's successor, "never lacked decision" is odd, for if any criticism of Clinton is valid, it is that as commander in chief he was an inactive procrastinater.

Although not a precise military history of the Revolution, this is a pleasant and vivid account of that crucial period in our history.

> John R. Alden, "Great Deeds and Grievous Errors," in The New York Times Book Review, July 3, 1955, p. 5.

EARL W. FOELL

In "**Roll Shenandoah**" historical novelist Bruce Lancaster himself rolls through the climax of the Civil War's decisive Shenandoah Valley campaign with impressive skill. Mr. Lancaster

is an expert at re-creating history, as his recent non-fiction account of the Revolutionary War, "**From Lexington to Liberty**," showed. And now he uses this flair for recapturing bygone atmosphere to disguise a facile romantic plot in a tumult of realistic battle scenes and terse reports on behind-the-lines strategy sessions.

Through his hero, Ellery Starr, a demobilized officer turned war correspondent, Mr. Lancaster views the symptoms of various rifts that threatened to tear the young nation asunder. . . .

As in his earlier Revolutionary War novels, Mr. Lancaster injects Intrigue and Romance into the exciting milieu he has carefully re-created from fact. Starr is fascinated by demure Gillian Westlake. Gillian is the daughter of itinerant lay preacher Joseph Westlake. Westlake, a fiery John Brown of a man, is suspiciously present whenever defeatism burgeons behind the Northern lines. Gillian believes in her father's near-treasonable doctrines. Ellery believes in Gillian. Where will it all end?

No experienced reader of historical novels need be in doubt about this question. Romance and the Union are the victors.

> Earl W. Foell, "Novelist's Eye on the Civil War," in The Christian Science Monitor, September 12, 1956, p. 9.

EARL W. FOELL

["**Night March**," the] latest fiction-coated history from Mr. Lancaster recounts Colonel Ulric Dahlgren's unsuccessful cavalry raid on Richmond in 1864. . . .

Mr. Lancaster's reconstruction of Civil War history is here just as careful as it was in his last outing. . . . But the fictional superstructure he has added is built out of coincidence and women's magazine romance. The hero is unbending and can't see the affection growing in the heroine's eyes. The heroine is a spitfire who keeps running into the hero all over the war. . . .

Mr. Lancaster is an able popularizer of history, as his excellent Revolutionary War volume, "**From Lexington to Liberty**," showed. And he has previously displayed some talent for stirring fictional characters into serious historical chronicles without distorting the facts. But "**Night March**" is hampered by the kind of contrived romance which simply doesn't stir in well. As a result the book flounders along in two layers; its history creditable; its romance, never quite credible, floating woodenly on top.

> Earl W. Foell, in a review of "Night March," in The Christian Science Monitor, May 22, 1958, p. 15.

WILLIAM B. HILL, S. J.

Bruce Lancaster, who has made several fictional but well authenticated escursions into American history, was working on *The Big Knives* when he died. . . . [True] to his own form of narrative but different from almost everything else that is being written; it is, to be brief, an old-fashioned book, straightforward in its narration, naïve in its heroics, absolutely romantic and, to tell the truth, somewhat refreshing.

There are two focal points in *The Big Knives*. The real hero is George Rogers Clark, defender of Virginia and Kentucky, brilliant leader of frontiersmen, brother of William Clark of Lewis-and-Clark fame. The story is, however, the story of Markham Cape, a fictional Bostonian who accidentally joins one of Clark's expeditions. Mr. Lancaster uses Cape to the fullest advantage—he makes him a tough, resourceful man who can handle himself well in the wilderness, but he also makes him a merchant whose dealings give us an insight into the politics and economics of our revolutionary war. . . .

The march on Vincennes, one of the fascinating bits of our early history, makes the most interesting part of the novel. The ground was actually flooded for many miles, and every soggy mile, it seems, is accounted for. There was so much water that Clark knew that the British would not be expecting him; they were not. With his small force, with some expert marksmanship, and with a few stratagems, Clark induced the British commander to yield the fort at Vincennes. There the book ends. (p. 74)

All in all, we have here a rather boyish, certainly unsophisticated novel, idealizing the frontiersman, giving him superb strength, unfailing resourcefulness, unbounded determination, fierce loyalty, and even religious tolerance. . . . The idealization, though there is some basis for it, is so intense as to give this novel that refreshing but unreal buoyancy which comes from an uninhibited joy in valor; it is a reading of history which is more enthusiastic than discriminating but is nevertheless pleasant. After all, the deeds upon which this piece of fiction is based were themselves heroic. (pp. 74-5)

> *William B. Hill, S. J., in a review of "The Big Knives," in* Best Sellers, *Vol. 24, No. 4, May 15, 1964, pp. 74-5.*

Fran(ces Ann) Lebowitz

1951?-

American essayist, journalist, and critic.

Lebowitz became a literary celebrity with the publication of *Metropolitan Life* **(1978), a collection of humorous essays written while she was a columnist for** *Mademoiselle* **and** *Interview* **magazines. Lebowitz aims her droll satire at contemporary urban lifestyles, particularly those of her fellow New Yorkers.** *Social Studies* **(1981) presents more of her frank and witty appraisals, in addition to comic vignettes about her adjustment to her new role as a best-selling author. Although most reviewers found this work less successful than** *Metropolitan Life,* **several praised Lebowitz's sharp analyses of human character.**

(See also *CLC,* **Vol. 11;** *Contemporary Authors,* **Vols. 81-84; and** *Contemporary Authors New Revision Series,* **Vol. 14.)**

© 1985 Thomas Victor

ARTHUR LUBOW

The attitude [of such humorists as Fran Lebowitz and Cyra McFadden] is illustrated perfectly by an ad for the *Animal House* movie which shows cast members thrusting their middle fingers toward the camera. This is the time of screw-you humor.

Its practitioners like to trace the roots of screw-you humor back to culture heroes like Oscar Wilde, Dorothy Parker and Lenny Bruce. Certainly, they have learned much from their predecessors. Bruce's vicious vulgarity cleared the path for the *Lampoon* stampede. Wilde and Parker maintained a cultured arrogance that Lebowitz and McFadden both affect. But in studies of literary heredity, it's important to keep track of what has dropped out of the gene pool. The elders were infected with a humility that often festered into self-loathing. As a consequence, even their sharpest jokes were tinged with compassion. Although they were cultural elitists, Wilde, Bruce and Parker were also political leftists. They reserved their contempt for the wealthy and the philistine. *Lampoon* humor is less fastidious. It picks off the easiest targets: usually women, blacks and homosexuals. It victimizes society's victims. (p. 19)

Lebowitz names as her heroes Oscar Wilde and, ''20,000 miles below,'' Mark Twain and Evelyn Waugh, but she is a smart, funny New York woman and the obvious comparison is Dorothy Parker. In her disparaging use of the word ''lady,'' in her distaste for ambitious fools and tacky furniture, in her fascination with telephones, liquor and parties, Lebowitz owes Parker a large debt. The debt is unacknowledged, and Lebowitz can be forgiven, because the differences are more interesting than the similarities. Beneath Parker's laughter, the attentive listener can hear a shriek of despair. The typical Parker protagonist is a clever, sophisticated woman who has been shamefully treated by a stupid, handsome, thoughtless man. Although her women realize the absurdity of their situation, they are helpless. They are victims of the human condition—usually, the war between the sexes.

Lebowitz's heroines are victims of domineering house plants, digital clocks and editors who respect deadlines. The pathos is gone. The beautiful brutes who tormented Parker's women have become prettyboy ''tricks'' of Lebowitz's gay companions: their sin is to annoy her by foolishly believing that the first amendment allows them to speak at dinner. Lebowitz says she envies tricks: ''The best thing in life is to be beautiful.'' But her life isn't bad. Friends, fame and fortune are a good start. Her writing expresses no pain stronger than a hangover headache. She is often hilariously funny, but it is a brittle humor, drained of sentiment or compassion.

Like the *Lampoon* writers, Lebowitz never makes fun of herself. An occasional wry self-disparagement, perhaps; but the reader never doubts that Lebowitz is the arbiter of style, and style is what counts. She writes: ''The three questions of greatest concern are: Is it attractive? Is it amusing? Does it know its place?'' Not surprisingly, this queen of meritocratic snobs comes from the world of fashion. ''Everything about the fashion world I find entertaining,'' she says. ''It's the ultimate artificial business. The things that are funniest are the least real and the least weighty.'' (pp. 20-1)

One wonders who reads Lebowitz and who laughs at her jokes. Fire Island Pines has few bookstores. Dress designers are not notorious bibliophiles. The secret to her amazingly broad appeal is her sensibility, which may be called, in an imperfect phrase, a gay sensibility. ''It's a certain irresponsibility at not being married or having children,'' Lebowitz says. ''I wouldn't call it lightheartedness, but superficiality. I don't care if the planet blows up after I'm dead. And I don't think other people who don't have children care either. You'd only care if someone you love would be alive then. In a certain way, it's like being a kid.''

Kids make fun of people who are different from them. Kids don't care what they break because they know someone will clean up after them. Kids join clubs and laugh at those not allowed to join. Kids pick on weaklings. Kids relish violence. Kids snicker at sex. Compare the shallow and childish level of the new screw-you humor to the competition. The leading humorist in America today is Woody Allen. Allen's recent essays tower above the products of his younger rivals. Unlike the bright young crowd at the *Lampoon*, he has read philosophy, not college philosophy reading lists. His subjects are death, despair and paranoia. And his results are genuinely funny. (p. 21)

In the early days, the *Lampoon* aimed at many worthy targets. But satire without purpose is like a rifle without a marksman—pointless and dangerous. Allen comes out of a tradition of Jewish humor, the comedian as victim. The *Lampoon* is something else. It is rich white humor, the comedian as oppressor. *Lampoon* jokes are the sort that gave the Cossacks a good chuckle after a night at the pogroms. It is fed by a confluence of two streams of thought: the Harvard arrogance represented by the *Lampoon*'s father, the *Harvard Lampoon* . . . and upper-class Catholic wit. . . . McFadden and Lebowitz are neither male, Catholic nor Crimson, but they share the *Lampoon*'s vantage point. They ridicule from a distance. They never turn the epee toward their own hearts. . . . Their humor is not profound and their targets are too easy. Like the *Lampoon*, their work is kids' stuff. (pp. 21-2)

> Arthur Lubow, "Screw You Humor," in The New Republic, *Vol. 179, No. 17, October 21, 1978, pp. 18-22.**

JAMES WOLCOTT

[*Social Studies*] shows the strain of trying to be too effortlessly knowing and droll. In the opening chapter, Lebowitz offers this nugget of advice: "The only appropriate reply to the question: 'Can I be frank?' is 'Yes, if I can be Barbara.'" That's dangerously close to a Neil Simonism. Lebowitz's first collection, *Metropolitan Life*, was a success not only because its sarcasm and urban sass were genuinely funny but because the book was full of quotable nifties. . . . Unlike *Metropolitan Life*, *Social Studies* doesn't have wisecracks that instantly engrave themselves on your memory; instead, the entries dribble off into wordiness and fey displays of whimsy, scattering like shavings from Oscar Wilde's tombstone.

The problem with *Social Studies* is that Fran Lebowitz doesn't seem to have any new subjects other than those created by the unanticipated success of *Metropolitan Life*. . . . Lebowitz, I think, needs to have a cultural beat to cover—television, perhaps, or movies—so that she can train her satirical gifts on some large and recognizable target. In *Social Studies*, she draws almost entirely on her own career for the book's humor and comes up dry. She's sucking through an empty straw.

> James Wolcott, in a review of "Social Studies," in Esquire, *Vol. 96, No. 2, August, 1981, p. 24.*

GLENN COLLINS

The sour cream sensibility that made Fran Lebowitz New York City's most sought-after export in 1978, when **"Metropolitan Life"** was published, still animates [**"Social Studies"**]. . . . Consider, for instance, the deftness of her Emily Post rendition, in **"Tips for Teens"**: "Remember that as a teenager you are at the last stage in your life when you will be happy to hear that the phone is for you.''

All is not as it once was for Miss Lebowitz, however, in the old apartment in the Village. She explains that, ''owing to some rather favourable publicity, I came into what is known as a little money.'' She looks for a maid, but feels ''An apartment, like a sweater, should be sent out to be cleaned.'' (p. 7)

Miss Lebowitz's wit will not be appreciated by all of the people all of the time. Having left the ranks of the truly poor, she devotes a chapter to advising the rich about the ways of ''the poorer person.'' It is a bit of writing that Marie Antoinette might have sincerely admired, with snappy sections like **"Breaking the Ice With Poorer People"** and **"What Not to Say to Poorer People."** . . . Despite the guide-to-the-rich rubric, her merriment at the state of the disadvantaged is less than charming. (pp. 7, 20)

All right, this Fran Lebowitz is not exactly brimming over with human compassion. Hers is not an Up-With-People view of personkind; as she says, ''Everybody talks about people, but nobody ever does anything about them.''

But here's what you're really wondering: Is **"Social Studies"** a worthy successor to her first book? In other words, as Miss Lebowitz asked last time out, is it attractive, is it amusing, does it know its place? Yes, yes and yes. The shock of acerb surprise is gone this time—we open the book already knowing she'll be funny—but the writing is more relaxed; she's not working quite so hard for the orthographic rush. And there is even a bit of delving into the Lebowitz past. . . .

In a nation where the arbiters of what is deemed funny are Beverly Hills programming executives, whose idea of humor is to play tennis in ''Superman III'' T-shirts, Fran Lebowitz's book is for real. As she puts it: ''Life is just one damned thing after another: and death is a cabaret.'' (p. 20)

> Glenn Collins, "The Sour Cream Sensibility," in The New York Times Book Review, *August 23, 1981, pp. 7, 20.*

VIC SUSSMAN

Those unfamiliar with Lebowitz might think her a moralist, an elitist, a snob. She is all those. But she is an equal-opportunity snob, venting her disdain regardless of one's race, disability, sexual persuasion, or for that matter, species.

When told, for example, that her wish to bar all dogs from New York would deprive ''the blind and pathologically lonely,'' she suggests that ''the lonely lead the blind.'' . . .

Lebowitz is a curmudgeon of classic proportions. Her work echoes H.L. Mencken, Dorothy Parker, and Robert Benchley—especially the latter when she's cranking out epigrams, lists, and rules for the betterment of the social order. Unlike Benchley, however, Lebowitz's humor lacks warmth or empathy. She is astringent, snide, and smarmy. And like the New York scene she chronicles, she makes no excuses. . . .

Not all of the 26 essays in *Social Studies* succeed. But as in her first book, . . . Lebowitz packs a lot into a little book and hits far more than she misses. Her elegant, finely honed prose can make you laugh out loud while wincing at her devastating images of America the Inane. . . .

Alone in her lifeboat on a sea of decadence, Lebowitz also does a marvelous job of spoofing herself, with her prissy devotion to propriety in conduct, clothing, food, and smoking, the last being "if not my life then at least my hobby. . . . Smoking is, as far as I am concerned, the entire point of being an adult."

Lebowitz is unashamedly Lebowitz, thank goodness, a funny, urbane, intelligent one-woman bulwark against cultural tickytack, creeping mellowness, and the excesses of what Mencken dubbed *"boobus Americanus."*

> *Vic Sussman, "An Equal-Opportunity Curmudgeon," in* Book World—The Washington Post, *August 30, 1981, p. 5.*

PETER GRIER

Miss Lebowitz is a professional New Yorker. . . . Her first book, **"Metropolitan Life,"** contained such penetrating essays as **"The Right of Eminent Domain Versus the Rightful Dominion of the Eminent"** and **"Why I Love Sleep."** It brought its author acclaim and a better level of creature comfort. **"Social Studies,"** her second collection, is not a junior high textbook. Rather, it attempts to answer the question "How can we find meaning in a world where the word 'collectible' is often used as a noun?" . . .

Her first book was peppered with remarkable aphorisms, including the memorable "the outside is something to pass through on your way from your apartment to a taxicab." This new volume seems to have fewer such bits, though the best ones are as good as any of her work. Many deal with general advice about the problems we encounter in modern society. Bulging waistline? Try reading **"The Fran Lebowitz High Stress Diet."** Confused about your role as a parent? Remember, "never allow your child to call you by your first name. He hasn't known you long enough." About to take a trip? "If you're going to America, bring your own food."

This last tip does raise a crucial point. Lebowitz is, above all, a New Yorker; as far as she is concerned, America is a foreign country. A hardship post, to boot. Not everyone likes New York, and not everyone may think Fran Lebowitz is funny. To find out your Lebowitz Tolerance Quotient, take the following simple quiz:

1. Do you think Woody Allen really isn't amusing at all?

2. Do you enjoy watching made-for-TV movies?

3. Is "quiche" the name of an exotic breed of lap dog?

4. Do you decorate your correspondence with cute crayoned drawings?

5. Were you the last on your block to stop wearing a leisure suit?

If you marked all five of the above "no," congratulations. A very funny experience awaits.

But if you answered "yes" to three or more, **"Social Studies"** might offend you.

Then again, as Lebowitz says, "Being offended is the natural consequence of leaving one's home."

> *Peter Grier, "W. C. Fields, Move Over," in* The Christian Science Monitor, *September 14, 1981, p. B4.*

BARRY GEWEN

Fran Lebowitz had a surprise bestseller . . . in *Metropolitan Life,* a collection of humorous pieces about the esthetic existence in New York City. . . . Her targets were phoniness, fatuity and anything cute. If it was warm and cuddly, it gave her a chill. A down-and-outer taking potshots at the pretensions of the avant-garde art world, she wrote with a topsy-turvy hauteur that led thousands who laughed at her barbs to conclude W. C. Fields was alive and well and living in the Big Apple.

Lebowitz' new collection, *Social Studies* . . . , is more of the same—though not the same, for irascibility wears about as well as sandpaper. Lebowitz can still be very funny. . . . At her best, she also can write about everyday annoyances better than almost anyone else. Her **"Diary of a New York Apartment Hunter"** will bring a guffaw of sympathy to any reader who has ever engaged in the most discouraging activity short of looking for a job. . . . (p. 14)

Success, however, does not become her. The contemptuousness on which so much of her humor depends here seems uncalled-for, unearned, her scornfulness merely the arrogance of the lumpen-sophisticate. The haughtiness that was genuinely funny when she was a struggling survivor in New York's lower depths has become, now that she is a bestselling author, a pose, a vehicle for gags, so that even where she is being amusing, the falseness of the tone makes the humor sound strained.

Worse, indeed disastrously, large portions of *Social Studies* aren't clever at all. Too often, Lebowitz relies for laughs on easy reversals and substitutions—her greediest cases an echo of the New York *Times'* neediest cases; instructions on how to marry a poor person instead of a millionaire; an autobiography of the comic as garment manufacturer: "I started with a humor pushcart on Delancey Street. . . ." Since the technique itself is the joke, these pieces are about as amusing as a Levi-Strauss anthropological transformation. Before long, one finds oneself skimming, winnowing out the good lines from this chaff.

Apparently *Social Studies* is on its way to being as much of a success as *Metropolitan Life.* Anyone considering buying the book, though, would be better advised to spend a half hour or so reading it at a bookstore. The wisecracks are few and easy to spot. The rest is scarcely suitable for the remainder shelves. (pp. 14-15)

> *Barry Gewen, "America in Three Contexts," in* The New Leader, *Vol. LXIV, No. 20, November 2, 1981, pp. 14-15.**

RUSSELL DAVIES

Miss Lebowitz is a perfectly recognisable and familiar kind of hard-pressed writer. Almost all humorists are brain-rackers and space-fillers, a large part of whose mental energy is fed to the consuming question 'What the hell do I write about this week?' Inevitably, this question does not always get flushed away with the rest of the waste matter once composition has actually begun. Sometimes it survives right through the process, so that in the end procrastination is still left sitting there, the unacknowledged subject of the whole thing.

So [*Social Studies*] is not without pieces about writing pieces—in fact it is rounded off with one, a fantasy in which a news item about the selling of notional books (millions paid for paperback and movie rights to novels as yet unwritten) prompts Miss Lebowitz to seek financial recognition for several non-existent books of her own, which her writing has prevented her from writing. (p. 22)

It's more or less accepted on both sides of the Atlantic that 'professional' humour is largely complaint re-channelled into other forms of exaggeration. The natural home of this contention, however, must be New York, where the inhabitants seldom relax their efforts to make exasperation an art-form. Miss Lebowitz lives in New York City, and her pieces are full of its little local difficulties. Finding a decent apartment isn't so much a subject for her as a perpetual undercurrent; it, or the memory of it, keeps bubbling up into everything.

And when Miss L. isn't undertaking a mental survey of Great Apartments she has walked away from . . . , she is discovering new attitudes to apartments in general. 'It was apparent to me that an apartment, like a sweater, was impossible to clean if one was in it. Following this logic, it was then equally apparent that an apartment, like a sweater, should be sent out to be cleaned.' The next step, of course, is to imagine that the cleaners give her the wrong apartment back. . . . Here again, the re-application of the familiar outcome to the impossible situation proves that Miss Lebowitz has got something. (pp. 22-3)

Incidentally, if there's one thing in this that differentiates Miss Lebowitz's comic practice from the English tradition at present, it's the phrase 'following this logic', which draws attention to the mechanics of the joke in a way our local operators would be embarrassed to do. But some of Miss Lebowitz's stuff takes the form of an itemised critique of life: she enjoys letting the joins show. Some of the bits are all joins. She is a great list-maker and cataloguist. This may arise from too-diligent study of real-estate blurbs, or copies of *Consumer Reports* left about in otherwise unwelcoming apartments. (It may also arise from the old enemy, desperation. A great rule for humorists is: when desperate, concoct an Alphabet of Something.) The *pièce de resistance* in this line is **'The Frances Ann Lebowitz Collection'**, an illustrated auction catalogue of worn artifacts from the author's estate—most of them domestic/dingy in aspect ('Broil King Toaster Oven Early/Late Nineteen-Sixties') and dating evidently from Miss Lebowitz's 'poor' period.

There is a good deal of rich/poor tension in the book. . . . Her **'Guide for the Misfortune Hunter'**, one of the few pieces whose outrageousness is already stated by the premise, but presented in characteristically tabulated questionnaire-cum-guidebook form, includes a **'Short Glossary of Words Used by Poorer People.'** . . .

In lasting humour, it seems to me, there is always some element that turns away from reasonableness—the very thing Miss Lebowitz fundamentally, is clinging to. I do not expect you to accept this point, however, if you are a gay landowning Californian telephone-operator with a taste for hats. *You* will find Miss Lebowitz sufficiently unreasonable as she is. (p. 23)

Russell Davies, "Joinery," in New Statesman, *Vol. 103, No. 2657, February 19, 1982, pp. 22-3.*

DUNCAN FALLOWELL

Miss Lebowitz wears New York on her sleeve and she is therefore distinguished by an amusing, fretful, trivial mind which will sacrifice the truth—and the whole truth alas—for a joke whenever the two find themselves in conflict. So voracious is the American appetite for new luminaries that she has been 'forced' by the media there, as one might force celery, and this has exposed her weaknesses, the cool thinness of content, the unsatisfactory nature of an intellect crisp to the tooth but pale green and watery in all other respects. Unless they be possessed of higher powers, all stars need time because stardom is the ability to live outside time and duration is the customary method for accumulating proof. This is especially true in a fast age like our own when change is the only constant, and the only stability is gyroscopic.

So in five minutes' time she might be very good. At the moment these pieces [in *Social Studies*] are so slight and the book contains so few of them that one wonders where they have come from, what magazines she is writing for, and in what way. (p. 26)

Despite her cynical New York Jewish tone, the Goddam world view, Miss Lebowitz is a sentimentalist and very much in love with the romance of freelance journalism—cigarettes, coffee, deadlines, blood pressure, fistfuls of hair—and her fundamental comic technique is to use the mock heroic in the expression of this neurosis. There is something endearing and old-fashioned about it. She is perhaps Dorothy Parker's predecessor. But clearly she is being advised to dissociate herself from café society journalism and swim into the aristocratic air of statement. Her form is the one-liner. Since she is not a Chinese sage and has a column to fill, this often has to be stretched to three lines, sometimes five, and the padding shows. Sometimes she hits the bull's eye. . . . Sometimes she misses completely. . . . And one is left with the sickly aftertaste of a little cleverness with its back to the wall. Someone should hit her because it's there, and it is running to waste hidden away in all these tight-arse, smart-alec defence mechanisms. The final enquiry is: how do you compose a book of only 147 pages in post-modernist layout with gaps between paragraphs a yard deep and a smattering of ugly visuals and still come up with padding? In striving for Minimalism, Fran Lebowitz has so far achieved only Lessness. (p. 27)

Duncan Fallowell, "Lessness," in The Spectator, *Vol. 248, No. 8015, February 20, 1982, pp. 26-7.*

CAROLE MANSUR

Fran Lebowitz, author of *Social Studies,* is decidedly in control of her world, with no husband, children or dogs to tug at her apron-strings and topple her from the pinnacle of independence from which she surveys with a satirical eye American, and more particularly New York life.

Not that feminist or indeed American rhetoric prejudices our enjoyment of this collection of twenty-six humorous pieces, for the liberty she exercises in drawing a knife through urban society, dissecting its pretensions and puncturing its sensitivities, is not that of a liberated lady but of a liberated writer; what surely discomforts readers and embarrasses her still-closeted fellows is her reckless exposure of the indulgences of her profession, her unashamed declaration that she rises late, spends the remainder of her day reading, and her evening not writing.

On occasion this overweening self-confidence leads her to abandon her stance as social observer and she trips into fantasy. . . .

For the most part, however, she is right on target, bursting the overblown bubbles of city sophisticates' self-esteem with an impish mischievousness. She ridicules joggers lapping the reservoir, people who call movies films, order in French at restaurants and live high-stress lives in high-tech homes. Her methods are those of the academic cataloguing and analysing data, breaking behaviour down into codes and proceeding from the premise that all people are alike, apart from their feet and the way they like their eggs cooked. . . .

Less frivolous are the ironical case studies of a social worker, each concluding with an appeal for cash aid to the victims of free-market capitalism. The last of these, the traveller stranded in the airport baggage-claim area, hopelessly searching the carousel for her seven suitcases crammed with designer clothes she knows to be lost, is the most concentrated image of metropolitan man's condition. (p. 323)

> *Carole Mansur, "Out of School," in* Punch, *Vol. 282, No. 7371, February 24, 1982, pp. 322-23.**

Andrea Lee
1953-

American nonfiction writer, novelist, and short story writer.

Lee is best known as the author of *Russian Journal* (1981), a highly praised work based on a diary Lee kept of her trip to the Soviet Union in 1978 with her husband, who had won a fellowship to study in Moscow and Leningrad for ten months. In addition to her candid impressions and observations of the country, Lee's sketches of several young Soviet students and workers are regarded as entertaining and informative stories about life in an authoritarian society.

Lee's first novel, *Sarah Phillips* (1984), was originally published as a series of short stories in *The New Yorker*. The novel is a partially autobiographical account of a privileged and rebellious young black woman and her prominent family. While traveling in Europe, the protagonist, in an extended flashback, recalls the conflicts she encountered as the daughter of a prominent minister and civil rights leader. Lee was praised for her sensitive dramatization of the dilemma faced by upper- and middle-class blacks who have become assimilated into mainstream society yet struggle to maintain their cultural heritage.

PETER OSNOS

Lee writes very well. There is a warmth and freshness about her style that makes reading [*Russian Journal*] effortless. She takes us wherever she is, conveying a feeling of place and atmosphere that is the mark of real talent. . . .

In fact, it was probably Lee's innocence that gave her the gall to undertake a work like this in the first place. An aspiring Sovietologist would be daunted by the need to draw conclusions and make judgments. Knowing how much one doesn't know can be debilitating when it comes to taking on a subject as broad as Soviet life today.

Yet, in most respects, Lee succeeds. Her descriptions of what it is like to be Russian are right on technical details and sensitive to cultural patterns. Her visits to the public baths and farmers' markets, her accounts of Sundays spent with friends or of an encounter with Soviet-style hippies strike responsive chords in someone, like me, who has the same memories. Moreover, humanizing the Russian people is especially important in politically tense times such as these.

What is best about the book—what distinguishes it from other books about the Soviet Union published in recent years—is her accounts of friendships with young people. . . . Her insights into the materialism of Russian youth, the conservatism of some, the nihilism of others, tell us a lot about the coming generation of Soviets. This is valuable because the people she met include leaders of the next generation, who are Muscovites, many of them enrolled at Moscow University. A certain selectivity is at work in her sample. Lee's friends are people either authorized to mingle with foreigners or daring enough to do so. Foreigners tend to meet a preponderance of disenchanted or rebellious Soviets; that, evidently, was Lee's experience too.

© Jerry Bauer

There is one slightly awkward problem with the book. Andrea Lee, it turns out, is black. The only indication of this comes in a single sentence describing her meeting with an Ethiopian student. "Toward me," she writes, "he showed the absolute lack of interest with which many Africans greet American blacks." Later she quotes the student as saying that the Russian "masses call us black devils and spit at us in the street." There is nothing else in the book about Lee's experiences as a black. She writes in considerable and intimate detail about Russians, but tells us nothing about the part race may have played in her relationships with them.

Lee's husband is white. Interracial couples in the Soviet Union are extremely rare. That this did not lead her into some interesting encounters is hard to believe. Apparently, she feels that her blackness has nothing to do with her time in the Soviet Union. That is her business. But she never even says as much. Discovering that Andrea Lee is black gave me the feeling that, for all of its candor, *Russian Journal* is holding some things back. . . .

For all its charm, *Russian Journal* is no more than it self-effacingly claims to be: a gifted young writer's impressions of a relatively short time in a new and very different world. That she got as far as she did in that world is a tribute to Andrea Lee.

Peter Osnos, *"Blue Jeans in Red Square: An American in Moscow,"* in Book World—The Washington Post, *October 25, 1981, p. 10.*

SUSAN JACOBY

["**Russian Journal**"] is such a subtly crafted reflection of both the bleak and golden shadings of Russian life that its tones belong more to the realm of poetry than journalism. . . .

I was the same age [as Miss Lee] when I spent two years as a journalist in Russia, a decade before Miss Lee's sojourn. The mid-20's are an ideal time for a foreigner to experience Russia: One is young and unexhausted enough to confront the taxing mixture of beauty, frustration and ambiguity without collapsing, but old enough to make important distinctions between the real life of *homo sovieticus* and romanticized images of the "suffering Slavic soul."

The failure to make such distinctions has landed many Western observers of Russia in a swamp of *poshlost,* an untranslatable word whose meanings Vladimar Nabokov summarized as "corny trash, vulgar clichés, Philistinism in all its phases, imitations of imitations, bogus profundities."

The romanticization of material deprivation is a form of *poshlost* that has always appealed to foreigners in Russia, but Miss Lee did not fall into the trap. She does describe the intensification of her own esthetic responses in the absence of the easy stimulation provided by Western advertising and consumer goods. There is, she observes, no routine sensory fix to be derived from the crowds, streets and shop windows of Moscow—"only the rarer, more demanding pleasures of nature and architecture. . . ." (p. 11)

The absence of color, pleasing graphic design and satisfying textures from everyday life is no small matter; it makes Russians pathetically eager for the lowliest products of wasteful capitalism. Miss Lee is about to throw out a dunning letter from her university alumni association when a Russian friend grabs it in order to save the letterhead. "It's so beautiful," the Russian says. Later, Miss Lee finds the letter pinned up over the friend's bed.

The subject matter of this journal is highly idiosyncratic; it in no way provides a survey of Soviet life—or even of the limited portion of Russian society accessible to a foreigner. What Miss Lee offers are the people, places and experiences that touched her most deeply. (pp. 11, 22)

In Leningrad, the great blues singer B. B. King is able to dislodge the audience out of the stiffness and rote applause that are the norm at Soviet ballets and concerts. In the end, the Russians are moved to tears. "B. B. King astounded me," says one man. "This blues music—it's not like jazz. He poured his whole heart and soul out there on the stage. Such feeling is very Russian—we believe in emotion, in the soul. I never thought an American could feel that way."

There is one regrettable omission in "**Russian Journal.**" Miss Lee is a black American—a fact that even an alert reader might miss, because it is mentioned only once, in an oblique reference late in the book. The author obviously made a conscious decision not to use her race as one of the prisms for reflecting Russian life. This choice may have been motivated by an understandable fear that her book would be merchandised as an ethnic curio piece.

There may also have been another factor at work. Miss Lee is so light-skinned that many Russians would not identify her as a black American. In my experience, most Russians held extremely rigid racial and ethnic stereotypes. (I was constantly interrogated about the "discrepancy" between my Jewish-sounding last name and my blond hair and blue eyes.) A famous (and otherwise brilliant) Russian writer once told me that racial prejudice was inevitable because the sight of a black person immediately arouses fear of the dark. A freckle-spattered, sand-toned complexion like Miss Lee's is not the image that springs to mind when a Russian thinks of "blacks."

Nevertheless, the high quality of Miss Lee's writing and the acuity of her perceptions make it especially regrettable that she chose to avoid racial issues. If her Russian friends didn't know that she was black, she must have been exposed—sometimes with an assumption of fellow feeling—to the sort of prejudice in which the Russian word for "black" (*chyornii*) is used as a pejorative for all Soviet Central Asians. If her Russian friends did know she was black, that knowledge must have affected their perceptions (and Miss Lee's) in some way. Miss Lee's responses would surely have been as interesting as the rest of her observations, and I wish she had included them. (p. 22)

Susan Jacoby, *"One Year in Moscow,"* in The New York Times Book Review, *October 25, 1981, pp. 11, 22.*

MARY LOUISE PATTERSON

[In *Russian Journal,* what Andrea Lee] has written most about are the disaffections of those people whom she apparently spent most of her time seeking out and befriending—dissident Jews and black marketeering Russian youth. Strange. All of these people are deeply alienated from Soviet life and society, seem primarily concerned with acquiring Western friends, clothing, phonograph records and mannerisms (like gum chewing), and dream incessantly of the bygone Russian aristocracy or of escaping to the "free world." The Soviet Union in all of its political and cultural complexity, contradictions, historical richness and profound importance in today's world was not emcompassed by Ms. Lee's tunnel vision. Moreover, it is regrettable that the author has placed her excellent and colorful command of the English language in service to the cause of misrepresenting her perceptions as "facts" and then beguiling the reader into accepting them. (p. 116)

Ms. Lee states at the outset that she arrived in the USSR free of political bias, even much endeared to the country based on her fond memories of the many Russian fables she heard during her childhood. Constantly and cleverly, she strains to maintain this fiction of impartiality and political innocence throughout the book. Thus, she is shocked by her dormitory room's "Orwellian" radio, which can only be turned down to an inaudible level and not off—although such radios are frequently found in hotel rooms in the United States, Mexico and Europe. At another point, she mentions that she smuggled letters for Russian dissidents into Moscow, that she and her husband house-sat in Moscow for a vacationing U.S. diplomat, and that she and her husband were State Department approved. Unbiased?

The book lacks any self-questioning or self-examination with respect to the meaning of her Soviet experiences. She doesn't even relate her Afro-American identity to the story. The pretention of honesty is exposed as fraudulent early on when she describes a Friday night dance at the U.S. Embassy, an event into which she and her husband sneaked in a Russian student.

She writes: "When I . . . stand in the embassy commissary, with its rows of peanut butter jars and boxes of sugared cereal, or walk among the big shiny Detroit cars in the embassy driveway, or talk to the earnest, affable bureaucrats who work in the offices, I feel as if I'm seeing part of a dream America. The dear, blind, brash, innocent America of television shows and commercials—the kind of vision that we simple souls in exile would naturally long for, and unfailingly recreate." Does Ms. Lee honestly believe that *all* of us *simple* souls would recreate that vision, including us Black folk, if we were abroad? And would we all feel that we were "in exile"?

Andrea Lee's highly subjective views paint a picture of the Soviet Union that has the net effect of reinforcing the fanatical anti-communism, warmongering and bellicosity so much in vogue currently. I don't doubt her experiences or that she met the people she describes. But the journal reminds me of the fabled blindfolded man who, led to the elephant, feels its leg and describes a tree. (pp. 116-17)

> Mary Louise Patterson, *"Subjective, Narrow View,"* in Freedomways, *Vol. 22, No. 2, second quarter, 1982, pp. 116-17.*

CHRISTOPHER BOOKER

Since 1917 there must have been several hundred books by Western visitors describing visits to the Soviet Union—the vast majority falling into one or two clearly defined categories. On the one hand, as landmarks in the history of self-deception, were those stereotyped eulogies of the 1930's and 1940's, extolling the heroic collectivism of an imaginary paradise in the making. On the other, right from the start, has been a very different, much more personal type of book, by authors ranging from H. G. Wells and Malcolm Muggeridge to Laurens van der Post and George Feifer. And despite the enormous variety of their styles and points of view, not the least interesting feature of this second group of books is how often they also have seemed to describe a familiar pattern of experience. (p. 23)

A distinguished addition to this second group of books is *Russian Journal* by Andrea Lee, a black American girl . . . who four years ago spent ten months in the Soviet Union. . . . (pp. 23-4)

She does not attempt any sweeping analysis of Soviet life or 'the Russian character'. She merely observes, with what, if our contemporary novelists wrote so well, one might be tempted to call 'a novelist's eye' - through some 35 almost self-contained vignettes of people and places. We visit scenes familiar and unfamiliar—Moscow student life, a Moscow peasant market, a bath-house full of giggling Muscovite ladies letting their hair down like children; further afield, Stalin's birthplace in the little Caucasian town of Gori, a Leningrad nightclub (from where they were driven home by a taxi-driver singing Verdi arias at the top of his voice). We join Miss Lee and her husband as they take part, with a 'worker' friend Petya, in the great May Day parade past Lenin's tomb, catching a rare close-up glimpse of Brezhnev and other members of the Politburo. . . .

Some of the longer episodes read like vivid short stories, such as a chilling Christmas Day visit to the luxurious *dacha,* where [journalist] Victor Louis holds court with his upper-middle class English wife Jennifer; or a strange encounter with Tikhon Khrennikov, the unspeakable Chairman of the Union of Soviet Composers, who invites them to a premiere of some of his music. . . . Then there is the moving profile of Ibrahim, a proud, sad Ethiopian, brought to Moscow like so many of his young countrymen to be educated as a loyal Marxist, who has conceived such a passionate hatred of the Soviet Union that he wishes only to return to fight with the anti-Soviet Eritrean nationalists. His brother has already died in this cause, and when Ibrahim requests in a session of table-tapping to speak to his brother's ghost, the answer to his first unspoken question comes back, 'Death'. What did you ask, a girl timidly enquires. 'I asked my brother what I could expect when I get home'.

The dark, oppressive underside of Soviet life is constantly present in the background, but all the more forcefully for being so understated. An old woman sneaks past the guard into the brightly-lit Aladdin's cave of a *beriozka* (hard-currency shop), just to take a look at the forbidden plenty on the shelves before being hustled out. Andrea and her husband go up onto the Lenin Hills with Petya to watch a fireworks display, and are shocked to be brusquely pushed by armed guards into a tiny stockade. Even the loyal Petya is forced to comment 'it embarrasses me to have you see that. Our government is awfully afraid of riots, you see. People gathered together make revolutions, and we can't have another of those'.

In common with so many predecessors, Miss Lee finally records how, when they left Soviet soil, she and her husband were flooded with elation. But they had undoubtedly left behind some part of themselves with the unforgettable people they had met in that poignant land—even with Grigorii, their 'informer', who makes his last appearance taking them out into the woods of the Lenin Hills, in his 'bureaucrat's suit', to hear the nightingales. . . . What a country! (p. 24)

> Christopher Booker, *"Russia Revisited,"* in The Spectator, *Vol. 248, No. 8031, June 12, 1982, pp. 23-4.*

MICHAEL IRWIN

The entries [in *Russian Journal*] are chronologically ordered: there is little theorising and no thesis. Andrea Lee likens them to 'a set of photographs taken by an amateur who is drawn to his subject by instinct and capricious inclination'. This unpretentiousness is one of the great strengths of her book. She obviously has no interest in selecting or distorting evidence to make out a case.

It is her general good sense which inspires confidence. . . . [She] is neither complacently nor guiltily American. She recognises that as a Westerner, physically and sartorially, she becomes an automatic focus of attention, an inevitable influence on the scenes in which she takes part: in that sense, what she sees tends to be atypical. It is by no means an irrelevant factor that, in so far as her personality emerges from the notes, she seems friendly but shrewd, always prepared to like people and to enjoy herself but not to the detriment of her alertness. Although she hasn't come looking for bad news, she isn't going to be conned or intimidated. She also wins credit for her refusal to adopt a pose of detachment, to imply that she herself is immune to the pressures she sees as deforming the lives of her acquaintances. When she comes under surveillance as a result of running English classes for a group of Soviet Jews on the verge of emigration, she grows conscious 'of an intense anger forming like a stone in my guts . . . a personal anger based on fear'. At first she is put out by the devouring stares of subway passengers fascinated by her clothes, but later, starved of ready visual stimulation in Moscow, she becomes a starer herself whenever she encounters 'a well-cut dress (terribly rare), a handsomely bound book (still rarer), or an attractive face.' She is all the more persuasive an observer for implicating herself in what she observes. . . .

Andrea Lee brings to these vignettes a novelist's talent for conveying moods in very few words. While avoiding grandiose diagnoses she makes many incidental remarks that catch the attention. When describing Yura, a hunchbacked librarian in Leningrad, she reflects that the physically and mentally defective seem far better integrated into the social system than are their American counterparts: 'Deformed by nature or age, they are very often the strictest guardians of social form, many of them, like Yura, deeply patriotic. For him, life does seem good, perhaps the best it could be in any country.' After an evening with some Moscow hippies she comes to the surprising conclusion that their life-style 'isn't as much a rebellious departure from the social norm as it was for hippies in the United States'. Economic pressures and the shortage of housing have made even the most respectable Russians accustomed to pooling resources or dossing down in one another's houses.

Given her astuteness, it is a pity that Andrea Lee isn't prepared to speculate a little more ambitiously. She glances at several issues which she could profitably have explored further. In discussing the deletion of sex-scenes from foreign films she mentions 'the odd mental talents a diet of such films must develop: an ability for elision, for constant suspension of logic'. But comparable deficiencies exist at every level of life in a Communist society. What views can the Soviet citizen hold on housing or agriculture or disarmament if he distrusts the party line but has no alternative source of fact or theory? What profitable occupation can there be for the mortal and intellectual energies that in a democracy are expended on political controversy? The freak diet on which the Russian has to subsist must surely foster not only 'odd mental talents' but odd mental limitations of several kinds. What Andrea Lee remarks in passing she could well investigate at large. . . .

The book suffers from one or two other minor limitations, most of which the author herself would no doubt acknowledge. She describes only a narrow social spectrum. The friends she makes are students, artists, dissidents, professional people, the great mass of those she sees in the streets remaining inscrutable: 'glum workmen in grimy quilted jackets, fantastically fat old women in shawls, girls with exhausted faces under their make-up'. It must be conceded, even of the class she knows best, that the Russian who will consort with a visiting Americans is likely, by definition, to be unrepresentative.

Her husband, Tom, is said to speak 'near-native' Russian. She herself lays claim to 'a far slighter knowledge of Russian strengthened only by a good ear for language'. It would be reassuring if she admitted to the possibility that she might have misunderstood a conversation or misconstrued its subtext. Arguably she sees too simply, too clearly. She can make participation in the private problems of Russian life sound implausibly unproblematic. She seems to accept her involvement in the crises of her new friends with the amiable unself-consciousness of a David Copperfield. Some episodes seem too neat, too 'finished'. . . .

This may seem an over-elaborate reaction to a work that is deliberately simple in manner and scope. But the modest truthfulness which Andrea Lee aspires to is most difficult to attain, requiring precariously delicate adjustments of attitude and tone on the author's part. A more theoretical book could stand or fall on the theory: *Russian Journal* must win assent by the authenticity of all its parts. To note the author's few miscalculations is to suggest the difficulty of an ostensibly undemanding enterprise. *Russian Journal* is a considerable exercise in observation, empathy and personal and literary tact.

Michael Irwin, "Hidden Privilege," in London Review of Books, *September 16 to October 6, 1982*, p. 20.

SUSAN RICHARDS SHREVE

The central concern of **"Sarah Phillips,"** Andrea Lee's first novel, is with a young black woman's quest to invent her own history in the long shadow of a powerful inheritance. Sarah is from a serious and prosperous family involved with civil rights and the problems of underprivileged people. She is a smart, clear-eyed, rebellious young woman who has been given the same schooling as any upper-middle-class white girl and wishes at once for her family's absolute disapproval and the comfortable warmth of their society. The book is a series of short pieces, primarily about childhood, some of which have appeared in the New Yorker, as did Miss Lee's first book, **"Russian Journal."** The stories read like an unsentimental autobiography in which the narrative thread is the mind's landscape of significant memory.

"Sarah Phillips" is, of course, more than a single life. Sarah's story is representative of the changing history of blacks in America. For several generations, the leadership of the black people has been primarily vested in preachers providing their congregations—which have extended beyond the church—with a sense of unity and dignity and a future. But their children, like Sarah and Matthew, her brother, have been educated for a new kind of leadership. They are expected to "make it" in the white, middle-class establishment and at the same time to see that world clearly, without romantic illusions. Sarah is not consciously grappling with issues of history in these pieces but it is clear that Miss Lee intended her to be a child of the civil rights movement, representative of a new black woman, educated, sassy, worldly, harshly critical, somewhat self-deprecating and bound for a kind of glory. . . .

The "formal precision" with which Andrea Lee informs us of the fine balance between experience and the development of self is surprising and sharp. One is struck by the sometimes chilling objectivity Sarah has toward her life. The point of view is that of a writer who is at once a part of an experience and an observer of it. **"Sarah Phillips"** is a work of fiction; nevertheless, the author is certainly examining the relationship between a writer and her life, the "I" and experience. In the chapter in which the Reverend Phillips dies, the event of his death and the emotional detachment implicit in Sarah's recording of it are compelling and disturbing. She is pleased with her dress for the funeral and writes, "When I saw how expensive and beautiful I looked, I was filled with a surge of self-congratulatory excitement, and with the feeling of assuming a glamorous new character with the clothes. Once seated in the gray interior of the big black car, I leaned my head against the window glass in an affected manner, hoping that passers-by in the March night would see and admire me as a tragic heroine."

The difficulty with the narrative is that the book reads like connected short stories instead of a coherent novel; the central character moves through a series of emotional epiphanies that sometimes don't take off. A further problem is that Sarah's intellectual distance, which is part of her character, prevents us from ever catching her off guard. We don't know her well enough to be moved deeply by her insights. We do know her parents, however, and they are quite marvelous, as are many of the minor characters.

"**Sarah Phillips**" is finally a pilgrimage through childhood in which a young woman, frightened as we all are of the powerful emotions of the past, discovers in that past the unlimited contours of her life. Andrea Lee's authority as a writer comes of an unstinting honesty and a style at once simple and yet luminous.

Susan Richards Shreve, "Unsentimental Journey," in The New York Times Book Review, *November 18, 1984, p. 13.*

LAURA OBOLENSKY

"What matters is that something—at last—has happened to me!" remarks a young traveling companion to Sarah Phillips, the eponymous narrator of [*Sarah Phillips*]. . . . It's hardly a startling outburst coming from a recent college graduate long numbed by the tedious business of growing up. And the opening chapter makes it clear that Sarah, taking that remark as her cue, has made something happen to her life. Late out of Harvard, black "but light-skinned . . . with a lively appetite for white boys," she is five months into a European romp which has her bouncing between Paris, the French countryside, and London. She also "plays the queen" in a loose ménage-à-quatre whose other participants are her full-time lover Henri, "an illegitimate child raised outside Paris by his mother and adopted only recently by his rich uncle," and Henri's two childhood cronies—Alain, who comes "from a large and happy petit-bourgeois family," and Roger, a student sprung "from the pettiest of petty nobility" (Sarah isn't coy about her class consciousness)—both of whom she sleeps with occasionally "in a spirit of Brüderschaft." (p. 41)

Indeed, something has happened to Sarah—something light-years removed from her middle-class Philadelphia upbringing, something which would surely raise the eyebrows of her recently deceased, civil rights activist, Baptist minister father, and of her prim, once schoolmarm mother. Which presumably was the whole point of the escapade. But youthful rebellions can be a punishing business, and by the end of the first chapter Sarah clearly senses that her own binge is turning into a bore. When at the end of a bibulous lunch Henri teases that she is the offspring of a mongrel Irish-woman raped "by a jazz musician as big and black as King Kong, with sexual equipment to match," Sarah expediently concludes her Parisian spree has been "nothing more than a slight hysteria," and calls it quits. (Never mind that until then she has delighted in coaxing poor wisecracking Henri into telling her "nigger jokes.")

The balance of the narrative consists of successive flashbacks to Sarah's growing years which, though intended to justify her subsequent Parisian "hysteria," fall a bit short of the mark. By her own admission, Sarah and her peers are "the overprotected or horribly spoiled products of a comfortable suburban childhood." . . . In keeping with their middle-class circumstances, the Phillipses seem to have a penchant for conspicuous consumption. Though said to "worship thrift," mother vacations in Europe and shops at Saks, Aunt Emma exudes whiffs of Arpège, and Sunday dinners are invariably "massive" or "extravagant." Brother Matthew goes to summer camp in the Poconos while Sarah heads for Camp Grayfeather in "Wyeth Territory," Delaware; and after the obligatory stints at exclu-

sive private schools, it's Swarthmore for Matthew and Harvard for Sarah. Nothing out of character for any self-respecting affluent suburban family here. Or is there? Well, yes, sort of.

After all, the Phillipses are black, and it's the turbulent early 1960's; though close to being won, the fight for civil rights goes on as does discrimination. Through Reverend Phillips—Lee's strongest characterization apart from that of the narrator herself—we catch glimpses of the Struggle, for this spellbinding preacher, who can throw an occasional member of his mostly female flock "into fits of rapturous shrieks," is also a passionate civil rights activist. When not hectoring from his pulpit, he turns to hectoring the conscience of a refractory America from the airwaves; predictably, he also organizes boycotts and multitudinous marches.

Though she clearly idolizes him, Sarah doesn't quite know what to make of this crusading father. When he lands in an Alabama jail after a more exalted act of civil disobedience, she admits to being "privately embarrassed." . . . And the tokenism that she experiences firsthand when she becomes the first black student to be enrolled at the exclusive Prescott School for Girls leaves her more thrilled than wretched: "It's a little like being in a play," she tells her mother "looking for a laugh"; "everyone's watching me all the time." To her credit, Lee doesn't shy from daubing the Phillipses with the brush of the very racism against which the good Reverend is constantly inveighing. When sitting with her mother in the evenings, Sarah remarks, "Daddy . . . would talk unflatteringly about negroes," and rail against their propensity "for spoiling a community." And when later in the book Matthew brings home his Jewish girlfriend for the parental once-over, it's a reverse case of *Guess Who's Coming to Dinner*.

For all its insight into the little-known world of upper-class blacks, however, *Sarah Phillips* is not the novel it is touted to be, and Lee's forte lies more in the hundred-yard dash of the short story . . . than in the intricately plotted long-distance narrative. (pp. 41-2)

Sarah Phillips makes for a disconcerting read. Despite its talk about rebelling against a childhood during which "civil rights and concern for the under-privileged (were) served up . . . at breakfast, lunch, and dinner," Andrea Lee never really dramatizes the dilemma. And what remain deeply troublesome sociological issues are treated tangentially, or with a tone of detachment often bordering on the sardonic. The moral and emotional conflict that should rend her narrator as she struggles between two worlds, neither of which really claims her allegiance, is never demonstrated. Instead, what Lee proves once more is that affluence is a powerful equalizer—that no matter how adept the irony, and no matter what her ethnicity, a young lady who behaves like an elitist snob and thinks like an elitist snob is an elitist snob. (p. 42)

Laura Obolensky, "Scenes from a Girlhood," in The New Republic, *Vol. 191, No. 21, November 19, 1984, pp. 41-2.*

CHRISTOPHER LEHMANN-HAUPT

["**Sarah Phillips**"] is set in "the hermetic world of the old-fashioned black bourgeoisie—a group largely unknown to other Americans, which," as Sarah reflects, "has carried on with cautious pomp for years in eastern cities and suburbs, using its considerable funds to attempt poignant imitations of high society, acting with genuine gallantry in the struggle for civil rights, and finally producing a generation of children educated in newly integrated schools and impatient to escape the outworn rituals of their parents.''

We are satisfied with the eloquence and brilliant clarity of detail with which Andrea Lee describes Sarah's childhood as the daughter of an upright Baptist minister and the ambiguities of growing up a member of a proud and privileged minority. If her fiction strikes us as intensely autobiographical it tells us a story we would want to read no matter what its form.

The only hitch is that Miss Lee—who is the author of one previous book, a highly praised report on Soviet life called **"Russian Journal,"** . . . revisits Sarah's past only through the exercise of memory. She never reveals how Sarah acts once she has recalled her origins. Probably this is for Andrea Lee to explore in her future fiction, but one can't help wondering if her imagination will prove as powerful as her memory. Most of what is so good about **"Sarah Phillips"** suggests that for now, at least, straightforward autobiography is more useful to her than fiction. Still, however she decides to tell the stories of her life in the future, the results should fulfill our hopeful anticipation.

> *Christopher Lehmann-Haupt, in a review of "Sarah Phillips," in* The New York Times, *December 6, 1984, p. C22.*

ISA KAPP

[The heroine of *Sarah Phillips* is] a black American heiress of all the ages.

To be so much a child of privilege is apparently, for a black girl in the '60s, not the easiest of fates. It seduces her into many kinds of snobbery; she turns away from the school cook when he waves at her, and she dreams of ways to scandalize the bourgeoisie—a temptation the author herself cannot quite resist. Andrea Lee begins the book in Paris, where an expatriate Sarah is living in a swank apartment near the Bois de Boulogne, juggling several bedmates.

Ironically, for the reader, it is precisely the history of an intelligent black girl growing up in an atmosphere of propriety and cultivation, not her impulse toward mutiny, that is engrossing. The time has come for the black novel to move beyond the recall of poverty and prejudice that has given it distinction up to now, and deal with the challenges in an era of integration. Although Lee takes a transitional step in this direction, she is somewhat awkwardly preoccupied with the posture her heroine ought to assume in any given circumstance. (p. 7)

> *Isa Kapp, "The First Time Around," in* The New Leader, *Vol. LXVII, No. 22, December 10, 1984, pp. 5-8.**

FRANCIS GOSKOWSKI

If Ms. Lee is indubitably a writer, is she likewise a novelist? To this, the answer is a "yes" with qualifiers. *Sarah Phillips* is engaging, witty, and, in spite of its episodic structure, coherent. We begin in Paris, where Sarah Phillips is living a deeply longed for exile's existence, something she had been moving toward all her previous years. France, however, is anything but foreign. The racist oafs she takes up with in Paris resemble no one so much as the pampered children of the white American middle class Sarah thought she had left behind for

good. . . . By chapter's end she knows she must leave France. Chapter two, however, does not carry the story forward to any new adventures in exile but back to the Philadelphia suburb of Sarah's youth. This and the rest of the novel's chapters tell us how and why Sarah has made her way to France. . . .

When, at the end of the novel, Sarah attends her father's large, public funeral, she realizes that the event marks a turning point in her life, and, like Joyce's Stephen at the end of *Portrait of the Artist as a Young Man,* chooses flight rather than a return to the familiarities and predictabilities of the suburbs.

But we know that this is not really the end of the story. The first chapter, we remember, has described Sarah's French sojourn unsympathetically—her French lover has convinced her of "the hopeless presumption of trying to discard my portion of America"—so we are left finally in some doubt as to what Ms. Lee is trying to say in this novel. Have we just left Sarah "in the midst of things" as she searches for identity? Or is the book more of "a gesture of indefinite revolt," to use Edmund Wilson's phrase about F. Scott Fitzgerald's *This Side of Paradise,* than a rounded narrative of exile and return? Should the reader take the whole of Sarah's account ironically or as a sincere statement of alienation? However it is explained, this thematic ambiguity blurs the novel's focus and softens its impact.

Finally, we should note the absence of genuine anxiety or pressure in this novel. What Sarah actually seems to be rebelling against is not so much social or religious tyranny as the overwhelming blandness of American life. On the evidence of her memoir, Sarah is not compelled to do much of anything. Even her refusal to be baptized does not elicit anything more than raised eyebrows and some laboriously gentle prodding from relatives. We miss, in other words, some of the more dramatic conflicts that have dominated novels of this sort in the past.

Nevertheless, all strictures aside, we must recognize the emergence of a major novelistic talent in *Sarah Phillips.* Without a doubt, Ms. Lee will be heard from again, and she will command our attention.

> *Francis Goskowski, in a review of "Sarah Phillips," in* Best Sellers, *Vol. 44, No. 11, February, 1985, p. 408.*

PATRICIA VIGDERMAN

[The form of] **Sarah Phillips** is deceptive: its twelve chapters at first seem to be merely a dozen neatly crafted short stories . . . ; and because the tale it tells is written in the first person, it has the feel of a memoir. But the formal model for this novel is neither of these. The young heroine of the title grew up on such literary fare as the Melendy family [of Elizabeth Enright's novels] and E. Nesbit's Bastable children, and Lee has given her story a structure very like that of those wonderful children's "novels." Each chapter is a separate adventure, but the book as a whole constructs another world—one that could be your own but is, well, more exciting. Sarah's adventures, like those of the Melendy family, bring to life a clever and well-loved young person who longs to take possession of the wider world. The crucial difference between Sarah and the Melendys, though, is that Sarah's family is black.

What gives Sarah's story its special resonance is the way her race both does and does not define her. Her cultural heritage is as much a matter of the Melendys and Macbeth as it is of anything specifically black or Afro-American. Her family is generations removed from the South; they are professional people "not too dark of complexion" and not given to shouting in church. Sarah is essentially destined for Radcliffe from birth, and the racial component of her identity is extremely subtle.

Born in the North in 1953, Sarah Phillips embodies a dream of color blindness—it's Martin Luther King, Jr.'s dream, to be precise—a dream held for generations before she was born. Like most dreams come true, of course, she is somewhat different from what the dreamers had in mind. Sarah and her older brother Matthew grow up to have a sophistication about being black in America that is far beyond the civil rights ethic or the bitter jokes of her parents' generation. When Sarah is denied the part she deserves in the play at her fancy white prep school and is cast instead as a black maid (it's 1965 in the Philadelphia suburbs), she says, "After that life at Prescott was easier for me. It was simply . . . a matter of knowing where you stood." The new knowledge comes to her as a physical sensation—a giggling fit. . . . For a daughter of that dream, then, the real moment of puberty is the one on which she sees where she stands in relation to white America—and it's a moment of laughter, not tears or rage.

Only two years earlier, as a child who is still reading *The Melendy Family*, she doesn't yet have that cool understanding. Indeed, when her father takes her with him to Washington, D.C., where he is helping to plan the march that took place in August of 1963, she sees a smile of complicity pass between him and a black taxi driver. "Something began to burn and flutter in my chest: it was as if I had swallowed a pair of fiery wings." Emotionally stirred, she sees the march as a crusade, or maybe the French Revolution. But her parents don't take her with them to the march (too many strangers, too many germs) and she and Matthew watch it on TV. They fight about whether or not it means anything. . . . (pp. 23-4)

It is not until her senior year at Radcliffe that her confident understanding of where she stands is seriously challenged. The spring before her graduation she is called home to her father's funeral. Her father was a spiritual and social leader, and his death is public property. But she is a kind of arrow shot out of the community that he led, and she is completely unable to respond to the massively attended funeral. Dressed like the heroine of a novel, she sleepwalks through the event, deciding it is easier to "pretend to be a heroine" than to begin dealing with either her grief or the torch that is passed on to her by this death.

This is not a story we read every day. Because Sarah has been set firmly into white America, this novel does not fit easily into the Afro-American tradition, and may even meet with some disapproval. "Until we have put something on (the white man's) streetcorner that is our own," the novelist Zora Neale Hurston wrote in 1934, "we are right back where we were when they filed our iron collar off." Hurston spoke for a distinctly black cultural identity and ridiculed the black intellectuals of her own day who seemed to be imitating white culture. But Sarah is not imitating anything. She is as firmly in possession of the culture we share as (white and middle-class) I am. Like Sarah, as a child I "fell away into a remote dimension when I opened a book"—and we read the same books. Andrea Lee's novel describes one girl's journey from that remote dimension to a story of her own. It's a very grace-

fully written book about black identity that makes what Sarah and I share seem more important than what we don't. It puts us on the streetcorner together. (p. 24)

Patricia Vigderman, in a review of "Sarah Phillips," in Boston Review, *Vol. X, No. 1, February, 1985, pp. 23-4.*

BRUCE VAN WYNGARDEN

The first thing to be said about . . . [*Sarah Phillips*] is that it contains writing of surpassing skill. It is a coming-of-age remembrance in which detail and insight are delightfully, and sometimes poignantly, blended. The second thing that must be said is that *Sarah Phillips* is not really a novel. It is a chronological gathering of self-contained vignettes. . . . The problem is that the seams show. I was never quite able to shake the notion that I was reading well-written short stories that had a common narrator. . . .

[Sarah's] childhood, we learn, was at the same time unique and typical. She lived in a fine house in a tree-lined neighborhood, attended private schools and camps, and for the most part was a normal, if precocious kid. Typical. But, there's a kicker: Sarah is black. Her father is a prominent Baptist minister who is a leader in the sixties' civil rights movement. Sarah is in a rather unusual position: She observes her father fight for the rights of her "people"—rights that, for the most part, she already enjoys. Not to say that she doesn't experience bigotry, it's just that the prejudice she encounters is of a subtler sort. As the only black child in a previously all-white school, no one calls her "nigger," she is just not invited to come to the Friday night dances with the neighboring boys school.

As Sarah grows older, there is less of even this sort of slighting. In most of the later chapters prejudice is seldom a factor except in sort of an inside-out way, as when her brother Matthew brings home a white girl for dinner. By the end of the meal, their mother is unable to hide her feelings any longer and wonders aloud "why her children can't stick to their own kind." Matthew's reaction seems the crux of *Sarah Phillips:* "You are just incredible! You and Daddy spend all of your lives sending us to white schools and teaching us to live in a never-never land where people of all colors just get along swell, and then when the inevitable happens you start talking like a goddam Lester Maddox!"

Since Andrea Lee was born in Philadelphia and attended Harvard, it is probably safe to assume that much of *Sarah Phillips* is autobiographical. Most first novels are. A young writer has little else to work with but the raw material of their own life. As I neared the end of this slender book, I found myself hoping we were eventually going to go back to Paris and find out what happened *after* Sarah's decision to leave. Instead, the book ends at the point just before her Paris adventure. In essence, the first chapter should have been the last. If, however, Andrea Lee's intention was to leave the reader wanting more, she has succeeded wonderfully. *Sarah Phillips* is an engaging and promising start.

Bruce Van Wyngarden, "Pieces of the Past," in Saturday Review, *Vol. 11, No. 1, February, 1985, p. 74.*

Laurence (James) Lieberman

1935-

American poet, critic, and editor.

Lieberman's poetry combines the particular and the visionary in its celebration of the physical world. The long, flowing lines and eloquent language of his poems set them apart from the works of his contemporaries. Noting the similarity between Lieberman's language and classical music, Peter Serchuk described his poetry as "full of sound and rhythms, continually resonating shades of feeling and meaning." Lieberman's powers of observation, his Whitmanesque joy in life, and his smooth narratives are also cited as strengths of his poetry. Many of his poems reflect his travels. His first two collections, *The Unblinding* (1968) and *The Osprey Suicides* (1973), describe the wonders of life in the underwater coral reefs of the Caribbean, as well as his personal experiences and perceptions as a traveller. Similarly, *God's Measurements* (1980) reflects the time he spent in Japan with his family, and in *Eros at the World Kite Pageant: Poems 1979-82* (1982) Lieberman further explores his vision of the Orient and the Caribbean.

Unassigned Frequencies: American Poetry in Review, 1964-1977 (1977) collects Lieberman's reviews of the works of many important contemporary poets. Rejecting various critical standards, Lieberman relies on personal criteria for determining poetic worth. Although faulted for selectivity, a tendency to overpraise, and the lack of a unifying principle, Lieberman has been commended for his insights into the poets he prefers and the enthusiasm with which he unravels the complexities of their work.

(See also *CLC*, Vol. 4; *Contemporary Authors*, Vols. 17-20, rev. ed.; and *Contemporary Authors New Revision Series*, Vol. 8.)

© 1985 Thomas Victor

J. D. McCLATCHY

It is a welcome convenience to have gathered together [in *Unassigned Frequencies: American Poetry in Review, 1964-77*] a dozen years' worth of Laurence Lieberman's reviews of and essays on contemporary American poetry.... Lieberman is not a distinguished stylist, nor is he eccentric, original, or daring in either his preconceptions or conclusions. In his Preface he remarks: "I adopted early on the policy of dealing only with those books which somehow spoke to the purity of being in me." Likewise he invokes the vague rubric of "spiritual intellect" by which to measure a poet's vision, and the "rhythm of experience" by which to judge his voice. I have no idea what either of those criteria might be. Occasionally a moralistic tone intrudes, probably encouraged by the critic's feeling himself embattled in the face of the "absolute and irrevocable moral vacuity" and the "political machinations of our day." He is neither intrigued by intellection nor charmed by elegance.... [He] seems impatient with those poets he considers extremists of one sort or another—the confessionalists or formalists, the personalists or surrealists. And it is strange, considering the forty-five poets he discusses, that Lieberman has omitted—because they did not speak to his purity of being?—such indispensable figures as Elizabeth Bishop, Robert Penn

Warren, Sylvia Plath, Richard Wilbur, Adrienne Rich, James Merrill, and Robert Lowell.... (p. 439)

But to those poets who do engage his interest—especially James Dickey, David Wagoner, Mark Strand, W. S. Merwin, and John Ashbery—Lieberman brings a passionate advocacy. His strength as a critic is the degree to which he takes such poets seriously, *very* seriously.... He admires poems that abut or defy or transcend their historical conditions, but even more he singles out those poems that take risks.... I presume he is quoting Rilke when, in defense of James Dickey's "supernal healthiness," he declares that "the more tragic emotion—suffering, bitterness, despair—art can absorb and transmute into joyousness of being, the healthier it is." Though this all strikes me as a rather overheated esthetic, it is appropriate for a critic whose touchstones are Roethke and Yeats.... What remains curious about a reader so convinced by Yeats, or even by the muscled delicacy of Roethke, is that he wants poetry to move us to respond to ourselves and the world, but not to poetry itself.... I am surprised that, a poet himself, Lieberman does not count words, too, as things of this world; indeed, the world of poetry is nothing but. But I am not surprised—am, in fact, heartened—to see the strong, heady love that calls this unacknowledged legislator to the things of this world, and to their poetic reimaginings. (pp. 439-40)

J. D. McClatchy, "Lives of the Poets," in The Yale
Review, *Vol. LXVII, No. 3, Spring, 1978, pp. 431-40.**

CHARLES MOLESWORTH

Laurence Lieberman fashions his criticism out of his sensibility, ignoring theory and literary history. His book [*Unassigned
Frequencies*] is a compendium of reviews done for various
journals, though he claims he was determined to "fashion and
refine" the review-essay, and to "mold a full-fledged art genre
in its own right." This may sound inflated, and of course it
is, for the fashioning that extends these pieces is essentially
enthusiasm.... [Lieberman's language] is close to the language of advertising hype: the awkward figures of speech that
verge on the ridiculous (the suction that freezes, the hot ice),
the grasping adjectives ("gloveless, perishable"), the reliance
on the unutterable as the source of power ("we can hardly
locate"), and so forth. Needless to say, it tells us little about
the poems, and if our estimation or appreciation of [the talent
of the poet under review] is less than enthusiastic, such hyperbole only diminishes our interest. We may come to suspect
that it is only through such uncritical adulation that the poetry
can be accepted, and therefore reject both poetry and criticism.

When read in bulk, or reread for specifics, these essays cloy
badly, and—like much enthusiasm—they can seem more pointless the closer we examine them. Why compare James Dickey
to Yeats on any grounds? Why feel under any circumstances
that Ashbery is "the only author in [your] life"? ... After a
while, all of Lieberman's poets merge into one meta-poet: a
figure of the most intense vision possible, fierce in his commitment to craft, extending his powers in each successive volume, conquering his demons, etc., etc. (pp. 461-62)

Lieberman's approach is somehow both dogged and erratic.
The twenty-eight brief reviews that are gathered in the middle
section of the book never add up to anything like a coherent
statement, and the sensibility they reflect has no center, and
barely any markings, so rooted is it in mere opinion. Lieberman
has much of the language of literary criticism at hand, and is
as likely to discuss structure as theme or tone or imagery, but
no intelligible set of concerns or approaches informs the effort.... [One] wonders at all those diverse poets tossed aside,
and whether their "own poetic art" got attention elsewhere.
Many will say he was right: given the welter of books published, the only guide is fierce commitment. But commitment
to what? ... [Since he] admits to not reviewing some good
books, and demonstrates the narrowness of his approach, hasn't
he in effect described why he might be a fine *reader* of poetry,
but rather a disqualified *reviewer?* His Rousseauistic "purity
of being" might be worth advertising, but I can't see it's clearly
or deeply enough expressed to be worth applauding. (pp. 462-63)

*Charles Molesworth, in a review of "Unassigned
Frequencies: American Poetry in Review, 1964-77,"
in* The Georgia Review, *Vol. XXXII, No. 2, Summer,
1978, pp. 461-63.*

DAVE SMITH

Laurence Lieberman's *Unassigned Frequencies* dignifies poetry. However, as one professor once told me, regarding such
scholarship, it is *only* paracriticism. Lieberman's interest lies
in helping readers to understand and, perhaps, to love contemporary American poetry. He grinds only one axe: quality....

Of 44 poets examined, there are dramatic absences: Warren,
Levine, Lowell, Bly, Sexton, Plath, Black Mountain, etc....
There are, arguably, imbalances. Of his choices Lieberman
says the books "had somehow chosen me, rather than I them."
In the main, those considered seem our most important poets....

Lieberman's language matches the poetry he admires. He sees
his task as "encountering the great adventure," an experience
both revolution and revelation.... His poetry's values are
originality, energy and passion. His artist is the cultural pioneer
of inwardness; art is "a strange kind of intimacy, a blood
brotherhood, between the artist and himself.... No one else
can help." (p. 377)

Because he believes we live in moral and spiritual decay, in
a poverty of the communal dream-life, Lieberman's poets are
prophets with a moral song. Their explorations will discover
two things; first, that "the persona becomes a medium through
which the author can release and realize possibilities in the
self," in which case the single personality may expand to the
universal personality; second, that this process will lead to "a
new inner light by which all things beheld are observed to
glisten with a ghostly luster."

The judgments in the book are wise and durable. Lieberman
is exceptional on Ammons, Richard Howard and Jean Gar-
rigue.... All of the poets are well-served by his comments,
if sometimes overpraised. He will face consternation (wrongly)
for his words on Kinnell, (rightly) Viereck and Snodgrass. He
writes too little about Miller Williams and is, I think, mistaken
about growth in Mark Strand's *The Story of Our Lives.*...
(pp. 377-78)

The most impressive work, however, is in Lieberman's longer
essays. No one has written with more intelligence about William Stafford, James Wright, David Wagoner, and James Dickey.
Lieberman includes four pieces on Dickey and two remain the
best discussions of that poetry to be had. His was the first
observation of James Wright's pursuit of a domestic and moral
dream language. He reveals the hard ground beneath Stafford's
sometimes predictable pastoralism. And no contemporary critic
offers more help with our enigmatic visionary, W. S. Merwin.

But Lieberman's monument is surely his essay on Ashbery.
Its focus is "Self-Portrait In A Convex Mirror," a poem which
stuns, baffles and deflects readers. Ashbery emerges as Lieberman's supreme example of the contending self, the "soul
surgeon," whose personal struggle heralds great social and
cultural change.... For the many readers puzzled by Ashbery,
Lieberman makes an extraordinary guide about whom some
will chafe and mutter. But all will find him indispensable in
this territory.

Books about contemporary poetry, in process and in print, are
many and diverse. None will make the poets of our time more
available to serious readers than *Unassigned Frequencies*. We
might wish this one were truly representative and it would be
good to have had Lieberman's personal synthesis of our poetry's strengths and weaknesses, for he writes throughout with
a needed intelligence, sympathy and clarity. But we must be
glad for what he has given us, for this splendid performance.
(p. 378)

*Dave Smith, in a review of "Unassigned Frequen-
cies: American Poetry in Review, 1964-77," in*
Western Humanities Review, *Vol. XXXII, No. 4,
Autumn, 1978, pp. 377-78.*

PETER STITT

The poems in *God's Measurements* are so expansive, both in form and content, as to look Gargantuan beside the works of most poets. It is a method that Lieberman developed in his second book, *The Osprey Suicides,* which forms a kind of bridge between *The Unblinding* and the current volume. One doesn't easily forget a poem like **"The Skeletonizers,"** where the poet's wit and inventiveness can be seen almost in the very process of expanding to fill the enormous frame he has built. It is in that poem that a priest, nipped by piranhas, is described as "a forked turnip / of waterlogged driftwood." The spirit (tone, mood) of this body of work is what chiefly arrests us—a joyous and encompassing tone, one that takes (or makes) pleasure seemingly in everything. The poems are life fulfilling, even life generating.

God's Measurements is the result of Lieberman's year-long stay in Japan in 1971, and could almost be subtitled travels, adventures, observations. It is amazing how trivial—but accurate, real, unadorned, unromanticized—is the action which takes place. And although many monuments, sites, scenes, ceremonies are described, the poems do not take their life from these but from their speaker, our surrogate traveler and guide. . . . Most poets try to earn our regard through the assumption, whether explicit or implicit, of a special role, usually that of wise man or seer, sometimes that of warrior or superstar, sometimes that of wit or cleverman. Lieberman throws all that away in this book; his guise is that of poet as tourist, observer. . . . Refreshing—and productive of humor.

Lieberman's greatest strength may be his descriptive ability, which operates through a broad range . . . , applied to objects enormous, minute, and human in scope. . . . [What makes his description] so impressive is its language. Lieberman's long lines are not wordy, loose, and profuse; what he is aiming for is precision—precision within profusion—and so he doubles and redoubles his phrases in order more accurately to nail down his exact meaning.

We see that Lieberman invests the world with a sense of sacredness, a holiness that inheres within the physical. This is only to be expected of a statue of the Buddha, of course, but exists elsewhere as well. . . . The tone of [**"In Pursuit of the Angel"**]. . . is so buoyant, so energetic—the speaker takes such pleasure in everything he sees and does. It is an attitude that permeates the volume, in every poem, on every level. What Lieberman gives up in intensity he makes up in accuracy and good humor. He writes in the tradition of Whitman, but without the diffuse metaphysics; his closest kin among current poets may be Gerald Stern. *God's Measurements* is an excellent book. (pp. 892-94)

> *Peter Stitt, "Dimensions of Reality," in* The Georgia Review, *Vol. XXXIV, No. 4, Winter, 1980, pp. 887-94.**

PETER SERCHUK

[In *God's Measurements*] Lieberman's immersion into a foreign land takes place not so much in the mind but in the skin. It is a blood consciousness, an animal sensation, felt through the skin before it is seen or heard, long before the mind can put on the constraints of knowledge. In this sense Lieberman's poems are a nerve pulse of reaction, the spirit set spinning by visceral and sensual electricity. It is not surprising that several of these poems take place inside and around the metal-stone

skins of ancient buddhas, the very form of the poems often resembling their shape. (pp. 274-75)

There is something more deeply moving in Lieberman's poems beyond their fantastic skin-consciousness. Lieberman's poetry conveys the quality which makes Yeats's verse immediate and emphatic: it is in a perpetual state of self-becoming, a celebration of all things, physical and spiritual, constantly evolving. . . . Even the smallest occurrences become body-soul experiences—train rides, the moon's reflection on water—the poet surprised and delighted by what is. Things don't have to *be something:* they simply have to be. (pp. 275-76)

Without a doubt the driving force behind Lieberman's work is his language. I know of no other poet now writing whose language is so closely matched to his experience, so perfectly in tune to the content it carries and creates. In this sense it's much like classical music, full of sound and rhythms, continually resonating shades of feeling and meaning.

This dimension sometimes makes Lieberman difficult to read. We are not used to hearing the American tongue so flexed in full expression, so jubilantly invested with full breath. Having been numbed by the poetry of shorthand in recent years, we require several readings to catch up with Lieberman's cascading composition, to be reminded that our American language is rich with music if we would just open our ears to its possibilities. (p. 276)

> *Peter Serchuk, "Confessions of Travelers and Pilgrims," in* The Sewanee Review, *Vol. LXXXIX, No. 2, Spring, 1981, pp. 271-78.**

HARRY THOMAS

Lieberman is *the* documentary poet, "viewy," "descriptive," the poet as transcribing retina in love with light and with the things light illumines. The poems in *God's Measurements* constitute nothing less than a glorification of sight, of *seeing.* . . . [His] is the language of the ecstatic eye. What is interesting is that Lieberman seldom lapses into chant or, what is worse, into giving the mere statistics of attention. Rather, he hopes that at some moment his photography will be transformed into painting, his statistics into insight. When this happens, as it does in **"The Washroom Ballet," "Flamingos of the Soda Lakes," "Yoshino: False Dawn of the Cherry Blossom," "The Human Bomb," "The Sea Caves of Dogashima,"** and in the poem translated from the Japanese of Ryuichi Tamura, **"The Beacon Light of Oshima,"** the outcome is staggering. (p. 203)

About ten years ago Lieberman began to experiment with syllabic meters, arranging his lines in strange, oversized, geometric stanzas reminiscent of Marianne Moore's poems. Every reader of Lieberman has noticed the resemblance. It exists, it is slight, and it is connected to two more important resemblances: the documentary eye (though Lieberman's field of observation is entirely different than Moore's), and an interest in the exotic. The dissimilarities between them are more numerous. To start with, Lieberman lacks "compression," which Moore said, in addressing a snail, was "the first grace of style." . . . [Lieberman's lines are refusals] of prosodic chastity, of syntactic delicacy, of the tendentious. In all these he differs from Moore. Overall his effect is less precise, less pointed than hers and his diction obeys fewer, if any, constraints. This last characteristic, though generally admirable, has made it possible for Lieberman to write some of the most atrocious lines ever. About plankton seen while diving, he effuses: "Minuscule / acrobatics whirl in refracted light, the tiny lives / spinning upon themselves— / dazzle to dim, sparkle to fade—dancing and effervescing, / luminous as fireflies." To her credit Moore printed no dazzlings to dim. (p. 204)

As a chronicle of a tourist's impressions, [*God's Measurements*] is by far the best I have read. Still, I am bothered by a baffling absence of *thinking*, of *querying* in some of the poems. We can attribute this poverty of ideas to Lieberman's sanguine dislike of sententia or, less kindly, to his inability at times to bring his details into focus. Or we can attribute it to a pure avidity for recording. . . . (p. 205)

> *Harry Thomas, "Poets and Peddlers: New Poetry by Hopwood Winners," in* Michigan Quarterly Review, *Vol. XXI, No. 1, Winter, 1982, pp. 200-17.**

ROBERT W. HILL

Eros at the World Kite Pageant is divided into three sections, the first two set in Japan: "I. Songs of Leave-Taking" and "II. Kashikojima Quartet." These are, in a chronological sense, trailers from *God's Measurements,* but, more significantly, they are a farewell and tribute to a country and impressions that have informed some of the best poetry Lieberman has made. In Part I, he deals with individual characters at a much closer distance than in *God's Measurements.* . . . [In *Eros*] the Dionysian energies of Americans on the move relay a different sort of reverence, a respect for the age-old human *context,* a Chaucerian tolerance that has no place or need in the divinely placid *God's Measurements. Eros* is more humorous, not side-splittingly but gently, as with good friends in a strange place. Picture-snapping, children playing incongruously among the ancient scenes and scapes, the poet . . . less in awe and more familiar, but also more aware that going home is near.

Part II, the "Quartet," on the other hand, is the majestic tribute, paradoxically rich and austere at once. These poems bring the poet back to awe, but now overwhelmed by men and men's made things more than by the implicit or explicit divinity in the preceding book. . . . "The Roof Tableau of Kashiko-jima" and, much longer, "The Tilemaker's Hill Fresco" demonstrate the expansive vision—literal *seeing*—so characteristic of Lieberman's work; the stanzas are regularized as to line-count and typographical shape in order to replicate to some extent the patterned view the poet has from his vantage point above the buildings. (p. 123)

Here it is fit to ponder "On the Life That Waits," dedicated to James Wright, the conspicuously different poem in this book (which is also dedicated to Wright and to Lieberman's wife, Binnie). Its narrator aspires to an atypically (for this poet) mystical union with nature. Obviously indebted to Wright for its tone, its delicate tensions, and its quietly active natural creatures, this poem is perhaps the most touching of all in *Eros*. The narrator is so plainly a writer, so starkly self-critical, and yet so anachronistically plangent that the simple lines are almost shocking. . . .

Part III, "Runaways" (actually over half the book), is comprised of six poems set in the Caribbean. The first, "Dominican Shoe Tinkers," recalls "five small figures" who are determined to ply their trade: "Each stoops / to inspect our boots and sandals— / rattle off / agendas of defects in shoe— / handicrafter's / lingo, offers repairs and shine." The narrator seems only slightly ill at ease over such poverty-driven enterprise, but the energetic good humor of the tinkers short-circuits too

glib social interpretations. "Eros at the World Kite Pageant" (Santiago, Dominican Republic) is a poetical circus involving festive people, illusions of puppetry aloft, dramatic interplay of kites engaged in outrageous erotic maneuvers, judges and clergy aghast, disqualifications and final awards. Lieberman's generous flow of line and language is especially suitable for this exuberant scene. "Moonlighters" and "Saltcod Red" are shorter, more tightly constrained studies of wood sculptors and a cockney-accented fish dealer. . . . "Song of the River Sweep" (Dunn's River Falls, Jamaica) is a twenty-page cinematic depiction which begins with the observer-narrator high above the scene below—a characteristic Lieberman stance. By the time the poem has wound its way to a conclusion, the reader's senses have been entirely engaged by the rush of water, the physical exertion of climbing, and the panoramic overview of historical and cultural material. The culminating image of a hurricane tears through the final few pages of the poem, ripping things apart and reconstituting them like collage art. Perhaps the most remarkable accomplishment of Lieberman's language is its ability to shift like real-world elements, wind and weather, to incorporate and to discriminate in the sensorium of the mind. (p. 124)

> *Robert W. Hill, in a review of "Eros at the World Kite Pageant: Poems, 1979-82," in* The South Carolina Review, *Vol. 16, No. 1, Fall, 1983, pp. 123-25.*

JAMES FINN COTTER

In his fourth book of poems [*Eros at the World Kite Pageant: Poems 1979-82*], Laurence Lieberman creates his own psychodramas of confrontation and recognition in a style that is classically disciplined and yet openly modern. His broken-lined free-verse forms lend themselves to flowing narration that builds at its own pace to acute insights into our relation with earth, the past, and one another. In his title poem, Lieberman begins by describing the scene of a massive kite-flying contest in the Dominican Republic; the different kites become mythic monsters of an adventure-trip through the sky. . . . The poet's lines become a kite tugging and dancing skillfully in a suspended state: will he lose control? will the poem plummet to earth? No problem. . . . Lieberman masters his craft by identifying himself with it. In "The Tilemaker's Hill Fresco," he recreates the daylong labor of a tilesmith and his assistant as they replace the roof of a hilltop temple. The act of seeing is the progress of the poem. . . . The artisan imposes pattern and color on the whole scene: "A mathematics that endures (oh, steadfast cosmos!), / and survives—like inner light—." In "The Grave Rubbings," the poet's children also draw out from the rock the design waiting to be transcribed: the tombstone art comes alive in "story-pictures of local sights." The poems move from Japan to Jamaica, from the cubist vision of Cézanne to the exotic abstracts of Jackson Pollock. The final poem, "Ode to the Runaway Caves," takes us underground for a tour of a prehistoric, subconscious world of darkness, lakes, and wall-paintings. Blind bats, huge salamanders, eels, crayfish, and even a stray buzzard confront the awestruck hikers in this strange cavern, where the guide boasts only of his friendship with Sean Connery from filming the cave-like scenes for *Dr. No.* Primitive mystery surrounds us but we see nothing of its presence. Lieberman rejects no path to the unseen, however. . . . Hand in hand, the poet leads the reader on his highly personal, deeply felt quest into the steep mesas and lush landscapes which he has observed, absorbed, and articulated. (pp. 720-21)

James Finn Cotter, "Poetry Encounters," in The Hudson Review, *Vol. XXXVI, No. 4, Winter, 1983-84, pp. 711-23.**

MICHAEL McFEE

Twenty years ago, Laurence Lieberman wrote, "The extended lyric is one of the most fertile and inviting territories for the poet of today." He has proceeded to prove it in his own work, especially the recent distinctive widespread poetry, where the lyric is extended not merely in length or height, to exceed the standard sheet, but also in breadth, with cantilevered lines staggering across the page, and even in depth. Reading Lieberman, a volume of poetry becomes a poetry of volume, as he—eager guide and interpreter—leads high and wide and deep, underwater, into caves, along cliffs and roofs, up in the air. It is a splayed, roomy poetry. Lieberman extends the lyric in every dimension, and the measure of line, sentence, and stanza strains to match the measure of the "fertile and inviting territory" he blazes. It's easy to be distracted from this formal inventiveness by the persona Lieberman has adopted to keep his finger on "the lovely pulse of the universe," a somewhat comic figure best described as a tourist-enthusiast, a voyager-voyeur, an exuberant traveler given to marveling exclamation. But that character takes his life from his lines: without Lieberman's innovative measurements, the voice of his poems would never gain momentum.

It's hard to describe a Lieberman poem on the page. Some look like a kind of weaving, the line shuttling back and forth in a variable though finally regular pattern. Others resemble a DNA molecule model, with great helixes of genetic-poetic material twisting down the leaf. To borrow the subjects his poems describe—and, in part, imitate—they are by turn collages, tile mosaics, shifty schools of fish glancing away, rivers cascading down cliff-ledges, with the antic poet now kite-flyer, now spelunker, now scuba artist. (pp. 367-68)

No historical precedent [to the form of Lieberman's poems on the page] leaps to mind. Marianne Moore skewed her poems precisely, of course, though according to factors of rhythm and rhyme which Lieberman apparently eschews. (A very early "shaped" poem, **"Orange County Plague,"** in his first book, *The Unblinding,* did rhyme; but none have done so since, on that sustained scale.) The unaligned poetry of earlier centuries was also shaped by ear and not eye. Among contemporaries, Ammons is perhaps first cousin to Lieberman in radical formalism, especially in discursive lyrics like "Visit" or "Uh, Philosophy." But these are not nearly the length of **"Eros"** or other poems in [*Eros at the World Kite Pageant: Poems 1979-1982*] And when Ammons, of more anarchic temperament, really began to extend his lyrics, he left the involved shaping impulse behind for more abstract matrices and configurations, consummated in *Sphere* and destroyed in *The Snow Poems.* Dickey has been known to sprawl, and Lieberman has hymned him in essays and imitated his impulsive gap-prosody in poems; but Dickey has never been obsessive enough to sculpt such an elaborate template as the one used in **"Eros."**

Whatever the influence, if there must be one, it is a fact that Lieberman has always inclined toward extended measure in his best lyrics. (Even his *books* are long, averaging about 100 pages each.) Many of the poems in his first two books slumped fashionably against the left-hand margin, their form basically justified by type. But Lieberman could rouse himself and resist that sinister tyranny, resulting in poems distinctively his own

in tone and form—**"The Porcupine Puffer Fish,"** in *The Unblinding,* or the title poem and most of Section I of *The Osprey Suicides,* a luminous bestiary of Laurence's whelks and lobsters. The bouyant structures of these poems may have been inspired by the tropical water or air of their settings. *God's Measurements* was definitely inspired by *its* setting: Japan. Lieberman, decorously, evoked the tone of oriental craft—flat, colorful, outlined, intricate in a way that the westernized haiku-sneeze fails to suggest. He made his lines dance, sometimes centered in a stately ensemble, other times shuffled in a more complex rhythm. There was more movement than before, less invitation to pause and savor: his visual measure, "caught between form and flow," like an unfolding calligraphic scroll, balanced flux and continuity with Buddhist shrewdness. And finally, in *Eros,* whose first half concludes the Japanese cycle, and whose final section (including the title poem) commences a Caribbean sequence, he stretches the lyric to its limit, each stanza-unit a brilliant tile laid for the viewer, the whole expansive mosaic designed for appreciation in close-up or long shot.

Another lapse into metaphor. . . . Does that indicate false wit, Lieberman's measure indefensible except as fancy figure of speech? Not necessarily. Lieberman has never excelled as a poet of logic and incision, despite the apparently chiseled template. He is most satisfying as a descriptive poet of the senses, and his discovered measure serves that talent beautifully, winding sinuously down the page, the process of sight and mind made tangible. In his poetry, like the diver in *The Osprey Suicides,* "We hear / With our skins." His poems are "skin songs." And even when the scene is static, little more than tableau—people in a washroom, a park at night—the measure gives it movement and spirit. It's possible to play the pedantic trick of setting a poem flush left, or justified as prose, to show how prolix Lieberman's style may sound *en masse;* but that only proves the initial point, that voice and form are tightly integrated in his poems.

For all their length, the subjects of Lieberman's lyrics—true to tradition—are not complex. **"Eros,"** a ten-page poem, is typical. After some exposition . . . , the poem is chiefly devoted to description, vivid pictures of the various kites and contestants, the comic-erotic drama in the sky. And that's his basic narrative pattern: exposition, description, and occasional reflection, often distinguished by italics. The poems aren't particularly contemplative, at least in the mode of Ammons' longer lyrics, though Lieberman manages a visionary gleam every now and then. His method is inclusive, not reductive: rather than boil his poems down to spare lyric essence, or contrive a dramatic scheme for plain details, he simply looks and talks, preserving the conversational insulation other poets might excise. In the paradox of "extended lyric," Lieberman's interest is in the extension, the teasing-out of the poem's stuff, rather than the lyricism; his are lyrics with the stuffing sewn back in, bulky and companionable. The images are there, as well as fine strokes of phrase, but preserved in their common context, not framed and hung on the stark museum wall of the page. (pp. 370-71)

Lieberman's great risk and attraction [is] his transparency. Not that he bares his soul in any confessional manner: quite the opposite. He is wholly, perilously at the service of the world, encountering, absorbing, and assimilating with such sympathy that he threatens to dissolve himself. In his poems, he repeatedly performs the miracle celebrated at the conclusion of Richard Howard's wonderful "Saintly Hermits in a Landscape":

"Look! A man may vanish as God vanished, / by filling all things with created life." (The same self-effacement characterizes the reviews in *Unassigned Frequencies*: Lieberman is best not as a critical critic, but as an appreciator.) And there's the cunning in Lieberman's choice of voice, in his persona. Rather than affect sophistication, Lieberman cheerfully admits his ignorance, adopting in fact one of the most helpless and bathetic poses possible, that of an American tourist in foreign cultures—in Japanese *Gaijin*, foreigner, alien. He is not the world traveler but *boobus americanus,* fumbling with camera or Berlitz phrasebook, thirsting (in his own words) "for contact with the local populace!"—a kind of Derek Walcott in reverse. (pp. 372-73)

This pose is hardly without guile. Armed with Nikon or binoculars, Lieberman knows he is the watcher, the watcher watched, and exploits that self-consciousness. But it avoids certain pitfalls. In the hands and feet of many poets, travel becomes a means of condescension, an imperialistic plundering for sake of allusion. Places, works of art, afternoons in cafés or evenings in bars—the poet on the road collects anecdotes, superior data, to amuse other aesthetes. Lieberman doesn't need their sensitive airs, can't afford them in fact on his **"Chamber of Commerce Tour."** He has to keep his insights common, even in such a dazzling and "artistic" poem as **"The Tilemaker's Hill Fresco."** (p. 373)

Such moments of ecstasy [as in **"My Love Shooting the Buddha"** in *God's Measurements*], when Lieberman completely loses his "foreigner" consciousness, are rare. More often than not, the extended lyrics in *Eros* merely crumble away into ellipses, the poems overlapping, not really ending, and certainly not with the final haiku-like explosions and exclamations common in *God's Measurements*. If the dominant metaphor in *God's Measurements* is dance, in *Eros* it seems to be film, frame, camera. The poems fade out and in. Lieberman exhibits a documentary willingness to sprawl, to allow the poem's film to run unhindered through the sprockets of its form, as in a Mekas "diary" piece. This may irritate some readers. One poet complained to me that Lieberman had become a bit windy and lacking in dramatic concision. He probably thinks Lieberman's 22-page poem on a cave trip, **"Ode to the Runaway Caves,"** could have been a lot less travelogue and a lot more insight, image, and historical vision. Others may be exasperated by Lieberman's phrasing and syntax, sometimes quite jazzy or goofy, like a comic strip or S. J. Perelman—"the suntranced duo," "my comely models," "spun cat innards" (for koto strings), "savage curs," "Oh, no quarrels / have I!'', "little guessed he," "do they not scoff at the host of vacationers / in polkadotted / and beflowered swimwear? . . ." Why is he willing to sound lax, even dopey? Again, it inheres in his *measure*. (p. 375)

Lieberman is looking for . . . [a] high-stress flexible measure, with room for the lyric's self-conscious intensity as well as more prosaic interludes. He wants to write a metamorphic poetry that "sweeps / from form to form: glorious / interchange!" Lieberman is achieving "the unbroken flow" he admired in Ammons and Dickey, as described in the title essay of *Unassigned Frequencies*:

> Many a contemporary poet handles language like a mason laying a foundation for a house— the words are so many concrete blocks to be cemented into a wall. Dickey and Ammons treat language with special attention to tone, modulation, and breathing space; all are suavely

managed. Particular words and phrases rarely call attention to themselves; they must swing with the abiding rhythm and movement. It is hard to conceive of this poetry being composed slowly, word by word. There is too much continuity and rhythmic sweep.... It will take some doing to offset the movement toward fragmentation of experience set in motion by the shorter lyrics of William Carlos Williams in the twenties, and to initiate a return to structures that are large enough to cope with our most important experiences.

Lieberman's structures have that amplitude, and his spirit seems ideally suited to dealing with those experiences. His poems are devoted to the re-integration of "the common life and commonplace," as Ammons called it. Lieberman's family is the immediate agent of that life, and also his protection from the superficial introspection of the *Gaijin*-alien. He—*"demented foreigner, father to harebrained louts"*—is too busy worrying about his children on the train, at the falls, on the cliff edge, fearing the worst, fantasizing rescue. They keep him truly human. His delight in his family, his "creative brood," as in the world itself, is apparently inexhaustible. In the title poem of *God's Measurement,* he walks with his son on his shoulders around a stupendous Buddha:

> Now, wobblingly, we stalk: you, stiltjack,
>   in love with instant towers sprung from the idiot body's
> endlessly stretchable elastic of flesh, I
>   half scaffold, half anchor,
>   the two of us a father-son hobbling hinge—
>   telescope of our bones, joined end to end,
>   not doubled up
>   in laughter or loss of balance but bending
>   and unbending into beatitudes. . . .

"Bending and unbending into beatitudes": a fit description of the movement of Laurence Lieberman's mind and poetry at its best. In temperament as well as measurement, to quote the poet from his cliff-top perch, *"I / am open and take the gift of life."* (pp. 376-77)

Michael McFee, "Gaijin's Measurements," in Parnassus: Poetry in Review, *Vol. 11, No. 2, Fall-Winter, 1983 & Spring-Summer, 1984, pp. 367-77.*

THOMAS SWISS

As he so successfully did in *God's Measurements,* Laurence Lieberman continues in his new book [*Eros at the World Kite Pageant: Poems 1979-1982*] to explore the culture of Japan; in addition, in the third and longest section of the book, he writes about a visit to the Caribbean. Lieberman makes the perfect poet-traveler. Astutely observant, he notes even the smallest— and sometimes the most telling—details of two very different cultures. Lieberman plays both sociologist and naturalist, but what focuses these poems for the reader is the persona's involvement in the book's strong narrative dimension.

As a teller of stories Lieberman chooses occasions for the poems that are alive with potential: he explores their full weight, examining a spectrum of literal and metaphoric possibilities. Unlike some poets who write another kind of meditative verse, placing a heavy burden on invention and the self, Lieberman is always willing to step outside of himself.... The poems are subject-oriented, and there are no great associative leaps that can sometimes leave a poem emptied of everything but rhetoric and style. As the persona in **"On the Life That Waits"** says, "It is important to look close"; and Lieberman looks closely at many things. . . .

In these poems there are a generosity of spirit, an openness to experience, and a willingness to search for connections that lie beneath the surface in order to link interpretation with perception. A recurring word is *convergence,* and in many poems the persona seems to glide back and forth between dream and waking states, allowing these crossed connections to transform his vision. (p. lxx)

Laurence Lieberman is fond of the long poem, and his new work is now reaching epic length. The final poem in *Eros,* **"Ode to the Runaway Caves,"** runs to over 8000 lines. . . . Long poems invite certain risks—among them the dangers of repetitiveness and poetic overreaching; but Lieberman, a practiced craftsman, has solved most of these problems. The long poem enables him to incorporate a wide range of techniques— dialogue, description, commentary, speculation—that all serve the narration and enlarge the drama.

As the length and organization of the poems work against fragmentation and *for* convergence, so does his evolving poetic line. Words on the page, whole stanzas, zigzag in a syncopated manner that has become Lieberman's technical signature. As stanzaic patterns emerge in surprising but justifiable fashion, we are swept up in Lieberman's forceful style.

Eros at the World Kite Pageant is a fine collection. If it signals less of an advance in Lieberman's career and more of a honing of earlier subjects and a further refinement of style, these are no minor accomplishments. (p. lxxi)

> *Thomas Swiss, "Convergences," in* The Sewanee Review, *Vol. XCII, No. 3, Summer, 1984, pp. lxx-lxxi.*

David (John) Lodge

1935-

English novelist, critic, short story writer, and dramatist.

Lodge began writing during the late 1950s and has steadily gained respect both for his critical works dealing with literary theory and for his novels satirizing religious and academic practices. His novels blend farcical action with serious themes and present sincerely moral characters who are perplexed by the conflicting social attitudes of contemporary Western society. While his fiction is consistently realistic, Lodge's critical works explore both traditional and experimental forms of the novel, often focusing on the role of language in literature.

In his novels, Lodge draws extensively on his Roman Catholic upbringing and his experiences as a soldier, a graduate student, and an English professor. His first novel, *The Picturegoers* (1960), is about a young man who loses his faith temporarily but later becomes a priest. His second novel, *Ginger, You're Barmy* (1962), depicts England's peacetime army and reveals Lodge's resentment toward his military experiences. This work centers on two young men—one passive and uncommitted, the other idealistic and confident of his own religious integrity. Lodge's next novel, *The British Museum Is Falling Down* (1965), typifies his fiction. The novel humorously portrays a chaotic day in the life of a young graduate student attempting to fulfill his academic responsibilities as well as his obligations as a Catholic. It satirizes, among other things, the efforts of Catholics to cope with their church's ban on contraception.

Changing Places (1975) solidified Lodge's reputation as a leading writer of "campus novels." This work, in which a British and an American professor of literature exchange teaching positions, explores social, literary, and political differences between England and America during the 1960s. *Small World* (1984), a sequel to *Changing Places*, is set ten years later and examines changes in social attitudes and academic life. In the novel *How Far Can You Go?* (1980), Lodge concentrates on themes related to Catholicism as he follows a group of Catholic friends from childhood to adulthood. The characters respond in different ways to the doctrinal developments that liberalized social and moral views in the Catholic community during the 1960s. *How Far Can You Go?* is generally considered Lodge's most accomplished fictional work.

The Language of Fiction (1966), in which Lodge emphasizes the primacy of language in fiction, introduces the predominant concerns of his approach to literature. Whereas some critics judge a work by its moral or social content, Lodge argues that the content should be viewed primarily in terms of language and stylistic devices. In *The Modes of Modern Writing* (1971) and *Working with Structuralism* (1981), Lodge deals with various aspects of structuralism. Critics generally consider his discussions to be useful introductions to contemporary literary theory. They especially appreciate his analyses of several major novels of the nineteenth and twentieth centuries.

(See also *Contemporary Authors*, Vols. 17-20, rev. ed. and *Dictionary of Literary Biography*, Vol. 14.)

Photograph by Mark Gerson

MAURICE RICHARDSON

[*The Picturegoers* is] arbitrarily constructed, but lively. The framework, very loose, is provided by the local cinema, a squalid dream-pit losing the battle against television, relying on the sale of ice-cream. Its habitués include a bemused priest, and a teddy boy seat-slasher with horror-comic fantasies. Several of the characters are Roman Catholics in varying stages of sin and grace. The main focus eventually pinpoints Mark Underwood, a young lower-middle-class intellectual lodging with the cheerful Mallory family, whose daughter, Clare, was once a novice. His attempts to seduce her cause eavesdropper's agony to her devout Irish cousin. It is a bit disconnected but a lot of it is quite funny. Mr Lodge has a strong squalorological bent but he generally relents just before actually rubbing your nose in it.

Maurice Richardson, in a review of "The Picturegoers," in New Statesman, *Vol. LX, No. 1533, July 30, 1960, p. 165.*

CHRISTOPHER RICKS

[In *Ginger, You're Barmy*] David Lodge gives an authentic picture of the sordid futility of National Service, and this background really shoulders aside the story we're meant to be watching—the contrast between the narrator Jonathan (fluent and accommodating) and his friend Mike (religious and bouncing with integrity). Jonathan gets Mike's girl, which doesn't turn out to be much of a bargain. But he also gets a conscience, as a result of Mike's troubles. Some of this is forced, and it often seems to condone Mike's murderous side—he almost kills a wicked corporal—simply on the grounds that Mike's soul is in the right place. But the army life is absolutely right. . . . Perhaps people who haven't been in the army won't much care that pyjamas are thought effeminate, that boots are bulled with hot spoons, and that trousers must not be perfected with lead weights. But I found the total recall agreeably unnerving. (p. 675)

> *Christopher Ricks, "Noises," in* The New Statesman, *Vol. LXIV, No. 1652, November 9, 1962, pp. 674-75.**

CHAD WALSH

[David Lodge] wrote his first novel, *The Picturegoers,* while doing his two-year hitch of peacetime Army service. [With *Ginger, You're Barmy,* he] has now, one hopes, got those two years out of his system by adding to the ample bookshelf of novels on the woes refined souls undergo when dragooned into the armed forces.

The standard characters are all there: sadistic officers, the rebellious Mike Brady, who escapes and joins the Irish Republican Army; frail Percy Higgins, who accidentally (or is it accidentally?) kills himself; assorted reluctant soldiers with provincial accents, the silver-spoon public school boys destined for commissions. And finally the hero-narrator, Jonathan Browne, who has an A.B. in English from the University of London and no desire to bear arms. . . .

[Browne] foregoes the chance to become an officer, and concentrates on living through the two years as blandly as possible.

Mr. Lodge presents a convincing enough world of petty tyranny and senseless brutalities. His characters lack depth but are real as far as they go. The trouble is simply that the story has been told so often that merely to tell it again is not enough.

> *Chad Walsh, "Peace Stories," in* Book Week—New York Herald Tribune, *July 25, 1965, p. 14.*

THOMAS P. McDONNELL

If the reader doesn't too much mind, I should like to sneak into this review of David Lodge's second novel, *Ginger, You're Barmy,* by way of retrospect. For the book reminds me of those far-off halcyon days when people were reading John Galsworthy's *The Forsyte Saga,* and when I languished for weeks, like any other very young and pre-War romantic, over the death of Soames Forsyte in the interlude called "Indian Summer."

Old Soames Forsyte has vanished forever, I'm afraid, and so has his saga, and all that concern with upper-class manners. I cannot say in his going that England has not itself lost a certain grace and style of life. But had we ever really seen England in any but a lit'ry light? And, until the "invasion" and national encampment of our arms placed many [American] soldiers there, had we ever been aware that the Midlands existed at all? . . .

[The] Britain we saw in Lincolnshire was not Galsworthy's England, surely, not even Robin Hood's of Nottingham: it was a contemporary England that we had never seen in print until

the angry young men, so-called, came along after the war. (p. 249)

I wonder if Americans have come anywhere near to knowing the British Army—I mean, of course, somewhat this side of Rudyard Kipling and, in our own day, the Evelyn Waugh of *Men at Arms.* Evelyn Waugh's work is superlative, certainly one of the best in the last several decades of English writing, but it is Forsyte all over again in upper-class arms.

Now I should not be so downright insane as to place David Lodge's second novel against what seems to be the final achievement in fiction of Evelyn Waugh, but I would maintain that *Ginger, You're Barmy* is the British Army in ways that Waugh's officers and gentlemen are not. At the conjunction of both views, however, lies the point and price of man's civility in the modern world—in Evelyn Waugh, its diminishment and death; and in David Lodge, its quiet and, yes, noble struggle for survival.

For Corporal Jonathan Browne, drafted into Britain's peacetime Army, is, I think, a quietly noble figure. His indignities are never so wildly comic—or so self-inflicted—as the possession, loss, search, and recovery of a gentleman-officer's thunder-box in *Men at Arms*, but to endure the process of dehumanization is the only victory that the peacetime soldier can claim. The recovery, not of a thunder-box but of the private person—this, in fact, is the only victory that matters to him at all.

Some reviewers have passed off *Ginger, You're Barmy* as the same old thing about life in the army, but it is a much better book than they are readers. They are certainly unknowing in the ways of military life if they do not realize that extreme regimentation all but forces a reversion to types. . . . (pp. 249-50)

In closing, it is again slightly appalling that several hurried—and possibly harried—"New York" professional reviewers have given *Ginger, You're Barmy* such a poor reading. They have missed, certainly, that it is a beautifully written book, and that its marvelously controlled first-person orientation lifts it out of the mere melodrama that they were no doubt expecting to read in just another book about life in the army—that lowercase universal army which, whether British or American, almost at every point challenges the right of the human being to exist as a human being.

Mostly, I think, they have missed in *Ginger, You're Barmy* a poignancy in crisis and denouement, no less, that you will be hard put to it to find anywhere in the reams of overblown nihilism which passes for fiction today. (p. 250)

> *Thomas P. McDonnell, in a review of "Ginger, You're Barmy," in* Commonweal, *Vol. LXXXIII, No. 8, November 26, 1965, pp. 249-50.*

C. B. COX

The virtue of David Lodge's new book [*The Language of Fiction*] is that it attempts to find a *via media* between linguistic analysis and evaluative criticism. He begins with an extremely intelligent description of the nature of literary language and its relation to reality. In his view, the novelist's words deserve the same kind of close attention we are accustomed to give to poetry. (p. 376)

If language is so important, what methods are available for analysing the verbal texture of a novel? Lodge acknowledges that in measuring the success of literary devices we must fall back on subjective reactions, but argues that these must be related as closely as possible to analysable stylistic effects. By such means we may approach to some unanimity of judgment, even if this is not finally attainable. He examines the contributions to stylistics made by continental scholars such as Spitzer and Ullmann, and concludes that when they relate a particular literary effect to a particular ordering of language, their criticism takes a significant step forward from impressionistic appreciation. Novels bring special problems because their length makes them difficult to hold as a totality in the mind. Lodge believes 'the perception of repetition is the first step towards offering an account of the way language works in extended literary texts.' In the second section of his book he applies this theory to six novels, *Mansfield Park, Jane Eyre, Hard Times, Tess of the D'Urbervilles, The Ambassadors* and *Tono-Bungay*, examining key-words such as 'judgment' in *Mansfield Park* or 'fire' in *Jane Eyre*.

This critical section justifies his arguments for the importance of the novelist's words, but his emphasis on repetition fails to convince. In *Jane Eyre* he finds 'about eighty-five references to domestic fires (plus about a dozen separate references to "hearths"), about forty-three figurative allusions to fire, about ten literal references to fire as conflagration (in connection with Bertha's incendiarism), and four references to Hell-fire.' This sounds like a bad PhD thesis. Fortunately, he does not confine himself to this approach and provides excellent interpretations of *Tess* and *The Ambassadors*.

He analyses the 'sensuous relish,' enforced by rhythm and alliteration, in Hardy's description of Tess walking in the garden of Talbothays Dairy: 'She went stealthily as a cat through this profusion of growth, gathering cuckoo-spittle on her skirts, cracking snails that were underfoot, staining her hands with thistle-milk and slug-slime, and rubbing off upon her naked arms sticky blights which, though snow-white on the apple-tree trunks, made madder stains on her skin. . . .''

The conventional response of revulsion is checked by a note of celebration of the brimming fertility of the weeds. From this perceptive analysis Lodge proceeds to a brilliant study of Tess's relationship with nature. Such detailed studies of important passages, leading to evaluation of main patterns of meaning, provide a more rewarding critical approach than the counting of key-words. When in *Tono-Bungay* he discovers repeated words associating England with disease and decay, this proves nothing about the novel's literary value. In this chapter, if we examine Lodge's own style, we find, instead of precise criticism, repeated use of words such as 'vivid,' 'powerful,' 'eloquent' and 'skilful' to browbeat us into accepting a high estimate of the novel.

Lodge concludes with a fascinating account of Kingsley Amis's use of language, though his theories make him too sympathetic to *I Like It Here*. This chapter is typical of the whole book—perceptive, full of ideas, but not finally convincing. (p. 277)

> *C. B. Cox, "Words and the Novelist," in* The Spectator, *Vol. 216, No. 7187, March 25, 1966, pp. 376-77.*

DON CRINKLAW

[In *The Language of Fiction*] English critic David Lodge points out that inherent in [the] failure to confront the problem of language in the novel is the view that the novelist's medium is not language but life, his literary activity not arranging "proper words in their proper order" but a convincing organization and

evaluation of reality. According to this attitude, the novelist's language is "merely a transparent window through which the reader regards life—the writer's responsibility being merely to keep the glass clean."

What is really at issue here, as Lodge realizes, is the old argument of form-versus-content. It is a commonplace that the writer, unlike the composer or painter, works with arbitrary tools; a writer's "style" is no more than his choice of words, and words cannot be freed of their cargo of meaning as if they were color-combinations or note clusters. In this case, as C. S. Forster observed, "the envelope *is* the message."

Lodge devotes the first quarter of his book to an attempt to correct the impression that the novel is a word-structure in which words do not matter. Inadequately summarized, his resolution of the form-content problem is achieved through a demonstration of the non-paraphraseability of *all* imaginative writing, and through a refinement of principles laid down by I. A. Richards, who proposed a division of language into *scientific* (used for pure explication) and *emotive* (used for eliciting emotional reactions) and thus, by implying that the novel illustrates the first and poetry the second, did his bit to muddy the waters. Lodge reasonably argues that these are not two *types* but rather two overlapping *functions* of language, and proposes to view language as a continuum moving constantly between the two extremes, assimilating both the end and the means, the envelope and the message. And he asks that we realize that a bad great writer has been forgiven, after all, only so much bad writing, and a novel, because it depends upon "these words in this order" also, survives translation no more comfortably than a poem.

Lodge can write clearly and well when he wishes, but for too much of this section he chooses to write in a rather murky style, and he has brought such a ponderous load of academic artillery into his argument that this section will be of interest only to specialists. The more casual reader may wish to scan it only as preparation for the more intriguing parts to follow, in which Lodge formulates a technique whereby a novel may be persuaded to yield up its secrets by an examination of its linguistics, and proceeds to apply his technique to seven novels, ranging from *Mansfield Park* to *Lucky Jim*.

Lodge begins this section of the book by reminding those critics who judge a novel according to its moral (or cultural, or psychological, etc.) truth, that their "judgment of such truth must be controlled and modified by aesthetic experience," since "critics can claim special authority not as witnesses to the moral value of works of literature, but as explicators and judges of effective communication, of 'realization.'"

But author Lodge is not, as that statement might suggest, about to burn with a "hard, gemlike flame," for his technique is inoperable without active engagement with the "moral dimension" of the novel. What he proposes is a variation on the "structural" approach to criticism, whereby "a cluster of images, or value words, or grammatical constructions" is traced throughout a novel. It is not a word-count or an image-catalogue Lodge suggests—in that case a computer could criticize quite well—but rather an understanding of the novel's vision of life brought about by an examination of the words that evoke it.

The seven essays that conclude the book are genuinely remarkable: closely reasoned, lucid and rich with new and, it seems to me, valid, insights. (pp. 645-46)

Don Crinklaw, in a review of "The Language of Fiction," in Commonweal, Vol. LXXXIV, No. 23, September 30, 1966, pp. 645-46.

MARTIN PRICE

David Lodge's *Language of Fiction* has the subtitle, "Essays in Criticism and Verbal Analysis of the English Novel." "All novel-criticism," he writes, "is carried out in the teeth of methodological difficulties"; and he does his best to clarify and meet some of these in a first part of almost a hundred pages. The remainder of his book consists of essays on various kinds of verbal problems in Jane Austen, Charlotte Brontë, Dickens, Hardy, James, Wells, and Kingsley Amis. . . . Mr. Lodge writes a clear, urbane style that is capable of great delicacy in argument and analysis. Although he does not cite modern linguistic philosophers at first hand, he is clearly affected, at whatever remove, by the work of Wittgenstein and Austin. Even more, he has read the relevant criticism published in America, notably the work of W. K. Wimsatt, Wayne Booth, and Ian Watt. The analyses are more interesting, as it turns out, than the introductory discussion, for that is devoted largely to clearing away misconceptions and to establishing the legitimacy of his concentration on language in the novel. Because of his sharp awareness of the suppleness of linguistic devices and of their dependence upon larger structures of meaning, Mr. Lodge avoids the limiting of field that impoverishes so much stylistic criticism. The verbal skill of a novelist "can only be demonstrated when the language is 'about' something. To handle words is necessarily to handle meanings; and in the case of fiction we summarize such meanings in such concepts as 'plot' and 'character.'" Mr. Lodge points out that the very evidence critics collect to demonstrate the expressiveness of an author's style may be used to convict the author of monotony or obsession. Explication can lead to informed criticism, but it must serve critical judgment in turn.

Mr. Lodge refuses, then, to limit himself rigorously to verbal effects. They provide departure and goal; he runs the risk of circularity, but the results provide ample justification. In treating *Mansfield Park* he shows how the "subtle and untiring employment" of a "vocabulary of discrimination" prepares us to accept Fanny's moral passion. It is a vocabulary, moreover, which must discriminate constantly between the moral order of value and the social; the ambiguity of a "secularized spirituality" imposes exacting tests of judgment, tests that only Fanny, if even she, can fully meet. (pp. 299-300)

Finally, to choose only the most striking of Mr. Lodge's analyses, there is a fine discussion of Kingsley Amis's rejection of the symbolistic and complex art of the "modern" for the "ordinary prose discourse" of the "contemporary." But the breakdown of the comic ease of *Lucky Jim* provides the most interesting observation: "His language, turned back at the metaphysical frontier, returns to sabotage the positivist, common-sense epistemology at the center of his work, producing that sour, spoiling comedy which creates such dissonances in *Take a Girl Like You*."

The very range of problems Mr. Lodge can open by the study of language suggests that he is interested in the full depth of the novels more than in methodological purity. He is a humane and lively critic, and his precision never withers into arid measurement. If he does little to advance the theory of the novel, he offers us good practical criticism by which to test theories.

For theory must always be tested by how much awareness it shuts out in return for what it admits. (p. 301)

Martin Price, "Theories of the Novel," in The Yale Review, Vol. LVI, No. 2, December, 1966, pp. 294-301.*

PAUL WEST

[Humor] has become the English novelist's means of distracting us from his own omissions, evasions, and incapacities—an opiate for jolly, shy readers who, when they want a serious novel, turn to the fey or solemn unpretentiousness of Spark or Snow respectively. (p. 371)

Campus novels, British-style, keep on coming, and so does the spy and paramilitary stuff; but there's precious little really searching fiction. . . . Some of us are trying, however, and there is no other direction than up.

David Lodge is trying, for example. True, his new novel [*The British Museum is Falling Down*] contains a good many sportive and deliberate set-pieces meant, I suppose, to tickle us to death; comedifications I call them, and here are three, rated according to Ha-ha: (1) Lecherous girl unzipping man only to discover his loins are girded in his wife's lace panties—Ha, ha; (2) furtive Catholic in surgical-goods shop being watched by a priest—Ha; (3) London butchers in a basement conversing in Hemingwayese—Ha 2.

But there is also, precipitating the escapades, a far from trivial theme, and that is the Catholic's prospect of creating so many children he doesn't know what to do. Adam Appleby, a young Catholic graduate student who toils in the Reading Room of the British Museum, awakes one morning only to have his wife tell him she thinks the rhythm method has failed again: a fourth child looms. From this point on, Adam reels and meanders through a fuliginous London, trying to cope with the flunkeys, goons and monomaniacs who beset him during his unsalaried working day. Being jobless, neurotic and nowhere near completing his Ph.D. thesis on "The Structure of Long Sentences in Three Modern English Novels" (he hasn't even chosen his three novels), he is almost unhinged by the prospect. He discovers that what is absurd isn't that one day of his own life can include a false fire alarm, a Catholic club lunch, a sherry party with academics, a rich American wanting to buy the Museum, two bouts with a hot virgin, one with a cool matron, a communist Chinese delegation invading the Reading Room, his own scooter catching fire, not to mention all kinds of hallucinations in corridors and tunnels and jittery phone conversations with his wife (whom, in spite of it all, he wants to go home to and make love to).

No: the absurdity he finds is the cosmic, natural one of timing married love according to two thermometers and meticulous entries in a little Catholic diary. . . . (pp. 371-72)

Mr. Lodge has created a clown whose compulsive sorties across London are just as mechanical, just as impersonal, as Mother Nature herself. The clowning has a frantic quality (I dare not say Dada-like), not so much relieving the seriousness and the pain of the theme as assimilating Nature's indignities into the human dignity of mocking oneself (who, after all, has complete right to his own flesh?). As Adam's wife says to herself in the long Molly-Blooming reverie that, in the form of one ironic enormous sentence, ends the novel, "you could spend your whole life preparing to get into bed." It's a life-affirming book, but only just; and that is enough to save it from being an arid or merely tribal caper. The wife's night-reverie, after a day of alarm clinched by the arrival of her period, twists the preceding comedy by the tail, gives it a depth and a resonance that mitigate even the hackneyed quality of Adam's eventual rescue by millionaire (a part-time job offered him out of the blue). Funny—both laughable and daunting-peculiar—how life contrives to keep going on, utilizing alike those who love it fractionally more than they hate it, those who hate it fractionally more than they love it.

Some wan literary jokes apart ("C. P. Slow," "Mormon Nailer"), *The British Museum is Falling Down* is a pert fable, discomfiting and yet warm. It could, I think, have been less hectic, less giddy, without becoming miserable or flat. . . . (p. 372)

> *Paul West, "Denying the Ecstasies along with the Agonies," in* Commonweal, *Vol. LXXXVI, No. 13, June 16, 1967, pp. 370-72.*

JOHN P. WHITE

[In *Out of the Shelter*] Timothy Young ("Godfearing and Immature"?) is blitzed from innocence at five, passes through Catholic schools, "resigned to a life of humble obscurity", and ends with a pretty wife, a brace of children, and a post in Environmental Planning and Design. His true reveille, the core of the novel, comes at sixteen, when he holidays in Heidelberg with his older sister Kate, employed as a secretary by the American Occupation Army. There, and on swinging trips to luxury resorts, Timothy accepts the patronage and the confidences of Kate's circle: Vince and Greg, Rudolph the war-injured houseporter, Don the American intellectual who hungers for a place at LSE. Timothy does some discovering of his own: smuggled by his sister into a women's hostel he gets rescued from a locked cupboard by the woman whose love-making in the adjacent bedroom he had been eavesdropping on, and who nearly seduces him. He has an inchoate affair with an American teenager after a party. Finally—though no irony seems to supervene—he Keeps the Aspidistra Flying. . . .

This book has more energy and truth than its predecessor, *The British Museum is Falling Down*. But Timothy never falls far; and while it is easy to see from what he has escaped—the constricted life of an inner London suburb—what he has escaped to is less readily defined. Perhaps the wild party near the end defines it, when the guests dress in a collection of German military uniforms, until the snapped-on electric light uncovers the sinister tawdriness behind the charade. There the book might have stopped. Mr. Lodge's Epilogue—fifteen years later—unnecessarily reasserts a bourgeois sanity that lowers the voltage of a novel that will nonetheless keep you at it for all three hundred pages.

Mr. Lodge's devices of retrospect, for all their subtlety, do not hide the comic freshness of the presentation. Particularly sharp is his rendering of the five year old Timothy's perceptions. And the background of the Blitz with its wartime chat is *experto crede*, in the tone of truth.

> *John P. White, "Innocent Abroad," in* The Tablet, *Vol. 224, No. 6801, October 3, 1970, p. 956.*

JONATHAN RABAN

David Lodge's [*The Novelist at the Crossroads*] has a comfortably home-grown air; like an Amis hero, he is cautious about abroad, relies on common sense to get him through, and comes to grief when he tangles with dangerous foreign notions. His last book, *Language of Fiction,* might have been read as a novel about an English liberal who discovers that linguistics isn't nearly as ferocious as it looks. His new one—a potpourri of articles and reviews—assimilates, with much the same ease, a Kermodious theory of fictions. He is excellent on writers like Greene and Wells, who are relatively close to his own temperament; and writes a lively, argumentative, splendidly unprofessionalised prose. But on neo-modernism he might be Exhibit A in Josipovici's case against English critics who play, embarrassedly, at taking the whole awful business seriously. His essay on Beckett, 'Some Ping Understood', drearily confirms one's worst suspicions about its facetious title. It rises to a marvellously squeamish climactic sentence: 'However, the possibility of some allusion to Christ cannot, I think, be discounted.' It makes him sound like someone eating a large plate of tapioca pudding under the eye of a baleful aunt, but I suppose I had better admit that my own reading of *Ping* induced much the same tepid and dutiful sensation. (pp. 864-65)

> *Jonathan Raban, "Desperate Reveries," in* New Statesman, *Vol. 82, No. 2126, December 17, 1971, pp. 864-65.**

PATRICK PARRINDER

Dr Lodge's *Language of Fiction* (1966) was a militant statement of the primacy of language in the criticism of the novel. Its author combined a tenacious theoretical argument with a series of bold rhetorical analyses of major English novels, in what became one of the most widely-read books on the novel of recent years. It should be said at once that *The Novelist at the Crossroads* is a less important work. The essays collected here date back to 1966, and several are already well known. If they have a common theme, it is that of opposition to the radical 'neo-modernistic' fiction of Barth and Burroughs, and the revaluation of more conventional novelists like Graham Greene and Muriel Spark. To state it like this is to risk doing violence to the scrupulousness and precision of Dr Lodge's analyses, but it is clear that his overall theme is not an original one. The main interest of these essays as collected is accordingly to be found in their tone and stance. Dr Lodge's approach has mellowed since his earlier book, and he reaffirms the primacy of language (in an essay reprinted from *Novel*) in such broad terms as to constitute not a prescriptive framework, but only an enabling theory designed not to interfere with the critic's task. At times he pursues his earlier 'key-word' method of rhetorical analysis, often on very brief texts; the book reprints three short stories (by Hemingway, Beckett, and the author himself) in their entirety. Nowhere does he take on a work of the dimensions of the classic novels explored in *Language of Fiction*.

A key-word of Dr Lodge's own current criticism is 'pluralism'. Where this is used (as in the Preface) to describe his own position, one might prefer the word 'eclecticism', for it is not the end—the ultimate standpoint or source of values—which varies in his essays, but rather the means, the critical technique. 'Pluralism' refers also to the state of contemporary criticism and the arts in general, and Dr Lodge's usage here is an index of his own standpoint. His manner is eminently temperate and reasonable, his methods carefully empirical, his outlook based on an inbuilt tolerance. I detected only one really rash assertion in the whole book (on page 249), and that, significantly, expressed an undue complacency about the state of present-day criticism. Dr Lodge's whole strategy is an appeal to consensus, and a bid for centrality. It is in these terms that his endorsement of post-war English realism in opposition to the radical and schismatic forms of 'fabulation' and the non-fiction novel must be understood. (p. 878)

> *Patrick Parrinder, in a review of "The Novelist at the Crossroads and Other Essays on Fiction and Criticism," in* The Modern Language Review, *Vol. 67, No. 4, October, 1972, pp. 878-79.*

NEIL HEPBURN

I hope nobody will be put off buying David Lodge's hugely funny new novel [*Changing Places*] by hearing that it has some quite serious things to say about some quite serious things. I cannot remember having laughed aloud so much at a book since *Lucky Jim*.

It is 1969: student rebellion and women's liberation are no more than rumours in England, if robustly functioning in California. By a series of accidents, the victims of a university exchange scheme are tough, radical, aggressively publishing New Critic, Morris J. Zapp (of Euphoria—'Euphoric State'—near Esseph on the West Coast), and put-upon, unpublished, unambitious Philip Swallow (of Rummidge, redbrick Midlands). With the simultaneous taking-off of their aeroplanes begins a pattern of synchronisation between their lives. They suffer separate but equal culture-shock and defeat at the hands of locals, they interfere with each other's families, sleep with each other's wives, flourish strangely in each other's environments, which themselves come more and more to resemble each other.

Through the jokes you are invited (but you can decline, and just laugh) to look at a series of reflections, both on and of the two worlds—reflections on symmetry, on the novel as a reflection of reality, on the way real troubles like Vietnam and the Prague Spring are reflected in unreal ones like student unrest, on narrative techniques and literary styles (brilliant parodies, convincing wisecracking for Zapp and allusive irony for Swallow), and, finally, on America and England as reflections of each other. No funnier or more penetrating account of the special relationship is likely to come your way for a long time. (p. 286)

> *Neil Hepburn, "Fathering," in* The Listener, *Vol. 93, No. 2395, February 27, 1975, pp. 285-86.**

MARTIN PRICE

David Lodge is one of the ablest critics and theorists of the novel at work in England. It is especially interesting, therefore, to see him come to terms with structuralism. [In *The Modes of Modern Writing: Metaphor, Metonymy, and the Typology of Modern Literature*, Lodge] draws upon Roman Jakobson's scheme of the two axes of language, metaphor and metonymy, or, one can say, association through resemblance and through contiguity. Most literary structure is then seen as an interplay between these two processes, with one or the other predominating. It is the predominance of metaphor that Mr. Lodge uses to characterize "modernist" writing and the predominance, to a different degree, of metonymy that he takes to characterize both the realism that precedes modernism and the "postmodernist" writing that follows. In the last part of his book Mr. Lodge tries to locate much English and American writing of our century on a scale between the pure forms of metaphor

and metonymy, and he provides close study of a number of works in the process. (p. 254)

Professor Jakobson traced the full polarization between the metaphoric and metonymic in two forms of aphasia. In most language, we see the interplay of the two polar forces but the predominance of one. As Mr. Lodge remarks, "it may be asked whether anything that offers to explain so much can possibly be useful, even if true." But he answers the question at once: "I believe it can, for the reason that it is a binary system capable of being applied to data at different levels of generality, and because it is a theory of dominance of one quality over another, not of mutually exclusive qualities." This system calls to mind the many dialectical theories of poetry, such as Coleridge's, that stress a reconciliation of opposites. To apply terms at different levels of generality may require that they be somewhat elastic, that is to say, vague or ambiguous. Apart from the fundamental contrasts of similarity (metaphor) and contiguity (metonymy) or of selection (substitution) and combination (contexture), we find in Jakobson's scheme such contrasts as drama and film, montage and closeup, symbolism and condensation or displacement in dreams, poetry and prose, lyric and epic, romanticism or symbolism and realism. (pp. 255-56)

The use of an axis is somewhat troubling. I tend to see the two axes of which Jakobson speaks as the x and y axes along which we plot the coordinates of a curve. One can then see the curve moving predominantly along one axis but swerving as it is governed by the other, itself the resultant of their pressures. I am not at all sure that this is an adequate way of imagining the scheme, especially when I see Mr. Lodge say, "he must be *doing something* with the axis of combination which he appears to follow in such a straightforward way." I would propose that we see selection and combination at work in both metaphor and metonymy. In the latter we must select representative details rather than hope to be exhaustive. We cannot provide the full context but only the relevant context, and different modes of representation will require different degrees of relevance and selection. What becomes fascinating is how the very process of selecting a telling detail leads to synecdoche and can, with very little further pressure, convert the detail into metaphor. There is a kind of realism (I would cite Ibsen as well as the early Joyce, whom Mr. Lodge treats brilliantly) which is always at the point of shifting, or switching, to symbolism. There is an iridescence that allows us to see a detail from one angle as a bit of plausible representation, from another as the outward reaching of thematic assertion, that is, of metaphor and symbol. (p. 257)

The final chapter deals at some length with postmodernist fiction, starting with Samuel Beckett's refusal "to settle into a simply identifiable mode or rhythm, thus imitating, on the level of reading conventions, the resistance of the world to interpretation." That resistance gains its full import from a "poignant demonstration of the human obligation to attempt such interpretation, especially by the process of organizing one's memories into narrative form." Mr. Lodge distinguishes a variety of methods by which postmodernist writers frustrate our expectations of form. They tend to reject the traditional choice between metaphor and metonymy as a principle of progression. What one finds is the suggestion of a form, whether realistic or modernist, and the simultaneous rebuff of any effort to pursue it. The forms of the rebuff may be contradiction, permutation (an exhaustive but finally pointless canvassing of all possibilities, as in Beckett's comedy), discontinuity ("Between these apparently discontinuous passages the bewildered but exhilarated reader bounces and rebounds like a ball in a pinball machine, illuminations flashing on and off, insights accumulating, till the author laconically signals TILT''), randomness, excess (''overloading the discourse with specificity''), and the short circuit. Mr. Lodge provides a caution: if the idea of order were finally to be expelled or disposed of, we should lose ''the norms against which we perceive its derivations. A foreground without a background inevitably becomes the background for something else.''

It may be that the last sentence is one of the laws of literary history: the triumph of a form is the beginning of its displacement. One can see something of this in the last century of painting, with Cézanne's late structures or post-impressionist color generating more abstract forms whose full vigor was still marked by a sense of what they were uncreating. Representational painting returns in somewhat modified forms, self-consciously insisting upon the banality of the ''context'' it readmits. Photo-realism alludes to billboards but also reaches back behind the attenuation of images that marked the coming of abstraction.

I have departed from Mr. Lodge's concerns only to indicate how provocative are the questions he raises. Yet I wonder how much he has explained by his use of the metaphor/metonymy distinction. It explains, he says, ''why at the deepest level there is a cyclical rhythm to literary history, for there is nowhere else for discourse to go except between these two poles.'' This seems to me to require that we direct our attention to the interpenetration of the two modes, as Mr. Lodge does with brilliance in his final chapter or as Gérard Genette, whom he cites, has done with Proust. To concentrate upon these middle ranges makes the pattern of oscillation less cogent. It raises questions about how our sense of context changes from one age to another; what might seem metaphoric in one culture becomes metonymic in another. So, too, there are cultures or subcultures that stress the verticality of experience, the sense of divided and distinguished worlds that generates metaphor so readily. But these are matters that the book helps one perceive.

Mr. Lodge's book is a very good one. It is bold and ambitious but always lucid and explicit, and it returns again and again to specific texts by way of both illustrating and testing its assertions. Mr. Lodge is happily incapable of being vatic, pompous, or arch. I am not sure that they always order this matter better in France. (pp. 258-59)

> *Martin Price, ''Metaphor and Metonymy,'' in* The Yale Review, *Vol. LXVII, No. 2, December, 1977, pp. 254-59.*

PETER CONRAD

Criticism used to be an applied science, a practical aid to the reading; now it has triumphantly purified itself of that subordination, despises texts which are drearily 'readerly', and limbers up in the void. The subtlest critics have outgrown literature altogether, and prefer a self-soliciting enumeration of their own skills. David Lodge practises a terminal species of terminological criticism, sharpening his rhetorical terms and exercising his hermeneutic techniques, but more for self-delight than to aid an engagement with literature.

The Modes of Modern Writing does contain a conventional historical argument about modern literature, but that matters less than its para- (or, as Mr Lodge would say, 'meta-') critical

quality, its theoretical exhibitionism. Mr Lodge's thesis, encoded in a concrete poem on the book's cover, is that modern writers have renounced metonymy for metaphor—but this is no more than the truism that art has abandoned realism for symbolism, in a new camouflage of jargon. Mr Lodge's apologetic parentheses admit as much: 'In the modernist writers discussed so far we have observed a general tendency to develop . . . from a metonymic (realistic) to a metaphoric (symbolist or mythopoeic) representation of experience.' Strip 'modernist' of its pretentious suffix, cancel out the array of alternatives Mr Lodge produces from his rhetoric-manual, and an argument the publishers commend as 'bold and original' recoils into an innocuous old saw. However, just as in the modern works Mr Lodge admires content exists only to license the antics of form, so the appearance of historical narrative in his own book is no more than a convenience, which exists to provide opportunities for the deployment of new and ever more garish terminology.

Mr Lodge's critical language, distended by pretension, demonstrates the sad law of inflation and devaluation. The ordinary tokens of critical argument have lost all import, and need to be ponderously reflated. The trick generally is to equip them with affixes. The limp and sorry word 'modern' needs one fore and aft: having first been blown out into 'modernist', it then grows another ungainly appendage to become 'postmodernist'. 'Realism' spawns a trio of clamorous alternatives: on the laden shelves of the jargon-market, 'unrealism', 'nonrealism' and 'irrealism' compete for our attention. Verbs and adjectives are propped up as substantives: among Mr Lodge's grammatical mutants are the unlovely terms 'transcribability' and 'literality'. On occasion Mr Lodge concedes the irrelevance of this high style of learned obscurantism, as when he calls an Orwell essay (or 'text' to use his jargon word) 'self-sufficient, self-authenticating—autotelic, to use the jargon word', or when he winsomely confides that the portentous terms of his subtitle mean nothing new: the mud in *Bleak House* is 'a kind of metaphorical metonymy, or as we more commonly say, a symbol'. Then why not use the common word? Because jargon is a device for mystification, a mimicry of a value which doesn't exist. Critics these days are a priestly caste who guard their activities by conducting them in a cabbalistic language impenetrable by the laity. Hence Mr Lodge slips every so often into French, a language more amenable to the invention of bogus substantives than our own blunt idiom. (p. 821)

The nasty thrill with which Mr Lodge announces that he has reduced novels to figments of language, 'defamiliarising' (his word) the world we know and exterminating character, alerts us to the aggressive dislike of literature which criticism of this kind often betrays. This is criticism as a vengeful decreation. The world exists to be turned into a book; books exist to be interpreted, not to be read. Mr Lodge's favoured texts are those which boast of being 'nonreaderly' (which is to say, in the vernacular, unreadable): *Finnegans Wake* or Gertrude Stein's *The Making of Americans*. Though contemptuous of readers, writers are required to stand in awe of critics, their redeemers, and Mr Lodge issues sharp rebukes to Isherwood, who reveals a reactionary hostility to academic criticism in *A Single Man*, and Thomas Pynchon, whose *V* impiously 'mocks interpretation'. Various humiliations are visited on literature for its stubborn suspicion of criticism. If there's nothing to literature but words, then there are no barriers between it and other, meaner linguistic activities: Mr Lodge therefore exerts himself to demonstrate the literariness of *Guardian* articles and a desk encyclopedia. The most alarming snub threatens to reduce literature to a symptom of brain disease. Mr Lodge shares Jakobson's admiration for the linguistic inventiveness of patients with speech disorders, and perversely praises Gertrude Stein's refusal to use nouns because it makes literature aspire to the disabled, chaotic condition of aphasia.

English empiricism, it seems from this book, has altogether lost its nerve, and, sooner than risk the accusation of being old-fashioned, has capitulated to the deconstructing, obfuscating hierarchs of what Mr Lodge calls 'the *nouvelle critique*'. Things have come to a pretty pass. (p. 822)

> Peter Conrad, "Untranscribability," in New States-man, Vol. 94, No. 2438, December 9, 1977, pp. 821-22.

PAUL ABLEMAN

On page 73 of [*How Far Can You Go?*], David Lodge suddenly pokes his head up out of the narrative and starts boasting. This struck me as an unseemly intrusion and I fretted impatiently. But on the next page, sheer incredulity supervened when I came to a fan letter from a Czech admirer that Mr Lodge had seen fit to include. Damned cheek! Bloody narcissism! I snapped the book shut and took a turn in the garden in order to regain that lofty impartiality that so becomes the reviewer's craft. (p. 23)

Having recovered something like a state of critical grace I returned to the book and again found, as I had been doing before wading into the Bog of Self-Satisfaction, that it was enjoyable. True, ego-tremors continued to generate shudders of revulsion but the work had much to commend it. On the penultimate page the reason for David Lodge's curious cavortings became clear although remaining unjustified. In a final section that brings the story of his main characters up to date, Mr Lodge comes clean and states: 'I teach English literature at a redbrick university and write novels in my spare time, slowly, and hustled by history.' This admission, allied to hints throughout the text, exposed the book as being a sociological account of a group of young Catholics, one of whom is the author, rather than fiction.

We first meet the ten principals in a gloomy church 'South of the Euston Road' in 1952. They are all members of the College Catholic Society. We get a brief character sketch of each, polarised between religion and sex which remain the dominant themes throughout. Mr Lodge is good on sex and excellent on religion, at least as regards observance, and the tension of his book derives from the torque exerted by the former on the latter. Before our very eyes, the Holy Catholic Church is warped round by the human reproductive system, and notably the formidable challenge of birth-control, until what was once Baroque puritanism has become something like a cross between Protestant fundamentalism and a three-ring circus. I have to take this evolutionary process on trust although rumours of the marvels of the charismatic movement have reached me from books and friends.

Mr Lodge manages to be funny about Catholicism without, as far as I can judge, either heresy or offence. His tone is in marked contrast to that of convert Catholics like Evelyn Waugh and Graham Greene whose belief seems to be a counterweight to a burden of sophistication that renders simple belief impossible. Credo quia impossible est. But Mr Lodge's 'cradle Catholics' believe because, as a result of conditioning, they find it impossible not to. (pp. 23-4)

One of the ten chief agonists is queer, and does more than his share of agonising as a result, but most of the rest marry, some to Catholics and some to outsiders. Before long the amourous couples begin to discover that the Rhythm Method, their sole permitted defence against the onslaught of posterity, doesn't work very well. No matter how religiously they maintain their abstruse charts and measure their rectal temperature they give birth with about the frequency of Portuguese peasants. All their non-Catholic friends have the statutory two and a half babies and big cars while they produce monster families and minis.

After the papal encyclical of 1968, which sternly reiterates the prohibition against effective birth control, revolt flares up. Soon afterwards, and virtually without a rumble, Hell simply vanishes—and all Hell breaks loose. Soon Catholics are necking in church and there's little to choose between nuns and a chorus line. Mr Lodge is finely attuned to the nuances of Catholic doctrine and shows how immeasurable transformations in practice may result from what seem to be trivial adjustments in interpretation. Indeed he makes the whole vehicle seem so precarious that the loosening of a single bolt could easily send it lurching over a precipice. But then one reflects that the great gaudy cart has nevertheless trundled on for 2000 years across very varied road surfaces. (p. 24)

> Paul Ableman, "Role 'n' Roll," in The Spectator, Vol. 244, No. 7921, May 3, 1980, pp. 23-4.

NICHOLAS SHRIMPTON

David Lodge is a gifted clown who suffers from an irrepressible urge to play Hamlet. On this occasion he puts aside the motley in order to assume the still more unlikely role of Father Hamlet, S.J. *How Far Can You Go?* is a social and doctrinal history of middle-class Roman Catholicism in England from 1952 to 1979, presented as a cisatlantic version of Updike's *Couples*. From doubts about propriety at the College Cath. Soc. Hop, to scruples about group sex in a Swinging Seventies sauna, Lodge's characters chronicle the changing life of the church in what is best summed up as a series of conjugal rites.

The boisterous comedy which made *Changing Places* such a treat is not, of course, entirely abandoned. . . . Father Austin Brierley, suffering from impure thoughts, is told by his ecclesiastical superior to 'try ejaculations' ('My Jesus, mercy, Mary help!'). The same character, suffering later from life in a sociology department, gives a splendidly witty sketch of fashionable intellectual nostrums from Kant to McLuhan, from which only Wittgenstein's 'whereof we cannot speak, thereof we must remain silent' emerges with credit. Unfortunately not all the philosophical material is integrated so flawlessly. A lot of the jokes are in-jokes. . . .

Much of the intellectual material is, in fact, not integrated at all. Lodge's problem here was, obviously, the prospect of a non-catholic audience. Readers who share the novelist's faith, age and background will probably devour this book with an engrossed, or possibly enraged, sense of self-recognition. The rest of us need to be helped. But I am far from convinced that such help is best provided in the form of six-page summaries of papal encyclicals, introduced with the words 'Patience, the story will resume shortly' and tacked back on to the narrative with the brisk cliché 'enough of this philosophizing'. David Lodge, cunning craftsman as he is, prepares us for these theoretical inserts by establishing a highly intrusive narrative personality from the very first page. But inserts they remain.

How Far Can You Go? is at its best at those moments when an intimate link is established between theological debate and personal life. The real hero of the novel is the pill, and Lodge's picture of these couples struggling to come to terms with it hovers delicately between tragedy and farce. One extremely sombre note is struck by the reiterated assertion that the Rhythm Method actively promotes the birth of deformed or mongoloid children. At the other extreme there is the marvellous picture of a belatedly liberated Adrian striding into a chemist's shop and demanding, with vague memories of his National Service days, 'a gross of sheaths prophylactic'. The consequences of *Humanae Vitae* for English Catholics, as David Lodge sees them, are less atheism than a rejection of authority. His characters find themselves making their own moral decisions and becoming accustomed to the consequent psychological adjustments.

Despite its epigraph from Hans Küng, in other words, this is not really a religious novel, certainly not the religious novel as, say, Piers Paul Read writes it. The reflections on fundamental questions of faith are brief and occasional. The essential purpose is to write a social novel about a sub-group which happens to be defined by its creed. What makes the group interesting, of course, is that its members feel with peculiar intensity the great change in English manners and morals which has taken place in the last twenty five years. . . . The pity is that this humane and humorous theme is weighed down with so much incidental lumber. When David Lodge submits social detail to direct comic scrutiny, as in his vision of the reverse-action contraceptive machine in the Catholic Teachers Training College he has few rivals. But *How Far Can You Go?* could do with a lot more writing like that.

> Nicholas Shrimpton, "Conjugal Rites," in New Statesman, *Vol. 99, No. 2565, May 16, 1980, p. 749.*

TERENCE HAWKES

Structuralism has been around quite long enough for us to be used to it. So the clamour of its recent head-on collision with the English academic consciousness possibly represents something more complex than a row about literary criticism. A clue lies in structuralism's blatant foreignness. The current 'crisis' in English studies clearly has some of its roots in the crisis in the notion of Englishness which such studies were invented to serve. Since the war, many forces—Welsh and Scottish nationalism, the continuing nightmare of Ulster, television-fuelled regional cultures, black and Asian subcultures, the slow explosion of the 1944 Education Act—have all exerted their disintegrating pressures on that confident, unified sense of English identity which validated and was validated by a particular notion of English literature. In this context, structuralism meets a ready-made response. The invader, bent only on pillage and defilement, must be repelled at all costs, the castle doors slammed firmly in the garlic-scoffing face.

Fortunately, the castle's inhabitants are not all of one mind. David Lodge, for instance, has been sitting in the courtyard with his suitcases packed for some time. *Working With Structuralism* confirms him as a cautious but committed traveller, ready and willing to cross the moat and treat with the foreign devils.

His response to the present chaos in criticism (not unlike the state of physics after Einstein and Heisenberg, he claims) is appropriately workmanlike, with its calm and level-headed buckling down to practical issues. Reassuringly, Lodge goes

out of his way to preserve continuity with older and more familiar terminologies, patiently and persuasively aiming to talk us down from the heights of abstract theory to the firm ground of specific works of art. A taming, domesticating exercise perhaps, but one which derives its impetus from the entirely sensible recognition that structuralism (a too-elastic label covering 30 or more years of still developing and often contradictory activity) won't just go away. . . .

Some luggage has already gone in advance; notably Lodge's impressive account of the implications for fiction of Jakobson's distinction between metaphor and metonymy in *The Modes of Modern Writing* (1977). Most of that book's good qualities, its sure-footed lucidity, the crispness of its exposition, also enhance the present volume. Any residual angularity can reasonably claim consonance with the 'workshop' character proclaimed in the title. The first section, 'Applying Structuralism', offers careful and fertile analyses of *Hard Times,* of Hemingway's 'Cat in the Rain', and of one of Lodge's own stories: work which amply demonstrates the extensive productivity of what has been learned from Barthes, Todorov, Genette, Greimas and others. The metaphor-metonymy distinction operates revealingly throughout, becoming the basis for a fruitful 'map' of the modern period in which the oscillation of writers between these poles emerges as cognate with their modernism or antimodernism. Other ventures include a number of courageous attempts, written for a variety of occasions, to assimilate structuralism's impact without 'paying the price of incomprehensibility'. They don't pay it and as a result they acquire a sprightly introductory function. Less successful are the essays on Evelyn Waugh, Ted Hughes, Tom Wolfe and Marin County's 'psychobabble'—not for any lack of intrinsic interest, but because they seem not so much provocatively 'counter' to structuralist theory (a claim the Preface too boldly makes) as simply deprived of it.

Lodge's interest in structuralism remains, he cheerfuly admits, limited largely to its earlier 'classical' modes in which it aimed to do for literature (or any other human system such as food or fashion) what grammar does for language. Later, more politically committed developments, as in the work of Foucault, Lacan and Derrida, which seek to analyse cultural institutions as agents of ideology, are perhaps too resolutely shunned. His book's inventive energy, its conviction and its resourcefulness offer immediate rewards nonetheless and they should attract readers to the cause. (p. 19)

> Terence Hawkes, "Critics in Their Castle," in New Statesman, *Vol. 101, No. 2623, June 26, 1981, pp. 19-20.* *

LeANNE SCHREIBER

["**Souls and Bodies**"] is an ostensibly comic protest novel whose target is the Roman Catholic Church of recent decades. When I say ostensibly comic, I don't mean to suggest that this book doesn't make you laugh out loud. It does. But beneath the humor, and sometimes subverting it, is the author's very serious effort to give shape to the confusion, sadness and anger of those Catholics who feel that they sold their souls and bodies to a church that later reneged on its part of a hard bargain. And like most protest novels, it will no doubt offend and unsettle many of those whose lives it attempts to represent.

The novel begins with nine University of London students attending 8 o'clock mass one dark, drizzly Thursday morning in 1952. . . .

"**Souls and Bodies**" ends 23 years later with most of the same group attending an outdoor Easter festival complete with dancing nuns, Pentecostal prayer sessions, a lecture on liberation theology and announcements of meeting times for Catholic Marriage Encounter Groups. Between opening and closing scenes, we follow the fortunes of 10 characters—the nine students and their college chaplain—as they are buffeted by one of the most tumultuous periods in their church's long history.

When the author first parades them before us, all 10 are "sexually innocent to a degree that they will scarcely be able to credit when looking back on their youth in years to come." . . . The men and women alike conceive of salvation as a kind of immortal board game, a high-stakes Snakes and Ladders in which a plenary indulgence can send you shooting up the rungs and a mortal sin can send you slithering back to Square 1—or worse.

Over the years, of course, this innocence and certainty will be lost. One of the 10 will go mad. One will stop repressing his homosexuality. One will mourn the loss of two children and his faith. One will write a popular column of very secular advice to the lovelorn. One will enter a convent. The priest will marry. All will suffer on the rack of the church's teachings on birth control. And all will prove that baptism in the Roman Catholic Church does indeed leave an indelible mark on the soul.

If this sounds a bit agitprop, it is. For David Lodge is a forthrightly didactic British novelist who does not hesitate, for instance, to interrupt his narrative for a lengthy disquisition on the origin, evolution and current implications of Catholic doctrines on sexuality. And he delivers it in his own voice, because he obviously feels that these are matters of too much practical and moral urgency for him to be entrusted to anyone as unreliable as a fictional narrator.

But even those who generally subscribe to the common wisdom that lectures on religion have no place in the well-made novel are unlikely to wish this section out of the book, because it is one of the most cogent explanations of church doctrine to be found in or out of fiction. And certainly the wittiest. . . .

By drafting his characters—"our friends"—into service as prototypes of every variant of Catholic experience, the author does at times lose something vital, but, in recompense, we get a very thorough crash course in modern Catholicism, including an introduction to process theology, the charismatic movement and the debates over priestly celibacy and the ordination of women.

The author takes pokes at various forms of orthodoxy—psychiatric, political and literary, as well as religious—but he is equally ironic, if more compassionate, about the various forms of reaction against them. He seems to believe that if authority can be cruelly repressive, efforts to escape it are likely to be foolishly misguided. For him, both orthodoxy and self-indulgence are inadequate responses to the one, true, unholy and inescapably catholic authority, death, which is the unstated subject of this novel and its ultimate object of protest.

Mr. Lodge has written a book full of his own energy, intelligence, wit, compassion and anger. "**Souls and Bodies**" does not cohere, but each of its parts offers enough satisfactions to make that normally damning statement a quibble.

LeAnne Schreiber, in a review of "Souls and Bodies," in The New York Times, *January 1, 1982, p. 17.*

PAUL THEROUX

"**Souls and Bodies**" is about as chatty as a novel can be. Polly, Dennis, Angela, Adrian, Ruth, Miles, Violet and the others are merely excuses for the novelist to dramatize recent history. He had his theme long before he had his characters, and though this is an example of a highly serious postmodernist approach to novel-writing, it does have its drawbacks. At one point, Dennis is conscripted into the British Army, but after a tentative description of army life come the sentences "I have described it in detail elsewhere. So have others. It is always the same."

Elsewhere means another novel, but is it always the same? This sounds a little like literary despair. At another point, the subject of marriage and birth control is raised, and in the middle of the paragraph is the sentence "I have written about this before," followed by a description of the earlier novel and a little disquisition on a fan letter Mr. Lodge received from a reader in Czechoslovakia.

The problem is not that the book is wild and wide-ranging in the narrative line; it is not wild or wide-ranging enough. Mr. Lodge strives after effects that sound something like Mary McCarthy being rewritten by Tom Robbins—not everyone's novel, and certainly not mine, thanks. It is the kind of fictional anomaly that ends up having its throat slit and its entrails slung out on the dissection table at the University of Birmingham (England), where the author teaches.

When Mr. Lodge forgets he is Professor of Modern English Literature, ditches the arch tone and all the mannerisms and begins to believe in these characters, the effect is refreshing and often effortlessly funny. There is an episode about some business (wisecracks, nudity, and is that cardiac arrest?) in a sauna with Jeremy and Miriam and Michael and Polly that is less an example of the technique of fiction than a tap on the funny bone, and that's how it ought to be.

English reviewers found a great deal to admire in this novel, and a great deal in it is admirable—but it shares with most Kingsley Amis novels a culture-bound set of references that will ring no bells for the American reader: National Service, Profumo, the "Lady Chatterley's Lover" trial, Colin Wilson, CND and the Aberfan disaster. Mr. Lodge, who addresses his readers in a matey way ("Gentle reader"), ought really to understand—if he wants his books to travel—the necessity of saying, "Gentle reader, the 'Blue Peter Special' that I've just mentioned is a television program."

So much for social history. Catholicism is more catholic, and all churchgoers will recognize the theological references to *Aggiornamento*, the vernacular mass, the encyclical *Humanae Vitae* and so forth. But these are the obvious paraphernalia of faith, the odd-seeming props of people who practice a religion. Satirizing such things is a bit like satirizing Hasidic side curls or the prayer mats of Islam. This gentle comedy has nothing to do with spirituality but a great deal to do with the gang mentality of the Catholic Youth Organization; it is not about belief, but lack of it.

I kept thinking throughout "**Souls and Bodies**" of how this subject has been tackled better in the past, for example, with grim hilarity in the stories of J. F. Powers, and with a crackling zest by Peter De Vries (remember his religious show on ice, the Christ Capades, in "Mrs. Wallop"?). (pp. 3, 23)

Paul Theroux, "A Novel of Catholicism in England," in The New York Times Book Review, *January 31, 1982, pp. 3, 23.*

JOHN PODHORETZ

Souls and Bodies is a novel about a group of unremarkable people. These twelve Englishmen and Englishwomen are Catholics; they meet in 1952 when they all join a New Testament study group in college. We first see them dutifully attending a rigorous early Thursday morning mass. At book's end, all but two are present at a "Paschal Festival" sponsored by an organization one of them has founded, the Catholics for an Open Church. At this festival people speak in tongues and spend their time in encounter-group sessions discussing the falsity of the doctrine of papal infallibility and the immorality of the Church's conservative stand on birth control. In between, Lodge guides us through three decades; we witness the changes in his characters' beliefs and the tenuousness of their faith through the great struggles of adulthood.

David Lodge is an English novelist and critic known slightly in this country for his last novel, *Changing Places*. That novel is an hilarious satire of academic life, both English and American. The new book is also frequently funny, but quietly searing. Like his characters, Lodge is searching for his faith and his religion; he himself appears frequently in the novel, delivering neat little essays on the moral impact of available contraception and sexual freedom.... Lodge is, he makes clear, as much a subject for contemplation as his characters. This is a disquieting and daring step for an author to take, but Lodge's subject, after all, is *faith*. Only the completely faithful or faithless writer could, without seeming disingenuous or false, exclude himself from such an issue. *Souls and Bodies* is a passionate book; its author seeks the answers to the problems of religious faith on every page....

We have grown so accustomed to those highly praised novels in which adolescents discover sexual freedom, irrational violence wreaks its consequences on a wise but hapless hero, and the struggle of life is reduced to a battle between superego and id, that a good novel about a few people merely trying to *get by* may seem a rather small achievement. If so, then perhaps we have lost sight of the value and purpose of fiction. A great deal happens in this short novel, yet in Lodge's view human action and consequence are subsidiary to the questions raised by human action and consequence: *How far can you go? Where are the limits? What—who—defines the limits?*

When John Irving shows us T. S. Garp's wife's lover's castration during fellatio, he tells us nothing about the lover or the wife or, most important, about Garp himself. When John Updike's Rabbit bemoans his middle-aged flesh and weary member, it feels like we are being asked to watch him masturbate. When Dennis, in *Souls and Bodies,* falls miserably into the arms of his love-starved secretary, we wonder not *How good was it?* but *Has he gone too far?* When Father Brierly insists that transubstantiation is purely symbolic, we wonder not *Is he right?* but *Has he gone too far?* When Michael, once so worried about the Hell awaiting him for his onanism, gazes with fascination at Swedish sex films in Piccadilly Circus, we wonder, along with him, *Has the world gone too far? Where are the limits now?* (p. 37)

When everything one does or thinks is "subject to spiritual accounting," as in the case of Lodge and his characters, the needs of the soul are more important than the needs and desires of the body. The modern popular novel has devoted itself to the body alone; Lodge joins an honorable and great tradition by restoring the primacy of the soul in fiction. (p. 38)

John Podhoretz, "How Far Can You Go?" in The New Republic, *Vol. 186, No. 14, April 7, 1982, pp. 37-8.*

MARTIN RAPISARDA

Lodge makes it clear [in *Working with Structuralism*] that he appropriates the orthodox or "classical" line of structuralism established by Jakobson, Levi-Strauss, and Todorov. He makes it exceptionally clear that he wants little to do with those renegades of structuralism, the poststructuralist horde of Derrida, Foucault, and Lacan. That he willfully adopts this tack closes off his work to the continuing debate among these representatives of the structuralist movement (movement suggesting a highly consolidated attack). For example, Lacan's critique of Jakobson's theory of metaphor and metonymy, the latter theorist so central to Lodge's periodization of the novel, is most regrettably absent from this present book. In ignoring this development of Jakobson's theory, Lodge deprives his own argument of some needed adjustments.

In fact, structuralism as it is presented in this book is restricted to just Jakobson's theory of metaphor and metonymy. Other vestiges of the structuralist theory are concealed. This theory is utilized as the basis for two chapters: "Modernism, Antimodernism, and Postmodernism" and "Historicism and Literary History: Mapping the Modern Period," perhaps the only structuralist (properly so-called) chapters in the entire book. Metonymy as the trope of contiguity of elements informs the realist novel, which in the modernist period exhibits a recalcitrant antimodernism. Bennett's *Old Wives' Tale* serves as an example of antimodernism in that it "tends to imitate, as faithfully as discourse can, the actual relations of things to each other in space-time."... Metaphor as the trope of substitution and selection informs modernist texts, such as *Ulysses,* which are "based on a similarity between things otherwise dissimilar and widely separated in space and time." So far, the bipolar arrangement "works" well, but enter the postmodernist text to upset the neat symmetry. Postmodernism short-circuits the whole structuralist system by not abiding by the oppositional extremes of metaphor versus metonymy; rather, it works by a series of contradictions, permutations, and discontinuities. Using Jakobson's theory provides a handy framework to help categorize the manifold discourses within modernism. But Lodge fails to answer what alterations and critiques of Jakobson's distinction result from postmodernism's disruption of the bipolar syntax. That he continues to use the theory elsewhere without addressing this question indicates a serious drawback.

The other chapters contain various topics: an essay on a Hemingway short story, a biographical sketch of Waugh, an assessment of Tom Wolfe's New Journalism, a discussion on pessimism in *Jude the Obscure,* and an explication of one of Lodge's own short stories. Each chapter presents more of a fine-tuning of New Critical interpretation than it exemplifies structuralist praxis. This short catalog of chapter topics should raise the question of the extent to which this book is indebted to structuralism at all. Sadly, Lodge's domestication and assimilation of structuralist terminology merely undergirds new critical readings, thereby providing ample evidence for the contention of structuralism being a Trojan Horse within the old paradigm. As an example of what a critic can do when faced with an assortment of texts and topics, this richly informative book serves admirably well. In structuralist matters, it is just another sequel. (pp. 362-63)

Martin Rapisarda, in a review of "Working with Structuralism: Essays and Reviews of Nineteenth- and Twentieth-Century Literature," in Modern Fiction Studies, *Vol. 28, No. 2, Summer, 1982, pp. 362-64.*

ANTHONY THWAITE

A few years ago, David Lodge's **'Changing Places'** travelled a hilarious route to and fro between Euphoria, US, and Rummidge, GB, charting the complicated intertwined fortunes of Philip Swallow temporarily in the former and Morris Zapp temporarily in the latter. The Groves of Academe were translated into a parodic Forest of Arden, in which destinies, actions and fortunes were seen through the eyes of equally parodic comic picaresque.

Now, in **'Small World,'** Lodge has both underlined his present intention (the sub-title is 'An Academic Romance') and vastly extended his geographical range. He has also made it in part a sequel to the earlier book: Swallow and Zapp are near the top of the cast-list, along with Swallow's wife Hilary and Zapp's ex-wife Désirée. But now the cast is as global as the topography: dozens of academics (British, American, French, German, Italian, Turkish, Japanese, etc, etc) thread its pages, many of them constantly travelling the world, jetting in and out of conferences and seminar rooms from Tokyo to Jerusalem, clutching their many-times-used papers on Deconstruction, Metaphor and Metonymy, Genre—and Romance.

The result is a wonderful tissue of outrageous coincidences and correspondences, teasing elevations of suspense and delayed climaxes, all of them interlaced with tongue-in-cheek literary and literary-critical allusions. A French homosexual academic's favourite toilet-water is called *Tristes Tropiques;* quotations from 'The Waste Land' (itself of course a cento of quotations) form a casual, and sometimes farcical, *leitmotif;* even Molly Bloom's ecstatic onomatopoeia takes on new life, the recurrent frenzied cry of jets as they carry their learned—and often ferociously ambitious—passengers hither and yon.

In all this mêlée, the central characters, transcending Swallow and Zapp, are a young innocent, Persse McGarrigle, a junior lecturer at the dim University of Limerick, and the enigmatic and beautiful Angelica Pabst. Angelica is Persse's Grail, *belle dame sans merci,* and all the rest of it. She, like several others in the book, actually defines Romance, though more outrageously than some, e.g. a Turkish lecturer's wife who simply says, 'You should be happy. It is like a fairy story.' **'Small World'** is that and more: a very happy, lively, exhilarating, funny and ingenious display of innocently experienced high spirits.

Anthony Thwaite, "Travelling People," in The Observer, *March 18, 1984, p. 23.**

HARRIET WAUGH

Like many satirists, David Lodge makes ridiculous those things that are close to him. So far, readers of his novels have been beguiled with an unexpected view of the British Museum Reading Room, an examination of American and English campus life during student unrest in the late Sixties, and the effects of Vatican II on Roman Catholic behaviour. In *Small World,* David Lodge goes back to academic concerns, only this time on a global scale. . . .

In the sense that some of the same characters reappear, *Small World* is a sequel to *Changing Places.* Ten years on, Professor Swallow is still professionally dim, but now he sports a beard, looks distinguished, heads his department at the dismal English University of Rummage and travels the highways of the air from God-knows-where to Turkey, expounding very boringly on Hazlitt, about whom he has written a dull book. While Professor Zapp from Euphoria State University in America has given up sex, been divorced by his wife, who has written a best-selling feminist novel on the horrors of being married to him, and as he juggles fashionable post-structuralist ideas at international literary forums with his peers, is busy intriguing for the best-paid academic post in the world.

All this junketing takes place inside the form of a literary romance. The romantic hero, an innocent abroad, is an Irish poet called Persse McGarrigle who teaches literature at an agricultural college in Limerick. He chases his muse, Angelica Pabst, a beautiful, clever, literary conference groupee around the world from one literary convention to another. Angelica, an orphan of the airways—she was abandoned at birth in an aeroplane lavatory—is, needless to say, doing a doctoral dissertation on Romance. Persse, chaste and holy as an Arthurian knight, tries for his lady's love against some entirely modern foes—pre-marital sex, aeroplanes, and independent womanhood. The quest is all and, as Angelica would explain, gives narrative tension. (p. 29)

As in all David Lodge's novels, the characters in *Small World* are instantly forgettable. There is no savagery in his satire or real malice in his wit. Instead, his novels engender a flowing sense of fun. The reader is given a very enjoyable time at nobody's expense. It makes him feel good. In this, David Lodge comes close to the effect of P. G. Wodehouse's writing, though he does not have his genius for creating entirely original characters or possess his unique facility with the English language. His wit, however, like that of Wodehouse, froths around and out of characters whose behaviour seems as sweetly absurd as the antics of playful puppies. If his characters lack Bertie Wooster's inner life, this is hardly a serious complaint.

Some of the jokes are likely to be lost on those who are not part of the literary academic *cognoscenti,* and others are there to make you feel well-read if you can catch them in passing. . . . Now and then when David Lodge broke into pastiche, I knew it was happening but was too ignorant to recognise where it came from. On the whole, when I miss things in books, I prefer to be unaware of their passing, as it distracts from having a good time. However, it would be mean-spirited to resent a novelist flexing his literary muscles merely because one's own are not as developed. *Small World,* despite such minor irritations, is the best constructed, the most gripping and the funniest of his novels to date. There are few writers I look forward to reading as much as I do him, and this novel is hugely enjoyable. (p. 30)

Harriet Waugh, "Grand Lodge," in The Spectator, *Vol. 252, No. 8126, April 7, 1984, pp. 29-30.*

MICHAEL ROSENTHAL

As **"Small World,"** an exuberant, marvelously funny novel demonstrates, no one is better able to treat the peripatetic quality of current academic life than the British writer David Lodge. Jet travel has brought all academics within reach of every meeting, and a current passport is as essential a part of every professor's baggage as an updated curriculum vitae. . . . "The day of the single, static campus is over,'' Morris Zapp, one of Mr. Lodge's itinerant professors, declares, prompting the acute question, ''And the single, static campus novel with it, I suppose?'' Zapp's retort neatly defines both structure and theme of **''Small World''**: ''Exactly! Even two campuses wouldn't be enough. Scholars these days are like the errant knights of old, wandering the ways of the world in search of adventure and glory.''

The exploits of these errant knights have come down to us through the romance, and as the novel's subtitle, ''An Academic Romance,'' indicates, this is the form Mr. Lodge has playfully chosen for his tale of professors on the make. **''Small World''** is veined with humorous allusions to Ariosto, the Grail romances, Spenser, Keats and others as Mr. Lodge follows his questing scholars from one literary conference to another as they search for amorous adventures and critical acclaim from their peers. In keeping with the nature of romance, it is a world of wonderful characters and strange events, of mistaken identities and people coming back from the dead, all presided over by the unflagging energy and wit of a superb comic novelist. The book's texture is perhaps best summarized by Cheryl Summerbee, the checker for British Air, who in the course of the novel moves from reading trashy true romances to an appreciation of ''The Faerie Queen'' and ''Orlando Furioso.'' Describing the contents of ''real romance,'' she describes at the same time the experience of reading **''Small World''**: ''It's full of adventure and coincidence and surprises and marvels, and has lots of characters who are lost or enchanted or wandering about looking for each other, or for the Grail, or something like that. Of course, they're often in love too . . .''

Two separate kinds of quest structure Mr. Lodge's romance— that of Persse McGarrigle for Angelica, the beautiful and brilliant graduate student he meets at the novel's opening conference at a British provincial university and then pursues all over the earth trying in vain to catch another glimpse of her, and that of a dazzling variety of scholarly knights for trysts, fame and, most important, the Unesco chair of literary criticism, which carries with it a tax-free salary of $100,000 and no responsibilities other than to think.

The ingenuous, virginal Persse remains throughout his trials uncontaminated by the randy, calculating academics surrounding him. As his name suggests, and as countless funny parallels make clear, he is the Percival of the Grail legends, innocently making his way through a fallen, sterile world, which only he can redeem by asking the questions that will set the Fisher King free from whatever it is that ails him and restore the land to its former fertility. The Fisher King in this instance is Arthur Kingfisher, the eminent literary critic, who has experienced

neither a fresh thought nor a sexual stirring for many years, the latter despite the inexhaustible ministrations of his devoted Korean graduate student Song-Mi Lee. Watching pornographic movies while reviewing the latest book on hermeneutics, Kingfisher remains in sorry shape.

The most distinguished theorist of his time, however, he has the power to designate the first recipient of the Unesco chair, and as such commands the interest of all who seek it. Mr. Lodge's contenders for the position occupy the entire spectrum of current critical opinion. Depicted in all their idiosyncratic splendor, every foible, jargon-filled phrase and flaw exposed, they constitute an irreverent, acute commentary on the contemporary literary scene. . . .

Despite the novel's breathless narrative pace, profusion of incident and geographic scope, Mr. Lodge never loses control of his material. His deliberately outrageous manipulation of character and event is entirely successful. Moments of fine comic inventiveness abound, like Persse's fumbling efforts to buy contraceptives in anticipation of his consummation with Angelica, only to find, as he excitedly unwraps his prize in the London underground, that through the shopkeeper's confusion of ''Durex'' with ''Farex'' he has purchased instead a medium-size box of baby food. . . .

As befits an academic romance, **''Small World''** concludes at the most august of all literary conventions, the Modern Language Association's annual meeting right after Christmas at which thousands of teachers of literature gather to meet friends, renew affairs, give papers and—if unemployed—get jobs. Here, Mr. Lodge takes the many tantalizing thematic strands he has been developing and brings them to full, satisfying comic resolution. Some quests are terminated, others renewed. It would be unfair to reveal the specifics of the ending, beyond saying that, unlike the Grail heroes, Persse does indeed ask the question—in the grand ballroom of the Hilton during the forum on ''The Function of Criticism''—which liberates the Fisher King from his malaise and has remarkable consequences.

Breathing comic life into a form that one would not immediately think appropriate to the contemporary academic world, David Lodge suggests that despite the depredations of critics, the capacity of art to give pleasure still endures. **''Small World,''** rich with resonances of the past, argues that case more effectively than could any of what Gulley Jimson of the ''The Horse's Mouth'' would call ''literary crickets.''

Michael Rosenthal, ''Randy Roads of the Professoriat,'' in The New York Times Book Review, *March 17, 1985, p. 7.*

Norman (Alexander) MacCaig

1910-

Scottish poet and editor.

MacCaig is considered one of Scotland's most important contemporary poets. His poetry is written in English, but it is deeply rooted in his native land and often describes the landscape, weather, people, and animals of the Scottish highlands. MacCaig has been praised for his keenly observant eye and accurate illustrative power. He relies heavily on metaphor and simile, and he frequently anthropomorphizes objects and concepts of the natural world. Critics have noted a commitment to the ordinary in MacCaig's poems, which rarely espouse social or political ideals, historical influences, or passionate personal feelings. However, reviewers also point to the warmth and humanity in MacCaig's work, attributing it partly to his wit and mildly self-mocking tone.

MacCaig's first two books, *Far Cry* (1943) and *The Inward Eye* (1946), are highly rhetorical and laden with metaphors. *Riding Lights* (1955), MacCaig's next collection, more closely represents his successive work, conveying the wit, observant power, and affection for the natural world evident in most of his verse. The poetry collected in these volumes as well as in the next four—*The Sinai Sort* (1957), *A Common Grace* (1960), *A Round of Applause* (1962), and *Measures* (1965)—are formally rhymed and metered. Although he never completely abandoned the structured form, MacCaig began to employ a free verse style with *Surroundings* (1966). Some critics suggested that the change was an unfortunate concession to current tastes, but most contended that it brought greater range and depth to MacCaig's work.

MacCaig's later poems delve into more philosophical subjects. *Surroundings* and *Rings on a Tree* (1968) explore aesthetics and the nature or act of observing. MacCaig's playfulness and self-irony remain constant in these volumes as well as in *A Man in My Position* (1969) and *The White Bird* (1973). Critics have also noted a move toward the personal in MacCaig's later poetry, a trend motivated by the deaths of several of his close friends during the 1970s. *The World's Room* (1974) and *Tree of Strings* (1977) contain poems which express the sorrow and loss he felt after these deaths. In *A World of Difference* (1983) MacCaig deals not only with the deaths of friends but also with the prospect of his own death.

(See also *Contemporary Authors*, Vols. 9-12, rev. ed.; *Contemporary Authors New Revision Series*, Vol. 3; and *Dictionary of Literary Biography*, Vol. 27.)

DONALD HALL

Norman MacCaig is a Scottish poet of distinction. Though he is now published in this country—his **"Riding Lights"** was recently published [here] . . .—it will probably take time for American readers to accept him, since he is British. . . . MacCaig at his best combines a philosophical toughness with an unstrained extravagance of language. In **"Instrument and Agent,"** **"Morning,"** and **"By Comparison"** he pursues this union of sense and color with special success. If you look for a word to name his characteristic diction you may find yourself calling

Courtesy of Norman McCaig

it "apocalyptic"; yet MacCaig is blessedly seldom so strained and unpleasant as the peusdo-school of the Apocalypse directed by Treece and Hendry. There is a largeness to his extravagance, a genuine size which minimizes the feeling of cunning derangement. . . . The grace and speed with which MacCaig accomplishes the difficult make him a poet to be read by anyone concerned with the poetry being written in the language.

> Donald Hall, "Philosophic Toughness, Unstrained Extravagance," in The Saturday Review, *New York, Vol. XXXIX, No. 52, December 29, 1956, p. 28.*

G. S. FRASER

[Mr. MacCaig is] an intrinsically difficult poet. [In *The Sinai Sort* he] seeks in the visible world and in personal relationships some more or less impersonal core of meaning which will rescue him from imprisonment in his own subjectivity:

> What our eyes say to us is fields
> Are there for us to weave in baskets
> To take a thought of murder home in;
> Or they're a pool where silence beckons . . .
>
> All that the eye names is disguises. . . .

Disguises, but disguising what? Mr. MacCaig cannot quite put it into words:

> . . . I'd tremble to discover
> That special, stubborn thing, that must forever
> Lie hooded between no and yes. . . .

Thus, these careful poems, strongly if sometimes rather stiffly shaped, are essentially exercises towards the definition of something recalcitrant. . . . Mr. McCaig demands a lot of effort (and the fashionable poem today is not the difficult poem but the poem that makes a simple situation *look* difficult); it seems to me he repays the effort. (p. 650)

> *G. S. Fraser, "Parnassian Grades," in* The New Statesman & Nation, *Vol. LIII, No. 1366, May 18, 1957, pp. 649-50.**

LEAH BODINE DRAKE

Norman MacCaig blends insight with craftsmanship, a daring use of words with traditional form, and lyric warmth with a wry, shrewd humor, all of which make his new book, **Riding Lights** . . . , a pleasure to read. . . .

He is a master of the pungent phrase and the exact if startling image. . . .

MacCaig's world, like that of the Georgians he resembles, is a morning world in which simple, familiar things—haystacks, hedges, horse troughs, and herring gulls—are seen in a clear light, not transcendental, but that of common day. . . .

Perhaps MacCaig seems overoccupied with death—actual death, no spiritual defeat as is Muir's concern—but he isn't bitter about it and means to make full use of his time upon earth. . . .

Many of [the poems in **Riding Lights**], underneath their nimble, gift-o'-the-gab richness of imagery, ring rather hollow. Some of the sophistication seems posed. But they are evidence of a subtle mind and of a capacity for transmitting experience.

> *Leah Bodine Drake, in a review of "Riding Lights," in* The Atlantic Monthly, *Vol. 199, No. 6, June, 1957, p. 77.*

ROBERT CONQUEST

Mr. MacCaig was an original member of the much-abused 'New Apocalypse,' which has taken such a lot of the blame for the genetically unsound mutants who shambled around in the Forties. He was always a much better writer than most of his associates and his new book [**The Sinai Sort**] is full of genuine and unassertive symbolist verse, with most of its difficult virtues, and few of its easy faults. Though his very successes show the limitations of the method, we must admire this poetry's integrity and concentration. (p. 787)

> *Robert Conquest, "A New Major Poet?" in* The Spectator, *Vol. 198, No. 6729, June 14, 1957, pp. 786-87.**

HUGH MacDIARMID

Dr. Kurt Wittig, in his recent volume, *The Scottish Tradition in Literature,* points out that Scottish poetry is a classical and not a romantic poetry, with a scrupulous regard for form, in contradistinction to English poetry, and opines that 'Never since the time of the Makars have the Gaelic and the Scots

stream of Scottish culture been so close to each other.' Mr. MacCaig's poems above all manifest the truth of these judgments. There is nothing of the 'Celtic twilight' here. We are back in the Gaelic sunshine. No contemporary poet has revived that high tradition with anything approaching the success of Mr. MacCaig. His work improves with each successive volume and is . . . at its best [in *A Common Grace*]. But it is extremely unlikely that it will ever achieve the popular appreciation it deserves. In his detachment from the crucial problems of his time, in the limitation of his appeal to the *literati*, there is a danger that his place will finally be found to be, no matter how accomplished his poems, in what Quasimodo calls 'the tradition of the voices which seem to be crying in the wilderness but which in reality are gnawing at the non-truth.' It seems ungrateful in the presence of these brilliant poems, those of a scholar not only in Gaelic but in Greek, and of one who has not only a sensitive and searching nose but a fine ear for the niceties of *piobaireachd*, to hope so urgently for an extension of his range. . . . It seems to me that that is all—the little more and how much it is—that is needed now to make Mr. MacCaig a poet of immediate international consequence.

> *Hugh MacDiarmid, "Noses," in* The Spectator, *Vol. 205, No. 6895. August 19, 1960, p. 288.*

P. N. FURBANK

Norman MacCaig belongs to the 'epistemological' school, whose ancestors are Valéry and Wallace Stevens. Their aim is to trace in the description of an outward scene the lines of some technical problem of philosophy—appearance and reality, the one and the many, flux versus permanence, the part versus the whole. Their poems bite their own tail: the particulars with which the poem opens make a return appearance later as the general. Behind the technique of the verse lies the imagists' desire that their work should *be* the thing it describes; several of MacCaig's poems [in *A Common Grace*] begin as statements about landscape and end as propositions about language. He depends heavily on the kind of word-play which links the particular and the general, the concrete and the abstract. . . . His poems are all knitted neatly together by . . . puns and alliterations and use of homonyms; they resemble a tidy semi-abstract canvas in the contemporary manner. He is, on the other hand, an attractive and not a difficult poet. His neo-metaphysical conceits—like that of the divided fisherman whose legs under the water seem like a separate creature wading—are often charming. . . ; indeed his easy-going and fanciful temperament has by nature little in common with the passionate pursuit of congruities, the devoted excavation of the paradigm, of his masters.

> *P. N. Furbank, in a review of "A Common Grace," in* The Listener, *Vol. LXIV, No. 1646, October 13, 1960, p. 651.**

JOHN PRESS

[*The essay from which this excerpt is taken was originally presented as part of The George Elliston Poetry Foundation Lectures at the University of Cincinnati in 1962.*]

Unlike Roy Fuller, who has attempted to survey the ramifications of contemporary society and to diagnose the sickness of man as a political animal, Norman MacCaig seldom makes any reference to current affairs or hazards a generalization about the state of the world. He concentrates his attention upon certain basic metaphysical problems, such as the nature of identity, the relationship of the perceiver and the perceived, the power of the mind to endow a landscape or an object with shape and meaning. Even in his love poems he is intent on analysing the mode of love's operation, the ways in which it can transform a person's inner life, either by creating order, unity, and peace out of chaos, or by shattering the principle of harmony in the mind so that chaos is come again. The self in its relations with one other individual; the self in its perception of the visible world and in its consciousness of the universe: these themes occur in poem after poem. (p. 172)

[MacCaig] is, in both senses of the term, a metaphysical poet. His wit, his reliance upon the conceit, his delight in playing with paradox and antithesis, his fondness for a close-knit argument as he teases out the thread of a subtle philosophical disquisition, his skill in maintaining a perilous equilibrium while dancing along the knife-edge of a daring speculation—all these are signs that he has studied to good effect the practice of the Metaphysical poets. There is no question of pastiche in his vocabulary, in his images, in his rhythms, or in the texture of his verse; but he owes much to his reading of the Metaphysicals and he has clearly fallen under the spell of John Donne, being one of those whom, to quote Mario Praz, 'the rhythm of thought itself attracts by virtue of its own peculiar convolutions'. (p. 173)

Some of MacCaig's most beautiful poems are descriptions of a landscape or a seascape. He portrays with a vivid immediacy the exact physical contours of a scene and of the objects in that scene, evoking their sensuous qualities with an unfailing accuracy. Yet even in his most direct transcriptions of the visible world he is never content merely to reproduce a physical likeness: he wants to make us aware that the simplest objects are part of a marvellously complex system of interrelationships, which we can explore by means of our five senses and by letting our minds play upon this elaborate network. What might degenerate into a pretentious and arid piece of scholastic logic-chopping is saved from this disaster by the alertness of MacCaig's observation and by the vivacity of his five senses. He is, moreover, no bookish recluse, but a man who knows and loves the countryside, who has fished the lochs and rivers, climbed the mountains, and studied the wild life of his native Scotland.

The enchanting wit, the melodic ease, the rhythmical subtlety of these descriptive poems do not readily lend themselves to analysis. There comes a point when criticism can no more anatomize the felicities of language than it can dissect the shape of a tune. (pp. 173-74)

It is hard to illustrate the nature and the quality of MacCaig's love-poetry by means of short extracts, because any abbreviation of his slowly unfolding, ruthlessly exploratory argument, diminishes its forensic impact. His love-poems never describe the physical characteristics of the beloved; they seldom portray her moral features; nor do they attempt to suggest the range of emotions awakened by the sexual act, to sketch the lineaments of gratified desire. They are, primarily, metaphysical inquiries into the essence of love, and into the painful intricacies of a unique relationship between two people.

MacCaig sees love as a force charged with supernatural energy that can transfigure a mode of life, or even bring into existence what formerly slept in embryo or in chaos. (p. 176)

The danger of this method, which leans so heavily on the riddling paradox, is that the ingenuity of the conceits, the

tortuous progression of the argument, may stifle the emotional life of the poem. (p. 177)

Perhaps MacCaig's most original poems are those in which he speculates on certain key problems of metaphysics, without either relaxing the rigour of the argument or letting his verse become slack and arid. The nature of time, of existence, and of identity, the meaning of chaos, the omnipresence of mortality which involves every creature and every inanimate object—such are the themes on which he composes his variations. (pp. 178-79)

MacCaig lacks Wordsworthian piety nor has he any feeling of warm sympathy with Nature, any belief in her reconciling, beneficent power; but his poetry takes on a Wordsworthian solidity and depth when he acknowledges himself to be part of a universal process into which everything is drawn, and which overwhelms all creation. Wherever man looks he discovers his identity with all that exists in the cosmos. . . . (pp. 179-80)

MacCaig's territory may not be large, but it is densely populated with good poems which are memorable for their alert Metaphysical wit, their sensuous energy, the closeness of their texture and the elegance of their pattern. He owes much to Donne, and something to Yeats; in one or two poems—**'Blue Chair in a Sunny Day'** and **'Country Bedroom'**—there are echoes of Wallace Stevens. . . . He owes even more to the keenness of his senses and to his innate philosophical turn of mind; but his greatest debt is to his native country: for his sense of being rooted in Scotland, with its tradition of metaphysical inquiry, its sombre, rich scenery, its pride in its ancient culture, has given his poetry an integrity of purpose, an air of aristocratic breeding, an austere but exhilarating strength, that distinguish it from the work of all but a few of his English contemporaries. (pp. 180-81)

> *John Press, "Metaphysics and Mythologies," in his* Rule and Energy: Trends in British Poetry since the Second World War, *Oxford University Press, London, 1963, pp. 159-201.**

EDWIN MORGAN

Norman MacCaig's new collection [*A Round of Applause*] is a good one, though mainly within the limitations we have come to expect. Most of the poems continue his favourite themes of exploring the effects of Highland landscape, the shifting, evasive boundaries between appearance and reality, the place of the human observer in the scheme of things. It's a pleasure to find such sharp and unexpected perceptions of the natural world: the rain-drop on the fence-wire turning "from apple to stretched-out pear", the mass of sheep half in and half out of the steading making "a white hourglass in the sun", the black wave that "bangs on timber and slavers past". Occasionally a device is overworked, like the many reminders that things are not what they seem: a cork turns out to be an otter's nose, a purse turns into a toad, a dead fish rots in the air—"A cloud it was, really". And the poems which attempt to delve most deeply into the question of appearance and reality, poems such as **"Loch na Bearraig"** which discuss whether a landscape, like a poem, should mean something or only be something—these don't always convince. I think the reason is that the experience behind the poem doesn't seem to be deep enough to bear the large intellectual statements the poem wants to make. The step from observation to comment, so temptingly open and easy, is in fact crucially tricky, because it involves a poet's beliefs, and I'm not at all sure, after reading these poems, what MacCaig believes, or if he believes, anything. (p. 41)

The best poems in the book are usually those which avoid or skirt these problems: mainly descriptive, vivid, atmospheric pieces often including animals or figures in a landscape: poems like **"Moorings"**, **"Spraying Sheep"**, **"Poachers Early Morning"**, **"Thaw on a Building Site"**, **"Byre"**. These have a mixture of wit and sensuous and pictorial clarity that's refreshing and attractive.... In spite of a few poems like **"Culag Pier"** and **"Ordinary Homecoming"**, human beings and human relationships take a very minor place in MacCaig's world of cows, waterfalls, and oystercatchers, and this is not unconnected with a certain unloving note, a scornful presence which sometimes appears to chill the verse.... I earnestly hope that the slight signs of greater human interest which do appear in this volume will be developed. (p. 42)

> *Edwin Morgan, "Three Scottish Poets," in* The Review, *No. 8, August, 1963, pp. 41-5.**

D. J. ENRIGHT

'Culag Pier', among [other poems in *A Round of Applause*], is reminiscent of the superior kind of documentary film, really clever camera work, the sharp eye and the ingenious intellect in nimble partnership.

In **'Still Life'** Mr MacCaig argues that

> martyrs in their fire,
> Christs on their crosses, fêtes and massacres,
> When purified of their small history,
> Cannot surpass, no matter how they struggle,
> Three apples (more than likely) and a jug.

Perhaps not—when purified of their small history—if 'purification' means forgetting or ignoring. In which case a viewer without a history is viewing a picture without a history. I cannot wax enthusiastic over the thin nerveless theory of art or of life which seems to be implied here, but happily Mr MacCaig's practice is generally otherwise: his poetry develops, not reduces, it reveals, not erases.... There is little of the still life about his **'John Quixote'** and less of the abstract. At times the effect is still somewhat inbred, I feel, a small orgiastic circle of object, avaricious eye and lusting wit. But there is strong, condensed stuff in *A Round of Applause,* best taken in small, satisfying doses, and it seems to me his most rewarding collection to date. (p. 21)

> *D. J. Enright, "The Greater Toil," in* New Statesman, *Vol. 65, No. 1660, January 4, 1965, pp. 21-2.**

FRANCIS HOPE

Patrolling the Scottish countryside [in *Measures*] Norman MacCaig comes across animals, landscapes, arrangements of clouds—even happenings, such as an electric transformer struck by lightning. But

> I, in a safe place, as I always am,
> Was, as I always am, observer only.

An observer of great verbal skill, though, whose poems make their immediate impact by sheer aptness, by painterish turns of phrases. 'A floating owl unreels his silence'; mosses 'plump their fat cushions up'; 'mouse stops being comma and clockworks on the floor.' One can't help seeing these, or the boat with arms akimbo' or the limpet 'snuffed by its hat', and taking

pleasure in them. But such observations of nature can notoriously lead to metaphysics. Mr MacCaig's claim to be 'observer only' isn't quite substantiated. Wordsworthian considerations of pattern and scale obtrude; these poems are 'measures' in various ways, yardsticks as well as rhythms.... Not everyone may feel that the bridge between description and exegesis is perfectly achieved. Mr MacCaig is minutely concerned with the way stuff gets differentiated into natural forms (so that even a heron 'stands in water, wrapped in heron'); his descriptive metaphors show a taste for essences as much as an eye for similarities. This might suggest—and is used to do so—the underlying choices and wishes of a Creator or a Scheme of Things, but it might, after all, just be the poet searching for the right word. (And usually finding it.) An analogy is made to serve as an argument. Those who think that poetry, and / or the world, demands an act of faith should be well satisfied; those who don't may find that some of these elegant, coolly vivid poems arouse expectations they don't quite fulfil. (p. 688)

> *Francis Hope, "Suffer and Observe," in* New Statesman, *Vol. LXIX, No. 1781, April 30, 1965, pp. 687-88.**

IAN HAMILTON

[For] a poetry that feeds so insistently and with such flashes of devout detail on a fairly narrow range of pictorial data, there is surprisingly little in Norman MacCaig's new book [*Measures*] to really catch and excite the eye. His scene-setting is efficient enough; there is a modestly deliberate air about it that seems to promise, at the very least, a spare fidelity to the concrete. It is significant, though, that the first two lines of his poems are invariably his best, precise, uncluttered, nicely poised; they seek out what he is fond of calling the 'perfect' moment in nature, a moment that is glassily static or, without excitement, suddenly fulfilled:

> As though defects were disallowed
> By some huge order that would not
> Permit a disobedience.

These lines, which follow the opening description of this **'Perfect Morning,'** show what usually happens next; 'defects,' 'disallowed,' 'disobedience,' 'some huge order'—are we really supposed to give any serious weight to such concepts, or is it all something of a game?

Only rarely does MacCaig allow his imagery to work for itself, to be responsible on its own concrete terms for those 'meanings' which he devotes whole knotty, abstract stanzas to claiming for it. His usual manner is to set up the scene, to lean back and in a curiously meandering, inconclusive way to puzzle over what he has made, or—worse—to make it seem much more puzzling than it is. The result is that images blur into explications and neither force upon us any serious or passionate claim; throughout there is this suspicion that both nature and the poet's mostly commonplace notions about it are being toyed with and entangled more in the interests of the neat stanza and the contented paradox than to serve any genuine poetic feeling. He plays around with **'Likenesses,'** a favourite sport, then asks:

> Why do I add
> Such notions up, unless they say what's true
> In ways I don't quite see, of me and you?

The question is not, finally, as rhetorical as MacCaig seems to think, but it is typical of the snug theoretical rut that his poems seem always to be digging for themselves. Part of his subject, of course, is that the 'inner' and the 'outer' eye ought not to trust each other, but believing this need not involve such an abject distribution of the spoils; here, surely, is one pact that poetry can arrange. Poems like, **'Sleet,' 'Summer Waterfall, Glendale'** and **'Sandstone Mountain'** are direct and richly texured enough to persuade that MacCaig is aware of this and that he has no real need to keep retreating into these happy deadlocks and trite self-questionings:

> Why should I drench them with false light?
> Why should I soar to make them tiny
> Or grovel to make them huge?

Good questions, certainly, but this is the easy way to ask them and expects no answers. (pp. 695-96)

> Ian Hamilton, "Questions and Answers," in The Spectator, Vol. 214, No. 7144, May 28, 1965, pp. 695-96.*

DAN JAFFE

Norman MacCaig is practically unknown in the United States. I have no notion of his earlier work, but his new book, *Measures* . . . reveals a poet whose English sounds natural and colloquial even to an American. His metaphors enliven; he satirizes with compassion; his wit doesn't flinch. Norman MacCaig can write the simple line that startles more each time one reads it. Something that matters happens in every poem in this book. That makes a book matter. (p. 31)

> Dan Jaffe, "An All-American Muse," in Saturday Review, Vol. XLIX, No. 42, October 15, 1966, pp. 29-31.*

C. B. COX

[Norman MacCaig's] concern is with the nature of poetic language. He is famous for the astonishing virtuosity in his choice of images: 'Like an orange pip squeezed from between fingertips The roebuck shot from the bracken bush,' 'Long weeds in the clear Water did Eastern dances, unregarded By shoals of darning needles.' In [*Surroundings*] (in which he experiments in free verse) he seems reconciled to the failure of words ever to come close to the true identity of things and people: 'I can describe only my own inventions.' . . . At his best MacCaig freewheels through conceits with a rush of inventiveness comparable to the extravagances of Donne. He accepts that he is playing a game with words, and in the process re-creates the unique actuality of a river, the sacred value of a personal relationship. But his distrust of words can become self-destructive. After seven lines of ornamental description of a glacier, he turns round and says this is all lies. His 'self' or 'mind' blunders in to make argumentative comments in dead language. In his best poems he is content simply to display 'how extraordinary ordinary things are.' (p. 522)

> C. B. Cox, "Fastidious Poets," in The Spectator, Vol. 217, No. 7217, October 21, 1966, pp. 522-23.*

JOHN CAREY

[In *Surroundings*] Mr MacCaig stalks the elusive images and, as usual, brings home some eyecatching specimens: the sea a 'fat-fingered facemaker' on the beach, frogs as freefall parachutists. His cult of the object precipitates a Keatsian unravelling of the self into the various components of a landscape.

He becomes excited at the prospect of union with a Scotch mist, and gives his ingenuity a pleasant run. The tone, though, cannot always keep up, and the lines begin to titter at their own whimsicality. The modification of object by observer offers another sidetrack for speculation. Mr MacCaig prods, a bit laboriously, at the difference between water trickling down a wall and a wall being trickled down by water. Some of his new poems undertake social comment. In one, **'King of Beasts,'** whimsy intervenes again, and leaves it hopping around between soap-box and nursery. But others find a genuine direction and follow it sharply. The best is about a dwarfish cripple begging outside the church at Assisi while a priest explains to tourists how clever it was of Giotto to make his frescoes reveal God's goodness to the illiterate. (p. 633)

> John Carey, "Durrell's Drift," in New Statesman, Vol. 72, No. 1859, October 28, 1966, pp. 632-33.*

ALAN BROWNJOHN

In *Rings on a Tree,* Norman MacCaig's presence in the foreground of his poems, greedily picking up and touching up detail—and over-manipulating his metaphors—restricts him to the realm of whimsical fancy. His latter-day free verse is more relaxed than all those tight, glib stanzas of the past, yet there is an increasing prosiness and the same struggle at the end of many poems to parcel up all the scraps into a snappy conclusion. But there is an eccentric vitality sometimes and a weirdly entertaining quality about a lot of the poems. (p. 363)

> Alan Brownjohn, "Repetitions," in New Statesman, Vol. 76, No. 1958, September 20, 1968, pp. 362-63.*

PETER BLAND

Like most of us Norman MacCaig is growing, as he gets older, 'to hate metaphors—their exactness and their inadequacy'. . . .

It is his love of gentleness that comes out strongest in **'Rings on a Tree'**. Being saddled with a rhyme-scheme is inclined to give most poets more words than they need, but, more than most, MacCaig has always been able to wear a formal dress lightly. Earlier poems like **'Feeding Ducks'** show how well he can stretch a formal pattern without splitting its seams. The gain in this new collection has perhaps been in a revival of impulse that his interest in freeing-up has allowed him. A more distinctly personal voice can be heard. The pair of observing eyes that one always admired in MacCaig at his best, has grown a face. It is a modest, outdoor, gentle, likeable face. It invites us into its personal life with charm and good grace. Among the bric-à-brac and the travel albums is a life well-worth knowing. 'Because I see the world poisoned / by cant and brutal self-seeking, / must I be silent about / the useless waterlily, the dunnock's nest / in the hedgeback?' The answer is no. Poems like **'Holy Moon'**, **'Estuary'**, **'Sleeping Compartment'** are full of detailed observation and muted feeling. **'New England Theocritus'** with its 'excess of moderation' succeeds in heightening sentiment to the level of a genuine love poem.

> Peter Bland, in a review of "Rings on a Tree," in London Magazine, Vol. 8, No. 9, December, 1968, p. 97.

ALAN BROWNJOHN

Norman MacCaig's verse in *A Man in my Position* has all the old suspicious fluency and variety, that superficially dazzling (and ultimately disappointing) way with unconsidered trifles which has always been his principal talent and his greatest weakness. Nothing here is less than agreeable, he can pull off triumphant snatches of submetaphysical wit and surprise (see the opening of **'Spring Tide'**), and he has certainly loosened up a lot since the time when he was doing everything with a rather too conspicuous formal neatness and finish. But when all the cleverness is said and done, what remains? One longer poem here. **'A Man in Assynt'**, and some lapses in the shorter ones ('And your hand is as cool as moonlight / and as gentle'), reveal some pretty routine romantic thinking, as if the brilliance of the others concealed the absence of any kind of hard core. Occasionally in earlier volumes MacCaig has shown signs of digging down more deeply: he has done a few really haunting and disquieting poems. In the new book he comes up with one or two which disturb the overall impression of an accomplished, attractive light verse writer—**'The Unlikely'**, **'In My Mind'**, and the title poem—but they are still swamped by what he calls, only too joyfully, his 'coloured ideas.' (p. 20)

> *Alan Brownjohn, "Meditations," in* New Statesman,
> *Vol. 79, No. 2025, January 2, 1970, pp. 18, 20.**

IAN HAMILTON

'Too happy to be sad. What / a pleasant, what a terrible / exclusion' writes Norman MacCaig, amiably contrasting himself with perhaps weightier authors, and this is more or less the note he strikes throughout *A Man In My Position*. More relaxed and unpretentious than in earlier books, he indulges himself with leisurely speculative fancies, small ironic musings. Most of it is agreeable enough, though it tends to leave the faintest, most forgettable, of impacts. But at least MacCaig is now working, with ease and skill, within his limitations. And there is one poem, a longer work originally commissioned by BBC-TV, of real quality. A Scots Nationalist lament, it is exact, unmelodramatic and in parts genuinely moving. And on the purely technical level, it is something of a model for media-poets—in conversational free verse, it moves with much vigour and caution, and is impressively difficult to interrupt.

> *Ian Hamilton, "Loads of Heavy Thinking," in* The
> Observer, *January 18, 1970, p. 34.**

DEREK STANFORD

Selected Poems by Norman MacCaig is made up of pieces chosen from the eight volumes published by him since 1955, numbering, in all, 87 compositions. Taken together, they reveal Mr MacCaig as a poet of consistently inventive ingeniousness: an artist who resorts to playfulness not only because he enjoys the fanciful but because it may also be employed to help the poet come at an aspect of meaning in some basic subject (such as love or death) as readily at times as seriousness. An instance of this is his poem *The Root of It.*

If I were asked what were Mr MacCaig's most dexterous verbal instruments, I should reply: the choice epithet, the original simile, the deft epigram—all of which he handles with the skill of a precision-tool worker. He writes, for example, of 'Straws like tame lightnings'; of water in a horse-trough 'Green as glass'; of nine ducks that 'go wobbling by'; and of time adding 'one malice to another one'. (pp. 64-5)

> *Derek Stanford, in a review of "Selected Poems,"*
> *in* Books and Bookmen, *Vol. 16, No. 12, September,*
> *1971, pp. 64-5.**

DOUGLAS DUNN

It comes as a mild shock to realise that Norman MacCaig is not much younger than Auden. In 1930 MacCaig would have been twenty. What happened to the poems of his twenties, in that era when talents grew so quickly? His new *Selected Poems* (and how welcome this book is) starts with *Riding Lights,* the volume published in 1955. Before that, MacCaig contributed to *The New Apocalypse* and *The White Horseman*—that fact in itself indicates the kind of poems he wrote then—and there were two volumes after that, *Far Cry* (1943) and *The Inward Eye* (1946). His rejection of the lavish verbalism of the 'forties was complete; in his nine years' silence his writing matured into the elaborated observation, wit and mental dexterity for which he is now known, a development parallelling the trend in English poetry as represented by The Movement. Yet MacCaig remained something of an exotic, even if a peculiarly Scottish one. . . . His powers of observation free the writing from the limitations that metaphysicising usually impose, although it is wrong to hang on to the sensuous visual quality of his word-pictures as if nothing else happened in his poems. However, it is the sameness of method that can be criticised. MacCaig is a "noticing mind", and from what he observes he tries to make generalisations that expand to as wide an inclusiveness as possible. (p. 68)

In his later poems MacCaig has adopted free verse, but not, I think, with any great success. More successful are the formal poems in his collection *A Man in My Position,* poems such as **"Structures"**, or **"Green Stain"**, but especially that perfect short poem **"So Many Summers"**, which is less concerned to say the teasingly difficult thing, or make surprising leaps, or coax out conceits. Above all, personal experience is involved to a greater extent than is generally the case. (p. 69)

> *Douglas Dunn, "King Offa Alive and Dead," in*
> Encounter, *Vol. XXXVIII, No. 1, January, 1972, pp.*
> *67-74.**

ALAN BROWNJOHN

The White Bird is Norman MacCaig's twelfth volume, and since he seems unlikely, now, to change his manner—always sparking out bright, neo-metaphysical fancies in short bursts—it seems churlish to reiterate one's disappointments with his repetitions, more appropriate to consider real, if rather limited, virtues, and be grateful for them. The artificial finish many of his poems have (often rounding things off, after a good start, with a banality) is compensated for by slants which only MacCaig manages, things distinctly and inimitably his; such as gulls which cry like

> a corkscrew singing in the morning
> or the leading contralto in a choir of tombstones,
> or a shell-less egg, or a terrified slate,
> or the hinges of a door in the Hospital for the Insane,
> or a moonbeam mewing in its forest, or an icicle
> arguing with an icicle.

'Inward Bound', an ambitious poem about Edinburgh, about spiritual journeys and creative endeavours, and about himself, is impressively sustained, witty and touching. The love poems in the book vary greatly in quality: the last one, **'In the Mist'**, provides a simple and moving trope to end with. (pp. 701-02)

Alan Brownjohn, "Uneasy Does It," in New States-man, Vol. 85, No. 2199, May 11, 1973, pp. 701-02.

DOUGLAS DUNN

MacCaig is an inventive writer, full of the assurance that makes it possible to get away with artificial figures and properties such as sustained metaphors, rapid associations and similes. Many effects of that kind come closer to journalese than parts of a serious contemporary poetic. In his long poem **"Inward Bound"**, full of good writing, lines such as these take the heat off his seriousness:

> Swans still go over, seaplaning down
> to Dunsapple, and geese
> squeezing the bulbs of oldfashioned motor horns
> waver high over the Queen's Bath House.

Observations tarted up and enlivened by a mind quick to detect metaphorical possibilities in almost anything are standard writerly tricks. The trouble is that by now we have come to believe that MacCaig is too adept at that sort of effect for his own good, and that he indulges his talent for making unlikely associations too frequently. Similes and metaphors flash all over his poems, and, though often pleasing in themselves, constitute a superfluity the poem must somehow carry in order to get to its destination.

On the other hand, when his powers are under proper control, when his verbalising gifts have been subordinated to the expressive necessities of the poem, he can write with severe ingenuity:

> And the window,
> that pale psychiatrist, stands watching it all,
> and coming to dreadful decisions.

Entire poems, however, are sometimes based on amazing and empty conceits flogged half to death, as in his celebratory poem **"Musical Moment in Assynt"**. MacCaig has written more poems about Ben Suilven than men have climbed it.

Plainer and better poems are **"Milne's Bar"**, **"The White Bird"** and **"Ugly Corner"**, while in **"Behind a Shut Door"** he writes with the formal elegance and cunning he exemplified so often in his many earlier books. A more recent aspect of his work has been a degree of unease and fright, self-examination in a humane rather than intellectual situation. Bitterness in **"Behind a Shut Door"** is expressively and poetically in contrast with the charm of how the poem is written, while in **"Country Dance"** and **"New Tables"** he writes a puzzling, tight and intelligent surrealism. Free verse is now one of his basic procedures, and, like most poets who have originally leaned back on the skills of rhyming and scanning, he uses the seemingly more relaxed manner with a decent concern for the integrity of individual lines, and the overall control that gives a poem in free verse shape and style. MacCaig is one of the most intelligent and clever poets we have, and *The White Bird* is full of interesting subjects handled with skill, if not always economy. (pp. 80-1)

Douglas Dunn, "Mechanics of Misery," in Encounter, Vol. XLI, No. 2, August, 1973, pp. 79-85.

PETER PORTER

Norman MacCaig's skill almost overreaches itself in *The World's Room*. He has always been adept at keeping several balls in the air: his chief manner nowadays is to describe a natural scene while subjecting the very language of the description to semantic analysis as it goes along. The result can be too many fireworks for the reader, yet it is this virtuosity which makes the best poems so successful.... Throughout the book, in easy and in difficult poems, words turn into different versions of themselves while you read. The feeling is in the audacity of the tangents MacCaig uses to approach his subject. The effect is original and strange.

Peter Porter, "In Search of England," in The Observer, December 15, 1974, p. 27.

DOUGLAS DUNN

[Norman MacCaig's *The World's Room*] presumably takes its title from the border ballad "Edward"—"The world's room, let them beg through life." If beggary suggests independence and enterprising improvisation, then these have been virtues of MacCaig's poetry for years. Recently he has loosened up his forms and put more faith in free verse than would have seemed likely to a reader of his earlier books. As an artificer of hard lines, regular stanzas, rhymes, MacCaig is less self-consciously brilliant than used to be the case. A characteristic poem by MacCaig holds sensuous invention and intellectual resourcefulness together as part of the one ploy. His gleeful cunning in the use of words, though now less gleeful and less cunning than in the past, is still a practice he obviously enjoys....

Always attentive to turning reality upside down, inside out and outside in by a process of verbal wit, this has meant in MacCaig's work a fidelity to inspiring landscapes and places rather than social conscience. The poetry does not suffer because of that. The pictorial triumph that ends **"Blackbird in a Sunset Bush"** is proof enough—

> The gravity of beauty—
> how thoughtfully, how pensively he puts it,
> charcoal philosopher
> in his blazing study—

which has the disinterested charm and detachment that marks his best work. Interestingly, it survives his adoption of freer forms, which does say something about rhyme and metre.

> I can praise
> What never was tortured between true and false,

he says in **"One Way Journey."** Much of MacCaig's poetry fits into that area, an amoral, imaginative territory of mind, landscape and creatures. In **"Progress"** and **"Aesthetics"** he is more critical, attempting to dissociate himself from the obstructively mundane. The imaginative-intellectual harmony he wants, and in his best poems achieves, has led him into a colloquial surrealism in **"Between Two Nowheres."** A civilised dignity about his writing prevents him from taking even that tentative surrealism to the lengths that might be possible for a younger poet. *The World's Room* is the best of his recent collections.... (p. 74)

Douglas Dunn, "Natural Disorders," in Encounter, Vol. XLIV, No. 5, May, 1975, pp. 73-6.

RUSSELL DAVIES

[MacCaig] has an odd way of giving his brain hallucinatory things to do on the surface, while emotion goes on in ground-swells and undercurrents below. When the undercurrents are for any reason cut off, MacCaig is left in mid-air with a silly grin on his face, but this doesn't often happen in *Tree of Strings*, which is a satisfying replica of MacCaig's earth, 'Rolls-Royc-ing round the sun with its load of gangsters'. (p. 449)

Russell Davies, "Ah Well," in New Statesman, *Vol. 94, No. 2428, September 30, 1977, pp. 448-50.**

DOUGLAS DUNN

Mr MacCaig was noted in the past for a crisp, plain rhymed verse in which his tough-minded clarity and intellect gelled in the objects of his acute concentration. Only two poems in *Tree of Strings* rhyme. Throughout the book his writing is mostly in a jaunty free verse. It has developed in his poetry in the last ten years and he appears to have given himself over to it almost entirely.

His free verse has always struck me as second-rate in comparison with the excellence of his rhymed, formal poems. There have been times when I've wondered at *why* so accomplished a verse-maker should *want* looser forms of writing when the technique already developed in successive books was satisfyingly achieved. At the same time, it suggests a tendency to look upon the Scottish gift of resting on old laurels as a sin. His poetry has not been kept up to date by it, though a more naked, clearer honesty is revealed by Mr MacCaig's more recent style, as well as a more noticeable subjectivity. His imagination and inventiveness are also consistent enough for him to gain his newer style without sacrifice of artistry. His mind has the same, perhaps greater, freedom of play, even if the niceties which rhyme and metre once offered him are less intriguing as a result.

> . . . for I am the last of my race
> as you are, and she, and he is.

Lines like these have perhaps made MacCaig a difficult taste for nationalist readers to acquire. Presumably they acquire his nationality, and prefer his highland landscape poems—now increasingly elegiac—his background instead of his foreground. His attitude to nationality is implicit in an overall concern for the individuality of all persons and things and phenomena. Everything in his poems is a special case. His sense of delight is uncommon in contemporary poetry, and no less beguiling now than ever it was. (pp. 92-3)

Douglas Dunn, "Young Fools, Old Fools," in Encounter, *Vol. XLIX, No. 4, October, 1977, pp. 89-94.**

ERIK FRYKMAN

Norman MacCaig's poetical world can be easily defined first in some negative terms: it is not a public world of social commitment or indignation, nor one of strong passions whether of love or hatred. Geographically it is in one sense restricted: with the exception of a handful of poems set in Tuscany and in New York, the background is Scottish - Edinburgh townscapes and, usually, Highland landscapes.

But in another sense the background is not restricted: we are often in a world of wide, clear space, of seafronts opening on distant horizons, of monumental hills and mountains, of high winds and dynamic darknesses, seagulls, eagles, hawks and herons.

As often, or rather more often, we are in the presence of intimately observed, close-at-hand scenery: hayfields, country roads, lonely crofts and wells, cows and bulls, ducks and crows and sandpipers; or, for that matter, grimy streets and house-sparrows.

It is a world peopled pre-eminently with the poet himself and, in some cases, a woman addressed lovingly but often with feelings of bafflement and frustration mixed in; peopled also with a few admired Highland characters, a few eccentrics, a handful of individuals ironically or even spitefully observed. It is a world of intimately analysed states and changes of mind which seldom appear really disturbing, although this also happens. A very frequent pattern is for a description of scenery to turn subtly—sometimes rather too subtly—into one of an inner landscape, and for correspondences to be thus established between the physical and the mental. This is done with an obvious gift for metaphor which at times becomes over-ingenious; but also with great economy: almost without exception MacCaig's books of verse contain about sixty pages and very few poems are more than a page in length. It seems to me that of all the books *Rings on a Tree* is the one in which the lust for metaphor-making is most restrained and also the tendency, conspicuous here and there throughout his oeuvre, to express somewhat precious thought. Some of the poems are infused with deep sympathy for other people, others—particularly in the New York suite—are slightly ironical and satirical, and there are fine examples of pure, sensuous description. (p. 7)

Two other general characteristics should be added here. . . . One is the fact that throughout his career MacCaig has dared to be Scottish without writing in Lallans or even noticeably sprinkling his poems with dialect words. . . .

The other is that whereas there are few topicalities mentioned in the poems, they are nevertheless usually about the present: some are overtly reminiscent, but not very many. There are poems in which MacCaig brings in (of some one is tempted to say drags in) the time and space concepts, often in a somewhat vague manner. He does have a few more precise meditations on history and bygone times in some memorable poems, and in several cases he also adds a time dimension through his use of mythological imagery. (p. 9)

In all MacCaig's books of verse published so far there is only one poem that stands out by its length: **"A Man in Assynt"** in *A Man in My Position*. . . . It is a declaration of love for the Western Highlands—at the same time a quiet-toned paean, a lament, and an expression of guarded hope. It is characterised throughout by sensitively graphic pictures of the scenery and un unsentimental celebration of the country and what remains of its people. It is in several ways typical of MacCaig's manner of writing, of the way he takes in and marshals impressions, and of his views on life around him.

It begins and it ends with long views, in time and in space and, fittingly, with the two elements of scenery that MacCaig so often uses to convey grandeur and spaciousness: mountains and the sea. The introductory stanza is an evocation, half factual, half metaphorical, of the geological creation of the landscape; the end of the last stanza is a vision of a hoped-for future, a time of repopulation metaphorically expressed in terms of an incoming tide.

Into his scenery MacCaig introduces himself, as he normally does, and, also characteristically, in a manner that is not very obtrusive, unspoilt by emotional self-display. . . .

He sees himself as placed somewhere between the vast spaces and the near-at-hand objects of nature, an observer and a lover-in-vain:

> . . . And I,
> somewhere between them,
> am a visiting eye,
> an unrequited passion.
>
> (p. 63)

As always, he celebrates the grandeur, the quietness, the remoteness and unsulliedness, the natural dignity of place and people; but as always the sense of space is accompanied by the sense of nearness and intimacy. . . .

The tendency to juxtapose concrete and abstract elements of the objects observed is also in evidence:

> Greenshank, adder, wildcat, guillemot, seatrout,
> fox and falcon—the list winds through
> all the crooks and crannies of this landscape, all
> the subtleties and shifts of its waters and
> the prevarications of its air—. . . .

One also finds the typical transition from pure to metaphorical description, or vice versa:

> Hard labour can relax.
> The salty smell outside, which is made up
> of brine and seaweed
> and fish, reaches the pub door but
> is refused admittance, Here,
> men in huge jerseys drink small drinks.

This quotation also illustrates the ubiquitous anthropomorphising device, practised here as elsewhere on objects and concepts great and small. . . . (p. 64)

Physically, the centre of MacCaig's poetical universe is normally the Highlands, although Edinburgh sometimes intrudes; in time, the centre is normally the present, with occasional intrusions of the past. Not surprisingly, urban civilisation is brought into this poem, but only briefly . . . as a contrast, and without any jeering at its inferiority: there may be a note of regret in the observation that the land "sells itself" to tired townsfolk who outnumber the natives in the holiday season; but the passage develops into a celebration of the "natural decorum", the acceptance of the visitors on the part of the local people, and a celebration of jollity and fellow-feeling.

History is likewise brought in almost in passing, first as an observation on the Highland Clearances and the concomitant emigration. Whom does "this dying landscape" belong to? Is it to the dead?

> . . .
> to men trampled under the hoofs of sheep
> and driven by deer to
> the ends of the earth - to men whose loyalty
> was so great it accepted their own betrayal
> by their own chiefs and whose descendants now
> are kept in their place
> by English businessmen and the indifference of a
> remote and ignorant government.

History makes a second brief appearance, less pointed, more as a spectacle seen through the wrong end of the telescope, clear but far away. Although the brief vision is of battles long ago. MacCaig does not emphasise meaninglessness and destruction here. . . . [It] is with the present that the poem is mostly concerned. In view of its general character of a large, comprehensive view, it is not surprising that it should not contain any individualised portraits. . . . [A] general picture is conveyed, unsentimentally, of hard work, pub relaxation, witty gossip, sardonic commenting on local politics, and flocking on the Sabbath to the "bare stone box" of a kirk . . . , to the sharing of "the bitter honey of the Word". Here MacCaig develops the stanza into an unorthodox, almost Whitmanesque credo of acceptance, and of joy in the manifoldness of the creation. It seems characteristic of his general outlook on life and may serve as a fitting summing-up of much that he stands for:

> Ten yards from the sea's surge
> they sing to Him beautiful praises
> that surge like the sea,
> in a bare stone box built
> for the worship of the Creator
> of all colours and between-colours, and of
> all shapes, and of the holiness
> of identity and of the purifying light-stream
> of reason. The sound of that praise
> escapes from the stone box
> and takes its place in the ordinary communion
> of all sounds, that are
> Being expressing itself—as it does in its continuous,
> its never-ending creation of leaves,
> birds, waves, stone boxes—and beliefs,
> the true and the false.
>
> (pp. 65-6)

> *Erik Frykman, in his* "Unemphatic Marvels": A Study of Norman MacCaig's Poetry, *Acta Universitatis Gothoburgensis, 1977, 70 p.*

ROBERT GREACEN

On the death of Hugh MacDiarmid, Norman MacCaig became the most important living Scottish poet, so replacing a craggy experimentalist with a traditionalist who has mostly preferred to use established verse patterns. In recent years he has veered towards free verse. MacCaig's poetry is witty, compressed and fairly accessible to the general reader. His latest collection [*The Equal Skies*] opens with twelve poems in memory of a friend. These are intensely moving in their restraint. They are wholly untouched by sentimentality even when MacCaig is writing of his dead friend's collie: 'Do you remember your name was Mephistopheles, / though (as if you were only a little devil) / everyone called you Meph?' A handful of the remaining poems are on specially Scottish themes (**'Highland Games', 'The Kirk'**) and several of the most striking on animals: puffin, toad, earwig, ape. The poet sees himself as a guillemot 'that still dives / in the first way it thought of: poke your head under / and fly down'. MacCaig may lack MacDiarmid's rough power and allusive sweep but he is a much more original observer of the natural world and a more kindly poet to have around.

> *Robert Greacen, in a review of "The Equal Skies,"* in British Book News, *August, 1980, p. 498.*

DONALD CAMPBELL

All the poems [in *A World of Difference*] are short and pithy, full of insight and razor-sharp wit, and many of them demonstrate yet again MacCaig's abiding love affair with the Scottish Highlands. There are poems about animals and birds (one about a bullfinch and another, magnificent one about a bull), Scottish history, metaphysical poems, funny poems, poems in which MacCaig indulges in his favourite trick of ascribing contemporary characteristics to the classical figures of literature and mythology. Most prominent of all, however, are a number of poems which seem to be concerned with old age and the approach of death. If this is unsurprising in a poet who is now in his seventies, it is also a little deceptive. Although, in **'Old Man'**, MacCaig tells us that 'my bow is broken / my arrows without flight feathers', there are enough poems in this book (including that one) to provide us with evidence that this statement is far from being true. MacCaig's excoriating wit may have mellowed with the years—although it is hilariously to the fore in a poem about John Brown and Queen Victoria—but his gift for the memorable phrase and the fresh and telling image is as faultless as ever. Perhaps, then, the prevailing, valedictory tone is the opposite of what it seems—not a contemplation of death, but an acknowledgement of the enduring and rich possibilities of living.

> *Donald Campbell, in a review of "A World of Difference," in* British Book News, *October, 1983, p. 641.*

DONALD DAVIE

A World of Difference is good enough, seductive enough, to provoke a look over this poet's performance through the years. This should have happened with MacCaig's *Selected Poems* in 1978: but if such a 'retrospective' was then attempted, I missed it. What one finds in the career as a whole is development indeed, but unspectacular and not always welcome. What happened, for instance, to the elaborate baroque formality of some love poems in the third collection, *A Common Grace* (1960)? An idiom then splendidly mastered seems to have been discontinued since. These poems are epistemological at the same time as they are amorous; hence a title like **'Standing in My Ideas'**. . . . MacCaig no doubt, sensing which way the wind was blowing, dismantled the admittedly cumbrous machinery of such writing so as to fall into line with the more seemingly artless procedures that then came into vogue. But the virtues of such Herbertian or Drydenesque writing are undeniable and irreplaceable; and when the wheel of fashion has come full circle, they will be esteemed once again.

In any case, even as MacCaig wrestled into his verse such bold and abstruse conceptualising, he never lost touch with sensuous perception. . . .

In the more stripped and apparently casual style that he has practised since, MacCaig reached his peak, I think, in *Measures* (1965). It's in that collection that we find the momentous and uncompromising poem, **'Aspects'**. . . . 'Ancestors have no place . . .' MacCaig means it: the recorded human past is for him squalid and nonsensical, no patterns can be found in it such as might determine the present and point to a future, or a choice of futures. Thus in *A World of Difference* Clio, 'the Muse of history, yawning with boredom . . . has long since failed to be amused':

> Sighing, she licks her finger
> and wearily
> turns over another page . . .

In a poem called **'Queen of Scots'** MacCaig cocks a snook at the historical past as cheaply as if he were soliciting the suffrage of an uneducated and unremembering public. But even when the sentiment is expressed with more dignity, as in **'Aspects'**, it is still facile, surely. For one thing, it is a sentiment that no one can hold to consistently: if MacCaig really thinks that *all* history is squalid, how can he write as he does, a poem of finely melancholy indignation about the chapter of history that we call the Highland Clearances? It's impossible not to compare MacCaig, on this score, with MacDiarmid. If MacCaig's thoroughgoing scepticism about history has saved him from the self-contradictions, the absurdities and the duplicities that punctuated MacDiarmid's career, readers across the political spectrum may yet agree that MacDiarmid's engagement with history is one of the things we expect of a great poet, or of a poet ambitious to be great. And MacCaig's consistent refusal thus to engage himself cannot help but count against him.

> *Donald Davie, "Retrospective," in* London Review of Books, *February 2 to February 15, 1984, p. 10.*

JOHN MOLE

For Norman MacCaig, in his latest collection *A World of Difference,* "experience teaches/that it doesn't." It always has. MacCaig delights in the variousness of things and rings every possible change on them. A number of his recent poems have been preoccupied with themes of death, but they are as inventive as ever and the vigour of their conceits gives the Old Boy a run for his money. . . . MacCaig is for the ascendency of quick-witted invention in the face of mortality, and his brilliance with metaphor is a kind of escapology. If at times he seems just too prodigal for words, so that his language crumbles into those whimsical "flibbertigibbet fripperies" he claims to cherish in **"How to Cover the Ground"**, it is impossible to dislike these excesses. They come with the man, and, besides, they don't come too often. (pp. 51-2)

> *John Mole, "The Reflecting Glass," in* Encounter, *Vol. LXII, No. 3, March, 1984, pp. 46-52.**

DICK DAVIS

A great many of Norman MacCaig's poems are about cutting heroes down to size . . . , or puncturing the pretensions of myth and rhetoric. He opens one poem [in *A World of Difference*]—

> *In folds of fire*—there's a fine sounding
>   phrase.
> The reality
> Is different

and this is his strategy in almost every poem—set up a resonant Aunt Sally and then knock it down. This gets to seem cheap after a while and hardly worth doing (to say of Aeneas 'he was not only pious, he was stupid' is to say very little except that you don't like Virgil, and that is your loss, not Virgil's). MacCaig is best when he avoids myth and the modern world, both of which make him nervously glib. The poems about personal memories are the most convincing and moving because they are relatively free of his need to show that he is not being taken in.

> *Dick Davis, "Screggy and Co.," in* The Listener, *Vol. 112, No. 2867, July 19, 1984, p. 25.**

William Mastrosimone

19??-

American dramatist.

Mastrosimone's plays center on sexual conflicts. Through the employment of shocking, often grotesque action, Mastrosimone heightens dramatic tension and evokes a strong emotional response from his audience. His most widely recognized play, *Extremities* (1983), begins with an attempted rape. When the victim-assailant relationship is abruptly reversed, the audience responds by applauding the female character's vengeance. As her vigilante justice becomes increasingly sadistic, however, Mastrosimone raises pertinent questions about the social conditions that produce violence and limit basic human rights. A number of critics faulted the play's conclusion as melodramatic or unresolved, but most agreed that the power of *Extremities* results from Mastrosimone's ability to maintain audience involvement by exploring extreme circumstances which can provoke barbarous responses from civilized people.

Mastrosimone has written two other plays that focus on tense male-female confrontations. *The Woolgatherer* (1980) centers on two lonely people who attempt to overcome their anxieties, and *The Undoing* (1984) concerns the volatile relationship between a widowed alcoholic woman and the disfigured man who tries to help her.

JOHN SIMON

[*The Woolgatherer*] is a kind of blue-collar *Voice of the Turtle*. In it, a randy, fast-talking truck driver meets Rose, a dime-store salesgirl who spins romantic fantasies behind her candy counter and gathers the wool sweaters of men she brings to her eerie and pitiful hole-in-the-wall (the sweaters, in turn, have holes in the wool), where, apparently, she has a way of not consummating the affairs.

Here is the play's first problem. It makes Rose's present, crazy as it is, believable, but, despite long and sometimes tiresomely precious monologues, leaves her past unduly shrouded. Has she always been so naïve, so virginal, so too-good-and-pure-and-bonkers for this world? If so, how could she accumulate all those woolly mementos of pickups past? Or even cross a street with impunity? If, however, her sexual past is a reality, and she still floats about in all this fey, wheyey innocence, there is something curdled and bloodcurdling about her.

As for Cliff, he seems far too verbal, clever, sophisticated to have remained a trucker for this long. Though he evokes his past, both on the soul-flattening highways and on the rocky road through marriage, with compelling eloquence, it is his present I cannot believe. This witty and articulate young man (who, quite inconsistently, is given a few double negatives to make his collar bluer) could, at the very least, be climbing up in an ad agency and bedding down with fashion models rather than with a Rose who isn't a rose isn't a rose isn't a rose.

Aside from this, Mastrosimone writes consistently witty and sometimes lyrical dialogue, seems to have experienced and understood many of the things he writes about, and would

have, if he omitted the supererogatory second act, a more than respectable one-act play. (pp. 49-50)

John Simon, "A Different Drummer," in New York Magazine, *Vol. 13, No. 25, June 23, 1980, pp. 49-50.**

EDITH OLIVER

A new playwright named William Mastrosimone has made a very heartening beginning with **"The Woolgatherer."** ... A young truck driver, whose truck has broken down in South Philadelphia, picks up a girlish young woman working behind a candy counter and is invited back to her room. All the action takes place in that shabby, sparsely furnished room, and all the action is the interplay between the two of them. She is an innocent whose whole life is a matter of reveries and daydreams—the woolgatherer. He is tough and witty and, it soon becomes apparent, just as lonely and starved for love and sex as she is, and, for all his roughness and put-downs, just as frightened and tentative. ... There is no plot to speak of, but the surge of sexual longing propels the action at least three-quarters of the way through, when Mr. Mastrosimone seems to run out of play; the strength is in the characters and also in the dramatist's considerable humor. ... [The candy vendor's] role is less substantial and convincing than ... [the truck driver's], and more sentimental. At one point, she tells him, in a monologue, of seeing a gang of tough boys at a zoo stone and kill some wailing cranes—an experience so brutal that it has almost addled her wits. This anecdote, I think, should have been allowed to take its chances with the audience, instead of being repeated and stressed and pushed at us, for all its meaning or non-meaning. The truck driver, something of a woolgatherer himself, also has a long monologue, about his life on the road and his harassment by inspectors. ... **"The Woolgatherer"** could easily have been an actor's exercise, but the force of Mr. Mastrosimone's talent has made it a play. (pp. 100-01)

Edith Oliver, "Present Conditional and Past Perfect," in The New Yorker, *Vol. LVI, No. 29, September 8, 1980, pp. 100-01.**

FRANK RICH

The near-rape of the opening scene [in **"Extremities"**] is all too credible. Marjorie ... is lolling about the New Jersey farmhouse she shares with two female roommates who are off at work. It's a sunny day, so the screen door is unlatched. In walks Raul ..., an ill-shaven, ill-spoken, soiled-looking young man. After a few preliminary words, he is wrestling with the scantily clad Marjorie on the floor, smothering her with a pillow, demanding that she say "I love you" and worse. Much to everyone's credit, the scene is not exploitively staged. Only the sick could find it titillating; the response that's demanded and gotten is abject revulsion.

It is giving nothing away to say that Marjorie, through remarkably fortuitous circumstances, manages to escape Raul's clutches in a few minutes, at which point she binds and gags him, then stashes him in her living room fireplace. The rest of "Extremities" concerns the heroine's decision to take the law into her own hands. Marjorie feels that there's no point in calling the police, because it is impossible to present legal evidence that will prove a charge of attempted rape: judges and juries only believe women in court, she believes, when they are "dead on arrival." Rather than risk the possibility that her intruder will get off scot-free on technicalities, she decides to torture Raul and maybe even bury him in her garden.

As you can see, Mr. Mastrosimone is dealing with serious issues here, about both the pathology of rape and the inequities of the criminal justice system. But "Extremities" ultimately blurs the issues rather than illuminates them because the story is pure, contrived melodrama. The play begins to lose touch with reality as soon as Marjorie miraculously escapes her formidable tormentor and drifts further and further afield from credible human behavior as its revenge story proceeds.

Mr. Mastrosimone's method for making his story plausible is to tell it as tersely as possible and to fill it with ciphers. That way we won't have time to question the narrative logic, and we won't have complex human feelings and motivations to examine and perhaps dispute. "Extremities" practically speeds along from one plot point to the next, and, the rapist excepted, gives us characters who are defined by a few opaque personality traits.

It may be that Mr. Mastrosimone just doesn't yet know how to write female roles—that was the one failing of his admirable previous work, "The Woolgatherer." In this effort, all we learn about Marjorie is that she's unemployed, is "a typical Leo," reads Glamour magazine and tends to dress in a sexually inviting manner. Her two roommates, who return home to argue against Marjorie's course of action for much of the evening, are a psychobabble-spouting parody of a bleeding-heart liberal . . . and a dim-witted loser . . . who was once herself a rape victim.

The roommates are quickly and easily manipulated by the grotesque, crude-mouthed Raul into taking pity on him and siding against Marjorie—one of the many manufactured developments that we have to take on faith. The only real motivation for this surprising demarcation of battle lines is that it gives the playwright the means to launch a debate about civil liberties, vigilante justice and the social forces that spawn sexual aggression. But because the people doing the arguing aren't real, the debate seems synthetic—a hypothetical argument with too many fictional variables to persuasively plead or even define any case.

What Mr. Mastrosimone finally ends up with is a reverse-gender variation on "Death Wish," with a slightly higher patina of sociological sophistication, wit and pungent dialogue. It's reasonably inoffensive, all things considered, until we reach the most unfortunate final scene. It's then that the author abandons all pretense of seriousness. He provides a ludicrous fairy tale ending that ducks a stand on any issue, that happily resolves the fate and relationships of all three women and that concludes with the sentimental suggestion that rapist and rape victim alike are bound together by a common humanity.

Frank Rich, "Miss Sarandon in 'Extremities'," in The New York Times, *December 23, 1982, p. C14.*

ROBERT BRUSTEIN

After trying to make a case for the production of neglected American plays in the belief that they are at least equal to recent imports, I am embarrassed by the one example under review this week. William Mastrosimone's *Extremities* . . . has more knuckles than fingers, a crude fist of a play being punched through a highly melodramatic production. After a relatively convincing beginning involving an attractive woman being terrorized by a brutal would-be rapist in an isolated rural house, the evening settles into a series of incredibly contrived twists and turns, proceeding on the implausible premise that, having subdued the thug and manacled him in the fireplace, the woman would rather commit murder than call the police (her argument is that the courts would inevitably acquit him and charge her with assault). Having made this bizarre determination, she sprays his eyes with Raid, scalds him with boiling water, tortures him with a paint roller, wraps an electric cord around his throat and pulls, pours gas over his body and threatens to ignite it, and finally decides to finish him off with a hammer (the vocal reaction of the audience to these various acts is more edifying than the events). . . .

It is the playwright's intention, apparently, to show how relatively mild people can be changed into murderers and tyrants in extreme situations, but since none of these people has any character outside the event, the theme is no more convincing than the plot. . . . *Extremities* is the melodramatic equivalent of a TV sit-com—call it a sit-dram. It exists not for its own sake so much as for the response it can manipulate from the spectator. But I think I prefer a laugh track to the kind of vindictive animal noises being squeezed out of audiences [during *Extremities*]. . . . (p. 28)

Robert Brustein, "The British Conquest," in The New Republic, *Vol. 188, No. 6, February 14, 1983, pp. 26-8.**

GERALD WEALES

Extremities begins with an attempted rape in which the intended victim, a can of bug spray happily at hand, turns the tables on her tormentor. At the first blackout (scene break), the man is blinded and the woman is strangling him with the wire of the telephone he earlier pulled out of the wall. The audience with which I saw the play went wild with approval. There are a variety of ways of reading that unstinting applause. The audience may have wanted to show its admiration for [the actors], whose performances were graphically convincing. It may have been yelling for a rescue as children did when I was a boy whenever the cavalry rode in to save the beleaguered wagon train. I think the response was as much visceral as theatrical, that the audience, full of people who had been mugged if not raped or whose close friends had so suffered, was signaling their desire if not their ability to fight back.

The opening scene and the response to it allowed the play to get off to a rousing start, to carry the audience through the long stretch of verbal fencing between Marjorie and the man whom she has imprisoned in the fireplace. (p. 180)

Raul is a despicable man, a rapist and murderer, who preys on the helpless. In a confession scene at the end of the play, he and the playwright suggest that he is helpless himself, a prey of his compulsion, but this psychological sentimentality is not portrayed through most of the play. The man we see is cruel and dangerous, but he is also inventive, manipulative, a bad but dedicated liar with a taste for ethical and therapeutic clichés and a twisted talent for comic lines. He has a way of besting Marjorie, forcing her to respond with an act or a threat of violence. At the beginning of the play we have seen Marjorie react to a wasp bite by first killing the insect and then burning it with her cigarette. For most of the play, we watch her behaving in a way that makes her seem more malevolent than her prisoner. I think that Mastrosimone wants to make a point . . . about the way the extremities of contemporary life bring to the surface the violence and anger that were once held under by what used to be called civilizing forces.

The character of Raul, however well conceived, is essentially a device, an occasion for Marjorie to reveal herself and, more important, to show her in concert and in conflict with the two women with whom she shares the house. Patricia is presumably a professional of some kind (she carries a briefcase)—a teacher, a social worker, a personnel director. She is the parodied voice of reason and liberal understanding, a comic figure in a non-comic situation, quite certain that the problem of Raul can be taken care of by orderly discussion. Terry, once a rape victim, would prefer to hide, to separate herself from what is going on; she is essentially cheerful, very uncertain, given to oblique bursts of rebellion against the dominance of both Marjorie and Patricia. Raul uses one woman against another, eliciting sympathy from Terry and Patricia, casting himself as the innocent victim of the vicious Marjorie. The audience, having witnessed the opening scene, knows that Marjorie's view of the rapist is a correct one, but the other two characters, who can see only an implacably murderous Marjorie and a blinded, trussed-up wheedling man, come to doubt their roommate. The irony of their responses, the implicit comment on our tendency to judge people and situations from the self-assurance of inadequate information, has a particularly ugly overtone here. What surfaces is the distrust, the dislike, the envy that the two other women feel for Marjorie; they respond in ways that are usually considered stereotypically male, assuming that Marjorie's habitual manner is an invitation to rape. The disintegration of this group of women is the best thing about Mastrosimone's play. Effective not simply as the dramatic presentation of three specific women, it suggests the precariousness of any relationship in which the shared sympathy and congeniality (which exists here too) is tested by a disorienting crisis.

The ending of *Extremities* is an ambiguous and, I think, a weak one. I had read Mastrosimone's script a few years ago, and one of my fellow playgoers, caught up in the drama, said at intermission, "Oh, you know how it comes out." I suddenly realized that I knew no such thing, that I had forgotten the ending. The reason is that there is no way, short of cataclysm, to bring this play to a close. Mastrosimone's is more of a way out than an inevitable finish. Raul, having been forced into a confession by the knife-wielding Marjorie, is left alone with her while the other two women go for the police. He asks if he can return to the fireplace, crawls blindly to his cage which is now his sanctuary and curls up in the fetal position, singing crazily to himself. Marjorie sits beside the fireplace, discards her weapons and begins to cry. Who are the tears for? The unfortunate Raul? Herself and the creature she has become? The empathetic audience, fellow inhabitants of a world gone awry? All of this? Described this way the final image may seem to be a rich and elusive one, but to me it looked like a trick, a too neat solution to a difficult problem, stage gesture as a substitute for emotional and artistic force. I found myself thinking back to other moments in which the playwright or the director was too intrusive, upstaging the seriousness of the play. That is unfortunate, for *Extremities* is more than a flashily staged, very well-acted evening of theater. Mastrosimone and his characters have some scary things to say about friends and enemies and the uneasy line between them. (pp. 180-81)

Gerald Weales, "What's A Friend For?" in Commonweal, *Vol. CX, No. 6, March 25, 1983, pp. 180-81.*

CHARLES BROUSSE

The press release calls it "a romantic comedy," but *The Woolgatherer* stretches the meaning of that description to its limit— if this is romantic comedy, so is Tennessee Williams' *Streetcar Named Desire*. There are funny moments, to be sure, mainly deriving from apt one-liners in the dialogue, but the overall atmosphere is heavy with sexual turmoil and forebodings of dark revelations to come. The audience, rather than remaining disconnected . . . , is invited to enter an emotional hothouse in which the basic question is why the characters on stage can't physically consummate what is quite obviously a shared psychic need.

William Mastrosimone, author of *The Woolgatherer,* is a young Eastern writer who made his mark recently with a play called *Extremities,* currently enjoying successful runs in both New York and Los Angeles. My reference to *Steetcar* was not accidental since Mastrosimone's preoccupation with repressed desire and his manner of expressing it in dramatic terms have been compared with Williams, the undisputed master of the genre.

Charles Brousse, in a review of "The Woolgatherer," in Pacific Sun, *Year 22, No. 2, January 13-19, 1984, p. 19.*

DAVID R. GOETZ

"The Undoing" was the sharpest and most compelling play in a strong repertory at Actors Theatre of Louisville's Humana Festival of New American Plays. . . .

The setting of "The Undoing" is the slaughter room of a poultry market where the owner, an alcoholic woman in her mid-30s, kills off chickens and liquor with grim determination and little enthusiasm. . . .

A stranger, a damaged man with a limp and an eyepatch, comes to fill an opening at the market and in the owner's bed. He's a recovered alcoholic and is determined to help her stop drinking and to make things right again. (That's the sense of the title, the wish to undo what has been done.)

Mastrosimone relentlessly blurs the distinctions between realism and absurdity. The stormy owner's last name is Tempesta, two neighborhood crones drop in to gather eggs from the chicken coops and to feed on her emotional problems, the pantomimed killing of chickens is a constant center of focus throughout. But he never leaves reality too far behind and his little dips into the absurd are dynamic. (p. 91)

David R. Goetz, "Works By Mastrosimone, Mann Top Louisville Play Festival," in Variety, *April 4, 1984, pp. 91-2.**

M. D. AESCHLIMAN

A skeletal description of *The Undoing* is unpromising and even distasteful. The play uses large elements of extremity, melodrama, and the grotesque. . . . *The Undoing* is set in the slaughtering room of a big-city poultry business that Lorraine is trying to keep going after the death of her husband at the hands of a drunk driver. She is rapidly drowning in alcoholism, despair, and guilt, when a mysterious, crippled stranger appears on the scene, apparently looking for a job. Out of these common, gloomy, and depressing elements, William Mastrosimone has fashioned a play of power and poignancy. The raw squalor and horror not only feel true, they work to some purpose. Only superficially and initially does the play resemble the mindless avant-garde, in which rage, shock, and obscenity are required for the *succès de scandale*. Instead, Mastrosimone is dealing honestly and convincingly with guilt and expiation, and also, not incidentally, with the inexorability and the dignity of work, a Conradian theme and a true one: work as a support for sanity, work as a means of expiation, work as a form of hope. (p. 45)

M. D. Aeschliman, "The Violent Bear It Away," in National Review, *Vol. XXXVI, No. 9, May 18, 1984, pp. 44-5.**

PATRICIA KEENEY SMITH

Some of the finest recent dramatic writing encompasses an admirably stringent and compassionate response to both the economic and emotional extremes of modern life. William Mastrosimone's *Extremities,* which I saw in London, is about rape, the law, victims, loyalty and treason, terror and strength and finally, astonishingly, about humanity. With a cast of four, a simple set, immediately accessible language and situation and [powerful acting] . . . *Extremities* is a knockout. . . .

There is humour in the play. The intruder manufactures stories with the alacrity of a standup comic and swears oaths like a terrified little boy, half mocking, half afraid. "I watched you riding your bike in those little white shorts, and you looked at me like I was a dead dog." . . .

Marjorie's two roommates return from work. They are stereotypes that really sting. One is a paranoiac young woman wearing current attitudes like armour, because once, when small and dressed up as Tinker Bell, she was raped. Since then, she's done "what all good little girls do: nothing!" Roommate number two bleats out the jargonistic propaganda of situational ethics and the inviolability of "relationship," on the naive assumption that there is no evil in the world, just bad upbringing and wrong interpretation. Morality, legality and female solidarity desert them both at the first sign of trouble, leaving Marjorie at the mercy of sheer survival tactics. "You don't have a case," she's told by her reasonable, traitorous friends, who also suggest she "dresses loose." "No, but I do have a hammer." It is, finally, Marjorie's hammer of independence, integrity and deep, if beleaguered humanity, that bangs the audience into thinking and feeling for itself, rather than merely attitudinizing.

With such specimens as *Extremities* and Marsha Norman's *'night Mother,* contemporary drama in plain, honest garb illustrates its ability to communicate the individual dilemmas produced by a violence that has become as commonplace as dirty dishes. Ill-served by theatrical exaggeration, by spurious and often costly attempts to entertain an audience with visuals or histrionics, these plays live or die on timing and subtext; that is, on the work of scrupulous theatre professionals whose main aim is to exhibit the truth of the text. These plays will not yield to burlesque satire or salaciousness. The lives they convey are ordinary to the point of boredom, but perilous, too. This is not a danger, however, that finds justification in either the thrilling or the illicit; it is simply sordid. The genius of these dramatic pieces lies in their surprising revelation of humanity through the inarticulate. They play out, physicalize, the world of tension behind the words, behind the eyes, behind the body's attacking lunge or draped defence. To do this requires consummate theatrical skill. (p. 38)

Patricia Keeney Smith, "Theatre of Extremity," in The Canadian Forum, *Vol. LXV, No. 748, April, 1985, pp. 37-8, 40.**

John McPhee

1931-

American journalist and nonfiction writer.

McPhee's witty and informative nonfiction pieces on a variety of subjects have earned him critical and popular acclaim. His diverse topics include former basketball player Bill Bradley; oranges; the Pine Barrens of New Jersey; nuclear bombs; and the state of Alaska. McPhee's books contain a plethora of facts, yet he is consistently praised for his clear, concise language and his entertaining prose style. *Coming into the Country* (1977), about McPhee's journey across Alaska, is among his most popular works and is considered by many critics to be his finest book. A staff writer for *The New Yorker*, McPhee bases most of his books on essays originally published in that magazine.

George Core wrote that "the essence of McPhee's fascination with the actual world is revealed in his attachment to character." McPhee's first two books, *A Sense of Where You Are* (1965) and *The Headmaster* (1966), profile respectively Bill Bradley and Frank Boyden, the headmaster of Deerfield Academy. In later works, McPhee's subjects are sometimes placed in physical or ideological conflict with one another. In *Levels of the Game* (1971) he recounts a tennis match between Arthur Ashe and Clark Graebner; more important than his description of an athletic contest, however, is McPhee's exploration of each player's personality and how it influences his playing style. The protagonist of *Encounters with the Archdruid* (1971) is George Brower, a dedicated conservationist. In this work McPhee presents Brower's meetings with three men who each want to develop wilderness land for human benefit. In each of these books as well as in other works, McPhee celebrates an individual's or a group's dedication to a particular ideal, avocation, or profession. For example, *Basin and Range* (1981) and *In Suspect Terrain* (1983) are based on his experiences with geologists who studied rock formations in the western and northeastern United States.

Several of McPhee's books collect his essays on a variety of subjects. These include *A Roomful of Hovings and Other Profiles* (1968), *Pieces of the Frame* (1975), *The John McPhee Reader* (1977), and *Giving Good Weight* (1979). Richard Horwich stated that McPhee's success is due to his powers of description, which "are such that we often feel the shock of recognition even when what is being described is totally outside our experience. . . . McPhee penetrates the surface of things and makes his way toward what is essential and unchanging."

(See also *Contemporary Authors*, Vols. 65-68.)

THE NEW YORK TIMES BOOK REVIEW

If you think 149 pages of oranges are more oranges than you need, you are right. Not even John McPhee, one of the better new non-fiction writers, can remove the pulp from [his book titled "**Oranges**"], which ran as a two-part series in The New Yorker last year. At the time, it was almost a parody of New Yorker subject matter (trivial) and manner (leisurely). It should have been allowed to rest there, an unread filler for the slick ads, but instead a book was squeezed out of it. So we have

© Nancy Crampton

. . . everything to delight the passionate orange lover. For the others, it will seem sheer navel-contemplation.

> A review of "*Oranges*," in The New York Times Book Review, *February 26, 1967, p. 45.*

RODERICK COOK

[*Oranges*] is a surprising book. You may come to the end of it and say to yourself, "But I *can't* have read a whole book about *oranges*!" But the chances are you will have done so, for Mr. McPhee takes this one simple fruit and makes a compote out of it. He writes like a charm, and without being cute, gimmicky, or in any way dull, he just tells you a lot about oranges. . . . It's a delicious book, in a word, and more absorbing than many a novel.

> Roderick Cook, in a review of "*Oranges*," in Harper's Magazine, *Vol. 234, No. 1402, March, 1967, p. 139.*

PAMELA MARSH

John McPhee ought to be a bore. He has all the qualifications. With a bore's persistence he seizes a subject, shakes loose a cloud of more detail than we ever imagined we would care to hear on any subject—yet somehow he makes the whole procedure curiously fascinating. . . .

[The five essays in **"A Roomful of Hovings and Other Profiles"**] are what the title of the book says they are—profiles, not biographies. There is a little life-history mixed up in every one of them, but obviously Mr. McPhee intends to show his subjects as they are now, though of course the past has some bearing on that. The impression given is that the book is telling us only what an intelligent listener could learn about the man if he had him to himself for an hour (or even a day) or so.

In **"A Roomful of Hovings"** Mr. McPhee is applying his own particular blend of microscope and telescope to show us Thomas P.F. Hoving (. . . a Director of the Metropolitan Museum); Fuell Theophilus, wild-food expert . . . ; Robert Twynam, groundsman at Wimbledon; T. H. Fielding. Several of MIT's Fellows in Africa share a chapter between them. . . .

[Mr. McPhee serves up] endless minutiae with a raconteur's flair. It is a gift that has a lot to do with enthusiasm. . . .

Pamela Marsh, *"The Lively Snippet, the Appetizing Trifle,"* in The Christian Science Monitor, *February 1, 1969, p. 9.*

CAROLYN F. RUFFIN

John McPhee writes a good announcer's script for the games people play.

His account of the political and social overtones of a tennis match between Arthur Ashe and Clark Graebner—**"Levels of the Game"**—has the feel of a good swift forehand slice.

If only for the style, the book is worth encountering. It's terse almost to the point of being cryptic. Mr. McPhee's athletic prose moves the attention deftly back and forth from the family background, upbringing, trials, political leanings, dress habits, and temperamental quirks of Ashe to those of Graebner.

Sometimes he swings into a long lob of biographical material. At other times he concentrates strictly on the tension that can mount in a match played by two men who have grown up in the tennis world together and who know each other more than well.

Whatever his approach, he so varies and paces his style that he holds the reader by his sheer technical skill. **"Levels of the Game"** has its own rules. It doesn't pretend to be "real." It only serves to test the skill of the writer over the circumstance he sets up. Mr. McPhee set his task this way: Don't be chronological. At whatever point, Ashe's or Graebner's background or temperament is reflected in the game, put it into the action as a kind of flashback.

For instance, talking about Ashe's cool manner during a tight spot in the set, Mr. McPhee quotes Graebner. . . .

After a few paragraphs on Ashe's early experience in tennis, Mr. McPhee is back describing the semifinal match of the first United States Open that is the setting for the book.

Mr. McPhee has the control to pull the whole feat off again and again. He exercises such restraint—balancing Graebner with Ashe and Ashe with Graebner—that it would seem the book should end in a tie.

But Ashe is black. And he emerges as the underdog, gets most of the cheers, works hard for his win, and wins. Also he plays flamboyant tennis and takes chances. That gives him, at least

as a literary character in the hands of Mr. McPhee, a certain advantage of glamour. Graebner plays conservative tennis.

In the meanwhile, Mr. McPhee succeeds in displaying the levels of more than tennis. He puts his style to work on the classes of American society and the way people "make it." He sets individuals up with a cool wit and undercuts them with their own words. . . .

Mr. McPhee pits the homespun philosophy of Ashe's father against the superficial bragging of Graebner's father. By the juxtaposition he accomplishes a kind of psychological crunch on middle-class America.

"Levels of the Game" isn't just a tennis book; though even for one who isn't a fan it is a fascinating sports account. Mr. McPhee's book is a compact sociology. It has the tone of a coolly executed drama about intertwined loyalties. And it scores well on all levels.

Carolyn F. Ruffin, *"Tennis in a Writer's Net,"* in The Christian Science Monitor, *December 24, 1969, p. 13.*

NEIL MILLAR

[In **"The Crofter and the Laird,"** John McPhee] has given us journalism rather than literature, and it is first class of its kind.

If it reveals little, it reports much, and the much is interesting—even fascinating. The pages do not hurl us forward on breakers of mental music, and that was not intended; the cool, accomplished, comfortable prose saunters into our attention, strolls about its subject, and is still sauntering, still reminiscing, when the last period falls like a blunt instrument on the last fraught sentence. . . .

[Mr. McPhee] has shown us a tiny world on the world's edge, and if his landscapes seem all background, his figures—mostly in the middle distance—breathe and talk. . . .

Their talk is more—or less—than talk, they gossip. Mr. McPhee reports a good deal of the gossip, and with considerable effect. Humanity has always interested itself, and islanders possess sharp eyes, quick tongues, ready ears. Their gossip is almost a communal art form:

"What is said in these places will frequently include a high proportion of factual incorrectness, but truth and fiction often seem to be riding the same sentence in such a way that the one would be lonely without the other."

This mixture, of course, can be found in other places than the Hebrides; fact and "factual incorrectness" (Mr. McPhee's typewriter can sport a delicate half-smile) form many a little tangled skein in the great knot of the world. **"The Crofter and the Laird"** gives so many gossip-samples on any one topic—and they often contradict each other so thoroughly—that we are saved from jumping to conclusions. We either jump to confusions or wade to conclusions.

Mr. McPhee is meticulous. He takes no sides; and if he did take sides he would certainly put them back where he found them, when he had finished with them.

The book offers us glimpses, watchings, and encounters, the past and present of a place in which the 20th century is still arriving and the 18th still departing. Coolly, cleanly, unromantically, honestly, we are shown a hard-faring life and a firm Highland people. The book may or may not lure us along the Road to the Isles, but it does show what we might see if we went there with our eyes open.

> Neil Millar, *"His Heart's in the Hebrides,"* in The Christian Science Monitor, *July 9, 1970, p. 15.*

JOHN HAY

After I finished reading **Encounters with the Archdruid,** what predominated in my mind was the idea of power, though it is not a part of the book's tone at all. John McPhee writes with conscious balance and sophistication. In writing about four men—or three played off against David Brower as protagonist—the author is purposefully noncommittal, though his admirations creep in. Anyone looking for good and evil, heroes and villains, moral lessons, and so on, will go away scratching his head.

These encounters between a crusading conservationist and three other men [Charles Fraser, Charles Park, and Floyd Dominy] who got their success from a different kind of religion with respect to nature—one that sees man first—take place in continental settings of great splendor: in the Glacier Peak Wilderness, on the Colorado River, on untouched Cumberland Island off the Georgia coast. Here they hurl their ironies at each other, they state their cases, they give way to silence; but the authority behind them is the land. The half-spoken theme is the conflict in men between their power to extract rewards from nature, considered as an end in itself, and another impulse in man which is to save nature, even to propitiate it. Nature in the long run will set its own terms, but we go on contending over her as usual, while the thunderclouds gather overhead.

You may come away convinced that Brower is America's most effective conservationist and a great man; or that he is an aesthete, a "preservationist"—which is the so-called practical man's epithet—or that he is hopelessly nostalgic. McPhee leaves you to draw your own conclusions. (p. 4)

It is hard to predict the outcome in the encounter between the great American plunder machine, and our lakes, rivers, and forests. As this book subtly suggests, there are many human sides to the problem. (p. 7)

> John Hay, *"In Defense of Wilderness,"* in Book World—The Washington Post, *August 15, 1971, pp. 4, 7.*

THE NEW REPUBLIC

[**The Deltoid Pumpkin Seed**] is the success story of a failure, tracing the invention, development, testing and completion of a wingless aerobody—neither airship nor airplane—by a group of dedicated amateurs. It comes complete with historical background, on-the-spot descriptions of the key events and capsule biographies of the many unusual men involved. . . . John McPhee can make almost any subject interesting. . . . Here his primary subject is the aerobody . . . , a strange structure deriving from the blimps and rigid airships with which many of its developers were once associated, and his discussion is often larded with the technical terms of aerodynamics and flight. But as usual his interest focuses not on the mechanical facts but on the human issues involved, the personalities of a handful of unusual men who mix their technical expertise with an almost obsessive affection for unusual aircraft, and the two theologically oriented men who successively directed the enterprise to its curious end. We explore their motives, their interactions, their hopes

and their varied forms of resignation . . . and meanwhile McPhee skillfully maintains suspense over whether or not the final model . . . will manage to pass its long-delayed testing. . . . What McPhee manages so deftly should not be laid out with drab explicitness in a review; at the risk of leaving the subject up in the air, one will say only that McPhee has done for the pumpkin seed what he did for the orange.

> A review of *"The Deltoid Pumpkin Seed,"* in The New Republic, *Vol. 169, No. 9, September 1, 1973, p. 33.*

SANDRA SCHMIDT ODDO

John McPhee has an eye and an ear and a typewriter that operate like the camera and full crew of a documentary film studio. Give him a theme and he comes up with a picture: edited, cross-cut, spliced and orchestrated, specific and full of the facts and the atmosphere of that theme. The picture, like a good documentary, carries its own emotional impact as well as, in this case, an urgent imperative.

McPhee's style is Journalism 101 elevated to the ranks of Art. He uses short sentences, no passive verbs, paragraphs that pursue their subjects with flat-statement, singleminded intensity. He uses them—the art of it—with easy grace, fluidity; and he has the courage to drop raw observations into seemingly unrelated contexts and leave them there reverberating as signals for the reader to interpret. He is also very, very good at breaking down specialized jargon into plain English, at interpreting the ways of scientists for the layman, at understanding and enjoying processes of thought, of invention, of human behavior.

> Sandra Schmidt Oddo, *"How Not to Make an Atomic Bomb,"* in The New York Times Book Review, *June 23, 1974, p. 4.*

ANN D. FOLEY

The **"Curve of Binding Energy"** is a collection of gossip and sensationalism; it is neither a journey into the "awesome and alarming world of Theodore B. Taylor," as its jacket proclaims, nor a reliable handbook on the vulnerability of weapons-grade nuclear material. Half biography, half essay with scant documentation, its main purpose seems to be the publication of a simplified blueprint for building a backyard atom bomb. . . . [John McPhee] does justice neither to Taylor, a truly remarkable man, nor to the very serious problems involved in the vulnerability of the nuclear industry to terrorist attack and diversion of materials.

> Ann D. Foley, *"Another Warning,"* in Bulletin of the Atomic Scientists: a magazine of science and public affairs, *Vol. XXX, No. 8, October, 1974, p. 49.*

EDWARD HOAGLAND

My own favorite among McPhee's books is **"The Pine Barrens"** (1968). This is a direct loving look at the people and social and natural history of the piney belt of New Jersey, beginning with a chatty old bachelor cranberryman whom we meet lunching on raw onions. It's boyish but masterful. . . . [**"Encounters With the Archdruid"** (1971) focuses on] . . . the conservation warrior, David Brower, and the book, besides being a more difficult project to undertake, wound up more urbane, edited and neutral in tone than his paean to the Pine

Barrens. I found it a little too much so, but McPhee may have been trying to obviate the most telling complaint I have heard against him: that of hero-worship.

His early study of the basketball star, Bill Bradley ["**A Sense of Where You Are**" (1965)], is marred in this way, according to followers of the sport—Bradley being not nearly the player McPhee describes, so that the book's central presupposition betrays him. His account of Frank Boyden of Deerfield Academy, "**The Headmaster**" (1966), records all the good things that might have been said for the man and the school but few of the bad . . . with the result that although McPhee writes more gracefully than Peter S. Prescott, who wrote about Choate in "A World of Our Own," Prescott's book is a truer profile of a prep school. . . .

The late pieces in this collection ["**Pieces of the Frame,**" as well as] "**Travels in Georgia**" and "**Ruidoso,**" and "**The Survival of the Bark Canoe,**" which appeared in The New Yorker too recently to have been included here, come close to being matchless. McPhee writes about people whose company he enjoys . . . and one has the sense always with him of a man at a pitch of pleasure in his work, a natural at it, finding out on behalf of the rest of us how some portion of the world works. He is most comfortable side by side with a chum rather than alone with his thoughts, but is preeminently a student of how people who are good at something do what they do: of craftsmanship, and people who in a private way thrive. (p. 3)

As a magazine specialist . . . he must constantly skirt the temptation to be clever and quick, if not glib, to be neat, not ambitious, in scale, to be understandable immediately, pat in staging his material, readable backwards or forwards or sideways—to be liked and to entertain. One has the feeling, in fact, that too many of his subjects have found his pieces pleasing. . . . And so one wants him, now in midlife, to blast out, leave the "editorial counsel" and his familiar Princeton environs behind, be less the passive photographer, and seek his fortunes on harsher ground. This is not to suggest he should abandon his posture of optimism for some groupie's variety of nouveau pessimism, running with the herd—only that he should test it further.

"**Pieces of the Frame**" is an interim collection of the sort that can't do much one way or another for an author's career. It contains several comely potboilers about Scotland presumably written to pay for vacations there, some trivia about basketball in the Tower of London from his Timewriter days, magazine "fact" pieces about gathering firewood and canoeing, a fine action montage about Wimbledon, and a curious roam through Atlantic City, draped on the frame of a game of Monopoly. This last, which is called "**The Search for Marvin Gardens,**" is saved from being meretricious by its unexpected seriousness—he actually does "Go To Jail." (pp. 3, 26)

Anchoring the book at the end is "**Ruidoso,**" which is one of those essays any writer might hope to have in his hand in that split-second when he presents himself for judgment at St. Peter's Gate and must overbalance all of his life's little shabbinesses with a single swift piece of work. This one is about quarterhorses and racing people and is written with the special omniscience McPhee has mastered as a technique, and of course with love, always his strong suit. (p. 26)

> *Edward Hoagland, "From John McPhee with Love and Craftsmanship," in* The New York Times Book Review, *June 22, 1975, pp. 3, 26.*

RICHARD HORWICH

Judging from *Pieces of the Frame,* [John McPhee has] a romantic temperament, which often inclines him toward the rough, wild places—the swamps of rural Georgia; . . . the savage Nantahala River in North Carolina, where canoeing (one of McPhee's passions) "is like going down the New Jersey Turnpike in a fog"; Ruidoso Downs, in the mountains of New Mexico, where 10 horses compete for three-quarters of a million dollars in a race that lasts 22 seconds; Loch Ness, in whose opaque depths men search for what may turn out to be the world's biggest worm.

Yet McPhee is a civilized man, at home in big cities. . . . He's a lover of sports and social pastimes, as addicted to Monopoly, tennis and basketball as he is to forests and rivers. The contrast between the worlds through which he moves—between the natural and the artificial, the real and the symbolic, the enduring and the ephemeral—is the thread that runs through these 10 essays. . . .

There is a view of the world implicit in all this. . . . To the novice canoemen of "**Reading the River,**" a fast stream may seem "a chaos of flow and spray," but, as the title suggests, there are those who can navigate it, and McPhee celebrates their craftsmanship, discipline and self-sufficiency wherever he finds it. . . .

Of course a writer's personal vision isn't worth much unless he can lend it to us. But McPhee's powers of description are such that we often feel the shock of recognition even when what is being described is totally outside our experience. I have never played Laver (thank God), but I know exactly what McPhee means, in "**Centre Court,**" when he speaks of a forehand drive that comes over the net "fast, heavy, fizzing with topspin." Sometimes it seems that McPhee deliberately chooses unpromising subjects, just to show what he can do with them. In "**Firewood,**" for example, he tells us that "firewood, in essence, is mysterious" and then makes good on that unlikely claim in an unlikely way—by explaining to us the chemistry of combustion. . . . The result is that fire, approached through science, seems magical, a sort of pyrotechnical alchemy in which "incandescent carbon particles, by the tens of millions, leap free of the log and wave like banners, as flame."

The appeal of fire is basic, primordial. Here and in most of these pieces McPhee penetrates the surfaces of things and makes his way toward what is essential and unchanging. He draws us to an appreciation of those things that seem simply to endure: birchbark canoes, Lew Hoad ("weathered and leonine"), the last oak of the original Birnam Wood, a 35-year-old cask of The Glenlivet, the Loch Ness monster. "The lumber of the giant sequoia is terrible," he writes. "Be good for nothing if you want to live forever is the message of the giant sequoia." Fortunately for us, it's advice that McPhee himself has steadfastly ignored.

> *Richard Horwich, "Civilized Man," in* The New Republic, *Vol. 173, Nos. 1 & 2, July 5 & July 12, 1975, p. 30.*

EDWARD HOAGLAND

[In "**Coming into the Country,**" John McPhee] says repeatedly that he will never see such wild grandeur again, speaking for all of us, of course. Professionally, he must have been looking for a place where he could apply all of his enthusiasms at once.

He was after a big, long, permanent book, written while he was still in the midst of life and could go after it, because in peripatetic journalism such as McPhee's there is an adventurous, fortuitous element: where the writer *gets himself* and what he *stumbles on*. McPhee had not always been notable as a risk-taker; had published several books that were essentially magazine articles between book covers. But here, presumably, he made his will, took the gambit; and in so doing, he introduced a new generosity of tempo to his work, a leisurely artfulness of organization he has not had before. And since it is a reviewer's greatest pleasure to ring the gong for a species of masterpiece, let me say he found it. . . .

Alaskans demand the right to make the same mistakes that we made in the Lower Forty-Eight. The land they threaten to ravage is our land—geographically one-sixth of the United States—but so is their freedom to ravage it our birthright freedom. The questions posed are complicated, like the tentative settlement of them proffered under the catchall Alaska Native Claims Settlement Act passed by Congress in 1971, whose specifics are being thrashed out still. McPhee goes into this matter, siding less than in the past with simply whomever he happens to be riding around with. My main objection to his other books has been that he was too aloof with the reader about himself—almost neurotically so—and not aloof enough about some of the subjects of his pieces, over-admiring them, taking them just at their word. Here he lets down his own hair a bit, and includes a running commentary from neighbors, enemies and friends about most of the people in the book.

Usually a champion of conservation causes, he finds so many friends among the solo miners . . . that he too starts to think of conservationists as posy-sniffers. "In the eco-militia, bust me to private. . . . For myself, I am closer to the preserving side"—preserving the miners. (p. 48)

It's high time for McPhee to have his day in the sun. In any case, journalism needs him. Investigative reporters—large, medium and small—have held the floor since Vietnam. Sword-of-God journalists, I call them, because of the air of righteous arrogance that has come to pervade much of their work. With their love of the bloodbath, their taste for gaudy deals, they have over-ripened under the klieg lights; they need some time in a root cellar.

This is the sort of book that was its own reward. (pp. 48-9)

> Edward Hoagland, "Where Life Begins Over," in The New York Times Book Reivew, *November 27, 1977, pp. 1, 48-9.*

SPENCER BROWN

John McPhee is journalist rather than essayist, not the only journalist though one of the best. McPhee rejoiceth not in uniquity but rejoiceth in the truth. Perhaps his vision of truth is what makes him appear unique. (p. 150)

McPhee's range is so extensive that it is astonishing how one man can encompass it. Surely no one could be an expert in tennis and basketball, nuclear physics, irrigation and river control, urban blight, the wilderness, and artistic treasures and forgeries—a partial summary of *The McPhee Reader*. Presumably his interest in each field is what originally dictates his choice of subject. Once made, the choice demands total research and total recall, since so much material comes from conversations and scenes that could not be fully noted on the spot. . . . Like a top-flight novelist McPhee has the knack of

creating at least the illusion of mastery, through his skill in setting down characteristic speech and his excellence in narrative.

Ernest Hemingway says that the extent and accuracy of a writer's knowledge of some activity will altogether determine the quality of his writing about it. The slightest ignorance will betray itself or will make the reader uneasy. . . . McPhee writes as if he subscribes to this principle. He seems to sound the depths of whatever he studies, yet his approach is almost always through a person rather than directly toward a subject. His exposition depends on the methods of fiction, and his best pages remind us forcibly of the best stories of Kipling, or the marvelous technical descriptions in Richard Hughes's *In Hazard*—the same clarity and offhand savoir faire. McPhee makes every reader wish to be an expert in each field of discourse. He is both a stimulator of intellectual curiosity and a showman who plays on the gee-whiz emotion. (pp. 150-51)

["**The Curve of Binding Energy**" and "**The Deltoid Pumpkin Seed**"] demonstrate McPhee's peculiar strength and also a weakness in the *Reader*. Wishing to show as many sides of McPhee as possible in a compendious book, Howarth [the editor] has necessarily limited the length of each selection. Consequently a reader unfamiliar with the whole work thus abridged may easily be confused. The fault is partly McPhee's: it is nearly impossible to figure out (even in the original length) what happened and what would happen to the Deltoid Pumpkin Seed—though I doubt if many readers stop reading, so compelling is the narrative drive. But this book does have the inevitable defect of an anthology of fragments: it cannot but distort.

Many of McPhee's pieces resemble the biographical sketches in Dos Passos's *U.S.A.*—in overwhelming richness of detail, in speed, in absorption with the person. But Dos Passos is more outside his character, usually satirical, always detached. And though McPhee is well aware of his characters' flaws, he so sinks himself into another man that his own vigorous personality vanishes; it comes as a shock when *I* appears *in propria persona*, complete with glinting wit.

His ability to merge with a character can lead him astray. In his study of Frank Boyden, "**Headmaster**," McPhee's admiration climbs through the words, and a kind of preachiness takes over; he forgets to *show* us and *tells* us instead. We are less than convinced. Somewhat similar is "**A Roomful of Hovings**." Hoving is no doubt a genius; but some of his mental feats here recorded stretch credulity; and not everything he and his family have done is admirable. (pp. 151-52)

McPhee's "nature is subdued to what it works in, like the dyer's hand." If this is sometimes a defect, it can also account for the superb coloring of everything he does. The material is the style—seemingly only functional yet possessed of sharp individuality. If you chance to open the *New Yorker* in the midst of a McPhee profile, you spot it at once: the direct, subject-verb, connectiveless sentences; the infallible vocabulary; the richness and speed. Like the Colorado River through the canyon in his unsurpassed description, he sweeps you along. (p. 152)

> Spencer Brown, "The Odor of Durability," in The Sewanee Review, *Vol. LXXXVI, No. 1, Winter, 1978, pp. 146-52.**

ROBERT COLES

[*Coming into the Country* tells] us about ourselves by documenting what life is like in, and what we are doing to, an enormous nation, far removed from our mainland, that happens to be one of our states—Alaska. John McPhee's approach, justly celebrated, brings to us the dramatic terrain—a subcontinent of empty tundra, untamed rivers, forbidding mountain ranges, treacherous ice fields—and the relative handful of human beings, Eskimos and Indians, who have for generations struggled to survive the extremes of Arctic weather. He does so, in large measure, through the eyes of a number of off-beat Americans who have left "the lower forty-eight," a common Alaska phrase, in search of a frontier kind of personal destiny. . . .

John McPhee has enough confidence in his angle of vision, and the subtlety and competence of his writing, to shun large statements, portentous generalizations—those important conclusions and interpretations so many social observers feel constrained to come up with, lest they feel, or be regarded as, not especially profound. He has enormous respect for his readers; he assumes they can get various messages without being beat on the hand, or confronted with brandished fists. He assumes that Thoreau's mode of inquiry is still possible today—the details of life's everydayness as important clues to the nature of man and a particular civilization. His descriptions of a kayak trip down the Salmon River, of the search undertaken for Alaska's new state capitol, of daily events in Eagle, a bush community of 100 souls, are rendered quietly, patiently, meticulously, suggestively. We can get what we want from the author—an education about a given stretch of natural landscape, an evocation of a kind of life once the norm in this nation, or an intimation or two of God's scheme of things. Those human creatures McPhee stalks—diminutive as in a Japanese or Chinese painting against the largeness of the land, the water, the hills, the trees—have their own ironic grandeur. To face down a demanding, consuming external world is to be on to something psychologically, spiritually—existence converging toward essence. By showing us what Alaska is like, McPhee reminds us what we have become. We have come a long distance historically, and Alaska gives us a chance to look at our past as it unfolds a second time around. . . . (p. F1)

> *Robert Coles, "Alaska, the State That Came in from the Cold," in* Book World—The Washington Post, *January 22, 1978, pp. F1-F2.**

LARRY McMURTRY

["**Giving Good Weight**"] is replete with the reportorial virtues for which John McPhee is so much respected. . . .

A constant element in Mr. McPhee's best reporting is his own wide-ranging curiosity, which often seems to center on people who are capable of sustaining intricate actions. The capacity some people have for being able to integrate or orchestrate complex sequences of actions—and actions in which something is at stake, if only a basketball game or a good meal—seem to fascinate him. It may be that he shares this fascination with most writers, whose most intricate action is apt to be changing a typewriter ribbon, but in Mr. McPhee's case the search seems in the main to have become a search for sufficiently challenging actions to describe.

This interest in action, evident throughout his career, has gradually enlarged to accommodate a Balzacian curiosity about the contexts of action. When curiosity finally exposed him to an authentically vast context—Alaska—Mr. McPhee more or less burst through the normal structure of the New Yorker profile and produced "**Coming Into the Country**," a wonderful book.

Of the five pieces reprinted here, the least engaging is about a project that has so far not reached the action stage: an attempt by New Jersey utilities to build two floating nuclear power plants off the Jersey shore. The complexity of the proposed undertaking offered Mr. McPhee an ocean of abstruse detail; like the project itself, he neither sank to clear defeat nor swam to clear victory. He is better at describing things happening before his eyes—Chef Otto beating an octopus [in "**Brigade de Cuisine**"], for example—than vast undertakings that have yet to cohere.

The title article, about the Greenmarkets in and around Manhattan, is better. Mr. McPhee has always been an inspired list-maker, and in the Greenmarket article this ability is so successfully brought to bear on vegetables that some readers may be tempted to rush off and buy a farm. (p. 3)

The ideal subject for Mr. McPhee is a man who practices an unusual, manually demanding craft, preferably in a wilderness. Skills absorb him; the attempt to describe them accurately prompts his most intense concentration. Skills that must operate in response to certain external pressures, such as the need to cook three-star meals for 40 customers a night, are for him the most interesting of all. The mastery of such skills, their maintenance and their relation to character occupy him time and again, so much so that Hemingway's old formula—grace under pressure—would describe a fair portion of his concerns.

Fortunately, he is not blind to the fact that pursuits which many might think trivial—pinball, for example—can require skills on a level that only obsession can achieve. Included in this collection is a short-short about a pinball shoot-out between two esteemed New York journalists, in which skill-testing is carried to a height just shy of parody. It might not be something one would want to save a whole New Yorker for, but it's nice to have it handy in a book. (p. 45)

> *Larry McMurtry, "Chef Otto and Friends," in* The New York Times Book Review, *November 18, 1979, pp. 3, 45.*

STEPHEN JAY GOULD

Basin and Range is a series of disparate but organically connected chapters recording McPhee's personal journey. Some are loosely sequential, as McPhee travels with geologists from the fossilized fracture zones of New Jersey to the active topography of Nevada. Others explore the consequences of plate tectonics. . . .

Where McPhee's style works—and it usually does—he triumphs by succinct prose, by his uncanny ability to capture the essence of a complex issue, or an arcane trade secret, in a well-turned phrase. (p. 26)

Where it doesn't work, at least not for me, McPhee sometimes seems to forget a principle he himself enunciates midway through the book: history is interesting when it presents a pageant of irreversible change, less so when it cycles and recycles the same kinds of physical events, and the events themselves are neither markers of time nor determiners of subsequent states. The history of life is a pageant; the history of rocks and landforms is not, unless the scale is broad enough, and events tell a coherent story framed within theories of geological change. . . . McPhee presents too much descriptive history of rocks and topography. However interesting to local *aficionados*, a regional sequence of repeatable events lacks the grandeur of true history.

To present a more serious objection, I think that McPhee has been beguiled by the mystique of field work. No geologist worth anything is bound to a desk or laboratory, but the charming notion that true science can only be based on unbiased observation of nature in the raw is mythology. Creative work, in geology and anywhere else, is interaction and synthesis: half-baked ideas from a barroom, rocks in the field, chains of thought from lonely walks, numbers squeezed from rocks in a laboratory, numbers from a calculator riveted to a desk, fancy equipment usually malfunctioning on expensive ships, cheap equipment in the human cranium, arguments before a roadcut.

This mythology leads to serious, but unfortunately conventional, misrepresentations of the past, a tradition that McPhee follows in the historical section of his work. (pp. 26-7)

> *Stephen Jay Gould, "Deep Time and Ceaseless Motion," in* The New York Review of Books, *Vol. XXVIII, No. 8, May 14, 1981, pp. 25-8.**

ROBERT D. HATCHER, JR.

In Suspect Terrain consists of a multitude of stories effectively welded into a coherent book by John McPhee's writing style. McPhee presents the development of several concepts that are either fundamental in geology or controversial because they lack supporting data or are very new. The book also outlines the nature, background, and motivation of geological scientist Anita Harris, who has made important contributions to our knowledge of sedimentary rocks and, particularly, of the movement of hydrocarbons in front of a thermal gradient. Written in the usual flowing McPhee style that integrates digressions to other subjects or times, this is a book you cannot put down. (p. 92)

The reader not versed in the terminology of geology runs some risk of becoming bogged down in jargon. The solution is to obtain a glossary or a good introductory geology text to keep at hand while reading *In Suspect Terrain*. This will add immensely to the reader's understanding of McPhee's accomplishment—a sterling effort integrating concepts, history, and the way one geologist thinks about the way she does her work. (p. 93)

In Suspect Terrain provides a great deal of information about the way many geologists think about science, about scientists'

skepticism of each other, about the necessity of a multitude of opinions on any concept, and about the necessity for continual questioning and revising of new and old ideas. This is the best way science can remain healthy and continue to grow. The book should be enjoyable for most of us and probably should be required reading for all geology students. (p. 94)

> *Robert D. Hatcher, Jr., "Layers of Time," in* Natural History, *Vol. 92, No. 4, April, 1983, pp. 92-4.*

BEAUFORT CRANFORD

What's especially notable about McPhee . . . is that his longer nonfiction is as good as his essays and less-wordy books. Well, with two exceptions—his forays into geology, *Basin and Range* (1981) and *In Suspect Terrain* (1983). Not even McPhee, alas, could consistently elevate that dismal subject above avalanching tedium.

La Place de la Concorde Suisse is undoubtedly McPhee's finest piece of work since *Coming into the Country* (1977), his chronicle of an inquisitive journey through Alaska. This time the happy wanderer hies off to Switzerland for a brief attachment to, of all things, the Swiss Army. Most people probably know of the Swiss Army as the source of nifty red knives. But to know the Swiss Army is in fact to know Switzerland, for—in the words of one of its officers—"Switzerland does not have an army, Switzerland *is* an army." . . .

This little book is an accomplished performance of observation and a splendid example of the sort of personable, plain-language reporting for which McPhee is justly famed. That he neglects to translate random French references may be annoying to people who read only English, but that's a minor quibble. . . .

Few of us—especially those who aren't spies—may care much about Switzerland or the Swiss Army, however well it promises to work should it need to. But when McPhee's up to snuff, which he certainly is here, his subject in a sense becomes secondary to his ability to illuminate and glorify it. Though he may have met his match in geology, he is very much at home in the craggy alps. Lucky readers, to have as splendid a stylist as McPhee to go prospecting for us.

> *Beaufort Cranford, "Quills in the Hills," in* The Detroit News, *May 13, 1984, p. 2M.*

Howard Nemerov

1920-

American poet, critic, novelist, short story writer, nonfiction writer, editor, and dramatist.

A significant American poet, Nemerov writes verse which is noted for its technical excellence, intelligence, and wit. Written in a variety of forms and styles—including lyrical, narrative, satirical, and meditative—his poems are, according to Phoebe Pettingell, "concerned less with the nature of things than with how we perceive them." Nemerov tends to focus on the individual consciousness and how it is affected by the external world. Because of his detached stance, his firm grounding in formal verse, and the sententious voice some reviewers have detected, he has frequently been labeled an academic poet. Yet his poetry is often marked by humor and occasional use of slang. Critics have noted that although it sometimes descends into mere wittiness or preciousness, Nemerov's humor provides a counterbalance to the urbanity and intellectual weight of his poems.

The Collected Poems of Howard Nemerov 1947-1975 (1977) won both a National Book Award and a Pulitzer Prize. This work includes poems from all of his previous major volumes and has generated considerable critical reevaluation of his poetry. The earliest poems in the collection—those from *The Image and the Law* (1947) and *Guide to the Ruins* (1950)—evidence the variety of forms Nemerov has always employed, as well as his adherence to traditional standards of rhyme and meter. In *The Salt Garden* (1955) and *Mirrors and Windows* (1958) Nemerov began to write less rigid verse and to explore the nature of perception and the relation of humanity to the world. The poems in *The Next Room of the Dream: Poems and Two Plays* (1962) and *The Blue Swallows* (1967) are simply written, thematically strong, and emphatic. Nemerov's penchant for short, witty epigrams, or "gnomes," predominates in *Gnomes and Occasions* (1972), while *The Western Approaches: Poems 1973-1975* (1975) returns to the formal approach and gentle pathos of his earlier poems. Despite the variety of forms and differing characteristics of his individual collections, Nemerov has, as Phoebe Pettingell observes, "displayed no dramatic conversion of style, method or outlook, but rather a gradual intensifying of a unified perspective." Poems in his more recent collections, *Sentences* (1980) and *Inside the Onion* (1983), include examples of both his ironic wit and his serious, lyrical meditations.

Nemerov is also a widely respected essayist. In a review of *Figures of Thought: Speculations on the Meaning of Poetry and Other Essays* (1978), Joyce Carol Oates noted the connection between Nemerov's essays and his poetry, observing that the essays "give flesh to speculations obliquely raised in the poems." *Poetry and Fiction: Essays* (1963), *Reflexions on Poetry and Poetics* (1972), and *Figures of Thought* collect Nemerov's writings on such subjects as the similarities between jokes and poems, computer poetry, and teaching literature, as well as critical essays on other writers. *Journal of the Fictive Life* (1965) records Nemerov's thoughts while he tried to write a novel. These works have been praised for their readability, humor, and intellectual depth.

© Rollie McKenna

(See also *CLC*, Vols. 2, 6, 9; *Contemporary Authors*, Vols. 1-4, rev. ed.; *Contemporary Authors New Revision Series*, Vol. 1; *Dictionary of Literary Biography*, Vols. 5, 6; and *Dictionary of Literary Biography Yearbook: 1983.*)

HAROLD BLOOM

[Howard] Nemerov is a study in the serenity of influence. He is humane, talented, witty, and sometimes eloquent. The puzzle is that his [*Collected Poems*] . . . should be so genial an echo-chamber: Frost, Stevens, Yeats, Auden, Eliot, and Tate sound forth everywhere. When I read Nemerov's **"Mrs. Mandrill,"** am I to read it as a loving parody of Stevens's "Mrs. Alfred Uruquay," or an involuntary and unknowing victim of Stevens's more powerfully comic poem? Something like the same question hovers over most of Nemerov's more ambitious efforts. It might have been better if their form had been more of an achieved poetic anxiety and their essence less of a human serenity.

Harold Bloom, in a review of "Collected Poems," in The New Republic, *Vol. 177, No. 22, November 26, 1977, p. 24.*

PHOEBE PETTINGELL

[In his *Collected Poems*] Howard Nemerov beautifully justifies Allen Tate's dictum that all of a poet's books should ultimately be regarded as one work by including the nine volumes of his verse to date. From *The Image and the Law* (1947) to *The Western Approaches* (1975), Nemerov has displayed no dramatic conversion of style, method or outlook, but rather a gradual intensifying of a unifed perspective. Along the way, the elaborate metaphysical casuistry occasionally evident in his early writing also has been reduced to gnomic riddles that astound by their unanswerable simplicity. . . .

Nemerov's theme never varies—it is always man's sometimes tragic, sometimes ludicrous relation to history, death and the universe. But he treats these characteristic concerns in an array of styles. At the very outset, he proved himself a master parodist, with a facility for burlesquing the foibles of fellow-poets. **"On the Threshold of His Greatness, the Poet Comes Down with a Sore Throat"** is surely the funniest spoof of Eliot's *The Waste Land* ever written (though its final line, "Metaphysics at mealtime gets in my hair," takes a respectful shot at Stevens, too). . . .

Nemerov uses imitation to pay tribute as well as to mock. His **"Ahasuerus"** is an "homage to George Herbert," specifically that poet's daring "The Sacrifice," wherein Christ describes the Passion in progress, and the moving refrain in both poems is, "Was ever grief like mine?" (p. 14)

Even flippancy is grist for Nemerov's poetic mill, as is fitting for one who has written on "the likeness of poems and jokes." In one of the brief witticisms he calls "gnomes," there is an anecdote that tells of consulting "the Old Ones deep in the graves" about the origins of language: "'We got together one day,' they said, / 'And talked it over among ourselves.'" This mind-teasing tautology offers the paradox that to invent something, one must have a conception of it beforehand. In **"The Painter Dreaming in the Scholar's House,"** among Nemerov's most beautiful and profound poems, the same theme is developed more fully as a theory of the creative process. The painter's art must bring into being what already exists but is unseen: "His work is not to paint the visible, / He says, it is to render visible." When he paints a tree, its seed, growth and decay, and ideas about other trees are simultaneously present to him. (pp. 14-15)

Howard Nemerov has the gift to be simple, the art to embody complex ideas in homely images and language. In an era where fashion dictates that poetry should alternate between emotional extremes of euphoria and bitterness, he avoids both with an ironic stance born of a tragic vision of life. Tragedy is the song that rises out of human suffering, and Nemerov is one of its finest singers. (p. 15)

Phoebe Pettingell, "Irony, Tragedy and Violence," in The New Leader, Vol. LX, No. 24, December 5, 1977, pp. 14-15.

HELEN VENDLER

[The essay from which the following excerpt is taken originally appeared in The New York Times Book Review, *December 18, 1977.]*

When Stevens wrote about his *Collected Poems* as "The Planet on the Table," he meant that a life's poetry, like a terrestrial globe, reproduces (though in a reduced scale) the whole world.

The world as Howard Nemerov knows it is revealed, prophetically, in the title of his first (1947) volume, *The Image and the Law.* The world comes to us in images; the mind seeks a law in the heterogeneous information infiltrating the senses. A late poem shows Nemerov as a boy confronting **"The Book of Knowledge,"** "a luxury liner on [a] sea unfathomable of ignorance," with poetry "as steady, still, and rare / As the lighthouses now manned and obsolete." These three things—our already immeasurable knowledge of the world, our nonetheless profound ignorance of its ways, and our landmarks and beacons in the productions of consciousness—are Nemerov's constant subjects. . . . [Nemerov's] mind plays with epigram, gnome, riddle, rune, advice, meditation, notes, dialectic, prophecy, reflection, views, knowledge, questions, speculation—all the forms of thought. His wishes go homing to origins and ends. Any natural fact—a tree, for instance—becomes instantly symbolic in his eye's gaze: its seed summons up "mysteries of generation and death," its trunk and branches recall "the one and the many, cause and effect, generality and particulars," its movement from roots to trunk to branches will serve as a metaphor for "historical process," and so on. . . . (p. 175)

However, Nemerov has struggled increasingly, in the course of his life, with his philosophical instincts, urging his poetry into moods that will accommodate fact and dream as well as wisdom. There is a touching poem (**"Beginner's Guide"**) that recalls his persistent, if never entirely successful, pursuit of the proper names—through bird books, flower books, tree books, star books—of things as they are, "to make some mind of what was only sense." Nemerov is not innately hospitable to fantasy and imaginative waywardness, though his wit is elusive, mischievous, and teasing. His masters in youth—Stevens, Auden, Frost and Yeats—shared in different ways his discursive and philosophic stance. He is drawn to Breughel and Klee for their allegories of dark whimsy. . . . Nemerov's paradox—"the mindfulness that is in things"—takes on flesh in his many surprising lines that make us see the obvious-but-till-now-unsaid. We have all, in the newspapers, read the engagements and the obituaries, but it remained for Nemerov to see that the papers printed "segregated photographs / Of the girls that marry and the men that die." (p. 176)

The morose humor that pervades the *Collected Poems* takes its rise from Nemerov's contemplation of various grim spectacles: the will's rebellion against necessity, history's repetitions, the pitfalls of the literary life, and the perpetual discrepancy between hope and event. Sometimes Nemerov's irony can itself seem contrived, a too orderly dismissal of life. But on the whole, the irony is mixed with a rueful pleasure, as Nemerov is distracted from wisdom by some natural phenomenon. He fends off his tendency to solemn periods with a jaunty colloquiality. . . .

The world causes in Nemerov a mingled revulsion and love, and a hopeless hope is the most attractive quality in his poems, which slowly turn obverse to reverse, seeing the permanence of change, the vices of virtue, the evanescence of solidities, and the errors of truth. Dreams lie with death and mathematics, forgeries invade art museums, a green and silent cherry tree shades "the bloody stones, the rotting flesh" of its fruit, and the "translucency of leaf" of the ginkgo filters "a urinary yellow light." The sensibility mapped by such phrases is one permanently unsettled and bent on making a law out of its unease.

As the echoes of Nemerov's *grands maîtres* fade, the poems get steadily better. The severity of attitude is itself chastened by a growing humanity, and the forms of the earth grow ever more distinct, as by small increments of reality. Nemerov brightens his lonely algebraic world, beset by the First and Second Laws of Thermodynamics. (p. 177)

If the ravens of unresting thought (as Yeats called them) swarm blackly through these pages, they find a series of living boughs on which to perch. The sadder poems about nature and life are, on the whole, the most memorable, but since one of the accidental services performed by any *Collected Poems* is to exert pressure on anthologies, anthologists of the future should not forget Nemerov's forceful, comic, and bitter topical poems, ranging from World War II to Vietnam, and embracing even such unpoetical matters as loyalty oaths. (pp. 177-78)

> Helen Vendler, "Howard Nemerov," in her Part of Nature, Part of Us: Modern American Poets, *Cambridge, Mass.: Harvard University Press, 1980, pp. 175-78.*

SUSAN WOOD

The publication of *The Collected Poems of Howard Nemerov* is ... something of a mixed blessing. One comes away with a renewed appreciation for how very good indeed he is at his best; yet one is also reminded of the unevenness that has always marked Nemerov's work, of how often wit and irony become mere devices for evasion, suppressing his exceptional lyric and meditative voice....

In the postwar decades characterized by several highly visible "schools" of poetic thought, Nemerov remained largely independent of those alliances, rooted in the more formal tradition of rhyme and meter, though writing poems with an extraordinary variety of style and subject matter, from light satire to the brilliant dream record **"The Scales of the Eyes."** In fact, within any given volume of his work one can isolate a number of particular kinds of Nemerov poems: political poems, satires, dramatic or dialogue poems, proverb poems, brief lyrics which take as their subject an event in nature, meditative poems, and so on.

This variety is, in reality, a weakness in Nemerov's work; it becomes a means of avoiding emotion, true feeling, of refusing to set his imagination free. I suspect this is a product of Nemerov's psyche, of a divided spirit who tries to hide a profound uncertainty behind a mask of reason and the polished surface of metaphysical wit.

When, however, Nemerov allows his creative mind a moment of freedom from the tyranny of his rational mind, he rises to heights of freshness and lyricism equal to anything in contemporary poetry, whether in poems of lucid meditation or ecstatic celebration. What moves us in these poems is the tension of the divided spirit he too often tries to hide, a tension in the evanescent identity of work and spirit....

Nemerov seems to have reached the height of his poetic powers in the '60s with *The Next Room of the Dream* (1962) and *The Blue Swallows* (1967). The books which followed, *Gnomes and Occasions* (1973) and *The Western Approaches* (1975), seemed weighted down with a kind of weariness, a desire to back off from further experience, that leads the poet to conclude, in *"Thirtieth Anniversary Report to the Class of '41"*: "What is there to discuss? / There's nothing left for us to say of us."

One can only hope that no final judgment is necessary, that Nemerov will find more to say....

> Susan Wood, "A Poet Collected in Tranquility," in Book World—The Washington Post, *December 25, 1977, p. H3.*

ROBERT B. SHAW

The great simplicities, the essential themes, sound trite in summary, and the challenge to the poet is to insure that they will not sound trite when he invokes them in his poem. [In his *Collected Poems,* Howard] Nemerov repeatedly meets this challenge in exploring the classically problematic relationship of the self to the world, of the perceiving eye to the objects perceived. To what extent, he repeatedly wonders, is the world we see our own creation? ... Is the poem a mirror reflecting the appearances of the world in responsible detail, or is it a window, a transparent medium through which we may see, perhaps, some reality beyond the usual appearances that hem us in? Or might it begin as the one and with care and luck become the other?

Nemerov never fully unravels these aesthetic and metaphysical knots. They provide him the material for endless reflection. "Reflection," with its possibilities as image and pun, is a favorite word of Nemerov's, one of whose solider volumes was entitled *Mirrors and Windows.* He prefers the spelling "reflexion," which gives perhaps an additional punning facet to the word. It means for him not random musing but a strenuous mental exercise: as an athlete might flex his muscles, he takes the occasion of writing a poem to give his mind a workout.

A key episode in Nemerov's argument with himself over his favorite questions comes in *"The Blue Swallows"*: the poet delightedly watching the configurations made by the flying birds becomes aware of how his mind "Weaves up relation's spindrift web, / Seeing the swallows' tails as nibs / Dipped in invisible ink, writing...." At this point skepticism bursts in:

> Poor mind, what would you have them
>   write?
> Some cabalistic history
> Whose authorship you might ascribe
> To God? to Nature? Ah, poor ghost,
> You've capitalized your Self enough.

This killjoy voice proceeds to reduce the scene to "The real world where the spelling mind / Imposes with its grammar book / Unreal relations on the blue / Swallows." But the poet isn't content to let reductive rationalism have the final word. In the last lines he addresses the birds whose darting paths provoked his speculations:

> O swallows, swallows, poems are not
> The point. Finding again the world,
> That is the point, where loveliness
> Adorns intelligible things
> Because the mind's eye lit the sun.

This yearning to find again a world both beautiful and intelligible has, of course, a religious dimension. The question of design leads to the question of a Designer. On this point Nemerov is thoughtfully noncommittal: his agnosticism has, I should say, more spiritual depth than the faith of many conventional believers.... The oscillation in **"The Blue Swallows"** between a hunger for ultimate significance and a self-accusing skepticism that suspects that appetite of sentimentality or obscurantism is present in many of his poems, lending intensity to his ongoing dialogue with nature.

To turn from theme to technique, Nemerov's encounters with the appearances he finds so lovely and so enigmatic are precisely rendered, frequently memorable. . . . In his better poems Nemerov shares the gift that Frost had in *his* better ones, a sort of tact which keeps a proper distance from the scene observed, an instinct for finding a vantage point neither too close nor too far away. The presences of nature and the presence of the poet alike have room to make themselves felt; the verse itself (often a blank verse which like Frost's is relaxed, flexible, but ultimately true to form) gives a sense of spaciousness in which the mind can pursue its explorations freely.

Nemerov is a more versatile poet than I may thus far have indicated. Besides his most typical meditative colloquies with nature, he has written some fine narratives ("**The Pond,**" "**A Day on the Big Branch**") as well as some brainy metaphysical lyrics that make their points without an evocation of landscape ("**A Clock with No Hands,**" "**Moment,**" "**Celestial Globe**"). There are also a great many satirical verses of various lengths. Lately Nemerov has relied heavily on the epigram, or as he likes to call it, the "gnome," as a favored instrument of ridicule. These little squibs, like the heavier artillery that preceded them, batter their targets in a highly satisfying way. (pp. 213-14)

I have always enjoyed the wit and trenchancy of these pieces in the past, and thought them a bracing complement to the poet's less topical contemplations. Seeing them amassed in the present volume, however, I find myself noticing that the targets are in most cases predictable (U.S. foreign policy, the consumer society, passing fads and persistent fatuities) and that they sometimes repeat themselves with diminishing force. . . . I am glad he has written in this vein, giving voice to his urbane humor and justly provoked asperity. But these gnomes are probably a mite too populous, especially in the latter part of the collection where they may distract one from due attention to the fine recent work in serious modes.

I have few other reservations regarding this book. The two verse plays on biblical themes remain blank spots to me. And the poems in the first two volumes included here are admittedly derivative, bearing the typical influences of their period—Yeats and Auden, in particular. Yet these are honestly crafted, and interesting as background to Nemerov's mature achievement. His distinctive voice first emerged in parts of his third book, *The Salt Garden* (1955), and reached its dominant declaration in *Mirrors and Windows* (1958).

He continues to exercise mastery in exploring his perennial themes; it is remarkable to notice how many of his most recent poems are among his strongest. It is as though his mind, from regarding nature with such steady and respectful attention, had been blessed with something of nature's own capacity for self-renewal. (p. 214)

Nemerov's contribution to our literature—as a gifted writer of fiction and critical prose, but pre-eminently as a poet—does not seem to me to have received as much celebrity as it deserves. Perhaps this is because he is so determinedly unhistrionic, refusing to equate feeling with noise. . . . Nemerov's virtues are all in fact unfashionable ones for our time: vivid intelligence, an irreverent sense of humor, a mastery of formal verse, an awareness of mystery. One can only hope that the climate may have changed enough for this collection to attract a wide audience of "wondering beginners." Such readers can expect to be charmed by the easy flow of Nemerov's reasoned discourse, and moved by those fine moments in his poems in which reason is overcome by awe. (p. 215)

> *Robert B. Shaw, "Making Some Mind of What Was Only Sense," in* The Nation, *Vol. 226, No. 7, February 25, 1978, pp. 213-15.*

TOM JOHNSON

Howard Nemerov is a poet known to most readers just well enough to be stereotyped. There are, in fact, two stereotypes regularly pasted upon his work. The first casts him as a good academic poet, which means that he teaches and writes criticism and that his poems are competent, intellectual, usually difficult, and usually dull. The second is by comparison unflattering; it is caught in the remark of an acquaintance who is an associate professor of English in a state university: he described Nemerov as a competent suburban poet. By which he meant, presumably, marginally competent, stuffy, hopelessly middle-class in concerns, unintellectual, and usually dull. This second attitude we shall dismiss, for the evidence will be seen to contradict all its points. (p. 445)

The origins of the first attitude, which does represent some truth, are easy to discover. Nemerov is a teacher, and he writes criticism: the publication of *Figures of Thought,* his third collection of critical essays and addresses, close upon the release of the *Collected Poems,* is auspicious. Furthermore his poems are technically competent. Technical excellence is hard to come by among the poets of any age, but in ours the denial of it has often become a fetish. So let there be no ambiguity here: Nemerov is a master of the craft of poetry, and that is the way the highest praise must begin. (pp. 445-46)

The impression that Nemerov is intellectual begins in the observation that there are ideas in his poems, and the impression that he is usually difficult begins in the opinion that there are too many ideas. To build one's own poetry entirely out of his ideas is a dangerous business: it adds a high wind to what is already a long tightrope walk. That someone (Stevens) in our own century has got away with it has set, for too many, a fatal precedent. But Nemerov never goes this far. He merely accepts Stevens's proposition that one's ideas are quite properly an essential part of his life and therefore of his art. In Stevens's poems and essays the greatest word is imagination, which stands for everything that is valuable; in Nemerov's the word is thought, and it stands for—well, thought. There is always something more.

Not all Nemerov's ideas are easy ones. Sometimes there are more of them than a poem can handle. Frequently it seems that he is out to make a metaphor of everything in a poem, every image fitting into one scheme of reference and beginning another at the same time. This quality does make many poems difficult, and makes others seem more difficult than they really are; but it is not (as has often been said) the source of Nemerov's failure or of his success. In the scale of the *Collected Poems* we see this density of symbolic speech in both good poems and broken ones, and recognize it for what it is: part of his character, not one of his gimmicks: the essence of first-rate intelligence.

One of the hardest literary lessons of this century was that it is all right for poems to be difficult. Still every poet must qualify for this dispensation himself. And the indictment against Nemerov is even longer: he writes about aesthetics, writing itself, and painting; his poems contain a density of allusion just as striking as their density of metaphor; he mixes funny things in with the serious ones. If we do object to the first of these we are in effect objecting to intelligence. (pp. 447-48)

The matter of humor is a touchy point. The last century to stress wit and high seriousness in its aesthetic was the eighteenth—altogether too intellectual a time for modern tastes. Nemerov and his critics have squabbled over his frequent irreverent intrusions of humor for years, and he has confessed that he has "sometimes found it a strain to suffer critics gladly upon this issue in particular." Too much has been made of it. A few of Nemerov's best poems and several of his good ones are built on direct humor, usually as irony. . . . Still the majority of his best poems, even though they may contain irony, do not rely on it; nor on puns or inversions. Seldom, in fact, have the critics who objected flatly to humor been distinguishable from the ones who claimed that in otherwise sound poems the humor had degenerated to wit, that is, to cleverness and slyness for their own sake. If humor is important to Nemerov (and it is), that is none of our concern; we are concerned with the poems themselves. And without entering the battle over specifics in the larger poems, I will admit, by way of abandoning this issue, that many of Nemerov's short poems, his throwaways, are merely witty. But wit, like other forms of cleverness, is an indulgence of intelligence; and if wit is a triviality, we should add that all poets produce trivial pieces and that most of these have not even wit to recommend them.

Because densely metaphorical speech becomes a natural expression for Nemerov's continuously flowering thought, complexly interacting metaphors using recurring images . . . are favorites of his. He varies the import of his images in much the same way that a composer performs variations on a theme. This technique is explicitly set out in two fine long poems, **"The Scales of the Eyes"** and **"Runes,"** in both of which the variations are separated into numbered sections. The first of these is called a "text and variations," and its diction and meters are formal, precise, and highly charged—

> The quiet pool, if you will listen,
> Hisses with your blood, winds
> Together vine and vein and thorn,
> The thin twisted threads red
> With the rust of breath.

—poetry in the grand, which is to say the Miltonic, manner. **"Runes"** is more relaxed, quietly meditative:

> This is about the stillness in moving things,
> In running water, also in the sleep
> Of winter seeds, where time to come has tensed
> Itself, enciphering a script so fine
> Only the hourglass can magnify it, only
> The years unfold its sentence from the root.

The working out of these ideas is not so intricately formed as in **"The Scales of the Eyes"**; the loose-hanging threads are manifestly part of the design. And so it is like our own experiences. In the smooth insistent pervasion of its reorderings, the poem itself embodies that ineffable mixture of form and flow which is our lives. (p. 449)

[His poems] are not metaphysical speculations. If some of them are difficult, and some are, it is because life is difficult to apprehend. But then, as Nemerov frequently shows, that is why it remains interesting. We perceive, if only through the persistence of irony, that his strongest sense is both humanistic

and pessimistic. . . . He trusts reason by default, like an existentialist who would rather have believed. The many religious images are part of the great striving. The loss of a usable rationalism is our common tragedy. . . .

In poems such as **"First Snow," "Drawing Lessons,"** and **"The First Day"** Nemerov has written more incisively of science and its place in our imaginations than anyone else has yet managed to do in good (or even readable) poems. And in poems such as **"A Spell before Winter"** he has succeeded in writing about nature at once sharply seen and felt, as both Emerson and Frost tried to do and failed. (p. 450)

What is common to these themes is not abstraction, but rather, consistently, the most human of concerns—the difficulty of our decisions, of our sharing, of our knowing; the certainty of our suffering. The breadth of accomplishment and depth of insight are one's most striking impressions from first readings of the *Collected Poems,* enriched later by the humor, the intricacy, the grace. (pp. 450-51)

> Tom Johnson, *"Ideas and Order," in* The Sewanee Review, *Vol. LXXXVI, No. 3, Summer, 1978, pp. 445-53.*

DAVID PERKINS

[The poems and essays in *Collected Poems* and *Figures of Thought: Speculations on the Meaning of Poetry & Other Essays*] give much pleasure, and have the special, additional interest that Nemerov seems representative. Just what he represents is hard to say. Auden noticed in a late poem that the "guttural tribes" are crossing the Rhine. The civilized language of clear, rational intelligence is ceasing to be spoken, and even poets and critics voice "haphazard oracular grunts." But there are many who still cling to the straw of reason, or reasonableness. The world would hardly go on without them. . . . [Nemerov] is the intelligent questioner, burning with thought and with thought about thought. Heir to all the ages, he is disinherited of positive, major commitment. Naturally he wants sometimes to pose as the American Adam, starting over again in the blessed "paradise" of "ignorance and emptiness" (**"The Loon's Cry"**), in Eden before things were named. Tamed but wanting to be wild (**"The Salt Garden"**), he writes in his *Journal of the Fictive Life,* "I hate intelligence, and have nothing else." (p. 351)

He began [his career] by saying, in *The Image and the Law* (1947), what he had found in his twenty-seven years of living up till then in school, and college, and the war, when he was a pilot: "spastic motions of despair," frozen horror, famine, lust, viciousness, ennui. In short, he had found other people's poems. He had looked a bit into his own experience, and maybe into his heart, but mostly into Eliot, Stevens, Auden, Empson, *et al.,* and he had descried the Waste Land.

So had many of his contemporaries. Where do you go from there? In *Guide to the Ruins* three years later (he has always been inventive and fertile), Nemerov was still in the same place. The war was still going on even though it was over, for the war in its horror was the world, life (**"Redeployment"**). But there were signs that Yeats was guiding him amid the ruins to something paradoxically positive: the heroic, Romantic self rejoicing in its lonely strength to be (**"A Song of Degrees," "Phoenix"**). In **"The Lives of Gulls and Children"** this self was figured in the first of his gulls; the bird embodies the Atlantic emptiness and fierceness of the world and also the fierceness of being that briefly defies and masters the cold "unhavening air" and ocean. Refusing the children's impulsive attempt to offer comfort, the dying gull stares at them "Out of a steady and majestic eye / Like a sun part baffled in cloud." Henceforth in Nemerov, however hopeless the human scene, however much human consciousness with its infinite analyses and divisions is shown to be out of touch and going nowhere, there is likely to be a gull in the offing, that is, an other, a symbol of the uncontrollable, dynamically changing reality that is forever beyond our knowing. We may call it nature. It is a thought to escape into when we despair at the sight and thought of the human. Though it is also terrible in its way, it is a kind of hope.

So what Nemerov said in these first books was what the great generation before him had said. Learning his art, he was assimilating the conventions of his time, the ways of saying and the things to say. He was recording possibilities of emotional experience and *Weltanschauung* that were open in twentieth-century poetry. Every young poet does this. But Nemerov did it with special talent. His early poems are good.

The Salt Garden (1955) was better, and remains Nemerov's finest single volume. Such poems as **"Winter Lightning," "The Scales of the Eyes," "I Only Am Escaped Alone to Tell Thee," "The Goose Fish," "The Vacuum," "The Quarry," "Deep Woods,"** and the title poem put Nemerov among the best of his generation. These poems were still composed in partnership with other poets. **"The Salt Garden"** is admirable and moving "Yeatsiana," as Randall Jarrell put it. **"The Scales of the Eyes"** learns from Roethke. Frost is in **"The Pond,"** a meditative story, and in several others, such as **"The Quarry"** and **"Deep Woods."** . . . (pp. 351-52)

Sounding like Frost, Nemerov was of course rebelling against the complication of style, the intensity and compression of the high Modernist mode. . . . His gradual rejection, from the 1950s on, of the high Modernist legacy was typical of almost all American poets at this time, but Nemerov made this transition less successfully. His new mode is meditative, relaxed, and risks a simplification of reality for the style's sake. It resembles Frost's, or the later Auden's, or a cross between them, but there is much variety, and Nemerov has his own voice. In general he is plain, thoughtful, uncompressed, and rather sad.

He turns out superlative poems from time to time. **"Trees"** is almost perfect for what it is, a one-sentence meditation of all that trees may suggest or symbolize. **"Storm Windows"** is marvelously fresh and delicate. **"Brainstorm"** and **"Writing"** are memorable. **"Going Away"** is clean, lucid, emotionally equable, accomplished. **"Runes"** is a dense, ingenious, moving sequence that ought to be studied closely and rarely is. . . . And many another of his poems in the 1960s and 1970s is also fine. Still, Nemerov was a more intense, vital, troubled, and interesting poet when he was younger and the Modernists spoke through him. His satiric poems of the last ten years are witty and pleasant, but too often they bite straw men not very hard. One has the impression of a distinguished talent running down, from the pose and semblance of the casual and simple to the reality of those qualities.

But I was asking myself what he has to say, and the question becomes in some ways more interesting and important with *Mirrors and Windows* (1958) and the five volumes since, partly because in them he may be speaking more for himself than out of the modern tradition and also because we naturally want to see what he is finding now, in our present moment of history.

In **"Death and the Maiden"**—it is a small point, but we must start somewhere—he asks, in the course of saying something else, whether "things / that happen can be said to come to pass, / or only happen." It is one of those nice questions that implicate cosmic ones. But Nemerov doesn't know the answer. When he tries to give answers, we see that the world is not quite a Waste Land in the old way, but a place where everything repeats itself boringly, and runs down gradually, and "nothing surprises us / Nor can delight" (**"Watching Football on TV"**). . . . In short, Nemerov has gone from looking on the Waste Land (seen from books) to living in it. As a dweller there, he has something of the attitude and feeling of Eliot's three Thames-daughters—"I made no comment," the second daughter sums up. "What should I resent?" His longest and maybe most impressive answer comes in the familiar **"A Day on the Big Branch."** In this narrative some poker players, having played all night, drive north in the morning to a natural place of cold clear water and stones—a "stream in the high hills." Symbolically they are returning to a source, seeking the oracle in the depths of nature, and they have to struggle toward it up "the giant stair of the stream," like Wordsworth climbing Mount Snowdon. Within the Romantic conventions the poem activates, a revelation is expected at the top. It comes and it doesn't. The middle-aged poker players find themselves uncomfortable lying about on the rocks; the rocks are just "modern American rocks," they don't mean anything. But still there are sermons in stones, at least, there are vague examples and suggestions. The stones just endure—"weathering . . . being eroded, or broken"—and they induce a sort of stony peace in the souls (if we may use the word) of the poker players. They come to recognitions, inner settlements, resolves, which are that they will go on playing poker, and drinking, and smoking. Generalizing we may say that they stoically accept their lives as they are.

An honest, depressing, dusty answer. Perhaps we shouldn't have asked the question. (pp. 353-54)

It seems to me that the greatest poets of our century thought they had something important to say. . . . [In] their poetry they sought, tested, and imparted a comprehensive and profound truth on the basis on which life, they hoped, could be enjoyed or endured or redeemed. . . . That Nemerov has no such truth to tell limits the excitement and impact of his poetry. So also with the majority of his contemporaries, the ones who do not mistake peculiarities of sensation for mystical experience. Nemerov has ended with a rather flat, factual, minimal, stoic response, a very honest response in a disinherited age. Perhaps it is more essentially sane, authentic, clear-eyed and in touch with the truth of our time than the interesting commitments of Eliot, Pound, Yeats, or Stevens. (pp. 354-55)

David Perkins, "The Collected Nemerov," in Poetry, Vol. CXXXII, No. 6, September, 1978, pp. 351-55.

THE VIRGINIA QUARTERLY REVIEW

[In *Sentences*] Howard Nemerov gathers together some epigrams, lyrics, riddles, and meditations in an uneven work. Many of these poems, as the title suggests, are experiments to see how prose syntax can shape a metrical line. Of course, Nemerov still rewards us with some poems of paradox and startling humor, but too many poems, especially the topical ones, have neither the charm of seriousness nor the subterfuge of cleverness. Only a handful remind us of Nemerov's emotional range, rhetorical finesse, and social power.

A review of "Sentences," in The Virginia Quarterly Review, *Vol. 57, No. 3 (Summer, 1981), p. 95.*

DAISY ALDAN

I opened *Sentences* with expectation and anticipation and found part one, called "Beneath," really beneath the level of Nemerov's previous work. In fact, if part one had to be included at all—and it is my opinion that the book would have been complete and worthy without it—then it would have been more in place as part three, for it is very likely that other readers of this book will lay it aside and thereby deprive themselves of the delight which part two, called "Above," and part three, called "Beyond," may bestow. The so-called epigrams and riddles are neither witty nor clever enough, unlike the delightful **"The Author to His Body on Their Fifteenth Birthday, 29 ii 80"** in part three.

Nemerov is at his best when he is recording (delicately) his observations of nature rather than when he is commenting on the weaknesses and foibles of humanity, for whom it seems he has little compassion. (pp. 475-76)

It is difficult to believe when one reaches part two that the same poet was responsible both for the gorgeous lyrics it contains and for the tasteless **"An Ace of Hearts"** in part one. The poem **"In Zeno's World"** indeed remains in one's mind, a poem with "inward spirit" and delicacy, utterly integrated in sound, idea, form, image. Here is Nemerov at his best. Then there are the evocative and awe-inspiring **"Acorn, Yum Kippur," "During a Solar Eclipse," "The Dying Garden," "A Christmas Storm"** and **"Easter,"** the last of which tells us simply and with reverence, "Death has been vanquished again, / What was a bramble of green barbed wire / Becomes forsythia," with the Resurrection and the Crown of Thorns inherent in the silence. In poems such as these a seeming ambiguity concerning the Divine seems resolved, and this adds enormous power to the works mentioned. . . .

Part three has the nostalgic sequence **"By Al Liebowitz's Pool."** An awareness of aging becomes evident, and also regret for past youth; but there is no "raging against the dying of the light," for Nemerov states in **"Thanksgiving"** that he has been fortunate to have avoided all the major tragedies which beset mankind, has had love and good fortune, and now, though he will "be sorry to let go when I let go," is reflective and mellow. Nemerov has mastered classical structure: there are sonnets and villanelles and lots of iambic pentameter. Rarely are "contemporary" structures employed. While the nature lyrics integrate beautifully with the old structures, sometimes, in caustic commentaries on life and our "evil" times, the classical structures seem imposed rather than outgrowths of the poems' demands.

On the whole, excluding part one, there is beauty, skill and intelligence if not passion in Nemerov's volume. We learn little of his "weals and woes"—an exception in our time of so much "confessional" poetry—and this is a welcome relief. (p. 476)

Daisy Aldan, in a review of "Sentences," in World Literature Today, *Vol. 55, No. 3, Summer, 1981, pp. 475-76.*

MARY KINZIE

The last poem in Howard Nemerov's new *Sentences* is called **"Because You Asked About the Line Between Prose and Poetry."** It is about rain gradually turning into snow, but still acting like rain (only somehow lighter and thicker), until—there is suddenly snow flying instead of rain falling. The poem rhymes as a quatrain and a couplet and is composed in Howard Nemerov's own pentameter, an organism we recognize by the off-handed inversions of sentence order that sound at once decorous and colloquial; by that studied freedom of address and careful familiarity with old puns ("clearly flew"); and by the chill, dry precision of analogy ("gradient . . . aslant . . . random"). To these idiosyncratic marks of character, Nemerov adds the unassuming realism of the plot: you recognize only much later the poet's providence in having put something dark, living, and winged into the background.

> Sparrows were feeding in a freezing drizzle
> That while you watched turned into pieces of snow
> Riding a gradient invisible
> From silver aslant to random, white, and slow.
>
> There came a moment that you couldn't tell.
> And then they clearly flew instead of fell.

Formally, the poem is masterful, reassuring in its regularities, disturbing in its hints of chaos—those twin impulses that make up at least the necessary conditions of great verse. In Nemerov's rhymed poems, there is more activity in the final feet than in his unrhymed; the hints of chaos in **"Because You Asked . . . "** are whispered by the rhyme-dissonances between "drizzle" (the end of the fifth-foot amphibrach) and "invisible" (whose four syllables make up the two regular iambs of the fourth and fifth feet, with no supernumerary unstressed syllable at the end). Although DRIZ- rhymes with -VIS-, and although both DRIZZLE and INVISIBLE have final Ls, these rhyming sounds fall in different metrical places. We swallow the last two syllables of INVISIBLE—naturally, because the main accent falls on -VIS-, and in Nemerov's lines, because we are half-consciously trying to make the metrically nonparallel words match.

This rhyming on words that are, so to speak, cross-woven metrically, and the swallowing of certain lines (which necessitates the elongation of others) are parts of a larger design in which are also woven sentence and pause. For as the words unfold forward within the abstract metrical frame, they also pick up unaligned threads of grammatical periods and endings, which then hitch back across those lines, and even back across whole stanzas. If the metaphor of fabric-weaving applies to the making of verses, we must imagine either the warp as regular and the shuttle as uneven, or the warp as erratic and the voice of the shuttle as constant. The process in either case must accommodate both glide and tug, both smooth progress and lurching regress. The subject of the sentence that forms the quatrain of Nemerov's poem is "Sparrows," but the burden of the quatrain's theme is the "drizzle" that turns (for two-and-a-half lines) to "pieces of snow." A further twist is that, while "drizzle" is technically in command of the syntax for only one-half line, it is still continuing to fall through the ensuing transformations.

Because poetry moves backwards and forwards at once, the bit of cloth you wind up with is irregular, full of holes, yet also peculiarly complete, like a cat's cradle held on one hand by an adult and on the other by a child. Even the "symmetry" of the Popean couplet depends on radical asymmetries in the puns and in their disposition among parts of speech and in non-matching metrical places. In Nemerov's poem the adjectives "aslant" and "slow" do not inhabit the same semantic realm; yet for the moment of their expression, they are parallel in their doubleness: both render both shape *and* speed. Indirectly, "silver aslant" shows us rain razoring down quickly, while "random, white, and slow" suggests how the snow is starting to coast lethargically, scoot sideways, move anyway but straight down.

Even so bald a device as the choice of poly- over monosyllabic words in a metrical line is an indispensable means of varying speed, sentence structure, and texture. Compare the second line, "That while you watched turned into pieces of snow," with its commanding monosyllables, and the rhopalic series of polysyllables in the third line, "Riding a gradient invisible," which is softer, more rapid (because of weak secondary stresses on the last two words), more abstract, and syntactically unfinished.

In support of diction, syntax, and meter, Nemerov also employs a hovering effect, based sometimes on ambiguity, and sometimes on error. For example, I might revise his final couplet to expose the grammatical clumsiness of the final line:

> There came a moment when you scarcely knew.
> And then instead of fell they clearly flew.

But in Nemerov's couplet, with its authoritative rhyme, the ungrammatical use of "fell" is largely concealed, perceived by us only as a dull after-throb. In addition to softening the awkwardness in the last line, Nemerov also invigorates the meanings in the penultimate. By using "that" instead of "when," he divides the reference between time and quality: (1) There came a moment during which you could not tell which was which; (2) There came a moment that you couldn't tell about. Of course the poem is about not being able to pinpoint delicate change; but it is also about not being able to describe how something got itself changed from rain into snow, prose into poetry, while watcher and writer know very well what the final state has come to: "And then they clearly flew."

What clearly flew? Clearly, the pieces of snow, now soft and crowded flakes. But in the poem's updrafts are also borne aloft those feeding sparrows—not literally, rather as part of the suggestive warrant for any kind of flight. In other words (the words of the title), so is the poem launched. Not going straight to its goal—not falling like rain—a poem imperceptibly thickens itself out of the visible stream of prose. It crosses a line, before which it was transparent, following which it is opaque, by being *in lines*, displaying the words it holds in common with prose so that these are increasingly bracketed, thereby more choice, but also more free.

That poetry holds words in common with prose is a truth for which Howard Nemerov gives especially profound warrant in his poetry (which now numbers roughly 600 pages). He is a master of blank verse in the brief lyric and the middle-length poem, and has molded the unrhymed iambic pentameter line into some of the subtlest formal bodies we have. His forbear in this is Frost, but Nemerov is less heavily stressed and less the rural *poseur*. Not that Nemerov lacks his poses; on the contrary, he can be most irritating in his roles as watcher-of-broadcasts, man-walking-dog, suburban-stroller, visitor-of-parks. He lets the bourgeois into his satiric poetry, but also in his lyrics, he lets in (in less censored or censorious fashion) the world of solitary privilege. The finest poem in *Sentences*, "By Al Lebowitz's Pool," provides a protected bell jar for Neme-

rov's meditations on time, light, youth, distance, and correspondence. It is a superior poem, but also one that depends on our *liking* the moneyed reserve of the middle classes. . . . [In "**By Al Lebowitz's Pool**," the] poet observes the untouchable and undesired daughters swerving like fish through the water, on which surface, on other days, float only beach balloons or a wasp. The summer wanes. The speaker usually has a drink in hand. Idly, the poet roves among these details, which seem to provide at last, in each of the poem's five sections, the hypnagogic abstraction necessary for elegy. (pp. 344-46)

But in contrast to other masters of the typical like Frost, Auden, and Cunningham, Nemerov is not, even in his sublime poems, always able to decide what he should do with the prosaic side of feeling. His worldly poses are often double-jointed—excuses for personal pathos where we expect the satirist's probity. His jokes frequently protest their humor. Since his first poems, *The Images and the Law* (1947), his books have been marred by gnomes too glib and constructed to be true. He tries to be playful, but sounds grim. And when he wants that grimness to be prophetic, he sounds inward and crotchety. . . . I suspect that Howard Nemerov desires to be viewed as a poet who can range, with indulgence, majesty, or fury, over a broad geography of subjects and moods. This is not the case. His best mood, the one that brings out the tenderest and most credible language, is that mood of pitying praise in the presence of natural law and intellectual construct. In another age, Nemerov would have been bard to the Royal Society or an enclave of Thomists. He was framed to celebrate the edifice of mind from a gargoyle's niche; he depends, that is, on a tradition of shared intellectual achievement to which he can pay orthogonal homage in the form of tears. (p. 347)

[His] is blank verse both cerebral and melodious, yet what moves us is not that balance, but the frailty of fame and the doomed circularity of poetic endeavor. The breathing shapes and stops, the vowels and consonants, are the foundations of shifting Babels whose magic is ephemeral. . . . [All] of Nemerov's best poems are strangely sad. Encumbered with habitual self, they rise to plateaus of nostalgic obedience to the world, on which a natural, rich simplicity is flexed by mutability. . . . (p. 349)

Sentences is a disappointing and self-indulgent volume on the whole, but has some landmark poems. In these serious poems, not only has Nemerov continued to accommodate himself to the literary tradition without falling back on parody; he has also in this handful of poems extended the resources of blank verse beyond what any modern practitioner, himself included, has managed to do. This extension comprises more than a mere prosodic advance; it is a rhetorical and imaginative advance. "**By Al Lebowitz's Pool**," "**The Makers**," "**Monet**," and "**A Christmas Storm**," for example, are dazzling in their very naturalness, especially when we take into account that the last two are single, elaborated sentences, each of which encourages all the digressive ribbons and falls of thought, as the poet draws them back into coherent movements of syntax and line. No one since Frost has done as much to move blank verse forward from where Wordsworth and Coleridge had left it. (p. 350)

> *Mary Kinzie, "The Judge Is Rue," in* Poetry, *Vol. CXXXVIII, No. 6, September, 1981, pp. 344-50.*

BONNIE COSTELLO

Nemerov's distance is classical—marmoreal, brisk, and witty, it works in a clear light, approaching feeling through intelligence. In measuring man he has many instruments at his command. His clean sense of decorum, in diction and idiom, allows him to violate our expectation for sharp effects; his penchant for epigram and aphorism gives a rhetorical truth value to his statement; his base of plain speaking weights his lilting measure. Writing for the occasion, with a marksmanship of line and phrase, he is, in a way, the latest of the sons of Ben.

Like all classicists, Nemerov thinks in ranks. [The three sections of *Sentences*]—Beneath, Above, Beyond—mark off, respectively, poems of low diction and subject (our social sphere of sex and power), poems of higher diction and subject (metaphysics and poetry), and those of middle diction and subject (our origin and fate). These categories are not pure, of course, but distinct enough that crossings shock us.

We are naturally inclined toward what is above or beyond, but even granting this prejudice, most of the poems in "Beneath" are best passed over. The wit is not quick enough to ballast the stooping manner. (p. 176)

The satirist's chief weapons of inversion and incongruity deflate exalted motives and, as in **"The Ace of Hearts,"** expose the asinine beneath the sentimental. But the build up doesn't fuel the one-liner in this case.

> My darling, all these sentiments and signs
> Of love, what difference posting through the town
> The purple hearts, the bloody valentines,
> If all are only asses upside down? . . .

Wit probes to the lowest common denominator, and following this simple principle Nemerov finds his strength. **"The Serial,"** a sonnet, takes a wide view from the most reductive of images: the "dramatis personae" of the telephone book. Each line reinforces or expands the endless, impersonal serialization of "persons parted, who as they leave the stage / Get quietly stood in for, page by page." **"Four Soldiers,"** one of the best in the book, takes on a complex of major themes—war, mortality, art—through the associative richness of a single image, an iron sculpture by David Smith. The sculpture becomes a monument and the verse an epitaph. . . . From Smith, who turned iron to irony, weapon to expression, thus life to art, Nemerov has learned a deep poetic justice, a delicate classical balance: "That way may the machine redeem the part / And nature for some time consent to art." (pp. 177-78)

While the best poems of "Above" glance toward heaven for their ideas of order, Nemerov makes their arguments by the design or puzzle in nature. The eye gathers knowledge if the intellect shapes it and art must repeatedly bow to life. . . . **"A Christmas Storm"** holds the breath through 39 lines of tugging syntax to record the transformations of a winter scene in gorgeous detail which is never gratuitous. Nemerov earns the crescendo "diamonded display" of the world in sunlit ice, not only in the prelude of the cruel storm, but in the benevolent consolation that, if suffering is discriminate, beauty knows no class.

The more metaphysical poems of "Above" sometimes echo George Herbert, which comes as a surprise after the Augustan tones of "Beneath." "So brief, so brave, so April pale" in **"First Things, and Last"** has the cadence of Herbert's "Sweet day, so cool, so calm, so bright" of "Virtue." Like Herbert, Nemerov delights in reading the book of nature. And like Herbert, he recognizes the virtue of simple diction and syntax in presenting the stance of childlike surprise. . . . (pp. 178-79)

But Nemerov has too much urbanity to play Herbert's score for long. His puns, unlike Herbert's, are a little tongue in cheek. **"Drift,"** which as it opens could be Hopkins, Herbert's closest heir ("A drive diminishing, a sigh between lift / and sift"), becomes saturnine with the sudden intrusion of slang, "You get my drift?" Nemerov is happier in the mode of Frost where irony and pastoral combine, as in **"Morning Glory"** which "seating gardeners" call "the Devil's Guts": "it's tied whole hedges up in knots. . . / And started to ambition after trees." But suddenly "It opens out its own pale trumpet-belled / Five bladed blooms. . . / . . . so frail they fall / At almost a touch." Nemerov's penchant for aphorism, like Frost's, has the mark of Yankee independence; his narratives are designed to prove exceptions to rules. (pp. 179-80)

The poems in "Beyond" are generally longer meditations on the body / soul debate. Addressing his own decaying body, he has the savage indignation of Yeats, the Yeats descended from Swift:

> Now we approach the Ecclesiastian Age
> Where the heart is like to go off inside your chest
> Like a party favor, or the brain blow a fuse
> And the comic-book light-bulb of Idea black out
> Forever, the idiot balloon of speech
> Go blank, and we shall know, if it be knowing,
> The world as it was before language once again

But Nemerov lacks Yeats's conviction and his closing is not irony but hard pastoral: "Homely animal, in sickness and health, / For the duration; buddy, you know the drill." (p. 180)

The poet feels most intensely the loss of poetry's Adamic freshness, recorded in **"The Makers."** No one remembers "those first and greatest poets," those natural geniuses who "worded the world." Yet in reaching back to the moment when flesh became word he makes those simple ancient sounds "star, water, stone. . . / wind and time and change. . . / love, death sleep . . . bread and wine" seem young even as echo. The first great poets, Nemerov reminds us, were also "the first great listeners," not simply filling the void, but giving it form. Certainly this master of metronome and pitch, who can astonish with a twisted syntax, a missed or added syllable, has learned as much about hearing as about saying from these "makers." "Interval, relationship and scale" are closer to his art than talk. (p. 181)

"Al Lebowitz's Pool" abounds in . . . breathing shapes and stops of breath, even while its mood is more reflective than declarative. Its casual passive-receptive voice and loose structure pass through sudden rightnesses, as a gradient of o's play along the line ("these globes / Of color bob about") or a ripple of syllables skips through the rhythm ("shimmering frequencies of waterlight"). Nemerov draws the reader into his revery, "imagine this," for revery is a kind of reading, taking thought "Up out of water and light and shadow and leaf / Doing the dance of their dependencies." The mind delights in its pool of correspondences, gently lapping with the motions of the eye. Such "mystery of pure relation" always looks right, though "the world is a misery, as it always was." (pp. 181-82)

"By Al Lebowitz's Pool" is the closest Nemerov comes in this volume to personal meditation, but even here the appeal is less of sympathy than of wit, less of sentient, intuitive knowledge than of seasoned thought and verbal precision. All Nemerov's lines reach confidently across the page, setting us on a clear route to the truths of the intellect. They speak with authority, filtering experience into statement, statement into verse. (pp. 182-83)

Bonnie Costello, "Sympathy and Wit," in Parnassus: Poetry in Review, *Vol. 9, No. 2, Fall-Winter, 1981, pp. 169-83.*

J. PATRICK LEWIS

[Howard Nemerov's] much admired romantic/realist dualism is shown to full effect in *Inside the Onion,* whose social-satirical poems are crafted masterfully. For all his early brooding tinged with bitterness, Nemerov has mellowed: "May it be our hope appropriate to grow / Into the next phrase as into the former ones, / And go upstairs about as often as down, / And to as many times a day as fro." Elsewhere, he writes that "the fury of knowledge fades," but happily not here, not in these fine poems.

J. Patrick Lewis, in a review of "Inside the Onion," in Library Journal, *Vol. 108, No. 22, December 15, 1983, p. 2335.*

PHOEBE PETTINGELL

The poems of Howard Nemerov concern themselves less with the nature of things than with how we perceive them. *Inside the Onion* . . . contains ruminations on a macrocosm revealed by the microcosm of **"A Sprig of Dill"**; the effect of the Equal Rights Movement in the Church, whereby "the pin-up girl becomes the Nail-up Lady"; **"Striders"** who walk on water but can't swim; a putative letter from Dante's long-suffering wife to Ann Landers, complaining about Beatrice; and comparable examples of Life's little ironies. . . .

[Nemerov] feels the continuity between past and present strongly. He converses with dead poets as with old friends. "Slow, dear Marvell? Vegetables are slow?" he questions the author of "To His Coy Mistress" incredulously, contemplating the uncontrolled growth of beans and squash running riot in his garden. **"In Memory of the Master Poet Robert Browning"** ruefully wonders about the death of Grand Opera and former ideals. Calling to mind Browning's mordant "A Tocatta of Galupi's," also a *carpe diem,* the modern poet concludes, "When things are over that's what they are, over. Master, I too feel chilly and grown old."

Art, for Nemerov, boils down to the tales, scribblings, tunes we make up about a universe too vast to comprehend: "A story many times told in many ways, / The set of random accidents redeemed / By one more accident, as though chaos / Were the order that was before creation came." He loves jokes, puns and small conundrums he calls "gnomes" because they tie the seemingly unrelated together, forming a new link unperceived before. Similarly, he finds comfort in the ritual progression of seasons. . . .

Nemerov writes some of his best poems about painters, since he shares their keen eyesight and fascination with form. **"A Blind Man at the Museum"** is guided by his wife, who pushes a pram containing speechless babies past "grazing cows and crucifixions and / Self-portraits where the painter's mirrored eyes / Reflect themselves unseeing in the plane / Eternity of art, unable to look out." The poet likes to imagine that the blind man used to be an authority on these very pictures. . . .

Nemerov uses [a] . . . "dumbshow of predicaments" to represent our fragmentary comprehension. Like blind men, each

feeling a different part of the elephant, we cannot predict the whole from what little we grasp. Yet such misapprehensions may themselves result in an imaginative act. *Inside the Onion* is not really about our inability to know. Instead, it stresses the mysterious connections we invent to make sense of things. Between the universe and our five senses "lies language, our fluid coupling with the world." (p. 17)

Phoebe Pettingell, "Frozen and Fluid Images," in The New Leader, *Vol. LXVII, No. 8, April 30, 1984, pp. 16-17.*

JAMES FINN COTTER

[Howard Nemerov's new collection] arrives to cast a cold eye on the contemporary scene. The title poem, **"Inside the Onion,"** strips away the layers to analyze the mathematics of our imperfections. Nature, **"Mad Housewife,"** has made the onion "One and the same throughout the in and out," and that is cause for tears. **"Reading Pornography in Old Age"** reminds the poet, ironically, of life in Eden before the Fall, "when we were beautiful / And shameless," and not yet driven out "to the laboring world / Of the money and the garbage and the kids." Many poems smack of sour grapes, but the satire tastes right in **"Imprecated upon a Postal Clerk"** (a surly attendant behind a counter), **"Disseverings, Divorces"** ("weddings that went / From woo to woe, from courtship through the courts"), and **"Facing the Funerals"** ("Men have their faiths as coffins have their handles, / Needed but once, but handy to have them"). Religion takes some hard raps in **"Last Things," "Prayer of the Middle Class at Ease in Zion,"** and **"An Act of God."** **"She"** is a funny bit about Dante's wife writing to Ann Landers on her husband's obsession with a dead woman. Toilet graffiti and Chinese scrolls provoke uncommon responses. Of the temperate poems, **"The Present Past"** is most eloquent: "But brief as flowering / Has always been, our power to attend / Is briefer by far, and intermittent, too." Nasty or nice, Nemerov remains in top form. (p. 500)

James Finn Cotter, "Poetry Marathon," in The Hudson Review, *Vol. XXXVII, No. 3, Autumn, 1984, pp. 496-507.*

PENNY BOUMELHA

[In *Inside the Onion,* Howard] Nemerov writes with a keen and explicit awareness of his poetic forerunners (Browning, Dryden and Marvell are among those invoked), of critics (a set of **'Gnomic Variations for Kenneth Burke'**), and of the conventions and techniques of poetry (one poem, indeed, is called **'Poetics'**). The effect is wryly self-knowing, disarmingly self-questioning, yet marks a confident claim to a place in this tradition, the title **'This My Modest Art'** notwithstanding. The writing is elegant, never less than accomplished, but sometimes so finished as to suggest a class assignment or a rhetorical exercise. The intellectual formality of the conceits and meditations is broken up by occasional shock tactics of slang and sex. Lust, in fact, seems to be dancing attendance on Nemerov's entry into old age, though accompanied by resignation rather than rage. For me, the predominant tone of this undramatically eschatological collection is caught in a phrase from the poem **'Graffiti'**:

> every saying is a compressed cry
> For the last things of love.
>
> (p. 11)

Penny Boumelha, "Princess Diane," in London Review of Books, *February 21 to February 27, 1985, pp. 10-11.*

Ngugi wa Thiong'o

1938-

(Has also written as James T(hiong'o) Ngugi) Kenyan novelist, dramatist, essayist, short story writer, journalist, and critic.

As a spokesman for his people and a chronicler of Kenya's modern history, Ngugi is widely regarded as the most significant writer in contemporary East Africa. *Weep Not, Child* (1964) was the first novel written in English to be published by an East African. His account of the Mau Mau Emergency, *A Grain of Wheat* (1967), was the first work to present the African perspective on this complex armed revolt against British rule during the 1950s. In addition, Ngugi wrote the first modern novel in his native Kikuyu language. He has also been influential in education in East Africa and is recognized as a humanist deeply interested in the growth and well-being of his people and country.

Ngugi's fiction reflects his abiding concern for the poor of Kenya who have been displaced first by white colonialists and later by the black opportunists who seized power after independence. His early works, *Weep Not, Child, The River Between* (1965), and *A Grain of Wheat,* present the harmful effects of colonialism, yet they also reflect Ngugi's optimism that Western education would address the inherent problems of colonialism and its legacy. However, as internal friction and class division widened following Kenya's independence in 1963, Ngugi's stance became increasingly Marxist, culminating in *Petals of Blood* (1977). In this novel Ngugi attacks capitalism and accuses wealthy landowners and bureaucrats of exploiting the poor and working classes. Various other themes are interwoven with the economic and political issues, including Christianity as opposed to tribal religions, youth versus the aged, and old cultures making way for the new.

Many of the essays in *Homecoming: Essays on African and Caribbean Literature, Culture, and Politics* (1972) emphasize the important social functions of literature. Due to Ngugi's efforts to restructure the way literature is taught in his country, more attention is now given to African writers than to previously stressed Western authors. Ngugi was also involved in building a local community center at Kamirithu and establishing an adult literacy program there. In collaboration with Ngugi wa Mirii and other members of that program, Ngugi wrote and staged the play *Ngaahika ndeenda* (1977; *I Will Marry When I Want*), which examines social, religious, and economic exploitation of the Kikuyus.

The production of *I Will Marry When I Want* in Ngugi's hometown of Limuru resulted in his arrest and a year's detention in prison, although no official charges were made. While in prison Ngugi wrote *Caitaani muthara-Ini* (1980; *Devil on the Cross*), the first modern novel to be written in his indigenous language. The book is an allegory intended to make peasants and workers more aware of the political forces that shape their lives. *Detained: A Writer's Prison Diary* (1981) recounts the circumstances of Ngugi's arrest and detention as well as his life since being released. At the time of his arrest in 1977, Ngugi was head of the department of literature at the University of Nairobi; he has yet to be reinstated.

(See also *CLC*, Vols. 3, 7, 13 and *Contemporary Authors*, Vols. 81-84.)

ANGUS CALDER

[*Homecoming*] has no pretensions to seem more than what it is: a collection of occasional essays on African and Caribbean writers and on cultural situations in the non-white world. But its tone, and the ideas which it sketches, are splendidly refreshing. Though he does inexplicably use the scholar's pedestalled 'we' on a couple of occasions, Mr Ngugi, a Kenyan, is immune to the fashionable trivialities of academic criticism. For him the bearing of a book towards society, the capacity it may lend us to cut down oppression, is all important. His comments on Achebe, Soyinka and Naipaul are, accordingly, the most valuable I've seen. The clarity with which he writes stems from complete conviction and from two prime sources of authority.

Firstly, when he says that 'the writer . . . lives in, and is shaped by, history,' he offers not dogma, but his own experience. His study of the Mau Mau Emergency, *A Grain of Wheat,* is arguably the best, and certainly the most underrated, novel to come from Black Africa. While at times he uses other people's books bluntly to illustrate his own social criticism, he doesn't confuse novels with pamphlets, or a writer's effects with his intentions.

He is, secondly, a subtle and resolute Marxist humanist. He builds on the achievements of older men—Fanon, Richard Wright, Nyerere and many more—who suffered in the vanguard of black literature and politics. . . .

His belief in the capacity of poor people to control their own lives has a strength which is oddly rare among African intellectuals, and this informs the view of culture which he sets out in several stimulating essays.

So does the earlier history of his Kikuyu people. They had no kings; no writing; no monuments. And hence their culture was their whole present and changing way of life, its songs, its rituals, its sustaining religious ideas. Christianity, propping up colonialism, destroyed their faith in what they had had. Mau Mau, for all its shortcomings as a movement (and Mr Ngugi admits them) was a reassertion of faith. However, what has happened has happened. 'No living culture,' Mr Ngugi says, echoing Fanon, 'is ever static.' He tells artists (and Christians) to work with political direction so as to re-establish the communal character of the old culture on new plans, pan-tribal, pan-African, pan-'Third World':

> Ideally, our social and economic life should be so organised that each village and each section of our cities is an art centre, a music centre, a drama centre.

Then, in the sense intended by the book's title, man will have 'come home.' (p. 562)

Angus Calder, "Fresh and Whole Vision," in New Statesman, *Vol. 84, No. 2170, October 20, 1972, pp. 526-63.*

ADRIAN ROSCOE

[In Ngugi wa Thiong'o's fiction there is] an abiding concern with the soil and man's relationship to it, not as some Lawrentian dream of giving industrial man an anchor for his sanity, but as the central factor in an equation guaranteeing the economic, social, psychological, and spiritual survival of a people. Urban-dwelling strangers must not underestimate this point about land. Ngugi might not have explored it, might indeed have written a different kind of fiction, if colonialists had not taken his land and post-colonialists not failed justly to redistribute it. The soil is also portrayed in its extra-economic aspects, in its aesthetic and artistic role as landscape and background, as a milieu of hills, valleys, and ridges in which Ngugi's characters are born and live their lives. Other African writers have a feeling for landscape and paint it well. . . . But one's sense of a landscape's beauty and its meaning for an author and his people are vitally more present in Ngugi than in most. Where often it is simply a felt background or backcloth to a narrative, as it is in, say, Achebe or in the Malawian novelist Kayira, here it is a palpable shaping influence on the physical and spiritual lives of the characters. . . .

Religion too is never far from Ngugi's mind. As everywhere else in African writing, Christianity is identified as a deeply potent element in the encounter between local society and the West. But its treatment here transcends the superficial levels found too often elsewhere and becomes deep sensitive investigation. Ngugi's work is the best account yet of how Christianity not only gnawed away at tribal values (the standard

charge against it), but how it actually resonated with deep elements in the hearts of the people. (p. 171)

Ngugi's work bears the marks of surprise and disappointment that the world is not as he once thought, that the goodness he perhaps sees in his own nature does not predominate in the affairs of men. It records the response of a sensitive Christian soul who discovers, sadly, that he has been serving an unsatisfactory cause. (p. 172)

A trinity of themes is achieved with 'education', or more exactly schooling in a western mode. This is important, for Ngugi's main characters (those whose consciousness we get close to) are men who see beyond their own milieu, who understand the forces at work on a world rather than tribal scale, and have an awareness of comparative justice, economic fairness, and grand political intrigue. Their mode of training, which Ngugi consistently calls 'education' (ignoring Kenyatta's caveat and inviting the suggestion that traditional Gikuyu education does not merit the name), is seen as a catalyst to development, the moulder of new leaders who will guide the clans through the complexities of the modern world, a way of achieving the possibles of political theory. Like Christianity, however, it has also the side effect of creating class divisions, of disrupting tribal unity and alienating individuals from their peers and families. Hence the agonising position of Njoroge in *Weep Not, Child,* and John in the short story **'A Meeting in the Dark'.**

If these are main themes in Ngugi's writing, what holds them together? What constitutes the shaping vision behind them? Politics is an obvious answer, and more specifically the doctrines of Marxism. If ever the point was in doubt, Ngugi's **Homecoming** records how deeply his world view has been influenced by Marx. The niceties of land disputes, cultural vertigo, and spiritual chaos are well enough; but behind and beneath them all, as if in explanation of them, lies the framework of ideas which are the parameters of Marxism.

While some may doubt the importance of the relationship between a writer and his beliefs, Ngugi gives his own views in very plain terms. The boundaries of a writer's imagination, he says, are limited by his 'beliefs, interests, and experiences in life, by where in fact he stands in the world of social relations'. . . . Ngugi's creative work clearly shows that for all his sensitivity to political and social issues, human relations are what he cares about most passionately. His vision includes a horror at what has been done, and is being done, to human relationships in Africa, political convictions about why this is happening, and a dream of 'a true communal home for all Africans'.

Ngugi is regularly compared with Achebe . . . , and Conrad's influence is also rightly canvassed. But his general growth as a writer, and especially his espousal of 'political art', brings him closer to Orwell than to either of these. Ngugi and Orwell are both shy, burningly honest men, provoked by injustice; defenders of the weak, public figures through circumstances rather than inclination. . . . Coming from Ngugi's novels, with their care about love and human relationships, their concern for 'the surface of the earth', it is easy to conclude that he too is an artist who, in a less revolutionary age, would have written differently; or at least that his work would have been the result of a slightly modified equation of egoism, aesthetics, and the rest. If Mau Mau had never happened, if Kenya had won its freedom in peace, if independence had been marked by political virtue with the peasant gaining from land reform, Ngugi would have had to work with different material. Meanwhile, like

Orwell, he is not a propagandist in the crude sense, but a committed literary artist.... Ngugi espouses politics, the science of the possible, because he believes that change can occur: he remains, therefore, a hurt optimist rather than a defeated Jeremiah.

But neither politics nor large issues guarantees successful fiction; and while critics argue ... whether Ngugi qualifies for such exalted titles as Genuine Socialist Novelist, the question whether he possesses the basic skills of his craft seems too infrequently raised. Fortunately, he is strong in all those necessary areas of scene-setting, plot, structure, characterisation, and firmness of prose without which his books would be either unreadable or mere political ephemera.

The River Between's hero is described as having eyes that are 'delicately tragic'. A happy phrase, it evokes a pervading quality in Ngugi's vision and in his prose. Neither heavily proverbial like Achebe's nor crisply economic like Oyono's, Ngugi's prose is unpretentious, neither over-refined nor casually rough-hewn. It is free of the excesses associated with rhetoric, for despite a slow hardening of tone, Ngugi seems to agree with Dennis Brutus that rhetoric tends to falsify experience. Hence his quiet-voiced prose, one-speed and steady, never racing out of control, and possessing a clarity that keeps event and character always plainly visible. An honest, sensitive style, it neither cavorts nor strikes attitudes; nor will it court the vanities of over-dressing. Its measured pace allows for silences, giving Ngugi's writing a reflective quality, as if the consciousness producing it is still, as it articulates, puzzling over human experience, trying honestly to interpret it aright, wanting to understand and record it all exactly, and thus needing pauses, a stillness, to do it properly. (pp. 172-76)

The author's rendering of the shape, colour, and texture of the landscape is important on two special counts. First it marks him as a true Gikuyu who has not entirely lost his own bond with the soil. Secondly its deep sensitivity confounds all those scholars, black and white, who, despite massive literary evidence to the contrary, argue that African people have no feeling for landscape, ignore its beauty, see it only as so much soil to hoe. The affectionate pictures of Gikuyuland are also a sign of how Ngugi, though an African novelist in the broadest sense of being a spokesman for the whole continent (and even for the black race) is basically working as a regional novelist, like Achebe and Beti, or Laye and Hardy. Though universal in appeal, he portrays a particular people in a particular locale. His canvas is restricted to Kenya's Central Province.... Only the upland ridges and valleys of Gikuyuland are chosen for evocation.

The bond between character and land is especially strong in *The River Between,* where Waiyaki, soon after his second birth, goes with his father to visit one of the clan's sacred places.... We cannot understand the individual, social, and spiritual significance of either character outside their relation to the landscape. Chege's whole life has been moulded by the land. His maturity, his fulness as a human being, are owed to it. Only when Waiyaki too has been initiated into a full understanding of the land, reborn into a full relationship with it, will he in turn become a mature member of his people.... Ngugi's is one of the few genuine voices of the land in English-language writing anywhere; and he is spokesman for a people whose sacred bond with the soil caused them to undertake a bloody uprising against the colonial power. (pp. 177-178)

Three colonial products which Ngugi frequently identifies are loneliness, class divisions, and guilt. Loneliness is common in all three novels, and in the short stories. We are meant to see this, I think, not as reflecting a modern existentialist infection but as a palpable result of the fracture of an old order by the engines of capitalism, the Puritan ethic, and the progress myth.... Ngugi's men and women are lonely, and feel lonely, in a new way; and it is clearly, from textual evidence, a result of their encounter with Europe. A simple exercise is to read Kenyatta's *Facing Mount Kenya* before approaching the fiction of Ngugi. The change worked on the Gikuyu people since Kenyatta wrote in the Thirties is astonishing. The first is a picture of tight cohesion where men and women acknowledge a common cause in a highly democratic society. The second is a picture resembling Picasso's Guernica ..., where all is fragmentation and anxiety as members of the same group cut throats and betray friends, all in a chaotic fight for selfish enrichment. (pp. 180-81)

Both the fragmentation of Gikuyu society and the loneliness it breeds reach their highest pitch in *A Grain of Wheat,* whose picture of isolated guerrillas operating in a hit-or-miss way in scattered areas, with little sense of a home base and frequently slaughtering their own people, is the most poignant evidence for the fracture and isolation that haunt Ngugi's imagination. Figures like Mugo, an only son anxious for solitude and prepared to betray the tribe to achieve it; figures like Gatu and Gikonyo; and Kihika, the Messianic figure so loved by his people, a man essentially alone in his special level of spiritual and military involvement—they are all victims of a condition Ngugi laments.

A predictable result of Westernism and its accompanying new economic order is the growth of social class in what Kenyatta once described as an extraordinarily egalitarian society. As the new order fosters individualism, offering excessive rewards to those who can get trained, social competition begins. Men get ahead of their fellows, build their own fortress and drop the portcullis—raising it only for their own children to sally forth to gain the same privileges and the same rewards. Men are set against men, groups emerge with special interests whose solidarity is based on money and the command of strategic areas of the economy. (p. 183)

A factor which compounds the hardships of land deprivation and social fragmentation is the enormous guilt load Ngugi's people seem doomed to carry. Whether this is a general truth about the Presbyterian impact on Gikuyu society or a generalisation of Ngugi's personal experience (the artist imagining that others must feel the world in the same manner as himself) one does not know. Yet the amount of guilt gnawing away at the minds of Ngugi's characters in all three novels and in such short stories as **'A Meeting in the Dark'** is extraordinary. (p. 188)

Ngugi's strengths have been acknowledged widely. It is argued, with little contradiction, that his skill at structure and characterisation increases throughout the three novels; and while some might argue, as undergraduates do, that *A Grain of Wheat* has too complex a structure, none denies that this is an advance on the symmetrical apprentice-work structures of the first two books. Ngugi has also achieved the difficult task of fusing the 'artistic' with the 'political' so that we have here creative literature and not simply a propaganda sheet. One suspects, however, that he began his career simply reporting life as he found it, portraying his society as it really was, and then later discovered that Marxist theory crystallised his thoughts, confirming his own hunches and providing a theory about why matters were the way he saw them. This schedule would explain why the tone of *Homecoming,* especially the 'Author's Note', is palpably at odds with the restrained, patient prose of the novels. This sounds like a new Ngugi, strangely bitter, like the Achebe of *A Man of the People,* losing his patience but finding a cause.

Ngugi's special achievement is partly to have analysed sharply a people's agony at a particular moment in their history and also to have given us a powerfully honest reading of human nature. (pp. 189-90)

The result of this honesty is that Ngugi's level of character portrayal is second to none in Africa. There is a constant prodding beneath the skin of his figures, a picking over the entrails of emotion, fear, and motive: and these he relates to the great backcloth of historic circumstance, the movement in time of a whole society and its world view. Why did Gikonyo confess the oath? Why did Mugo betray Kihika? Why did Mumbi yield to Karanja? Why did Koinandu rape Dr. Lynd? Why did Waiyaki and Nyambura drift apart? Why was Ngotho content to work for Howlands? Why did Thompson behave the way he did? That questions like these are raised without being given simple answers reflects the complex nature of life as Ngugi sees it.

Finally, what has developed over the three novels is not simply Ngugi's ability to draw character but to handle, over a distance, the careers of a range of different figures. *A Grain of Wheat* is particularly important for this. But ultimately what counts is the vision of the author himself. Here is a reflective, moral artist whose outlook and prose tone are summed up in that phrase he himself chose for one of his characters: 'a tragic delicacy'. (p. 190)

Adrian Roscoe, *"Prose,"* in his Uhuru's Fire: African Literature East to South, *Cambridge University Press, 1977, pp. 168-214.**

LEWIS NKOSI

Powerful works of literature usually break out of some great national trauma or personal obsession; the Mau Mau freedom struggle with its attendant sacrifices, its triumphs and betrayals, has become Ngugi's own personal preoccupation. His first published novel, *Weep Not, Child* (1964), and his third, *A Grain of Wheat* (1967), are prolonged meditations on the theme of national struggle, the courage, sacrifices and loyalties it requires, and not surprisingly some of the opportunism and failure of nerve which are brought to the surface by such momentous events.

Indeed, *A Grain of Wheat,* which seems to me a much better novel in its structural balances and tensions than his latest work, *Petals of Blood* (1977), has sometimes been criticised for not being "ideologically correct" by some socialist commentators who are depressed by a novel which has only traitors for its heroes; except that in Ngugi's defence it must be said that many readers may see this as a more or less valid metaphor for the disappointed hopes of those in Kenya who expected more from their leaders.

A Grain of Wheat is built around a series of ever-widening concentric circles of guilt and betrayal: from the most obvious case of Karanja who once flirted with the freedom movement but later turned administrative chief for his area during the Mau Mau; to Gikonyo who broke down during detention at Yala Camp and confessed the oath he had taken; to Mumbi, Gikonyo's wife, who yields to Karanja's sexual advances; right to the final revelation of the biggest betrayal of all, when Mugo, who when chosen to lead the Uhuru celebrations, confesses to

have given away to the British authorities Kihika, the hanged hero of the forest fighters. On the last page of this carefully constructed novel, which takes as its framework Conrad's *Under Western Skies,* Mumbi might have been talking for the entire community when she tells the husband:

> People try to rub out things, but they cannot. Things are not so easy. What has passed between us is too much to be passed over in a sentence. We need to talk, to open our hearts to one another, examine them, and then together plan the future we want.

Talking is what Ngugi has been doing ever since. Quite clearly what he is talking about is what a lot of people in higher places in Kenya today would rather not have it talked about. *Petals of Blood* is not so much a novel as an attempt to think aloud about the problems of modern Kenya: the sharp contrast between the city and the countryside, between the "ill-gotten" wealth of the new African middle-class and the worsening plight of the unemployed workers and peasants. Sometimes the novel veers very sharply, as many such novels tend to do, toward the fable, albeit a socialist fable, with capitalists carrying such unlikely names as "Sir Swallow Bloodall".

I think Ngugi's latest fiction fails because the author is so conscious of not having written a "socialist novel" before that he gives up concrete observation, which is the correct starting point of all true materialists, in favour of a fable-cum-satire-cum-realist fiction in order to illustrate class formations in modern Kenya. To do this he is impelled to create characters who are so unreal as to invalidate a great deal of what Ngugi sets out to prove. (pp. 334-35)

There are some fine touches in *Petals of Blood,* as in the scene in which Wanja, now a rich brothel-madam, is keeping a rendezvous with Karega, an old acquaintance (or lover) who has become an important trade union leader. Asked why she still maintains the old hut although she now owns a palatial mansion, Wanja replies: "I don't want to forget old Ilmorog. I never shall forget how we lived before the Trans-Africa Road cleaved Ilmorog into two halves."

The line not only rings true because all over the world there are many prostitutes and members of the nouveau riche who feel that way about their background, but because the statement also illustrates the heart-rending contradictions that people who prostitute themselves have to live through. It is a small example of how well Ngugi can dramatise these contradictions when he becomes more concrete and is prepared to delve into his characters.

What becomes clear in *Petals of Blood* is a major shift in Ngugi's work, ideological in nature, from the earlier emphasis on nationalism and race questions to a class analysis of society. In *The River Between,* for instance, Ngugi was concerned with the conflict between tradition and modernism, a trite theme in modern African literature, with a rather overheated love affair to give the story its glossy "Romeo & Juliet" finish. His short story, **"The Village Priest"**, contained in *Secret Lives,* is an attempt to dramatise this conflict by pitting a Christian convert with a wily medicine man who causes the rain to fall after a long drought, thus proving the old gods are still more powerful than the new.

In *Petals of Blood* the perspective shifts from concerns with nationalism and cultural identity to the overriding question of class conflict and internal exploitation. When Wanja says to

Karega, "You used to argue that the past was important for today", the trade union leader answers: "...We must not preserve our past as a museum: rather, we must study it critically, without illusions, and see what lessons we can draw from it—no. Maybe I used to do it: but I don't want to continue worshipping in the temples of a past without tarmac roads, without electric cookers, a world dominated by slavery to nature." (p. 335)

Lewis Nkosi, "A Voice from Detention," in West Africa, No. 3162, February 20, 1978, pp. 334-35.

GOVIND NARAIN SHARMA

Ngugi's *Petals of Blood* is a complex and powerful work. It is a statement of his social and political philosophy and an embodiment of his prophetic vision. Ngugi provides a masterly analysis of the social and economic situation in modern Kenya, a scene of unprincipled and ruthless exploitation of man by man, and gives us a picture of the social and moral consequences of this exploitation. He diagnoses it with the skill and penetration of a seasoned social thinker, but refuses to be disheartened by the depressing nature of the situation. Like a poet-prophet in the tradition of Blake and Whitman, he sees the past, present and future as a continuum, and is confident that the future is full of hope and promise and that the Kingdom of God will come. That a new earth, another world, can be created, is the vision revealed to the hero, Karega, only if man could avoid sliding into the slough of cynicism and succeed in sustaining faith and hope. He tries to inspire others with this vision. The wish of another leading character, Munira, is to "re-create the past so that one can show the operation of God's law [?], the working out of God's will, the revelation of His will so that now the blind can see what the wise cannot see." ... He too comes to share Karega's belief in the creation of a new world, though his conception of the means by which it would come is different. *Petals of Blood* is thus scientific in its social analysis, eschatological in its historical framework and prophetic in its moral and spiritual attitude. Ngugi's outlook is deeply influenced by the two great traditions of thought, Marxism and Christianity. He makes use of Marxist and Christian concepts to delineate the predicament and trace the moral and spiritual evolution of his characters as well as to portray the general condition of society, and of the two myths to trace the historical pattern of his apocalypse. But African utopianism constitutes the matrix of his apocalyptic vision.

Though there is plenty of direct social and political comment, Ngugi's fictional technique is to convey, as he had done in *A Grain of Wheat,* the meaning and significance of the outer struggle in society through the inner turmoil it creates in the minds, hearts and souls of certain key individuals who are members of this society. What distinguishes them from others is that they are intelligent, sensitive and considerate, have certain ideals and principles, dream dreams and have visions. Having a tender social conscience, they are reluctant to throw themselves wholeheartedly in the unprincipled pursuit of wealth, position and power which is the sole concern of the new élite in the country. They provide a fairly representative cross-section of Kenyan society, based on their social origins as well as their political, social and religious orientations. The world of *Petals* is that of post-independence Kenya, a world of "naked, shameless, direct, brutal exploitation" and moral and cultural decadence in which a select few are enriching themselves at the expense of the workers and peasants of the land. The promises of pre-independence days have long since been forgotten. . . . Whereas traditional religious and moral thought has attributed exploitation and injustice in the world to human wickedness and folly, Ngugi, analyzing the situation in Marxist terms, explains these as "the effect of laws of social development which make it inevitable that at a certain stage of history one class, pursuing its interests with varying degrees of rationality, should dispossess and exploit another." . . . Ngugi, like Marx, traces the various stages in the evolution of society: feudal, bourgeois-capitalist and proletarian, the capitalist stage being characterized by the simplification of the class antagonism between bourgeois and proletariat. Since Ngugi is a firm believer in Africa's glorious past, he cannot fully agree with Marx in his attitude towards the past; but he shares Marx's millennialism and knows that however long and arduous the struggle of his people for total liberation may be, victory is certain. (pp. 302-03)

The struggle, however, is going to be a long and hard one, for it involves recovering fully from the damage that capitalism, colonialism and "its religious ally, the Christian Church," have done to the minds and souls of the African people. (p. 304)

The self-alienation of the African is even more acute than of the worker in other parts of the world because he has been the victim of both colonialism and racism. The onslaught of an alien culture and religion has fostered in him a dislike of his own colour, his own traditions and culture. The problem therefore is nothing less than that of restoration of his psychological, moral and spiritual integrity, his self-image as an individual, free, healthy and whole, well-integrated with his culture and society; and the metaphor which Ngugi uses for this restoration is that of "homecoming." (p. 305)

This problem of restoring them to their home or of building a new home, "a true communal home for all Africans," is Ngugi's main concern in *Petals of Blood.* In his understanding of alienation, of the way human consciousness is affected by the operation of socio-economic forces, Ngugi has been influenced deeply by Marx, but when it comes to the portrayal of the alienation and projection of his vision of a new society he relies even more on the language and myths of Christianity. Ngugi's attitude to Christianity is highly ambivalent. Christianity as an organized religion is corrupt and hypocritical. . . . (pp. 305-06)

But Ngugi accepts the Bible as a definitive myth embodying great truths about the regeneration of the individual and society, a single archetypal structure extending from creation to apocalypse, and it is the major informing influence on his symbolism in *Petals of Blood.* (p. 306)

Petals of Blood is Marxist in its portrayal of alienation and of socio-economic factors which contribute to this alienation. It is Christian in its typology and symbolism, and Ngugi's spirit of prophetism makes it a judgement as well as a call to action in the manner of the book of Revelations and the *Manifesto of the Communist Party.* Both Christianity and Marxism, with their messianism and promise of a millennium, reinforce Ngugi's faith in the certainty of salvation, both personal and social, and of their mutual interdependence. But it is African utopianism which gives content and meaning to his apocalypse. (p. 313)

Govind Narain Sharma, "Ngugi's Apocalypse: Marxism, Christianity and African Utopianism in 'Petals of Blood'," in World Literature Written in English, Vol. 18, No. 2, November, 1979, pp. 302-14.

MICHAEL ETHERTON

The play which sets out to delineate the true folk hero is *The Trial of Dedan Kimathi* by Micere Mugo and Ngugi wa Thiong'o. Kimathi, one of the most important leaders of the guerrilla war for independence in Kenya, called Mau Mau, has been the subject of a number of books, . . . but none has been written with such intense political commitment, as well as a commitment to make Kimathi's life and death meaningful for modern Kenya, as Mugo's and Ngugi's imaginative play. The focus of the drama is Kimathi's trial; but the play ranges freely forwards and backwards in time in order to contain in the first instance the story of how a female peasant activist, simply called 'woman,' attempts to help the imprisoned Kimathi and in the process wins over to the cause of freedom two young people who in the final scene of the play make their brave act of commitment. In the second place the play contains the temptations of Kimathi. The Indian banker, the Kenyan business executive and politician, the priest, all try to bribe him, in various ways, to give up the struggle, and are, to a certain extent, symbolic of the Kenya which has emerged since independence. Finally the play also deals with the heavy burden of responsibilities which the leader of a popular revolution has to face. . . . (p. 68)

The play as a whole weaves these various strands together, culminating in a climax which is so theatrically effective that at its first performance in Nairobi the audience at the end are reported to have danced out of the theatre into the street. There can be no doubt that the play is very effective in the theatre. It has moved away from naturalism . . . and makes a determined effort to bend all the resources of the modern theatre to the aim of political awareness and commitment. (p. 69)

Despite the successful theatricality, the play is still basically literary in its conception; and its social commitment is also a literary commitment—as the authors indicate at the end of their preface:

> In this we believe that Kenyan literature—indeed all African Literature and its writers are on trial . . . African Literature and African Writers are either fighting with the people or aiding imperialism and the class enemies of the people.

This literary commitment extends to the theatre, particularly a theatre staging the plays of writers:

> We believe that good theatre is that which is on the side of the people, that which, without masking mistakes and weaknesses, gives people courage and urges them to higher resolves in their struggle for total liberation. So the challenge was to truly depict the masses (symbolised by Kimathi) in the only historically correct perspective: positively, heroically and as the true makers of history.

This view of the nature of historical theatre contains an explicit criticism of an historical theatre which eulogizes the generals and ancient traditional rulers—the romantic heroes like Chaka and Kurunmi—as much as of the theatre which deals naïvely with the colonial period.

It suggests a way forward, by means of literary drama with all its potential élitism, to a theatre which manages to address the mass of the people. In Mugo's and Ngugi's own terms, 'good theatre' is not necessarily performed inside well-equipped theatre buildings. (pp. 69-70)

Michael Etherton, "Trends in African Theatre," in African Literature Today, *No. 10, 1979, pp. 57-85.**

EUSTACE PALMER

Ngugi wa Thiong'o's latest novel, *Petals of Blood*, is easily his most representative. It incorporates all the major preoccupations of his career as a novelist. . . . Of all African novels it probably presents the most comprehensive analysis so far of the evils perpetrated in independent African society by black imperialists. It subsumes several other aspects of Ngugi's earlier novels—the widespread and effective use of symbols and images, the concern with education and religion, the resourceful and morally courageous women and the indecisive young men who are called upon to play a major role in society, but are unable to do so successfully because they are plagued by a sense of insecurity or guilt. Even the narrative technique seems to be a conglomerate of the methods of *A Grain of Wheat* on the one hand, and *The River Between* and *Weep Not, Child* on the other. The novel is constructed on grand epic proportions, but it is an epic, not just of the East African struggle, but of the entire African struggle. (pp. 153-54)

The narrative technique of *Petals of Blood* is not as complex or subtle as that of *A Grain of Wheat*. Most of it is told in the form of reminiscences rather than flashbacks. The story starts in the present with the four main characters—Wanja, Karega, Abdulla and Munira—in jail on suspicion of being implicated in the murder of the three African directors of the theng'eta brewery. It really takes the form of Munira's recollections as he sits down in his cell writing copious notes in order to clear his own mind about the significance of the events and satisfy the demands of the probing police inspector. Thus from the present the story goes back twelve years to Munira's recollections of his first arrival in Ilmorog. It periodically returns to the present and Munira in his cell, and on one or two occasions goes even further back in time to his experiences while at school at Siriana in the 1940s and the Mau Mau uprising of the 1950s. Otherwise the novel moves progressively forward from Munira's first arrival to the present, and to the resolution of the murder riddle. It would be inaccurate to say that *Petals of Blood* makes use of shifting chronology. The narrative method consists for the most part of reminiscences which nevertheless progress sequentially.

The novel's title, *Petals of Blood*, points to the centrality of the symbolism in the elucidation of the meaning. One dominant symbol cluster relates to flowers and other forms of vegetation. At times these suggest regeneration, fecundity, and luxuriance; but more often, as in the poem by Derek Walcott with which Ngugi prefixes the novel, they suggest destruction, corruption, evil, the unnatural, and death. . . . [In] the body of the novel itself we discover that the flower with the petals of blood belongs to a plant that grows wild in the plains and . . . is itself the victim of evil. Its innocence, like that of Blake's sick rose, has been destroyed by the agents of corruption. The flower thus becomes a symbol of the entire society Ngugi is concerned with—potentially healthy, beautiful, and productive, but its potential unrealized and itself destroyed by the agents of corruption and death.

The plant with the petals of blood is actually the theng'eta plant which grows wild on the plains that are associated with luxuriance, vitality and vigour. It is also a plant that is associated with Ilmorog's pristine traditional splendour, for it was used in making the drink which inspired the old seers, poets, and players. It also symbolizes truth and purity, for the flower with the four red petals was used to purify the drink and the drink itself had the remarkable quality of forcing people to confront the truth about themselves: 'Only you must take it with faith and purity in your hearts.' Therefore, when the people of Ilmorog, under the leadership of Nyakinyua, that staunch upholder of traditional values, decide to re-engage in the production of theng'eta, it symbolizes a decision to return to the purity of their traditional values, and the transformation of theng'eta into a debased modern spirit by the capitalists suggests the erosion of traditional values and the destruction of traditional innocence by the corrupt and depraved agents of modernism.

The drought is another pervasive symbol in the novel. Here Ngugi has used an actual historical and ecological fact—the recent disastrous drought in most of Africa—for symbolic purposes with telling effect. The drought symbolism is often juxtaposed with rain symbolism suggesting the fecundity and luxuriance which the region, under normal circumstances, ought to enjoy. . . . The drought generally refers to the people's deprivation of all those things which should make life meaningful.

Then there is the symbol of maiming which also relates to the people's spiritual condition. The one-legged but very resourceful Abdulla is the most concrete symbol in the novel of man's inhumanity to man. But the physical maiming, which the Ilmorogians almost extend to his donkey on one occasion, also relates to a spiritual condition, for the people all carry maimed souls. Abdulla's lame leg is therefore merely the physical manifestation of a general spiritual fact.

The scene of most of the events of the novel is the community of Ilmorog which grows from a small traditional village into a modern capitalist complex. But Ilmorog could easily have been any other Kenyan village. It is a microcosm of Kenyan society as a whole and its experiences are a paradigm of what happened to a number of similar Kenyan communities. (pp. 154-56)

Ilmorog is soon transformed into a capitalist complex with all the attendant problems of prostitution, social inequalities, and inadequate housing. It has been twice exploited and destroyed; once by the white imperialists, and now by their successors, the black imperialists.

The hero of the novel is Munira, the teacher who decides to settle in Ilmorog. Devotees of Ngugi cannot fail to recognize in him reminiscences of Ngugi's three earlier heroes—Njoroge in *Weep Not, Child* who pins his faith on education and refuses to face the world of adult responsibility, Waiyaki who in spite of his admirable qualities fails to attain the stature of a manly hero through his indecision, and Mugo who is tortured by a sense of guilt and insecurity. In fact Munira is an anti-hero, an ultra-sensitive young man whose life is a failure. (p. 158)

Ngugi demonstrates sure psychological insight in the presentation of his hero [in *Petals of Blood*]. We have not only his thoughts and actions, but the forces which have conditioned him. His shrinking introspective personality is an unconscious reaction partly to his overbearing, contemptuous, and superbly successful proprietor-father, and partly to his materialistic and no less successful brothers and sisters who have been able to carve niches for themselves in the highly competitive capitalist Kenyan society. But although Munira possesses a certain measure of idealism, it would be a mistake to suppose that his withdrawal from involvement is due to an idealistic revulsion against his corrupt society; it is due more to cowardice than to idealism.

Like Waiyaki in *The River Between,* Munira succeeds in becoming accepted and idolized by the people as a teacher. He thus achieves a sense of fulfilment at last and his love for Wanja also draws him into involvement. The sexual prowess he demonstrates in his love-making helps give him that sense of mastery and masculinity that he has completely failed to manifest in the world of adult affairs. But it is the association with Wanja which reveals the cracks in his personality and eventually leads to his disintegration. (p. 159)

To a large extent *Petals of Blood* concentrates on the post-independence disillusionment which had only been hinted at at the end of *A Grain of Wheat*. It gives a most comprehensive picture of what the author sees as the evils pervasive in Kenya under black rule. . . . Ngugi also shows tremendous concern about the clash between the old traditional values and the decadent values of a modern capitalist society. In particular, he exposes the tendency of the modern capitalists to debase those values, as when they convert the time-honoured songs of the initiation ritual into obscene entertainment at their parties, or pervert the oath-taking custom for the most sordid ends. (pp. 161-62)

Organized religion also comes in for some very savage satire in this novel. Christianity, which in earlier novels was shown to exercise a firm hold over the lives of the people, is presented here as oppressive, unsympathetic, and hypocritical. Munira's father, who is a patriarch of the church as well as a pillar of the state, is actually a capitalist and black slaver of the most rabid sort. . . . Like Joshua's in *The River Between,* his religion is a life-denying force which has stifled the life in Munira's wife and children. Essentially he is an irreligious and godless man who cannot see that his Christianity ought to preclude the taking of an oath geared towards the consolidation of tribalism. (p. 165)

Ngugi has often been accused of not doing enough to impart an African flavour to the language of his novels. This charge could certainly not be laid against *Petals of Blood,* where Ngugi makes extensive use of proverbs and songs, rendering them directly, at times, in the indigenous language. In fact the extensive use of the oral tradition in this novel reinforces one's sense of a society that used to be cohesive and dignified, and in most cases the relevance of the songs and legends can be demonstrated.

Petals of Blood has been described by one reviewer as a rambling novel. This is unjust. Nevertheless, on putting down the novel the reader has an uneasy feeling that Ngugi has been too ambitious, that he has attempted to do too much within the compass of a single novel. There are both thematic and stylistic reminiscences here, not just of Ngugi's own earlier novels, but of Ousmane, Armah, Ouologuem, Achebe, Soyinka, and others. Such a work is bound to be uneven in quality. There are brilliant scenes, superbly realized, alternating at times with rather more tedious ones. This is partly due to the fact that Ngugi's chosen method of narration—the use of reminiscences—involves much more telling than showing. There seems to be a preponderance of narration and assertion over detailed scenic demonstration. We hear people talking about their past experiences rather than see them enacted before our eyes. How much more effective it would have been to have seen Karega's trade union activities enacted than to be told about them by himself! It is also a pity that Ngugi decided to place at the centre of events a hero like Munira who is not only spineless, but succeeds eventually in totally alienating the reader's sympathy. Mugo, in spite of his self-confessed treachery towards Kihika, never loses the reader's sympathy, because of his basic courage and honesty. There seems to be a certain uncertainty about Ngugi's attitude towards his hero. At the start he gives him a certain measure of idealism, but then suggests that his non-involvement is due not to idealism but to cowardice, and at the end he makes him a villain. This element of mistiness surrounding the hero seriously impairs the novel's impact on the reader. Nevertheless, no one can fail to acknowledge its importance and relevance. It is indeed a major publication. (pp. 165-66)

> Eustace Palmer, "Ngugi's 'Petals of Blood,'" in
> African Literature Today, *No. 10, 1979, pp. 153-66.*

G. D. KILLAM

Ngugi writes in the preface of *Secret Lives* that the stories form his creative autobiography, that they touch on ideas and moods that affected him at the same time he was writing the novels and that his writing in general is 'an attempt to understand myself and my situation in society and in history'. There is a good deal of overlapping between the novels and the short stories in terms of theme and character. Often the short stories have characters, incidents and plots that have their counterparts in the novels or represent variant treatments of the same incidents and characters in the larger works. (p. 73)

The themes one finds in the stories and the order he imposes on them in the collection reflect Ngugi's development as a novelist: the treatments become progressively more contemporary. The stories deal with the nature and moral worth of various aspects of original Gikuyu culture, of the effect of Christian teaching both in schools and the churches on the quality of African life; of the development of capitalism, class-consciousness and human alienation as a new Kenya develops out of the independence struggle. Ngugi's position in the stories as in *A Grain of Wheat* and *Petals of Blood* is that of a humane socialist whose stories provide an account seen over the perspective of probably fifty years of relations between individuals, usually two, in a world of moral, ethical and religious uncertitude. Political Africa, in the widest sense, is the background to the stories, and what happens to the characters in the stories can be taken as a metaphor of what is happening in the land.

The first three stories in the book . . . tell of relations between mothers and children. The first two stories, **'Mugumo'** and **'And the Rain Came Down!',** tell of women who are childless and embittered because of it. Mukami is the youngest of Muthoga's four wives. She has been the favourite until it is discovered that she is barren. No longer able to bear his bitter beatings and the scorn of the other wives, she leaves in the dead of night. . . . [She] finds sanctuary under the 'Sacred Mugumo—the altar of all-seeing Murungu'. There she falls asleep and has a dream vision of Gikuyu and Mumbi, 'Mother of the Nation'. She awakes, restored, determined to return to her husband and home. She has learned from Mumbi the lesson

that for strength there must be unity in the family. To secure the point Mumbi has made Mukami pregnant in the arbour of Mugumo.

In the association of Gikuyu and Mumbi with Adam and Eve, the occasion of the immaculate conception in the arbour of the fig tree, in the language he employs, Ngugi exploits the similarities between Gikuyu and Christian legends and strengthens the points of his story—that strength comes from unity, from a compassionate understanding and from tolerance and co-operation. When these qualities in human relations disappear, the result is social and moral chaos. Drawing on legends from the past to make a comment on the present Ngugi offers implicitly a plea for a return to basic human values. (pp. 73-5)

The stories in the second part of the book treat of events in the period defined by the coming of the white man through to his departure from Kenya. In these seven stories we find a number of familiar faces, both black and white, in circumstances strongly reminiscent of the novels. Ngugi focuses his attention on the secret lives of characters in circumstances which produce a good deal more tension than in the first group. This is because two worlds come into collision in the situations.

Decent values, usually associated with original African values, suffer as a result of coming into contact with imported ones. The irony which informs the stories in this group proceeds from human relations and is not, as was the case in the first group, the irony of fate (or of magic). It is a mordant irony moving toward the scathing irony Ngugi adopts in the third and final section. (p. 76)

In **'The Black Bird'**, Mangara sacrifices a promising career in medicine, the love of a beautiful and faithful woman, and his life, to lay the curse placed on his family by 'the Black Bird'. . . .

The irony is that the generations succeed each other in assuming the responsibility of their forebears. Ngugi leaves the various implications of the story to the musings of the reader. In this story he is at his least explicit.

We meet another stern Christian in **'A Meeting in the Dark'.** The irony of this story is one found elsewhere in his writing— that the message of Christian love and compassion will provide a decent and upright life too often prompts the opposite behaviour. We have seen that this is so in *The River Between* and in *Petals of Blood,* in 'The Black Bird' and in subtle, less explicit ways in *Weep Not, Child* and *A Grain of Wheat.* Here we meet John, the son of a Christian preacher whose religion is arid and who, incapable of love himself, engenders only fear in his son. (p. 77)

Ngugi understands the beliefs that have made John the moral cripple he is. But he has neither pity nor compassion for him. And this is rare in Ngugi. It accounts as well for this being the least successful of the stories. Everything here is too pat. There are no ambiguities of character. And despite the nature of the ending, little tension. But the story does show Ngugi moving toward the creation of characters such as we find in the final three stories—the type of modern Kenyan who, through education and ambition based upon imported values, adopts a Christian name, a self-serving personal morality which is hollow at the core. (pp. 77-8)

The remaining stories in Part II deal with the emergency and post-emergency period and **'The Martyr'** is the best of the three, possibly the best in the collection. Ngugi offers a microcosm of Kenya at the time of the emergency and in it we are afforded points of view which are both English and African.

Mrs Hill lives on a plantation she and her husband established. She lives alone—her husband has died and her children are 'at home' in England. Castigated by her friends Mrs Smiles and Mrs Hardy, who between them purvey all the cliches associated with the white civilizing mission, Mrs Hill nevertheless prefers to treat in a kindly fashion her 'houseboy', Njoroge. She cannot know that for Njoroge she is the embodiment of those forces which have driven him from the land and forced on him the humiliation of working as a servant. . . .

Ngugi is dealing with the pain and shame occasioned by injustice. The irony of the story proceeds from Njoroge's reflection, as he castigates himself for going against his plan to betray Mrs Hill: 'If only he had not thought of her in human terms!' When he does he seeks to save her; when she thinks of him in human terms she has to kill him. (p. 78)

The last four stories are set in modern Kenya and show the consequences of historical process initiated by the introduction of modern values and methods in education, religion, and business. Ngugi's claim in **'A Mercedes Funeral'** that 'Wahinya's progress from hope to a drunken despair is the story of our times' can be taken as a motto (if the adjective 'drunken' is omitted) of all the stories in Part III of the book. Each of the principal characters in the stories progress from hope to despair. Even the outwardly successful sense, in their secret hearts, that but for a trick of fate they might be in the place of the destitute and forlorn. These are stories, then, about victims and their purpose is to upbraid and castigate the new bourgeoisie, that Wabenzi tribesmen, who take on imported names and clothing, drive expensive imported cars and make victims of their own people. Ngugi's irony has a cutting edge to it: there is a little ambiguity in the way he tells tales. The objects of his scorn, the objects of his pity are plain to see. Two of the stories— **'Wedding at the Cross'** and **'A Mercedes Funeral'** are as good examples of satiric writing as one can find in recent African writing. (pp. 79-80)

Ngugi's stories, in the final section of the volume, are centred in the human losses that follow in the wake of modernization that produces both cultural and spiritual rootlessness in the characters, none of whom is able to make a satisfactory response to life. All of these people are victims, though not all of them have yet found it out.

Ngugi's statement that 'I don't think I'm particularly good' at writing short stories shows shrewdness of judgement. There is some unevenness in the treatment, the ironic endings do not always succeed and some of the stories lack tension, thus interest. At times there is bad writing—a curious use of English idiom and sometimes grammar that cannot be deliberate. But for the most part the narrative line is always clear, the characterization—whether realistically or symbolically created—precisely observed and sharply portrayed. Except in one or two cases a decisive climactic moment is achieved. Moreover, the stories, because of their correspondence with events and characters in the novels, serve to elaborate the larger works and intensify the artistic purposes of their creation. Ngugi is concerned with the new Africa—with the quality of life in the here and now. And while he portrays the past as a time of unity of sensibility, he does so without sentimentality or nostalgia. If his contemporary landscape is bleak and without hope at least he has given his readers the materials with which to contemplate it through an honest rendering, both in physical and emotional terms. (p. 86)

G. D. Killam, in his An Introduction to the Writings of Ngugi, *Heinemann, 1980, 122 p.*

JAMES CAMPBELL

Because of its subject matter, [*Detained: A Writer's Prison Diary*] cannot fail to be interesting, yet it feels like a patchy book, inflated with letters and a long account of the author's subsequent battle with the university which had arbitrarily dismissed him. In the longest section, 'Prison Notes', it is often unclear what was actually written in prison (there is scarcely any evidence of the 'diary' of the title) and what was composed later, developed out of the experience of detention. There is a shrewd account of the reasons behind Kenyatta's popularity—it was Kenyatta's death which occasioned the detainees' release—and some of the historical evaluation is informed and perceptive, but Ngugi lacks the type of mind which can compress history into metaphors, maybe the most effective way for a writer who is not a historian to write about history.

It makes for better reading, however, than *Writers in Politics*, far too much of which is bombast of the 'Down with Imperialism' variety, a fault shared by his earlier book of essays, *Homecoming*. There are essays here protesting against the suppression of indigenous Kenyan culture, protesting against repression in South Korea, protesting against the moderate tradition in Afro-American literature and thought. Are the essays in *Writers in Politics* literature or protest? This question is not the astonishing irrelevance it may seem to Ngugi, coming from one whose values he doubtless would see as being conditioned by a bourgeois society. Protest, whatever its effect on the streets, invariably seems like bombast on the page. And bombast is what usually results from a failure of argument, or simply from a lack of argument. As essayist, Ngugi is often little more than an enthusiast of Marxism or an articulate protester, and the pieces which result lack the main justifications of the essay form, which include anecdote and dialectical argument as well as opinion. The best of them concern Kenyan culture and (surely no coincidence) were written for the page, unlike the rest which were originally delivered orally. Ngugi is a convert to Marxism, and no one is more zealous than a convert; but unlike one of the writers he criticises unfairly in these pages, James Baldwin—whom, along with Martin Luther King and Ralph Ellison, he accuses of being a 'sellout'—Ngugi is not always aware that even if all literature is protest, all protest is not literature.

James Campbell, ''Protestations,'' in New Statesman, *Vol. 102, No. 2627, July 24, 1981, p. 21*

JOHN POVEY

[Ngugi's *Writers in Politics*] confirms that he sees himself as a spokesman for the radical Third World.

Ngugi is convinced that ''writers must choose one side or the other side in the battlefield: the side of the people or the side of those social forces and classes which try to keep the people down.'' Those tired clichés exemplify what is so dismaying about this book. No matter what one's general sympathy for much of Ngugi's view, his diction is banal, and that is a devastating accusation to launch at a writer. But use of secondhand phrases from socialist tracts, as George Orwell properly reminded us, is not accidental but is clear evidence of avoiding original thought. There are excellent reasons to teach Kenyan children in Swahili rather than in English, as Ngugi advocates. His recommendation carries less credence when couched in slogans such as ''Neocolonial profit hunting adventures'' or ''imperialist cultural domination in the cultural struggle.'' The only familiar animal I missed was the legendary ''fascist hyena.''

Marxist attitudes intrude even when Ngugi directs his attention to literature. Does it really add much to our appreciation of Jane Austen to be told she provides "a wonderful picture of the leisurely parasitic landed middle classes in eighteenth century England?" Do we admire Brontë more because *Wuthering Heights* gives us "a most incisive examination of an industrial bourgeois class?" . . .

No artistic advance occurs in this present collection. Whether a reader responds with "right on!" or merely "oh dear" depends upon prior assumptions unlikely to be modified by the jargon in this book.

> *John Povey, in a review of "Writers in Politics," in* World Literature Today, *Vol. 55, No. 4, Autumn, 1981, p. 717.*

VICTORIA BRITTAIN

Professor Ngugi's novels, whether written at Makerere, Leeds or Nairobi Universities, have all sprung from an imagination fired by Kenyan politics. But with *Detained* and *Devil on the Cross* he has entered into direct confrontation with the regime, and his art has become the vehicle for his political purpose. His earlier novels were set against the conflicts produced in Kenya by British colonial society. The female circumcision crisis of the Thirties (*The River Between*) and the Mau Mau rebellion (*Weep Not, Child*) pointed up the dilemmas of families split between old and new. These novels established his reputation in Europe and America as a craftsman and a storyteller who introduced non-Africans to African personalities and preoccupations. East African writing had previously been the preserve of white settlers. None of these had created a truly African protagonist. In *Writers and Politics* Ngugi is scathing about the narrowness of such well-known writers as Elspeth Huxley and Karen Blixen whom he places in 'the tradition of great racists like Hume, Trollope, Hegel and Trevor-Roper, all arch-priests of privilege, racism and class snobbery'. . . .

Writers and Politics gives a strong sense of the man and his political evolution during the 1970s: 'For me,' he says, 'it was a decade of tremendous change, towards the end I had ceased being a teacher and become a student at the feet of the Kenyan peasants and workers.' In Europe this may read like posturing, but when Ngugi says it, it seems a natural and modest description of his politics. *Petals of Blood,* published three years ago, prepared the way for his detention by President Kenyatta: it is an ambitious novel which portrays post-colonial Kenya as a cruel, materialistic society in which the weak and poor are mercilessly exploited by the rich and powerful, who include politicians and churchmen as well as businessmen. . . .

Devil on the Cross takes up the same theme, putting a stronger emphasis on the part played in modern Kenya by foreign capital. It was written on lavatory paper in prison and it is clear from *Detained* that the creation of Wariinga, the heroine, was Ngugi's main resource in enduring the detention without trial which he could only expect to end with the death of Kenyatta. . . . Wariinga is a classic portrait of a young Kenyan urban woman caught in a pattern of exploitation by a male-chauvinist society. She is made pregnant by the sugar daddy who waits for her after school, leaves the baby with her parents back home in the village, tries to contribute to its upkeep by working as a secretary in Nairobi, but is sacked from her job for refusing to sleep with her boss, and evicted from her miserable lodging by a rapacious developer. She and her boyfriend, Gatuira, a teacher from Nairobi University, are caught up by

chance in a gathering, in the town of Ilmorog . . . , of all the great crooks of Kenya meeting to compete for the title of the greatest crook of them all. The meeting, the centrepiece of the novel, sways between satire, farce and nightmare as one businessman after another boasts to the company, fellow crooks and foreign observers, about his skills in selling nothing for something to the poor.

Selling bottled air to peasants is exactly what Ngugi believes Kenyan capitalism is capable of. The one weakness of the book is Wariinga's transformation into a radical, liberated motor mechanic who forces respect and comradeliness from her fellow workers (male). Perhaps Ngugi meant it as fantasy, like the bottled air, but it detracts from her appeal in the first part of the novel, when she knows there is no way out.

The key to the character of Wariinga is to be found in Ngugi's work at the community centre at Kamirithu, the village outside Limuru which was the focus of his life for 18 months before his detention. In *Detained* he tells for the first time in print the story of the community centre and the adult literacy classes he taught. In six months 55 workers and peasants learnt to read and write, and, in a village whose only previous entertainments were the bar and the church, they wanted to put on a play. Ngugi and a university colleague wrote it and the newly literate peasants spent two months rewriting and altering it. . . .

The play, *Ngaahika Ndeenda* ('I shall marry when I wish'), was written in Kikuyu and acted by non-intellectuals in the countryside. Its theme—that the fruits of independence have gone to those who collaborated with the British rather than to those who fought for it—was considered a threat to public security. *Petals of Blood* had presumably escaped the censor because it is a long, difficult novel written in English. *Ngaahika Ndeenda* appealed to a mass audience and was a dramatic cultural departure for Kenya—too dramatic for the Government. (p. 19)

Detained describes the degradation of life in detention—poor food, little exercise, the sadistic use of ill-health to break the prisoners' spirit. Ngugi himself suffered agonising toothache which was not treated for more than a month. And the book includes a letter from another prisoner who, for two and a half years, instead of getting electrotherapy for a bad back, was treated for mental instability. The book is a wonderful testimony to friendship as Ngugi describes his growing admiration for various detainees who had been there for years before he arrived. (pp. 19-20)

> *Victoria Brittain, "Kenya's Dissident," in* London Review of Books, *June 3 to June 16, 1982, pp. 19-20.**

NICHOLAS HYMAN

More consciously achieved than his already remarkable if earnest *Petals of Blood,* [Ngugi's *Devil on the Cross*] has the effect of a human symphony. It pierces Kenyan injustices, yet rallies to individual choices and potentially alterable societies, anchored in the development of a range of characters plus what Ngugi has called "tasty" language. . . .

A competition among robbers is the centrepiece of *Devil on the Cross,* with representatives of multinationals as honoured guests, in suits made of dollars or yen. The boasting of the kings of the Kenyan midden brings gesture, proverb and juicy cant together.

Articulate, not quite ordinary yet certainly representative men and women seek to oppose the crooks' convention, much to the outrage of the police. The town of Ilmorog, where a luxuriously appointed cave is the setting for the gloaters' testimony, contains every facet of a contemporary Third World society.

The dust and pavements of Nairobi also figure in this rich though compact novel, whose sense of place is as powerful as the conviction, effortlessly sustained, that these representative half-saints and sinners affect our waking and dreaming lives.

Chosen roles take over identities partly ascribed by class or sex stereotyping. Thus a composer who succeeds in his quest for national music, from the community of world and precolonial sources, is at the end stymied by accepting a show of reconciliation with his oppressive, *parvenu* father. The mafioso violence, of engineered car crashes and Rachmanite evictions, is never wanton. Rather, Ngugi implies, such brutality is part of the very process of the "primitive accumulation of capital."

Devil on the Cross pinpoints the overcoming of sexism and some redistributive road of industrialisation as twin priorities. Opting for these follows a realisation of what is wrong: the peasant and industrial worker processions are generally at the stage of merely knowing their lot, rather than perceiving an alternative path.

Here is one of those rare books which show, and help to transform, a range of lives.

> Nicholas Hyman, "Bandits in Power," in Tribune, Vol. 46, No. 26, June 25, 1982, p. 8.

B. W. LAST

In Ngugi wa Thiong'o's plays, a political commitment that grew out of a historical experience provides the basis for the creation of a work of art. The plays are interesting because of this commitment to a specific ideology, communicated with a passion that says much about Ngugi's own feelings about his subject matter; although the plays are less well known than the novels, they offer examples of how Ngugi treats his themes, which are specific and political in reference. (p. 511)

Ngugi is concerned with "the struggle for freedom" in his writing; this struggle might be against the colonial power, or against bureaucracy in general, but there is always blame attached, and a call for a firm stand against the common enemy. In *This Time Tomorrow* we are meant to feel sympathetic towards the common people in Uhuru market who find themselves about to be turned out of their homes. . . . There is anger here and there is blame. The anger comes from the refusal of the authorities to allow the individual to pursue his own life because of the pressure of external forces, as though foreign capital still dictated local events. This, in turn, is related to blame, since both the local authority and the external powers are too distant from the common people; this leads to a lack of comprehension for their needs and aims. The Shoemaker develops this idea; in the following speech, he denounces the way in which his liberty has been impinged upon from above:

> It is not that I don't want to move. But the government should give me a place to go. After all, I deserve it. I was a member of the Party— an active member, you might say. I took the oath in 1950. I felt a new man. Who did not? I mean, of those who took the oath? We were

> fighting for freedom. We were fighting for our soil. We used to sing: "Even if they deride me, and beat me, and kill me, They shall never make me forget." This is a black man's country, I was arrested and sent to Manyani, Manyani—you have not heard of it? A concentration camp. See? I came home after the emergency. The whiteman had not gone. No job for me, no land either. . . .

This particular man's plight may be one with which we can sympathize, but we are also asked to see his criticism as an explanation of the country's problems. There is a feeling of disenchantment with the past and the present administrations, as though the situation has not changed over the past twenty years. The "freedom" for which he had been fighting seems as remote as it ever was, and so the blame must lie with the people who are, or were, in a position to administer that freedom. The Shoemaker's anger is, then, one which stems from disappointed ideals, and from a discovery that internal and external forces have similar motives. In an attempt to answer the problem that is posed in the play, Ngugi introduces the character of the Stranger. He appeals to the people to resist the police and stay on their "property." . . . The appeal for unity, however, is a vain one and the play ends on the sad words of Njango, who laments, "If only we had stood up against them! If only we could stand together!" Although the play is often crude in expression and even over simple in attitude, it does place Ngugi's theatre in its proper context as an influential vehicle by which political consciousness may be aroused through a consideration of specific political events. The anger and the blame that are solicited because of this again occur in *The Black Hermit*. In this play the hero, Remi, must find his political stance and act upon it. At the beginning he is in the "city"—in fact, he is "swallowed up by the pleasures of it." The absence of Remi from the village way of life and the "traditional" involvement with the tribe is viewed with consternation by the elders. . . . [The elders fear] that education will eventually destroy traditional life and turn the black man into one subservient to and dependent upon the whites. The answer is simple to the elders and concerns fighting back through politics and accepting the responsibility of leadership. The elders of the tribe have to persuade Remi to take an active part in their struggle; passivity in the city is an idle trade.

Given this basis, the play works its message into the mind by a direct emotional appeal to "struggle" for independence of mind and action, despite the white stranglehold. . . . The anger with the "new government" is once again part of the total disappointment after the disappearance of the whites. To the village elders, Remi is seen as a "saviour" who will bring "freedom" to the people and "restore the tribe to its land"; but the precise nature of the salvation is never fully explored, since these concepts are never truly realized during the course of the play. True, the figure of the Pastor is a foil by which the hollowness of the new way of life is indicated, but his platitudes are easy to knock down. He proposes lack of action— ("He [Remi] must be kept away from politics")—which is precisely the status quo against which the play kicks. So when Remi turns to him and says, "Pastor, you and your religion never did anything for our people. It's only divided them and made them weak before the whiteman," . . . this too comes across as a platitude since there has been no dramatic struggle towards this conclusion. Like the previous statements it has an emotional appeal, intended to have an immediate effect.

Remi's speech when he finally decides to return home is an interesting one, for it includes much of the political and cultural dilemma that an East African must have felt as the new era seemed to dawn. . . . [The] "freedom" is not one that includes merely the new religion and customs; this is a mere external force. It includes also the internal structure of the tribal system, which contributes towards the "manacles" in which the people find themselves. Remi's struggle will be against all of the "pieces of superstition," for he has concluded that the total structure is wrong, not simply parts of it. This must lead to a clash of values; as the Woman says, "the peace and solitude [of the village] will now be torn by strife and sorrow." However one might view Remi's political stance, there is no denying that it contains passion and force. To equate Remi with Ngugi is perhaps too simple a leap, but both have the dedication, passion and anger of the committed intellectual. The question that is raised in the play—precisely how to act in the face of a political and cultural crisis—is Remi's dilemma. Ngugi attempts to answer this in a later play, *The Trial of Dedan Kimathi,* written in collaboration with Micere Githae-Mugo, a fact which adds to the dramatic, emotional, and political success of the play. The authors sketch in a historical and contextual background:

> There is no single historical work written by a Kenyan telling of the grandeur of the heroic resistance of Kenyan people fighting foreign forms of exploitation and domination, a resistance movement whose history goes back to the c15 and c16 centuries when Kenyans and other East African people first took up arms against European colonial power.

Placed in this context, the play extends points made in Ngugi's other works; it is made plain that the "dreams" of the two authors were made real by a combined intellectual effort on their part. Their efforts also meant that they had to go in search of the "real" Kimathi, and by doing so discovered that his name meant something to the people to whom they spoke. This inspired the authors with "fire and enthusiasm," and Kimathi came to be representative of the struggle of the people over the whole continent. Ngugi and Mugo use devices from Ngugi's earlier plays, but try to extend the impact of this one. In some respects, then, *Trial* can be seen to go back to *This Time Tomorrow,* but the anger in the later play is more bitter, and direct blame is laid. . . . [The] blame lies squarely on the shoulders of the exploiting foreigners. Ngugi's answer to this exploitation, or, rather, retaliation against it, lies in the desire to reform the minds of the people—his audience—by educating them through the media of drama. This accounts largely for the scenes in the first movement of the play in which the "Black Man's History" takes place and which culminates in the repetition of the slogans: "Away with oppression! Unchain the people!" . . . These are familiar enough emotions to any reader of Ngugi, but what he does in this play is to attempt to find an answer to the question of the nature of the combat in the face of apparently insurmountable odds. Ngugi finds his answer in the character of Dedan Kimathi, who is a symbol of the masses and whose example must be followed so that the people become, in Ngugi's words, "the true makers of history." (pp. 511-16)

By making Kimathi a symbol of the masses—and enlightened masses at that—Ngugi has solved another problem. Although the man may die, the spirit of the revolution continues within the minds of the people, who appear at the end singing "a thunderous freedom song." The message is clear: the masses must continue the struggle; hope for the future lies with the youth of the country. This is why, when Kimathi is sentenced to death, he laughs, for he knows that he has instilled hope into the minds of his followers. The domination of the foreign exploiters may be breaking down; so the play ends on a positive note: a man already committed to change has convinced his people that to struggle is the only way to defeat the imperialist forces. The struggle between Kimathi and imperialism is personalized by Ngugi in the confrontation between Kimathi and the judge. It is a simple statement of opposites, and a clash between two different world views. . . . The pattern is typical of Ngugi: set up a situation in which political slogans may be used to initiate an emotional response in the spectator. The words "property," "foreign" and "exploiter" in contrast to "the people" occur over and over again in Ngugi's plays and establish a base from which the foreigners and the exploiters may be attacked. The plays are structured around the equation of opposites, and direct comments about the nature of contemporary events are made. Ngugi and Mugo see Kimathi as a symbol of a more universal struggle against exploitation, but still they structure the events around a specific point in time. So the resistance movement to which they refer in the preface is in a sense just beginning; their duty is to educate the people to this fact. The colonial factor remains the important factor because of its emotional and intellectual appeal. (pp. 516-17)

> B.W. Last, *"Ngugi and Soyinka: An Ideological Contrast,"* in World Literature Written in English, *Vol. 21, No. 3, Autumn, 1982, pp. 510-21.**

DAVID COOK AND MICHAEL OKENIMKPE

[Through his writings Ngugi has emerged as] a man who identifies himself unequivocally with a progressive, radical line of thought concerning all the pressing social issues of his time, and who eagerly deploys every means at his disposal to further the views and policies that he advocates. (p. 232)

So vigorously has Ngugi related his art to social issues that it closely mirrors the changes that have taken place in his reformatory and political thinking. In the process of writing his earlier novels, short stories and plays, Ngugi was still formulating his stand on various issues agitating his society. While the facts of the writer's upbringing and personal experiences form the staple of his subject matter, literary values are not questioned. It is part of the universal heritage of literature that it should seek to highlight the problems which burden, manacle and maim mankind. For the youthful Ngugi these problems included, at one level, family afflictions such as childlessness, marital strife and kindred feuds; and at another level, communal adversities such as droughts or floods, and the vast societal dilemmas of colonialism, confrontation between different religions, creeds and patterns of behaviour, and Mau Mau. Resolution is sought in term of man's enduring spiritual values. The author's voice is muted; and the manner in general shuns harshness and violence of language or approach. (pp. 232-33)

In the middle period, during which *A Grain of Wheat* is the principle literary work, Ngugi's stand on social issues becomes steadily more radical, but as an artist he is still controlled by his aesthetic awareness. His aim is to embody a major statement on public affairs as the primary theme in an essentially literary artefact. His reinterpretation of past events is conveyed by implication and suggestion rather than by direct statement. The whole history of the Kenyan struggle, particularly Mau Mau's heroic stand during the Emergency, is elevated to the status of a popular mass uprising. So the evil machinations of the MP who out-manoeuvres the land-co-operative are seen as thwarting the popular will. This symbolizes the whole conduct of political authority in independent Kenya, rendering the long-awaited, hard-fought-for independence hollow and meaningless. For all this, the socio-political message takes second place to the fate of the individual upon which literature has most often focused.

In the latest period, a rebellious Ngugi seems tired of sifting his message through a genre to which each reader may react differently. So he makes attempts to modify his medium and render it less arbitrary. Logically his new outlook is dynamically expressed in his first language both in *Ngaahika Ndeenda* and *Caitaani Mutharaba-ini,* which as a later priority he translates into English [as *Devil on the Cross*] to join *The Trial of Dedan Kimathi* and *Petals of Blood.* During this period also he twice employs drama as the mode most immediate in its impact.

Had Ngugi turned to Gikuyu earlier in his career, it would have been because of his opposition to the colonial legacy and his desire to redevelop traditional African culture: we recall the cry from his undergraduate journalism for the replacement of English by Kiswahili in East African schools. Now his primary motivation is the need to reach the masses, with whose problems he identifies himself and whose spokesman he has become: developing an indigenous language is an important but secondary aim.

The Trial of Dedan Kimathi seeks to mobilize the popular will against neo-colonialism and the new capitalism which are widening the gap between the Kenyan rich and poor. The play redefines for the whole population—but in particular for the ordinary man and woman—the role which the Mau Mau insurrection played in gaining Kenya's political sovereignty. It depicts the upheaval as a class reaction against repressive political and economic control, in terms of popular Marxist-inspired social conceptions. Ngugi has evidently come to see his earlier works as too reticent on the true nature of the uprising, so that now he rights the imbalance. His choosing to put this message on the stage points to his urgent desire for communication at grass roots.

In pursuit of the same goal of harnessing popular indignation against corrupt, oppressive power-groups, and so instigating revolutionary action by the peasantry and the workers, *Petals of Blood* adopts a new idiom. We are now brought face to face with a world gasping for breath in the grip of neo-colonialist capitalism. We are shown the oppressor and the oppressed, the overfed and the starving, the predators and their victims, the degenerate city and the desolate village. Among the exploited poor are a few architects of change who will lead the populace in redesigning society. Ngugi no longer minces his words or speaks in parables. Corruption and injustice are openly denounced: characters are clearly prototypical across the whole conspectus of this sagging society; the imagery is unambiguous. Ngugi spells out the desperateness of the situation and urgency of the need for change.

In *Devil on the Cross* Ngugi adds laughter as a new weapon to undermine and expose the profligacy of the elite, expecting that a wide audience will eagerly take part in the satiric unmasking of their overlords. By contrast the sufferings and the triumphs of individuals struggling against their debased environment are seriously, even earnestly, portrayed. The burlesque self-exposure of the demi-gods of neo-colonialism pro-

vides, Ngugi realizes, a suitable stylized setting for the directly didactic fictional statement. The sheer daring of the project carries both the denunciation and the revolutionary exhortation to extremes which we might formerly have thought impossible within the framework of a novel, however unconventional. (pp. 233-34)

[From] Ngugi's earliest writings such concepts as a people's government, the power of the proletariat, mass-controlled means of production and distribution and the need for egalitarian social services are the implicit premises of his fiction. In the latest period his entire thinking and writing are cast in the mould of anti-capitalist revolutionary doctrine.

Two important convictions characterize this new phase. First, there is the total rejection of the possibility of rebuilding African societies on old colonialist foundations. To build an egalitarian society is not to cleanse outmoded institutions of corruption and make them function more efficiently, but to destroy them altogether, make a fresh beginning, and create new systems. Secondly, Ngugi is disillusioned about reforming those who are at the power bases of society; he virtually despairs of rousing the consciences of the rich. He now concentrates all his efforts on developing among the poor an awareness of the inequalities which are at the root of their sufferings, and of urging them towards a revolution which alone can set the whole situation in the country to rights. This is the impulse behind *Petals of Blood, Devil on the Cross,* the recent plays and the latest stories in *Secret Lives.* The social doctrine which has been long maturing is at length comprehensive and coherent: control of the many by the few is blatantly immoral: history is on the side of the oppressed and will ensure their inevitable victory. There is a new sharpness and militancy in the call on the poor to engineer their own deliverance. Whereas Waiyaki and Njoroge meant well but fumbled, and even Kihika was too ill-informed to prevail over the handicaps that constrained him, Karega and Muturi now know how to marshal the collective will of the work-force in labour organizations, ready to dominate the battle looming ahead in this tense environment. The middle class is parasitic. Far from being relied on to realign the class system, it should itself be dissolved in the eventual restructuring of society. (pp. 234-35)

[In] *Petals of Blood* Ngugi felt the need in certain passages to be more explicitly didactic than he had been hitherto. . . . As a novelist Ngugi was taking a calculated risk. He was prepared to jeopardize the 'suspension of disbelief' in order to ensure that his ideas stood out absolutely plainly. He deliberately sidestepped certain conventions of the well-made novel as they had for long been understood in the West, though he had not yet made radical modifications in the mode of his own fiction.

The stylistic leap on which Ngugi ventured in the composition of *Devil on the Cross* is thus a logical development in his search for an effective pattern for the committed novel. Taken out of its whole context, the story of Wariinga is Ngugi's most uncompromisingly didactic piece of straight fiction to date, while the debates centred on Muturi in the matatu and after the workers' rally only thinly veil the author's teaching voice. . . . [The] formal control required for the extended parody in the novel creates a fictional world in which the almost equally stylized serious narrative is more readily acceptable than it might otherwise be. Nevertheless, if we consider this part of the fable simply as it stands, we find ourselves face to face with a new Ngugi who has chosen a much balder, and consequently more self-conscious manner of story-telling.

We have now reached the point at which we must ask point blank whether it is, in general, legitimate or effective to employ literature as a means of expounding and promoting a social doctrine, and how successful Ngugi has been in doing so. (p. 235)

As his socio-political ideas became more and more cogent and forward-looking, Ngugi's wrestle with his materials has become fiercer and more demanding. The first reactions to *Petals of Blood* by many of us steeped in literary principles and criteria . . . was to see it as a step backwards from *A Grain of Wheat* since in place of the almost perfectly controlled form and texture of the earlier novel, the intellectual skeleton grins through the vital literary flesh in a number of places in *Petals of Blood*. Readers preoccupied with radical political ideas, on the other hand, readily saw *Petals of Blood* as a big step forward in its uncompromising rejection of capitalist exploitation together with the old class structure, and its definition of the struggle towards a juster society by concerted communal effort. It would be a pity to be carried away entirely to either extreme. A middle position might paradoxically be put like this: *A Grain of Wheat* is the more perfect novel, but *Petals of Blood* is arguably the greater. . . . *A Grain of Wheat* reconciles the two sets of claims, literary and socio-political, by somewhat muting the latter: not through any dishonesty, but because Ngugi's social view was less fully developed. The new surge of righteous but clear-sighted political anger in *Petals of Blood* tends to pull the literary frame somewhat out of true but not enough to dim its claim to be a major, complexly structured novel. *Petals of Blood* thus stands as a rare literary achievement: with all its faults upon it, a skilfully articulated work which in no degree compromises the author's fully fledged radical political viewpoint.

The same is true of *Devil on the Cross,* though in adopting an entirely new mode it shakes itself free from some of the previous problems and in doing so creates its own. But the solutions to these new problems are in part inherent in the genre. Satire is by definition a means of being entertainingly didactic. The comic inversion involved shifts the basic tone away from the ponderously moralistic, towards the scandalously sensational. . . . Ngugi has avoided the major pitfall of satire, the monotony of a repetitive pattern, and in doing so he has at the same time ensured that his message is not only varied but is maintained at a level which is generally comprehensible. He has surveyed the many and various aspects of economic exploitation without losing a large part of his readership in technical detail. What is more remarkable is the way he has combined this ironic extravaganza with the simplified revolutionary idyll of a prototypical victim of the system. Wariinga grows out of a bewildered imitation of bourgeois values into a trained radical self-awareness. Her origins are in the class borderland between the workers and the white-collared pen-pushers. If Gatuiria sadly represents a falling back at the moment of crisis into stereotyped reactions implanted by a conditioned childhood, Wariinga shows how individuals—men or women—can shake themselves free of their past and prepare to participate in what they envisage as a different kind of future. Readers will vary in how far they can accept this formalized parable, much of it written in a newly formalized style which may at times seem rather forced, and even flat after what we have been accustomed to. . . . Ngugi will no doubt judge the success of his moral fable by its impact on the general readership he has aimed at, rather than by any critical consensus. But an unbiased view will hardly deny the boldness and force with which he has handled this fresh experiment in committed fiction.

In both *A Grain of Wheat* and *Petals of Blood* Ngugi has, in a more established fictional manner, embodied his major themes in his characters, his patterned imagery, his story and his setting. Cabral, in modifying and extending Marxist theory through the process of analysing a situation fundamentally different from that in Europe but common throughout the ex-colonial world, makes a clear distinction between the struggle for independence and the later campaign for national liberation. The former takes place in a colonial situation and is the essential subject of *A Grain of Wheat*. . . . (pp. 236-38)

The novel shows how untrained men like Kihika made a determined effort through Mau Mau to provide an alternative vanguard class. But we further see how, having made a crucial contribution to the ousting of colonialism, this group is suppressed to allow the MP who double-crosses the land co-operative and his fellows to negotiate a 'fictitious political independence'. These ideas are implicit in their positive and negative aspects in the narrative as it relates to Kihika and Thompson, Gikonyo and Karanja, Mumbi and Mugo. There is almost no overt didacticism. The points are silently emphasized as events comment on each other by juxtaposition. The novelist's control and craftsmanship are of a very high order throughout. We are led to see for ourselves the necessity of moving on to a *true* independence by the awakening of 'the consciousness of broad popular strata' and the reuniting of 'the population around the ideal of national liberation'.

When Ngugi turns to expose the iniquities and needs of neo-colonialist Africa in *Petals of Blood,* he himself is now unreservedly outspoken. . . . (p. 238)

Petals of Blood and *Devil on the Cross* both embody such themes but in contrasting styles. In the former these motifs are developed, as in *A Grain of Wheat,* by familiar fictional methods through the narrative, characterization, interrelationships, imagery and setting. They are related to the emotional needs, problems and intertwinings of the human situation. . . . In exaggerating and concentrating the same ideas, *Devil on the Cross,* on the other hand, alternates deliberately between outlandish satire and a highly formalized narrative. (pp. 239-40)

The socio-political motifs in *Petals of Blood* remain for the most part implicit in the narrative. . . . [There are] exceptional passages in which the author through the Lawyer or by other means becomes more directly didactic. These interventions are clumsier than the more extreme methods adopted in *Devil on the Cross* since they are not an inherent part of the manner of the work. The norm of *Petals of Blood* is the integration of story and ideas. Wanja's testimony is at once a vivid depiction of her life-story, and a revelation of all that someone at the mercy of this society suffers; Abdulla's epitomizes both his own heroism and betrayal, and those of the Mau Mau movement as a whole. Such accounts are vividly personalized, full of action, and are central threads in the story which the novel sets out to tell.

The overt didacticism of *Devil on the Cross* is not isolated in occasional passages. It is of the very essence of the book, both in its satirical exposures and its more sober demonstrations. The novel stands or falls as a whole by the success or failure (for each individual reader) of its bold experiments. It sets out directly to deploy literature as a means of encouraging specific social reactions. (p. 240)

The central irony of the disastrous 'development' of the township in Part Four is the very life-blood of the novel as a novel. The palaces and slums of this now soulless boom-town are again sketched in as a backcloth for *Devil on the Cross*. To the uninitiated, Ilmorog appropriately here takes on the sad, characterless blur of Anytown, but to those familiar with *Petals of Blood* the setting adds another detailed dimension to disillusionment. In the earlier novel, figures that make up our picture of the place are known to us in depth throughout the length of their lives and back through their distant ancestry.

In *Petals of Blood* furthermore, the detective investigation provides Ngugi, especially in the last part, with a structure enabling him to develop fully every aspect of the social scene that he wants to depict in a thrilling and gripping sequence. The bare, stark, high-pitched drama of *Devil on the Cross* brings out the features of the same society differently in grim silhouette.

The wedding of theme and story can be traced right down to individual sentences as well as to individual characters in *Petals of Blood*. (p. 242)

This subtle, implicit emergence of theme from the heart of the story itself is foreign to the satiric and explicitly didactic methods of *Devil on the Cross*. Here little is left to the imagination. The artistry lies first in laying bare social evils which normally lie snugly concealed by rationalizations and apologia, so that their monstrous absurdity in human terms is clearly exposed; and secondly in lending to revolutionary idealism a new plausibility and human warmth. The familiar inversion of all morality in the conduct of public affairs no longer seems inevitable. A juster alternative appears far from coldly intellectual or impossibly visionary. Single sentences which we might pick out from *Devil on the Cross* . . . will not therefore reveal and confirm how the narrative crystallizes certain themes. Rather will they be the culmination of ideas which are meant to be plainly evident throughout. (pp. 242-43)

Certainly if a critical balance sheet is to be drawn up either for *The Trial of Dedan Kimathi* or for *Petals of Blood,* there will be far more on the credit than the debit side. In our lordly critical presumption, we may detect here and there, as in virtually any major work, deviations from the ideal blending of theme and mode. But Ngugi has courageously and successfully set out to mould both the novel and—in collaboration—the drama into his own burning socio-political testimony, without over-simplifications, by gearing the most dynamic features of the art of fiction to his passionate purpose.

In *Devil on the Cross,* it is true, he has stormed across the usually recognized bounds of fiction into the realms of rhetoric, open satire and didacticism, and in so doing has dared to challenge our established assumptions about literary genres. Yet this is no more radical an approach than that adopted by many novelists across the world in the second half of this century in attempting to revitalize 'the novel', whose funeral oration has been prematurely read by numerous critics.

No doubt Ngugi would agree with, but reinterpret, Dr Johnson's assertion that there are 'laws of higher authority than those of criticism'. In fact, until he ventured on *Devil on the Cross* he had rarely in the novel sidestepped the principles of literature any more than those of socialism. And indeed even in the prison novel he is more concerned to rethink literary criteria than to reject them. So we can justly say that Ngugi seems at all times to have sought the ultimate goal of any committed writer: to harness the 'laws' of art to the dictates of his own conscience. (p. 243)

David Cook and Michael Okenimkpe, in their Ngugi wa Thiong'o: An Exploration of His Writings, *Heinemann Educational Books Ltd., 1983, 250 p.*

REED WAY DASENBROCK

Devil on the Cross is a fascinating if uneven work. Ngũgĩ never leaves his politics behind, but the compelling parts of the novel are those in which he manages to transmute his politics into the stuff of imaginative fiction. The key episode in the novel, for instance, is a truly bizarre scene in which all the chief robbers in Kenya (read capitalists) gather together in a cave in order to compete for the honor of being considered Kenya's greatest thief. Scenes such as this establish an inventive, even wacky new mode of political fiction in Ngũgĩ's work, somewhat reminiscent of contemporary Latin American fiction or Wole Soyinka's *Season of Anomy*. *Devil on the Cross* is told as an oral tale, at times modulating into song, and is presented as the song of a Gĩcaandĩ player, a Kenyan equivalent to a minstrel or balladeer. The story he tells is that of a young woman, Warĩĩnga, who ends up killing her former lover, a rich man whose son she hoped to marry. The plot has a number of points of contact with that of Ngũgĩ's last novel, *Petals of Blood* . . . , which is set in the same town of Ilmorog and whose plot also turns on a sexually related murder of some rich men. This parallel is a disturbing one, for it is not at all clear what Ngũgĩ's attitude is toward these isolated though political acts of violence. Nevertheless, *Devil on the Cross* is a far more interesting work than *Petals of Blood* because of its greater flights of fancy, its greater zaniness. Better magic realism than socialist realism. Ngũgĩ has come a long way since *Weep Not, Child,* and *Devil on the Cross* is the first evidence that he has gained as well as lost in the process.

Reed Way Dasenbrock, in a review of "Devil on the Cross," in World Literature Today, *Vol. 58, No. 1, Winter, 1984, p. 153.*

Peter (Richard) Nichols

1927-

English dramatist, scriptwriter, and autobiographer.

Nichols writes plays about the mores, anxieties, and institutions associated with the English middle class. He exploits both the serious and the comic sides of his themes, often making extensive use of black humor to lighten what might otherwise be deeply troubling plays. Nichols is regarded as a master of dramatic techniques; his characters often directly address the audience, and he also combines music-hall type sketches with serious dramatic action. His subjects are usually topical, often painful, and, with one exception, autobiographical. Nichols's first stage play, *A Day in the Death of Joe Egg* (1967), is an overtly autobiographical work that is considered one of his most important dramatic achievements.

Nichols began his career writing television plays. He turned to theater for *A Day in the Death of Joe Egg*, believing the play's comic approach to its subject would be deemed inappropriate for television. This play tells the story of a married couple whose daughter, nicknamed "Joe Egg," is spastic and mentally retarded. While Joe's mother finds satisfaction in nurturing Joe and continues to hope for her recovery, she also accepts her husband's need to joke about the situation. The couple conduct imaginary conversations with their mute daughter and playfully reenact scenes from their life with her. Although the play centers on a severely handicapped child, most critics noted that *A Day in the Death of Joe Egg* is really about the way a marriage is affected by an unforeseen burden.

In his other plays that examine marriage and family life, Nichols consistently presents destructive marital and parent-child relationships. Set in the World War II era, when Nichols was a teenager, *Forget-Me-Not Lane* (1971) is a nostalgic yet bitter rendering of Nichols's turbulent family life. The historical action of the play is commented upon by the adult Nichols persona, who twenty-five years later finds himself established with a family very much like that from which he had wanted to escape. "We're all in the genetic trap," he concludes. *Chez Nous* (1974) is a lighter domestic comedy about two married couples sharing a vacation home. The discovery at the beginning of the play that one of the men has fathered a child with the other's teenage daughter catalyzes conversation about marriage, sex, fidelity, and love in modern times. Nichols stated that *Chez Nous* is "about the irksomeness of marriage and the family, and the way people grow out of one family only to will themselves into another. All my married men are a bit like that—they feel trapped, and want to be free, but realize they probably couldn't make it on their own." *Passion Play* (1981), one of Nichols's most inventive plays, also revolves around a middle-aged man's adultery. Both the unfaithful man and his wife have alter egos representing their natural, unrepressed selves. While humor is derived from this device in the first act, act two is bleaker; the spirits of both characters seem broken, and the marriage neither thrives nor ends.

In addition to writing about marital and familial concerns, Nichols has also explored other contemporary institutions in works which Benedict Nightingale labeled Nichols's "public plays." *The National Health (or Nurse Norton's Affair)* (1969)

Photograph by Mark Gerson

uses a hospital as a microcosm of society and juxtaposes two versions of hospital life. The "real" version is set in a male ward and chronicles the interaction and suffering of several patients. Although Nichols's characteristic gallows humor lightens this portion of the play, death is a constant presence and the mood is somber. Nichols included *Nurse Norton's Affair*, a spoof of a romantic soap opera originally written as a one-act play for television, to further lighten the script. *The Freeway* (1974) satirizes the belief in cars as a key to freedom. Set in futuristic Britain, the play presents a massive, three-day traffic jam as a microcosm of British life. Nichols's other public plays include *Privates on Parade* (1977), a musical comedy about an entertainment troop in Malaysia at the end of World War II, and *Poppy* (1982), Nichols's only play that is purely historical rather than autobiographical. The form of the play—a musical pantomime—is also a departure for Nichols. *Poppy* focuses on the unsavory efforts of the British to promote opium addiction among the Chinese in the early nineteenth century.

After the production of *Poppy*, Nichols declared his intention to give up writing for the theater and to write novels instead, thereby avoiding the interference of actors, producers, and directors. In his autobiography, *Feeling You're Behind* (1984), he explains his disillusion with the theater and also discusses his father, whose strong personality greatly influenced Nichols's life and work.

(See also *CLC*, Vol. 5; *Contemporary Authors*, Vol. 104; and *Dictionary of Literary Biography*, Vol. 13.)

CLIVE BARNES

A strange thing happened to me leaving the theater last night. I passed a lady wrapped round in what I perhaps generously imagined to be musquash, saying to her escort: "It's not funny, it's not tragic, it's not meaningful—it's nothing." The good lady was referring to Peter Nichols's comedy "**A Day in the Death of Joe Egg.**" . . .

To an extent I suppose the lady was right—ladies in even pretend musquash usually are. The play's humor, its tragedy and its meaning might seem less to musquash than to humanity, and Mr. Nichols's command of playwriting skills, for all his beautiful ear for speech, and his daring willingness to try anything, is, on occasion, rough around the edges. Yet "**Joe Egg**" (to use its shortened title) is an immensely moving, even profound play about love and marriage. No it's not funny—it has wit, a bitter, excoriating wit. No it's not tragic—it is ironic, as ironic as the uncalled-for domestic accident, the unexpected death in incongruity. And, certainly, no, it's not meaningful—only critics, poor devils, have to be meaningful, not playwrights.

What "**Joe Egg**" attempts, and I think, to a surprising extent achieves, is the analysis of a relationship, the dissection of human feeling, the laying bare of people.

The people are commonplace enough. Because Mr. Nichols is English and lives in Bristol, his people are English and live in Bristol—but they could just as well be American. The hero, Bri, is a schoolteacher. Spoiled by his mother, he depends upon a self-defensive, antic jokyness to get by in life. Sheila, his wife, is a kind of earth mother, bestowing her love promiscuously upon tame fish, cats, budgerigars, and, of course, Bri. And their 10-year-old child, Josephine, the Joe Egg of the title.

A normal enough couple—but with an abnormal child. Joe is a spastic, subject to fits, virtually unable to move, to see, to talk. As a Viennese doctor who sees Joe says: "She is a vegetable." This is the vegetable love between Bri and Sheila, the thing they have to live with, equate to and, somehow, cope with. "It would have been a good enough marriage," as Bri says toward the end, "except . . ."

How do you face a child that is a vegetable? It is not a nice subject, is it? More like a skeleton in the back of people's minds, lurking unspoken, than a fit subject for entertainment? Bri accepts it with bitter, corrosive laughter. To be himself he has to be outrageous.

With his wife he taunts God (whom he characterizes as "a manic-depressive rugby footballer") in a series of jokes. Between themselves they act out absurd playlets, self-searching exposés of their relationship with their "living parsnip." . . .

The wife plays these games because their self-inflicted, mocking lacerations soothe Bri. . . . But beneath the fabric of the marriage, its workings are wrecked. Sex is something they share, but even this has the undertones of their failure to conceive more children, other than Joe.

Mr. Nichols handles this part of the play with considerable imagination. He uses both the direct, vaudeville-style soliloquy (complete with band combo to introduce it, isolating it from the conventional narrative of the rest) and a technique of exaggerated revue sketches to map out the child's life. In all this the audience is used as a kind of mass marriage counselor, where Bri expounds his problems, and Sheila, with much less self-pity, tries to help. . . .

It is an aspect of the play worth noting perhaps that its dialogue has more the pure naturalism of a screenplay than the heightened manner of dramatic dialogue—lines are tossed away as if to a camera. Partly as a result, the play seems more episodic than might a theater work more carefully shaped, and at times the play has the totally honest inconsequentiality of dialogue that all but demands a camera to keep it company and give it depth.

There are flaws here, but then we live in a fascinating era of the un-well-made play. Certainly I think few plays this season will prove as provocative or as moving. . . .

"**Joe Egg**" is not a comfortable evening, and definitely not a perfect evening, but it is very much worthwhile.

Clive Barnes, "'A Day in the Death of Joe Egg'
Opens," in The New York Times, *February 2, 1968,*
p. 26.

HAROLD CLURMAN

It has been said that Peter Nichols' *A Day in the Death of Joe Egg* . . . is about the breakup of a marriage that has produced a spastic child. If this were all there was to it, I doubt that I should find the play interesting or even tolerable. It would be clinical and much too special.

The child, the sight of which we are more or less spared, serves as the play's fulcrum. But to confuse the device with the theme would be grossly to misunderstand it. Its value and fascination lie elsewhere.

The child's deformity . . . should be seen as the misfortune of a particular marriage. But many marriages are weighed down and sometimes destroyed by terrible burdens. . . . In *Joe Egg* the child who plagues the marriage of Bri and Sheila is the peculiar burden they have to bear; the play's scheme dramatizes the different kinds of adjustment the various characters make to it.

The situation is painful, but the play is a comedy; it provokes considerable laughter. It is an odd comedy: everything about it is wrong, its form is askew. It oughtn't to work. But it does. That is its originality.

The curtain is up as we enter the theatre, but instead of the stylization one might expect in that case, we see a fairly realistic setting. A musical combo ambles across the stage and disappears. . . . Then Bri (short for Brian) appears, dresses down the audience as if it were a prep school class. Bri is a teacher. He then moves into the household setting and the play proceeds for a bit as a normal naturalistic piece.

Bri's address to the audience has set up a convention. From time to time, each of the characters (including the spastic girl) breaks away from the others and speaks about him or herself and the rest of them; for the most part, these monologues are quite funny. At the end of the play Bri, who has twice attempted to bring about the child's death, finally succeeds in doing so. He then abandons his unsuspecting wife.

Shocking or pathetic, you might suppose; not at all. One observes the play with eyes much more sardonic than tearful. But it is just in this, our impassivity, that the artistic victory lies. The method is not Brechtian. Brecht's soliloquies (usually songs) do not make any personal comments on the "story"—they stand apart from it—and function as the drama's oblique reflection. In Nichols' play the action would scarcely be intelligible if the characters did not explain their attitudes and behavior. For example, Bri tells us beforehand that he is going to leave his wife. Sometimes he and his wife enact past events necessary for exposition and then as actor-characters add further comment on what we have just seen happen, as if the whole episode and the play itself were a public demonstration.

Nichols intends the audience to take a cold, if you will a heartless, view of the matter. He demands no commiseration or identification with his characters: he wants you to regard them as phenomena—objects for the entertainment of your intelligence. He doesn't expect you to do anything about it: how can you? It's a show. Brecht wishes your understanding to rouse you to judicious steps of social consequence. Nichols might be following Coleridge's "law" which runs: "There ought never to be more pain than is compatible with coexisting pleasure, and to be amply repaid by thought."

Nichols' disposition is eminently contemporary and thoroughly English. It is at least as representative of England today as Osborne's *Inadmissable Evidence*. It is a new wrench to the proverbial British "stiff upper lip." In a larger sense *Joe Egg* makes a point about present middle-class life almost everywhere. (pp. 247-48)

What Nichols implies but never declares is that the cream of this disastrous jest is that life is absurdly empty unless it is confronted and embraced in all its inherent anguish. Only in that way can living be good. But the rule of "common sense"— which the English are presumed to have in abundance—leads only to wretched farce. (p. 248)

A sharp and perceptive play, *A Day in the Death of Joe Egg* makes a remarkably sobering evening in the theatre. (p. 249)

> *Harold Clurman, in a review of "A Day in the Death of Joe Egg," in* The Nation, *Vol. 206, No. 8, February 19, 1968, pp. 247-49.*

CHARLES MAROWITZ

[*Privates on Parade*] is full of solid, old-fashioned virtues. There is a maze of story-line; a lot of sympathetic, clearly-delineated characters; an unmistakeable sense of location; tenderness, conventional morality, comedy, high-spirits and human reassurance.

Set in the environs of Malaya during the so-called 'emergency' period and following the fortunes of a squad of performing militia-men (the south-east Asia ENSA brigade), the show strongly resembles the war-films from which so much of its nostalgia is derived. In those larky capers of the 40s, a sense of impregnable camaraderie managed to resolve all conflicts indirectly attributable to 'the enemy'. . . .

These films were invariably filled with colourful characters who, despite their outward flippancy, were cast in the heroic mould. . . . They were as distinct as Commedia del Arte types. . . . It was a universe as ordered as Shakespeare's; as

circumscribed by Christian values as the Elizabethans were by the chain-of-being. (p. 22)

Nichols' play is rooted in that kind of simplicity, and to pretend that it is questioning the British presence in South East Asia or delving into the deeper issues of the emergency years is unadulterated bunkum. It isn't, nor does it need to. Mainly it is demonstrating a kind of playwriting which hasn't been around for a very long time, which, indeed, has fallen out of fashion, and which, when it was in fashion, was the mainstay of those uncomplicated movies which are regularly revived to oohing-and-aghing audiences at the National Film Theatre.

As a piece of comic engineering, one must salute the ingenuity that could construct such a play in the 1970s. To be so profoundly tuned into the ambiance of another time and to be able to work it to your advantage, is no mean feat. Although it is not uncritical of those halcyon years, it is palpably affectionate about them, and to encounter a play motivated by affection rather than social loathing or class prejudice is itself a rarity these days. It falters only in the second half when it gets bogged down in jungle-safari plots and begins to reiterate itself. *Privates On Parade* is a displaced Ealing comedy; a delayed legacy from the Boulting Brothers. It is 'the play of the film' and if nostalgia, now waning, ever gets a second wind in England, it could be . . . [a] big cinematic blockbuster. In so being, it will have found its most natural form. (pp. 22-3)

> *Charles Marowitz, in a review of "Privates on Parade," in* Plays and Players, *Vol. 24, No. 7, April, 1977, pp. 22-5.*

HAROLD HOBSON

Privates on Parade is hilariously funny. But its essence is not the brilliant display of theatrical fireworks which it gives us, dazzling though this is. . . . No, the essence of the play, the factor in it which makes it worthy of an attention comparable with that called forth by [Robert Bolt's] *State of Revolution*, is to be found in a brief scrap of conversation, halfway through the play, between the officer commanding an entertainment unit of the British Army in Malaya and a decent (well, comparatively decent) young private who has recently come out on National Service.

The commanding officer, Major Flack, is a Communist-basher; the young man, Private Stephen Flowers . . . is well-meaning, eager, and weak, but promising. Flack has cast a favourable [eye] upon him, and makes him a serjeant. He then says, 'We've got to believe in something. Those fellows do. What is it these Communists believe in?' The question is largely rhetorical, but Flowers answers it swiftly. 'They believe in equality and social justice'. . . . The major disregards the reply, and goes on: 'If we don't believe in something, we have no justification here. At best we are unwelcome visitors, at worst unscrupulous invaders'. Behind all the high jinks, the larks, the quiddities of character, the jokes and the gags, Mr. Nichols is asking a question of vital importance. What has Western civilisation to offer in place of what is offered (or rather, of what simple-minded people think is offered) by Communism?

Mr. Nichols is a genial man. He likes everybody, even his villain, who is engaging in illicit commerce that nobody really believes in, and . . . [Captain Terri Dennis, a] posturing homosexual is immensely likeable. His lower ranks have filthy tongues, but they are kindly fellows, and at a moment when a comrade is in distress, as in a small but touching incident when one of them loses his glasses and gropes for them on the floor, they are capable of unexpected sensibility. (p. 39)

But Mr. Nichols is not deceived. These are all degenerate people. They have no principle, they have no belief, they have nothing to sustain them. What the British army has become—in face, too, of a profound body of passionate, crusading conviction—is, like Cromwell's army before he created the New Model, an amiable but futile rabble. There is no hope for western society here.

The only man in the play who has any body of doctrine in him is the character whom the audience is most ready to ridicule, that is, Major Flack. Major Flack is a kindly but woefully conventional Christian. Yet he believes in his conventionality. When he makes his fundamentalist, public school little speeches the audience laughs at them. They represent a world universes away from our own permissive society. . . . [At] the end he has his moment of triumph, all the greater because he is not thinking of triumph, but of sincerity. The foulest-mouthed of the play's characters is killed, and the Major pronounces over him the last words of *The Pilgrim's Progress*. Nothing could be more ludicrously inappropriate. . . . But they do not seem ludicrous to the Major. . . . I am sure that Mr. Nichols himself does not believe that the Major's Christianity is any answer to the faith of Communism. But if it is not, has the West any answer at all? Everything in *Privates on Parade* (and not in *Privates on Parade* only) would suggest that it has not. That is why, after an evening as richly packed with side-splitting entertainment as anyone could desire, we leave the [theatre] sorrowful rather than comforted. (p. 40)

> *Harold Hobson, in a review of "Privates on Parade," in* Drama, *No. 125, Summer, 1977, pp. 39-40.*

GORDON GOW

The safety valve of laughter functions usefully as one watches *Born in the Gardens;* and although this is no more than playwright Peter Nichols has by now conditioned us to expect of him, one cannot help but be a little bit surprised at the civilised sang-froid with which he returns to his usual sphere of current social comment after his recent and delightful excursion into the past in *Privates on Parade*. Even there, of course, the humour had a blackish tinge, and so does the fairly constant mirth of the new play, but Nichols possesses the dexterity to avoid toppling into the pit of gloom that has claimed certain other practitioners of his delicate craft. By inciting us to laugh at life's vicissitudes, he encourages us to regain the belief that living, for all its trials, is tolerable.

Ways of arriving at this desirable state of mind will vary, to be sure, according to individuals. In quirky old Maud and her curious younger son Mo (who is not as young as all that), Nichols has hit upon a couple of extreme cases to magnify the value of constructing mentally an edifice too little appreciated in a world grown bleakly realist, to wit the ivory tower, albeit in this instance a thin-walled one.

For a metaphor, Nichols chooses Alfred, the gorilla who was born in Bristol's zoological gardens, never having known the jungle freedom to which, in the common view, he was by nature entitled. Consequently he didn't miss it. Probably he was quite happy with it. Now Alfred is dead—stuffed, a museum piece . . . , and one might think that Maud and Mo are close to the same condition. Yet, while life remains to them, they have at least a comforting illusion of security in their self-imposed confinement, surrounded by their chosen and harmless tokens of grace.

Their cage is the family home, a Victorian house, sombre and vast, in Bristol, where the music room, which is all we see of the place, contains a set of drums and cymbals upon which Mo can accompany his beloved old records of bygone jazz, and a television set with the volume permanently turned off, to whose familiar faces Maud can chatter about anything that comes into her vagrant mind, without having to hear the possibly worrisome things the faces themselves might be saying. (pp. 25-8)

Satisfactory though the partnership of Maud and Mo indubitably is, time does not stand still for them, nor are they destined to be left entirely alone. Transience is emphasised by the presence in the music room, in an open coffin, of the corpse of Maud's husband, rouged to disguise the inroads of reality, and awaiting burial. For the funeral, Maud's two other children come to stay a short time, and to meddle.

Her elder son Hedley is a labour MP, dressed more like a Conservative (which Maud would prefer him to be, and has long deluded herself into thinking he is). . . .

The daughter Queenie has flown in from California, where she makes a libidinous home, sustains a rich tan, and has benefited from breast surgery. . . . In the continuing vein of social sniping, Queenie brings an outsider's eye to her native land, and likes nothing that she sees. . . .

Oddly, Nichols ends his first act with Queenie making a phone call without the realist prop: a cross between mime and monologue; and the second act begins with Hedley doing likewise. It is not, of course, the first time that Nichols has tried this degree of confrontation between character and audience, but it is a device that sits awkwardly in the context of *Born in the Gardens,* conveying little that could not have been brought out, if it needed to be brought out at all, in the otherwise admirable flow of dialogue. . . .

A quibble arises, too, in respect of a tendency to hang on to gags, repeating them in an old-fashioned way, as, for instance, in the protracted battle of Maud against the mites. . . . Nichols comes as near as dammit to being disarming, too, when he has one of his characters make a protest against the West End stage and the very type of play he is, so expertly, purveying. Since much of what he has to put across is dark, not to say pessimistic, I should perhaps stress again that the tone he uses is nearly always funny, and at its best quite engagingly wry. (p. 28)

> *Gordon Gow, in a review of "Born in the Gardens," in* Plays and Players, *Vol 27, No. 5, February, 1980, pp. 25-28.*

BENEDICT NIGHTINGALE

[In *Born in the Gardens*] the main problem . . . is how to reconcile state-of-Britain punditry and family politics. (p. 179)

[Maud and] her shambling, slovenly son [Mo], are absent-mindedly ensconced in Tudor Manor, a Victorian folly distinguished mainly for its exploding geyser and bust gadgetry. Enter [Mo's] two siblings, a well-meaning but (of course) ineffective Labour MP . . . and a contemptuous double-divorcée from wigged-out California. . . . The new arrivals' aim is to rescue, their victims to avoid being rescued. [Maud and Mo] want only to continue the same blithe descent into terminal eccentricity upon which (Nichols suggests with a mixture of nostalgia, affection and exasperation) many of us British-born lemmings are presently engaged. One trouble with the play is a lack of development and momentum, though there's an abundance of wry, funny lines to distract us from it. Another, as I've implied, is its general impression of being not one thing nor the other. As social analysis, it's sketchy and impressionistic, not to say jaded and biased; as a record of relationships, it has its moments of truth, but not so many and penetrating that we feel we're engaging with real people engaging with real life. Still, the same accusation could be made against Shaw's *Heartbreak House,* a comparison that is, I suppose, a sort of praise in itself. (pp. 179-80)

Benedict Nightingale, "Scribes," in New Statesman, *Vol. 99, No. 2250, February 1, 1980, pp. 179-80.**

VARIETY

["**Poppy**"] parodies the traditional British pantomime show for kids, with its principal boy and girl, "drag" dame and generally broad style of playing to and involving the audience. The books for such presentations are usually very loose and discursive versions of folklore figures and popular legends.

"**Poppy**" in short, is a children's show for grownups, a jovial, tuneful slice of cutthroat colonial history when the British got the Chinese hooked on opium for the oldest of reasons—money, or Anglo-Saxon greed rather than philanthropy. The show effectively makes its critical, relevant point about colonial treachery and chauvinistic arrogance, but not at the expense of consistent, lively, eyefilling entertainment as the first priority. . . .

Whether or not it's a particularly remote subject for a musical, "**Poppy**" turns out to be a surprising and almost endless delight of elaborately arranged settings, corny jokes, visual gags, lavish costumes, lively and appealing dance routines and witty, well-sung songs. . . .

It takes a few moments to adjust to what's afoot in this spectacle show but it's a treat the rest of the way.

Pit., in a review of "Poppy," in Variety, *October 13, 1982, p. 182.*

BENEDICT NIGHTINGALE

In his exasperation at the theatrical profession [Nichols] has, in effect, turned his guns upon himself and his audiences. He will, he says, write for the stage no more: a decision that even his severer critics will agree to be misguided, misdirected, indeed vandalistic. . . . Frankly, it thinks Peter has gone a bit bonkers, and would urge him to pull himself together, pick up his quill, and get writing pronto. To that end it has one final and, it thinks, irresistible argument to put: is Nichols really content to leave the theatre on the—and here we come to the point we've been assiduously avoiding—on the sheer disaster of *Poppy*? (p. 28)

The idea [of *Poppy*] . . . is to create an ironically slanted version of the kind of English panto that, as he tells us in a characteristically nostalgic programme note, Nichols enjoyed as a boy. There are comic horses, a chorus of frolicking yokels who change in hue and garb as the action moves further and further into the mysterious East, an Oriental potentate who produces magic bangs and flashes when he's vexed, a leggy and distinctively female principal boy, a tweedy and indisputably male Dame, several anachronistic and seemingly spontaneous jokes about Lord Lucan and the Barbican air conditioning, some

suggestive *double-entendre;* and all to inform us about the imperial atrocities inflicted by the drug-toting British upon the Chinese Circa 1840. . . . All the familiar conventions are introduced, and many are rendered . . . didactic. . . .

[The] pantomime, especially when the script evokes it with such love and in such detail, isn't a very satisfactory form for airing and exposing our ancestors' attempts to hook a nation on opium by means of bribes, threats and gunboats. Part of the idea presumably is to contrast the gallumphing innocence, callow moral certainties and essential insularity of a [*Dick Whittington*] with what the real-life mayors, aldermen and city magnates were perpetrating in the name of patriotism and profit; but that doesn't seem to take us far enough to justify parody so pervasive and persistent.

That more than this is meant is apparent from the claim of a spoof Queen Victoria, according to whom anyone who wants to understand her subjects 'could do worse than spend a little time deciphering the British pantomime'. In other words, Nichols is suggesting that there's something in the form which helps explain our national content, something in the panto which illuminates our arrogant, greedy and violent colonial history. But he never really makes that connection, or never makes it on any rational level. You could, I suppose, conclude that what crushed the Chinese were trite rhymes, bathroom jokes, audience participation, humanoid horses and general sexual ambivalence; but that can't be what Nichols intended.

The panto element adds little and, I fear, subtracts much. Without it, perhaps we might have had a more thorough investigation of a part of our collective unconscious we've preferred to keep suppressed. . . . The historians who concluded that the import of dope was only a surface pretext for Chinese hostility to British traders and diplomats can't all be blimps or knaves. . . . Besides, didn't China have its domestic crop, with which its officials seemed perfectly prepared to poison their own people? But *Poppy,* thanks partly to the intrusion of stereotypes from panto, almost always prefers the pontificating simplification to the inconvenience of qualification.

It would be excessive to conclude that Nichols is always better when he concentrates on love or marriage, personal relationships or, as in the case of *Forget-Me-Not Lane,* autobiography, than when he dons his prophet's loincloth and starts glumly deploring the state of the nation, past or present. I have to admit, though, that I myself prefer his more private work, such as *Joe Egg, Chez Nous* or *Passion Play* [performed in America as *Passion*], to his more public, such as *The Freeway* or even *The National Health,* pieces too sketchy and impressionistic altogether to succeed as social summations. Indeed, his more public plays seem to me bearable only when their private parts come plausibly to life, as happens for instance in *Born in the Gardens,* which Nichols clearly intended as a bleak comment on a representative sample of the derelict English, but which I, for one, remember for some splendidly eccentric scenes involving [Maud and Mo] . . . loonie mum and shambling, helpless son respectively. But there is no chance of such rueful humanity in *Poppy,* which is all caricature, moral superiority, showbiz dazzle and loud music. Let me rephrase my opening question. Is Peter Nichols, whom we value for the truth and warmth of his admittedly somewhat pessimistic insights into people, really intending to abandon the theatre on a note like *that*? (p. 29)

Benedict Nightingale, "Opium for the People," in New Statesman, *Vol. 104, No. 2691, October 15, 1982, pp. 28-9.**

CLIVE BARNES

Peter Nichols always has been one of the most fascinating of the contemporary playwrights, and in *Passion* . . . he has given us a savage comedy about love, sex and despair.

Perhaps most about despair—although that does not prevent it from being heartrendingly funny, particularly at first, before the blood starts to be drawn in earnest, and Nichols becomes too honest and too serious for simple laughter. . . .

What makes Nichols particularly interesting as a playwright is his sheer confidence with technique. He seems to have gone on record with some statement that this is to be his last play. I don't believe it for a single minute—and if I did I would be very sad—but certainly technically he has surpassed himself. And so simply.

Always he has been interested in moving theater in different directions. Ever since his *Day in the Death of Joe Egg* he has been pushing for some kind of duality of theatrical expression. Some way of standing outside that proscenium arch and—frankly—commenting.

The idea is to get a double input. It's partly Brechtian, so you see events reflected in the mirror-image of the characters.

Here he has come straight out with it. A story of adultery. But both the husband and the wife are played by two actors. At first he lets you think that this is simply ego and alter-ego—the kind of Jungian nonsense that Woody Allen would have thought of before he found Bergman—but it soon becomes far more complex.

By putting these two lives on these two different planes—and, in the second act, the crucial act, switching them around so even as audience, let alone as people, you're not quite sure who is who—you see a relationship in the whole gaudy, bloody, pattern of life.

Nichols is one of the great theatrical magicians. He fools you into a naughty, stultified, kind of amazement. He is a conjurer. But much more—although to be honest, I don't know that there is much more in the theater than a conjurer—he is a poet, certainly, and a juggler perhaps. But with Nichols we can settle for a conjurer.

In the first act, indeed, you settle for a very clever light comedy. But Nichols knows that life is not precisely a light comedy, and he starts to hurt quite outrageously.

Nichols has never been a playwright with a message—he is a playwright with a report.

Apart from his technical expertise—which I am possibly stressing unfairly simply because it is so evident—he has a way of picking up conversation. It is the art of finding character in the air of the way people disclose themselves as people. . . .

This is an important play. . . . [It] has the humor of the moment and it points out—intensely—the way people live, feel, think and love. At this last gasp of the season, it lights up Broadway.

> *Clive Barnes, "Nichols' Funny Romp Sizzles with 'Passion'," in* New York Post, *May 16, 1983. Reprinted in* New York Theatre Critics' Reviews, *Vol. XXXXIV, No. 9, May 23-May 30, 1983, p. 235.*

FRANK RICH

It really is true: There are no tired stories—only tired writers. In **"Passion"** . . . the English playwright Peter Nichols takes one of the oldest tales in the book—a middle-aged husband has an affair with a younger woman—and, with virtuoso writing and unsparing honesty, rocks the foundations of an audience's complacency. The gripping, recognizable world in this play is a barren contemporary landscape where husbands and wives can divorce easily, but where passion and suffering form an unholy union that no one can tear asunder. It's the most savage view of marriage yet from the author of **"A Day in the Death of Joe Egg"** and **"Forget-Me-Not Lane."** . . . In **"Passion,"** the playwright rethinks the eternal love triangle by using a strategy that reverses Harold Pinter's in the somewhat similar "Betrayal." Instead of fracturing time to create drama out of what his characters do not say, Mr. Nichols slows down time to force his characters to tell all.

His troubled married couple of 25 years, James . . . and Eleanor . . . , are shadowed by their private selves. . . . By giving literal second faces to two-faced characters, the author can reveal what James and Eleanor are really feeling; he can stage interior psychological debates that are usually beyond the reach of the theater. He can also, in the final stretch, pull the terrifying switch of letting the alter egos usurp the roles of the public James and Eleanor almost entirely: There's ultimately no privacy for people who enter the hell of inexorable self-destruction.

At first, the rewards of this double-image effect are farcical revelations of hypocrisy. . . . But soon the divided nature of the characters—and the juxtapositions of longing and heartbreak—become rending. When we watch the two Jameses draft a love letter to Kate at home, we simultaneously see both Eleanors learn about the letter's existence while dining at a restaurant. "Think of nothing," pleads the disintegrating private wife to the relatively composed public one, "or you'll cry."

Yet this technique—which has also been used well by playwrights like Brian Friel and Marsha Norman—isn't the sum of Mr. Nichols's achievement. In its Royal Shakespeare Company premiere in 1981, **"Passion"** was called **"Passion Play"**—and a neo-religious play it is. James and Eleanor are atheists, but they're haunted by the God they've killed off. . . .

James fools around with his mistress precisely to escape the 2,000-year grip of Christian morality: Kate is a product of a new, '60's generation that "disregards conventional values." But when the conventions are gone, what's left proves a "minefield of lies"—an abyss as devoid of clear codes as the blank, minimalist paintings that usually cross James's easel. . . .

Mr. Nichols isn't calling for a reinstitution of what a character calls "a rundown monogamy." He raises open-sided questions without answering them, finally to end his play at a Christmas party that bleeds into a chilling symbolic tableau—a resurrection for the couple's souls that is more nihilistic than New Testament. The play's flaws are of form, not philosophy. In Act-II, Mr. Nichols stretches the narrative and repeats points. He also fails to convince us that Eleanor and Kate would remain social acquaintances even as James bounces between them. . . .

"Passion," the last of the 1982-83 Broadway season's plays, is one of the best.

> *Frank Rich, "Frank Langella in 'Passion'," in* The New York Times, *May 16, 1983, p. c14.*

BRENDAN GILL

The subject of **"Passion"** . . . is the by no means novel one of marital infidelity. Mr. Nichols has given the subject a certain freshness and, in his clever first act, a certain piquancy as well by dividing the married couple with whom he is concerned into two pairs. . . .

[The first act] contains many agreeable turns and twists of plot and is so lighthearted that we feel no difficulty in laughing at what is, after all, a classically painful situation. This light-heartedness steadily drains away throughout the second act; we perceive that though the jokes continue the playwright is increasingly in earnest, even to the point of presenting us with an attempted suicide by the once spunky Nell, who is then encouraged to return to life by a panicky, solicitous Jim. How on earth, we wonder, has the anguished shadow of Anna Karenina happened to fall across this intricate suburban comedy? Nor is Mr. Nichols willing to send us out into the night with merry hearts; confronting us with the possible death of God and the sure old age, impotence, and death of his characters, he ends his play on a note of grim indeterminancy that is likely to set back the cause of adultery by twenty years.

Brendan Gill, "Perils of Wedlock," in The New Yorker, *Vol. LIX, No. 14, May 23, 1983, p. 103.**

JOHN SIMON

Passion Play by Peter Nichols, which, for reasons of titular conflict, is called *Passion* on Broadway, needs its British title desperately. . . . [It] rings every change on "passion" and "play," as well as on the medieval, religious meaning of "passion play" and all its conceivable contemporary lay equivalents. Life, according to Nichols, is a hectic mixture of, or contest between, passion and play: Marriage, love affairs, casual sex, work, religion, creation, recreation, everyday existence—all of them are a sort of, usually warring, aggregate of passion and play. The difficulty lies in sorting them out; the impossibility, in reconciling them. The history of this conflict is the record of an agony, a crucifixion: the love life, or just plain life, of an ordinary human being.

Kate was the mistress of Albert, James's friend and coeval. . . . But Albert died, and at his funeral, where the promiscuous Kate wore an expensive outfit meant to intoxicate James, that solidly married father of two grown and gone daughters began to fall for her. The rest of the play—and this is as much as I can divulge of a plot that depends all too much on surprises—concerns the permutations of this passion, which, unlike Freud's sexual act ("a process in which four persons are involved"), according to your mode of counting, involves three or five. That is because, alongside the basic trio, we get from Nichols the inward (or private, secret, unvoiced) selves of James and Eleanor, to wit, Jim and Nell. On stage, Jim and Nell are made to resemble their outward selves, but their words and actions express the hopes, longings, fears, and thoughts that James and Eleanor leave unexpressed.

The device has a long theatrical history. . . . [But] Nichols is much trickier than any of its previous users. At carefully calculated intervals, he springs on us, first, Jim, then, quite a bit later, Nell. (Where was she until then?) Thereupon he has Jim (who, by rights, should remain invisible and inaudible to anyone but James) anticipating some of James's doings, even calling up Kate on the phone. When the novelty of this wears off, Jim actually *becomes* the outward self, interacting with Eleanor, while James seems to become the inward one. After a while, Nell similarly takes over for Eleanor in a psychiatrist's office. This can be rationalized as the unconscious self receiving ther-

apy; but Jim's taking over from James in the middle of nowhere would require reams of casuistry to defend.

Thenceforth things become Gordianly entangled. You never know any more which is the outer, which the inner, self, with every self apparently interacting with every other one. (If that is the point, it is not susceptible to lucid dramatic realization.) As the stage action also frequently takes place in two different locations simultaneously, with one minor speaking character and six all-purpose mumbling extras likewise involved, the proceedings become so chaotic that I got more—though not much more—from a subsequent reading of the play than from seeing it. Yet since *Passion* is so plainly geared to enactment, to being visual fun (otherwise, why bother with the doubling device?), it is self-defeating: less clear and effective in the mode in which it wants to be more so. Two equally grave flaws are that it works up to an ending that is totally opaque, explicable in any number of ways, all equally unpersuasive; and that, as it proceeds, it does not shed much new light on marriage and adultery, monogamy and polygamy, fidelity and infidelity—passion and play.

It also cheats. For whereas James and Eleanor are made—thanks to their hidden alter egos, who are, as is the wont of hidden alter egos, more interesting than the public egos into dizzylingly complex persons, poor Kate is given an only quasi-artistic profession (photography) and a name that is already a nickname and diminutive, and denied a private Katie or Kate-let. This is grossly unfair. As a major part of the plot and even of a kind of subplot, or pre-plot, involving Agnes, Kate is jolly well entitled to her own private self. But the author, male and middle-aged, patronizes Kate into a pornographic fantasy figure: a girl of the mindless, unbridled younger generation, scarcely interested in anything but sex, and always ready to have it, straight or kinky, with any passing, passable stranger. Although a playwright can and must be selective, such tendentious oversimplification strikes me as dishonest and unworthy of the author of *Joe Egg* and *The National Health*. (p. 74)

Passion is an unsatisfactory play by an intelligent and gifted playwright, and so contains lines and passages of poignancy and grace. But it also has a great deal of manipulativeness and pretension, what with, for example, Mozart's *Requiem* and the *Saint Matthew Passion* (yes, I know, it's a passion play) being pumped into it periodically, along with Beethoven's Ninth, discussions of Christianity versus paganism, classical versus modern art, psychotherapy versus the right to refuse it, and sundry other topics not immiscible with the matter at hand but inadmissible when so self-consciously and perfunctorily dragged in and surrounded by all that gimmickry. We watch with an initially amused bedevilment that subsides into frustrated lassitude. (p. 75)

John Simon, "Double or Nothing?" in New York Magazine, *Vol. 16, No. 22, May 30, 1983, pp. 74-5.**

MERVYN JONES

In *Poppy,* for the first time, Nichols has gone outside his own experience and indeed his own period, and has written a historical play. The subject is the Opium War, about the least justified and most reprehensible war in world history; one knows enough about Nichols' political outlook to be confident that this is also his judgement of it. However, the dramatic momentum impels us to see the war as it was presumably seen by contemporaries—as an encounter between a civilised nation (Britain) and an incomprehensibly alien culture, as a natural expression of British energy and martial virility, and as an adventure to be reckoned, on balance, as jolly good fun. A European visitor to London, buying a ticket on the recommendation of his hotel porter and knowing nothing of the author, would probably regard *Poppy* as a manifestation of the mood of anachronistic jingoism and collective hypomania that came over the British in the year of the Falklands war. There must be something wrong.

It must have seemed a splendid idea—for Nichols, so congenial as to be irresistibly tempting—to depict the Opium War through the allegory of a pantomime. Joan Littlewood, in the unforgettable *Oh What a Lovely War,* had depicted the 1914-18 war through the allegory of a seaside concert party. . . . But what Littlewood and her team brought off has been achieved, to my knowledge, only that once; it was true theatrical magic, a kind of miracle. We saw a pierrot as still a pierrot, valiantly keeping up the bright cheerfulness of the role, and yet at the same time a soldier engulfed by the horror of the trenches. Alas, the Prince Charming, the pantomime dame and the soubrette of *Poppy* remained a Prince Charming, a pantomime dame and a soubrette. A few scenes, admittedly, struck a sombre note, but evoked only the facile pathos or the easy appeal to sentiment that find their allotted place in *Dick Whittington* or *Ali Baba.* The pantomime was never more than a pantomime. . . .

Many reasons for this sad outcome can be offered. . . . When allowance is made for all these factors,however, *Poppy* has to be remembered as the only play in Peter Nichols' record that crucially failed to give expression to its purpose.

It is difficult to write plays, no doubt about that; and it is immeasurably difficult for a writer with the seriousness, the complexity, and the vibrant inner tensions of Peter Nichols. If he has now reached the conclusion, after years of struggling with the dramatic form, that the problems of fully conveying his meaning through this form—and under available conditions of production—are too exhausting to yield satisfaction, the loss is ours. But if he is really going to write novels, I look forward very much to reading them. (p. 8)

> Mervyn Jones, "Peter Nichols, the Playwright Who Has Had Enough," in Drama, *No. 148, Summer, 1983, pp. 7-8.*

MILES KINGTON

[*Feeling You're Behind*], Nichols's account of his life up to the success of *A Day in the Death of Joe Egg,* is frequently unhappy and nail-chewing. . . .

Nichols is a Bristolian, and the key to his character lies in his provincial yet big city upbringing, which gave him aspirations without satisfying them. As a pure evocation of childhood the early chunk of the book is very satisfying, and so is the long section dealing with his RAF days in India and Singapore (which all seem part of his childhood; his continuing virginity comes over as more than just sexual). But it is the portrait of his father to which he returns so often that contains the biggest clue to his nature.

Most of the time, to be frank, he makes fun of his father. . . . An extrovert Cockney, he sprayed out pet phrases, monologues, mannerisms, stand-up comic acts and domestic routines which seem to have deeply embarrassed the young Nichols, yet which he comes back to again and again. When he cannot find the letters written to him in the Far East, he goes so far as to make up the kind of letters his father would have written.

Later he was to put his father on stage again and again—he once, he says, saw three actors sitting at the same canteen table, all of whom had portrayed his dad on stage. I leave some other delves into the subconscious to explain what all this means, but Nichols is engagingly frank about the way he has used his life and family to fuel his drama. The trouble is that the border line between the two is hopelessly blurred. He quotes freely from his plays to illustrate the way his family spoke, and quotes his family often to justify something from his plays. By the end of the book I wasn't sure which was real life and which was art. I'm not sure he was either.

So it's a troubling, sweet sour, undecided book. It's also an engaging, attractive, colourful and absorbing book. It's a confessional book, sometimes of unimportant things . . . sometimes of terrible things. . . .

But above all it poses the question—what does Peter Nichols do next?

> Miles Kington, "Peter Nichols: A Taste of Vinegar," in The Sunday Times, *London, May 20, 1984, p. 44.*

JIM HILEY

Confronted with the death throes of the Raj and the inanities of National Service simultaneously, Peter Nichols decided that he was a natural for the awkward squad and would probably remain so. . . .

Nichols went on to become what's known in the less imaginative quarters of the theatrical community as 'difficult'. For example, he doesn't mind arguing with directors. . . . And he walked out on his last play, *Poppy,* making the not completely outrageous claim that the Royal Shakespeare Company handles dead playwrights better than living ones.

Now he has quit the theatre altogether, and it is much the poorer for it. What makes his departure even sadder is that neither in this autobiography [*Feeling You're Behind*], nor elsewhere have his complaints been developed into a critique and thoroughly debated. Similarly, his plays have been tolerated rather than embraced and scrutinised. . . .

This seems to have discouraged him from telling us more about how he works. *Feeling You're Behind* takes in a period during which he wrote several TV plays, and concludes with the productions of his memorable first stage play, *A Day In The Death Of Joe Egg,* in London and New York. Characteristically, Nichols points out that the show's initial success was nothing like as great as legend has it. . . . But for a writer's autobiography, including as it does his years of self-education, there is disappointingly little about the process of writing.

In abundance, though, are the virtues found in his plays. He has an entertainer's compulsion to give the customers more than their money's-worth. Nichols the dramatist encases his essential (and essentially traditional) English naturalism with show-business razzmatazz—from the cod soap opera antics punctuating *The National Health* to the concert party routines of *Privates on Parade.* So it is with Nichols the first-person raconteur. This book is rich in comic turns, music-hall setpieces and one-liners, all expertly timed. But again, as in the plays, the feelings of the moment are always conscientiously laid bare, while more perennial truths are dealt with by hints and diffident speculation. . . .

Near the opening of the book, he informs us—with a shake of his head and a quick glance in Freud's direction—that his memory begins 'at about the age of 12'. His life before then is evoked with miscellaneous musings prompted by old snapshots, liberal slices of dialogue from his autobiographical plays, and a few remembered scenes in which he himself points out inconsistencies. This is as frustrating for the reader as for the author, but at least a savoury portrait of his father emerges in the early pages—as sickly fascinating and far more frightening than the stage version in *Forget Me Not Lane*. (p. 24)

'Puberty struck me harder than the war,' says Peter Nichols, and it is with these roughly coinciding events that the book really gets off the ground. . . .

Life and coincidence help him to keep up the entertainment value and a smattering of glamour. As a schoolboy, he was told by his father to 'develop the habit of feeling you're behind. Behind people like Tom Graveney'. It is typical of Nichols's tale that the swashbuckling cricketer just happened to be a classmate, and was invariably top of the form.

This is hardly the most penetrating of autobiographies. But it is less self-pitying, and much more stylish, than the title suggests. (p. 25)

> Jim Hiley, "The Awkward Squad," in The Listener, *Vol. 111, No. 2860, May 31, 1984, pp. 24-5.*

SYLVIANE GOLD

When "Joe Egg" came to Broadway in 1968, it seemed a daring amalgam of two divergent trends in British drama. With this flamboyantly theatrical vaudeville about a spastic child, Peter Nichols had married the social concerns of the "angry young men" of the 1950s with the outrageous black comedy of the 1960s.

That he would treat the subject at all, much less treat it without a smidgen of sentiment, was enough to give his play a certain shock appeal. . . .

[The] real glory of this revival is the opportunity it affords us for another look at Mr. Nichols's play, now that we're no longer startled by it, now that it can be separated from its historical context. And what we see is a complex, multilayered work that touches lightly but tellingly on some of the most disturbing issues of our time.

"Joe Egg" tackles doctors and Britain's socialized-medicine system with biting burlesque. In a tightly constructed comedy of manners, it takes aim at social and biological snobbery. Euthanasia is explored in a scene of door-slamming farce. And running all through the entertainment is a compelling, life-or-death argument between the conflicting claims of faith and reason, between hope and despair in the face of the incomprehensible.

Bri has embraced despair; Sheila clings to hope. He sees God as a "manic-depressive rugby footballer"—and himself as "the ball." She responds with all-encompassing good will that extends equally to plants, animals, the women in the local home for unwed mothers and, in fact, just about everyone but her mother-in-law.

Neither wins the argument. And always in the background is the daughter they have come to call Joe Egg. She functions in the play as both the very real daughter of a very real marriage and as a living, breathing personification of all the inexplicable burdens and nasty turns of fate we meet with as we go through life. Mr. Nichols's play, brimming though it is with theatrical invention and lively wit, is at bottom deeply philosophical.

It's no wonder we missed some of that back in 1968. But good plays are sneaky.

> Sylviane Gold, "The Return of 'Joe Egg'," in The Wall Street Journal, *January 15, 1985, p. 32.*

JOHN SIMON

A Day in the Death of Joe Egg may not be a great play, but it is, in many ways, awesomely and gladsomely good, and far better than anything you can find on Broadway today. . . . In fact, it is what the theater would be preponderantly like if we were lucky: made up of plays that seized our interest, hugged our emotions, made us laugh and cry (sometimes simultaneously), and gave us an abundance of things to think about on the subject of the play, on related issues, and indeed on life itself in the broadest, most searching terms.

That *Joe Egg* fulfills these requirements should compensate for an occasional dull patch, a not quite convincing ending, and language that is not, in the strict literary sense, first-rate. The play . . . must restore anybody's faith in the theater's ability to cut through nationality, social class, levels of intelligence and sophistication and hold the most diversified audience in a pulsating unanimity of involvement. The play demonstrates both (as Irving Wardle put it after the London premiere, in 1967) "the old truth which needs constantly to be rediscovered, that comedy has its roots in suffering" and that there are ways of combining realism and stylization that triumphantly bypass the pitfalls of plodding naturalism and dehumanizing fantastication. The wonderful thing about *Joe Egg* is that even if it does not point its finger at you like a recruiting poster, even if it deals with a matter whose specifics are alien to you, there is no way for you not to recognize that it is—deep down where it hurts, exhilarates, and exalts—about you. . . .

["Joe Egg", the spastic daughter of Brian and Sheila,] is kept at home out of excesses of love and guilt: She is the horribly askew centerpiece around which everything revolves, which keeps the marriage centripetal though troubled until it finally breaks up.

Nichols tries to persuade us that this marriage is doomed by the emotional disparity of the partners—that it would dissolve even without Joe. Of this he does not convince me. But no matter: The play is a marvelous demonstration of how people cope, or try to cope, with the impossible: how their small successes are heroic and heartwarming—and excruciatingly funny; how their failures are infinitely forgivable. But, in tiny and not so tiny ways, the play fibs. Bri and Sheila, like the Nicholses, who had such a child, play games to alleviate their pain. They reenact black-comedy encounters with doctors, clergymen, newscasters, and others who try or do not try to help, or variously exploit their predicament. The couple improvises absurdist, parodistic (but oh, so real!) skits about the past, as well as fantasies about the present and future—in some of which Joe becomes normal—without offending against good taste. For it is only through such breathtaking tastelessness that Joe can be endured in the household and given the exacting and distasteful care she needs, as well as what she would not get in a special hospital: love. (p. 60)

But the real Nicholses did send their daughter to a special hospital, and the marriage survived. I am the last person to ask drama to become a carbon copy of life; nevertheless, it is these two major departures from biography that most hurt the artistic authenticity of the play. In the end, Nichols cannot make Joe's staying on fully believable or Bri's escape from Sheila seem real enough, though I don't know whether this is a failure of artistry or of logic. What is ingenious, however, is the way absurdist comedy yields to and finally fuses with social satire in Act II, where Nichols introduces a friendly couple: Freddie, a wealthy, square, socialist do-gooder, and Pam, his idly rich, superficial and selfish, but amusing wife. These, and Grace, Bri's typical yet pungently non-cliché mother, round out a tragicomic view of bourgeois society that remarkably manages to be both ludicrous and touching. The interaction of characters and conversations, superbly orchestrated, makes *Joe Egg* the kind of first play that Nichols understandably has never surpassed, though, to his credit, sometimes equaled. (pp. 60-1)

This felt and thoughtful play allows each character to be relatively right and relatively wrong, relatively absurd and relatively heart-wringing. Yet far from being calculated and manipulative, these relativities spring full-fledged and alive from the author's honestly observant and inventive mind. They are above all—shudderingly, riotously, fastidiously—true. (p. 61)

> *John Simon, "The 'Egg' and 'I'," in* New York Magazine, *Vol. 18, No. 3, January 21, 1985, pp. 60-1.*

PAUL BERMAN

[*A Day in the Death of Joe Egg*] ought to be anything but cheery, you would think. An English schoolteacher and his wife kid each other around the living room, joshing and flirting and encouraging each other in their different hobbies. And we see with a bit of a shock that life and marriage aren't going well, for Mum and Dad have a 12-year-old daughter who's three-quarters dead with brain damage. The stuff of serious drama,

in short. One even thinks of Ibsen for a second, since Mom ascribes the child's defects to her own sexual past, which is the ghost of an Ibsenian theme.

How to live with such a tragic situation? Anyone with a good idea in *Egg* is shown to be a bad person, which rather incriminates the idea. Dad's old school chum, who advocates institutionalization, is an immoral hypocrite. The chum's wife favors euthanasia and should plainly be its first victim. The doctor is so crude as to talk about "wegetables," in his German accent. A minister is so trendy he's a joke. As for Mum, she expounds a bubble-gum philosophy of love for all living things. "Where there's life, there's hope," summarizes her view. But there isn't hope. Perhaps the play itself, the action on stage, will offer a way to understand the family tragedy? No such luck. Dad, cast down by Mum's lack of interest in sex, tries to murder the child in a backhanded way, and when that doesn't work, he skips town. This ought to drive home how inadequate all other responses to the tragedy have been, how truly awful is this family's situation. Dad's freak-out and flight ought to open a bleak window on reality. But not for a moment do we believe this ending—that nice old Dad would do in the wegetable; or that Mum would accept Dad back after the wegetable recovers; or that she would turn a new leaf by promising to make love more often, now that she knows Dad harbors murderous instincts.

And given this central failing in *Egg,* the failure to rise adequately to the household situation, what dominates the stage is somehow the comforting atmosphere of middle-class civility, the triumph of humor over a grim situation, the hope of family tenderness, the cheery upbeat theater spirit . . . the comfy sofa, the squeaky-clean living room. . . . The tone, the feeling is all too A-O.K. (p. 186)

> *Paul Berman, in a review of "A Day in the Death of Joe Egg," in* The Nation, *Vol. 240, No. 6, February 16, 1985, pp. 185-87.*

Edna O'Brien

1932-

Irish novelist, short story writer, dramatist, and screenwriter.

O'Brien's works focus on the lives of women, portraying their yearning for love and acceptance and their inevitable disappointment. O'Brien, who was born and raised in western Ireland, has spent most of her adult life in London. Both Irish village life during the 1940s and 1950s and contemporary urban settings are depicted in O'Brien's fiction. The influence of her Catholic upbringing is apparent in much of her work, even when it is furthest removed from the Irish Catholic milieu of her youth. The pleasure that O'Brien's heroines find in sex, for instance, is often mixed with guilt and shame. Her frank portrayal of female sexuality has drawn both praise and criticism and has caused her books to be banned in her native country. O'Brien's women are usually presented as martyrs whose dependence on men leads to unhappiness and sometimes results in tragedy; her men are often drunken, callous, and irresponsible.

O'Brien's first novel, *The Country Girls* (1960), was an immediate success and begins a trilogy that continues with *The Lonely Girl* (1962) and *Girls in Their Married Bliss* (1964). These books follow two young girls from a convent school in rural Ireland to Dublin and finally to married life in London. Like many of O'Brien's heroines, the girls are thwarted in their search for love, and the last novel ends on a bitter note. *August Is a Wicked Month* (1965) is similarly desolate. It concerns a vacationing divorced woman who seeks meaning and union with a variety of sexual partners. At the end of the novel, her young son dies during a camping trip, and she is further than ever from finding fulfillment. In *Casualties of Peace* (1966) O'Brien introduces an element of violence, as the protagonist is killed by her best friend's husband. O'Brien returned to a rural Irish setting for *A Pagan Place* (1970) and wrote directly about her own youth and Ireland's continuing influence on her in *Mother Ireland* (1976). An urban setting and implications of psychic and physical violence are again present in *Johnny I Hardly Knew You* (1977), in which a woman explores why she has murdered her lover.

O'Brien's short story collections present many of the same settings and themes as her novels. Her stories located in the Irish countryside are narrated by young girls observing their mothers, fathers, and neighbors. The narrators are often confused by the ties and conflicting passions that connect these people. As Lorna Sage observed in a review of *Returning* (1982), "The tales belong to an era of austerity, intensified by Irish puritanism." O'Brien has also written stories which, like her urban-centered novels, involve older, sophisticated women whose experiences with love and sex have left them disappointed. Both kinds of stories are represented in *A Fanatic Heart: Selected Stories* (1985). Oliver Conant notes, "When O'Brien turns from constrained, personalist Western Ireland to an urban culture of drifting hedonists, in which no one is known to anyone else . . . , something of her sureness of touch is lost." Many critics agree that her writing is most effective when it recreates the Ireland of her childhood.

© Jerry Bauer

(See also *CLC*, Vols. 3, 5, 8, 13; *Contemporary Authors*, Vols. 1-4, rev. ed.; *Contemporary Authors New Revision Series*, Vol. 6; and *Dictionary of Literary Biography*, Vol. 14.)

HAROLD HOBSON

"*Who's Afraid of Virginia Woolf?*" someone once asked ribaldly. Virginia Woolf, she was afraid of Virginia Woolf. She was afraid of sexual intercourse, she was afraid of her father, she was afraid to go to dances in her youth, or to receive journalists in maturer age, she was afraid of losing her inspiration, and above all she was afraid of going mad. The only thing she was not afraid of was going to aristocratic, intellectual parties, and these her husband debarred her from, because *he* was afraid of *them*. . . .

[In *Virginia* the] books come out, the clever friends are remembered, but the fear remains, withdraws for a moment, and then leaps forward yet more ferociously. The story is magnificent and terrible, and Edna O'Brien tells it impressionistically rather than in straight narrative, and doing so is able to invest it with a mystery, a horror, and a sense of evil that Henry James could not have surpassed.

Harold Hobson, in a review of "Virginia," in Drama, *No. 140, second quarter, 1981, p. 17.*

DIANA DEVLIN

If there is a danger in generalising about social groups, there is also danger in looking deeply into an individual as Edna O'Brien does in *Virginia,* a portrait in theatre of Virginia Woolf. The play is shaped round her moods which swirl around through happiness, vitality, despair, elation and bitterness. Events and characters are incidental allusions—I wonder how comprehensible it is without Quentin Bell's biography at your elbow. But it is compelling, a kind of emotional documentary drawing us into the frighteningly vivid mind of a creative woman trapped by her overpowering feelings, genius and madness mingling inextricably.

Diana Devlin, in a review of "Virginia," in Drama, *No. 140, second quarter, 1981, p. 55.*

LORNA SAGE

In **'Returning'** Edna O'Brien is back in her old parish—sitting round the kitchen table gossiping with Mother Ireland, inhaling the savours of oilcloth, soda bread and cocoa, and meditating on the tricks of memory. All nine stories hark back to a 1940s girlhood and have an autobiographical tinge, but there's little that is documentary about them, for the life she's recalling is a tissue of rumour, superstition and disappointed dreams which is already half-transmogrified into fiction. . . .

It's hard to get away, and hard once you do not to feel a stinging sense of betrayal towards figures who once loomed large but later pale to shadows. Miss O'Brien's childhood self, already 'on the run,' observes her world with the secret knowledge that she'll escape, and that the guilt of having done so will never leave her. **'Ghosts'** recalls the cramped, fantasy-swamped lives of three women, a crazy spinster, a sensual girl and a drudging, lonely wife . . . as somehow more real and, even, more glamorous than anything the 'free' world offers.

It's a masochistic thought—'It was clear to me then that my version of pleasure was inextricable from pain'—but on the whole the tone of **'Returning'** is uncharacteristically subdued. These tales belong to an era of austerity, intensified by Irish puritanism, and Edna O'Brien has shorn her style of its wilder curlicues to correspond. Surprisingly, perhaps, it suits her very well.

Lorna Sage, "Back to Mother Ireland," in The Observer, *April 25, 1982, p. 30.**

SARA MAITLAND

Edna O'Brien is quite simply a wonderful writer of short stories. She is evocative, sensual and technically subtle. Her writing is a real pleasure to read. She is also staggeringly consistent—making allowance for personal preferences in the reader, she continues over the years to produce story after story of a uniformly high standard, and never seems to fob her readers off with the occasional dud. . . . (p. 25)

[*Returning*] is bound together by a common theme: O'Brien's lost Irish childhood. 'Lost' though is perhaps the wrong word, as many of the nine stories explore a regret at having wilfully thrown away that childhood rootedness in exchange for a fantasy of worldly delights in a bigger, more cosmopolitan environment. The stories suggest that the bright promises have proved illusory, but that it is too late to return. . . . But this boggy melancholy never quite collapses into sentimentality. How O'Brien avoids this is a worthy question, but she keeps

her details so specific and material—smells, colours, objects rendered with a hard precision—that saves them from soft mistiness. And moreover the world of rural Ireland is seen honestly enough for what it is: something that anyone in their right mind would want to escape from, limited, limiting, and charged with a blight of cruelty and insanity. But the impossibility of going back there does not change the desires, and especially not the memories.

As the title suggests it is the moment of returning as an adult to the place of childhood that triggers and shapes the memories. Several of the best stories—**'The Doll'** and **'The Batchelor'** for example—are told from this angle. The narrator comes home after a period of detachment and understands things differently from how they appeared at the time. Guilt about infant obtuseness is mingled with sadness at what has been lost, and relief at escape. The stories are loaded with emotional innuendo and implication in a way that is both impressive and rewarding.

It has to be said however that Miss O'Brien does sometimes go over the top and plays to an audience expectation of Irish daftness. Under the shadow of the deplorable, and too often very funny, Irish joke, it is hard to write about the eccentricities, drunkenness and misdirected passions of Irish peasantry without being sucked into parody. There is an implicit 'begorrah' in a number of these tales which leaves me uneasy. Moreover in choosing to emphasise the Irishness of her childhood, Miss O'Brien does not explore as much as I would wish the other—perhaps more universal—aspect of her experience: its femaleness. In the last story **'Sister Imelda'** she moves in this direction, describing the illicit and sublimited relationship between a young nun and her convent-school pupil. I found this one of the most moving of all the stories, because, though fixed and specific in its details, it records an experience that is by no means exclusively Irish.

There is a strong and still vital tradition of short story writing from Ireland: elements of it have been reproduced throughout this country—a green nostalgia for a vanishing Catholic childhood within a close and closed community where 'rich characters' flourish, and bizarre encounters with the quasi-sexual are the daily lot of school-children (along with drunken impoverished fathers, Mass-attending houseproud mothers, disgraceful relatives and ambivalent clerical personalities.) Edna O'Brien is a worthy exponent of this tradition. She does it excellently; but is it grudging to wish that she would use her wonderful technical accomplishment to explore something that has not been done so often before? (pp. 25-6)

Sara Maitland, "Begorrah," in The Spectator, *Vol. 248, No. 8027, May 15, 1982, pp. 25-6.*

DARCY O'BRIEN

Nearly all of [O'Brien's] novels have been, one way or another, about breaking away—from home, family, marriage or love affair—and yet each is also testimony to the impossibility of the clean or permanent break. Childhood, family, husband, and lover live on to haunt heart and memory. Her settings may vary from Ireland to London to sunny Mediterranean isle, but one truth hovers continuously near the surface of her prose, and that is the persistence of memory, the impossibility of forgetting. No one ever gets over anything, she tells us; we carry with us till death each broken tie and love. . . . (p. 179)

Certainly for the urban reader it is difficult to imagine the protected, remote nature of [Edna O'Brien's childhood, which] spanned the distance from a tiny village in one of the least populated districts of an underpopulated island to a convent set by a lake in the next county. In their own ways these places are as intricate as London or New York, but to grow up in them, especially during a time when one's country was sealed off from the world by political and military neutrality, was to make inevitable severe shocks later on when the ways of the rest of the world were encountered. Perhaps we are all inclined to remember our childhoods as innocent but Edna O'Brien's childhood truly was innocent in the sense that it was protected from urban artifice and that it fostered more than most the clear-cut beliefs in good and evil, truth and falsehood, love and hate. Take someone from such a background, plant them in a modern city, and you can produce a mental case, an energetic entrepreneur, or an artist. Edna O'Brien turned out to be something of both of the latter two phenomena. Her art, dressed out just flamboyantly enough to be eminently saleable, evokes consistently and persistently an innocent past confronted with a brutal present. That she did not grow up a jaundiced, urban sophisticate is everywhere evident in the repeated attempts of her heroines to have it both ways and in their frustration and bitterness at having it neither.

It is easy enough to trace the realities of this childhood through Miss O'Brien's fiction. She describes the convent in *The Country Girls,* and we get glimpses of the village life here and there in the novels and in many of the short stories. . . . That her arrival in Dublin at the age of sixteen inspired her first novel is enough to suggest the intensity of the occasion. It was not the childhood itself but the confrontation of that childhood with a relatively modern city that was the catalyst, a clash of sights, sounds, feelings and values that would persist in her mind and continue to be the flashpoint of her sensibility and her art. (pp. 181-82)

Edna O'Brien is the first country girl to write of this experience and to make her own kind of poetry of it, and the bravery of the accomplishment ought not to be slighted. A country girl with literary pretentions in the Dublin of the late 1940s and early 1950s would have been a rude intrusion into the male, pub-centred world of the literati. . . . She had no literary predecessors, this Catholic, female, literary migrant. Certainly there had been Irish women writers before her—Maria Edgeworth, Lady Gregory, Somerville and Ross, Elizabeth Bowen— but they had been of the Protestant, Anglo-Irish ascendancy, with established families to back them up and with an entirely different, rather aristocratic slant to their lives and works. . . .

Her odyssey might serve any ambitious woman as a model of toughness and determination. She survived not only the literary spite and backbiting of Dublin but an unhappy marriage, childbearing, motherhood and uprootedness as well to become, by her thirty-fourth year, that rare thing, a writer earning a living by her craft. (p. 183)

It might be thought of as ironic that [O'Brien's] . . . first three novels, all of them with girls or a girl in their titles, all of them describing the vulnerability of the female at the hands of an insensitive or brutal male, were themselves the vehicles by which she travelled to independence. But if this be an irony, so then is most of Miss O'Brien's fiction, even after girls vanish from the titles, because again and again she writes of the vulnerable, mis-used female, girl or woman, wife or lover, left to dwell in recollections of embraces and of deep-sworn vows betrayed. But let us push irony aside and call it simply paradox, the paradox of the strong, independent woman writing of women as victims. (p. 184)

One of Miss O'Brien's heroines, Mary Hooligan of *Night* (1972), triumphs over these disappointments by means of a Molly Bloomian burst of lyrical energy and humour. Another, Nora of *I Hardly Knew You* (1977), smothers her young lover with a pillow. She goes to prison, feels what seems a great deal like self-pity, as many murderers do, but appears also to savour her act, as she did the weeks of lovemaking that preceded it. . . . If one had to choose an archetypal Edna O'Brien heroine, one could hardly do better than with Martha, who narrates the title story of a collection called *The Love Object* (1968). Separated from her husband and with two young boys to care for, Martha, thirty, falls for an older gentleman who is wealthy, famous and married for the third time. She loves him fiercely, although one is unsure why, because he seems more interested in his public life and in the proprieties of his marriage than in love. Their relationship diminishes, Martha is tortured by loneliness and a feeling that she has been used, and she contemplates suicide, pulling back from that brink only when she realises that her sick son needs her. Martha lives chiefly to be needed, and what she discovers with her lover is that he does not so much need her as choose to make use of her. Yet, long after their union has been reduced to occasional public encounters, she cherishes the memory of this man, because, she says, not to nourish the memory of him in her heart would be to live with nothing, and 'nothing is a dreadful thing to hold on to'.

That a woman has nothing more valuable inside of her than the memory of a broken love affair with a rather self-centred man may or may not be a valid glimpse into the female heart— of this one cannot and dares not speak. What matters here is that it is a condition typical of the Edna O'Brien heroine, and an effect of it is that these women end up looking more sensitive and less selfish than their men and yet also much weaker. The women endure, more or less, depending on this book or that, but the men hurry off to their social and professional engagements, seemingly not much bothered by a severance that may have left the woman close to self-destruction.

One's guess is that many if not most of Edna O'Brien's readers must have contemplated the relation between these heroines and their creator. Never mind whether such contemplation be indecent, speculative, out of proper bounds, or unworthy of the professional critic: it is a question that arises and begs to be addressed. Two answers to it occur. Either the strong, independent, worldly author is being insincere in her presentation of women as fragile and dependent on men, with only a remembered sense of loss to sustain them, or, alternatively, these heroines do reflect Edna O'Brien's sense of herself in relation not only to men but to the professional world which she inhabits and they control. Unlike her heroines, she has her writing, but like them she dwells on images of a paradise lost and perhaps never even gained. What this suggests is that even in her mature years she continues to see herself as the country girl, equal to the challenge of the city but much abused by it, intentionally innocent, greeting the world with open arms but forced to close up when battered by its aggression and coldness. (pp. 184-85)

Edna O'Brien has retained a reverence and wonder for the simple physical images of her youth, because they mean to her security and the peace that reigned before the fall, even if from time to time she writes a story about a lecherous priest or a drunken Irish father. More and more her novels have become prose-paeans to the pleasures of the country, the garden, the kitchen or the bed. . . . No surprise at all then that she, like her heroines, would feel abused by metropolitan life, whether or not she has endured and flourished professionally. Is sensitivity meant only for the failures?

Nothing is more telling of her background than her treatment of sex. Wholly unlike most of her contemporaries, male and female, she writes of sex explicitly but with a wonder and an awe that is completely at odds with the modern, urban sensibility, if it can be termed as such. She does not burden her books with the heavy theorising of D. H. Lawrence, but like Lawrence she infuses her sexual passages with a tremulous energy that can only be called reverence. Unlike Lawrence, however, she nearly always includes sensations or atmospheres of guilt which heighten the pleasure and the pain, generating a painful pleasure and an intensity that remind us of how much we lost when we decided that sex was normal and healthy and nothing more to worry about than bacon and cabbage. . . . One great advantage of her never having severed herself emotionally from her background is that she has been able to preserve a sense of mystery about sex as well as about landscape, weather and all of the mundanities that make up daily life.

It might be said further that all of Edna O'Brien's novels read like confessionals—and in the strict sense of a monologue revealing sins and crying out for absolution. We know from the start in *I Hardly Knew You* that Nora has murdered a lover and that she is talking to us from behind prison bars on the day before her trial. Why exactly she has killed the young man we are never sure, and this absence of credible motive hurts the novel, especially since the gratuitous violence prevalent during the heyday of existentialism has passed, mercifully, from the literary scene. The only way to understand the crime is to see it as the logical outcome, in Edna O'Brien's terms, of the sexual struggle that has been continuous throughout her novels and stories. . . . One has the discouraging sense that at last Miss O'Brien has wrung dry the withers of her themes, that she has, literally and figuratively, reached a dead end. (pp. 186-88)

Somehow Edna O'Brien must, in future, break free of the self-enclosure to which all of the virtues of her talents and sensibilities have led her. Her pre-lapsarian memory, which can lend to a seduction in a London flat all of the delicious anticipations, fears, guilts and resentments of a country girl fresh from the convent, has served her well but perhaps too long. At times during the past few years one has turned to the first page of a new Edna O'Brien story or novel and had the unexciting idea that one has been there before and often.

To wish for more and different from Edna O'Brien is merely an expression of hope that springs from past pleasures. One does not wish to denigrate a writer whose personal and literary courage has from the start been great and who has already contributed so much to contemporary fiction. But perhaps she should let her familiar fields lie fallow for a season and strike out on a new journey, taking her vivid, precise language and her music with her. She might even write about a man who is neither callous nor powerful: say for instance an abandoned husband. (p. 189)

> *Darcy O'Brien, "Edna O'Brien: A Kind of Irish Childhood," in* Twentieth-Century Women Novelists, *edited by Thomas F. Staley, Barnes & Noble Books, 1982, pp. 179-90.*

OLIVER CONANT

Half the stories in this collection by the gifted Irish writer Edna O'Brien [*A Fanatic Heart*] are about the hard agricultural life

and predominantly primitive, tradition-bound people in Western Ireland. The other half concern the modern life of restless, for the most part affluent, cosmopolites free from yesterday's moral and sexual constraints. Yet while the two worlds she presents are very different, O'Brien's farmers and villagers live as fully, if often incomprehendingly, in a recognizable present as do her London sophisticates. Unlike, say, Hemingway's Basques, they do not offer an idealized refuge from contemporary woes.

The farms, at least the more prosperous ones, are mechanized. Men work in quarries, drive trucks or scheme to market rustproofing compounds. The women clumsily but assiduously follow city fashions. Nor are terrorist violence and death lacking. Ireland's civil strife is reported with a casualness that serves to indicate how much a condition of everyday existence it is even in the green, peaceful-seeming valleys.

The resources O'Brien brings to her representation of rural life include an acute sensitivity to the beauties of the lakes, mountains and flora of Western Ireland; a seemingly effortless, unobtrusive lyricism; a simple but strong narrative sense; and an impressive understanding of her frequently odd, wayward characters that does not operate too quickly or completely. What is especially appealing about the tales of Western Ireland, though, is their quality of abundance.

Without any prettying or falsifying, the most impoverished surroundings are shown to accommodate some deep creature comfort, if only in the form of warm soda bread "dolloped with butter and greengage jam." . . . The feeling of abundance also arises from the linguistic fecundity of the Irish, with their ample stock of expressive idiom; and of course from the author's Joycean ear, her capacity to capture all that quotidian poetry.

O'Brien's own linguistic power is often quite breathtaking, too. She can note in passing the "cream blooms" of the horse chestnut tree "hung like candles merely waiting to be lit." Or she can encompass the whole of life in a single spare sentence: "Nothing happened except the land was plowed, the crops were put down, there was a harvest, a threshing, then geese were sent to feast on the stubble, and soon the land was bare again."

Since *A Fanatic Heart* consists of selected stories, the reader is able to glimpse O'Brien's developing ability, over roughly two decades, to render what she calls "her own part of the world." "Irish Revel," a relatively early story published in the 1968 book *The Love Object,* contrasts the purity of Mary, a shy young girl from a "mountainy farm," with the lechers and carousing drunks who live in the village below her remote little white-washed house on a hill. This is interesting, yet a bit too pat to be wholly effective. Narrated in the third person, the tale lacks the emotional depths that are uncoverd once the author begins to put herself in the scene, as she does in eight of the first nine stories here (initially issued in 1981 as a slim volume entitled *Returning*).

In "Irish Revel" the villagers . . . strike me as caricaturish, almost stock Irish, an easiness that eventually disappears. A related failing is a tendency to generalize in a distancing and distorting manner. Thus the writer observes of Mary's people that "they were hard . . . and it was only when someone died that they could give into sentiment and crying." Again, in the later stories, after the "they" becomes the "we" of O'Brien's own family, she is less absolute and more alert to the presence and nuance of feeling, however deeply hidden beneath rock-like layers of customary reticence.

To be sure, writing about one's childhood or employing the first person does not guarantee triumphs of memory and imagination. But O'Brien is careful to alternate the vividness of the child's perceptions with hard-won adult knowledge of human motives and situations. (p. 14)

The mature awareness presiding over O'Brien's narratives typically dispels illusions. In **"The Connor Girls"** it enables us to see through the allure of a well-to-do Protestant household that for the child seems an "exalted world." In **"The Doll"** it clarifies what to the child is the inexplicable meanness of a teacher who confiscates a treasured doll: "She kept the doll out of perversity, out of pique and jealousy." In **"Savages"** it shows how the most brutal intolerance and cruelty can have the sanction of church and respectable society. And in **"Sister Imelda,"** an evocative tale of a convent school—somewhat the equivalent of Stephen Dedalus' Clongowes—it demonstrates how religious fervor can stultify youth and instinct.

More crucially, the writer's mature awareness can attempt to come to terms with the very often terrible pain of her upbringing, pain the child can respond to only with great gusts of feeling, tantrums, bewilderment, or small rituals of self-punishment. It has one basic source: Both the child and the mother are deprived of the love of the father. Fathers in these stories tend to disappear, to go off on a "batter"—an endless drinking spell; if at home, they are violent, subject to fits of insane rage. To survive, emotionally and otherwise, mother and daughter become for a time a world unto themselves, as they do in the harrowing **"A Rose in the Heart of New York."**

When O'Brien turns from constrained, personalist Western Ireland to an urban culture of drifting hedonists, in which no one is known to anyone else—"Nobody ever says where we come from or what haunts us" she remarks of her companions in this world—something of her sureness of touch is lost. Granted, her gifts are such that she can write affectingly about the progress and disappointments of love no matter where these transpire—in orchards or fields, London flats or posh resorts. In the urban pieces there is a rather obsessive concentration on affairs with a succession of sleek married men. The affairs always begin deliciously and end miserably, possibly because the married men ultimately appear to fill the role of the absent father. Although the stories have an undeniable pathos that will appeal to a certain kind of female grievance, their characters, particularly the males, are hollow, interchangeable partners. In addition, the settings are barely detailed, an absence I find curious and frustrating in a writer otherwise so handsomely possessed of a sense of place.

O'Brien's imagination of society in West Ireland—including the love between men and women this society can admit, and some it can't—is the product of care and thought. Neither the same care nor the same thought seems to have gone into her investigations of people who are themselves careless and thoughtless. Perhaps the difference derives from portraying a way of life and portraying a life style. (pp. 14-15)

> Oliver Conant, "Edna O'Brien's Two Worlds," in The New Leader, *Vol. LXVII, No. 20, November 12, 1984, pp. 14-15.*

MARY GORDON

"I thought that ours indeed was a land of shame, a land of murder, a land of strange, throttled, sacrificial women," says the narrator of Edna O'Brien's story **"A Scandalous Woman."** Of Irish murder and Irish shame we have heard much, but the news has been in the mouths of men. Edna O'Brien tells the Irish woman's inside story. She has—as only the finest writers can—created a world; she speaks in a voice identifiably and only hers. No voice could be less androgynous or more rooted in a land. Her great subjects are childhood and sexual love; both themes come to flower in a soil teeming with lively and portentous objects. Clothes, stuffs, foods, medicines, in her hands turn into vessels brimming with meaning and value. And her language itself takes on the texture of a precious thing, precious and yet familiar, held close to the body, kept, always, in the center of the home. . . .

The narrator of many of the stories in **"A Fanatic Heart"** is a young Irish girl who lives the life of the overwrought, obsessively observant outsider. The world of adults she perceives is often incomprehensible to her. She watches adults move, as if in a trance, toward their destruction, propelled by a passion she finds beautiful and wishes to share in herself. Sex for these doomed creatures always brings tragedy: this is Ireland, and the love between men and women can only leave women worn out and men jaded, careless, longing to be away, or choked in a helpless romance unable to express itself. Everyone pays, but women pay the highest price. (p. 1)

[A] bank clerk is the cause of grief to Eily in **"A Scandalous Woman."** Eily is one of the town beauties: "She had brown hair, a great crop of it, fair skin, and eyes that were as big and as soft and as transparent as ripe gooseberries. She was always a little out of breath and gasped when one approached, then embraced and said, 'Darling.' . . . For one Advent she thought of being a nun, but that fizzled out and her chief interests became clothes and needlework."

This description—the gooseberry eyes, the breathlessness, the temporary religious vocation replaced by interests of a more ordinary girlish sort—is Miss O'Brien at her best. The physical detail burrows into the mind; how clearly one sees Eily—the breathless transparent one, bound for sex trouble. The girl who is the narrator of this story is younger than Eily, honored by her friendship with this beautiful, worldly creature and more than happy to be the go-between for her and her Protestant lover. Of course, Eily becomes pregnant; the town forces her lover to marry her. He is resentful and does his duty reluctantly, moving away from her emotionally until she goes mad. At the end of the story, the narrator, now a pregnant, unhappily married woman, sees Eily chastened, psychiatrically rehabilitated, a ghost of her former self.

Of course, not all Irish women so flagrantly and casually betray the secret of their sex; there are nuns and mothers in whom sex is concealed, or pressed into the service of another love. **"Sister Imelda"** describes the rapt, devoted love of a passionate, intelligent and lonely young nun and a young girl, equally passionate, intelligent and lonely. Their love, although partaking in aspects of the sexual, is more or less than that. It is the love of two sensualists caught up in a fantasy of asceticism; it is all about the dream of perfection and perfectibility, about self-denial and the areas of human life unable to be quashed despite good intentions and, indeed, holy vows. By the end of the story, the young girl grows out of her crush on the nun, becomes worldly, wears too much makeup, chases after boys. Always, though, in her mind's eye will be the image of the betrayed, mysterious one she had to leave if she was to have an ordinary life. . . .

The overwrought, observant girl in these stories grows into a woman who leaves the things she has loved and feared in Ireland. She becomes an exile: unmothered, unbefriended, torn from the land. Of course, she will try to find in the sexual love of men all she has left behind; she will look to romantic love for the placement she had in the home she could not wait to leave. And, of course, the romances will be doomed to fail; no human relation could bear so much freight. But in the failure, how splendid, and what a rendering of sexual life Miss O'Brien spreads before us in the stories about men and women that account for so large a part of her reputation.

In turning from the stories of childhood to the stories of sexual love, we lose the mocking humor whose source in the Irish stories is the provincial's insistent misapprehension of the larger world. The lovers in Miss O'Brien's stories are, for better or for worse, powerful citizens of the great world. They inhabit the glamorous professions; the women are journalists, poets, television stars; the men are wealthy businessmen dealing in interesting, valuable commodities. For these people, crossing the English Channel, or indeed the Atlantic Ocean, means no more than crossing to the next village meant to the people in the stories about Ireland. Actually, the larger journey is of less significance, for the people who cross the ocean are equally at home in any city they touch down on, whereas for the Irish villagers, to walk a mile down the road is to make a journey to the moon.

The women in these stories give themselves to love as a kind of self-immolation; to open themselves to love is to open themselves to madness, and each time, knowing this fully, they cannot resist. They are lifted up, these women, they are cruelly dropped down, and all their awareness does nothing to prevent them from their fate. Body and soul, they are taken over. . . .

These love affairs take place in carefully appointed houses of women whose houses mean a great deal to them, but domestic life has no place. The women try to do ordinary tasks—cook an ordinary meal, sew on an ordinary button—but the acts become incandescent. Every gesture, however innocently intended, turns into seduction and must lead the lovers out of the kitchen into bed. Children, in these stories, are absent: away at school, snatched from their mothers by their punitive fathers who declare their former wives unfit by virtue of the very passion that drives them to the husband of some other woman allowed to keep her children and to share her man.

Miss O'Brien, however, does not present us with another tired episode in the ancient history of "the other woman." Glimmering in these stories, like a gimlet in a swamp, is a pervasive ironic morality. The other woman, after all, is not so different from the wife; she is grasping, she is vengeful, she is greedy, and she has the will to hurt. In these stories no one is an innocent, and everyone must suffer. Ireland can be left, but the curse of sex hangs over the head of all the world.

Miss O'Brien combines the romantic's passionate feeling for language and the material world with the classicist's unerring sense of form. Each of her stories is shaped into a complete and satisfying whole; she has the courage and the sureness of vision to derive from the singularity of her characters' experience general truths about the world. It is a painful world, a vale of tears where ghosts jostle the beautiful fleshly living for a place in the fanatic heart. (p. 38)

> *Mary Gordon, "The Failure of True Love," in* The New York Times Book Review, *November 18, 1984, pp. 1, 38.*

JULIAN MOYNAHAN

[The best stories in Edna O'Brien's *A Fanatic Heart*] are powerful, bleak, and unforgiving; they draw on memories of her Irish upbringing from about age 9 to the end of her convent days and her departure for pharmacy school. The best of the English stories about love affairs don't come close in merit to these Irish stories, while the worst of them are merely chic and novelettish, something to read under the hair dryer.

Take "**Paradise,**" from her 1968 collection, *The Love Object*. A woman jets from London to a lavish Italian seaside villa where her host and lover, a morose older man of means, summons her to his bed on evenings when he is feeling up to it. The house is crawling with serving people and with discreetly tippling and pill-popping beautiful people. These leisure-class riff-raff spend their days boating and picnicking, but they are really there to provide background for the heroine's dogged efforts to master swimming in the villa pool. (p. 34)

The title story of this same collection, "**The Love Object,**" is only a little better, and it may be considered a paradigm of most O'Brien tales of the London love triangle. It provides a foot-of-the-bed fever chart of an affair between the narrator, who is 30, divorced, and a well-known face on English TV, and an elderly, "famous" married man who does something in the law. . . . The tone and mood of the account approach barely controlled hysteria as the man starts finding other ways of spending his free afternoons. It is all so stereotypically British. . . .

The final section of *A Fanatic Heart* is called "**Quartet: Uncollected Stories, 1979-1981.**" Here O'Brien writes four brief vignettes which attempt to abstract the essence, alembicate, or create a poetics of The Affair. If she is an English Colette in this way, then she is a failed Colette. In "**Violets**" the reader is privy to a seduction-in-progress at an elegant restaurant. "**The Call**" describes waiting for one's lover to telephone and fighting temptation to disrupt his domestic peace by phoning him oneself. "**The Plan**" entails a fantasy of making a friend and confidante out of the lover's wife. "**The Return**" is about flying back to London from a Greek holiday spent by oneself and anticipating resumption of the affair.

We know how it will end. Should we not, the mere title of an earlier story in the book, "**Over,**" from her 1978 collection called *A Scandalous Woman,* will tell us. In these stories of English passion among top people, Edna O'Brien manages to make the game of adultery dull and predictable.

Her Irish scene can be savage and cruel, but it is never dull. Her youthful narrator-heroine inhabits a cut-stone house in a Shannon-side hamlet where most of the neighbors are small farmers. The people are poor, slaves to custom, morally terrorized by a puritanical religious code they have internalized; and a surprisingly large number are crazy, or else afflicted with physical and mental defects and handicaps. An extra turn of the screw is supplied by the period background. It is World War II, when the Allied embargo imposed on Ireland as punishment for its neutrality caused severe shortages of food, other consumer goods, fuel, medicines, and machine parts, thus plunging the countryside into a deeper darkness and chill than would normally be the case. (p. 35)

[O'Brien's] fullest treatment of the theme of love and interdependence between mother and daughter in this volume is the fine story called "**A Rose in the Heart of New York**": "The mother said that there was no such thing as love between the sexes and that it was all bull. She reaffirmed that there was only one kind of love and that was a mother's love for her child." Significantly, this is followed by a moment "dense with hate" on the part of the daughter, and of course the close, supportive relationship leads to mutual bitterness and regrets after the daughter has grown up, gone abroad, and prospered. (pp. 35-6)

Virtually epical in its treatment of the mother-daughter bond from birth to death, **"A Rose"** must be judged a classic of the new literature that bears the mark of the women's movement. With it one might want to place the haunting nun's story, **"Sister Imelda,"** in which O'Brien's surrogate narrator finds a mother surrogate and near-lover at her convent school, only in the end to break the tie quite brutally as she comes to see that her ambitious future lies with the secular world. (p. 36)

Julian Moynahan, "Irish Girls, English Affairs," in The New Republic, Vol. 192, Nos. 28 & 29, January 7 & 14, 1985, pp. 34-6.

ADAM MARS-JONES

A Fanatic Heart is a collection drawn from over a decade of Edna O'Brien's career as a writer of short stories; it prints complete her 1981 volume *Returning* . . . as well as a "Quartet" of uncollected stories. . . .

The book opens with the *Returning* stories, set in Ireland during the Forties and Fifties. . . .

These stories reveal a particular sympathy for internal exiles, the casualties of convention, but at their best the stories themselves are impersonal. The central character is usually a young girl, but it is her best friend or sister that takes the risks and pays the penalties. Although the girl looks on intently, in some way she is not involved; to one of these characters, for instance, whose family has suddenly come down in the world, "the word 'pauper' sounded so beautiful, like some kind of Indian flower or fruit."

This unjudging receptiveness is compromised from time to time in the *Returning* stories by an inappropriate adult voice. This intrusive persona sees the stories as interesting only insofar as they throw light on her own background. The first story in the book, for example, **"The Connor Girls,"** deals faithfully with its subjects, a pair of sisters with great prospects and greater disappointments. They have been unable to choose a world to replace the one they were born into. But then, in the last paragraph, the narrator hijacks the story. Her husband, who is an outsider, is rude to the Connor sisters and "at that moment I realized that by choosing his world I had said goodbye to my own and to those in it. By such choices we gradually become exiles, until at last we are quite alone." End of story. This brutal extrapolation, quite at odds with what has gone before, violates the compass of the story. The depiction of other lives is suddenly unimportant, and the tale is prevented from working itself out in its own terms.

O'Brien's endings are not a strong point. Since she has an attaché case full of style (and then some), her final paragraphs are always beautifully written, but they aren't always appropriate. Even the most impressive stories in the book, both stories about terrible enclosure, one in a nunnery and the other in an unsuitable marriage, have endings that falter. **"Sister Imelda"** closes almost with flippancy. "In our deepest moments we say the most inadequate things." **"A Scandalous Woman"** makes the opposite mistake by driving home the moral with a theatrical intensity. ". . . I thought that ours

indeed was a land of shame, a land of murder, and a land of strange, throttled, sacrificial women."

The self-advertising voice from **"The Connor Girls"** recurs in a number of stories. It introduces **"Ghosts,"** a trio of essentially unconnected sketches, in the manner of a duchess opening a country fair, with a remark that the characters represent "defiance, glamour, and a kind of innocence that I miss in my later world." . . .

The composite Edna O'Brien heroine goes to sleep in her teens and wakes up after the breakup of her marriage. She is much changed by her hibernation. She has memories of childhood, but none of her life as a wife and mother; her life now gets its meaning from a sexual relationship with a married man. . . .

The setting of these later, very personal stories is most often London, and here too the outsides of things are lovingly described, but the social awareness is fragmented. Two of the stories deal with the actual breakdown of the heroine (**"Paradise"** and **"The House of My Dreams"**) but it is fair to say that these stories only exaggerate a general tendency. There are many ecstasies on display, and many despairs, but little to mediate between despair and ecstasy. Outside the charmed circle of love, nothing makes sense. There is only a difference of degree between the sane heroine of **"Over,"** who thinks her neighbor is "trying to impress me with her shouting and her car and her rainwear," and the unstable heroine of **"Paradise"** who attributes a fellow guest's radiant complexion to "constant supplies of male sperm." The world view of the O'Brien heroine is likely to be paranoiac in some degree.

Love is a state of grace, but an O'Brien heroine never falls for a man whose availability is unqualified. A life of ordinary piety as wife and mother leaves her untouched; she has set her sights on the martyr's crown, and wastes no sympathy on those who play the humbler parts. . . .

The pattern is foreseeable but O'Brien fails to foresee it, and is herself betrayed. Betrayal within marriage doesn't touch this writer's nerve; even those stories whose plots involve it give no details. (Interestingly, too, only once does a woman do the betraying, and then the betrayed party, Sister Imelda, is also a woman.) Edna O'Brien is good on the chronic disappointingness of men, and indefatigable in her charting of a woman's moods and desires, even if it is one particular woman at the expense of all others, and a woman at that who defines herself solely through her relationships with men.

With some of these stories Edna O'Brien gets stuck in a rut, and risks setting herself up as the patron saint of innocent temptresses. Even the most self-obsessed story has its trawl of detail and of fierce undignified truths, and many are enlivened by flagrantly excellent phrasing, but it is a pleasure to find, toward the end of the book, a growing detachment. The heroines of **"Christmas Roses"** and **"Ways"** both foresee the pattern and escape it; the heroine of **"Ways"** meets the wife in question before she meets the man in question, and manages in consequence not to seduce him. After what has gone before, this is some sort of breakthrough. (p. 17)

Adam Mars-Jones, "Women Beware Women," in The New York Review of Books, Vol. XXXII, No. 1, January 31, 1985, pp. 17-19.*

ROBERT MASSA

Virginia Woolf, [Edna O'Brien] said in an Arts and Leisure defense of her play-biography [*Virginia*], "scoffed at certain plodding writers who hauled their characters from lunch to dinner. Any work about her would have to follow the flow of her life . . .'' Following that flow, O'Brien writes long, rambling monologues for Virginia, coalescing the impressions of six decades, and intercuts them with dialogue scenes that proceed by the same kaleidoscopic logic. A venturesome approach, but it fails both as art and as biography.

As art *Virginia* fails because we are given too much undigested information. The play, oddly, snaps into clarity only during the madness scenes, when we don't expect Virginia to be coherent. The rest is like a greatest hits selection from Woolf's and her husband's diaries, favorite lines piled up on top of each other through such wispy associations they signify nothing. O'Brien is not sowing little grains of experience, but scattering them to the wind, hoping a few will fall on good soil. It seems less an homage to Woolf's delicate aesthetic than a parody of it.

As biography the play is even more problematic. Though she overwhelms us with information, O'Brien's selection manages to be curiously idiosyncratic. A full quarter of the play concerns Virginia's relationship with Vita Sackville-West, while her equally or more profound relationships with her sister Vanessa, her mother, and other women are relegated to parenthetical comments; Katherine Mansfield is mentioned only in a name-dropping litany of writers published by the Woolfs' press. The easily sensationalized relationship with Vita is considered so central that intermission comes as the two trundle off to bed,

an event which may not have happened, and probably would not have after such coy foreplay.

Similarly, what we are shown of Woolf's writing seems beside the point. Passages are read from *Orlando,* the satiric pseudobiography dedicated to Vita, but as the androgyny of the book's central character is not revealed in this play, its inclusion seems spurious. Meanwhile, *To the Lighthouse* and *The Waves,* clearly her masterpieces, are never mentioned directly. The political polemics of Woolf's later years, which more than the fiction were responsible for the renewed interest in her that began two decades ago, seem reduced to random sloganeering. This Virginia talks more about buying a new hat than about world wars.

Before her 50th birthday Woolf wrote, "I come to feel more and more how difficult it is to collect oneself into one Virginia." Any two-hour play will suffer next to all her books and all that has been written about her, but the slivers of her life given here finally are most dissatisfying because they unintentionally reinforce the stereotypes trumpeted by those who misread her. In both form and content, O'Brien has created a Virginia who strikes us most of all as a petty, reactionary, indulgent aesthete, drowning in herself long before she jumped in the river.

Robert Massa, "Sheep's Clothing," in The Village Voice, *Vol. XXX, No. 11, March 12, 1985, p. 79.*

Kenzaburō Ōe
1935-

Japanese novelist, short story writer, nonfiction writer, editor, and critic.

An author whose work is widely read in Japan, Ōe writes fiction which frequently explores the sense of betrayal and rootlessness experienced by many Japanese following World War II. Though postwar Japanese life informs his subject matter, Ōe's style and ideological content owe much to his study of European and American writers, particularly Jean-Paul Sartre and Norman Mailer. His style, which John Nathan describes as "wild, unresolved, but never less than vital," eschews the more delicate tendencies of the I-novels and other prewar Japanese conventions. Some scholars fault Ōe for weakening the integrity of traditional prose with Western structures, but others laud him as an important innovator in Japanese fiction.

Though the postwar democratic influence of the American occupation and the New Constitution generated hope for the defeated nation following its surrender in 1945, many Japanese continue to suffer a sense of social dislocation and loss of identity. Ōe's sensitivity to postwar circumstances and his acceptance of democratic ideals form the basis of his political beliefs and led to his association with Japan's New Left. He has written essays on political and social topics, often emphasizing the search for cultural and ideological roots. Ōe also is a militant spokesman against nuclear warfare installations in Japan.

Ōe gained national recognition while still a student at Tokyo University when his first work, a novella titled *Shiiku* (1958; *Prize Stock* or *The Catch*), was published. The novella tells of the friendship between a Japanese boy and a black American prisoner-of-war that is shattered by the brutal reality of war. The novel *Megumushiri kouchi* (1958) is an extended version of this work. Other early stories and novels explore modern youth's conflict with society, often manifested through sexual perversion. "Kimyō na shigoto" (1957), "Shisha no ogori" (1957; "Lavish Are the Dead"), and *Warera no jidai* (1959) feature protagonists who indulge in perverse sex and violence as means of escaping the emptiness of their lives.

In 1964 Ōe became the father of a brain-damaged child; in his succeeding work he turned increasingly to themes concerning retardation and related moral issues. Beginning with *Kojinteki na taiken* (1964; *A Personal Matter*), Ōe introduces the recurring motif of the retarded child as a metaphor for the human condition and as a reminder of the implications of nuclear warfare. Published simultaneously with *Hiroshima nooto* (1964), a collection of essays and interviews about the Hiroshima bombing, *A Personal Matter* relates the story of Bird, who struggles with the desire to escape responsibility for his deformed child. The first of Ōe's heroes to reject a desperate flight into fantasy, Bird eventually comes to terms with his circumstances. Such works as *Man'en gannen no futtobōru* (1967; *The Silent Cry*) and stories in the collection *Warera no kyōki o iki nobiru michi o oshieyo* (1969; *Teach Us to Outgrow Our Madness*) are similarly concerned with the relationship that develops between a father and his brain-damaged son.

(See also *CLC*, Vol. 10 and *Contemporary Authors*, Vols. 97-100.)

JAMES TOBACK

Until recently, Japanese literature had remained in hermetic isolation. . . . [No] major writer appeared to describe the hope, anger and despair that followed VJ Day. Then came Kenzaburo Oë. . . . [Since 1958, when he wrote his first novel, Oë] has written eight novels, several stories and two volumes of essays (expressing his New Left political orientation) and he has apparently become the literary hero of Japan's young intellectuals.

"A Personal Matter," his seventh novel, is the first to be translated into English. It owes obvious debts to Kierkegaard: the search for—and confrontation with—the self. Its urban surroundings, the classless misfits that populate it, and its vivid sexual descriptions make it seem socially and thematically similar to its Occidental counterparts. Unfortunately, it is a disappointment.

The protagonist is Bird, a 27-year-old cram-school instructor, once a Tokyo street fighter, now an exhausted, bored husband, frightened by the decline of his physical and phallic power. The imminent birth of his child represents to Bird a lock on the cage. The baby is born with a brain hernia, giving it the look of a two-headed monster. Bird decides that only through filicide will he be able to escape.

While he plans ways and means, Bird retreats frantically to a dream world of fantasy, alcohol and sex, all in the willing arms of Himiko, a widow, his former classmate and friend, who lives by—and quotes to Bird—the Blakean dictum "Sooner murder an infant in its cradle than nurse unacted desires." They take the baby to an abortionist friend of Himiko's and plan to flee to Africa, Bird's persistent image for freedom and recaptured youth. Suddenly, he sees that by abdicating responsibility, by seeking to transform illusion into reality, he is only destroying himself.

As a result of his reversal, Bird recognizes that his totally dependent infant will hone him for, rather than bar him from, a genuine quest for manhood. His old self is indeed dead, but a new and nobler self can be born from its ruins, a self constructed on the knowledge that nothing is strictly "a personal matter." This affirmative revelation, announced only in a brief epilogue and imposed with an abruptness that recalls the Euripidean *deux ex machina,* comes off as a disconnected and unearned moral lesson. . . .

The basic situation of **"A Personal Matter"** should have embodied the themes of freedom and responsibility, youth and maturation, loneliness and community, but it does not. It is further hindered by a style infected with bald metaphor, banality and circumlocution. One wonders whether part of the fault might not lie in translation. As it rests, a potentially moving story and a significant message have been seriously weakened.

> James Toback, *"Bird in a Cage," in* The New York Times Book Review, *July 7, 1968, p. 23.*

D. J. ENRIGHT

The blurb [introducing *A Personal Matter*] tells us that thirty-three-year-old Kenzaburo Oë is "the most dynamic and revolutionary writer to have emerged in Japan since the end of the War," . . . and that "he has wrenched Japanese literature free of its deeply rooted, inbred tradition and moved it into the mainstream of world literature." One would deduce from these descriptions that either Oë is Superman-san or else, enfeebled by centuries of incest, Japanese literature is peculiarly backward! What the blurb doesn't tell us is that fiction was somewhat doubtfully part of the Japanese literary tradition, and that because of its low status compared with poetry and philosophical writing, it showed a distinct tendency toward the pornographic throughout the nineteenth century. Thus, at the end of the War, Japanese writers of fiction had a good start: they were already "modern." . . . [Where] extreme situations in fiction are concerned Oë is no great pioneer. In truth he can only seem revolutionary to someone who still thinks of Japan in terms of priests chanting sutras and elegant geisha entertaining their cultured guests with readings. . . . (p. 35)

Oë's hero, a young man called Bird, becomes the father of a freak, a two-headed baby, or more exactly a baby with brain hernia. . . . Having been shown his baby son, he takes refuge with a girl he knew at the university, whose husband killed himself a year after their marriage, possibly because of her "deviate tastes." . . . We gather that Bird's father committed suicide too. Disgust is the prevalent if not exclusive condition of mind for the next 100-plus pages. Himiko, the girl, is chasing a bigger and better orgasm. Much of the time Bird isn't in a

fit state to lend any assistance. . . . A fantastic amount of vomiting goes on, . . . depicted in greater detail and with more feeling than one would expect from a Japanese; and when Bird isn't actually vomiting, his stomach is generally heaving or churning. It appears that his trouble is that he has lost his self-esteem—we wonder he hasn't lost his innards—while Himiko's trouble is that really she is just a romantic girl. . . . (pp. 35-6)

Together with the hospital staff, Bird connives at the death of the unfortunate baby by having it fed on sugared water. He refuses to let the brain surgeon operate on it, and he and Himiko take it to a back-street abortionist's, where it can be left to die quietly. They have trouble in finding the place (there is a passage of black humor with a policeman) and the baby catches pneumonia. Then suddenly, after some more vomiting, Bird decides that "all I want is to stop being a man who continually runs away from responsibility," so either he must strangle the baby with his own hands or else accept it and try to bring it up. He rushes back to the abortionist's, recovers the baby, and takes it to the hospital. Our final sight of Bird is as the young father in a family group, along with wife and parents-in-law and baby. The monster was not a monster; the brain hernia was not brain hernia; it was a case of a benign tumor. Says the young father,

> I kept trying to run away. And I almost did.
> But it seems that reality compels you to live
> properly when you live in the real world. . . .

Stirring words! The samurai spirit is not yet extinct. Bird is taking a new job (as a guide for foreign tourists, incidentally), he is going to save up for his son's future, he will have to drop his childish nickname. Maybe he'll even give up vomiting.

The only thing about *A Personal Matter* that might be said to be "revolutionary" is its happy-as-possible ending. The pity is that this is wholly incongruous; it is simply inconceivable that Bird could turn over so many new leaves in the space of the book's last few pages. Even the most avid admirers of the happy ending in fiction (and there must be quite a few by now) will find this one a miserable fraud. (p. 36)

> D. J. Enright, *"Days of Marvelous Lays," in* The New York Review of Books, *Vol. XI, No. 6, October 10, 1968, pp. 35-7.**

ARTHUR G. KIMBALL

There is an archetypal appeal about Bird, the diminutive hero of Kenzaburo Oe's *A Personal Matter.* It is that of the underdog, the little hero, the embattled champion confronting the overwhelming size of the giant enemy yet enduring and prevailing to victory. It is an appeal which transcends national boundaries and which the folktales, legends, and even comic strips of countless peoples illustrate. . . . The psychological appeal is deep; it roots in man's hope that despite appearances, or even current conditions, right will prevail over might, light over darkness. It is an affirmation, an insistence, that order will prevail over chaos.

But though the image of the small hero is almost universally admired, it has special appeal for the Japanese, whose history records their consciousness, especially in modern times, of being a small island nation surrounded by much larger rivals who all too frequently proved threatening. (pp. 140-41)

Small wonder that Oe's hero is popular. Nor is it strange that the novel once again records a quest for identity, for Bird must, in a complex, threatening world, find himself, convince himself of his role as a man, locate himself on the human map. The novel's central theme is this search for an acceptable self-image; Bird, from the opening pages, is concerned with his identity. . . . His brief series of adventures [includes] . . . : a change, an initiation into manhood, a growing out of self-preoccupation into mature responsibility. Birds are fashioned for flight; at the end of the novel the hero has outgrown his childish nickname.

What sort of a hero, then, is Bird? (pp. 142-43)

[Physical] description marks Bird as distinctively modern, the hero replete with such antiheroic qualities as physical flaws and (as it turns out) psychological tics, as well as a penchant for introspection. One can sympathize and identify with such a fellow traveler in his weakness. But Bird's compensating qualities are even more appealing. In his younger days, Bird has been a feared brawler. The fighting spirit of the samurai is apparent. . . . Bird is of course knowing, wise in the shadowy, tough ways of the world. . . . And he possesses sensitivity, that trait which makes a near-artist of so many modern heroes (and readers). Bird's distress when he attempts to make love with Himiko illustrates. It is not a sign of his inability, for he proves able after all; his problem marks, rather, his sensitive search for self-understanding. Indeed his success in satisfying Himiko suggests a crucial change in Bird, from the self-preoccupied and hence near-impotent to the less selfish and hence competent. . . . Even his desire to flee to Africa, though it is in part an escape wish, is a sign of sensitivity, the mark of the dreamer, of one who refuses to accept dully whatever circumstances bring. And Bird is intelligent; a teacher capable in the academic world, he yet resists its pretenses (he has quit graduate school). . . . Yet Bird proves himself ultimately responsible; pragmatically fortifying himself with something called "forbearance," he transfers his sensitive fighting spirit to a larger battleground than his own inner world.

The transfer suggests the irony of Oe's title, *A Personal Matter.* The Japanese original, *Kojinteki na Taiken,* has the meaning of personal and private, with perhaps secondary overtones of uniqueness and depth. It is of course very much a "personal" affair, a matter of Bird's identity as a person. It is unique not only in the sense that every personal experience is by definition unique, but in the dramatic, almost bizarre nature of the experience. In another sense, however, it is not merely personal but inter-personal. A bird, however much one may admire its qualities, is not a human. Oe's hero too must learn to identify himself with other persons. His obsession with himself and the seeming injustice of his fate must give way to a more human concern or it will end in isolation and flight. (pp. 143-45)

The birth of Bird's first child, an abnormal baby, precipitates his rebellious quest. For Bird, the strange object he glimpses in the hospital proves an ontological shock and he feels emasculated, stripped of his manhood. The baby with its suspected brain hernia is an appropriate symbol for an intellectually warped society; it suggests the unnatural product of an unnatural environment. There is too much head; the unstated implication, which applies to Bird, is that there may not be enough heart. Bird's reaction, expressed primarily in sexual terms, is equally appropriate. . . . His problem is how to recover his manhood or, in terms of the title, his role as a person. Bird and the baby at the beginning of the novel are both warped; at the end, they are becoming natural. The suspected hernia turns out to be a benign tumor; Bird's self-preoccupation becomes a responsible concern for others. Thus Bird and the baby are closely iden-

tified, a fact underscored throughout the novel by Bird's imitations of the child. . . . Oe maintains a careful balance or planned ambiguity with regard to the baby's role in relation to Bird. For an abnormal child is on the one hand an irrational event, a bolt of fate beyond one's control. On the other hand it is a part of its father, and the deep shame Bird suffers, and which the reader is first tempted to regard as unwarranted, proves to be only too appropriate after all. . . . Oe suggests that ultimately much of the responsibility is Bird's; to fail to accept it would be to deny himself. To destroy the child would be to commit spiritual suicide.

In his opening chapter Oe introduces major themes and hints at the novel's outcome. The narrative opens with Bird gazing at a map of Africa in a showcase.

> The continent itself resembled the skull of a man who had hung his head. . . . The miniature Africa indicating population distribution in a lower corner of the map was like a dead head beginning to decompose; another, veined with transportation routes, was a skinned head with the capillaries painfully exposed. Both these little Africas suggested unnatural death, raw and violent. . . .

Africa has a complex symbolic function for Bird. It represents, of course, a wish-fantasy, a place of escape, and the maps Bird purchases and pins to the wall above the bed signify what he regards as a ticket to freedom. But Oe's metaphors suggest a deeper significance. The showcase map hints at both Bird and the baby: the latter in the reiterated head-shape . . . , Bird in the reference to the "man who had hung his head," and both in the reference to "unnatural death." . . . One suspects, then, that Africa is as much Bird's own dark inner world as it is the Dark Continent, as much the unnatural society he is trapped in as the rapidly changing land of his dreams, and that his desire to go there is at its deepest level as much his desire to triumph over his own circumstances as an escape through flight. . . . Bird, like so many of his contemporary peers, feels trapped. Like John Updike's Rabbit, his impulse is to run. Unlike that protagonist, however, Bird finally decides to remain. . . . There is nothing to do but stand and fight.

That this is what Bird will do is foreshadowed in the opening chapter where he encounters the gang of teen-age toughs. Through a combination of quick wit, courage, and his own toughness, Bird manages to escape with only minor bruises. The episode is a microcosm of the novel's overall plot; Bird is shamed, suffers, but, with his back to the wall, faces his problem head-on and wins a victory. (pp. 149-50)

His triumph has a primitive, earthy appeal. It is a gory moment, but there is a healthy naturalness to Bird's action when he reawakens to the "joy of battle" and drives "like a ferocious bull" into his attacker's belly. . . . The action contrasts with the unhealthy, unnaturalness of the "outlandish establishment" where Bird first encounters the gang. Appropriately named "Gun Corner," this strange place suggests the hostility as well as the grotesque unnaturalness of society. (p. 150)

[Bird's] quest for identity is to a large degree expressed in terms of sexuality. Much of the quest takes place in the apartment of Himiko, an old girl friend from university days. Bird's sojourn with Himiko serves a number of functions, and the apartment . . . becomes the symbol of a complex psychological experience. In the first place, the messy apartment . . . is an emblem of chaos, reflecting the confusion, frustration, and rebellion in the minds of both Bird and Himiko. For Bird, the confusion shows in his deep-rooted fears over his sexual role. Shamed by the birth of his abnormal child and the symbolic experience in the "Gun Corner" (the name suggests yet another sexual indicator), Bird needs to assert his masculinity, but finds his desire matched by his dread. Bird seems to suffer from a kind of castration complex, and is at first unable to satisfy Himiko or achieve orgasm himself except in a perverse way. . . . Bird's father has committed suicide, one learns, and the fact that Himiko's frustration is due to her young husband's also having killed himself suggests the complexity of Oe's delineation here. Himiko, with keen insight, charges Bird with never having had satisfactory sexual relations.

Bird thus needs both to satisfy and be satisfied by Himiko. In part his desire is an escape, a retreat to the womb. . . . But Oe's metaphors suggest that the womb is more a symbolic place of self-discovery than of escape or comfort. And Bird's tendency to identify with his baby adds to the notion. . . . The discovery motif becomes more explicit later when Bird likens his experience to being in a cave like Tom Sawyer, but without Tom's success. (pp. 151-53)

But his initiation into self-discovery and maturity is more hopeful than he imagines at the time. One of the signs is his display of honesty in refusing to acknowledge his fit of vomiting in front of the cram school class to be other than it is . . . ; another is his later success in sexually satisfying Himiko; when, for once, he acts selflessly in accord with another's needs. His sexual coming-of-age is an important step toward maturity. (p. 153)

Bird's quest is of course not yet ended. During his stay with Himiko he has run the gamut of anxiety, experiencing by turns self-pity, shame, hostility, and masochistic urges; Bird's wife challenges his self-centeredness when she wonders if he is "the type of person who abandons someone weak" when that person needs him most. . . . And the wife's suspicions almost prove true, as Bird in a last desperate regression plans with Himiko to have a quack doctor kill the baby and then to flee to Africa, thus abandoning wife, child, and responsibility. Significantly, Bird and Himiko attempt to complete their plan in Himiko's red MG, apt image of her rebellious frustration. Like the "pluralistic universe" with which she tries to rationalize her despair, the red sports-car is a pathetic form of escape. . . . But with radio news reports of Soviet nuclear testing providing an ironic international background music to his own destructive urges, Bird decides to leave Himiko and his dreams of Africa, and claims his child.

Some critics find the end of the novel disappointing. "He takes responsibility and, in a weak ending, that is that," says Edward Seidensticker, adding that the conclusion is "comfortingly positive—and not really very convincing." Part of the trouble may lie in the abruptness of Bird's about-face. Oe tries, at least, to prepare the reader for the outcome by hints in the form of Bird's initiatory steps and by symbolic foreshadowings such as the fight with the teen-age gang. More important, however, is what the outcome suggests. The novel has been interpreted as an allegory of Japan's growth to maturity among nations, as well as a dramatization of the "essentially solitary and withdrawn nature" of one's existential choice. There is something Japanese in the feisty hero's sublimated samurai spirit, but there is more that transcends national interests. Bird, like a number of modern heroes, plumbs the depths of the existential pit only to emerge aware that one's existence involves other existences, that self-suffering is ultimately self-destructive. The

family to which Bird returns at the end, one suspects, is not so much Japanese as simply human, the matter not so much private as personal in a universal way. Contemporary man, dwarfed and threatened by the grotesque complexity of life, and bolstered more with forbearance than bravado, can yet be a man. (pp. 154-55)

> *Arthur G. Kimball, "A New Hero," in his* Crisis in Identity and Contemporary Japanese Novels, *Charles E. Tuttle Company, 1973, pp. 140-56.*

BRUCE ALLEN

[In *The Silent Cry*] two brothers return to the beleaguered village which conceals their past. The elder is a half-blind shell of a man, surrounded, and dulled, by idiocy, drunkenness, and suicide. The younger burns to resist "injustice." . . . They uncover startling truths about themselves, and their heritage in a feverish, clotted allegorical novel that seems to explore the conflict between simplistic activism and debilitating intellection. Character and action are quite unconvincing; dreams, symbols, and eerily repeating leitmotifs suggest that Oe means us to accept every scene for its abstract thematic weight.

> *Bruce Allen, in a review of "The Silent Cry," in* Library Journal, *Vol. 100, No. 5, March 1, 1975, p. 502.*

CHOICE

There are certain resemblances between [*The silent cry*] and *A personal matter*: each protagonist has a deformed child, is in a profession associated with the English language, is spiritually isolated from society, and is known throughout the book by a name borrowed from the animal world (The Rat in this novel; Bird in *A personal matter*). . . . *The silent cry* begins on a somber note: the deformed child has just been institutionalized, and a close friend of The Rat's has committed suicide. At this point, The Rat's younger brother returns from America and suggests that the brothers and The Rat's wife try to find their roots in their ancestral village where their forebears had been involved in a peasant uprising in 1860. The brothers' differing childhood memories and historical perceptions and the younger one's attempt to restage the earlier rising make up the body of the novel. The reading is long and hard. (p. 692)

> *A review of "The Silent Cry," in* Choice, *Vol. 12, Nos. 5 & 6, July & August, 1975, pp. 691-92.*

JOHN NATHAN

[Ōe's] first published story, **"An Odd Job,"** appeared in the May, 1957 issue of the [Tokyo] University literary magazine. It was about a bewildered college student who takes a part-time job slaughtering dogs to be used in laboratory experiments. (pp. xiv-xv)

[Like the college student], Ōe's early heroes have been expelled from the certainty of childhood, into a world that bears no relation to their past. The values that regulated life when they were growing up have been blown to smithereens along with Hiroshima and Nagasaki; what confronts them now, the postwar world, is a gaping emptiness, enervation, a terrifying silence like the eternity that follows death. They are aware of the consequences of submitting to life in such a world; the riddle they must solve if they are to survive, to discover freedom for themselves, is how to sustain their *hostility* in the face of bewilderment and, finally, apathy.... A more accessible battleground is violent sex, antisocial sex, what one of Ōe's characters calls "a fuck rife with ignominy." Sooner or later Ōe's heroes discover that the only *territory* they can reach beyond the emptiness of everyday life is what their society deems "sexual perversion." Consider J. in Ōe's 1963 novel *Homo Sexualis*. J. is a playboy whose first wife has been driven to suicide by his flirtations with homosexuality. He becomes what the Japanese call a "subway pervert," ejaculating against the raincoats of young girls in crowded rush hour trains.... J. is perhaps the bravest of Ōe's heroes, and one of very few who succeeds in the terms he proposes to himself. At the end of the novel, frightened and alone, he visits his industrialist father and asks to be restored to the family fold. His father happily consents and promises him a good job; J. leaves the office intending to move back into his father's house. He is about to climb into his Jaguar when he finds himself moving toward the subway. He ... plunges into a subway and ejaculates against a high school girl. He comes to his senses as he is being led off the subway by a policeman, and the tears streaming down his cheeks are "tears of joy...."

In 1964, when he was twenty-nine, Ōe's first child was born with brain damage, and the baby boy, whom he called "Pooh," altered his world with the force of an exploding sun. I won't presume to describe Ōe's relationship with the child, he has done that wondrously himself in a story included in this collection, **"Teach Us To Outgrow Our Madness."** Suffice it to say that over the years as Pooh grew up, a fierce, exclusive, isolating bond developed between father and son. (pp. xv-xvi)

Ōe's own perception of the child's destructive force, the metaphor that first presented itself to him, was a nuclear explosion. The year Pooh was born he wrote two books at once and asked his publisher to release them on the same day. One was *A Personal Matter* ..., the first of a series of novels whose central character is the young father of a brain-damaged child. The other was a book of essays about the survivors of Hiroshima, *Hiroshima Notes*. Ōe was of course asking that the books be considered together; in one he chronicled the survival of an actual atomic bomb, in the other he sought the means of surviving a personal holocaust.

The child's tidal pull on Ōe's imagination is already discernible in *A Personal Matter*. Bird, the protagonist, a stymied intellectual with a failing marriage, dreams of flying away to Africa for a "glimpse beyond the horizon of quiescent and chronically frustrated everyday life." There is nothing new about this fantasy; it is evidence that Bird is descended from Ōe's prototypical hero. But Bird's wife gives birth to a baby with a "cave for a head," a "monster baby" who threatens to destroy his dream. (p. xvii)

Bird is the first of Ōe's heroes to turn his back on the central fantasy of his life, the first to accept, because he has no choice, the grim substitution of forbearance for hope. Until the advent of his first-born child, the quest for self-discovery took Ōe's heroes beyond the boundaries of society into a lawless wilderness. Beginning with Bird, they turn away from the lure of peril and adventure and seek instead, with the same urgency, the certainty and consonance they *imagine* they experienced before they were betrayed at the end of the War. It was as if Ōe no longer had the heart to light out for the territory, not with the defenseless child that had become a part of himself. (p. xviii)

[Longing] for a *mythic homeland* was always there in Ōe; very likely it was engendered in him, along with his anger....

Certainly it is to be felt in one of his first and most beautiful stories, **"Prize Stock."** The mountain village in which a black American soldier is being held prisoner exists nowhere in actual Japan. Instead of paddies there are "fields," instead of hogs and cows, "wild mountain dogs." ... But the surest proof that Ōe is rendering myth and not reality is the scene near the end of the story, just before the child narrator is betrayed by the black soldier, when the village children lead him by the hand to the village spring for a "primeval" bath.... The ecstasy of this moment, its "repletion and rhythm," is the ecstasy of ritual, and ritual is the stuff myth is made of. Here for the first and only time in his telling of the story, the narrator must step outside the time frame in which the story occurs and cast his memory back in his attempt to convey the moment. That is because myth exists only in memory, in a remote "primeval" time before history, and can never be experienced.

In recent years, this mythical mountain village surrounded by a primeval forest has loomed ever larger in Ōe's imagination, his Yoknapatawpha county, a place to which his heroes are ineluctably drawn in search of themselves. (pp. xviii-xx)

[Certainty] is shared by all of Ōe's recent heroes. But none is more passionately certain that salvation is to be discovered in a mythic version of his past than the narrator of **"The Day He Himself Shall Wipe My Tears Away,"** ... Ōe's most difficult and disturbing work to date. The narrator lies in a hospital bed eagerly waiting to die of liver cancer, probably imagined.... In these days he insists are his last, his entire consciousness is channeled into reliving a moment in his past, just before the War ended, when he accompanied his mad father on a suicide mission intended to rescue Japan from defeat. On August 15, 1945 (that most emblematic day in Ōe's early life), his father has led a band of Army deserters out of their mountain village to the nearby "provincial city" which is to be the scene of their insurrection. On their way up the pass out of the valley to the "real" world, they sing, in German, the refrain from a Bach cantata they have learned from a record the night before, "And He Himself shall wipe my tears away." When the narrator asks the meaning of the words, his father explains that *"Heiland"* (German for "Saviour") refers to "His Majesty the Emperor." ... This first of many absurd distortions is meet, for the rebels intend to sacrifice themselves in the Emperor's name and believe, the small boy accompanying them most fervently of all, that the Emperor who is a living god will not only accept but consecrate their sacrifice. The culmination of the episode, which lives in the narrator's imagination as the single, exalting moment in his life when he knew precisely who he was and what he was about, occurs when his father, *a certain party*, is shot down, and a sign that his death has indeed been consecrated is mystically revealed.... (pp. xx-xxii)

In part, the fulsome prose is parody. Ōe wrote this in 1972, in the shadow of Yukio Mishima's suicide by hara-kiri. On one level it is an angry parody of Mishima, a remorseless grotesquing of the mini-insurrection which made it possible for Mishima to "cut open his belly and die." But there is more to this than anger. There is also longing, not so different in quality from Mishima's own, for the sweet certainty of unreasoning faith in a god. (p. xxii)

"The Day He Himself Shall Wipe My Tears Away" conveys more of Ōe's essence than anything he has ever written. The astonishing power of the work is the energy that arcs between the poles of anger and longing that are the central contradiction in his vision. Its formidable privacy—which is what makes it so very difficult to follow and prevented many Japanese readers from finishing it—reflects the fierce privacy which has isolated Ōe and his son increasingly from the outside world. Like his narrator, intent on reliving a moment in the past existing only in his imagination, Ōe has become a miner digging straight down toward the pain at the center of his private world. In a lesser writer this would be a fatal limitation. But Ōe has the power to make us feel his pain. Life as we know it may not be so bleak as he perceives it to be. But the dislocation and the anger and finally the madness ever before his eyes is there for all of us, never so far removed from our own experience that we are at a loss to recognize it. (p. xxiii)

> John Nathan, in an introduction to Teach Us to Outgrow Our Madness: Four Short Novels *by Kenzaburō Ōe, translated by John Nathan, Grove Press, Inc., 1977, pp. ix-xxv.*

IVAN GOLD

"Do you think I'm making this up? I'm a man dying of liver cancer, why should I have to tell made-up stories?" asks the central character in **"The Day He Himself Shall Wipe My Tears Away,"** the longest, most ambitious of the four short novels by Kenzaburo Oe which make up this remarkable book [*Teach Us To Outgrow Our Madness*]. The character (never named) wears green underwater goggles which had belonged to his dead, mad father, and rails away at someone who may or may not be his wife. Since no one confirms his diagnosis, since he may have cirrhosis instead, or some neurological ailment unconnected with his liver, his accuracy in all other areas may also be in question. But no matter. Lying in his hospital bed, raging, remembering, picking obsessively over his past, he leaves no doubt that he is telling the truths which exist for him, which exist for Oe. . . .

"Prize Stock," the second story in the book, relates through a child's eyes the capture by Japanese villagers of a downed American airman. The airman is black. He is referred to as "the catch," and is imprisoned in the cellar of the narrator's house, where it is decided that the townspeople will "rear him" until the prefecture decides how it wants to dispose of him. A strange, loving relationship, almost like that of a child for its pet, grows up between the narrator and the soldier, who is eventually given the freedom to wander the village. When the prefecture finally decides, ominously, that it will take the prisoner, the boy rushes to warn him. . . . But he succeeds only in causing the soldier to panic; the soldier seizes the boy and locks them both in the cellar. In the violent aftermath, the soldier is killed and the boy is severely wounded by his hatchet-wielding father. **"Prize Stock"** is a haunting story, probing the deeper places of the postwar relationship between citizens of the two countries; it remains in the mind.

In the title story, **"Teach Us To Outgrow Our Madness,"** Oe returns to the subject which was at the heart of his novel *A Personal Matter* . . .—the fierce bond which springs up between a father and his brain-damaged son. . . . The boy in the story is nicknamed "Eeyore" . . . but the father is referred to only as "the fat man": "Until his son began to peel from his consciousness like a scab, the fat man was convinced that he experienced directly whatever physical pain his son was feeling. . . ." No mere summary of the events of this brilliant story can convey the resonance and depth with which Oe is able to imbue the relationship.

"I had the feeling there was nothing to worry about so long as I was sufficiently obsessed," Oe has the narrator say in the fourth and final story, **"Aghwee The Sky Monster,"** which deals in its turn with a man's possible "solution" to the birth of a defective child. The narrator here is looking back on his first job, as companion to a composer who has gone a little mad; this man has connived in the death of his child, only to discover afterward that surgery would probably have saved it.

Obsession in and of itself is hardly a guarantee of literary quality, but Oe is a supremely gifted writer . . . able to "fictionalize" the most significant elements of his life as can few others, and his work has enormous impact.

> Ivan Gold, "A Ray from the Rising Sun," in Book World—The Washington Post, *September 11, 1977, p. E4.*

CHOICE

At least one of [the stories in *Teach us to outgrow our madness*], **"Prize stock,"** has appeared before in English (**"The catch,"** translated by John Bestor in *New writing in Japan,* 1972). Oe's place in Japanese letters appears to be secure, although it is to be hoped that something more compelling will emerge from his reworking of the same materials: madness, suicide, physical malformation, disease, and rural eccentricity. The stories in this collection include his third use (in English) of a man with only one eye and his third use of a brain-damaged child. Each story is moving in itself but seems to be only another study toward the master work. . . .

> A review of "Teach Us to Outgrow Our Madness: Four Short Novels," in Choice, *Vol. 14, No. 10, December, 1977, p. 1368.*

HISAAKI YAMANOUCHI

[*The essay from which the following excerpt is taken is a slightly revised version of a paper read at the European Conference on Modern Japan held at St. Antony's College in April 1973.*]

[The] major roles in the contemporary [Japanese] literary scene are played by postwar writers. Among these, we choose for discussion here two men whose choice of themes and innovation in literary methods make them particularly relevant to an understanding of modern Japan: Abé Kōbō (1924-) and Ōe Kenzaburō (1935-). (p. 153)

Despite the gap in their ages (Ōe being eleven years the younger), there are interesting similarities as well as differences between the two. Both are concerned with the solitude of men and women alienated from contemporary society and suffering from a loss of identity. Besides the thematic parallels in their works, Abé and Ōe agree in their deliberate deviation from the dominant trend of the prewar Japanese novels. They are completely free from the sentimentality or self-commiseration characteristic of the I-novelists. Their prose style is also a mark of their deviation from the Japanese tradition. Abé's style is objective, logical and lucid. Ōe, on the other hand, deliberately distorts the traditional syntax, but is incomparable in his use of vivid imagery. Comparisons are often odious, but Abé's literary world has a closer kinship with that of Kafka and some contemporary European writers than that of his countrymen. It is also evident that Ōe is greatly indebted to and has absorbed much of the writings of Jean-Paul Sartre, Henry Miller and Norman Mailer. (pp. 153-54)

Between the two writers there are parallels in more ways than one. Abé's earliest work came to be published through a recommendation by Haniya Yutaka (1910-) who was then a member of the magazine *Kindai Bungaku*. Practically the earliest of Ōe's short stories, 'A Strange Job' (**'Kimyōna Shigoto'**, 1957), was chosen for the University of Tokyo Newspaper Prize by Ara Masahito (1913-), who was also a founding member of *Kindai Bungaku*. Abé and Ōe thus share the qualities that must have appealed to the literary taste of their elders, who constituted one of the main forces of postwar Japanese literature. But these circumstances are in a way incidental. The link between the two must be defined in more fundamental terms. In Ōe's earliest short stories such as 'A Strange Job' and 'The Arrogance of the Dead' (**'Shisha no Ogori'**, 1957), the main characters are university students who are engaged in humiliating hack work for their livelihood. Unable to resort to political activities as their fellow students do, they find no way out from their present impasse. In this respect their condition may most appropriately be described as one of confinement, alienation and deprivation of freedom, which are all unmistakably Abé's major themes. (pp. 162-63)

[Abé and Ōe] are both concerned with the search for identity, each in his own way. (p. 172)

The search for identity presupposes a community in which the ego is to be realised as a social self. For Abé, however, a community is an illusory idea which he rejects outright. His works provide a picture of life in which man is utterly lonely, deprived of communication with his fellow men and determined by physical reality.... In contrast to Abé, Ōe seems to aspire to a community in which the personal identity is to be realised. The difference between the two in this respect is probably due to the fact that as a child one lived the life of an expatriate while the other was deeply rooted in his native rural community. However, it is extremely difficult for Ōe, now living in the midst of industrial society, to celebrate the pastoral. As a result he portrays characters overwhelmed by the strain of urban society, or else he is 'of the Devil's party': in depicting a tension between the social restraint and spontaneous impulse, he represents the latter by anti-social characters, such as juvenile delinquents, sexual perverts and criminals, who are apparently intended to be fallen angels. Ōe's dream of a pastoral community is expressed in such a way as to show the difficulty of its realisation.

The history of modern Japanese literature, as in other aspects of culture, has been streaked with the cross-currents of the native tradition and Western influence. There were writers, such as Tanizaki and Kawabata, who represent an almost spontaneous example of the traditional sensibility. Mishima's artificially acquired Western taste, on the other hand, was deliberately counter-balanced by his fortified Japanese consciousness. Abé differs from any of these predecessors. He was brought up as an expatriate in a place somewhat like a barren wilderness, where neither the culture of his homeland nor that of the West was available in tangible form. In such circumstances there was nothing for him but to conceive of culture, of whichever hemisphere, in the abstract. (pp. 173-74)

With Ōe it is a different matter. On the one hand he is Westernised in his attempts to assimilate various features of contemporary European and American authors. On the other, however, he presents his themes in a specifically Japanese context.... [He is concerned] with the communal identity to be sought in indigenous culture. This is likely to derive from his anxiety about his own and his countrymen's precarious footing in contemporary Japanese society, where the native tradition is jeopardised by the ever-accelerating modernisation which began

under Western influence in Meiji and has perhaps got out of hand.... [Ōe's work], despite its Westernised façade, houses sentiments that epitomise the present dilemma of the [Japanese] nation. In this sense, Ōe's is a search for the identity of the race as well as the individual. (p. 174)

> *Hisaaki Yamanouchi, "In Search of Identity: Abé Kōbō and Ōe Kenzaburō," in his* The Search for Authenticity in Modern Japanese Literature, *Cambridge University Press, 1978, pp. 153-74.**

MICHIKO N. WILSON

What is most innovative about Ōe's works is that he cultivates the techniques of Cervantes and Rabelais and follows in their footsteps. From 1964 on, by employing farce, travesty, satire, and "grotesque realism," which has debasement and laughter at its core, Ōe has challenged and turned upside down the notion of what Japanese literature should be. In contrast to Meiji-Taishō Realism, which is often characterized by a spirit of Confucian solemnity, Ōe tries to offer an alternative worldview by synthesizing in his artistic world the long-neglected elements of *gesaku*-like humor, the satiric, and especially the earthy qualities of folklore such as *Konjaku monogatari* (Tales of Modern and Ancient Times).

Ōe's originality also lies in the intensity of his message aimed at both the individual and the entire human race. Despite the extremely personal lyricism that runs through his works, his private universe, directed by what he calls "the Cosmic Will," offers immediacy and relevance to contemporary problems. Ōe believes that social, political, and environmental issues are as much "situations" created by man as man is the victim of his own "situations." For him "to outgrow" this insane world, grappling with the world's problems is the only way to survive. (pp. 23-4)

Four Western literary figures—Auden, Sartre, Mailer, and Rabelais—stand out among those whose philosophy and literary techniques have had profound influences upon Ōe's consciousness. He reminisces in the notes to Part III in *Solemn Tightrope Walking* (1965), the first of three collections of essays: "My literary ground was shaped like a triangle, the three points of which were Sartre, Norman Mailer, and postwar Japanese literature." Also, W. H. Auden often dominated Ōe's early discussions on literature in general.... [Three] important points which Ōe has continuously insisted on [include]: to promote social awareness, to demystify human behavior, and to liberate the human mind. With these issues in mind, Ōe struck upon [Auden], another mentor whose intent and undaunting spirit of continuity (*jizokusei*) became his own. (pp. 24-5)

Ōe shares Mailer's radical views on sex and politics. Politics interests Mailer so long as it is an integral part of man as a social being, that is to say, "politics as a part of everything else in life." While Ōe is encouraged by Sartre's statement that "one of the chief motives of artistic creation is certainly the need of feeling that we are essential in relationship to the world," he is also inspired by Mailer who believes that the purpose of art is "to intensify, even if necessary, to exacerbate, the moral consciousness of people." ... Parallel to this is the role of the artist, which, according to Mailer, is "to be as disturbing, as adventurous, as penetrating, as his energy and courage make possible."

One particular poem by Auden eventually came to represent the lifestyle of the prototype of Ōe's hero. It is entitled "Leap

Before You Look''; its first stanza sums up the young hero's sentiments and action.

> The sense of danger must not disappear:
> The way is certainly both short and steep,
> However gradual it looks from here;
> Look if you like, but you will have to leap.

For Ōe's hero, this sense of danger stimulates the need to act, the need to "intensify and exacerbate the moral consciousness of people." It is in this light that we are able to come to terms with the militant nature of Ōe's statement on the use of sex, which has often invited annoyance and dissatisfaction from Japanese critics. For example, he deplored the fact that his ambitious work, *Warera no jidai* (*Our Times*, 1959), was dismissed as a novel of sexual perversion.... In Ōe's narratives sexual terms and descriptions are meant to provoke the reader, to generate in his mind, as Ōe puts it, "an exaltation of an ideology''; by stimulating the mind and agitating the psyche, he hopes to dig "a vertical mine shaft" straight into the heart of the darkness of both the individual and of mankind. After all, sexuality is inseparably tied to what is at the root of human existence. What Ōe is aiming at is sobriety of mind with sex as a stimulant to one's consciousness, never sexual stupor.

Another Western literary mentor who has been a constant inspiration to Ōe is Rabelais.... *Gargantua and Pantagruel* by Rabelais foretells the direction [Ōe] would take a decade later in creating *The Pinchrunner Memorandum* (1976), a novel of satire, laughter, and regeneration. (pp. 25-7)

[*The Pinchrunner Memorandum*] is in many ways antithetical to post-Meiji realism and its succeeding literary traditions. It is in a way a violation of a taboo, in the sense that the combination of socio-political issues with Rabelaisian laughter, slapstick farce, satire, and "grotesque realism" has often been regarded as extraneous to the realm of "serious" literature, or *belles lettres*. Ōe also brings into the novel an element of the fantastic, which enjoyed considerable popularity among nineteenth-century Western writers. The result is that his work is remarkably free of cynicism, sentimentality, and pessimism. (pp. 27-8)

Michiko N. Wilson, "Ōe's Obsessive Metaphor, Mori, the Idiot Son: Toward the Imagination of Satire, Regeneration, and Grotesque Realism," in The Journal of Japanese Studies, *Vol. 7, No. 1, Winter, 1981, pp. 23-52.*

SANROKU YOSHIDA

The title of each story [in *Atarashii hito yo mezameyo*] is based on a line translated from William Blake's poems, and the title of the last, whose original English reads "Rouse up, O, Young Men of the New Age," is also the book's title. The themes of the stories, such as madness, fear of death and the nightmare of infanticide, are all evoked by that particular Blakean phrase which is used as the title. There is no plot per se in any of these stories, but the narration revolves around the life of the narrator/author and his idiot son, nicknamed Eeyore. The stories are organized by juxtaposing various episodes involving Eeyore's growing process, the interpretation of Blake's poems by the author and his reminiscences of past events in his life, all linked only by imagery.

Ōe conveys the message that the world is not only for the healthy but also for the handicapped like Eeyore, who tend to be ostracized in society.... The images of grotesque realism and hyperbolic distortion of reality to which Ōe resorted frequently in previous works such as *Dōjidai gēmu* (The Game of Simultaneity; 1979) and *Kōzui wa waga tamashii ni oyobi* (The Flood Unto My Soul; 1973) are nonexistent here. This book, the most recent of Ōe's works, is less complex linguistically and easier to read than those earlier, full-length novels and appears to mark the beginning of a new phase in Ōe's literary career.

Sanroku Yoshida, in a review of "Atarashii hito yo mezameyo," in World Literature Today, *Vol. 58, No. 2, Spring, 1984, p. 326.*

George (Ames) Plimpton
1927-

American nonfiction writer, editor, and author of books for children.

Best known for *Paper Lion* (1966), a highly acclaimed account of his experiences in a professional football training camp, Plimpton writes sports literature marked by sound reportage and elegant prose. He provides an unusual perspective on the sports world by relating his experiences as an amateur among professionals. Often compared to James Thurber's well-known character, Walter Mitty, Plimpton entertains grandiose dreams of competing against those who are masters of their sport. Whereas Mitty emerges triumphant in his daydreams, however, Plimpton invariably fails when given the opportunity to act out his fantasies. When asked why he chooses to write about sports as a participant rather than as a spectator, Plimpton stated: "I hope I am better able to tell something about the sport itself, the mystiques, the rituals, the athletes themselves." Critics agree that Plimpton captures the drama inherent in competitive sports, and they especially praise his apt character sketches and his authentic use of vernacular.

Plimpton achieved overwhelming critical and commercial success with *Paper Lion*. Posing as a rookie quarterback at the summer training camp of the Detroit Lions, Plimpton incisively recounts his misadventures and tells of his relationships with the players. Although quickly discovered to be an amateur, Plimpton developed an insider's rapport with the players which enabled him to delve into the psychology of the sport. One critic noted, "Mr. Plimpton's true vocation is writing, and the agility and imaginativeness of his prose transform his account of this daydream from a rather self-conscious adventure story into a classic of sports reporting." *Paper Lion* was later adapted for film.

Plimpton's other books similarly explore his exploits in various sports. His first full-length work, *Out of My League* (1961), describes a post-season baseball game in which Plimpton pitched to some of the sport's best players. Plimpton returns to football as his subject in *Mad Ducks and Bears* (1973) and *One More July* (1977), and he examines the golf circuit in *The Bogey Man* (1968) and boxing in *Shadow Box* (1977). These works often demonstrate an eclectic approach, mixing sports trivia and anecdotes with straightforward, journalistic material. *Fireworks: A History and Celebration* (1984) is a commentary on its title subject. Plimpton has contributed articles to many magazines and is an editor of *The Paris Review*.

(See also *Contemporary Authors*, Vols. 21-24, rev. ed. and *Something about the Author*, Vol. 10.)

MARIANNE MOORE

[The essay from which this excerpt is taken originally appeared in The New York Herald Tribune, *April 23, 1961.]*

A defeated pitcher—"a rather proud figure . . . peering into the depths of his glove"—and a passion for sport had planted in George "Prufrock" Plimpton a craving to pitch from the mound in the Yankee Stadium in an exhibition game. Much

time on the phone had resulted in no more than "a snort at the other end" or a "Whazzat? Let's go through that again, hey," and the dream of participating in a game at championship level might have come to nothing if Toots Shor, when consulted, had not proposed a thousand-dollar prize set up by *Sports Illustrated* to be divided by the team which got the most hits—Plimpton pitching. (p. 243)

Out of My League copes with the problem of the imaginary nightmare of walking every batter and the glittering triumph (the shutout) of striking them out, one after the other. . . . [After his stint as pitcher], hungry and thirsty, impatient to see the National League play the American, unrecognized as the pitcher for *Sports Illustrated,* neither ballplayer nor spectator, Plimpton found an empty seat in the upper deck of the stadium, bought two hot dogs, and was paying the vendor for a beer when evicted for having no ticket stub. He "crouched briefly in the aisle— . . . as nomadic as the youngsters who scuttle in without paying and are flushed like shorebirds and flutter down two or three sections to settle" until ushered further.

George Plimpton, as is already apparent, shines in simile—his great device; also in characterization. He has an ear for vernacular, says Willie Mays "has a pleasant face to start with," sometimes explodes in mighty laughter, and "his eyebrows (can) arch up," making him look "as if his manager had just finished addressing him at length in Turkish.'' Bob Friend, as magnetic as he was unaware that he was, said, ''I don't feel all that much at home either,'' in reply to Plimpton's ''It's all a little new.''

Verisimilitude? In *Out of My League* it is not so much easy to find as it is impossible to avoid. ''Frank Thomas' size made him look dangerous. . . . I imagined I heard the bat sing in the air like a willow switch.'' Ernie Banks, who won a Most Valuable Player award for ''his ability to lay off the bad pitches,'' was at the plate for such a long time that he ''seemed to recede into the distance, along with (Elston) Howard (catching), until the two of them looked like figures viewed through the wrong end of a telescope.'' Elston Howard's detachment, in contempt of a stodgy task, had been painingly apparent to Plimpton. Then as Stan Lopata hit foul after foul, ''lashing out like a cobra from his coil,'' Plimpton says, Howard ''began to rise from his crouch after every pitch and fire the ball back . . . with an accuracy that mocked my control, harder than I was pitching it to him,'' inflicting ''a deep bone bruise which discolored my left hand for over a week.''

Christy Mathewson says, ''a pitcher is not a ballplayer—he is a man in need of sympathy.'' Well . . . for a full-time man of letters, anonymity is a ''role,'' and the reader's emotion is envy, envy of a man who retired his first two batters and later achieved the fine moment of his afternoon ''when Mays hit that towering fly . . . forever available for recall.'' As Charles Poore says, ''in a world where athletes are always signing ghost-written books this turnabout, with a writer ghosting an athlete, is fair play.'' If in *Out of My League* triumph does not dominate nightmare, something is wrong with the reader—if the performance by George Plimpton, his satistician, and photographer, Garry Winogrand, has not earned them the triple crown with ''rim tucked under,'' for poetry, biography, and drama. (pp. 244-45)

Marianne Moore, ''A Writer on the Mound,'' in her A Marianne Moore Reader, *The Viking Press,* 1961, pp. 243-45.

MARK HARRIS

A few years ago, in Douglass Wallop's ''The Year the Yankees Lost the Pennant,'' the Devil, for his usual fee, permitted a middle-aged baseball fan to act out his fantasy of diamond heroism. In a more naturalistic context, the magazine Sports Illustrated has since permitted George Plimpton . . . to act out the same fantasy. The results are reported with such skill in **''Out of My League''** that immediately after reading the book I was seized with an excruciating recurrence of bursitis of the shoulder and was forced to bed for a week.

The Plimpton Plan was this: prior to a post-season exhibition game at Yankee Stadium between stars of the two major leagues, Plimpton would pitch to eight National League hitters and eight American, and whichever group hit for more total bases would receive a $1,000 purse donated by Sports Illustrated. The point was, as Plimpton explained it to Editor Sid James, ''that I would pitch not as a hotshot—that'd be a different story—but as a guy who's average, really, a sort of Mr. Everybody, the sort who thinks he's a fair athlete.''

Ah, yes, money was at stake! And comfort! Money is comfort in a game which (taking for granted, of course, the spiritual side of things) counts its moneys and its comforts in total bases, and the more the better, because the more the prouder, and

above all is pride. ''You could tell,'' wrote Plimpton when his shoulder healed, ''they were pleased their profession had treated me as roughly as it had.''

How the profession treated Plimpton, and why Plimpton required healing . . . everybody must read for himself. My shoulder simply cannot go through it again.

Mark Harris, ''On the Mound Was Mr. Everybody,'' in The New York Times Book Review, *April 23, 1961, p. 3.*

MYRON COPE

The literature of sports has been mainly an assembly line of shallow volumes aimed at the level of Little League readers. In recent years, however, it has shown signs of developing into maturity, as a succession of skillful authors, still hopelessly addicted to the games of their youth, turned the American athlete upside down to see what might fall out of him. The results have been surprisingly interesting. *The Long Season,* by pitcher Jim Brosnan, emancipated the baseball player from agate boxscores and brought him to life as a coarse but often winsome figure, capable of high humor in a profession beset by anxieties. Then Bill Veeck, former owner of the St. Louis Browns as well as the Indians and the White Sox, collaborated with Ed Linn to produce *Veeck—as in Wreck,* a free-wheeling account of front-office conniving and promotional gymnastics. If the reader could not exactly audit the ruthless mogul's books, he could at least reach out and squeeze his paunch.

George Plimpton's first venture into the new sociology of sports was **Out of My League,** in which he described his experience as an amateur of all-star pitching against major league players in a post-season game. The gimmick behind his new book [**Paper Lion**] was to persuade the management of a professional football team to let him pose as a rookie quarterback. From this vantage point he hoped to set down the responses of ''the average weekend athlete'' to life in a pro football training camp. (p. 1)

[**Paper Lion**] is possibly the most arresting and delightful narrative in all of sports literature. For the account of his gimmick soon gives way to solid reportage, in which he captures the sights and sounds of pro football with uncommon fidelity. Sportswriters tolerate training camp routine as a monotonous but undemanding vacation from the office, whereas Plimpton came equipped with the neophyte's advantage—an unashamed enthusiasm for his subject—as well as the artist's feeling for significant detail.

From the moment the author arrives in camp carrying a pair of tight football shoes he bought in an army-navy store, a Spalding football, and a manual of basic formations written by a high school coach, he skillfully tunes in to the mood and tempo of a squad rounding into condition for a campaign of violence. Soon each of the bulky inmates becomes distinct, one from the other. He writes, for example, of 300-pound line coach Less Bingamen: ''. . . down on the field he had a strange cry, like a bird's, to exhort his linemen, calling, 'Here we go,' which came out 'Hibby-go, hibby-go, hibby-go'—repeated endlessly.'' Such detail brings the reader directly on the field, where he can feel the morning sun on his neck and become aware of the insecurity that threatens each of these powerful and skillful men who are fighting for a job. The pathos of cutdown time is an old sportswriting theme, but *Paper Lion* presents the victims with a novelist's eye for depth. . . . (pp. 1, 13)

Plimpton strings together a succession of vignettes, sometimes moving, often hilarious. He is aided by art but also by fortune. For one thing, the Detroit Lions are a particularly hard-living, fun-loving team, a tradition which dates back to the influence of Bobby Layne, its brash quarterback of the '50s. Moreover, professional athletes as a group have a weakness for men of means, particularly movie stars and socialites. The rapport between Plimpton and the Lions was immediate, enabling him to move into the group and become, himself, a vivid camp figure.

But it is Plimpton's skill as an author that turns his flimsy scheme to play quarterback into a perfectly acceptable narrative device. (p. 13)

> Myron Cope, "Quarterback Sneak," in Book Week—World Journal Tribune, October 23, 1966, pp. 1, 13.

THE NEW YORKER

[Mr. Plimpton] prevailed upon the owners and coaches of the Detroit Lions, of the National Football League, to permit him to join their team of gigantic professionals as a third-string quarterback in summer training camp and then to appear briefly in an inter-squad exhibition game. . . . Fortunately, Mr. Plimpton's true vocation is writing, and the agility and imaginativeness of his prose [in *Paper Lion*] transform his account of this daydream from a rather self-conscious adventure story into a classic of sports reporting. His eyes and ears are wonderfully quick, and there is a memorable accuracy to his descriptions of a descending punt, the noise of enormous linemen colliding in scrimmage (it resembles, he says, a sack of Venetian blinds being shaken) and a pair of quarterbacks so bemused by their game that they remain on the field after practice to throw passes to schoolboys. Best of all are the long dormitory dialogues, over the tick of night lawn sprinklers and the plink of guitars, that bring alive the humor, cruelty, fears, sadness, and extraordinary professional intelligence of the courageous and variously complicated young men who make their living by public violence. Mr. Plimpton came away from his ordeal with feelings of affection and strong protectiveness toward the Lions; these are entirely convincing, for he has written about athletes without condescension or unwarranted awe, and by the end of his book it is possible to understand the mysterious process that builds a band of quick, gargantuan egotists into a selfless, inextricable, and dangerous mechanism called a team. . . . (pp. 245-46)

> A review of "Paper Lion," in The New Yorker, Vol. XLII, No. 38, November 12, 1966, pp. 245-46.

BRIAN GLANVILLE

There are worse ways of getting to know about a country than through its sports, and since America's two major national sports have been rejected by almost the whole of the rest of the world, they serve as an especially intriguing paradigm. The Japanese play baseball and play it badly, having produced just one major league player in sixty years—though on every other Tokyo streetcorner, a baseball thuds monotonously into a baseball glove. Canada alone has taken to that strange amalgam of ritual and brutality which is American football. In writing about it from the inside [in *Paper Lion*], a literate and observant Walter Mitty, George Plimpton tells us much about the game,

much about the United States, and a certain amount about himself. (p. 114)

At his best, there is no more satisfying sports writer in America than Mr. Plimpton, precisely because he is, first of all, a writer. . . . There is, however, little in *Paper Lion* to compare with Mr. Plimpton's bravura piece, published in *Sports Illustrated,* about the attempt of Cassius Clay and his trainer-acolyte, Bundini, to find restaurant service on a highway in the South. This is, I think, because the very nature of his enterprise implies a dichotomy; a need to run with the hare and hunt with the hounds.

It is certainly to Mr. Plimpton's credit that he should have undertaken his task without a vestige of patronage, as "one of the boys"; so much so that the footballers came gladly to accept him as one of themselves, wanted him to play in the public exhibition match against the Cleveland Browns, despite the management; repeatedly ask him back to training camp, even use him to represent them at player-drafts.

But Mr. Plimpton is *not* one of the boys, otherwise he would not have been able to write this book. He is a sophisticated literary gentleman with a boyish passion for sport, and the two qualities are constantly, in this book, pulling him in two different directions. Thus, there are tantalizing passages when he abandons his crisp, journalistic style of short, functional sentences, and takes wing. A passage toward the end evokes the scene out at the training camp as he leaves for home, passing two girls, youthful and pretty on the tennis court, while the sad, despairing cry of the Lions players wafts over the trees.

This is fine, and this is literature. But when Mr. Plimpton is exchanging wisecracks with the players, coming down—without condescension, it is true—to their jocular, jockstrap level—then he is inevitably diminished.

The book is loose and long, bearing the signs of its origin as a series of magazine articles, so that its more distinguished passages tend to get buried in straightforward reportage. But the picture of a professional footballer's world, however unsympathetic, comes out four square and three dimensional. Not that Mr. Plimpton means, for a moment, to be unsympathetic; he clearly likes most of what he sees. But the persisting adolescence, the hazing and the hierarchy of it all, are reminiscent of the nasty army world with which we have been familiarized by James Jones.

Much of this is attributable to the pernicious system of the draft, the annual influx of rookies. At the beginning of each season, every club brings in a troop of college footballers, who might laughingly be called amateurs. The veterans are thus immediately confronted by a series of challengers for their positions—and react accordingly. Mr. Plimpton shows us how they not only behave to the unfortunate rookies like bullies at an English public school, but studiously withhold the benefit of their experience, enjoying rather than correcting the newcomers' mistakes. It is, as I have said, the system which produces the situation, but systems do not happen by accident; they grow out of a country's character, its unconscious demands and aspirations. (pp. 116-17)

American football seems, like so many American folk-phenomena, hung-up on violence and a doubtful concept of masculinity. It was Christopher Isherwood who wrote, in *Lions and Shadows,* that for the genuinely strong man, there is no test; he merely sits at home while the weak man makes his moral way round by the killing Northwest Passage. All this

Mr. Plimpton shows us with great clarity, though without manifest intention.

He also shows us much which interests and even delights, presenting us with a wonderful gallery of grotesques, a glorious catalogue of hangers-on, exotically superstitious players, eccentric managers, peculiar fans. . . .

Mr. Plimpton's book deserves its popularity, satisfying as it does the fantasies of a million men in the stands, in prose and with an eye and ear which none of them could match. For the literary, it must be a tantalizing book, giving, as it does, so many evocative glimpses of how well Mr. Plimpton can write, how impressively he uses simile and metaphor, especially in passages like the one which describes the crowd's invasion of the field at Yankee Stadium.

He is a good writer; too good, one feels, for so antipathetic a game. May its life be nasty, brutish . . . and short. (p. 117)

> Brian Glanville, "The Brutal Sport," in Commentary, *Vol. 44, No. 4, October, 1967, pp. 114, 116-17.*

DICK SCHAAP

George Plimpton, who infiltrated professional football to write the fascinating **"Paper Lion,"** now has turned to professional golf; and to answer the inevitable question, **"The Bogey Man"** is no **"Paper Lion."** Except in the quality of the writing, which remains high, it isn't even close.

The difficulties begin with the title. **"Paper Lion"** was an inspired play on words perfectly reflecting both concept and content. **"The Bogey Man"** is a weak semi-pun which probably isn't even accurate. Plimpton does not particularly dwell upon his own golf scores, but of the ones he does mention, only a few sound like bogeys. More often, apparently, Plimpton was a double-bogey man.

The Walter Mitty touch that gave the previous book a fine feeling of insanity has vanished. In **"Paper Lion,"** Plimpton was an amateur posing as a professional; and although the Detroit players quickly pierced his disguise, he still went through the motions of impersonating a rookie, suffering many of the same agonies the pros suffered, eating the same meals, sleeping in the same dorm, risking physical damage to explore a territory no outsider had ever before penetrated.

But in **"The Bogey Man,"** Plimpton does not even pretend to become a touring golf pro. Golf has no equivalent of football's training camps, no course where only professionals may groom their skills, no sanctum where only professionals may enter, so Plimpton enjoys no singular experience. . . .

Plimpton is an excellent reporter, with an acute eye and a sharp ear, but his gifts alone cannot overcome the fact that pro golfers, generally speaking, are an introverted, secretive, solitary bunch. Plimpton looks and listens, but not a single contemporary golfer springs boldly to life in **"The Bogey Man."**

Night Train Lane, Carl Brettschneider, Joe Schmidt and a handful of other Detroit Lions emerged as distinct, vivid figures in **"Paper Lion,"** but they have no counterparts in **"The Bogey Man."** There is, early in the book, a frustrating attempt to share a friendly round with Sam Snead; and there is, late in the book, an equally frustrating attempt to interview Arnold Palmer, but each episode offers merely a glimpse, a hint, of an individual. Plimpton captures Jack Nicklaus talking about humming to himself on the golf course, and he captures half-

a-dozen golfers talking about the "yips," an attack of nerves on the green—fine vignettes—but no character grows during the book. No one becomes a person. . . .

The dominant character in **"The Bogey Man,"** understandably, is Plimpton himself, but even the self-portrait is incomplete. It is only George Plimpton the hacker, the would-be par shooter, and everyone who can read knows that there is also Plimpton the bon vivant, Plimpton the political campaigner, Plimpton the editor, Plimpton the intellectual, dozens of different Plimptons who never invade **"The Bogey Man."** . . .

"The Bogey Man" isn't nearly as much fun as **"Paper Lion,"** but **"Paper Lion,"** after all, was an exceptional book. Measured strictly against the average sports book, the average golf book, **"The Bogey Man"** could be considered a success. It is literate and intelligent, which closes out the match, two-up, against most of the competition.

Yet it would be unfair not to measure **"The Bogey Man"** against **"Paper Lion."** Plimpton always likes to put himself up against the best.

> Dick Schaap, "George Plimpton Off His Game," in The New York Times Book Review, *November 10, 1968, p. 8.*

C. MICHAEL CURTIS

[There] is a limit to the enthusiasm one can maintain for another man's fantasy life, and in [**"The Bogey Man"**] there is too much candor and self-consciousness in the Plimpton mirage to sustain the pretense of genuine insight or involvement. . . .

The presumption of the book . . . is that "the world of big-time golf" can be faithfully recorded by a sensitive sports nut with a handicap of 18, provided he spends a bit of time traveling with pros and vicariously sharing in their triumphs and eccentricities.

So what does one learn about Arnold Palmer? That he drinks Coca-Colas at two o'clock in the morning: Dorothy Kilgallen would have found that out in a great deal less time, and with considerably more gusto.

The point is not, however, that Plimpton is inadequate as a reporter. He is a great deal more diligent, and certainly more civilized, than most of the men who keep us in touch with our heroes. The problem is one of presumption. Plimpton pretends, more or less, to be something he isn't. And the very candor that keeps his fantasy in perspective prevents it from taking hold.

"The Bogey Man" is a very good book for people who want more from their sports reporters than a list of winners from the Buick Open. Within limits it may be the best reflective sports reporting available. But it is, nonetheless, a dismal waste of fine talent, and a thankless abuse of one man's claim to dignity.

> C. Michael Curtis, "Plimpton and His Latest Game," in The Christian Science Monitor, *December 5, 1968, p. 24.*

CHRISTOPHER LEHMANN-HAUPT

It goes without saying that sequels never live up to their originals . . . you can't go home again . . . time waits for no man . . . and all that. So of course George Plimpton's **"Mad Ducks and Bears: Football Revisited"** is not the book that his earlier football misadventure **"Paper Lion"** was. Of course the gimmick of the amateur competing with professionals has worn thin, the surprise gone, the drama dissipated. Of course the new book deserves to be called "Cub of Paper Lion" or "Paper Lion Recycled" or whatever. No, it's no shock that this new book is relatively disappointing: what comes as a surprise is that it isn't more disappointing, that it isn't altogether a bore, that it is in fact rather entertaining, all things considered, and that Mr. Plimpton has made the most of a bad situation. . . .

[If] one drift of the book is essentially somewhat aimless—it begins as a manual by Plimpton, [Alex] Karras, and John Gordy (another veteran Detroit Lion) on the fundamentals of line play, then collapses into Karras's and Gordy's reminiscences and other comic marginalia, and then resolves itself into yet another Plimpton misadventure (this time playing Baltimore Colt quarterback against the Detroit Lions for a television special)—well then its very aimlessness gives us a chance to see more closely Mr. Plimpton's unusual reportorial skills.

For though the point was easily overlooked in the entertainment of **"Paper Lion,"** Mr. Plimpton is more than an opportunist cashing in on clever gimmicks. He has a wonderful flair for comic descriptive writing. He has the patience to listen carefully to what others tell him; the imagination to visualize and ask interesting questions; and the persistence to cross-reference the best stories he is told, no matter how much time or travel may be involved. Best of all, he never patronizes, and thus has the power to draw intelligence from a stone.

And these talents of Plimpton's are evident throughout **"Mad Ducks and Bears"**—whether he is tracking down by long-distance phone and sympathetically questioning an errant fan who once in Plimpton's presence leaped out of the stands and dashed into the midst of a game in progress; whether he is exploring how Karras and Gordy made out in their playing days with money, practical jokes, women, coaches, and the fans; or whether he is simply describing Karras's golf-game. . . . So Mr. Plimpton's new book is never a disaster; it by no means falls flat on its face.

Still, it remains a sequel, and sequels never live up to their originals . . . you can't go home again . . . time waits for no man . . . and all that. A feeling of something missing pervades these pages, no matter how amusingly Plimpton and his friends cavort, we can't help but be reminded of the old grad in his attic wistfully waving a moth-eaten pennant. One trusts **"Mad Ducks"** was intended as an afterthought—one assumes Plimpton spun it effortlessly out of other projects that engaged him. And one hopes that, having finished it, he will now move on to new athletic endeavors, new charming misadventures, new fields on which to meet defeat.

Christopher Lehmann-Haupt, "Cub of Paper Lion,"
in The New York Times, *November 12, 1973, p. 31.*

BARBARA GRIZZUTI HARRISON

We are meant, it is fair to assume by the epigraph Plimpton has chosen—"rage, rage against the dying of the light"—to understand that [**"Mad Ducks and Bears"**] is a serious book. Indeed, at one point Plimpton temporarily departs from his I-am-a-tape-recorder approach to his subjects (who seem, when they're not smashing one another's heads, to live almost entirely in a world of laughter without warmth, practical jokes and instantly replayed one-liners) to declare, not unreasonably, that he has found himself "much less at ease with the violence

of football than before . . . because the second time around seems to require that I look at it more clinically and personally. . . .'' (pp. 24-5)

Fair enough. But Plimpton, unfortunately, is a victim of his need to be a good guy—a good gentlemanly guy, decent, reticent, modest, unobtrusive—in the eyes of the athletes of whom he stands in awe. (It is however, the aren't-they-marvelous sort of awe that is particularly related to condescension.) So he immediately blocks, as it were, his own metaphor: "It was very likely tedious," he says, "for the players to be asked so many questions about violence." He is neither clinical nor personal; he gives us, without the benefit of his own reflections, a grab-bag of anecdotes and reminiscences that demonstrate, at tedious length, what we already know: that pro football is composed of brutality, sentiment, and avarice—a volatile mix, but not the stuff of tragedy. . . .

"Mad Ducks and Bears" cannot make any real claim to being a serious book. There is no cohesive statement, nor is there any attempt to generalize from the rather parochial set of particulars. Plimpton is too busy playing Robin to the athletes' Batman, which doesn't stop him from slyly winking at his readers, who are presumably in on the joke—that being that the natives are quaint.

Is it an entertaining book? Well, I tried very hard, as I read it, to remember how I felt about the Brooklyn Dodgers when I was 12. . . . I was insatiable for details of the players' lives; no crumb of a fact would have struck me as having anything less than cosmic significance. Much of this book would have appealed to me then.

But for those of us who have outgrown that kind of worship—well, there are some good bits. I welcomed the hard stuff, like the accounts of the players' negotiating for higher salaries and bigger pensions. My interest was whetted—and my feminist ire aroused—by the little dollops of information about the players' wives. I was fascinated by the almost sexual, orgiastic nature of the violence of contact football (one of the players remarks that he'd rather stick than be stuck), the panting, the grunts, the exhortations, the visceral hate.

But when I felt called upon to exercise compassion for players, like Karras, forced against their wills to retire, I felt exploited. I did, in fact, respond to their rage and their bewilderment. But what, after all had they lost? The opportunity to suffer painful injuries and, fueled by their pain, to "knock someone's head off" while bellowing with their own hurt. They had lost the opportunity to humiliate and be humiliated and to make bad jokes about it. That isn't glorious, and it isn't tragic, either. It's sad and awful and ugly and grim and vicious. I wish Plimpton had told us something of how he felt about all of this—something more that is, than "Jeez," "Holy Smoke." Because he hasn't, **"Mad Ducks and Bears"** reads like a celebration of violence and mayhem by a gentleman whose pleasure it was to go slumming. And that isn't funny. (p. 25)

Barbara Grizzuti Harrison, "Football People," in
The New York Times Book Review, *January 6, 1974,*
pp. 24-5.

CHRISTOPHER LEHMANN-HAUPT

In **"One More July,"** George Plimpton has returned to the world of professional football, and one's first inclination is to protest that we had enough of it in **"Paper Lion"** and more than enough in **"Mad Ducks and Bears."** But what has drawn

Mr. Plimpton back this time is not another inglorious opportunity to get himself pasted to the turf at the quarterback position. It is the beguiling intelligence of certain professional football players, a characteristic that Mr. Plimpton not only can take credit for discovering and conveying to the world at large, but also may even be suspected of inventing. . . .

[The] football intelligence one meets in **"One More July"** belongs to Bill Curry, a former all-Pro center and president of the Players' Association whom Plimpton first met and befriended when he "was up to some participatory journalism with the Baltimore Colts." Since then, Curry has bounced around the National Football league for a few years, picked up a debilitating knee injury, and is now driving north from his home in Georgia to give his career one last shot with the Green Bay Packers, where it all began under the malevolent dictatorship of Vince Lombardi. Plimpton meets Curry at the airport in Louisville, Ky., climbs into his Volvo, switches on a tape recorder, and rides with him. The rest is mostly Curry, talking and reminiscing.

The result is a penetrating look into the world of professional sports. The conversation does amble through some well-worn territory—drugs, race relations, Howard Cosell, the idiosyncrasies of unusual players, the behavior of fans, the disappointment of being cut from the squad.

And there is the usual share of amusing anecdotes that one has come to expect in Plimpton's reporting. . . .

But what makes **"One More July"** especially refreshing is Bill Curry's unusual intelligence. After all that has been written about the violent game during the past decade, he still manages to tell us odd and original things about playing professional football. . . . More surprising still, he breathes new life into tired subjects, such as the fearsomeness of Vince Lombardi, who had such powers of command that he once ordered a frisking dog off the practice field and was immediately obeyed; or about why professionals really play the game for love and not for money. . . .

In fact, so involved did Bill Curry get me in the game that in the final chapter, where he and Plimpton finally arrive in Green Bay, Wis., and Curry conducts a tour of the places he used to live and play at in the old days under the now-deceased Lombardi, I actually felt a sense of elegiac nostalgia—a nostalgia for what he has earlier persuaded us was one of the most horrendous experiences of his career. Such is the ambiguous intensity of the professional football life; Bill Curry has caught it as well as anyone who has written before him.

Of course it is Plimpton who suggests that Curry describe the town of Green Bay as if he were the stage manager in Thornton Wilder's "Our Town." It is Plimpton who has drawn Curry out from start to finish, if only by muttering "What?" or "That's hard to believe," or "Well, I don't see how you went on with someone like that." I don't want to take anything away from him. I just mean to emphasize that this is a different sort of Plimpton football book; not a product of Plimpton the caperer, but of Plimpton the interviewer. In which role he is, as usual, at his very best.

> *Christopher Lehmann-Haupt, in a review of "One More July," in* The New York Times, *July 29, 1977, p. C17.*

JOE FLAHERTY

In the opening line of **"Shadow Box,"** George Plimpton gambles. "I never understood boxing," he writes, thus attempting to set up the reader for a sucker punch. The gambit is audacious, since boxing is the one sport that can bring out the prophet in a Quaker. Call it a literary right-hand lead. But then, as one gets deeper into the book, he realizes he has read very little about the actual *mano a mano*. What has been offered are some Plimpton misadventures, personality portraits observed first hand and culled from history, a smorgasbord of characters: boxers, writers, hangers-on and peripheral zanies. So the opening gambit becomes a query: *Does he really understand boxing?* . . . By this time, the reader is so charmed and beguiled that he frankly doesn't give a damn. (p. 9)

Plimpton has stock in setting himself up as a naif—it's a persona as carefully crafted as Mailer's. In his participatory journalism he has been described wrongly as a Walter Mitty, and he is doing nothing of the sort. This is no daydreaming nebbish. What makes Plimpton work is that he juxtaposes cultures.

When he writes of his preparation for a three-round bout with the light-heavyweight champion Archie Moore, he recounts that he went to the Racquet Club library on Park Avenue to read "The Art and Practice of English Boxing," published in 1807. The reader is chortling already. It is not incidental that Plimpton gives us a chapter on eccentric royalty who fancied themselves amateur boxers. It's the image he's after. He is a public man who has appeared on television, and many of us are familiar with his gangling, tweedy demeanor and Oxford accent. He plays the "fancy pants" to our outhouse Americana. My God! Imagine *him* messing it up with Moore or mucking with the Detroit Lions in **"Paper Lion."**

His book on pro golf, **"Bogey Man,"** didn't come off because his breed invented golf. But the baseball diamond (**"Out of My League"**), the ring and gridiron are perfect foils. He is not our latter-day Mitty but a retooled young Charles Laughton in "Ruggles of Red Gap."

He also is intrepid reporter enough to track down the conclusion of the heist that took place in Atlanta the night of Ali's comeback fight, and his account of the first Frazier-Ali go at the Garden (when he followed Ali to the hospital) is superb and thorough. And for his inventiveness, the marvelous Alex Karras I met in **"Mad Ducks and Bears"** was never in evidence on ABC's "Monday Night Football."

Sometimes, the persona becomes a little too farfetched and contrived. When he bruises the point of his helplessness, he seems to be shaking the reader by the lapels, shouting "What's a nice guy like me doing in a joint like this?"

But that is a minor carp. The only major disappointment is when the book ends. . . . Bloody good show, old sport. (p. 44)

> *Joe Flaherty, "Muhammad Ali Meets Ernest Hemingway," in* The New York Times Book Review, *November 6, 1977, pp. 9, 44.*

CRISTOPHER LEHMANN-HAUPT

What's the best story in George's Plimpton's latest book, **"Shadow Box,"** in which the anthologist of pros tries to do for pugilism what **"Paper Lion"** did for professional football? For my taste it's a little episode that occurred during the late 1950's in the library of New York's Racquet Club, where the author, while timorously reading "The Art and Practice of English Boxing" in preparation for a three-round bout he had finagled with the then light-heavyweight champion, Archie Moore, comes upon an especially provocative passage describing the effects of a punch below the ear, knocks over his footrest with a crash and stirs the entire library into a gentlemanly pother. But this is fairly subtle stuff, dependent for its humor on the Plimptonian turn of phrase. Other readers may well prefer the many stories about Ernest Hemingway's competitiveness, or the chapter in which Mr. Plimpton invites his writer acquaintances to fantasize their own deaths, or Truman Capote's diabolic plan for revenge on Kenneth Tynan for attacking "In Cold Blood."

Did I say that **"Shadow Box"** is a book about fisticuffs? It is, it is. It begins with Mr. Plimpton's famous bout with Moore, from which we learn firsthand the rigors of prize-fighting, and how hard it is just to keep one's arms in the air for three minutes, let alone move about and punch and defend oneself. It goes on to explore some peculiar highlights in the history of boxing—about other contests between professionals and amateurs and other writers who've been drawn into the ring. Finally, it picks up the career of Cassius Clay/Muhammad Ali, and follows it closely from the first fight with Charles (Sonny) Liston, in which he first won the heavyweight championship, all the way through his dramatic victory in Kinshasa, Zaire, over George Foreman, in which Mr. Ali regained the championship after his suspension by the boxing establishment for refusing to be drafted.

Moreover, a fairly serious theme threads its way through Mr. Plimpton's serendipitous narrative. Like many people, he felt Mr. Ali's suspension had been unjust—that the boxing "commissions had no right to deprive the boxer of his means of making a living—any more than a plumber should be prohibited from keeping at his job if he refused induction." He had vaguely tried to do something about it—had joined an informal writer's committee, had begun a letter to his Senator, had even complained to Howard Cosell, who pronounced himself afraid of assassination should he take a stand on the matter. But nothing much came of Mr. Plimpton's sense of injustice, except Plimptonian wool-gathering about friends who had committed themselves on other ethical matters. So he felt guilty, which brought him closer to Mr. Ali and made it doubly satisfying to him when the fighter won back his championship with his fists. And it is this involvement with the champion's fortunes that permits Mr. Plimpton to write a vibrant first-person-singular account of an event in which he himself was not the prime participant. . . .

[The] detailed and affectionate portrait of Mr. Ali . . . is the best thing about this book—and not only of him but also of his opponents, his friends and his entourage. But the [other] stories make for a book that will appeal to a wider audience than one of boxing fans. They add up to a book for fans of human nuttiness.

> *Christopher Lehmann-Haupt, in a review of "Shadow Box," in* The New York Times, *November 16, 1977, p. C27.*

ELLEN WILSON FIELD

["**Fireworks: A History and Celebration**"] is a gorgeous book, with photographs of fireworks displays, factories and the like, as well as drawings and paintings (also in both black and white and color) of great displays of the past, the artists ranging from newspaper illustrators to Currier and Ives to Winslow Homer.

Those interested in the art of making and displaying fireworks, though, will rejoice in the text, for **"Fireworks"** is far from just a picturebook. Mr. Plimpton researches the history and development of fireworks, interviews professionals, recounts great triumphs and disasters, and provides a glossary of terms. The subject is dear to his heart, and such enthusiasm is infectious.

> *Ellen Wilson Field, "Books: Pyrotechnics and Potboilers," in* The Wall Street Journal, *August 28, 1984, p. 20.**

FRED FERRETTI

When we are children we know *absolutely* that when we grow up we will be firemen, test pilots, policemen, railroad engineers, tugboat captains, nurses and Presidents. Most times, *when* we grow up, most of us are none of these. Yet we have our dreams. Then there is George Plimpton, our perennial child, a fellow with an apparently limitless capacity for play-acting, an indefatigable joiner, who manages to sell video games, pitch major league baseball, quarterback major league football, sidestep charging rhinos, conduct orchestras, ignite firecrackers and in general act out his childish fancies, then write about them, sharing them with us.

In his newest book ["**Fireworks**"] Mr. Plimpton tells us gleefully not only that he helps create and set off "bombs", which is what fireworks people like the Gruccis, the Zambellis and the Rozzis call their rocketing creations, but that he helped orchestrate the Reagan-Bush fireworks at the last inauguration and arranged the explosion in Florida of Fat Man II—a 700-pound firework that was the largest ever, according to "The Guinness Book of World Records."

There is much in this handsomely illustrated book about the history of fireworks. . . .

Nor does the book lack for arcane trivia. . . . Princess Diana's wedding fireworks were a disappointment. But the largest set piece of fireworks ever built, at Britain's Crystal Palace in 1898, a tableau depicting the destruction of the Spanish fleet in Manila Bay earlier that same year, was not.

This is a disjointed book; it is jottings really, and occasionally Mr. Plimpton writes with more than a touch of archness. But you forgive all that, just to listen to the little boy tell us about his role in getting Fat Man II fused, lighted and skyward.

> *Fred Ferretti, "The Bombs Bursting in Air," in* The New York Times Book Review, *September 23, 1984, p. 13.*

Mario Puzo

1920-

American novelist, nonfiction writer, scriptwriter, short story writer, and critic.

Puzo is best known as the author of *The Godfather* (1969), an enormously popular saga about an Italian-American crime syndicate and its rise to power. In addition to setting new sales records, the novel is the basis for two Academy Award-winning films, *The Godfather* and *The Godfather, Part II*. In this novel, as in his other work, Puzo presents a vision of society in which violent crime is often considered a necessity for survival. Money—its acquisition and the influence, power, and prestige that it can buy—dominates Puzo's work. Other prevalent themes include revenge, endurance, loyalty, and the exploitation of the weak by the powerful.

Puzo's early novels, *The Dark Arena* (1955) and *The Fortunate Pilgrim* (1965), earned him critical praise but were virtually ignored by the general public. *The Dark Arena* centers on the emergence of the new German republic during the post-World War II years as seen through the eyes of a former American soldier. *The Fortunate Pilgrim*, set during the Depression, concerns the problems faced by an Italian immigrant family as they attempt to escape the poverty and crime of the Hell's Kitchen section of New York City. Critics praised the book for its vivid depiction of ethnic communities struggling for survival.

After the commercial failure of his first two novels, Puzo decided to try for best-selling success by including such elements as sex, drugs, and violence in his next book. *The Godfather*'s popularity is widely attributed to the sensationalistic way in which Puzo combines these components, yet the novel also generated substantial critical approval for its lucid realism and its strong characterizations. Although many critics complained that the novel glamorizes organized crime, Don Vito Corleone and his sons were nevertheless accepted by the public and became near-mythical figures in popular culture. Lawrence Jay Dessner suggests that Corleone's greatness lies in the fact that "he is [an] ideal executive, so high in the corporate structure that his success is not measured in dollars and cents. . . . The Don is an apotheosis of the Executive. He resembles the prophetic Spirit, Christ the Son, and as his title implies, God, the Father."

Following the success of *The Godfather*, Puzo continued his examination of the criminal underworld. *Fools Die* (1978), his long-awaited exposé of the gambling world and its capital, Las Vegas, explores the growth of legalized gambling and its influence on American economy and society. Most critics viewed the novel's protagonist, a popular novelist-turned-scriptwriter, as a thinly disguised portrait of Puzo and his desire to be regarded as a serious writer.

Puzo returned to the milieu of the Italian underworld with *The Sicilian* (1984), a fictional account of the life of Salvatore Giuliano, who was regarded as a folk hero by the peasants in Sicily even though he was responsible for more than two hundred murders and other crimes. The novel, which can be viewed as a sequel to *The Godfather*, centers on Michael Corleone's attempt to recruit Giuliano into the Corleone

family. *The Sicilian* helped regain critical favor for Puzo, who was praised for his ability to capture the turbulent society and political history of Sicily.

(See also *CLC*, Vols. 1, 2, 6; *Contemporary Authors*, Vols. 65-68; *Contemporary Authors New Revision Series*, Vol. 4; and *Dictionary of Literary Biography*, Vol. 6.)

SEAN CALLERY

Mario Puzo's second novel ["**The Fortunate Pilgrim**"] eminently justifies the decade of literary limbo since the publication of his critically acclaimed and nearly totally neglected "**The Dark Arena**." The author has chosen to portray, or perhaps it might be more accurate to say, recall, a species of family romance, and to give a fervent and candid account of a people: the South Italian immigrants and their children living in New York's Hell's Kitchen during the depression and in the early days of the Second World War.

Lucia Angeluzzi-Corbo is an old-country Italian mother who survives the violent deaths of two husbands and the estrangement of her children—an alienation almost absolute, although conventional family piety masks the bitter truth. Her most exceptional trait is her tenacity in retaining the moral outlook of generations of impoverished peasants, whose defenses against a most precarious existence were cunning and intransigence in the face of an unremittingly cruel social order. The American-born children are strangers—loving and hating their elders, to be sure—but cut off from their experience of the past. (pp. 362-63)

"**The Fortunate Pilgrim**" is ornamented by fascinating bits of the milieu executed by an artist whose intimate knowledge of these people is always evident. The minor characters include a welfare worker who cheats the authorities for his clients, and enriches himself in the process; a German baker who despises Italian-Americans and pays dearly for refusing tribute to self-appointed protectors; a young doctor whose professional status removes him from the ghetto but cannot expunge his own feelings of isolation.

At the end of her story, and indeed, the beginning of the end of the community, Lucia removes the remnants of her family to Long Island. . . .

Mr. Puzo's brilliant novel is reminiscent, in setting and to a lesser degree style and point of view, of the early Farrell and of Di Donato's "Christ In Concrete." The narrative manner is florid, even operatic; to this reviewer's taste exactly right and appropriate to reproduce an era and a people so recently with us and yet gone and almost entirely unsung. (p. 363)

> Sean Callery, in a review of "The Fortunate Pilgrim," in Commonweal, Vol. LXXXII, No. 11, June 4, 1965, pp. 362-63.

ROGER SALE

Most schlock fiction in the last decade or so has been voyeuristic—glimpses into Hollywood, rock musicians, the jet set, corrupt politicians, replete with drugs, kinky sex, casual violence. Mario Puzo's *The Godfather,* of which more copies than the Bible have been in print during the last five years, lets us peep at the Mafia, as good a subject as any for this kind of thing. Most people who read it agreed that while yes, it was awful, it made a decent deal with its reader because it offered glimpses of Mafia life that were convincing and maybe even authentic. At the outset of *Fools Die* one seems to be in for much of the same. The scene is Las Vegas, a world any voyeur might want to have a look at. . . . [This book] is scenario writing, leaving Puzo or someone else little to do when turning *Fools Die* into a screenplay.

It is good, too, to have the man who hits the twenty-four straight passes win over $400,000 in one night and then go upstairs and shoot himself—that is what one wants in schlock fiction. Intermittently thereafter Puzo comes back to Vegas and tells us about how a big gambling hotel is run, how scams are discovered, how you can identify the true from the phony hustlers. . . . [This is] Hemingway and the bulls all over again, in bloated and repetitive prose. And as we should expect, the sex that goes with it is wholly without sensuality. . . .

But Puzo doesn't stick with Vegas and hustling; indeed, he doesn't stick with anything very long. There are perhaps certain advantages in this looseness or aimlessness for the writer of schlock; he can throw in gaudy effects without having to do more than sketch a backdrop, snap a few pictures, and move on: there are some bits to do with a Norman Mailerish writer, a stint in Hollywood for the minor novelist hero so we can learn all over again how awful *that* is, a quick trip to Japan to hijack a million dollars worth of yen to Hong Kong, a hustler

from Tennessee who wants to get a young gospel singer castrated so his profitable voice will never change, etc. . . .

All this should help to identify the kind of book *Fools Die* is, the reason it seems a publishing event rather than a novel. But to identify it as such is also somewhat misleading, since *Fools Die* has serious intentions. One senses this first when, after the novel leaves Las Vegas, one realizes there is not going to be any plot. One then sees that the characters aren't so much stick figures as hopelessly unrealized "real" people that Puzo would like to make clear for us, but can't because he hasn't skill enough. After the Vegas episode comes a long section about the hero, John Merlyn, who thinks he's a magician, but he's really just a guy, a writer, except we never learn what he writes about. . . . Even when he goes to work for the Mailerish novelist (who also runs America's leading literary review) and then to Hollywood after his second novel becomes a best seller, Merlyn is continually grim, no fun to have around. One begins to suspect that this is something quite unexpected in schlock—an autobiographical novel.

I don't know whether anything that happens to John Merlyn actually happened to Mario Puzo, but that hardly matters. What gives the book its mealy shapelessness is, clearly, a serious impulse—otherwise the book would have been more shapely, the characters more clearly drawn, the dull point more pointed. (p. 32)

As I stumbled my way through *Fools Die* I kept asking myself who could possibly enjoy reading such gloomy trash. Of course it will be a hit, because of *The Godfather.* . . . Does Puzo himself think *Fools Die* is a good novel? Unlikely though that may seem, it is possible. Producing a publishing event, he also wants to write a novel; so he has grafted inarticulate bits of experience that sound autobiographical onto his voyeuristic effects. He even tells parts of the book in the first and parts in the third person so as to distinguish the schlock from the serious writing, though the divisions aren't quite that neat.

Merlyn himself suggests how all this may have happened. All the fools in the book die, but Merlyn goes on living, guilty for how little he cares about life, and for how little he can connect with it. It's easy to see what his wife means when she says she is happier when he is away much of the time. Is Merlyn a version of Mario Puzo, a morose man who became hugely successful with a best seller and who longs to join the human family by writing a real novel?. . . [*Fools Die*] is bad writing, but not of the usual trashy kind; Merlyn, and perhaps Puzo too, really wants to say how unhappy he is. But he can't, except in language as crude as this, so Puzo ends up with a real monster of a book to show he thus wanted and thus tried. (p. 33)

> Roger Sale, "Portrait of the Artist," in The New York Review of Books, Vol. XXV, No. 16, October 26, 1978, pp. 32-3.

PEARL K. BELL

Nothing succeeds like success, and on the strength of Puzo's phenomenal killing with *The Godfather* . . . the fountain seems unlikely to run dry. One doubts whether government regulations about consumer fraud apply to the "gentleman's trade" of publishing, but it must be time they did. Like some brands of radial tire, this book should be recalled. What buyers of *Fools Die* will discover before they've yawned through ten pages is the dismaying fact that it is no *Godfather*—not even a good-bad book but a slovenly dud. There is no plot, no action beyond an inexplicable suicide early on, which is, I think, meant to swell in deep symbolic resonance throughout the book. But what it symbolizes beyond Puzo's inability to figure out what it symbolizes remains an untantalizing mystery.

Fools Die opens in Las Vegas, and Puzo does write at length about gambling, but that is not what this novel is about. What stirs Mario Puzo the writer is not the luck of the draw but rage against the high-handed literary big shots who have denied him the stature of an artist. In an effort to settle the score with these emperors of sensibility, he draws up a list of the ten "most ridiculous" books ever written (Proust, all of Hardy, no surprises here), pelts the reader with pithy *aperçus* about the labor of literary creation . . . and grinds out the obligatory caricature of Norman Mailer. . . . Though he makes some half-hearted feints at probing "the evil that lurked in the heart of man," Puzo is mired in the frustration boiling away in the heart of the millionaire *shlockmeister* who yearns for the sweet cultural delights of serious critical attention.

Since even the author of *The Godfather* can scarcely be cynical enough to assume that millions of readers will uncomplainingly swallow a novel that is nothing but a long and boring howl against the "classy literary world," Puzo stops gnashing his teeth now and again to grind out the expected goodies about sex, Hollywood, and gambling in Las Vegas. . . . Nothing he writes about Hollywood could not just as easily be happening in Flatbush, give or take a swimming pool or two. Indeed, the book is such a disorderly grab bag of random anecdotes that practically any of these nuggets could be omitted without making a particle of difference.

The single exception to all this floundering is Puzo's familiar pop-novelist urge to teach us things we would otherwise not easily learn. Like his fellow *mavens,* Puzo believes that specialized information about the customs of an arcane country, preferably lurid—first the Mafia, now gambling in Las Vegas—is a negotiable substitute for talent and bestows an air of high seriousness on low-minded kitsch. Thus *The Godfather* was not only a riveting story but a guided tour through the Sicilian "families" gunning each other down for control of the rackets. The fact that Puzo had no first-hand knowledge of the bloody underworld he charted with such seeming authenticity, that it was by hearsay out of imagination and much of it probably spurious, is beside the point of such books. If it sounds right, it *is* right.

In *Fools Die* the expert informs us at length about the inner workings and devious mores of the garish Vegas oasis. Since Puzo is apparently a Las Vegas regular, this time the lecturer is not in the least dependent on invention, and he tells us a great deal, often in impenetrable argot, about baccarat, roulette, crap shooting, scamming, hookers, and the protocol of croupier behavior. Soon dispelled, however, are any Dostoevskyan parallels which the wealth of gambling lore and Puzo's effort to explore the psychology of a "degenerate gambler" may be meant to suggest, for despite all the information he generously deals out, he does not begin to confront Dostoevsky's real subject, which was not the game itself but the tormented soul of the gambler.

Except for these gobs of fact, *Fools Die* is a tedious fake. The calculus of Puzo and his publishers, therefore, may have gone something like this: if multitudes could gobble up *The Godfather* without a qualm about its sentimental pornography of violence, why should the public balk at simple dullness? Yet it is precisely the crashing bore that may turn away customers looking for escape and excitement, not moral niceties. . . . At this rate, there may be so many duds like Puzo's littering the counters that the secret will out—these novels do not entertain—and no one will want to buy them. Popular novelists would then once again be forced to do the job right, with some measure of the "sheer skill" Orwell admired, because the iron law of diminishing returns would make it harder for the likes of Mario Puzo to get away with a book more accurately titled *Fools Buy.* (pp. 72-3)

Pearl K. Bell, "Good-Bad and Bad-Bad," in Commentary, Vol. 66, No. 6, December, 1978, pp. 70-3.*

JOHN DRUSKA

I admire Mario Puzo's perceptions of ethnic life (see *The Fortunate Pilgrim* and *The Godfather Papers*); I sympathize with his poor boy's sense of the unprivileged writer's struggle in commercialized and stratified America. And his bravado in concocting *Fools Die*—the stunts he pulls to support a structure on the immense scale he's conceived—reveals at least shadows of a real novelist's daring. I understand Puzo more than I do some of the critics who've panned this book because of its trash appeal; I share his feelings that a lot of those who've been set up to pass judgment on writers, to enshrine art for us, have gotten to do so because their privilege affords them this privilege. They might rap *Fools Die* as a bad novel; I'm more concerned that it's bad Puzo. . . .

Puzo's role in compiling this package marks him a degenerate novelist akin to those Vegas rollers he portrays as "degenerate gamblers." To direct his picaresque actions toward some semblance of an ending Puzo resorts to the old Hollywood tricks (stolen from classical tragedy and diluted through melodrama) of entrapping most of his characters in their foibles and/or the accidents of fortune, and punishing their missteps with death. As he lets death, with gratuitous regularity, level his actors for him and punctuate his novel much as it does the TV news, Puzo levels the practice of his craft and art to arch craftiness. (p. 93)

Mario Puzo started his career trying to crash the top floors of literary fame; he seems stuck now going around in that old revolving door of success, which leads to literature's bargain basement. If his middle-classifying of the novelist's art has been admirable in light of his turning Wasp-spun American dreams to an ethnic-outcast's uses, his demoralizing performance of *his* art today is reprehensible to the extent that it claims more and more, through his perpetuation of American pulp. Puzo's talents and conscience, reducing a calculated poorboy's con to another establishment scam, equating him with his sold-out characters.

Puzo's alter ego Merlyn, one of the few surviving stars in *Fools Die*, talks superciliously about fools dying, though he gets hemmed in a little himself by death at the end. But if Puzo's sort of fools deserve to die, Puzo-Merlyn the novelist, ego-tripping along, has been writing a while already on borrowed time. (pp. 93-4)

John Druska, "Poor Boy Makes Bad," in Commonweal, Vol. CVI, No. 3, February 16, 1979, pp. 93-4.

ELIOT FREMONT-SMITH

I never read *The Godfather.* I missed it when it came out in 1969, and later I didn't want to spoil the movie. Others, obviously, accepted the risk; . . . *The Godfather* is reputed to be the bestest-selling fiction ever. I also missed Puzo's two earlier novels, which are said to have been "critically acclaimed" and are reissued from time to time. I did try to read his next novel, *Fools Die* . . . , but gave up when it became apparent that nothing of any interest whatsoever was going to happen. This is all right, no hard feelings on any side: Puzo is not the kind of writer one must stick with in case dullness is only feigned and a big surprise is coming. What is adumbrated is what you get.

Which brings me to *The Sicilian,* and a surprise. The adumbration itself is what you get. Puzo isn't an action writer, at least not here—he's a foreshadower. The action in *The Sicilian* is neither vivid nor building, as toward some point or crescendo. It is full of secret deals, betrayal, and mayhem, but the scenes themselves are fuzzy, brief, and anticlimactic—as though Puzo were no more interested in them than he is in character invention or development, leaving all that to the presumably forthcoming film.

Yet I finished *The Sicilian* . . . and did not feel cheated. Oh, a little bit, maybe. It took me a while to realize I didn't have to keep all the names straight—new ones are forever being introduced, but they are mostly interchangeable with the old—or retain a grip on each and every strand of the interlocking webs of deceit, since one strand or web is very much like another. And I fretted needlessly over such possible hidden subtleties as the difference between the Mafia and the "Friends of the Friends." (I now believe there isn't any.) Too late for me (but not for you), I realized that I could have read the whole thing in half the time, just concentrating on the odd-numbered pages (or the even, to suit the mood). But these are tiny carps and rues, and hardly affect the overall pleasure of the book—the pleasure of constant expectancy. Along, of course, entirely familiar terrain.

It's important that *The Sicilian* is an insert; otherwise it would be inert. Without the Corleone connection and all that evokes—the classic movie images, the throbbing *Godfather* theme tune—the novel would just lie there, listless and flat, lacking both point and dimension. It would be in fact what it merely pretends to be, a saga (or outline of same, with padding) of the rise and demise of a freelance bandit who is too beautiful and brave and strong and big for his britches in the mountains of western Sicily, 1943-50. Fortunately it is more: it is a detail in Michael Corleone's life.

I emphasize this because some readers may find the connection a trifle skimpy—Michael is prominent in the book only at the beginning and the end, and for long stretches seems entirely forgotten—and conclude that it's a crass commercial gimmick to boost *Sicilian* sales. They could be right, technically. But for me, Corleone detail—that is, adumbration—has to be the name of the Puzo game. It is at once enough and essential. . . .

There is also . . . a history of Sicilian oppression and of the Mafia from Spanish Inquisition times—how Mussolini almost wiped it out, how it revived with the American invasion of 1943 (some ironic high jinks here), how church and state and the Friends of the Friends operate together in a continuous ballet of favor, blackmail, and betrayal, and how manner (the way in which understandings are conveyed and received, from

accommodations to threats to murder) is all-important. Old stuff to a *Godfather* fan, but tingly still.

And there are many more deceptions and double crosses than suggested here—about 218, I would guess. Hardly anyone isn't in secret service to someone else, and hardly anyone doesn't commit the dread crime of breaking silence, *omerta,* or doesn't deserve or have cause for vendetta. Even the devoted professor Hector Adonis respects two masters, his godson Turi [the protagonist] and Don Croce. Nor can cousin Pisciotta be entirely trusted when the chips are down. And the people! So many people, new ones every minute, and often their families, too. . . .

All of which keeps Turi very busy; he does manage a glimpse or two of the Sicilian landscape, and a lover not his wife—but Puzo's heart isn't in these things. (A scene in which Michael is said to enjoy Turi's mother's squid and spaghetti is unintentionally funny.) Puzo's interest is in portents, the foreshadowing of horrid events sooner or later to happen. For suspense is not the aim, but tragedy, and it's through adumbration that the events of *The Sicilian* can stake a claim to tragedy. That's why there are so many portents and repetitive events (each little section seems almost a new beginning): if one doesn't work, another may.

Given the grubby subject matter, the endeavor is certainly ambitious, and that it works at all is amazing. Turi's heroics and vaunted idealism (near the finale, he even envisions being elected head of Sicily) are almost incidental, since character as opposed to stereotype is not Puzo's forte. Short and simple sentences, and a childlike storytelling tone (with an ambiguous irony stuck in here and there) matter more. And the theme music in my head.

Is *The Sicilian* tragic? No, not in its present form. Will it be a best-seller? Yes. Will the filmed Corleone saga be further augmented with this insert? Hope so. Sometimes pure exploitation becomes a legend most.

> *Eliot Fremont-Smith, "What Becomes a Legend Most," in* The Village Voice, *Vol. XXIX, No. 47, November 20, 1984, p. 45.*

CHRISTOPHER LEHMANN-HAUPT

It seems that in his novel **"The Godfather,"** Mario Puzo did not tell the whole story of Michael Corleone's two-year exile in Sicily. It seems that just as he was about to set sail from Palermo, he received new instructions from his father, Don Corleone. . . .

Michael's orders, it seems, were to rendezvous with a Sicilian bandit named Salvatore (Turi) Guiliano, and bring him back to America. This was not a simple assignment, for the people Michael had to deal with were extremely sinister, and the streets through which he walked had "thin snakelike alleyways" running off them "like venom." Indeed, it was such a tricky, dangerous job that it takes an entire novel to explain. Thus Mr. Puzo gives himself a reason to revisit the milieu of what has proved to be his most successful fiction to date. Thus he writes **"The Sicilian,"** or what might more aptly be designated "The Godfather, Part 1½."

In a way, this is good news. It gives Mr. Puzo another chance to do what he seems to do best, which is to spin a yarn of treachery, violence, sex, sadism, revenge and bloody justice. Michael Corleone is a mere onlooker here, a device to frame the story of another romanticized killer, a handsome thug who robs from the rich and gives to the poor and at the same time fights the leftward deviating tendencies of postwar Italian political elections.

The story of Turi Guiliano also affords Mr. Puzo the opportunity to explain the Mafia historically. He even gives us [an] etymology. . . .

At the same time, as if in response to those who thought he over-romanticized the Mafia in **"The Godfather,"** Mr. Puzo scourges "the 'Friends of the Friends,' as they were called here in Sicily." For Turi Guiliano is not only waging war with the Carabinieri, or the Italian National Police, he is also fighting Don Croce Malo, the hugely fat Capo di Capi of the "Friends of the Friends."

But it's also a little sad that Mr. Puzo has felt it necessary to return to his Italian gangsters. He has said several times over the years that when he wrote seriously in his first two novels, **"The Dark Arena"** and **"The Fortunate Pilgrim,"** nobody paid much attention. It was only when he indulged in the sex and violence of **"The Godfather"** that he got rich and famous. The autobiographical novel that followed **"The Godfather," "Fools Die,"** didn't work. So here he is indulging again, and though **"The Sicilian"** is fun and compelling, it seems like an admission of defeat in a way.

It also seems a little undernourished compared with **"The Godfather"**—its characters all younger, paler cousins. . . .

They seem especially pale when Michael Corleone is on stage and Pete Clemenza is in Sicily to arrange for Michael's return to the States. And they almost disappear before Don Corleone himself, who has the last word in **"The Sicilian."** "Now listen to me," he says to Michael. "A man's first duty is to keep himself alive. Then comes what everyone calls honor."

"Always remember," he says, to "live your life not to be a hero but to remain alive. With time, heroes seem a little foolish."

One can just picture Marlon Brando delivering those lines. And that's another problem with **"The Sicilian":** even the familiar characters seem pale compared with their movie counterparts. . . . I guess I missed the sound of the mandoline.

> *Christopher Lehmann-Haupt, in a review of "The Sicilian," in* The New York Times, *November 22, 1984, p. C19.*

ROSS THOMAS

By now, Mario Puzo's two principal fictional characters, Vito Corleone, the Godfather, and his son, Michael Corleone, the deputy Godfather, have achieved an almost mythic status. . . . [Two] much praised films have been based on [*The Godfather*], and there is even a prosperous chain of pizza parlors that carries the name. The Godfather indeed lives.

So what if you combined this particular myth with a couple of other favorites: Robin Hood, for instance, plus a heavy dash of Charlemagne's two favorite knights-errant—those precursors of male bonding, Roland and Oliver. Well, that's exactly what Puzo has done [in *The Sicilian*] and what results is a novel about the Godfather trying to rescue Robin Hood. (p. 1)

[*The Sicilian*] is primarily a novel about Sicily and the Sicilians and not about those kinsmen who emigrated to America where they organized crime. Puzo's Sicily is a harsh, violent, dreadfully impoverished land ruled by a hierarchy composed in almost equal parts of church and state, crooks and cops. Although

corruption is everywhere, his peasants are almost uniformly proud, relentlessly noble, and I haven't read such artfully stilted dialogue since Hemingway put Robert Jordan up in those Spanish mountains with Maria, Pablo, Pilar, El Viejo and that bunch.

It is quite possible that *The Sicilian* may appeal to two types of readers. The first are the romantics who like to think that somewhere there really may be a Robin Hood. The second type are the realists who long ago got fed up with Roland after he refused to blow that damned horn of his at Roncesvalles despite Oliver's eminently sensible pleadings.

But it is quite possible that *The Sicilian* will appeal to both types. I know that it appealed to me. (p. 13)

> *Ross Thomas, "Robin Hood Takes on the Mafia," in* Book World—The Washington Post, *November 25, 1984, pp. 1, 13.*

GAY TALESE

It is to Mr. Puzo's credit . . . that he has resisted the temptation to write a second **"Godfather"** [with **"The Sicilian."**] He has reduced Michael Corleone to a minor figure while concentrating instead on the personal character of Giuliano and the character of the island that led him—and so many Sicilians before and after him—into selecting a career in crime as the route to affluence and respect in a land ruled by people without a strong social conscience.

More than a **"Godfather"** sequel, Mr. Puzo's new book may be regarded as a 20th-century follow-up to the 19th-century portrait of Sicily that Giuseppe di Lampedusa presented so magnificently in **"The Leopard."** As **"The Leopard"** reflects the forlorn view of the aristocratic family of the Prince of Salina in the wake of the 1860 invasion by Garibaldi's red-shirted revolutionaries and rowdy opportunists, Mr. Puzo's novel shows Sicily in the midst of the World War II invasion by Allied troops. And Mr. Puzo's somewhat coarse literary tone and cynicism could well represent, through Giuliano, the voice of a frustrated grandson of one of the Prince of Salina's servants.

Both novels exude a love of Sicily while at the same time they evoke a spirit of despair: crumbling monuments, remnants of lost battles and an awareness that the island has been virtually indefensible since the invention of the ship. But the two novels also celebrate Sicilian individualism, the ability to shift and flow with the crosscurrents of the Mediterranean, to serve all masters but remain truly loyal only to one's self.

If Mr. Puzo carries this message to the extreme, it is because he has chosen an extremist as his central character. And yet most of his fictionalized account of Giuliano's life and death—excepting his transposition of the "i" and the "u" in his hero's surname—is in accord with the facts already published by historians and journalists of the postwar period. In fact, many of the people described in **"The Sicilian"** bear the real names of individuals who were once influential in Giuliano's life—not only members of his immediate family, but also the *carabinieri* colonel who organized the Italian Government's final assault against Giuliano, the police captain who was credited with riddling Giuliano's body with a Tommy gun, and Giuliano's most trusted adviser and cousin who, in the opinion of most historians of Sicily and Mr. Puzo as well, not only ultimately betrayed Giuliano but was his actual murderer and was himself later murdered in prison. (p. 43)

Perhaps only an American writer with deep Sicilian roots and passions could have succeeded as Mr. Puzo has in symbolizing a desperate society through the deeds of a desperado, and in revealing how thin is the line that often separates a freedom-fighter from a terrorist. In many ways, the criminal Salvatore Giuliano, and the liberator of Italy, Giuseppe Garibaldi, were motivated by the same dreams and drives. Both killed many men in the name of righteousness and justice as they saw it; and the bodies of Giuliano and Garibaldi each had been pierced by bullets directed at them by the highest authorities in Italy. But Garibaldi survived to become Italy's leading 19th-century patriot, while Giuliano died as a celebrated 20th-century Italian outlaw. Although Mr. Puzo's book never compares the two men, his novel does suggest that Giuliano was born at the wrong place at the wrong time, and that his limitations were shaped less by a warped character than by the irreducible confinements of his island. (p. 44)

> Gay Talese, *"In the Land of the Godfathers," in* The New York Times Book Review, *December 9, 1984, pp. 1, 43-4.*

ROBERT ROYAL

Generally speaking, the modern novel is not so much an art form as a predicament. When belief in man as the rational animal wavers, as it often does in modern fiction, one or the other of two extremes predominates: angelism . . . or bestialism. . . . The result is a loss of true imaginative power in spite of the emotional, intellectual, and literary force of a given work. We get many fictions that are, in a word, effete.

You could not apply that term to Mario Puzo's *The Sicilian*. Puzo's deliberately commercial success with the bestial in *The Godfather* may lead many readers to assume that his new novel merely continues in the same vein. They would be mistaken. There is no gratuitous sex or violence here. Puzo has returned to some of the richer human material that won him critical acclaim for his early novels. He loses little of his basic animal vigor in *The Sicilian*, but he uses it in the service of a wider vision than might be expected. (pp. 52-3)

Stripped to its bare essentials, Puzo's story reads much like many another adventure tale. In many respects it is. Puzo's art is a popular one with few literary pretenses. . . . But *The Sicilian*, besides being simply a darned good read for its action and intrigue, has far stronger characterization, deeper insight, and more simple zest than most adventure stories. (p. 53)

Puzo's value as a writer does not consist in verbal niceties, but in the vitality he is able to capture in every character and in his whole story. There are some people who will dismiss this novel as "macho" posturing. (Sicilian culture is not macho, but merely possessed of strongly defined familial and social roles.) The same people will probably profess admiration of African art for its primitiveness. *The Sicilian* is hardly sicklied o'er with the pale cast of thought, but neither is it seeking refuge from sterility in the dark gods of the blood. In it the animal and the rational still exist in some kind of vital balance—not a subtle or surprising world, but an essential point of reference nonetheless.

Hilaire Belloc once suggested that if you are looking for the opposite of sentimental, try Villon. If you are looking for a current opposite of effete, try Puzo. (p. 54)

> Robert Royal, *"Try Puzo," in* National Review, *Vol. XXXVII, No. 6, April 5, 1985, pp. 52-4.*

Adrienne (Cecile) Rich

1929-

American poet, essayist, and critic.

Rich writes poetry that documents the changing image of women in American society and charts her own personal growth as a woman and a poet. Her early work is characterized by its formal structure, quiet tone, and modest concerns; her reputation, however, rests on her later work, which is looser in form and is noted for its direct, passionate exploration of personal and political issues. Speaking mainly to and for women, Rich strives to create a "common language" among women and, as Alicia Ostriker notes, to "organize a collective, not an individual, escape, in which the traditional dualisms of Western philosophy and literature will be transcended." Rich's later works have created controversy as a result of her increased interest in political and feminist concerns. Some critics have accused her of reverting to stereotypes in her portrayal of the evils of a patriarchal, capitalistic society, and her polemical, didactic tone has been faulted for detracting from the artistic value of her work. Yet many applaud Rich's poetry, citing the power and passion of her commitment as central to the strength of her verse.

Rich's first book, *A Change of World* (1951), published when she was an undergraduate at Radcliffe University, was awarded the Yale Series of Younger Poets Award. In his introduction to the book, W. H. Auden praised Rich for displaying "a modesty not so common at that age, which disclaims any extraordinary vision, and a love for her medium, a determination to ensure that whatever she writes shall, at least, not be shoddily made." The poems in this collection, as well as those in Rich's second book, *The Diamond Cutters and Other Poems* (1955), are formally rhymed and metered and differ significantly from the rest of her work. *Snapshots of a Daughter-in-Law: Poems 1954-1962* (1963) first evidences Rich's emerging feminist consciousness. Subsequent volumes, including *Necessities of Life: Poems 1962-1965* (1966), *Leaflets: Poems 1965-1968* (1969), and *The Will to Change: Poems 1968-1970* (1971), further delineate her growing dissatisfaction with contemporary society and reflect her increasingly complex personal and political beliefs.

Rich received the National Book Award for *Diving into the Wreck: Poems 1971-1972* (1973). Using the metaphor of a diver examining the ruins of a sunken ship, Rich, according to Wendy Martin, "explores the disparity between her personal experience as an active, accomplished woman and the priorities of the larger society" by attempting to "return to her primal origins, to plunge into the depths of her psychic and cultural past." The feminist outlook that permeates *Diving into the Wreck* is further developed in *The Dream of a Common Language: Poems 1974-1977* (1978), *A Wild Patience Has Taken Me This Far: Poems 1978-1981* (1981), *Sources* (1983), and *The Fact of a Doorframe: Poems Selected and New 1950-1984* (1984). Central to these works is the importance Rich places on a historical perspective, both individually and collectively. *A Wild Patience Has Taken Me This Far* includes references to the achievements and hardships of such women as Emily Dickinson, Susan B. Anthony, and Ethel Rosenberg, as well as Rich's own grandmothers, and in the book-length poem in

Sources Rich looks even closer at her own past for insight and understanding of her evolving identity.

Rich has also published three works of prose: *Of Woman Born: Motherhood as Experience and Institution* (1976), *Women and Honor: Some Notes on Lying* (1977), and *On Lies, Secrets, and Silence: Selected Prose 1966-1978* (1979). Like her poetry, Rich's prose embodies her quest for personal understanding, for a vision with which to approach the future, and for the "common language" she hopes to establish among women. Her continual struggle to assert the validity of women's history and experiences has placed her in the forefront of feminist literature. Rich's clear language, vivid detail, and disciplined thought has generated much praise. Reviewing *The Fact of a Doorframe*, Helen Vendler observed: "Rich's great virtue is her long struggle for authenticity. It has been endangered by self-pity and by writing for a cause. . . . [But] she will be remembered in literary history as one of the first American women to claim a public voice in lyric."

(See also *CLC*, Vols. 3, 6, 7, 11, 18; *Contemporary Authors*, Vols. 9-12, rev. ed.; and *Dictionary of Literary Biography*, Vol. 5.)

W. H. AUDEN

[*The essay from which this excerpt is taken originally appeared in 1951 as an introduction to Rich's first book of poems,* A Change of World.]

Radical changes and significant novelty in artistic style can only occur when there has been a radical change in human sensibility to require them. The spectacular events of the present time must not blind us to the fact that we are living not at the beginning but in the middle of a historical epoch. . . . (p. 125)

So long as the way in which we regard the world and feel about our existence remains in all essentials the same as that of our predecessors we must follow in their tradition; it would be just as dishonest for us to pretend that their style is inadequate to our needs as it would have been for them to be content with the style of the Victorians.

Miss Rich, who is, I understand, twenty-one years old, displays [in *A Change of World*] a modesty not so common at that age, which disclaims any extraordinary vision, and a love for her medium, a determination to ensure that whatever she writes shall, at least, not be shoddily made. In a young poet, as T. S. Eliot has observed, the most promising sign is craftsmanship for it is evidence of a capacity for detachment from the self and its emotions without which no art is possible. Craftsmanship includes, of course, not only a talent for versification but also an ear and an intuitive grasp of much subtler and more difficult matters like proportion, consistency of diction and tone, and the matching of these with the subject at hand; Miss Rich's poems rarely fail on any of these counts.

They make no attempt to conceal their family tree: **"A Clock in the Square,"** for instance, is confessedly related to the poetry of Robert Frost, **"Design in Living Colors"** to the poetry of Yeats; but what they say is not a parrotlike imitation without understanding but the expression of a genuine personal experience.

The emotions which motivate them—the historical apprehension expressed in **"Storm Warnings,"** the conflict between faith and doubt expressed in **"For the Conjunction of Two Planets,"** the feeling of isolation expressed in **"By No Means Native"**—are not peculiar to Miss Rich but are among the typical experiences of our time; they are none the less for that uniquely felt by her. (p. 126)

[Poems] are analogous to persons; the poems a reader will encounter in this book are neatly and modestly dressed, speak quietly but do not mumble, respect their elders but are not cowed by them, and do not tell fibs: that, for a first volume, is a good deal. (pp. 126-27)

W. H. Auden, *"Foreword to 'A Change of World',"* in *"Adrienne Rich's Poetry" by Adrienne Rich: Texts of the Poems, The Poet on Her Work, Reviews and Criticism, edited by Barbara Charlesworth Gelpi and Albert Gelpi, W.W. Norton & Company, 1975, pp. 125-27.*

MARGARET ATWOOD

[*The essay from which this excerpt is taken originally appeared in* The Globe and Mail, *November 1976.*]

Adrienne Rich is not just one of America's best feminist poets or one of America's best woman poets, she is one of America's best poets. Her most exemplary poems are read not because they are supposed to be good for us, but because they are good, and in some cases (which is all any poet can ask for) they are

very good. This is not to deny the feminist content of her poems, or their sometimes overtly polemical intent. At her best, Rich pulls off what few poets with the courage of their convictions can ever manage: she is eloquent, she convinces and inspires. She is a serious writer and an important one, and her prose book on the institution of motherhood [*Of Woman Born: Motherhood as Experience and Institution*] is a serious and important book.

"Motherhood?" The very word evokes the trivial. "It's a motherhood issue," we say, meaning that no one could be against it. "American as Mom and apple pie," we say, meaning banal, but comforting, permanent, healthy, a *given*. But it's the unexamined assumptions behind phrases like this that Rich is writing about. Such assumptions, she says, are unwarranted; in fact, *all* assumptions about "motherhood" are unwarranted, because it is something we really know very little about. (pp. 254-55)

Rich is writing about pernicious myths. One of the most pernicious, of course, is that mothering is an instinct, that it simply wells up in all "real" women who give birth to children (and according to the same myth, a woman who does not give birth to children is not a "real" woman; she is a cipher). . . . The very suggestion that mothering is not an instinct opens up a number of worm-cans that not only most men but most women prefer to keep tightly closed. To question the institution at all— that set of beliefs which requires mothers to be at once both superhuman and sub-human—is to evoke the most primal and deeply threatening fears going around, fear of rejection by one's own mother. Yet, as Rich says, we all have mothers; every adult in this society was raised by a person who was expected to be a "mother," to take primary and largely single responsibility for her children, who felt thwarted by this and projected her resentment onto her children to a greater or lesser degree. Many did not choose motherhood; it was thrust upon them by a society unwilling to provide either contraception or recognized and dignified opportunities for any other occupation but "housewife." If we learn mothering from our mothers, would it not be better to replace the present institution with one with less built-in resentment?

This seems to me the question at the core of the book, though Rich touches ground elsewhere. There are interesting chapters on historical motherhood, bits of information on such diverse but pertinent subjects as the development of obstetrical forceps, the takeover of midwifery by male doctors, puerperal fever (often caused because the attending physician had come straight from the dissection of corpses without washing his hands), the rise of the factory system and its effects on home life, the segregation of women and children from fathers by the institutions of "work" and "the home." (pp. 255-56)

This is an important book, but it is not flawless. One could quibble about many points. Some will question the historical and anthropological material, others the theoretical underpinnings. Some are bound to find the book too harsh on men: if women are objecting to being lumped together as Woman, cannot men be given credit for their individualities too? Aren't there any *nice* men? Don't some men love their children, too? I myself would question the rather sensationalistic last chapter, which takes off from the case of a woman who chopped up her two youngest children on the front lawn of her suburban house and goes on to suggest that such emotions and such actions are possible for all mothers under "the system." (pp. 256-57)

This is a book that can be quarreled with, but it cannot be ignored, or dismissed because of this or that fine point, this or that emphasis. To write a flawless book on this subject would be impossible; to write a popular one would be equally impossible, because Rich is saying a number of things many would rather not hear. However, it was not Rich's intention to write a flawless book or a popular one; rather, she wished to open a dialogue, a dialogue which must be pursued. There is really nothing less at stake than the future of the human race. (p. 257)

> Margaret Atwood, "Adrienne Rich: 'Of Woman Born'," in her Second Words: Selected Critical Prose, Toronto: House of Anansi Press, 1982, pp. 254-58.

LINDA W. WAGNER

[*The essay from which this excerpt is taken originally appeared in* The South Carolina Review *in 1978.*]

Adrienne Rich's most recent poems are interesting because they differ in several important ways from her work during the 1960s. . . . The concerns in [*A Change of World*] and the following *The Diamond Cutters* were often mythic, the themes and personae of the poems as clearly defined as their shapes. But even in Rich's *Snapshots of a Daughter-in-Law* (1963), her themes are often literary: "**Euryclea's Tale**," "**Antinous: The Diaries**," "**A Knight**," excerpts from "**The World Book, 1927**." Those that are not obviously derivative are somewhat hesitant in their personal identification as if, new to the business of organic form, Rich is also new to a more intimate relation between poet and persona. (pp. 224-25)

The poems in *Snapshots of a Daughter-in-Law* include some social satire, some philosophy, and some slight movement beyond those themes, as in "**The Roofwalker**," a poem dedicated to [Denise] Levertov which contains the strong lines, "A life I didn't choose / chose me" (even though the poem has a male persona). Such masking is also evident in the title poem, where Rich touches the beginning of feelings—"nothing hurts her anymore"—but then slides behind masks suggested by her use of lines from Dickinson, Baudelaire, Diderot, Mary Wollstonecraft, Simone de Beauvoir quoting Sophie Volland, and others.

Although the sequence poem "**Snapshots of a Daughter-in-Law**" is probably central to many of Rich's later poems in that it does recognize the problems of growing up female, and especially female artist, in America, it is a laboring version of what will appear twelve years later in the fully realized poem "**From an Old House in America**." . . . In easy rhythm, Rich traces lines of suicide, child-bearing, execution, and deprivation, one current of history of "an American woman." . . . Yet the tone of even the bleakest recounting is calm, sure; it seldom becomes artificial. . . . (pp. 225-26)

The strength apparent in Rich's controlled expression of some of the deepest themes of a woman's life is reflected also in "**The Fact of a Doorframe**," a 1974 poem about poetry. . . . Here, poetry has become a source of nourishment, an ancient talisman, no longer a literary artifact.

This sense of art as integral to life, basic and sustaining for life, seems new to Rich, one gift of the whole opening, changing process which her personae and her poems seem to have undergone. . . . As Rich explains . . . ,

> Today, I have to say that what I know I know through making poems. . . . the poem itself en-

genders new sensations, new awareness in me as it progresses. Without for one moment turning my back on conscious choice and selection, I have been increasingly willing to let the unconscious offer its materials, to listen to more than the one voice of a single idea. Perhaps a simple way of putting it would be to say that instead of poems *about* experiences I am getting poems that *are* experiences, that contribute to my knowledge and my emotional life even while they reflect and assimilate it.

(pp. 226-28)

Besides this shift in Rich's personal concept of the role of the poet, other changes in her poems from the sixties to the present are also apparent. She now seldom uses a mythic persona. The meanings of the poems are now expressed more directly (fewer poems depend on a prefatory epigram, for example), and those meanings are likely to be broader in application than those of any of the earlier poems, now that the "absolutist approach" has melted into the process of discovery. The sharp specificity of *Snapshots of a Daughter-in-Law* has given way to the announced generality of *Necessities of Life* and *The Will to Change*. "**November 1968**," the opening poem of the latter collection, presented the poet as "stripped," "beginning to float free," and yet being forced to question in a kind of mock surprise, "How you broke open, what sheathed you." . . . In "**From a Survivor**," a 1972 poem, the process of the opening of the persona's consciousness is described as "not a leap / but a succession of brief, amazing movements / / each one making possible the next."

Although Rich's feminine readers felt that she was speaking expressly for them, one interesting point about these poems of the late sixties and early seventies is that more often than not, the personae are either undetermined or masculine. The paradox of the strongest so-called feminist poetry is precisely that, it seems: that in their desire to create liberating experiences for women, feminine writers have also heightened their perception of the problems all human beings face. The best poems of feminism become poems of "community." Or, as Rich defined the "political" impulse in "**The Blue Ghazals**":

> The moment when a feeling enters the body
> is political. The touch is political.

By seeing *political* as a physical encounter and not an intellectual one, Rich attributes some of our strongest feelings to emotions rather than reason: in that attribution she may be feminine, but not in the range of her applicability. (pp. 229-30)

> Linda W. Wagner, "Levertov and Rich: The Later Poems," in her American Modern: Essays in Fiction and Poetry, Kennikat Press, 1980, pp. 221-30.*

SARA MANDELBAUM

For nearly a decade, Adrienne Rich's poetry has been rooted in a passionate belief in "thc will to change" and in a need to imagine "what *can* be." In *A Wild Patience Has Taken Me This Far*, she has not abandoned this aesthetic, but she does seem to have taken pause and given herself over to that "severer listening" she once described. Although her work has always been imbued with a keen sense and appreciation of history (if also a certain mistrust of it), these new poems are united in a fierce, exacting determination to pursue memory in order to "ease the hold of the past / upon the rest of my life / and ease my hold upon the past."

Disdainful of the nostalgia that she feels has gripped the peculiarly ahistorical moment in which we live ("Nostalgia," she writes, "is only amnesia turned around"), Rich beckons past ghosts as well as still-living family members to prod her memory and haunt her imagination. Susan B. Anthony, Jane Addams, Willa Cather, Emily Dickinson, Ethel Rosenberg, her grandmothers, her father, her mother-in-law, and sister are among those she summons—both to allow them to speak as they themselves would be heard, and to address them herself. In one of the strongest poems, **"The Spirit of Place"** (dedicated to her lover/companion Michelle Cliff), there is a section in which the poet attempts in a final address to rescue the memory of Emily Dickinson, whose life has been so oversimplified and trivialized by the "experts." Rich writes with affection:

> with the hands of a daughter I would
>   cover you
> from all intrusion even my own . . .
>
> with the hands of a sister I would leave
>   your hands
> open or closed as they prefer to lie . . .
>
> with the hands of a mother I would close
>   the door
> on the rooms you've left behind
> and silently pick up my fallen work
>
> (p. 21)

The familiar themes persist in this new volume: the omnipresent threat of "male dominion"; colonization and rape of the land, which she understands anew through the lens of Native American history and the southwestern landscape; the intellectual/activist mission that a woman has to embrace the complexity of experience, "needing to know better than the poem she reads / knowing through the poem . . ."; the conviction that the truth of women's lives not be obliterated yet again, as when she writes of the "matrices we weave / web upon web, delicate rafters / flung in audacity to the prairie skies / nets of telepathy contrived / to outlast the iron road . . ."; and of course, the daily, ordinary heroism of women everywhere.

Her journey into the past does not leave Rich's poetry unaltered. She has become, I think, less sanguine about the mind's freedom to choose unfettered from "the hawk wind / poised to kill" (in the poem, **"What Is Possible"**), and less likely to advocate change purely for its own sake. The radicalism of her vision, however, remains strong and invigorating; the writing as lyrical, polemical, and moving as ever—and even more honest. In addition, Rich leaves us with what few other living poets are able to offer their readers: the images with which to build a strategy for survival. (p. 22)

> *Sara Mandelbaum, in a review of "A Wild Patience Has Taken Me This Far," in* Ms., *Vol. X, No. 6, December, 1981, pp. 21-2.*

KATHRYN KILGORE

[Adrienne Rich's *A Wild Patience Has Taken Me This Far*] is a ritual of man-hatred. . . . She believes in sides: *"With whom do you believe your lot is cast?"* On the wrong side is "instantaneous violence ambush male." Since Rich is capable of writing phenomenal poetry, it's disappointing when she doesn't. Her new work is jumpy, confused, and murky, as though written in code for a few friends. As Rich becomes more political,

more the poet speaking for women—especially lesbians—she grows overly polemical. Women don't need more rhetoric, especially from a poet who is capable of the complex thoughts and images, insights and depths seen in Rich's earlier work. Worse, the rhetoric is sloppy—a statement like "I can never romanticize language again" is soon followed by the highly romantic: "If you can read and understand this poem / send something back: a burning strand of hair / a still-warm, still-liquid drop of blood," or ". . . you standing by the caldron's glare / rendering grammar by the heat / of your womanly wrath."
A Wild Patience Has Taken Me This Far is a feminist vision; there are love poems to women, and poems to friends, eulogies to early suffragists, pastiches of women's journals and letters, poems to Rich's grandmother and mother-in-law. The book revolves around history and its distortions; it touches on what it means to grow old, to study the detached objects of dead cultures, to learn to become empty of chattering preconceptions, to see nature. Rich sees herself as divided between "Anger and tenderness: my selves." Her former aim of becoming a camera "To record / in order to see" has been modified to serving as glasses for the near-sighted: the past, although full of failure, is still with us; Rich wants to enlighten those who don't see it, who aren't angry.

She examines the stereotyped roles our culture holds for women, and says "This is the war of images." . . . But her own images sound like limp Eliot, and her exaggerated nonstop anger almost turns poetry into parody. . . . (pp. 20, 30)

In the service of her politics, she is pointlessly rhetorical . . . as well as manipulative. Describing the arrest and beating of a young woman, Rich insists she was there, but that the scene was silent, like an early film, and she was "just beyond the frame." She puts herself in this powerless, irresponsible position, then assumes she can arouse our anger against the white male police without us noticing who is behind this scene, who controls the silence.

Many of these new poems come from that point slightly "beyond the frame," with Rich looking on, looking back, attributing to other women specific emotions of her own, her particular perspective, her simplified, purified life. She usually chooses to write about exceptional women and romanticize their strength. Because she uses anger to the point of obliterating it, her attempts to build on its intensity can fall flat; she states we should honor our foremothers "with grief with fury with action," but what does the word action mean alone, or the abstractions grief and fury? They evoke no emotion. Rich has drifted away from the details of "the thing itself." . . .

Still, Rich does have moments of examining complexity. She says, in **"The Spirit of the Place,"** "force nothing, be unforced / accept no giant miracles of growth / by counterfeit light." And in a poem for Ethel Rosenberg, she admits that "if I dare imagine her surviving / . . . I must allow her to be at last / political in her ways not in mine / . . . defining revolution as she defines it / or, bored to the marrow of her bones / with 'politics.'" It's a relief when she remembers these possibilities. It's unwise to shrink and knot up history, then recut it to fit in our pockets. If we are really doomed to repeat ourselves, I'd send Rich back to look at the wreck. (p. 30)

> *Kathryn Kilgore, "Rituals of Self-Hatred, Arts of Survival," in* VLS, *No. 3, December, 1981, pp. 20, 30.**

LE ANNE SCHREIBER

In 1951, W. H. Auden introduced Adrienne Rich's first volume of poetry by praising it for poems that "are neatly and modestly dressed, speak quietly but do not mumble, respect their elders but are not cowed by them, and do not tell fibs'' [see excerpt above]. Thirty years later, Adrienne Rich still does not tell fibs, but that's about the only phrase that can be salvaged from Auden's once apt description. Miss Rich has long since proclaimed herself her own authority, and sometimes even takes on the role of elder stateswoman. She has written through youth, fame, marriage, motherhood, separation, solitude, political rage, feminist awakening and lesbianism. In its broad outlines, if not in its particulars, her progress through the decades has paralleled that of her generation of women; of the major poets among them, she is the one who has survived to tell the tale.

In **"Diving into the Wreck"** (1973), her voice was that of a solitary woman taking inventory of her wounds. In **"The Dream of a Common Language"** (1978), she was healing, scarred but still whole, ready to celebrate the possibility of a new beginning. Now, at age 52, the poet seems ready to imagine herself entering history, and therefore ready to embrace as her flesh and blood those who already have.

Many of the poems in **"A Wild Patience Has Taken Me This Far"** have their source in the letters, journals and diaries of earlier generations of American women. Women whose memories we have twice abused, first by long neglect, more recently by turning them into icons, unblemished and unreal. Miss Rich, who herself knows something of what it is to be treated like an icon, is now intent upon restoring these women to their particularity. . . .

Several of the longer poems in this volume are conjuring acts in which the poet resurrects women like Elizabeth Cady Stanton, Susan B. Anthony, Jane Addams, Emily Dickinson. . . . Setting up a kind of dialogue between her own poetry and quoted excerpts of their writing, she explores the limits of her empathy, knowing that where her identification with them ends, their particularity begins. . . .

"A Wild Patience" also contains more directly personal poems, about the poet trying to come to terms with increasing physical disability, about trying to find a way to talk to her mother-in-law, about trying to salvage something from the wreck of a love affair that went down in bitterness. With few exceptions, these are not poems of experience tamed, solutions grasped; rather they reach toward the edge of some possibility for a larger, truer, more humanly satisfying reckoning with things. They're the kind of poems that keep you up late at night and then enter your dreams.

In recent years, Miss Rich's candor has made it easy for those who are so inclined to label her. Feminist. Lesbian. And, of course, polemical, which is often used as a euphemism for the first two labels. But it would be a shame to cordon her off. Because she is a poet trying to see deeply, think clearly and speak plainly about our lives—our past, our prospects. As a self-consciously American poet, Adrienne Rich is—cannot help but be—a daughter of Emerson and Whitman. Like them, she is half-crazy with dreams of Self-Reliance, Transcendence and Democracy. It's just that she doesn't want to be the daughter of a culturally broken home. And so, belatedly, she is unearthing foremothers, revising history to suit her needs, turning Elizabeth Cady Stanton into not an icon but a poet. Taking her 19th-century words and putting them into brand-new verse.

Whitman's barbaric yawp was for us all. So is Adrienne Rich's common language.

Le Anne Schreiber, in a review of "A Wild Patience Has Taken Me This Far," in The New York Times, *December 9, 1981, p. 22.*

HELEN VENDLER

One longs, reading [Adrienne] Rich's *A Wild Patience Has Taken Me This Far,* for the poem to take an unexpected byway, to reverse itself, to mock itself, to question its own premises, to allow itself, in short, some aesthetic independence. In Rich, the moral will is given a dominating role that squeezes the lifeblood out of the imagination. . . . The moral will is deplorably given to stereotypes. So Rich's mother-in-law appears as the stereotype of the discontented idle older woman who lives "on placebos / or Valium," and who appears incapable of understanding her son's strange and restless wife, whom she addresses in placating clichés:

> A cut lemon scours the smell of
> fish away
> You'll feel better when the children
> are in school

One might see these sentences as symbolic gestures of understanding, mutely, if awkwardly, helpful; but they do not satisfy Rich, who has an unholy desire to say the baldly exposed things she finds truer than deflected symbolic interchange:

> Your son is dead
> ten years. I am a lesbian,
> my children are themselves.
> Mother-in-law, before we part
> shall we try again? Strange as I
> am,
> strange as you are?

Though this seems even-handed (in the admission that they both are strange) the only true even-handedness, the only true imaginative play, would be for Rich to stop setting her own terms for family intercourse. She writes the script for what she wishes her mother-in-law would say to her (instead of the present vague "Tell me something"). . . . But these casual, and even prying, questions ("Is there anyone special?") are not the common coin of our mothers' more formal era; why should older women have to come into our own far too intrusive "confessional" mode? (pp. 32-3)

I take up this instance only to raise the question of Rich's inflexibility of stance. Elsewhere in these new poems we meet, as before, the innocent victimized woman, the brutal sadistic cop: "he pushes her into the car / banging her head . . . he twists the flesh of her thigh / with his nails / . . . he sprays her / in her eyes with Mace / . . . she is charged / with trespass assault and battery." And, as if to affix a stamp of authenticity, "This is Boston 1979," says the poem—as if the only attestation to the genuineness of art is a newspaper dateline.

This sort of propaganda poetry generates a counterproductive aesthetic result: the reader, comically enough, becomes an instant partisan of policemen and mothers-in-law. It is for the sake of Rich's own good intentions—to show the gulf between women of different generations, to protest the helplessness of the wrongly arrested citizen—that I wish she would consider more closely her aesthetic means. Stereotypes (the uncomprehending mother-in-law, the vicious cop) not only exist, but exist in sufficient numbers to have given rise to the stereotype; but they have no more place in art in their crude state than the grasping Jew or the drunken Irishman. . . . [The] dialectic of mutual violence (criminals to police, police to criminals—a system in which the brutalized police brutalize the innocent along with the guilty) is less present in Rich than it would be in a writer of more comprehensive imagination. In the sentimental black-and-white terms of these poems, men are exploiters, women helpless pawns who never chose their role:

> . . . when did we ever choose
> to see our bodies strung
> in bondage and crucifixion across
> the exhausted air
> when did we choose
> to be lynched on the queasy elec-
> tric signs
> of midtown when did we choose
> to become the masturbator's
> fix

This, from the title poem, begs many questions of biology, history, economics, and social change. But even if we assume that evolutionary roles (and women's complicity in them) could be changed overnight, this passage assumes that in the present women no longer (by seeing themselves as bargainers with sex) have any complicity in how men see them; and it equally assumes that men are always the victimizers, never the victimized. Later in the poem Rich has a chance to reflect on Christ as victim, male though he was; but she chooses to think only of his mother in her iconic form as Pietà. There follows an unrelenting indictment of form in art as a mystification of violence. If, Rich argues, a Pietà (or a Passion) has been rendered beautiful, art has performed a disservice; a disguise has been imposed, by a pattern "powerful and pure," on the reality of blood and sacrifice. . . . (pp. 33-4)

There is, as anyone can see, something wrong with this argument. In her first book, Rich had, rather wrong-headedly, praised Bach for his austerity, asserting that "a too-compassionate art is half an art." Now the argument claims that a too-beautiful art is half an art. This position would admit as proper art only the tortured and twisted crucifixions of the more gruesome Spanish masters, not the hieratic crucifixions of, say, the Byzantine tradition. The adamantly realist aesthetic of the on-the-spot news photo ("This is Boston 1979"; "This is Judea 33 AD") leaves out a great deal (chiefly the mediation of reflective thought) in its fascination with transcription *tout court*.

The dangers of unmediated transcription are accompanied, in this volume, by the dangers of self-dramatization. To call a poem "**Integrity**," to begin it with the theatrical sentence "A wild patience has taken me this far," to add that the "anger and tenderness" breathing in oneself are "angels, not polarities"—this is to make oneself one's own heroine. There are dangers in the melodramatic enshrining of one's own capacities. . . . In a moment of distraction, Rich misreads a title, THE HISTORY OF WOMAN SUFFRAGE, as THE HISTORY OF HUMAN SUFFERING, and ratifies her mistake:

> OF HUMAN SUFFERING: borne,
> tended, soothed, cauterized,
> stanched, cleansed, absorbed, en-
> dured
> by women

The last line is incomplete: it should read "by women and men"—otherwise it is a lie. Whitman tending the Civil War dead; Keats tending his dying brother; Arthur Severn tending the dying Keats; these and all their innumerable male counterparts rise to refute the sort of history Rich here retells. Truth

has its claims. And though Rich adapts Whitman's line, "I am the man, I suffer'd, I was there," to her own "I say I am there," her great predecessor said it of the sufferings of men and women alike, of runaway slaves, of the old and of children, of the ill and the deformed. It is hard to believe in an empathy reserved for one segment of humanity alone.

Rich's form in this volume is essentially the form of realist oratory. She presses points, she pursues an argument, she cites instances, and she pitches her voice above the conversational or narrative level—not always, but more often than not. Conscience, as she says, hurls questions at her; she hurls, in her turn, accusations at society. Her fierce Utopian desires are at their best when most unsettled, as in [her 1969 poem, "**Orion**."] (p. 34)

The line-form Rich uses in most of the new poems derives more from the older English alliterative line with a heavy pause in the middle than from the old seamless Norman pentameter. Rich's lines usually stop somewhere in the middle, halt, add a thought, pause at the end of the line, and take up the skein of thought anew as the line turns around. This halting progress suggests, interestingly enough, an intellectual process rather different from the one which produces Rich's intransigent diction and social cartoons; it may win out in the long run over more programmatic agitations. There are many more poems here than I can mention; all of them (and I do not except the poems putatively about "other people") strenuously pursue what it is to be Adrienne Rich in middle age—her investigations, her commitments, her memories, her outrage. I wish these poems were not so exclusively bound to that single realist vision. (p. 35)

> *Helen Vendler, "All Too Real," in* The New York Review of Books, *Vol. XXVIII, No. 20, December 17, 1981, pp. 32-6.**

MARJORIE PERLOFF

Two paradoxes have, in recent years, dogged the poetic footsteps of Adrienne Rich. . . . The desire to write a poetry that denies the mediation of language, the power of words to disguise and to transform experience, seems to go counter to the very need for poetry in the first place, a need that Rich herself expressed quite differently a decade ago:

> For a poem to coalesce . . . there has to be an imaginative transformation of reality which is in no way passive. And a certain freedom of the mind is needed . . . if the imagination is to transcend and transform experience it has to question, to challenge, to conceive of alternatives, perhaps to the very life you are living at that moment. You have to be free to play around with the notion that day might be night, love might be hate: nothing can be too sacred for the imagination to turn into its opposite or to call experimentally by another name. For writing is re-naming.

What inhibits this "free play" of the mind, this capacity to "conceive of alternatives," is, so Rich argued in 1971, the conventional role in which woman is cast. . . . But now, ten years later, that very imaginative transformation of reality which allows one to conceive of "the notion that day might be night, love might be hate," is repudiated in favor of what the poet construes as that which is "true for us." And what is "true for us'' turns out to be, predictably enough, the commonplaces of male oppression and female victimization. . . . (pp. 130-31)

Images of victimized women, from Emily Dickinson (**"The Spirit of Place"**) to the unnamed black student sadistically bullied and jailed by white policemen (**"Frame"**), haunt Rich's new book [*A Wild Patience Has Taken Me This Far*]. One could argue, in defense of such polemical and didactic poetry, that, at this particular moment in our history, what is needed is not the negative capability, the free play of the mind Rich formerly spoke of as a good denied to women by their secondary status, but a straightforward, readily comprehensible call to action. Curiously, however, that call to action is undermined—and this is the second paradox I mentioned above—by Rich's conservative rhetoric, a rhetoric indistinguishable from that of the Male Oppressor. It is as if Rich, the radical lesbian poet, cannot shed the habit, learned by the time she was 21, a Radcliffe graduate and the winner of the Yale Younger Poets Award for *A Change of World,* of having to write a poetry that would win the approval of the judges. Like Sylvia Plath, but unlike, say, Emily Dickinson or Gertrude Stein or Mina Loy or H. D., Rich has always produced work well within the parameters of the Establishment press. . . . Indeed, when we probe the imagery, the syntax, and verse forms of *A Wild Patience Has Taken Me This Far,* we find that the spirit presiding over the collection is less that of Emily Dickinson than of Robert Lowell. (pp. 131-32)

What does it mean to be so receptive to the style of a male poet who, from Rich's point of view, must surely be considered something of an enemy, the prodigal husband and demanding poet-lover, alternately needing his women and renouncing them in what Rich calls "the old way of marriage"? This is a question feminist critics have not sufficiently posed, as if subject matter were all. It is an especially important question in Rich's case for Lowell is by no means the only male presence in *A Wild Patience.* For one thing, her verse forms pay a curious homage to the male tradition: **"Heroines,"** for example, is written in the staggered tercet or three-step line first used by William Carlos Williams in the poems of his last decade. For another, certain poems read like updated versions of the English Classics. In **"What Is Possible,"** for instance, the poet's contemplation of "the clear night in which two planets / seem to clasp each other" recalls "Dover Beach." . . . (p. 135)

How does it happen that a poet as committed to radical feminism as is Adrienne Rich should cast her poems, perhaps quite unwittingly, in the very masculine modes she professes to scorn? Perhaps the problem is that Rich is so anxious to *teach* and to *persuade* that she tends to forget that form is itself a political statement. . . . The confessional-realistic mode that Rich has adopted demands, I think, a willingness to put oneself on the line, to expose one's own follies and errors, one's conflicting desires, as Lowell does in his best work. But Rich's polemicism, coupled with what is evidently a natural reticence precludes such self-exposure: she regularly positions herself *outside* experience, whether her own or that of other women; she is daughter, sister, daughter-in-law, lover, victim, but never quite the daughter of X or the lover of Y. Similarly, her characters remain abstractions—''heroines'' like Susan B. Anthony or Mary Colter; pathetic victims like her mother-in-law, who is presented as the stereotypical nagging housewife. . . . That this mother-in-law might have her own strengths and gifts is not considered a possible option, and one wonders whatever happened to Rich's earlier belief that the poetic imagination must "conceive of alternatives, perhaps to the very life you

are living at that moment." Alternatives are now subordinated to *the* Alternative, the Cause. The poet gives way to the teacher-scholar. . . . Rich, as anyone who has read her prose knows, is a powerful thinker, a brilliant intellectual. Her current impasse as a poet is that she has not yet found a form, a language that might be equal to her hard-won insights. (p. 136)

Marjorie Perloff, ''Private Lives/Public Images,'' in Michigan Quarterly Review, *Vol. XXII, No. 1, Winter, 1983, pp. 130-42.**

ADRIENNE RICH

Because of the attitudes surrounding me, the aesthetic ideology with which I grew up, I came into my twenties believing in poetry, in all art, as the expression of a higher world-view. . . . But my personal world-view at sixteen, as at twenty-six, was itself being created by political conditions. I was not a man; I was white in a white-supremacist society; I was being educated from the perspective of a particular class; my father was an ''assimilated'' Jew in an anti-Semitic world, my mother a white southern Protestant; there were particular historical currents on which my consciousness would come together, piece by piece. My personal world-view was shaped in part by the poetry I had read, a poetry written almost entirely by white Anglo-Saxon men—a few women, Celts and Frenchmen notwithstanding. Thus, no poetry in the Spanish language, or from Africa, or China, or the Middle East. My personal world-view, which like so many young people I carried as a conviction of my own uniqueness, was not original with me, but was, rather, my untutored and half-conscious rendering of the facts of blood and bread, the social and political forces of my time and place. (pp. 524-25)

I could hazard the guess that all the most impassioned, seductive arguments against the artist's involvement in politics can be found in Yeats. It was this dialogue between art and politics, that excited me in his work, along with the sound of his language—never his elaborate mythological systems. I know I learned two things from his poetry, and those two things were at war with each other. One was that poetry can be about, can root itself, in politics. Even if it is a defense of privilege, even if it deplores rebellion and revolution, it can and may have to account for itself politically, consciously situate itself amid political conditions, without sacrificing intensity of language. The other: that politics leads only to ''bitterness'' and ''abstractness'' of mind, makes women shrill and hysterical, and is finally a waste of beauty and talent: ''Too long a sacrifice / can make a stone of the heart.'' There was absolutely nothing in the literary canon I knew to counter the second idea. Elizabeth Barrett Browning's anti-slavery and feminist poetry, H. D.'s anti-war and woman-identified poetry, like the radical, yes, revolutionary work of Langston Hughes and Muriel Rukeyser, were still buried by the academic literary canon. But the first idea was extremely important to me: a poet—one who was, as it were, certified—could actually write about political themes. . . . (p. 527)

But there were many voices then, as there are now, warning the North American artist against ''mixing politics with art.'' I have been trying to retrace, to delineate, these arguments, which carry no weight for me now because I recognize them as the political declarations of privilege. There is the falsely mystical view of art, that assumes a kind of supernatural inspiration, a possession by universal forces unrelated to questions of power and privilege or the artist's relation to bread and blood. In this view, the channel of art can only become clogged and misdirected by the artist's concern with merely temporary and local disturbances. . . . This view of literature has dominated literary criticism in England and America for nearly a century. In the fifties and early sixties there was much shaking of heads if an artist was found "meddling in politics"; art was mystical and universal but the artist was also, apparently, irresponsible and emotional, and politically naive. (p. 531)

[We] are told that political poetry, for example, is doomed to grind down into mere rhetoric and jargon, to become one-dimensional, simplistic, vituperative; that in writing "protest literature"—that is, writing from a perspective which may not be male, or white, or heterosexual, or middle-class, we sacrifice the universal; that in writing of injustice we are limiting our scope, "grinding a political axe." So political poetry is suspected of immense subversive power, yet accused of being, by definition, bad writing, impotent, lacking in breadth. No wonder if the North American poet finds herself, or himself, slightly crazed by the double messages. (p. 532)

In my own case, as soon as I published—in 1963—[*Snapshots of a Daughter-in-Law: Poems 1954-1962*], a book of poems which was informed by any conscious sexual politics, I was told, in print, that this work was "bitter," "personal"; and that I had sacrificed the sweetly flowing measures of my earlier books for a ragged line and a coarsened voice. It took me a long time not to hear those voices internally whenever I picked up my pen. But I was writing at the beginning of a decade of political revolt and hope and activism. The conditions for becoming a consciously, self-affirming political poet were there, as they had not been when I had begun to publish a decade earlier. . . . Even before I named myself a feminist, or a lesbian, I felt impelled to bring together, in my understanding and in my poems, the political world "out there"—the world of children dynamited or napalmed, of the urban ghetto and militarist violence, and the supposedly private, lyrical world of sex and of male/female relationships. (pp. 533-34)

By the end of the 1960's an autonomous movement of women was gathering, and declaring that "the personal is political." That statement was necessary because, in other political movements of that decade, the power relation of men to women, the question of women's roles and men's roles, had been dismissed—often contemptuously—as the sphere of personal life. Sex itself was not seen as political, except for interracial sex. Women were now talking about domination, not just in terms of economic exploitation, militarism, colonialism, imperialism, but within the family, in marriage, in childrearing, in the heterosexual act itself. Breaking the mental barrier that separated private from public life felt in itself like an enormous surge toward liberation. For a woman thus engaged, every aspect of her life was on the line. We began naming and acting on issues we had been told were trivial, unworthy of mention: rape by husbands or lovers; the boss' hand groping the employee's breast; the woman beaten in her home with no place to go; the woman sterilized when she sought an abortion; the lesbian penalized for her private life by loss of her child, her lease, her job. We pointed out that women's unpaid work in the home is central to every economy, capitalist or socialist. And in the cross-over between personal and political, we were also pushing at the limits of experience reflected in literature, certainly in poetry.

To write directly and overtly as a woman, out of a woman's body and experience, to take women's existence seriously as theme and source for art, was something I had been hungering

to do, needing to do, all my writing life. It placed me nakedly face-to-face with both terror and anger; it did indeed *imply the breakdown of the world as I had always known it, the end of safety,* to paraphrase [James Baldwin]. . . . But it released tremendous energy in me, as in so many other women, to have that way of writing affirmed and validated in a growing political community. I felt for the first time the closing of the gap between poet and woman. (pp. 535-36)

> *Adrienne Rich, "Blood, Bread and Poetry: The Location of the Poet," in* The Massachusetts Review, *Vol. XXIV, No. 3, Autumn, 1983, pp. 521-40.*

SUSAN SHERMAN

Adrienne Rich's *Sources* is a book of names and naming. More precisely, it is a book of renaming, rediscovery, recognition. Adrienne Rich is a poet who believes in intrinsic meaning and believes in the possibility of change. The word "sources" in the title does not mean "beginnings" alone. It is the original Greek word *arche:* origin as sustaining force. Understanding, for Rich, is more than a one-directional movement into the future, it is also simultaneously a movement into the past. Understanding is not based in imitation of the changing forms of objects, but rather in the unchanging but chaotic, nameless, sources that sustain us. . . . In order to advance, Rich must not only return, she must re-define, re-find herself. To William Carlos Williams' "no poems but in things," Rich adds, no poem without the question that motivates the poem, that focuses the poet, that brings the poem into being. And for Adrienne Rich, the defining questions are: "With whom do you believe your lot is cast? / From where does your strength come?" . . .

Sources is a difficult poem. Looking into it deeply is like looking into a maze of mirrors, it is endless. And because of a depth which can be overlooked in its forcefulness, it can be deceptive. Beneath the obvious examination of identity (in this particular poem Rich's Jewish identity) lies the question of survival, the accompanying question of the price of survival, and beneath that the question of identity again—not as fact, but process. (p. 3)

It is interesting to compare this poem to an earlier one, **"Abnegation,"** which appears in *Poems: Selected and New, 1950-1974. Sources* begins sixteen years later. "The narrow, rough-gullied backroads almost the same." But something has drastically changed since the earlier poem. The red fox, the vixen of **"Abnegation"** is now long dead. The earlier symbol of survival is now an "omen" but no longer "sister"—at least not in the sense of the earlier poem—because the symbol of vixen, survivor without past, without history, with only instinct as root, is no longer enough. In the intervening sixteen years, Adrienne Rich has found a history, an identity, a name with which she can live—"woman"—and *grow.* The "immaculate present" no longer suffices, just as in 1983 the word "woman" itself is no longer enough. Just as the name "Jewish," when she comes to it, and I don't believe she actually comes to it herself in this particular poem, will not finally be enough. Because for Adrienne Rich, as for anyone actively involved in the process of change, "there is no finite knowing, no such rest. Innocent birds, deserts, morning-glories, point to choices, leading away from the familiar."

Sources is not a book of poetry in the usual sense—a collection of individual poems. It is one long poem of twenty-three parts. But it is, in a very real way, a compilation—an anthology of ideas and feelings, suggestions, questions, hints. It would be an act of violence to overanalyze a poem in critical form which is in itself an analysis in poetic form—a form most aptly chosen because the experiences related in *Sources,* the theme of *arche* itself cannot be torn from the strength of the language, the images of specific places and people that populate the poem. This is a beautifully written work, moving from poetic image to philosophical statement fluently and powerfully. It would be an act of violence to demand of this poem what it is not and, conversely, not to recognize it for what it is. (pp. 3-4)

Sources is a poem which has moved me, angered me, inspired me, thrown me back upon myself in a very special way. Ironically, it is its incompleteness that is one of its greatest strengths. It is a poem whose source is the heart of a woman who refuses to stay put, who is motivated by the necessity to change a world that is so full of oppression, of suffering. . . . It is a poem that, finally, rather than tracing a source *becomes* a source in itself. There are a hundred future poems in this one poem. A hundred new choices. The naming has only begun. (p. 4)

Susan Sherman, "Rich Roots, New Routes," in The Women's Review of Books, Vol. I, No. 3, December, 1983, pp. 3-4.

ALICIA OSTRIKER

[*The essay from which this excerpt is taken was originally published in a slightly different form in* The American Poetry Review, *July-August 1979.*]

Adrienne Rich is a poet of ideas.

In most poetic circles, it is unfashionable to espouse ideas—except, of course, for ideas about technique. (p. 102)

[Rich's poems] depend on the assumption that the writer's mind exists to embody the implicit meaning of a culture at a moment in time, the place history has marched to, intelligence at its keenest pitch; and to bring the reader there. They declare a state of awakened consciousness—the poet's—and claim that the present actual consciousness of the writer, and the latent consciousness of the reader, are identical.

Whitman asks us to think that we are innocent and great. Baudelaire asks us to think that we are guilty and wearily disgusted. Rich asks us to think that we need to give birth to ourselves. (p. 103)

The poet springs from the soil of Modernism. Her youthful writing in *A Change of World* (1951) and *The Diamond Cutters* (1955) reflects the ranking styles in postwar literary academe. From Frost and Auden in particular she inherits craftsmanly formalism, an analytical rather than emotional treatment of material, and a resigned sense of life as a diminished thing. (p. 104)

Failures of language, standing for failures of love, appear at key points in these first two volumes. Superficially, the young poet's handling of this theme seems conventional enough. . . . Rich has "the unsaid word" of a wife in loyal stasis while her husband ranges. There are uncommunicating parental figures in **"The Middle-Aged."** A woman who "thought that life was different than it is" goes down to old age mildly, unprotesting. **"Living in Sin,"** a poem of Lowellian distaste for shabby reality, depicts the tainting of romance by common grime; but the heroine says nothing.

Some of these poems tremble on the brink of indignation. They seem about to state explicitly the pattern they all share, of a connection between feminine subordination in male-dominated middle-class relationships, and emotionally lethal inarticulateness for both sexes. But the poetry in these two books is minor because it is polite. It illustrates symptoms but does not probe causes. There is no disputing the ideas of the predecessors, and Adrienne Rich at this point is a cautious good poet in the sense of being a good girl, a quality noted with approval by her early reviewers. (pp. 104-05)

Snapshots of a Daughter-in-Law (1963) [is] Rich's breakthrough volume.

The title poem of *Snapshots* was the first Rich wrote openly as "a female poet" although she had not found "the courage . . . to use the pronoun 'I'—the woman in the poem is always 'she.'" The young woman speaker sees all women as "pinned down by love," and thinks she is going mad. But her real subject is the woman of intellect. . . . "A thinking woman sleeps with monsters," Rich discovers. "The beak that grips her, she becomes." The culture of the past is a predator to a woman; an intellectual woman who absorbs it becomes her own enemy. Thus for the first time in this poem, Rich challenges the language of the past, quoting Cicero, Horace, Campion, Diderot, Johnson, Shakespeare—as the flattering, insulting, condescending enemies of women's intellect. . . . "Snapshots" consists of fragmentary and odd-shaped sections instead of stanzas, and has the immediacy and force Rich did not attempt earlier. (pp. 106-07)

After *Snapshots,* nothing inhibits Rich's intensity or integrity. The feeling of something inexplicably wrong has been transformed into cries that the house is on fire, and the mind of the poet is ablaze. . . . *Necessities of Life* (1966) concerns the necessity of personal withdrawal and reconstruction: "I used myself, let nothing use me," as a prerequisite for life in the world. . . . *Leaflets* (1969) and *The Will to Change* (1971) extend the field of struggle and intensify the sense of crisis. Confronting not only Vietnam but the barricades of class, race, sex, youth versus age, activist versus theorist, Rich cannot accept either a public or a private life not motivated by the will to change oneself, to change others, to change the world. . . . The tempo of the work speeds to reflect the speeding mind. Divesting herself of traditional formalities, the poet lets herself think in (apparently) disconnected streaks. "The notes for the poem are the only poem," she says. "The moment of change is the only poem." There are gestures in the direction of hope. . . . A few pieces—**"Women," "The Observer," "Planetarium"**—suggest strength through some connection between woman and the world of nature. But mostly the will is paralyzed by the monstrosity of evil it faces. Nothing seems alterable except by violence. (pp. 108-09)

By *Diving Into the Wreck* (1973), Rich's ideas have become systematically feminist, and she is assuming an influential position in an intellectual movement. . . . The constellation of institutions which comprise patriarchy is held responsible for all imperialisms, political and psychic. Our civilization's religion, philosophy, history, law and literature rest on the subordination of women and of the female principle in men, and our civilization is therefore finished:

> The tragedy of sex
> lies around us, a woodlot
> the axes are sharpened for.
> The old shelters and huts . . .

scenes of masturbation
and dirty jokes.
A man's world. But finished.
They themselves have sold it to the machines. . . .

The "compromised" woman who continues to live in this society finds herself envying

the freedom of the wholly mad
to smear & play with their madness
write with her fingers dipped in it. . . . . . .

She nevertheless continues to take the risk and suffer the pain of self-knowledge. . . . She identifies with other women and attempts to understand their common history in order to organize a collective, not an individual, escape, in which the traditional dualisms of Western philosophy and literature will be transcended. (pp. 109-11)

The poet thinks in images, and Rich's gift for vivid and energetic imagery has been one of her chief strengths since the beginning. Her range includes astronomy, modern technology, natural history, movies . . . , historical records, as well as the contemporary urban scene and domestic setting. She uses dream and fantasy images extensively. Her primary subject is herself battling "the beak that grips her," which is the male culture's denial of her identity, and her language functions at a level where her life and the lives of others evidently coincide. (p. 111)

Throughout the period subsequent to *Snapshots,* Rich questions the idea of language and the value of poetry, exemplifying the conflicts "a thinking woman," whose tools are words, undergoes when she wants expression of personal truth and communication of realities hitherto unrecognized. (p. 112)

What Rich does with this problem comes in three stages, corresponding to her phases of self-reconstruction, political engagement, and feminism. In the first two, I think she hits dead ends. In the last, she begins to discover an alternative. . . . In *Leaflets* and *The Will to Change,* the poet reenters the world with the desire to use language for healing, but is repeatedly defeated. **"Images for Godard"** sees "language as city" surrounded by shockproof suburbs and squatters awaiting eviction—a place out of touch with reality. **"A Valediction Forbidding Mourning"** has "my swirling wants. Your frozen lips. / The grammar turned and attacked me." **"The Burning Paper Instead of Children"** juxtaposes the idea of book-burning by two schoolboys, which has shocked a liberal neighbor, against the literal burning of Jeanne d'Arc and the napalming of Vietnam. . . . Attacking not only the formal language of the past but that of the present—however well intentioned—Rich prefers a child's semiliterate composition on poverty, or Artaud's *burn the texts.* "This is the oppressor's language / yet I need it to talk to you. . . . I cannot touch you and this is the oppressor's language," she concludes in desperation. Two years later, in the title poem of *Diving into the Wreck,* a new possibility opens. There is a breakthrough comparable to that of **"Snapshots."**

The poet in **"Diving"** reads but cannot use "the book of myths" in which "our names do not appear." She seeks "the thing itself and not the myth," which sounds like an extension of the anti-intellectualism of the *Leaflets* and *Will to Change* period. But this is a different sort of poem from anything earlier. For one thing, it is narrative. The poet does not remain trapped in stasis and analysis, helplessly acted upon. She makes a

move; she acts. For another, her language is revisionist. Out of the past, she invents an altered symbolism. (pp. 112-13)

If the source of an oppressor's language is a set of false perceptions of reality, it is necessary to begin at the beginning. The poem suggests a place, a scene, where our iron distinctions between perceiver and perceived, subject and object, he and she, I and you, dissolve. There it leaves us. (p. 114)

Why, in Rich's writing, does one find so little joy, so little sense of the power of joy? Why does the work come from a sense of unrelieved crisis in which nothing can be celebrated, nothing savored? Rich is not, one feels, a poet to whom love—untheoretical, undoctrinal love—comes easily, either toward herself or toward others. . . . She does not construct desirable fantasies. There is suffering, and then there is more suffering, with "no imagination to forestall woe," almost as if suffering itself were a value. . . . [But] Rich's readers need to know about the female equivalent of the burning bush, the voice of the covenant, the promised land. They need to know about the goddess. Lacking the imagination's projection of a world without victims, a self unvictimized, unmastered, complete—and it is for the poets to give us this, to articulate the delight that is *there,* latently, as much as women's despair is *there*—lacking this, the will to change is helplessly fettered.

A more dismaying aspect of Rich's work to me is her partisanship. Explicitly or implicitly, since *Snapshots,* Rich's position has depended on the idea of an enemy. Her "I" affirms by excluding, her communal "we" implies a hostile "they." Of course "we" know who "they" are. For a period after *Snapshots* the poet uses male figures sympathetically; there are poems of kindness and hopefulness addressed to her husband; there is Orion, her brother-double; there are friend/lover figures in *Leaflets,* and the male artists Chekhov, Ghalib, Rodin, Berrigan, Artaud, Godard in *Leaflets* and *The Will to Change.* In *Diving* the poet defines herself as the androgyne, the being who is at once female and male. But men in this volume are depicted universally and exclusively as parasitic on women, emotionally threatened by them, brutal—the cop is identified with the rapist—and undeserving of pity. "His" mind is a nightmare of possessiveness, conquest, and misogyny. (pp. 116-17)

I hope not to oversimplify this issue. Women's anger is real, and it is legitimate. We see it surfacing everywhere in women's writing, the best and the worst (I suppose it is missing only from the mediocre), like a scream from a mouth that has just been ungagged. This anger needs acknowledgment. Unacknowledged, it poisons and cripples. But when an angry woman implies that she fantasizes punishing her enemy purely for his own good, she begins to resemble the officer who said he burned the village to save it. (p. 118)

These elements in Rich's work dismay me, I must add, for several reasons. First, Rich is the strongest woman poet in the country, and a major influence. If she is in error, her influence serves error. Second, whatever distresses me in Rich—the joylessness, the self-pity, the self-righteousness, exists also within myself and within others. She is a mirror in which multitudes are seen as one. Third, she may not be in error. If this is the case, we are emerging from the tangled growths of the past, only to enter a desert which appears to stretch indefinitely before us, arid and stony, and none of us will see the end of it in our lifetimes.

The Dream of a Common Language at last gives us Rich as visionary. "Dream" implies this. "Language" means not only words, poetry—several of the poems are about "a whole new poetry''—but any form of communication, including the touch of bodies, and including silence. It means the ability ''to name the world'' essential for gaining strength in the world; and ''the drive / to connect,'' through symbols and in actuality, with each other, the world, and ourselves. ''Common'' language means a faith that attempts to communicate can succeed, that we can connect, not as privileged persons or under special circumstances, but in ordinary dailiness.

The core of the book is its exploration of loving woman-to-woman relationships. Rich speaks of mothers and daughters, literal and figurative sisters, cohorts in poetry, lovers, ancestresses. (pp. 119-20)

As a flute song of personal meditation, **"Sibling Mysteries"** is hauntingly lovely. As a myth of female sexuality, it is too narrow. Yes, women's initial erotic experiences are maternal-infantile. So are men's. Yes, perhaps mature sexuality attempts to recover and replay the blissful mother-child union. Perhaps all adult tenderness, all affection, finds its source and models itself on those memories. This idea could explain a great deal about human romance—not confined to love between women. For some women, the stereotypic dominant-father/subordinate-mother family pattern does not apply. For some, the physicality of our mothers never stopped being available. And for some, heterosexual experience has never meant terror or resignation. . . . (p. 121)

Three other poems in **Dream** excite my skepticism. The opening pieces on Marie Curie and Elvira Shatayev appear to romanticize feminine martyrdom; the latter is an all-female *liebestod.* Where is the portrait of a woman whose power kills neither others nor herself? **"Hunger"** seems marred by a naive belief that women's love, ''hosed'' on the world, would eliminate its literal and figurative famines. Those who believe in infallible feminine virtue may recall the comparable virtue of the American Worker in the 1930s.

These are comparatively tangential matters, not vitiating this volume's courageous spirit, its transformations, the beauty of its poetry. The force of love, negligible in her earlier books, here brings Rich a resolution to trust, to move from victimization toward responsibility and choice, and to reject (not withstanding the aura of the first two poems) martyrdom. . . . (pp. 121-22)

The most important poems break new ground metaphorically. **"Origins and History of Consciousness,"** opening in the poet's crisis-haunted room, moves to a dream of walking into water:

> My bare feet are numbed already by the snow
> but the water
> is mild, I sink and float
> like a warm, amphibious animal
> that has broken the net, has run
> through fields of snow leaving no print;
> this water washes off the scent—
> *you are clear now*
> *of the hunter, the trapper*
> *the wardens of the mind—*

This of course recalls **"Diving Into the Wreck,"** but the speaker of **"Diving"** needed props—rubber suit, knife, camera, book of myths, schooner, ladder—which this speaker, entering her animal nature, can discard. . . . Moreover, where **"Diving"** closes under water, **"Origins and History of Consciousness"** resurfaces. It returns from dream to reality. The pond in woods becomes the city of muggers. But the poet recapitulates her

decision of risked love as a descent ''in a darkness / which I remember as drenched with light,'' and resolves to move outward. The poem ends with a sense of introducing Eros into Civilization.

"Natural Resources," another poem of transformations, revives and synthesizes two metaphors from **Snapshots:** the aerial cargo of the new woman, and the ''abandoned mineshaft of doubt'' in **"Double Monologue."** (pp. 122-23)

The technique employed in these two poems is a kind of overlay of transparencies. Present and past, reality and imagination, the life of the self and the lives of other selves, the spatially enclosed and the spatially unenclosed, are held in a tenuous, luminous balance. . . . A philosophically developed feminism may mean an alternative idea of time and change, neither linear as in Hebrew tradition, cyclic as in classical philosophy, or juxtaposed against eternity as in Christianity. There is a flexing of the mind here, and no sense of an enemy. I am filled with curiosity to see more of what Rich can do along these lines, confident that whatever comes next will be an advance. What does not change is the pressure of Adrienne Rich's intelligence. . . . (p. 124)

> *Alicia Ostriker, "Her Cargo: Adrienne Rich and the Common Language," in her* Writing Like a Woman, *The University of Michigan Press, 1983, pp. 102-25.*

HOLLY PRADO

[In **Sources**] Rich moves her personal search for identity back to her own family and also to wider American roots, seeing all outsiders as part of this country and seeing the need to reconcile the roots with the present. Her language, as always, is clean—a fine balance of restraint and urgency. The book is too short, though, for such a depth of ''sources.'' This may be a beginning for Rich, a mature poet who can now continue her personal search but can also define for us a broadly human life. . . .

Some poets surrender to chaos; many see a way through it. This art which is ''so out-of-it, it's ridiculous'' still can leap and sing—and perhaps catch someone's ear who didn't intend to listen.

> *Holly Prado, in a review of "Sources," in* Los Angeles Times Book Review, *March 25, 1984, p. 9.*

WENDY MARTIN

In 1951, Rich graduated Phi Beta Kappa from Radcliffe and published her first volume of poems *A Change of World.* . . . (p. 174)

In 1955, two years after she was married, Rich gave birth to her first son, David, and published *The Diamond Cutters and Other Poems,* which received the Ridgely Torrence Memorial Award of the Poetry Society of America. . . . [As with *A Change of World*], Rich was commended for her graceful, feminine style, her poetic decorum, and her skill in the use of metrics, scansion, and rhyme. . . .

As a young poet, wife, and mother, Rich struggled to balance her domestic and aesthetic efforts. In contrast to her later work, her early volumes, *A Change of World* and *The Diamond Cutters,* are written from the perspective of a woman who tries to conform to the demands of a traditional society and whose power is measured by her ability to attract and please men. . . . (p. 176)

Snapshots of a Daughter-in-Law, published in 1963, records [Rich's] resentment and dismay about the disparity between her aspirations as an accomplished poet and the traditional social values. Rich's contemporaries, Sylvia Plath and Anne Sexton, also experienced considerable anxiety and distress due to their conflicting roles as women and as serious artists, but unlike Rich neither evolved an analytic approach that enabled them to understand the sociocultural roots of their guilt and despair. Rich's references in *Snapshots* to Mary Wollstone-craft, Simone de Beauvoir, and other autonomous women indicate that she was already working within a feminist framework that enabled her to recognize and reject self-destructive emotional responses. (p. 179)

Although more vigorous language and personal rhythms replace the careful formalism of her earlier poems, "Snapshots" is less forceful than Rich's later work. . . . *Snapshots* marks the beginning of a personal and political pilgrimage; subsequent works describe the stages of the journey. . . . (p. 181)

In *Necessities of Life: Poems, 1962-65,* which was published in 1966 and was nominated for the National Book Award, Rich pursues her exploration of the relationships between personal identity and the cultural context. In this collection, Rich articulates her emerging awareness that individual experience cannot be arbitrarily separated from its historic context, and there is a growing conviction that the tension she experiences between her personal values and larger social forms embodies the cultural schism between mind and body, nature and civilization, oppressor and oppressed, which she feels is the basis for patriarchal order. (p. 184)

[During her] years of teaching [from 1966 to 1973] in such diverse institutions as Swarthmore and City College, Rich became active in the protest against the Vietnam War; *Leaflets: Poems, 1965-68* reflects her growing awareness of the profound connection between private and public life. With her increased participation in institutional life and her growing visibility as a poet, Rich attained an identity that is dramatically different from that of [Anne] Bradstreet or [Emily] Dickinson. Unlike her predecessors, she has evolved a sense that she can not only shape the circumstances of her own life but that she can function as a spokeswoman for those people whose lives have not often been recorded in literature. In this regard, her prospects are more like Whitman's than Dickinson's.

In *Leaflets,* Rich writes of her desire to create public forms that are capable of meeting private needs, and she rejects traditional masculine aesthetics, which arbitrarily separates art and life. Asserting that poetry and politics are intertwined—that poetry has the power to transform lives—Rich writes, "I want to choose words that even you / would have to be changed by." Having decided that she cannot merely escape into apolitical aestheticism, she calls for a reintegration of the personal and the political in order to create new forms of civilization. (p. 185)

The poems in *The Will to Change: Poems, 1968-70,* which received the Shelley Memorial Award of the Poetry Society of America, chronicle Rich's increasing rage at the waste of human energies, especially those of women in patriarchal society, and continue to explore women's efforts to define their own reality. This volume also reflects Rich's decision to change her personal life. In 1970, she left her marriage. . . . (p. 187)

Adrienne Rich's effort to achieve a new understanding of her personal and political needs is perhaps best expressed in *Diving into the Wreck: Poems, 1971-72,* which was published in 1973. This volume won the National Book Award in 1974 and has been praised by Helen Vendler for its "courage in the refusal to write in forms felt to be outgrown" [see *CLC,* Vol. 7]. In this volume, Rich explores the disparity between her personal experience as an active, accomplished woman and the priorities of the larger society. (p. 188)

In contrast with *Snapshots of a Daughter-in-Law,* published a decade earlier, *Diving into the Wreck* represents a major shift in attitude. During the interval between the publication of the two volumes, Rich's poetry became less ironic and instead concentrated on emotional awareness and forceful self-presentation. *Snapshots of a Daughter-in-Law* is written from the perspective of an outsider—a daughter-in-law—who observes but does not affect the world around her. The voice in the poems of *Diving into the Wreck* is strong and resolute. . . . This volume expresses the concerns of the increasingly visible feminist movement of the 1970s. (pp. 196-97)

Poems: Selected and New, published in 1975, includes a sixteen-part poem, "**From an Old House in America**" (1974), in which a country house provides a metaphor for the lives of the women who lived in it. . . . [The] major events of the lives of these women occurred at home; their existence was shaped by the social and economic paradigm of differentiated spheres of female domesticity and of male commerce. The poem attempts to recapitulate the complex and varied history of American women with a montage of voices from the past that recalls the women who first came to America across the Bering Strait, and then with the Puritans. . . . (p. 199)

"**From an Old House in America**" blends a variety of styles, from portraiture ("in my decent collar, in the daguerreotype") to historical commentary ("I am an American woman / I turn that over") to fragments of monologue (*"I will live for others, asking nothing / I will ask nothing, ever, for myself"*). The poem combines direct, even blunt, lines (*"will you punish me for history* / he said / *what will you undertake* / she said") with highly lyrical phrases. . . . Moving back and forth between past and present, [this poem attempts] . . . to bridge the gaps between lucidity and darkness, isolation and community, suffering and reparation, primal power and its terrors. This excavation of prehistory is a process that parallels the function of consciousness-raising on a personal level. Just as the release of repressed memories increases the self-awareness of individual women, so the unearthing of ancient cultural forms opens up new social possibilities. This revisioning of the chthonic past, American history, and feminist ideals signals a change of emotional and poetic center for Adrienne Rich.

Since the publication of *Diving into the Wreck,* Rich has increasingly devoted her energy to recording women's history and to understanding the ancient and contemporary forms of female relationships. In *Of Woman Born: Motherhood as Experience and Institution* (1976), an extended analysis of the ways in which patriarchal institutions deny women control over their bodies and their lives, Rich searches the past for historical clues that can help women envisage a viable future. Attempting to recover the lost history of women, Rich examines the mythic and anthropological prehistory of motherhood in Western culture, the modern domination of the birth process by male physicians, the psychological roots of "matrophobia," and the nature of the mother-daughter bond—issues that were especially important to American feminists in the 1970s.

Throughout *Of Woman Born,* Rich cites specific incidents from her life to illustrate her analysis. Candid comments about her complicated feelings toward her own mother and her children, as well as astute historical analysis, are interspersed with quotes from her diaries and journals.... By including observations from her personal experience, Rich achieves an unusual blend of subjective insight and objective analysis, undercutting male genre hierarchies that accord more importance to the philosophical treatise than the diary. This combination of private and public discourse in order to eliminate arbitrary stylistic categories parallels her refusal to accept the transitional distinction between politics and poetry. (pp. 200-02)

As in *Of Woman Born,* Adrienne Rich's subsequent volumes of poetry, *The Dream of a Common Language* and *A Wild Patience Has Taken Me This Far,* attempt to reverse the classification of women and nature with the lower orders of being. *The Dream of a Common Language* is divided into three sections, each having a different emphasis: the poems in the first group, "Power," are concerned with the outstanding achievements of individual women; the second group, "Twenty-One Love Poems," is a lyrical testimony of female eros and the shared lives of women; the third group, "Not Somewhere Else, But Here," explores the effects of the past on the present, analyzing natural, social, and personal history in order to discover its implications for contemporary women's lives.

The Dream of a Common Language articulates Rich's belief in the need for a community of women based on shared values and goals. **"Origins and History of Consciousness,"** written over a two-year period from 1972 to 1974, excavates the experience of the modern woman who is no longer bound by the narrow emotional range of socially defined female self-images. Having won her freedom from *"the hunter, / the trapper / the wardens of the mind,"* Rich has decided that survival in an alien society is not enough. Insisting on the need for communication as the basis of companionship and of community, she declares, "No one sleeps in this room without / the dream of a common language." ... (p. 207)

Both *The Dream of a Common Language* and *Of Woman Born* are concerned with the suffering of women separated from community, the power of cooperation, the need to understand and name one's experience. In the title poem of the first section, **"Power"** (1974), Marie Curie's extraordinary achievement illustrates the paradoxical conditions of many women's lives in a patriarchal society:

Today I was reading about Marie Curie:
she must have known she suffered   from radiation
    sickness
her body bombarded for years   by the element
she had purified
It seems she denied to the end
the source of the cataracts on her eyes
the cracked and suppurating skin   of her finger-ends
till she could no longer hold   a test-tube or a pencil

She died   a famous woman   denying
her wounds
denying
her wounds   came   from the same source as her power
                                                        (p. 208)

[In the second part of *The Dream of a Common Language,* the] declarative unadorned, sometimes flat lines of [the] poems focus on the simple details of everyday experience.... In contrast to the tradition of Dante, Petrarch, and Shakespeare,

the tone of these poems is conversational, sometimes colloquial; the mood is lyrical, and there is no yearning for escape. Instead, the words weighted with consonance affirm the ordinariness of the present moment.... These are poems of ecstasy but not of flight. Behind the simple, proselike stanzas is Rich's commitment to reveal her erotic relationship with another woman. She asserts that private attachment must exist in the context of wider public life. Risking the possible censure of homophobic readers and critics, Rich refuses to settle for a closeted, secret existence.

The love poems are remarkably direct. There is no need to construct a myth of the mysterious other; instead, there is tender intimacy, unobscured by elaborate metaphors or opaque references.... (pp. 209-10)

"Twenty-One Love Poems" explores emotional complexity and ambivalence in addition to the pleasures and joys of a relationship, and these poems acknowledge the loneliness and separation that come from failed love.... (pp. 210-11)

"Not Somewhere Else, But Here," the third section of the volume, contains poems written over the three-year period 1974-77. The material in *The Dream of a Common Language* is not organized chronologically or even thematically. Themes and images reappearing throughout all the sections of the book create ever-widening spirals of intensified meaning. The need for relationship, for community, for the power of women is explored throughout the volume. The title poem of this section, written in 1974, serves as the companion poem to **"Origins and History of Consciousness."** Lamenting the failure of love to achieve fusion, the poem grieves for "Spilt wine   The unbuilt   house the unmade life." ...

The structure of these poems is no longer restrained by convention but reflects the poet's struggle to probe the depths of consciousness. The language, intense yet lyrical, is often punctuated by silences as weighted as the words. (p. 212)

A Wild Patience Has Taken Me This Far: Poems, 1978-81 continues to celebrate the accomplishments of women, extraordinary and ordinary, in an effort to create positive, public female images. (p. 217)

"Culture and Anarchy" (1978), with a title taken from Matthew Arnold's collection of essays first published in London in 1869, is a long poem that presents the female version of his pledge to "use ideas freely," to be "nourished not bound" by them. In contrast to Arnold's emphasis on the civilization that men have made, Rich sustains the lyrical celebration of nature and the power of women begun in **"Transcendental Etude"** [from *The Dream of a Common Language*].... Like the nineteenth-century suffragettes quoted in the poem, the poet lives in finite time that ultimately becomes history; the poem juxtaposes past and present in order to provide a comprehensive portrait of female friendship, female community, and female vision. (pp. 217-18)

Arrayed against the shared love and work of these women stand the controls ranging from social exclusion to rape that support patriarchal culture. These evils perpetrated against women are contrasted with the poet's delight in nature.... Quiet observation, careful attention to small details—this concentration of energy on coexistence with nature, like the sustained attentiveness and caring of a supportive friendship, is a true act of civilization. (pp. 218-19)

Insisting that women must find the appropriate syntax, images, and metaphors to create their realities, Rich asserts that women must actively work to create a vision that captures their organic connection to the deepest forms of life. And she feels that the conflict between feminist and patriarchal perspectives runs so deep that it affects the most basic perceptions of the human body and the environment: "this is the war of images." Rich states that "language is power" and that poetry can be "used as a means of changing reality." . . . Since poetry gives voice to our deepest experiences, it can change reality, but, as Rich observes, it must be a poetry that "will dare to explore, and to begin exploding, the phallic delusions which are now endangering consciousness itself." . . . (pp. 221-22)

The title of this volume comes from the first line of **"Integrity"**(1978): "A wild patience has taken me this far." This poem presents another portrait of a woman and her landscape. Again, the poem is concerned with wholeness. Prefaced with Webster's definition of the word, "the quality or state of being complete; unbroken condition; wholeness; entirety," the poet takes a solitary journey that in some respects parallels her earlier exploration of emotional and cultural origins in **"Diving into the Wreck."** However, this time the anger that impelled the poet to penetrate psychic and social depths has been replaced by "wild patience"—an untamed steadfastness—that enables her to find a mooring in the facts of her own experience. . . . The fear and uncertainty of **"Diving into the Wreck"** has become the quiet strength of a woman who knows herself and accepts the diversity of her experience. . . . (p. 223)

In 1982 Rich completed **"Sources,"** a twenty-three part poem that is among the most probing of her autobiographical and cultural explorations. Composed in a variety of styles from short lyrical stanzas and conversational phrases to staccato dialogue and long prose paragraphs, this poem contains characteristic images from past work—the blooming milkweed, Queen Anne's lace, the old country house. Questions of power, authority, the interior life versus the quest, phenomenological versus theoretical rendering of experience, and the importance of place versus abstraction resurface in this work. As in past poems, there are passages that capture the beauty of the New England landscape in an elegant mesh of assonance, consonance, and internal rhyme. . . . While acknowledging the influence and importance of New England's culture and geography on her life and work, for the first time Rich explores the influence of her Jewish heritage. (p. 225)

The poet ponders her own rootlessness, her involvement with "New" Englanders even to the extent of "believing their Biblical language / their harping on righteousness." . . . Then she acknowledges another biographical thread—that part of her related to the southern Jews of Vicksburg and Birmingham, and to extend the connection, that part of her connected to the Ashkenai, *the halutzot*, the Jews destroyed in the pogroms of World War II. Rejecting notions of special destiny—whether it be the Jews as "chosen people" or the Puritan "elect"— that have inspired repeated missions to build a city on a hill from Jerusalem to the New World, she dedicates herself to an "end to suffering" and vows to bring her intelligence and understanding to bear on her existence. . . . This poem outlines a female counter-quest—the mission is not to abandon the past in order to control the future but to remain connected to specific circumstances of experience while making personal choices that also shape the larger world. For Rich, vision means being able to see present life clearly as well as to imagine future possibilities.

From the disintegration of Rich's old life has come a new synthesis based on a commitment to write of women's actual lived experience. Choosing the particularities of everyday life over metaphysical imperatives, her emphasis on the quotidian and on nurturance constitutes a female response to the zealous elitism of the Puritan saints and the egotistical subjectivity of the male romantics. (p. 226)

Adrienne Rich's poetry serves a prophetic function by articulating the history and ideals of the feminist struggle. By recalling the ancient chthonic mysteries of blood and birth, by reconnecting daughters with their mothers, by drawing parallels between women today and their historical counterparts, and by envisioning the women of the future who will emerge from the feminist struggle, her poetry celebrates women's strength and possibilities. (p. 227)

> *Wendy Martin, in her* An American Triptych: Anne Bradstreet, Emily Dickinson, Adrienne Rich, *The University of North Carolina Press, 1984, 272 p.**

HELEN VENDLER

[Adrienne] Rich belongs to the school of plain-style poets, those who distrust, as evidence of mystification and hierarchy, ornament and embellishment in poetry. Plain-style poets ask to be judged on effectiveness, rather than on conventional ideas of "beauty": they make scant use of the elaborations of rhetoric, preferring the "horizontal" connections of contiguity to the "vertical" connections of metaphor. Though they affirm that their gaze is fixed on the actual and the historic, they are often utopian, and see the actual and the historic outlined against a Platonic social ideal. Their vision of a better world is entirely reactive, conceived as the opposite of the unjust world they perceive in the here and now. They are not lost in visionary radiance, and their language is not ecstatic but aggrieved.

Plain-style poets belong to the long chronicle of English and American Protestant dissent, with its history of political and religious reform. When Rich finds her own literary ancestors, she quotes women who used this Protestant voice (Susan B. Anthony, Jane Addams); she could equally well have named men like Thoreau in *Civil Disobedience*, William Lloyd Garrison, and Frederick Douglass. . . . In using this voice, Rich is writing in a central American tradition.

It is true of all literary voices that they have had fewer women than men practitioners. But in the case of the voice Rich uses, the disparity arises not solely from the relative numbers of male and female writers. Rather, it is caused chiefly, as many women writers have said, by the existence of a competing voice, one thought more "suitable" for women than this voice of Protestant personal and public drama, command, and reprobation. The competing choice is the one that Dickinson, Moore, Bishop, Sexton, and Plath repudiated as strongly as Rich repudiates it. It is the voice of girlishness, erotic pining, winsome coyness, religious submissiveness, and sentimental motherhood, the voice of the nineteenth-century woman poet. (p. 32)

Dickinson repudiated the "female" voice by blasphemy and pride; Moore, by learning and "observations"; Bishop, by homelessness and skepticism; Sexton, by parody and wildness; Plath, by anger and geometric chill. No one of these women, however, took upon herself the public voice of the political activist. (Perhaps Muriel Rukeyser is Rich's nearest predecessor in that respect.) The voice of "power"—a word Rich uses over and over again about writing—is a voice social in intent. And indeed, Rich's poetry is often treated as social poetry. I find Rich more often a personal poet, psychological rather than social. . . .

Most of the poetry in *The Fact of a Doorframe* has been previously published in book form. There are six new poems, and a few old "lost" or uncollected poems. The new poems, of which the most memorable is **"In the Wake of Home,"** continue to reexamine what Rich names the two poles of her nature, "anger and tenderness." It is the anger that has chiefly defined her as a mature poet, as her own private rage gradually attached itself to various oppressed groups—women, poor women, black women, lesbian women. . . .

Rich's own original rage, even if generated by an inborn temperament, was emotionally attached to her relationship with her father. . . . Her own solution had been not only to remember her primal anger but to bring it to bear on all other conceivable wrongs suffered by women at the hands of men. One wonders where Rich's anger would have led her if she had had a kind father, and a cruel mother. It is a question one wants to have her intelligence address. She looks hard and long at her own past, but she has not looked at it dispassionately, not yet. . . .

[In **"In the Wake of Home"**] Rich writes of the woman for whom "home" has been unsatisfactory. (p. 33)

[It] is written in a voice usable by everyone who can enter the "you" of Rich's general address. The danger of this "collective," "usable" address is that it can become so general as to be stereotypical, as I think happens when Rich invokes those ancillary figures of childhood who supplemented our unsatisfactory parents:

> And what of the stern and faithful aunt
> the fierce grandmother   the anxious
>   sister
> the good teacher   the one
> who stood at the crossing when you had
>   to cross
> the woman hired to love you

Rich is here as far away as possible from Lowell's idiosyncratic, not to say eccentric, family figures in *Life Studies*. Her aesthetic is stubbornly communal, "responsible," and "accountable" (her words in **"North American Time"**). Though she has irony, and knows personal exhaustion, she has no humor, and no historical skepticism about political effort. Her sternness, the sternness of a secular homilist, cannot allow humor; it is to Anne Sexton or Elizabeth Bishop that one looks for that. Rich's great virtue is her long struggle for authenticity. It has been endangered by self-pity and by writing for a cause, but she repeatedly has returned to self-scrutiny and acknowledged her findings. She will be remembered in literary history as one of the first American women to claim a public voice in lyric. And it is not only a political audience that she possesses (though she has that too). I have read, and not for political reasons, almost everything she has written. What Rich said of Emily Dickinson is true of herself; she has had to "retranslate her own unorthodox, subversive, sometimes volcanic propensities" into poetry. That is always an impossibly difficult translation, the more so since (as Rich says elsewhere, sounding like Wallace Stevens) "There is no 'the truth,' 'a truth'—truth is not one thing, or even a system. It is an increasing complexity." From a poet who believes this, all things are to be hoped. (p. 34)

Helen Vendler, "A Plain-Style Poet," in The New Republic, *Vol. 192, Nos. 28 & 29, January 7 & 14, 1985, pp. 32-4.*

CAROL MUSKE

With [Adrienne Rich's] **"The Fact of a Doorframe"** we confront 34 years of the "opinionated" poems of this complex and controversial writer, who began as poet-ingenue, polite copyist of Yeats and Auden, wife and mother. She has progressed in life (and in her poems, which remain intimately tied to her life's truth) from young widow and disenchanted formalist, to spiritual and rhetorical convalescent, to feminist leader, lesbian separatist and *doyenne* of a newly-defined female literature—becoming finally a Great Outlaw Mother. . . .

The next question, of course, looking at 34 years of her work, is: have Adrienne Rich's poems survived her opinions? At times her partisan views have outdistanced her poetry's inventiveness, but we must also consider that she has redefined "partisan," for what other poet in recent memory has spoken of creating a new language, unearthing a lost history, rewriting the sacred texts for her cause? If her tasks sound grandiose, her stated intent does not; it's almost funny. "To do something very common, in my own way."

"The Fact of a Doorframe" has an imposed, retrospective order, as if to give cohesion to autobiography, a common ground to the poems. But her placement of the title poem gives us more insight into her sense of personal history than do her introduction, her notes or the selection and arrangement of the work. Dated 1974, the poem is placed on the frontispiece, a door in a doorframe, inviting us into the nine books (two new since her last volume of selected poems appeared 10 years ago) and a quantity of older and recent uncollected poems. The title poem is about the suffering of entering—birth, death, writing—and it refers to the head of the talking mare, Falada, from the fairy tale, "The Goose Girl." The mare's head was a kind of poetical conscience for the goose girl (in reality a princess), expressing the heart's guilt, putting into language another's suffering. . . .

Like the head of the magical talking mare, poetry has always been both dilemma and animating principle for Adrienne Rich: "Now, again, poetry, / violent, arcane, common." Her writing has always lifted her naturally toward a unifying transcendental vision, a dream, but a dream simultaneously wrenched and weighted by its moral embodiment, called by her at different stages: love, truth, integrity, commonality, silence. She is a true metaphysical poet, made didactic by force of her politics. She cannot proceed without her principles (and who would ask it of her?) but the dialectical struggle that ensues between her heart and her imagination places her among the suffering she describes. The world she aspires to naturally in her poetry is not the world she must embrace for now. She writes in **"North American Time"**: "But underneath the grandiose idea / is the thought that what I must engage . . . / is meant to break my heart and reduce me to silence."

She has been, from the beginning, a poet of pathos. Even the highly formal and imitative volumes **"A Change of World"** (1951) and **"The Diamond Cutters"** (1955) endlessly tied and retied their charming lyricism to notions of truth. But in **"Moving in Winter,"** an uncollected poem from 1957, we begin to see a bolder integration of pathos. Where love has grown disillusioned, and truth simultaneously more commanding, this young poet of formal melody admits an insistent counterpoint (that of a wronged sensibility), and the poem is "shocked" into being. . . .

What fuels the poem (besides the skillful argument between form and content) is the poignant tug of war between anger and tenderness. It is this kind of poem, the dance of opposites, she does best.

There are many places in Adrienne Rich's work where anger has won the tug of war, and not to her advantage. Nonetheless, this furious passage from the poem **"Snapshots of a Daughter-in-law"** works well: "The argument *ad feminam*, all the old knives / that have rusted in my back, I drive in yours, / *ma semblable, my soeur!*" The outraged observation approaches glee in the punch line borrowed from Baudelaire and is more effective at its offhand feminization of "male" language than the following "revision" of Portia's speech, from **"Natural Resources"**: "But gentleness is active / gentleness swabs the crusted stump." The poem loses its dramatic tension as it degenerates into namecalling, with gentleness "bearing witness calmly / against the predator, the parasite."

Conversely, a rare moment of equanamity is denied in a more recent poem, **"The Spirit of Place,"** in which "the undamaged planet seems to turn / like a bowl of crystal," in Elizabethan beauty and order. The communion of the poet with nature is undercut by a political vigilance that distrusts even the stars: "All the figures up there look violent to me / as a pogrom on Christmas Eve in some old country." In passages like those above, she loses her own argument and the language goes flat, victimized by her ideological impatience.

But at other times her dialectical fire produces poems of transcendent beauty. Her music has not forsaken her, after all these years, through all the transformations. . . .

We are going to hear even more from this remarkable poet, whose passionate excesses, whose brilliant, terrifying leaps of faith often affect us more deeply than the ingrown successes of our assemblage of "approved" poets. The last poem in **"The Fact of a Doorframe"** ends with the line, "and I start to speak again," and we have no doubt that she will.

> *Carol Muske, "Lingua Materna: The Speech of Female History," in* The New York Times Book Review, *January 20, 1985, p. 5.*

Françoise Sagan

1935-

(Pseudonym of Françoise Quoirez) French novelist, dramatist, memoirist, short story writer, and scriptwriter.

Sagan's first novel, *Bonjour Tristesse* (1954), made her an international literary celebrity before she reached the age of twenty. The novel centers on a precocious teenager whose jealousy of her father's mistress leads to tragedy. Like most of Sagan's later characters, the young protagonist of *Bonjour Tristesse* is self-indulgent and restless, struggling with little success against the inertia that deadens her comfortable life. Sagan was credited with capturing the amoral, almost nihilistic mood of her generation, and her subject matter led critics to compare her with the French novelist Colette.

Most of Sagan's subsequent works echo the themes and characters of *Bonjour Tristesse*. Her prevailing concern has been the futility of love in a world where people are preoccupied with superficialities. Sagan's characters are often rich, bored, and disappointed in their pursuit of pleasure. Many of her novels explore the attraction between young and mature characters: *Un certain sourire* (1956; *A Certain Smile*) details the love affair of a young girl and an older man; *Aimez-vous Brahms?* (1959) depicts two middle-aged lovers who struggle against their desires for younger partners; and in *La femme fardée* (1981; *The Painted Lady*) a young gigolo falls in love with an older opera star. Although some critics have faulted her later work for being shallow and repetitive, most praise her subdued prose style and maintain that *Bonjour Tristesse* and her other early works evidence Sagan's literary talent.

(See also *CLC*, Vols. 3, 6, 9, 17; *Contemporary Authors*, Vols. 49-52; and *Contemporary Authors New Revision Series*, Vol. 6.)

© Jerry Bauer

ANATOLE BROYARD

In 1954, when Francoise Sagan came out with **"Bonjour Tristesse,"** she was like a teen-age French Joan Didion. Trés chic, very literary, she took the title of her first short novel from a poem by Paul Eluard. Her original choice, "Solitude With Narrow Hips," was also from Eluard and her publisher rejected it as too fancy.

For almost 30 years, in one novel after another, Miss Sagan had been getting less fancy, losing some of her youthful grace and the diffidence that had given her first book its economy. She seemed to have switched her literary allegiance from Eluard to La Rochefoucauld and Vauvenargues, from a mood of pleasant, rather evanescent poetry to the rumpled ironies of the bedroom.

What was particularly disappointing was the increasing conventionality of her ideas, her language and her novelistic technique. She seemed to have gone from a golden childhood to a gray middle age, without ever having passed through the voluptuous period between. People stopped taking her seriously.

Now, with her longest novel, **"The Painted Lady,"** she has been hailed by some critics in France as having made a trium-

phant comeback. One critic even compares her new book with "Tender is the Night." But these claims are only half true. There are good passages here and there, but out of the 12 characters in the book only three or four are well done.

Miss Sagan still has a poor ear for speech. Her characters talk as if they came not out of Paris but a bookstore. And she's heavy-handed, positively moralistic, in her distribution of bad and good characters. The bad ones are altogether humorless, which is surprising, for—in high society, at least—it's immorality that so often drives people to wit.

"Tender is the Night" is not the book that **"The Painted Lady"** reminds us of, but Katherine Anne Porter's "Ship of Fools". Each is a morality tale at sea and the resemblance extends even to the presence of an unpopular dog. . . .

Miss Sagan ends **"The Painted Lady"** with a concatenation of gratifications worthy of Dickens himself. From Paul Eluard to Charles Dickens—that's quite an evolution, even for a French woman.

*Anatole Broyard, in a review of "The Painted Lady,"
in* The New York Times, *January 27, 1983, p. C18.*

FRANCES TALIAFERRO

In *The Painted Lady*, her twelfth novel, Francoise Sagan attempts something more ambitious in scale than its slender predecessors. Relying on the familiar device of the voyage, she gathers together a company of worldly characters and puts them in conflict with each other.... [Plenty] of satisfyingly rich, naughty passengers have signed up for the Mediterranean "music cruise" of the luxury ship *Narcissus. Narcissus!* The name echoes clearly throughout the novel, lest any reader mistake the port from which this ship of fools has embarked....

The painted lady of the title is sad Clarisse, a beautiful, mysterious, unhappy heiress who hopes to disguise her alcoholism and her woe by slathering her face with layers of makeup. Her cruel husband, Eric, scorns his bourgeois origins and pretends to have risen from the working class to his present eminence as publisher of a leftist newspaper. This "cashmere communist" envies money and loves power of all sorts, particularly his ascendancy over his wretched wife. Yet there is something indomitable in Clarisse: her spirit cannot be crushed by her handsome, sadistic husband. The couple's companions on board are wealthy music lovers, parvenus, adventurers, philistines. The arriviste and the securely rooted, the callow and the weathered—each has his own reason for joining the cruise of the *Narcissus,* each longs somehow for the reassurance of love or power.

The action of *The Painted Lady* is confined to the changing alliances of these psychologically overlapping characters. According to the conventions of the shipboard genre, each person must eventually reveal his true self by word or deed. Most graphically, the unhappy Clarisse cries hard enough to dissolve her *maquillage:* "From behind the thick, baroque, almost obscene greasepaint emerged a superb new countenance, until now unknown...." Other characters disclose themselves less dramatically, but by the end of the voyage it is clear that no toad, no handsome prince, is quite what he seemed to be at the beginning of this fairy tale of metamorphoses.

The Painted Lady reads much better as civilized trash than as a serious psychological novel. Like an afternoon dalliance, it requires no real engagement; the reader must only be mildly curious and complaisant enough to accept the premise that this is how the very rich behave. Then one can be rewarded by melodrama.... (p. 74)

Unfortunately there are patches of real interest in *The Painted Lady,* honest moments that mar its consistency as an escape romance. Irony, Mlle. Sagan's natural mode, keeps breaking irrepressibly out, as if the soul of La Rochefoucauld could not be contained by the body of Jacqueline Susann. Mlle. Sagan is most herself in her passages of parody or rueful wit, as when she reflects that "That's what old age is ... to love only what you can love and desire only what you can have. It's called wisdom." Such maxims are the undoing of *The Painted Lady,* for they show us what an entertaining moralist the author might be if she abandoned such made-for-television silliness as the present work. (pp. 74-5)

> *Frances Taliaferro, in a review of "The Painted Lady," in* Harper's, *Vol. 266, No. 1593, February, 1983, pp. 74-5.*

ELAINE KENDALL

A Sagan novel is like a Chanel suit—instantly recognizable despite changes in accessories and hemline. The basic design remains the same year in and year out in all essential particulars, a style once radically innovative reduced to one predictable formula.

"The Painted Lady" is mid-calf length; the scene is shifted from Paris to the Mediterranean, the life depicted once again is the hermetic world of the bored and idle rich. The satire is mechanical, the tone weary, the symbolism heavy-handed; the prose is so brittle it threatens to shatter into parody.

Aboard the Narcissus for a deluxe music cruise are 10 passengers attended by Captain Elledocq and his purser, Charley Bollinger. Virtually everyone seems a reincarnation from early Sagan, a familiar type, a shadow of some former and more vigorous self....

We will be at sea for 10 days with two complaisant husbands, a pair of competitive and voracious older women, a poseur, a gigolo, a collection of potential dupes, an alcoholic, ... [a] mogul and his little friend, with only Elledocq and Charley to keep order. These people, meant to be a cross-section of the French upper-middle class, will board the Narcissus in one set of combinations and disembark in another, with some interim skirmishing along the way. Their sexual and financial rearrangements will constitute the entire plot; the prediction, discussion and analysis of the permutations will serve as dialogue.

Frequent gaps will be filled by rhapsodies to the sea, musings on death, remembrances of affairs past. During the course of the 450 pages, there will be a mild *frisson* or two as some of the passengers turn out to be more sensitive and intelligent than they seemed; others less so. These barely perceptible alterations constitute character development. People will change their clothes frequently, men as well as women; narcissism is a trait equally distributed between the sexes. They will make cruel remarks to one another, fraught with innuendo too fragile to survive in translation....

The artless style, the elliptical phrasing, the undifferentiated characterizations—all so appealing in a novel by an ingenue of 24—now seem merely haphazard, an encore languidly performed by a woman who has finally reached a certain age herself. The gulf between the satirist and her targets has dwindled and closed. Sagan's self-centered lovers and mistresses, indifferent husbands and restless wives, obediently re-enact their empty rituals of seduction and betrayal, deception and intrigue, for an observer as jaded as they: *tristesse,* now hardened into resignation.

> *Elaine Kendall, "Sagan: A Former Teen-Age Wonder, Now Dressed in Mid-Calf Middle Age," in* Los Angeles Times Book Review, *February 6, 1983, p. 3.*

NORA JOHNSON

"Already new dramas today?" asks one character of another halfway through ["**The Painted Lady**"]. "Something's always happening on this ship, and none of it straightforward and simple." In this French "Ship of Fools," intrigue is the order of the day among the 10 or so jet-set types aboard the liner Narcissus on its celebrated autumn music cruise. All or most of the passengers are very rich, very famous and, in the manner long ago perfected by the author, very, very bored....

Whether because of the translation or some sea change of the concept, for Miss Sagan boredom seems a grander term than mere monotony—one that includes loneliness and a kind of existentialist anxiety and is a more profound condition of the human spirit.

Yet in the end the people in this book are boring in both senses of the word. I found myself longing for the grace and freshness of her early novels, those slender tales of love between aged children and middle-aged burnouts that seemed so remarkable when they began appearing in the 50's. If she seemed to know everything then, now she appears to have forgotten some essentials. A story about superficial people usually ends up being superficial, and boredom, amusing in the young, becomes sad in middle age. I wish Miss Sagan would get off the yachts and turn her considerable talent to a more meaningful slice of her country's society; I felt she didn't care much about this crew, and as a result neither did I. I waited in vain for a moment with as much charm as the one in an early novel when a shy, sensitive young man slides up to a lone and lovely older woman during a concert intermission and asks, *"Aimez-vous Brahms?"*

> *Nora Johnson, "Bonjour Ennui," in* The New York Times Book Review, *February 6, 1983, p. 10.*

JOANNA RICHARDSON

Françoise Sagan, like [Colette], is fascinated by the endless permutations, the innumerable vicissitudes of love: by its boredom and its cruelty, its passion and calculation, its perversion and its powers of inspiration. She remains as fascinated as she was nearly 30 years ago, when she published her first book; but her own turbulent life has deepened her awareness, and it has perhaps made her more cynical.

In *The Painted Lady* she writes on a new and much larger scale, and she has chosen a subject of much complexity. . . .

In this massive novel, of some 450 pages, Françoise Sagan charts the course of [several] inter-related love-affairs; she does so with cynicism, compassion and understanding, with a rather cruel humour, and at moments with a touch of slapstick comedy. The result is an ungainly comedy of manners, and, to my mind, an uneven entertainment. With the exception of Andreas and the Painted Lady, none of the characters commands the reader's sympathy or their concern. They are spiteful, materialistic, constantly self-seeking (is the ship not called the *Narcissus?*); and they are not merely unpleasant, they tend to be caricatures. Besides, the account of their various infatuations is far too complex and far too long. Mlle Sagan is happier when she is working on a smaller scale. She is at her best in a novel of average length, in a novella or a vignette, where much remains unsaid and much is left to the imagination. *Bonjour Tristesse* is a novel of quite another order; the short stories expand like those Japanese paper flowers, opening out of shells in a glass of water: delicate, mysterious and poetic. *The Painted Lady* is a brash and cumbersome novel; it is like a large-scale poster done by an accomplished watercolourist. There is, one has to confess, a good deal of vulgarity about it.

> *Joanna Richardson, "Overblown," in* The Spectator, *Vol. 250, No. 8080, May 21, 1983, p. 25.*

LORNA SAGE

Françoise Sagan's problem has been that she has inhabited the same gilded cage ever since **'Bonjour Tristesse.'** She is forever the poor little rich girl of letters, trapped in her legend along with the same inevitable cast of characters—the unscrupulous, the irresponsible, the gamblers, the bankers, the divas, the gigolos, and so on. She has acquired almost no new mental furniture in the past 30 years. However, what she has done in

'The Painted Lady' is miraculously resurrect her *interest* in it all, and so render it glamorous all over again.

She has become expansive, gossipy, generously nostalgic, and sent her awful beautiful people on a Mediterranean musical cruise aboard the SS Narcissus—no expense spared, elaborate amorous intrigues laid on to keep everyone amused. We're still, of course, imprisoned in the legend: there's a nice moral disquisition on the vital importance of playing your part stylishly, gallantly, and to the bitter-end. Nevertheless—perhaps, indeed, because of its tear-jerking frivolity—**'The Painted Lady'** is great fun, and guaranteed to outclass the Krantzes and the Conrans on the right beaches this summer.

> *Lorna Sage, "Cryck in the Neck," in* The Observer, *May 22, 1983, p. 30.**

FAY WELDON

[C. J. Richards, who translated *Incidental Music* into English,] has ruthlessly rendered the Colette-ish richness, the sensuous subtleties of Miss Sagan's stories into a Zolaesque starkness, as if determined to demonstrate their irrelevance to the modern age. And one has some sympathy with her; these fictional essays in love—love lost, love discovered, love disowned, love betrayed—do seem to belong to another era, when beautiful married women had time to sit on park benches after lunch, waiting for their lovers, and didn't have to be back at the office like everyone else.

But Miss Richards, in taking up arms against this peculiarly Parisian version of love, has no business making Miss Sagan, its elegant proponent, ridiculous. To translate the very first sentence of the very first story in the book as "Angela di Stefano, who had spent the morning shouting in vain for her cat, Rascal, vanished in the narrow streets of the old quarter of Nice" is to be both inaccurate and misleading. It was the cat that vanished, not Angela. Surely there is someone at her publishers competent to point this out? **"The Cat and the Casino"** is so charming it deserves better.

All Miss Sagan's stories are charming, of course. She is the guest who sits at the dinner table and ravishes the assembled company with her beauty and wit but whose name cannot quite be remembered in the morning because nothing that was said was quite real, none of it quite related to actual experiences of life. . . .

In the opening sentence of . . . **"Partway Round the Course,"** Cyril Doublestreet begins, according to Miss Richards, to "feel sick." He doesn't, of course. *"Il se sentait mal à l'aise,"* which means "queasy" or "out of sorts" or "not quite himself" or, if we have to be literal, "ill at ease." The phrase has more involved connotations than "sick," including as it does a sense of spiritual discomfort.

Well, what's a poor translator to do? There's a deadline; the stories must be quickly rendered down, like a whole fresh delicious duck into boring duck soup. Anyway our Cyril, age 55, an American seen through Parisian eyes, a good ole boy puffing his way round a golf course, enjoys a sudden, unexpected amorous encounter and is, you'll be glad to hear, rejuvenated; one cares. The story survives the translation.

And in perhaps the most real, most powerful and most painful of the stories, **"One Year Later,"** an abandoned wife meets her husband and his new lover over dinner a year after their parting. She's had no option—if she wants to be asked out to dinner, that is, and not be shunned by her friends—but to pretend that she has passed efficiently from the role of happy wife to that of vivacious divorcée. But she has been and still is profoundly hurt. Since Miss Sagan believes in rather old-fashioned twists and turns of fate, our heroine overhears the new mistress rejecting her husband in just the same terms as she herself was once rejected by him and feels the better for it. Would that real life were so neat!

Nevertheless, the stories, even running in their English translation at a quarter of their potential richness, are well worth the reading. They have a fragile, classic grace; they are a reminder of that other world before liberation, when women of a certain class, a certain age, lived by love. I suspect that many still do and need their voice, and if it comes from Paris, why not? French remains, it seems, the language of love.

> *Fay Weldon, "Wives Who Live for Love," in* The New York Times Book Review, *March 11, 1984, p. 12.*

MYRNA J. McCALLISTER

In 1954, *Bonjour Tristesse* portrayed a bored, cynical, and amoral world that seemed to speak for the post-war generation. Then, at least some of Sagan's acclaim was due to her youth and promise. Three decades later, [the 12 stories collected in *Incidental Music*] still depict the same kind of world. The only noticeable difference is that now the characters have aged; all the women are "past their prime," though "still beautiful." Despite changes of setting (Paris, Detroit, Italy) and varying chronological settings (19th century, war-torn France, the present) there is a sameness to these views of middle-aged persons involved in fleeting, adulterous situations.

> *Myrna J. McCallister, in a review of "Incidental Music," in* Library Journal, *Vol. 109, No. 5, March 15, 1984, p. 598.*

THE NEW YORKER

[*Incidental Music* contains twelve] light, airy, mildly ironic stories about men and women falling in love, being in love, or, especially, falling out of love. The time and the place vary—Austria in 1883, the vanquished France of 1940, turn-of-the-century Baden-Baden, early-nineteenth-century Naples, contemporary Paris. But the people are almost always the same—people for whom romance (or sex) is everything—and so are the neatly (often transparently) plotted stories. . . . The book's title, with its suggestion of momentary, undemanding pleasure, is most appropriate.

> *A review of "Incidental Music," in* The New Yorker, *Vol. LX, No. 8, April 9, 1984, pp. 143-144.*

MARTHA DUFFY

Pity the genre novelist who embarks on a different course. For more than 25 years, Françoise Sagan has published brief, ironic tales of love lost or betrayed. She is a supremely confident writer, both in her resolute economy of style and in her command of the milieu she describes: the frivolous, overwrought bourgeois society where emotion can be both teased and indulged. (p. BT6)

[*Salad Days,* published in France as *Le Chien Couchant,*] has a radically different setting, the working-class world of a grim little town outside Lille, and the author has been lectured by French critics for attempting it. . . . The outline is familiar, maybe even a bit hoary: Gueret, a down-trodden bookkeeper, despised by his bosses and his landlady, stumbles upon a cache of jewels. They were lost in the course of a murder, which Gueret did not commit but Mme. Biron, the landlady, thinks he did. She is a retired Marseille moll, and in her eyes Gueret's bravado raises him from an irritating reminder of her reduced circumstances to a means of escaping from them. (pp. BT6-BT7)

How the American publisher came up with a blithe title like *Salad Days* . . . for this predictable little morality tale is hard to figure out. Sagan is writing against her strength. She seems to have little access to these pinched minds, so that her customary grace notes—sly humor, sheer oddity—are rarely struck. But the story is told in sure-handed fashion, and it is flawlessly paced. Gueret at least is a convincing character, and the author takes an unexpectedly hearty interest in his clumsy pursuit of Mme. Biron. The French critics are doubtless right that this is second-class Sagan, but there is enough here to justify her exploring the low road for once. (p. BT7)

> *Martha Duffy, "Pinched Minds," in* Time, *Vol. 124, No. 10, September 3, 1984, pp. BT6-BT7.*

PAUL STUEWE

[In *Salad Days*] a timid office clerk stumbles over some stolen jewellery, falls into unsavoury company, and finally plunges into the depths of degradation. Simenon used just this sort of simple, universally understood plot in crafting his classic thrillers, but Sagan definitely isn't in his league: she's much too sentimental about her characters, and her expository passages are cluttered with excessive and tension-reducing detail. Although these aren't serious defects in the romantic fiction Sagan usually essays, they become irritating when carried into the mystery-suspense field.

> *Paul Stuewe, in a review of "Salad Days," in* Quill and Quire, *Vol. 50, No. 11, November, 1984, p. 42.*

Siegfried (Lorraine) Sassoon

1886-1967

(Also wrote under pseudonyms of Saul Kain and Pinchbeck Lyre) English poet, novelist, memoirist, and editor.

Sassoon was one of several English poets, including Robert Graves, Edmund Blunden, and Wilfred Owen, who gained recognition during World War I. In his most highly regarded works, Sassoon used realism and bitter satire to express the suffering of soldiers and to dispel the traditional, idealistic image of war as a glorious and noble undertaking.

Unlike his wartime verse, Sassoon's early poetry is written in the Georgian style, a return to Romantic traditions in reaction to Victorian reason and realism. In general, Sassoon's language is archaic and his subjects are conventional. One exception is *The Daffodil Murderer* (1913), a long, blank-verse monologue which parodies John Masefield's *The Everlasting Mercy*. Of these early works, the title poem of *The Old Huntsman and Other Poems* (1917) stands out for its mellow, humorous reminiscences of the changes time had wrought on the title character and the world. In the same volume are a number of short poems which express Sassoon's outrage with war. Before Sassoon had experienced the trenches, he had remarked, upon reading Robert Graves's war poems, that war should not be written about so realistically. His own idealistic verses, including "Absolution" and "The Kiss," are sometimes called his "happy warrior" poems and employ the language and structure of his pastoral work. His opinions and his poetry changed after his experiences in the Somme offensive. His writing became blunt, unsentimental, colloquial, informal in style, and, as Sassoon said, "deliberately written to disturb complacency."

Sassoon was wounded and disabled a number of times and received the Military Cross for bravery, which he subsequently threw into a river in protest. During one of his recuperative periods, having become pacifistic, Sassoon declined to return to his unit, issuing instead a written protest which was widely printed and even read in the House of Commons. The result was not the court-martial that he had hoped for, but rather a hospital stay, ostensibly for treatment of shell-shock, arranged in part through the efforts of Robert Graves. During his time at Craiglockhart Hospital, he began writing the poems of *Counter-Attack* (1918), a graphic detailing of the physical and psychological effects of the war on its participants. Another volume, *Satirical Poems* (1926), chastizes politicians, media, "armchair generals," women, and the clergy for their tacit approval and even encouragement of participation in the war.

Critics of the time, including some of Sassoon's friends and fellow poets, disapproved of Sassoon's treatment of war, claiming that he dealt only with its immediate and startling aspects. They thought that his anger might invalidate his work aesthetically because his descriptions appealed to the senses rather than the imagination. Wilfred Owen, whom Sassoon met at Craiglockhart, concluded that Sassoon's poems did not expand and intensify the horror of war into a greater human context, but rather enjoined the reader to react to the moment. According to John Middleton Murry, there was a "lack of fin-

The Bettman Archive, Inc.

ished artistry" about Sassoon's work, a negativity that terrifies and then numbs so that the reader cannot absorb the full aesthetic experience. Virginia Woolf stated that Sassoon "deserted art in a compulsion to express the intolerable." Occasionally, however, he was able to see beyond his anger. The best example of this is "Everyone Sang," an often-praised lyric of joy and relief at the Armistice.

Sassoon wrote the majority of his prose between 1926 and 1945. The most successful of these works are the autobiographical novels *Memoirs of a Fox-Hunting Man* (1928), *Memoirs of an Infantry Officer* (1930), and *Sherston's Progress* (1937). *Memoirs of a Fox-Hunting Man* was widely read and gained Sassoon a reputation as an excellent prose stylist. It recounts the prewar life of the Sassoon persona, George Sherston, a prosperous country squire. The book's popularity assured an audience for the companion volumes, both of which deal with Sherston's experiences during and immediately following World War I. These three novels were eventually incorporated into one volume, *The Memoirs of George Sherston* (1937). A second group of autobiographical works employ first-person narrative. *The Old Century and Seven More Years* (1938) and *The Weald of Youth* (1942) are nostalgic looks at Sassoon's pleasant, sheltered youth. *Siegfried's Journey 1916-1920* (1945) elaborates on his experiences during and after the war.

Sassoon turned more and more to spiritual concerns in his poetry written after World War I. Much of this work demonstrates a belief in man's ongoing search for goodness. Poems in such collections as *The Heart's Journey* (1927), *Vigils* (1934), and *Sequences* (1956) are concerned with the search for self and for meaning in the universe. In these volumes Sassoon used the simple, direct, compact language of his wartime verse, but the tone and outlook are gentler and the poems are more introspective. These collections did not achieve the renown of the more powerful war poems, but some critics recognize them as significant achievements.

(See also *Contemporary Authors*, Vol. 104, Vols. 25-28, rev. ed. [obituary] and *Dictionary of Literary Biography*, Vol. 20.)

MARGUERITE WILKINSON

Wisdom is the shining power in the poetry of Siegfried Sassoon. To read it is to come face to face with indelible memories of unspeakable anguish. No palliatives are offered. The truth about warfare is told, as Mr. Sassoon understands it, with a vigor and insight that inhibit even the euphemisms of our own thoughts while we read. It is told by a poet who has refused to be blinded and benumbed by glamour and illusion, who will not describe as noble and beautiful that which was only horribly necessary. It is told by a man, a soldier, who will never forget this Calvary of the youth of our generation. (p. 142)

With this devotion to verity, which is the passion of the realist, Mr. Sassoon's poetry unites an intellectual poise and rectitude that belong to idealism. That, I believe, is why his presentation of the facts and emotions of warfare can be made with such acrid irony. He has found it necessary to set side by side with the hell of a young man's life in war the Paradise of a young man's visions. For this reason, he has become, to many of us, the chief interpreter of the meanings of the great war.

When his first widely-circulated book, "The Old Huntsman", was published in 1917, many poets and nearly all journalistic versifiers were writing about the war. Here and there, and usually one by one, good poems appeared. But most of what was written said the same old things in the same old way, with the same old rhymes and the rhythms supposedly martial. Men and women at the front wrote what they felt in the heat of excitement, without waiting to "recollect in tranquillity". Men and women at home, who had never heard a gun or smelt powder, wrote what they thought people ought to feel at the front, or what they thought would please those at home. There was much sentimentalism, honest and dishonest, and almost unlimited metrical propaganda. Then came Siegfried Sassoon with his poetry, strong as a gust of fresh wind, bringing both bitterness and fragrance. The bitterness was to be found in such sharply thought-out and exquisitely felt studies of the war as "They", "At Carnoy", "Special-Constable", "The Hero", "Blighters", and "The Kiss", probably the finest poem in the book. The fragrance was to be found in poems not about war, such brief and lovely lyrics as "A Child's Prayer" and "Wonderment".

But the bitter lyrics are the unforgettable ones. (pp.142-43)

[Consider] these lines from "The Kiss", addressed to "Sister Steel" and sharp with anger against the thing that can only be made endurable by anger:

> Sweet Sister, grant your soldier this:
> That in good fury he may feel
> The body where he sets his heel
> Quail from your downward darting kiss.

Following "The Old Huntsman", in 1918 came "Counter Attack", Mr. Sassoon's second book, with an introduction by Robert Nichols, who bids us read it again and again because it was written "for mankind's sake". In this introduction Mr. Nichols takes occasion to tell how much "The Old Huntsman" meant to the men who read it while they were still fighting in France.

In "Counter Attack" we find only war poetry. The fullness of realization has come to Mr. Sassoon, and he has little to say of the fragrant things of home and Paradise. The language is somewhat less smooth and fluent, nearer to the rough speech of the men with whom he suffered. Many of these poems are sketches, made in a few words, of happenings at the front, little stories about his friends. But they keep the same irony that stings consciousness in "The Kiss". (pp. 143-44)

[In Sassoon's third book, "Picture Show",] are to be found a number of his finest poems. There is no relaxation of spirit or technique, and, if there be any change in quality, it is in his increasing conciseness and lucidity, his growing power to use natural rather than literary rhythms. "I Stood With the Dead" has a grim directness and reality that only the profoundly felt rhythms of natural speech can give. . . . (p. 144)

> Marguerite Wilkinson, "Siegfried Sassoon," *in* The Touchstone, *Vol. VII, No. 2, May, 1920, pp. 142-45.*

S.P.B. MAIS

In *The Old Huntsman and Other Poems* [Sassoon] has collected some seventy-odd poems, which mark him out as one of the little group of young warriors who felt impelled to put their impressions of war into verse, one with them in his appreciation of the beautiful and his curiosity about the dead, but not in the least like any other of them in his manner of writing or the conclusions at which he arrives about the effect which fighting has upon him.

In the first place he is colloquial, pellucidly clear, simple, terse, and straightforward. He dwells rather on the ironic side of it all; as a satirist in verse he excels. He, least of all the younger poets, can find glamour and nobility in the war. He paints ruthlessly what he sees, and what he sees is no thin red line or charge of heavy or light brigade. For the most part he regards war as an intolerable waste of good material. (p. 131)

[Such a poem as *To Any Dead Officer Who Left School for the Army in 1914*] reads amazingly like prose, but the white heat of his indignation raises the simple theme of his thought up out of the ruck of ordinary commonplace, and the very ordinariness of it takes on the guise of something that is unforgettable; it may not be poetry, according to the critic's canon, but it strikes home and we feel, with the writer, "blind with tears" at the purposelessness of such wanton destruction.

In the poem which gives the title to the book we are shown an old huntsman living over again by his cottage fireside great days of old with the hounds. He ponders on his probable future when he is dead. . . . (p. 132)

[It is easy to] see why Mr Sassoon dedicated his book to Thomas Hardy. There is the same passionate love of the countryside, the same sympathetic vision of the rustic, the same keen irony and Swift-like detestation of frippery and unreality.

Mr Sassoon, like many other subalterns taking a hand in the "great game," is filled with loathing at war under modern conditions, and he is too courageous to pretend that it is otherwise with him. He can even dare to sympathise with and openly print the sentiments of the one-legged man, which would certainly be censored or else howled down by the nine-tenths of the fire-eating civilian population. . . . (p. 133)

Mr Sassoon is at one again with all the other poets of his time when he comes to write about his dead comrades. The unanimity with which the modern soldier-poets sing of the mingling of their lost companions with the glories of nature is worth the psychic's earnest attention: it is a phenomenon not the least marvellous in an age of amazing discoveries. . . . His anger at the war itself is as nothing compared with the fury into which he lashes himself when he writes of the way that the war is treated at home, in the music-halls for example. Perhaps the supreme example of this is to be found in *Blighters*. . . . (p. 134)

But it is not only upon the war that Mr Sassoon dwells: he has that deep passion for beauty without which no poet can hope for a permanent place in our hearts, beauty whether expressed in the petals of a rose or a sky at dawn or any other natural glory. . . . Mr Sassoon fulfils Wordsworth's conditions of keeping his eye on the object, and he heightens his effect by the strict accuracy of each stroke.

Many poets have (of late) tried to describe in poetry the romance of the train, but in *Morning Express* Mr Sassoon has, I think, eclipsed the others, partly because of his literal precision, his selection, and his simplicity, partly also because of his economy in the use of words: it is a severely reticent picture, austere, exact, and withal beautiful. There is something of the Pre-Raphaelite in his work here. . . . But by far the most precious quality about Mr Sassoon is that in spite of his righteous anger there is behind all this an indomitable courage and a splendid optimism. . . . Like his own old huntsman and Rupert Brooke he shows very clearly that he is a real lover of life, and furthermore that he is a devout lover of life. (pp. 135-36)

Poets of his calibre are rare indeed. . . . It will be the fervent wish of all those who read Mr Sassoon's work that he may be spared to fulfil the prophecies which the critics have ventured upon with regard to his powers, and continue to sing even more sweetly, more surely now that peace has returned. (p. 137)

> *S.P.B. Mais, "Siegfried Sassoon," in his* Books and Their Writers, *Dodd, Mead and Company, 1920, pp. 131-37.*

JOHN MIDDLETON MURRY

It is the fact, not the poetry, of Mr. Sassoon that is important. When a man is in torment and cries aloud, his cry is incoherent. It has neither weight nor meaning of its own. It is inhuman, and its very inhumanity strikes to the nerve of our hearts. We long to silence the cry, whether by succour and sympathy, or by hiding ourselves from it. That it should somehow stop or be stopped, and by ceasing trouble our hearts no more, is our chief desire; for it is ugly and painful, and it rasps at the chords of nature.

Mr. Sassoon's verses [in *Counter Attack and Other Poems*]— they are not poetry—are such a cry. They touch not our imagination, but our sense. Reading them, we feel, not as we do with true art, which is evidence of a man's triumph over his experience, but that something has after all been saved from disaster, but that everything is irremediably and intolerably wrong. And, God knows, something is wrong—wrong with Mr. Sassoon, wrong with the world which has made him the instrument of a discord so jangling. Why should one of the finest creatures

of the earth be made to suffer a pain so brutal that he can give it no expression, that even this most human and mighty relief is denied him?

For these verses express nothing, save in so far as a cry expresses pain. Their effect is exhausted when the immediate impression dies away. Some of them are, by intention, realistic pictures of battle experience, and indeed one does not doubt their truth. The language is overwrought, dense and turgid, as a man's mind must be under the stress and obsession of a chaos beyond all comprehension. (pp. 75-6)

[A description of the dead in the trenches, for example,] is horrible, but it does not produce the impression of horror. It numbs, not terrifies, the mind. Each separate reality and succeeding vision is, as it were, driven upon us by a hammer, but one hammer-beat is like another. Each adds to the sum more numbness and more pain, but the separateness and particularity of each is lost. . . . We are given the blurred confusion, and just because this is the truth of the matter exactly rendered we cannot apprehend it any more than the soldier who endures it can. We, like him, are 'crumpled and spun sideways.'

There is a value in this direct transcription of plain, unvarnished fact; but there is another truth more valuable still. One may convey the chaos of immediate sensation by a chaotic expression, as does Mr. Sassoon. But the unforgettable horror of an inhuman experience can only be rightly rendered by rendering also its relation to the harmony and calm of the soul which it shatters. . . . But in Mr. Sassoon's verses it is we who are left to create for ourselves the harmony of which he gives us only the moment of its annihilation. It is we who must be the poets and the artists if anything enduring is to be made of his work. He gives us only the data. There is, indeed, little enough harm in this; it is good that we should have the data; it is good that Mr. Sassoon should have written his book, and that the world should read it. But our concern here is with Mr. Sassoon the potential poet.

There is a danger that work such as his may pass current as poetry. It has the element of poetical popularity, for it produces an immediate impression. And since Mr. Sassoon is a young man, he may be hypnotized by popularity into believing that his work is done, and may end by wrecking the real poetic gift which at rare intervals peeps out in a line.

> 'The land where all
> Is ruin and nothing blossoms but the sky.'

The last five words are beautiful because they do convey horror to the imagination, and do not bludgeon the senses. They convey horror to the imagination precisely because they contain, as it were, a full octave of emotional experience, and the compass ranges from serenity to desolation, not merely of the earth, but of the mind. The horror is in relation; it is placed, and therefore created. But in the following lines there is no trace of creation or significance:

> A yawning soldier knelt against the bank,
> Staring across the morning blear with fog;
> He wondered when the Allemands would get busy;
> And then, of course, they started with five-nines
> Traversing, sure as fate and never a dud.

We choose these lines because they make a tolerable, if not a very distinguished, prose. Those that follow them in the piece which gives the book its name are more violent journalism. But why should such middling prose be ironed out into nominal blank verse lines, unless Mr. Sassoon imagined that he was, in fact, writing poetry? What he was doing was to make a barely sufficient entry in a log-book. (pp. 76-80)

John Middleton Murry, "Mr. Sassoon's War Verses," in his The Evolution of an Intellectual, *1920. Reprint by Jonathan Cape, 1927, pp. 75-84.*

EDWARD SHANKS

'Satirical Poems' has been awaited by many persons with varying degrees of eagerness for a considerable time, and now, when it appears, it bears on its dust-jacket the following rather chilling pronouncement from his publishers:

These satirical poems cover a period of nearly seven years. They will be followed by a book of entirely serious verse.

Entirely serious verse! And where has that a better place than in satirical poems? I do not doubt Mr. Sassoon's gifts as a poet, nor will I advance anyone to dispute his claim to be the most accomplished versifier of our time. But there seems to me to be in these simple phrases a confusion which has not been without a certain effect on the poet. . . .

There was a time when Mr. Sassoon seemed to be the only poet properly attuned to the difficult conditions of our times. Then he was a satirist and he was still "entirely serious." His strength lay, perhaps, in the fact that then he felt no necessity to make a dichotomy where none can properly exist. On one page the reader found that restrained, dynamite-like little poem which begins: "Good morning, good morning! the General said," on another the poem describing how a reassuring letter was sent home about the death of a useless panicking subaltern, and on another that best of all Armistice poems, 'Everyone suddenly burst out singing.' These pieces represented Mr. Sassoon's view of the war, in all moods, and though his view was not, and is not, universal, yet it existed in a mind that saw all around the subject and felt passionately about it. This new collection suggests a mind acalm with the sails idly flapping. Mr. Sassoon is, as I have said, perhaps the most accomplished versifier of our time, and, at worst, something more than that. His impressionistic powers are remarkable, as in [a] piece called 'Storm on Fifth Avenue.'. . . (p. 653)

Much of [it] is foreign, and yet for a little while the reader has sat through the New York thunderstorm with the poet. But, when one comes to the satirical note at the end, what does it mean save that Mr. Sassoon, looking at the modern world, feels he ought to be satirical? . . . This poem is not quite a fair, but it is a very striking, example of Mr. Sassoon's work as satirist. It is his practice to make an effective impressionistic picture in rather jaundiced colours and then to heave a sigh that things are no better, but this, without stronger passion, is not true satire, it is no more than poetic carping. . . .

Mr. Sassoon is a poet who has learnt a great deal from having been once a satirist. He was a satirist because there was a thing he hated very much—the War, and another thing, the way in which it was waged. The hatred sharpened his tongue and gave him to say certain poems which will not be forgotten. But the War passed and with it the power of hatred which it had engendered in Mr. Sassoon. Unfortunately he was left with the satirical bent, but not with the satirical justification. He hates nothing now. The nearest he comes to it is malicious amusement, and even that is shot with a streak of pity. Were one to judge by this book alone, one would say that there was no

wind left to fill his sails, but perhaps we ought to wait for the promised book of "entirely serious verse." (p. 654)

Edward Shanks, "Satire," in The Saturday Review, *London, Vol. 141, No. 3683, May 29, 1926, pp. 653-54.*

EDWARD SHANKS

[*Memoirs of a Fox-Hunting Man*] has caused no small amount of speculation among its readers. Who wrote it? Is it truth or fiction? The answer to the first of these questions was fairly obvious and is now confirmed. It is Mr. Siegfried Sassoon. As to the other question, I reply: Mainly truth, but neither all truth nor all the truth. And speculation here is in place, for on the results of such an analysis one's opinion of the book will very largely depend. . . .

[My] impression, derived from considerations of style and construction, [is] that the author set out to write a novel, autobiographical, to be sure, in its foundations, but still a novel, with a definite pattern and almost with a definite plot. As he proceeded, however, sheer delight in his recollections of the truth overcame him, and the pattern disappeared. From that point the book, which to begin with is rather disappointing, vastly improves. One could wish that the first two hundred pages or so were other than they are, but the remainder, with its fresh convincingness, its increasing serenity in a definite mental attitude, and, not least, its joyous descriptions of enjoyable experiences ought to become (I say this with diffidence) a classic of the hunting-field, and (this with less diffidence) a little classic of autobiography.

Edward Shanks, "A Little Classic," in The Saturday Review, *London, Vol. 146, No. 3807, October 13, 1928, p. 473.*

IRWIN EDMAN

The quality of Siegfried Sassoon's prose writing has by this time become an established and unique mode in contemporary English letters. Where else is the note of reminiscence, half-lyric and half-humorous realism, so delicately sounded? Who else evokes with such combined detachment and nostalgia the atmosphere of a vanished quarter-of-a-century ago, or the ardors and endurances of a poetic and (to use Mr. Sassoon's own phrase about his own early manhood) chuckle-headed youth? Where else can one find so precise and yet passionate an evocation of the very texture of the English sky and the English landscape, or where find so much good sense and freshening insight into so many figures, famous and obscure, in English society, politics and literature?

Mr. Sassoon has exhibited these delicious excellences in a now considerable series of memoirs with the same subject: himself. There were semi-fictional personal histories, told in a thinly-disguised third person, some of them well known a generation ago on both sides of the Atlantic: **"Memoirs of a Fox Hunting Man," "Memoirs of an Infantry Officer,"** and **"Sherston's Progress."** There is the now frankly first-personal story begun in **"The Old Century,"** continued in **"The Weald of Youth,"** and now in this volume before us, **"Siegfried's Journey,"** the only half-playfully named story of the author's journey through the war years and their immediate sequel. . . .

Mr. Sassoon in his memoirs has created a form of his own and achieved a tone in its combined simplicity, and psychological subtlety unlike that of any autobiographer I know. The prose itself, never obtrusive or fancy, remains in itself a peculiar treasure. It is the prose of a writer—and a man—who has never ceased to be a poet. And it is not only in the surface of the prose or in its texture that the poet is felt. Events, even trivial ones of long ago, become for Mr. Sassoon essences beheld. They are themes for ruminations, always modest and always succinct. The passages of **"Siegfried's Journey"** become parables of more than his own person. These memoirs are reflections on the society, the culture of England, and—in this volume—of the United States, by a man who, for all his self-deprecations, is a poet with a mind.

This section of the memoir begins in the midst of the last war. Siegfried . . . has just been invalided home from the Western Front. . . .

He is made welcome at the beautiful country house "in the shadow of lofty elms" by a brilliant and eminent titled lady. He visits an old uncle, for whom the war is something remote fought by gallant and proper nephews. After a few weeks of this sort of thing, young Siegfried felt he must write something "that would give comfortable civilians a few shocks." He did—his famous anti-war poems.

On a second invalided leave, this time because of a wound, Siegfried's anti-war opinions crystallized; he felt that the war had become a meaningless slaughter. There are entertaining and touching accounts of what happened when he reduced his opinions to writing, not in verse—which had already attracted both highly favorable and some morally adverse opinion—but in prose. . . .

Winston Churchill is only one of the famous figures who dot these pages, none introduced for the sake of their celebrity but for the part they played in shaping the imagination of the young soldier-poet. There are vignettes of Thomas Hardy at Max Gate, which give a firmer, fresher image of that great writer, whom Sassoon regards above all as a poet, than any I have ever seen. There is the same sort of rememberable account of meetings with T. E. Lawrence, Masefield, the Sitwells, Galsworthy, Robert Bridges, then Poet Laureate. None of these portraits is mere reverence or "official" portraiture. Each is the image, obviously authentic, registered by a poet's eyes and remembered with an artist's fidelity in these pages. Equally good, but more amused, are the American portraits. . . . His notes on his stay in America are proof to an American of his ability to evoke the authentic aspects of things and persons. Robert Frost comes quite as alive as Masefield, and midtown New York as much as Sussex. Only the rooted affection for the English scene is lacking in these American pages.

Like the previous volumes, this book is a unique record of a personality whom only England could have in one person. A fox-hunting man, a soldier, and a meditative and humorous poet all in one. And few writers today take the care to achieve the exact and musical beauty of Sassoon's simple and noble prose.

> Irwin Edman, "Mr. Sassoon Continues His Auto-biography," in The New York Times Book Review, March 24, 1946, p. 4.

ROBERT HILLYER

Siegfried Sassoon's [*Collected Poems* comes] as a revelation even to one who has followed his work, both prose and verse, through the past thirty years. His position (shared, perhaps,

by his friend Wilfred Owen) as the foremost poet of World War I, left the reader with established notions that single volumes could not quite dispel. Now, with the whole range of his poetry before us in one volume, we see every part of his performance in relation to the whole. He stands forth as a major poet.

The collection truly presents an autobiography. The personality is well-nigh complete and deeply impressive; not a great poet only, but a civilized man. Humor, kindness, taste, and righteous anger are here, each in its just place and nowhere in recent literature more eloquent. Yet, though the book is personal, it is not romantically self-centered. . . .

The mood of Browningesque monologue in **"The Old Huntsman"** quickly gives way to the stung indignation of the poems written during the first war. Considering these, we are struck with the number of good pieces such as **"When I'm Among a Blaze of Lights"** and **"The General,"** which have remained obscure amid the selections so often repeated in the anthologies. Neither their irony nor that of the more familiar protests has rusted with time because all Sassoon's poems are populated: the swirl of people and actions embodies anger beyond the one situation that roused it. Furthermore, the untiring, quick-eyed observation of others precludes self-pity. The contrast here to the poets of World War II is lamentable. . . .

Because of Sassoon's dramatic presentation of his material he calls Hardy to mind. I find him a better poet than Hardy, broader in sympathy, less contrived, happier in conclusion, and in technique incomparably more polished. Sassoon is, with all else, an interesting poet. He summons our attention and holds it by the variety of his episodes and responses.

We are fortunate to have this perspective of all Sassoon's poetical work in a single volume. No modern collection could be more valuable.

> Robert Hillyer, "Great and Civilized," in The Saturday Review of Literature, Vol. XXXII, No. 5, January 29, 1949, p. 28.

JOSEPH COHEN

Robert Graves, while naming the modern writers he considered to be in the "small, clear stream of living" poetry, said he found it "remarkable that the extraordinary five years of Siegfried Sassoon's poetic efflorescence (1917-21) should be utterly forgotten now." At a time when Graves' own autobiography of his wartime experiences, *Goodbye To All That*, has been reissued, along with Edmund Blunden's *Undertones of War* and Wilfred Owen's *Poems*, it is indeed remarkable that Sassoon's poetic achievement during the Great War is now forgotten, and even more remarkable that Sassoon, who has published his poems in every decade of this century, is largely unknown by the present generation and ignored by its critics. Like a decommissioned man-of-war, he rests quietly at anchor in poetry's mothball fleet.

I believe that Sassoon's poetic decommissioning is largely self-determined; that it has resulted from an amalgamation about 1940 of two roles he had played fully to that time, those of angry prophet and country gentleman, into a third role: the self-effacing hermit. (p. 169)

Sassoon's enthusiasm for his role of angry prophet is amply recorded in his prose accounts of his war experiences, *The Memoirs of George Sherston* and *Siegfried's Journey 1916-1920;*

but the intensity with which he responded to the role and developed it during the war years and afterward is revealed only in his poems. The prose accounts are of emotions recollected in tranquillity; the war poems are the raw unchecked emotions themselves. In the two dozen or so war poems first collected into *The Old Huntsman and Other Poems* . . . , Sassoon unleashed the exasperation, the horror, the fear, the disillusionment, and the bitter cynicism that came to characterize the poetry of the trenches in the war's last two years. . . . Sassoon abstracted the futility, despair, loneliness and mockery of the war, and with fury thrust it into the faces of his unsuspecting countrymen, safe and snug in England.

His approach was direct and his technique simple: he emphasized and re-emphasized the contrast between the relative comfort and safety of the homefront and the misery and insecurity of the trenches. While the poetic worth of his formula was questionable, its communicative potential was unlimited. Sassoon exploited, without hesitation, the shock value obtained from exposing the superficial optimism of those whom the people set in authority. (pp. 170-71)

Moreover, Sassoon's poetry is filled with warnings and predictions, both general and specific, of dire judgments, and of death by fire and sword for those who insist on fighting wars.

With these versified admonitions, Sassoon quickly established his reputation. Like most prophets, he soon became a controversial figure and in many quarters an unpopular one. (p. 172)

Sassoon was also subjected to strong literary censure. . . .

Nonetheless, Sassoon was encouraged by the public reaction to his war poems in *The Old Huntsman* despite the unfavorable response to much of it. Certain friends, critical of the government's conduct of war, like Robert Ross, and outspoken pacifists, like Lady Ottoline Morrell, applauded him. His quickly achieved fame suggested to him that he had developed a new voice more cogent, more powerful, and more significant than any his poetry had known previously. (p. 173)

It must be recognized, in retrospect, that Sassoon's war poetry suffered from his indulging too much in the role of prophet, for once he decided that it was proper for him, he entered upon the role with so much exuberance that he permanently hurt his reputation as a poet. True, he pleaded effectively for the combatants and just as effectively castigated those whom he held responsible for the suffering of the soldiers. But his verse pleadings and remonstrances reduced his efforts to political propaganda. Though he foresaw and foretold the misery involved in the prolongation of the war, his rash attacks alienated many whom he might otherwise have induced to accept his point of view. Most of all, he lacked the compassion which gave needed balance and restraint to the works of two other poets of the war, then unknown, Wilfred Owen (whom Sassoon discovered while in hospital), and Osbert Sitwell.

A comparison of the war poems of Owen and Sassoon, particularly, will reveal that a strong spirituality underlies the war poems of the former but is lacking in the war poems of the latter. Sassoon is preoccupied with justice and the futility of sacrifice, whereas Owen tempers justice with mercy and describes sacrifice in terms of Christian love. (p. 175)

Sassoon has himself recognized the absence from his war poems of that spiritual essence which would have engendered pity. While writing in *Siegfried's Journey* of the poems he composed in the war he observed, "Unconsciously, I was getting nearer to Wilfred Owen's method of approach. (For it was not until

two years later [1920] when I edited his poems, that I clearly apprehended the essentially compassionate significance of what he had been communicating)." Yet Sassoon's poems composed in the 1930's when, in my opinion, he reached the fulness of his prophetic powers, remained untempered by compassion in their relentless attack on man's propensity to fight.

When World War I ended, Sassoon continued to write satirical poems, castigating hypocrisy, vanity, and political corruption. His brief flirtation with the Labor Party right after the war provided him with some new material, but he failed to sustain his interest in local politics. He subsequently directed his thrusts mainly at the big-time "rumour breeders," the newspapers, whom he regarded as irresponsible molders of public opinion. (pp. 176-77)

When the war clouds reappeared over Europe and the arms race began that culminated in World War II, Siegfried Sassoon, the angry prophet, spoke once more to the people to warn them of destruction to come, of death to be rained down from the heavens, of cities to be leveled. These prophecies appeared chiefly in two volumes: *The Road to Ruin* (1933), and *Rhymed Ruminations* (1940). (p. 177)

In *The Road to Ruin* Sassoon predicted death by fire, gas, and disease. He offered no hope for mankind. He anticipated and elaborated both of the great fears of World War II, chemical and biological warfare. . . . Of course, he was not alone in sounding prophecies and no monopoly is claimed for him here, but he was playing masterfully a role he had determined for himself years before. (pp. 177-78)

Sassoon came to the end of the role of prophet in 1940. After World War II broke out, he stopped his warnings and paid as little heed as possible to world affairs. Strangely, when he used the war for a subject, his approach contained none of the earlier prophetic anger. He did not attack the government for misrepresentation or the people at home for indifference. His **"Silent Service"** is so unlike the poems which made him famous that it is difficult to accept the fact that he composed [its] lines. . . . We are impressed, indeed, by the resemblance between this poem and Sassoon's **"Absolution."** . . . No longer the prophet, he has become instead an apologist for a government whose policies had long been anathema to him (p. 178)

Like the prophets of antiquity, who sometimes became disillusioned, Sassoon in his old age has thus ceased to be concerned directly with the affairs of this world, and he has begun to contemplate eternity. The prophet in Sassoon has turned into the hermit. . . .

Shortly before World War I started, Sassoon began to develop in his poetry the role of country gentleman. Since he did not publish *The Old Huntsman and Other Poems,* which reveals the presence of this role, until 1917, it was prematurely eclipsed by his immediate acceptance as prophet. Yet Sassoon believed at the time of publication that his long blank-verse title-piece, **"The Old Huntsman,"** was more important than either the war poems or a third section he included, made up of lush romantic lyrics composed between 1908 and 1916. He had written **"The Old Huntsman"** in desperation in 1915 when he realized that he was nearly thirty years old and had not yet found his own voice. He knew that the romantic lyrics with their distillations of his childhood reveries . . . were not only inconsequential but lacking in authenticity. In 1913 he had heard, for the first time, his authentic voice when he composed a parody of John Masefield's *Everlasting Mercy*, called *The Daffodil Murderer*.

This poem . . . impersonated a jailed Sussex farmhand awaiting trial for homicide. . . . (p. 179)

Two years later Sassoon recognized that the Sussex farmhand was a figure more familiar to him than the ghosts of his childhood dreams, and "**The Old Huntsman**" began to take shape. The struggling poet found it easy to develop in a lifelike portrait the central figure of this poem just as he had the similar one in the Masefield parody, giving his hero—and here the huntsman is his hero rather than the foot-soldiers of the war poems—an authenticity he had not achieved before. Part of this authenticity comes from allowing the old rustic to develop a series of pastoral images in his simple musings. . . . (pp.179-80)

Understandably, the war poems in the *The Old Huntsman* commanded all the attention, and the title-piece was subsequently ignored by the public. Having himself become preoccupied with the war, Sassoon did not return to the themes of hunting and riding to hounds, but nature remained for him a constant source of inspiration. When the war ended and the public tired of refighting its battles, Sassoon was among the first to attempt to revive the Georgian devotion to nature and pastoral sports. (p. 180)

For one who knew death as intimately as Sassoon did in the trenches, this would seem to be little more than a superficial pose. Yet it was that close association with wholesale human destruction that crystallized for the poet what was of fundamental importance to him: the pleasures of a youth spent in a pastoral setting. Consequently, as he got farther and farther away from the war, he moved ever closer to the re-creation of the rustic wonderland of his mother's country estate. Not only did the Great War ultimately push Sassoon into the past; it disengaged him from the normal activities of a machine-filled world. (pp. 181-82)

It remains only to be noted that with the publication of each succeeding volume, Sassoon's relationship with nature becomes more individualized, and his poems more personal. Occasionally, this close identity produces a poem of much charm. . . . (p. 182)

At other times, Sassoon sees so little outside of his immediate association with nature that his poems become banal. (p. 183)

Banality is not the only result of individualizing too much one's relationships with nature in a machine-dominated century. To de-emphasize the value and the necessity of machines and, more important, of human contacts, in favor of birds, horses, dogs, butterflies, stars, and trees is to invite hermithood. Just as the disillusionment of the unheeded prophet pushed Sassoon toward the role of hermit, so has overindulgence in the role of the country gentleman.

To live the role of the hermit one needs a forest, a cell, a candle, a bed, and an inclination to live alone. In *Sequences,* which Sassoon published in 1956, he documents his acceptance of hermithood by describing his whole existence in these terms. Moreover, he possesses an appropriately introspective melancholy. . . . (pp. 183-84)

But the poet-hermit is no longer troubled with politics like the angry prophet, or concerned with pastoral sports like the country gentleman. His interests are largely metaphysical. . . .

[The] emphasis is almost always on the personal quest for immortality, and Sassoon addresses his own "unscientific selfhood" to "Ask the night sky for intimations of God." His contemplative answer is that of the typical hermit: God exists,

but man has a long and difficult journey to travel in order to reach Him. . . . (p. 184)

Consequently, for his recent verses, and for his way of life, Sassoon is everywhere regarded today as a hermit. . . .

But while Hardy, and Henry Vaughan too, have helped to shape Sassoon into the hermit, the role he plays at present is rather the product of his life experience: the transformation of the angry prophet and the country gentleman into the self-effaced hermit.

In playing all three roles, Sassoon has recorded poetically the crumbling of the old order and the disappearance of a way of life better than the one which replaced it. In this respect, Sassoon is more like Proust than like Vaughan or Hardy. Like Proust, who was also the product of a mixed religious and social union, he has sealed himself off and written compellingly from the bed of his mind, his "remembrance of things past." It is for this achievement, I believe, that Robert Graves is justified in including Sassoon among those in the "small, clear stream of living poetry." (p. 185)

> *Joseph Cohen, "The Three Roles of Siegfried Sassoon," in* TSE: Tulane Studies in English, *Vol. VII, 1957, pp. 169-85.*

C. E. MAGUIRE

John Middleton Murry, writing in 1918 [see excerpt above] with the stern authority only the very young critic can achieve, decided that Siegfried Sassoon's *Counter Attack,* then enjoying best seller status, was "not poetry." . . . Not only was the language overwrought, dense and turgid, but the verse failed to express the relation of war's horror to "the harmony and calm of the soul which it shatters." . . . Sassoon simply presented the data of desolation, which the reader had to relate to some serenity before art could be achieved. What was missing Murry thought obvious: it was a philosophical background which might have allowed Sassoon to grapple with his experience and comprehend it. This background would give some "intellectual remoteness" to the verse, and save it from presenting mere brute fact.

It is difficult to quarrel with this estimate, especially since Sassoon's subsequent literary career seems like a (characteristically) docile attempt to remedy the faults Murry points out. (p. 115)

Although he always wanted to be a poet, he spent almost three decades of his life happily untouched by, or cautiously evading, intellectual influences. His school career was undistinguished, his university course cut short. His law notes were "more physical than mental exercise." Released from bondage, he devoted himself almost exclusively to fox hunting. With this sport he so identified himself, [that he called] his first "novel" *Memoirs of a Fox-Hunting Man* and his first well known volume of verse *The Old Huntsman.* . . . Hunting was for him a poetic apprenticeship akin to Wordsworth's early communing with nature. It combined adventure, beauty, comradeship. He was not coming to conclusions about people or events, but saturating his senses with the feel of things. He was not exactly becoming mature, either mentally or emotionally; his reaction to the war proves this. He was, as Murry might put it, accumulating data.

The war turned him into a rebel, though not all at once. Robert Graves reports that before he had seen action, he told Graves the latter's poems were "too realistic, and that war should not be written about in a realistic way." . . . When he and Graves talked of peace, Sassoon defined it "in terms of hunting and nature and music and pastoral scenes." . . . But the cumulative effect of the war's horrors broke both the physical strength he had built up in the hunting years and his emotional balance. When in 1917 he was invalided home, he was "a beastly wreck and in a rotten state of nerves." Out of this experience grew the horror poems of *Counter Attack,* which made his reputation as a fierce anti-war propagandist.

It is ironical that this aspect of his writing and his personality should be the only one remembered, for it was a brief and uncharacteristic interlude. (pp. 116 17)

> *C. E. Maguire, "Harmony Unheard: The Poetry of Siegfried Sassoon," in* Renascence, *Vol XI, No. 3, Spring, 1959, pp. 115-24.*

DONALD DAVIE

Graves and Sassoon—it's not any accident of publishers' or reviewers' time-tables which brings them up for judgment together [with Sassoon's *Collected Poems 1908-1956* and Graves's *More Poems, 1961*]. One hardly thinks of the one without the other. And of course it's Sassoon who comes off worse. Two poets who set out together with the same shoddy late-Victorian equipment: one of them in mid-career discarded the unserviceable inheritance, bag and baggage, the other still carries the whole dead weight of it; one of them may be the most important British poet now writing, the other seems an anachronism.

What Graves rejected, what Sassoon hung on to, was not just the lumber of inadequate language and inadequate conventions in verse, but also, and necessarily, the lumber of inadequate sentiments and attitudes. Graves, by rejecting this, was able not just to write 20th-century poetry but to live a representative 20th-century life. Sassoon, backward-looking, refused. And yet, in another sense, it is Graves who looks backward much farther, and that is his strength. For the language in his poems reverberates with the whole of its history from earliest times to the present; whereas the English that Sassoon writes knows of nothing before 1840 as well as nothing since 1914.

At least, however, Sassoon has been consistent all through. One sees this, reading his *Collected Poems* as a whole. And it's important. For remembering **'Blighters'** and **'Base Details'** and **'The General'** and **'Everyone Sang'**, the justly famous anthology pieces from 1914-18, one had surmised (and surely it's been said) that the trenches shocked Sassoon into the 20th century and gave him perceptions which he later went back upon. This isn't true. Those poems . . . represent splendidly brave and decent actions by the human being, but not any breakthrough by the poet. They are memorable human achievements, but not properly speaking poetic achievements at all. . . . Thus, after the war, Sassoon had nothing to go back on. (pp. 958-59)

But in any case this volume deserves better than to have future anthologists picking it over; it has, and will have, extraordinary value as a representative document, of one sort of English decency struggling in terms of its decencies to come to terms with our world. (p. 959)

> *Donald Davie, "Poets and Improvisers," in* New Statesman, *Vol. LXI, No. 1579, June 16, 1961, pp. 958-59.**

HOWARD SERGEANT

After the first few weeks of fighting [in World War I] a veritable flood of war poetry and verse was produced by established and unestablished poets, soldiers and civilians alike. (p. 37)

After several months, however, there was a distinct change of tone in the work of most of the poets on active service, and with it a truer presentation of war itself, based, of course, on personal experience. The emphasis was switched from the heroic sacrifice of the combatants to the conditions under which they were compelled to perform the duties assigned to them. Even where the original note of dedication to a noble cause was still evident, it was far more restrained than before and frequently identified with a spirit of comradeship. In place of the vague abstractions and lofty sentiments which characterised the opening phase of hostilities, we find realistic accounts of particular engagements, of the daily routine at the Front, and of the life shared by the soldiers in and behind the Lines; in place of public laments "for the fallen" in general, poems prompted by the deaths of intimate comrades.

A second and more significant change in the attitude of the combatants was noticeable after the disastrous Battle of the Somme in the summer of 1916. For some months previous to that engagement the men in the trenches had been growing more and more conscious of the difference in outlook between the civilian population at home and themselves. Experience had taught them that war was not the romantic adventure they had conceived it to be, and that neither the physical agony and violent death they had witnessed nor the suffering and hardship they had themselves endured, were to be expunged from their memories by the seemingly complacent iteration of such euphemisms as "reported missing" and "our glorious dead".

The war poems of Siegfried Sassoon clearly illustrate this changed attitude. . . . Like his contemporaries, he had joined the army in a spirit of devotion to duty, and though he had resisted the temptation to indulge in the high-souled extravagancies of Rupert Brooke, whom he greatly admired, he had been as convinced as the rest of his generation of the heroic nature of the task to be performed.

The realities of trench warfare, then, broke upon him as a complete contrast to anything he had known or imagined of the soldier's life, and so outraged his sensibilities that he could no longer write in his former innocent manner. His deep sympathy for his comrades strengthened his determination to tell the truth about the war, to expose it, with all its inhumanity and intolerable waste of life, for the monstrous evil he had discovered it to be, and, above all, to shock the civilians at home out of their state of complacent ignorance. . . . (pp. 37-8)

To achieve his object he made use of a colloquial style owing much to the experiments of John Masefield, and was at first inclined to allow his anger to rise unchecked so that his verse became the vehicle for emotional outbursts. After he had recovered from the initial shock of his experience of front-line conditions, however, his lyrical impulse began to assert itself in a new way and this, combined with his talent for ironic statement, added an extraordinary power to his work. With his emotions under control he was more able to crystallize his thoughts into pungent phrases—to select his targets with greater discrimination and, hence, to give his satire a keener edge than when he was rebuking unimaginative bishops. The poems which immediately followed, reaching a magnificent climax in *Everyone Sang,* are the finest of his whole poetic career. In them his natural tenderness . . . his realistic attention to detail . . .

and the intensity of his feeling for his comrades of the trenches, as well as his most effective irony, are fittingly conveyed and co-ordinated.

It may well be maintained that the experience of war galvanized him into creating genuine poetry, for afterwards he was never able to recall the spirit which had moved him during the turbulent years of warfare. Nor could he go back to his earlier pastoralism; the world had irrevocably changed and he had changed with it. . . . It was as if he had completely exhausted the capacity for strong feeling (at least, so far as his poetry was concerned) and, seeing little cause for hope in the contemporary scene, was growing more and more dependent upon his memories . . . , turning to history for solace and searching among the "barrows of the century-darkened dead". Again and again in the lyrical poems of *The Heart's Journey* (1928) and *Vigils* (1935) we find him listening for "vanished voices". . . . (pp. 39-40)

The best of his later satirical pieces . . . are amusing as casual verse, but lack the sting and the urgency of his satire of the First World War. By the time that hostilities broke out again with the war of 1939-45 the poet who, in 1917, had protested so bitterly against "the callous complacency with which the majority of those at home regard the continuance of agonies which they do not share, and which they have not sufficient imagination to realise", could speak of war in the following terms:

> In every separate soul let courage shine—
> A kneeling angel holding faith's front-line. . . .

The keynote of his *Sequences,* published in 1956, is to be found in a poem appropriately entitled *Ultimate Values*. . . .

Memories and awareness of the past inform most of the poems in this volume with a philosophical mellowness wrung from experience. Now somewhat bewildered by the atomic age in which we live, yet steadfast in his religious faith, Sassoon turns with obvious relief to watch a coal-tit in a tree or to observe . . . [the appearance of the first day of spring]. (p. 40)

His failure to sustain his poetic intensity and his detachment from the social and political conditions of the twenties and thirties may have been due to the disillusionment of the inter-war period, but they can also be explained as the incidental developments of the very attitude which informed his poetry of protest. No-one was more deeply moved than Sassoon by awareness of human suffering, but he was concerned with the immediate and obvious effects of the War—widespread suffering, in fact, and the tragedy of wasted life—rather than with the circumstances which had made such a conflict possible. (pp. 40-1)

> Howard Sergeant, "Siegfried Sassoon—Poet of War," in Contemporary Review, Vol. 202, July, 1962, pp. 37-41.

BERNARD BERGONZI

Apart from the transiently popular Nichols, Sassoon was the one soldier poet to be widely read during the course of the war. In 1917 *The Old Huntsman* made an impact on civilians because of the originality of its themes, and on soldiers because of [its] authenticity. . . . And in the following year, the searing poetic manifesto of *Counter-Attack* attracted a large number of admiring readers, among them—rather disconcertingly for Sassoon—Winston Churchill.

There was nothing in Sassoon's early life and background to suggest a potential rebel and a defier both of public opinion and military authority. . . . Sassoon typified an *echt*-Georgian state of mind: whatever radicalism he manifested during the war was forced upon him by events, not temperament; and in his moments of most bitter anger his poetic methods remained traditional, however startling his sentiments. (p. 92)

As Sassoon indicated, the impulse behind the more mature war poems in *The Old Huntsman* was strictly realistic, even naturalistic, a desire to show things as they were without any haze of patriotic sentiment. In some ways Sassoon was not particularly well equipped for the role of ruthless realist; his basic, strongly Georgian sensibility and background were very inclined to see man and his surroundings in some kind of harmony, no matter how precarious. In such a poem as '**At Carnoy**', for instance, he traces this harmony on the very edge of its imminent dissolution. . . . Here the subjoined date—two days after the opening of the Somme offensive—is an intrinsic part of the poem's meaning. It was circumstances rather than temperament that made Sassoon a realist; unlike some of his fellow soldier poets he could not be content with using scenes of rural English life as a compensation and balance for the brutality of life at the Front: in '**The One-Legged Man**' Sassoon thrusts the two together in angry and shocking juxtaposition. The poem begins as a deceptive pastoral piece. . . . But in the final couplet the unexpected point is hammered home with unsubtle force. . . . In other, similarly epigrammatic poems Sassoon directs an impulse of pure anger across the constantly growing gulf that separated the unthinking civilian world of the Nation at Home with its jingoistic slogans from the embattled Nation overseas. (pp. 95-6)

Elsewhere in *The Old Huntsman* collection Sassoon made a more radical onslaught on traditional attitudes than he may have realized; as in '**The Hero**'. . . . In this poem—based all too probably on authentic happenings—the image of the hero is undermined with the energy of a Thersites. Sassoon has observed of this poem and '**The One-Legged Man**': 'These performances had the quality of satirical drawings. They were deliberately written to disturb complacency.' This sums up very well the quality of Sassoon's war poetry; it has a deliberate simplicity and hard outline that recalls the impact of good poster art. He is usually regarded as a smaller, because less compassionate and universal, poet than Owen; and this is certainly true. Satire does not reach the heights achieved by Owen's generalized lyric pity; but the comparison is not an easy one, and within the limitations of his satirical mode Sassoon is a brilliant performer. In those poems, however, in which he attempts something closer to Owen's manner, Sassoon's treatment is less assured. (p. 96)

In *The Old Huntsman* one can follow the transformation of Sassoon's war poetry from early conventional idealism to the severe realism of the poems based on his note-book entries; and here the tone is often didactic rather than realistic in any detached documentary fashion: Sassoon was increasingly dominated by the desire to use poetry as a means of forcibly impressing on the civilian world some notion of the realities of front-line life. In his next collection, *Counter-Attack,* . . . we find Sassoon's most powerful and memorable war poetry. But between the publication of the two books Sassoon underwent the experience that he has described in detail in *Memoirs of an Infantry Officer* . . . : his revolt against military authority, his one-man campaign against the continuation of the war. (p. 97)

In [the poems of *Counter-Attack*] Sassoon completes the transformation of documentary realism into an angry didactic outcry. Although he was never a poetic modernist or even, like Owen, a conscious experimenter, Sassoon was forced by the need for exactness in registering front-line experience into a degree of colloquial language and a conversational tone that was still a novelty in contemporary verse. (p. 102)

Yet despite the extended range in *Counter-Attack,* Sassoon remains fundamentally a poet of narrow but direct effects: his language is hard, clear, sharply defined, rather than suggestive or capable of the associative effects of a poet of larger resources. On the whole, Sassoon remained aware of his limitations and did not attempt a profundity that was beyond him: his gifts were, pre-eminently, those of a satirist, and it was in satire that he excelled. . . . The principal target for Sassoon's satire was the civilian population, and in particular, figures like politicians and journalists, who issued exhortations or encouragements to the troops without having any real conception of what they were enduring. (p. 105)

Counter-Attack secured Sassoon's reputation as a poet. By 1918 the public mood was ready for what he had to say, and his attacks on the Nation at Home were accepted with a possibly masochistic fervour. It found admirers in unexpectedly high places. . . . Thus, Sassoon's anti-war outcry had been transformed . . . into a subtler form of pro-war propaganda. The Establishment has always been adept at incorporating rebels, and Sassoon—now once more a serving officer—saw something of the process when he was invited to meet Churchill and good-humouredly treated to a set speech on the militaristic virtues. (pp. 106-07)

If the poems in *Counter-Attack* were, in fact, regarded as inspired shell-shock symptoms, as psychological evidence rather than moral statements, then it seems as if Sassoon's public protest was blunted, just as his attempt at a personal protest had been. Nevertheless these poems, expressing a mood of anti-heroic revolt with such fervour and harsh wit, strike a new and incisive note in the literature of war.

Throughout the 'twenties, when he continued to have left-wing leanings, Sassoon wrote sharp, epigrammatic verses that sniped at authority and conventional attitudes. In this respect he was at one with his age . . . , and sometimes these poems rise to an unusual level of poetic intensity. . . . As with other writers who narrowly survived the Great War, it was to remain Sassoon's one authentic subject; it, or the emotions stemming from it, inspired his best poems, and his admirable prose works. When Sassoon attempted to write straightforward poems on subjects remote from the war, he dwindled to the stature of a minor Georgian survival: the bulk of his later poetry, sententious or laxly pastoral, is carefully written and overpoweringly dull. He continued to write pungently satirical poems into the 'thirties, but in 1940 he commemorated the feelings of the time in one or two flatly conventional patriotic poems. . . . But it is the poems of 1916-18 that count, and that represent Sassoon's ineradicable contribution both to English poetry and the records of the Great War. (pp. 107-08)

> Bernard Bergonzi, *"Poets III: Sassoon," in his He-
> roes' Twilight: A Study of the Literature of the Great
> War, 1965. Reprint by Coward-McCann, Inc., 1966,
> pp. 92-108.*

PETER LEVI

How wonderful that Siegfried Sassoon is eighty, and that we should still have a poet whose taproot reaches the nineteenth century. One can experience in his poetry the slow, restless ripening of a very great talent; its magnitude has not yet been recognised. He has been after all really important in the history of modern poetry, and the importance is not over; both personally and as an influence, a doctor of the language, he is one of the few poets of his generation we are really unable to do without. The serious and absolutely authentic tone of his voice now is as different from the false Georgianism into which English poetry has relapsed as his early poems were different from the thick green Georgian atmosphere of his youth.

The secret seems to me to be sheer intelligence and truth to nature and his own nature, and to be summed up in the influence of Hardy and of Henry Vaughan. . . .

[The] strength and compassion and the human decency of English poetry at the end of the war came to life through Sassoon, and it seems to be due to the marvellous instrument of language and of feeling which had been prepared and developed by Hardy. . . .

The war was important for Sassoon's poetry chiefly in making it more urgent and opening in him a level of absolute seriousness, but he was not simply a war poet; in *Counter-Attack* (1918) he published with poems like *The General* and *Suicide in the Trenches*, a beautiful and tranquil elegy for a fellow-foxhunter. Sassoon's very strong feeling for riding and the countryside is a large part of what has made him in the past thirty years an unfashionable poet. . . . (p. 171)

Yet all this time, regardless of fault or fashion, every book of Sassoon's poetry has had a serious claim on the world's attention. . . . It was not just that in *Counter-Attack* he had published some important poems which were still direct and exciting; it was not his instinctive or temperamental principles; it was nothing to do with a rusticated lyrical tradition. It was directness, an evocative honesty of the eyes, and a harshly sweet resonance reminiscent of a violoncello.

It is particularly in his later poems that the seriousness and the musical noise have at last worked themselves out. His poetry divides roughly into three periods: the early rustic awakening with the astonishing new dimensions of his war poetry; a satiric period which was linguistically interesting for the combination of casual bite with an admirably fibrous Hardyesque verbal texture; and a ruminative and metaphysical period, a late autumnal flowering. The first period led directly into the second, but the position from which the peacetime satires opened fire was neither as strong as Pope's nor as deeply entrenched as Hardy's; and the satire foundered. Perhaps its spirit was exorcised in prose.

The third period began restlessly and unhappily. Like most other metaphysical poets, Siegfried Sassoon has given the impression of many times replaying the same themes, and then suddenly against all the odds enunciating them with a simple clarity. He has worked throughout his life on resistant material, and in the last period of his poetry as in the first, he has opened the possibility through a few unique and extraordinary poems of a particularly truthful style and tone of voice that without him might have been impossible. His late poems have had a brooding delicacy that fits particularly closely to the thought-rhythms of an ageing, meditative man, his mind and words sharpened by a lifetime of genuine, personal poetry.

There is a sense in which Sassoon is not a major poet; but in this sense there is a specially high degree of honesty and individuality which belong exclusively to minor poets. He has achieved this degree.

There is still a temptation, which at times he seems to have found seductive as a self-image, to equate his poetry with the sober, beautiful world of nineteenth-century topographical artists. . . . But one should compare the received religious conceptions of his early poems . . . with the colder meditations which overcame them. Something essential in him, an instinctive movement to lament, an early shaking of hands with failure and with the idea of God, comes to its meaning only in the final handful of sparse, hermetic poetry, like a few leaves on an old tree.

What strength and what interest there is in the enormous oak-tree of his poems, in the depth of its root and in its final crown of leaves: *de l'arrière-saison la rayon jaune et douce.* (pp. 172-73)

Peter Levi, "Sassoon at Eighty," in Poetry Review, *Vol. LVIII, No. 3, Autumn, 1966, pp. 171-73.*

PAUL FUSSELL

What is unique in Sassoon is the brilliance with which he exploits the dichotomies forced to his attention by his wartime experience and refines them until they become the very fiber of his superb memoir of the war.

One of the most flagrant of dichotomies is that between prewar and postwar Sassoon, between the "nice" unquestioning youth of good family, alternately athlete and dreamer, and the fierce moralist of 1917, surging with outrage and disdain. (p. 90)

Between the ages of nineteen and twenty-six he published privately nine volumes of dreamy Keatsian and Tennysonian verse, and it is this body of work that Blunden has in mind when he observes that, oddly, "no poet of twentieth-century England, to be sure, was originally more romantic and floral than young Siegfried Sassoon from Kent."

The war changed all that. (pp. 90-1)

What Blunden calls Sassoon's "splendid war on the war" took place initially in the pages of the *Cambridge Magazine*, which published many of the anti-war—or better, anti-home-front—poems collected in the volume *The Old Huntsman* in May, 1917. Two months later he issued his notorious *non serviam*, **"A Soldier's Declaration."** (p. 91)

By the time of the Armistice he was exhausted and trembly, sleepless and overwrought, fit for no literary work. He found peace and quiet again in Kent, but nightmares kept intruding. By 1926, however, he had recovered sufficiently to begin work on the obsessive enterprise which occupied most of the rest of his life, the re-visiting of the war and the contrasting world before the war in a series of six volumes of artful memoirs. The writing took him from one war to another: he finished the job in 1945. The first three volumes (later collected and titled *The Memoirs of George Sherston*) comprise *Memoirs of a Fox-Hunting Man* (1928), *Memoirs of an Infantry Officer* (1930), and *Sherston's Progress* (1936). This trilogy deals with elements of his life from about 1895 to 1918. In the next volume, *The Old Century and Seven More Years* (1938), he went back to his infancy and boyhood and with less fictional concealment covered the years 1886 to 1909. In *The Weald of Youth* (1942), he focused on that part of his prewar life, the "indoor" and "London" part, which for the sake of artistic coherence he had largely suppressed in the "outdoor" *Memoirs of a Fox-*

Hunting Man. In *The Weald of Youth* he depicts his hobble-dehoy country self in embarrassed contact with literary and stylish London from 1909 to 1914. The final volume, *Siegfried's Journey* (1945), deals with his literary activity during the Great War and with his first two postwar years, from 1918 to 1920, from the viewpoint of the Second War. The whole autobiographical labor consumed almost twenty years of nervous concentration. . . . (pp. 91-2)

Of all those for whom remembering the war became something like a life work, Sassoon is the one whose method of recall, selection, and expression seems to derive most directly from the polarities which the war pressed into the recesses of his mind. (p. 92)

To see what Sassoon does with such insistent polarities, to see the way they determine his whole lifetime mental set and become the matrices of his memory, we must turn to the three works constituting *The Memoirs of George Sherston*.

In *Memoirs of a Fox-Hunting Man* Sassoon has rearranged events to emphasize a polarity between his "Aunt Evelyn," with whom he lives in "Butley," Kent, and Tom Dixon, her groom. To simplify and clear the ground for this operation, he gets rid of his own parents, saying, "My father and mother died before I was capable of remembering them" . . . , although in *Siegfried's Journey* his mother is still living when he's thirty-four. Being raised by "Aunt Evelyn" is a way of not writing about one's real mother, a way of turning a deeply emotional actuality into something close to romantic comedy. Aunt Evelyn is comic and innocent and likable, fearful of "George"'s breaking his neck one day on those horses. The groom Dixon, on the other hand, finds his main pleasure in shrewdly slipping round Aunt Evelyn's wishes and introducing George to serious, risky horsemanship. Sherston tells us of his loneliness and his yearning for a "dream friend," whose failure to materialize made his early life "not altogether happy." . . . (pp. 92-4)

Four-fifths of *Memoirs of a Fox-Hunting Man* is pastoral romance, but pastoral romance complicated by criticism from the forty-year-old Sassoon. Looking back with affectionate pity at young Sherston's innocence, and with some sorrow at his social snobbery, Sassoon manages to assay him while summarizing one particularly exciting day of hunting: "All the sanguine guesswork of youth is there, and the silliness; all the novelty of being alive and impressed by the urgency of tremendous trifles." (p. 94)

If the theme of the "peaceful" part of the book had to be expressed as an infinitive, it would be *to be alive,* or *to be glad,* that is, not to know the "secret meaning" of Love and Death. (p. 95)

One large prevailing irony never overtly surfaces, but the whole course of events implies it. This is the fate of cavalry in the unanticipated war of static confrontation. The whole first part of *Memoirs of a Fox-Hunting Man* prepares us, as it prepares George, to expect for him a brilliant career in the cavalry, which was still, in the days of his youth, virtually the equivalent of "the Army." What is going to happen instead is just hinted in the little participial phrase about motoring here: "Dixon had taken (George's favorite horse) Cockbird to Downfield the day after mobilization, and had returned home just in time to interview some self-important persons who were motoring about the country requisitioning horses for the Army." . . . The joyous comings and goings of horses and riders which make the early part of the book a celebration of utterly unrestrained movement stop abruptly, to be replaced by their opposite, stasis in fixed trenches.

Memoirs of an Infantry Officer, the second volume of the trilogy, exhibits a similar overall ironic structure. But here the irony underlines not only the futility of the war, but—surprisingly—the futility of polarizing one's opposition to it. If the target of hatred in the first volume was the war itself, the target of a wonder verging on ridicule in the second is George Sherston himself, and especially his habit (from which the first volume has so notably benefited) of facile antithesis.

The dynamics of *Memoirs of an Infantry Officer* are penetration and withdrawal: repeated entrances into the center of trench experience, repeated returns to the world of "home." . . . From the repeated ins and outs and the contrasts they emphasize, George learns "the truth about the war": that it is ruining England and has no good reason for continuing. (pp. 96-7)

George notes everywhere a new cynicism about the war and observes in himself an increasing confusion of attitudes about it. His own personal poles are widening daily. As Graves says of Sassoon, "He varied between happy warrior and bitter pacifist." In April George's battalion is committed to the line near Arras, and his intellectual and political awareness begins to sharpen. The sight of "an English soldier lying by the road with a horribly smashed head" triggers one of his first political perceptions. "In 1917," George says, "I was only beginning to learn that life, for the majority of the population, is an unlovely struggle against unfair odds, culminating in a cheap funeral." . . . Although he is not moved quite to Lear's

O, I have ta'en
Too little care of this!

he is now able to understand how for some the war is simply a continuation of "life" by other means, a mere intensification of the gross state of nature which is their normal lot. They are always engaged in what George recognizes in *Sherston's Progress* as the 'battle of life.'" . . . (pp. 98-9)

He is about to be wounded and to go out of the line for what seems the last time. . . . In hospital, he stokes his bitterness by gobbling up liberal reading matter like "Markingtons'" *The Unconservative Weekly* (H. W. Massingham's *The Nation*). Sent to convalesce at "Nutwood Manor," Lord and Lady Asterisk's country seat (actually Lord and Lady Brassey's, in Sussex), he grows even angrier as he contrasts the tenor of letters from his battalion with his hostess's highminded but vague Theosophical optimism.

On June 7, at the very moment the attack on Messines is in progress, he lunches—a gross polarity!—with Markington at his London club and hears him hint that Britain's war aims have now become crudely acquisitive. In consultation with "Thornton Tyrrell" (Bertrand Russell) and now brimming with zeal and self-righteousness, he composes his statement of mutiny and defiance. He launches his gesture from the recesses of Butley, where he carefully overstays his month's leave. He mails copies to newspapers and sends one direct to Clitherland Camp to "explain" his non-appearance there for re-posting. The statement itself perceptively asserts the hopeless division that has opened between the two Britains, but Sassoon's presentation of George writing it is satirical and ironic; he speaks of "working myself up into a tantrum" . . . and of convincing himself that, through his agency, "truth would be revealed." . . . The rhetoric of the statement, which busily divides all things into twos, admits of few shadings or qualifications:

. . . I believe that the war is being deliberately prolonged by those who have the power to end it.

I believe that this war, upon which I entered as a war of defense and liberation, has now become a war of aggression and conquest. . . .

On behalf of those who are suffering now I make this protest against the deception which is being practiced on them; also I believe that I may help to destroy the callous complacence with which the majority of those at home regard the continuance of agonies which they do not share, and which they have not sufficient imagination to realize. . . .

But what he discovers when he finally presents himself at Clitherland, rigid with self-consciousness, is not at all the adversary proceedings he has been soliciting. To his astonishment, everyone there is very pleasant to him, if a bit embarrassed by his imprudence. He has expected to encounter the enemy in a melodramatic court-martial. Ironically, the authorities decline to accept the role of enemy that George insists they assume. Slipping out of the binary trap that George has contrived for them, they convene a Special Medical Board, pronounce him shell-shocked, and send him, with all good wishes, to a benign sanitarium. (The convalescent David Cromlech has been their shrewd intermediary.) Their solution is one which George has not even entertained as a possibility; it is a gentle rebuke not so much to his mutinous pacifism as to his habit of simpleminded binary vision, and Sassoon's treatment of that habit from a distance of thirteen years bespeaks his awareness of its intellectual and emotional and artistic limitations, even if he has invited it to dominate the structure and texture of his memoir. Sassoon is being critical of his art as well as of his wartime character. He is pointing to the defect both owe to their origin in something so exaggerated, mechanical, and overwrought as the Great War.

In the final volume, *Sherston's Progress,* George makes, as he says, a "definite approach to mental maturity." . . . He learns that the world-wide disaster implicating him is beyond his understanding and thus surely beyond his influence or control. A severe critic would find the texture of *Sherston's Progress* the least artistic among the three volumes: there are signs of impatience and fatigue. One such sign is the frequent and sometimes embarrassingly self-conscious auctorial intrusions which shatter the verisimilitude, like this chapter opening: "Sitting myself down at the table to resume this laborious task after twenty-four hours' rest, I told myself that I was 'really feeling fairly fresh again.'" . . . Another index of fatigue is Sassoon's leaving seventy-three pages in something close to their original form as diary, without troubling to transmute them into something closer to fiction. The book was written in four months at the end of 1935, and Sassoon was doubtless distracted and disheartened both by the Depression and by signs in Europe that the Great War was about to come alight again. But whatever its weaknesses in its smaller elements, the book in its overall structure is as tellingly ironic as its predecessors. (pp. 99-101)

As I have indicated, the trilogy is elaborately structured to enact the ironic redemption of a shallow fox-hunting man by terrible events. If the delights of mindless sport are warmly and straightforwardly celebrated in the first volume and recalled with pleasure even in the last, the intervening events make

George at the end an illustration of William Shenstone's mid-eighteenth-century dictum: "The world may be divided into people that read, people that write, people that think, and fox-hunters." It is to reveal George's new capacity for understanding this—and the cost of that understanding—that the trilogy is written. The trilogy, that is, enforces a "moral" point; Sassoon's own life at the time makes no moral point at all.

For during the years covered by the *Memoirs* Sassoon was most conspicuous not as a fox-hunter but as a publishing poet excited by his literary career and careful always to advance it. This was the center of his life, but we hear nothing of it whatever in the *Memoirs*. To find out about it we must go to *Siegfried's Journey*, where he confesses that "Sherston was a simplified version of my 'outdoor self.' He was denied the complex advantage of being a soldier poet." (pp. 102-03)

I think the reason is that Sassoon wants his contrasts to be as bold and dramatic as possible. A poet is a contrast to an infantry officer, all right; but there is an even greater contrast between a fox-hunter brimming with health and a puling neurasthenic.

I must emphatically disagree, then, with Arthur E. Lane, who says: "*The Memoirs of George Sherston* is in no way fictional, unless one balks at the use of pseudonyms such as Thornton Tyrrell (for Bertrand Russell) and David Cromlech (for Robert Graves)." I would say that the *Memoirs* is in every way fictional and that it would be impossible to specify how it differs from any other novel written in the first person and based on the author's own experience. (pp. 103-04)

Even if we allow that in Sassoon's *Memoirs* historical events and personal fiction do walk hand-in-hand, it is clear that what is presiding throughout is not fidelity to fact but workmanship. (p. 104)

Paul Fussell, "Adversary Proceedings," in his The Great War and Modern Memory, *Oxford University Press, 1975, pp. 75-113.**

P. J. KAVANAGH

Siegfried Sassoon, as [*Diaries: 1920-1922* shows], finished up after the First World War as a literary star of magnitude difficult to imagine today. Not only was he physically (Military Cross) and morally (his public stance against war's continuance) courageous, his poems were clear, the anger in them comprehensible and they were also good. Today they ring as true as they ever did; it is difficult to see how they could be better.

So we find him in 1920, when these diaries begin, settling down to write some more; courted, flattered, genuinely befriended by just about all the great literary figures of the time and by his contemporaries too, those of them who had survived.

What could be more pleasant? No material worries, talent, and great fame: the only trouble was, he could no longer write good poems. There is not the slightest reason to feel superior to Sassoon because of this; what he had done, and was later to do in prose, can speak for itself. But a poet who can no longer produce the stuff is in a miserable position. . . .

So there is the interest (if that is what it is) of literary frustration. But there is the greater interest of glimpsing what literary life in London, in the early Twenties, was like; the vastly comfortable way that even moderately successful writers passed their days. They all seemed to live in each other's pockets.

Sassoon's own life, in its surface rhythms, makes one want to spit with envy. An unattached bachelor of private means, he has two rooms in W. J. Turner's house in Westminster, with Turner on hand for conversation about poetry (or about sex) whenever Sassoon feels like it. Lunch at the Reform, a concert in the afternoon, the *Ballets Russes* in the evening, supper tête-à-tête with Arnold Bennett or H. G. Wells, W. H. Davies dropping in, and Frank Swinnerton, and Robert Graves . . . week-end in the country with Thomas Hardy. There is nothing forced or organised about this. In London all the lions seem to inhabit the same postal district, and tread the same pavements, go to the same theatre on the same evening. . . . And so on, almost every day. It should have been fun.

Alas, apart from the agony of unwritten or empty poems, and apart from the homosexuality which, though unremorseful, seems a sad tale of romantic passion followed at once by resigned, friendly disillusion, other splits begin to appear. He vanishes to Cirencester to his hunting friends, he enjoys this, and enjoys them, but they are too unthinking for him, whereas his London friends cannot share the physical excitements he craves. These are matters he writes marvellously about later in his prose-books, but not here. He is still bewildered.

There is something worse; this self-aware, fêted rebel is unconsciously trapped, and the trap is social. He belongs to the unconventional, artistic, upper-class and he sees too much of them. One can say that with confidence because he says so himself. Even when he escapes, to Germany, to Italy, he bumps into them all the time. He even wastes his time cutting Osbert Sitwell in the Piazza San Marco (having already done so in Munich). Why, the contemporary reader asks himself, why the *blazes* didn't he go somewhere else? Or change his acquaintance? It is almost as though he believes there *is* no other world.

P. J. Kavanagh, "Slow Decline," in The Spectator, *Vol. 247, No. 7997, October 17, 1981, p. 21.*

DAVID MONTROSE

Siegfried Sassoon never disguised the fact that his autobiographies and his three 'George Sherston' novels were based on diaries. So when, in 1981, the first instalment of those diaries (1920-1922) picked up exactly where his third and last volume of autobiography, *Siegfried's Journey*, had broken off, it looked like an editorial admission that all earlier material had been thoroughly plundered by the author. Rather surprisingly, then, the second instalment [*Diaries 1915-1918*]—opening, in late 1915, when Sassoon joins his regiment in France, closing with the Armistice—harks back to the writer's active service: the period that, as fictionalised, began in the final chapter of *Memoirs of a Fox-Hunting Man* and continued straight through *Memoirs of an Infantry Officer* and *Sherston's Progress*. The first half of *Siegfried's Journey,* too, falls within its ambit. If anything, the congruence between the diaries and the novels is even greater than expected: there is little reordering of incident, and large portions have been transplanted almost entire. In fact, so finely-written is Sassoon's original that these portions often represent the trilogy's more striking passages.

That, as a poet, Sassoon was at his most prolific during 1915-1918 is amply reflected. Poems were copied into the diaries as they were completed; there are almost 60 here, ranging from Sassoon's best to his worst: nearly half of them were left uncollected. The poems' relationship to the diaries differs from that of Sassoon's other works. They were written concurrently, rather than years afterwards, and represented an alternative method of observation that usually complemented the day-to-day journalising instead of deriving from it. The diaries refute the critical opinion that Sassoon, when recreating his exploits for the trilogy, tempered the grim vision embodied in his poetry. Certainly, as John Lehmann has stated, several episodes from the poems undergo 'mollification of effect' in translation to the novels, but this is scanty evidence from which to draw inferences: Sassoon's novels seldom borrowed from his poetry. The diaries better indicate how faithfully experience was cast into fiction. Comparison reveals that a few harsh comments were softened, some diaristic terseness diffused, inevitably, through expansion into conventional prose; on the whole, though, the correspondence of tone is remarkable. Remembering, too, that Sassoon's outstanding poems were polemics designed to shock non-combatants at home, it seems likely that they represented a distillation, rather than the novels a dissipation, of the writer's increasing resentment.

Together with . . . [the] arrangement of the war poems—which allows them, for the first time, to be read in order of composition—the diaries . . . reinforce the existing picture of Sassoon's progress from, in Robert Graves's terms, 'happy warrior' to 'bitter pacifist'. . . . The trenches, as Graves predicted, changed Sassoon's style: a more realistic presentation of events was soon evident. Nevertheless, as the diaries demonstrate, Sassoon still tended to treat trench warfare as another, if bloodier, field sport: his fearlessness was a byword.

In fact, the 'bitter pacifist' was not completely formed until late 1916. Sassoon had been invalided home that August with trench fever. At the front, his declining belief in the war had manifested itself through reckless bravery. A common pattern: fighting loss of faith by reaffirming it all the more strongly. In England, though, it proved more difficult to avoid brooding. Unfortunately, the diary for that sick-leave is missing, but both *Memoirs of an Infantry Officer* and *Siegfried's Journey*—which is Sassoon's only autobiography to deal with the war but, significantly, does not commence until August, 1916—confirm the pivotal importance of those months. During this time, too, his poetry acquired an edge that eventually peaked in the savage indignation of **'Blighters'**, **'Base Details'** and **'Does It Matter?'**

Even more unfortunately, a second gap in the diaries coincides with the culmination of Sassoon's disillusionment: his celebrated protest against the war in July, 1917, and ensuing consignment to Craiglockhart War Hospital for shell-shocked officers. These events are, admittedly, presented in Sassoon's books, while Hart-Davis has included letters written and received by the author throughout the period; but one still misses the day-to-day evidence of Sassoon's thoughts that the diaries could have provided. Particularly so because, having delivered his protest, Sassoon failed to carry it through after being convinced that he would never receive the court-martial (and publicity for the pacifist cause) he had envisaged.

> *David Montrose, "Three-Way Stretch," in* New Statesman, *Vol. 105, No. 2719, April 29, 1983, p. 31.*

CHRISTOPHER LLOYD

Unlike the period 1920-2, which without the evidence of the [*Siegfried Sassoon Diaries 1920-1922*] was for the most part *terra incognita*, the years [covered in *Siegfried Sassoon Diaries*

1915-1918] are closely associated with Sassoon's first three prose works—*Memoirs of a Fox-Hunting Man* (1928), *Memoirs of an Infantry Officer* (1930), and *Sherston's Progress* (1936). Whereas, therefore, the content of the [1915-1918 diaries] . . . was not difficult to anticipate—indeed sections are quoted verbatim in *Sherston's Progress*—a more fascinating issue lies in the intrinsic merits of this section of the diaries. These can now be seen to exist on several levels.

First, the diaries provide a fine descriptive account of the 1914-18 war to be read both as historical evidence and as literature. Secondly, they are a vivid record of an intensely personal reaction to the experience of war, combining prose passages of considerable literary power interspersed with outpourings in various poetic forms. Sassoon's diaries are, in effect, his notebooks incorporating such material as trial set-pieces and reading-lists in addition to the entries themselves. Yet the dispassionate tone and the precision of the writing in adverse conditions or during periods of mental torment attest a highly distinctive literary talent. There is, for instance, the marked contrast between the heightened response to the essentially rural setting of the 1914-18 war and the stark horrors experienced by those involved with the fighting. . . . [He writes] lyrical passages in praise of nature, offset by terse, simply phrased, but deeply effective accounts of trench warfare. . . . Even more revealing is the unfolding of Sassoon's own character. What emerges is the desire for self-fulfilment, the growth of independence of mind and the search for a specific identity both as a man and a poet. It is for their introspective qualities that the diaries should be read with the greatest attention, for these years were crucial to Sassoon's development. They are, in short, a vital point of reference for establishing the proper context in which the often misunderstood preoccupations of his early life should be seen and for the birth of many of the themes found in his later poetry, much of which is ignored. Sassoon began the war in 1915 consciously acting a part in which he did not wholly believe: 'Puff my pipe in the tent and read Hardy and wait for tidings of the battle' (14 July 1916), and he speaks of his reputation as one of 'the cheery, reckless sportsman—out for a dip at the Bosches' (16 July 1916). Yet by those dates Sassoon had already begun to write his poems protesting against what he called on 14 March 1917 'the spectacle of Youth being murdered', whilst 'Grey-haired colonels with fierce eyebrows lingered over a chicken casserole with the tenderness of a lover' (27 February 1917). His anger culminated in the official statement made to the authorities in June 1917, which was much admired by some, but was diagnosed by Arnold Bennett as spiritual pride and was soon somewhat nullified by Sassoon's own decision to return to the front.

Thirdly, the diaries of 1915-18 are important for an appreciation of Sassoon's rather complicated working methods. Admittedly, . . . the diaries allow a more accurate chronology of the poems to be established, but for the prose the matching of passages with later published reworkings raises certain problems. It will have to be calculated how much the writer expands and reduces, or in what ways he rearranges the material, quite apart from prompting such questions as the significance of the passing of time in Sassoon's world, or the author's persona. (pp. 263-64)

> *Christopher Lloyd, in a review of "Siegfried Sassoon Diaries: 1915-1918," in* The Review of English Studies, *Vol. XXXV, No. 138, May, 1984, pp. 263-64.*

Tom Sharpe
1928-

English novelist.

A comic novelist who is popular in England, Sharpe has been described as a successor to P. G. Wodehouse. Sharpe's novels frequently contain farcical plots in which he makes extensive use of slapstick and black humor; his targets for satire include modern attitudes about sex, education, culture, and politics. He achieves farce by detailing the adventures of grotesque characters who become involved in outrageous, often violent incidents. Many critics find Sharpe's observations on human behavior and modern society uncomfortably truthful.

Sharpe's first two novels, *Riotous Assembly* (1971) and *Indecent Exposure* (1973), were praised for their humorous yet reproachful depiction of the effects of South Africa's apartheid policies. These works are set in the fictional town of Piemburg, which is modeled on Pietermaritzburg, South Africa, where Sharpe lived and worked for several years. The novels have several characters in common, and in both books Sharpe ridicules psychiatry and other modern medical practices as well as the excessive power wielded by police. He also equates deviant sex with the drive for political and social power, a motif that recurs in Sharpe's later works. Basically concerned with such vital human rights as liberty and equality, *Riotous Assembly* and *Indecent Exposure* are generally considered his most serious works.

Sharpe's subsequent novels are set in England, where he has resided since his deportation from South Africa. These works include *The Throwback* (1978), *Ancestral Voices* (1980), *Vintage Stuff* (1982), and a trilogy comprising *Wilt* (1976), *The Wilt Alternative* (1979), and *Wilt on High* (1984). These works satirize various aspects of contemporary English society and culture.

(See also *Contemporary Authors*, Vol. 114 and *Dictionary of Literary Biography*, Vol. 14.)

© Jerry Bauer

AUBERON WAUGH

The highest praise anyone can give to a novel which has a humorous intention is to say that it made him laugh out loud. . . . Well, this reviewer laughed out loud about ten times, in Tom Sharpe's first novel [*Riotous Assembly*], when sober and without any external stimulus. . . .

Farce is one of the most difficult things to write successfully. Wit and craftsmanship are the ingredients required, and the two very seldom go hand in hand. If one must be strict, Mr Sharpe is by no means faultless on either score: jokes are sometimes repeated once too often; the timing is occasionally wrong; a few of the jokes are embarrassingly unfunny. But his farce is of the black variety, which makes it easier to overlook occasional failure. There is basically only one joke in the book, which is the time-honoured South African character of Farmer Van Der Merve. In this case, he is not a farmer but a number of South African policemen. . . .

Where Mr Sharpe leaves the basic situation-joke of horrible old South Africa and starts playing around with jokes about

rubber fetishism he is on much less certain ground. But the grand finale, a set battle between patients in a mental hospital re-enacting, as part of their therapy, the great battles of the Zulu war, is a masterpiece of black farce, and makes me suppose that there is a true comic genius here. If Mr Sharpe does not allow the praise which this first novel will quite deservedly excite to go to his head, if he worries a bit more over his characters, takes a little longer to develop his situations without running after every joke on the horizon, . . . if he can do all these things he seems assured of a place in the neglected, despised and backbiting world of English letters. . . .

Satirical purists would probably say that the book is a failure in that it falls between two stools—savage political satire and loathing of man's brutality etc on the one hand, slapstick on the other. They would be right to say that the book falls between two stools, but wrong to say that it is therefore a failure. It is extremely enjoyable to read and therefore a success. Its imperfections are only relative to its many excellences.

Auberon Waugh, "Lancing Farce," in The Spectator, *Vol. 226, No. 7455, May 15, 1971, p. 671.**

PIERS BRENDON

Riotous Assembly has done for the South African police what *Catch-22* did for the American Air Force. It has treated the *apparatchiks* of apartheid to a murderous ridicule infinitely more destructive than the polemical pleading or passionate abuse to which they are normally subjected in literature. Just as Joseph Heller exposed the ulcerous absurdities of militarism, so Tom Sharpe has illuminated the squalid lunacies of racialism.

This is no mean feat in view of South Africa's apparent determination to burlesque its own best endeavours. Since 1965, for example, 12 white men have been acquitted on charges of contravening the Immorality Act while their black sexual partners have been found guilty. It is difficult to trump aces of sick humour like that. Mr Sharpe has done it in this important first novel, a black comedy to which the South African government will undoubtedly apply the most rigorous colour bar. (p. 42)

At the most obvious level he has created a hilarious farce which is peopled chiefly with vicious, moronic and grotesque gendarmes who are made to jump through a number of lurid hoops. As such the book is very funny—I cachinnated so continuously into the small hours that my wife complained she couldn't get any sleep. But it also works at a more profound and symbolic level. The farce is so violent, extravagant and unremitting; it contains such a wealth of bestial ferocity and technicolor perversion that there is a distinctly manic flavour about it. Mr Sharpe cleverly eschews overt propaganda, concentrates firmly on the particular garish details of his story and gives us the minimum of explicit help in understanding his more serious general purpose. One therefore needs to make a determined effort of will to see *Riotous Assembly* (terrible title) for what it really is, to assimilate its full, horrific implications. Hidden behind the camouflage of uproarious slapstick is a complex allegory of South African life. (pp. 42-3)

Riotous Assembly has its faults, of course. The marriage between boisterous low comedy, by itself entirely successful, and the more sophisticated humour of punning, circumlocution and verbal misunderstanding is often less than happy. The writing seems hasty and uneven in places. The characters are slight and sketchy and not always self-consistent. But these are minor flaws in what deserves to be a triumphant best-seller. . . . From its admirable dedication to 'all those members of the South African Police Force whose lives are dedicated to the preservation of Western Civilisation in Southern Africa', to its hair-raising conclusion in the hanging shed of Piemburg Gaol, this book is an outstanding *tour de force.* (pp. 43-4)

> *Piers Brendon, in a review of "Riotous Assembly," in* Books and Bookmen, *Vol. 16, No. 9, June, 1971, pp. 42-4.*

STANLEY REYNOLDS

Tom Sharpe's new novel about the charms of the South African police force, *Indecent Exposure,* has all the usual serious purpose of social satire, but into it he has woven the bright thread of farce which keeps the action moving along with mirth and the characters cartwheeling cartoon fashion backwards out of the frame. The police Kommandant has had a heart transplant. Now possessing an Englishman's heart he goes all Anglophile, getting involved with a Littlewoods Pools' winner who pretends he is a British Colonel of the old flag-waving school. Meanwhile, the Kommandant's deputy, Luitenant Verkramp, is out to do his boss in and get his job. A wild fandango of a plot unravels with Sharpe striking out with all fours at every conceivable aspect of South African society plus, as a sort of comic make-weight, hitting several more universal modern items on the button.

If civilizing South Africa is an honourable advocation these days, banning cricket tours may be one way of doing it but Tom Sharpe's remorseless mockery is a lot more fun.

> *Stanley Reynolds, in a review of "Indecent Exposure," in* Punch, *Vol. 264, March 21, 1973, p. 401.*

ANTHONY THWAITE

I missed Tom Sharpe's first novel, **'Riotous Assembly'**. . . , but I put that right after reading its sequel **'Indecent Exposure.'** Clearly Mr Sharpe is a formidably equipped satirist, with something of the cruel farcicality of early Evelyn Waugh and the po-faced propriety of pre-war Anthony Powell; but he is very much his own man. This is partly because of the narrow localising of his setting—a South Africa where all the concepts and practices of apartheid are pushed to their absurd and bloody conclusions.

A characteristic ploy of Mr Sharpe's is to let a semantic misunderstanding grow and accelerate in a shower of *double-entendre*—one of the 'Carry On' techniques, but here handled with altogether finer skill and inventiveness. . . .

Ruthlessness and muddle collide at every point and, as in **'Riotous Assembly,'** all ends in carnage and chaos. Mr Sharpe is a very funny writer, with an exuberant and yet beautifully controlled sense of devastating farce.

> *Anthony Thwaite, "Freewheeling Fantasies," in* The Observer, *March 25, 1973, p. 36.**

ANTHONY THWAITE

With **'Riotous Assembly'** and **'Indecent Exposure,'** Tom Sharpe carved out for himself a special niche as the savagely funny chronicler of Piemburg, a dreadful South African place where farcical happenings drip with blood and where the pitfalls of linguistic misunderstanding are spiked with deadly consequences. To say of these books 'I laughed myself sick' is not just the tired old reviewer's hyperbole but a fair account of their physical effect. Laughter becomes a painful rictus, and the purging has a good deal of terror about it.

Now, with **'Porterhouse Blue,'** Mr Sharpe has come home—to Cambridge, in fact, which, on the evidence of this novel, was hardly his most kindly nurse. Porterhouse College is as squalid and intrigue-ridden as Piemburg; or, put another way, it's as if the ponderous Royal Academy of 'The Masters' had been parodied by Breughel or even Bosch. The Fellows gorge their way through sumptuous food and drink; the undergraduates are rich—*Dives in Omnia* is the college motto—and candidates are scrutinised for wealth rather than wisdom; and the notion of change is sacrilege. Sloth, grossness and stupidity are the marks of a Porterhouse man.

Into this reactionary backwater a new Master, Sir Godber Evans, erupts like an irritating dyspeptic bubble. A political appointment, he means to sweep away the centuries of inertia. But of course his chosen task is hopeless. Even the porters, such as the ancient Skullion, are passionate about the sacrosanct Porterhouse traditions. . . . The wretched Zipser, the sole research graduate in this haven of non-scholarship, is too obsessed with his sexual problems to get involved, even if he had the power.

But everyone *does* get involved, and such is Mr Sharpe's skill that each strand is inextricably linked with all, until the whole mesh turns into a garotte. . . .

Mr Sharpe's characteristic style, so verbally quick and yet polished, is difficult to convey in short quotations; the whole effect, stylistically and through incident, is a cumulative one, a toppling house of comic cards that knock you flat. He is the funniest new writer to have emerged for several years, and I tremble to think what his next setting will be. He has certainly made the transfer from South Africa to England with consummate ease.

Anthony Thwaite, "Capers on the Cam," in The Observer, *April 14, 1974, p. 31.*

JONATHAN RABAN

No one, unfortunately, could be much annoyed by Tom Sharpe's *Porterhouse Blue,* a genial romp through an imaginary Cambridge college, complete with well-tried fictional worthies like a deaf chaplain . . . and a morose virgin of a graduate student called Zipser. Billed as a "Rabelaisian comedy", its closest affinities are really with *Dad's Army* and *All Gas and Gaiters;* its most noticeable loss is the absence of a studio audience to keep one chuckling when the jokes grow old and thin. Its final gag, the elevation of Scullion the cantankerous porter to the position of Master of the College, has both a simplicity and a conservatism that hold the book far short of the black farce which it seems to be half-heartedly trying to become. (pp. 76-7)

Jonathan Raban, in a review of "Porterhouse Blue," in Encounter, *Vol. XLIII, No. 1, July, 1974, pp. 76-7.*

PETER ACKROYD

Tom Sharpe has raided that Madame Tussauds of English writing, the comic novel, and has come out with a comfortable, nostalgic but amiable joke. *Blott on the Landscape* is to the contemporary novel that Ruskin Spear is to painting or Philip Larkin to poetry. It is better than it really ought to be. In his earlier novel, *Porterhouse Blue,* Mr Sharpe nudged us sharply in the ribs with the University Joke—in *Blott* he knocks us all over with the Stately Home Joke. Sir Giles Lynchwood and Lady Maud Lynchwood are daggers drawn. Sir Giles will not "do his duty by" Lady Maud and, to add insult to lack of injury, he intends to run a motorway right through their hate-nest, Handyman Hall. With the help of Blott, the Willing Gardener, Lady Maud Puts a Stop to It and to those Meddling Civil Servants. There are some extremely funny scenes, which actually seem funnier in retrospect than they did at the time, and over it all hangs the air of mild prurience which is so necessary in matters of humour.

Of course you can see most of the situations developing—in fact you could do so from several miles away with an inverted telescope—but Mr Sharpe's dialogue is nifty enough and he has the knack of combining predictability with risibility. And like all nice, old-fashioned comedy there is a nice, old-fashioned moral to buttress some of the wilder moments of nostalgia: "What had Sir Giles done for the future? Nothing. He had desecrated the past and betrayed the future. He deserved to die. Blott took his shotgun and went round to the garage." It is one of the more charming characteristics of light comedy that it can accommodate murder and rapine without apparent

discomfort. *Blott on the Landscape* is imaginative enough to be enjoyable, and it is fanciful enough to be taken seriously.

Peter Ackroyd, "On the Road," in The Spectator, *Vol. 234, No. 7665, May 24, 1975, p. 637.*

PETER BUCKMAN

[*Blott on the Landscape*] features a dastardly baronet with masochistic fantasies, sexually impotent but something of a financial wizard, intent on diddling his large and unlovely—but not unlovable—wife out of her inheritance and the people of his constituency out of an area of natural beauty. He plans, in short, to have a motorway driven bang through his wife's ancestral home, and will stop at nothing to get his way. Such blackguardism arouses in his wife the aggressive cunning of her forbears, and with Blott the gardener as her agent she thwarts her husband—he gets eaten by lions—and enforces a happy ending. But Mr Sharpe cannot be compared to Wodehouse merely because he writes about rural England. There is about his characters the same air of unreality, but none of Wodehouse's balmy fantasy. Mr. Sharpe's characters have no virtue about them: all are nasty in varying degrees. Doubtless this is a proper reflection of our own neuroses, and anyway no writer of Mr Sharpe's inventiveness will want to live under another writer's shadow. Suffice it to say that he can indeed be very funny, but the screams you may hear are not of mirth, but pain. (p. 995)

Peter Buckman, "I Only Laugh When It Hurts," in Punch, *Vol. 268, June 4, 1975, pp. 994-95.*

ANTHONY THWAITE

Tom Sharpe's new novel, **'Wilt,'** . . . [might be described] as an anti-permissive sexual comedy, or a reactionary filthy farce. Clearly Mr Sharpe very much disapproves of what his protagonist, Henry Wilt, refers to as 'this sexual liberation kick' with its jargon-ridden chat about 'open-ended free-wheeling sexual options.' Wilt is a low-grade lecturer in Liberal Studies (a malign term in itself) in a low-grade technical institute in the Fens. . . . His wife Eva (about whom he fantasises murder) is a large woman with febrile enthusiasms. To her, Henry is a dull creep. . . .

In some characteristics Henry is the archetypal Donald McGill butt—the sexually inadequate little man menaced by vastly endowed predatory women; his surname could hardly be more explicit. But the fact that in the end he triumphs over the hideous obstacles put in his path (a lifesize inflated doll that looks like a real woman is the most hideous and persistent obstacle) makes him a hero, and specifically an anti-sexual hero: cant—together with its near-homonym—is his enemy, and both are finally trounced. A rancorous and foul-mouthed detestation of phoneyness in education and in sex wins through to the headship of Liberal Studies for Henry, fertile-fulfilment for Eva, and therefore an even placidity for both.

Laughter is obviously what Tom Sharpe is after: disgust or boredom are what many readers may feel. . . . His four earlier books used sex incidentally, as what one could call disgrace notes. In **'Wilt,'** it's almost his sole theme, followed with his usual pertinacious verbal energy; but a lot of the time what hovers behind the words . . . seems to be a bilious coarseness and an obsessive fear. It needs a Swift to cope with such murkiness or—in another way—the black genius of a Joe Orton. Under its hilarities, **'Wilt'** is a lowering book.

Anthony Thwaite, "We Are Not Aroused," in The Observer, *February 29, 1976, p. 27.**

NEIL HEPBURN

It is refreshing to find an accomplished writer taking as his hero a man who actually despises the idea that his life is defined by his sexuality: This is not the only bonus in *Wilt,* in which Tom Sharpe lacerates and leaves for dead such bogey-men as liberated Americans proselytising for 'touch therapy', the academic establishment, bullyingly certitudinous policemen and sandwich-coursing artisans. . . .

Wilt is fed up with it all, and the entanglement with a life-size inflatable doll, all too realistically feminine, . . . is the last straw: his fantasies of murdering his wife boil over into an actual dress rehearsal—with the doll—of a corpse-disposal.

His wife departs, and he is soon delivered into the hands of the police as her suspected murderer. His eventual triumph over all these enemies marks the beginning of a tremendous growth in his self-confidence. Shades of *Lucky Jim.* Yet it is not Kingsley Amis but P. G. Wodehouse to whom Mr Sharpe has been tediously compared; and he was, I used to think, in real danger of being trapped in that master's empty room, too small to swing his vicious gifts in. *Wilt* is at least halfway to breaking out of that cosy den into the ferocious satire for which Mr Sharpe's gifts best fit him. (p. 286)

Neil Hepburn, "Latin-Americans in Paris," in The Listener, *Vol. 95, No. 2447, March 4, 1976, pp. 285-86.*

MELVYN BRAGG

Tom Sharpe's greatest gift is to pile Pelion on Ossa, double it, and play it again. When he gets up a head of steam, he can set off a multitude of explosions which crackle across page after page of sharp and comic prose. In *The Throw Back* he brings off one extremely funny and long sequence of disasters which turn a tranquil and discreet suburban street in London into a blitzed, corpse-glutted comic wasteland.

The Throw Back is an excellent notion. Lockhart Flawse, brought up in the borders by his grandfather, inhabits a world stuck somewhere in the late 18th century. He's a hunter, a fearless warrior, independent, chaste, a romantic and a poet, completely out of touch with everything modern from electricity to expense accounts. But he soon learns—when true (unconsummated) love pitches him into the great Wen and he finds himself ejected by a society which cannot endure his honesty and truthfulness. It is the revenge of Lockhart Flawse on the society which is the book's dynamo.

Sometimes the pile of tricks begins to wobble and seem as if it might collapse on itself. And I could have done with one or two more of the quieter parts of the book. When Lockhart, for example, goes in pursuit of the identity of his father he meets an old friend of the family and that scene was a refreshing contrast. Refreshing because for once it was not sucked instantly into yet another lunatic spin. Lockhart Flawse himself, ridiculous as the idea of him might seem at first, becomes not only enjoyable but very convincing. Tom Sharpe clearly relishes what his hero stands for and puts his heart into a character who has the energy of Flashman and the nerve of a border riever.

Sharpe is one of the funniest contemporary novelists writing in Britain today and *The Throw Back* sees him in top form, piling jokes on comic inventions with all the skill of the literary illusionist.

Melvyn Bragg, "Greene & Sharpe," in Punch, *Vol. 274, March 22, 1978, p. 505.**

FRANCIS KING

In Tom Sharpe's *The Throwback* sex is usually—and unusually—repellent: a libidinous nonagenarian makes his middle-aged bride feel 'like a cross between a sexual colander and a cess-pit'; a doctor has a spontaneous ejaculation while examining a virgin; a dildo, manipulated by two previously innocent spinster sisters, shoots half-a-pint of double cream and egg-white across the room when the vicar's wife makes an unexpected call. The aggression consists largely of brutal practical jokes: a lecherous colonel pulls on a condom filled with oven-cleaner; a dog is dismembered and placed piecemeal in a house to fill it with a stench of corruption; another dog is given LSD and goes berserk. . . .

Often a mishearing or a misunderstanding of a word provides the basis for a joke. The greens of a golf-course are taken for vegetables; someone wonders why he was told to have his head examined when 'it wasn't even bleeding.' Even that hardy stand-by 'queer' is pressed into service.

Humour is like drink: one can never be sure how it will take one. Although I doubt if I should ever have applied to Mr Sharpe's previous novels the reviewers' superlatives quoted on the back of this one—'a gust of raucous fun', 'a toppling house of comic cards', 'explosively funny'—I certainly enjoyed them. But in the case of this latest offering I felt as though I were marooned at one of those parties where the drink, so exhilarating to everyone else, only makes one feel more and more morose. In such circumstances, the wise party-goer slips away unnoticed. But what can the reviewer do except stick it out to the end? (p. 21)

Francis King, "Wise-Cracks," in The Spectator, *Vol. 240, No. 7812, March 25, 1978, pp. 20-1.**

PETER KEMP

Like some belligerent eccentric in a bath-chair, an old-fashioned English silliness is let rip in Tom Sharpe's book, *The Wilt Alternative.* Creaking painfully but urged on by peppery indignation, the narrative careers all around the place as it seeks out louts and lefties it can knock for six. Wet progressives, gabbling trendies, bolshy union-men, and international terrorists are all pursued with apoplectic snorts and mercilessly flailed with whimsy. . . .

Besieged with some hostages in the Wilt household, a trio of terrorists soon find they are fighting to retain their mental balance as they slither round on pickled onions vomited by the hero's brood of monster quads, quail from the saggily adipose spectacle of his nude wife wading vengefully towards them, and are driven frenzied by the spry put-downs of his next-door neighbour, a game old bird who wears bullet-proof corsets. Weathering this barrage of pottiness, they eventually fall prey to a violent instance of the lavatory humour that pervades the book. Mrs Wilt's organic lavatory explodes and, as they flee the house, it is apparent that the terrorists 'had taken the full force of the bio-loo and were perfect examples of the worth of their own ideology.' 'Shits in shits' clothing,' a character obligingly explains in case the point has not been noted.

Overkill of this kind typifies the book. Characters are crudely placarded with names like Bilger, Symper, Frackas, Schautz Exasperated lurches of exaggeration, coupled with inaccuracy (an apparent belief that the Tupamaros are Argentinian terrorists, for instance), enable the targets of this book's attack to escape any real damage. And this is a pity. There are many amongst them that it would be a pleasure to see spiked. But, in order for this to happen, something more pointed than Sharpe's blunt instruments would need to be applied. (p. 159)

> Peter Kemp, "Idylls and Hells," in The Listener, Vol. 102, No. 2622, August 2, 1979, pp. 158-59.*

ROBERT NYE

Sharpe is to [Arno] Schmidt as Wodehouse is to Joyce—simpleminded farce touching fingers with a rich comic vision, I suppose.

Well, let's not despise the craft evident in *The Wilt Alternative,* in which Sharpe's hero is the liberal conscience in full impotent flight from modern terrorism in every form. I enjoyed the succession of incidents enormously, and there is something marvellously English about the ignorance and innocence of the central character.

On a technical level, I observe that Sharpe is still confining his real efforts to dialogue—when he describes action or seeks to enact thought he is an amateur, and awkward, with far too many adverts to the square inch.

But this is to carp at Wilt himself, and Wilt should not be carped or sneezed at. To have created a character of such infinite ridiculousness is an achievement. His wife and his mother are well-observed too, and generally it might be said that Sharpe improves on Wodehouse in the depiction of female comic-cuts.

> Robert Nye, "Comic Violence, Violent Comedy," in The Guardian Weekly, Vol. 121, No. 6, August 5, 1979, p. 22.*

NICHOLAS SHRIMPTON

Sharpe's central character [in *Ancestral Vices*], Walden Yapp, is an opinionated know-all who teaches 'Demotic Historiography' at a plate-glass university and reduces all experience to the frigid orthodoxies of Marxist sociological jargon. But some experiences are more easily subdued than others. Sitting in the cells, awaiting a life sentence on a false charge of murdering a dwarf in order the more easily to enjoy improper intimacies with his mentally sub-normal wife, Yapp is gripped by a terrifying sense that his ideological moorings are coming adrift. . . .

This grotesque moment is as close as *Ancestral Vices* ever comes to seriousness, but one should not presume from it that the book is a right-wing attack on socialist theorising. Sharpe's satire is astonishingly, at times almost worryingly, even-handed. At one moment he's laying into lefty academics; at the next, with equal enthusiasm, he's berating big business and the aristocracy. Occasionally he comes close to direct contradiction. . . . The truth is that everything is grist to Mr Sharpe's comic mill and he doesn't believe in thinking too hard about his raw material before he tosses it in.

What results is another bawdy and brutal romp of the kind which he does so well. If you like jokes about dwarfs called 'Little Willy' and chefs who mishear the first consonant of an order for sucking pig, then you'll lap it up. There's an interesting attempt to establish the verb 'to thorpe' (to decline to give evidence at one's own trial) in the English language. But on the whole Tom Sharpe's conception of the still sad music of humanity is a protracted Bronx cheer and he plays it loud and long.

> Nicholas Shrimpton, "Cold Feet in Moscow," in New Statesman, Vol. 100, No. 2590, November 7, 1980, p. 30.*

MARY HOPE

There are more things in the heaven and hell-on-earth than are dreamt of in the philosophy of Walden Yapp, the unfortunate hero—for want of a better word—of [*Ancestral Vices*], Tom Sharpe's latest excursion into the anarchical-fantastical-satirical. Yapp is a lefty identidon from a new university, so programmed into ongoing confrontation situations that he is chosen by the appalling, foul-mouthed Lord Petrefact to write the history of the capitalistic misdeeds of the Petrefact family in order to spite the other members of the tribe. . . . Since what the family is trying to hide is not breadline wages and back-to-back tied cottages, but the fact that the cheerful workers are earning splendid remuneration at a Mill which has been converted into a booming fetish factory, the stage is set for the usual Sharpe high jinks and contorted confusions. . . .

The scatter effect of Sharpe's satire gives the lie to the theory that all satire is reactionary. Though the description of Kloone University, where the members of the SCR 'brought with them an evangelical fervour for the experimental, the radical, the anarchic and the interpersonally permissive . . . far in advance of their students' is wickedly, wonderfully accurate, as anyone who ever breathed the air of Sixties academe will know, the tables are turned at the end of the book where the old repressive establishment forces are marshalled back into action, enmeshing hapless Yapp in ill-understood confusions. The moral is that the world is a random place, a constant struggle between conflicting and dangerous idiocies, opposing certainties which are equally blind to the vagaries and unpredictabilities of the real world.

What Sharpe is saying through this manic rigmarole is that the drunkenness of things is always pretty various and that we'd all better realise it: 'if Yapp were to allow himself to be seduced by the random and chaotic nature of existence he would lose the assurance fostered so carefully over the years, that history was imbued with purpose and that the happiness of mankind was ultimately guaranteed . . .'. The only happiness that Sharpe guarantees is fleeting but helpless laughter at the savage foolery of each camp: a plague on both your houses.

> Mary Hope, in a review of "Ancestral Vices," in The Spectator, Vol. 245, Nos. 7594 & 7595, December 20, 1980, p. 34.

STANLEY REYNOLDS

Tom Sharpe, Britain's leading practitioner of black humour, is said to have gone off lately. Certainly since he was forced to leave South Africa his novels have lacked the political edge of those first two satires, *Riotous Assembly* and *Indecent Exposure*. But a funny writer doesn't have to be political. All he has to be is funny and with *Vintage Stuff* . . . it is clear that the Sharpe wit has not dulled.

The idea behind *Vintage Stuff* is one of those dreadfully simple notions which seem to be behind all the best good comic writing. The anti-heroes of the book, young Peregrine Clyde-Browne and his housemaster, Mr Glodstone, at the appalling Groxbourne school, love old-fashioned adventure stories like *The Prisoner of Zenda* and *The Thirty-Nine Steps*. More than that. They read nothing but these sort of books and, what's more, they believe every word in them. . . .

Mr Glodstone, with his glass eye in which he wears a monocle, is a true romantic. . . . He hates the modern world. He longs for the old, the good and the true as opposed to the new, the bad and the false. When you come to think of it, this should make Mr Glodstone a totally admirable character and Tom Sharpe making fun of such a noble fellow should be ashamed of himself.

But Mr Glodstone is mad. . . . He is not alone at Groxbourne. There are many madmen there. Not the least of these is Slymne, the geography master, who is Glodstone's arch-enemy although Glodstone does not know it.

Seeking to revenge himself on Glodstone, Mr Slymne . . . lays a terrible trap for him. He invents the plot of a real-life adventure yarn: a French Countess, the mother of one of the students, held captive in her own castle. Slymne counterfeits notes from the Countess begging Glodstone to rescue her.

It is marvellously funny following Glodstone and young Clyde-Browne in their rescue-bid, seeing the admirable but outdated values of Richard Hannay and Bulldog Drummond come up against the modern world. Anyone who enjoys a rattling good yarn won't be able to put down *Vintage Stuff,* although *The Thirty-Nine Steps et al* will probably never seem the same again. (p. 743)

> Stanley Reynolds, "The Sharpe End," in Punch, Vol. 283, No. 7407, November 3, 1982, pp. 743-44.*

JONATHAN KEATES

This is the age of the Knowing Novelist, the guy who gives it you straight from the shoulder, with no illusions and a liberal supply of sardonic nudges. The reader, unless he is the proverbial blind horse, feels flattered at being let in on the secret, and the itch for authenticity, part of a venerable tradition stretching back to Defoe and beyond, is triumphantly scratched. . . .

[One] in the know is Tom Sharpe. Nothing the fellow can't tell you about what goes on down at the Tech. A circus Malcolm Bradbury with a false nose and a pom-pom on his hat, he pulls the rug out from under anything that moves. [In **'Wilt on High,'** fans] will relish the gamy imbroglio, complete with peeping Toms in the loo, comic American air force officers (hyper-authentic, these), a cod Greenham Common and a herbalist whose preparations, lacing Wilt's homebrew, induce an irrepressible erection.

What Sharpe actually knows is the art of tapping all the most fundamentally English springs of fun. Lavatories are good for a laugh, so is sex in its more Chaucerian guises, and policemen are especially risible for their peculiar blend of oafishness and brutality. Wilt's return is indeed accompanied by that of his ancient enemy Inspector Flint, from whose bladder trouble the author gets handsome comic mileage.

Just as hoarily native is Sharpe's prodigality of detail. Nothing escapes him which can give definition and perspective to these well-worn shapes of farce and slapstick. The brothel madam turned children's story writer, however, or the pregnant hamster on the stairs or the knee-jerk to the groin learnt at a Rape Resistance class are sideshows more distracting than the central knockabout.

> Jonathan Keates, "Whelk in the Soup," in The Observer, September 30, 1984, p. 20.*

FRANCIS KING

In retrospect, it may be seen as prophetic that Tom Sharpe's fifth novel should have been called *Wilt*. After the exuberant ejaculations of that work and its predecessors, there followed depressing indications that this author found it increasingly difficult to keep it up. Now any hopes raised by the title *Wilt on High* are all too soon dashed. So far from Wilt being on high, he has reached a new low. . . .

The plot, which is certainly ingenious, is concerned with the manner in which Wilt becomes prime suspect in the course of a police enquiry into drug dealing. An overdose of heroin causes the deaths, first of a girl student, daughter of the Lord Lieutenant of the country, at the College, and then of a gang-boss to whom Wilt has been giving classes in English Literature at the local gaol in which he has been incarcerated. A connection is established, and in no time at all an overzealous police-officer is giving directions for the wholly innocent Wilt to be kept under close surveillance. His house and car are bugged; and subsequently it is the discovery of not one but two bugs bleeping away in his Ford Escort that arouses the suspicion of a security officer at the US airbase where he also lectures and leads to him being confined as a possible terrorist or spy.

Mr Sharpe's speciality is not human comedy but inhuman farce. It is a cold eye that he casts on the pitiful absurdities of existence and a rough hand with which he manipulates the puppets chosen to demonstrate those absurdities. Fortunately, he has here abandoned the cloacal obsession that in some of his other novels threatened to submerge everyone and everything under its malodorous tide. In its place, there is now an obsession with sexual performance, of the same kind that so often finds anguished expression on late-night phone-ins. . . .

[Wilt's wife] Eva, exasperated by the problem of too little, not too much, nooky, consults . . . [a] doctor, who provides an aphrodisiac. Ingested by Wilt in large quantities in the beer that Eva has used as the dilutant, it induces a priapism so extreme that his unavailing attempts to bring a prolonged erection even to half-mast lead him first to introduce cold cream into his penis with his wife's icing syringe and then to apply a restraining bandage and a cricketer's box before setting off for his lecture at the American airbase.

For me, all this is too gruesome to be funny—as are the scenes involving the death of the girl student and the subsequent discovery of her corpse in the College boiler-room. . . .

Mr Sharpe is not a verbally exciting writer in the manner of P. G. Wodehouse or Peter de Vries. When he does attempt some verbal frolic, it is usually in the form of a *double entendre* of the kind that I have attempted, in a spirit of emulation, at the outset of this piece. . . .

In this increasingly frenetic novel, Mr Sharpe reminds me of one of those immensely skilled directors of farce, a Ray Cooney or a Mike Ockrent, who devise for their players such a remarkable wealth of business that it takes the audience a long time to realise that the piece itself is wholly empty. Perhaps Mr Sharpe should now write a serious novel. I have always been convinced that to achieve success in a serious novel is easier than in a comic one.

Francis King, "Keeping It Up," in The Spectator, *Vol. 253, No. 8157, November 10, 1984, p. 28.*

L. J. DAVIS

Tom Sharpe's chronicles of Henry Wilt have attracted something of a cult in his native Britain, but he has yet to attract much of a following on this side of the pond, a deplorable situation that the present publication of *Wilt on High* should do much to dispel. . . .

As we join Wilt at the beginning of his latest misadventure, he has risen to the headship of the department of liberal studies at the Fenland College of Arts and Technology. . . .

[Sharpe's style of] writing requires a clear if baleful eye, a controlled awareness of the outrages inflicted by ordinary life, and a narrative mind swimming forever and valiantly against a competing logical system that needs, as they say, no introduction; the experience is not unlike reading science fiction about the present. Wilt arrives equipped with a quartet of appalling prepubescent daughters and an exomorphic earth mother of a wife who immediately proceeds to poison his beer with aphrodisiac, and he shortly acquires a shadow in the form of the chief of the local narcotics squad, a maniac who believes his unwitting quarry is leading him to the lair of a criminal mastermind. Up to this point, and despite a few loose ends (such as why Wilt remains married to the wretched woman), the book is a sockdolager that fairly begs to be read aloud. Great stuff, this.

It fails, I think, because of three surprisingly commonplace mistakes: a curiously British notion that there is something inherently uproarious about male genitalia, a compulsion to arrange a finale of surpassing hilariousness in the manner of a West End farce, and a by no means exclusively British belief that once you know a foreigner's nationality, you know something useful about him.

Wilt on High ends with a colossal ball-up at a nearby American Air Force base; I'm sure we'll all admit that there are few things funnier than an American. . . . The confrontation has its moments—Sharpe is too talented and generous a writer to blow completely even the most unpromising of material—but I guess you had to be there. The wonder is that the book actually survives the experience, rather like a favorite uncle in his cups. No matter what he does now, only a few moments ago he was absolutely marvelous.

L. J. Davis, 'A Farce on the Trendy Side," in Book World—The Washington Post, *March 3, 1985, p. 5.*

Jim Shepard

19??-

American novelist.

Shepard's first novel, *Flights* (1983), is marked by subtle humor and a spare yet evocative prose style. The novel explores a young boy's emotional growth as he seeks to establish his independence. Critics admired Shepard's ability to transcend the clichés usually associated with the coming-of-age theme. They also praised his understanding of family pressures and the confusions peculiar to youth. Tom Paulin echoed the critical consensus in his assertion that "*Flights* is a stunning and highly professional first novel."

PUBLISHERS WEEKLY

For some readers, this first novel [*Flights*] may call to mind two other memorable debuts: *Ordinary People* and *Birdy*. Skillfully written and often moving, Shepard's story of a young boy growing up in Connecticut contains elements of both of those novels as it explores the world of Biddy, a 13-year-old who is prone to all the small woes of any young boy.... Although the novel doesn't soar quite as high as it might have after the promise of the book's carefully developed exposition, it is nonetheless an exhilarating experience and Biddy is a character not easily forgotten.

A review of "Flights," in Publishers Weekly, *Vol. 223, No. 25, June 24, 1983, p. 53.*

TOM PAULIN

We're all familiar—boringly familiar—with the kind of novel which describes a male adolescent's sexual fantasies, initiation and subsequent adventures. First novels especially tend to treat this theme and the reader has by now a right to reject modern-day versions of *Tom Jones* on sight. Jim Shepard's first novel concerns a 13-year-old boy growing up in Connecticut, but it in no way belongs to the overworked genre I've just described. *Flights* is a subtle, brilliant, beautifully-wrought fiction which succeeds because it chooses Biddy Siebert's pre-adolescent consciousness as its focus and center. Shepard has cleverly elected to write about boyhood, rather than youth, and in doing so he has made that relatively unexplored hinterland seem uniquely his own.

Biddy Siebert's consciousness is precisely that of a boy who feels that he exists on the fringes of other, more powerful lives. He moves through the landscape of a small town, a place of salt marshes, wired perimeters and narrow blacktops that lead to the Sikorsky aircraft works and the local airport with its derelict "melancholy Windsock Restaurant." Very astutely, Shepard creates a personality which is ordinary and unassertive—Biddy is neither passive nor rebellious, just an occasionally delinquent "normal" boy. He's interested in baseball and airplanes, serves as an altar boy and sings in the choir. He appears to have no distinctive qualities or talents and yet he is in no sense a null or boring figure to watch. Like Henry James' Maisie he seems to be acted upon by a coarse and often insensitive adult world which he is powerless to alter or un-

derstand. Here, Shepard's gnomic epigraph—"Children are the eyes and hands of a family"—deftly suggests just how kids of Biddy's temperament exist in a family. Like eyes and hands, they are the instruments of an invisible will power—in this case, of the currents of a difficult, though unexceptional marriage.

Biddy's family is neither private and nuclear, nor large and extended, and this means that Biddy and his sister, Kristi, are the victims of the tense and shifting definitions which his parents seek to impose....

By consistently understating and by rejecting all intrusive commentary Shepard neatly allows the reader to deduce character and psychology from small but significant actions and snatches of casually perfect dialogue. His deceptively simple prose-style and low-key narrative manner conceal a cool, exacting artistry.

One of the outstanding features of *Flights* is the dreamlike precision with which action and landscape are described. Biddy's fatalistic numbness and intense self-absorption refract a bizarre reality which is both banal and strange, ordinary and marvelous. This muted atmosphere is particularly effective in an early scene where Biddy's family and friends gather on the Siebert lawn one Labor Day to watch an air show. A parachutist detaches himself from the diamond pattern which the rest of his team is making, the group watches and comments casually, and then the atmosphere is charged first with surprise, then fear. ''He could be coming here,'' someone says, and then the parachutist is seen ''coming in low and hard, still pulling, not floating at all, swooping, and Biddy could see the frustration on his face and the shine on his boots.'' Biddy's father swears and begins to herd the women out of the way, the parachutist dips lower, hits the roof, bounces and then comes twisting down again ''catching a TV tray with watermelon on it and kicking it up over the clothesline in a rain of pink chunks and seeds.'' Shepard narrates this episode with studied poise and we're reminded of it later when Biddy goes to the restroom during a wedding celebration and catches a vague smell ''of melon and urine.'' It's as though Biddy is sensitive to mysterious fragments of experience which he is as yet incapable of understanding or giving shape to.

Jim Shepard, however, has succeeded wonderfully in building a sharp, enigmatic, highly intelligent fiction from what at first appeared an unpromising subject. Shepard is gifted with a wise and unforced insight into the shifting politics of family life, and he is able to move his story to its climax of momentary independence and escape without any appearance of conscious plotting. It would distort his achievement, if I were to reveal just what that climax is—this novel needs to be savored moment by moment for its benign artistic cunning and sheer imaginative wisdom. *Flights* is a stunning and highly professional first novel and we may safely predict a most distinguished future for its author.

> Tom Paulin, *''Taking Flight from the Troubles of Childhood,''* in Book World—The Washington Post, *September 25, 1983, p. 4.*

FREDERICK BUSCH

''Flights'' is the story of Biddy Siebert, a boy who at 13 knows more than he can cope with, sees more than he can comprehend, wants more than he has and seizes more than he can grasp. It is a first novel about growing up, and it is a very good one. Its achievement is in no small way the result of the author's ability to generate and respond to human warmth.

The novel is shaped by Biddy's school year and his family's gatherings in Connecticut, near Long Island Sound, where we meet his father, mother, sister and a large, loud crowd of relatives and friends. All these people, including Cindy, the sexy daughter of his godfather Dom, Ronnie her fiancé and the nuns who teach Biddy, have expectations of the boy. He tries to please them all, but feels that he is failing those who rely on him. They frequently agree. Only God and the priest in the confessional don't complain, and he wishes they would.

The men of the novel exert the most pressure, even in ordinary moments, as when they counsel him on how to play baseball: ''Get to the bag and concentrate on the throw. And get your legs up if the runner's coming in high.'' Of course, Biddy botches everything the men try to teach him, and they tell him so. He even fails when playing imaginary second base for the Baltimore Orioles or safety for the Minnesota Vikings; in his reveries, he fails, in skill and courage, at each crucial play. (p. 15)

The novel is often funny in its celebration of the buzz of middle class family life. It offers a realistic sense of children. Biddy matters enough to us to keep us reading with concern as his life mounts up around him, and as we wait—thanks to Mr. Shepard's talent we can feel it coming—for Biddy's big move.

The writing is excellent. At one point, Biddy, receiving stitches after cutting his finger on a tuna fish can, feels ''the two halves of his skin being pulled together like the sides of a sneaker.'' The sports talk is right, the family quarrels marvelously evoked—they are overheard from life, we feel, and they are effortlessly rendered.

Meanwhile, something is born in Biddy when he rides with his parents in their friend's small plane. He begins to acquire books about aviation and navigation, to ask questions about flying and to store up gear, courage and the desire he will need to steal the friend's airplane for a solo flight. When he receives his F in math (to him, in life), he departs. He cons the owner of the plane and acquires the keys; then he rapidly readies for takeoff out of sight of the control tower and, undetected, he takes off. After he lands, he leaves the cockpit on his own, rather than waiting to be pulled out. The novel demonstrates with this act that Biddy knows he is on his way to something important: a grown-up life that he must try to shape.

I wish that there had been more of Biddy's flight, and more detailed description of his preparation, and that it had come earlier in the novel, for these events are unconvincingly thrust upon us at the last minute. And I must also question Mr. Shepard's lyrical, moving last line—''He'd come this far, he had a way to go, and he wanted to be ready by the time they arrived.'' By itself, the line is splendid, but in the context of the novel it seems superfluous.

The line shows how Mr. Shepard feels about Biddy, but the words don't reflect Biddy's thoughts. Mr. Shepard is like an overprotective father here. His motive is love. But the boy speaks most clearly in this novel when he dreams and acts on his own. Without that handsome line, the novel would end with the description of an act done by a boy who is aware that he is taking control of his life and becoming a man. I wish that it had.

There are other times when Mr. Shepard demonstrates his talent at the expense of Biddy's consciousness and allows the writing to focus on the author instead of the boy. When Biddy sees the pilot whose plane he later will steal, the beginning of his dream is felt by the reader, but not in Biddy's terms. Mr. Shepard writes about ''the very idea of that much spatial freedom—the ability to go, free of the confining limits of even roads or tracks.'' But how did Biddy think about all that, and in what terms?

Still, overall, this is a well-made, well-written and splendidly-imagined novel. **''Flights''** is impressive in its hard earned simplicity and thrilling in its compassion. (pp. 15, 33)

> Frederick Busch, *''Failing Math and Life,''* in The New York Times Book Review, *October 9, 1983, pp. 15, 33.*

MARK M. McCAFFERY

James Shepard is brilliant. [In *Flights* he] writes with a clear, fresh style with an economy of words. By this very crispness, his style highlights and complements the swift action of the plot. He depicts the emotional and spiritual maelstrom around Biddy with a startlingly simple, yet moving, clarity.

Shepard's characterization is especially well done. The characters are at once intricate and almost serpentine in their complexity, and yet simply understood. All are emotional cripples whose only fault is attempting to do what they think is best, something that actually stifles, if not crushes, Biddy. Even the only truly nasty character, the closest thing *Flights* has to a villain, Biddy's younger sister, Kristi, evokes more compassion than hatred.

Shepard's style, the multifarious paradoxes of character and the magnificent fusion and interweaving of fantasy within Biddy's mind make *Flights* one of the most memorable and interesting novels I have read in a long time. It is a wonderful first novel and I predict a long and fruitful career for Shepard. I also highly recommend the book for anyone who has himself yearned to escape from the world for a time.

> Mark M. McCaffery, in a review of "Flights," in
> Best Sellers, *Vol. 43, No. 8, November, 1983, p.*
> *286.*

TOM ALESSANDRI

It has been too many years since I visited the Glass Family. And I miss their energy, eccentricity, dressing gowns, medicine cabinet—their life-confirming struggles. Fortunately, and until J. D. Salinger decides to return us to Seymour and Buddy's bedroom, we have the Sieberts [of *Flights*]: Dad, Mom, Kristi and a Holden reborn, Biddy. . . .

Flights is a rousing success for what it does *not* do. It avoids pandering to our current taste for flash, chase and perversion. Rather, in its sensitive realism, it examines a comfortably ordinary family in Connecticut, as they survive events through four holidays one year. *Flights* is a dramatic exercise in the sheer panic of growing up, and a palatable treatise on happiness.

The centerpiece is 13-year-old Biddy. The nun who teaches him in seventh grade describes him as a smart boy who thinks too much and doesn't do his best. Biddy has been told life should be fun, exciting and happy, but he feels empty. All Biddy's traditional touchstones seem to be crumbling. His parents are in a mid-life crisis; friends drop him for no apparent reason, or grow up and away. His school life is no longer the clear, steady course of good behavior, good grades; he becomes preoccupied with his teachers' foibles. And, though it does at times still enwrap him in a mysterious warmth, Biddy's Catholicism has lost its sway. Confession seems more a perverse game than a sacrament. His baseball and football fantasies have lost their power and he comes to see them as childish diversions

from real life. Slowly he creates a concrete challenge for himself—a dream to be made tangible: flight. Biddy's resolution is not to run away, escape or merely soar above in a stolen Cessna. Rather, his aim is to make himself, at long last, accountable *to* himself.

Flights has its moments of high comedy: Sister Theresa, for example, conducts a spelling bee which conjures up visions of the Spanish Inquisition. But Biddy's serious questions find echoes in his family as well. The Sieberts's problems are not melodramatic, but they are intriguing. Biddy's questions are not earthshaking, only fundamental. Shepard's novel smacks of Judith Guest's *Ordinary People,* drawing dramatic interest from the everyday.

In its soaring conclusion, *Flights* wonderfully documents Biddy's decision to put his life together—like Jimmy Stewart in *The Flight of the Phoenix*—out of odds, ends, patches, pieces, a rudder here and an aileron there. Biddy, like the Hucks and Holdens before him, takes responsibility for himself. The result: happiness? Maybe—but certainly, at least, a *way* to happiness.

> Tom Alessandri, in a review of "Flights," in Amer-
> ica, *Vol. 149, No. 18, December 3, 1983, p. 360.*

LARRY DOMINGUES

[*Flights*] tells the story of one boy's attempt to flee, both in fantasy and in reality, from the confusion of his world. . . . While he lives in the midst of much emotional suburban blight, Biddy understands little of it, or of the effect it has on his own stability. When the young protagonist finally labors to gain control of his life and plans his escape, readers will be both heartened by the attempt and saddened by its possible futility. Young adults will like this simple but likable character, as well as the themes of escape, adolescent pain and loneliness. Many readers, though, may not understand the author's oblique character and plot development. One of the most dramatic episodes is written skillfully, but its connection to later events may not be evident to some readers. The themes are developed slowly and there is little action in the beginning. Even so, *Flights* dramatizes a modern adolescent experience to which many young adults will relate. (pp. 87-8)

> Larry Domingues, in a review of "Flights," in School
> Library Journal, *Vol. 30, No. 10, February, 1984,*
> *pp. 87-8.*

Wole Soyinka

1934-

(Born Akinwande Oluwole Soyinka) Nigerian dramatist, poet, novelist, critic, translator, editor, and autobiographer.

Soyinka is considered one of the most important contemporary African dramatists writing in English. Blending modern European dramatic form with such African elements as Yoruba tribal myth, folklore, dance, and music, Soyinka infuses the Western stage with new dramatic possibilities while commenting on modern Nigeria's political and social realities. Unlike many African writers, Soyinka rejects the notion of négritude, a literary concept which urges blacks to ignore European aesthetics and honor instead their own racial values and roots. For Soyinka, the artist "has always functioned in African society as the record of the mores and experience of his society and as the voice of vision in his own time." Soyinka's ability to perceptively explore Nigeria's problems without attaching specific blame to a single cause or source has helped establish his reputation as an artist committed to social awareness.

Soyinka began his career writing poems for the Nigerian literary magazine *Black Orpheus* while studying at the University College of Ibadan. His early dramas focus upon dichotomies of good versus evil and progress versus tradition. *The Swamp Dwellers* (1958) condemns African superstition in its story of religious leaders who use the fears of their townspeople for personal gain, while the comedy *The Lion and the Jewel* (1959) affirms positive African values and rejects incongruous European elements. *The Trials of Brother Jero* (1960) and *Kongi's Harvest* (1964), two of Soyinka's sharpest satires, also address cultural contradictions.

Soyinka's dramas often examine such metaphysical issues as birth and death. The theme of sacrifice, particularly that of the artist who martyrs himself for the moral benefit of his society, is also evident in many of his works. *A Dance of the Forests* (1960), a drama written for the Nigerian Independence festivities, denounces the violence and opportunism of Nigeria's past and cautions against future recurrences. The hero is confronted with the apparition of a dead child, which symbolizes the endless spiritual cycle of birth, infant death, and rebirth in a damned society, and condemns himself in the hope of ending the cycle and bringing peace to both the dead and the living. In *The Strong Breed* (1964), the protagonist offers himself as a substitute for an idiot his village intends to sacrifice as part of their annual fertility ritual. *The Road* (1965) is an absurdist drama in which a deranged "Professor," who earns his living from automobile accidents, gropes spiritually toward "the essence of death." Death on the road becomes a sacrifice to progress, a notion Soyinka regards with incredulity.

Soyinka is also an important voice in African fiction and poetry. His first novel, *The Interpreters* (1965), is praised by Bernth Lindfors as "the most complex narrative work yet written by an African." Through use of dislocations in time and shifts in viewpoint, Soyinka relates the story of a group of young Nigerian intellectuals who contemplate their country's uncertain future. Soyinka's personal commitment to his own country's future was tested in 1967, when his efforts to curtail the Nigerian civil war resulted in his arrest and im-

prisonment without trial by the Federal military government. The poems included in his collection *Idanre and Other Poems* (1967) contemplate events leading to the Nigerian crisis and pay tribute to members of the Ibo tribe slaughtered in Biafra by Soyinka's fellow Yoruba tribesmen. *A Shuttle in the Crypt* (1972) includes two poems smuggled from Soyinka's cell and published as *Poems from Prison* (1969). The claustrophobic nature of the poetry symbolizes both Soyinka's imprisonment and his determination to retain his sanity. In this volume and in the prison notes which comprise *The Man Died* (1973), Soyinka celebrates his own humanity and indicts the racism and fascism engendered by militarist rule.

Since his release from prison following the defeat of the Biafrans, Soyinka's work has assumed a darker, more militant tone. The satirical drama *Madmen and Specialists* (1970) and Soyinka's second novel, *Season of Anomy* (1973), explore the destructive aftereffects of war, specifically the tyranny and internal corruption of "reformed" governments. *A Play of Giants* (1984) is an absurdist satire in which four African heads of state meet to discuss plans for their nations. Soyinka's autobiography of his early years in western Nigeria, *Aké: The Years of Childhood* (1980), is a departure from his typically angry postprison works and focuses upon light recollections and humorous family experiences.

(See also *CLC*, Vols. 3, 5, 14 and *Contemporary Authors*, Vols. 13-16, rev. ed.)

MARTIN TUCKER

For a long time . . . [African] writers have been trying to connect African literature with European culture. The results have often been impressive. . . . The initial enthusiasm for African literature was largely social and political—African literature became the expression of a self-conscious national and continental identity. With the growth of independence, the focus of feeling dissipated. No longer was there one thing to look forward to—the one thing had come, and, having come, had splintered into a hundred new themes, foci and quests. (p. 510)

The leading playwright of Nigeria . . . is one example of this complex evolution of spirit. Wole Soyinka identifies himself with this split in . . . [the title poem of his *Idanre and Other Poems*], praising the slave who rolled a rock down on his complacent master and, in the smashup that followed, created a multiple godhead. Soyinka also refers to the "Mobius split"—which he identifies in a note to the poem as "a mathe-magical ring, infinite in self-recreation into independent but linked rings and therefore the freest conceivable (to me) symbol of human or divine (e.g., Yoruba, Olympian) relationships."

In this long poem, Soyinka captures his country's experience of bloodshed, horror and hate. **"Idanre"** was written before the civil war, but Soyinka had seen enough massacres of Ibos and other peoples to know the bite of pain and remorse, to feel the sting of sympathy. As Soyinka says in the preface, the poem is built of two separate experiences: one was a visit to the hills of Idanre, the petrified rocks of supernatural force and shape, and the other was a walk through a rainstorm, "three years later and some two hundred miles away." The second experience brought back the meaning of the first, or rather gave the two experiences a total meaning. In the drenched quiet that follows the destruction by both fire and rain, Soyinka finds his measure of calm. It is, in spite of the reign of storm and havoc, a pacific poem.

Soyinka wrote the poem some time ago. . . . The poem has its African identities: the dominant deities are Ogun (the Creative Essence), god of war, iron and metallurgy, and Sango, god of lightning and electricity. Ogun, who cleared a path of earth and then attempted to retire to his godlike heights, is trapped by liquor and ire into fighting a battle with other, more jealous gods. In his drunken stupor he murders his own men, and in shame re-enacts his crime every year. Warring gods are the province of many poets; African poetry is not unique in this respect. Yet what **"Idanre"** and other poems in . . . [this collection] reveal is a quieter, less assertive kind of statement: this African poetry is lyrical and pained, it is a head bowed not in defeat but in supplication.

One of Soyinka's most beautiful poems, **"The Hunchback of Dugbe,"** may remind some readers of Dylan Thomas' "The Hunchback in the Park." The moods of the poems are similar, the images come from shifting shades of light and darkness: shut out from the beauty of the conventional world, the hunchbacks create their own world of beauty. (pp. 510-11)

Soyinka has other similarities to Thomas: the sharp thrust of sensual imagery, a "perverse impalement" of sexuality, the belief in a regenerative universe, the obsessive awareness of death.

Yet these similarities are not the result of direct influence so much as the shared use of techniques and imagistic insights available to all poets. Indeed, it is probably time to recognize the similarity of African to other poetry. It then becomes more apparent what variety of forms and vast cultural apparatus African poets bring to their work. The two encounters related in Soyinka's poem, **"Civilian and Soldier,"** convey and fuse the dilemmas of Vietnam, of Biafra, of Russia in 1917. The first encounter is between a captured civilian and a soldier. The civilian pleads for his life, arguing that he is not a warrior, he is a part of his land. . . . The second encounter is imaginary. The civilian hopes one day to meet the soldier and shoot him. . . .

In the past, Wole Soyinka has been lively, forceful, demonstrative, certainly playful. In this volume he is meditative and understated, willing to contemplate himself as well as grant others their expressions. This quiet dignity is a new center to Soyinka's work.

Soyinka's plays, on one level, are about the conflict between past and present, between tribal beliefs and modern expediency. He was both critical and appreciative of both ways of life. What he was most attached to were those universal features of character that distinguish a man no matter *when* he was born. . . .

In his earlier work he granted vitality and shrewdness to his tribal chieftains and their beliefs in animism and spirit, particularly when they were in opposition to dry Western rationalizations of universal mysteries. He reveled in his peasant showing up the poorly educated African, the pompous schoolman stuffed with British abstractions. In this present volume there is still something of this jollity: **"To My First White Hairs"** is a mock-praise poem celebrating the coming of his old age. But mostly the poems convey a new quality of acceptance: a lyricism about life has replaced the enthusiasm for it. Even in **"Abiku,"** a poem about those legendary changeling children who die only to return and plague their mothers, the poet's eye is on the *unchanging* quality of pain, the inevitability of suffering and death. . . .

It is almost as if Soyinka's expansiveness has contracted. His spirit is not broken, but it has retrenched for watering. . . . Until the time of his imprisonment by his fellow Yoruba tribesmen and their powerful allies, the Hausas, he was a free spirit able to jibe and love all comers. Now the love remains but the stimulus for fulfillment, the desire for experience, has diminished. (p. 511)

> *Martin Tucker, "African Genesis," in* The Nation, *Vol. 209, No. 16, November 10, 1969, pp. 510-12.*

ELDRED D. JONES

If Wole Soyinka had never written another line, he would probably always be remembered in one version or another of his duiker-duikritude, tiger-tigritude, Negro-negritude quip. In many minds, particularly minds unfamiliar with his work, Soyinka is permanently installed as the arch opponent of negritude, while in fact his work exhibits all that negritude was essentially about, bar the shouting. Few writers have used the totality of African experience to greater purpose or with more effect. No African writer has been more successful in making the rest of the world see humanity through African eyes.

Using his African background, he explores the human condition. His experience—even as it appears in his work—is not entirely confined to his local environment, but this is his main inspiration and his starting-point. He makes the fullest use of Yoruba mythology, the Nigerian landscape—mountain, stream and forest—as well as its steel bridges, power stations, night clubs and tenement houses. The local pantheon of deities, the shrines in which they were and are worshipped, the animals, the plants, the rocks, all form the environment against which Soyinka treats his essential subject, *homo sapiens,* in his constant struggle of adjustment to this changing environment. *Homo sapiens* may be dressed for the nonce in a black skin and live in the sun and rain of Africa, but being essentially human he would still be recognizable if he decided to change both habit and habitat.

Soyinka is a conscious but not a self-conscious artist—this explains his impatience with too much philosophizing about being an African. That he can afford to just be himself is the result of two things. The first, which has to be stated with some care since it has been stated so often without enough definition, is that Soyinka is the product of British colonialism which differed from French colonialism, particularly in the area of education. The differences between the two systems have been exaggerated. Neither system was designed to produce an African who would be proud of being African. In this contempt for the African heritage, no Briton in the nineteenth century, when it most mattered, would have yielded an inch to a Frenchman. The British, because they are a reticent people, not given to clear-cut pre-definitions, did not talk about their intentions quite so much. They just went ahead and established what they knew the African needed—good, barefoot English public schools. Because some of these schools were very good in their way, and because African institutions were condemned mostly by implication and the cold shoulder, the message escaped many Africans who were able to go on being African while also playing cricket. . . . They were not compelled by the system to submit their names for the ballot and take out club membership. The French system encouraged a more overt discarding of African values as a qualification for the French club card. Therefore the French subjects felt the need to burn their cards in public when they found themselves compromised by their membership.

This leads to the second reason why Soyinka could afford to be himself in the fifties and sixties. It is simply that by that time the repudiation had taken place—by Senghor and Césaire and others in France in the thirties and forties. But, to repeat— in so far as the aim of negritude was to use the African experience meaningfully in art, the movement could have found no better exponent than Soyinka. (pp. 113-14)

There is in the negritude writers a kind of worship of Mother Africa which is absent in Soyinka's work. For him the 'ancients' were no better than the 'moderns' even though the former built greater empires. . . . For Soyinka, the gods were and still are often guilty of either callousness or caprice in their dealings with men, so that one is forced to bring them too to judgment. . . . This is where his greatest value lies—and his greatest personal danger; he is an irritant to complacency and a wet blanket to romance. (p. 114)

Throughout his works Soyinka is rejecting false solutions and in as late a work as *The Interpreters* he is still engaged in showing how one set of people avoid the struggle by holding on to old beliefs and avoiding conflict, while others try to face the complexities of life. In works early and late he is concerned with the individual's struggle with his environment. In this struggle he has first to try to know himself, body and soul, and then to face the world with the help of other men if this

is forthcoming, in spite of other men when this is necessary; with the help of the gods when this is available, and in desperation without even this. It is in this sense that his interpreters in the novel of that name are truly on their own, battling their way against themselves and the world. (p. 115)

Soyinka's look into Africa's glorious past in *A Dance of the Forests* is as disillusioning as his look at the present and the future. There is no false resting-place there either. The almost disdainful way in which Aroni refers to the glorious past is itself a sign that we are not going to see demi-gods in the African past. To Forest Head's request: 'Remind me, how far back are we?' the reply is

> About eight centuries. Possibly more. One of
> their great empires. I forget which.

Hardly a way to introduce a glorious epoch! What Adenebi the Council Orator was expecting was quite different: 'Mali. Songhai. Perhaps a descendant of the great Lisabi Zimbabwe. May be the legendary Prester John himself. . . . I was thinking of heroes like they.' (This inventory slyly suggests historical confusion in Adenebi's mind.) The court of Mata Kharibu provides an anti-climax to Adenebi's expectations. It contains all too familiar characters. Soyinka heightens the comparison with our imperfect present by making the human characters in the play double as both contemporary and historical characters, thus making the point that the more men change, the more they remain the same. The specific guise or garb may change but the basic human characters remain fundamentally unaltered. (pp. 119-20)

The theme of sacrifice . . . pervades Soyinka's work. In their own way, Chume, Igwezu, the Captain in *A Dance of the Forests,* the five interpreters, Oba Danlola, and of course Eman in *The Strong Breed.* The whole of Soyinka's work, like the road which he so often uses as a symbol of both sides of the coin of progress, is strewn with the debris of sacrifice. This theme appears so often and in so many different ways that it needs a special mention.

The Road as an insatiable receiver of victims is one of Soyinka's most common images. No doubt the Lagos-Ibadan road on which the author must have made innumerable hazardous journeys, and which is strewn with the wreckage of uncountable crashes, must have burned this particular form of sacrifice into his brain. One of his poems, **'Death at Dawn',** is a direct result of an actual occurence, and in this poem the image of sacrifice is the dominant one. The involuntary sacrifice of the white cock which should have appeased the road, the folk augury, and the fruitless prayer, all suggestive of attempts to appease the gods, are found in [the prayer which ends the poem, ''May you never walk when the road waits famished'']. . . . (pp. 125-26)

In *A Dance of the Forests* the theme of death on the roads is combined with that of municipal corruption when the smoky truck nicknamed 'Chimney of Breko' becomes a funeral pyre for sixty-five of the seventy-five luckless souls who trusted themselves to its overloaded body. In *The Interpreters,* Sekoni loses his life in a road accident (the language is reminiscent of **'Death at Dawn'**). . . . (pp. 126-27)

All these deaths on the roads may be called involuntary sacrifices to progress. . . . The victim of the road as unwilling victim is only one facet of Soyinka's treatment of the theme of sacrifice. Throughout his work there are voluntary sacrifices when the victim walks to an avoidable fate with his eyes open, urged on by a compelling inner prompting which makes a fatal end almost inevitable. Such is the sacrifice of Eman in *The Strong Breed*, the most obvious example of this theme in Soyinka's work.

Eman is a martyr to society. He offers his life to an ungrateful society when, by just doing nothing, or obeying the voice of an easy prudence (represented by Sunma) he could have gone on living. Time after time Sunma tries to drag him away.... (p. 127)

When the actual ordeal comes Eman's body flinches, but in the end, having offered himself in Ifada's place, he is sacrificed. Eman is represented in the play as a Christ-figure; the parallels are obvious: he is willing to die for a thankless people, at the end he flinches at the physical ordeal, and he dies lifted high on a tree. It would have been uncharacteristic for Soyinka to prolong the play in order to show a people totally repentant and converted as a result of witnessing Eman's sacrifice. Yet he does give a faint glimmer of hope. According to tradition, the villagers were supposed to cast their evils on their selected victim by cursing him. They would have done this cheerfully to the idiot Ifada, an unwilling victim. But at the sight of a willing victim, one who had done only good to the village,

> One and all they looked up at the man and
> words died in their throats.... Not one could
> raise a curse.

They sulk away from their leaders who have to have strangers for victims and dare not sacrifice themselves. Eman's death had at least sown doubt. Perhaps what he could not achieve by his life he could begin to achieve with his death. Eman made the ultimate sacrifice which not everyone is called on to make, but there are lesser sacrifices to society's demands throughout Soyinka's work.

In his poem **'The Dreamer'** there is another Christ-figure whose sacrifice seems to have a glimmer of hope. The poem starts with the figure (one of three) mounted higher than trees, an obvious reference to the Crucifixion, and ends with the bitter flowering of seeds sown by the act of sacrifice.... (pp. 127-28)

We are reminded of Tertullian's words, 'the blood of martyrs is the seed of the church'. Like the church, society's flower too seems to need stronger nourishment than water. It often demands blood. We seek for life in death....

Most of the themes which appear in Soyinka's work find room for expansion in his only novel to date, *The Interpreters*. The five principal young men, Sagoe, Bandale, Egbo, Kola and Sekoni, represent a new generation equipped with new skills, striving to get to grips with themselves and their environment. With them may be coupled other characters in the novel trying to battle their way into a personal understanding of themselves and the world, while still trying to live in it. (p. 129)

The strong vein of social criticism and comment which is found in Soyinka's work appears in full flower in *The Interpreters*. There are roughly two sorts of characters in the society that the novel portrays; the establishment figures, and the mavericks who do not accept without question the rules which in fact only govern surface appearances. This is indeed the crux of the matter. To a large extent, the mavericks are what they seem, while the establishment figures, on close examination, merely present a façade that does not represent their real selves. Since the mavericks so openly reject the insincerity of the establishment, and the establishment so thoroughly rejects the irreverence of the mavericks, the two groups are irreconcilable.

The case of Professor Oguazor's daughter neatly exemplifies the double standards of the establishment.... (p. 130)

What the novel implicitly rejects is not so much the fact that Oguazor has a daughter by his housemaid, but the insincerity which makes him totally suppress that fact, a process which makes him totally uncompassionate when he discovers that a young student at the university is pregnant. When he decrees punishment for the young man responsible, his 'meral' tone is uncompromising....

It is this blatant hypocrisy and its accompanying total lack of compassion that the novel seeks to expose in figures like Professor Oguazor. (p. 131)

This is Soyinka's technique of demolition. The values of the pillars of society are shown to be unreal. The interpreters on the other hand are engaged in finding a life which would be consistent—from which the pretences would be stripped. This so far society will not tolerate. This is the confrontation which *The Interpreters* presents. It is not an 'African' problem. Events all over the world have shown in the new generation a similar dissatisfaction with what to them is a façade concealing a rotten structure. Thus Soyinka, using a Nigerian setting, has portrayed a universal problem. This is what makes both this novel and the whole corpus of Soyinka's work universally valid. Through the particular and the local he sees through to the basic universal human problems. (p. 132)

> *Eldred D. Jones, "The Essential Soyinka," in* Introduction to Nigerian Literature, *edited by Bruce King, 1971. Reprint by Africana Publishing Corporation, 1972, pp. 113-34.*

JOHN COLEBY

In *Death and the King's Horseman* Wole Soyinka turns again to the Yoruba tradition and contrasts its ritual and mystique with the pragmatic paternalism of the last years of British rule. He appears for the time being to have abandoned the immediacy of *Madmen and Specialists,* for an exploration of the deeps of his ancestors' beliefs, maybe *reculer pour mieux sauter*.... He warns against oversimplification in performance and urges would-be producers to the risky and difficult task of 'eliciting the play's threnodic essence.' They should take his advice.

The play is based on an actual event in 1946, slightly adapted for 'minor reasons of dramaturgy'. It is akin to his earlier work *The Strong Breed*. The Yoruba King has died on the thirtieth day of mourning; his Horseman, an hereditary office-holder, must die too, so that he can escort his sovereign into the next world. Technically a suicide, the death is to be in fact a powerful act of will by the Horseman, Elesin Oba, supported by his tribal peers. The reaction of the District Officer, Simon Pilkings, when he hears what is in the wind, is what might be expected. The unlooked for but inevitable reappearance of Elesin's son Olunde from England whither he had gone to train as a doctor, sponsored by Mr. and Mrs. Pilkings, engages dramatic overdrive. The climax is very beautiful. The power and the glory of Yoruba honour stand fully revealed. One would like to see this play given the production it deserves....

> *John Coleby, in a review of "Death and the King's Horseman," in* Drama, *No. 119, Winter, 1975, p. 87.*

ELAINE JAHNER

[In *Myth, Literature and the African World,* one] major issue underlies all the rest and keeps recurring throughout all the essays, with Wole Soyinka's entire book devoted to the explorations of its implications. In Soyinka's words, that issue is the "simultaneous act of eliciting from history, mythology and literature, for the benefit of both genuine aliens and alienated Africans, a continuing process of self-apprehension." . . . His writings show that he continues to develop in his understanding of the crucial significance of the issues he presents in his most recent essays. He assumes that his readers are willing to understand that the most insidious and prevalent form of racism is that which forces African concerns into a non-African frame of reference and then judges the African lacking. The effects of this particular form of racism are far-reaching and they account for many of the tensions in African political life, a fact that Soyinka as writer and as political activist has come to know well.

In the essays under discussion here, Soyinka has not indulged in strident political rhetoric; rather, he competently and intelligently explores the matrices of African systems of communication, especially aesthetic communication. He shows how genuine understanding of a culture must embrace the reference points taken from within the culture itself and resist the temptation to begin with external reference points that so often lead to the African's betrayal. . . . Soyinka rejects all "externally induced fantasies of redemptive transformation in the image of alien masters," but such massive ground clearing is briefly accomplished so that he can . . . show how myth and ritual dramatize the process of self-apprehension and provide the energy for the regeneration of African aspirations on all levels of life.

Several of Soyinka's own dramas show that he knows how to press the indigenous gods into service on behalf of African freedom because he knows that the essence of the gods is not only human but social and that the dramas of the gods are media of communal recollection and cohesion. When Soyinka writes about the stage as a center of radical energy, he is discussing the power of basic cultural symbols to unite people in their understanding and ability to participate in the individual and communal struggle for an ongoing sense of purpose. Within this context, the power of myth and ritual are revealed as a part of the daily political reality and the discussion of the relationship between ideology and social vision follows naturally from one about myth and ritual drama.

Soyinka engages in some nimble defining of words as he discusses the link between ideology and African literature. Readers have to be alert to the particular semantic features of Soyinka's concept of ideology in order to grasp the point of his essays. According to him, any literary ideology is the result of literary activity having been set apart from other aspects of social life as an autogenous phenomenon, cut off from the human phenomenon it is supposed to reflect. Such truncation has not occurred in Africa so Soyinka can state the reasonableness of his claim that a literary ideology traditionally has had little to do with the actual process of creating literature in Africa. But clearly African literature is guided by concepts of an ideological nature and Soyinka needs terms to describe such guidance. He recruits the phrases "visionary projection of society" and "literature of social vision"; then he uses the expressions to delimit certain types of literature that crystallize "the most important function of the genre, the decongealment of the imaginative function by past or present reality, even in

the process of reflecting on them." With his definition of literature as social vision as his point of departure, Soyinka can then go on to a trenchant commentary on the effectiveness of selected writers' attempts to help Africans understand themselves and the world to understand Africa. . . . [Even] a cursory reading of commentary on African writers and critics can show the non-African propensity to embrace a single writer as an infallible spokesperson for all of the many cultures of Africa. To bestow such a status on Soyinka would be to miss the whole point of his book which is that the world must be attentive to the specific features of the many African statements about African life. (pp. 131-33)

Elaine Jahner, "African Culture Today," in Book Forum, *Vol. III, No. 1, 1977, pp. 130-35.*

BERNTH LINDFORS

[Today Soyinka] is widely regarded as one of Africa's most original creative artists. He has defined his own distinctive idiom in drama, poetry, fiction and criticism, never allowing himself to fall too deeply under the sway of alien or autochthonous traditions of expression. In the marketplace of modern literature, where many convertible currencies are freely available, Soyinka owes surprisingly few traceable debts.

Yet in recent years he has published two plays that are undisguised adaptations of well-known European masterworks: *The Bacchae of Euripides,* which Soyinka "conceived as a communal feast, a tumultuous celebration of life," and *Opera Wonyosi,* an Africanization of John Gay's *The Beggar's Opera* and Bertolt Brecht's *The Threepenny Opera.* . . . What is interesting to observe in both of these adapted works is the degree to which Soyinka modified the original texts in order to achieve his own ends. We might well ask, how much did he blatantly retain and how much did he transform in obedience to independent creative stresses?

The Bacchae of Euripides has already been commented on by a number of drama critics and scholars, the consensus view being that Soyinka succeeded in reinvesting the play with greater dimensions and complexity by introducing African elements that harmonize with the original theme but do not radically alter the nature of the drama. In other words, though he extended its basic structure and rearranged its furnishings, he did not tamper with its original design. . . . One might venture to say that in form as well as content Soyinka's *Bacchae* remains [a European drama]. . . . (p. 22)

The same kind of statement could be made about *Opera Wonyosi,* which follows Brecht rather slavishly in places and transforms far less of *The Threepenny Opera* than Brecht's play transformed of John Gay's eighteenth century musical drama, *The Beggar's Opera.* Soyinka seems content to pour local palm-wine into European receptacles rather than devise wholly new containers for his home-brewed spirits. *Opera Wonyosi* is a very topical Nigerian satire, but it gains much of its thrust and momentum by delivering its message in a dependable, racy vehicle of foreign manufacture. Indeed, at times Soyinka looks more like a hitchhiker than a trailblazer.

Take the "character structure" of the opera, for instance. Soyinka does not bother to change the names of a number of his dramatis personae, retaining the traditional Captain Macheath (i.e., Mack the Knife), Hookfinger Jake, Police Commissioner "Tiger" Brown, Jimmy, Polly, Jenny, Sukie and Lucy. Even when he does introduce a new name, the name iself does not necessarily signal a change in the role or personality of the character to whom it is given. . . . The only new characters of any significance are representatives of various professions: a military man, colonel Moses; a university academic, Professor Bamgbapo. . . . One comically inflated character readily identifiable as a notorious contemporary personage is Emperor Boky, a hilarious caricature of Emperor Jean-Bedel Bokassa of the Central African Republic, whose imperial coronation, like that of the Queen in Brecht's rendition, serves as the occasion for Macheath's royal reprieve at the end of the melodrama, thereby providing the happy ending that Gay, Brecht and Soyinka sardonically agree light opera demands. (p. 23)

The songs Soyinka used in *Opera Wonyosi* came from a variety of sources, hardly any of which were African. He grafted new words onto well-known Euro-American tunes, much as Gay had done with old English airs in *The Beggar's Opera*. For instance, he borrowed Kurt Weill's famous score for the theme song, the "Moritat of Mackie the Knife," but changed Brecht's lyrics to suit his Nigerian audience. . . . Other melodies recognizable from Soyinka's lyrics include such popular favourites as "The Saint Louis Blues," . . . and at least one Nigerian "highlife" tune, but there is no evidence that any traditional African songs or indigenous musical instruments were utilized. Musically *Opera Wonyosi* was an eclectic Western medley.

This is not to say that Soyinka's effort to adapt an alien art form was unsuccessful. *Opera Wonyosi* may have retained a Brechtian structure and a Gayish agility of wit, but Soyinka managed to turn the flavour of the farce into something characteristically African. Indeed, though all the action is presented as taking place in the Central African Republic, it is not difficult to identify specific Nigerian targets of his satire. . . . Military rule itself is mercilessly lampooned, and the charges brought against Colonel Moses at his trial—charges of arson, rape, assault, and murder . . . —have an uncomfortably close correlation with real happenings in postwar Nigeria. . . . Soyinka was tweaking some very prominent public noses, just as John Gay had done 250 years before. (pp. 24-5)

Soyinka's purpose in writing this opera was to satirize Nigeria in the mid-1970's, a period marked by military rule and an economic boom fueled by oil. . . . *Opera Wonyosi* apparently was meant to restore human communication. . . . Soyinka attempted to do this by holding up to ridicule and scorn many of the social atrocities committed in the morally confused postwar era. The story of Mack the Knife was a convenient peg on which to hang his charges against his countrymen, for the underworld ambience of such a traditional villain-hero was sufficiently distanced in time and place to provide a large-scale perspective on the subject of human depravity, thereby imbuing the dramatic action with a semblance of "universality," yet at the same time that ambience resembled so closely the cutthroat, dog-eat-dog atmosphere of the "high period of Nigeria's social decadence" that Mackie could be easily assimilated as a local folk-hero/villain. Nigerian audiences would not be likely to question the stylized squalor of the beggar's world portrayed in this opera, for that would be tantamount to denying the surreal dimensions of their own corrupted world. Soyinka had chosen an excellent warped mirror to reflect the absurdities of an unbalanced age. (p. 30)

It may be no mere coincidence that both Brecht and Soyinka reworked the story of Mack the Knife in a postwar era, for both must have felt that their countrymen had learned nothing from the horrors of the holocaust. Man's unreluctant return to depravity after such catastrophe must have struck them as dan-

gerously idiotic. To show up this dark, benighted side of human nature, both turned to light opera, sugarcoating the bitter message they wished to convey to a complacent populace. By making people laugh at something absurdly close to home, they sought to make them think.

Brecht, however, fashioned his opera as a comment on the evil inherent in all mankind and reinforced by manmade institutions. . . . Soyinka, on the other hand, spoke primarily of the evils visible in Nigeria. Like Gay, he was striking out at specific targets in his own society, so his was a more topical satire than Brecht's. But whereas Gay was content to expose social evils without denouncing them or inquiring into their origins, Soyinka was interested in provoking his audience to raise questions about what their world was coming to and why. . . . Soyinka thus stands in a middle ground between Gay and Brecht. He has more social commitment than Gay but less pessimism than Brecht. He appears to believe that reform is possible so long as one can recognize and speak out against the evils that man brings upon man. *Opera Wonyosi* is his attempt to contribute to the reform of contemporary Nigeria through song, dance, and satirical laughter. (pp. 31-2)

> *Bernth Lindfors, "Begging Questions in Wole Soyinka's 'Opera Wonyosi'," in Ariel, Vol. 12, No. 3, July, 1981, pp. 21-33.*

DON SHEWEY

[*Aké: The Years of Childhood*], Nigerian playwright Wole Soyinka's childhood memoir, is a superb act of remembrance, recreating with dazzling clarity such Everychild mysteries as the proper engineering of birthdays, the significance of domestic landmarks like the Wash-Hand Basin, and the jumble of treasures stashed in the "insatiable cavern" underneath Mother's bed. But Soyinka's ironical sensibility and his unsentimental attitude toward childhood also transform an unusual autobiography into a tale of haphazard education that is comically true to life.

Growing up in the '40s under British colonial rule, the second son of an English-speaking schoolteacher and a fanatically Christian shopkeeper, young Wole . . . had more to explain to himself than the average munchkin. He had to deal with culture-clash at every turn: European/African, ancient/modern, Christian/pagan. Is it any wonder that he confused the vestments of St. Peter in stained-glass windows with the hooded robes of the *egúngún,* ancestral priests masquerading as spirits of the dead?. . . The egúngún, the Wolf Cubs, saints, termites, His Master's Voice, Christianity, class, race: these are all mysteries of faith to *Aké*'s narrator, who ages from three to 11 in 230 pages, and he questions each one.

A skillful dramatist even as a child, Soyinka instantly sees his tempestuous mother and fastidious father as characters, whom he dubs "the Wild Christian" and "Essay" (from S.A., meaning H.M., Headmaster). Much of the book's abundant comedy springs from the collision of Essay's imperturbable elegance and the pathetic unruliness of lesser mortals. . . . Many such characters make vivid appearances, but next to Essay and the Wild Christian, the largest role in young Wole's life is played by food. (p. 40)

The detailed menus, the survey of wildlife, the litany of place names add a sensual edge to the book's sense of childlike discovery. And the few times the adult Soyinka intrudes to compare today's Aké with the past, his comments dwell on the sensual. He mourns that the smell which once dominated the marketplace has been overcome now by sound—the sound of raucous vendors and ghetto-blasters—while the delicacies he snacked on as a youth have been replaced by nutritionally inferior fare like ice cream and popcorn. Soyinka's bitterness at the invasion of the ''global waste industry'' is sharp but well placed. . . .

Sometimes Soyinka leaves his mysteries too unexplained, like the ankle-cutting ritual that his non-Christian grandfather secretly administers, and other times he shows his hand too much; his fascinating account of the Egba women's tax revolt comes off as a little pat, a Good Ending. But, on the whole, reading *Aké* has an enchanting effect.

> *Don Shewey, in a review of ''Aké: The Years of Childhood,'' in* The Village Voice, *Vol. XXVII, No. 35, August 31, 1982, pp. 40-1.*

JAMES OLNEY

[''Aké''] is destined to become a classic of African autobiography, indeed a classic of childhood memoirs wherever and whenever produced.

What Mr. Soyinka makes most vividly present is the living landscape of Aké, the Nigerian village where he grew up on a parsonage compound. . . . It is from the wonderfully colorful, agitated, aroma-laden markets, the likes of which one finds all across West Africa, that Mr. Soyinka distills the essence of the Aké of his memories. . . .

In one of the finest chapters of ''Aké,'' Mr. Soyinka eulogizes the markets of his childhood. His memory is remarkable; he still seems able to hear the sounds, taste the flavors and smell the aromas of 35 and 40 years ago. Every sound and smell blended together in the evenings of Mr. Soyinka's childhood to form ''part of the invisible network of Aké's extended persona.'' They are gone now, but once he could be sure of ''Ibarapa's sumptuous resurrection of flavours every evening.''. . .

Throughout his previous work, Wole Soyinka has insisted on the dual nature of the role performed by the African artist. The artist ''has always functioned in African society . . . as the record of the mores and experience of his society *and* as the voice of vision in his own time.'' In ''Aké'' Mr. Soyinka rehearses his own vision even as he traces its roots in the experiences and people of his African childhood. The world that Mr. Soyinka recalls in ''Aké,'' that he creates or re-creates from memories of the past (for it is sadly different now), is a world of pervasive, indwelling spiritual presences.

A sense of these presences is felt as Mr. Soyinka recalls the people among whom he grew up: his mother and father . . . ; his paternal grandfather, who was crucially important to Mr. Soyinka's education in Yoruba traditions. . . . But the importance of the spiritual world is seen more obviously in the descriptions of the *egúngún*, ancestral spirits who return in all their power and vitality when their masks are danced in festive procession and who represent the extended being of parents, grandparents and elders. Indeed, the *egúngún* even assert their presence through the organ in the Christian church. . . . (p. 7)

There is more than a little method in this mingling of African ancestors and the Christian deity. Mr. Soyinka sees this and other ritual performances as more or less successful attempts (Yoruba more successful, Christian less) at restoring to a condition of unity and cosmic balance the three interpenetrating, interdependent worlds of his traditional Yoruba (and more generally African) belief: the ancestors, the yet unborn and the living.

In addition to these three realms Mr. Soyinka distinguishes a ''Fourth Stage,'' and throughout his work we find symbolic figures, spirits and objects that have an especially intimate tie to the stage that he calls ''the numinous area of transition.'' The *egúngún*, who make the transition and bind the worlds of the living and the dead together with the dancing of their masks, belong to this Fourth Stage. But in ''Aké'' there are other examples: There is the girl named Bukola, who is an *àbikú* (''a child which is born, dies, is born again and dies in a repetitive cycle''); there are the wood spirits around the parsonage compound; there is Mr. Soyinka's little sister, whose death, on her first birthday, makes him expect some sort of universal cataclysm; there is the guava tree that Mr. Soyinka imagines to be *his* tree, inhabited by spirits that he can command. . . . Such symbolic figures and incidents in ''Aké'' perform the function of ordering and vitalizing the cosmos that they do in Mr. Soyinka's other work, whatever the mode. (pp. 7, 18)

For all its seriousness, ''Aké'' is not at all a solemn book. On the contrary, it is full of high good humor and a lyric grace. The book's structure is largely one of strung-together sketches and anecdotes. . . . But even these sketches and anecdotes are used to describe and realize a world to which Mr. Soyinka's mature understanding and his dozen or so volumes of fiction, drama and poetry are deeply committed. . . .

Through recollection, restoration and re-creation, he conveys a personal vision that was formed by the childhood world that he now returns to evoke and exalt in his autobiography. This is the ideal circle of autobiography at its best. It is what makes ''Aké,'' in addition to its other great virtues, the best available introduction to the work of one of the liveliest, most exciting writers in the world today. (p. 18)

> *James Olney, ''The Spirits and the African Boy,'' in* The New York Times Book Review, *October 10, 1982, pp. 7, 18.*

NADINE GORDIMER

Soyinka, an elegant writer, has in his recent novels tended to be an overly self-conscious one. For the best of reasons—he is never complacent, always searching out the most striking and complete way to say what he has to say—he sometimes produces the bad result of making the reader aware of the writer's unresolved choices. Too many words, too many inversions, too many clamoring clauses which punctuation cannot handle intelligibly. . . .

It is not surprising, then, that his approach to his years of childhood [in *Aké*] should have more in common with *Tristram Shandy* than with Proust or Laye. . . . For the first ninety pages or so, the tone is waggish. The ''worked-up'' anecdotal dialogue of his parents and others reads like inventions based on what are really family sayings—whose origin is germane, a whole view of life rather than a response to a single happening. It is hard to believe that a boy under five thought of his mother as ''Wild Christian'' although the fact that everyone referred to his father as ''HM'' (headmaster) would have made it natural for him to see that as a name for intimate use, and not a title. It is hard to accept that a three-and-a-half-year-old's sassy ripostes were as well phrased as the supremely articulate adult now "hears" them in memory. And as for rediscovering the time dimensions of childhood, the scrappy organization of the first part of the book does not at all express the child's extended time spans and the size of events that swell with these, measured neither by seasons nor by dates. . . .

When the people in his village of Aké begin to be aware of the distant 1939-1945 war, the small boy Wole does seem to take over the interpretation of his own experience, maybe because by then he was just old enough to have sorted the hot and cold of sensuous impressions into some order available to memory. One forms the oblique picture of him for oneself, without the interference of the adult Soyinka's artifice. Wild Christian and HM are no longer ideograms of idiosyncrasy, but those most mysterious beings of our lives, parents. In the loving daily battle between the mother (who dispensed Christian charity and discipline as practically as the contents of her cooking pots) and father (scholarly agnostic toward both Christian and Nigerian gods) and their unpredictable child, he emerges as original innocence; not original sin, as his parents sometimes seemed to believe. . . .

Parents are generally the scapegoats for all our adult inadequacies. Was there, then, something about Wole Soyinka's childhood, some security that produced the courage both physical and intellectual, and prepared him for the outlandish demands his era was to make of him? Yet his environment is revealed not as the natural paradise lesser writers edit . . . from the footage of reality. To begin with, his parents were middle-class, his mother a shopkeeper and debt-collector as well as a wild Christian, his father more interested in books than traditional status possessions; and the middle, in modern African societies, is the ground of the tug between the African way of life and the European way in which, as Chinua Achebe has definitively chronicled, things fall apart. (p. 3)

Like a piece of *etú*, the rich locally woven cloth, social relations were a garment whose ceremonial weight was at the same time cosily enclosing. The child was never overawed by it. . . . The different coordinates—which style of life goes with which class, which conventions with which kind of respect, which snobbishness with which pretension—are the source for non-Africans, who (of course) know only the styles of life that go with *their* social categories, of a fascination that takes hold with the hand of the child.

When the not-quite-heaven that was Wole's natal village of Aké extends, along with the parental relationship, to his father's natal territory at Isara, the fascination becomes complete. The grandfather, with a painful scarification ceremony, puts the boy in the care of the god Ogun just as Wild Christian has put him in the care of Christ. Again, the result is not a trauma but greater security for the child. And the writer finds his way to him with a felicity of evocation and expression of the "axis of tastes and smells" along which the preparation of foods provides a family genealogy, a wonderfully sensuous *first* sense of self, other, and belonging. The whiff of identical flavor in dishes prepared by different hands, different generations, is the child's own historiography and system of kinship. . . . The pleasures of entering Wole Soyinka's childhood, for a stranger, consist not only in differences but in correspondences as well. (pp. 3, 6)

Nadine Gordimer, *"The Child Is the Man,"* in The New York Review of Books, *Vol. XXIX, No. 16, October 21, 1982, pp. 3, 6.*

TANURE OJAIDE

In **"Four archetypes,"** Soyinka displays his poetic gift as he expresses strong views about himself, his country, and human existence at a critical period in Nigerian history. To give universal validity to the events in Nigeria during the civil war, he uses Joseph, Hamlet, Gulliver, and Ulysses as masks to express his predicament at the time. His voice and viewpoint deserve to be heard.

"Four archetypes" is the second section of *A Shuttle in the Crypt,* a collection of Soyinka's poems about the Nigerian crisis between 1966 and early 1971 and his own detention by the federal authorities for allegedly sympathizing with the secessionists. The four archetypal figures are analogues of the poet. Though unique in some ways, these four personae have certain similar qualities, and the poet sees their experiences as reflecting his own during the Nigerian crisis.

All four are strangers in the situations in which they find themselves; they are lonely, and hanker after truth and ideals. Joseph and Gulliver are imprisoned, Ulysses is detained by Circe, and Hamlet is exiled from Denmark to England. Through these personae, the poet identifies the values he seeks and cherishes. He thus uses the archetypes to universalize his condition. His loneliness is not unique because he is one of many wanderers. His problems of isolation, alienation, persecution, and pain are human and natural. In the course of dramatizing his condition, the poet indicts the military establishment, which was responsible for his arrest and detention.

Two kinds of voice are heard in these poems: the self-dramatizing and the critical. The voice is self-dramatizing when the poet defends himself against false accusations and when he explains his idealistic motivations. The voice is critical when he denounces the federal establishment as hypocritical, tyrannical, and mean. In both voices, there is passion because of the personal involvement of the poet. It will be clear that the two voices heard in these poems belong to one personality with a unified sensibility because pursuit of ideals inevitably results in rejection of negative values. In these poems, especially **"Joseph"** and **"Gulliver,"** the poet seems to write with a motive . . . aimed not simply at sociopolitical criticism but at history—a determination as a witness, to get down a record of the abuses of the violators of his person and society. (pp. 58-9)

The poem **"Joseph"** is indebted to the story of Joseph and Potiphar's wife in Genesis. Joseph, the eleventh and favorite son of Jacob, is known for two major qualities: discipline in resisting the temptation of his master's wife and insight in interpreting dreams. **"Joseph"** is a dramatic monologue, and its speaker is pungent in his denunciation of the hypocrisy of "Mrs. Potiphar." He denies the charge of sexual harassment Potiphar's wife levels against him. By presenting herself as the victim, and hiding the fact that she is a victimizer, she lays claim to a virtue she does not possess. The speaker shifts from accusing Potiphar's wife of hypocrisy to rejecting the quality of sainthood associated with Joseph. Since saints are agents of divine fulfillment, they are passive and patient, but the speaker [believes] . . . there should be no passivity in evil times because action is needed. Since he curses and wants quick solutions, he is unlike those holy men who are pious, passive, and patient. He accepts martyrdom, dying for a cause, which is not necessarily a saintly act; he is interested in moral responsibility, not holiness. (p. 59)

The poet employs many poetic devices to achieve vindication of himself and castigation of the establishment. In the Biblical story, Potiphar's wife is left holding the clothes she has herself torn in order to fabricate evidence for the rape. In the poem, irony and metaphor are particularly effective in exposing the hollowness of the woman's chastity.... She rests on a "whitened couch of bones," another underscoring by the poet to expose her hypocrisy. Irony, metaphor, possessives, and negative epithets puncture Potiphar's wife's claim to virtue and expose her for what she really is....

"**Joseph**" is both self-dramatizing and anti-establishment, a mixture of self-defense and satire. It is an analogue of Soyinka's situation during the Nigerian Civil War: the federal military government is like "Mrs. Potiphar" lying against the dutiful, honest, and foresighted poet; and Joseph's imprisonment is akin to ... [Soyinka's] solitary confinement because he was neither tried nor given an opportunity to defend himself. The poet succeeds in defending and universalizing his predicament in a self-dramatizing and critical voice....

Written in the third person singular, "**Hamlet**" does not attempt to achieve the dramatic voice of "**Joseph.**" Instead, it presents a controlled, introspective, and impassive voice analyzing what spurs Hamlet into action in the very last moments of his life. Before Hamlet makes up his mind [to kill his uncle, Laertes], doubts halt and lame his "resolution on the rack"; his desire to avenge treachery and villainy is dampened by caution.... He is "passionless" as he does not betray his motives—he is controlled, disciplined, and deliberate. "Passion" is repeated to draw attention to the contrast between Hamlet's self-control and the king's lack of emotional restraint. Furthermore, it is ironic, and yet appropriate, that he uses passionless behavior to expose the guilt of passion. (p. 60)

To Soyinka, the discovery of further treachery spurs one to decisive action.

Soyinka uses certain techniques to shape voice and viewpoint. The poet is distant to avoid sentimentality. While it is apparent that Hamlet is a metaphor for the poet, the analogy is drawn in a rather cold way. The poetic distance and use of rhyme and stanzas reflect Hamlet's self-control, a fusion of poetic art and theme.... The repetitions of "passion" and "doubts" and the pun on "still" and "steel" help to draw attention to Hamlet's vacillation and sudden action.

Though it is the poet who speaks about Hamlet, unlike Joseph, who speaks for himself, "**Hamlet**" and **Joseph**" both concern treachery against innocent individuals.... Hamlet would not have acted decisively after resolving on his uncle's guilt if he did not have final evidence of treachery. Somehow, he is an agent of divine justice.

"**Hamlet**" is a mask through which Soyinka expresses his position during the Nigerian crisis. Soyinka believes that the January 1966 coup formed a good basis for positive changes in Nigeria.... The poet thus sees the July 1966 counter-coup as a form of political betrayal.... It is possible the poet sees the counter-coup as a form of murder of his father and the usurping of his mother, Nigeria, by the Gowon administration—hence the Hamlet analogy.

"**Gulliver**" has as its background Gulliver among the Lilliputians in Swift's classic. After being washed ashore in Lilliput, Gulliver is secured by Lilliputians and is later freed on certain conditions.... [Four] articles of impeachment are brought against Gulliver: urinating in the palace precincts, refusing to join the killing of the innocent people of Blefuscu for conscience sake, having good relations with ambassadors of Ble-

fuscu, an enemy state, and trying to leave for Blefuscu with only oral assurance, not with a legitimate permit.

Gulliver's plight is analogous to the Nigerian situation that gave rise to Soyinka's detention and to this poem. Lilliput seems to be Nigeria and Blefuscu, Biafra. Soyinka would not support the federal side, and he went to Biafra without permission from the Lagos authorities. He also fraternized with such people as Victor Banjo and Christopher Okigbo, who could be metaphorically described as ambassadors of Biafra. With this double background of *Gulliver's Travels* and the Nigerian crisis in mind, the maudlin, complaining, and denouncing voice of the poet who is victimized for being far-sighted can be better understood.

From the first line of the poem, one gets the impression of a satire, especially with the symbolic "ship-(of state)-wreck." This wrenched cliché has political overtones in its apparent reference to the Nigerian state wrecked by crises. The word *necropolis*, the allusion to Lethe, the Latinate *obtruding* and *famished,* and the many compound words in the first verse paragraph create a sophisticated and learned voice. The poet uses antithesis to convey the contrast between Gulliver-himself and the Lilliputian-Nigerian rulers.... In *Gulliver's Travels* and this poem, physical stature is an exteriorization of moral standing.

The speaker describes the opposing side in negative terms.... His urinating to extinguish the flame [of the empress' apartment] is paradoxical.... This "indecent act" produces positive results.... [The] poet sees the end result as paramount. The means, indecent behavior and violence, are geared towards highly positive results.

As the poem progresses, the self-vindicating voice becomes more articulate.... Not long after [Gulliver] was pardoned, war broke out between Lilliput and Blefuscu. The speaker mocks the Lilliputians, who were the aggressors.... The Lilliputians' false claim to superiority is subtly presented. They talk of "Us," starting with a capital U, a sign of egotism; and the "you" of the "Blefuscoons" starts with a small y .... The Lilliputians are racists and fascists. Soyinka seems to be throwing jibes at the current rulers of Nigeria, whom he sees as arrogant.

During the war, Gulliver "pressed a reasoned course / Of temperate victory," but the Lilliputians (like the federalists of Nigeria) would not accept a "temperate victory" as enough. He turned to arbitration, but the belligerent Lilliputians were bent on wiping out the enemy. This is a kind of self-justification and self-absolvement from the crimes associated with the war. This section of the poem recalls Soyinka's trips to the northern part of Nigeria and to Biafra. After his arbitration efforts were spurned, old accusations were brought up as an excuse to get rid of a peacemaker. The speaker is accused of being a blasphemer and an arsonist. The antithetical views of the speaker and the Lilliputians are emphasized in the speaker's being too big intellectually to abet their petty ideas.

The speaker is condemned to "capital doom" because his elimination would save those to whom he had been a threat, but the Court Hygienist voices a dread: that the speaker could even in death infect others with his disease. Since the poet's death could incite antigovernment activities, there is need for a compromise. At this stage, the poem has gone beyond its Gulliver-in-Lilliput base to a Soyinka-in-Nigeria poem.... The Court Hygienist is a political-internal security adviser, perhaps an inspector general of police or director of prisons, who weighs the pros and cons of government action against a dissident.

The final verse paragraph is ironic. The speaker is condemned, and his "fault is not in ill-will but in seeing ill." "Seeing" and sight-related words are repeated to emphasize the "offense" of the so-called culprit. The good qualities of foresight and insight are considered dangerous in this state. The sentence is not based on justice or law, but on the whims and caprices of the tyrannical state. (pp. 61-4)

"**Ulysses**" is related to a long literary tradition. Ulysses is the Greek Odysseus, who helps to take Troy and is known for his travels, resourcefulness, endurance, and experience. He is also an agent of salvation; Circe transforms his men into swine, but with the help of Hermes he avoids personal dehumanization and brings his men back to their human shape.... In Joyce's novel, he is a kind of Everyman. In Soyinka's poem, the references to sea, wind, rocks, straits, and Circe are Odyssean.

The speaker of "**Ulysses**" is involved in an internal quest, and his voice is introspective.... The poet allegorizes the human condition, which is full of cyclic attempts to create immortal values out of painful experiences.

The speaker reveals that he had been toying with "concepts." His theoretical "concepts" in the classroom were a "crystal cover on the world," and everything was held in suspension until the storm of experience came with its thunder and broke things into fragments. (After all, the poem is subtitled "Notes from here to my Joyce class.") He implies that previously he was living in a world of concepts, but that now he is going through the reality of those ideas. There is some connection between the classroom and his prison, between the concept and the reality; but the harsh reality of experience is more telling to the poet.

The latter part of the poem concerns the speaker's quest. He is a lone wanderer, and the quest takes him to and through various difficult experiences.... These anecdotes are relevant to Soyinka's position during the Nigerian crisis. He was detained like Ulysses and like him he survived dehumanization, while others turned to human swine. The poet's mental activity, a kind of Odyssean resourcefulness, saved him from the fate of others. The choice between Scylla and Charybdis is that between facing trouble in criticizing the military rulers and drowning in the corruption of the government.... Despite the dangers and pain of the quest, it results in a new awareness, "our lighted beings."

Like "**Gulliver**," "**Ulysses**" ends with images of light and darkness. To the poet, a lonely quest leads to knowledge, and pain brings wholesome effects. The meaning of life comes from experiences gained in action or involvement, not the theoretical talk in the classroom. (pp. 64-6)

The experiences of the four archetypes are analogous to Soyinka's during the Nigerian crisis. The working out of the kinship between the poet and the four figures reveals Soyinka's poetic imagination, learning, and genius. Each persona is an objective correlative of the poet's state. The intellectualization elevates the voice from that of a common victim to that of the victimized hero. Joseph, Hamlet, Gulliver, and Ulysses are all heroes; and the poet implies that he too is heroic, having gone through the same kind of experience.

The two kinds of voice—the self-dramatizing and the critical—are interrelated, since expressing one's personal predicament in a political context involves criticism of one's persecutors.

By assuming the mantle of the questing hero who has been arbitrarily imprisoned and betrayed, the poet denigrates the establishment that persecuted him. There is ..., especially in "**Joseph**" and "**Gulliver**," a strong satirical edge in the self-dramatization as the speakers in the poems hammer at hypocrites, traitors, and perverters of justice. There are some shades to the self-dramatizing, such as the passivity in "**Hamlet**" and the dialectic in "**Ulysses**," but in each case the poet defends his position. In "**Four archetypes**," the voice of the poet is passionate and firm and relays the views he wants to be heard. (p. 66)

> *Tanure Ojaide, "The Voice and Viewpoint of the Poet in Wole Soyinka's 'Four Archetypes'," in* Research in African Literatures, *Vol. 14, No. 1, Spring, 1983, pp. 58-67.*

ARTHUR RAVENSCROFT

Soyinka's new play [*A Play of Giants*] is a political statement in the sense that it seeks to show, as unambiguously and as physically as is feasible in the theatre, the motivations of neo-colonialist African tyrants.... *A Play of Giants* is a work of bitter anger, a denunciation of what is monstrous and dehumanizing not only in Africa and the Third World generally but in the other two suave worlds as well. The 'giants' are four African heads of state (freely modelled upon Nguema, Bokassa, Mobutu and Amin) discussing and exercising the mechanics of absolute power, while they pose in the Bugaran UN embassy in New York for a life-size group sculpture that President-for-Life Kamini wants installed in the United Nations building. The crudity of their thinking is conveyed by the crudity of their language, and they regard human beings as mere maggots or ants to be squashed, zombies to be controlled 'from birth to death ... in thousands of millions'. The witty, elegant political satire of Soyinka's *Kongi's Harvest* ... and *Madmen and Specialists* ... here gives way to dialogue and action that have the caricature dimensions of farce, while the four major characters ... are presented not as individuals but, very appropriately, as if they were carnival masks personating tyrannical systems. By such means Soyinka powerfully converts the diabolical into the despicable, but even as the audience will be moved to guffaw at the absurd antics of these 'giants', it will be chilled by the realization that the same antics are enactments of the helpless being crushed by the powerful. The full stage business of numerous and rapid entrances and exits by various functionaries ... emphasizes the farcical mode while involving super-powers and other industrial nations in the monstrous, orgasmic power-lust that allows mindless brutality to flourish. It is Soyinka's angriest play, and by no means the least of his works for the theatre.

> *Arthur Ravenscroft, in a review of "A Play of Giants,' in* British Book News, *December, 1984, p. 757.*

GERALD WEALES

[*A Play of Giants*] was a disappointment to an admirer like me who prefers Soyinka when he modifies traditional African ritual to express his contemporary ideas (*The Road, Death and the King's Horsemen*). Yet, even when Soyinka's theatrical inventiveness is not used to its fullest, he has important things to say about Africa in particular, the world in general.

The giants in the play that Soyinka subtitles "A Fantasia on the Aminian Theme" are four African dictators, based on Bokassa, Mobutu, Ngeuma, and Idi Amin. Soyinka's genre this time is conventional political farce, and his satiric method is the overstatement of *Kongi's Harvest*. One might argue that it is impossible to overstate men like Bokassa and Idi Amin, outrageously comic and outrageously bloody, but grotesque caricature in life is different from that on stage. Not only in its four dictators, but in the Russian and American U.N. delegates . . . , the self- and other-deluding black American professor and politician, and the Swedish apologist/mistress, *Giants* makes no attempt at subtlety. It is sometimes funny, sometimes blunt satire, . . . [artificial] without being effective in its use of that artificiality, as Soyinka has been on other occasions. . . . Too often, in *Giants,* Soyinka shrinks his skills as a marksman by making his targets too large.

There is no doubt about Soyinka's serious intentions in *Giants*. . . . His immediate butts are not only such African rulers, but also the great powers whose acquiescence helps sustain them. Beyond that, his larger theme is "the taste of absolute power." The play's repetitions, in act and word, tend to weaken the bite in the satire. His most effective statement of theme is the device which both defines the chief character and gives the play whatever plot it has. Kamini (the Idi Amin figure) is presented as vain and sentimental, sly but obtuse. In scene after scene, incapable of following any but the simplest remarks, he lifts a single word or phrase out of a speech whose import has escaped him, builds a response on it—often a cruel one—and settles back in self-congratulatory complacence at his correctness. It is altogether proper, in the farcically violent worlds of the play and international politics, that he take his titles literally, his rhetoric as reality, and the letter of international law as binding (the Bugara Embassy is Bugaran territory), and builds them into an explosive finale which presumably destroys not only him and his fellow giants, but the American and Russian delegates and the Secretary General as well. The incidental music is from Wagner's *The Twilight of the Gods,* but for Soyinka its use is probably not only a joke, but wishful thinking. (p. 86)

Gerald Weales, "Cultural Mixes," in Commonweal, *Vol. CXII, No. 3, February 8, 1985, pp. 85-6.*

Lisa St. Aubin de Teran

19??-

English novelist.

Teran married an exiled Venezuelan while still a teenager, and her novels reflect her subsequent initiation into both the Latin-American culture and an expatriate lifestyle. South America looms as an antagonistic presence throughout her works; the landscape she portrays is riddled with insects, drought, and disease. Yet Teran also reveals the haunting beauty and rich, magical folklore that characterize the region. Many critics praise the subtlety and refinement of Teran's prose style.

Teran's first two novels are largely autobiographical. In *Keepers of the House* (1982) a young Englishwoman returns with her husband to his ancestral home in Venezuela, where she learns and records centuries of his family history. *The Slow Train to Milan* (1983) explores the fugitive lifestyle as the heroine accompanies her husband and two other men who are trying to escape from the law. Although the action of this novel takes place in Europe, the aristocratic element of Latin-American culture is represented in the cultivated and aloof characters of the three men. Teran returns to Venezuela for the setting of *The Tiger* (1984). Using supernatural elements, she describes a young man whose domineering grandmother is able to control his life even after her death.

© Jerry Bauer

ANNE SMITH

[The heroine of *Keepers of the House*], like the author herself, has married a South American ranch owner at sixteen, and gone to live with him on his estate in the Andes. As drought slowly destroys the land, and her husband fades away with a kidney complaint, Lydia listens to tales of the valley, an anecdotal account of her husband's family history, from an old retainer. She puts these together chronologically for the record before she leaves, pregnant with the last heir.

Keepers of the House [published in the United States as *The Long Way Home*], is a sub-Marquezian fiction, which has something of Marquez' power of depicting in microcosm the cruelties and catastrophes, the endemic corruption, and the feudal relationship with death and the supernatural that characterise South American life. Occasionally the stories are anecdotes, familiar everywhere; occasionally the author gets carried away with the exuberance of her adjectival prose and actually contradicts herself—as when she describes an eighty-nine-year-old peasant as looking and moving like a man of fifty, then in the next paragraph tells us that he 'teetered rather than walked' . . .—and the framework of Lydia's narrative is somewhat fragile; but the portrait of life in the valley rises above such immaturities of technique and style with the haunting quality of folktales.

Anne Smith, "Mirrors," in New Statesman, Vol. 104, No. 2676, July 9, 1982, p. 23.*

HERMIONE LEE

[*Keepers of the House* is an] exceptional first novel, richly evocative and cunningly crafted. Like her author, Lydia is transformed, by her marriage to a saturnine Venezuelan landowner, Diego Beltran, from teenage English schoolgirl to 'La Doña' of a vast decaying avocado farm and sugar plantation in the Andes. While her husband lies gripped by 'a sleeping sickness of the heart,' Lydia becomes, in all senses, the last 'keeper of the house.' She bears the last heir to the Hacienda La Bebella, she struggles to rescue it from ruin, and she inherits, from the stories of an aged servant, the savage chronicle of the Beltrans, 'leaders in a land of impossible odds.'

The stories horribly manifest what V. S. Naipaul, writing of Argentina in 1972, lists as the ingredients of the Latin American nightmare: poverty, violence, 'protest, despair, faith, machismo, magic, *espiritismo*, revenge.' . . . Locusts, maggots, weevils, running sores, goitres, amputated limbs, rotting avocados, litter the book with an almost boisterous abandon. . . . This 'grand guignol' is part of the book's charm and verve. Like [Carlos] Fuentes, Ms. de Teran is writing about narrative. Her chronicler, inheritor of an oral tradition, finds images for the stories in the eighteenth-century tiles which covered the treasure of the house, or in the five mill-wheels, or in the bones which strew the valley. The energy which has drained from the Beltran family is reborn in the vivid, strenuous telling of their tale.

Hermione Lee, "Nightmares from the New World," in The Observer, July 11, 1982, p. 29*.

JOHN MELLORS

Lisa de Terán is a spellbinding storyteller, and most readers will be fascinated by the exotic and often horrifying tales of generals and peasants and virgins and whores [in *Keepers of the House*]. Wisely, the author lets most of the extravagances speak for themselves. A great-great-uncle caught leprosy (from cheese!) and sentenced himself to 20 years' solitary confinement in a room in his house, speaking only through a screen and becoming an oracle to the country people who sought his advice. Lisa de Terán has a way with words when she decides to assert herself: of a badly wounded soldier, 'even his fingers felt as though they would vomit.' *Keepers of the House* is as much memoirs as novel, but, fact or fiction, the book enthrals.

John Mellors, "Mirror Writing," in The Listener, *Vol. 108, No. 2772, August 5, 1982, p. 22.**

ROBERT TAUBMAN

[*Keepers of the House*] is the work of a young English writer drawing on her own experience of a remote valley in Venezuela, but recording it with an eye more on the bizarre or appalling than on ordinary life. Even the domestic details seem hardly ordinary—such as vulture's eggs for supper, or catching leprosy from the cheese. The family history of the Beltran family who rule the valley goes back 200 years, some of them highlighted by feud or massacre, or by locusts, drought and pestilence. Only rarely is it mentioned, in a couple of tributes, that the Beltrans have had among them creative minds, inventors and innovators who in the 19th century brought prosperity to the valley. This interests the novelist much less than the literary tradition that sees South America as a metaphor for hell. Not that she has an antecedent in Graham Greene: her stark portraits of the eccentric and afflicted would be more at home in Dante's *Inferno*. General Mario, a national hero who has also devised a new way of making sugar and built a hospital, is celebrated here for his 23 years of dying alone of leprosy. Arturo Lino, until he's put away, expresses his disgust at the tediousness of the valley in a series of murders. Cristobal, 110 years old on the last page—'his shock of wild hair became a blaze of gold, and around his head there was a strange halo'—is a one-legged tramp whose other leg was amputated by brothers jealous of his energy. Lisa St Aubin de Teran isn't writing fantasy—only, one suspects, exaggerating. Successful exaggeration gives some of these characters a superhuman grandeur, compounded of their energies and obsessions, but it's less than enough to make them humanly interesting.

Robert Taubman, "Playing," in London Review of Books, *August 5 to August 18, 1982, p. 19.**

MARION GLASTONBURY

The Slow Train to Milan is Lisa St Aubin de Teran's second autobiographical novel, and an invitation to travel first class with a very special first person: 'Strangers still come up to me sometimes in Paris or London or Caracas. And they say, "You were one of the four, weren't you?"' This inaugural hint of international renown and exclusive intimacy admits us to the charmed circle of mysterious adventurers with whom Lisaveta, half-waif, half-heiress, dreamy, cosmopolitan, and absurdly young, drifts around Europe. The year is 1970 and her three exiled Venezuelan companions are wanted by Interpol, though their shoplifting is more closely documented than their bank-robberies, and their political commitment is manifested only in peremptory scorn for democracy, communism, religion, clerks, waiters and the unemployed. . . .

Elias has genius, Otto is writing a book about Sartre, Cesar is a wealthy landowner of ancient lineage, and all are gifted with aesthetic and temperamental qualities that leave policemen gasping, hoteliers thunderstruck and old ladies infatuated. Their loves and hates are operatic. They wear their diseases like signet rings. Perpetually menaced by violence and privation, they are credited with the ravaged grandeur of the landscapes through which they pass: the corroded angels of Venice, the scorched facades of Bologna, the snow of the Alps spread about 'like crumpled damask.' Perhaps the nostalgic romance of the slow Italian train is merely a metaphor for the languorous passage of food and drink through these sacred monsters whose very hangovers are epoch-making and illustrative of aristocratic hauteur: 'His kidneys refused to eliminate the alcohol from his body and kept it in him for days and days.'

Meanwhile Lisaveta, universally adored and swathed, by turns, in silk, fur and blood-stained blankets, starves and suffers bitter-sweetly, tends a scrofulous kitten, misses Harrods. She also describes the ups and downs of her gangsters' odyssey in a style so fluent, merry and felicitous that even the most reluctant and charm-resistant reader is, finally, glad to have gone along for the ride.

Marion Glastonbury, "Charmed Circle," in New Statesman, *Vol. 105, No. 2712, March 11, 1983, p. 27.**

PHILIP HORNE

[*The Slow Train to Milan* is narrated by] Lisaveta, who starts the action as a schoolgirl, and tells of her marriage to the much older César and their travels in Europe with his friends Otto and Elias. . . .

Early on in her relation to [these] three South American friends we find Lisaveta 'examining their habits with the detachment of a sociologist,' and the growth of her affection for them never takes the mild chill off her sad observations—partly perhaps in tribute to the coming-on of something like the desolation conveyed by *Keepers of the House,* partly perhaps because the dialogue is mostly translated back into a language remote from the original Spanish or Italian. Events often repeat themselves into habits in Lisaveta's retrospect—'We went from town to town so many times that it is hard to remember the first time as an isolated event'—and many of her self-contained paragraphs note strategems for order in the unstable behaviour of a group whose period of exile, as one of them sharply says, '*is* a waste of time'.

Lisa St Aubin de Teran is a fine writer, and her subtle prose looks best when it looks, unblinking, at the oddity of the dealings of out-manoeuvred men so courageous and ridiculous. Thus, of Elias: 'He always dressed informally, except for his pale suede shoes which were, he said, de rigueur,' where, cunningly, a strictly personal formality looks the same as anyone else's informality. Or of César's obsession with exactly the right watchstrap: 'It often became a question of pride for a jeweller to produce the very one. . . . But each time, César would take it or leave it, and toss it into a box that he kept for the purpose. They were never right.' The indifferent phrase 'take it or leave it' jars back into perplexing life from its misfit with 'and toss it;' 'for the purpose' mocks the illogic of the sentence and the procedure, the cross-purposes of action and attitude. The language here is twisted into a fine strain. We get a similar witty surprise from a quite law-abiding sentence in Chapter One, where Lisaveta has been trying to say goodbye to the foreigner following her. 'When all my farewells failed, I gave up and shut the door in his face, only to find that he had his foot wedged in the frame.' 'And shut the door in his face,' like 'and toss it' above, gives the sentence a turn after the misleading 'gave up,' a wry curl in the deadpan expression. She gives up, not resistance, just polite resistance.

Such enjoyable finesses are not infrequent in *The Slow Train to Milan*. Elias is arrested in Italy for a minor offence, but is sought by Interpol for great ones: his friends can thus find themselves grateful for a terrible prompt brutality. 'The very police had punched his face to an unrecognisable pulp.' 'Unrecognisable,' usually a violent hyperbole, picks itself out here with delightful precision. Yet the charm and poise of a manner can become mannerism, and Lisa St Aubin de Teran's attentiveness sometimes slips into an embarrassing self-attention, an allusive display of sophisticated intentions. . . .

[The] glittering, precious prose advertises nothing so much as its own knowledgeableness; it recalls the book's unfortunate first sentence, which lets drop that 'strangers still come up to me sometimes, in Paris, or London, or Caracas.' The tedium of travel, most of us know, can be real enough: but the reiteration of its ordinariness and the casual mention of foreign facts . . . usually arouse a justifiable suspicion of designs to impress, and such doubts are never quite allayed in this novel. The length at which the itinerary is gone over, elaborately circumscribing a central emptiness (César's misery in exile), seems to indicate a wishful reliance on the power of an oblique method to convey a state of genuine pathos—the predicament of heirs cruelly dispossessed of their country. The book tries to live off the same interest as *Keepers of the House,* but at such a distance from the South America powerfully gone into there that all the felicities it grasps—its moodiness and cross-purposes, its passages between motion and stillness, the fear always sensed under the lethargy and the perilous trust which cements the group—feel like broken promises of a true unity of impression. (p. 14)

> *Philip Horne, "Maids," in* London Review of Books, *April 1 to April 20, 1983, pp. 14-15.**

BEN PLEASANTS

A favorite theme of European novelists is the decline of great families. Galsworthy, Proust, Balzac and Thomas Mann, to mention a few, have filled thousands of pages with splendid genealogies all headed toward the abyss. Lisa St Aubin de Teran, taking a shorter route and a page from South American writers, creates her Andean chronology [**"The Long Way Home"**] . . . in less than 200 pages.

The author, who managed her husband's sugar plantation in the Andes, confesses early on that this is her task. Her fictional servant Benito says, "Fate has brought you here to chronicle our decay. Our history is like the history of a whole country; you have come to save it from the sand."

Lines like that spray from the works of Sidney Sheldon when he is pausing between murders and seductions to philosophize on matters of importance. Sheldon, however, writes of the relentlessly upward-moving middle class; St Aubin de Teran is a genuine aristocrat, a member of that forever-fading class

that enjoys, most of all, decaying in public like Blanche Dubois on the Broadway stage.

What makes St Aubin de Teran an artist and Sheldon a writer of best sellers? Simply her desire to expand myths and textures, to explore events until they reveal specific rather than generic characters. One could argue that the blood feuds that take place in this book, the savage massacre of the Beltran family by a general whose new wife-to-be is less than honest about her lack of virginity, are really Homeric. . . .

The book has a romantic tinge and pictures the family as a good friend to the peasants, which seems complete nonsense and flaws the work. . . .

Still, there is a curious, haunting quality to this book; it is the smell of heliotrope carried across the slave quarters of a rotting plantation. There is an essence here as well as a stench.

> *Ben Pleasants, "Down the Andes: A Family Decline," in* Los Angeles Times Book Review, *April 10, 1983, p. 12.*

NORMA B. WILLIAMSON

The Long Way Home is a short book, but in its pages a dying land and its rich past are evoked in a multi-hued tapestry woven from the births and deaths, triumphs and disasters of the ancient Beltrán family. The Beltráns arrived in the Momboy Valley of the Andes Mountains with the Conquistadores, and their estates flourished in its rich soil. Diego, a political exile and heir to the family estate, returns with his wife, Linda, a young woman in love with the past, and the two attempt to return the estate to its former productivity. . . . *The Long Way Home* deals with people who live passionately and who are too busy dealing with the realities of maintaining life to have time to question its meaning. It is a refreshing departure from the preoccupation with alienation and change of so much recent fiction. A day arrives when Linda must leave the Momboy Valley, and as she views it for the last time she feels the child in her womb "turn and slide until the weight of its head rested in her groin, and it seemed symbolic that it should have been so crowned before leaving the land of its ancestors; and it seemed like a good sign of her child who was thus laden with history before it was born." It seems a good sign to me that there are still writers who recognize the connection of the living with the past.

> *Norma B. Williamson, in a review of "The Long Way Home," in* National Review, *Vol. XXXV, No. 16, August 19, 1983, p. 1033.*

MADISON BELL

"**The Slow Train to Milan**" is a rambling travelogue with little in the way of a destination. Lisaveta, a 16-year-old British schoolgirl, falls in with César, an aristocratic 35-year-old Venezuelan exile she meets in London. For no expressed reason she marries César and spends the next couple of years drifting around Italy with him and his two eccentric South American friends Otto and Elias, going nowhere and doing not much. . . . Their motives are most unclear, and Lisaveta's lack of curiosity about them at first astounds and finally irritates, for nothing is ever explained. . . . Matters seem to take a . . . serious turn when Elias is arrested and tortured, but this plot line trails off into oblivion after his release, as do all the others. At the end of the novel we are informed in a single paragraph that Lisaveta accompanies César to Venezuela and spends seven years raising avocados; why she should do so remains inexplicable. This blend of fiction and memoir has its charms, but its unrelieved ambiguities ultimately fail to intrigue.

Madison Bell, in a review of ''The Slow Train to Milan,'' in The New York Times Book Review, *April 22, 1984, p. 14.*

ANATOLE BROYARD

Imagine three men in their middle 30's, political exiles from Venezuela, attractive, bold and cultivated. Because it's not safe for them to stay too long in one place, they move restlessly through Europe, shunting back and forth on the local train between Paris and Milan. With them is a 17-year-old English girl who has impulsively married Cesar, one of these three men, who picked her up in a London street.

This is the plot, if you can call it that, of **"The Slow Train to Milan."** It's preposterous, but in the sense of being consciously so, an argument, so to speak, for preposterousness. Like the author's name, Lisa St Aubin de Terán, **"The Slow Train to Milan"** has a good deal of style. It's four characters are all originals, to the point where you feel that your tolerance for originality is being tested. When César proposes to Lisaveta, her first answer is ''Perhaps when I get to know you better.'' He replies ''You will never know me,'' and this is true. We don't get to know him either, but we see all around him, so that we identify him by elimination.

After so many books about people knowing one another all too well, there is a certain novelty in **"The Slow Train to Milan."** One is almost tempted to ask whether it is necessary, or desirable, to know people so intimately, to lose the opportunity for projection. The characters in Miss St Aubin de Terán's book remind us of a time when people preserved a certain distance, a certain formality. . . .

Like so many unusual characters in modern novels, Lisaveta and César love the movies. When they aren't in the movies, he sleeps and she frets. Otto and Elias come and go in answer to mysterious imperatives. Not every reader will see these activities as significant. Nor is it easy to see them as symbolic. Yet it can be argued that there is more purposeful behavior here than in some of Samuel Beckett's novels.

The three men dislike explanations, which they consider inelegant. It is as if they feel that they have left explanations behind them, in Venezuela. Yet they are honorable in their eccentric way, and proud. They are Latin, in some unmistakable sense. Miss St Aubin de Terán doesn't seem to like explanations either, and she may have written **"The Slow Train to Milan"** to show us how superficial they are. Like her characters, her book is protected by its elegance.

Anatole Broyard, in a review of ''The Slow Train to Milan,'' in The New York Times, *April 25, 1984, p. C19.*

THE NEW YORKER

[**"The Slow Train to Milan"** is an] aimless story narrated by a rich man's daughter who quits cramming for her Cambridge entrance exam and marries an exiled Venezuelan political radical—a guilt-stricken landowner—who introduces her to two other South American outlaws. . . . At one point, one of the outlaws warns the girl that she is like a piece of barley sugar,

which is unlike an aniseed ball: at least ''an aniseed ball has an aniseed inside it.'' The warning can be applied to her story as well.

A review of ''The Slow Train to Milan,'' in The New Yorker, *Vol. LX, No. 12, May 7, 1984, p. 159.*

JONATHAN LOAKE

All the jokes about Lisa St Aubin de Teran's exotic name have done little to inhibit her exotic approach to the novel. In spite of her last book, *The Slow Train to Milan,* she has more in common with the novelists of South America, her home for seven years, than with English or even European literary traditions. Reading *The Tiger,* however, I began to question her effectiveness at conveying the experience, rather than merely the oddity, of the life she observes. The imaginative impact of the Venezuelan climate and culture is undeniable (and probably irresistible if you have lived in the place in the way that she has). But do her books really come alive?

The Tiger revisits some of the extraordinary physical and spiritual landscapes which distinguished *Keepers Of The House.* It tells the story of Lucien, a man blessed with miraculous luck at roulette, who uses his winnings to create the legend of himself. (p. 16)

The Tiger is episodic and closer to legend than conventional fiction. It describes a violent world of wealth, drought, poverty, the unwinnable battle against insects, disease, and death, and the sheer weight and weariness of time. Her ability to portray so vividly the spiritual oppressiveness of this environment is Lisa St Aubin de Teran's great imaginative achievement.

But *The Tiger* has another kind of heaviness. Whereas *Keepers Of The House* had the curiosity value of transparent autobiography, *The Tiger* relies more on the writer's ability to arouse sympathy for characters other than herself. In this department, she shows her limitations. Her characters seem distant, the subjects of a tale handed down and exaggerated in the retelling. Although this is to be expected in legend, it is also true that good legends arouse our sympathy notwithstanding their unreality. The various significances which attach to Lucien (the man set apart, the man with a mission, perhaps man as artist) cannot bring him alive. Not only does he have few relationships with other characters; he has no relationship with the reader. His career is reported to us but not effectively realised, and if the protagonist is uninteresting, the other merits of the book become more difficult to appreciate.

The overall effect is rather like many people's experience of museums. At first, they show some interest in the exhibits. After trailing around, however, they long for the tearoom, where people talk to each other. If pressed, they'll admit that one dead marvel is much like another, whatever it says on the printed cards. (p. 17).

Jonathan Loake, ''Lifeless Legends,'' in Books and Bookmen, *No. 348, September, 1984, pp. 16-17.*

VALENTINE CUNNINGHAM

A landscape of weird fears and muttering hysterias, Lisa St Aubin de Teran's South America may for its part sport the occasional ironic turn but little in it makes for amusement. What concerns her in *The Tiger* are questions of inheritance. The land of Venezuela itself is young Lucien's prime burden, an antagonistic place and climate that infect, sicken and decay.

But into this rebarbativeness is also inserted the brutality of his strange grandmother's legendary German ancestors. Misia Schmutter, tight-corseted and tight-fisted, stern patroness of whips and scorpions, poisons and bumpings-off, a demonic tyrant with mythic energies and fabled witch-powers, a woman terribly embittered by Germany's First War defeat, battened on Lucien in her vast old age to be the recipient of her malevolent wisdoms.

The scars of what he then boyishly received haunt him like the TB spots on his lungs or as the relentless tiger of his racking asthma. . . . The family evils get confirmed in the anti-semitism of the ancestral German places Lucien visits in the Thirties and the tortures he's subjected to when he is imprisoned back home for cannibalism (a crime of which he may in fact be innocent).

There remains something oddly unstated and only part-focused at the heart of this novel's mysteries. But it still makes extraordinary headway against the perennial difficulty of providing would-be mythic characters like these with a presence awesome enough for the reputations which their author seeks to assign them. And the novel's dark fabulations jut and seep into the imagination as strongly almost as anything by the well-known band of South American fabulators, Carlos Fuentes, say, or Cabrera Infante, even (occasionally) Gabriel Garcia Marquez himself.

> Valentine Cunningham, "Landscapes of Looniness," in The Observer, *September 16, 1984, p. 20.**

FRANCIS KING

[*The Tiger*] is like some turbid dream of all the South American fiction that has come one's way in the last 20 years.

The setting, except when the hero, Lucien, travels to his German fatherland or, on his way back from there, passes through Brazil, Surinam and Guyana, is a Venezuela black with vice, suffering and oil; but it might be any area of South America transformed by a febrile imagination into a never-never-land of mystery, magic, cruelty and beauty.

Lucien's grandmother, Misia Schmutter, known as 'the Empress of Orinoco,' is a proud, cruel despot, bending everyone— her lazy, lascivious son, her terrified grandchildren, her awe-stricken servants—to her iron will. (pp. 28-9)

Yet, as Lisa St Aubin de Terán describes all the enormities committed by this monster, one's hackles somehow fail to rise. She has no ordinary weaknesses, vanities, moments of contrition or impulses of tenderness and therefore, being so wholly inhuman, evokes no response from our own humanity. This response only comes when, hideously swollen with a seemingly miraculous pregnancy that eventually turns out to be a fatal tumour, she stoically descends, step by step, into the waiting darkness.

Dead, Misia Schmutter continues to cling to her grandson, Lucien, like a tiger on his back, dominating his thoughts and actions as she did in her lifetime. . . . But precisely what the author wishes to convey by the presence of the dead tyrant as

a burden that Lucien must constantly carry about with him, is never wholly clear. Does this tiger on his back represent his Prussian ancestry, with its savage discipline, its stoical endurance and its love of beauty and order? Or does it represent the training that, whipped into him as a child, he is powerless to abjure? One has the feeling that the author herself is not certain.

Misia Schmutter has all her life been a votary of chance, represented by the roulette board at which she and Lucien gamble together. Lucien, in his years of unparalleled prosperity— squandering money in his gothic mansion on people whom he knows to be worthless—is the darling of chance. Then chance deserts him, and he finds himself as helpless as an athlete stricken with cramp or an actor stricken with amnesia. But here again, though there is a lot in the novel about chance, as there is about self-control, quite what the author is attempting to say is never clear.

For all her wickedness, the old grandmother has the power to affect miraculous cures; and . . . Lucien has the same power. But in each case the origin of this power—is it divine or is it diabolic, and are grandmother and grandson to be seen as representatives of the forces, by turns healing and destructive, of nature?—remains ambiguous.

There is no doubt of the depth and range of this author's talent. The book contains innumerable haunting descriptions of human folly, cruelty and degradation, and it evokes with extraordinary clarity its desolate landscapes of dust, sun and cactus. From time to time it presents some life-and-death confrontation that freezes the blood. But at the end of it all, the question puts itself with all the implacability of Misia Schmutter herself: So what? At the centre of all these turbulent, capricious events, there seems to be a blank.

My guess is that here is a case of an author fatally misjudging her natural and very real talent. It is as though someone with the kind of fresh, true voice ideal for folk-song had decided to emulate Flagstad singing Isolde in the vast opera-house at Manaos. The gulf between ambition and achievement is sadly apparent. (p. 29)

> Francis King, "Turbid Dream," in The Spectator, *Vol. 253, No. 8151, September 29, 1984, pp. 28-9.*

MARION GLASTONBURY

Noted elements of the author's previous work recur [in *The Tiger*]: travel, illness, extremes of affluence and squalor, all couched in stately prose that confers an aura of distinction, connoisseurship, savoir vivre, on a bunch of richly caparisoned nonentities. Neither heirlooms nor dynastic traditions nor premonitions of doom can raise Lucien to the mythic stature and epic significance sought by his creator. He exists by rumour and hearsay, the figment of a vacuous gossip column, the talk of a phantom town.

> Marion Glastonbury, "Bells of Hell," in New Statesman, *Vol. 108, No. 2794, October 5, 1984, p. 30.**

Melvin B(eaunorus) Tolson

1900?-1966

American poet, journalist, and dramatist.

Tolson is regarded as one of America's leading black poets. During his lifetime, however, his poetry received little attention outside academic circles. Tolson was accused of not writing for the "black folk," even though the major emphasis in his work was to illuminate the lives of those black Americans for whom, he believed, "color is a birthmark and poverty is a birthright." Critics also faulted his use of intricate metaphors as esoteric and difficult to comprehend. Nevertheless, Allen Tate recognized Tolson's importance as the first black American poet to assimilate "completely the full poetic language of his time, and, by implication, the language of the Anglo-American tradition."

Tolson's first collection, *Rendezvous with America* (1944), offers a wide variety of poetic forms, from sonnets to free verse. Although this volume received little attention, the poem "Dark Symphony" was praised by one critic for its "vigor of thought with intensity of emotion but without violence." In 1947, Tolson was appointed Poet Laureate of Liberia and was commissioned to write a poem commemorating the African nation's centennial. The result, the epic poem *Libretto for the Republic of Liberia,* was published in 1953 and helped place Tolson among the prominent figures in black American literature. Although the poem was praised highly for its style and effectiveness, which several critics have compared to Hart Crane's *The Bridge* and T. S. Eliot's *The Waste Land,* some questioned Tolson's use of traditional structure and contended that it should have been written in Negro dialect. Tolson answered those inquiries with his next volume, *Harlem Gallery: Book I, The Curator* (1965), in which he fused black idioms with the classical style of his earlier poems. Tolson originally planned *Harlem Gallery* as a five-volume epic poem chronicling the history of blacks in America from the early 1600s to the present. Only *The Curator* was completed before his death, and it earned him the critical appraisal which many critics believed his work had long deserved. Basically a humorous look at life in Harlem during the 1920s and 1930s, the poem also contains a serious consideration of the role of black artists in a predominantly white society, focusing on the problems they face in creating works for the enjoyment of both cultures. *A Gallery of Harlem Portraits* (1979) contains early versions of the poems included in *Harlem Gallery.* Although not as polished as the later poems, Robert Farnsworth describes these poetic portraits as "brashly vivid . . . [and] meant to give an epic cross-section of the city of Harlem."

In the late 1930s and early 1940s, Tolson authored a weekly column for *The Washington Tribune* called "Caviar and Cabbage." These articles, as Robert Farnsworth has written, "reveal Tolson's thought and feelings much more directly and immediately than does his more carefully wrought poetry." Ranging from national politics to popular culture, these pieces were collected and published in 1982 as *Caviar and Cabbage.* Tolson received the National Institute of Arts and Letters Award in 1966, affirming his success at capturing in his work the complex relationships between African, black American, and Western cultures.

(See also *Contemporary Authors,* Vols. 89-92 [obituary].)

THE CHRISTIAN CENTURY

[Melvin B. Tolson] speaks with one of the clearest, strongest voices now to be heard in verse. His long poem, "Dark Symphony," which is included in [*Rendezvous with America*], won the national poetry contest held in connection with the American Negro Exposition in Chicago. Like "Rendezvous with America," . . . it belongs in the category of what is being currently called "American scriptures." Here is vigor of thought with intensity of emotion but without violence; a tragic sense of life redeemed from despair and restrained from bitterness by breadth of sympathy and an unshaken faith in democracy. This is poetry which at once unveils some of the "problems" of our society and gives magnificent expression to the spirit of America as men of vision dare to hope that it really is. (pp. 1078-79)

A review of "Rendezvous with America," in The Christian Century, *Vol. LXI, No. 38, September 20, 1944, pp. 1078-79.*

NATHANIEL TILLMAN

It is fitting that . . . [the] publishers of Dunbar's poems forty years ago, should bring out *Rendezvous with America,* a volume of poems from the pen of Melvin B. Tolson, one of the most articulate Negro poets of the present generation. Dunbar was the poet-interpreter of a people still somewhat primitive but struggling to throw off the thwarting effects of years of slavery. Tolson is the full-throated voice of a folk that feels its power surging up and that has come to demand its place in a country it helps to make great and free. Much of the promise indicated in the best of the formal English poems of Dunbar reaches its fulfillment in the poetry of Professor Tolson. (p. 389)

Professor Tolson in his two sustained poetic efforts, "**Rendezvous with America**" and "**Dark Symphony**," catches the full and free rhythmic swing and the shifting tempo of the verses of Walt Whitman—or of the late Stephen Vincent Benét. Both poems exhibit genuine poetic feeling, facility of expression, and vividness. The title poem, which is especially strong in imagery, is so apt an interpretation of and challenge to America that it deserves a lasting place in the anthologies of American literature. (p. 390)

To me Professor Tolson seems to show a finer mastery of traditional poetic form than most of the recent Negro poets. He handles the quatrain, long or short line, with virtuosity. And he exhibits excellent technique in the twelve Shakespearean sonnets which comprise a section of the volume. . . .

Some readers will doubtless find a few of the poems difficult reading in spots, for, as a teacher of English, Tolson is fairly well saturated with literary allusions; and, occasionally, his vocabulary naturally has a tendency to be learned. But most of the poems in the present collection can be understood and enjoyed by a wide public; and they deserve a wide public. For here is poetry with pleasing melody and rhythm, maturity of expression and imagery, and personal depth and universal interest. *Rendezvous with America* establishes Tolson as a substantial American poet. (p. 391)

Nathaniel Tillman, "The Poet Speaks," in PHYLON: The Atlanta University Review of Race and Culture, *Vol. V, No. 4, Fourth Quarter, 1944, pp. 389-91.*

ALLEN TATE

[There] is a great gift for language, a profound historical sense, and a first-rate intelligence at work in [*Libretto for the Republic of Liberia*] from first to last. . . . (p. vii)

The poem is in eight sections mounting to a climax which is rhetorically effective but not I think quite successful as poetry. The last section begins in a six-line stanza which is controlled with considerable mastery, but the movement breaks down into Whitmanesque prose-paragraphs into which Mr. Tolson evidently felt that he could toss all the loose ends of history, objurgation, and prophecy which the set theme seemed to require of him as official poet. Nevertheless even this part of the poem is written with great energy. I point out what I consider its defects only because the power and versatility of other parts of the poem offset them, and enjoin the critic to pay the poem the compliment of very severe scrutiny.

What influence this work will have upon Negro poetry in the United States one awaits with curiosity. For the first time, it seems to me, a Negro poet has assimilated completely the full poetic language of his time and, by implication, the language of the Anglo-American poetic tradition. I do not wish to be understood as saying that Negro poets have hitherto been incapable of this assimilation; there has been perhaps rather a resistance to it on the part of those Negroes who supposed that their peculiar genius lay in "folk" idiom or in the romantic creation of a "new" language within the English language. In these directions interesting and even distinguished work has been done, notably by Langston Hughes and Gwendolyn Brooks. But there are two disadvantages in this approach: first, the "folk" and the "new" languages are not very different from those that White poets can write; secondly, the distinguishing Negro quality is not in the language but in the subject-matter, which is usually the plight of the Negro segregated in a White culture. The plight is real and often tragic; but I cannot think that, *from the literary point of view,* the tragic aggressiveness of the modern Negro poet offers wider poetic possibilities than the resigned pathos of Paul Laurence Dunbar, who was only a "White" *poète manqué*. Both attitudes have too often limited the Negro poet to a provincial mediocrity in which one's feelings about one's difficulties become more important than poetry itself.

It seems to me only common sense to assume that the main thing is the poetry, if one is a poet, whatever one's color may be. I think that Mr. Tolson has assumed this; and the assumption I gather has made him not less but more intensely *Negro* in his apprehension of the world than any of his contemporaries. . . . But by becoming more intensely Negro he seems to me to dismiss the entire problem, so far as poetry is concerned, by putting it in its properly subordinate place. In the end I found that I was reading *Libretto for the Republic of Liberia* not because Mr. Tolson is a Negro but because he is a poet, not because the poem has a "Negro subject" but because it is about the world of all men. And this subject is not merely asserted; it is embodied in a rich and complex language, and realized in terms of the poetic imagination. (pp. viii-ix)

Allen Tate, "Preface to 'Libretto for the Republic of Liberia'," in Libretto for the Republic of Liberia *by Melvin B. Tolson, Twayne Publishers, Inc., 1953, pp. vii-ix.*

JOHN CIARDI

Certainly the most ambitious and in some ways the most compelling of the new books is M. B. Tolson's "**Libretto for the Republic of Liberia.**" . . .

With a prodigious electicism, and with a percussion as has not been heard since Hart Crane's "The Bridge," Tolson constructs a vision of Africa past, present, and future, . . . and—as Tolson sees it—the last new continent and future of the world, "Futurafrique." There are times when Tolson's heaping on of image after image and of phrases from German, Spanish, French, and from African languages as well, leaves the reader knocked out: too much is happening too fast, and the result seems to be not exaltation but dizziness. When Tolson succeeds, however, one feels a force of language and of rhythm as breathtaking as anything in the range of American poetry.

This is obviously a book to return to. The blast of language and vision is simply too overwhelming for first judgments. It seems a reasonable guess, however, that Tolson has established a new dimension for American Negro poetry.

John Ciardi, in a review of "Libretto for the Republic of Liberia," in The Nation, *Vol. 178, No. 9, February 27, 1954, p. 183.*

KARL SHAPIRO

A great poet has been living in our midst for decades and is almost totally unknown, even by the literati, even by poets. Can this be possible in the age of criticism and of publication unlimited? It is not only possible but highly probable. Poetry today is an established institution which has many of the characteristics of a closed corporation. . . . Poetry as we know it remains the most lily-white of the arts. A novelist and pamphleteer like Baldwin is world famous; Tolson, easily the literary equal of any number of Baldwins, is less honored in his own country than the most obscure poetaster.

Yet not all poets and critics are at fault. Tolson has been recognized by eminent men of letters for a long time and at the extremes of the literary spectrum. Allen Tate paid homage to him in an introduction to *Libretto for the Republic of Liberia* [see excerpt above], an essay which is more famous than the poem. . . . Theodore Roethke, Selden Rodman, John Ciardi, Robert Frost, and Stanley Hyman have tried to bring Tolson to the general literary consciousness, but with little success. (pp. 11-12)

In a time when black skin is the literary rage, poetry by Gentlemen of Color continues to be ignored. And it is ignored far out of proportion to the common indifference to the art.

It is one thing to accept an artist on the grounds of his art (regardless of race and creed) as long as the artist can adjust to the ruling "Graeco-Judaic-Christian" culture. It is another to accept an artist who contravenes that culture. Tolson belongs to the second category; he is in effect the enemy of the dominant culture of our time and place. He is, to use the term he prefers, an Afroamerican poet, not an American Negro poet accommodating himself to the Tradition. It is probably for this reason that the *Libretto,* despite its *succès d'estime,* failed to tickle the sensibilities of the literati and professoriat. The *Libretto* pulls the rug out from under the poetry of the Academy; on the stylistic level, outpounding Pound, it shocks the learned into a recognition of their own ignorance. [*Harlem Gallery: Book I, The Curator*] pulls the house down around their ears.

Tolson writes in Negro. (p. 12)

It is not enough to equate Tolson, as his best critics have done, with Eliot or Hart Crane, the *Cantos* or *Anabase.* To make him equal is to miss the point, just as it would be to make him *better than.* Tolson writes and thinks in Negro, which is to say, a possible American language. He is therefore performing the primary poetic rite for our literature. Instead of purifying the tongue, which is the business of the Academy, he is complicating it, giving it the gift of tongues. Pound, Eliot, and Joyce did this, but with a pernicious nostalgia that all but killed the patient. Tolson does it naturally and to the manner born. . . .

The history of the American Negro places him linguistically at the center of the American culture, as it does no other nationality or "race." Negro survival has depended upon the mastery of the gradations of English; the Negro has in his possession a *Gradus Ad Parnassum* of our culture which no other minority or majority can conceivably encompass. This is the significance of Allen Tate's salute to Tolson's *Libretto.* (p. 13)

The *Harlem Gallery* will not make matters easier. Massive as it is, it is only a beginning of a greater work. . . . The *Gallery* returns to basic themes of the *Libretto.* One of these is the accusation of Gertrude Stein that the Negro "suffers from Nothingness." Written in a style conforming to the ode form

of the earlier poem, it is in fact a narrative work so fantastically stylized that the mind balks at comparisons. The milieu is Harlem, from the Twenties on. The dramatis personae comprise every symbolic character, from the black bourgeois babbitt and the Lenox Avenue poet to the alienated Negro Professor and sage who sits in the bar and elaborates, along with The Curator and others, a Platonic dialogue. (p. 14)

But like so many great works of poetry it is a comic poem. It is funny, witty, humoristic, slapstick, crude, cruel, bitter, and hilarious. The baroque surface of the poem modifies none of this. The *Harlem Gallery* is as if improvised by one of the great architects of modern poetry. It may be that this work, like other works of its quality in the past, will turn out to be not only an end in itself but the door to poetry that everyone has been looking for. (pp. 14-15)

> *Karl Shapiro, in an introduction to* Harlem Gallery: Book I, "The Curator" *by M. B. Tolson, Twayne Publishers, Inc., 1965, pp. 11-15.*

GWENDOLYN BROOKS

Melvin Tolson offers [*Harlem Gallery: Book I, The Curator*] as preface to a comprehensive Harlem epic. Its roots are in the Twenties, but they extend to the present, and very strong here are the spirit and symbols of the African heritage the poet acknowledges and reverences. He is as skillful a language fancier as the ablest "Academician." But his language startles more, agitates more—because it is informed by the meanings of an inheritance both hellish and glorious.

You will find in this book a much embroidered concern with Art; many little scheduled and cleverly twisted echoes from known poetry . . . , a reliance on clue-things, the things-familiar; Harlemites of various "levels" and categories; humor and wit that effectively highlight the seriousness of his communiques. (p. 51)

Although this excellent poet's "news" certainly addresses today, it is very rich and intricate news indeed, and I believe it will receive the careful, painstaking attention it needs and deserves when contemporary howl and preoccupation are diminished. (p. 52)

> *Gwendolyn Brooks, in a review of "Harlem Gallery: Book I, The Curator," in* Negro Digest, *Vol. XIV, No. 11, September, 1965, pp. 51-2.*

LAURENCE LIEBERMAN

[*The essay from which this excerpt is taken was originally published in* Hudson Review, *Autumn 1965.*]

Karl Shapiro, in his introduction to *Harlem Gallery* [see excerpt above], makes the highest possible claim for Tolson: "A great poet has been living in our midst for decades and is almost totally unknown, even by the literati, even by poets." He says further that Tolson's art has been ignored mainly because he is an enemy to the "'Graeco-Judaic-Christian' culture" of our ruling establishment: "He is, to use the term he prefers, an Afroamerican poet, not an American Negro poet accommodating himself to the tradition. . . . *Tolson writes in Negro.*"

It may well be that my problem in reading this book is that I am not Negro. Well, I have just spent a year teaching at the college in St. Thomas. The student body here is about 90 per cent Negro. . . . I have tried to get the students . . . to become interested in reading Tolson's book. They do not understand him. He simply does not speak their language. How then can it be said that Tolson writes *in Negro*?

Perhaps this is an unfair criterion; it may be that poetry in our time is for The Few, and this handful of readers is an intellectual elite that prevails over racial or religious or national barriers. For my own part, as a reader, I feel that *Harlem Gallery* does have some of the hallmarks of an important work of art, and I share the sort of literary wishful-thinking that makes me want to support Mr. Shapiro's enthusiastic response.

The book has astonishing linguistic range, a vital new imagery, and much technical excitement. It is a strange hybrid of many dialects. But there seem to be only traces of *Negro* slang and dialect. The characters are literary oddities: they sparkle like ornaments in the vast mosaic of the poem. The book is weighed down with literary allusions; it is top-heavy with the tradition and special learning. While it is true that often Tolson successfully ridicules the cultural establishment from which he derives so much of his imagery, more often he is too steeped in that tradition to work against it. There are many passages that are cluttered with references to poets, painters, composers—and their works. . . . Some lines are so thick with allusions that they become opaque; a reader cannot find his way into their meanings, their sayings. The tradition that the poem supports *is* basically that of the "Graeco-Judaic-Christian culture," and not a distinctly Negro heritage. I think Tolson defines his own difficulty in breaking away from the dominant culture of America in a few lines of the poem:

> I was a half-white egghead with maggots on the brain.
> I ate my crow,
> for the unconscious of the artist
> cannot say to itself *No*.

The literary milieu which gave him birth now refuses to set him free. (pp. 252-53)

Harlem Gallery is intended as a prelude (*Book I: The Curator*) to a much larger work. There are some sections that suggest in their clarity and razor-sharp irony that Tolson has it in him to become, and may well be on the way to becoming, a satirist of the first order. If he can find his position and his voice more distinctly outside the cultural fortress he is failing to undermine from within, I will be among the first to cheer as the walls come tumbling down. (p. 254)

> Laurence Lieberman, "M. B. Tolson and A. R. Ammons: Book-Length Poems," *in his* Unassigned Frequencies: American Poetry in Review, 1964-77, *University of Illinois Press, 1977, pp. 252-56.*

JOY FLASCH

During his sixty-six years, Melvin Beaunorus Tolson, an outstanding black poet, produced only three books of poetry which were published; but he is recognized today as a unique and challenging poet by those acquainted with his work. An artist who espoused a difficult poetic style at a time when such a style was not the "fashion," particularly for a black poet, he was willing to sacrifice popularity during his lifetime and trust the "vertical audience" of the future to recognize the true value of his work. (p. 7)

There are those, of course, who cannot comfortably read Tolson's vivid descriptions of the accomplishments of the black man, despite centuries of atrocities and humiliations inflicted

upon him by the "Great White World." In like manner, his work is not popular either with those black Americans who recognize themselves in his picture of the hypocritical "Black Bourgeoisie" because of their materialistic, white middle-class values or with those proponents of the "Black Esthetic" who resent his addressing his poetry to all who will read and appreciate it rather than his restricting his audience to black readers.

Tolson had courage. Unable to abide fence straddlers, neither could he side with extremists whose views he found simplistic. As a black poet, he wrote with pride about his people—their past, present, and future—but his standards and integrity as an artist required freedom so that his poetic style could flower in the manner which would permit fullest development. The resulting intellectual, allusive, philosophical style addresses itself to all who recognize the wit, the humor, the satire, the memorable characters, the metaphors, and the sheer poetry of his work. Ever mindful of his heritage and of his responsibility as a black poet, he nevertheless made clear the necessity of the artist to develop without limitations of any kind on his artistic imagination. (pp. 7-8)

Though a divided opinion exists about Tolson's work among both black and white critics because of its undeniable difficulty, its limited quantity, and its candid criticism of various large segments of American society, it is a contribution which cannot be ignored. (p. 144)

What exactly then is the contribution Tolson has made to contemporary literature? First, *Rendezvous* contains several excellent poems which are being recognized more each year by editors of anthologies. Although few of Tolson's poems have been set to music. *Rendezvous* contains many lyrical lines which would lend themselves to a musical background, such as certain sections of **"Dark Symphony,"** as well as **"Ballad of the Rattlesnake"** with its up-to-date theme of racial frustration, hatred, violence, revenge, and the consequences. In *Libretto,* Tolson has taught the history of the courageous little African republic in symbolic, allusive language; but he also shows the motives of those who originated the idea of founding Liberia, the first "victims" who established the colony, the greedy nations who fed on its narrowing boundaries—all in the impressive intellectual style which was his trademark from this time on.

In *Harlem Gallery,* he succeeded in creating, through representative types, dramatic scenes, and philosophical discussions, a community of black Americans who offer an education to all who meet them in the one hundred and seventy-three pages of their existence. In this book, his style is somewhat relaxed in comparison with *Libretto*—though it is also intellectually stimulating and challenging. In much of *Harlem Gallery* he employs the dramatic scene, which he enjoyed writing and wrote effectively. A former dramatist, Tolson, like Frost, had "a great love of people and of talk." Tolson ranges easily from the level of intellectual word play on down. The allusions and special learning are still there, but the sometimes strained quality of *Libretto* is gone. In this work, Tolson truly found his voice as he juxtaposed the literary and literal worlds in which he lived. (p. 147)

Perhaps the chief handicap in Tolson's style lies not in any inability on his part but in the fact that, by the time he had developed it, the poets who had introduced the stress on intellectualism, symbolism, and allusion had abandoned in large part these techniques. . . .

Certainly Tolson was aware of the change which Eliot, Yeats, and the other poets whom he read closely had made, but he could not abandon the style in which he had discovered he could best express himself. If this style was outmoded, it would not exclude him from his place among twentieth-century poets, he believed; for the true artist writes for the future. (p. 148)

Had Tolson completed the five-volume epic poem of *Harlem Gallery* relating the story of the black man in America, and had he sustained the caliber of Volume I, *The Curator,* he would have accomplished one of the most extraordinary feats of any poet in the twentieth century. (p. 149)

His sensitivity as a black poet dictated the subjects and themes of his work; his artistic imagination and intellect determined his technique. He had done what he had to do. There are those who find fault with his work; but there are many who agree with Spector, Shapiro, and others who say that, regardless of his reputation in the "present critical climate," he stands "firmly as a great American poet." The final evaluation of his contribution as a poet will be determined in years to come by that "vertical audience" for which he wrote—by both black and white scholars who have scarcely penetrated the surface of the complex poetry waiting to be mined; but there are hundreds of people whose lives he touched as professor, lecturer, and friend who are ready to testify now as to the impact he made on them. (pp. 149-50)

> *Joy Flasch, in her* Melvin B. Tolson, *Twayne Publishers, Inc., 1972, 175 p.*

ROY P. BASLER

[*The essay from which this excerpt is taken was originally published in a slightly different form in* New Letters, *March 1973.*]

Tolson is perhaps the poet of our era who best represents, or comes nearest to representing, in his comprehensive humanity, the broadest expanse of the American character, phrased in the richest poetic idiom of our time. Better than his contemporary peers, at their latitudinal and longitudinal extremes, he knew the span from low-brow to high-brow in both life and literature, and he loved the American English language, from gutter to ivory tower, more intimately than any of them. His poetic diction is a natural blend of home words and hall words where *hearth* and *bema* sing side by side. He is the natural poet who cultivated his nature, both root and branch, for the flower and the seed, for it was the seed even more than the flower, Ruskin to the contrary, that Tolson the poet believed art grew for.... (pp. 149-50)

What Tolson undertook, I think with great success, was to liberate the allusive, scholarly poetry Eliot created from the service of Eliot's sterile tradition and philosophy. While embellishing it with large humor, he put it to use as a vehicle for his own "prospective" view of human history. (p. 154)

It has been said by recent black writers that the black writer today must write primarily for black readers. It has also been said that the black writer must also write for white readers, or have few readers. Tolson recognized in his blood and bones as well as in his head that such statements are partial truths, and he set about writing for any reader who would take as much trouble to enjoy the reading, as he took to enjoy the writing, of poetry. Karl Shapiro has said that Tolson "writes Negro" [see excerpt above]. True perhaps to some extent, but what does it mean when Tolson sounds to me more like Tolson (as Whitman sounds like Whitman) than he sounds like a Ne-

gro, and more like a man than a member of any race? It happens he was Negro-Irish-Cherokee, with as much or little as any of us to be proud of in the matter of ancestry. And intellectually he was more of the basic Jeffersonian tradition than most white Americans have ever been since Jefferson himself. For he believed in equality of "the man inside." . . . (pp. 154-55)

Tolson's unfinished masterpiece was planned to be a major epical work, of which only the prologue, "**Book I: The Curator**" was published in 1965 as *The Harlem Gallery.* . . . Although one can only speculate about the overall plan, which called for four books—Egypt Land, The Red Sea. The Wilderness, and The Promised Land—to follow "**Book I: The Curator,**" the latter stands alone as a unique work for which traditional poetic terminology has no entirely adequate word. It is not an ode, as was the *Libretto,* though in some respects like it, but rather a kind of lyric-dramatic narrative sermon in verse. In any event, it is as carefully, and often as intricately, structured as a Tantric mandala, but swinging with Harlem rhythm and sublimely mingling the idiom of bedroom, street slang, scholarly diction, Shakespearean metaphor and foreign tongues with a controlled abandon that only a poet who had observed all levels of life and touched all aspects of language could command. (p. 157)

It is not *The Waste Land* or *The Four Quartets,* I think, which limn the present or light the future with the past so well that scholars salvaging libraries of this era may someday guess what manner of men were we. Nor is it even Sandburg's *The People, Yes,* nor William Carlos William's *Paterson,* but rather Tolson's *The Harlem Gallery,* where the heart of blackness with the heart of whiteness lies revealed. Man, *what* do you think you are is not the white man's question but the black man's rhetorical answer to the white man's question. No poet in the English language, I think, has brought larger scope of mind to greater depth of heart than Melvin Tolson in his unfinished song to the soul of humanity. (pp. 158-59)

Poetry provided for M. B. Tolson what research, teaching, writing and publication failed to provide for his black counterparts in the world of science, education, and learning—an opportunity to employ his intellect and project his identity as a man in a realm where skin color was nonsignificant. . . .

One might find himself forced to be a Negro historian, but not a Negro poet. One could be a man, and proudly a Negro, and especially a poet, without specializing in being primarily the Negro on the one hand, nor apologizing for being one on the other. This M. B. Tolson felt, believed, declared, and demonstrated. To my mind, this is a supreme accomplishment of an individual human spirit in America in our day, to which moonwalking as the supreme collective accomplishment of our engineering know-how shines like a candle in broad daylight. (p. 160)

Tolson has written of American life as it is, and will be. He has taken our white-black culture and imagined it into a new thing more representative of the modern human condition than any of his contemporary peers among poets has managed to create, and it is not "negritude," although he has plenty of that, but "humanitude" that enabled him to accomplish the feat. (p. 161)

> *Roy P. Basler, "The Heart of Blackness: M. B. Tolson's Poetry," in his* The Muse and the Librarian, *Greenwood Press, 1974, pp. 148-61.*

ROBERT M. FARNSWORTH

Harlem was a seed that grew and flourished in Tolson's literary imagination. (p. 259)

A Gallery of Harlem Portraits [written during the early 1930's] reveals Tolson's early fascination with Harlem's "El Dorado of racial dissimilarities." He does not generalize ambitiously about the significance of this cultural diversity as he will later in *Harlem Gallery, Book I.* At this point, he makes no great claims explicitly, but there is implicit pride in his fascination. He dramatizes the lives of Harlem people very directly and immediately so that the reader experiences the joys and pains, the frustrations and intensity, the impoverishment and the ingenuity, in short the style of Harlem life.

Tolson frequently used the public world of the Harlem Renaissance in drawing his portraits, but he usually deliberately altered names and specific biographical information so that his portraits became generalized or "type" figures rather than incisive comments on particular personalities. (p. 261)

The typescript of *A Gallery of Harlem Portraits* suggests that the opening poem, "Harlem," may well have been written later than the other portraits in an attempt to give the entire book focus and some coherence. It only partially succeeds, but the effort indicates the direction in which Tolson's imagination is later to develop *Harlem Gallery, Book I.* In "Harlem," Vergil Ragsdale, consumptive poet working as a dishwasher, has written an epic poem, "An African Tragedy." Acknowledging his own rapidly approaching death, he sketches roughly the historical transformation of Harlem that he will not live to observe. This editorial gnomic observation follows:

> The Curator has hung the likenesses of all
> In *A Gallery of Harlem Portraits*

The character of The Curator is not developed in this poem or anywhere else in this manuscript. There *is* a later poem-portrait of Vergil Ragsdale. Ragsdale's role in this manuscript suggests the roles to be played in the later *Harlem Gallery* by Mister Starks, the suicide musician poet, author of *Harlem Vignettes,* and Hideho Heights who gives the bravura public tributes to John Henry and Louis ("Satchmo") Armstrong, but whose more ambitious and private poem, *E. & O. E.* so moves and disturbs The Curator—the latter reference is an oblique advertisement for Tolson's own critically neglected poem by the same name.

In *A Gallery,* probably under the influence of *Spoon River Anthology,* the concept of a series of poetic portraits is kept relatively simple and the formal implications of the relation between poetry and painting are left relatively unexamined. In *Harlem Gallery,* Hideho Heights challengingly declares that in the beginning was the word, but The Curator, an ex-professor of art, along with the trenchant African, Doctor Nkomo, persist in trying to reconcile the claims of painter, poet, and musician, as artists who clarify and give meaning to the profusion and confusion of human experience in any historical time. (p. 262)

The blues is such an implicit part of Tolson's experience and writing that at the time of making the . . . statement [that such poets as Edgar Lee Masters, Robert Browning, and Walt Whitman influenced the writing of his poems in *A Gallery of Harlem Portraits*] it apparently did not warrant [Tolson's] conscious recognition. However, in his master's thesis he identifies the particular poetic achievement of Langston Hughes, who in "The Weary Blues" "catches the undercurrent of philosophy that pulses through the soul of the Blues singer and brings the

Blues rhythms into American versification." . . . This use of the blues indicates to Tolson that Hughes "understands the tragedy of the dark masses whose laughter is a dark laughter." The profound racial message of the blues carries for Tolson, as it did for Hughes, significant proletarian overtones. The dark laughter of the blues permeates *A Gallery of Harlem Portraits* as well. (pp. 263-64)

The blues . . . [in *Harlem Gallery*] are incorporated into a more symphonic idiom and structure. The stories of John Laugart and Mister Starks are blues stories, but they are not given in the more readily recognizable blues idiom so frequently used in *A Gallery of Harlem Portraits.*

The blues root Tolson's poetry in the experience of black America, and they provide a literary means of expressing some of his most deeply felt social contradictions. He is fascinated with cultural fusion, and he sees in the Harlem experience a cultural pluralism and sophistication of extraordinary promise. But the dark laughter is always there, a sometimes bitter but strangely tonic laughter that keeps the painful but fortifying awareness of the history of the black American ever present even in the most optimistic and imaginative speculations on his future.

A few of the poems in *A Gallery* may also surprise Tolson readers with their blatant political propaganda. (pp. 265-66)

Some of the poems in *A Gallery* suggest that Tolson was not so certain in the thirties as he was in the sixties of the relation between art and politics. A poem as propagandistically banal as "Hilmar Enick" can hardly be defended on any grounds, but scattered through the latter portion of the manuscript there are a few tired poems, and not all of them are concerned with political sermonizing. "Harold Lincoln," for example, is also deadly flat. Fortunately, these poems are few and far between. (pp. 266-67)

One cannot help but be struck by the variety of topical references in *A Gallery of Harlem Portraits.* The thirties were a period of intellectual stretching and testing for Tolson, but he was also acutely interested in the changes that were occurring in the American social fabric. . . . *A Gallery* reflects the commitment of a passionately engaged, if often whimsically ironic imagination. (p. 267)

Melvin Tolson frequently asserted an "I-ness" that could not be encompassed by his "Negro-ness," but he never needed to think of himself as white, and he was proud of the ability of his people to survive and achieve. He knew that it took wit, courage, and sophistication, and he believed that the world was wide open for him to learn from, or if it was not wide open he was going to do his damnedest to make it so for him and those to follow. (p. 271)

Tolson's literary career suggests that this admonition constantly sounded in his own mind. He traveled on and up an extraordinary distance. Did he wander from the true path by listening to the Siren strains of Eliot and the New Critics, or did he break through to an advanced level of achievement and artistic sophistication with which the literary world has not yet caught up? It is too soon to answer that question with final authority and confidence. Those who have appreciated and understood how far he traveled have been too few, but they have often been persons of discernment and literary authority. We need to walk the roads Tolson actually did travel with greater attention to his signposts and his destination. (p. 272)

Robert M. Farnsworth, in an afterword to A Gallery of Harlem Portraits *by Melvin B. Tolson, edited by*

Robert M. Farnsworth, University of Missouri Press, 1979, pp. 255-72.

ROBERT BONE

[*A Gallery of Harlem Portraits*] is not simply an early version of *Harlem Gallery*. Early and late in his career Tolson sought to capture, as if on canvas, the panorama of Harlem life in the aftermath of World War I. But the two attempts, thirty years apart, were radically different in aesthetic mode and poetic idiom. . . . (p. 65)

Like the Masters poem, *A Gallery of Harlem Portraits* depends primarily for its effects on a strategy of ironic reversal: Illusions momentarily prevail, only to be punctured. Stylistically, both poems display a flair for epigram and a predilection for simile over metaphor. The free verse line employed in common tends to be prosaic, even cacophonous, being dominated by narrative rather than musical considerations.

But Tolson never stops at mere imitation. A poet of cultural fusion, he strives characteristically for a blend of Euro-American and Afro-American forms. In the present instance he draws on the folk form of the blues ballad to impart an ethnic flavor to his art. The ballad is a poem that tells a story and as such is well suited to a series of narrative sketches. The blues ballad . . . tells a story from the unique comitragic perspective of the blues. (p. 66)

For the blues dimension of his art Tolson was indebted to the poetry of Langston Hughes. . . . The structural property of the blues that fascinated Tolson was its basic pattern of repetition and variation, culminating in a terminal surprise. This "snapper" is a distinguishing mark of Tolson's Harlem sketches.

A second source of inspiration from contemporary black writing was George Schuyler's satirical novel, *Black No More* (1931). This haymaker, aimed at the maw of American racism, is responsible for much of Tolson's tone. Both works strive to cure the national disease by a combination of ridicule and laughter. Both castigate white patrons and philanthropists no less than outright rednecks. Both provide a bottoms-up perspective on interracial sexuality. And both reserve their sharpest barbs for the black bourgeoisie, who are portrayed as so intent on social climbing that they have lost touch with their ethnicity. . . .

The more proximate sources of the poem are to be found in Afro-American history. They have to do with the mass migration of World War I that brought nearly half a million southern Negroes to Harlem in quest of a better life. . . .

The human cost of this migration was appalling: Hopes were dashed, values rendered obsolete, institutions shattered, family ties disrupted, and individuals destroyed as the black community struggled to reconstitute itself in an urban setting. Disenchantment with the Promised Land is the crux of Tolson's poem. . . .

[The] theme of disenchantment leads in the direction of a cosmic irony. For irony springs from the perception of discrepancy, incongruity, non sequitur: "Life kin take a Lindy Hop, Black Boy, an' mess you up." Throughout *A Gallery of Harlem Portraits* a pervasive irony underscores the disparity between ideal and actuality, dream and disposition, intention and result. Above all the poem comments on the gap between the promise and performance of American democracy, where the lives of its black citizens are concerned. Tolson's satire thus remains

as pointed in 1979 as when it was conceived nearly half a century ago.

Despite its satirical bite, however, the poem will endure as a celebration of Harlem life. For Tolson it represented a homecoming, an embracing of his blackness, an expression of love for his people. Though he was born and bred in middle America, Harlem became his spiritual home. (p. 67)

Robert Bone, "A Poet with a Fame Deferred," in Change, Vol. 11, No. 7, October, 1979, pp. 65-7.

MARIANN RUSSELL

Tolson was much impressed by the paradox of Harlem. . . . It was for Tolson, as *Harlem Gallery* exemplifies, in such gathering places as the Chitterling Shop and the Zulu Club, in such characters as Hideho Heights and Dr. Nkomo, in such rites as Heights's recital of his poem and the Zulu Club dialectics, a center of black life and achievement. At the same time, the life that flourishes arises from the strictures of the ghetto, as Harlem and the racial situation limit the expression of its life. Poverty, exploitation, and racism limit the possibilities and shape the psyches of the ghetto residents. From this duality, Tolson fashioned his poem, which is not about the balancing of tragic and comic elements in the ghetto, but about the fashioning of individual and communal identity within the limitations of "this place" and "this time." The synthesis that Tolson anticipated was that of the blues, where disparate elements and modes are held in tension.

In stressing again and again the diversity, the variety of Harlem life, Tolson referred to it as a *comédie larmoyante*. "Harlem is a multiple jack-in-the-box. No Negro novelist has yet pictured Harlem in its diversity—not James Baldwin, not Ralph Ellison, not Richard Wright. It will take a black Balzac to do Harlem's *comédie larmoyante*." This view of Harlem as a *comédie larmoyante* is obliquely related to the concept of ghetto laughter. In discussing the humor in *Harlem Gallery* . . . , Tolson equated "dark laughter," *lachen mit yastchekes*, and "*ghetto laughter*." He referred to Stanley Hyman's explanation of *galgenhumor*, "gallows humor." In *The Tangled Bush*, Hyman pointed out that self-destructive humor is "characteristic of all oppressed peoples. Negro humor is so similar that the Negro poet Melvin Tolson characterizes it with the Yiddish phrase *lachen mit yastchekes*, 'laughing with needles stuck in you.'" Such humor, a type of gallows humor, is, according to Hyman, "life-affirming, and greatness of soul consists in cracking a joke with the needles in you, or the noose around your neck, or life almost impossible to endure." Tolson thus related the tragicomic sense of his poetry and of black life to the affirmativeness of gallows humor. (pp. 104-05)

From Tolson's Notebooks, one can see that dark laughter was stressed as a response to the strictures of the status quo. The ambivalent laughter of the ghetto not only embodies a personal response to pain but is linked to a communal defiance of the limitations that restrict the black man. Thus, "the ghetto's dark guffaws / that defy Manhattan's Bible Belt!" . . . and the "dark dark laughter" of Harlem's "immemorial winter" are associated with the coming of the "new New / Order of things." . . . This new order, an affirmative response springing from the confinement of ghetto living, either literally in Harlem or figuratively in black America, is captured in the penultimate stanza of the ode:

> In the black ghetto
> the white heather
> and the white almond grow.
> but the hyacinth
> and asphodel blow
> in the white metropolis!

The tragicomic becomes a communal and an individual response that presages the race's ultimate role in the "Great White World."

This pattern—established in the content of the ode of the tragicomic, or ambivalence, of the white "flowers of hope" finally springing from the black ghetto—is repeated to some extent in the form of the ode. Of course, the convention of the greater ode itself dictates a progressive movement among its parts as one section, with its imagery and mood, is juxtaposed with other sections with different, often opposing, imagery and mood, and the movement of the whole proceeds to a final unity. The imagery and tone associated with the concreteness of ghetto life (as in the Zulu Club) are juxtaposed with the imagery and tone of The Curator's discursive musings on art and man. The public self with its images plays against the private self and its images. The whole is united by the psychological process of The Curator's making his statement, defining his self, envisioning his ode. However, Tolson's language is the most prominent feature of his artistic performance, and that elaborately constructed language working against and through the concreteness of ghetto life is an embodiment of the "phoenix riddle" that Tolson sees in Harlem. (pp. 105-06)

Elements of the Tolson style are reminiscent of a modern poetic tradition. Tolson, like the modernists, tried to squeeze all verbiage from his poetry. He juxtaposed the colloquial and the literary. He used irony and wit. His diction included the use of puns. All in all, the complexity and allusiveness, together with the concreteness and precision of modern verse, can be seen in the Tolson style. Tolson's use of internal rhyme, half-rhyme, infrequent rhyme, and, rarely, no rhyme at all, and his use of such linking devices as alliteration, assonance, consonance, and repetition, and his lines with sometimes a trace of regular meter but most often rhythm derived from a freer sense of verse, all hark back to the usage of some modern poets.

Tolson, however, melded these elements from modern tradition into his own ideal of the "S-Trinity of Parnassus"—the linking of sound, sight, and sense in poetry. Since Tolson composed his lines to be read aloud. . . , the importance of such devices as internal rhyme, alliteration, and assonance, as well as occasional rhyme, becomes evident. The tone of the orator, the voice of the actor, are sometimes heard in the rhythms of his verse. The centered placement of words on the page is a device that appeals to sight as, generally, the words are so placed as to visually heighten significant phrases or words. *Sense* refers to meaning and to the image's appeal to the senses so that memory and sensual evocation are integrated into the total performance of the ode. Tolson, having worked through the masters of modern poetry, used the devices he found therein as the basis of his peculiar style. . . . (pp. 106-07)

Tolson's distinctive voice can be heard, for instance, in his use of allusions. For one thing, the allusions in his poems are not exclusively or chiefly literary. . . . Further, his allusions do not form a pattern of reference to an older tradition conceived as more valid than the present, or to a world larger or smaller than our own, but are intended to extend and complicate the language itself; are, in fact, an element of wordplay. (p. 107)

Another element of Tolson's performance is his use of similes and metaphors. . . . Although some of his similes depend on startling, generally unremarked similarity between objects, Tolson characteristically yoked startlingly disparate objects at their one point of contact—generally in the word itself—so that the simile generally and the metaphors less frequently act as extended puns in an almost metaphysical sense. (pp. 108-09)

The energy of Tolson's performance is visible in the verbal feat of *Harlem Gallery.* Tolson tried to compact his language, to make, as his son observed, every line a great one. Naturally, he failed, sometimes slipping into obscurity or congestion, but the effort is there in every line, and many a sinuous line detaches itself from the context and remains fixed in the memory.

Tolson, through The Curator, declared "Metaphors and symbols in Spirituals and Blues / have been the Negro's manna in the Great White World." . . . He also said in his Notebooks: "I have hidden my identity as a Negro poet in Words. Thus I am more militantly a Negro." Tolson evidently felt that his use of words, metaphors, and symbols was expressive of his Negro identity. Therefore, the complicated verbal feat of *Harlem Gallery* can be related in form as well as in content to the Afro-American experience. That Tolson's language can be said to capture the speech of the ordinary ghetto inhabitant is indeed questionable, but it may be said that Tolson's idiosyncratic voice reveals both a "possible American language" and the lyric impulse of the blues. More importantly, the whole poem arising from the Harlem inspiration is itself an analogy or metaphor for that stubborn life that Tolson saw surviving and ultimately triumphing in the Harlems of this world.

Arthur Davis's comment—"If the poem . . . is to be taken as a serious attempt to depict Harlem (and, by extension, the Negro world), then it is a failure—a brilliant failure, perhaps, but still a failure"—provokes a central question. After an examination of Tolson's performance in *Harlem Gallery,* and some consideration of its Harlem roots, what comment can be made about the relationship between the two? On the one hand, the Harlem roots, the acutely observed and felt participation in black life in America and in Harlem, undoubtedly contributed to the strengths of *HG.* Tolson's style and manner are not offset but enhanced by involvement in the concrete, tough, unexotic life of the ghetto. On the other hand, Tolson both succeeded and failed in his attempt to capture the many-sided variety of the Harlem community. He himself noted that neither Ellison nor Wright nor Baldwin has captured Harlem life; and neither has he. Perhaps Harlem life is, finally, unrecapturable. Its kaleidoscopic life, shifting with the decades like the life of the Afro-American, like the substance of America, may be ultimately beyond summing and can only be evoked by an authentic voice here or a keen observer there. But as an *evocation* of Harlem and its life, Tolson surely succeeds, for each one who has inhabited or visited Harlem has his own Harlem to recall. Tolson's Harlem may not be that of the Harlemite who said, "I love this place; this is my turf" (for all Tolson's love and exploration, Harlem was not Tolson's "turf"), but, as one who had an extraordinary capacity to participate in and observe the life of the black man in Harlem and elsewhere, Tolson managed to render an extraordinary vision of the significance of Harlem yesterday and today. And if the single vision is not the complete vision, it is one rendered in a performance as extraordinary, daring, and bold in its mode as any enacted on those Harlem streets. (pp. 110-11)

Mariann Russell, in her Melvin B. Tolson's "Harlem Gallery:" A Literary Analysis, *University of Missouri Press, 1980, 143 p.*

CHOICE

Caviar and Cabbage reveals another side of the complex black poet Melvin B. Tolson.... Here one meets Tolson not as abstruse poet, but as sharp-shooting and sardonic journalist whose weekly columns in a black newspaper, the *Washington Tribune,* were radical in political persuasion and sermonic in rhetorical style. Here one also encounters the Tolson whose debating students at black Wiley College in Marshall, TX, occasionally defeated the Oxford University team. Witty, urbane, very tough in sheer argumentation, Tolson's columns are valuable for their own sake. But they also record with eloquence a very turbulent period in American history.

> *A review of "Caviar and Cabbage: Selected Columns by Melvin B. Tolson from the 'Washington Tribune', 1937-1944," in* Choice, *Vol. 20, No. 2, October, 1982, p. 271.*

Michel Tournier

1924-

French novelist, short story writer, essayist, and editor.

Tournier writes intellectually challenging, provocative fiction that blends myth and symbolism in realistic settings. Many of his novels and short stories are retellings of myths or legends adapted to contemporary circumstances, and they frequently contain elements of sexual deviance and grotesquerie. They often involve children as major or minor characters; critics have noted that the loss of innocence is a central theme in Tournier's work. His writing, which is densely detailed and philosophically speculative, has been faulted by some reviewers for being verbose and pretentious. Although the importance of his work has been debated in both his own country and abroad, Tournier has gained considerable stature in France as the recipient of two prestigious literary prizes: the Grand Prix du Roman from the Académie Française for *Vendredi; ou, les limbes du Pacifique* (1967; *Friday*), and the Prix Goncourt for *Le roi des aulnes* (1970; *The Ogre*). In recent years several more of his works have been translated into English.

Tournier gained immediate renown in France with his first novel, *Friday*. In this work, a retelling of Daniel Defoe's *Robinson Crusoe*, Tournier uses modern philosophical and anthropological theories to reinterpret the myth, arriving at conclusions about human nature in isolation that differ markedly from Defoe's assumptions. Similarly, in *The Ogre* Tournier combines legend and reality to create an ironic story which strongly emphasizes allusion and symbolism. Partly based on Johann Wolfgang von Goethe's poem "Erlkönig," the novel revolves around a man who procures young boys for Hitler's military academies. *Les météores* (1975; *Gemini*), about a set of twins and their homosexual uncle, examines duality, narcissism, and sexual deviance.

Two other noted works, *Gaspard, Melchior et Balthazar* (1980; *The Four Wise Men*) and *Gilles et Jeanne* (1983), continue Tournier's practice of reworking fables and tales in unexpected ways. *The Four Wise Men* is an adaptation of the Biblical story of the Magi. Tournier uses religious symbolism and philosophy to explore the motives and desires of the kings, and he adds a twist by focusing on a fourth king, who arrives too late to see the Christ child. Although some reviewers considered the novel overly stylized, most praised Tournier's detailed, lyrical prose and his imaginative depiction of this Christian legend. *Gilles et Jeanne* is based on the historically documented acquaintance of Joan of Arc and Gilles de Rais, a nobleman who was also executed for heresy. Focusing more on Gilles, the novel portrays his devotion to Joan and his strange behavior after her death.

Like his novels, Tournier's short stories center on disturbing obsessions and abnormalities that are rendered more powerful by the realistic context in which they are developed. Danièle McDowell called the stories in *Le coq de bruyère* (1978; *The Fetishist*) "lucid and realistic in the midst of fantasy," and of the same collection Victor Brombert observed: "Horror is never distant, especially when the world evoked seems at first reassuringly familiar. But the devouring ogre is lurking; daydreams swiftly turn into nightmares. The grotesque reintro-

© *Jerry Bauer*

duces into the commonplace the troubling and revelatory dimension of myth."

(See also *CLC*, Vols. 6, 23; *Contemporary Authors*, Vols. 49-52; *Contemporary Authors New Revision Series*, Vol. 3; and *Something about the Author*, Vol. 23.)

GEOFFREY STRICKLAND

[Michel Tournier] has claimed that when a story comes right, it is then just right for children; when it lacks perfection it is only good enough for adults. The use of ready-made tales like *Robinson Crusoe* in *Vendredi* (1967) or Goethe's *Erlkönig* in *Le Roi des aulnes* (1970) and of the most conventional narrative devices—omens, especially, and dramatic suspense and coincidence—characterise all his adult fiction. He uses them, it is true, with a conscious gusto and hence with what could always be taken as an air of self-parody which recall not so much the novels of the nineteenth century as those of Gide, a writer he resembles in many ways. [In *Gaspard, Melchior et Balthazar*, his] use of the story of the Nativity as told by St. Matthew and of a Russian Orthodox legend concerning a fourth pilgrim king is certainly no new departure. . . .

Gaspard is a black African travelling to escape from the humiliation and grief he has suffered from a white concubine, his slave, who has shown disgust at the blackness of his body and been caught in the arms of her white so-called brother. Haunted by the sense of his own negritude and the poignant love of the slave he is unable to kill, he accepts the advice of an astrologer and follows the star of Bethlehem northward to Judaea. Here he meets Balthazar of Nippur, the Hellenised aesthete whose museum of artistic treasures gathered over a lifetime has been destroyed by an iconoclastic mob, whipped up by his own High Priest. It is Balthazar who brings to the baby king in the stable the gift of myrrh, since his deepest love is for the fragile timelessness of art. Melchior, Prince of Palmyre, has only a gold coin. He is a refugee from a palace *coup* travelling incognito, though at the court of Herod it is revealed that his movements, like those of his new companions, are known to the Judaean secret police, which serves an authoritarian state atrocious in its dealings with possible contenders for power but beneficial to commerce and the ordinary citizen. Herod himself is a tragic monster living in opulence but discharging a minutely described cancerous vomit and excrement. (p. 239)

The fourth king whose story is told is Taor of Mangalore, a lover of Turkish delight, who travels to Judaea in search of a special recipe. Here he learns of the prophecy of the birth of Jesus but arrives too late at the stable and then spends thirty-three years at work in the salt mines of Sodom. On his release, he journeys to Jerusalem hoping to meet Jesus and finds his way to the house where the last supper has just been eaten. He is in time only to consume the last of the bread and wine. The novel ends with his being raised on angels' wings to Heaven.

In the *Times Literary Supplement* [see *CLC*, Vol. 23] . . . , John Sturrock sees the Tournier of this novel as 'a forthright moralist' who has 'given us his reasons for esteeming the Christian scheme on social, aesthetic and political grounds'. The four kings, after all, find their deepest needs resolved, clarified and transformed in the stable of Bethlehem while Taor of Mangalore, who has entered his salt mine voluntarily to replace another prisoner, learns both the 'existence of evil and the supreme value of self-sacrifice'. Mr Sturrock's review is admirably and rightly enthusiastic but I find it difficult to agree that the novel's virtues are of this straightforwardly ethical variety. I mentioned Gide earlier on as a novelist whom Tournier resembles at least in his tendency to self-parody. . . . Like Gide, Tournier is never closer to facetiousness than when he is at his most sentential. As in Gide too, the freedom from actual solemnity or the need or desire to insist goes with a release of imaginative energy. . . . (pp. 239-40)

Tournier's novels, in fact, like Gide's, raise acutely—and this is one of the many fascinating things about them—the question of whether the novel can ever be, in intention at least, morally sustaining or edifying without sacrificing its essential freedom. The 'irresponsible plastic way' of seeing 'figures and situations' which, for James, was the condition of 'a free aesthetic life' and which he found lacking in George Eliot is Tournier's way, as it was Gide's *par excellence* and if he is a far more confident, resourceful and prolific novelist than Gide it is conceivably because he enjoys an actual freedom that was denied to Gide himself. There is no deeper joy, he writes in *Le Roi des Aulnes,* than when a man has discovered his true perversion. Sexual deviation features prominently in all Tournier's fiction, though not in the latest novel itself. One has only to think of Robinson Crusoe's coupling with his own island (in spite of a temporary setback when he is stung by a spider), the paederastic or, more precisely, paedephoric passion of Tiffauges in *Le Roi*

des Aulnes, the explicit homosexuality of Alexandre in *Les Météores.* Tournier writes for a permissive age. The evident inhibitions of Gide the novelist in this respect and his earnestness as an essayist are those of an earlier age, though Tournier himself in *Le Roi des Aulnes,* finds it necessary to dissociate himself from what might seem like imaginative sympathy with the Nazis by whom his French hero is employed and his portrait of Goering, for this reason, has a caricatural grotesqueness which, in this context, seems merely dutiful and perfunctory. (pp. 240-41)

The miraculous ending of the story of the fourth king in [*Gaspard, Melchior et Balthazar*] is, however, perfunctory in another way. It is nothing other than blasphemous, all the more so in that it is done with a lack of scruple, either artistic or religious. Myth, Tournier has said on a number of occasions, is by its nature subversive: especially, one might add, with the latest novel in mind, myth candidly recognised or presented as such. There is a much deeper subversion, none the less, which Tournier's pursuit of the question: what do men really want? induces; and which makes the very plausibility and inventiveness with which he answers it an effective *mise en cause* of the novel itself. . . . The question: what do men want? what is their actual destiny? resolves itself always for Tournier into the question: what is their obsession? (p. 241)

Geoffrey Strickland, "The Latest Tournier," in The Cambridge Quarterly, *Vol. X, No. 3, 1981-82, pp. 238-41.*

D. KEITH MANO

Fable is often a rather precious genre. Ingenuousness, repetition, fantastic plot are humored as they would not be in any other form. Preciouser yet, when fable dilates on material with which we have had a long and sensitive relationship: the Nativity in [the case of *The Four Wise Men*]. . . . Even flat, unadorned references can hit you like a sucking chest wound. The fabulist, moreover, will expect his reader to collaborate. "Legends live on in our substance. They derive their truth from the complicity of our hearts." Dissatisfaction, therefore, might be attributed to emotional incompetence in a critic. Beyond that, Tournier's writing is sensuous as *Salammbô* and authoritative as concordances. . . . By page 15 I was prepared to follow Tournier through a Babylonian captivity.

Yet, after that promise-cramful start, *Four Wise Men* seems caught in formal gridlock. The narrative is, simply, not well-structured. Fables have to build amperage, build expectations: they are, after all, a teaching device and should be pointed. Like the joke or the fairy tale, their force deploys best in upward progression: most often a sequence of three. You know, his oldest son went out, then his middle son . . . Each will be found less inadequate, more spontaneous-mature until the youngest-last. Tournier has cut material around that pattern pretty well, adding a fourth (and last and youngest) wise man, Prince Taor.

This Taor chronicle fills more than one-third of the text. Tournier meant it to be his most profound and repercussive segment. In fact, though, Taor is predictable and not nearly as engaging as Balthasar and Gaspar. The book, shaped so, seems to flame out. (There is, midway, a discursive 25-page monologue by Herod. It will disabuse number three, Melchior, of his obsession with political power. Unfortunately, it also pushes the narrative architecture yet further from plumb.) And around young Taor, Tournier has written his most preachy and sentimental fiction. . . . Childlikeness and childishness are very different. Occasionally Tournier can abut on the latter. . . .

Still, though *The Four Wise Men* might not be a Narnia Chronicle, I don't mistrust Tournier's devotion. Christian reverence has suffused his fable: it is absolute, fierce, and of great clarity. Through unembellished retelling the redemption miracle barrels at us, a holy *tour de force*. And that, too, in quite another sense, is precious. (p. 1291)

> *D. Keith Mano, "Precious and Preciouser," in* National Review, *Vol. XXXIV, No. 20, October 15, 1982, pp. 1290-91.*

JONATHAN BAUMBACH

In his first novel, **"Friday,"** the highly regarded French novelist Michel Tournier reversed the relationship between Robinson Crusoe and Friday, with Friday, who is less limited than Crusoe, emerging as the ascendant figure. The novel, which transcended the cleverness of its idea, reimagined Defoe's fable into a resonant fable of its own. In **"The Four Wise Men,"** Mr. Tournier again shows himself to be a philosophic novelist who likes to work with received material—the story of the Magi in this case—and play ironic variations on his subject, a writer for whom paradox and irony become a source of vision.

Each of the title figures in **"The Four Wise Men"** presents himself directly to the reader. Gaspar, King of Meroë, opens the novel by announcing: "I am black, but I am a king. One day, perhaps, I shall have this paraphrase of the Shulamite's song—I am black but beautiful—engraved on the tympanum of my palace. For what greater beauty can there be than a king's crown? To my mind that was so solidly established a certainty that I did not so much as think of it. Until the day when blondness burst into my life." The stylized rhetoric of the voice does not invite us to empathize. Mr. Tournier's language, a mix of modern idiom and literary diction . . . enforces distance. These Wise Men are emblematic figures rather than particularized characters.

The blondness that bursts into Gaspar's life is, in one of its manifestations, the blonde slave girl, Biltine, with whom he becomes infatuated and by whom he is deceived and deeply disillusioned. Coincidence becomes omen. One blond symbol leads to another; the comet that prefigures the birth of the Christ Child appears to Gaspar like a head with flowing blond hair. But the diminishing of self-love that comes with rejection opens Gaspar to the possibility of divine love. In each of the separate stories that comprise this novel, we are made aware of the uncanny connection of seemingly contradictory experiences.

The wisest of the Wise Men, Balthasar, King of Nippur, is an esthete, a collector of exquisite objects. . . . Mistaking image for reality, Balthasar marries a woman he has never met on the basis of her portrait and then finds her less compelling than her picture. After becoming disillusioned with marriage, Balthasar travels around the world collecting art treasures, which he houses in a museum called the Balthasareum. The musuem becomes an extension of his pride, the justification, as he says, "of my whole life." When the musuem is destroyed by rioters, Balthasar's life is also destroyed. The king turns old with magical suddenness. . . . Catastrophe becomes the occasion of wisdom and renewal. Balthasar moves from beauty to Beauty, the Child representing to him (as it does to each of the others) the most perfect example of his heart's desire.

All of the Wise Men's stories have the same configuration: Profound loss leads to greater gain. It is through inventive detail that Mr. Tournier must distinguish the stories—and the characters—from one another. Melchior, Prince of Palmyra, is a king without a kingdom, his throne (like Hamlet's) usurped by his uncle after his father's death. A wanderer and exile, the young prince has to beg from door to door for his livelihood. He is often rebuffed because of the proud look on his face—a manifestation of his sense of himself as wronged king. Privation eventually engenders a certain humility. Melchior comes to realize "that king, bandit and beggar have this in common: living ouside the usual workaday world, they acquire nothing by toil or exchange." After he sees the Child, Melchior is content to renounce his earthly kingdom.

Although retold with considerable wit, there are few surprises in the stories of Gaspar, Balthasar and Melchior. The tour de force of Mr. Tournier's novel is the invention of a fourth Wise Man, Taor, Prince of Mangalore—also known as the Price of Sweets. A pampered dilettante with a sweet tooth, Taor embarks on a long, quixotic journey, ostensibly to locate the recipe of a delicacy called pistachio *rahat loukoum*. It is an absurd—really absurdist—Grail quest, and his mission predictably comes to grief. He arrives too late to see the Child, whom he conceives as the Divine Confectioner, and finds himself ultimately in the hellish landscape of Sodom on the edge of the Dead Sea. Through an act of sacrifice, the most apparently trivial of the kings emerges as the most substantial and humane. Taor's career embodies aspects of the careers of the other three kings (and that of Christ as well). His story, which is the most affecting of the four, serves to unite the disparate fables of the novel.

Almost every episode in Mr. Tournier's novel reduces itself to stunning paradox. As Balthasar tells us and the novel illustrates over and over again, "the answer consisted in the impossible opposites." **"The Four Wise Men"** is a work of extraordinary clarity, but it is a clarity born, I suspect, of preconception and formulation. . . . [Its] limitations—its reductive simplicity—become . . . obvious. The great novels engender discovery as they go along, surprise themselves as they surprise the reader. **"The Four Wise Men"** knows everything it knows before it starts out on its journey. (pp. 14, 34)

> *Jonathan Baumbach, "But Taor Had a Sweet Tooth," in* The New York Times Book Review, *October 24, 1982, pp. 14, 34.*

PETER LaSALLE

[*The Four Wise Men*] is a novel of high achievement. Tournier works to assert an apologia of Christianity and its underlying message of love, and he does so with finely paced arguing, well-balanced counterarguing and, most importantly, genuine intellectual energy. But again the reader isn't overwhelmed by the philosophy (with a good measure of theology in this case) because the literary content is solid, and it all makes for a very engrossing story. The writing is suspenseful and humorous, one of the more entertaining sections being the ass's rather cockeyed first-person (first-animal?) recounting. The prose throughout is lush and satisfying in itself, often building on lists and precise sensual evocations, as in this sentence describing the temple of a tree-worshipping tribe encountered by Taor in his wanderings: "The thick thatch roof, the absence of windows, and the tangle of climbing plants—jasmine, ipomea, passion flower—all conspired to keep the interior in a deliciously cool half-darkness." . . .

This may be more than a novel of high achievement, in fact; it may be the best work so far of a truly daring writer. (p. 298)

Peter LaSalle, in a review of "The Four Wise Men," in America, *Vol. 147, No. 15, November 13, 1982, pp. 297-98.*

LEWIS JONES

This first part of [*The Four Wise Men*] is essentially an argument about the possibility of Christian art. It is lively, poetic and funny, but it is too abstract to attain the incarnate, legendary quality it extols. And the power which sustains it is apparently withdrawn by the testimony of the Ass. To borrow his own metaphor, Michel Tournier weaves for himself a cocoon, comprising theology and cunning French critical theory, and appears to die within it. But in the second half of the book the industrious grub breaks out of its chrysalis and takes brilliant flight. The bare bones of the novel are brought miraculously to life. . . .

Though it may sound, in summary, to be merely an existentialist hagiography, *The Four Wise Men* struck me as a true masterpiece.

Lewis Jones, "Hatching Out," in New Statesman, *Vol. 104, No. 2696, November 19, 1982, p. 27.*

ROGER SHATTUCK

Both by modifying the events and by alternating a third-person omniscient narrative with Crusoe's log, Tournier's first novel, *Friday* [published in England as *Friday; or, The Other Island*], shifts Defoe's story from a tale of stolid survival to a drama of high intensity. Crusoe falls into a state of wallowing, hallucinating bestiality (*la souille*) before pulling himself together and civilizing his solitude into a caricature of the social order complete with charter, penal code, calendar, water clock, palace, and public inscriptions from Franklin's *Almanac*. Friday, when he arrives years later, fits uneasily into this thoroughgoing culture and literally blows it up by inadvertently igniting Robinson's cache of gunpowder.

That mammoth explosion triggers an even more devastating earthquake. Afterward, emerging from the rubble, Friday gradually initiates Crusoe into a new existence more responsive to the spiritual poetry of air and sun than to cultivating an earthly garden. Friday stretches a goat's hide into a huge kite and mounts its skull as a wind harp high in a dead cypress. Then the two residents of the island wait for a suitably stormy and moonlit night in order to participate in a ritual. For twenty pages after Crusoe has first sensed "a hidden unity" in Friday's behavior, Tournier has been preparing this scene:

> The wind blew with increased strength as they drew near the singing tree. Tied on a short string to its topmost branch was the kite, throbbing like a drumskin, now suspended in trembling immobility, now swerving around wildly. Andoar-the-flier hovered over Andoar-the-singer, seeming both to watch over him and to threaten him. . . . And over all sounded that powerful, melodious song, music that was truly of the elements, inhuman music that was at once the deep voice of earth, the harmony of

the spheres, and the hoarse lament of the dead goat. Huddled together in the shelter of an overhanging boulder, Robinson and Friday lost all sense of themselves in the splendor of this mystery wherein the naked elements combined—earth, tree, and wind joined in celebrating the nocturnal apotheosis of Andoar.

The passage assembles a number of Tournier's most characteristic themes: the physical and symbolic power of the elements . . . , the different forms of throating or shouting by which human beings attempt to answer the elements, and the precious union or communion achieved under rare conditions of effort and circumstance, and lasting only for a short space. Twenty-eight years after Crusoe's wreck a ship stops for water and finds an Englishman gone native living with an English-speaking native. Crusoe has become so attached to his "solar metamorphosis" in which he has overcome both solitude and insanity that he decides to stay. Friday, fascinated by the ship, joins the crew and leaves in his place a cabin boy whom Crusoe names Thursday. Tournier thus transposes Defoe's story into a vehicle for both symbolic action and philosophic reflection. The double point of view permits striking meditations not only on God, religion, and morality as in Defoe, but also on perception, identity, and the temptations of oblivion.

Tournier's fourth and most recent novel turns to a story both closer to us and more remote from us than Selkirk's shipwreck off Chile. *The Four Wise Men* accepts the three names and three gifts recorded as far back as the sixth century in a Nativity account attributed to the Venerable Bede. For some reason Tournier makes Gaspar black instead of Balthazar. Considering the freedom of his version I wonder why Tournier adopted the traditional royal status of the Magi, whereas that ancient Chaldean word designates priestly augurers, occult knowledge, and suspicious status akin to charlatanry. Nonroyal Magi of dubious origins would have suited one of Tournier's strongest concerns: good as the twin of evil. Instead, Tournier's novel concentrates the power and fascination of evil in the world-weary, desperately ill, cruel figure of Herod. These two hundred pages of subtly stylized prose sprinkled with humor and concrete detail create a strong awareness of coincidence as the other face of destiny. At the hub of history, timing is all. . . .

[When the] kings reach the stable in Bethlehem, Tournier, instead of raising the tone of his prose to majesty or hushing it to piety, has the ass tell the story in a vernacular account that finds its level between the reverence of a stain-glass window and the rudeness of a comic strip. (pp. 10-11)

Friday and *The Four Wise Men* are Tournier's most accessible and successful novels. He makes those old bottles hold new wine. Both novels include episodes that explore the limits of plausibility and fantasy. (p. 12)

Having expressed my admiration for Tournier's first and fourth novels, I must not neglect his two other substantial works of fiction. In *The Ogre* [published in Great Britain as *The Erlking*] World War II carries Abel Tiffauges from a Paris garage to three different sites in Germany where, as a somewhat privileged prisoner of war, he approaches closer and closer to the awful heart of Nazism. From the start he knows he is an ogre, "issued from the mists of time," a benevolent, virtually sexless monster dreaming of an earlier androgynous condition in which man, woman, and above all child inhabit one body.

The intricately plotted narrative gradually reveals Tiffauges as a modern stock bearing two legendary grafts: Saint Christopher, who gave his life to save the infant Jesus by carrying him across a river; and the fearsome death figure of the Erl-King immortalized in Goethe's poem. Feeling sympathy toward many aspects of German history and life, Tiffauges discovers the full horror of the Nazi system only when he has become half implicated in it. He extricates himself by saving a Jewish boy prisoner and carrying him to safety at the cost of his own life.

The net of religious, political, philosophical, and historical meanings that traverses every page of *The Ogre* has its counterpart system in *Gemini,* the story of an ultimate couple, a pair of identical twins. When Jean leaves their nest-prison in modern Brittany, Paul can only follow his other half in a desperate Platonic quest that turns into a latter-day version of *Around the World in Eighty Days* and ends at the Berlin Wall. With a little detachment *Gemini* begins to sound like a systematically dialectic work generated by the concepts of identity and otherness, of individuality and twinship. But the central story line is almost usurped by the portrait of Uncle Alexander. This flaming homosexual and King of Garbage Men comes so close to taking over the novel that Tournier has to kill him off halfway through. *The Ogre* and *Gemini* are highly ambitious novels of ideas in contemporary settings. . . .

[Tournier describes his style] as "hyperrealist"—"objectivity pushed to the point of hallucination." Too often, however, especially in *The Ogre* and *Gemini,* Tournier fails to impose the formal and stylistic discipline he prescribes for himself. The narrative energies overflow the channels of the action, and the style sometimes follows suit. He indulges in too many "untimely interventions by the author," a practice he himself condemns as interfering with the reader's responsibility to assemble the pieces of the story. Tournier is an incorrigible pedagogue, and, having decided not to innovate or experiment with the traditional form of the novel and to maintain the advantages of clear language, falls occasionally into excessive didacticism.

But Tournier remains immensely readable despite his lapses. The question we can no longer avoid is just what ends are served by this powerful literary phenomenon of attractive exterior. What is this new *paideia?* The most direct and abrupt way of addressing the question may be to grab hold of the extreme accusations aimed at Tournier by his French detractors, usually veiled when in print, yet often blurted out uncompromisingly in conversation. He is a pervert, he is a fascist. Or presumably his books, if not the living author, deserve those qualifiers.

Perversion. Tiffauges in *The Ogre* obeys a tender, nonsexual attraction to young children of both sexes that is mistaken by characters in the novel itself for child molesting. Several other dubious inclinations accompany Tiffauges's pedophilia—inchoate coprophilia, vampirism, and fetishism. They combine into the gentle, polymorphous perversities of a modern ogre. *Gemini* will strain most readers' sensibility even more. After an initiation combining sex acts with Christian ritual and fencing exercises, Uncle Alexander carries his homosexuality with an arrogant flourish of moral superiority. But homosexuality is a flimsy makeshift compared to the dyadic cell of twinship, the ultimate incestuous-homosexual unit. Jean and Paul practice "oval love" (sic) from a very early age, and their existence for each other as the perfect doubles permitting unnaturally close physical and spiritual relations both defines and destroys their identities as separate individuals. In *The Four Wise Men* the residents of Sodom defend their erotic practices as an effective means of diverting sex away from propagation into

stimulation of the entire organism. Yet only Crusoe appears to have achieved a happy love life; for him, "sex difference has been surpassed."

Fascism. "Returned to the state of nature, the goats no longer lived in the anarchy to which domestication reduces them. They formed into hierarchial flocks commanded by the strongest and wisest rams." These lines from *Friday* may be Tournier's most succinct refusal to espouse the ideal of a classless (or homogenized) society. In *The Ogre* Tiffauges accommodates to the Nazi system of which he is a prisoner more than he rebels against it, and participates in some ghoulish, SS-sponsored race experiments that fascinate him as strongly as they repel him. (pp. 13-14)

All these elements are present in Tournier's writings. They do not represent the dominant features of his moral and political thought, nor do they constitute adequate evidence to associate his work with perversion or fascism. Such scurrilous charges (perversion from the right, fascism from the left) conspire further to prevent us from reading Tournier without prejudice. Even if we can do so, it is not easy to survey and describe the new dispensation toward which his works seem to converge. For in most ways Tournier takes the world as it comes and preaches few reforms. . . .

The most compact and eloquent expression of Tournier's philosophy can probably be found in the last chapter of *Le Vent du Paraclet,* where he deplores the disappearance of *Sophia,* the ideal wisdom, a slowly acquired, personal compound of knowledge and experience. Rousseau's "conscience" and Kant's "good will" killed the ancient wisdom by shattering it into science, formal morality, and mere information. And in the same chapter Tournier rejects the collective security of both Catholicism and Marxism and defends the stern rewards of solitude and self-reliance: Crusoe elected to remain on his island.

I dissent from much of Tournier's thinking about the world and our conduct within it. But his chosen themes have led him to write impressive novels. Tournier returns us to the universe of Melville, Conrad, and Tolstoy where, despite a straining toward myth and patches of overwriting, something humanly significant is continually at stake.

Tournier's books may claim one's attention for another reason. Without placards or fanfares, keeping their comedy and their anomaly behind a decorous exterior, his four novels acquiesce in the widely announced disappearance of the avant-garde. Insofar as they adapt existing legends and celebrate earlier forms of wisdom, his works leave behind the preoccupation with originality that has propelled the arts for the last two centuries. Tournier's turning toward history and traditional questions of philosophical dispute does not of itself grant him classic stature of effectiveness as a novelist. But by sparing himself the need to innovate in form, he has been able to direct his inventive powers simultaneously toward elaborating a story line and toward marshaling a powerful style that is by turns descriptive, narrative, and expository. (p. 14)

Tournier is a writer of superb gifts and major achievements from whom we shall be hearing more. When asked who was the greatest French poet, André Gide found himself obliged to answer, "Victor Hugo, *hélas.*" If asked today who is the most exciting novelist now writing in French, I would answer with alacrity, or perhaps, "paradoxically," "Michel Tournier, *heureusement.*" (p. 15)

Roger Shattuck, "Why Not the Best?," in The New York Review of Books, Vol. XXX, No. 7, April 28, 1983, pp. 8, 10-15.*

L. S. Roudiez, in a review of "Gilles & Jeanne: Récit," in World Literature Today, Vol. 58, No. 2, Spring, 1984, pp. 240-41.

ANGELA McROBBIE

Michel Tournier's *The Fetishist and other stories* is, apparently, a best seller in France. Its point of reference is the literary ponographic tradition so perfectly epitomised in the writing of Bataille. But, for me, this collection figures not so highly in this convention of perverse writing. At their most interesting, the stories re-work well known myths and fables: Adam and Eve; Robinson Crusoe; Tom Thumb. Alternatively, they explore the private, obessional world of male sexual fantasy. 'The Fetishist' itself is a dramatic monologue from inside the asylum—an account of the rise and fall of a man who loves only frills and knickers and who has to pay the cost. **'The Red Dwarf'** heaps together all the trimmings of classic male sexual psychopathology. He, a Paris clerk, is small, rejected, and ultimately murderous—which is to say that he gets his own back at the expense of his sole female (but unfaithful) lover.

Tournier's is a carefully written book which travels over a familiar erotic landscape. My disengagement from it derives not so much from its unsurprising sexual politics as from its failure as erotic writing, within a particular tradition, to leave sufficient spaces in between. Ultimately, *The Fetishist* is both over-written and over-literal, reflective only, I suspect, of current tastes in coffee-table perversity. (p. 25)

Angela McRobbie, "Hand-Me-Downs," in New Statesman, Vol. 106, No. 2751, December 9, 1983, pp. 25-6.*

L. S. ROUDIEZ

The overrated Michel Tournier has now given us a narrative [*Gilles et Jeanne: Récit*] that attempts to bring together the destinies of Joan of Arc and Gilles de Rais. . . . Emphasis is placed on their close companionship up to Joan's unsuccessful assault on Paris and Gilles's vow to follow her anywhere, in heaven or hell, and on their being charged with heresy (among other accusations) and eventually being burned at the stake. The parallel leads to the suggestion that, since Joan was later rehabilitated and canonized, the same might happen in the case of Gilles. The idea is interesting enough, but the intellectual world teems with ideas while accomplishments are few.

Tournier veils his fiction with a semblance of authenticity by quoting what one assumes to be extracts from the actual testimony of witnesses at Rais's trial and appending five footnotes to the narrative. He nevertheless must twist the facts if the reader is to give credence to his thesis. He thus suggests that Rais was burned rather than hanged and conveniently forgets that Rais was not condemned to death by a Church court, for under the threat of excommunication he did confess and received absolution; the ecclesiastical court was incompetent to examine the accusation that he tortured and murdered young boys, and the death sentence was handed out on the authority of the Parliament of Brittany. But all that would skew the parallelism he needs.

As usual, Tournier's writing is undistinguished. It can be vulgar or pretentious by turns; it is mostly stereotyped. In short, *Gilles & Jeanne* may be skipped without loss. (pp. 240-41)

NICHOLAS SPICE

In English nurseries little boys are known to be made of frogs and snails and puppy dogs' tails. Little girls . . . are made of sugar and spice. And all things nice. . . . Prickly, the infant protagonist of the sixth story in this collection of 14 [*The Fetishist and Other Stories*] by Michel Tournier, would agree. Maleness repels, femaleness attracts him. Papa is grizzled, tobacco-smelling, stiff and, above all, stubbly: rebarbative, in fact. Mama—soft, creamy, sweet-scented, supple Mama—summarises all things nice. Much else in the adult world reinforces these categories for Prickly. Including the public conveniences in the park which he goes to some afternoons with Marie his nanny. On the left, the Gents: foul-smelling and incommodious; on the right, the Ladies: perfumed, decorative and sumptuously furnished; in the middle, Mamouse, the large lady caretaker who sits 'like the dog Cerberus' at the gates of hell, watching over her *pourboires* and her pot of simmering chicken-giblet broth. Prickly's chief aim in life is to sneak past Mamouse into the Ladies, where behind closed doors, and without having to stand up (a position which inhibits him), he can pee in peace. When Mamouse gets wise to this Prickly seeks advice from his friend Dominique, who is older than him and who passes in and out of the forbidden zone with mysterious immunity. At the centre of the park maze Dominique reveals how this can be: 'Next, opening them wide, he pulled down the red underpants he had exposed. His smooth, white stomach ended in a milky slit, a vertical smile in which there was just a trace of pale down.' The logic of the situation begins to dawn on Prickly. The vexatious problem of peeing like a man, Marie's threats to have his willie cut off if he doesn't stop wetting his bed, the curious statue in the park of Theseus and the Minotaur where Theseus, dressed like a girl, is apparently about to cut off the Minotaur's willie, the hideous vision of a man's genitals glimpsed one day in the urinals ('the quantity of swarthy, flabby flesh he was trying with difficulty to cram back into his fly was incredible'), those chicken giblets in Mamouse's pot . . . it all adds up. Prickly no longer wets his bed. His mind is made up. He takes Papa's cut-throat razor and pre-empts the inevitable. He cuts off his willie himself. The outcome of **'Prickly'** is a shock because it is unforeseen, but also because it is not unforeseeable. Prickly's self-mutilation precipitates the sudden recognition of an awful congruity in everything that has led up to it, and we experience a sudden rush of meaning to the brain. This effect is typical of Tournier's control of the short story form.

When Prickly's mother goes out for the evening, Prickly begs her to leave him her black kidskin gloves. 'They were as supple and warm as fresh, living skins, and the child swathed his body in their empty hands, Mama's hands, and fell asleep under their caress.' This is a solace that Martin, the fetishist, would keenly appreciate. It is in a glove, so to speak, that he experiences his first sensual encounter with Antoinette, the love of his life: 'that little fabric hand that I could squeeze in *my* hand, put in my pocket, Antoinette's hand'. But his romance only really takes off with Antoinette's panties, which a comic and curious turn of events brings into his rapt possession. We meet Martin long after this fateful occurrence. He is on day release from the mental hospital where he has been an inmate for the past twenty years. While his attendants are having a drink in a nearby bar, he talks to us for an hour. . . .

Properly speaking, Martin is not a fetishist but a synecdochist, since his speciality of mind is to discover the whole in the part—a woman in her underwear, a person in his shoes, a man in his wallet. Instances of synecdochism and related mechanisms of cathexis crop up all over Tournier's stories. In 'The Lily of the Valley Lay-By', for example, it's an articulated lorry that gets charged up with emotional energy; in 'Tristan Vox' a radio personality is displaced by his voice; and in 'The Red Dwarf' a woman identifies her lover as 'a walking penis'. Synecdoche, Tournier shows us, is a standard figure in the rhetoric of consciousness. It is only the intensity of this habit in Martin that marks him off from his fellow men.

The form of 'The Fetishist' as a one-man play accentuates an essential characteristic of Tournier's creative personality: his generosity towards his characters, his willingness to grant them full autonomy. Tournier justifies Martin by letting Martin justify himself. Even the subsidiary characters in Tournier's stories are given the freedom to exist in their own right, so that we often get the sense that it is merely chance that has allotted them a minor role in the action. Viewed from another perspective, we feel, the story could be theirs. This has the effect of making the stories replete with possibilities, while in no way disturbing their tightness as dramatic actions. . . .

[Distilled] from their embodiments as stories, Tournier's subjects may appear outlandish and bizarre. The fact that in their worked-out form the stories have the credibility of things discovered and merely mediated is partly due to the way Tournier incorporates into them experiences familiar to us all, experiences we recognise and can identify with: watching a cat jump onto a wall ('she ran at it as if it were flat on the ground'), eating breakfast early on a spring morning in the dark ('he gazed at the black rectangle of the window in front of him'), padding around the bathroom in a bathrobe or trying to make one's way along the top of a slippery wall. By locating the normal within the abnormal Tournier renders the force and tyranny of these concepts redundant.

Nicholas Spice, "Spicy," in London Review of Books, March 15 to April 4, 1984, pp. 20-2.*

PAUL BERMAN

Having read *The Ogre*, I was naturally eager to see a play called *The Fetishist* by the same author. This time the obsession turned out to be women's underclothes. The fetishist is mad for women's underclothes. He steals money to purchase them in quantity and one day attacks a woman in the métro to acquire her fetching garter. The escapade lands him in a psychiatric ward, where the question becomes, Is the fetishist insane? Or merely a man of unusual taste? Certainly not insane, not in Tournier's presentation. Fetishism is nothing but normality, concentrated. It is more erotic than normality because it's so sharply focused. And it illuminates the landscape. One day the fetishist's affections extend to well-worn franc notes, which he loves for their underclothing-like quality as well as for their ability to be exchanged for actual underclothes. Consumed with this new passion, he launches a pick-pocketing spree. This definitely isn't insane; it's what everyone does. Normal people fetishize money like mad, and make money a focus of erotic impulse, and loot and pillage to their heart's content to get more and more. But the form their fetish takes is socially acceptable, and they never notice it in themselves.

The Fetishist is like *The Ogre*, then—another subversive assault on sexual repression, capitalism and authority. But it is better than *The Ogre*, shrewder, funnier, briefer (if not quite brief enough). It seems to me better written. . . .

Paul Berman, in a review of "The Fetishist," in The Nation, Vol. 238, No. 25, June 30, 1984, p. 810.

VICTOR BROMBERT

In one of the most haunting stories [in "The Fetishist"] by Michel Tournier—arguably France's finest novelist today—a photographer destroys her male model by devising a method that immerses him directly in a developing bath of chemicals, enswathing him like a corpse in a shroud to achieve on the cloth the photographic equivalent of a funerary frieze. Does art feed on death? In another story, life seems to take its revenge. The golden, incorporeal voice of a spellbinding radio announcer with the mythical name of Tristan Vox is destroyed by banality itself—in the form of a jealous secretary and a jealous wife. Art and life seem to be interlocked in a deadly struggle.

Mr. Tournier is a disturbing virtuoso. His technical range is stunning. His prose is sensuous and muscular; it can be colloquial, stylized, restrained, exuberant. Tones shift, as he quickly moves from realism to irony to the whimsical to the violently preposterous. His dialogues and situations often have the flavor of the theater of the absurd. His rhetoric is at once opulent and precise. . . . Mr. Tournier has a sense of comedy, but even his jokes are grim. His humor shakes the edifice of received ideas and casts a light of suspicion on the games we play. . . .

Horror is never distant, especially when the world evoked seems at first reassuringly familiar. But the devouring ogre is lurking; daydreams swiftly turn into nightmares. The grotesque reintroduces into the commonplace the troubling and revelatory dimension of myth. Mr. Tournier's starting point is often the routine of daily life, with its layers of boredom. . . . Mr. Tournier's world is . . . akin to that of the fairy tale—a world of monsters, deviations and metamorphoses, which exorcise our old fears and initiate us to new ones. But the stories he writes are fairy tales for adults only. (p. 7)

In "The Fetishist," a collection of 14 widely different short texts, Mr. Tournier demonstrates what a literary artist can do in the concentrated form of the story, tale or novella. Whether he stylizes a concrete situation or derives plots from an abstract idea (he shuttles back and forth between the two formulas), Mr. Tournier produces dramatic narratives whose impact is directly related to the economy of means. The "knot of hatred" that leads a dwarf to kill the beautiful woman whose lover he has become, the obsession with women's underwear that leads the fetishist to acts of violence, the lethal artistic experiments of the photographer—these are some of the situations Mr. Tournier exploits to illustrate how the literary craft can at the same time project and tame an omnipresent irrationality. . . .

Some readers may find hard to take what Mr. Tournier himself described to a reporter as his attraction to the "sordid supernatural." When his first novels appeared, there were those who took offense at the mixture of scatology and fantasy. More serious, in an artistic perspective, might be the charge that his writing is at times forced, didactic, culturally overdetermined, burdened with literary and legendary referents. While these traits may be seen as flaws, they in fact enhance the thematic richness of Mr. Tournier's stories. Some themes are favored:

the painful initiation into a masculine world, nostalgia for lost innocence, the childlikeness of the adult, the affinities between the monster and the clown, the even greater bond between the ogre and the child, the fascination with triviality raised to the level of the demonic.

Mr. Tournier, whose novel **"The Ogre"** has more than a marginal relation to the Holocaust, doubtless projects a far-reaching malaise induced by the traumas of modern history and the politics of ideologies. This malaise comes across most powerfully in those stories in **"The Fetishist"** where suicidal instincts are revealed through metaphysical yearnings. Transcendence is ultimately always seen as lethal. (p. 9)

> Victor Brombert, *"Grim Jokes and Poetic Gore,"* in The New York Times Book Review, *September 9, 1984, pp. 7, 9.*

JOHN WEIGHTMAN

[Tournier] came to literature by way of philosophy, and all his writing is sensuously epistemological or phenomenological; that is, he is primarily concerned with our emotional-cum-intellectual grasp of reality which, for each of us, turns the world, if not into "a forest of symbols" in the Baudelairean sense, at least into a sharply idiosyncratic pattern of poetic responses, either positive or negative. . . .

The hero of the story or dramatic monologue [*Le Fetichiste (The Fetishist)*] is certifiably mad, since his whole life has been eaten up by his obsession with female underwear. . . . He has no being outside his sexual instinct, and that instinct has narrowed down to a fixation on certain shapes and qualities of material, which tyrannize him for reasons totally beyond his understanding. He is, in fact, a tragicomic hero of particularized phenomenology, whom the doctors are trying to bludgeon into "normality" with electroshock treatment.

I don't know whether such extremely specialized people exist in reality, but Tournier's intention in describing a completely polarized instance is both clear and valid. He is implying: "Tell me what your fetish is and I'll tell you who you are." A further point, which can be easily deduced, is that the misfortune of this particular fetishist could, through a slight change of emphasis, have been transformed into a fortune, had he been a sculptor, say, obsessed not with what covers breasts and buttocks, but with the amorous carving of such roundnesses, or a photographer absorbed in the suggestive presentation of underwear for luxury magazines. This is to say that the difference between the neurotic person and the successful artist may be a very narrow one; the neurotic lives his neurosis directly as a phenomenological doom, whereas the artist stands at one or two removes from his and, through the therapeutic process of symbolic transfer, maintains his balance and may, incidentally, earn his living through appealing to, and satisfying, the neuroses diffused throughout the "normal" public.

To put it another way, which is amply illustrated in the rest of the volume, normality is only a statistical mean to which none of us wholly belongs. (p. 25)

Tournier's examples are taken from various points on the normal-abnormal spectrum, but with a preference for the abnormal end. The hero of *Le Coq de bruyère* [*The Woodcock*] is exceptional in being archetypically French, as if he belonged to a Maupassant short story. A retired army officer, he prides himself on his fencing and his prowess as a rider, which are the necessary accompaniments of his extra-marital adventures, since

they confirm his virile equality with much younger men. All goes well until, with the onset of old age, he loses his grip slightly and openly establishes a young mistress in the town, to the distress of his tolerant wife, who then develops psychosomatic blindness as a phenomenological defense against such a breach of good manners. Various peripeteia ensue, demonstrating the hero's inability to progress from the stylish physicality of sexual performance to genuine understanding, and he is last seen half-paralyzed and in a wheelchair, being pushed by his now cured wife. This reversal has something of the trick ending frequent in short stories (Tournier is not averse to such devices), but the text is raised above the level of a routine narrative by the author's mastery of concrete detail and his impeccable ear for the niceties of speech. (pp. 25-6)

Most of the other stories are concerned with characters more closely related to the fetishist in the sense that they are "monsters" or "ogres" (to use a term that Tournier himself is fond of), whose phenomenological adjustment to the world is biased by some physical peculiarity or mental twist with which they can, or cannot, come to terms. . . .

Here we have several . . . examples: a little boy who is so innocently disgusted by male sexuality that he spontaneously cuts off his penis to drop it among similar fleshy odds and ends stewing in a pot; a girl whose only escape from the existential nausea of living is to accumulate possibilities of death; a noose, poisonous mushrooms, a gun, and, finally, a custom-built, living-room-size guillotine; a wife who falls in love with her husband's voice as a radio announcer and establishes a crazy dichotomy between the unprepossessing physical man and the vibrant, though abstract, persona; a truck driver, torn between the rival claims of a love affair and his deeply sensuous commitment to his truck and the phenomenology of the open road; a gifted pianist who, because of his near blindness and general ugliness, accidentally makes a fortune as a comic turn, when what he really wants to do is to play Bach. . . .

Tournier fills out the sinister framework of each story with so much everyday detail, brilliantly and wittily expressed, that the dominant tone is one of wild hilarity at the inextricable blend of ordinariness and strangeness in the world, a tone very unlike the gothic solemnity which now makes Poe, for instance, seem rather old-fashioned. . . .

Opinions may vary, admittedly, about the level of seriousness on which Tournier is writing. Is he a solid literary figure, or is he, perhaps, just another "ludic" writer like Robbe-Grillet, who has replaced the latter's maniacal parsimoniousness by the opposite tendency, a jackdaw-like fascination with all the glittering possibilities of modern intellectualism, which he exploits for his own, and our, entertainment, without really welding them into a durable artistic whole? These short stories are very nicely shaped, but their form depends perhaps too much on the trick ending, which governs the preceding narrative and gives them something of the air of phenomenological exercises or diversions. On the other hand, the four big novels (the latest, *Gaspard, Melchior et Balthazar,* translated as **The Four Wise Men,** is a virtuoso performance, a lavish retelling of the nativity story in the style of Flaubert's *Salammbo*) bulge with content, but not all of it, to my mind, is equally convincing. I also find them ultimately shapeless: they seem to break down in retrospect into brilliant fragments, preselected, as it were, for some future anthology of "poetic prose."

Perhaps a key to this central uncertainty lies in Tournier's repeatedly expressed obsession with children and childhood, since the child discovers the world as an undifferentiated phenomenological blur, before he sorts it out more or less according to the sterner values of the social context of adulthood. Tournier, the artist, is no doubt reflecting Tournier, the man, who, on his own admission, is no ordinary adult, but a sort of child-man, still happily floundering in the blur without any great urge to grow up in the usual way, a perverse, polymorphic Peter Pan with a gift of style. (p. 26)

John Weightman, "Polymorphic Peter Pan," in The New York Review of Books, *Vol. XXXI, No. 17, November 8, 1984, pp. 25-6.*

SVEN BIRKERTS

Tournier is one of the few novelists alive who deserves to be called "visionary." From one book to the next, he has been developing and extending a set of themes that are radically at odds with the common views of Western society. To the rationalist/Christian scheme he opposes a sensual Gnosticism; in the face of the "social contract" he flings an imperious, anarchic individualism. This is his real crime. In another age he would have been burned at the stake.

Friday or The Other Island (1967), Tournier's first novel, is relatively mild and playful in its heresies and is, for that reason, the most accessible of the four that have been translated. Already, though, the project of re-reading the world has been undertaken, and the key principles sketched: character as destiny, material reality as a Baudelairean "forest of symbols," the survival in the psyche of a lost wholeness, and the possibility given to the man of recovering this state through exceptional deeds of self-attainment. Mythic or textual reverberation is here, as in future novels, a crucial structural element....

In all of Tournier's novels, man is presented as a being reft from some original unity, condemned to wander in a world where the order of things has been scrambled and ciphered, as if by some calculating archfiend. But like the Gnostics, Tournier believes that a gleam of the pure light is still buried in our being. By this light one can make out the guiding signs, possibly even discover what pattern they make. There is no place for social order in this—social order is the very paradigm of the fallen condition. Only the private sense of destiny, the obscure proddings of self-intuition, can be relied upon. (p. 39)

[In *The Ogre*] we are asked to accept the convergence of private self and outer world and to stand in the shower of portents and symbols that marks Tiffauges's "particular history." We are a long way from Crusoe's island: the track of Tiffauges's destiny will carry him down through the rings of a symbolist's inferno and into the sulfurous maw of Nazi Germany.

Tiffauges is the proprietor of an auto garage in Paris. When a shop accident one day incapacitates his right hand, he discovers that he can write a perfectly fluent but very different script with his left. What's more, the discovery prompts, *compels* him to set down his reflections and memories. The "accident," like Crusoe's shipwreck, signals the eruption of a hitherto buried identity....

The Ogre is in many ways a shapeless book. Its narrative hews to the logic of obsession, private and, later, collective. We follow along as Tiffauges abandons, stage by stage, all belief in volition, until he finally obeys only the configuration of events and his reading of signs....

The Ogre has been reviled both for its attentiveness to the unseemly—the book is full of anatomical fetishism, prolonged caresses, coprological excitements—and its cool, unflinching depiction of Tiffauges as a Nazi yes-man. Tournier plunges his ogre into a hell, but the fellow flourishes, witnessing and enacting horrors with little trace of remorse. But to interpret this as authorial sanction is foolish. *The Ogre* is a Gnostic fable. It may be peculiar, but it is redemptive as well. For the whole to succeed, Tiffauges must be fully immersed in the corrupted element—only then can he achieve his apotheosis. As Dante had to penetrate to the deepest cavity of hell before he could pass through Lucifer's thighs and see the stars again, so Tiffauges must bear the growing weight of Ephriam right into death before he can see the symbolic triumph of spirit.

With *Gemini* (1975), Tournier took his obsessions in new directions. Destinies and mysteries of inversion were still dominant, but the field of research was now that of human identity. The tale of the perfect geminate pair, Jean and Paul, is played off against the bizarre homosexual adventures of their uncle, Alexandre. The plot instigates and survives every kind of improbability.... Pattern folds into pattern until the most provocative ideas come to life. The divided twins become the drifting halves of the sacred whole that Diotima described in *The Symposium*. Alexandre's priapic search becomes the reverse of Jean's, its profanation. And so on. On the surface we see the deft play of mirrors; at the root we are caught up in an interrogation of the foundations of the psyche. Tournier is interested above all in locating the source of the primal imbalance that sponsors our relentless bonding and mating....

What *does* the author finally believe? What is the basis of his vision of destinies? The spiritual need is certainly at the core of each of the novels: we are always hovering on the brink of hidden orders, superior realities, transcendent states. But for all that, there is little that refers to any orthodoxy, even such as the Gnostics—in spite of their hatred of orthodoxy—might have unwittingly held. Christian allusions abound, but invariably they seem to be more a part of a mythic substratum than hints of a proffered solution. *The Four Wise Men,* the fourth of Tournier's novels, hardly dissolves this impression of heterogeneous spiritual drives.

In *The Four Wise Men* (1980), Tournier presents us with yet another retelling. This time he has adapted the Bible story of the journey of the Magi, refurbishing it completely with the addition of an apocryphal fourth traveler. With his singular narrative gifts, he animates a time and place and brings to life four very different—and very troubled—men.... Is Tournier making sport, playing versions on a sacred text, or is he trying to shake the scales from our eyes, to make us see the grace embedded in the rough matter of creation? Is he mocking or pointing? How we answer will depend largely upon how skewed or straight we believe the order of things to be.

There is much to question in Tournier's enterprise, and many, out of refinement or faith, will not approve it. But I can think of nothing that matches the verve and daring of these imaginings. They open the sluices wide to the unconscious materials that are the very stuff of art's pity and terror. His way of transforming these into the legends of spirit restores to the novel a sense of "high stakes" that has long been missing. (pp. 40-1)

[The Stories in *The Fetishist*] progress in vivid flashes and have little of the recondite speculation that makes the novels at times forbidding.

Tournier has a way of tricking us into the realm of the perverse. We accept and absorb some deviant tic, our curiosity is piqued— and then, all at once, we are caught up in the strange logic of compulsion. . . . Too bizarre even to summarize, every one of these 14 stories in some way extends Tournier's Gnostic attack on order. He manipulates relentlessly the anxieties with which we surround the taboo. Where we repress, he exalts. Where we discern only darkness, he finds illumination. By flipping the underside of the psyche up into the light, he achieves the desired inversion—we stare at the world as if it were a negative that has yet to be printed. (p. 42)

Sven Birkerts, "Ogres and Oracles," in The New Republic, *Vol. 192, No. 6, February 11, 1985, pp. 39-42.**

Fay Weldon

1933-

English novelist, dramatist, scriptwriter, and short story writer.

Weldon's novels focus on the troubles of women in contemporary society. Weldon emphasizes the oppressiveness of marriage and the exploitative role of men within this social institution, yet she also analyzes the ways in which women are responsible for their own situations. Although Weldon explores serious problems, the outlandish plots of some of her works and the witty remarks of her characters often result in a comic tone. Her style is also playful; she uses such techniques as authorial intrusion to directly address the reader or the characters, translation of spoken dialogue into its unspoken meaning, delineation of dialogue in script form, and composition of extremely short paragraphs separated by wide spaces.

In her early novels Weldon examines the successes and failures of sisterhood by creating female characters related through blood or friendship. While she generally presents a dark picture of the female condition, Weldon usually ends these works on a note of hope. Esther, the heroine of *The Fat Woman's Joke* (1967), regains her self-respect and her husband's appreciation during a separation from him. In *Down Among the Women* (1971) Weldon portrays three generations of oppressed women; rebellion and hope for female independence is embodied in the third generation, represented by the heroine's illegitimate daughter. *Female Friends* (1975) tells of Chloe's difficult decision to leave her mean, manipulative husband and raise her five children alone. Chloe's relationship with two close friends, portrayed mostly through flashbacks, provides essential support in her marital crisis, yet a less-than-total loyalty among the women is also revealed. In all of these books, children are shown to be of primary importance to women, and motherhood is a central theme in *Remember Me* (1976) and *Puffball* (1980). In the former, the ghost of a divorced woman haunts her husband's second wife until the wife begins to take her obligations as a stepmother more seriously. *Puffball* also includes a supernatural element—a jealous witch named Mabs who attempts to interfere with her neighbor's pregnancy. The novel ends happily: the neighbor delivers a healthy baby, Mabs conceives a child, and both women become more generous. In keeping with her interest in women, Weldon includes detailed information about pregnancy in *Puffball*, the theme of which is, according to Francis King, "the tyranny of women's biological functions."

In her recent works, Weldon continues to explore the plight of women in inventive ways. *The President's Child* (1982) was labeled by several reviewers as a combination feminist novel and "airport novel," an epithet which refers to its thriller-like plot. In *The President's Child*, a woman who became pregnant as a result of an affair with a politician finds that his supporters, fearful that public knowledge of the liaison will hurt his presidential aspirations, are trying to kill her. Several reviewers noted that in this novel, as in much of her work, Weldon fails to develop her male characters as fully as her female ones and portrays them unsympathetically. *Life and Loves of a She-Devil* (1984) is a revenge fantasy carried to extreme lengths. Having been called a "she-devil" by her husband in a moment of anger, Ruth decides to act like one

© Jerry Bauer

and exacts complete revenge on her husband and his beautiful mistress. *Letters to Alice on First Reading Jane Austen* (1984) is an unusual work by Weldon in that it blends literary and feminist themes. The book combines the adventures of a college girl with letters to the girl about the merits of Jane Austen's work from her "Aunt Fay." As a means of exploring the nature and value of fiction, the letters contain analyses of Austen's work, biographical and historical information about Austen and the era in which she wrote, and advice to aspiring writers. In addition to fiction, Weldon has also written more than fifty television scripts, including two for *Upstairs, Downstairs* and a dramatization of Austen's *Pride and Prejudice*, which aired in Great Britain in 1980.

(See also CLC, Vols. 6, 9, 11, 19; *Contemporary Authors*, Vols. 21-24, rev. ed.; *Contemporary Authors New Revision Series*, Vol. 16; and *Dictionary of Literary Biography*, Vol. 14.)

JOHN NAUGHTON

Fay Weldon's fiction is generally bleak territory for the male chauvinist psyche. But [*Watching Me, Watching You*] reminds one that feminism is not just an anti-male creed, and that she wears hers lightly, preferring to string her male characters along rather than string them up, relying on them to collapse under the weight of their absurdity or greed or selfishness or pomposity, rather than feeling the need to bury them under piles of authorial invective.

One candidate for sarcastic entombment is Martin, freelance designer and husband of long-suffering Martha, around whom one story, **'Weekend',** revolves. An account, on the face of it, of how a working wife and mother copes with the incessant demands of a middle-class lifestyle, it really serves to establish Martin's candidature for the Shit of the Year award. For, like many of his kind, he wants everything his way, all the time, with no exceptions: the affluence which comes from a second income, for example, plus the ministrations of a 'full-time' wife and mother; or a lavish weekend's entertainment at the couple's country cottage—but without any exertion on his part. . . .

Is this another parable about the traditional (and, to some feminists, contemptible) conniving martyrdom of Woman? Or is it about the admirable acceptance of responsibility for keeping life going, a further affirmation of the social importance and maturity of women and, conversely, of the irresponsibility and immaturity of men? The subtlety of Fay Weldon's story is that you can, validly, read it either way. But its artful ambiguity is nevertheless carefully circumscribed, for it precludes the possibility that Martin will emerge from it looking anything other than a cad.

However, I suspect that's because he's Martin, rather than because he's a male. Certainly there are other stories in this collection where Ms Weldon gives ample evidence of being able to think herself into male characters. The best is, I think, **'Christmas Tree',** a 20-page life of a playwright, risen from the working classes but uneasy in his success. There is a marvellous economy of style and structure here, and an enviable knack of capturing the tone of her characters. In this case it's the glib, aphoristic style of contemporary English dramatists— by Stoppard out of Raphael, delivered by Conti. 'A writer,' says the playwright at one point, 'is gigolo to the Muse, not lover.' Fay Weldon's own abilities, however, belie that.

John Naughton, "Family Lives," in The Listener, Vol. 105, No. 2714, May 28, 1981, p. 717.*

JAMES LASDUN

Retaliatory sexism is one way of describing the stories in Fay Weldon's **Watching Me, Watching You.** The Weldon Male is as rigidly rôle-bound as any of our most misogynist writers' females. He works in the Arts or Media, believes himself to be a patient, rational liberal but invariably proves himself a fascist brute in sexual politics; he tends to have an ex-wife whom he left as soon as he became successful and desirable to other women; he treats his present wife like a slave—beating her or threatening her with psychiatric treatment if she rebels; and he has a knack of making himself seem the injured party as he reduces his women to miserable wrecks.

To begin with, the effect of reading these stories is one of persuasive aversion therapy against the male sex. After a while, however, the relentlessness with which Fay Weldon has her vulnerable, long-suffering women ground into the dust by her ghastly men, becomes counter-productive, and one begins to wonder whether the depressing world these characters inhabit is not ultimately, for all its similarities with the real world, an entirely private creation.

Be that as it may, Fay Weldon damns her men with efficiency, and these stories remain extremely compelling. A measure of their success is the panache with which they survive flaws such as overstatement, a heavy-handed use of symbols (for example, a man's monopoly of power in his marriage is represented by his invincibility on the monopoly board), repetition of effects (girls who dye their pubic hair green, ghosts, a lot of china-breaking and drink-spilling at significant moments) and 'tacked-on' happy endings—flaws which would be disastrous for any less talented writer.

James Lasdun, "Pig Stys," in The Spectator, Vol. 247, No. 7983, July 11, 1981, p. 22.*

FRANK RICH

The heroine of . . . **"After the Prize"** is a particle physicist who has just won the Nobel Prize. Its author . . . is no scientist, but she might as well be. **"After the Prize"** is so diagramatically written, in its characterizations, thematic strategies and dramatic structure, that it is less a living play than an open-and-shut equation. . . .

"After the Prize" begins as a contemporary gloss on the Tracy-Hepburn "Woman of the Year." After the physicist, Wasp . . . wins her prize, she discovers that her husband, Edwin . . . , is less than overjoyed to play consort to a famous wife. But it's soon clear that Miss Weldon really wants to write her own version of Simon Gray's "Otherwise Engaged." Like Mr. Gray's publisher-hero, the brainy yet self-destructive Wasp deploys stinging wit and maddening logic to avoid dealing with anyone's feelings, including her own. . . .

Miss Weldon's heroine is never as clever as everyone, including the author, seems to think. Wasp may be intelligent—or at least polysyllabic—but she's mainly a selfish, chilly boor whose nonstop bons mots fall flat. She doesn't even seem all that passionate about her science, and we never do learn why the vaguely written Edwin has heretofore loved her for 18 years. By the time Wasp arrives at her inevitable catharsis— in which she must at last confront her utter loneliness—the audience has long since been otherwise engaged.

Up until that point, Miss Weldon has taken us through a plot that is relentlessly didactic. Wasp has a twin sister . . .—named Bee, no less—who is the heroine's exact opposite: she's all heart and no brain. . . . The heroine contrives a one-night stand between Bee and Edwin, so that, by proxy, she might fill her husband's unsatisfied emotional needs. Meanwhile, Wasp also tries to retrieve her own lost passion, again by proxy. . . .

In her rhythmic, A-plus-B-equals-C fashion, the playwright shows us each nocturnal tryst—neither of which reveals much about any character—before bringing wife and husband back together for their final confrontation. Because the writing is as brittle and calculating as the central character, **"After the Prize"** becomes an Alan Ayckbourn farce, minus the humor or feeling or surprise. To liven things up, Miss Weldon also throws in a farfetched melodramatic plot twist, involving the paternity of Wasp and Edwin's unseen son. This allows the playwright to shatter the couple's marriage by artificial narrative fiat rather than by doing the harder work of actually dramatizing the collapse of their relationship.

Frank Rich, "Fay Weldon offers 'After the Prize'," in The New York Times, November 24, 1981, p. 22.

JOHN SIMON

[*After the Prize*] is rather like munching on peanuts while waiting for a drink that never arrives: Eventually you find yourself stuffed with something you didn't want and still high and dry. . . .

[The plot is] more geometry than dramaturgy, and must have been written on graph paper slanting across a drawing board. The dialogue could also have been spewed out by a medium-inspired computer: It has the ring of wit and wisdom, but not their substance. Thus we hear about people "thinking of quarks and antiquarks instead of what's going on in their bodies," and others who let "sex suffuse their lives." "Then how do they concentrate on what they're doing?" "They don't, I suppose." "Exactly!" This has the unmistakable snap and crackle of epigrams about it, but gets no closer to them than to Rice Krispies. At other times, the chatter flows on evenly, filled with a mild, bored animus, like souls in a civilized sort of hell in an eternal Plutonic dialogue. . . .

[Everything] is so neatly balanced: the two antithetical sisters, Wasp and Bee, and the two men who might as well have been called Sheep and Wolf. There is one somewhat artificial revelation, and an ending that, true, isn't quite symmetrical. Or an ending. . . .

I didn't care a particle about any of it. (p. 162)

John Simon, "Soldiers and Sisters," in New York Magazine, Vol. 14, No. 48, December 7, 1981, pp. 159, 162.*

MARY CANTWELL

Were Fay Weldon's novels and short stories as well known in this country as they are in her native Britain, she might by now have attained the status of writer-most-quoted in contemporary essays on women vis-à-vis men. She is witty, pithy and a talented aphorist, as useful a peg on which to hang a paragraph as Jane Austen, but without Austen's generosity. If the latter's lucidity is warmed by tolerance, Miss Weldon's is chilled by rage. The more one reads Fay Weldon—and her output is considerable—the more one is aware of her terrible anger. By itself, a Weldon novel or story evokes laughter; read in conjunction with her others, it evokes unease. For all its humor, her picture of male and female together is unrelentingly grim, and each new work adds another shadow. . . .

"**Watching Me, Watching You**" consists of 11 short stories . . . and her first novel, "**The Fat Woman's Joke**." . . . All of them are about men and women—as husbands, wives, lovers, haters, oppressors, victims. They are never friends: male-female friendship is impossible in Miss Weldon's world. Its inhabitants, to lift a line from an old Nichols and May routine, have lots of proximity but no relating.

In "**Holy Stones**," for instance, a recently married middle-aged journalist takes his adored young wife to Israel, a trip he hopes will teach her "the dangers of irrational belief." She, however, remains faithful to religion; he in turn and in revenge, becomes unfaithful to her. "He, who had been prepared to worship his wife, had married a woman who worshipped strange gods instead of her husband." (This kind of nail-and-hammer ending is typical of Miss Weldon; there is no way in which the reader can miss her point.) . . .

These are moral tales, and the practical lesson conveyed is that since men and women live in two eternally separate territories, he or she who strays onto the other's turf must be armed. At least the female must be armed and cautious; the male can afford confidence, his never-failing weapon being her own fear of losing the status and security given by marriage. He is her enemy, but then so is she.

Miss Weldon can be curiously careless about details . . . but her diction is invariably exact. Within her confines she is a dazzling writer, but those confines are increasingly claustrophobic.

"**The Fat Woman's Joke**" [originally published in the United States as "**. . . And the Wife Ran Away**"] is a case in point. Alan and Esther Sussman have a long marriage cemented by food. They go on a diet, the cement crumbles, Alan has an affair with his long, lean secretary, and Esther moves out. "It will all be over for you as it is for me," she tells her friend Phyllis, who attempts to roust her from the seedy flat in which she sits stuffing herself. . . .

Esther, Alan, Phyllis, Phyllis's husband, the Sussmans' son and Alan's mistress embark on a sexual rondelay. Things happen, nothing's resolved, the characters come full circle. Along the way Miss Weldon, through Esther, delivers herself of some brilliant perceptions. So do the others for that matter: Miss Weldon's people are always carrying messages.

Everything that is to concern Fay Weldon in her later work is already sprung full-blown in "**The Fat Woman's Joke**." And although each book is, if anything, more clever than the last, she is still treading the same, very narrow path. What Miss Weldon does, she does very well—but it is more than time for so clever a writer to move out of the house.

Mary Cantwell, in a review of "Watching Me, Watching You," in The New York Times, December 21, 1981, p. 23.

LEWIS JONES

The President's Child is a feminist novel; it is addressed to the sisterhood and it is about men giving women a hard time, conspiring to do them in. . . . But it is also, as its title suggests, a parody of the 'airport' novel (written about and, usually, for money: banking or politics, expensive women and ingenious violence). The combination of genres is an audacious one, interestingly extreme, and it makes sense: after all, men give women a hard time in airport novels as well as in feminist ones. Is this unlikely marriage, if you will excuse the metaphor, a successful one?

The story is told by a blind woman called Maia to her female neighbours in Wincaster Row, Camden Town. They live in 'an island of privilege in an under-privileged city sea'; they are professional people, most of them working in the media. Maia speaks for them, as well as to them. . . .

The story she tells is about Isabel, a woman who used to live in Wincaster Row. Isabel was brought up in the outback of Australia by her eccentric mother. . . . Isabel leaves Australia for England, attaching herself to a series of rich men. She becomes a successful journalist. She tricks her way on to the maiden flight of Concorde (one notes the feminist irony), and it is here, appropriately, that the 'airport novel' begins. She finds herself sitting next to a handsome man called Dandy Ivel, who, as it happens, has been chosen by a group of rich men as a future President of the USA. They fall in love; but Dandy's 'people', especially Pete and Joe, his two 'goons', disapprove of the liaison (they think Isabel is 'an insult to the sweet name of womanhood'—not a suitable First Lady) and manage to break it up. Isabel returns to England and bears Dandy's child, a boy. By the time he is six, the boy has become imperious and difficult and the spitting image of his father. Dandy's people have been keeping an eye on Isabel. They think it's time to act.

The novel, then, is an ironic combination of complementary conspiracy theories. The 'airport' parody is both funny and relevant; the feminism is not mere agitprop (it is acknowledged that men may be kind and that women may be unkind); Ms Weldon combines them effectively. But the novel is rather slapdash. This is reflected in the details. Here she is on feminism: 'Here and now, sisters. Here and now. Build your houses strong and safe, love your children, and die for them if you have to and try to love your mothers who didn't.' This kind of thing can only be described as crass.

Lewis Jones, "Airport," in New Statesman, *Vol. 104, No. 2688, September 24, 1982, p. 30.**

HARRIET WAUGH

Fay Weldon has delighted and irritated critics and readers for some time now. Women, on the whole, give her the thumbs up sign, men are sometimes inclined to be more ambivalent in their appreciation. It is not difficult to see why she gets such different reactions. She has a happy facility to write entertainingly about women and female concerns in a stylish manner. Humour constantly breaks through what otherwise might be a rather relentless moan about the shape of life and the effects of sexuality. She concentrates her thought on women's experience of being women in a world governed by the doings of men. About men she has little to say. They are merely frightful gargoyles conjured up by women, just in case women should mistakenly think that by being born they have inherited paradise. . . . The plots follow a simple pattern. The heroine is lined up at the start of a race. She is all set to go with her egg firmly or sometimes precariously balanced on her spoon. Then she runs leaping, ducking and weaving through obstacles mainly consisting of men. The fun for the reader is in the excitement of the race; will the heroine reach the touchline with her egg intact, will it fall plop, or when it does fall is it going to be magicked into an india rubber ball and bounce back on to the spoon again? Fay Weldon, with only a few exceptions, tells a very good story even if the individual novel is merely a flourish in her general thesis about women's tribulations. As to the newest of these stylish flourishes, *The President's Child* is an amusing and exciting thriller presented as a fable. (p. 24)

Fay Weldon has created a cross current in the novel to add to its other virtues, depth and seriousness. Isabel's story is told by a blind female 'Listen with Mother' narrator who lives in Wincaster Row and was a friend of Isabel when she lived there. Isabel's life is presented by her as a fable. The reader is not necessarily supposed to suspend disbelief as you do in a naturalistic novel. Not only does the narrator tell the neighbours whom she addresses that she may not be telling it truly, but the story is itself deliberately unbelievable although exciting and engrossing. The fable shows how a woman is brought up against the male dynamo that in its relentless movement, shakes, breaks and destroys. At the end the blind woman is herself swallowed into the fable. This strand does add point and substance to the novel but unfortunately the narrator is an intensely irritating creation. When not dealing with the main thrust of the story she utters short paragraphs as though out of a con-

tracting womb bursting with female poetic sensibility. Unless you are far gone into infantile regression it makes tiresome and contrived reading. . . . The trick is to skim lightly over these episodes reading just enough to get the gist of it and so know the angle you are meant to have on things. (p. 25)

Harriet Waugh, "Unbelievable," in The Spectator, *Vol. 249, No. 8047, October 2, 1982, pp. 24-5.*

CAROL STERNHELL

For the last decade, Weldon, our most intelligent archivist, has been preserving women's lives in brittle, ironic prose; like a feminist Jane Austen, she has a sharp eye and tongue for the least romantic side of human relationships. Weldon's men have never amounted to much; indeed, critics frequently complain (to quote Joyce Carol Oates) that Weldon denies "subtlety and humanity to roughly one-half the population." *The President's Child* may be Weldon's mocking response to years of such criticism, for with this novel she takes her refreshingly unromantic portrait of men several steps further into a nightmare vision of male conspiracy, an international alliance against Isabel and, in a sense, against all women: "She was not to be allowed to live, because she was a source of danger, moral and physical, to her son. Perhaps all fathers feel like this, in their hearts?" Where the male characters in such earlier Weldon books as *Remember Me* and the glorious *Female Friends* were variously insensitive and ineffectual . . . , the men in Isabel's life are quite literally the enemy.

On one level, *The President's Child* can be read as an unfolding mystery—we quickly learn that Isabel's son looks remarkably like a leading U.S. Presidential candidate, and people are inconveniently beginning to notice it—but the apparently realistic plot soon becomes too surrealistic (like a dream) and hyperrealistic (like a comic book). Isabel's life on pleasant Wincaster Row . . . seems safely part of a familiar Weldon landscape; Isabel and her women friends chat, raise children, manage jobs, make love. This comfortably detailed real life, however, is merely "a reproduction . . . a sham, a mockery, an insult to the original"; at the core of Isabel's existence is a lie, what she sneeringly calls "the secret falsehood at the heart of every mother." . . .

Characters seem to have stepped randomly from the pages of divergent literary genres. Isabel's psychiatrist, for instance, seems surreal, calmly macabre, well aware of the two attempts so far on Isabel's life, he can still advise Homer that the problem is entirely hers. . . . On the other hand, Dandy Ivel's "goons," Pete and Joe—whose nicknames are Kitten and Hot Potato, who have learned their lessons from Watergate, who kill because they enjoy it—are comic book figures, works of Pop Art painted in primary colors. The story is narrated by Maia, Isabel's blind neighbor, a Camden Town Tiresias; as is fitting in a novel about the inevitable ambiguities and dangers of the parent-child bond, a tale about Homer and Jason ("Jason! What a name"), Maia speaks for the Greek chorus of women on Wincaster Row. There is nothing organically wrong with her eyes; she simply chooses not to see. . . .

Fay Weldon, that master of realism, character, and textual richness, insistently experiments with fantasy. In *Remember Me,* one major character was a ghost; *Words of Advice,* spun a weirdly modern fairy tale; *Puffball,* her last book, was primarily a parable about nature. Now *The President's Child,* despite its elaborate, lively plot and up-to-the-minute dialogue, is as much ancient fable as it is contemporary novel. Since my favorite Weldon works tend to be the least experimental—*Down Among the Women, Praxis,* and especially *Female Friends*—I resisted the story of Isabel, wanting more complex characters and less philosophy, wanting to think less and feel more. When I succumbed, and I did, it was not to the mystery of the plot but to the greater mysteries of the telling. Like Isabel, Weldon speaks as "a servant of the truth," looking always for new truths and new ways to express them. In *The President's Child,* the questions she raises are old ones, of motherhood, self-sacrifice, and power. "The male-female struggle never really was an issue, Isabel," Homer tells his wife near the end. "Real power, real influence, is a secret thing." The novel's most authentic voice is that of Maia, who knows that "the struggle is eternal, and dreadful." . . .

> Carol Sternhell, *"Fay Weldon's Dangerous Dreams,"* in The Village Voice, *Vol. XXVIII, No. 29, July 19, 1983, p. 34.*

PADDY KITCHEN

When I finished *Letters to Alice,* I had an image of Fay Weldon as conjuror, whipping a cloth from a generously laden table and leaving the plates of food and glasses of wine mysteriously undisturbed. It came unbidden, and does not suffer too close an interpretation. Crudely, I think the cloth represents literary subsidiaries like college English departments, while the table stands for good novelists and the repast their works. The thought of her as a conjuror reflects the combination of interpretation, autobiography and fiction in these . . . pages—comparable to producing a pack of cards, 12 silk scarves and a dove out of one flat pocket.

Alice is a fictional niece, who has just started a college course in English literature and has written to her Aunt Fay remarking that she finds Jane Austen "boring, petty and irrelevant". Aunt Fay's half of the subsequent correspondence forms an epistolatory novel which, as the blurb says, "echoes a series of letters that Jane Austen actually did send to her niece who was trying to become a novelist, and which summed up her views of what was important in life and literature". What Aunt Fay thinks is important in life *is* literature. . . .

I wish she'd been around in her present guise when I was studying *Emma* for A level 30-odd years ago. As a stroppy, horse-riding 16 year-old, I found the novel every bit as boring and petty as punk-haired, liberated Alice does. Yet if only I'd known some of the things she tells her fictional niece, I might have been much more receptive. . . .

When I likened English departments to dispensable tablecloths, I did not mean that Fay Weldon wants them done away with. She does not believe that Alice "would do better out of their care than in". But she warns her against the continual analysis of novels by those who cannot write them. . . .

The conjuror's sleight of hand occurs when Alice, who has been struggling to write what we are led to believe will turn out to be a thoroughly incompetent novel, fails her exams and immediately has her book accepted for publication. It is true that she *may* continue to study English elsewhere, but as the novel looks like becoming a bestseller, this probably won't happen.

Either way, her aunt has introduced her to the concept of the City of Invention, which "lies at a mid-way point between the Road to Heaven and the Road to Hell", and "glitters and glances with life, and gossip, and colour, and fantasy". Its

buildings are the Houses of the Imagination created by writers. . . . "If you plan to build here," she urges Alice, "you *must* know the city." The conjuror has made the fictional a reality, defying all who have said—since Jane Austen first reported them—"Oh! it is only a novel!"

To make much of the art form one practises, to celebrate it, to glory in it, arouses disapproval in some quarters—particularly if it is done in straightforward language, with unmixed enthusiasm. Fay Weldon's credentials are intact: she is a good writer whom thousands of people willingly read, and she travels widely and awarely in the City of Invention. She is an aunt the would-be novelist may trust.

> Paddy Kitchen, *"Conjuror's Trick,"* in The Times Educational Supplement, *No. 3541, May 11, 1984, p. 27.*

LORNA SAGE

Letters to Alice on first reading Jane Austen is an improbable act of collusion: Aunt Fay writing to a fictional niece who's contemplating a novel (as Austen wrote to one of her real nieces) offering sensible thoughts on moral guidance and keeping fantasy under control.

The result is a set of literary sermons only perfunctorily disguised by irony ('I hate . . . these sweeping assessments . . . and yet. . . . Put me in a pulpit and I know I too . . .'). Niece Alice, an ex-punk Eng.-Lit. student, provides a pretext for Fay Weldon to throw together some careers advice for the woman writer. For example, that the 'domestic arts' should be properly valued as they were in Aunt Jane's day. . . . Aunt Fay, these days at least, preaches a kind of 'separate spheres' pragmatism. Her past in advertising seems to be surfacing in her style, in the propaganda for making the best of things ('given the general dreadfulness of the world') and taking male awfulness for granted, like Aunt Jane. It's on the grounds of being a realist that she claims kinship. But this in turn produces a painful contradiction, since one can't help but be aware throughout the book that she is one of our main contemporary experts in registering fashionable myths and catching trends. A most professional knitter. We're supposed to find it surprising, and ironic, when Alice, despite being put through her Austen course, produces a trendy bestseller called 'The Wife's Revenge,' but it's simply not.

What Alice has learned is opportunism: she's into the new celibacy, as, seemingly, is Fay Weldon. A pity, since the strengths of her fiction (whatever her market researchers may suggest) are largely a product of her unruly Gothic imagination.

> Lorna Sage, *"Aunt Fay's Sermons,"* in The Observer, *May 13, 1984, p. 23.*

IAN HISLOP

Fay Weldon, the famous novelist, writes a series of letters to her imaginary niece, a would-be novelist, on the subject of Jane Austen, the great novelist. [*Letters to Alice on first reading Jane Austen*], as you may have realised, is a book about novels. In fact it is a witty, convincing and spirited defence of the practice of reading and writing fiction.

"Do not abandon Eng. Lit. for Social Studies", the aunt begs her niece, as Alice complains about having to read Jane Austen at College. The letters are sent to explain why the work of Jane Austen is so highly valued, and attempt further to explain why Literature, "with its capital L", is at least as useful as Social Studies. The result is both a fascinating study of Jane Austen and a novelist's enquiry into her own art. This she calls 'Invention' and alongside the discussion runs an Invention about Alice, an epistolary novel in the form of a campus farce: Young Alice falls for her professor, leaves her boyfriend and ends up with the professor's wife when her boyfriend goes off with the professor's sister. To complicate matters further this becomes the basis for Alice's novel which becomes a best-seller. As I said, it is a book about novels.

The premise is that Alice finds Austen boring and irrelevant. Fay Weldon needs to bring her alive. She first gives a resumé of social conditions at the time, detailing in particular the great hazards to women of sex and childbirth. . . . She adds to this a broader historical summary and then answers the old question of why none of this history ever appears in the novels. A brief biography shows that contemporary events *did* influence the Austen family closely but the author chose to write about something smaller yet, Weldon argues, more important. (p. 16)

The novels themselves are then discussed and since Fay Weldon is not in the Eng. Lit. Business, as she calls it, her analyses seem refreshingly direct. They are a novelist's interpretation and manage to demystify the writing without diminishing it. . . . Fay Weldon is very aware of the dangers of speculation in literary biography. She admits it when she is guessing, and backs this up with known details of the family, letters and the like to create her picture of Jane Austen.

Constantly progressing from defending one author to defending Fiction as a whole, Fay Weldon develops her central metaphor of The City of Invention, where houses equal books, and the traveller to the realm of fiction wanders through the suburbs and districts of a city filled with houses. It is a pleasing analogy with bus-driver critics conducting tours of the city in the shadows of the great Castle Shakespeare. The city is an alternative reality that leaves the visitor changed on his return to life. In answer to the question "Why read Fiction?", Weldon gives a simple answer. To practice empathy. . . . It is this concise expression of what confirmed readers of fiction vaguely believe but rarely formulate that is so appealing. The novel may not be as central to the history of Civilization as Weldon believes but she persuades you that it is at least important. Even her excess on its behalf is rather inspiring: "And yet I do believe though all else fails, the City of Invention will stand."

Jane Austen wrote a series of letters to her niece in which she discouraged her from attempting to become a novelist. Fay Weldon in this modern fictional version actively encourages her niece to write. By the end there are three novelists, one alive, one dead and one fictitious to convince you of the worth of the novel. I was convinced. (pp. 16-17)

Ian Hislop, "Writing about Novels," in Books and Bookmen, *No. 345, June, 1984, pp. 16-17.*

VALERIE SHAW

Described as an 'epistolary novel', *Letters to Alice* presents a series of letters from the novelist and playwright Fay Weldon to a fictional niece, the aim being to persuade the girl (an eighteen-year-old college student) that Jane Austen is well worth reading. . . . As generous with her advice as with her well-earned money, the writer cannot avoid seeming unbearably superior as she steers her protegée through what she calls the 'City of Invention', sometimes offering insights into her own

life as a successful novelist, sometimes merely retelling Jane Austen's stories, but invariably leaving the impression that she understands literary matters better than anyone else. . . . As a fantasy, this book offers its own brand of harmless fun, but there are enough pronouncements about the role of fiction in the modern world, about the novelist's responsibilities and freedoms, and in fact about Fay Weldon's own work, to suggest that she intends *Letters to Alice* to be, in part at least, an apologia. Whether or not this is so, it is a shame to see Jane Austen used as a pretext, for this is what she remains here. Despite attempts to vivify her image and to document her age, Austen's individuality is overshadowed by the letter-writer's presence, and one is left wishing that Fay Weldon had gone all the way and written entirely about herself. The pretend niece might have been no less intrigued, and those literary critics and earnest 'Eng. Lit.' students so scorned by her aunt might have been challenged and stimulated in ways that this book leaves totally, and somewhat smugly, out of count.

Valerie Shaw, in a review of "Letters to Alice on First Reading Jane Austen," in British Book News, *August, 1984, p. 495.*

MICHIKO KAKUTANI

By now, Fay Weldon's readers know pretty much what to expect in her novels: marital infidelities, suburban angst and large helpings of female rage. The heroine of her first novel—**"The Fat Woman's Joke"**—was a middle-aged woman named Esther who had traded in her philandering husband for the dubious satisfactions of the single life, and most of Miss Weldon's subsequent heroines have shared both Esther's plight and her talent for gaining weight and complaining. Ruth, the "she-devil" in [**"The Life and Loves of a She-Devil"**], is no exception. . . .

Although Miss Weldon has a good, observant eye for social and physical details, her obsession with sexual warfare tends to turn her characters into one-dimensional figures in a feminist cartoon strip—figures defined almost entirely in terms of their erotic conquests and ability to dish out emotional pain. The men are all variations on this year's model of The Male Chauvinist Pig; they are into success and money and perfectly shaped women—they want good sex, good cooking and no strings. As for the women, they are either air-brained temptresses, eager to sell their sisters out for the affections of a well-endowed man, or oppressed housewives, victims of a double standard who suddenly sees the light.

How do we know this? Well, most of the time Miss Weldon's characters turn to the reader and start spouting a stream of clichés and psycho-babble. "Out there in the world," says Ruth, "everything is possible and exciting. We can be different women. . . ."

In his angry leave-taking, [Ruth's husband] Bobbo had called Ruth a "she-devil," and Ruth has decided to try to live up to her real nature. She declares, "I want revenge. I want power. I want money. I want to be loved and not love in return." Her pursuit of these goals is single-minded—and occasionally very funny. Unfortunately, Miss Weldon's gift for irony and wit is over-shadowed by her didacticism, and the initial energy of her preposterous plot soon trails off into predictable wackiness.

Ruth's quest for revenge entails her assuming one alias after another—each of which puts her in a position to stir up trouble in the personal and professional lives of Bobbo and [his mistress] Mary Fisher. As a "she-devil" she does not employ any real magic—just lots of freewheeling malice. Still, she does bear a peculiar resemblance to the heroines of John Updike's recent novel, "The Witches of Eastwick."

Like those scheming women, Ruth becomes something of a parody of the "liberated" woman—a bitter harridan bent on using her sexual wiles and a 1970's license for self-indulgence to inflict hurt on others. Her final act—having extensive plastic surgery that makes her irresistible to men—actually seems like a capitulation to the male values she says she despises. Given Miss Weldon's previous work, one would assume that she did not set out in **"The Life and Loves of a She-Devil"** to write an unforgiving parody of the women's movement—but that's the net result.

> *Michiko Kakutani, in a review of "The Life and Loves of a She-Devil," in* The New York Times, *August 21, 1984, p. C17.*

CAROL E. RINZLER

"I want revenge. I want power. I want money. I want to be loved and not love in return." [In *The Life and Loves of a She-Devil*] Ruth identifies her goals, then sets her plan in motion. (p. 1)

Ruth and her revenge are a potent combination, scary and awesome, and, in the hands of a lesser writer, *She-Devil* might have become a feminist diatribe. Fortunately, Weldon's control is near total; she manages a tone that is wry rather than shrill as she expresses a fantasy most women have entertained, if not in such loving detail, *viz.*, What I'd *really* like to do to that bastard.

Weldon's Ruth, as she metamorphoses from good-wife into witch, is unlike most of the heroines who have populated fiction in the last decade or so, those laudable, slice-of-life ladies who create an instant shock of recognition. Ruth is more caricature than character, larger than life, so to speak. Her actions and reactions are gigantic, grotesque, creating a more delayed but more shocking shock of recognition.

She-Devil is reminiscent of Lois Gould's *A Sea-Change*, one of the more under-recognized books of the last decade. Like Gould, Weldon takes chances and makes a leap into fiction of the imagination, exciting, at times thrilling, certainly threatening. And, like Gould, Weldon may be accused of writing a book that is anti-male, a charge both silly and simplistic.

One certainly may view the book as fiction with a message, the message perhaps depending more on receiver than sender. What matters more and what makes this a powerfully funny and oddly powerful book is the energy of the language and of the intellect that conceived it, an energy that vibrates off the pages and that makes *She-Devil* as exceptional a book in the remembering as in the reading. (pp. 1-2)

> *Carol E. Rinzler, "Hell Hath No Fury," in* Book World—The Washington Post, *September 30, 1984, pp. 1-2.*

ROSALYN DREXLER

In her remarkable tour de farce, **"The Life and Loves of a She-Devil,"** Fay Weldon has taken the subject of revenge and given it play. Let me say, right off, that there are no lovable characters in this fable, and so what! A book is not a massage, it is some kind of message: particularly when the book *is* a parable written to illustrate a moral and to demonstrate the witty ins and outs of the author's mind. Why else write such a tale of woe?

"The Life and Loves of a She-Devil" has all the earmarks of a feminist novel, and we know what kind of ears those are: they are put to the ground to catch even the slightest whisper, they are seldom pink, and they collect the wax of eloquence in bitter hunks. Ruth is a bitter hunk: first, she was born ugly. . . . But why call her a she-devil?

One evening she drops the soup during dinner, the dog and cat go wild, her dinner guests (Bobbo's parents) begin arguing and Bobbo's reverie about Mary Fisher, the woman he has a hankering for, is interrupted. Ruth runs upstairs to the bathroom and locks herself in. Bobbo follows. He says: ". . . I don't think you are a woman at all. I think that what you are is a she-devil!"

Ruth thinks about this and agrees that she is a she-devil. "But this is wonderful! This is exhilarating! If you are a she-devil, the mind clears at once. The spirits rise. There is no shame, no guilt, no dreary striving to be good. There is only, in the end, what you *want*. And I can take what I want. I am a she-devil!" . . . (pp. 1, 47)

[Whatever] Ruthie wants, Ruthie gets, and that includes Bobbo, by novel's end a broken man—petitioner, appendage, whipping boy, hanger-on, doormat, love slave—all the things Ruth used to be. And she vanquishes the enemy (the other women) too. She even moves into the High Tower at the edge of the sea where Mary Fisher and Bobbo lived together. But it is a bitter victory, not without sympathy for Mary (a nice touch): ". . . She is a woman: she made the landscape better. She-devils can make nothing better, except themselves. In the end, she wins."

Personally, I'd rather be a she-devil than, say, a gardener, and I think if one can manage to make *oneself* better (whatever better means to one) that should suffice. We can't change the world, can't protect those we love, or exert mind-control over those whom we would like to love us. Therefore I can't agree with Ruth when she says, regarding Mary Fisher: "In the end, she wins." To my way of thinking, Ruth won: she took revenge as far as it would go. She was mad as a hatter, but never mind, one must do what one must do.

"The Life and Loves of a She-Devil" is devilishly delightful. It affords a scintillating, mind-boggling, vicarious thrill for any reader who has ever fantasized dishing out retribution for one wrong or another. If, however, you are one of the lucky ones who does not carry a grudge, who has no chip on her / his shoulder, who does not contain seeds of discontent (ready to sprout), who is not made of the fiery material of rebellion, then read the novel just to keep in touch with the rest of us. (p. 47)

> *Rosalyn Drexler, "Looking for Love After Marriage: 'The Life and Loves of a She-Devil'," in* The New York Times Book Review, *September 30, 1984, pp. 1, 47.*

John Edgar Wideman

1941-

American novelist, short story writer, and nonfiction writer.

Wideman is best known for his novels and short stories which trace the lives of several generations of families in and around Homewood, a black ghetto district of Pittsburgh where Wideman grew up. Wideman's major theme involves the individual's search for self-discovery amidst the memory of both a personal past and black history in general. As Kermit Frazier has stated, "The characters in Wideman's fiction can escape neither collective nor personal history and memory, so they are forced to deal with them in some way—be it successfully or ineffectually." Wideman's concern for family heritage binds the past and present in his narrative, and his blend of European and black literary traditions makes for a distinctive voice in American literature. Robert Bone has called Wideman "perhaps the most gifted black novelist of his generation."

Wideman attended the University of Pennsylvania before being selected as an Oxford University Rhodes scholar. At Oxford he immersed himself in eighteenth-century literature and the early development of the novel. Wideman's first two novels, *A Glance Away* (1967) and *Hurry Home* (1969), reflect this formal training and his own early experiments with narrative technique. During this period, Wideman focused little upon racial or exclusively black issues; both novels involve a search for self by protagonists who are confused and controlled by their pasts. In *A Glance Away*, a rehabilitated drug addict returns to his home and renews his family and social ties while trying to avoid readdiction; in *Hurry Home*, a black law school graduate seeks cultural communion with white society by traveling to Europe and then reaffirms his black heritage by going to Africa. These characters find hope for the future only by confronting their personal and collective pasts. In *The Lynchers* (1973), Wideman directs his interests toward the conflict between blacks and whites in the United States during the 1960s. Wideman attributes this shift toward black-oriented themes and his use of myth and dialect to his growing awareness of such modern black writers as Richard Wright and Jean Toomer.

In *The Homewood Trilogy* (1985), which comprises the short story collection *Damballah* (1981) and the novels *Hiding Place* (1981) and *Sent For You Yesterday* (1983), Wideman uses shifting time frames, rich dialect, and rhythmic language to transform Homewood into what Alan Cheuse terms "a magical location infused with poetry and pathos." The interrelated stories of *Damballah* feature several characters who reappear in the novels and tell of the descendants of Wideman's maternal great-great-great grandmother, Sybela Owens. *Hiding Place* concerns a boy's strong ties to his family and his involvement in a petty robbery which results in an accidental killing. *Sent For You Yesterday* won the 1984 PEN/Faulkner Award for fiction. Through the characters of Doot, the main narrator, and Albert Wilkes, the outspoken blues pianist, Wideman suggests that creativity and imagination are important means of transcending despair and strengthening the common bonds of race, culture, and class.

Wideman describes his recent nonfiction work, *Brothers and Keepers* (1984), as "a personal essay about my brother and

myself." It recounts his brother's imprisonment for his involvement in a murder similar to that described in *Hiding Place*. Combining Wideman's literary skill with his brother's street wisdom, the book sensitively explores the consequences of decisions and how the brothers arrived at such dissimilar fates.

(See also *CLC*, Vols. 5, 34; *Contemporary Authors*, Vols. 85-88; *Contemporary Authors New Revision Series*, Vol. 14; and *Dictionary of Literary Biography*, Vol. 33.)

HARRY ROSKOLENKO

Like a scenario exploding during its 24-hour time-span, ["**A Glance Away**"] follows 30-year-old Eddie Lawson, a Negro ex-postal worker, who has entered an institution for a year to cure himself of the drug habit. . . . At home, in the East, there are his loving sister; his patient mother; his uncertain, fearful mistress; Brother, an albino Negro friend; and, eventually, Robert Thurley, a white professor and secret homosexual. We reach the climax in Eddie Lawson's and Professor Thurley's interior dialogue, as each one battles to conquer himself; one has the fear of going back to dope; the other, to his own compulsion.

Tight, compact and shining with verbal and dramatic skill, the novel shows Eddie meeting his mother and sister. . . . Brother, ugly, albino, weak, but always the good friend, hangs on like a waltzing shadow of the underworld.

Professor Thurley, on the other side of the tracks, picks up Negro kids. . . . For solace, Thurley drinks Southern Comfort, and accompanies . . . [a] colleague to church to hear his music. But he dreams of sailors, beatings, sad encounters, the terror of his condition. He is, he assures himself, "an aesthetic Catholic, in politics a passive Communist, in sex a resigned anarchist." . . . Every transgression leads him to more spiritual discoveries, to emotional digressions regarding his alienation from the world of women.

It is, however, the Negro's world in a boxed-in town that draws him. Here is the American underground, a hapless, hopeless condition, drink, dope and perversion. You are hooked or hooking. When Eddie plays blackjack with his last 50 cents, and wins from his white friends, he must make a run for it, or get a going over. When he calls on his implacable girl friend, it is for a bitter bout in bed while protesting that he loves her—not dope. When he goes to church on Easter Eve, he recalls what the doctor said at the institution: "All we can do is to restore you to yourself." When he visits an after-hours joint, and is introduced to Professor Thurley by Brother, he's once again ready for a bag of dope.

The novel of Jewish life has steadied itself, and Jewish novelists occasionally manage to get away from their interior monologue. A similar extension is taking place among many of our new Negro writers. Some are still compulsively Negro in their affirmations. This book, however, develops an enormous objectivity in its characterizations. Mr. Wideman has written a powerfully inventive novel.

> *Harry Roskolenko, "Junkie's Homecoming," in* The New York Times Book Review, *September 10, 1967, p. 56.*

ROGER EBERT

John Edgar Wideman's *A Glance Away* does not completely disguise the traces of the writer at work. His craft and plan occasionally become visible at the surface of the novel, blurring the characters beneath. They are three: Eddie Lawson, a Negro drug addict who has returned home after a year of therapy; Robert Thurley, a homosexual English professor; and Brother, an albino Negro who is by turns Thurley's lover and Eddie's closest friend.

Wideman cuts back and forth between the actions of his characters during a single day. . . . He explains the sense of uselessness and defeat held by both Thurley and Eddie, and then he brings them together through Brother for a reconciliation with life.

Wideman has the materials of a good novel, but his command of language is concealed by a bagful of stylistic tricks. He makes no distinction between quotes and narrative, and while I suppose there's nothing wrong with that, I can't understand why anyone would want to do it now that the innovators of the 1920's have shown it can be done. At the novel's end the three characters come together, drunk, in a hobo jungle, and Wideman presents their thoughts at random. The technique fails; one is not moved but simply confused. . . . There are other signs of the phantom English professor lurking in and behind the author: Eliot is quoted, as are nursery rhymes and

spirituals; and one scene suddenly turns into a fragment of a play. Emerging intact from the confusion, however, is the well-drawn character of Thurley, who is memorable and sympathetic. . . . (pp. 684, 686)

> *Roger Ebert, "First Novels by Young Negroes," in* The American Scholar, *Vol. 36, No. 4, Autumn, 1967, pp. 682, 684, 686.**

JOHN LEONARD

[In **"Hurry Home,"** Cecil Braithwaite is] a black man, sometime janitor, graduate of law school, deserter of the wife who sustained him during his academic endeavors. Webb is a middle-aged white man, an exhausted writer, a kind of ambulatory culture bag, seeking in America and Europe the son he sired on a black woman and has never seen, gambling that coincidence will somehow supply him with the one person capable of forgiving him. Webb finds Braithwaite in a New York museum and takes him to Spain. In Spain, and in France, and in Italy, and in Africa, Braithwaite discovers that he must go home again.

Such are the simple terms of an immensely rich and complicated novel. The complications are both stylistic and conceptual. **"Hurry Home"** employs a number of literary devices to tell the story of Cecil Braithwaite: flashback, flashforward, first person, third person, journals, identity exchange, interior monologue, dreams (historical and personal), puns, epiphanies. At times the devices seem a thicket through which one must hack one's weary way toward meanings arbitrarily obscure. . . .

But John Edgar Wideman is up to much more than storytelling. Braithwaite's struggle is not only with a divided self (ghetto vs. the white society symbolized by his law degree), with the death of his baby boy Simon, . . . with the seeking of black kings (the Moors who conquered Spain) and therefore a historical identity. . . .

Braithwaite's struggle is also with Western culture, white history, painting, architecture, literature, music. Mr. Wideman is capable of moving from ghetto language to Joyce with a flip of the page, and while one sits admiring the motion, a suspicion slips into the mind: Another kind of motion is also going on, a shift of gears down from the macro, to the micro, down to a basic unit of two; down from the madness of a culture that fingerpaints its masterpieces in human blood, that employs the majesty of art as an excuse for crimes; a culture built, like the economy, on sacrifice. Thus Braithwaite's journey into the gospels, Africa, language and art is a journey through culture to another reality beyond it—of smoke, death, spring. . . .

Webb seems so clearly a T. S. Eliot, or that aspect of Eliot that was Prufrock, rolled trousers and wave-combing mermaids and all, that he almost reeks of ether. . . . Other writers appear like apparitions to be snuffed out with a word-twist—Voltaire, Proust, Joyce—along with Christian saints, desperate painters, sick poets, betrayed kings. "There is no Africa." There is, then, no history, except of violation. Braithwaite might even be Webb's son—we never learn of his origins—but denies the father, the past; denies even the future, for with one son dead he will not wish another into the nullity.

What seems, then, a crushing fatalism—Braithwaite beginning as a janitor hauling bags of garbage down the stairs; ending as a janitor, presumably to go on hauling—might be read as something more savage. The garbage ("the forlorn crusts of pleasure") is cultural. . . .

There is no laughter in Braithwaite, the illegitimate child of history. There is an immeasurable emptiness, a black sea.

John Leonard, "There Is No Africa," in The New York Times, April 2, 1970, p. 37.

JOSEPH GOODMAN

["**Hurry Home**"] offers much in the way of technical competency and thematic depth, but frustrates our desire for immediacy. While many of the scenes take place in the urban ghetto of the mid-sixties, the ambience is that of an earlier, less volatile decade. Little or no mention is made of such timely realities as mass violence, and the protagonist, an educated and articulate man, is chary of all but the most conciliatory politics.

It is unfair, of course, to demand a polemical stance from either a black fictional character or an actual black author, but there is a limit to our objectivity. When, for instance, a conversation in a barbershop seems a sophisticated version of an Amos and Andy script, we cannot help cringing, and thinking of the many Afro-Americans who—in the real world—are using the rhetoric of Marx and Mao. . . .

[This] is not to say that "**Hurry Home**" is a bad novel; many of its pages are packed with psychological insight, and nearly all reveal Mr. Wideman's formidable command of the techniques of fiction. Moreover, the theme is a profound one—the quest for a substantive sense of self.

At 35, Cecil Braithwaite still wonders a great deal about who he is. Obsessed with potentialities, but unable to choose among them, he is trapped in spiritual limbo between his desires and his limitations. Ambivalence permeates his life. He works as a janitor in an apartment building, is married to a devout and ignorant woman, and spends a fair amount of time rationalizing his refusal to become part of the white world. Despite his philandering and drinking, he is obsessively intellectual, committed to continual introspection and self-effacing dialectic.

Like other heroes of modern literature, Cecil must suffer the angst of spiritual ambiguity. In his particular case, the anguish is intensified by the fact of blackness. . . .

Eventually, he flees to Europe, his trip paid for by an aging and dissolute writer who is guilt-ridden over a son he has fathered by a black mistress. . . . They are a pair well met, the one seeking to "know that I am someplace seen," the other "dreaming a Prufrock dream of himself." Yet, for all their tongue-and-groove dependencies, they cannot fulfill each other's needs. Not unexpectedly, Cecil's journey is circular. He returns home, reunites with his wife, and takes a job in "Constance Beauty's straightening parlor." Rather than face a life of perpetual flux, he—quite naturally—opts for obscurity.

Since the locus of "**Hurry Home**" is Cecil's consciousness, Mr. Wideman employs an appropriately elliptical style. Chronological plot and consistent point of view are abandoned, and the authorial voice is submerged in diaries, letters and journals. The prose, paratactic and rich with puns, flows as freely as thought itself. . . .

It is a dazzling display. While ingenious devices of style sometimes act as a scrim, blurring the contours of a story, we can have nothing but admiration for Mr. Wideman's talent. Admiration, and the hope that he will eventually find a subject worthy of his gift.

Joseph Goodman, in a review of "Hurry Home," in The New York Times Book Review, April 19, 1970, p. 41.

KERMIT FRAZIER

[Two] major concerns in Wideman's fiction [are] the significance of history in our lives and the ever-presence of a working imagination. In fact, these concerns are entangled in a kind of symbiotic relationship. The imagination tries to sort out and come to grips with history—with the past—in order to make viable the present and make possible the future. History, in turn, influences how the imagination perceives the present and how it projects itself into the future.

"Racial memories exist in the imagination," Wideman says. "I believe that there are certain collective experiences that get passed on." . . . The characters in Wideman's fiction can escape neither collective nor personal history and memory, so they are forced to deal with them in some way—be it successfully or ineffectually. (p. 19)

Wideman's novels—*A Glance Away, Hurry Home* and *The Lynchers*—take on forms that are quite suited to an exploration of memory and the imagination. Although there are distinctly realistic elements in them, the preponderant formal qualities are lyrical, surrealistic and expressionistic. . . . Thematically, however, the novels are firmly based in the very realistic northern urban environment and wrestle with fundamental Black experiences, even though Europe is important to *Hurry Home*. Hence, we have three novels that develop through a weave of realistic and experimental elements—novels that keep alive histories so real that the characters must continually grapple with them, while presenting imaginations so active that only an experimentally fluid style can render them. (p. 20)

[The] progression in each of these novels is as much through the imaginations of the characters as it is through their physical activity. This kind of progression bears association stylistically with stream-of-consciousness techniques, particularly with the theories of Henri Bergson. . . . The basic concepts of stream-of-consciousness writing are probably familiar enough, one significant idea being the view of time as durational with regard to the rendering of reality rather than simply projected spatially in terms of hours, days, months, and years. . . . Wideman's concern for the imagination and memory and his use of shifting points of view and tenses, ellipses, and long, loosely constructed sentences and associative metaphors are the keys to the structure of his novels. (pp. 21-2)

Durational time, unlike spatial time, often involves the juxaposition of simultaneous activities, be they physical or mental. Such juxtaposition, along with the connected flow of images, is common to Wideman's fiction. At the beginning of *Hurry Home* the narrator follows Cecil as he takes out the garbage and then slips into the apartment of an enticing white tenant, follows Esther as she goes to the basement to wash, and follows Esther's Aunt Fanny as she keeps her usual vigil in Cecil and Esther's apartment. The narration brings their activities together. . . . (p. 25)

A more intricate example of juxtaposition comes toward the end of *The Lynchers* and through the point of view of Anthony, the young hospital attendant. The physical state: Anthony is in the locker room of the hospital with Porter and Clement, two full-time attendants who like to kid him about his youth, his being a student and his possible sexual innocence. The mental state: Anthony is thinking about his white history teacher, Miss Collins, toward whom he has an attitude of respect and shyness. . . . [We] see a combination of innocence and sexuality and get a better insight into Anthony's mixed feelings about who Miss Collins is and what he might represent to her. (pp. 25-6)

Despite the emphasis on thought processes, however, there is still a fair amount of dialogue in Wideman's novels, with two stylistic differences from the dialogue in more conventional fictional forms: dashes are used instead of quotation marks and dialogue often weaves without warning through thoughts, emotional responses and descriptions. . . . These stylistic differences mean that it is sometimes difficult to distinguish speakers in a scene involving several characters. Roger Ebert, in reviewing *A Glance Away* [see excerpt above], considers Wideman's making "no distinctions between quotes and narrative" merely a 1920's stylistic trick. But Mr. Ebert misses the point. By making it necessary for the reader to concentrate even more when following dialogue, Wideman gives him the opportunity to know the characters not only by what they think and do but also by what they say: the reader learns to identify characters by the words they use, by their attitudes and intonations. Such a technique has been used effectively by writers as different as Joyce and Ernest Hemingway.

All of these stream-of-consciousness techniques can sometimes be overbearing. Sometimes it seems that style might be present simply for its own sake. . . . But when the stylistic techniques work well with imagination and memory, the results are stunningly lyrical—scenes crackle with a mental action that is an exciting collage, one similar to the better montage effects in film. (pp. 27-8)

Wideman paints a very bleak picture of the Black and white fears strangling urban life in this country. These fears lie just under the surface in his first two novels but explode into violent frustrations in *The Lynchers*. The ghetto, the Black family, the guilts and fears, the press of history and memory on the imagination: These are the concerns that run through Wideman's novels, and the progression can be seen through the central characters—Eddie Dawson, Cecil Braithwaite and Thomas Wilkerson.

Eddie's guilt and dilemma in *A Glance Away* center more on family history than on social history. It is his family that causes him pain, that has crumbled around him. . . . With [Eddie's father] Clarence's drunken death, Eugene and Eddie are left to carry the family legacy. But the big, powerful, active Eugene is cut down by the white man's war (a war that Eddie survives), leaving the more introspective Eddie to brood and dream in a house filled with women clinging to memories of how it used to be. Eddie cannot keep a job and his turn to dope only intensifies his mother's lack of love and respect for him. (p. 32)

Others will not let him escape his past. Alice, his old girlfriend, still blames him for having slept once with a willing, curious white liberal who was in her dancing class. As a result of that and of her own frustrations with her lack of achievement, Alice has become whorish, forcing the angered, rejected Eddie to rape her as a whore because she won't let him love her as a woman and his possible savior. His mother will not let him forget that his past is a string of failures. Her bitterness makes him suggest to his sister that they leave her in the suffocating atmosphere of their old home before they all rot. His mother, hearing this from a vantage point at the top of the stairs, falls

to her death in a scene heightened by sets of ambiguous wish-fulfillment.

Eddie flees the house and ends up in the old Sanctified Church, both crying from guilt and remorse and trying to recapture the best of his past. . . . After encountering an old man on a back bench who offers him bread that he refuses and who then mocks his grief, Eddie stumbles out of the church. In a bar, he and Brother meet Thurley—a Thurley who has stumbled from his own church service and who comes to feel that he can help get Eddie through the night of his grief. There is a question, however, of whether any of the three characters huddled around their hobo's fire will ever be able to resurrect themselves out of their roles of the misfit, the outsider, the one who has failed. Their disordered pasts are too much with them.

That which continually swirls in Cecil's mind in *Hurry Home* is not necessarily his past but more the past of a whole people, for he is an educated Black man vague about a sense of himself, but who goes imaginatively to Black culture in search of a much more solid base. When Cecil leaves Esther and then accepts Webb's invitation to go to Spain, he has embarked on his journey, his quest. The recurring question for Cecil is: "Why did you do it?" And his major interest is history, with the image of the slave ship etched indelibly on his mind. . . . (p. 33)

One interesting thing about Cecil's concern for the effects of slavery is that his relationship with whites in Spain sets up certain metaphors for slavery, which make the reliving even more vivid for him in his imagination. There is Webb, who has some of the qualities of the white liberal master, who often had Black mistresses and fathered Black sons. By accepting Cecil as a substitute for that Black son, Webb can take him to Europe to set him free and educate him to the world. . . . (p. 34)

Spain is also the seat of the Moorish influence, the history of the Black kings, their power and riches. Cecil dreams, becomes a king himself, calls himself "El Moro." The contrast is clear. At home, when Cecil walked down the streets of a Black neighborhood, the local people had taunted him subtly as an uppidy nigger—"Magistrate Cecil parading." . . . They push him into a ritualistic judgment game (according to Wideman, structured around St. John's version of the Passion) that begins when a shoeshine boy agrees to shine his shoes free of charge because Cecil only has enough borrowed money to pay for his haircut. After the shine, the street people gang up on him, declaring that he has cheated the boy. The boy sides against him and the indignant crowd forces him to give up a quarter. What the scene amounts to is a rejection by his own people. But in Spain, Cecil discovers painless haircuts: he is the dark foreigner who reminds the people of those who once ruled.

Nonetheless, Cecil returns to the States after three years, comes back to the city and to a job in Constance Beauty's straightening parlor, entrenched in the heart of the Black community. And he tells his story to his Uncle Otis, whose first name is Cecil's middle name, Cecil's one important family link. He tries to explain to his uncle why he left, what he has been seeking, and his uncle is sympathetic and reminiscent. . . . Yet the novel closes ambiguously, at a point that comes chronologically before its beginning. It ends at midnight: Cecil is dreaming . . . and Aunt Fanny is sitting in her chair like a ghost, having set the table for herself and for the four sons and a husband who are only history and memory in her imagination.

By the time we get to *The Lynchers* we have reached the 1970's. Blacks and whites are more separated than ever, and more and more Blacks have become trapped in decaying cities. Both family history and cultural history are important, and Thomas Wilkerson finds it difficult to cope with them both. He is caught in the middle of his parents' arguments and frustrations. . . . The press of cultural history is just as great as those family conflicts, and although Wilkerson enthusiastically teaches his Black students about Africa and their roots and has taken to wearing an Afro and dashikis, there is sometimes a hint of reticence, a sense that he is not yet comfortable enough with what he is doing. The elimination of such reticence, of such intellectual uncertainty and ambiguity, is one of the reasons why he listens to Littleman and goes along with the lynching plan. Wilkerson needs Littleman's finely tuned rhetoric, his forthright sense of purpose; he wants to be bolstered by it, to be moved to action.

Littleman—the public speaker, the spinner of words, the self-proclaimed messenger of history in the novel—continually runs down to his fellow conspirators the realities that he believes make the lynching necessary, realities he feels all Blacks and whites must come to acknowledge: It is a matter of power and control, a matter of overwhelming the enemy with action; and descriptions of the conspirators moving like brooding ghosts through the rotting streets and the desperate, inert masses of people make a powerful case for action. . . . To solidify such a nation the lynching must be ceremoniously public and Black people must be willing to die for the master plan. (pp. 35-6)

But the conspiracy fades . . . because Wilkerson, at bottom, remains reticent. He goes to see Sissie, the cop's Black whore who will be killed as a means to a greater end, to make sure, to try to prove to himself that her life is worth sacrificing. When he encounters Lisa, Sissie's young daughter, reciting a Black storybook rhyme to herself in front of the crumbling apartment building where she must live, he recalls his father teaching him such rhymes. . . . Wilkerson comes to believe that which Littleman has insisted he cannot afford to believe: that an individual should not be deliberately sacrificed for the sake of some notion of his people's history. Wilkerson hurries away without seeing Sissie, and the plan is doomed, for Littleman lies helpless in the hospital, unable to support the plan with his words.

The Lynchers pulsates with frustration from beginning to end. . . . It ends with young Anthony smashing the life-giving bottles and vials on top of the nurses' station in the crazy ward of the hospital. It is his reaction to the Black death, insanity and hopelessness around him. These kinds of frustration first spawn and then consume the lynching plan—a plan that was to avenge the older generation and become a legacy for the younger ones. . . . The process of the imagination at work is most important to Wideman, and the flow of history and memory is an integral part of that process. (pp. 37-8)

To be sure, Wideman's fiction is difficult and places great demands on the reader, which is probably why his novels are not popular. But he is an exceptional writer of keen insight who is certainly worth reading and following. (p. 38)

> *Kermit Frazier, "The Novels of John Wideman," in*
> Black World, *Vol. XXIV, No. 8, June, 1975, pp. 18-38.*

JOHN LEONARD

["**Damballah**" and "**Hiding Place**"] are two new books—a collection of related short stories and a novel about a few of the characters we meet in those short stories—by John Edgar Wideman. They are original paperbacks . . . , and I wish Mr. Wideman the most massive of markets because he is a fine writer.

But his earlier books had hard-cover publishers, back when being a black writer was fashionable. Can it really be that whole chunks of people, black or female or Jewish or Italian or Sapphic, go in and out of style according to a phase of the cultural moon? . . . Are we going to spend the next 30 years, as we've spent the last 30 years, waiting for Ralph Ellison to be less invisible? Is each aggrieved sector of our society permitted a single stiff spokesman? Is there in the 1980's a new "esthetic" of bad faith?

Mr. Wideman pertains because, like so many gifted moderns, he is ambivalent. He grew up in black Pittsburgh and got out via a Rhodes scholarship. He has been teaching ever since. He says out loud that he is "too self-conscious" to like watermelon; he would prefer James Joyce. And yet he has been drawn, in novels like "**Hurry Home**," back to the ghetto, as if to testify. He has become a black Boccaccio in search of "a history we could taste and chew." He is much more than an adjective. That his two new books will fall apart after a second reading is a scandal. . . .

The hero of "**Damballah**"—the title refers to a voodoo god, "the good serpent of the sky," who specializes in a kind of speechless but benevolent fatherhood—is John French. One sour apple on his family tree, Tommy, takes over in "**Hiding Place**." Tommy is running away from a murder conviction and from history. He is not one of those angels for whom "not hurting nothing is their nature"; maybe we need some hurting. He is taken in by Mama Bess. She is family, and what family does is to try to put together the "scars" and the "stories"; family, which forgives, is the opposite of history, which is haunted and denies itself. . . .

[In "**Hiding Place**," Tommy is] aware: "He will suffer for whatever he knows. Maybe that's why he forgets so much." Whereas Mr. Wideman, in ["**Damballah**"], his epic poem of black faces on severed heads, of gospel speech, of signifying, refuses to forget anything. . . . He goes home in these two books, stolen and seamed.

Isn't this what hard-cover books used to be about—the mind that is stolen and reclaimed, the home we have to go back to, a writer who belongs in our permanent library?

> *John Leonard, in a review of "Damballah" and "Hiding Place," in* The New York Times, *November 27, 1981, p. 25.*

MEL WATKINS

[In "**Damballah**" and "**Hiding Place**"] the high regard for language and craft demonstrated in [Wideman's] previous books is again evident. While "**Hiding Place**" is a novel set in present-day Pittsburgh, "**Damballah**" is a collection of interrelated stories that begins in Africa and traces the fortunes of one black family in the United States through slavery, escape and settlement in the North. . . .

To invoke [the African deity Damballah], according to Maya Daren's "Divine Horsemen: The Voodoo Gods of Haiti," is to "stretch one's hand back . . . to gather up all history into a solid, contemporary ground beneath one's feet"—to "gather up the family." And that is precisely the intent of Mr. Wideman in this collection of stories. This is something of a departure for him, and in freeing his voice from the confines of the novel form, he has written what is possibly his most impressive work.

The central character in the introductory story [of **"Damballah"**], which is set mainly in the antebellum South, is Ryan, a slave who is labeled a "crazy nigger" because of his refusal to abandon the customs of his African ancestors. His intransigence leads to his torture-murder at the hands of his master. From this point the book jumps in time to the late 1800's, where in **"Daddy Garbage"**—the story of two men who find a dead baby in a garbage heap—we are in Homewood, the black section of Pittsburgh that is the setting for the remaining stories. . . .

In **"Lizabeth: The Caterpillar Story,"** Lizabeth muses about the time her father, John French . . . , finds that she had eaten part of a caterpillar and eats the rest himself: "I got the most of it then," he says. "And if I don't die, she ain't gonna die neither." **"The Songs of Reba Love Jackson"** achieves a satiric edge through the confrontation between Reba, a devout, God-fearing gospel singer and the glib, irreverent radio announcer who interviews her. The last of these stories introduces the characters who are central to the plot of the simultaneously published novel **"Hiding Place."**

But each story moves far beyond the primary event on which it is focused. The prose is labyrinthine—events and details merge and overlap. (p. 6)

It is not mere coincidence that in one story Mr. Wideman quotes Jean Toomer's description of white faces as "petals of dusk." **"Damballah,"** with its loosely connected sketches and stories, is indebted structurally to Toomer's "Cane" (1923), and in turn to Sherwood Anderson's "Winesburg, Ohio." But the kinship with "Cane" is much more direct. Like Toomer, Mr. Wideman has used a narrative laced with myth, superstition and dream sequences to create an elaborate poetic portrait of the lives of ordinary black people. And also like Toomer, he has written tales that can stand on their own, but that assume much greater impact collectively. The individual "parts" or stories, as disparate as they may initially seem, work together as a remarkably vivid and coherent montage of black life over a period of five generations.

Mr. Wideman employs the same narrative technique in **"Hiding Place,"** but not nearly so effectively. The novel depicts the events of a few days during which Tommy, grandson of John French, hides in the squalid shack in which his great-grandmother's sister Bess has isolated herself. Essentially this is a tale of two lost souls: "Crazy, evil" Bess, who, because of the death of her husband and son, has severed all family ties to live a reclusive life in a ramshackle house atop a hill overlooking Pittsburgh; and Tommy, who is on the run after a scheme to rob a ghetto hoodlum ends in murder. Through extended interior monologue we learn of the events that precipitated both characters' estrangement and led them to their rendezvous. But despite some arresting passages in which Mr. Wideman displays his command of the language and of the voices of his characters, this is a static novel.

After the evocative richness of **"Damballah,"** **"Hiding Place"** is something of a disappointment; the novel's minutely focused view of the relationship between Bess and Tommy simply does not mesh well with its ornate style. Still, taken together, these books once again demonstrate that John Wideman is one of America's premier writers of fiction. That they were published originally in paperback perhaps suggests that he is also one of our most underrated writers. (pp. 6, 21)

> *Mel Watkins, "Black Fortunes," in* The New York Times Book Review, *April 11, 1982, pp. 6, 21.*

WILFRED D. SAMUELS

Hiding Place and *Damballah* are set for the most part in Wideman's boyhood community, Homewood, which is located in the eastern edge of Pittsburgh, Pennsylvania. His family, including Sybela Owens, his maternal great, great, great grandmother, were among its first settlers. Amidst Homewood's rich landscape and cityscape, Wideman weaves his tale around the fascinating progeny of Sybela Owens, most notably Mother Bess and Aunt May, two matriarchs who serve as griots of the family's history.

Hiding Place focuses primarily on the relationship that develops between Mother Bess and Tommy, Sybela's great, great, great grandson, who commits a robbery during the course of which a man is killed. Though innocent of the actual shooting, Tommy flees Homewood. . . . When boredom drives him to return to Homewood, however, Tommy is discovered and chased. Although he returns to Bess's home while in flight, as far as Bess can tell from the shooting and sirens which assault her sleep, Tommy is killed before she can offer him a hiding place. Because she believes Tommy has been killed, Bess resolves to . . . return to Homewood to tell his story.

Wideman's concern with history, salience of family, and culture seem to merge in *Hiding PLace,* where they are powerfully presented through Mother Bess. In her role as griot, she knows and recites the family's history, telling Tommy his lineage. Throughout the novel, Mother Bess exudes a will and strength which allow her to take her place in the canon of Afro-American literature next to Miss Jane Pittman of Ernest Gaines's *The Autobiography of Miss Jane Pittman* and Eva Peace of Toni Morrison's *Sula.*

Damballah, too, examines the importance of family and culture. Published in concert with *Hiding Place* . . . , *Damballah* presents Wideman's use of the short story to explore the individual experiences of Sybela's offspring: Elizabeth, Geraldine, Carl, Martha, etc. In **"Solitary,"** for example, he explores Elizabeth's story. In the family, she is known as the baby that survived a near tragic birth when Aunt May thrust her naked body in the snow. . . . Elizabeth is now the mother of five children; she spends her weeks visting her imprisoned son Tommy. The emotion-ridden experience causes her to lose, for a brief moment, her faith in God. . . . By the end of the story, however, her faith is restored rather than destroyed.

Most powerfully drawn, through, are the stories narrated by Aunt May, for through her Wideman brings mythology (folklore) and facts together, and he imbues her with the flair and dramatic abilities of the African storyteller. (p. 12)

With *Hiding Place* and *Damballah,* Wideman reaches the zenith of his concern with the themes that have been fundamental to his work since the appearance of *A Glance Away.* He continues his interest in experimenting with form, as is evident in his use of stream of consciousness and interior monologue, especially in *Hiding Place.* Critics will undoubtedly find similarities between Wideman's work and Faulkner's, especially *The Sound and the Fury* and *As I Lay Dying.* Wideman's Clement in *Hiding Place* demonstrates that the inarticulate's world is more complex than it appears on the surface to be, much in the same way that Faulkner's Benjy does. His Homewood community, with its history, place and people, is not unlike Yoknapatawpha County, which Faulkner based on fact.

By going home to Homewood, Wideman has found a voice for his work and consequently a means of celebrating Afro-American culture and further validating the Afro-American experience in literature. (pp. 12-13)

> *Wilfred D. Samuels, in a review of "Hiding Place" and "Damballah," in* The American Book Review, *Vol. 4, No. 5, July-August, 1982, pp. 12-13.*

JONATHAN YARDLEY

Brothers and Keepers is a book guaranteed to shock and sadden, for it is the story of a gifted and intelligent man whose thoughtless and unwittingly self-destructive behavior led him ultimately to a state penitentiary. It is also a depiction of the inexorably widening chasm that divides middle-class black Americans from the black underclass, a chasm that has terrible effects both for specific individuals and for the larger society.

The imprisoned man is Robert Wideman. He is now in his mid-thirties and is 10 years younger than his brother, the author. Both grew up in Homewood, the black ghetto in Pittsburgh that is often the setting of Wideman's fiction. . . . [Robby Wideman] drifted out of high school into a street life of drug-dealing and robbery that climaxed with his involvement in a fatal encounter; he is now serving a life sentence without parole at Western State Penitentiary in Pennsylvania, his only hope for freedom lying in the slender possibility that someday his sentence may be commuted by a forgiving governor.

This book is the elder Wideman's effort to understand what happened, to confess and examine his own sense of guilt about his brother's fate (and his own), perhaps also to make a case for his brother's eventual release. . . .

There are two voices in *Brothers and Keepers*. The principal one is Wideman's own; though at times it expresses the anguish he feels, for the most part it is cool, analytical, judicious, skeptical. The other is Robby's, mostly as heard by his brother in visiting hours at the prison; it too is cool, but this is street cool, and the language is that of the street. It is a language that sounds utterly alien to most white Americans, that is rarely heard in the novels Americans write, and it speaks of a world the sit-coms never show. Here, for example, is Robby talking about "the life" that is the stuff of street dreams:

"Straight people don't understand. I mean, they think dudes is after the things straight people got. It ain't that at all. People in the life ain't looking for no home and grass in the yard. . . . We the show people. The glamour people. Come on the set with the finest car, the finest women, the finest vines. . . It's glamour. That's what it's about." . . .

It was this dream—"that Superfly fantasy," Robby calls it—that led him to deal dope (and of course to use it), to walk off legitimate jobs when the mood suited him, to participate in various small-time heists and scams. One of these took place in November, 1975, when with two pals Robby attempted to out-hustle another petty crook; the trouble was that the petty crook got killed, and after a few months of flight Robby and his pals got caught. John Edgar Wideman sees the whole gloomy story as virtually preordained. . . .

No, it won't do to say: You made it out of the ghetto, so why should we excuse your brother's failure to do so? Wideman

knows that the story is far too complicated to fit so simplistic a formula. The elder brother knows that moving out of the ghetto into the white world is a process that requires excruciating compromises, sacrifices and denials, that leaves the person who makes the journey truly at home in neither the world he has entered nor the world he has left. He knows further that . . . for urban black males who came along a decade later than he did there was a whole new set of circumstances with which to contend, not least of these being that the civil-rights revolution had raised expectations that the realities of ghetto life only mocked and dashed.

Wideman is no apologist for the shady life to which his brother aspired or for the terrible, stupid act in which he participated; he merely wants us to understand—and wants himself to understand as well—what it is like out there in "the life" and what it can do to those who try to live it. He further wants us to understand what it is to be in prison, under the cold surveillance of the "keepers." . . . In the end, this is what Wideman says: To himself, that the life his brother has lived is inextricably part of his own; to the rest of us, that unless we are morally bankrupt we cannot close our eyes to this life or our own complicity in its unhappy course.

> *Jonathan Yardley, "The Prisoner Within," in* Book World—The Washington Post, *October 21, 1984, p. 3.*

CHRISTOPHER LEHMANN-HAUPT

Near the end of ["**Brothers and Keepers**"] . . . John Edgar Wideman interrupts his narrative to raise a couple of esthetic problems.

First, he has found something missing in the portrait of his brother, Robby, at least as it emerged in an earlier draft of the present book. . . . Acknowledging his brother's history means facing the dark side of himself, presumably—the ghetto self he escaped by attending the University of Pennsylvania and becoming the author of six published works of fiction. . . .

Second, he doesn't know how to end his book with a sufficiently dramatic flourish. He dreams of a denouement that will achieve Robby's release and put an end to the evils of prison life in America, but he knows this to be out of the question. Short of an apocalypse, he is momentarily stymied.

Neither of these dilemmas is especially interesting in itself; Mr. Wideman's raising them is really a device for self-examination. But I was relieved that he introduced such words as "esthetic" and "dramatic shape" to so angry and ideological a book. It makes me feel less precious for finding that the one thing I can praise about "**Brothers and Keepers**" is its success as a job of storytelling.

For Mr. Wideman has done well at intertwining the two voices of his narrative, his own and Robby's—the one a blend of black American self-consciousness and white education, the other as fluently black as the asphalt in a burning ghetto. He has brought a novelist's skill to his telling and retelling of Robby's crime—each time with a degree of detail that leaves the reader wanting to read more.

And he has solved the problem of his ending. Judgment Day is not at hand. Robby is still interminably confined, but he has been asked to deliver the commencement speech on the occasion of his having earned "an associate degree in engineering technology.'' And the moving text of his address is what constitutes the final section of "**Brothers and Keepers.**"

The problem is, this raises a contradiction. Mr. Wideman has earlier insisted on the dehumanizing nature of the American prison system. He has impressed upon us that convicted black criminals have no rights whatever, that, indeed, Robby stands little chance of surviving. He has persuaded us that his brother spends most of his prison term in persecutory solitary confinement—the hole. It comes as a revelation not only that he has won a degree, but that he has also found time to take a course of studies, as well as read, write, watch television, eat, exercise, worship in a Sunni Juma and find employment in the prison hospital. Where, one ends up wondering, did he find time to spend in "the hole." . . .

Other contradictions are more damaging to his case. If [the author] himself made it out of the Pittsburgh ghetto, then how can he claim that his brother's only guilt as a criminal was being black in a white man's world? His brother's explanation, implicitly endorsed by Mr. Wideman, is that the role of family athlete and scholar had been preempted by the older brother, so the younger one, a rebel in too much of a hurry to become a star, felt he had to make it "in the streets." But sibling rivalry can hardly be blamed on white society. White men, too, have occasionally been known to have Robby's problem. . . .

So Robby was a statistic, Mr. Wideman seems to be arguing. But that is a cop-out. People don't perceive themselves as statistics, except to rationalize their moral choices.

Fortunately, the complexity of "**Brothers and Keepers**" is such that one isn't put off for long by its many whining, posturing passages. Far more interesting than his indictment of white society for rigging the game against all black people is the author's self-accusation for being jealous of his brother's "badness." But what Mr. Wideman hasn't come to terms with is his discomfort for having achieved success in the so-called white world. One might even go so far as to call him a guilty liberal.

> *Christopher Lehmann-Haupt, in a review of "Brothers and Keepers," in* The New York Times, *October 29, 1984, p. C21.*

ISHMAEL REED

"**Brothers and Keepers**" is John Edgar Wideman's gripping account of the events, social pressures and individual psychological responses that led his brother Robert to prison for murder and him to a middle-class life as a professor of English at the University of Wyoming in Laramie. By combining his own literary skill with the candor and vitality of his brother's street style, Mr. Wideman gives added power and dimension to this book about the contrary values and goals of two brothers. It is a rare triumph in its use of diverse linguistic styles; the result is a book that has the impact of reading Claude Brown's powerful "Manchild in the Promised Land" and James Weldon Johnson's elegant "The Autobiography of an Ex-Colored Man" in alternating paragraphs. (p. 1)

Although "**Brothers and Keepers**" is, above all, a sensitive and intimate portrayal of the lives and divergent paths taken by two brothers, John Wideman's visits to prison are the source of some powerfully written scenes in which he conveys his impressions of American prisons. He never allows his narrative to become merely a sociological tract on prison reform, but he does share his insights concerning a society that would allow the abominable conditions existing inside prisons. . . .

Occasionally, the guards promote or carry out death sentences against prisoners they consider to be "trouble makers." Mr. Wideman refers to one guard as a "Nazi Gestapo Frankenstein robot," a characterization that might disappoint those who saw the author as merely another bland, genteel, malleable and mumbling token writer and professor. . . .

Mr. Wideman remembers times in his life when he wanted to punch or to murder someone instead of tolerating the insults. In "Black Like Me," John Howard Griffin, the white journalist who "passed" for black in order to see how it felt, wrote that the rudeness and hostility that black men faced in everyday life were what surprised him the most. Mr. Wideman was almost thrown in jail himself for being an accomplice to the crime committed by his brother and his friends, and he was questioned about his possible involvement in another robbery that his brother was suspected of. "I was black. My brother was a suspect. So perhaps I was the fourth perpetrator. No matter that I lived four hundred miles from the scene of the crime. No matter that I wrote books and taught literature and creative writing at the university. I was black. Robby was my brother." (p. 32)

> *Ishmael Reed, "Of One Blood, Two Men," in* The New York Times Book Review, *November 4, 1984, pp. 1, 32.*

Lanford Wilson

1937-

American dramatist.

Wilson's plays are performed more often than those of almost any other dramatist currently writing in the United States. His stature is attested to by many prestigious awards and by the enthusiasm and respect with which critics appraise his work. Although Wilson's first plays were performed in experimental Off-Off-Broadway theaters, his major works differ from those of many of his colleagues in their use of conventional dramatic forms. The labels "poetic realist" and "American realist" have been applied to Wilson, yet he often uses such nonrealistic devices as monologue and direct address of the audience by his characters. Wilson's plays frequently bring together large ensembles of characters, many of whom are misfits or outcasts, and he is noted for the compassion with which he treats even the least attractive of them. He is also considered a superlative writer of authentic dialogue. Among Wilson's best known works are *The Hot l Baltimore* (1973) and his series of plays about the Talley family, which typify Wilson's interest in the social landscape of America.

Wilson's initiation as a playwright coincided with the inception in the 1960s of the Off-Off-Broadway movement. Most of his early plays were produced at the Caffe Cino or at La Mama Experimental Theatre Club. Wilson's works for these two stages, most of which are one-act plays, often focus on destitute characters similar to those in the work of Tennessee Williams. Two of Wilson's most enduring works from this period are *The Madness of Lady Bright* (1964), in which an aging homosexual transvestite is driven mad by the loss of his beauty, and *Home Free* (1964), about a brother and sister who live as a married couple in a fantasy world. Wilson's first full-length play, *Balm in Gilead* (1965), impressionistically recreates life in the underworld of New York City. Often compared to William Saroyan's *The Time of Your Life*, this play is set in an all-night diner in which prostitutes, drug dealers, and hustlers reveal their individual personalities and histories through monologues and interaction with each other. *This is the Rill Speaking* (1965), a one-act play, and *The Rimers of Eldritch* (1966) use a similar, montage-like technique to reproduce life in small-town Missouri.

The suicide in 1967 of Joe Cino, producer at Caffe Cino, represented a major setback for Off-Off-Broadway theater. Wilson turned to regional theaters to produce his next few plays: *Lemon Sky* (1968), *Gingham Dog* (1968) and *Serenading Louie* (1970). He eventually found a permanent outlet for his talent in the Circle Theater, later known as the Circle Repertory Company, which he helped found in 1969 and for which he is still playwright-in-residence. Both Wilson and Circle Repertory scored their first major critical and commercial success with *The Hot l Baltimore*. Most of the play's characters are the residents and staff of a condemned hotel located in a decaying urban neighborhood. Wilson's concerns in *The Hot l Baltimore* are typical of his work as a whole: protest against the demolition of the past in the name of progress, revelation of the poetic nature and the humanity of characters who are usually considered "low life," and affirmation of the importance of having dreams. *The Hot l Baltimore* set a performance

© Diane Gorodnitzki

record for Off-Broadway theater and became the basis for a television series of the same name. Another critically successful Circle Repertory production was Wilson's *The Mound Builders* (1975). Wilson's affection for the past is again demonstrated as a group of archaeologists attempt to protect their discovery of an ancient civilization from commercial development. Ironically, the site is destroyed not by developers but by a local man whose jealousy and vengeance are aroused by the archaeologists.

5th of July (1977) is the first of five projected plays in Wilson's series about the Talley family. Set in Wilson's birthplace, Lebanon, Missouri, the series revolves around several generations of the Talley family, from the Civil War era through 1977, the year in which *5th of July* takes place. In this play, Ken Talley, Jr., a disaffected, paraplegic veteran of the Vietnam war, must decide whether or not to sell "the Talley place" to friends who want to turn it into a recording studio. Assembled for an Independence Day gathering, the cast includes these friends as well as Ken's homosexual lover, his sister and her daughter, and his Aunt Sally. The latter group ultimately persuades Ken to keep the place in the family, a decision which amounts to an affirmation of the value of the old over the new. Wilson was praised for creating several memorable characters, one of whom, Aunt Sally, appears as a young woman in *Talley's Folly* (1979). A short, two-character play which is introduced to the audience as "a waltz," *Talley's Folly* is set on Independence Day, 1944, and tells the simple yet affecting story of an unlikely match between Sally and Matt Friedman, a Jewish accountant who is rejected by Sally's narrowminded family. The play was extremely popular and marked Wilson's first success on Broadway. *A Tale Told* (1981) takes place on the same night as *Talley's Folly* and introduces other members of the Talley family—bigoted, anxious, greedy people who in the course of the evening decide to sell the family garment business to a conglomerate. Discussing the Talley series, Michiko Kakutani notes: "As far as Mr. Wilson is concerned, recording contemporary history . . . has always been an animating concern," and Wilson explains, "If I can get it down accurately, it's going to reflect something larger than the microcosm we're dealing with."

Wilson interrupted the Talley saga with *Angels Fall* (1982), which involves six people confined to a mission in New Mexico during a minor nuclear accident. The play's theme is articulated by a priest, who tells the others to consider the question, "What manner of persons ought we to be?" Critics noted that the "lifeboat" or "snowbound" device, in which the pressure of confinement brings out the true natures of the characters, has been overused, but most agreed that in *Angels Fall* Wilson's skillful handling of dialogue and characterization render this fact unimportant.

Interest in Wilson's plays has increased following his many recent successes. In 1984, both *Balm in Gilead* and *Serenading Louie* were revived. Among the awards Wilson has received are the New York Drama Critics Circle Award for *The Hot l Baltimore*, Obie awards for *The Hot l Baltimore* and *The Mound Builders*, a Pulitzer Prize for *Talley's Folly*, and the 1974 American Institute of Arts and Letters Award.

(See also *CLC*, Vols. 7, 14; *Contemporary Authors*, Vols. 17-20, rev. ed.; and *Dictionary of Literary Biography*, Vol. 7.)

CLIVE BARNES

Over the years with *Talley's Folly* and *The Fifth of July*, Wilson has been trading off the Talley family tree, which existed, or so he says, in Lebanon, Mo., and he has created a place, an ambiance, and now a family that is part of the legend of the American Theater rather in the way of those grand-scale plans of Eugene O'Neill.

What Wilson is interested in is people in transition. He has the same concept of change that once characterized the plays of Chekov. His people are agonized, dependent, and lost in some desperation of soul, but they're also people totally linked to their time and place. This is eventually the total link with Chekov.

It is a passage of reality immortalized into art. This kind of reality, this kind of impressionism, is what Lanford Wilson is trying to achieve in his Lebanon series of plays. He has taken the Talley family as a sample of American life.

It is not that they are typical; indeed, they are certainly not typical. But through their pains and ecstasies, they reflect the America we have known during the past, say, 50 years.

Wilson's Broadway hit *Talley's Folly* was only part of the story. Something is happening in life, but all the time something is happening elsewhere. For every arrival, there is a departure. In Wilson's *A Tale Told*, we are seeing what is happening in the Talley household at precisely the time that Sally Talley is

finding her love and destiny in the play *Talley's Folly*. This is the complete reflection of that play.

With Wilson, and the comparison with Chekov is not only unmistakable but essential, he conceives a period of change, at times in which lives suddenly emerge and die.

It is no mistake that these two plays, *Talley's Folly* and *A Tale Told* are so closely interlinked that a character from one can come into the other. Even more, they both are absolutely independent but complementary. . . .

[This] play has to be seen essentially in relation to *Talley's Folly,* where Wilson is making the point that life may be publicly impossible yet personally viable. . . .

This is possibly, very possibly, Wilson's best play to date. . . . Wilson is writing today as a man totally possessed and obsessed with the concept of the American history that formulated his own character. I have always considered that if any artist put down on paper or in the air the total feelings of himself and his time, nothing but greatness could evolve. So few of us, hardly any of us, have the courage and the honesty to do that seemingly simple thing. Wilson has it, and Wilson is creating an image of American history, an image of our presence and past, commanding to us that we will never forget.

Clive Barnes, "Wilson's 'Tale' Told Brilliantly," in New York Post, *June 12, 1981. Reprinted in* New York Theatre Critics' Reviews, *Vol. XXXXII, No. 14, September 7 - September 13, 1981, p. 185.*

FRANK RICH

There are a dozen characters in **"A Tale Told,"** Lanford Wilson's long-awaited third play about the Talley clan of southern Missouri, but I'm afraid only one of them is worth caring about. I'm equally sorry to report that the single exception, Sally Talley, isn't on stage too long. Sally pops up only in the play's waning moments, when she sneaks into her family's mansion to grab a suitcase and skip town.

So why do we care about her? It has nothing to do with her retrieval of that suitcase, but it has everything to do with some other baggage she is carrying. Sally is the one character who has appeared in all three Talley plays. . . . In both previous works, this woman is firmly and beautifully drawn, and that's why we're so glad to see her again here. When she finally appears in **"A Tale Told"** . . . she inevitably carries with her our fond, weighty memories of fully realized Wilson plays past.

Were it not for those memories, even Sally wouldn't come alive in **"A Tale Told."** The other 11 characters, having no such ballast, don't stand a chance. While Lanford Wilson is one of our theater's very best writers, his new play . . . seems written out of obligation rather than inspiration. No, his perfect ear for American speech hasn't failed him. . . . But this time Mr. Wilson's lush language . . . [has] been applied to a theatrical vacuum.

The play is about three generations of Talleys who are squabbling over the family garment business while Sally and Matt (who doesn't reappear) are planning their elopement down at that boathouse. Does the playwright really have anything pressing to say about the often venal business folk he focuses on here? I doubt it. Most of them are superficially defined, at times by a single character trait. Their familial relationships, loving or contentious, are so thinly sketched that we rely on the program's family tree to remember who is whose sibling or spouse. Indeed, one doesn't even believe in the relationships that tie this play to the others. Could the totally abject young couple we meet in **"A Tale Told"** actually be the parents of those strong-willed Berkeley renegades, June and Kenneth Jr., of **"Fifth of July"**?

The evening's plot, which involves revelations of sordid business and sexual affairs, appears to be Mr. Wilson's playful but ill-designed homage to such old-time melodramas as "The Little Foxes," "The Magnificent Ambersons" and just maybe "Peyton Place." The narrative holes might be tolerable if the story led to any greater revelation. Alas, Mr. Wilson mounts a conventional attack on hypocrisy and greed. Because the Talleys' innocent working-class prey are also one-note figures, the battle between the amoral haves and saintly have-nots never gathers what little fire it might.

There are some other concerns here, too—including radiation poisoning, no less—but they're often either thrown-in or unconvincing. Mr. Wilson brings on the awkward ghost of a dead Talley . . . , just killed in overseas battle, to deliver some forced-fed voice-of-history monologues debunking the romantic myths of war. As the family is considering selling its company to a big corporation, much is made of the decline of entrepreneurial craft and pride that will come with the growth of conglomerate America. Mr. Wilson's lament for the passing of small business seems disingenuous, to say the least, given his equally low regard for both the self-made Talleys and their out-of-town buyers.

Throughout the play, there are also prophetic comments about the social changes that will sweep the nation once World War II ends; they're not nearly as witty as Matt's related speeches in **"Talley's Folly."** The unflattering comparisons between **"A Tale Told"** and its predecessors don't end there. Sally's favorite relative here, a rebellious aunt . . . proves to be a flat rewrite of Sally herself. The potential sale of the family business—which parallels the potential sale of the family estate in **"Fifth of July"**—here is milked for melodramatic ends, rather than elliptical, Chekhovian poetry. In keeping with this unfortunate descent into obviousness, there are too many signposting lines that speak portentously of graveyards, the totaling up of lives and the symbolic decline of the Talley house. . . .

[We] can't help wishing we were elsewhere—back at the boathouse, tripping through the moonlight with our beloved Sally and Matt.

Frank Rich, " 'A Tale Told,' Part 3 of Talley Family Story," in The New York Times, *June 12, 1981, p. C3.*

JOHN SIMON

With *A Tale Told,* Lanford Wilson reaffirms his position at the forefront of American dramatists. I find this third of the projected five plays of the Talley cycle less entertaining than *Fifth of July* and less enchanting than *Talley's Folly,* but somehow more imposing, more commanding of respect, than either of its predecessors. This is not a lovable play, as the others are; there is something mundane or even dour about most of its characters, and their very intensities and eccentricities tend to be less than appealing. But why not? Such people exist in large, indeed overwhelming, numbers and demand to be anatomized on the stage. Let's say that in *Fifth of July* Mr. Wilson wears his Chekhov hat; in *Talley's Folly,* his Giraudoux beret;

in *A Tale Told,* his Ibsen stovepipe. They all fit him equally well, and he makes them convincingly his own. But hats, though they may help make the dramatist, do not make the man; underneath them, Lanford Wilson remains headily himself. (p. 46)

[There are twelve characters in *A Tale Told*], some of them treated only marginally, but all of them glaringly alive and kicking and being kicked; interacting, intriguing, injuring or getting injured; and, every so often, extending a helping hand instead of giving one another the finger. I have [not] . . . quoted their dialogue, which is always idiomatic, frequently racy, and sometimes penetrating. If I did not copy out chunks into my program for reproduction here, it is because I did not want to miss the next Talley sally.

There are some weaknesses. Lottie's motivation could be gone into more incisively and revealingly; the business aspects—financial finaglings and the impending sale of the mill—might be made clearer; the minor characters could perhaps be given a little more to do and be. Most troubling of all is Timmy's ghost, who seems to have wandered in out of a play by David Rabe—a supernatural, or merely theatrical, device that jars in such an expertly managed piece of naturalism. Of course, the character has his legitimate use, opening a window as he does on the greater cataclysm beyond the intramural shattering of the Talleys. But couldn't this have been achieved by realistic means? To some of my strictures it might be objected that there are two more plays to come, that the completed Talley tally may fill in all the gaps. But, surely, each play must also stand on its own feet, as the previous two have so firmly demonstrated.

Yet the strengths are equally patent and rather more pertinent. *A Tale Told* is spread across a larger canvas even than *Fifth of July,* with business, war, and family matters, as well as a sort of Buddenbrooksian decline of acumen over three generations cannily sketched in. These characters benefit both from their local color, which pricks and tickles our attention, and from the archetypal sharpness of their contours, which compels universal recognition and self-identification. At a time when most playwrights can produce only chamber music, Wilson can write for a whole orchestra. Indeed, he uses both complex harmony and moments of grating discord to excellent advantage. And his range is, as usual, wide: He possesses that Dickensian or Balzacian knowledge of many professions, activities, modes of being that puts the narrowness of a David Mamet and even the inspired monomania of a Sam Shepard to ultimate shame. (pp. 46-7)

John Simon, "All in the Family," in New York Magazine, *Vol. 14, No. 25, June 22, 1981, pp. 46-7.**

GERALD WEALES

A Tale Told is a companion play to *Talley's Folly.* . . . While Sally Talley and Matt Friedman are getting engaged—the action of *Folly*—the rest of the Talleys are up in the Talley Place splashing around in a bath of revelation. Something seems to have happened to the clan. Except for old Mr. Talley, a cutthroat Christian, at once self-righteous and ruthless . . . , the family members are blandly nasty, built out of 1940s realistic touches and caricatured bigotry. Buddy, home on emergency leave—he helped drive Matt off the place before the curtain went up—tells about tasting Italian coffee and having to spit it out on the ground. In the real world, many an anti-Semite likes kosher pickles and many an anti-Italian likes Italian coffee: but in Wilson's Talley world, narrowness is always complete—political, economic, social, gustatory. These characters, who have a certain credibility when we hear them described in a sentence or two in *Folly* or *July,* become animated platitudes when they walk the stage for more than two hours. . . .

Aside from the escape of Sally, who appears briefly at the end of the play, the main action in *Tale* is the decision to sell the clothing factory to a conglomerate . . . , an act of both community and professional irresponsibility. . . . There is a subplot about an illegitimate daughter of Eldon Talley (father of Sally and Buddy), but it seems to be as pointless as it is uninteresting. Perhaps it is supposed to illustrate the way Eldon "has allowed his morals to be eroded by his business sense," as a publicity throwaway put it, but Eldon is the spokesman for quality rather than quick money, and therefore moral in business if not in private life. The fatal telegram, so laboriously set up early in the play, gives the family a momentary jolt, the play a sentimental moment, but the death of Timmy on Saipan is lost in the general flurry of discovery and recrimination. Would be lost, that is, if Wilson did not insist on sending the character on stage to describe his death and make a point about the cosmetics of home-front propaganda, the integral use of which point would not be clear even if it were convincingly presented.

All in all, *A Tale Told* is a standard family package (adultery, illegitimacy, potential incest, greed, generation gap, sibling rivalry, death by cancer, death on the battlefield), but the characters elicit neither the distaste they might command as types nor sympathy as human beings. . . . (p. 500)

> Gerald Weales, "Flawed & Fascinating," in Commonweal, *Vol. CVIII, No. 16, September 11, 1981, pp. 500-02.*

FRANK RICH

Time is . . . on the mind of Mr. Wilson in . . . **"Thymus Vulgaris."** So, for that matter, is thyme: the herb's stifling scent overruns a Southern California house trailer that belongs to the heroine, a baggy, much-married woman named Ruby. . . . **"Thymus Vulgaris"** is about the homecoming of Ruby's daughter, Evelyn . . . , a hooker who plans to go straight by marrying a grapefruit tycoon she met at work. . . .

[The] women are campy cartoons—vulgar and stupid right down to their taste in junk food, underwear and platinum hair. The play's imagery (the San Andreas Fault, Schwab's drugstore) and message ("We all come to bad ends") are as prefab as Ruby's home. But Mr. Wilson does try to cover his bets. Evelyn boasts, unconvincingly, of "the beautiful and wonderful things" in her heart. The women call for their own music and light cues—a device the playwright also used in **"Talley's Folly"** and that here seems to be an apology for the brittle stylization of his characterizations.

Still, Mr. Wilson's characteristic and touching powers of empathy break through at the end, when the women suddenly gain some self-awareness. At that point, the author's theatrical tricks pay off, too, for he cleverly turns them inside out to illuminate his own esthetic credo as a dramatist. And if his writing doesn't move you, Mr. Wilson has one last card to play: **"Thymus Vulgaris"** ends with Willie Nelson's recording of 'Someone to Watch Over Me.'' . . . (p. 360)

["**Thymus Vulgaris"**] is a hilarious vignette about two generations of frowziness sharing their illusions, their self-deceptions and fears in the depressingly sunny atmosphere of a mobile home in southern California. This is not exactly new territory, but Wilson has given the play a new dimension by constantly making reference to the voyeurism implicit in the relationship of characters and audience, particularly characters whose psychic and physical disarray is bound to give so much pleasure to middle-class theatergoers.

In addition to playing with the complex relations created by the stage, Wilson constantly calls attention to the devices of exposition and the tricks of stagecraft that mold our sympathies with a play and its people. Despite the self-consciousness of these gestures, the play is wonderfully moving. . . . (p. 361)

> Frank Rich, " 'Confluence,' 3 One-Acters, at Circle Rep," in The New York Times, *January 11, 1982, p. C14.*

JOHN SIMON

[*Thymus Vulgaris*] takes place in a California trailer park where Evelyn, a prostitute about to marry a grapefruit millionaire, seeks out Ruby, her much-married, slatternly mother, outside whose pigpenish trailer thyme (*thymus vulgaris*) grows abundantly, drenching it with its scent. Two symbols for the price of one: Thyme stands for time—the years in which mother and daughter have grown apart, the short or long future still to be filled up or depleted, and the now in which decisions could be planted; *vulgaris* stands for the crudeness of the women, their common human vulgarity, and the ability of such coarseness to survive when all the other herbs around the trailer have long since perished.

But the symbolism doesn't end here: The San Andreas Fault is also dragged in, and the very trailer, anonymous amoung other faceless trailers, sidles toward symbolism. Then come the Pirandellian devices as in *Talley's Folly.* The three characters (there is also a state patrolman, written or directed for utter absurdism) address the audience or the lighting technician, or look at themselves from outside their skins. This is a heavy burden of portentousness for a semi-rowdy, semi-wistful farce. . . . [*Thymus Vulgaris* comes] to grief as wispiness and weightiness, naturalism and stylization refuse to be grafted together.

> John Simon, "Slow Flow," in New York Magazine, *Vol. 15, No. 4, January 25, 1982, pp. 56-7.*

FRANK RICH

"Sometimes I am amazed at how human everyone is," says the Roman Catholic priest . . . at the center of Lanford Wilson's new play, **"Angels Fall."** He may be amazed, but we're not. By now we've come to depend on Mr. Wilson's talent for finding the humanity in everyone he places on a stage, whether the setting be the Hotel Baltimore or the Talley family's Missouri farm. With equal depth, this writer can draw young people and old, men and women, Jews and Christians (both faithful and lapsed), hetero- and homosexuals, idealists and cynics. Mr. Wilson is one of the few artists in our theater who can truly make America sing.

Though **"Angels Fall"** . . . is not a successful play, its unmistakable flaws are often drowned out by the moving sound of its author's tender, democratic voice. There are six Wilson characters on view in this work—all different, all fully realized in the writing . . . . One is grateful to be among them even if they've been brought together by dubious means.

We meet them in a sun-baked mission in remote, northwest New Mexico, where the priest, named Father Doherty, does his good works with the sometime aid of his unofficial foster son, an Indian . . . who's soon to pursue a brilliant medical career. On the day "Angels Fall" unfolds, this tranquil sanctuary is invaded by two September-May couples. A psychologically unraveled, middle-aged Ivy League art-history professor . . . arrives with the young wife . . . who is taking him to a plush sanitarium in Phoenix. They're soon joined by a wealthy local widow . . . and her new "boy toy" of a lover . . . , an aspiring tennis star.

What these people have in common is that they are all spiritually confused. What keeps them together for the length of the play is a device: a nuclear accident occurs in the midst of New Mexico's nearby atomic complex, trapping everyone in the mission for its duration. This premise allows Mr. Wilson to stage what is called "a little rehearsal for the end of the world" and to raise a Biblical question: if the apocalypse is really around the corner, "what manner of person" are we all to be? "Angels Fall" is a series of debates and crises that propels each troubled character into making that choice.

The play's ailments, a few cheap jokes aside, are built in. Mr. Wilson can't escape the contrived nature of his plot gimmick; it seems like double overkill that his lost souls find themselves in both a real-life apocalypse and a church as they grapple with their crises of faith. And along with the locked-room format come the creaky conventions of the well-made play. The path from exposition to catharsis to resolution is too predictable; it's implausible as well as sentimental that all six characters would neatly arrive at individual ephiphanies by the final curtain.

Yet the human spirits bottled up in the play's artificial enclosure are real. Mr. Wilson is a master at confounding our expectations about characters who, at first glance, might appear to be stereotypes. Initially, one might mistake Father Doherty for a typical . . . leprechaun: he's a jolly, liberal clergyman who enjoys top-40 radio music, tolerates profanity and serves his visitors both jokes and lemonade. . . . But there are unmistakable creases of pain at the corners of [Doherty's] dancing eyes, and the playwright ultimately explains them by showing that even the good Father is capable of unsaintly vanity.

> *Frank Rich, "'Angels Fall,' Lanford Wilson's Apocalypse," in* The New York Times, *October 18, 1982, p. C15.*

JOHN SIMON

Angels Fall, by Lanford Wilson, is a lovely bit of atmosphere that may not quite coagulate into a play. . . .

There may not be much action, but there is a rich set of imbricated themes. What can we do for others? For ourselves? About mortality? About our fallibility? And what are the various forms of love? Are any of them authentic? Or even truly feasible? And also: Is this too great a load for so delicate, slender-shouldered a play? Yes, but the wonder of it is that Wilson writes with such insight and tact, such respect for his flawed but flavorous characters, such sprightly dialogue that only seldom forces its humor or dawdles over its pathos, and such (what shall I call it?) intelligent decency, that the absence of plot, the slight contrivedness (a mission amid potential holocaust, the neatly complementary relationships), the problems

that nuzzle triteness take on a new glow. Well, glow may be too strong a word; a crisp cleanliness, then, as of a bed of freshly laundered sheets. We slip into this play as between ozone-exhaling linen, and feel refreshed, renewed.

Wilson's range, both in his *oeuvre* and in this relatively slight play, is imposing. He has a good deal of factual information on a number of subjects to purvey with deftness; he has a sense of all kinds of places and activities, and uncovers both their extraordinariness and their ordinariness with acuity and joy; and, best of all, he knows people of every stripe, in the manner of someone with the rare gift of inspired observation. And not only observation, but also synthesis and dramatic confrontation, for these people, even if they precipitate no great events, nag and nibble at, and make dents in, one another. Yet the denting is wistful and melancholy rather than abrasive, and we leave *Angels Fall* with a sense that we are all falling, if not fallen, angels, but with hope for something around and inside us to break the fall—thus quick, bright things come to contusions rather than concussions. (p. 81)

Angels Fall has its little blemishes—misfiring jokes and overcalculated tidinesses—and may be the sort of play you don't find yourself usually liking. But it puts you absolutely *there:* into its problems, into the ways of caring and coping, into people touched by the holiness of a place. It is a play you may find yourself—unusually—loving. (pp. 81-2)

> *John Simon, "Too Much Heart? Too Much Brain?" in* New York *Magazine, Vol. 15, No. 43, November 1, 1982, pp. 81-3.**

GERALD WEALES

Father William Doherty—Father Bill to his Indian parishioners—picks up his Bible midway through Lanford Wilson's *Angels Fall* and searches for a proper text for the situation, a proper epigraph for the play. . . . [He] finds what he needs, both a description of the end of the world which might have been written with nuclear destruction in mind and a posing of the play's central question. What manner of persons ought we to be? [Saint] Peter seems to be concerned with how one prepares for eternal salvation, Wilson with how one lives best in a troubled world, but perhaps these are the same thing.

Angels Fall is another of those Wilson plays in which the dramatist brings together a disparate group of people, beset by anxiety, and allows them to talk—sometimes wittily, always articulately—while they try to cope with exterior pressures and interior doubts. . . . Although the talk contains a great deal of definition and self-definition, there is never a sense—as there is with Argia in *The Queen and the Rebels* that the talk is the means to the realization of the necessary person. Tennessee Williams once said, explaining his preference for the original ending to *Cat on a Hot Tin Roof,* that he did not believe that "a conversation, however revelatory," could bring an immediate change in a person. Williams is probably correct, and Wilson, letting his people talk and then proceed to their original destinations, is closer to real life than Ugo Betti. Yet, unless words have consequences, artistically speaking, why should we listen? What manner of conversation ought a play to be?

There is, as usual in Wilson, event to punctuate the talk. . . . And there is a central action of sorts. The young man decides to take a lucrative (and perhaps socially useful) position in cancer research instead of staying, as Father Bill wants him to, to work on the medicine-poor reservation. That is, he decides at the end to do what he has already decided to do at the beginning, which means that *Angels Fall* lacks the kind of development that leads to the destruction of the archaeological research in *The Mound Builders* or even the decision not to sell the farm in *The Fifth of July*. Even more than usual, the gathering of Wilson characters is pushed before the examining eye of the playwright and the audience by an artificial device.

The play's answer to Peter's question is that a person should follow his vocation. The most extended exposition of this point is given to the young tennis player, a comic figure of the athlete as hypochondriac, of the kept man as more child than stud. The preacher and the teacher . . . will stick to their calling; in fact, they preach and teach throughout the play. The doctor's choice of laboratory over reservation may violate the image Father Bill wants to force on him, but it emphasizes the play's assumption that the individual has to make his own decision. (p. 690)

Sometimes, as in *A Tale Told,* Wilson works in obvious stereotype. At his best, he does what realists have always done; he uses the details of everyday life to provide a believable surface for his people. The two main characters of *Angels Fall* are essentially stereotypes—the crochety, fey priest and the histrionic professor—who are supposed to transcend mannerism and display the pain, need, uncertainty that give depth to the cliché. (pp. 690-91)

Lanford Wilson needs a strong metaphorical or thematic structure to bring substance to the recognizable surface of his characters. Although Peter's question is an important one—perhaps, *the* important one—the answer here, even in the person of Father Doherty, smacks more of neatness than necessity. (p. 691)

> *Gerald Weales, " 'Angels Fall': Epistle of Peter to New Mexico," in* Commonweal, *Vol. CIX, No. 22, December 17, 1982, pp. 690-91.*

WALTER KERR

Sometimes a playwright can see a professional reef rearing up right in his path and feel obliged to risk heading for it anyway. For instance, I imagine that when Lanford Wilson sat down to write "Angels Fall," . . . he knew perfectly well that the first thing he'd be accused of was copying the format of what we can call the "snowbound" play. A "snowbound" play is any play in which a group of strangers, constituting something of a social cross-section, is forced by natural or unnatural means to remain where it is until the weather or the gunsmoke clears, by which time some or all members of the imprisoned party will have undergone character transformations. Got it? . . .

Actually, you can make a case that says "Angels Fall" doesn't belong to the category at all. Of its six characters, momentarily relaxing in a New Mexican church because a nuclear accident has closed the roads directly ahead, only two actually qualify as true passers-by. . . .

What's brought them into the building is the presence of a payphone in the vestibule, and, having made their calls, they choose to sit and talk. It's nice that they do, because the talk is good. And lively.

But that brings us to the real point. When the talk is good, when the talk is lively, it doesn't really matter whether the presence of the principals is rigged or not. You can *justify*

arrivals until you're blue in the face, but if what comes out of the actors' faces isn't fascinating, forget it. Conversely, the people can come from the moon, or from whatever planet may have spawned E.T., and if we're glad to make acquaintance we'll stop asking questions. We should remember that *all* drama is artifice. The only thing that counts is the imaginative use that's made of it.

Mr. Wilson's used it nicely in "Angels Fall."

> *Walter Kerr, "The Hazards and Pains Plaguing an Actor's Life," in* The New York Times, *February 3, 1983, p. C15.**

ROBERT ASAHINA

[Wilson] represents a distinctly American tradition—of downhome naturalism, firmly rooted in stubborn particularity while rising (or at least commendably aspiring) to compelling universality. And his best plays—*Fifth of July*, for example—deftly balance the competing claims of several shrewdly sketched characters whose lives mesh in a complex and revealing drama.

The drama in *Angels Fall*, however, is merely blatant contrivance. As many reviewers have noted, this is a "lifeboat" play in which the characters are thrown together by more or less arbitrary circumstances, beyond their control, which force them to question themselves and one another. . . .

The play proceeds along the familiar lines of recriminations prompting revelations and further recriminations prompting further revelations. (p. 231)

What drama there is results from a few not too surprising twists in some of these characterizations. Don is revealed to be not a run-of-the-mill M.D. but a brilliant researcher with a chance to leave the reservation for a university job, much to Father Doherty's distress. Zappy is not a gigolo; he truly loves Marion, who is not the ditsy broad she appears to be, but a successful gallery owner dedicated to her late husband's memory.

Unfortunately, the two main characters, Father Doherty and Niles, remain mostly the same from beginning to end. (Vita remains little more than her husband's passive adjunct throughout.) The priest is avuncular and philosophical, a shrewd but kindly man of the same cloth as Barry Fitzgerald; the professor is arrogant and neurotic, a rationalist "victimized by a sense of irony" and tortured by doubts about his scholarship and his teaching. . . . Religion versus reason, faith versus skepticism—the schema is simply too predictable.

We are hardly surprised when Father Doherty says of the accident—nuclear: how is that for fate?—that has brought the characters together: "The only benefit of these little accidents, these rehearsals for the apocalypse, is that they force us to get our act together." Which means asking ourselves, the priest continues, "What manner of persons ought we to be?"

True to the conventions of the lifeboat genre, an insight into that existential problem is forthcoming from the idiot savant on board, Zappy, whose epiphany occurred at age ten, when he discovered he was a natural at tennis. As he puts it, "That's magic, when you know what you're supposed to be." (p. 233)

At the end of *Angels Fall*, the nuclear accident turns out to be of less than apocalyptic dimensions; the roads are reopened, and the five travelers are free to leave, fallen angels who have presumably found some measure of redemption. It would be nice to think that they could so easily come to terms with their uncertainties, that all it took was a few therapeutic hours of forced intimacy with strangers in the shadow of possible doom. But that kind of sentimental pseudopsychodrama belongs in made-for-TV movies, where everything works out okay in the last fifteen minutes, not in a serious stage play by a serious playwright. (pp. 233, 35)

Robert Asahina, in a review of "Angels Fall," in The Hudson Review, *Vol. XXXVI, No. 1, Spring, 1983, pp. 231, 233, 235.*

CLIVE BARNES

Two marriages that have lost their way, four people adrift from their moorings, an America in flux—that is just about the emotional floor-pattern of Lanford Wilson's play, *Serenading Louie.* . . .

The women do nothing except keep house and support their husbands' psyches. The husbands work off-stage. It is a domestic drama. A domestic tragedy.

Wilson's play is very tidy. Even its scream at the end is almost politely suppressed.

These are well-heeled, well-bred, well-witted people. They lack involvement, they have no commitments, except to their essentially chilly selves, and they are doomed figures, lost in the American identification chaos that was eventually the middleclass contribution to the Vietnam War. . . .

They are similar people. With a frank, theatrical flourish, Wilson, with no apology or explanation, has them differently inhabit the same house—to show a kinship that is almost more than spiritual. And, as the play at the end breaks free of its stylized good manners, the two men can talk to one another without time or geographic boundaries. There is theatrical fantasy in the play's dramatic realism.

What Wilson is doing is providing us with the psychological background to what will become a newspaper's filler story of a suburban tragedy, the explanation behind the shocked-neighbor faces that will briefly appear on the TV screens expressing disbelief. He is trying to describe the private pain underpinning a public melodrama. . . .

This is a good, sometimes funny play, a thoughtful, thought-provoking play. It has a life of its own after the curtain. Its limitations are those of its characters. They are cold and boring. One sees what they wanted, but does not really care that they didn't get it.

Clive Barnes, "Two Marriages & No Communication," in New York Post, *February 3, 1984. Reprinted in* New York Theatre Critics' Reviews, *Vol. XXXXV, No. 3, January 28-February 6, 1984, p. 365.*

FRANK RICH

If you pay attention to its plot, Lanford Wilson's **"Serenading Louie"** is another play about marriage and adultery in the suburban upper middle class. Mr. Wilson's characters—two couples in their mid-30's, all longtime pals from Northwestern University days—are caught up in the usual cycle of betrayals, guilt and angry recriminations. Much of the play takes place

at that late hour when husbands and wives, having had too much drink or too little sleep, make war, not love.

Yet Mr. Wilson digs well beneath the surface of this familiar domestic battleground. Though his setting is an elegant home in the "Ordinary People" country north of Chicago, a character isn't wrong to describe this suburban terrain as a "Wilderness." Like the people in Mr. Wilson's **"Fifth of July"** or **"Angels Fall"**—who inhabit rural outposts—those of **"Louie"** are quintessential modern American drifters, desperate to connect to anything that might give their lives meaning. If they can't connect to one another, then they'll rummage through the past or peer into the future searching for ideals or for some notion of community that might fill the desolate vacuum of the present. . . .

[**"Serenading Louie"** was last seen] in 1976. The author has revised the text for the current revival. . . . The play still has its problems. Almost all the offstage characters—a child, a mysterious stranger, illicit lovers—seem artificially designed. The bleak denouement is unconvincing melodrama that leaves the evening stranded on an unearned sociological limb.

These obvious flaws are outweighed by the wounding honesty of much of the writing and the excellent production. . . .

As the play goes on, Mr. Wilson expands . . . [the] crises rather than resolving them, finally to push each character into a solitary corner of the shared living room. Alex decides that love is just "a neurosis" that two people "agree to share"—and we eventually realize that his commitment to public life is an escape from his inability to commit to a private one. The characters' retreats into the happier past only leave them more disoriented. . . .

"There's got to be a way of giving each other what we want," says Alex—but to find those ways, one must look to Mr. Wilson's later work. Here the only hope is Alex's wish that the first half of his life has been "just a dry run" for the "real life" yet to come. **"Serenading Louie"** can be as harrowing as quicksand. . . .

The warmer breezes come from the author's unfailing compassion, and from the performers.

Frank Rich, "Stage: 'Serenading,' by Lanford Wilson," in The New York Times, *February 3, 1984, p. C3.*

JOHN SIMON

Serenading Louie, the second revision of a 1970 play, is sensitive, serious, honest, funny, unsatisfying, and tremendously worthy. It is about everything and nothing, which means that if there were a catalogue of themes, it would have to be filed under "Life, the meaning of." More specifically, it is about two affluent suburban-Chicago couples on the cusp between youth and middle age. . . . Oversimplifying, I could say it is about four persons who want to feel more than they do, but who, because of something in themselves or in their spouses, are prevented from doing so. I could also say that the time is Halloween, when imps and goblins are rampaging—not around but inside these people. And they suffer—one wife has been cheating on her husband, and one husband has been Platonically unfaithful with a girl of seventeen—and they talk. But the talk and the suffering do not quite mesh; they cannot, as some of those triangles in our geometry textbooks did, cover each other. And awful things happen.

I cannot promise that you will like this play or these characters; certainly you won't love them. But you owe it to yourself to see their thrashings about, their helpless attempts at feeling more, and at being felt in return. These failures and their verbalizations—also, essentially, failures—have something exemplary and heroic about them, something that dares to take on universal concerns. Why is success a kind of failure? the play asks. Why must love die, and yet not die completely? Why can't we succor each other or even ourselves? Why is solicitude apt to be an involuntary but insidious torture? Wilson's string quartet—the play is very much like music, with the four characters, even when they are not together, flowing into one another because they inhabit the same space, the same set representing both domiciles—is indescribably intense and incisive, with nuances as fine and haunting (Halloween again!) as this from a wife about her husband: "I don't actually think that I loved him then, but I loved him then—now." I can't think of any other living American playwright who could have written a line this subtle and penetrating, this pregnant and this painful, in such utterly simple, denuded language. It is heartbreaking.

But the play is imperfect—very, very imperfect. Only one character is fully realized: Gabrielle. . . . (p. 68)

I repeat, something is gravely amiss. *Serenading Louie* does not quite find a sufficient shape and adequate action to embody its states of soul, and what action there is is crammed into the last moments. And though at its best the talk is magnificent, there may be a bit too much of it. This is, finally, a play about obsessions that we never fully get to share. But we do experience—indeed, learn—much along the way. (p. 69)

John Simon, "Playing with Fire," in New York
Magazine, Vol. 17, No. 7, February 13, 1984, pp.
68-9.*

JOHN BEAUFORT

Mr. Wilson is now a well-established, prizewinning dramatist with such works as **"The Hot L Baltimore,"** **"Talley's Folly,"** and **"Fifth of July"** to his credit. The subjective attitude that connects these very different later plays to Mr. Wilson's first full-length theater piece is an implicit concern for the human condition. However down and out and disreputable the social castoffs of **"Balm in Gilead"** may be, the playwright still regards them as human beings. If it were not so, the garish theater piece would be mere sensationalism.

While the time of the action has now been updated to 1972, the irony of the title remains that there is no balm in this Manhattan Gilead. There is instead the vulnerable companionship of outcasts, destructive delusion of drugs, and pursuit of sordid pleasures. The play's realistic setting . . . is a coffee shop in the lower depths of Upper Broadway—an oasis for its contentious patrons, an urban way station that may be slept in but is never swept out, an all-night spot whose managers must also serve as bouncers.

Mr. Wilson is primarily interested in atmosphere and characters (drifters, derelicts, prostitutes of both sexes, addicts and pushers). At the same time, **"Balm in Gilead"** contains an incidental plot concerning Darlene . . . , a naive young hooker from Chi-

cago, and Joe . . . , a drug pusher who falls fatally behind in his payments.

"Balm in Gilead" is in some respects a verbal folk opera with set pieces for arias recited by several of its 29 characters.

John Beaufort, "Definitive Revival of Lanford Wilson's First Full-Length Play," in The Christian Science Monitor, *June 18, 1984, p. 22.*

SYLVIANE GOLD

Sure, there are eight million stories in the naked city—but are there any that haven't yet been told? Judging by Lanford Wilson's slice-of-street-life drama, **"Balm in Gilead,"** the answer is no. . . . (p. 249)

[In **"Balm in Gilead"**] there are 25 junkies, hookers and assorted lowlifes disporting themselves in and around a seedy all-night coffee shop on Manhattan's Upper West Side. . . . **"Balm"** is less a play than a maudlin frieze. . . . There are no relationships, only brief transactions. "Hey, did you pay?" is the refrain that keeps ringing out from behind the counter.

Similarly, there are no characters in the play, only emblems. . . .

[Only one character] has anything even remotely affecting to tell us.

She is the foolish, gawky newcomer to New York. . . . Darlene is riddled with contradictions and unlikely naivete. But in a long, rambling monologue . . . the playwright conveys Darlene's pathetically constricted world. He also tips his hand. He's after pathos here, easy pathos. It's what he's always been after, even in his later plays, like **"Talley's Folly"** and **"Fifth of July."** (p. 250)

Sylviane Gold, "A Fondness for Freaks," in The Wall Street Journal, *June 20, 1984. Reprinted in* New York Theatre Critics' Review, *Vol. XXXXV, No. 9, May 21-May 27, 1984, pp. 249-50.*

ROBERT BRUSTEIN

Balm in Gilead is a work from the playwright's early period, before a wistful romanticism began to soften his writing. It is a closely observed sociological study of hookers, hustlers, pimps, pushers, and dopers of every sexual persuasion converging on each other in an all-night coffee shop on Halloween—Gorki's *Lower Depths* transferred to Upper Broadway. For most of its length, the play avoids plot, theme, or purpose, but eventually two figures break free from this sketchily drawn crowd of twenty-nine characters to make a story; Joe, a part-time heroin pusher who wants to escape his profession, and Darlene, a well-intentioned good-time girl from Chicago. At the climax, after mating briefly with Darlene in her hotel room, Joe is stabbed to death by a hood sent by the gangster for whom he works, an event barely noticed by the other denizens of the coffee shop. A casual murder, it emerges nonetheless as a highly melodramatic event, one which seems contrived when contrasted with the usual low pressure of the narrative. Like all naturalistic works, *Balm in Gilead* is persuasive and authentic only as long as it is pointless and meandering. (p. 28)

Wilson's play, for all its strengths, still falls short of being a satisfying work of art—not just because it fails to transcend its own naturalism and not because it is formally abrupt and incomplete, but because it somehow manages to contradict its own impulses. Wilson is almost Saroyanesque in his treatment of the lost and the dispossessed—whatever their habits and failings, almost all of his characters are basically good-hearted, with the exception of the hood who kills Joe. As in Saroyan's Manichean *Time of Your Life,* this is a contained society disrupted by external evil; the romantic sentiment hidden in the tough shell of Wilson's later plays, beginning with *Hot l Baltimore,* is just one step away.

Still, whatever the seeds it may be planting, *Balm in Gilead* is neither sentimental nor romantic . . . so let us be grateful. (pp. 28-9)

Robert Brustein, "Post-Naturalist Triumph," in The New Republic, *Vol. 191, No. 19, November 5, 1984, pp. 27-9.*

Appendix

The following is a listing of all sources used in Volume 36 of *Contemporary Literary Criticism*. Included in this list are all copyright and reprint rights and acknowledgments for those essays for which permission was obtained. Every effort has been made to trace copyright, but if omissions have been made, please let us know.

Killam, G. D. From *An Introduction to the Writings of Ngugi*. Heinemann, 1980. © G. D. Killam 1980. Reprinted by permission of Heinemann Educational Books Ltd.

Kimball, Arthur G. From *Crisis in Identity and Contemporary Japanese Novels*. Tuttle, 1973. Copyright in Japan 1973 by Charles E. Tuttle Co., Inc. All rights reserved. Reprinted by permission of Charles E. Tuttle Co., Inc., Tokyo, Japan.

Lieberman, Laurence. From "M. B. Tolson and A. R. Ammons: Book-Length Poems," in *Unassigned Frequencies: American Poetry in Review, 1965-77*. By Laurence Lieberman. University of Illinois Press, 1977. © 1965 by Laurence Lieberman. Reprinted by permission of the publisher and the author.

Mais, S.P.B. From *Books and Their Writers*. Dodd, Mead and Company, 1920.

Martin, Wendy. From *An American Triptych: Anne Bradstreet, Emily Dickinson, Adrienne Rich*. University of North Carolina Press, 1984. © 1984 The University of North Carolina Press. All rights reserved. Reprinted by permission.

McCann, Garth. From *Edward Abbey*. Boise State University, 1977. Copyright 1977 by the Boise State University Western Writers Series. All rights reserved. Reprinted by permission.

Moore, Marianne. From "A Writer on the Mound," in *A Marianne Moore Reader*. By Marianne Moore. The Viking Press, 1961. Copyright © 1961 by Marianne Moore. All rights reserved. Reprinted by permission of Viking Penguin Inc.

Murry, John Middleton. From *The Evolution of an Intellectual*. R. Cobden-Sanderson, 1920.

Nathan, John. From an introduction to *Teach Us to Outgrow Our Madness: Four Short Novels*. By Kenzaburō Ōe, translated by John Nathan. Grove Press, 1977. Copyright © 1977 by John Nathan. All rights reserved. Reprinted by permission of Grove Press, Inc.

O'Brien, Darcy. From "Edna O'Brien: A Kind of Irish Childhood," in *Twentieth-Century Women Novelists*. Edited by Thomas F. Staley. Barnes & Noble, 1982. © Thomas F. Staley 1982. All rights reserved. By permission of Barnes & Noble Books, a Division of Littlefield, Adam & Co., Inc.

Ostriker, Alicia. From *Writing Like a Woman*. The University of Michigan Press, 1983. Copyright © by The University of Michigan 1983. All rights reserved. Reprinted by permission.

Pacifici, Sergio. From *The Modern Italian Novel: From Pea to Moravia, Vol. 3*. Southern Illinois University Press, 1979. Copyright © 1979 by Southern Illinois University Press. All rights reserved. Reprinted by permission of Southern Illinois University Press.

Press, John. From *Rule and Energy: Trends in British Poetry since the Second World War*. Oxford University Press, London, 1963. © Oxford University Press 1963. Reprinted by permission of Oxford University Press.

Rawson, Judy. From "Dino Buzzati," in *Writers & Society in Contemporary Italy: A Collection of Essays*. Edited by Michael Caesar and Peter Hainsworth. St. Martin's Press, 1984. © Michael Caesar and Peter Hainsworth 1984. Reprinted by permission of St. Martin's Press Inc.

Roscoe, Adrian. From *Uhuru's Fire: African Literature East to South*. Cambridge University Press, 1977. © Cambridge University Press 1977. Reprinted by permission.

Rose, Mark. From *Alien Encounters: Anatomy of Science Fiction*. Cambridge, Mass.: Harvard University Press, 1981. Copyright © 1981 by the President and Fellows of Harvard College. All rights reserved. Excerpted by permission.

Russell, Mariann. From *Melvin B. Tolson's "Harlem Gallery:" A Literary Analysis*. University of Missouri Press, 1980. Copyright © 1980 by the Curators of the University of Missouri. All rights reserved. Reprinted by permission of the University of Missouri Press.

Schwartz, Kessel. From "The Isakower Phenomenon and the Dream Screen," in *Critical Views on Vicente Aleixandre's Poetry*. Edited by Vicente Cabrera and Harriet Boyer. Society of Spanish and Spanish-American Studies, 1979. © copyright, Society of Spanish and Spanish-American Studies, 1979. Reprinted by permission of the publisher and Kessel Schwartz.

Shapiro, Karl. From an introduction to *Harlem Gallery: Book I, "The Curator."* By M. B. Tolson. Twayne, 1965. Copyright 1965 by Twayne Publishers. All rights reserved. Reprinted with the permission of Twayne Publishers, a division of G. K. Hall & Co., Boston.

Tate, Allen. From a preface to *Libretto for the Republic of Liberia*. By M. B. Tolson. Twayne, 1953. Copyright 1953 by M. B. Tolson. All rights reserved. Reprinted with the permission of Twayne Publishers, a division of G. K. Hall & Co., Boston.

Taylor, John Russell. From *The Second Wave: British Drama for the Seventies*. Hill and Wang, 1971. Copyright © 1971 by John Russell Taylor. All rights reserved. Reprinted by permission of Hill and Wang, a division of Farrar, Straus and Giroux, Inc. In Canada by A. D. Peters & Co. Ltd.

Appendix

Cumulative Index to Authors

This index lists all author entries in the Gale Literary Criticism Series and includes cross-references to other Gale sources. References in the index are identified as follows:

Author Index

Author Index

Author Index

Author Index

Author Index

Cumulative Index to Critics

Critic Index

Critic Index

Critic Index

Critic Index

Critic Index

Critic Index

Critic Index

Critic Index

Critic Index

Critic Index

Critic Index

Critic Index

Critic Index

Critic Index

Critic Index

Critic Index

Critic Index

Critic Index

Critic Index

Critic Index

Critic Index

Critic Index

Critic Index

Critic Index

Critic Index

Critic Index

Critic Index

Critic Index

Critic Index

Critic Index

Critic Index

Critic Index

Critic Index